DATE DUE

FLOWERING PLANTS

OF THE NEOTROPICS

FLOWERING PLANTS

PUBLISHED IN ASSOCIATION WITH THE NEW YORK BOTANICAL GARDEN

OF THE NEOTROPICS

Edited by

- *Nathan Smith*

- *Scott A. Mori*

- *Andrew Henderson*

- *Dennis Wm. Stevenson*

- *Scott V. Heald*

PRINCETON UNIVERSITY PRESS • PRINCETON AND OXFORD

Copyright © 2004 by

The New York Botanical Garden

Published by Princeton University Press,

41 William Street,

Princeton, New Jersey 08540

In the United Kingdom: Princeton University Press,

3 Market Place, Woodstock,

Oxfordshire OX20 1SY

Library of Congress Cataloging-in-Publication Data

Flowering plants of the Neotropics / edited by

Nathan Smith . . . [et al.].

p. cm.

Includes bibliographical references and index.

ISBN 0-691-11694-6

1. Botany—Latin America. 2.

Plants—Identification.

I. Smith, Nathan, 1974–

QK205.F66 2003

581.98—dc21   2003045968

British Library Cataloging-in-Publication

Data is available

This book has been composed in postscript Times

Roman with Helvetica Neue and Perpetua display

Printed on acid-free paper. ∞

www.nathist.princeton.edu

Composition by Bytheway Publishing Services,

Norwich, New York

Printed in Italy by Eurographica

10 9 8 7 6 5 4 3 2 1

C O N T E N T S

403 Monocotyledons

PREFACE

THE DIVERSE FLORA of tropical America is reflected in the rich lexicon that American Indians developed for the plants that surrounded them. In 1648, Georg Marcgrave was one of the first Europeans to provide a written record of plants along the eastern coast of Brazil. However, it was not until the mid-1700s that scientific description of the Neotropical flora received its first great impetus when large numbers of species new to Western science were described by Jean Baptiste Christophe Fusée Aublet, Nicolaus Jacquin, and Carolus Linnaeus. Since then there have been many contributions to our knowledge of this rich flora, but perhaps the most significant is Carl Friedrich Philipp von Martius' *Flora Brasiliensis*, of which the first part appeared in 1840 and the last in 1906. The incredibly detailed botanical illustrations and descriptions in *Flora Brasiliensis* are useful in helping to identify Neotropical plants and bear testimony to the continuing utility of floras over time. The variety of Neotropical checklists and floras is too extensive to enumerate here but is summarized by geographic region in Frodin's recently published *Guide to the Standard Floras of the World*.

In the *Flowering Plants of the Neotropics*, our goal is to provide an authoritative reference to plant families that are known to occur in tropical America. Although Heywood's *Flowering Plants of the World* covers most of the families in this region, it is difficult to isolate information about plants found in the neotropics from this scholarly work. It is only in Maas and Westra's *Neotropical Plant Families* that a guide dedicated to the flowering plant families of the American Tropics can be found. This publication is an excellent reference to the Neotropical flora but lacks much of the detailed information and color images that *Flowering Plants of the Neotropics* provides. On a smaller geographic scale, Gentry's *A Field Guide to the Families and Genera of Woody Plants of Northwest South America* and Ribeiro et al.'s well-illustrated *Flora da Reserva Ducke* are exceptional references to Neotropical plants.

We enlisted the help of as many specialists as we could to describe the plant families of the neotropics. The treatments include a technical description of the family, a discussion of its place among the flowering plants, information about its ecology and economic uses, and entry into the technical literature. A glossary of terms applicable to the rich vocabulary used to describe Neotropical plants and aids to the identification of an unknown family are found at the end of the book.

Our wish is to provide a book reflecting current knowledge of the flowering plants of the neotropics that can be used by amateur and professional biologists alike. Through its use, we hope to stimulate an interest in the diversity and beauty of the flowering plants of tropical America, and, thus, promote their appreciation and conservation.

Nathan Smith, Scott A. Mori, Andrew Henderson,
Dennis Wm. Stevenson, and Scott V. Heald
The New York Botanical Garden

CONTRIBUTORS

Jim Affolter, The University of Georgia, Athens, GA 30602-0002, USA.

Victor A. Albert, Botanic Garden, Universiteteti Oslo, Oslo, Norway.

Ihsan Al-Shehbaz, Herbarium, Missouri Botanical Garden, P.O. Box 299, St. Louis, MO 63166-0299, USA.

William Surprison Alverson, The Field Museum, 1400 S. Lakeshore Drive, Chicago, IL 60605-2496, USA.

William R. Anderson, University of Michigan Herbarium, 3600 Varsity Drive, Ann Arbor, MI 48108-2287, USA.

María Mercedes Arbo, Herbario, Inst. de Botánica del Nordeste, Casilla de Correo 209, 3400 Corrientes, Argentina.

Alberto Areces, Botanical Park Inés Mendoza, R.R. 2, Box 5, San Juan, Puerto Rico 00926.

Wayne Armstrong, Herbarium, Life Sciences Department, Palomar College, San Marcos, CA 92069-1487, USA.

Daniel Atha, Institute of Economic Botany, The New York Botanical Garden, Bronx, NY 10458-5126, USA.

Sandy Atkins, Herbarium, Royal Botanic Gardens, Kew, Richmond, Surrey TW9 3AE, England, U.K.

Daniel F. Austin, Arizona-Sonora Desert Museum, 2021 N. Kinney Road, Tucson, AZ 85743-9719, USA.

Gerardo A. Aymard C., UNELLEZ-Guanare, Herbario Universitario (PORT), Guanare Edo. Portuguesa 3323, Venezuela.

Henrik Balslev, Herbarium Juntlandicum, Botanical Institute, University of Aarhus, Bygn. 137, Universitetsparken, DK-8000 Aarhus C, Denmark.

Rupert Barneby† (1911–2000). Formerly: Institute of Systematic Botany, The New York Botanical Garden, Bronx, NY 10458-5126, USA.

Spencer C. H. Barrett, Botany Department, University of Toronto, 25 Willcocks Street, Toronto, Ontario M5S 3B2, Canada.

Kerry Barringer, Herbarium, Brooklyn Botanic Garden, 1000 Washington Avenue, Brooklyn, NY 11225-1099, USA.

Hans T. Beck, Northern Illinois University, Department of Biological Sciences, DeKalb, IL 60115-2861, USA.

C. C. Berg, Herbarium, Botanical Institute, University of Bergen, Allégaten 41 N-5007 Bergen, Norway.

Amy Berkov, City College of New York, Department of Biology, J526, Convent Avenue @ 138 Street, New York, NY 10031-9198, USA.

Paul E. Berry, Botany Department, University of Wisconsin, 132 Birge, 430 Lincoln Drive, Madison, WI 53706-1313, USA.

Brian Boom, CERC, Columbia University, 1200 Amsterdam Avenue, New York, NY 10027-7003, USA.

Jason Bradford, Missouri Botanical Garden, Center for Conservation and Sustainable Development, St. Louis, MO 63166-0299, USA.

Jerald S. Bricker, Department of Biological Sciences, Cameron University, 2800 W. Gore Boulevard, Lawton, OK 73505-6377, USA.

John L. Brown, 30 Mill Pond Road, Bethlehem, CT. 06751-1912, USA.

Kenneth M. Cameron, Institute of Systematic Botany, The New York Botanical Garden, Bronx, NY 10458-5126, USA.

Lisa M. Campbell, The New York Botanical Garden, Bronx, NY 10458-5126, USA.

Lars W. Chatrou, Herbarium, Institut für Botanik, Universität, Rennweg 14, A-1030 Wien, Austria.

Flor Chavez, The New York Botanical Garden, Bronx, NY 10458-5126, USA.

Eric Christenson, 1646 Oak Street, Sarasota, FL 34236-7536, USA.

Steve Clemants, Herbarium, Brooklyn Botanic Garden, 1000 Washington Avenue, Brooklyn, NY 11225-1099, USA.

Lincoln Constance† (1909–2001). Formerly: University Herbarium, University of California, Berkeley, CA 94720-2465, USA.

Mireya D. Correa A., Smithsonian Tropical Research Inst., Unit 0948, APO AA 34002-0948, USA and Herbarium, Universidad de Panamá, Estafeta Universitaria, Panamá, Panama.

Thomas B. Croat, Herbarium, Missouri Botanical Garden, P.O. Box 299, St. Louis, MO 63166-0299, USA.

Garrett E. Crow, Department of Plant Biology Rudman/ Spaulding Hall, University of New Hampshire, Durham, NH 03824-3518, USA.

Douglas C. Daly, Institute of Systematic Botany, The New York Botanical Garden, Bronx, NY 10458-5126, USA.

Jerrold I. Davis, Herbarium, L. H. Bailey Hortorium, 462 Mann Library, Cornell University, Ithaca, NY 14853-4301, USA.

Piero G. Delprete, Institute of Systematic Botany, The New York Botanical Garden, Bronx, NY 10458-5126, USA.

Ernest T. DeMarie, c/o Christopher Columbus High School, Science Dept., 925 Astor Ave., Bronx, NY 10469-5126, USA.

Miriam L. Denham, Gesneriad Gardens, 10353 N. 65th Street, Longmont, CO 80503-9018, USA.

STEFAN DRESSLER, Forschungsinstitut Senckenberg, Senckenberganlage 25, D-60325 Frankfurt/M, Germany.

UNO ELIASSON, Department of Evolutionary Botany, Botanical Institute, Göteborg University, Box 461, SE 405 30 Göteborg, Sweden.

ROGER ERIKSSON, Botanical Institute, Göteborg University, Box 461, SE 405 30 Göteborg, Sweden.

ROBERT B. FADEN, United States National Herbarium, Botany Department, MRC-166, P.O. Box 37012, Smithsonian Institution, Washington, D.C. 20013-7012, USA.

CHRISTIAN FEUILLET, United States National Herbarium, Botany Department, MRC-166, P.O. Box 37012, Smithsonian Institution, Washington, D.C. 20013-7012, USA.

BEAT FISCHER, BAB—Büro für Angewandte Biologie, Depotstrasse 28, 3012, Bern, Switzerland.

ENRIQUE FORERO, Instituto de Ciencias Naturales, Facultad de Ciencias, Universidad Nacional de Colombia, Apartado 7495, Santafé de Bogotá, D.C., Colombia.

HARALD FÖRTHER, Ludwig-Maximilians-Universität, Institut für Systematische Botanik, Menziger Straße 67, D-80638, München, Germany.

DAWN FRAME, University Herbaria, University of California, Berkeley, 1001 Valley Life Science Building #2465, Berkeley, CA 94720-2465, USA & Herbarium, Institut de Botanique, 163, rue A. Broussonet, 34090 Montpellier, France.

PETER W. FRITSCH, Department of Botany, California Academy of Sciences, Golden Gate Park, San Francisco, CA 94118-4599, USA.

DAVID FRODIN, Herbarium, Royal Botanic Gardens, Kew, Richmond, Surrey TW9 3AE, England, U.K.

PAUL A. FRYXELL, Section of Integrative Biology, SBS, Biological Sciences Bldg., Room 311, University of Texas at Austin, Austin, TX 78712-1104, USA.

MARIA A. GANDOLFO, L. H. Bailey Hortorium, 462 Mann Library, Cornell University, Ithaca, NY 14853-0001, USA.

KARLA GENGLER-NOWAK, Department of Biology, Denison University, Granville, OH 43023-1359, USA.

FAVIO GONZÁLEZ, Instituto de Ciencias Naturales, Facultad de Ciencias, Universidad Nacional de Colombia, Apartado Aéreo 7495, Bogotá, Colombia.

CAROL GRACIE, Institute of Systematic Botany, The New York Botanical Garden, Bronx, NY 10458-5126, USA.

SHIRLEY A. GRAHAM, Department of Biological Sciences, Kent State University, Kent, Ohio 44242-0001, USA.

PETER GREEN, Herbarium, Royal Botanic Gardens, Kew, Richmond, Surrey TW9 3AB, England, U.K.

CLAES GUSTAFSSON, Botanical Institute, Göteborg University, P.O. Box 461, S-405 30 Göteborg, Sweden.

MATS H. G. GUSTAFSSON, Department of Systematic Botany, Institute of Biological Sciences, University of Aarhus, Nordlandsvej 68, 8240 Risskov, Denmark.

BARRY E. HAMMEL, Herbarium, Missouri Botanical Garden, P.O. Box 299, St. Louis, MO 63166-0299, USA.

CHRISTOPHER R. HARDY, Institute for Systematic Botany, Zollikerstrasse 107, CH 8008 Zurich, Switzerland.

ROBERT R. HAYNES, Director of the Herbarium, Box 870345, The University of Alabama, Tuscaloosa, AL 35487-0001, USA.

SCOTT V. HEALD, Institute of Systematic Botany, The New York Botanical Garden, Bronx, NY 10458-5126, USA.

ANDREW HENDERSON, Institute of Systematic Botany, The New York Botanical Garden, Bronx, NY 10458-5126, USA.

PAUL HIEPKO, Botanisches Museum Berlin—Dahlem (B), D-14191 Berlin, Germany.

HARTMUT H. HILGER, Freie Universität Berlin, Institut für Biologie, Systematische Botanik und Pflanzengeographie, Altensteinstraße 6, D-14195 Berlin, Germany.

PETER C. HOCH, Herbarium, Missouri Botanical Garden, P.O. Box 299, St. Louis, MO 63166-0299, USA.

MARIA HOFMANN, Freie Universität Berlin, FB 23, WE 2, Altensteinstraße 6, D-14195 Berlin, Germany.

NOEL HOLMGREN, Institute of Systematic Botany, The New York Botanical Garden, Bronx, NY 10458-5126, USA.

BRUCE K. HOLST, Marie Selby Botanical Gardens, 811 South Palm Avenue, Sarasota, Florida, 34236-7726, USA.

LARRY HUFFORD, Marion Ownbey Herbarium, Washington State University, P.O. Box 644238, Pullman, WA 99164-4238, USA.

JACQUELYN KALLUNKI, Institute of Systematic Botany, The New York Botanical Garden, Bronx, NY 10458-5126, USA.

MARIA LÚCIA KAWASAKI, Department of Botany, The Field Museum, 1400 S. Lakeshore Drive, Chicago, IL 60605-2496, USA.

CAROL ANN KEARNS, Environmental, Population, and Organismic Biology and Baker Residential Academic Program, UCB 176, University of Colorado, Boulder, CO 80309-0001, USA.

EGON KÖHLER, Institut für Biologie, Spezielle Botanik und Arboretum, Humboldt-University Späthstrasse 80/81, D-12437, Berlin, Germany.

ROGIER DE KOK, Centre for Plant Biodiversity Research, Australian National Herbarium, C.S.I.R.O. Plant Industry, GPO Box 1600, Canberra ACT 2601, Australia.

KLAUS KUBITZKI, Institut für Allgemeine Botanik, Ohnhorststraße 18, 22609 Hamburg, Germany.

JOB KUIJT, Department of Biology, University of Victoria, Victoria, BC, Canada V8W 3N5.

THOMAS G. LAMMERS, University of Wisconsin, Oshkosh, 800 Algoma Boulevard, Oshkosh, WI 54901-3551, USA.

DAVID L. LENTZ, Chicago Botanic Garden, 1000 Lake Cook Road, Glencoe, IL 60022-1168, USA.

DONALD H. LES, Department of Ecology and Evolutionary Biology, University of Connecticut, U-43, Storrs, CT 06269-3043, USA.

AMY LITT, 706 Kline Biology Tower, Department of Molecular, Cellular & Developmental Biology, Yale University, P.O. Box 208103, New Haven, CT 06520-6614, USA.

LÚCIA LOHMANN, Herbarium, Missouri Botanical Garden, P.O. Box 299, St. Louis, MO 63166-0299, USA.

PIERRE-ANDRÉ LOIZEAU, Conservatoire et Jardin Botaniques

de la Ville de Genève, ch. de l'Impératrice 1, Case postale 60, CH-1292, Chambésy/Genève, Switzerland.

JULIO ANTONIO LOMBARDI, Departamento de Botânica, Instituto de Ciências Biológicas, Universidade Federal de Minas Gerais, Avenida Antônio Carlos 6627, 31270-110 Belo Horizonte—MG, Brazil.

JIM LUTEYN, Institute of Systematic Botany, The New York Botanical Garden, Bronx, NY 10458-5126, USA.

HARRY E. LUTHER, Marie Selby Botanical Gardens, 811 South Palm Avenue, Sarasota, Florida, 34236-7726, USA.

PAUL J. M. MAAS, Herbarium, Inst. of Systematic Botany, State University of Utrecht, Postbus 80102, 3508 TC Utrecht, The Netherlands.

SANTIAGO MADRIÑÁN, Dept. Ciencias Biológicas, Universidad de los Andes, Apdo. Aéreo 4976, Santafé de Bogotá, D.C., Colombia.

ALAN W. MEEROW, United States Department of Agriculture, Agricultural Research Service, National Germplasm Repository, 13601 Old Cutler Road, Miami, FL 33158-1334, USA.

RENATO DE, MELLO-SILVA, Instituto de Biociências, Universidade de São Paulo, Caixa Postal 11461, 05422-970 São Paulo SP, Brazil.

JOHN D. MITCHELL, Institute of Systematic Botany, The New York Botanical Garden, Bronx, NY 10458-5126, USA.

LUIS EDUARDO MORA-OSEJO, Academia Colombiana de Ciencias Exactas, Físicas y Naturales Carrera 3a A No. 17-34 Piso 3 & deg, Bogotá, D.E., Colombia.

SCOTT A. MORI, Institute of Systematic Botany, The New York Botanical Garden, Bronx, NY 10458-5126, USA.

MARK E. MORT, Department of Ecology and Evolutionary Biology, Museum of Natural History/Biodiversity, University of Kansas, Lawrence, KS 66045-0001, USA.

CYNTHIA MORTON, Herbarium, Section of Botany, Carnegie Museum of Natural History, 4400 Forbes Avenue, Pittsburgh, PA 15213-4080, USA.

LYTTON JOHN MUSSELMAN, Department of Biological Sciences, Old Dominion University, 45th Street, Norfolk, VA 23529-0266, USA.

MICHAEL NEE, Institute of Systematic Botany, The New York Botanical Garden, Bronx, NY 10458-5126, USA.

LORIN I. NEVLING, JR., Illinois Natural History Survey, 607 East Peabody Drive, Champaign, IL 61820-6917, USA.

KEVIN C. NIXON, Herbarium, L. H. Bailey Hortorium, 462 Mann Library, Cornell University, Ithaca, NY 14853-4301, USA.

ELAINE M. NORMAN, Herbarium, Biology Department, Stetson University, P.O. Box 8261, DeLand, FL 32720-3761, USA.

ROBERT ORNDUFF† (1932–2000). Formerly: University Herbarium, University of California, Berkeley, CA 94720-2465, USA.

DONALD J. PADGETT, Department of Biological Sciences, Bridgewater State College, Bridgewater, MA 02325, USA.

TERENCE D. PENNINGTON, Herbarium, Royal Botanic Gardens, Kew, Richmond, Surrey TW9 3AE, England, U.K.

CLAES PERSSON, Botanical Institute, Göteborg University, P.O. Box 461, S-405 30 Göteborg, Sweden.

C. THOMAS PHILBRICK, Department of Biology, Western Connecticut State University, Danbury, CT 06810-6826, USA.

DUNCAN M. PORTER, Massey Herbarium, Biology Department, Virginia Polytechnic Institute and State University, Blacksburg, VA 24061-0406, USA.

GHILLEAN T. PRANCE, The Old Vicarage, Silver Street, Lyme Regis, Dorset DT7 3HS, England, U.K.

JOHN PRUSKI, Herbarium, Missouri Botanical Garden, P.O. Box 299, St. Louis, MO 63166-0299, USA.

QI LIN, Herbarium (PE), Institute of Botany, Chinese Academy of Sciences, 20 Nanxincun, Xiangshan, Beijing 100093, P.R., China.

RICHARD RABELER, University of Michigan, 3600 Varsity Drive, Ann Arbor, MI, 48108-2287, USA.

HEIMO RAINER, Institut für Botanik, Universität Wien, Rennweg 14, Vienna, Austria A-1030.

NELSON RAMÍREZ, Centro de Biología Tropical, Universidad Central de Venezuela, Aptdo. 20513, San Martín, Caracas, Venezuela.

ALESSANDRO RAPINI, Pós-Graduação de Botânica, Departamento de Ciências Biológicas, Universidade Estadual de Feira de Santana, Av. Universitária s/n, CEP 44031-460, Feira de Santana, Bahia, Brazil.

SUSANNE S. RENNER, Herbarium, Missouri Botanical Garden, P.O. Box 299, St. Louis, MO 63166-0299, USA. & Dept. of Biology, University of Missouri, St. Louis, Natural Bridge Road 8001, St. Louis, MO 63121-4499, USA.

ANDREW S. ROBERTS, The New York Botanical Garden, Bronx, NY 10458-5126, USA.

PAULA RUDALL, Royal Botanic Gardens, Kew, Richmond, Surrey TW9 3AE, England, U.K.

DANIEL SABATIER, İRD (Institut de Recherche pour le Développement), UMR AMAP, Boulevard de la Lironde, TA 40/PS2, 34398 Montepellier cédex 5, France.

GISELA SANCHO, División Plantas Vasculares, Museo de La Plata, Paseo del Bosque s/n, La Plata, 1900, Buenos Aires, Argentina.

CLAUDE SASTRE, Herbier, Laboratoire de Phanérogamie, Museum National d'Histoire Naturelle, 16 rue Buffon, F-75005 Paris, France.

JULIO SCHNEIDER, Research Institute Senckenberg and J.W. Goethe-University, Senckenberganlage 25, D-60325 Frankfurt/Main, Germany.

DAVID S. SEIGLER, Herbarium, Plant Biology Department, University of Illinois, 505 South Goodwin Ave., Urbana, IL 61801-3795, USA.

BERYL B. SIMPSON, Section of Integrative Biology, University of Texas, Austin, TX 78712-1104, USA.

NATHAN SMITH, Institute of Systematic Botany, The New York Botanical Garden, Bronx, NY 10458-5126, USA.

DJAJA DJENDOEL SOEJARTO, PCRPS, College of Pharmacy, University of Illinois at Chicago, 833 S. Wood Street, Chicago, IL 60612-7229, USA. & Botany Department, The

Field Museum, 1400 S. Lakeshore Drive, Chicago, IL 60605-2496, USA.

Douglas E. Soltis, Department of Botany, University of Florida, Gainesville, FL 32611-7800, USA.

Cynthia Sothers, Herbarium, Royal Botanic Gardens, Kew, Richmond, Surrey TW9, 3AB, England, U.K.

Rodolphe Spichiger, Herbarium, Conservatoire et Jardin botaniques de la Ville de Genève, Chemin de l-Impératrice 1 Case postale 60, CH-1292 Chambésy/Genève, Switzerland.

Clive A. Stace, Department of Biology, University of Leicester, Leicester LE1 7RH, U.K.

Bertil Ståhl, Gotland University, SE-62157 Visby, Sweden.

Rodrigo Duno de Stefano, Real Jardín Botánico de Madrid-CSIC, Plaza de Murillo 2, Madrid, Spain 28014.

Dennis Wm. Stevenson, The New York Botanical Garden, Bronx, NY 10458-5126, USA.

Janice Wassmer Stevenson, Institute of Economic Botany, The New York Botanical Garden, Bronx, NY 10458-5126, USA.

Lena Struwe, Rutgers University, Cook College, New Brunswick, NJ 08901-8551, USA.

Mark Tebbitt, Brooklyn Botanical Garden, 1000 Washington Avenue, Brooklyn, NY 11224-1099, USA.

Oswaldo Téllez-Valdés, Herbario Nacional, Departemento de Botánica, Instituto de Biología, UNAM, Apdo. Postal 70-367, C.P. 04510, México.

Wm. Wayt Thomas, Institute of Systematic Botany, The New York Botanical Garden, Bronx, NY 10458-5126, USA.

Carol Todzia, Plant Resources Center, Department of Botany, University of Texas at Austin, Austin, TX 78713-7640, USA.

Benjamin M. Torke, Missouri Botanical Garden, P.O. Box 299, St. Louis, MO 63166-0299, USA.

Gordon Tucker, Department of Botany, Eastern Illinois University, Charleston, IL 61920-3099, USA.

Dieter Wasshausen, United States National Herbarium, Botany Department, MRC-166, P.O. Box 37012, Smithsonian Institution, Washington, D.C. 20013-7012, USA.

Grady Webster, Herbarium, Botany Department, University of California, Davis, CA 95616-8500, USA.

Maximilian Weigend, Institut für Biologie, Systematische Botanik und Pflanzengeographie der Freie Universität Berlin, Altensteinstraße 6, D-14195 Berlin, Germany.

Peter H. Weston, Royal Botanic Gardens Sydney, Mrs. Macquarie's Road, Sydney, New South Wales 2000, Australia.

Pam White, Institute of Systematic Botany, The New York Botanical Garden, Bronx, NY 10458-5126, USA.

Dieter Wilken, Santa Barbara Botanic Garden, 1212 Mission Canyon Road, Santa Barbara, CA 93105-2126, USA.

Thomas K. Wilson, Herbarium, Botany Department, Miami University, 79 Upham Hall, Oxford, OH 45056-3653, USA.

George Yatskievych, Herbarium, Missouri Botanical Garden, P.O. Box 299, St. Louis, MO 63166-0299, USA.

Thomas A. Zanoni, Institute of Systematic Botany, The New York Botanical Garden, Bronx, NY 10458-5126, USA.

Georg Zizka, Research Institute Senckenberg and J.W. Goethe-University, Senckenberganlage 25, D-60325 Frankfurt/Main, Germany.

ACKNOWLEDGMENTS

WE ARE GRATEFUL to the Beneficia Foundation and the Samuel Freeman Charitable Trust for their financial contributions to this project.

This book would not have been possible without the contributions of the many botanists who prepared the family treatments, and we sincerely thank them for their efforts. In addition, we are grateful to Eileen Schofield for her numerous editorial contributions and Myrna Alvarez, Michael Balick, David Barrington, Paul Berry, Douglas Daly, Piero Delprete, Priscilla Fawcett, Sandi Frank, Carol Gracie, Ray Harley, John Janovec, Gregory Long, Paul J. M. Maas, John D. Mitchell, William S. Moye, Michael Nee, Amanda Neill, Michael Sundue, Wm. Wayt Thomas, Mathias Tobler, and P. Barry Tomlinson for their numerous contributions. We are grateful for the helpful comments of the reviewers and our Princeton University Press editors, especially Robert Kirk, Dale Cotton, and Sandra L. Sherman, who so patiently guided us through this project.

We thank those who provided images. They are credited in the figure and plate captions, but we wish to give special recognition to Bobbi Angell for most of the line art, Carol Gracie for the majority of the color photos, and Michael Rothman for the cover art. In addition, we thank the journals in which many of the images were originally published for allowing us to reuse them. The journals are credited in the captions. The full names of those who contributed color images are provided here: Alberto Areces, Joseph Beitel, Piero Delprete, Uno Eliasson, Karla Gengler-Nowak, Guenter Gerlach, Lawrence Gilbert, Carol Gracie, Andreas Gröger, Marion Jansen-Jacobs, Jacquelyn Kallunki, Tatyana Lobova, James L. Luteyn, Paul J. M. Maas, John D. Michell, Scott Mori, Michael Nee, John F. Pruski, Susanne Renner, Daniel Sabatier, Rudolf Schmid, Nathan Smith, Lena Struwe, Wm. Wayt Thomas, Carol Todzia, Lubbert Westra, George Yatskievych, Rodrigo Bernal, Lisa Campbell, Instituto Nacional de Pesquisas da Amazônia/Department for International Development (INPA/DFID), Dennis Wm. Stevenson, and Michael Sundue.

We are grateful to Anne and Tom Hubbard for their support of systematic botany at The New York Botanical Garden.

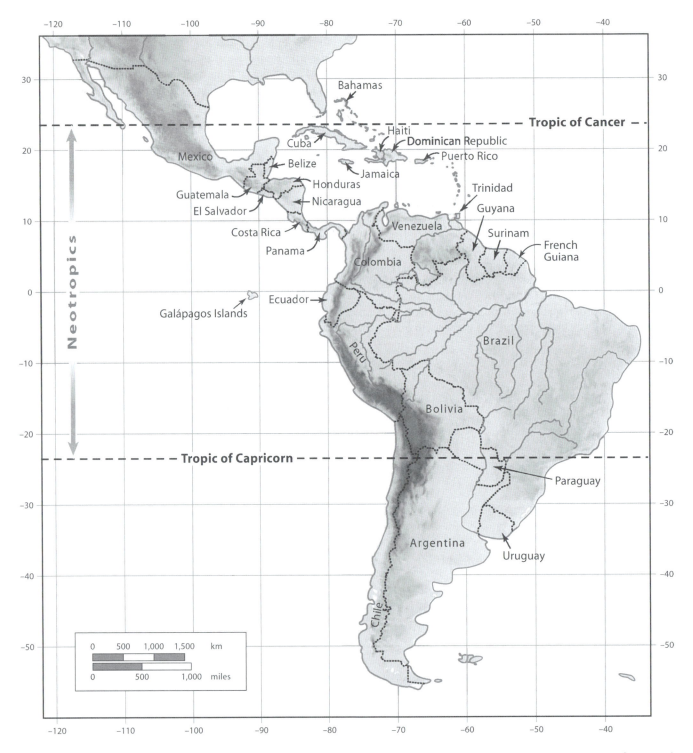

Map illustrating the boundaries of the neotropics and countries within this region. The neotropics is a region delimited by the tropics of Cancer and Capricorn, and is that part of the Western Hemisphere between 23°27′N and 23°27′S.

INTRODUCTION

TROPICAL AMERICA (or neotropics) is home to approximately 30 percent of the known flowering plant genera and species on Earth (table 1). This region, delimited by the tropics of Cancer and Capricorn, is that part of the Western Hemisphere between 23°27'N and 23°27'S. Extending over much of the Americas, the neotropics is composed of many habitats, ranging from the deserts of Mexico, to the vast lowland rain forests of Amazonia, to the cloud forests and *páramos* of the Andes. Much of the plant and habitat diversity is due to the incredible variation in elevation and rainfall. These factors, combined with millions of years of geological change, have led to an infinite number of microclimates and habitats such as the *tepuis*, where many genera and species are endemic (e.g., *Heliamphora* of the Sarraceniaceae and *Tepuianthus auyantepuianthus* of the Tepuianthaceae). Other families represented in this region are pantropical (e.g., Lecythidaceae and Sapotaceae), with genera and species occurring throughout the world but only in tropical regions, and numerous families are cosmopolitan or nearly so (e.g., Asteraceae and Orchidaceae), with taxa occurring throughout most of the world.

Botanists can only estimate the number of families, genera, and species that occur within the neotropics because many, if not most, of the taxa in this region have not been adequately studied. As a result, there are many species that still remain to be discovered and named and countless species that have not been studied for many of their taxonomic and ecological attributes, especially their molecular constitution.

Agreement on plant classification at all taxonomic levels is often controversial and, because of advances in the use of molecular data and tools for phylogenetic analysis, many changes in long-standing systems of classification are being proposed. Although these new concepts are summarized by the Angiosperm Phylogeny Group (1998) and Judd et al. (2002), there is still a long way to go before the new data can be integrated into a comprehensive and relatively stable system for the classification of the flowering plants. Although we have elected to base the *Flowering Plants of the Neotropics* on the Cronquist (1981) system for the dicots and the Dahlgren et al. (1985) system for the monocots, the concepts of the families in these systems have often been modified by the authors of the family treatments (see discussion on family classification, p. xxi).

The estimates of species numbers we provide in our tables vary according to the system of classification and the philosophy of taxonomic specialists. Moreover, for some large and complex families, such as the Fabaceae *sensu lato* and the Orchidaceae, it is difficult to even estimate the number of Neotropical taxa.

Many of the largest flowering plant families found in tropical America are also the largest flowering plant families on Earth (e.g., Asteraceae, Orchidaceae, Poaceae, Fabaceae *sensu lato*, and Rubiacae; table 2). Other families, such as the Aizoaceae and Brassicacae, are large families but do not have a strong presence in the American Tropics (table 3). Of the 284 native families recognized in this book, 42 are endemic to regions within the Western Hemisphere (tables 4, 5), 11 are nearly endemic to the neotropics (table 6), and 25

Table 1. Family, genus, and species diversity for the world and the neotropics. (*) Approximation excludes genera and/or species counts for the Orchidaceae, Lamiaceae, and Smilacaceae. Western Hemisphere counts were used for Agavaceae, Crassulaceae, Fabaceae, Gesneriaceae, Linaceae, Malpighiaceae, Myrtaceae, Poaceae, and Sapindaceae. (—) Approximation not available. FPN = this book.

	Worldwide angiosperm approximation (Thorne, 2001)	Worldwide angiosperm approximation (Takhtajan, 1997)	Worldwide angiosperm approximation (Cronquist, 1981)	Worldwide angiosperm approximation (Dahlgren et al., 1985)	Worldwide angiosperm approximation for families treated in FPN	Neotropical angiosperm approximation (FPN) (native taxa only)
Angiosperm families	490	591	383	—	—	284
Dicot families	376	458	318	—	—	225
Monocot families	114	133	65	101	—	59
Angiosperm genera	13,678	13,300	—	—	12,600	4,300 *
Angiosperm species	257,400	260,000	215,000	—	260,000	78,800 *
Dicot genera	10,900	10,500	—	—	10,350	3,500 *
Monocot genera	2,778	3,000	—	—	2,450	800 *
Dicot species	ca. 199,500	195,000	165,000	—	204,000	64,300 *
Monocot species	57,900	65,000	50,000	—	55,300	14,300

Table 2. Worldwide families well represented in the neotropics. Table ordered from the family with the largest number of tropical American genera to the smallest number of tropical American genera. (*) Numbers are for Western Hemisphere. (—) Approximation not available.

Family	Approximate # of genera worldwide	Approximate # of species worldwide	Approximate # of genera in tropical America	Approximate # of species in tropical America
ASTERACEAE	1,535	23,000–32,000	580	8,040
ORCHIDACEAE	700	20,000	—	—
POACEAE	650	10,000	375 *	3,300 *
FABACEAE *sensu lato*	650–700	18,000	272 *	6,700 *
RUBIACEAE	650	13,000	217	5,000
EUPHORBIACEAE	300	9,000	105	1,800
MELASTOMATACEAE	155	4,500	100	3,000
BIGNONIACEAE	120	800	80	600
ARECACEAE	189	2,000	67	550
SOLANACEAE	95	2,200	63	1,575
MALPIGHIACEAE	65	1,260	50 *	1,110 *
CYPERACEAE	60	5,300	40	1,000
ARACEAE	105	3,200	39	2,372
LAURACEAE	52	2,750	27	1,000
NYCTAGINACEAE	32	400	23	180
PODOSTEMACEAE	48	270	19	165
LYTHRACEAE	31	600	16–19	384
OCHNACEAE	30	500	16	300
LOASACEAE	20	330	15	180
PHYTOLACCACEAE	17	72	14	64
MARANTACEAE	31	550	13	350
POLYGALACEAE	22	950–1,000	11	400
LECYTHIDACEAE	20	292	10	204
CHRYSOBALANACEAE	18	521	8	417
XYRIDACEAE	5	375	5	250
PASSIFLORACEAE	18	700	4	500
PIPERACEAE	10	1,500–2,000	4	1,000
TURNERACEAE	10	190	4	170
VELLOZIACEAE	7	250	4	220
CECROPIACEAE	6	170	3	132
COSTACEAE	4	100–120	3	63
LENTIBULARIACEAE	3	280	3	129

are fully endemic to the neotropics (table 4). These 25 endemic families represent almost 9 percent of the angiosperm families native to tropical America but less than 0.75 percent of the species estimated to occur in the region. An aspect of these endemic families is the range in number of genera and species that occur among them. The two largest families, the Cyclanthaceae and Marcgraviaceae, account for nearly half of the species of all of the endemic families. Sixteen (64%) of these endemic families are monogeneric, and five families are monotypic. Thus, the relatively high percentage of endemic families (ca. 9%) probably reflects differences in opinion of what constitutes a family (e.g., the relatively speciose Cyclanthaceae and Marcgraviaceae vs. segregate families such as the Pterostemonaceae and Alzateaceae with only one to two species). Nevertheless, within the neotropics there are numerous endemic genera and species that sometimes represent many of the taxa in a family (e.g., Lecythidoideae of the Lecythidaceae); therefore, at the species level, endemism in tropical America is thought to be considerable, having been estimated by Heywood and Davis (1997) to be greater than 50 percent.

Table 3. Examples of worldwide families not well represented in the neotropics. Families in alphabetical order.

Family	Approximate # of genera worldwide	Approximate # of species worldwide	Approximate # of genera in tropical America	Approximate # of species in tropical America
AIZOACEAE	127	2,500	7	20
BRASSICACEAE	330	3,400	22–34	175–200
CORNACEAE	11	100	1	4
DIPTEROCARPACEAE	17	500	2	2
HAMAMELIDACEAE	30	100	3	6
PROTEACEAE	79	1,700	6	86
SAXIFRAGACEAE	30	500	3	7
ZINGIBERACEAE	46	1,300	1–5	55

Table 4. Families endemic to the neotropics. Table ordered from the family with the largest number of genera to the smallest number of genera.

Family	Approximate # of genera	Approximate # of species	Family	Approximate # of genera	Approximate # of species
CYCLANTHACEAE	12	180	EUPHRONIACEAE	1	3
MARCGRAVIACEAE	7	130	LISSOCARPACEAE	1	5
THEOPHRASTACEAE	6	95	PELLICIERACEAEE	1	1
QUIINACEAE	4	51	PHYLLONOMACEAE	1	4
EREMOLEPIDACEAE	3	12	PLOCOSPERMATACEAE	1	1
MUNTINGIACEAE	2–3	3	PTEROSTEMONACEAE	1	2
CARYOCARACEAE	2	25	RHABDODENDRACEAE	1	3
PERIDISCACEAE	2	2	TEPUIANTHACEAE	1	6
PICRAMNIACEAE	2	46	TICODENDRACEAE	1	1
ALZATEACEAE	1	1	TOVARIACEAE	1	2
BRUNELLIACEAE	1	65	CANNACEAE	1	10
COLUMELLIACEAE	1	4	THURNIACEAE	1	3
DUCKEODENDRACEAE	1	1			

Table 5. Neotropical families, with extra-Neotropical taxa, endemic to the Western Hemisphere. (*) Recent studies suggest taxa should not be recognized as separate families. Table ordered from the family with the largest number of tropical American genera to the smallest number of tropical American genera.

Family	Approximate # of genera worldwide	Approximate # of species worldwide	Approximate # of genera in tropical America	Approximate # of species in tropical America
AGAVACEAE	8	300	8	300
CALYCERACEAE	6	60	2	18
NOLINACEAE*	4	50	4	50
ALSTROEMERIACEAE	3	280	3	200
MARTYNIACEAE	3	17	3	17
TROPAEOLACEAE	3	89	1	60
CYRILLACEAE	3	14	2	13
LACISTEMATACEAE	2	14	2	14
ACHATOCARPACEAE	2	6	1	5
LENNOACEAE	2	4	1	1
DESFONTAINIACEAE	1	1	1	1
FOUQUIERIACEAE	1	11	1	8
KRAMERIACEAE	1	18	1	12
LEPUROPETALACEAE	1	1	1	1
MALESHERBIACEAE	1	24	1	13
NOLANACEAE*	1	18	1	15
SETCHELLANTHACEAE	1	1	1	1

Table 6. Examples of Neotropical families with only a few extra-American taxa. Table ordered from the family with the largest number of tropical American genera to the smallest number of tropical American genera.

Family	Approximate # of genera worldwide	Approximate # of species worldwide	Approximate # of genera in tropical America	Approximate # of species in tropical America
BROMELIACEAE	56	2,900	56	2,899
CACTACEAE	125	1,900	100	1,300
RAPATEACEAE	16	80	15	79
HUMIRIACEAE	8	65	8	64
VELLOZIACEAE	7	250	4	220
VOCHYSIACEAE	7	200	5	197
CARICACEAE	4	33	3	31
LEPIDOBOTRYACEAE	2	2	1	1
MAYACACEAE	1	4–10	1	3–9
GARRYACEAE	1	14	1	12
HELICONIACEAE	1	200	1	200

EDITORS' NOTE

THE dicotyledons and monocotyledons are grouped separately with the former coming before the latter (Cronquist, 1981), but this placement should not be interpreted as indicating evolutionary relationships. The monocots are hypothesized to be monophyletic and the dicots paraphyletic; yet, the separation of the monocots from the remainder of the flowering plant families makes identification of Neotropical plants to family a great deal easier.

There currently are many changes in our previous understanding of flowering plant relationships. Families once thought to be related—for example the Lecythidaceae and Dilleniaceae or the Vochysiaceae and Polygalaceae—are no longer believed to be related. The likelihood that more changes are to follow was the primary reason that we elected to use an alphabetical rather than a phylogenetic arrangement of the families. An alphabetical listing has the disadvantage of separating closely related families, but the very distinct advantage of allowing one to find a plant family without having knowledge of hypothetical relationships such as those outlined in Appendices I, II, and IV.

Each family treatment is divided into a **Bullet list; Numbers of genera and species; Distribution and habitat; Family classification; Features of the family; Natural history; Economic uses;** and **References**. The references include literature related to the family and usually are not repeated in the "Literature Cited" at the end of the book unless they are cited in the text. General references that were useful for providing information for numerous family treatments are mentioned in the discussions of the sections below. The complete reference for these citations can be found in the "Literature Cited." Because the literature on most families is so extensive, we have limited the references to those that will lead the reader to the more detailed and technical literature.

Section 1: Bullet List

The bullet list provides characters useful for identification of the families. Most of the features are based on Neotropical taxa; however, characters for naturalized taxa are included if they are frequently encountered in the neotropics.

As an aid to the initial identification of plant families, we provide dichotomous keys that lead to a single plant family or group of plant families (Appendix V). Once the number of families of an unknown plant has been limited through use of the aids to identification, the bullet lists should be consulted to confirm or further identify an unknown plant to family.

General references useful for providing additional character information used in the identification of Neotropical plant families are: GENTRY 1993; KELLER 1996; MORI et al. 1997, 2002; RIBEIRO et al. 1999.

Section 2: Numbers of Genera and Species

This section contains both worldwide and Neotropical counts for genera and species. Species numbers for the largest and, in some cases, for all of the genera found in the world and in tropical America are provided. The numbers of genera and species in many families are still not known, so this section may include only approximations. For some families, approximations of the number of taxa in the neotropics were not possible, and, in those cases, genus and/or species numbers for the Western Hemisphere or for specific regions in the neotropics are given.

General references useful for establishing the number of taxa in the neotropics are: MAAS AND WESTRA 1998; MABBERLEY 1993; THE PLANT NAMES PROJECT 1999; THORNE 1992, 2001; TROPICOS (Missouri Botanical Garden); WIELGORSKAYA AND TAKHTAJAN 1995; and WILLIS 1973.

Section 3: Distribution and Habitat

In this section, information on distribution is usually followed by a discussion of habitat. Most treatments begin with a general statement on worldwide distribution followed by discussions of the tropical American ranges of the family, genera, and sometimes species. Treatments of large families do not include information for all genera, but usually discuss the larger ones.

General references useful for understanding the distribution and habitat of Neotropical plants are: BROWN AND LOMOLINO 1998; MABBERLEY 1993; THORNE 1992, 2001; WIELGORSKAYA AND TAKHTAJAN 1995; and WILLIS 1973.

Section 4: Family Classification

This section covers information on familial and intrafamilial classification. Systematic botany is assimilating data derived from molecular biology and phylogenetic analyses and comprehensive classification systems including these data have not been developed fully for Neotropical angiosperm families. As in any scientific endeavor, classifications change through time as a result of the acquisition and application of new knowledge. Plant families are constructed based upon an understanding of genealogical lineages, and, as such, they are hypotheses of relationships. Because there is a constant search for new knowledge that allows testing of hypotheses, changes in classifications are often dictated by new information.

Flowering Plants of the Neotropics generally follows the systems of Cronquist (1981) and Dahlgren et al. (1985). In some instances, our authors deviate from them by splitting (e.g., Desfontainiaceae and Gelsemiaceae from Loganiaceae *sensu* Cronquist) or lumping (e.g., Apocynaceae and Asclepiadaceae *sensu* Cronquist) taxa. These and similar changes are discussed in this section and listed in Appendices I and

II. We include a summary of the major Neotropical families covered in Judd et. al. 2002 and have indicated where the tropical American plant families are placed according to them (Appendix III). We also have incorporated comments into the family treatments that reflect the most current information covered in Judd et al. 2002.

General references useful for understanding flowering plant relationships are: ANGIOSPERM PHYLOGENY GROUP 1998; CHASE et al. 1993, 1995, 2000; CLIFFORD AND YEO 1985; CRONQUIST 1981, 1988; DAHLGREN 1980; DAHLGREN et al. 1985; DOYLE et al. 1994; EHRENDORFER et al. 1968; ENDRESS 1994, 1995; HUTCHINSON 1926, 1959, 1967, 1973, 1980, 1993; JUDD et al. 1994, 2002; MABBERLEY 1993; RUDALL et al. 1995; SAVOLAINEN et al. 2000a, 2000b; SOLTIS et al. 2000; STEVENSON AND LOCONTE 1995; STEVENS 2001 onwards; TAKHTAJAN 1980, 1997; THORNE 1992, 2001; WATSON AND DALLWITZ 1992 onwards; and WIELGORSKAYA AND TAKHTAJAN 1995.

Section 5: Features of the Family

This section provides a technical description of the important morphological characters of the flowering plant families of the neotropics based on native and naturalized taxa and always includes information on habit, leaves, inflorescences, flowers, fruits, and usually seeds. Additional information is placed at the end of this section. Because many authors contributed to this book, some inconsistencies in terminology and formatting occur among sections of different families. For example, both hair and trichome are used to describe the indumentum; however, use is consistent within each family, and both terms are defined in the glossary.

References in which technical descriptions and morphological features used to describe Neotropical plant families can be found are: BELL 1991; ENDRESS 1994; ESAU 1977; FRODIN 2001; GENTRY 1993; GIFFORD AND FOSTER 1989; HEYWOOD 1993; KELLER 1996; KUBITZKI 1998a, 1998b; KUBITZKI et al. 1993; KUBITZKI AND BAYER 2003; KUIJT 1969; MAAS AND WESTRA 1998; and WEBERLING 1981.

Section 6: Natural History

This section provides information about the pollinators and dispersers of species of the family. For the most part, the information applies to Neotropical taxa but, for some families, descriptions of pollination and dispersal from outside the neotropics are included because this information may provide clues to pollination and dispersal in the taxa of the neotropics. Usually only the common names of pollinators and dispersers are provided, but occasionally technical terms are used and defined in the glossary. Other ecological information about a family, such as special adaptations of species to survive extreme environmental conditions, is sometimes provided.

General references useful for determining the pollinators and dispersers of Neotropical plants are: FAEGRI AND PIJL 1979; PIJL 1982; PROCTOR et al. 1996; RIDLEY 1930; ROOSMALEN 1985; and VOGEL 1968, 1969.

Section 7: Economic Uses

This section provides information about the major economic uses of each family from a worldwide perspective, but with an emphasis on the economically important plants of the neotropics. We elected to include information from outside of the neotropics because the history of economically important plants often includes their movement from one region into another with ecologically similar conditions. The introduction of plants often leads to greater productivity in the area of the introduction because natural diseases and predators have been left behind. Examples—such as coffee, a native of Ethiopia, in Brazil; rubber, a native of the Amazon, in southeast Asia; and the potato, a native of the Andes, in temperate regions throughout the world—are more the rule than the exception. In addition, especially in the search for new medicines, the knowledge that a plant family has economically important species outside of the neotropics may prompt a more careful search for species with similar uses in the neotropics.

General references useful for determining the economic uses of plants are: BALICK AND COX 1996; BERNAL AND CORRERA 1989–1992, 1994, 1998; CORRERA AND BERNAL 1989, 1990, 1992, 1993, 1995; HILL 1937; SCHERY 1972; SIMPSON AND OGORZALY 1995; SMITH et al. 1992; UPHOF 1968; and WIERSEMA AND LEÓN 1999.

Section 8: References

References specific to each family are included at the end of each treatment. However, references with information about numerous families, such as floristic treatments, are not listed.

Abbreviations of journal titles follow Bridson and Smith 1991 and Lawrence et al. 1968, and titles of books follow Stafleu and Cowan 1976–1988 or are spelled out.

Glossary

We include a glossary of terms used in the descriptions of Neotropical flowering plants in this book. Many glossaries are available, but among the most useful are: BORROR 1985; GLEDHILL 2002; HARRIS AND WOOLF HARRIS 1994; HICKEY AND KING 2000; KIGER AND PORTER 2001; LAWRENCE 1951; and STEARN 1992.

Illustrations and Color Images

This book is illustrated by 258 line drawings and 308 color photographs. In the captions of the line drawings, credit is given to the artists and to the original publications in which they were published. If an illustration was published previously, specimen vouchers are not listed, but if it is published herein for the first time, we usually cite the specimens upon which it is based.

DICOTYLEDONS

Traditionally, the dicotyledons have been treated as plants that have: two cotyledons; root systems of a persistent primary root; stems with vascular bundles borne in a ring enclosing a pith; leaves that are usually net-veined; flowers with parts (when of definite number) typically borne in sets of five, less often four, or seldom three (carpels often fewer); and pollen typically triaperatureate, or of triaperatureate-derived types. These general characters (taken from Cronquist, 1988) define the dicotyledons within the Cronquist (1981) angiosperm classification, the base system followed in this book (see appendix I).

Current molecular and morphological studies suggest that the dicotyledons treated in this traditional sense form a paraphyletic group and that many of the characters listed above were present earlier in seed plant evolution (Judd et al., 2002).

ACANTHACEAE (Acanthus Family)

DIETER WASSHAUSEN

Figures 1, 2; Plate 1

- *usually herbs or shrubs*

- *nodes usually swollen in young stems*

- *leaves usually opposite and decussate or sometimes quaternate, simple; cystoliths often present*

- *inflorescences often with leaflike bracts*

- *flowers sympetalous; stamens usually 2 or 4; locules generally 2*

- *fruits usually elastically dehiscing loculicidal capsules*

Numbers of genera and species. Worldwide, the Acanthaceae comprise approximately 240 genera and 3,240 species. In the Western Hemisphere, there are approximately 85 genera and 2,000 known species, with 75 genera and 1,780 species in tropical America. About eight genera, including the two largest, *Justicia* (450–600 species) and *Ruellia* (300 species), are pantropical. Of the remaining 77 genera in the Western Hemisphere, 33 are monotypic and 14 others possess only two or three species each. Genera of Acanthaceae are often distinguished on relatively minor characters such as anther configuration and pollen sculpture, and, therefore, there are numerous taxonomic problems at the generic level. Until these problems are resolved, it is difficult to infer phylogenetic relationships and geographical patterns in the family.

Distribution and habitat. Species of Acanthaceae occur almost exclusively in the Tropics and subtropics with five major centers of diversity and richness. The Indo-Malaysia region is distinguished mainly by numerous taxa of *Strobilanthes* and of the tribe Andrographideae. From this center radiate regions that possess few endemics, so that Japan and China have mostly widely distributed species. In Afghanistan and still farther removed in the Mediterranean region are found only xerophytic taxa (e.g., *Acanthus* with 50 species) and finally, Australia has only 57 native and naturalized species. A second center of diversity, which is at least as rich in taxa as Asia, is tropical Africa and Madagascar. This region possesses a large number of endemic genera.

The remaining three centers of diversity occur in the Western Hemisphere. The Andes of South America are especially rich in Acanthaceae. Examples of genera with extensive species diversity in this region are *Aphelandra* (180 species), *Justicia* (600), *Sanchezia* (50), and *Pachystachys* (13), as well as a number of monotypic genera. The second South American center of diversity is Brazil. Its vast and diverse flora is especially rich in species of *Mendoncia* (85 species) and *Ruellia* sections *Dipteracanthus* and *Physiruellia* (250).

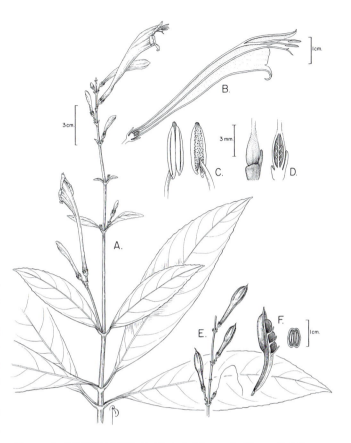

Figure 1. ACANTHACEAE. *Polylychnis fulgens*. **A.** Stem with inflorescences. **B.** Medial section of flower. **C.** Adaxial (left) and abaxial (right) views of anthers. **D.** Lateral view of intact ovary (left) and medial section (right) of ovary; note nectary. **E.** Part of infructescence. **F.** Lateral view of open fruit (left) and transverse section of fruit (right). Reprinted with permission from Mori et al. (2002). Artist: Bobbi Angell.

Genera and species from this center of diversity radiate to the north into the Guianas and to the south into northern Argentina. The third center of diversification in the Western Hemisphere is tropical Mexico and Central America. More than 350 species in 40 genera occur in Mexico alone. Representatives of the tribes Aphelandreae and Odontonemeae reach their highest level of development in this region.

Species of Acanthaceae occur in almost every type of habitat, in forests, swamps, and meadows. Some species are found on rocky outcrops and others in deserts. Above 3,000 meters, the family is found only in habitats that are favorably protected from the cold and that receive sufficient rainfall, such as the eastern slope of the Cordillera in Bolivia.

Family classification. The Acanthaceae are placed in the Scrophulariales by Cronquist. The family has traditionally been divided into four subfamilies, the Mendoncioideae, with two genera and 88 species in tropical western Africa, Madagascar, South America, southern Mexico and Central

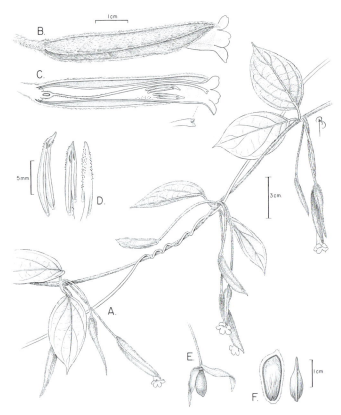

Figure 2. ACANTHACEAE. *Mendoncia hoffmannseggiana.* **A.** Stem with leaves and pendent inflorescences twining around another plant. **B.** Lateral view of flower. **C.** Medial section of flower. **D.** Adaxial (left and center) and abaxial (right) views of anthers. **E.** Lateral view of fruit subtended by two bracteoles. **F.** Medial section of fruit showing seed (left) and seed (right). Reprinted with permission from Mori et al. (2002). Artist: Bobbi Angell.

cystoliths that characterize the Acanthaceae. In the subfamily Nelsonioideae, the retinaculum is less developed, papilliform or lacking, definitely not forming a jaculator, and the cystoliths are absent. This subfamily seems to possess characters that suggest an intermediary link between the Scrophulariaceae and the subfamily Acanthoideae, sometimes leading to its inclusion in the former family. Finally, 93 percent of the species and all but nine of the genera of Acanthaceae belong to the well-marked subfamily Acanthoideae. It is widely accepted by most monographers in the family that this subfamily represents a monophyletic taxon.

Recent molecular studies using parsimony analyses of *ndh*F and *rbc*L sequences have demonstrated that *Elytraria* and *Thunbergia* are successive sister taxa to all Acanthaceae taxa that have retinacula and explosively dehiscent fruits. These studies further demonstrated that taxa with both retinacula and explosively dehiscent fruits can be subdivided further into two monophyletic groups that correspond to taxa with and without cystoliths. Within the group with cystoliths, three putatively monophyletic groups correspond to taxa possessing quincuncial, leftcontor, and ascending-cochleate corolla aestivation patterns.

Another recent study used molecular sequence data from nuclear ribosomal internal transcribed spacers and the intron and spacer of the *trn*L-*trn*F chloroplast region to estimate phylogenetic relationships within the large, wide-ranging, and taxonomically difficult tribe Justicieae. Analysis of the combined data set provided a highly resolved hypothesis of relationships that supported the Justicieae as being monophyletic; within the tribe, five lineages and one paraphyletic grade are recognized. A novel aspect of this study notes that the large genus *Justicia* (450–600 species) is not monophyletic, that the members of the Eastern Hemisphere form a grade and the members of the Western Hemisphere are monophyletic only if a number of other genera (*Harpochilus, Megaskepasma,* and *Poikilacanthus*) are included.

Features of the family. Habit: mostly terrestrial, rarely aquatic, perennial herbs, shrubs, rarely trees or twining vines. Stems when young terete to quadrate, often with bracts, or bracteoles, the nodes usually swollen, spines sometimes present, the spines derived from reduced leaves. Intercellular concretions present (cystoliths), usually of calcium carbonate, appearing as white streaks in epidermis of leaves, the cystoliths absent in subfamilies Nelsonioideae, Mendoncioideae, and Thunbergioideae, and in the tribe Aphelandreae of subfamily Acanthoideae. **Indument:** herbs and shrubs glabrous or pubescent, the trichomes eglandular or glandular. **Stipules** absent. **Leaves** usually opposite and decussate or sometimes quaternate, simple, sessile or petiolate; blade margins entire, rarely spiny-toothed. **Inflorescences** terminal or axillary, of solitary flowers or arranged in spikes, racemes, cymes, or thyrses, often densely clustered, frequently in axils of conspicuous bracts; bracts often leaflike, brightly colored, sometimes enclosing corolla tube, sometimes becoming spinose; 2 bracteoles often present. **Flowers** actinomorphic (*Ble-*

America; the Thunbergioideae, with a single genus and about 90 species in Africa, Madagascar, Tropical Asia, Australia, and naturalized in the southeastern United States to South America; the Nelsonioideae, with six genera (three monotypic) and 62 species in tropical and subtropical regions of both the Eastern and the Western Hemispheres (southeastern and southwestern United States, Mexico, Central America, West Indies, South America, southeast Asia, Malaysia, Australia, Africa, Madagascar, and the Philippine Islands); and the Acanthoideae, the largest subfamily, with 230 genera (many monotypic) and about 3,000 species mainly native to the tropics and subtropics of both the Eastern and the Western Hemisphere and also found in the United States, Australia, and the Mediterranean Region of Europe.

The subfamilies Mendoncioideae and Thunbergioideae have sometimes been treated as distinct families (e.g., Mendonciaceae *sensu* Cronquist) and the subfamily Nelsonioideae has at times been referred to the Scrophulariaceae. The reason that the first two subfamilies are sometimes recognized as distinct is that they each lack the hook-shaped retinacula or jaculators (the specialized mechanism of seed dispersal) and *chum, Ruellia, Pseuderanthemum*) or zygomorphic (*Aphelandra, Dicliptera, Stenostephanus, Justicia*) or somewhat intermediate (most of remaining genera), bisexual, sometimes large and showy; calyx synsepalous, the sepals 5, usually deeply 4- or 5-lobed (or entire to multilobed or toothed in Mendoncioideae and Thunbergioideae), the lobes equal or unequal in length, sometimes partially or completely fused with one another and forming heteromorphic segments; corolla sympetalous, the tube cylindric or funnelform, sometimes twisted 180° (i.e., corolla resupinate as in *Hypoestes* and *Dicliptera*) or 360°, the limb 5-lobed or 2-lipped, the upper lip of bilabiate corollas usually with 2 lobes, the lower lip with 3 lobes, these imbricate or contorted in bud; androecium usually with 2 or 4 stamens, the stamens epipetalous and included in corolla tube or exserted from mouth of corolla, often didynamous, the filaments distinct or connate in pairs basally, the anthers sometimes with basal appendages, the thecae 1 or 2, parallel to perpendicular when 2, collaterally attached to filament or superposed or widely separated by modified connective, dehiscing by longitudinal slits; staminodes sometimes present, then 2 and made up of minute projections or sterile filaments; nectiferous annular disc usually present around base of ovary; gynoecium syncarpous, the ovary superior, the carpels 2, the locules generally 2, the style simple, filiform, included within corolla tube or exserted from corolla mouth, the stigma funnelform, 2-lobed (or sometimes 1 lobe suppressed); placentation axile (or parietal in subfamily Nelsonioideae), the ovules 2 to many in each locule. **Fruits** capsules or drupes, the capsules loculicidal, explosively dehiscent, stipitate or estipitate, 2-valved (subfamilies Acanthoideae, Nelsonioideae, Thunbergioideae), in some capsular genera (e.g., *Dicliptera*) the septa with attached retinacula separate from inner wall of mature capsule, the drupes fleshy (subfamily Mendoncioideae). **Seeds** 2—many in capsules or 1 in drupes, borne along length of fruit or only basally or distally in capsules, each seed usually subtended by a prominent hook-shaped retinaculum or jaculator, the seed globose to lenticular, often asymmetrically notched at base, glabrous or pubescent, the trichomes often hygroscopic or becoming musculaginous when moistened, the seed coat smooth or variously ornamented.

The two small genera of trees are *Bravaisia* (3 species) and *Trichanthera* (2 species) both reaching 4–20 meters tall. The vines belong to *Mendoncia* and *Thunbergia*, the latter naturalized in the neotropics.

Natural history. A great array of diverse floral forms is evident in Acanthaceae. Characteristically, the flowers are protandrous, nectar-yielding, brightly colored, and often arranged in large and showy inflorescences. When the stigma is receptive, it lies directly above the already dehiscent anthers. Insects, hummingbirds, and bats strike the downward-directed tips of the pollen sacs and are dusted with pollen. The pollinator then transfers the pollen to the projecting stigmas of other flowers. Because only one or two flowers per inflorescence are open daily, the inflorescences are visited on consecutive days. Toward early afternoon, the stigmas of all flowers, whether pollinated or not, characteristically arch downward, thus making direct contact with the inwardly dehiscing anthers and ensuring self-pollination in the absence of previous cross-pollination. Speciation in Acanthaceae appears to be pollinator driven. Floral visitors observed and reported include carpenter bees (on *Thunbergia grandiflora*, an introduced ornamental); euglossine bees (on *Aphelandra scabra* and *Justicia stipitata*); bats (on *Ruellia exostema* and *verbasciformis*); butterflies (on *Tetramerium* and *Pseuderanthemum*); and hummingbirds in species with long, tubular, red flowers (e.g., *Pachystachys spicata* and *Justicia secunda*). Furthermore, the spicate inflorescences of numerous species (e.g., *Ruellia proxima*, *Stenostephanus longistaminus*, *Pachystachys ossolaea*, and *P. puberula*) are covered extensively with scale insects and ants. Exudate immediately surrounding the scale insects may attract the ants, which protect these species of Acanthaceae against herbivores.

A developing capsule is normally evident within a few days after pollination and fertilization. In most genera, the seeds are dispersed up to 5 meters from the parent by the explosive dehiscence of the ripe capsule. This mechanism has been attributed to the progressive loss of water from the maturing fruit. In numerous species, the seeds are covered with minute hairs that, when moistened, become erect and musculaginous; this may be an adaptation to help disperse the seeds and anchor them to a suitable substrate. The seeds of some widespread disjunct species, such as *Dicliptera sexangularis*, may stick to the feet of waterfowl and other birds and, thus, have been transported over long distances.

Economic uses. The most common use for members of the Acanthaceae is as ornamentals. No less than 36 genera are ornamental plants in tropical and subtropical regions of the Western Hemisphere, and many escape cultivation. One of the brightest blues of tropical gardens is provided by the corolla of *Thunbergia grandiflora*, the blue trumpet vine or skyflower. This native of India and southeastern Asia is a vigorous vine that has become naturalized in many areas of the tropics. About a dozen or more species of *Thunbergia* are cultivated in the American Tropics and in warm temperate regions, and some have become naturalized. *Thunbergia alata*, the black-eyed Susan vine, is found commonly in temperate zones. Other cultivated species of *Thunbergia* are *T. coccinea*, bearing drooping clusters of scarlet flowers with a yellow throat; *T. erecta*, king's mantle or bush clock vine, a woody twiner or shrub with solitary, blue-purple flowers; and *T. fragrans* with long, white, fragrant flowers.

The Neotropical genus *Sanchezia*, consisting of shrubs with glossy, white- or yellow-veined leaves and spikes of bright yellow flowers, is represented in cultivation by *S. speciosa* and *S. parvibracteata*; the latter has smaller bracts and larger calyx lobes.

The prominently veined leaves; nerved bracts; and long, tubular, blue corollas of *Eranthemum pulchellum*, known as the blue sage and native to the Indo-Pakistan subcontinent, have made it a popular ornamental in Neotropical gardens, from which it occasionally escapes.

Barleria cristata, the Philippine violet native to India and Burma, is a pubescent shrub with spiny bracts enclosing blue or white flowers and *B. lupulina*, a thorny species called hophead and native to Mauritius, possesses attractive black-green foliage, hoplike spikes on maroon stems, and yellow flowers. Both are grown as ornamentals and sometimes become naturalized in disturbed areas.

The large decorative leaves of species of *Acanthus* have played important roles in both the arts and ancient horticulture. The "acanthus" ornamental leaf pattern (based on *A. spinosus*) was a favorite decoration in classical sculpture. According to legend, this use of the leaf originated about 430 B.C., when a Greek sculptor adopted it as a distinct element in the decoration of columns for Corinthian temples. Virgil described an acanthus design embroidered on the robe of Helen of Troy. Species of *Acanthus* also have been used medicinally. An extract of the boiled leaves of *A. ebracteatus* (sea holly) is used as a cough medicine in parts of Malaya, and the roots of *A. mollis* (bear's breech) are used to treat diarrhea in some parts of Europe.

Crossandra infundibuliform (firecracker flower) is cultivated commonly in gardens in Neotropical regions and is a favorite houseplant in the United States. The genus *Crossandra* (50 species) is distributed mainly in tropical Africa, Madagascar, Arabia, and the Indo-Pakistan subcontinent. *Crossandra infundibuliform* has a four-sided, terminal, flowering spike with bracts from which the orange flowers arise. Two additional species can be found in cultivation: *C. nilotica*, a pubescent plant with red and orange flowers, and *C. pungens*, with extremely dense flowering spikes of yellow flowers and spiny bracts.

At the turn of the twentieth century, a number of species of *Aphelandra* were reported from the greenhouse trade. Today, only *A. squarrosa*, the zebra plant native to coastal Brazil, is a popular houseplant. The creamy yellow markings on the glossy, dark green leaves and the four-sided spikes of bright yellow bracts tinged with red give the zebra plant a special appeal long after the yellow flowers have faded. *Asystasia gangetica*, known as coromandel and native to tropical Africa, Asia, and Malaya, is now naturalized in the neotropics. It is distinguished by the pale lavender or yellowish flowers growing along a trailing stalk.

Members of the genus *Pachystachys* are known best for their ornamental beauty, and many may be found in botanical gardens. Their prominent terminal spikes with bright red, purple, or white flowers and bright yellow bracts, are impressive sights. The common red-flowered species is the cardinal's guard, *P. spicata* (usually erroneously called *P. coccinea*), and the species with yellow bracts and white flowers is the golden yellow lollipop plant, *P. lutea*.

Pseuderanthemum carruthersii (*P. atropurpureum*), the purple false eranthemum, is probably native to Polynesia. It often is cultivated for ornament because its leaves are purple or sometimes green and variously marked with yellow along the veins.

The polka-dot or measles plant, *Hypoestes phyllostachya*, commonly cultivated as a houseplant, also is grown as an ornamental in temperate regions. However, its tropical origin in Madagascar necessitates that it be confined indoors in winter months.

The Mexican species *Odontonema cuspidatum* (firespike) is cultivated commonly. This handsome plant with a terminal thyrse and bright red, tubular flowers is planted frequently by local peoples in the neotropics, where it sometimes escapes. It is related closely to *O. tubiforme* (*O. strictum*), and in some parts of Mexico, the two species are difficult to distinguish.

Two species of *Fittonia*, both low-growing forest herbs native to Colombia, Ecuador, and Peru, are well known in horticulture as shade-loving houseplants with attractive foliage.

The shrimp plant (*Justicia brandegeana*), a native of Mexico, is admired for its curving or drooping clusters of long, terminal spikes with downy bronze or rose to yellow bracts overlapping the white, red-spotted flowers that suggest the curved tail of a shrimp. White shrimp plant (*J. betonica*) has white or green bracts. King's crown, *J. carnea*, a native of southeastern Brazil, has thin and sometimes velvety leaves. This vigorous branching plant produces a handsome, dense terminal crown of prominent bracts enclosing rose-purple or pink flowers.

In Mexico and Central America, leaves of species of *Justicia spicigera* (*mohintli*) and *J. colorifera* are crushed and placed in hot water to yield a bluing agent used in laundering to whiten clothes. *Justicia spicigera* also is known as Mexican indigo because it is a source of blue dye. Because of their household uses, these species are cultivated commonly from Mexico to Colombia.

Justicia pectoralis, is reported to have numerous medicinal, hallucinogenic, and economic uses throughout its wide range. The sweetly fragrant, dried leaves are pulverized by some South American Indians and added to their *Virola*-based hallucinogenic snuff, possibly merely as a flavoring.

Recently, species of *Ruellia* and other Acanthaceae have been reported in pharmaceutical journals to possess anti-infective and antimicrobial properties.

Some species of Acanthaceae are widespread weeds in the Tropics and subtropics. These include *Nelsonia* (3 species), *Blechum* (± 10 species), and *Thunbergia*.

References. BARKER, R. M. 1986. A taxonomic revision of Australian Acanthaceae. *J. Adelaide Bot. Gard.* 9:1–286. BREMEKAMP, C. E. B. 1965. Delimitation and subdivision of the Acanthaceae. *Bull. Bot. Surv. India.* 7:21–30. CORRERA Q., J. E., AND H. Y. BERNAL. 1989. Acanthaceae. In *Especies vegetales promisorias de los países del Convenio Andrés Bello*, Tomo I. Bogotá, D. E., Colombia: Secretaria Ejecutiva del Convenio Andrés Bello. DANIEL, T. F. 1983.

Carlowrightia (Acanthaceae). *Fl. Neotrop. Monogr.* 34:1–115. DANIEL, T. F. 1993. Mexican Acanthaceae: diversity and distribution. In *Biological diversity of Mexico: origins and distribution*, eds. T. P. Ramamoorthy, R. Bye, A. Lot, and J. Fa, 541–58. New York: Oxford University Press. LINDAU, G. 1895. Acanthaceae. In *Die Natürlichen Pflanzenfamilien*, A. Engler and K. Prantl, 4(3b):274–354. Leipzig: Wilhelm Engelmann. LONG, R. L. 1970. The genera of Acanthaceae in the southeastern United States. *J. Arnold Arbor.* 51:257–309. MCDADE, L. A., T. F. DANIEL, S. E. MASTA, AND K. M. RILEY. 2000. Phylogenetic relationships within the tribe Justicieae (Acanthaceae): Evidence from molecular sequences, morphology, and cytology. *Ann. Missouri Bot. Gard.* 87:435–58. SCOTLAND, R. W., J. A. SWEERE, P. A. REEVES, AND R. G. OLMSTEAD. 1995. Higher-level systematics of Acanthaceae determined by chloroplast DNA sequences. *Amer. J. Bot.* 82:266–75.

ACERACEAE (Maple Family)

NATHAN SMITH

- *trees*

- *leaves opposite, simple or 3-foliolate*

- *flowers with petals absent; stamens usually 4–6; carpels 2*

- *fruits schizocarps, the mericarps 2, winged*

Numbers of genera and species. Worldwide, the Aceraceae comprise two genera and approximately 180 species. In tropical America, there is a single genus, *Acer*, and two native species, *A. negundo* subspecies *mexicanum* and *A. saccharum* subspecies *skutchii*.

Although extratropical, *A. saccharum* subspecies *grandidentatum* reaches its southern limit in the mountains of northern Mexico. *Acer negundo* (ranging from temperate North America to Guatemala), as well as other species, has been used ornamentally in other montane regions of the neotropics.

Distribution and habitat. The Aceraceae are mostly a north temperate family with the greatest diversity in China, where many species of *Acer* and a second endemic genus, *Dipteronia* (two species), are found. Species of *Acer* are also found in Japan, as well as Asia, Europe, and North America.

In tropical America, *A. negundo* subspecies *mexicanum* occurs in montane forests of Mexico (e.g., Chiapas and Veracruz) and Guatemala, and *A. saccharum* subspecies *skutchii* is found in similar habitats of Mexico (Chiapas and Tamaulipas) and Guatemala.

Family classification. The Aceraceae are placed in the Sapindales by Cronquist. Recent molecular studies show the Aceraceae as being close to the Hippocastanaceae. Many authors feel that these two families are better placed within the Sapindaceae *sensu lato* (see Sapindaceae).

The family differs from the Sapindaceae in having opposite versus often alternate leaves, usually simple versus usually compound leaves, two versus usually 3 carpels, 2 ovules per carpel versus usually 1, usually colpate versus rarely colpate pollen, a samara versus berrylike, drupelike, or samaralike fruits, exarillate versus often arillate seeds, and differences in phytochemistry.

Features of the family. Habit: trees. Stipules absent. Leaves opposite, simple or 3-foliolate in *Acer negundo*; when simple blades lobed, the margins entire; leaflet margins serrate; venation pinnate in *A. negundo* or palmate. Inflorescences terminal or lateral, corymbose, racemose, or fasciculate. Flowers actinomorphic, bisexual or unisexual (plants dioecious or polygamodioecious), small; sepals usually 4 and inconspicuous (*A. negundo*) or 5 (*A. saccharum*) and connate; petals absent; disc absent in *A. negundo* or present, then extrastaminal; androecium usually of 4–6 stamens, exserted, the filaments distinct, the anthers dehiscing by longitudinal slits; gynoecium syncarpous, the ovary superior, the carpels 2, the locules 1 per carpel, the styles distinct (at least above base); placentation axile, the ovules 2 per locule. Fruits schizocarps, the mericarps 2, winged. Seeds 1 per mericarp.

Natural history. The flowers of *Acer* are wind- or insect-pollinated, and the fruits are wind-dispersed.

Economic uses. Species of *Acer* are grown commonly as ornamentals. The wood is often used in construction and for fuel. In northeastern North America, the sap of *A. saccharum* (sugar maple) is boiled down to make maple syrup and sugar. Some species (e.g, *A. campestre* and *A. pseudoplatanus*) also provide nectar used by bees to make honey.

References. DELENDICK, T. J. 1981. A systematic review of the Aceraceae. Ph.D thesis. City University of New York. DELENDICK, T. J. 1990. A survey of foliar flavonoids in the Aceraceae. *Mem. New York Bot. Gard.* 54:1–129. GADEK, P. A. et al. 1996. Sapindales: molecular delimitation and infraordinal groups. *Amer. J. Bot.* 83(6):802–11. GELDEREN, D. M. VAN, P. C. DE JONG, AND H. J. OTERDOOM. 1994. *Maples of the World.* Portland, OR: Timber Press. MURRAY, A. E. 1970. A monograph of Aceraceae. Ph.D. thesis. Pennsylvania State University. RODRÍGUEZ, L.-C. 1985. Aceraceae. In *Flora de Veracruz*, fasc. 46:1–7. Xalapa, Mexico: Instituto Nacional de Investigaciones sobre Recursos Bióticos.

ACHATOCARPACEAE (Achatocarpus Family)

MICHAEL NEE

Plate 1

- *shrubs or small trees, deciduous*

- *stems often armed with spines*

- *leaves alternate, simple, often turning black when bruised or dried; blade margins entire*

- *flowers with petals absent*

- *fruits berries, whitish, translucent*

- *seeds 1 per fruit, large, dark*

Numbers of genera and species. The Achatocarpaceae comprise two genera and about six species. One genus, *Achatocarpus*, with five species is found in tropical America.

Distribution and habitat. The Achatocarpaceae are restricted to the American Tropics and subtropics. The family is distributed in areas of dry thorn-scrub vegetation, with *Achatocarpus* ranging from Mexico to Argentina and *Phaulothamnus* from Texas to northern Mexico.

Family classification. The Achatocarpaceae are placed in the Caryophyllales by Cronquist, and this placement is supported by recent analyses. The family is very close to, and often merged with, the Phytolaccaceae. The compound, unilocular ovary is the technical character used to justify its separation.

Features of the family. Habit: shrubs or small trees, deciduous. **Stems** often armed with spines. **Stipules** absent. **Leaves** alternate, simple, somewhat fleshy, often turning black when bruised or dried; blade margins entire. **Inflorescences** axillary, racemes or panicles. **Flowers** sometimes produced when leaves are fallen, unisexual (plants dioecious); sepals 4 or 5, persistent in fruit; petals absent; androecium of 10–20 stamens; gynoecium syncarpous, the ovary superior, the carpels 2, the locule 1, the styles 2; placentation basal, the ovule 1. **Fruits** berries, whitish, translucent. **Seeds** 1 per fruit, large, dark, visible in semitransparent whitish pulp of fruit; aril small, at hilum; embryo curved.

Unlike many other Caryophyllales, the wood has normal secondary growth.

Natural history. Species of this family may form a prominent part of the vegetation, for example, in the Gran Chaco of Bolivia.

The insignificant flowers with many stamens and protruding stigmas apparently are wind-pollinated. No information is available about dispersal biology.

Economic uses. Other than use for firewood, the family has no documented economic value.

References. BITTRICH, V. 1993. Achatocarpaceae. In *The Families and Genera of Vascular Plants*, eds. K. Kubitzki, J. G. Rohwer, and V. Bittrich, 3:35–36. Berlin: Springer-Verlag. GIANASI, D. E., G. ZURAWSKI, G. LEARN, AND M. T. CLEGG. 1992. Evolutionary relationships of the Caryophyllidae based on comparative *rbc*L sequences. *Syst. Bot.* 17:1–15. OLMSTEAD R. G., H. J. MICHAELS, K. M. SCOTT, AND J. D. PALMER. 1992. Monophyly of the Asteridae and identification of their major lineages inferred from DNA sequence of *rbc*L. *Ann. Missouri Bot. Gard.* 79:249–65.

ACTINIDIACEAE (Kiwi Family)

Djaja Djendoel Soejarto

Figure 3, Plate 1

- *usually trees or shrubs*
- *leaves alternate, simple; blade margins often serrate*
- *inflorescences axillary, thyrses*
- *flowers actinomorphic; perianth often 5-merous*
- *fruits usually berries*
- *seeds numerous, black*

Numbers of genera and species. Worldwide, the Actinidiaceae consist of three genera, *Actinidia*, *Clematoclethra*, and *Saurauia*, with a total of 300–325 species. *Saurauia*, with more than 270 species, is the only genus found in tropical America, where at least 71 species occur.

Distribution and habitat. The family is found in the tropics and subtropics of America and Asia, and extends to the temperate zone in Asia. In the American Tropics, the greatest number of species are found along the Central American mountain chains and on the slopes and in the valleys of the Andes.

The largest genus, *Saurauia*, is represented in both tropical America and tropical Asia. In the Americas, species of *Saurauia* are found from Mexico to Bolivia. The genus has not been recorded from the Caribbean or the Amazon basin. *Actinidia* occurs in East Asia, with its center of distribution in China, while *Clematoclethra* is endemic to northwestern China.

The Actinidiaceae primarily grow in cool and humid habitats at 500–2500 (–3000) meters elevation.

Family classification. Traditionally, the Actinidiaceae have been placed in the Theales (e.g., *sensu* Cronquist) and considered to be closely related to the Theaceae and the Dilleniaceae; however, results of molecular studies point to a close relationship with members of the Ericales, and the family may be a basal offshoot of that order.

Previous classifications have included *Sladenia* in the family, but this genus has now been placed in the Theaceae. Some taxonomists have suggested that *Saurauia* should be placed in its own family, the Saurauiaceae.

Features of the family. Habit: usually trees or shrubs; raphides present. Stems often pubescent when young. Stipules absent. Leaves alternate, simple; petioles often present; blades variable in shape and size, coriaceous to papery, frequently pubescent, usually green but pubescence may give appearance of brown to gray or bluish-gray color, the mar-

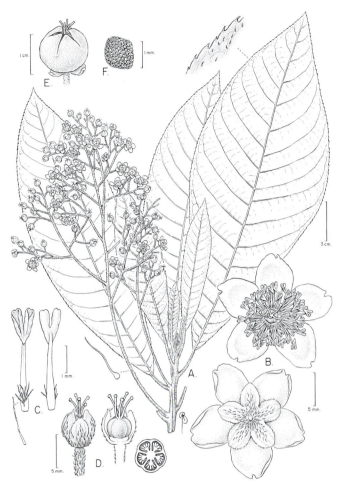

Figure 3. ACTINIDIACEAE. *Saurauia spectabilis* (A, Solomon 7494; B–D, Beck 2809; E, F, Feverer 6427a). **A.** Stem with inflorescences and leaves showing detail of margin (above). **B.** Apical (above) and basal (below) views of flower. **C.** Adaxial (left) and abaxial (right) views of stamens and detail of trichome (lower left). **D.** Lateral views of immature fruit surrounded by sepals (left), gynoecium partially surrounded by sepals (center), and transverse section of ovary (right). **E.** Oblique-apical view of young fruit surrounded by sepals. **F.** Seed. Original. Artist: Bobbi Angell.

gins often serrate. **Inflorescences** axillary, thyrses, with few to numerous flowers (up to 500 in South American *Saurauia*), the terminal axes in dichasia. **Flowers** actinomorphic, unisexual or bisexual (plants dioecious or polygamo-dioecious); sepals (3–4)5, imbricate, frequently green to pale green; petals (3–4)5, imbricate, often white (crimson red in *Saurauia napaulensis* and brownish yellow in *Actinidia latifolia*); androecium of 15–50(–240) stamens, the stamens sometimes fasciculate, and adnate to petals (*Saurauia* species), the filaments white, the anthers yellow; gynoecium syncarpous, the ovary superior, the locules (3)5(30); placentation axile. **Fruits** usually berries, loculicidal capsules in some *Saurauia*. **Seeds** numerous (as many as 1,000 or more per fruit), black.

Some species of *Saurauia* (e.g., *S. tomentosa*) become large trees and all species are evergreen.

Natural history. Pollination is accomplished mostly by insects, especially beetles. No information is available about dispersal biology.

Economic uses. The most important product of the Actinidiaceae is the fruit of the kiwi or Chinese gooseberry (*Actinidia chinensis*), which is now grown in several countries and is sold widely throughout the world. Fruits of most species of *Saurauia* contain a sweetish, clear, mucilaginous pulp, which is consumed locally. A number of species of *Actinidia* have been cultivated as ornamentals in temperate regions. Wood of *Saurauia* is important locally for use in construction and as firewood. Several species of *Saurauia* are used locally for medicinal purposes, including treatment of snakebite.

References. DICKISON, W. C. 1972. Observations on the floral morphology of some species of *Saurauia*, *Actinidia* and *Clematoclethra*. *J. Elisha Mitchell Sci. Soc.* 88:43–54. GILG, E., AND E. WERDERMANN. 1925. Actinidiaceae. In A. Engler and K. Prantl, *Die Natürlichen Pflanzenfamilien*, 2nd ed. 21:36–47. Leipzig: Wilhelm Engelmann. HUNTER, G. E. 1966. Revision of Mexican and Central American *Saurauia* (Dilleniaceae). *Ann. Missouri Bot. Gard.* 53:47–89. KELLER, J. A., P. S. HERENDEEN, AND P. R. CRANE. 1996. Fossil flowers and fruits of the Actinidiaceae from the Campanian (late Cretaceous) of Georgia. *Amer. J. Bot.* 83:528–41. LI, H.-L. 1952. A taxonomic review of the genus *Actinidia*. *J. Arnold Arbor.* 33:1–61. SOEJARTO, D. D. 1980. Revision of South American *Saurauia* (Actinidiaceae). *Fieldiana, Bot.*, n.s., 2:i-vii, 1–141. TANG, Y.-C., AND Q.-Y. XIANG. 1989. A reclassification of the genus *Clematoclethra* (Actinidiaceae) and further note on the methodology of plant taxonomy. *Acta Phytotax. Sin.* 27(2):81–95.

AIZOACEAE (Fig-marigold Family)

DENNIS WM. STEVENSON

Figure 4, Plate 1

- *succulent herbs or subshrubs*

- *leaves opposite, less often alternate, simple; blade margins entire*

- *inflorescences cymose or flowers solitary*

- *flowers actinomorphic*

- *fruits capsules*

Numbers of genera and species. Worldwide, the Aizoaceae comprise 127 genera and approximately 2,500 species. In tropical America, there are seven genera and about 20 species.

Distribution and habitat. The center of diversity of the Aizoaceae appears to be Southern Africa. The monotypic genus *Cypsela*, is endemic to the Western Hemisphere and is found in the West Indies, southern North America, and coastal areas of northern South America. The Pantropical genera that occur in the neotropics are *Sesuvium*, *Tetragonia*, and *Trianthema*. Many ornamental species have become naturalized after invading disturbed areas with Mediterranean climates. Thus, the original distribution of many genera and species are not readily ascertainable. Genera of the Eastern Hemisphere that are naturalized and commonly found in the neotropics include *Aptenia*, *Malephora*, and *Mesembryanthemum*.

The Aizoaceae grow in the drier parts of the subtropics and Tropics, often in sandy coastal soils that receive the winter rains of Mediterranean climates.

Family classification. The Aizoaceae are placed in the Caryophyllales by Cronquist and its position within the order remains enigmatic. The most recent treatment of the family recognizes five subfamilies. Two subfamilies, Mesembryanthemoideae and Ruschioideae, have an apparent perianth of numerous, brightly colored segments and a base chromosome number of $x = 9$, whereas the other three subfamilies, Aizooideae, Sesuvioideae, and Tetragonioideae, have fewer perianth segments and a base chromosome number of $x = 8$.

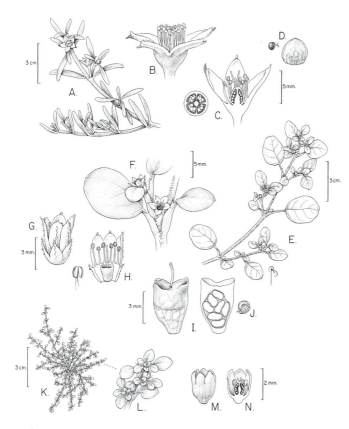

Figure 4. AIZOACEAE. *Sesuvium portulacastrum* (A–D), *Trianthema portulacastrum* (E–J), and *Cypselea humifusa* (K–N). **A.** Stem with leaves and flowers. **B.** Lateral view of flower. **C.** Tranverse section of ovary (left) and medial section of flower (right). **D.** Seed with funicle (left) and lateral view of capsule (right). **E.** Stem with leaves and flowers. **F.** Detail of flowers in leaf axils. **G.** Lateral view of flower. **H.** Longitudinal section of flower (right) and anther (left). **I.** Fruit with persistent style (left) and medial section of fruit (right). **J.** Seed. **K.** Plant showing habit. **L.** Part of stem with leaves and flowers. **M.** Lateral view of flower. **N.** Medial section of flower. Reprinted with permission from Acevedo-Rodríguez (1996). Artist: Bobbi Angell.

Features of the family. Habit: herbs or subshrubs, annual or perennial, succulent. **Stipules** usually absent or small.

Leaves opposite, less often alternate, simple; petioles usually absent; blades commonly with connate basal sheath, often with conspicuous surface wax, the margins entire. **Inflorescences** cymose or flowers solitary. **Flowers** actinomorphic, bisexual; tepals (3–)5(–8), variously connate basally; androecium with 5–many stamens, the outermost often variously petal-like; gynoecium syncarpous, the ovary superior to inferior, the carpels 5, the locules and styles equal to number of carpels, the stigmas papillate; placentation axile, the ovules 1–many per locule, basal when solitary. **Fruits** capsules, loculicidal, rarely septicidal or circumscissile. **Seeds** 1–many per locule.

Natural history. The family often exhibits adaptations (such as crassulacean acid metabolism) to high light and dry conditions. The leaves are generally succulent and adapted for water storage; extreme adaptations occur in the Old World "living stone" plants, such as *Lithops.*

Pollination is effected by the wind and various insects, including bees, wasps, and butterflies. Plants are generally self-incompatible, but unopened self-pollinated flowers exist. Hygrochastic capsules are known for some genera, whereas, in others, especially those with circumscissile capsules, the seeds are "splashed out" by raindrops.

Economic uses. Aizoaceae are widely cultivated as ornamentals and a considerable horticultural industry specializes in living stones (*Lithops*) and ice plants (*Mesembryanthemum*). However, ice plants have become widespread invasive weeds in California. A few species contain alkaloids and are used locally as medicinals. *Tetragonia tetragonioides* (New Zealand spinach) is used widely as a vegetable.

References. HARTMANN, H.E.K. 1993. Aizoaceae. In *The Families and Genera of Vascular Plants*, eds. K. Kubitzki, J. G. Rohwer, and V. Bittrich, 2:37–69. New York: Springer-Verlag. RETTIG, J. H., H. D. WILSON, AND R. MANHART. 1992. Phylogeny of the Caryophyllales: gene sequence data. *Taxon* 41:201–209.

ALZATEACEAE

SHIRLEY A. GRAHAM

Figure 5

- *shrubs or small secondary hemiepiphytic trees*
- *leaves opposite, simple; blades coriaceous, the margins entire*
- *flowers with pinkish-white anthers, these fleshy, resembling petals*

- *fruits loculicidal capsules, dry, bilaterally flattened, horizontally striated*
- *seeds membranous-winged*

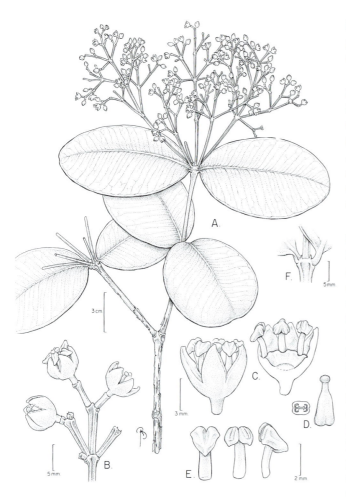

Figure 5. ALZATEACEAE. *Alzatea verticillata* (A–E, Luteyn et al. 15307; F, Baldeon et al. 2997). **A.** Stem with leaves and inflorescence. **B.** Detail of inflorescence. **C.** Lateral view of flower (left) and longitudinal section of flower with gynoecium removed (right). **D.** Transverse section of ovary (left) and lateral view of gynoecium (right). **E.** Abaxial (left), adaxial (center), and lateral (right) views of stamens. **F.** Detail of node showing stipules. Original. Artist: Bobbi Angell.

Numbers of genera and species. The Alzateaceae consist of a single species, *Alzatea verticillata*. Two subspecies are recognized, the northern *amplifolia* and southern *verticillata*. These are minimally distinct with partially intermediate representatives occurring near the Ecuador-Peru border.

Distribution and habitat. The Alzateaceae are found in Central America and Andean South America. *Alzatea* was known only from Bolivia and Peru until 1936 when it was collected in a low montane forest in Costa Rica. In 1978, it was discovered in Panama, and subsequently it has been collected in the Chocó of Colombia and in Ecuador near the Peruvian border.

In Central America, *Alzatea* occurs at elevations of 1,000–2,200 meters in montane forests. The genus occurs in South America on the eastern escarpment of the Andes in montane wet forests at elevations from 900 to 2,200 (–3,000) meters.

In Panama, *Alzatea* has been observed growing as an epiphyte in tall trees and as a diminutive shrub to 2 meters in elfin cloud forest.

Family classification. The Alzateaceae are placed in the Myrtales near the Lythraceae by Cronquist. Comparison of specialized morphological attributes and sequence data from the *rbc*L gene indicate that *Alzatea* belongs near the small African myrtalean families Rhynchocalycaceae, Oliniaceae, and Penaeaceae. The Alzateaceae share the greatest number of derived morphological characters with the Rhynchocalycaceae.

Features of the family. Habit: shrubs or small secondary hemiepiphytic trees. **Stipules** present, axillary. **Leaves** opposite, simple; petioles absent or poorly developed; blades obovate, elliptic, or oblong to oval (closely resemble those of *Clusia* [Clusiaceae], with which it commonly grows), lustrous, coriaceous, the margins entire. **Inflorescences** paniculate-cymes, 10–30 flowers. **Flowers** actinomorphic, bisexual; floral tube present, campanulate, coriaceous, 4–6 mm long, the (calyx) lobes 5(6), valvate, fleshy, persistent; corolla absent; nectary broad (extending to sinuses of floral tube lobes); androecium of 5 stamens, the stamens alternate with calyx lobes, the anther connectives fleshy, conspicuous, heart-shaped, pinkish white, becoming exserted between calyx lobes at anthesis, resembling petals; gynoecium syncarpous, the ovary superior, the carpels 2, the locules 2, bilaterally flattened, the style 1 mm long, stout; placentation parietal. **Fruits** loculicidal capsules, dry, bilaterally flattened, horizontally striated. **Seeds** 40–60, membranous-winged, fragile.

Other notable features are vestured pitting of the vessel elements and internal phloem, a combination that supports placement of the Alzateaceae in the Myrtales. The family is unusual in the order because of its bisporic *Allium*-type embryo sac and stems with trilacunar, three-trace nodes. Branched sclereids occur in the leaf palisade tissue.

Natural history. Flowering of *Alzatea* in Central America occurs throughout most of the year. In Peru, it occurs from August to October, and in Bolivia, flower buds have been collected in November.

Neither nectar production nor insect visitors have been reported for the genus, although the petal-like appearance of the anthers suggests that they function in insect attraction. No information is available about dispersal biology.

Economic uses. No economic uses are known for this family.

References. ALMEDA, F. 1997. Chromosomal observations on the Alzateaceae (Myrtales). *Ann. Missouri Bot. Gard.* 84: 305–08. CONTI, E., A. LITT, P. G. WILSON, S. A. GRAHAM, B. G. BRIGGS, ET AL. 1997. Interfamilial relationships in

Myrtales: molecular phylogeny and patterns of morphological evolution. *Syst. Bot.* 22:629–47. GRAHAM, S. A. 1984. Alzateaceae, a new family of Myrtales in the American tropics. *Ann. Missouri Bot. Gard.* 71:757–79. GRAHAM, S. A. 1995. Two new species in *Cuphea* (Lythraceae), and a note on Alzateaceae. *Novon* 5:272–77. SILVERSTONE-SOPKIN, P. A., AND GRAHAM, S. A. 1986. Alzateaceae, a plant family new to Colombia. *Brittonia* 38:340–43.

AMARANTHACEAE (Amaranth Family)

MICHAEL NEE

Figure 6

- *herbs, less frequently semiwoody or soft-woody vines*
- *plants often growing in disturbed areas*
- *flowers usually subtended by a scarious single bract and two bracteoles; tepals dry, scarious or membranous; placentation usually basal or free-central*

Numbers of genera and species. Worldwide, the Amaranthaceae comprise 70 genera and about 1,000 species. In tropical America, there are 21 native genera and about 300 species, and about four naturalized weedy African species of *Achyranthes* and *Cyathula* that are now widespread. The largest genera in the neotropics are *Alternanthera* (100 species), *Gomphrena* (60), *Iresine* (40), *Pfaffia* (30), and *Amaranthus* (25).

Distribution and habitat. The Amaranthaceae are nearly cosmopolitan, missing only from the Arctic. The Tropics and subtropics contain the majority of the genera and species.

Many species colonize disturbed areas in nearly all habitats and are often roadside weeds. The few forest species are usually found in seasonally dry or thorn forests.

Family classification. The Amaranthaceae are placed in the Caryophyllales by Cronquist. The family is closely related to the Chenopodiaceae, but differs by the scarious bracts and the less succulent nature of its species. Recent molecular studies suggest that these two families should be combined to form a single monophyletic group. The family is divided into two subfamilies, the Amaranthoideae and the Gomphrenoideae.

Most genera in the Amaranthaceae are in need of taxonomic revision, and the generic placement of various species is problematical. The morphology of the filament tube and the presence and shape of the pseudostaminodia are crucial for defining the genera, but the general aspect of species in *Alternanthera*, *Gomphrena*, and *Pfaffia* do not always correlate with the staminal characters, so a realignment of species and reconsideration of these genera may be in order.

Figure 6. AMARANTHACEAE. *Amaranthus viridis* (A–D), *Achyranthes aspera* (E–J), and *Alternanthera tenella* (K–O). **A.** Stem with leaves and inflorescence. **B.** Lateral view of pistillate flower. **C.** Lateral view of fruit subtended by persistent sepals. **D.** Seed. **E.** Stems with leaves, an inflorescence (left), and an infructescence (right). **F.** Detail of inflorescence. **G.** Lateral view of flower with subtending bracteoles. **H.** Lateral view of flower with part of perianth removed. **I.** Medial section of gynoecium. **J.** Lateral view of seed with persistent upper part of fruit. **K.** Stem with leaves and axillary inflorescences. **L.** Flower with subtending bracteoles. **M.** Lateral view of medial section of flower subtended by bracteoles. **N.** Lateral view of stamens and interstaminal appendages. **O.** Lateral view of seed with persistent upper part of fruit. Reprinted with permission from Acevedo-Rodríguez (1996). Artist: Bobbi Angell.

Features of the family. Habit: herbs, less frequently semiwoody or soft-woody vines, often succulent. **Stipules** absent. **Leaves** alternate or opposite, simple; blade margins usually entire. **Inflorescences** cymes, sometimes compound, often grouped together into panicles, thyrses, or dense heads or spikes; bract 1, scarious; bracteoles 2, the bract and bracteoles often almost equal to tepals in size and shape. **Flowers** usually actinomorphic, bisexual or rarely unisexual, small (sometimes some are sterile and modified into hooks or bristles); tepals (generally considered to be sepals) 3–5 (seldom fewer), dry, scarious or membranous; petals absent; androecium of 3–5 stamens (generally equal in number to tepals), the stamens opposite tepals, the filaments free or united into tube, often with apical lobes or teeth (pseudostaminodia), alternating with anthers; gynoecium syncarpous, the ovary superior, the carpels 2 or 3, the locule 1, the style 1, often lobed at tip; placentation frequently basal, sometimes free-central, rarely apical, the ovules 1 (several), rarely pendulous. **Fruits** often small capsules (with 1–several seeds), nutlets, achenes, or berrylike (*Pleuropetalum*). **Seeds** black, shiny, the embryo curved.

Natural history. The Amaranthaceae generally are found in soils high in nutrients (e.g., nitrogen). Many species are herbs adapted to take advantage of disturbed environments with little competition. For these reasons, the family has been very successful at invading cultivated land.

No information is available about pollination and dispersal biology.

Economic uses. Species of *Amaranthus* provide many important edible plants. Several species of "grain amaranths" (included in the "pseudo-cereals") have been domesticated for their small but nutritious fruits. One of the first domesticated plants of Mexico was *A. hypochondriacus*, but it is now only a very minor crop. Several *Amaranthus* species are used as potherbs, but this practice is less widespread in the Western Hemisphere relative to Africa or Asia.

Ornamentals in the Amaranthaceae include *Celosia argentea*, *Alternanthera bettzickiana*, *Gomphrena globosa* (globe amaranth), and species of *Amaranthus* with colorful inflorescences.

References. BURGER, W. C. 1983. Amaranthaceae. In Flora Costaricensis, ed. W. Burger. *Fieldiana, Bot.*, n.s., 13:152–80. CORRERA Q., J. E., AND H. Y. BERNAL. 1989. Amaranthaceae. In *Especies vegetales promisorias de los países del Convenio Andrés Bello*, Tomo I. Bogotá, D. E., Colombia: Secretaria Ejecutiva del Convenio Andrés Bello. ELIASSON, U. H. 1987. Amaranthaceae. In *Flora of Ecuador*, eds. G. Harling and L. Andersson, no. 28:1–138. Göteborg, Sweden: Department of Systematic Botany, University of Göteborg. ELIASSON, U. H. 1988. Floral morphology and taxonomic relations among the genera of Amaranthaceae in the New World and the Hawaiian Islands. *Bot. J. Linn. Soc.* 96:235–83. TOWNSEND, C. C. 1993. Amaranthaceae. In *The Families and Genera of Vascular Plants*, eds. K. Kubitzki, J. G. Rohwer, and V. Bittrich, 2:70–91. New York: Springer-Verlag.

ANACARDIACEAE (Cashew Family)

JOHN D. MITCHELL

Figure 7, Plate 2

- *usually trees or shrubs*
- *clear or viscous to milky sap (often poisonous and drying black)*
- *leaves alternate, frequently pinnate, sometimes simple*
- *flowers small, inconspicuous, actinomorphic; intrastaminal disc often present, fleshy*
- *fruits indehiscent*
- *seeds 1 per locule*

Numbers of genera and species. Worldwide, the Anacardiaceae comprise approximately 78 genera and more than 700 species. In tropical America, there are approximately 33 genera and 170 known species. *Rhus* is the largest genus in tropical America, with about 25 species.

Distribution and habitat. The Anacardiaceae are native to the Western Hemisphere (north to southern Canada, south to Patagonia), Africa, southern Europe, temperate and tropical Asia, tropical and subtropical Australasia, and most of Oceania. The primary centers of diversity of the Anacardiaceae are in Mexico, South America, southern and equatorial Africa, Madagascar, Indochina, and Malesia. The Eastern Hemisphere is richer in species than the Western Hemisphere. *Rhus* is most diverse in Mexico, with only one species extending to Costa Rica and western Panama.

The family is found in dry to moist, mostly lowland habitats. In the neotropics, the typical habitat of *Anacardium*, *Antrocaryon*, *Spondias*, *Tapirira*, and *Thyrsodium* is lowland moist forest. Certain genera such as *Apterokarpos*, *Cardenasiodendron*, *Cyrtocarpa*, *Pseudosmodingium*, and *Schinopsis* are found only in drier vegetation types including tropical deciduous forest, tropical arid scrub, and savannas. *Mauria* and the monotypic *Ochoterenaea* can be found in

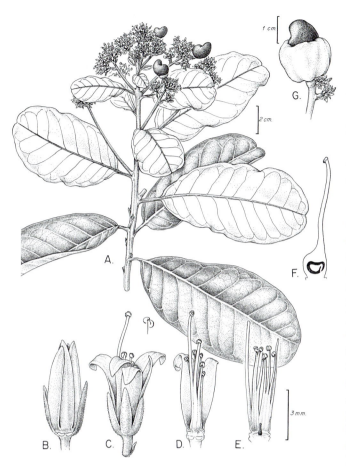

Figure 7. ANACARDIACEAE. *Anacardium spruceanum*. **A.** Stem with leaves, inflorescences, and developing fruits; note that the fruit enlarges before the hypocarp develops. **B.** Lateral view of flower bud. C–E. Three lateral views of staminate flowers: **C.** Intact. **D.** With most of perianth removed. **E.** With staminal tube opened; note pistillode. **F.** Medial section of gynoecium. **G.** Lateral view of fruit subtended by hypocarp. Reprinted with permission from Mitchell (1997). Artist: Bobbi Angell.

the montane and premontane forest of the Andes, with the former genus extending north to Central America. The large, mostly southern cone-centered *Schinus* is the only genus to occur naturally above 3,000 meters.

Family classification. The Anacardiaceae are placed in the Sapindales by Cronquist, and this is supported by recent molecular phylogenetic analyses. A single ovule within each locule distinguishes the Anacardiaceae from the very similar and closely related Burseraceae. The family has traditionally been divided into five tribes: the Anacardieae, with eight genera (an unnatural group if the aberrant Paleotropical genera *Androtium* and *Buchanania* are included); the widespread Rhoeae (including the Julianiaceae), with approximately 44 genera, some of which require reassignment; the Semecarpeae, with five genera restricted to tropical and subtropical

Asia, Malesia, northern Australia, and Oceania; the Spondiadeae, with approximately 19 genera, which are pantropical and very likely monophyletic; and the Dobineae (sometimes suggested as a separate family, the Podoaceae), with one or two genera of subshrubs to small trees restricted to continental Asia.

Preliminary published and unpublished phylogenetic analyses of selected DNA sequences suggest that the tribe Spondiadeae is monophyletic and the various genera of the Anacardieae and Semecarpeae are nested within the heterogeneous Rhoeae.

Features of the family. Habit: trees or shrubs, less frequently vines, scandent shrubs, or lianas (e.g., *Toxicodendron* in part); resin canals present, clear or viscous to milky sap present (in some genera the sap may turn black after exposure to air), often poisonous. **Stipules** absent. **Leaves** alternate, often clustered at ends of branches, frequently pinnate, sometimes simple. **Inflorescences** terminal and/or axillary, paniculate, thyrsoid, spicate, racemose, fasciculate, or of solitary flowers. **Flowers** actinomorphic, bisexual, or unisexual (then the plant dioecious, polygamous, or andromonoecious; e.g., *Anacardium* and *Mangifera*), small, inconspicuous; perianth rarely absent (e.g., pistillate flowers of *Amphipterygium* and *Orthopterygium*), usually biseriate; sepals 3–5, usually imbricate, rarely valvate in bud, usually basally connate, the lobes distinct; petals 3–5 (rarely more or absent), imbricate or valvate in bud, green, whitish, yellow, or pale pink to deep reddish purple; androecium with 5–10 (–12) stamens, usually diplo- or haplostemonous, actinomorphic or rarely zygomorphic (*Anacardium* or the introduced *Mangifera* in which one or more of the stamens are much larger than the others), the filaments usually distinct, rarely basally fused into a tube (e.g., *Anacardium*), the anthers longitudinally dehiscent, usually dorsifixed, rarely basifixed; staminodia present in female flowers; hypanthium rare (*Thyrsodium*); intrastaminal disc usually present (absent in *Anacardium* or inconspicuous in some genera), nectar secreting; gynoecium syncarpous, sometimes pseudomonomerous, the ovary superior (in neotropical taxa), the carpels 3–5, the locules 1–5, the styles prominent or absent to very short, distinct or basally fused, usually terminal, occasionally lateral, the stigmas usually capitate; placentation apical to basal, the ovules 1 per locule, anatropous, either apically, basally, or laterally attached to wall (via prominent funicle). **Fruits** indehiscent, usually drupaceous, occasionally samaroid, rarely subtended by a large fleshy hypocarp (as in *Anacardium*). **Seeds** 1 per locule, usually lacking endosperm, the cotyledons usually entire, plano-convex.

The cashew genus *Anacardium* includes three species of subshrubs with xylopodia (underground trunks) that are restricted to *cerrado* vegetation in Brazil, Paraguay, and Bolivia. The tallest tree of the Neotropical Anacardiaceae, *A. excelsum*, attains a height of 60 meters.

The introduced mango tree (*Mangifera indica*) is the only

species in the Western Hemisphere with an extrastaminal disc.

Natural history. Members of the Anacardiaceae usually are pollinated by insects, frequently bees and moths. *Amphipterygium* and *Orthopterygium* are wind-pollinated.

The fruits of several genera are modified in various ways for wind dispersal. *Astronium* and *Myracrodruon* fruits are subtended by enlarged winglike sepals; *Loxopterygium* and *Schinopsis* fruits have a single lateral wing; *Cardenasiodendron* and *Pseudosmodingium* fruits are encircled by a marginal wing and resemble *Ulmus* (elm) samaras; and *Actinocheita* and *Ochoterenaea* fruits are completely or marginally covered with very long trichomes. The majority of Anacardiaceae fruits are fleshy drupes, which are dispersed by birds and mammals. The enlarged fleshy hypocarp or cashew apple of most *Anacardium* species attracts bats, primates, some terrestrial mammals, and large fruit-eating birds as dispersal agents.

Economic uses. The sap of several Neotropical genera (e.g., *Anacardium, Comocladia, Lithrea, Loxopterygium, Mauria, Metopium, Pseudosmodingium,* and *Toxicodendron*) is poisonous and may cause severe cases of contact dermatitis in sensitive individuals. The dermatitis-causing compounds are usually catechols or resorcinols.

Spondias (e.g., *S. dulcis, S. mombin, S. purpurea, S. tuberosa*), *Antrocaryon amazonicum,* species of *Cyrtocarpa,* and the introduced mango tree (*Mangifera indica*) provide edible fruits.

The cashew of commerce (*Anacardium occidentale*) is a major, worldwide, trade commodity because of its edible seeds ("nuts"). The cashew apples (hypocarps) of *A. occidentale* are eaten fresh, made into preserves, candied, juiced, or used as ice cream flavoring. Those of *A. giganteum* also are consumed locally. The fruits of the Brazilian pepper tree (*Schinus terebinthifolia*), a species that has been widely introduced and is now established as an invasive weed worldwide in the Tropics and subtropics, are the "pink peppercorns" of *haute cuisine. Schinus molle* (including *S. areira*), the molle or California pepper tree, is planted as an ornamental or shade tree throughout the highlands of Central Mexico and the Andes.

Several genera include important timber trees, such as *Astronium, Loxopterygiuim, Myracrodruon,* and the tannin-rich species of *Schinopsis* (*quebrachos*), the latter of the dry forests of northeastern Brazil, Paraguay, Bolivia, and Argentina.

References. BARFOD, A. 1987. Anacardiaceae. In *Flora of Ecuador,* eds. G. Harling, and L. Andersson, no. 30:11–49. Göteborg, Sweden: Department of Systematic Botany, University of Göteborg. BARKLEY, F. 1937. A monograph of the genus *Rhus* and its allies in North and Central America including the West Indies. *Ann. Missouri Bot. Gard.* 24:265–498. BLACKWELL, W., AND C. DODSON. 1967. Anacardiaceae. In Flora of Panama, eds. R. E. Woodson, Jr., and R. W. Schery. *Ann. Missouri Bot. Gard.* 54:350–79. BORNSTEIN, A. 1989. Anacardiaceae. In *Flora of the Lesser Antilles: Leeward and Windward Islands,* ed. R. Howard, 5: 93–104. Jamaica Plain, MA: Arnold Arboretum, Harvard University. CORRERA Q., J. E., AND H. Y. BERNAL. 1989. Anacardiaceae. In *Especies vegetales promisorias de los países del Convenio Andrés Bello,* Tomo I. Bogotá, D. E., Colombia: Secretaria Ejecutiva del Convenio Andrés Bello. ENGLER, A. 1883. Anacardiaceae. In *Monographiae Phanerogamarum,* eds. A.L.P.P. de Candolle and A.C.P. de Candolle, 4:171–500. Paris: G. Masson. MILLER, A. J., D. A. YOUNG, AND J. WEN. 2001. Phylogeny and biogeography of *Rhus* (Anacardiaceae) based on its sequence data. *Int. J. Plant Sci.* 162(6):1401–07. MITCHELL, J. D. 1990. The poisonous Anacardiaceae genera of the world. *Advances Econ. Bot.* 8:103–29. MITCHELL, J. D. 1995. Anacardiaceae. In *Flora of the Venezuelan Guayana,* eds. P. Berry, B. Holst, and K. Yatskievych 2:399–412. Portland, OR: Timber Press. MITCHELL, J. D. 1997. Anacardiaceae. In *Flora of the Guianas,* eds. A.R.A. Görts-Van Rijn and M. J. Jansen-Jacobs, ser. A, fasc. 19:1–79. Richmond, Surrey, U.K.: Royal Botanic Gardens, Kew. MITCHELL, J. D., AND S. A. MORI. 1987. The cashew and its relatives (*Anacardium:* Anacardiaceae). *Mem. New York Bot. Gard.* 42:1–76. YOUNG, D. A. 1976. Flavonoid chemistry and the phylogenetic relationships of the Julianiaceae. *Syst. Bot.* 1:149–62.

ANISOPHYLLEACEAE (Anisophyllea Family)

MATS H. G. GUSTAFSSON

Figure 8

- *trees or shrubs*

- *leaves alternate, in 2 or 4 rows, simple, often dimorphic*

- *flowers often with fringed or divided petals; ovary inferior; styles 3 or 4, distinct*

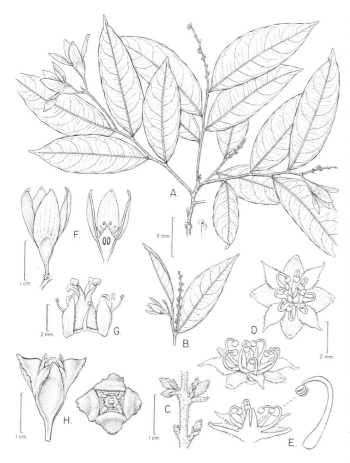

Figure 8. ANISOPHYLLACEAE. *Polygonanthus amazonicus* (A–G, Zarucchis et al. 3115; H, Silva 4486). **A.** Stem with leaves, inflorescences, and developing fruits (left). **B.** Part of stem with inflorescence and developing fruit. **C.** Part of inflorescence with flowers in bud. **D.** Apical (above) and lateral (below) views of flowers. **E.** Medial section of flower (left) and lateral view of stamen (right). **F.** Lateral view (left) and medial section of young fruit (right). **G.** Lateral view of young fruit with stamens and two petals. **H.** Lateral (left) and apical (right) views of mature fruits. Original. Artist: Bobbi Angell.

Numbers of genera and species. Worldwide, the Anisophylleaceae comprise four genera and approximately 30 species. *Anisophyllea* is by far the largest genus, with around 25 species. In tropical America, there are two genera, *Anisophyllea* and *Polygonanthus*, with two species each.

Distribution and habitat. *Anisophyllea* occurs throughout most of the Tropics, but is most species-rich in the Eastern Hemisphere. *Polygonanthus* is found only in Amazonia. Of the remaining genera in the family, *Combretocarpus* is restricted to Borneo, and *Poga* to West Africa. The family grows in wet, primary, tropical forests and swamps.

Family classification. The Anisophylleaceae have often been treated as a part of Rhizophoraceae, perhaps on the basis of similar petals, and wood anatomy. Numerous other characters (e.g., flower morphology and embryology) are very differ-

ent from the Rhizophoraceae, and there is now wide agreement that the two families are not closely related. Based on morphology, a position in the Myrtales or Rosales (as by Cronquist) has been suggested, but molecular data indicate that the Anisophylleaceae belong in the Cucurbitales.

Features of the family. Habit: trees or shrubs. **Stipules** absent. **Leaves** alternate, occurring in 2 or 4 rows, simple, often dimorphic; blades with base asymmetric, the margins entire. **Inflorescences** axillary, racemes or panicles. **Flowers** actinomorphic, unisexual (the plants dioecious) or bisexual (or appearing so), inconspicuous; sepals (3)4(5), the lobes valvate; petals (3)4(5), valvate, often fringed or divided, entire in *Polygonanthus*; androecium of (6)8(10) stamens (twice as many as petals); nectar disc present, surrounding ovary base, deeply lobed; gynoecium syncarpous, the ovary inferior, the carpels equal to number of locules, the locules (3)4, the styles (3)4, distinct; placentation axile, the ovules 1 or 2 per locule, pendulous. **Fruits** fleshy drupes (*Anisophyllea*) or dry, woody, strongly winged (*Polygonanthus*), crowned by much enlarged and persistent calyx lobes (*Polygonanthus*). **Seeds** 1 per fruit (*Anisophyllea*); endosperm absent, the cotyledons reduced or absent.

The leaves of *Anisophyllea* occur in four rows, and, on the horizontal branches, the leaves of the upper two rows are very reduced in size. The leaf venation in the majority of *Anisophyllea* is characterized by 2 or more very strong sideveins departing from the midvein near the base and nearly reaching the apex of the blade.

Natural history. The Anisophylleaceae are known to accumulate large amounts of aluminum. No information is available about pollination and dispersal biology.

Economic uses. In the Eastern Hemisphere, some members of the family (*Combretocarpus* and *Poga*) are important timber trees. *Poga* also yields edible seeds, which are pressed to produce an oil used in cooking and medicine. The West African species *Anisophyllea laurina* has fleshy, edible fruits referred to as monkey apples.

References. DAHLGREN, R.M.T. 1988. Rhizophoraceae and Anisophylleaceae: summary statement, relationships. *Ann. Missouri Bot. Gard.* 75:1259–77. JUNCOSA, A. M., AND P. B. TOMLINSON. 1988a. A historical and taxonomic synopsis of Rhizophoraceae and Anisophylleaceae. *Ann. Missouri Bot. Gard.* 75:1278–95. JUNCOSA, A. M., AND P. B. TOMLINSON. 1988b. Systematic comparison and some biological characteristics of Rhizophoraceae and Anisophylleaceae. *Ann. Missouri Bot. Gard.* 75:1296–1318. PIRES, J. M., AND W. A. RODRIGUES. Notas sôbre os gêneros *Polygonanthus* e *Anisophyllea*. *Acta Amazon.* 1(2):7–15. SCHWARZBACH, A. E., AND R. E. RICKLEFS. 2000. Systematic affinities of Rhizophoraceae and Anisophylleaceae, and intergeneric relationships within Rhizophoraceae, based on chloroplast DNA, nuclear ribosomal DNA, and morphology. *Amer. J. Bot.* 87(4): 547–64.

ANNONACEAE (Soursop Family)

Lars W. Chatrou, Heimo Rainer, and Paul J. M. Maas

Figure 9, Plate 3

- *plants woody; bark fibrous, often emitting spicy aroma when cut; wood with fine tangential bands of parenchyma*

- *leaves alternate, usually distichous, simple*

- *flowers generally with 3-merous perianth; stamens numerous; gynoecium apocarpous*

- *fruits usually apocarpous, rarely syncarpous or pseudosyncarpous*

- *seeds with ruminate endosperm*

Numbers of genera and species. The Annonaceae comprise some 135 genera and more than 2,500 species worldwide. In tropical America, there are 40 genera and around 900 species. Of the 40 genera, 19 have five species or less. Monotypic genera include *Duckeanthus*, *Pseudephedranthus*, and *Ruizodendron*. Middle-sized genera, such as *Rollinia*, *Unonopsis*, and *Xylopia*, contain 40 to 70 species. The largest genera are *Annona* (150 species), *Duguetia* (95), and *Guatteria* (265). *Guatteria* is one of the largest Neotropical genera of woody plants.

Distribution and habitat. The Annonaceae are pantropical. Two genera of the Western Hemisphere, *Asimina* and *Deeringothamnus*, are confined to subtropical and temperate regions in the United States and Canada. Four Neotropical genera also occur on other continents. *Anaxagorea* is unique for its distribution in tropical America and Asia. *Annona* and *Duguetia* are predominantly Neotropical, but each has four representatives in Africa. *Annona glabra* is the only species of the family naturally distributed on two continents. *Xylopia* has the widest geographical distribution, as it is found in tropical America, Africa, Madagascar, and Australasia, and some Pacific islands (e.g., New Caledonia, Fiji).

Annonaceae occupy all habitats, from forest to shrub- and grasslands. Their main occurrence, however, is in lowland rain forests, where they constitute one of the most important families of woody plants in terms of individual abundance and species richness. A few specialized taxa occur on white sand (Amazonian *caatinga*), on sand plains (*restinga*) along the Atlantic coast, and in sclerophyllous scrub (semidesert in northeastern Brazil, and the Caribbean). *Annona glabra* occurs in the back-vegetation of mangroves and is widely distributed along the Pacific and Atlantic mangrove belt. Only a few species (in *Guatteria* and *Raimondia*) occur above 2,000 meters.

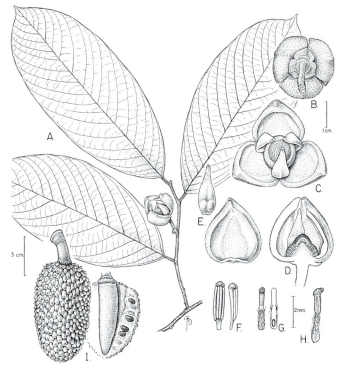

Figure 9. ANNONACEAE. *Annona prevostiae*. **A.** Stem with leaves and partially opened flower. **B.** Basal view of flower. **C.** Apical view of flower showing both whorls of petals. **D.** Medial section of flower. **E.** Adaxial views of inner petal (above) and outer petal (below). **F.** Adaxial (left) and lateral (right) views of stamens showing shieldlike apical expansion of connective. **G.** Lateral view (left) and medial section (right) of a carpel. **H.** Sterile carpel with thickened stylar region. **I.** Mature fruit (left) and longitudinal section of fruit (right) showing thickened receptacle. Reprinted with permission from Mori et al. (2002). Artist: Bobbi Angell.

Family classification. The Annonaceae are placed in the Magnoliales by Cronquist. The historical classification by Fries was based primarily on floral characters. Position of the inflorescence, aestivation, relative size of the perianth, features of the elongated tongue-shaped to dilated shieldlike anther connective appendage, placement and number of ovules, and apo- versus syncarpy was used to divide the Annonaceae into two subfamilies, three tribes, and 14 genus-groups. However, analyses of pollen ultrastructure and molecular data from plastid DNA refutes the higher-level taxonomic units in the family proposed by Fries. Many of the recent phylogenetic studies focus primarily on informal genus-groups. These genus-groups incorporate extant hypotheses on intergeneric relationships, although their composition has been derived after phenetic analyses.

Phylogenetic analyses on the basis of morphological, palynological, and molecular data agree on the position of *Anaxagorea* as sister to the rest of the family, which is essentially divided into two main clades. The first clade is suppported by inaperturate pollen. The basal lineages within this clade are mainly Neotropical and include *Guatteria*, *Xylopia*, all genera with (pseudo)syncarpous fruits, and *Cymbopetalum*, *Trigynaea*, and related genera. Sister to this clade is a small clade that contains *Tetrameranthus* as the sole Neotropical representative, supported by the presence of a third integument in the seed. The second main clade contains genera with monosulcate and disulcate pollen. This predominantly Asian clade comprises all Neotropical genera with imbricate sepals, one basal ovule, and apocarpous fruits, such as *Cremastosperma*, *Malmea*, and *Oxandra*.

Features of the family. Habit: shrubs, small to medium-sized trees, rarely canopy trees (*Duguetia surinamensis*, *Onychopetalum amazonicum*), subshrubs, or lianas. **Bark** fibrous, easily torn off in long strips (resembles bark of Lecythidaceae); often emits spicy aroma when cut. **Wood** with fine tangential parenchyma bands forming reticulate pattern with 4–8-seriate rays (in cross section). **Stipules** absent. **Leaves** alternate, distichous (spiral in *Tetrameranthus*), simple; indument of simple trichomes, less often stellate trichomes or lepidote trichomes (*Duguetia*); blades with midvein adaxially sunken, sometimes raised; domatia rarely present (*Annona*). **Inflorescences** axillary or terminal (sometimes shifting to leaf-opposed or infra-axillary), rhipidiate. **Flowers** actinomorphic, bisexual, or rarely unisexual; perianth generally 3-merous; calyx sometimes cup-shaped, the sepals 3, generally smaller than petals, distinct, or connate at base to fully connate (*Hornschuchia*, *Xylopia pro parte*); petals 6, usually in two whorls, usually distinct, variable in size, often fleshy, thick (in most *Anaxagorea*), chartaceous (in *Sapranthus*), cream, white, or yellow (at maturity), rarely red or purple; androecium with numerous stamens (only 6–11 in *Bocagea*), the stamens spirally arranged, distinct, the filaments short, the anthers relatively large, the connective expanded above thecae, shieldlike; staminodes uncommon (found only in *Anaxagorea*, *Fusaea*, *Xylopia*); gynoecium apocarpous, the ovaries superior, the carpels often numerous (often reduced to one in *Trigynaea* and *Tridimeris*), the stigma usually sessile (*Fusaea* possesses a distinct style); placentation basal or lateral, rarely apical, the ovules 1–many. **Fruits** usually apocarpous, then often composed of distinct stipitate fruitlets (monocarps), the fruitlets 2–200, often fleshy, usually indehiscent, rarely syncarpous (*Annona*, *Fusaea*, *Raimondia*, and *Rollinia pro parte*) or pseudosyncarpous (*Duguetia*). **Seeds** 1–many (per monocarp); endosperm ruminate (useful for generic delimitation), sometimes arillate (*Cymbopetalum*, *Xylopia*).

Subshrubs with a subterranean, irregular, woody stem (xylopodium) are abundant in savannas, and include some species of *Annona*, *Duguetia*, and *Guatteria*. Lianas are rare in the neotropics (*Guatteria scandens*, *Annona* section *Pilannona pro parte*). The total number of Neotropical liana species is less than ten, which is 1% of the total number of Neotropical species. This portion is very low compared to the 33% liana component in African and Asiatic species.

The leaf indument is mostly made up of simple hairs. All species of *Tetrameranthus*, a few species of *Annona*, *Rollinia*, and *Anaxagorea*, and roughly half of the species of *Duguetia* are provided with stellate hairs. *Duguetia* is the only genus with lepidote hairs, which are often intermingled with stellate hairs.

Domatia, consisting of tiny cavities often covered by tufts of hairs, are present in *Annona* in the axils of the secondary veins and midvein.

Ramiflory is quite common, and cauliflory (e.g., *Klarobelia cauliflora* and *Xylopia benthamii*) is less frequent. Flagelliflory is found in *Anaxagorea floribunda*, three species of *Duguetia*, and four species of *Hornschuchia*.

Unlike in African and Asiatic species, only a few deviations from the trimerous and tricyclic perianth occur in Neotropical Annonaceae. *Duguetia phaeoclados* is an oddity because of the variable number of unequal petals, arranged spirally, and no clear distinction between sepals and petals. *Anaxagorea sylvatica*, *Malmea dimera*, and *Tridimeris* are dimerous. *Tetrameranthus* and one species of *Asimina* (*A. tetramera*) have tetramerous flowers. In some sections of *Annona* and *Raimondia*, the inner whorl of petals is lacking or rudimentary.

The petals vary in size from a few millimeters, like in *Bocageopsis* and *Oxandra*, to more than 18 cm in *Sapranthus violaceus*. The two whorls of petals are more or less equal in length, but in some genera, like *Xylopia*, the inner ones are often smaller, whereas in *Heteropetalum* the outer petals are smaller than the inner ones. Petals of *Cardiopetalum*, *Fusaea peruviana*, *Rollinia*, and a few species of *Annona* are connate to some extent. The peculiar winglike appendages of the outer petals of *Rollinia* give the flower a propeller-like appearance. In *Cymbopetalum* the inner petals are often boat-shaped with distinctly involute margins.

Good examples of apocarpous, indehiscent fruits are *Guatteria*, *Malmea*, and *Unonopsis*. Dehiscent fruits occur in *Anaxagorea*, *Cymbopetalum*, and *Xylopia*. The former genus is unique among the family due to its apically and explosively dehiscing monocarps.

Natural history. The stigmas of Annonaceae secrete an exudate that links the distinct carpels together and provides a suitable substrate for the germination of the pollen grains and the migration of the pollen tube. Pollination is accomplished by various beetles, thrips, and flies, depending largely on the size of the flowers. Pollinators of small-flowered species are mainly sap beetles and thrips. A peculiarity of the large-flowered species of Annonaceae is the formation of a pollination chamber (e.g., some *Annona* and *Duguetia*) that, together with the production of heat and concomitant emission of scent, attracts relatively large scarab beetles. The common occurrence of food tissue on the inner side of the petals (e.g., *Duguetia*, *Mosannona*, and *Porcelia*) may be considered as a coevolutionary feature of beetle pollination.

Fruits of the Annonaceae are dispersed by birds, mammals, and fish. The hard and thick fruit wall of some species from dry vegetation types serves as a germination chamber. In these fruits, moisture accumulates during the colder hours of the day and is preserved through the hotter periods, thereby facilitating germination and seedling survival.

Economic uses. A few species of Neotropical Annonaceae are cultivated throughout the Tropics and subtropics because of their edible fruit, such as *Annona cherimola* (custard apple, *cherimoya*), *A. muricata* (soursop), *A. squamosa* (sugar apple, sweet apple), and *Rollinia mucosa* (*biribá*). Others are only of local interest; e.g., species of *Fusaea* and *Porcelia*.

The strong and fibrous bark often is used for making rope. Some species of *Duguetia* are named *tortuga caspi*, meaning "turtle wood" because of the hardness. The wood often is used for firewood and for making poles, canoes, and bridges. The only species commercially exploited are *Oxandra lanceolata* (lancewood) in the Caribbean and some related species of *Oxandra* in the Amazon Basin and Panama. The sapwood is used for special items such as fishing rods and billiard cues.

Some Annonaceae are receiving attention in pharmaceutical research because natural compounds in the leaves and bark, such as acetogenins and alkaloids, have potential to inhibit fungi and bacteria and the growth of cells (as in tumors).

References. CHATROU, L. W., J. KOEK-NOORMAN, AND P. J. MAAS. 2000. Studies in Annonaceae XXXVI. The *Duguetia* alliance: where the ways part. *Ann. Missouri Bot. Gard.* 87:234–45. CORRERA Q., J. E., AND H. Y. BERNAL. 1989. Annonaceae. In *Especies vegetales promisorias de los países del Convenio Andrés Bello*, Tomo I. Bogotá, D. E., Colombia: Secretaria Ejecutiva del Convenio Andrés Bello. DOYLE, J. A., P. BYGRAVE, AND A. LE THOMAS. 2000. Implications of molecular data for pollen evolution in Annonaceae. In Pollen and spores: morphology and biology, eds. M. M. Harley, C. M. Morton, S. Black, et. al., 259–84. Richmond, Surrey, U.K.: Royal Botanic Gardin, Kew. DOYLE, J. A., AND A. LE THOMAS. 1997. Significance of palynology for phylogeny of Annonaceae: experiments with removal of pollen characters. *Pl. Syst. Evol.* 206:133–59. FRIES, R. E. 1959. Annonaceae. *Die Natürlichen Pflanzenfamilien*, A. Engler and K. Prantl, 2nd ed. 17aII:1–171. Leipzig: Wilhelm Engelmann. JOHNSON, D. M., AND N. A. MURRAY. 1995. Synopsis of the tribe Bocageeae (Annonaceae), with revisions of Cardiopetalum, Froesiodendron, Trigynaea, Bocagea, and Hornschuchia. *Brittonia* 47(3):248–319. KESSLER, P.J.A. 1993. Annonaceae. In *The Families and Genera of Vascular Plants*, eds. K. Kubitzki, J. G. Rohwer, and V. Bittrich, 3:198–201. Berlin: Springer-Verlag. KOEK-NOORMAN, J., A. K. VAN SETTEN, AND C. M. VAN ZUILEN. 1997. Studies in Annonaceae XXVI. Flower and fruit morphology in Annonaceae. Their contribution to patterns in cluster analysis. *Bot. Jahrb. Syst.* 119:213–30. MAAS, P.J.M., L. Y. TH. WESTRA, AND COLLABORATORS. 1992. *Rollinia. Fl. Neotrop. Monogr.* 57:1–188. WEBBER, A. C. 1996. Biologia floral, polinização e aspectos fenologicos de algumas Annonaceae na Amazonia Central. Thesis, Universidade do Amazonas, Manaus, Brazil.

APIACEAE (Carrot or Parsley Family)

LINCOLN CONSTANCE† AND JAMES M. AFFOLTER

Figure 10

- *predominantly herbs, less often woody*
- *leaves often pinnately or palmately dissected*
- *inflorescences usually in umbels, less often in heads*
- *flowers with 5 sepals (or apical teeth of sepals), petals, and stamens; ovary inferior, the carpels 2*
- *fruits schizocarps, the mericarps 2*

Numbers of genera and species. Worldwide, the Apiaceae are estimated to comprise 455 genera and 3,600–3,751 species. The largest genera are *Bupleurum* (180–190 species), *Eryngium* (more than 200 species), *Ferula* (170 species), *Hydrocotyle* (130 species), *Peucedanum* (100–120 species), and *Pimpinella* (150 species). Most of these genera require further study. In tropical America, there are 48 genera and about 500 species.

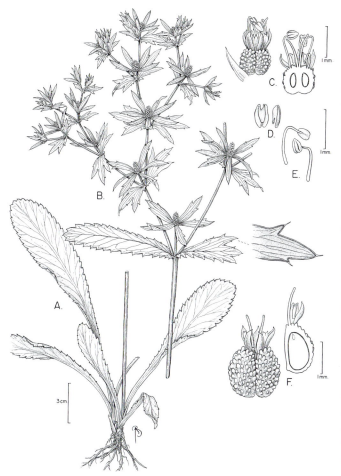

Figure 10. APIACEAE. *Eryngium foetidum*. **A.** Basal part of plant with leaves. **B.** Upper part of stem, inflorescences, and leaves with detail of margin (right). **C.** Entire flower (left) and medial section of flower (right). **D.** Adaxial (left) and lateral (right) views of petals showing reflexed apices. **E.** Abaxial (left) and lateral (right) views of stamens. **F.** Lateral view of whole fruit (left) and medial section through one mericarp (right). Reprinted with permission from Mori et al. (2002). Artist: Bobbi Angell.

Distribution and habitats. The Apiaceae are cosmopolitan, even reaching the Arctic of Eurasia and North America and the Antarctic islands south of the Strait of Magellan and New Zealand. Many genera are circumboreal, none is circumaustral except by cultivation, and only *Hydrocotyle* and *Centella* are truly pantropical. Although less evident than in much of Eurasia, the Apiaceae form a significant part of the vegetation of Mexico and subtropical America.

There are relatively few north-south connections in the Western Hemisphere; these connections are more abundant between Eurasia and sub-Saharan Africa. Each of the austral areas has its own characteristic genera, but there is some affinity between those of southern South America and Australia and New Zealand. Species of *Oreomyrrhis* form a chain around the southern Pacific from Mexico to Taiwan.

Apiaceae are predominantly temperate-zone or high-altitude plants that largely avoid the lowland Tropics.

Family classification. The Apiaceae (or Umbelliferae) are placed in the Apiales by Cronquist with the Araliaceae. Recent morphological and molecular analyses suggest that these two families are better placed together to form a more broadly defined Apiaceae.

The Apiaceae may have been the first group of flowering plants recognized as a family; it was first monographed in 1672. In a treatment that placed heavy emphasis on characters of the fruit, Drude recognized three subfamilies (Hydrocotyloideae, Saniculoideae, and Apioideae) and 18 tribes. Although Drude's classification has been criticized for using subtle or poorly defined characters, no generally acceptable revision has been worked out during the past century. Recent investigations based on a variety of molecular characters suggest that the Apioideae and Saniculoideae are monophyletic sister groups while the Hydrocotyloideae are polyphyletic (containing some members more closely allied to the Araliaceae *sensu stricto* and others to the Apioideae and Saniculoideae).

Features of the family. Habit: predominantly herbs, less often shrubs or shrublike, creeping plants, or tuberous or cushion-forming plants, rarely trees or treelike. **Stipules** rarely present. **Leaves** alternate, rarely opposite, simple, or compound, often large, a basal sheath common; petioles often present, rarely modified into phyllodes; blades often pinnately or palmately dissected. **Inflorescences** axillary or terminal, usually in umbels, less commonly heads, compound or simple, conspicuous; involucre often present at base of umbel, involucels (bracteoles) common below umbellets; the flowers often densely crowded. **Flowers** small, actinomorphic, often bisexual, if unisexual then many species andromonoecious, the lateral and late-developing flowers often unisexual; sepals 5, often reduced (prominent in *Eryngium*), frequently only apical teeth of sepals apparent; petals 5, usually white, yellow, blue, or red-purple, the base clawed, tapered, the apex usually incurved (acute or obtuse in Hydrocotyloideae); androecium of 5 stamens, the anthers basi- or dorsifixed, dehiscing longitudinally; gynoecium syncarpous, the ovary inferior, the carpels 2, the locules 2, the styles may be swollen into stylopodium, this often nectar secreting; placentation axile, the ovules 1 per locule. **Fruits** schizocarps, dry, usually compressed or flattened, less often globose or cylindrical, the mericarps 2, with costae (ribs) 5(10), obscure, threadlike, or prominently extended into wings, or prickles. **Seeds** 2 (1 per mericarp), rarely 1, the commissural surface flat, variously concave, or grooved (an important distinction among subfamilies); endosperm often copious, the embryo usually small, the cotyledons linear to very broad.

Myrrhidendron is the most treelike of Neotropical genera, but some Mexican genera, such as *Arracacia, Coaxana,*

Coulterophytum, Enantiophylla, Neonelsonia, Prionoscia-dium, Mathiasella, and *Dahliaphyllum* also contain substantial amounts of secondary tissue.

The leaves of Apiaceae are extraordinarily diverse. They range from the round peltate leaves of aquatic *Hydrocotyle* to the segmented tubular leaves of many *Eryngium, Lilaeopsis,* and *Ottoa* to the entire, toothed, or lobed cushion leaves of *Azorella.* Most apioid leaves, some of them huge, are pinnately or palmately dissected. Species occurring in arid habitats frequently develop prickly foliage; true succulence is rare.

Availability of mature fruit is a virtual necessity for satisfactory identification since the classification of Apiaceae centers on the three-dimensional shape and compression (or lack of it) of the fruit, and the ornamentation or modification of its external surface.

After anthesis, the two mericarps commonly separate from each other but remain suspended from the center of the fruit by a 2-parted projection called the carpophore. The carpophore remains attached to the parent plant after the mericarps have been shed. Less frequently, carpophore halves may remain attached to and fall with the individual mericarp.

The exterior surface of each mericarp is provided with ribs or costae that extend from the base of the style to the stalk supporting the fruit. The ribs of an individual fruit may be subequal or some may be highly developed and the others not. The fruits are often compressed or flattened either dorsally (in the same plane as the carpophore and the internal or commissural surface) or laterally (at right angles to the commissure).

The mericarp is more than a seed because it is surrounded by one or more layers of tissue derived from the ovary wall. These layers may be more or less differentiated from each other in the presence or lack of sclerification, number, and thickness. The ends of resin canals that permeate the whole plant body may be observed between the seed coat and pericarp.

Natural history. Published information on breeding systems in the Apiaceae is nearly lacking. The exposed nectar and abundant insect visitors indicate that promiscuous pollination, as well as self-pollination, would be the rule. Observation in the field however, suggests, that although a certain amount of reproduction results from pollination by generalized insect visitors, this is not necessarily the prevalent pattern. Variations in flower color (usually white, yellow, blue, or red-purple) and nectar availability due to physical barriers within the flower (e.g., the narrow tube formed by incurved petals and filaments in *Eryngium*) can restrict the types of effective pollinators. No information is available about dispersal biology.

Economic uses. The family is the source of many important herbs and spices (e.g., parsley, fennel, dill, coriander, cumin, caraway, and anise), as well as several vegetable crops (e.g., carrots, parsnips, and celery). Most of these originated in temperate Eurasia and the Mediterranean region but are now used and cultivated on a widespread basis. Native and introduced species of Apiaceae also have been incorporated in local systems of traditional medicine in temperate and tropical America, where they are used to treat a variety of ailments.

The commonly cultivated and weedy Neotropical native known as false coriander (*Eryngium foetidum*) has strongly scented foliage and is used as a substitute for coriander. An important Andean root crop, arracacha (*Arracacia xanthorrhiza*), may be the only member of the family domesticated in South America. Approximately 30,000 hectares are devoted to *arracacha* cultivation in Brazil, Colombia, Ecuador, and Venezuela, and it is grown widely in Peru and Bolivia as a subsistence crop.

References. BELL, C. R. 1971. Breeding systems and floral biology of the Umbelliferae as evidence for specialization in unspecialized flowers. In *The Biology and Chemistry of the Umbelliferae,* ed. V. H. Heywood. London: Academic Press. CERCEAU-LARRIVAL, M.-T. 1971. Morphologie pollinique et corrélations phylogénétiques chez les Ombellifères. In *The Biology and Chemistry of the Umbelliferae,* ed. V. H. Heywood. London: Academic Press. CONSTANCE, L., AND D. E. BREEDLOVE. 1994. *Dahliaphyllum,* a new arborescent umbellifer from Guerrero. *Acta Bot. Mex.* 26:83–87. DOWNIE, S. R., D. S. KATZ-DOWNIE, AND M. F. WATSON. 2000. A phylogeny of the flowering plant family Apiaceae based on chloroplast DNA RPL16 and RPOC1 intron sequences: towards a suprageneric classification of subfamily Apioideae. *Amer. J. Bot.* 87(2):273–92. DRUDE, C.G.O. 1897–1898. Umbelliferae. In *Die Natürlichen Pflanzenfamilien,* A. Engler and K. Prantl, 3(8):61–250. Leipzig: Wilhelm Engelmann. HERMANN, M. 1997. Arracacha (*Arracacia xanthorrhiza* Bancroft). In *Andean Roots and Tubers: Ahipa, Arracacha, Maca, and Yacon,* eds. M. Hermann and J. Heller, ser. Promoting the conservation and use of underutilized and neglected crops, 21. Rome: IPGRI. FRENCH, D. H. 1971. Ethnobotany of the Umbelliferae. In *The Biology and Chemistry of the Umbelliferae,* ed. V. H. Heywood. London: Academic Press. MATHIAS, M. E. 1971. Systematic survey of New World Umbelliferae. In *The Biology and Chemistry of the Umbelliferae,* ed. V. H. Heywood. London: Academic Press. MORISON, R. 1672. *Plantarum umbelliferanum distributio nova.* Oxford. PIMENOV, M. G., AND M. V. LEONOV. 1993. *The Genera of the Umbelliferae.* Richmond, Surrey, U.K.: Royal Botanic Gardens, Kew. PLUNKETT, G. M., D. E. SOLTIS, AND P. S. SOLTIS. 1997. Clarification of the relationship between Apiaceae and Araliaceae based on *mat*K and *rbc*L sequence data. *Amer. J. Bot.* 84(4):565–580.

APOCYNACEAE (Dogbane or Milkweed Family)

ALESSANDRO RAPINI

Figures 11, 12, 13; Plate 4

- *herbaceous or woody*

- *latex present*

- *leaves usually opposite, simple; blade margins entire*

- *flowers 5-merous (except gynoecium usually bicarpellary); styles united at apex forming an enlarged head*

- *fruits usually paired follicles*

- *seeds usually comose*

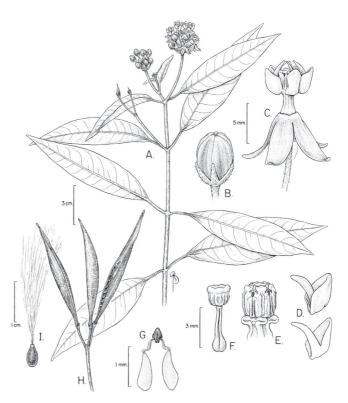

Figure 11. APOCYNACEAE. *Asclepias curassavica*. **A.** Stem with leaves and inflorescences. **B.** Lateral view of flower bud. **C.** Lateral view of flower. **D.** Intact hood and horn (above) and medial section of hood and horn (below). **E.** Lateral view of gynostegium. **F.** Lateral view of gynoecium with capitate stigma. **G.** Pollinia. **H.** Part of infructescence. **I.** Seed with coma. Reprinted with permission from Mori et al. (2002). Artist: Bobbi Angell.

Numbers of genera and species. Worldwide, the Apocynaceae comprise 250 to more than 550 genera, and between 3,700 and almost 5,100 species. In tropical America, there are nearly 100 accepted genera and about 1,500 species. A few genera such as *Cynanchum* may very from 200 to more than 400 species; others, such as *Nautonia*, are monotypic (*N. nummularia*).

Distribution and habitats. Species of Apocynaceae are found on all continents except Antarctica. Most species occur in tropical regions, but a few can reach 61°N or 50°S. The family comprises both widespread species, such as *Asclepias curassavica* (a pantropical weed), and narrowly endemic species, such as *Ditassa diamantinensis*, restricted to the region of Diamantina in the state of Minas Gerais, Brazil.

Species of Apocynaceae grow in various habitats, from tropical rain forests to semiarid regions. They occur from sea level to mountain tops, mainly on dry soils, but also on rocks or in flooded areas, and sometimes river margins (e.g., *Matelea pedalis*).

Family classification. The Apocynaceae are placed in the Gentianales by Cronquist. Several systems of classification varying at the taxonomic ranks have been proposed. Apocynaceae, as here circumscribed, was traditionally divided into two families: Apocynaceae *sensu stricto* and Asclepiadaceae *sensu lato*, distinguished by the absence or presence of translators, respectively. Apocynaceae *sensu stricto* included two subfamilies: Rauvolfioideae (Plumerioideae), with anthers completely fertile, distinct from each other, and free from the style; and Apocynoideae (Echitoideae), characterized by partially sterile, connivent anthers fused to the style. Two subfamilies were recognized in Asclepiadaceae *sensu lato*: Periplocoideae, comprising 50 genera and about 200 Palaeotropical species with tetrasporangiate anthers, pollen grains in tetrads or in pollinia, and spoon-shaped translators with a

sticky terminal disc (it is sometimes treated as a family but now considered by some authors to be more related to groups included in Apocynaceae *sensu stricto*); and Asclepiadoideae, with bisporangiate anthers, pollen in pollinia, and translators with two arms and one corpusculum, except in tribe Secamoneae (tetrasporangiate anthers and translators without arms) and *Fockea* (translators without arms).

Cladistic studies based on morphological and molecular data have not supported maintaining Apocynaceae and Asclepiadaceae as separate families. Asclepiadaceae *sensu stricto* (excluding Periplocoideae) is a monophyletic family; however, if segregated from Apocynaceae, the latter becomes paraphyletic. Therefore, we include the Apocynaceae *sensu stricto*, the Asclepiadoideae, and the Periplocoideae in a broadly defined Apocynaceae.

The Apocynaceae are among the 10 largest families of flowering plants. The main difficulty for the delimitation of the taxa is related to the great diversity and wide distribution of the family associated with the need of globally based studies.

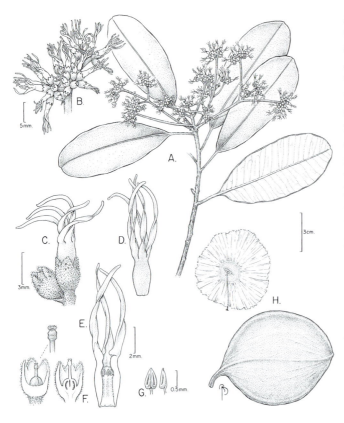

Figure 12. APOCYNACEAE. *Aspidosperma album*. **A.** Stem with leaves and inflorescences; leaf at bottom right turned to show abaxial surface. **B.** Part of inflorescence. **C.** Lateral views of flower (right) and calyx (left). **D.** Lateral view of corolla. **E.** Medial section of corolla showing adnate stamens. **F.** Longitudinal section of basal part of flower (far left) with detail of style head (above), and medial section of basal part of flower (right). **G.** Adaxial (left) and lateral (right) views of stamens. **H.** Lateral views of fruit (below) and seed (above). Reprinted with permission from Mori et al. (2002). Artist: Bobbi Angell.

Features of the family. Habit: herbs, shrubs, trees, vines, or lianas rarely deciduous or with reduced leaves (during flowering periods; e.g., *Metastelma scoparium*); colleters frequently present; internal phloem present. Latex present, often milky. Stipules usually absent. Leaves usually opposite, less frequently whorled (e.g., *Rauvolfia*, *Hemipogon*), or alternate (e.g., *Aspidosperma*, *Vallesia*), simple; blade margins entire. Inflorescences determinate, terminal or nodal, paniculate, racemose, corymbiform, or umbelliform, rarely flowers solitary. Flowers actinomorphic or nearly so, bisexual, usually 5-merous (except gynoecium); sepals 5, connate (at least at base); internal colleters often present, basal or joined alternately with sepals; petals 5, connate (at least at base), funnelform, salverform, campanulate, urceolate, rotate, or reflexed, convolute; corolline and/or gynostegial corona often present, the lobes distinct or fused; stamens 5, alternate with petals, united to corolla-tube, the filaments short, distinct to fused into tube around gynoecium, the anthers basifixed, fertile or partially sterile, free or fused to gynoecium (then forming

gynostegium), the thecae usually 2, dehiscence longitudinal or apical; meiotic divisions of pollen mother cells simultaneous or successive; pollen grains granular, in tetrads (e.g., *Apocynum*) or pollinia; polliniaria (of Neotropical species) with 2 pollinia of adjacent stamens connected by a translator, translator secreted by stigmatic region, comprising a corpusculum and 2 translator arms; nectaries present, distinct or fused (then forming a disc), surrounding base of gynoecium, or in stigmatic chambers (on gynostegium, alternate with stamens); ovary superior, rarely semi-inferior (e.g., *Plumeria*), the locules 1(2) (2 in *Ambelania*), the carpels 2 (–8 in tribe Pleiocarpeae, a non-Neotropical group), usually distinct, less often connate (e.g., *Ambelania*), the styles united at apex forming enlarged head, the stigmatic region well developed; placentation marginal, parietal, or axile, the ovules numerous, rarely 1 or 2 per locule, usually anatropous, pendulous. Fruits usually paired follicles, often only 1 develops, rarely fused (e.g., *Mandevilla* spp.), capsules (e.g., *Allamanda*), berries (e.g., *Couma*), or drupes (e.g., *Thevetia*, *Vallesia*). Seeds 1–numerous, usually comose, less often winged (e.g., *Allamanda*, *Plumeria*, *Aspidosperma*) or arillate (e.g., *Tabernaemontana*), the endosperm nuclear, oily, the embryo straight.

The Apocynaceae produce various chemicals, including iridoid compounds, cardiac glycosides, and alkaloids, especially of the complex indole (derived from tryptophane or tryptamine), pyrrolizidine, steroid, and pyridine groups.

Natural history. Pollination takes place by a variety of insects (or rarely birds in a few Paleotropical species), which are reflected in the great diversity and complexity of the flowers. The main pollinators are bees and wasps (Hymenoptera), butterflies and moths (Lepidoptera), and flies (Diptera). They usually visit the flowers for nectar produced by nectary-glands surrounding the gynoecium, or, in the most specialized groups, behind the anthers in the stigmatic region of the gynostegium. The nectar accumulates internally, often with the aid of the corona. In several species, trichomes on the inner side of the corolla and the corona, as well as the shape of the anthers, guide the proboscis or the legs of pollinators to ensure that pollen grains or the corpusculum of the pollinium get attached to them.

A few experiments have shown that pollen grains deposited outside the stigmatic region or not released from the anthers are capable of fertilization; therefore, contrary to what was believed, the pollinia and the clefts between the anthers apparently do not have a key-lock function, and autogamy in the family is not uncommon.

Most genera of Apocynaceae have gynoecia that combine the advantages of a functionally syncarpic ovary and an apocarpous fruit. This specialization attains its highest level when associated with agglutination of pollen grains into pollinia. When pollinia reach the stigmatic region, they can fertilize the ovules of any carpel, thereby resulting in production of numerous seeds from a single pollination.

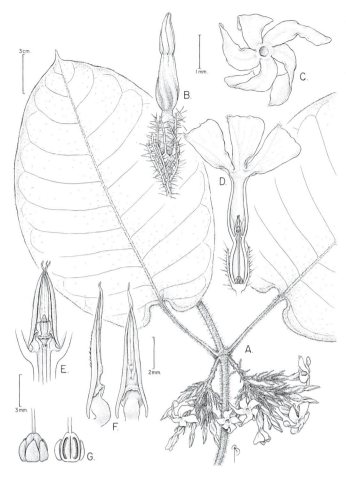

Figure 13. APOCYNACEAE. *Macropharynx spectabilis*. **A.** Stem with leaves and inflorescences. **B.** Lateral view of flower bud. **C.** Apical view of corolla. **D.** Longitudinal section of flower. **E.** Longitudinal section of throat of corolla showing stigma surrounded by anthers. **F.** Lateral (left) and adaxial (right) views of anthers. **G.** Lateral view of ovary surrounded by glands (left) and medial section of ovary (right). Reprinted with permission from Mori et al. (2002). Artist: Bobbi Angell.

The seeds are dispersed predominantly by wind but, in the cases of indehiscent fruits or arillate seeds, animal dispersal is indicated.

One of the best studied plant-animal interactions is that between *Danaus plexippus* (monarch butterfly) and *Asclepias curassavica* (blood-flower). The caterpillars of this butterfly often feed on the leaves of this plant and accumulate considerable amounts of cardiac glycosides. When fully developed, the butterflies remain inedible for birds.

Economic uses. In indigenous cultures, *Apocynum cannabinum* (Indian hemp) is utilized as a source of fiber for ropes and cords for handicrafts. The resistant and flexible branches of *Funastrum clausum* are used as fishing poles, and arrow poisons are extracted from a few species (e.g., some *Matelea*).

Rubber and chewing gum are produced from the latex of

Apocynum (dogbane) and *Asclepias* (milkweed). The downy hairs of the seeds are used as filling (e.g., in pillows).

Some arborescent species, especially of the genus *Aspidosperma*, provide wood for construction, furniture, and tools. The ridges of the grooved trunks of some *Aspidosperma* species are especially prized for making ax handles.

Because of the profusion of secondary metabolites, the family is an important source of bioactive compounds. The most utilized in medicine are the indole alkaloids. In *Catharanthus roseus*, more than 95 compounds have been identified, especially vincristine (leucrocristine) and vinblastine (vincaleucoblastine). These substances interrupt cellular division and are used in chemotherapy for cancers, including Hodgkin's disease and acute leukemia. Vincamine, extracted from *Vinca minor*, increases blood flow to the brain and is used for the treatment of cerebrovascular problems, especially in older people. Reserpine, obtained from *Rauvolfia serpentina* (snakewood), was used to treat high blood pressure, and its cardiac glycosides were previously important in the treatment of cardiac diseases, but both compounds have been replaced by more effective substances. A few species are extremely toxic and may cause death when accidentally consumed by cattle or children.

The Apocynaceae are widely cultivated as ornamentals, and some species are now naturalized in many regions. These include *Nerium oleander* (oleander), with more than 400 cultivars, 175 of which are commercialized; *Catharanthus roseus* (Madagascar periwinkle); *Vinca major* (greater periwinkle) and *V. minor* (lesser periwinkle) from the Mediterranean region; *Allamanda carthatica* (alamanda), *Plumeria rubra* (frangipani), and *Thevetia peruviana* (yellow oleander), Neotropical species grown in gardens and along streets in tropical cities; and some Paleotropical plants such as *Ceropegia* and *Hoya* (wax plant).

References. BERNAL, H. Y., AND J. E. CORRERA Q. 1989. Asclepiadaceae. In *Especies vegetales promisorias de los países del Convenio Andrés Bello*, Tomo II. Bogotá, D. E., Colombia: Secretaria Ejecutiva del Convenio Andrés Bello. CORRERA Q., J. E., AND H. Y. BERNAL. 1989. Apocynaceae. In *Especies vegetales promisorias de los países del Convenio Andrés Bello*, Tomo I. Bogotá, D. E., Colombia: Secretaria Ejecutiva del Convenio Andrés Bello. ENDRESS, M. E., AND P. V. BRUYNS. 2000. A revised classification of the Apocynaceae s.l. *Bot. Rev.* 66:1–56. KUNZE, H. 1991. Structure and function in asclepiad pollination. *Pl. Syst. Evol.* 176: 227–53. KUNZE, H. 1993. Evolution of the translator in Periplocaceae and Asclepiadaceae. *Pl. Syst. Evol.* 185:99–122. NICHOLAS, A., AND H. BAIJNATH. 1994. A consensus classification for the order Gentianales with additional details on the suborder Apocynineae. *Bot. Rev.* 60:440–82. ROSATTI, T. J. 1989. The genera of suborder Apocynineae (Apocynaceae and Asclepiadaceae) in the southeastern United States. *J. Arnold Arbor.* 70(3):307–401; 443–514. SENNBLAD, B., AND B. BREMER. 1996. The familial and subfamilial relationship of Apocynaceae and Asclepiadaceae evaluated with rbcL data. *Pl. Syst. Evol.* 202:153–75. STRUWE, L., V. A. ALBERT, AND B. BREMER. 1994. Cladistics and family level classification of the Gentianales. *Cladistics* 10:175–206.

SWARUPANANDAN, K., J. K. MANGALY, T. K. SONNY, K. KISHOREKUMAR, AND S. C. BASHA. 1996. The subfamilial and tribal classification of the Asclepiadaceae. *Bot. J. Linn. Soc.* 120:327–69.

AQUIFOLIACEAE (Holly Family)

PIERRE-ANDRÉ LOIZEAU AND RODOLPHE SPICHIGER

Figure 14, Plate 4

- *trees or shrubs*

- *leaves usually alternate, simple*

- *flowers unisexual; staminodes present in pistillate flowers and a pistillode present in staminate flowers*

- *fruits drupes, usually containing 1–6 pyrenes*

Numbers of genera and species. Worldwide, the Aquifoliaceae comprise a single genus, *Ilex*, and more than 500 species. In tropical America, there are about 300 species. Three small Old World genera, *Oncotheca*, *Phelline*, and *Sphenostemon*, have sometimes been included in the Aquifoliaceae, but they are now treated as separate monogeneric families. *Nemopanthus*, with a single species native to eastern North America, is currently included in *Ilex*.

Distribution and habitat. The Aquifoliaceae occur mostly in the tropics but extend into temperate regions to 63°N (America, Eurasia) and 35°S (America, Africa). There are only two or three species in Europe, one in Australia, one in Africa, and the remainder occur in America (most in South America) and Asia (most in southeast Asia).

In tropical America, species of *Ilex* are found from lowland to montane forests (disturbed or primary) to 4,000 meters elevation in the Andes. The family is usually found in humid habitats.

Family classification. The Aquifoliaceae are placed near the Celastraceae in the Celastrales by Cronquist. Recent molecular studies propose placement of the Aquifoliaceae into a clade among the asterids containing mostly sympetalous plants in a position basal to most of the Asterales.

Features of the family. Habit: trees or shrubs, usually evergreen, seldom deciduous. **Stipules** present, often caducous, small. **Leaves** alternate, rarely opposite or sub-opposite, simple, rarely pubescent (then with simple and unicellular hairs), heterophylly occurring in some species (see text below); blades sometimes punctate, the margins entire to spiny. **Inflo**-rescences axillary, cymes arranged in solitary dichasia, thyrses, fascicles, or thyrsoids. **Flowers** actinomorphic, unisexual (the plants dioecious), often 4–6(–23)-merous; sepals valvate, ± connate at base; petals imbricate, 1–10 mm long, often white or cream, rarely green, yellow, pink, purple, red, or chocolate-colored, the base usually connate, forming tube up to one-half length of corolla, less often distinct; stamens alternate with petals; staminodes present in pistillate flower and pistillode in the staminate flower; gynoecium syncarpous, the ovary superior, the locule 1 per carpel, the style terminal, usually short or absent, the stigma pronounced; placentation apical-axile, the ovule usually 1 per locule. **Fruits** drupes, containing 1–6(–23) pyrenes. **Seeds** 1–6(–23), small; endosperm abundant, oily, proteinaceous.

Heterophylly may occur with leaf margins spiny or entire in the same species (e.g., *Ilex dipyrena* and *Ilex dimorphophylla*), or on the same plant (e.g., *Ilex aquifolium*).

The presence of staminodes in the pistillate flower and an aborted ovary in the staminate flower has caused some authors to misinterpret the flowers of *Ilex* as bisexual.

Natural history. Pollination usually is accomplished by insects attracted by nectar produced at the base of the petals. The seeds are dispersed by birds. In cultivation, germination often requires 1–2 years or more.

Economic uses. The leaves of more than 60 species of *Ilex* are used for beverages. The most widely known is a tea made from *I. paraguariensis*, the *Yerba Maté* or Paraguay tea. This species is native to Argentina, Uruguay, Paraguay, and Brazil, but the tea is consumed throughout South America. It is prepared in a gourd or a cow horn and sipped through a

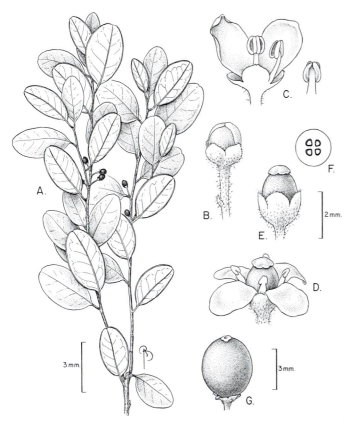

the Andes, as an emetic and stimulant; *I. cornuta* from China, as a tonic or for treating kidney diseases (leaves and bark); *I. cymosa* from southeastern Asia, for treating fever (roots); *I. mitis* from Africa, as an enema for treating colic in children, as a purgative, and for use in witchcraft rituals.

The wood was or is used for handles of guns and various tools (*I. colchica*, a substitute for ebony), mallets, bolts and locks, pulley blocks for ships (*I. aquifolium*), furniture, ceilings, brake blocks, railway sleepers, and firewood (*I. cissoidea*, *I. mitis*).

Birdlime (a sticky substance to snare small birds) has been made from the bark of *I. aquifolium* and *I. latifolia*. Large quantities of *I. aquifolium* formerly were shipped from the English Lake District to the East Indies for use as an insecticide.

Many *Ilex* (hollies) are cultivated in parks and gardens throughout the world for their foliage and decorative berries (e.g., *I. aquifolium*, *I. opaca*, *I. cornuta*, *I. crenata*, and *I. purpurea*).

Figure 14. AQUIFOLIACEAE. *Ilex urbaniana*. **A.** Stems with leaves and fruits. **B.** Lateral view of flower bud. **C.** Medial section of flower (left) and apex of stamen (right). **D.** Lateral view of pistillate flower with sterile stamens. **E.** Lateral view of pistillate flower with petals and staminodes removed. **F.** Transverse section of ovary. **G.** Lateral view of fruit. Reprinted with permission from Acevedo-Rodríguez (1996). Artist: Bobbi Angell.

References. ALIKARIDIS, F. 1987. Natural constituents of *Ilex* species. *J. Ethno-Pharmacol.* 20:121–144. ANDREWS, S. 1989. A checklist of the Aquifoliaceae of Bahia. *Rodriguésia* 63:36–44. BAAS, P. 1974. The wood anatomical range in *Ilex* (Aquifoliaceae) and its ecological and phylogenetic significance. *Blumea* 21:193–258. CORRERA Q., J. E., AND H. Y. BERNAL. 1989. Aquifoliaceae. In *Especies vegetales promisorias de los países del Convenio Andrés Bello*, Tomo I. Bogotá, D. E., Colombia: Secretaria Ejecutiva del Convenio Andrés Bello. GALLE, F. C. 1997. *Hollies. The Genus Ilex*. Portland, OR: Timber Press. LOESENER, T. 1942. Aquifoliaceae. In *Die Natürlichen Pflanzenfamilien*, A. Engler and K. Prantl, 2nd ed. 20b:36–86. Leipzig: Wilhelm Engelmann. LOIZEAU, P.-A. 1988. L'or vert du Paraguay. *Mus. Genève*, n.s., 287:16–20. LOIZEAU, P.-A. 1994. Les Aquifoliaceae péruviennes. *Boissiera* 48:1–306. LOIZEAU, P.-A., V. SAVOLAINEN, S. ANDREWS, AND R. SPICHIGER. Aquifoliaceae. In *The Families and Genera of Vascular Plants*, ed. K. Kubitzki. (In prep.). POWELL, M., V. SAVOLAINEN, P. CUÉNOUD, J.-F. MANEN AND S. ANDREWS. 2000. The mountain holly (*Nemopanthus mucronatus*) revisited with molecular data. *Kew Bull.* 55: 341–347. SAVOLAINEN, V., J.-F. MANEN, E. DOUZERY, AND R. SPICHIGER. 1994. Molecular phylogeny of families related to celastrales based on *rbc*L 5' flanking sequences. *Molecular Phylogenetics and Evolution* 3:27–37. SAVOLAINEN, V., R. SPICHIGER, AND J.-F. MANEN. 1997. Polyphyletism of celastrales deduced from a chloroplast noncoding DNA region. *Molecular Phylogenetics and Evolution* 7:145–57. SPICHIGER, R., V. SAVOLAINEN, AND J.-F. MANEN. 1993. Systematic affinities of Aquifoliaceae and Icacinaceae from molecular data analysis. *Candollea* 48:459–464.

straw. The leaves of several taxa prepared as substitutes for tea are known for their stimulating or emetic effects; e.g., *I. tarapotina* from Peru and Colombia, the *Yaupon* (*I. vomitoria*) from southeastern North America and Mexico, the *Shui-cha-tz* or water tea (*I. yunnanensis* var. *eciliata*) from the Sino-Tibetan border areas, and the T*arajo* (*I. latifolia*) from Japan or China.

Baie de Houx is produced in the Alsace region of France from *I. aquifolium*. The berries are fermented with sugar for seven years to produce one of the rarest and most expensive fruit brandies.

Several species are known for their medicinal properties; e.g., *I. aquifolium* from Europe, for treating smallpox, catarrh, and pleurisy (leaves); *I. colchica* from East Bulgaria, Turkey, and the Caucasus, for treating fever and stomach ailments (leaves) or coughs (bark and roots); *I. guayusa* from

ARALIACEAE (Ginseng or Ivy Family)

DAVID FRODIN

Figure 15

- *shrubs, trees, lianas, occasionally herbs, sometimes hemiepiphytic*

- *stipules sometimes becoming elongate, fused and ± ligulelike*

- *leaves alternate (spiral), sometimes ± crowded toward shoot ends and even forming rosettelike flushes, often palmately compound, sometimes simple; leaf bases often ± sheathing stem*

- *inflorescences often compound, generally umbels or heads*

- *flowers actinomorphic, small; ovary inferior, surmounted by distinct disc surrounding styles or stylar column*

- *fruits drupaceous or, less commonly, baccate*

Numbers of genera and species. Worldwide, the Araliaceae comprise approximately 50 genera and 1,420 described species, but many additional species, particularly in *Schefflera*, await description. In the Western Hemisphere, there are ten genera (eight of them native) and 475–525 species. The largest genera therein are *Schefflera* (250–300 species), *Oreopanax* (150), and *Dendropanax* (70), but estimates for the two latter genera are problematic. Only *Sciadodendron* (if kept separate from *Aralia*) is monotypic. Reduction in the total number of species of *Oreopanax* is likely with further revision.

In tropical America, there are seven genera (five native) and 460–510 species. Native genera include *Aralia, Dendropanax, Oreopanax, Schefflera,* and *Sciadodendron*. *Hedera* and *Tetrapanax* have become established, while several "fancy" cultivars from *Polyscias* section *Polyscias* are widely grown in warmer areas.

Distribution and habitat. The Araliaceae occur throughout most of the more humid tropics, with some found in seasonally dry regions as well as in north and south temperate zones. They are also found on many islands in the Indian and Pacific Oceans, from Madagascar to Hawaii, the Austral Islands and Rapa Iti, but in the Atlantic the Araliaceae occur only on the Azores, the Madeira group, and the Canaries. The family is most speciose in the Americas and the Indo-Pacific regions, with prominent centers of generic diversity in monsoonal Asia, Malesia, and the Pacific Islands; Africa and the Americas have few genera. Of the three largest genera, *Schefflera* has the widest distribution, being pantropical (although with few species in Africa), but its major infra-

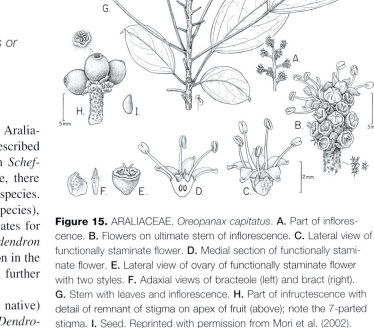

Figure 15. ARALIACEAE. *Oreopanax capitatus*. **A.** Part of inflorescence. **B.** Flowers on ultimate stem of inflorescence. **C.** Lateral view of functionally staminate flower. **D.** Medial section of functionally staminate flower. **E.** Lateral view of ovary of functionally staminate flower with two styles. **F.** Adaxial views of bracteole (left) and bract (right). **G.** Stem with leaves and inflorescence. **H.** Part of infructescence with detail of remnant of stigma on apex of fruit (above); note the 7-parted stigma. **I.** Seed. Reprinted with permission from Mori et al. (2002). Artist: Bobbi Angell.

generic groups are largely regional; *Polyscias* (along with *Gastonia* and related Pacific genera) extends unevenly from Africa to Hawaii and the Society Islands; and *Oreopanax* (excluding *Sinopanax*) is exclusively American.

In tropical America, *Schefflera, Dendropanax,* and *Oreopanax* are more or less found throughout, while *Aralia* (including *Sciadodendron*) has a patchy presence from Mexico and Cuba to Argentina and southern Brazil. *Pseudopanax* is confined to extratropical Chile and Argentina, and *Oplopanax* and *Panax* to temperate North America. The Asian, Euro-Mediterranean, and Macaronesian *Hedera* and Asian *Tetrapanax* have become established in parts of the Americas. Within *Schefflera*, Brazil is dominated by members of the formerly separate *Didymopanax*, the Guayana uplands by the *Crepinella* and *Cheilodromes* groups, the Andes by the

Sciodaphyllum group (this extending to Nicaragua and Jamaica), while the *Attenuatae* group is prominent in Central America and the West Indies. *Schefflera morototoni* (formerly *Didymopanax morototoni*) is by far the most widely distributed species. Within *Oreopanax*, the *O. capitatus* alliance is most strongly represented in Central and northwest South America; elsewhere, only *O. capitatus* is found. In the *Aralia* alliance, the *Sciadodendron* group (including *Aralia rex*, *A. soratensis* and *A. warmingiana*) is widely distributed, but the distribution of *A. humilis* and its relatives is limited to Central America, Mexico, and the southwestern United States.

Neotropical Araliaceae are generally montane, although they have been recorded from sea level to nearly 4,000 meters elevation. Few, however, are encountered in Amazonian rain forests. The forests and scrub of the Andes and Central America are the home of most species of *Oreopanax*, where they may become prominent. Some species of *Schefflera* may also assume dominance or co-dominance as, for example, *S. attenuata* (*aralie montagne*) on high ridges and slopes in the Lesser Antilles. Species of *Schefflera* are also common on many of the high sandstone *tepuis* of Guayana; elsewhere, they play a semi-important role in the *mata atlântica* and *cerrado* formations of Brazil. *Aralia warmingiana* (*carobão*, *lagarto*) forms part of the canopy in subtropical forests in Paraguay, northeastern Argentina, and parts of southern Brazil. Many species are pioneers in forest gaps, edges, abandoned land, cuttings, and on landslips.

Family classification. The Araliaceae, along with the Apiaceae, were placed by Cronquist and Takhtajan in the Apiales, an opinion followed here. The order (an alternative name for which is Araliales) is on current evidence best limited to these taxa, whether expressed as one, two, or more families. Its nearest relative in the Americas is the extratropical *Griselinia* (Griseliniaceae or Cornaceae *sensu* Cronquist).

Within the Araliaceae, as conventionally circumscribed, there are four tribes, the Hedereae (or Schefflereae of Harms), Aralieae, Myodocarpeae, and Mackinlayeae, and a number of genera of uncertain affinity (including *Tetrapanax*). All American genera except *Tetrapanax* belong in the Hedereae and Aralieae. No infrafamilial classification (save for that of Harms) has ever become widely adopted; moreover, resolution of relationships is complicated by their being, together with Apiaceae, part of a well-known and classically interesting "family pair." The Myodocarpeae (inclusive of the unusual New Caledonian genus *Myodocarpus*) and Mackinlayeae are evidently nearest to the polyphyletic subfamily Hydrocotyloideae (historically part of Apiaceae). Wen et al. have argued for retention of two families but with circumscriptions different from that of Harms and most other authors since at least the latter half of the nineteenth century. They call for inclusion of most of the former Hydrocotyloideae in Araliaceae, with even the insertion of some of its genera (e.g., *Centella* and *Micropleura*) into the Mackinlayeae. Additional studies, moreover, suggest that *Stilbocarpa* is

best referred, along with the remaining hydrocotyloids (e.g., *Schizilema*, *Azorella*, and *Bowlesia*), to Apiaceae. Such proposals are, however, premature on the evidence so far presented. Alternatives to the upkeep of two families in Apiales are their union—already proposed in the nineteenth century and again advocated in one recent systematics textbook—or recognition of perhaps as many as ten families, with all native tropical American genera remaining in a reduced "core" Araliaceae.

Much interest has also centered on wider relationships of the Araliaceae/Apiaceae. In the past, a perceived relationship with Cornaceae, and, more broadly, the rosids, was fashionable, but current evidence suggests a closer relationship with Asterales. The Apiales, together with Asterales and Dipsacales, is now seen to form part of a monophyletic though internally unresolved clade in the "Euasterids II" alliance by the Angiosperm Phylogeny Group.

Features of the family. Habit: shrubs or trees (to 35+ m tall in *Schefflera morototoni*), sometimes lianas or sprawling (e.g., *Hedera* and *Oreopanax capitatus*), occasionally rhizomatous herbs (e.g., *Aralia bicrenata*), sometimes hemiepiphytic (as in *Oreopanax capitatus* and some species of *Schefflera*), often with thick, pithy stems, the stems and leafy parts sometimes armed (e.g., *Aralia elata*). **Stipules** strongly developed in many species, at least partly united with petiole, the free portion usually connate and at times extending into a conspicuous stipular ligule (many Andean *Schefflera*), or scarcely developed and the base not obviously sheathing (most commonly in *Dendropanax*). **Leaves** alternate (spiral), sometimes ± crowded toward shoot ends and even forming rosette-like flushes, often compound (usually palmate), sometimes simple, small to large (sometimes 1+ m long); petiole short to very long, often of varying lengths, round or vertically elliptical in cross section; petiolules if present short (*Aralia*) or ± elongate (*Oreopanax*, *Schefflera*), usually in proportion to length of leaflets; simple leaves with entire or palmately lobed margins, the lobes shallow (as in *Oreopanax sanderianus*) to deeply so (as in *Oreopanax dactylifolius*) or all but entirely divided (as in *Oreopanax echinops*); leaflets often ranging greatly in size on same plant, usually palmately (*Schefflera*, *Oreopanax xalapensis*) or pinnately arranged (*Aralia*), rarely a mixture (as in *Schefflera diplodactyla*), the leaflets in single planes or rarely in fascicles (e.g., *Schefflera robusta* and *S. sciodaphyllum*); venation usually pinnate, often ± palmate in simple blades (e.g., *O. capitatus*). **Inflorescences** terminal, often compound, usually conspicuous, generally umbels or heads, less often in racemes or spikes (as in *S. fontiana*), racemules or spicules; bracts subtending branches, small to large, promptly or more tardily deciduous; pedicels continuous with calyx (native genera) or jointed just underneath (in *Polyscias*). **Flowers** actinomorphic, bisexual or unisexual in *Oreopanax* (the plants dioecious), small; calyx fused to ovary for all or most of length, scarcely extending beyond it, the free portion merely forming a flush, flanged, or toothed rim surrounding disc; corolla with 5–

10(12) petals, these broad at base, usually distinct or sometimes ± fused and corolla falling as a whole (*Schefflera*, *Sciadodendron*), valvate (Hedereae: *Dendropanax*, *Oreopanax*, *Schefflera*), or imbricate (Aralieae: *Aralia*, *Sciadodendron*); androecium usually with as many stamens as petals or corolla lobes and alternate with them, rarely more numerous, the filaments filiform or straplike, the anthers dorsifixed, opening by longitudinal slits; disc always present, more or less fleshy, elevated or not, ± nectariferous; gynoecium syncarpous, the ovary inferior, the carpels 2–10(12), the locules (1)2–10(12), the styles distinct (*Schefflera japurensis*, *S. quindiuensis*), ± fused into distinct column, or ± sessile and reduced to level of disc, the stigmas then padlike; placentation axile, the ovules solitary, pendulous, anatropous; raphe ventral. **Fruits** drupaceous or, less commonly, baccate, normally lacking oil-cells or vittae or a carpophore, the exo- and mesocarp usually fleshy (sometimes thickly so), often shrinking considerably on drying, the endocarp hard (in *Dendropanax* and *Schefflera*) or relatively thin (in *Oreopanax*), the hard endocarps and enclosed seeds together commonly known as pyrenes, each 1-seeded. **Seeds** usually 2 or more per fruit (rarely 1, as in *Schefflera monosperma*), laterally compressed; endosperm copious, oily, uniform or variously ruminate, the embryo small, near hilum.

Seed germination is epigeal and is soon followed by the first seedling leaves. These are normally simple but species with compound leaves usually soon become divided. In some species there may be a "juvenile" phase wherein the leaves are morphologically different from those of the adult. This heterophylly is particularly striking in *Schefflera morototoni*; the juvenile leaflets are therein delicately textured and silvery beneath, while in adult trees they are entire, more or less coriaceous, and variously coppery-sericeous on the under surface.

Branching varies from orthotropic to plagiotropic, but shoots are developmentally not that specialized. Stems of smaller species and branches in larger species are capable of lateral or replacement growth from latent buds, though under forest conditions branching is initially or always sparse. In some species with sparse or no branching (as in *Tetrapanax papyrifer*), new stems may arise from a spreading underground system to form stands. This may be an adaptation to episodic severe frost or other traumatic events. Other species, particularly the larger trees, exhibit more profuse branching with age. Rhythmic growth with some phenological leaf specialization has been reported in *Oreopanax*.

In certain species, such as *Schefflera diplodactyla*, the inflorescence can reach an immense size with the elongate main axis bearing 50–60 or more long primary branches. As many as six orders of branching are seen in the compound umbels of *Schefflera chimantensis*, but two or three orders are common. In species with unisexual inflorescences, the male ones are normally larger than the female, while in bisexual ones, lower peduncles or secondary branches may sometimes be entirely or partially male.

Natural history. Most species are more or less evergreen, but *Aralia warmingiana* and *Sciadodendron excelsum* are seasonally deciduous. Shoot growth and initiation of flowering are irregular or distinctly seasonal (in *A. warmingiana* and *Schefflera morototoni*). *Schefflera* and *Oreopanax* include some hemiepiphytic species, such as *O. capitatus* (*aralie blanc*), which may grow on the walls of old buildings and ruins as well as trees), whereas other species of *Schefflera* are climbers. Pollination is achieved principally by bees, wasps, and flies seeking nectar, and seed dispersal is mainly by birds.

Economic uses. The wood in Araliaceae is generally light and easy to work but is not durable or resistant to decay. *Schefflera morototoni* (*ambay-guazú*, *cacheta*, *luciferhout*, *mandioqueira*, *morototó*) and related species such as *S. angustissima*, *S. calva*, and *S. navarroi* (all known in Brazil as *mandioqueira*) are used for timber and for making plywood and matches. In Argentina, plywood is also made from *Aralia warmingiana*. In both those genera as well as *Oreopanax*, the wood is used as fuel. Furthermore, species of *Oreopanax* (*pumamaqui*) have potential for use in reforestation at higher elevations.

The swollen roots of ginseng, a product mainly of two north-temperate species, *Panax ginseng* (northeast Asia) and *P. quinquefolius* (eastern United States and Canada), yield well-known aphrodisiacs and antioxidants.

Several tropical American species are actual or potential ornamentals, notably *Oreopanax xalapensis* (*macuilillo* or *pata de gallo*), *O. peltatus* and its allies, and *Schefflera morototoni*. Of species native elsewhere, *Hedera* (ivy) and *Tetrapanax* (rice paper tree), as well as *Schefflera actinophylla* (umbrella tree, from Australia and southern New Guinea), are widely cultivated ornamentals. The value of Neotropical Araliaceae as horticultural subjects was recognized from as early as the late eighteenth century, when they were introduced into cultivation in Europe. Several species of *Oreopanax* of ornamental value have subsequently proved hardy in southern Europe and North Africa. Elsewhere, *O. xalapensis* is sometimes used as an ornamental in the United States, particularly in California, and *O. peltatus* is grown in the Hawaiian Islands.

References. BORCHSENIUS, F. 1997. Oreopanax (Araliaceae) in Ecuador. *Nordic J. Bot.* 17:373–96. CANNON, M. J., AND J.F.M. CANNON. 1989. Central American Araliaceae: a precursory study for the Flora Mesoamericana. *Bull. Brit. Mus. (Nat. Hist.), Bot.* 19:5–61. FRODIN, D. G. 1975. Studies in Schefflera (Araliaceae): the Cephaloschefflera complex. *J. Arnold Arbor.* 56:427–48. FRODIN, D. G. 1995. Neotropical montane Araliaceae: an overview. In *Biodiversity and Conservation of Neotropical Montane Forests*, eds. S. P. Churchill et al., 421–431. New York: New York Botanical Garden. FRODIN, D. G., AND R. GOVAERTS. 2002. *World Checklist and Bibliography of Araliaceae*. (World checklists and bibliographes, 7.) Royal Botanic Gardens, Kew. HARMS, H. 1894–1897. Araliaceae. In *Nat. Pflanzenfam.*, eds. A. Engler and K. Prantl, III(8):1–62. Leipzig: Wilhelm Engelmann. PHILIPSON, W. R. 1979. Araliaceae, I. In *Flora Malesiana*, ed. C.C.G.J. van Steenis, I (9):1–105. Leiden: Flora Malesiana Foundation. RODRÍGUEZ C., R. L. 1971. The relationships of the Umbellales. *Bot. J. Linn. Soc.* 64(suppl. 1):63–92. WEN, J. 1993. Generic delimitation of Aralia (Araliaceae). Brittonia 45:47–55. WEN, J, G. M. PLUNKETT, A. D. MITCHELL, AND S. J. WAGSTAFF. 2001. The evolution of Araliaceae: a phylogenetic analysis based on ITS sequences of nuclear ribosomal DNA. *Syst. Bot.* 26:144–67.

ARISTOLOCHIACEAE (Dutchman's Pipe or Birthworth Family)

FAVIO GONZÁLEZ

Figure 16, Plate 5

- *lianas or vines, less often herbs or shrubs*
- *flowers frequently smelling of carrion; perianth zygomorphic, pitcherlike; gynostemium present; gynoecium (5)6 carpellate*
- *fruits capsules*
- *seeds usually numerous, winged or arillate*

Numbers of genera and species. Worldwide, the Aristolochiaceae comprise seven genera and about 550 species. Most authors treat *Aristolochia* in its wide sense; however, as many as 15 genera have been segregated on the basis of perianth and gynostemium morphology. Here only three of these are recognized as monophyletic genera, *Endodeca* (2 species), *Isotrema* (ca. 40), and *Pararistolochia* (ca. 33). *Aristolochia sensu lato* (i.e., including *Euglypha* and *Holostylis*) has approximately 350 species worldwide. *Thottea* (ca. 27 species), *Asarum* (ca. 100), and *Saruma* (1) are the other genera.

In Tropical America, there are two genera, both from the subfamily Aristolochioideae, *Aristolochia sensu lato* (with ca. 200 species in the neotropics) and *Isotrema* (ca. 15).

Distribution and habitat. The Aristolochiaceae are predominately tropical or subtropical, with some species reaching temperate latitudes. *Aristolochia sensu lato* is remarkably diverse in the tropics of Asia and America. A considerable number of endemic species grow in Brazil, Hispaniola, and Mexico. *Isotrema* has a disjunct distribution in North and Central America, and East Asia. Among the extra-Neotropical genera, *Pararistolochia* has a disjunct distribution in West and Central Africa and Australasia; *Thottea* is restricted to tropical East Asia; *Asarum* is confined to north temperate regions of both hemispheres, and *Saruma* is endemic to central China.

The family is found in various habitats including tropical rain forests, gallery forests, dry forests, and savannas.

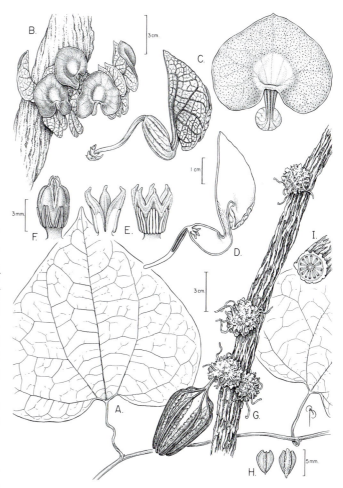

Figure 16. ARISTOLOCHIACEAE. *Aristolochia bukuti.* **A.** Stem with leaves. **B.** Cluster of cauliflorous flowers. **C.** Lateral (left) and frontal (right) views of flower. **D.** Medial section of flower. **E.** Medial section of young gynostemium (left) and young gynostemium in pistillate phase (right). **F.** Older gynostemium in staminate phase. **G.** Corky stem with dehisced fruit. **H.** Seeds; the view on right shows the raphe. **I.** Transverse section of stem. Reprinted with permission from Mori et al. (2002). Artist: Bobbi Angell.

Family classification. Cronquist placed the Aristolochiaceae in a monofamilial order, the Aristolochiales. The family has been considered to be closely related to either (a) the Annonaceae, (b) the Rafflesiaceae, or (c) the so-called paleoherbs, especially the order Piperales and the monocots. The first hypothesis is based on the presence of P-type sieve-element plastids, oil cells, aporphine alkaloids, flowers with several carpels, and well-developed petals in *Saruma*. The second hypothesis has been proposed because of the similarities in floral structure, particularly the presence of a simple, fleshy perianth, a gynostemium, and an inferior, pluriovulate ovary. In the third hypothesis, it is suggested that the Aristolochiaceae are closely related to the paleoherbs because they share adaxial prophylls, trimerous flowers, monosulcate or inaperturate pollen, and type PIIc sieve-element plastids. Molecular data support a close relationship between Aristolochiaceae and the Piperaceae, Saururaceae, Lactoridaceae, and Hydnoraceae. These data reveal an unexpected close relationship with *Lactoris* (Lactoridaceae *sensu* Cronquist) and taxa of the Hydnoraceae, but these connections have not been definitively established.

Currently, two subfamilies are recognized, the Aristolochioideae (*Aristolochia, Endodeca, Isotrema, Pararistolochia,* and *Thottea*), and the Asaroideae (*Asarum* and *Saruma*). The Aristolochioideae are mostly woody, with hooked hairs, silicified cells, an inferior ovary, and a constriction between the perianth and the ovary that serves as an abscission zone for the caducous perianth. The Asaroideae are mostly herbaceous, lack hooked hairs and silicified cells, possess a semi-inferior to inferior ovary, and are without a constriction between a noncaducous perianth and the ovary.

Features of the family. Habit: lianas or vines, less often perennial herbs or shrubs, aromatic, often rhizomatous. **Stipules** absent. **Leaves** alternate, distichous, simple; prophyll single, adaxial, sometimes adnate to the parental axis and resembling a stipule (the so-called pseudostipule); venation often palmate. **Inflorescences** usually axillary, or cauliflorous, fasciculate, racemose, or cymose, the racemes short or branched with long internodes, the cymes usually rhipidia. **Flowers** zygomorphic, bisexual, protogynous, frequently smelling of carrion; perianth formed by 3 petal-like sepals, these reddish, purple, yellow, or pink, fused and pitcherlike; androecium of 5 or 6 stamens, in single whorl, the anthers extrorse, longitudinally dehiscent, fused to styles to form (3,5)6(–12)-lobed gynostemium; gynoecium syncarpous, the ovary inferior, the carpels usually 6 (5 in pentandrous species of *Aristolochia* from southern United States, Mexico, Belize, the Bahamas, and Cuba), the locules 5–6(4 in *Thottea*); placentation submarginal, the ovules often numerous, anatropous. **Fruits** septicidal or septifragal capsules, dehiscing acropetally (basipetally in *Isotrema* and the pentandrous *Aristolochia* species). **Seeds** usually numerous, usually winged or with sticky arils; embryo tiny, the endosperm abundant, oily, sometimes starchy.

Natural history. In the both the Western and Eastern Hemispheres, Aristolochiaceae have coevolved with swallowtail butterflies of the family Papilionidae. The butterflies use these plants to lay their eggs, and the larvae feed exclusively on leaves (and sometimes flowers) of the family, especially species of *Aristolochia, Endodeca, Isotrema, Pararistolochia,* and *Thottea*. The larvae are able to tolerate and sequester the toxic aristolochic acids, which make them poisonous to predators. In the neotropics, the larvae of two Papilionidae genera, *Battus* and *Parides*, feed only on species of *Aristolochia, Endodeca,* and *Isotrema*.

Flowers of most Aristolochiaceae are fly-pollinated. In *Aristolochia, Endodeca,* and *Isotrema*, the flowers are protogynous, and most species apparently require cross-pollination. The perianths of these three genera, as well as that of *Pararistolochia*, exhibit remarkable plasticity in shape (uni-, bi-, or trilobed) and size (the lengths ranging from 2 centimeters in *Aristolochia nummularifolia* to 105 centimeters in *A. grandiflora*), perhaps in response to different pollinators.

Methods employed to attract pollinators are: odors produced from specialized structures located on the inner surface of the perianth; the purple and yellow or greenish color patterns of the perianth; a transluscent "window" at the base of the perianth, which guides the insects to the gynostemium; and the frequent presence of white, reddish, or purple conical trichomes around the entrance of the perianth. These trichomes also are present on the inner surface of the floral tube. They remain rigid and facing downward during anthesis, thereby temporarily retaining the insects inside the flower until the pollen is released. Then the trichomes relax, and the insects escape. All these mechanisms are present in *Aristolochia* and *Pararistolochia*, but conical trichomes are entirely lacking in *Endodeca* and *Isotrema*.

Seed dispersal usually involves a combination of wind and water (streams), except for species with sticky arils, which may attach to the bodies of animals.

Economic uses. The Aristolochiaceae are known widely for their ancient uses in traditional medicine, mainly for inducing abortion, counteracting inflamation, lowering blood pressure, and lessening muscle convulsions. Some species of *Aristolochia* possess antitumoral activity, but with toxic side effects. The name *Aristolochia* (from Greek *Aristos*, better, and *lochios*, the uterine discharge that occurs after childbirth) alludes to the alleged properties of extracts of species of the genus in facilitating childbirth and the expulsion of the placenta.

References. CORRERA Q., J. E., AND H. Y. BERNAL. 1989. Aristolochiaceae. In *Especies Vegetales Promisorias de los Países del Convenio Andrés Bello*, Tomo I. Bogotá, D. E., Colombia: Secretaria Ejecutiva del Convenio Andrés Bello. DUCHARTRE, P.E.S. 1864. Aristolochiaceae. In *Prodromus*, ed. A. de Candolle, 15(1):421–98. Paris. GONZÁLEZ, F. 1990. Aristolochiaceae. In *Flora de Colombia*. Monografía no. 12:1–184. Santafé de Bogotá: Instituto de Ciencias Naturales, Universidad Nacional de Colombia. GONZÁLEZ, F. 1991. Notes on the systematics of *Aristolochia* subsection

Hexandrae. Ann. Missouri Bot. Gard. 78(2):497–503. GON-ZÁLEZ, F., AND P. RUDALL. 2001. The questionable affinities of *Lactoris*: evidence from branching pattern, inflorescence morphology, and stipule development. *Amer. J. Bot.* 88(12): 2143–50. GONZÁLEZ, F., AND D. W. STEVENSON. 2000. Perianth development and systematics of *Aristolochia*. *Flora* 195:370–91. GONZÁLEZ, F., AND D. W. STEVENSON. 2002. A phylogenetic analysis of the subfamily Aristolochioideae (Aristolochiaceae). *Rev. Acad. Colomb. Cienc.* 26(98):25–60. HOEHNE, F. C. 1942. Aristolochiáceas. *Flora Brasílica* 15(2):3–141, t. 1–123. São Paulo, Brazil. HUBER, H. 1993. Aristolochiaceae. In *The Families and Genera of Vascular Plants*, ed. K. Kubitzki, J. G. Rohwer, and V. Bittrich, 2: 129–37. Berlin: Springer-Verlag. MASTERS, M. T. 1875. Aristolochiaceae. In *Flora Brasiliensis*, ed. C.F.P. von Martius, 4:77–114, t. 17–26. NICKRENT, D. L., A. BLARER, Y.-L. QIU, D. E. SOLTIS, P. S. SOLTIS, AND M. ZANIS. 2002. Molecular data place Hydnoraceae with Aristolochiaceae. *Amer. J. Bot.* 89(11):1809–17. PFEIFER, H. W. 1966. Revision of the North and Central American hexandrous species of *Aristolochia* (Aristolochiaceae). *Ann. Missouri Bot. Gard.* 53: 115–96. SCHMIDT, O. C. 1935. Aristolochiaceae. In *Die Natürlichen Pflanzenfamilien*, eds. A. Engler and K. Prantl, 2nd ed. 16b:204–42.

ASTERACEAE or COMPOSITAE (Aster or Sunflower Family)

JOHN F. PRUSKI AND GISELA SANCHO

Figures 17, 18; Plate 5

- *herbs, shrubs, less commonly trees or vines*

- *leaves alternate, opposite, or less commonly whorled, usually simple; blades entire to finely dissected*

- *inflorescences with flowers congested on a common receptacle and subtended by a series of bracts (phyllaries), forming a primary inflorescence called a capitulum, the capitula solitary or arranged in secondary inflorescences (the capitulescence)*

- *flowers usually 5-merous; corolla sympetalous; stamens epipetalous, the anthers united into tube (syngenesious), dehiscence introrse; gynoecium syncarpous, the ovary inferior, the carpels 2, the locule 1, the style 2-branched; ovules 1 per ovary*

- *fruits cypselae; pappus distal, of (1)2–many scales, awns, setae, or bristles, or sometimes absent*

Numbers of genera and species. Asteraceae are among the largest families of flowering plants with approximately 1,535 genera and 23,000–32,000 species worldwide (about 8–10% of the angiosperms).

In tropical America, there are approximately 580 genera and 8,040 species. These figures are based on counts from several representative herbaria (e.g., Museo Universidad Nacional de La Plata, Argentina; Missouri Botanical Garden; The New York Botanical Garden; and U.S. National Herbarium, Smithsonian Institution) and include the segregates of *Aster, Eupatorium, Senecio,* and *Vernonia.* A second estimation of 8,403 tropical American species, from the combined totals in somewhat mutually exclusive (at the species level)

areas of Brazil, Venezuela, Peru, Mesoamerica, Mexico, and the West Indies, is congruent with the herbarium count. A cumulative generic count from the literature for these areas, however, would be highly artificial, since many genera occur across these six broad areas. The counts and literature references for these six regions are: 1) Brazil (Baker 1873–1884; 150 genera and 1,290 species); 2) Venezuela (Badillo 1994; 195 genera and 786 species); 3) Peru (Beltrán and Baldeon 2001, *fide* M. Dillon, pers. comm.; 245 genera and 1,530 species); 4) Mesoamerica (checklist of J. Pruski, unpubl.; 255 genera and 1,375 species); 5) Mexico (Turner and Nesom 1993; 387 genera and 2,861 species); and 6) the West Indies (checklist of P. Acevedo, pers. comm.; 163 genera and 529 species).

Some of the larger genera of Asteraceae in the neotropics are: *Baccharis* (300–430 species) and *Diplostephium* (ca. 110) in the Astereae; *Ageratina* (250–290), *Chromolaena* (166), *Mikania* (400–430), and *Stevia* (ca. 235) in the Eupatorieae; *Calea* (154), *Verbesina* (ca. 300), and *Viguiera* (ca. 180) in the Heliantheae; *Gochnatia* (68) in the Mutisieae; *Gynoxys* (ca. 60), *Pentacalia* (ca. 220), and *Senecio* (ca. 500) in the Senecioneae; and *Critoniopsis* (ca. 85), *Lepidaploa* (ca. 120), and *Lessingianthus* (101) in the Vernonieae.

Distribution and habitat. Asteraceae occur on all continents except Antarctica. The family is very speciose in temperate regions (especially in Russia and the United States), where, perhaps, more than half of its species occur. Asteraceae are also well represented in tropical America, where all five subfamilies are found. Of these subfamilies, only the Barnadesioideae are restricted to tropical America. Seven tribes are found wholly or largely in the neotropics (Barnadesieae, Eupatorieae, Helenieae, Heliantheae, Liabeae, Muti-

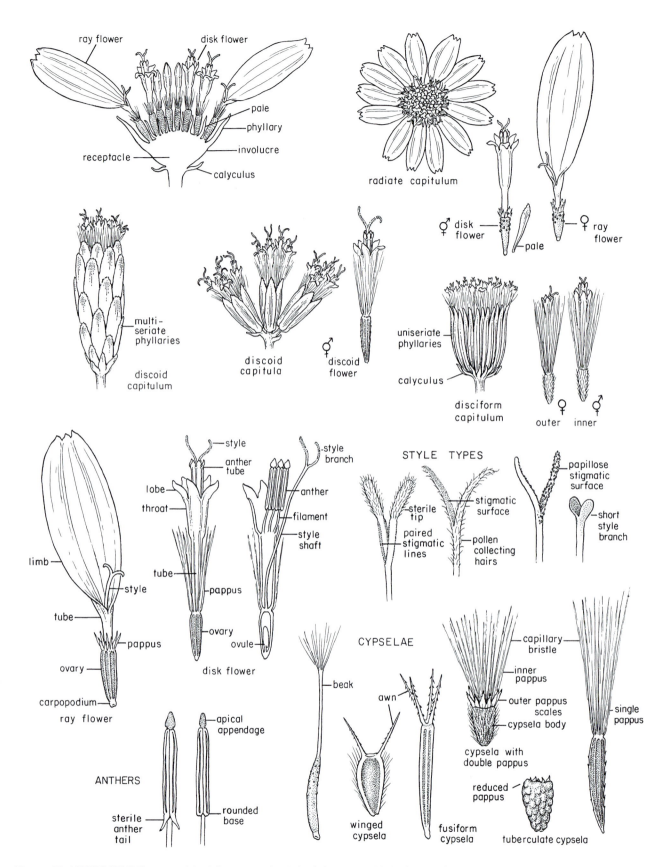

Figure 17. ASTERACEAE. Features of the inflorescence (capitulum), flowers, and fruits (cypselas) used in the classification of Asteraceae. Reprinted with permission from Mori et al. (2002). Artist: Bobbi Angell.

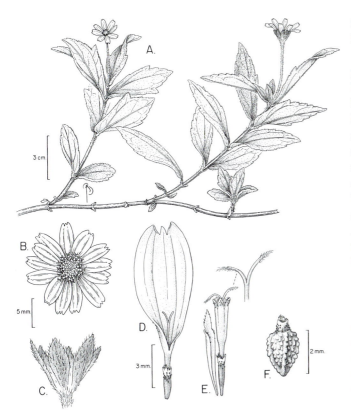

Figure 18. ASTERACEAE. *Sphagneticola trilobata.* **A.** Stem with leaves and capitula. **B.** Apical view of capitulum. **C.** Lateral view of involucre. **D.** Adaxial view of ray flower. **E.** Lateral view of disk flower (right) with subtending pale (left), and detail of style branches (above right). **F.** Lateral view of cypsela. Reprinted with permission from Acevedo-Rodríguez (1996). Artist: Bobbi Angell.

sieae, and Tageteae). Eight tribes (Anthemideae, Astereae, Cardueae, Gnaphalieae, Lactuceae, Plucheeae, Senecioneae, and Vernonieae) are partly represented by native species in the neotropics, but these tribes are mostly nontropical American. Four tribes (Arctoteae, Calenduleae, Echinopeae, and Inuleae) are not native to the neotropics.

Of the tribes found wholly or largely in tropical America, approximately 90 species of the small tribe Barnadesieae are restricted to South America and are well represented in planaltine Brazil and Andean Bolivia, but have only a single species in Guayana. The Mutisieae have centers of basal taxa in Guayana and planaltine Brazil, but are also well represented in the Andes, Mesoamerica, and the West Indies. Members of the small tribe Liabeae are most diverse in the central Andes but are also found in the Greater Antilles and from Mexico through Central America. The Heliantheae and Eupatorieae are closely related and most likely originated in the Western Hemisphere, where the majority of taxa occur. Both groups include fairly weedy members and account for much of the diversity of the family in the drier regions of Mexico and Brazil. Helenieae largely occur within and north of Central America. Tageteae range from the southern United States to Brazil, with most taxa distributed in the xeric highlands of Mexico.

In South America, some groups are most diverse in Guayana, in the Planalto (largely within Brazil), or in the Andes. Within the family, the Amazon Basin largely serves as a barrier to large-scale migration between the Guayanan and Brazilian Shields, and possesses relatively low species diversity of Asteraceae. In some groups, for example the Mutisieae, taxa occur both north and south of the Amazon. The ancient Guayanan and Brazilian shields have a largely different flora from that of the geologically more recent Andes. The Brazilian Shield has a flora rich in species of Vernonieae and Heliantheae. By contrast, one fourth of the Guayana Asteraceae is made up of species of Mutisieae, with Heliantheae poorly represented except for *Calea*, one of the two largest genera in Guayana.

In Central America there are fewer endemics than in Mexico where 1,813 species of the 2,861 species reported are endemic. Certain South American-centered genera (e.g., *Oritrophium* and *Werneria*) are disjunct to some high mountains in northern Central America and Mexico, but not in Panama or Nicaragua. On the other hand, some groups (e.g., *Talamancalia* and some Astereae) occur only on high peaks in Costa Rica, Panama, and the northern Andes.

Certain South American-centered groups are also well represented in the West Indies (e.g., *Gochnatia*, *Liabum*, and *Piptocoma*). Many West Indian groups are endemic, especially those restricted to particular islands of the Greater Antilles. Occasionally predominantly African genera (e.g., *Crassocephalum*) are disjunct to the West Indies, but rarely are found in Central America.

In tropical America, species of Asteraceae are found in most habitats. Although species are usually found in less forested or disturbed areas, such as low-elevation savannas, *cerrado*, *tepui* meadows, *páramo*, and *puna*, the family has also successfully invaded forest habitats. Most Neotropical Asteraceae are perennial herbs or shrubs. In the Brazilian and Bolivian Planalto, fire-adapted subshrubs with xylopodia are common. Tall climbing and arborescent species also occur in the American Tropics. For example, species of *Mikania* (Eupatorieae) and *Pentacalia* subgenus *Pentacalia* (Senecioneae) may be forest lianas; *Critoniopsis* and *Vernonanthura* (Vernonieae), *Stenopadus* (Mutisieae), and *Aequatorium* (Senecioneae) are arborescent; and *Stenopadus andicola*, a tree to 26 meters, is the tallest American Asteraceae.

Family classification. Asteraceae are the sole family placed in the Asterales by Cronquist. On the other hand, thirteen families were placed in Asterales by the Angiosperm Phylogeny Group, with a monophyletic Asteraceae grouped as a paired terminal taxon with the small South American family Calyceraceae, the currently acknowledged sister group of Asteraceae. The Asteraceae are considered monophyletic because they store carbohydrates as polyfructosan, notably inulin, rather than starch, have an extensive resin-duct system, and unique flowers congested on a common receptacle to form a capitulum. The advanced tribes are commonly very speciose and have a diverse secondary metabolite chemistry that may have led to the great success of the family.

For much of the last century, Asteraceae were treated by both de Candolle and by Bentham and Hooker as has having thirteen tribes. These were placed within two subfamilies by de Candolle. The first subfamily, the Tubuliflorae, was composed of twelve tribes. The second subfamily, the Liguliflorae, contained only the Cichoraceae (now Lactuceae) and was characterized by articulated laticifers. However, in the 1960s and 1970s dramatic realignments in the subfamiliar classification of Asteraceae were proposed. Carlquist also recognized two subfamilies, but grouped the component tribes in new ways. For example, tribes with ligulate, bilabiate, pseudobilabiate, and discoid flowers (with continuous stigmatic surfaces) were aligned together in Cichorioideae, whereas tribes with radiate flowers (mostly with 2-banded stigmatic surfaces) were aligned together in Asteroideae.

The next major development in the subfamiliar classification of Asteraceae was the elevation of Mutisieae subtribe Barnadesiinae to subfamily rank as the Barnadesioideae, the third widely recognized subfamily of Asteraceae. The recognition of a third subfamily was based on molecular findings that stressed the significance of the 22 kilobases chloroplast DNA inversion found in all Asteraceae surveyed, except Mutisieae subtribe Barnadesiinae, which, by lacking this inversion, has cpDNA that is colinear with virtually all other land plants. Furthermore, the Barnadesioideae are characterized by a unique floral trichome type ("barnadesioid" hairs, described below in the key to tribes). Bremer stressed that the Cichorioideae (including the earlier Carduoideae) was paraphyletic. To address the paraphylly of Cichorioideae, Bremer (in Hind and Beentje) excluded Mutisieae (which lacks pollen-collecting or sweeping hairs on the styles) and Cardueae (perhaps closely related to some Mutisieae, such as *Ainsliaea* and *Dicoma*) from Cichorioideae. In the classification recognizing five subfamilies, the more advanced Cichorioideae and Asteroideae are similar by having a deletion in the *ndh*F gene and by often having spiny pollen, and the Asteroideae are monophyletic by having 2-banded style branches and duplication in the *rbc*L gene.

Our treatment follows Bremer and provisionally uses five subfamilies and nineteen tribes of Asteraceae. The tribes are only slightly modified from those of H. Cassini (see Bremer).

The ancestor of Asteraceae is unknown, but has been cited by Cronquist as perhaps being in the Rubiaceae. However, Cronquist also considered close relations between Asteraceae and Calyceraceae, Campanulaceae, and Goodiniaceae. Many modern workers consider the nearest relative of Asteraceae to be South American Calyceraceae, and South America and the Pacific are suggested centers of origin of Asteraceae.

Because most tribes of Asteraceae are larger than the average plant family, a key to the tribes of tropical American Asteraceae is included below. The five subfamilies (in phylo-

genetic order) and nineteen tribes (arranged alphabetically) recognized here are outlined first.

Subfamily BARNADESIOIDEAE. Tribe: Barnadesieae.
Subfamily MUTISIOIDEAE. Tribe: Mutisieae.
Subfamily CARDUOIDEAE. Tribe: Cardueae (includes Cynareae).
Subfamily CICHORIOIDEAE. Tribes: (Lactucoideae)– Arctoteae (provisionally includes Eremothamneae), Echinopeae (includes Carlineae), Lactuceae (includes Cichorieae and Gundelieae), Liabeae, and Vernonieae. The genera *Adenocaulon*, *Moquinia* (including *Pseudostifftia*), and *Tarchonanthus* are incertae sedis.
Subfamily ASTEROIDEAE. Tribes: Anthemideae (includes Ursinieae), Astereae, Calenduleae, Eupatorieae, Gnaphalieae, Helenieae (provisionally including Bahieae, Chaenactideae, Madieae, and Perityleae) Heliantheae (including the Coreopsideae), Inuleae, Plucheeae, Senecioneae, and Tageteae.

Key to the native and naturalized tribes of tropical American Asteraceae.

1. Leaves commonly alternate. Stigmatic surface continuous over inner surface of style branches, never divided into two separate lines. Capitula discoid, ligulate, bilabiate, or pseudobilabiate. Flowers with disk corolla lobes (when present) long and narrow; ray, bilabiate, pseudobilabiate, or ligulate corolla limb (when present) 5-lobed; anthers with flat apical appendages and fertile spurred (calcarate) or sterile tailed (caudate) bases; pollen sometimes lophate (Subfamilies Barnadesioideae, Carduoideae, Cichorioideae, and Mutisioideae).
   2. Latex abundant, colored or milky. Flowers all ligulate . . . LACTUCEAE.
   2'. Latex usually absent, or rarely present but not milky. Flowers rarely ligulate.
      3. Plants usually with nodal spines on stems. Capitula often pseudobilabiate. Floral pubescence of "barnadesioid" hairs (2-celled trichomes associated with a large thick-walled basal or footcell) . . . BARNADESIEAE.
      3'. Plants without spines or, when present, on the leaves. Capitula discoid or bilabiate, rarely ligulate. Floral pubescence never of "barnadesioid" hairs.
4. Flowers with style branches commonly short and style shaft glabrous.
   5. Leaves usually spiny. Capitula discoid. Receptacle bristly or glabrous. Styles with a ring of hairs in the upper part of the shaft below point of bifurcation. Filaments often papillose or pilose . . . . CARDUEAE.
   5'. Leaves not spiny. Capitula often bilabiate. Receptacle glabrous and epaleate, rarely weakly paleate. Styles with smooth, papillose, or hairy branches but without a ring of hairs in the upper part of the shaft. Filaments glabrous . . . MUTISIEAE.
4'. Flowers with style branches long and upper style shaft evenly pubescent or papillose
   6. Leaves opposite or in rosettes. Flowers with corollas usu-

ally yellow or reddish. Capitula usually radiate. Pappus usually uniseriate . . . . LIABEAE.

  6'. Leaves usually alternate. Flower corollas not yellow. Capitula discoid; pappus often biseriate . . . . VERNONIEAE.

1'. Leaves opposite or alternate. Stigmatic surface commonly in paired lines (2-banded) on the inner surface of style branches. Capitula radiate or discoid. Flowers with disk corolla lobes usually short; ray corolla limbs (when present) 3-lobed; anthers commonly with boat-shaped apical appendages and rounded, less commonly spurred or tailed bases; pollen never lophate; (subfamily Asteroideae).

  7. Involucre with primary phyllaries 1-seriate, equal in length, sometimes calyculate.

    8. Leaves opposite, often pinnatifid, the lower surface and phyllaries dotted with large embedded oil glands. Capitula radiate. Fruits with pappus often of scales . . . . . . TAGETEAE.

    8'. Leaves alternate, not commonly pinnatifid, the lower surface and phyllaries without large embedded oil glands. Capitula radiate, discoid, or disciform. Fruits with pappus of capillary bristles . . . . SENECIONEAE.

  7'. Involucre with primary phyllaries 2–many-seriate, commonly unequal in length.

  9. Phyllaries papery. Anther bases tailed (caudate). Cypselae never with carbonized walls.

    10. Flowers with style branches apically acute, the shaft sometimes pubescent; anther bases distinctly tailed . . . . PLUCHEEAE.

    10'. Flowers with style branches apically truncate, the shaft not pubescent; anther bases with minute tails . . . . GNAPHALIEAE.

  9'. Phyllaries scarious or herbaceous. Anther bases rounded or truncate. Cypselae sometimes with carbonized walls.

    11. Style branches with sterile appendages. Pappus of bristles (rarely scales or absent).

      12. Capitula discoid with corollas white, blue to violet, never yellow. Leaves opposite . . EUPATORIEAE.

      12'. Capitula radiate, rarely disciform, or when discoid with yellow corollas. Leaves alternate ASTEREAE.

    11'. Style branches without sterile appendages. Pappus usually of scales, a crown or absent.

      13. Receptacle paleate, only occasionally epaleate. Anthers usually blackened or reddish . . . . HELIANTHEAE.

      13'. Receptacle usually epaleate. Anthers pale.

        14. Leaves usually opposite. Cypselae with carbonized walls. Phyllaries herbaceous, rarely scarious . . . . HELENIEAE.

        14'. Leaves alternate. Cypselae without carbonized walls. Phyllaries with dry scarious margins . . . ANTHEMIDEAE.

The biggest recent changes at the generic level in classification of Neotropical Asteraceae have been the splintering of the traditional genera *Aster*, *Eupatorium* (both largely based on floral microcharacter differences), *Vernonia* (largely based on differences in capitulescence type and pollen morphology), and *Senecio* (largely based on features of the styles branches and anthers). As now defined, *Aster*, *Eupatorium*, and *Vernonia* have no or very few species in the neotropics, whereas at least 400–500 Neotropical species of *Senecio* are still recognized.

Features of the family. Habit: annual or perennial herbs, shrubs, less commonly trees or lianas, sometimes epiphytes, rarely aquatics. Indument various, sometimes absent, the trichomes glandular or eglandular. Stems mostly subterete and nonwinged. Stipules absent. Leaves usually cauline, sometimes in basal rosettes, alternate, opposite, or less commonly whorled, simple, infrequently compound (e.g., *Coreopsis*, *Ericentrodea*, *Hidalgoa*, some *Mikania*); blades entire to finely dissected. Primary inflorescence a capitulum; capitula solitary or grouped into a capitulescence, generally distinct from each other, but occasionally fused (syncephalous) into supercapitula; capitulescence maturing in determinate manner, composed of 2–many, variously cymose, corymbiform, thyrsoid-paniculate, racemose, sessile or pedunculate capitula. Capitula (compact heads) of sessile flowers (florets) maturing in an indeterminate manner, on common, naked or paleate, generally glabrous receptacle, the receptacle surrounded by cylindrical to globose involucre; bracts (phyllaries) (1)2–many, generally persistent, often imbricate and graduate, in 1–several series, the capitula (1)2–many-flowered, the corollas of outer flowers radiating and zygomorphic (radiate, ligulate, bilabiate, and pseudobilabiate capitula) or the corollas of all flowers nonradiating and actinomorphic (discoid or disciform capitula), homogamous (with a single flower type) or heterogamous (with 2 flower types); homogamous capitula discoid (with bisexual, rarely unisexual, actinomorphic, tubular to filiform florets), ligulate (with bisexual, zygomorphic florets), bilabiate (with generally bisexual, zygomorphic florets, corolla with a bifid opposed inner lip, occasionally also with actinomorphic, or nearly so inner bisexual florets, the corollas of capitulum thereby heteromorphic with two corolla shapes), or pseudobilabiate (with bisexual, zygomorphic florets, corolla with a single opposed inner lip, occasionally also with actinomorphic or nearly so inner bisexual florets); heterogamous capitula radiate (with zygomorphic, pistillate, or neuter outer ray florets and actinomorphic, bisexual, or functionally staminate central tubular florets) or disciform (with pistillate, nonligulate generally filiform outer florets and bisexual central tubular florets). Flowers (florets) bisexual, unisexual (plants then monoecious or less often dioecious), or sterile (perianth remains but both pollen and ovules aborted), (3)5-merous; calyx absent or modified into pappus (see fruit description); corolla sympetalous, actinomorphic or zygomorphic, the zygomorphic corollas with basal tube and bilaterally symmetric upper portion, radiate (pistillate or neuter with a single, usually 3-lobed limb), ligulate (bisexual with a single 5-lobed limb), bilabiate (generally bisexual with an outer 3-lobed limb and an opposed inner 2-lobed lip), or pseudobilabiate (bisexual with an outer 4-lobed limb and an opposed inner 1-lobed lip), the actinomorphic (=disk) corollas with basal tube tubular to filiform, generally broadening above into (3)5 lobes, the lobes usually equal; androecium with stamens as many as and alternate with corolla lobes, epipetalous at junction of tube–throat, the filaments distinct, the anthers united into tube surrounding style (syngenesious), rarely not so, mostly oblong, the base commonly blunt or with sterile tail (caudate) or fertile spurs (calcarate), the apex often variously appendaged, the dehiscence introrse; gynoecium syncarpous, the ovary inferior, the carpels 2, the locule 1, the style often immersed (basally) in cupular nectary at ovary apex, filiform, 2-branched, the branches with continuous or 2-banded stigmatic surface, the branch apices fertile to tip or sterile and appendaged distally, variously shaped, commonly papillose or ornamented with pollen-collecting or sweeping hairs; ovule 1 per locule, basal, erect. **Fruits** cypselae (achenes), terete to compressed (usually radially so), often obconical, fusiform, or cylindrical, less commonly plump or flattened, sometimes with a slender neck or beak, often black or brown, glabrous to tomentose or sericeous, pubescence commonly of twin-hairs, generally much shorter than corolla; carpopodium (foot of cypsela) radially symmetric or bilateral, sometimes sculpted; calyx sometimes absent, often persistent distally, commonly forming pappus of (1)2–many scales, awns, setae, or bristles, the pappus segments commonly subequal in a single series, less commonly unequal or in distinct inner and outer series, minute to often nearly as long as corolla, the margins smooth, scabrid, barbellate, or plumose, or rarely of "barnadesioid" hairs. **Seeds** with fatty oils; endosperm absent (nuclear), the embryo straight.

The chromosome numbers of Asteraceae range from $n = 2$ (in *Haplopappus gracilis*, the lowest number in the plant kingdom) to $n = 114$.

Natural history. Most species of Asteraceae are pollinated by insects. Bird pollination is sporadic in the Cardueae, Heliantheae, Senecioneae, and also occurs in some species of Barnadesieae and Mutisieae. Bat pollination has been reported in *Gongylolepis jauaensis* of the Mutisieae. The family also includes genera (e.g., *Ambrosia* and *Artemesia*) that are secondarily adapted to wind pollination. Among the insects, bees, which usually collect pollen and nectar, are the most important pollinators of Asteraceae in the neotropics. Many other insects have been reported visiting the capitula of Asteraceae, but the efficacy in pollination by insects other than bees has been demonstrated only a few times.

The clustering of flowers into a capitulum and its correspondent efficiency with regards to insect pollination are believed to have contributed to the success of the family. Hind and Beentje suggest that the variety of corolla shapes, sexual arrangements, and capitula types are a response to the centripetal development of capitula, leading to development of radiating florets more attractive to pollinators, and subse-

quent sexual specialization. The capitulum is functionally equivalent (with regards to pollination) to a single simple flower, and there has been an evolutionary tendency toward production of radiating outer florets to attract pollinators. The pollen presentation by Asteraceae flowers is both passive and active. Passive pollen presentation occurs when the growth of the style pushes the introrsely dehisced pollen distally from the anther cylinder (pump-type mechanism or plunger-pollination). Active pollen presentation occurs when the contraction of the filaments, in response to stimulation by a pollinator, pulls down the anther cylinder and thus exposes some of the pollen to the pollinator.

Dioecy, uncommon in the Asteraceae, is independently derived and occurs sporadically in genera such as *Lycoseris* (Mutisieae), *Podanthus* (Heliantheae), and *Baccharis* (Astereae). Although dioecy does not seemingly correlate with pollination mechanisms, a correlation with wind pollination has been suggested.

Fruits of Neotropical Asteraceae are commonly wind-dispersed, but species of a few genera (e.g., *Acanthospermum*, *Adenostemma*, *Bidens*, *Cosmos*, and *Xanthium*) have sticky knobs or retrorsely barbed awns and are dispersed after sticking to the fur of animals. These species have become weedy pests in the paleotropics. *Tilesia baccata* has fleshy fruits eaten and dispersed by birds. Birds are thought to have facilitated the widespread distributions of species of *Gongylolepis*, *Oritrophium*, and *Stenopadus* and to have caused the disjunct distributions of taxa (e.g., *Blennosperma*, *Grindelia*, *Lasthenia*, *Psilocarpus* at the genus level; *Agoseris coronopifolia*, *Madia gracilis*, *M. sativa*, *Malacothrix coulteri*, *M. floccifera*, *Microseris pygmaea*, *Perityle emoryi*, and *Thelesperma megapotamica* at the species level) between western North America and southern South America.

Asteraceae are notable for having a diverse secondary chemistry consisting primarily of sesquiterpene lactones and polyenes (=polyacetylenes). These compounds discourage predation and are, thus, considered an important factor in the evolutionary success of the family. The basal elements of the family, the Barnadesieae and the Mutisieae, lack complex polyenes and sesquiterpene lactones, but have secondary metabolite chemistries based mostly on triterpenes. These are not effective in defense; however, these groups have developed mechanical means of defense: spines in the Barnadesieae and coriaceous leaves in the Mutisieae.

Economic uses. In tropical America, Asteraceae are commonly used as vermifuges (e.g., *Calea pinnatifida*), derived from the well-developed secondary metabolite chemistry of the family. Many Neotropical Asteraceae are used for a variety of medicinal purposes. Venezuelan *Calea divaricata* is used as a cold remedy, Mesoamerican *Calea ternifolia* (often reported as *C. zacatechichi*) is employed as an auditory hallucinogen, and South American species of *Acmella* and the Mesoamerican *Salmea scandens* are used to relieve toothaches. Popular herbal remedies are extracted from species of *Arnica*, *Calendula*, and *Echinacea*. Several species of *Mi-*

kania are widely used as snakebite remedies. A few Neotropical Asteraceae are used as fish poisons, including species of *Clibadium*, *Ichthyothere*, *Neurolaena*, and *Chromolaena* (*C. odorata*). *Tagetes* is used commonly throughout much of the neotropics as a tea as well as a pesticide. Species of *Tagetes* are also cultivated for their yellow-orange pigments extracted from the flowers. *Chrysanthemum coccineum* is the species from which pyrethrum (a natural insecticide) is derived. *Stevia rebaudiana* has been traditionally used in Paraguay as a sweetening agent, and its extract, stevioside, is now also used in Japan.

Important foods derived from Asteraceae include lettuce (*Lactuca sativa*), sunflower seeds (*Helianthus annuus* and relatives), chicory (*Cichorium intybus*), artichoke (*Cynara scolymus*), and chard and salsify (the young flowering shoots and roots of *Tragopogon porrifolius*, respectively). Safflower (*Carthamnus tinctorius*) is used as a red dye. Wormwood (*Artemesia absinthium*) yields absinthe, once widely employed as a liqueur flavoring. Species of *Parthenium* yield a rubber substitute called *guayule* in small quantities.

Perhaps Asteraceae are best known for its ornamentals, such as asters and daisies (formerly *Aster sensu lato*) and sunflowers (*Helianthus*). Most cultivated tropical American Asteraceae have the local common name of *margarita*. Other common ornamentals are wedelia (*Sphagneticola*), chrysanthemum (*Chrysanthemum*), dahlia (*Dahlia*), callistephus (*Callistephus*), coreopsis (*Coreopsis*), gazania (*Gazania*), gerbera (*Gerbera*), flame vine (*Pseudogynoxys*), stokesia (*Stokesia*), helichrysum (*Helichrysum*), marigold (*Tagetes*), zinnia (*Zinnia*), and black-eyed susan and coneflowers (*Rudbeckia*).

Many ubiquitous weeds are species of Asteraceae. Among them are *Tessaria integrifolia*, a fast growing soft-wooded species often occurring in dense stands in upper Amazonia and elsewhere in tropical America, and species of *Bidens*, *Chromolaena*, *Gamochaeta*, *Pseudelephantopus*, *Struchium*, and *Tridax*. The pollen of ragweed (*Ambrosia*) is one of the major causes of hay fever. *Sphagneticola trilobata* and other species contain sesquiterpene lactones that are known to cause dermatitis in humans.

References. Badillo, V. M. 1994 [1995]. Enumeración de las Compuestas (Asteraceae) de Venezuela. *Revista Fac. Agron. (Maracay)* 45:1–191. Baker, J. G. 1873–1884. Compositae. In *Fl. Bras.* 6 (2,3), ed. C. F. P. Martius. Stuttgart. Beltrán, H., and S. Baldeon. 2001. Adiciones a las Asteraceas del Peru. *Dilloniana* 1(1):9–14. Bentham, G., and J. D. Hooker. 1873. *Genera Plantarum*, vol. 2. London: Reeve & Co. Bernal, H. Y., and J. E. Correra Q. 1991. Compositae (Asteraceae). In *Especies vegetales promisorias de los países del Convenio Andrés Bello*, Tomo VI. Santafé de Bogotá, D. E., Colombia: Secretaria Ejecutiva del Convenio Andrés Bello. Bremer, K. 1994. *Asteraceae: Cladistics & Classification*. Portland, Oregon: Timber Press. Candolle, A. P. de. 1836. *Prodromus Systematic Naturalis Regni Vegetabilis*, vol. 5, Paris: Treuttel and Wurtz. Carlquist, S. 1976. Tribal interrelationships and phylogeny of the Asteraceae. *Aliso* 8:465–92. Correra Q., J. E., and H. Y. Bernal. 1990. Compositae (Asteraceae). In *Especies vegetales promisorias de los países del Convenio Andrés Bello*, Tomo V. Bogotá, D. E., Colombia: Secretaria Ejecutiva del Convenio Andrés Bello. Heywood, V. H., J. B. Harborne, and B. L. Turner (eds.). 1977. *The Biology and Chemistry of the Compositae*. London: Academic Press. Hind, D. J. N., and H. J. Beentje (eds.) 1996. Compositae: Systematics, Vol. 1. *Proceedings of the International Compositae Conference, Kew, 1994.* Royal Botanic Gardens, Kew. Hind, D. J. N., C. Jeffrey, and G. V. Pope (eds.). 1995. *Advances in Compositae Systematics: Compositae Systematics, Biology, Utilization*. Royal Botanic Gardens, Kew. Pruski, J. F. 1997. Asteraceae. In *Flora of the Venezuelan Guayana*, Araliaceae-Cactaceae, eds. J. A. Steyermark et al., 3:177–393. St. Louis, Missouri: Missouri Botanical Garden. Rzedowski, J. 1978. Claves para la identificación de los géneros de la familia Compositae en México. *Acta Ci. Potos.* 7:5–145. Turner, B. L., and G. L. Nesom. 1993. Biogeography, diversity, and endangered or threatened status of Mexican Asteraceae. In *Biological Diversity of Mexico: Origins and Distribution*, eds. T. P. Ramamoorthy et al., 559–75. New York: Oxford University Press.

AVICENNIACEAE (Black Mangrove Family)

Nathan Smith

Figure 19, Plate 6

- *trees of mangrove habitats*

- *pneumatophores often present*

- *leaves opposite (decussate), simple; petioles basally grooved, the margins of the grooves lined with hairs*

- *flowers bisexual; sepals 5; corolla lobes and stamens 4; placentation free-central, the ovules pendulous*

- *fruits single-seeded capsules; bracteoles and sepals persistent*

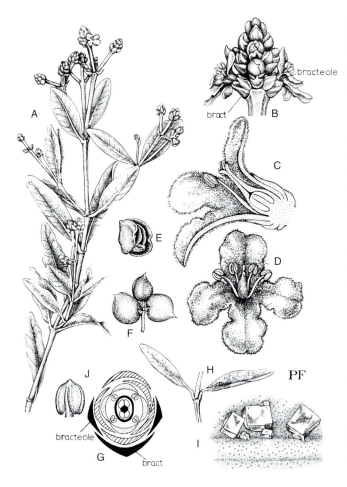

Figure 19. AVICENNIACEAE. *Avicennia germinans.* **A.** Stem with leaves and inflorescences (x⅔). **B.** Part of inflorescence with two flowers at anthesis (x2). **C.** Medial section of flower (x4). **D.** Apical view of flower (x4). **E.** Seedling before expansion (x⅔). **F.** Lateral view of fruits (x⅔). **G.** Floral diagram. **H.** Node (x⅔). **I.** Salt crystals on leaf blade surface (x13). **J.** Anther (x18). Reprinted with permission from Tomlinson (1980). Artist: Priscilla Fawcett.

Numbers of genera and species. Worldwide, the Avicenniaceae comprise a single genus, *Avicennia*, and about eight species. In tropical America, there are at least three species.

Similarities in morphology suggest that *Avicennia africana* (of West Africa) and *A. germinans* may be the same species.

Distribution and habitat. The Avicenniaceae are essentially pantropical. Species of *Avicennia* are found in coastal maritime habitats. In the Western Hemisphere, *Avicennia germinans* ranges from southern Florida and the West Indies and throughout Central America to the coasts of Peru and northern Brazil. *Avicennia bicolor* is found in Central America and in Colombia near the mouth of the Buenaventura River and *A. schaueriana* grows in the Lesser Antilles and along the Atlantic coast of South America to Uruguay.

Family classification. *Avicennia* was placed in the Verbenaceae by Cronquist within the Lamiales. More recent classifications have placed this genus in the Lamiales as its own family based on differences in leaf anatomy, placentation, seedling morphology, incipient vivipary, pollen, and anomalous secondary growth. Recent phylogenetic studies suggest that *Avicennia* should be placed in the Acanthaceae.

Features of the family. Habit: trees of mangrove; branchlets articulate, terete to 4-angled. **Roots** often horizontal and extended, these giving rise to conspicuous pneumatophores. **Stipules** absent. **Leaves** opposite (decussate), simple; petioles short, basally groved, the groove (often only the margins) lined with hairs; blades ovate to narrowly elliptic, the abaxial surface glaucous, often tomentose and covered with salt crystals, the adaxial surface usually glabrous, conspicuously more green, with minute punctations, the margins entire. **Inflorescences** axillary or terminal, spicate or subcapitate, pubescent, the flowers subtended by a single bract and a pair of bracteoles. **Flowers** slightly to very zygomorphic, bisexual, protandrous, often pubescent; sepals 5, distinct, ovate, imbricate; corolla basally connate (forming tube), white, yellow, or white with yellow throat (*A. bicolor*), glabrous/glabrescent (*A. schaueriana*), or pubescent adaxially, the lobes 4; androecium of 4 stamens, the stamens included or excluded, in slightly or very unequal pairs; gynoecium syncarpous, the ovary superior, the carpels 2, the locules 4, imperfect; placentation free-central, the ovules 4, pendulous. **Fruits** capsules, coriaceous, sometimes beaked, with persistent bracteoles and sepals. **Seeds** 1 per fruit.

Natural history. Species of *Avicennia* have developed a unique root system that allows respiration during periodic saturation of the soil. Horizontal roots give rise to small (usually <30 cm long) roots that perpendicularly stick out of the ground to allow the exchange of gas through lenticels. Although these pneumatophores are conspicuous characters for *Avicennia*, they are not always visible (e.g., during high tide) and also occur in other Neotropical species such as *Laguncularia racemosa* (Combretaceae).

Pollination is accomplished by bees. Research suggests that species of *Avicennia* growing together flower at different times, thus keeping competition between species low as well as providing pollinators with nectar for a more extended period. Dispersal of seeds and seedlings is by water.

The seeds of *Avicennia* are known to germinate within the fruit while still on the parent plant. Unlike true vivipary, which occurs in some Rhizophoraceae, the seedling does not emerge until the fruit has fallen. The germination of *Avicennia* is thought to be a strategy that helps the seedlings establish themselves more quickly in tidal environments.

Economic uses. Species of *Avicennia* are valuable resources because they stabilize coastal soils. In southern Florida, honey is made from the nectar of *Avicennia germinans*. The bark of this species has been used to tan leather, and the wood has been used for construction and fuel.

References. MOLDENKE, H. N. 1960a. Materials toward a monograph of the genus *Avicennia*. I. *Phytologia* 7(3):123–68. MOLDENKE, H. N. 1960b. Materials toward a monograph of the genus *Avicennia*. II. *Phytologia* 7(4):179–232. MOLDENKE, H. N. 1960c. Materials toward a monograph of the genus *Avicennia*. III. *Phytologia* 7(5):259–93. SCHWARZBACH, A. E., AND L. A. McDADE. 2002. Phylogenetic relationships of the mangrove family Avicenniaceae based on chloroplast and nuclear ribosomal DNA sequences. *Syst. Bot.* 27:84–98. TOMLINSON, P. B. 1986. *The Botany of Mangroves*. Cambridge, U.K.: Cambridge University Press.

BALANOPHORACEAE (Balanophora Family)

FAVIO GONZÁLEZ

Figure 20, Plate 6

- *plants parasitic on roots, achlorophyllous*
- *vegetative parts often subterranean*
- *leaves greatly reduced*
- *inflorescences funguslike, emergent*
- *flowers very small, unisexual; locules absent*

Numbers of genera and species. Worldwide, the Balanophoraceae comprise about 18 genera and 43 species. The largest genus, *Balanophora*, is confined to the paleotropics. In tropical America, the following seven genera occur: *Corynaea* (1 or 2 Neotropical species), *Helosis* (1), *Langsdorffia* (3, with 1 Neotropical), *Lathrophytum* (1), *Lophophytum* (3), *Ombrophytum* (4), and *Scybalium* (4).

Distribution and habitat. The Balanophoraceae are mostly pantropical, with some members reaching subtropical areas. The greatest diversification of the family occurs in Asia and the neotropics. The Neotropical members generally inhabit lowland and moist, montane, undisturbed forests in shaded habitats from sea level to 4,000 meters. Six of the seven Neotropical genera are endemic to tropical America: *Corynaea* to montane cloud forests from Costa Rica to Bolivia, often between 1,000 and 2,000 meters; *Helosis* to rain forests of Mexico and Central and South America, from sea level to 2,000 meters; *Langsdorffia* to montane, cloud forests of Mexico, Central America, and tropical South America (another species occurs in Madagascar and another in New Guinea); *Lathrophytum* to montane and premontane forests in the Rio de Janeiro area, Brazil; *Lophophytum* to wet lowland forests below 1,000 meters in tropical South America; *Ombrophytum* from wet lowland forests to dry montane thickets and *punas* in Ecuador (including the Galápagos Islands), Peru, Brazil, Bolivia, Chile, and Argentina; and *Scybalium* to montane cloud forests of the Greater Antilles, Colombia, Ecuador, and Brazil.

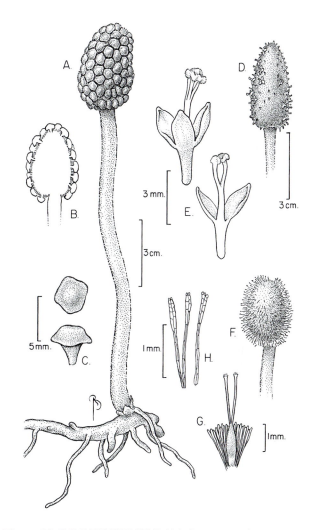

Figure 20. BALANOPHORACEAE. *Helosis cayennensis* var. *cayennensis* **A.** Plant showing aerial portion of plant and part of subterranean portion. **B.** Medial section of inflorescence. **C.** Apical (above) and lateral (below) views of peltate bracts from inflorescence. **D.** Inflorescence with a few staminate flowers. **E.** Lateral view (above) and medial section (below) of staminate flower with one anther removed; surrounding hairs not shown. **F.** Lateral view of inflorescence covered with ciliate hairs during pistillate phase. **G.** Lateral view of pistillate flower with perianth and some of surrounding hairs removed. **H.** Detail of three trichomes. Reprinted with permission from Mori et al. (2002). Artist: Bobbi Angell.

Family classification. There are three main opinions about the placement of the Balanophoraceae: 1) included as members of the Magnoliidae (*sensu* Takhtajan) near Hydnorales and Rafflesiales; 2) placed in the subclass Rosidae as members of the order Santalales (*sensu* Cronquist), mainly because of its parasitic habit and pistillate floral reduction; and 3) related to *Gunnera* of the Gunneraceae. Because of sequencing difficulties, molecular data have not been useful in establishing relationships of the Balanophoraceae.

Three of the six subfamilies are present in the neotropics: the Scybalioideae (*Helosis*, *Corynaea*, and *Scybalium*), the Lophophytoideae (*Lathrophytum*, *Lophophytum*, and *Ombrophytum*), and the Balanophoroideae (*Langsdorffia*). The subfamilies are distinguished mostly on the basis of floral characters. The flowers of both Scybalioideae and Lophophytoideae have two styles; however, the flowers are embedded in a layer of filiform trichomes in the Scybalioideae and not embedded in filiform trichomes in the Lophophytoideae. The Balanophoroideae differ from the latter two subfamilies in having one style.

Features of the family. Habit: obligate root parasites; achlorophyllous; vegetative parts often subterranean, attached to host by an amorphous tuber formed by tissues of both host and parasite, except in *Helosis*, *Scybalium*, and *Lophophytum* (as well as in other extra-Neotropical members) in which the tuber is formed from parasitic tissue only; epigeous part of plant tomentose, squamose, or naked, whitish, yellowish, pink, red, or purple. Leaves usually present and numerous (lacking in *Ombrophytum* and *Lathrophytum*), alternate (spiral), simple, usually reduced to scales, clasping, lacking stomates. Inflorescences funguslike, emergent, terminal, racemose, spikelike, sometimes globose (shape may vary by sex; e.g., *Langsdorffia*), sometimes branched, yellowish to purple, the stalk scaled or bracteate (in *Langsdorffia*, *Lophophytum*, and *Scybalium*), naked or much reduced (in *Corynaea*, *Helosis*, *Ombrophytum*); bracts peltate, scale-like, or clavate (in *Ombrophytum*), tighly covering flowers and falling before anthesis. Flowers very small (some of smallest in angiosperms), numerous, actinomorphic, unisexual (the plants monoecious or dioecious), embedded in layer of filiform hairs (paraphyses) in Scybalioideae. Staminate flowers aggregated (in many branches; e.g., *Ombrophytum*), rarely solitary (*Lathrophytum*); perianth lacking (e.g., *Ombrophytum*) or with a 3(8)-lobed perianth; androecium with stamens usually equal in number and opposite perianth lobes, variously fused into synandrium (common in *Langsdorffia*), the anthers dehiscing longitudinally. Pistillate flowers lacking perianth or perianth reduced; gynoecium with superior ovary, the carpels 2–3, the locules absent, the style 2-lobed (entire in *Langsdorffia*), the stigmas capitellate, smooth, secretory; placentas reduced, the ovules 1–3, ategmic. Fruits achenes, tiny, sometimes aggregated into funguslike infructescences. Seeds small; endosperm oily, the embryo undifferentiated.

During development, the inflorescence breaks out of a cu-

pular envelope, which remains as a collarlike "volva" around the base. The "volva" represents the protective cover of the tuber or rhizome which is ruptured by the emerging inflorescence. The "volva" of species of *Ombrophytum* grows into a large, spathelike sheath at the base of the inflorescence.

Several inflorescences are borne directly from a tuber in *Corynaea*. The inflorescence may be conspicuously branched, as in subfamily Lophophytoideae, or apparently unbranched as in subfamily Balanophoroideae (*Langsdorffia*). In the Scybalioideae, the ultimate flower-bearing branches are subtended by peltate bracts that have been interpreted as modified peltate leaves.

A remarkable feature of the family, unusual among flowering plants, is the gynoecium which lacks locules and possesses poorly differentiated, ategmic ovules embedded in gynoecial tissue.

Natural history. Most of the hosts of the tropical species of Balanophoraceae are trees or shrubs, but host specificity is still unknown. *Ombrophytum subterraneum* is reported to be a root parasite of several herbaceous species of *Medicago* and *Nicotiana* and to be entirely subterranean, even during flowering and fruiting.

Pollination, seed dispersal, and germination are poorly known. Flies (Diptera), bees (Hymenoptera), and beetles (Coleoptera, especially Chrysomelidae and Curculionidae) have been observed as floral visitors of species of *Corynaea*, *Lophophytum*, and *Ombrophytum*, as well as of extra-Neotropical species of *Balanophora* and *Sarcophyte*. Ant dispersal has been reported in extra-American species, and water has been suggested to be another dispersal agent in the family.

Economic uses. Wax produced from Asiatic species is burned as a source of light. Extracts from species with phallic inflorescences have been suggested to possess aphrodisiac properties. The inflorescences of several species of *Langsdorffia*, *Lophophytum*, and *Ombrophytum* are consumed by humans.

References. DePamphilis, C. W. 1995. Genes and genomes. In *Parasitic Plants*, eds. M. C. Press and J. D. Graves, 177–205. London: Chapman and Hall. Eichler, A. W. 1869. Balanophoreae. In *Flora Brasiliensis* 4(2):1–74, t. 1–16. Monachii: Lipsiae, Apud R. Oldenbourg in Comm. Hansen, B. 1976. Pollen and stigma conditions in the Balanophoraceae s. lat. *Bot. Notiser* 129:341–45. Hansen, B. 1980. Balanophoraceae. *Fl. Neotrop. Monogr.* 23:1–80. Hansen, B., and K. Engell. 1978. Inflorescence in Balanophoroideae, Lophophytoideae and Scybalioideae (Balanophoraceae). *Bot. Tidsskr.* 72:177–87. Hooker, J. D. 1856. On the structure and affinities of Balanophoreae. *Trans. Linn. Soc. Lond.* 22: 1–68. Kuijt, J. 1969. *The Biology of Parasitic Flowering Plants* Berkeley and Los Angeles: University of California Press. Kuijt, J., and W. X. Dong. 1990. Surface features of the leaves of Balanophoraceae—a family without stomata? *Plant Syst. Evol.* 170:29–35. Nevling Jr., L. I. 1960. Balanophoraceae. In Flora of Panama. *Ann. Missouri Bot.* *Gard.* 47:303–08. Richard, L. C. 1822. Mémoire sur une nouvelle famille des plantes, les Balanophorées. *Mém. Mus. Hist. Nat.* 8:404–35.

BALSAMINACEAE (Balsam Family)

David L. Lentz

- *herbs*

- *stems translucent, watery, ± succulent*

- *leaves simple*

- *flowers zygomorphic, resupinate; lowermost sepal with spur-nectary; anthers fused into ring arching over ovary, falling off when touched*

- *fruits loculicidal capsules, dehiscence explosive*

Numbers of genera and species. Worldwide, there are two genera and 450 species. In tropical America, there is one genus, *Impatiens*, with two native species and several naturalized species. All but one of the species in the family belongs to *Impatiens*. *Hydrocera* has one species native to Asia.

Distribution and habitat. Species of Balsaminaceae are found in Europe, Asia, the East Indies, Africa, Madagascar, and North and Central America. The family is especially widespread and diverse in the paleotropics. Only *Impatiens mexicana*, and *I. turrialbana* are native to the neotropics, but at least three species, *I. balsamina*, *I. bakeri*, and *I. walleriana*, have become naturalized along roadsides and other disturbed areas.

Species of the family grow in moist understory habitats. *Impatiens mexicana*, endemic to Orizaba, Mexico, grows up to 2,300 meters in humid ravines covered by tropical deciduous forest. *Impatiens turrialbana* is known only from moist valleys on slopes of the Turrialba and Irazu volcanoes in Costa Rica.

Family classification. The Balsaminaceae are placed in the Geraniales by Cronquist. Takhtajan places the Balsaminaceae in a separate order: the Balsaminales. Recent studies based on molecular data, however, place this family in an expanded Ericales.

Features of the family. Habit: herbs, annuals or perennials, usually glabrous. **Stems** translucent, watery, ± succulent, often with raphide-sacs. **Stipules** absent or represented by pair of tiny petiolar glands. **Leaves** alternate or opposite, simple, often with raphide-sacs; petiole vascular bundles arc shaped; blades with margins toothed or entire; venation pinnate. **Inflorescences** axillary, racemose, cymose, geminate, or solitary (racemose or geminate in *Impatiens mexicana*, and *I. turrialbana*); pedicels twisted. **Flowers** zygomorphic, bisexual, resupinate; sepals 3, uppermost 2 obsolete, lowermost petal-like and saccate, bearing abaxial spur-nectary; petals 5, side petals fused (*Impatiens*), forming 2 lateral pairs, the fifth separate, concave, sepal-like; androecium of 5 stamens, the filaments, short, broad, apically connate, the anthers tiny, fused into caplike ring, arching over ovary, falling off when touched; gynoecium syncarpous, the ovary superior, the carpels 5, the locules 5, the style 1, the stigmas 1–5. **Fruits** loculicidal capsules (*Impatiens*), valves 5, dehiscence explosive. **Seeds** very small, the endosperm limited, the cotyledons relatively large.

Impatiens mexicana is distinguished from other *Impatiens* by its yellow flowers, large spur, dentate leaf margins, eglandular petioles, and alternate leaves while *I. turrialbana* has purple to scarlet flowers and opposite leaves.

Natural history. The native Neotropical species of *Impatiens* are rare annuals. In general, species of touch-me-nots are pollinated by bees, butterflies, moths, and hummingbirds. The funnel-shaped flower is arranged so that an incoming pollinator must push past the anthers and the stigma to insert its proboscis into the recurved nectar spur. Seeds are expelled from the capsule when it bursts open or "explodes" upon drying.

Economic uses. Several species of *Impatiens* (touch-me-not), notably *I. sodenii*, *I. balsamina*, *I. walleriana*, and hybrids, are cultivated widely as garden ornamentals or as pot plants.

References. Barringer, K. 1991. Balsaminaceae. In *Flora de Veracruz*, eds. A. Gómez-Pompa and V. Sosa, Fasc. 64: 1–8. Xalapa, Mexico: INIREB. Elias, T. S. 1967. Balsaminaceae. In Flora of Panama, eds. R. E. Woodson, Jr., and R. W. Schery, *Ann. Missouri Bot. Gard.* 54(1):21–24. Rydberg, A. 1910. Balsaminaceae. *North American Flora* 25(2): 93–96. Wilson, P. 1995. Selection for pollination success and the botanical fit of *Impatiens* flowers around bumble bee bodies. *Biol. J. Linn. Soc.* 55:355–83.

BASELLACEAE (Madeira Vine Family)

ROGER ERIKSSON

Figure 21

- *vines, usually fleshy to succulent*
- *leaves alternate, simple*
- *flowers small (perianth 1–7 mm long); sepals 2, petal-like*
- *fruits nutlike, partly or completely surrounded by persistent perianth*

Numbers of genera and species. Worldwide, the Basellaceae comprise four genera and about 20 species. In tropical America, there are four genera and 15 species. All species of *Anredera*, *Tournonia*, and *Ullucus* are native to the Western Hemisphere, and one species of *Basella* (*B. alba*) has been introduced and is locally naturalized.

Distribution and habitat. The Basellaceae are native to tropical and subtropical parts of America, southeastern Africa, and Madagascar. The main center of diversity is in South America. Most species of Basellaceae occur in dry and open areas, from sea level to above 4,000 meters elevation in the Andes. Only a few species, such as *Anredera tucumanensis*, prefer more humid forests.

Family classification. The Basellaceae are placed in the Caryophyllales by Cronquist. The family is probably monophyletic, and shares supposedly derived features with certain genera of the Portulacaceae, thereby indicating a close relationship with this family.

The family is sometimes divided into two tribes; one tribe contains *Basella*, *Tournonia*, and *Ullucus* and is probably paraphyletic; the other tribe contains *Anredera*. *Tournonia* and *Ullucus* are both monotypic and probably form a monophyletic group.

The present generic and infrageneric circumscriptions of *Basella* and the largest genus, *Anredera*, are not satisfactory. *Basella paniculata* from southeastern Africa strongly differs from the other species in the genus, and further studies may show that it is better placed in a (sub)genus of its own. *Anredera* is here treated in the broad sense, including *Boussingaultia* and *Tandonia*. Traditionally *Anredera* only included *A. vesicaria*. Preliminary phylogenetic studies indicate that *A. vesicaria* forms a monophyletic group with *A. floribunda* that may merit formal recognition. If this is done, *Boussingaultia* and *Tandonia* may have to be re-evaluated.

Features of the family. Habit: vines (some cultivated species erect with more compact growth), perennial, usually fleshy to succulent, trailing to scandent, the vegetative growth

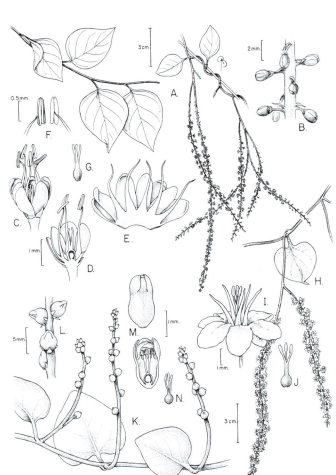

Figure 21. BASELLACEAE. *Anredera vesicaria* (A–G), *A. cordifolia* (H–J), and *Basella alba* (K–N). **A.** Stem with leaves (left) and stem with leaves and inflorescences (right). **B.** Detail of inflorescence. **C.** Lateral view of flower. **D.** Medial section of flower. **E.** Corolla spread open to show connate filaments. **F.** Adaxial (left) and abaxial (right) views of anthers. **G.** Lateral view of gynoecium. **H.** Stem with leaf and inflorescence. **I.** Lateral view of flower. **J.** Lateral view of gynoecium. **K.** Stem with inflorescences. **L.** Part of inflorescence. **M.** Lateral view (above) and medial section (below) of flowers. **N.** Lateral view of gynoecium. Reprinted with permission from Acevedo-Rodríguez (in prep.). Artist: Bobbi Angell.

sometimes tinged with red. **Stems** herbaceous, or occasionally suffruticose, short-lived, often annually renewed from aerial or subterranean tubers, or thickened stem base. **Stipules** absent. **Leaves** alternate, simple; petiole usually distinct; blades often more or less elliptic, ovate, or cordate, the margins entire (except *Tournonia hookeriana* with dentate margins and small marginal glands). **Inflorescences** axillary or terminal, spikes (*Basella*), dichasia (*Tournonia*), few-flowered racemes (*Ullucus*), many-flowered racemes or panicles (*Anredera*); bracteoles 2, frequently subtending flower, opposite. **Flowers** small, actinomorphic (except calyx), usually bisexual, rarely functionally unisexual (*Anredera vesicaria* and perhaps other species); perianth 1–7 millimeters long, greenish, whitish, reddish, or yellowish at anthesis; sepals 2, petal-like, opposite, alternating with bracteoles, adnate to petals at base; petals 5, imbricate, usually connate only at base (>1/3 of length in *Basella alba*), the apex obtuse or conspicuously caudate (in *Ullucus tuberosus*); androecium of 5 stamens, epipetalous, the filaments connate at base or into tube (*Basella alba*), the anthers with longitudinal slits, or with porelike slits (in *Ullucus tuberosus*), dehiscing apically; gynoecium syncarpous, the ovary superior, the carpels 3, the locule 1, the styles 1–3; placentation basal, ovule 1. **Fruit** nutlike, indehiscent, partly or completely enclosed by persistent perianth, the perianth often somewhat accrescent, pale to brownish or purplish black, membranous, or thick, rarely very thick and juicy (*Basella alba*).

The homologies of the bracteoles, sepals, and petals have been much debated, and a number of terms have been proposed for these structures. The perianth may actually be truly biseriate, and is here treated accordingly. The sepals of some species of *Anredera* have characteristic, dorsal structures in fruit; e.g., the inflated gibba of *A. ramosa* or the broad wing of *A. vesicaria*.

Most Basellaceae have spherical pollen with a spinulose and foveolate surface and six or more apertures. Unusual reticulate and perfectly cubical pollen is found in *Basella alba*.

Natural history. The pollination of the Basellaceae is largely unknown, but the small and sweetly fragrant flowers of *Anredera* probably attract insects. Some species of *Basella* are cleistogamous.

Fruits enclosed by a persistent and often thickened perianth occasionally may be dispersed by birds. The fruits of *A. vesicaria* that are enclosed by winged sepals are certainly wind-dispersed.

Economic uses. Several species of Basellaceae are cultivated worldwide. Species of *Anredera* are grown as ornamentals, including *A. cordifolia* (Madeira vine). *Basella alba* (Malabar spinach) is grown mainly for its edible leaves and the fleshy perianth enclosing the fruit yields a dark violet dye used in food.

Ullucus tuberosus subspecies *tuberosus* is an important food crop in the high Andes from Venezuela to northern Argentina and has been cultivated for its edible tubers for several thousand years. It is propagated vegetatively, and about 50–70 distinct cultivars are known. The starchy tubers usually are consumed boiled, and either fresh or rehydrated ones that have been dried for long-term storage can be used.

References. BOGLE, A. L. 1969. The genera of Portulacaceae and Basellaceae in the southeastern United States. *J. Arnold Arbor.* 50:566–98. ERIKSSON, R. 1996. Basellaceae. In *Flora of Ecuador*, eds. G. Harling and L. Andersson, no. 55:55–83. Göteborg, Sweden: Department of Systematic Botany, University of Göteborg. MOQUIN-TANDON, A. 1849. Basellaceae. In *Prodromus Systematis Naturalis Regni Vegetabilis*, ed. A. de Candolle, 13(2):220–30, 462. Paris: Victor Masson. SPERLING, C. R., AND V. BITTRICH. 1993. Basellaceae. In *The Families and Genera of Vascular Plants*, eds. K. Kubitzki, J. G. Rohwer, and V. Bittrich, 2:143–46. Berlin: Springer-Verlag. ULBRICH, E. 1934. Basellaceae. In *Die Natürlichen Pflanzenfamilien*, A. Engler and K. Prantl, 2nd ed. 16c:263–71. Leipzig: Wilhelm Engelmann.

BATACEAE (Saltwort Family)

MICHAEL NEE

Figure 22

- *subshrubs of ocean shores, somewhat succulent*

- *leaves opposite, simple*

- *bracts subtending flowers*

- *flowers reduced*

- *fruits drupaceous*

Numbers of genera and species. Worldwide, the Bataceae comprise one genus with two species. A single species, *Batis maritima*, is found in tropical America.

Distribution and habitat. *Batis maritima* inhabits Pacific Ocean shores from California to Peru, the Galápagos, and Hawaiian Islands, and on the Atlantic from Florida to Brazil, including the Caribbean islands. The recently discovered *Batis argillicola* is found on the south shores of New Guinea and northern Australia.

The Bataceae grow along ocean or other saline shores, and are well adapted to high insolation and saline soils. They often grow in association with mangroves, but not in tidal water more than a few centimeters deep.

Family classification. The Bataceae are placed in the Batales, along with the Gyrostemonaceae, by Cronquist. The

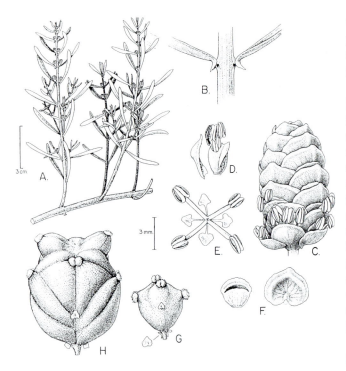

Figure 22. BATACEAE. *Batis maritima*. **A.** Stems with leaves and inflorescences (x½). **B.** Node showing lobate leaf bases (x5). **C.** Lateral view of staminate inflorescence (x8). **D.** Lateral view of staminate flower subtended by bract and enclosed by saccate organ (right) and bract (left). **E.** Apical view of staminate flower (x8). **F.** Adaxial view of saccate organ that encloses staminate flower (left) and adaxial view of bract subtending flower (right; x8). **G.** Lateral view of pisillate inflorescence (right) and adaxial view of bract (left; x8). **H.** Lateral view of pistillate inflorescence at large scale (x16). Reprinted with permission from Cronquist (1981). Artist: Bobbi Angell.

The family has also been associated with catkin-bearing plants such as found in the Betulaceae, Fagaceae, and Salicaceae because of the very reduced and seemingly wind-pollinated flowers.

Features of the family. Habit: subshrubs of ocean shores, to 1 meter tall, somewhat succulent, yellowish green. **Stems** arching, weak. **Stipules** small, caducous. **Leaves** opposite, simple; blade base lobate, the margins entire. **Inflorescences** axillary or terminal, spikes, small, the female spikes with fewer flowers; bracts subtending flowers present (smaller on female plants). **Flowers** reduced, unisexual (the plants dioecious in *Batis maritima*); male flowers from bilobed structure (origin unknown, possibly bracts or sepals), smaller than bracts; sepals 4 (male flowers), may be considered staminodes, or absent (female flowers); petals absent; androecium of 4 stamens, the filaments exserted from bracts; gynoecium with ovaries connate at base, the carpels 2, the locules 4, the stigmas 2; placentation parietal-basal, ovule 1 per locule. **Fruits** drupaceous. **Seeds** 4, each enclosed in a pyrene.

Natural history. No information is available about pollination and dispersal.

Economic uses. No economic uses are known for the family.

References. BAYER, C. AND O. APPEL. 2003. Bataceae. In *The Families and Genera of Vascular Plants*, eds. K. Kubitzki and C. Bayer. 5:30–32. Berlin: Springer-Verlag. GOLDBLATT, P. 1976. Chromosome number and its significance in *Batis maritima* (Bataceae). *J. Arnold Arbor.* 57:526–30. MABRY, T. J., AND B. L. TURNER. 1964. Chemical investigations of the Batidaceae. *Taxon* 13:197–200. MCLAUGHLIN, L. 1959. The woods and flora of the Florida Keys. Wood anatomy and phylogeny of Batidaceae. *Trop. Woods* 110: 1–15. RODMAN, J. E., ET AL. 1996. Molecules, morphology, and Dahlgren's expanded order Capparales. *Syst. Bot.* 21(3): 289–307.

presence of mustard oils suggests affinities with Cronquist's Capparales and recent studies place the family near taxa of this order (e.g., Brassicaceae and Tovariaceae). Although habit and habitat of the Bataceae are similar to *Sarcobatus* and *Salicornia* of the Chenopodiaceae, the floral and chemical characteristics of the Caryophyllales are lacking in *Batis*.

BEGONIACEAE (Begonia Family)

FAVIO GONZÁLEZ

Figure 23

- *usually herbs*

- *leaves alternate, simple; blade base asymmetrical; venation palmate*

- *flowers unisexual; ovary usually inferior*

- *fruits 3-lobed, usually winged*

Numbers of genera and species. Worldwide, the Begoniaceae comprise three genera and about 1,000 species. *Begonia sensu lato* is the only genus in tropical America where an estimated 500 of its 1,000 species occur. The Hawaiian *Hillebrandia* is monotypic and the New Guianean *Symbegonia* (sometimes placed in *Begonia*) contains 11 species.

At least two other small genera have been segregated from

Begonia: *Begoniella*, consisting of at least four Colombian species, and *Semibegoniella*, containing three species from Ecuador.

Distribution and habitat. The Begoniaceae are widespread in tropical and subtropical regions, missing only from Australia and some islands of the Pacific. In tropical America, *Begonia sensu lato* is highly diverse in northern South America.

The family is most diverse in humid forests from 1,000 to 3,000 meters elevation. Some species, however, grow in lowland vegetation.

Family classification. The Begoniaceae are placed in the Violales by Cronquist, close to Cucurbitaceae and Datiscaceae. Wood anatomy and *rbc*L data support the relationship of these families.

Features of the family. Habit: herbs or small shrubs, perennial, terrestrial or epiphytic, erect, climbing, or creeping, often pubescent, frequently succulent, sometimes acaulescent. Stipules large, membranaceous, persistent. Leaves alternate,

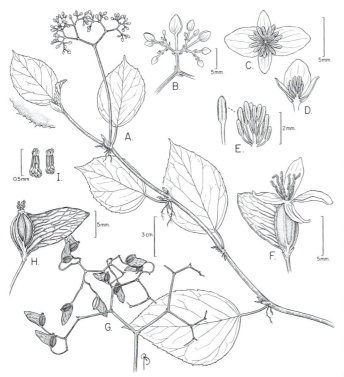

Figure 23. BEGONIACEAE. *Begonia glabra.* **A.** Stem showing rooting at the nodes, leaves, and immature inflorescence with detail of margin (upper left). **B.** Detail of part of inflorescence. **C.** Apical view of staminate flower. **D.** Medial section of staminate flower. **E.** Part of androecium (right) and detail of stamen (left). **F.** Lateral view of pistillate flower. **G.** Infructescence. **H.** Lateral view of fruit. **I.** Seeds. Reprinted with permission from Mori et al. (2002). Artist: Bobbi Angell.

simple; blades frequently lobed, the base asymmetrical, the margins serrate; venation palmate. **Inflorescences** commonly axillary, cymose, often asymmetrical, showy. **Flowers** usually zygomorphic, unisexual (the plants monoecious), pink, reddish, or white. **Staminate flowers**: sepals 2, petal-like; petals 2, usually smaller than sepals; androecium of 4–many stamens, the stamens resembling stigmas, the connective pronounced, the anthers basifixed, longitudinally dehiscent. **Pistillate flowers**: perianth uniseriate; tepals 4–5; gynoecium syncarpous, the ovary inferior or semi-inferior, often winged or horned, the wings sometimes unequal, the carpels (2)3(6), the locules (2)3(6), the styles usually 3, the stigmas usually 3, papillose, often bifid, twisted; placentation parietal or nearly so (in nonseptate species), or axile (in species possessing complete septa), the placenta sometimes lobed, the ovules many, anatropous. **Fruits** loculicidal capsules, asymmetrical, 3-lobed, usually winged. **Seeds** numerous, tiny, reticulate, operculate, the endosperm lacking, the embryo straight.

The shape and structure of the ovary, including the type of placentation, and the micromorphology and surface of the seeds, are important in the classification of the family.

Natural history. Staminate flowers often open before pistillate flowers, thereby promoting cross-pollination. Female flowers, which lack a pollinator reward, mimic male flowers, which offer pollen as a reward. Bees have been recorded as visitors of several species.

In American species, dispersal by both wind and animals has been observed.

Economic uses. Begoniaceae are cultivated widely as ornamental garden plants or houseplants. There are an estimated 10,000 hybrids and cultivars.

References. AGREN, J., AND D. W. SCHEMSKE. 1991. Pollination by deceit in a neotropical monoecious herb, *Begonia involucrata*. *Biotropica* 23:235–41. BARANOV, A. 1981. Studies in the Begoniaceae. *Phytologia Mem.* 4:1–88. BERG, R. G. VAN DEN. 1983. Pollen characteristics of the genera of the Begoniaceae, *in* J.J.F.E. de Wilde (ed.), Studies in Begoniaceae I, pp. 55–66. *Wageningen Agric. Univ. Pap. Wageningen*, The Netherlands. BOUMAN, F., AND A. DE LANGE. 1983. Structure, micromorphology of *Begonia* seeds. *Begonian* 50:70–78, 91. CARLQUIST, S. 1985. Wood anatomy of Begoniaceae, with comments on raylessness, paedomorphosis, relationships, vessel diameter, and ecology. *Bull. Torrey Bot. Club* 112:59–69. CHARPENTIER, A., L. BROUILLET & D. BARABE. 1989. Organogenèse de la fleur pistillee du *Begonia dregei* et de l'*Hillebrandia sandwicensis* (Begoniaceae). *Can. J. Bot.* 67:3625–39. GOLDING, J., AND C. E. KAREGEANNES. 1986. Begoniaceae, part II: Annotated species list. *Smithsonian Contr. Bot.* 60:131–584. GOLDING, J., AND D. C. WASSHAUSEN. 2002. Begoniaceae, Edition 2. Part I: annotated species list. Part II: illustrated key, abridgement and supplement. *Contrib. U.S. Natl. Herb.* 43:1–289. LANGE, A. DE, AND F. BOUMAN. 1992. Seed micromorphology of the genus *Begonia* in Africa: taxonomic and ecological implications, *in* J.J.F.E. de Wilde (ed.), Studies in Begoniaceae III, pp. 1–82. *Wageningen Agric. Univ. Papers,* Wageningen, The Netherlands. LE-CORFF, J., J. AGREN, AND D. W. SCHEMSKE. 1998. Floral display, pollinator discrimination, and female reproductive success in two monoecious *Begonia* species. *Ecology* 79(5):1610–19. MERXMULLER, H., AND P. LEINS. 1971. Zur Entwicklungsgeschichte mannlicher Begonienbluten. *Flora* 160:333–39. RONSE-DECREANE, L. P., AND E. SMETS. 1990. The systematic relationship between Begoniaceae and Papaveraceae: a comparative study of their floral development. *Bull. Jard. Bot. Natl. Belg.* 60:229–73. SMITH, L. B. 1973. *Begonia* in Venezuela. *Phytologia* 26:209–27.

SMITH, L. B., AND B. SCHUBERT. 1946. The Begoniaceae of Colombia I. *Caldasia* 4:3–38, 77–107, 179–209. SMITH, L. B., AND B. SCHUBERT. 1955. Studies in the Begoniaceae. *J. Wash. Acad. Sci.* 45:110–14. SMITH, L. B., AND B. SCHUBERT. 1958. Begoniaceae, in R. E. Woodson and R. W. Scherry (eds.), Flora of Panama, *Ann. Missouri Bot. Gard.* 45:41–67. SMITH, L. B., D. C. WASSHAUSEN, J. GOLDING AND C. E. KAREGEANNES. 1986. Begoniaceae, part. I: illustrated key; part II: Annotated species list. *Smithsonian Contr. Bot.* 60: 1–584. URIBE, L. 1955. Begoniáceas. *Flora de la Real Expedición Botánica al Nuevo Reyno de Granada,* 27: 99–131. Instituto de Ciencias Naturales, Universidad Nacional de Colombia, y Real Jardín Botánico, Madrid, España.

BERBERIDACEAE (Barberry Family)

LISA M. CAMPBELL

Figure 24

- *shrubs*
- *cauline spines present (in* Berberis*)*
- *flowers actinomorphic, bisexual; anthers dehiscing by basal valves; staminodia 6*
- *fruits berries*

Numbers of genera and species. Worldwide, the Berberidaceae comprise 15 genera and about 670 species. In tropical America, there are two genera and about 225 species. Approximately 200 of the more than 500 species of *Berberis* occur in the neotropics, as well as about 25 of the 100 species of *Mahonia.*

Distribution and habitat. Berberidaceae are especially diverse in eastern Asia and eastern North America. Species of *Mahonia* and *Berberis* are distributed throughout the Northern Hemisphere. In the Western Hemisphere, species of *Berberis* and *Mahonia* occur in North America, with *Mahonia* extending to Costa Rica and *Berberis* to Tierra del Fuego. In the neotropics, species occur in the highlands of Central America, the Andes, and southeastern Brazil.

Mahonia and *Berberis* are found in dry habitats and temperate deciduous and subtropical evergreen forests.

Family classification. The Berberidaceae are placed in the Ranunculales by Cronquist. Some authors consider Berberidaceae to be near the Ranunculaceae and related to the Lardizabalaceae, Menispermaceae, and Papaveraceae. Based on

features of the stamens and pollen, the base chromosome number, and molecular data, three groups of genera are recognized: 1) the woody Nandinoideae, comprising the single Asiatic species *Nandina domestica*; 2) the herbaceous Leonticeae and Epimediineae; 3) and the polymorphic Berberidineae, including the woody *Mahonia* and *Berberis* and *Ranzania japonica*, an Asiatic herb.

Features of the family. Habit: shrubs, perennial, evergreen or deciduous. Stems pachycaulous (*Mahonia*), short shoots and cauline spines present (*Berberis*). Wood often yellow. Stipules absent or vestigial. Leaves alternate, simple (*Berberis*) or imparipinnately compound (*Mahonia*); blade margins entire (*Berberis* and some *Mahonia*), or toothed or spiny (*Mahonia*). Inflorescences axillary or terminal, racemous, paniculate, or of solitary flowers. Flowers actinomorphic, bisexual; perianth of sepals; sepals 3–12; staminodia 6, petal-like, yellow, yellow-orange, or red-yellow (in South American *Berberis*); nectaries at base of staminodia; androecium with 6 stamens, the stamens opposite staminodia, the anthers dehiscing by basal valves; gynoecium syncarpous, the ovary superior, the carpels 3, the locule 1, the style short or absent; placentation basal, the ovules few. Fruits berries. Seeds 1–18, small.

Some authors include *Mahonia* in *Berberis*; the former is distinguished from the latter by its compound versus simple leaves.

The Berberidaceae contain many alkaloids, such as berberin, which imparts a characteristic yellow color to woody parts.

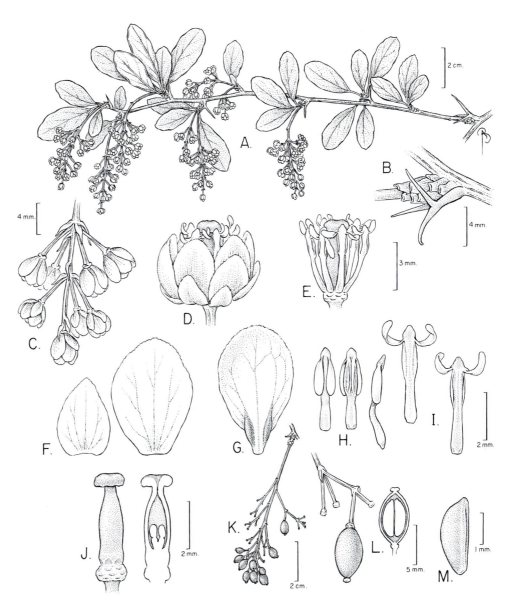

Figure 24. BERBERIDACEAE. *Berberis bumeliifolia* (A–J, Solomon 10987; K–M, Solomon and Nee 17940). **A.** Stem with leaves and inflorescences. **B.** Detail of node showing spine. **C.** Part of inflorescence. **D.** Lateral view of intact flower. **E.** Lateral view of flower with sepals and staminodes removed. **F.** Sepals. **G.** Nectariferous staminode. **H.** Abaxial (left), adaxial (middle), and lateral (right) views of stamens. **I.** Views of stamens showing dehiscence of anthers. **J.** Lateral views of gynoecium (left) and medial section of gynoecium (right). **K.** Infructescence. **L.** Lateral view (left) and medial section (right) of fruits. **M.** Lateral view of seed. Original. Artist: Bobbi Angell.

Natural history. Some species of *Berberis* are alternate hosts to the rust *Puccinia graminis*. Information on the basic biology of the Neotropical species, such as pollination mechanism and mode of dispersal, is lacking.

Economic uses. Berberin, found in *Berberis*, is an effective antibiotic and is used to treat eye infections. Compounds from *Podophyllum* are known to have anticancer activity and also are used to treat venereal warts. Neotropical species of Berberidaceae and related families produce many isoquinolines and may be underutilized locally for medicinal purposes. Species of *Mahonia* and *Berberis* (barberry) are cultivated as ornamentals. Fruits of these genera are made into jam, and *Berberis* is used as a honey plant in Russia.

References. AHRENT, L. W. A. 1961. *Berberis* and *Mahonia*. A taxonomic revision. *J. Linn. Soc., Bot.* 57:1–410.

BERNAL, H. Y., AND J. E. CORRERA Q. 1989. Berberidaceae. In *Especies vegetales promisorias de los países del Convenio Andrés Bello*, Tomo II. Bogotá, D. E., Colombia: Secretaria Ejecutiva del Convenio Andrés Bello. JACHEN, E. 1949. Die systematische gliederung der Ranunculaceen und Berberidaceen. *Akad. Wiss. Wien, Math.-Naturwiss. Kl., Denkschr.* 108:1–82. KIM, YONG-DONG, AND R. K. JANSEN. 1998. Chloroplast DNA restriction site variation and pylogeny of the Berberidaceae. *Amer. J. Bot.* 85:1766–78. KUMAZAWA, M. 1937. *Ranzania japonica* (Berberidac). Its morphology, biology and systematic affinities. *Jap. J. Bot.* 9:55–70. LECHLER, W. 1857. *Berberides Americae australis*. Stuttgart: Sumpibus librariae E. Schwizerbart. LEWIS, W. H., AND M.P.F. ELVIN-LEWIS. 1977. *Medical Botany: Plants Affecting Man's Health*. New York: John Wiley & Sons. LOCONTE, H. 1993. Berberidaceae. In *The Families and Genera of Vascular Plants*, eds. K. Kubitzki, J. G. Rohwer, and V. Bittrich, 2:147–52. Berlin: Springer-Verlag. LOCONTE, H., L. M. CAMPBELL, AND D. WM. STEVENSON. 1995. Ordinal and familial relationships of Ranunculid genera. *Pl. Syst.* *Evol., Suppl.* 9:99–118. MEACHEN, C. A. 1980. Phylogeny of the Berberidaceae with an evaluation of classification. *Syst. Bot.* 5:149–72.

BETULACEAE (Birch Family)

DAVID L. LENTZ

Figure 25

- *small trees or shrubs*

- *leaves alternate, simple; blade margins dentate*

- *inflorescences catkins*

- *flowers unisexual*

- *fruits nuts*

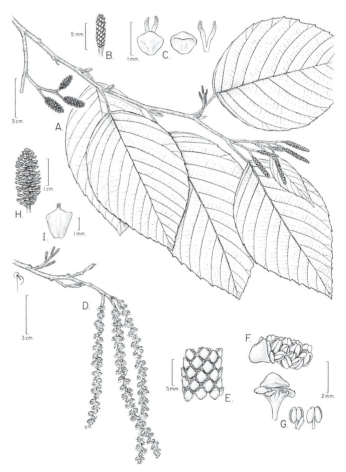

Numbers of genera and species. Worldwide, the Betulaceae comprise six genera and about 170 species. In tropical America, there are three genera and four species. *Alnus* has two species (*A. acuminata* and *A. jorullensis*), and *Carpinus* and *Ostrya* each has one species (*C. caroliniana* and *O. virginiana*).

Distribution and habitat. The Betulaceae are found mostly in northern temperate zones, but also occur in mountainous areas of Central America and Andean South America. The family prefers cool, moist habitats.

Alnus acuminata ranges from the Sierra Madre Occidental in Sonora, Mexico, to the Andean highlands of Bolivia from 2,000 to 3,200 meters. *Alnus jorullensis* is sporadically distributed from Mexico to Andean South America and is often found growing with oaks from 1,800 to 3,800 meters. *Carpinus caroliniana* is distributed from North America to as far south as Honduras; it is usually found in moist forests and along streams from 1,300 to 1,800 meters in Central America. *Ostrya virginiana* is widely distributed from North America to Honduras, where it occurs from 1,000 to 3,000 meters.

Family classification. The Betulaceae are placed in the Fagales by Cronquist on the basis of morphological and molecular data. The family is closely related to the Fagaceae.

Traditionally, the family has been divided into three tribes, the Betuleae, with two genera (*Betula* and *Alnus*) and 80 species; the Coryleae, with two genera (*Corylus* and *Ostryopsis*) and 17 species; and the Carpineae, with two genera (*Carpinus* and *Ostrya*) and 40 species. Recent molecular studies are largely congruent with the traditional intrafamilial classification.

Figure 25. BETULACEAE. *Alnus acuminata* (A–C, Moraes 2404; D, Nee and Atha 50004; E, F, Smith and Vasquez 4861; G, Fierro 359). **A.** Stem with leaves and male and female catkins. **B.** Lateral view of pistillate catkin. **C.** Abaxial view of female flower subtended by bract (left), adaxial view of bract (center), and bifid style (right). **D.** Stem with staminate catkins. **E.** Part of staminate catkin. **F.** Staminate flower. **G.** Bract from staminate catkin (left) and stamens (right). **H.** Lateral view of fruiting catkin. **I.** Fruit. Original. Artist: Bobbi Angell.

Features of the family. Habit: small trees or shrubs. **Bark** often smooth, peeling off in large thin layers. **Stipules** present. **Leaves** alternate, simple; blade margins dentate; venation pinnate. **Inflorescences** catkins (aments), pendulous (staminate catkins), or erect on stiff axis (pistillate catkins). **Flowers** unisexual (the plants monoecious); sepals (if present) 1–6, scalelike. **Staminate flowers** with androecium of 2–12 stamens. **Pistillate flowers** lacking vestigial stamens; gynoecium syncarpous, the ovary inferior, the carpels 2–3, the styles separate, the locules 2–3 below, 1 above, the stigmas dry; placentation axile, the ovules 1–2 per locule. **Fruits** nuts, small, laterally compressed, usually winged (*Alnus*), or ovoid, compressed and subtended by an aliform, persistent bract (*Carpinus*), or encased in saclike, vesicular bracts arranged into fruiting catkins that resemble hops (*Ostrya*). **Seeds** 1 by abortion; endosperm fleshy, the embryo large, thin.

Natural history. All species are wind-pollinated. The winged seeds (most *Alnus*) and fruits with winglike bracts (*Carpinus* and *Ostrya*) are dispersed by wind.

Economic uses. The sap of *Alnus acuminata, A. jorullensis,* and *Ostrya virginiana* are used to tan and dye leather. The wood is said to be excellent for furniture and for the manufacture of other artisanal products. Because the wood is extremely durable, it is used to make cross-ties for the Mexican railroad. Sometimes *Alnus acuminata* is planted to provide shade in coffee fields. The Mexicans make charcoal and/or firewood from *Carpinus caroliniana.* The leaves and bark of *Ostrya virginiana* are used for medicinal purposes in Mexico.

References. BERNAL, H. Y., AND J. E. CORRERA Q. 1989. Betulaceae. In *Especies vegetales promisorias de los países del Convenio Andrés Bello*, Tomo II. Bogotá, D. E., Colombia: Secretaria Ejecutiva del Convenio Andrés Bello. CARRANZA, E., AND X. M. SÁNCHEZ. 1995. Familia Betulaceae. *Flora del Bajío y de Regiones Adyacentes*, fasc. 39:1–21. Pátzcuaro, México: Instituto de Ecología, A. C. KILLEEN, T. J., E. GARCÍA E., AND S. G. BECK, eds. 1993. *Guía de Arboles de Bolivia*. St. Louis, MO: Missouri Botanical Garden. NEE, M. 1981. *Flora de Veracruz*, ed. A. Gómez-Pompa, fasc. 20:1–20. Xalapa, Mexico: Instituto de Ecologia, A.C. WEN, J., M. VANEK-KREBITZ, K. HOFFMANN-SOMMERGRUBER, O. SCHEINER, AND H. BREITENEDER. 1997. The potential of Betv1 homologues, a nuclear multigene family, as phylogenetic markers in flowering plants. *Molecular Phylogenetics and Evolution.* 8(3):317–33.

BIGNONIACEAE (Trumpet-Creeper Family)

LÚCIA G. LOHMANN

Figure 26, Plate 6

- *usually lianas or trees*
- *leaves usually opposite, compound*
- *tendrils derived from terminal leaflet often present in lianas*
- *flowers usually with showy corolla, sympetalous; stamens usually 4, didynamous (2 long and 2 short); stigma 2-lobed*
- *fruits usually capsules*
- *seeds often winged*

Numbers of genera and species. Worldwide, the Bignoniaceae comprise 120 genera and about 800 species. In tropical America, there are 80 genera and about 600 species. Of these, *Tabebuia, Jacaranda, Arrabidaea, Anemopaegma,* and *Adenocalymma* are the largest, and together accommodate almost half of the species in the family. The remaining genera are relatively small, with several being monotypic. The Bignoniaceae have one of the lowest species-to-genus ratios of all flowering plant families.

Distribution and habitat. The Bignoniaceae are mainly pantropical with only a few representatives found in temperate zones. Tropical America is the center of diversity of the family. The remaining tropical Bignoniaceae occur in Madagascar, Africa, and tropical Asia. The few temperate Bignoniaceae are distributed through North America, Europe, and Asia, however, the original distributions of some of these species is obscure because many are now widely cultivated (e.g., *Campsis radicans*).

Bignoniaceae are abundant in different tropical habitats, but are predominantly canopy trees and lianas of lowland forests. Many taxa also occur in dry-forests and dry open habitats, such as Neotropical savannas, such as the Brazilian *cerrado*, while others are abundant in mountainous regions with rocky outcrops and white sands. Except for the two monotypic Andean tribes (Tourrettieae and Eccremocarpeae), species of Bignoniaceae usually do not reach very high elevations.

Family classification. The Bignoniaceae are placed in the Scrophulariales by Cronquist, but in an expanded Lamiales that includes many of Cronquist's Scrophulariales by the Angiosperm Phylogeny Group. Molecular phylogenetic data support the monophyly of the family, excluding *Paulownia* (now Paulowniaceae) and *Schlegelia* (now Schlegeliaceae). These same analyses suggest that the Neotropical tribes Bignonieae and Crescentieae, as well as the African tribe Coleeae each form a monophyletic group and that the Pantropical

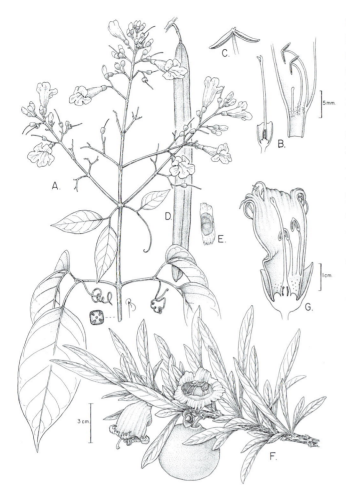

Figure 26. BIGNONIACEAE. *Arrabidaea chica* (A–E) and *Crescentia linearifolia* (F, G). **A.** Stem with leaves and inflorescence; transverse section of stem (lower left). **B.** Medial section of calyx and gynoecium (left) and medial section of lower part of corolla showing two of the four adnate stamens and the single adnate staminode (right). **C.** Apex of the stamen showing versatile anther. **D.** Lateral view of fruit. **E.** Winged seed. **F.** Stem with leaves, flowers, and young fruit. **G.** Medial section of corolla and gynoecium showing two of the four adnate stamens and the nectary at the base of the ovary. Reprinted with permission from Acevedo-Rodríguez (1996). Artist: Bobbi Angell.

tribe Tecomeae is paraphyletic. The Bignoniaceae includes seven tribes, divided on the basis of geographical distribution, habit, and fruit morphology. The most widely distributed tribe is Tecomeae, which is mainly Neotropical, but also includes representatives in Europe, North America, Africa, and Southeast Asia. Tecomeae comprise 250 species and 20 genera of trees, treelets, woody shrubs, and a few lianas (e.g., *Campsis radicans* and *Podranea ricasoliana*). The following four tribes are endemic to the neotropics: Bignonieae, Crescentieae, Tourrettieae, and Eccremocarpeae. The largest of these is Bignonieae, which accommodates all Neotropical lianas and shrubs with septicidal capsules, and includes approximately 350 species distributed among 50 genera. Recent molecular data, however, suggest that several of the

traditionally circumscribed genera of Bignonieae are not monophyletic. Crescentieae are centered in Central America and include three genera and 33 species of trees, treelets and shrubs with indehiscent fruits. Tourrettieae and Eccremocarpeae are both small and monogeneric. The tribe Tourrettieae has a single species, *Tourrettia lappacea*, an annual vine that occurs throughout the South American Andes and along the Central American cordilleras, while Eccremocarpeae include three species of Central Andean vines of the genus *Eccremocarpus*. All Malagasy Bignoniaceae are included in the tribe Coleeae which, like Crescentieae, possess indehiscent fruits. Coleeae are composed of approximately 75 species and six genera, five of which are endemic to Madagascar, and includes the monotypic *Kigelia pinnata*, which is restricted to Africa's grasslands. Species of Coleeae are predominantly cauliflorous treelets but can also be shrubs or small- to large-canopy trees. The Oroxyleae include four genera in the Eastern Hemisphere of trees, lianas, and shrubs with loculicidal capsules.

Features of the family. Habit: often lianas or trees, less frequently shrubs, rarely herbaceous, the trees often deciduous. **Stems** cylindrical or angled, frequently with interpetiolar glands and/or ridges, especially when young. **Stipules** absent; axillary bud scales frequently modified into stipulelike structures (pseudostipules). **Leaves** usually opposite, less often alternate, rarely simple; blades often compound (palmate, pinnate, 2–3-foliolate, or 2–3-ternate), with terminal leaflet modified into simple, bifid, trifid, or multifid tendril. **Inflorescences** terminal or axillary, panicles, cymes, thyrses, or sometimes of a solitary flower. **Flowers** usually zygomorphic, bisexual; sepals usually cupular, tubular, spathaceous, or urceolate, frequently bearing conspicuous glands; corolla often showy, sympetalous, usually funnel-shaped, 5-lobed, white, cream, yellow, orange, pink, purple, red, green, or bluish; androecium usually with 4 stamens (2 in *Catalpa* (Tecomeae) and *Pseudocatalpa* (Bignonieae), didynamous, the anthers usually with 2 thecae, rarely 1 (e.g., *Colea, Ophiocolea,* some *Jacaranda*); staminode 1, usually reduced, present in flowers with 4 stamens; disc usually present, surrounding ovary, often nectariferous; gynoecium syncarpous, the ovary superior, the carpels 2, the locules 2, the style elongated, the stigma 2-lobed; placentation axile, rarely parietal (Crescentieae and Coleeae), the ovules several to many. **Fruits** usually dry capsules dehiscent by 2 valves, sometimes hard-shelled pepos (Crescentieae and Coleeae). **Seeds** several to many per fruit, typically winged, less often corky, or embedded in pulp (Coleeae and Crescentieae); endosperm lacking.

Stems of most Neotropical lianas have anomalous secondary growth of their wood in which the xylem and phloem form a 4–32-armed crosslike structure as seen in cross section. This pattern results from failure of portions of the cambium to produce secondary xylem, which presumably gives higher stem flexibility to climbers.

Simple leaves are found in some members of several

tribes; e.g., *Amphitecna* and *Crescentia* (Crescentieae), *Catalpa* and some species of *Tabebuia* (Tecomeae), some species of *Arrabidaea* and *Distictella* (Bignonieae), and *Phylloctenium* and *Phyllarthon* (Coleeae). Alternate leaves are characteristic of the tropical *Amphitecna* and *Crescentia* and the temperate *Catalpa*.

Natural history. Members of the Bignoniaceae exhibit various patterns of flowering phenology—e.g., steady-state, modified steady-state, cornucopia, big bang, and multiple bang—and have various pollination strategies. Together, these are thought to allow the maintenance of high species diversity by allowing different species to share limited pollinator resources.

Bignoniaceae are mostly pollinated by bees and wasps, but also by hummingbirds (Western Hemisphere), sunbirds (Eastern Hemisphere), hawkmoths, butterflies, bats, and possibly lemurs (*Rhodocolea nycteriphila*, Coleeae). Flowers usually have a nectary that surrounds the ovary and produces a nectar reward for pollinators. Sometimes the nectary is absent, and mimetic pollination strategies that depend on bees scouting for new nectar sources have evolved in flowers that closely resemble nectariferous flowers occurring in the same habitat. In such flowers, nectar guides adapted for bee pollination are usually present, possibly to enhance pollinator attraction. The nectar produced by many species is frequently robbed by hummingbirds or carpenter bees that puncture the base of the corolla tube just above the calyx to access nectar without making contact with the anthers or stigma.

Chances of self-pollination are reduced by means of the "sensitive" stigma, which consists of two flaplike lobes that close together immediately after a pollinator has touched them (i.e., has left pollen from a previously visited flower). Thus, when the pollinator backs away from that flower (now carrying new pollen), it touches only the nonreceptive outer surface of the stigmatic lobes. Mechanisms of late self-incompatibility also have been reported for the Bignoniaceae.

Most Bignoniaceae fruits are dry capsules whose seeds are wind- or water-dispersed. The seed-bearing pulp of Coleeae and Crescentieae, however, may be eaten and dispersed by mammals. Many dry capsules are ornamented and stick to the bodies of animals (e.g., *Tourrettia lappacea* and many species of *Clytostoma*).

Several Bignoniaceae have specialized nectar glands on their leaves, stems, flowers, or fruits that attract ants, which, in turn, protect the plants against herbivores. Most liana species have extrafloral nectaries, and ants have been observed cleaning extraneous structures (e.g., insect eggs) from leaf surfaces, which may help protect the leaves. Other taxa, such as *Stizophyllum* and some species of *Tabebuia*, have hollow stems that provide housing for ants. The genus name *Tabebuia* actually was based on the Tupian Indian words for "ant" and "wood."

Vegetative parts of some Bignoniaceae have strong odors, reminiscent of garlic, almond, and clove, which supposedly act as repellents to herbivorous insects.

Economic uses. Many Bignoniaceae are very popular as ornamentals in the neotropics. Eight countries have Bignoniaceae species as their national tree, and *Jacaranda mimosifolia* is one of the most widely cultivated subtropical trees in the world. The wood of many Bignoniaceae, especially species of *Tabebuia*, is much prized for construction because of its great durability (due to large amounts of lapachol). Some fast-growing timber species have been tested for reforestation purposes (e.g., *Jacaranda copaia*). Although Bignoniaceae do not include many edible fruits, *Crescentia* seeds and pulp are eaten and used in Nicaragua to produce a drink called *semilla de Jicaro*. The garlic-scented species frequentyly are used as condiments throughout the neotropics. Several species have been reported to contain compounds active against major diseases such as cancer, diabetes, syphilis, malaria, hepatitis, rabies, and leishmaniasis. Other species have been reported to be extremely toxic and are used by local fisherman to poison fish and crabs. Several species produce dyes used by native peoples in the Amazon for body paint and to dye basket fibers. Some lianas are used as ropes. The fruits of *Crescentia cujete* were used in the past to carry and store water and, even today, fruits cut in half are used to bail boats.

References. BERNAL, H. Y., AND J. E. CORRERA Q. 1989. Bignoniaceae. In *Especies vegetales promisorias de los países del Convenio Andrés Bello*, Tomo II. Bogotá, D. E., Colombia: Secretaria Ejecutiva del Convenio Andrés Bello. D'ARCY, W. G. 1997. A review of the genus *Eccremocarpus* (Bignoniaceae). *Ann. Missouri Bot. Gard.* 84:105–11. GENTRY, A. H. 1979. Distribution patterns of Neotropical Bignoniaceae: some phytogeographical implications. In *Tropical Botany*, eds. K. Larsen and L. B. Holm-Nielsen, 339–54. New York: Academic Press. GENTRY, A. H. 1980. Bignoniaceae. Part I, Crescentieae and Tourretieae. *Fl. Neotrop. Monogr.* 25:1–130. GENTRY, A, H. 1990. Evolutionary patterns in neotropical Bignoniaceae. In Modes of reproduction and evolution of woody angiosperms in tropical environments, eds. G. T. Prance and G. Gottsberger. *Mem. New York Bot. Gard.* 55: 118–29. GENTRY, A. H. 1992. Bignoniaceae. Part II: Tecomeae. *Fl. Neotrop. Monogr.* 25(2):1–370. LOHMANN, L. G., J. BROWN, AND S. MORI. 2002. Bignoniaceae. In Guide to the Vascular Plants of Central French Guiana, eds. S. Mori et al. *Mem. New York Bot. Gard.* 76(2):118–39. LOHMANN, L. G., AND M.J.G. HOPKINS. 1999. Bignoniaceae. In *Flora da Reserva Ducke*: guia de identificação das plantas vasculares de uma floresta de terra-firme na Amazônia central, eds. J. E. Ribeiro et al., 608–23. Manaus, Amazonas, Brazil: INPA-DFID. SPANGLER, R. E., AND R. G. OLMSTEAD. 1999. Phylogenetic analysis of Bignoniaceae based on the *cp*DNA gene sequences *rbc*L and *ndh*F. *Ann. Missouri Bot. Gard.* 86:33–46. STEVENS, P. F. (2001 onwards). Angiosperm Phylogeny Website. Version 3, May 2002. http://www.mobot.org/MOBOT/research/APweb/. ZJHRA, M. L. 1998. Phylogenetics, biogeography, and pollination ecology of endemic Malagasy Coleeae (Bignoniaceae). Dissertation, University of Wisconsin—Madison.

BIXACEAE (Lipstick Tree Family)

SCOTT V. HEALD

Figure 27, Plate 6

- *trees, shrubs, or suffructescent herbs*

- *red or orange sap often present*

- *stipules present*

- *leaves alternate, simple, with stalked peltate trichomes* (Bixa) *and palmate venation*

- *flowers bisexual; sepals and petals 5; stamens numerous; gynoecium syncarpous, the ovary superior*

- *fruits loculicidal capsules.*

Numbers of genera and species. Worldwide, the Bixaceae comprise four genera and perhaps 18 species. The non-American *Diegodendron* is monotypic. In tropical America, there are three native genera, *Amoreuxia*, *Bixa*, and *Cochlospermum*. *Amoreuxia* has three Neotropical species, *Bixa* is variously treated as having one to five Neotropical species, and *Cochlospermum* comprises four Neotropical species.

Distribution and habitat. The Bixaceae are a pantropical family. *Amoreuxia* is native to the southwestern United States, Mexico, and in Central and northwestern South America. *Bixa* is native to the warm and humid American Tropics, and is now cultivated throughout tropical regions of the world. *Cochlospermum* subgenus *Cochlospermum* is generally found in seasonally dry, deciduous forests of tropical America, Africa, Asia, and Australia, while *Cochlospermum* subgenus *Diporandra* is restricted to tropical America. *Diegodendron* is endemic to Madagascar.

Most species are native to lowland, seasonally dry tropical forests. Small trees or shrubs of rapid growth and producers of abundant seed, the Bixaceae are common components of secondary vegetation.

Family classification. The Bixaceae are placed in the Violales by Cronquist. Opinions differ in the circumscription and ordinal alignment of the family. Cronquist lumped the Bixaceae and Cochlospermaceae and considered these allied with Flacourtiaceae and Cistaceae. He placed *Diegodendron* in the Ochnaceae because of its gynobasic style. Takhtajan emphasized wood anatomy in his placement of Diegodendraceae next to Sphaerosepalaceae and again with treating Bixaceae and Cochlospermaceae as separate families allied with the Cistaceae. Alverson et al., based on plastid *rbc*L sequence data, suggest that *Bixa*, *Cochlospermum*, and *Rhopalocarpus* (Sphaerosepalaceae *sensu* Cronquist) form a bixalean clade within an expanded Malvales. A similar result was achieved

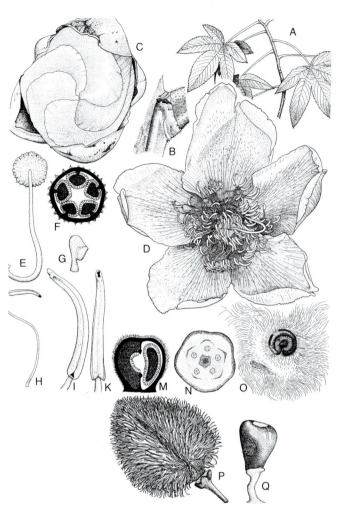

Figure 27. BIXACEAE. *Cochlospermum vitifolium* (A–O) and *Bixa orellana* (P, Q). **A.** Stem with leaves (x⅛). **B.** Node showing stipular scar (x4). **C.** Apical view of flower bud (x2). **D.** Apical view of flower (x1). **E.** Apical view of gynoecium (x2). **F.** Schematic transverse section of ovary (x4). **G.** Ovule (x24). **H.** Lateral view of stamen (x2). **I.** View of anther (x6). **K.** View of anther; note apical pore (x6). **L.** Missing in original plate. **M.** Schematic medial section of ovary (x4). **N.** Transverse section of receptacle below ovary, showing five vascular bundles leading to androecium (x2). **O.** Seed (x2). **P.** Lateral view of fruit (x1½). **Q.** Seed (x2). Reprinted with permission from Cronquist (1981). Artist: William S. Moye.

by Fay et al.'s analysis of *rbc*L data, though the placement of *Rhopalocarpus* and *Neurada* (Neuradaceae *sensu* Cronquist) is uncertain. These molecular studies are corroborated by similarities among the taxa in vegetative and fruit morphology, woody anatomy, seed anatomy, and embryology.

Features of the family. Habit: trees, shrubs, or suffructescent herbs, often with red or orange sap. **Indument** of unicellular, multicellular, or peltate (*Bixa*) trichomes. **Stipules** present. **Leaves** alternate, simple; blades with entire to deeply palmately lobed margins; venation palmate. **Inflorescences** terminal, thyrsoid or racemose, sometimes appearing before leaves. **Flowers** actinomorphic to slightly zygomorphic (*Amoreuxia*), bisexual; sepals 5, distinct, imbricate, with small nectariferous glands abaxially in *Bixa*; petals 5, distinct, contorted or imbricate, white to pink, or yellow; androecium of numerous stamens, distinct, the anthers straight or horseshoe-shaped (*Bixa*), opening by short, porelike slits; gynoecium syncarpous, the ovary superior, the carpels 2–5, the locules various owing to ± completely intruded partitions, the style terminal; placentation parietal to nearly axile (*Amoreuxia*), the ovules numerous. **Fruits** unilocular (incompletely partitioned in *Cochlospermum* and *Amoreuxia*) loculicidal capsules with 2–5 valves. **Seeds** numerous, straight or coiled, the seed coat glabrous, pubescent, or provided with a fleshy, bright red sarcotesta (*Bixa*); endosperm starchy (*Bixa*) or oily.

Natural history. Little is known about the natural history of the Bixaceae. In most cases, flowering and fruiting occurs in the dry season, often while the plants are leafless. Flower morphology suggests bees as pollinators and they have been observed visiting flowers. Most species of *Cochlospermum* are reported to be self-incompatible.

Economic uses. *Bixa orellana* (*sensu stricto*), a cultivated species apparently unknown in the wild, is grown widely as the source of the dye bixin. Likely in cultivation for centuries before Columbus' arrival in the New World, the plant was used by Amerindians for numerous therapeutic applications, as fuel and cordage, and as the source of a bright red-orange dye. Reported therapeutic uses include treatments for epilepsy, fever, dysentery, intestinal parasites, tumors, kidney diseases, and venereal diseases. Its widespread use in the Americas have led to such common names as *urucú* or *annatto* in Brazil and *achiote* in Spanish-speaking countries.

Today, the sarcotesta is still used to color cosmetics (principally lipstick) and food (e.g., butter and cheese) because it is nontoxic, nearly tasteless, and a source of vitamin A. *Bixa* and *Cochlospermum* (especially a double-flowered cultivar of *C. vitifolium*) are cultivated widely as ornamentals in tropical and subtropical gardens.

References. ALVERSON, W. S., K. G. KAROL, D. A. BAUM, M. W. CHASE, S. M. SWENSEN, ET AL. 1998. Circumscription of the Malvales and relationships to other Rosidae: Evidence from *rbc*L sequence data. *Amer. J. Bot.* 85(6):876–87. BAER, D. F. 1977. Systematics of the genus *Bixa* and geography of the cultivated annatto tree. Ph.D. dissertation, Los Angeles: University of California. Available from: University Microfilms International, MI. BERNAL, H. Y., AND J. E. CORRERA Q. 1989. Bixaceae. In *Especies vegetales promisorias de los países del Convenio Andrés Bello*, Tomo II. Bogotá, D. E., Colombia: Secretaria Ejecutiva del Convenio Andrés Bello. FAY, M. F., C. BAYER, W. S. ALVERSON, A. Y. DE BRUIJN, AND M. W. CHASE. 1998. Plastid *rbc*L sequence data indicate a close affinity between *Diegodendron* and *Bixa*. *Taxon* 47:43–50. NANDI, O. I. 1998. Ovule and seed anatomy of Cistaceae and related Malvanae. *Pl. Syst. Evol.* 209(3–4):239–64. POPPENDIECK, H.-H. 1980. A monograph of the Cochlospermaceae. *Bot. Jahrb. Syst.* 101(2):191–265. POPPENDIECK, H.-H. 1981. Cochlospermaceae. *Fl. Neotrop. Monogr.* 27:1–34. SMITH, J. H., ET AL. 1992. *Tropical Forests and Their Crops*. Ithaca, NY: Cornell University Press. POPPENDIECK, H.-H. 2003a. Bixaceae. In *The Families and Genera of Vascular Plants*, eds. K. Kubitzki and C. Bayer. 5: 33–35. Berlin: Springer-Verlag. POPPENDIECK, H.-H. 2003b. Cochlospermaceae. In *The Families and Genera of Vascular Plants*, eds. K. Kubitzki and C. Bayer. 5:71–74. Berlin: Springer-Verlag. SRIVASTAVA, A., Y. N. SHUKLA, S. P. JAIN AND S. KUMAR. 1999. Chemistry, pharmacology and uses of *Bixa orellana*—a review. *Journal of Medicinal and Aromatic Plant Sciences* 21(4):1145–54.

BOMBACACEAE (Baobab or Balsa-wood Family) (including the Bombacoideae clade and Matisieae clade)

WILLIAM SURPRISON ALVERSON

Figure 28, Plate 7

- *usually trees*

- *swollen or spiny trunks and/or buttresses often present*

- *leaves alternate, often palmately compound, less frequently simple or unifoliolate*

- *flowers medium to large, sometimes showy, bisexual; stamens partially or entirely fused into tube*

- *fruits usually capsules*

- *seeds surrounded by hairs in several genera*

Numbers of genera and species. Worldwide, the Bombacoideae clade comprises 18 or 19 genera and about 160 species. In tropical America, there are 16 genera and about 135 species of the Bombacoideae clade.

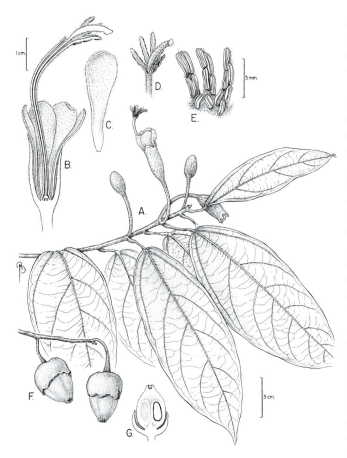

Figure 28. BOMBACACEAE. *Matisia ochrocalyx.* **A.** Stem with leaves, axillary buds, and flowers. **B.** Medial section of flower. **C.** Adaxial view of petal. **D.** Upper part of androecium surrounding style and stigma. **E.** Detail of upper part of androecium showing anthers. **F.** Part of infructescence with nearly mature fruits. **G.** Medial section of fruit. Reprinted with permission from Mori et al. (2002). Artist: Bobbi Angell.

The Neotropical genera of the Bombacoideae clade are *Aguiaria* (1 species), *Bernoullia* (2), *Catostemma* (10–15), *Cavanillesia* (3), *Ceiba* (12+, including *Chorisia*), *Eriotheca* (19), *Gyranthera* (2), *Huberodendron* (5), *Neobuchia* (1), *Pseudobombax* (20), *Pachira* (ca. 40, including *Bombacopsis* and *Rhodognaphalopsis*), *Scleronema* (5), *Spirotheca* (5–6), and probably *Ochroma* (1), *Patinoa* (4), and *Septotheca* (1). Three genera, *Adansonia*, *Bombax*, and *Rhodognaphalon* occur only in the Eastern Hemisphere, but the latter genus is not clearly distinct from *Pachira*.

In tropical America, the Matisieae clade comprises three genera and 70–80 species: *Matisia* (30 species), *Phragmotheca* (10), and *Quararibea* (30–40).

Distribution and habitat. Members of the Bombacoideae clade are pantropical but much more diverse in the neotropics, particularly in lowland Andean forests. A few species reach northern and southern subtropical areas. With only two exceptions, the Central and South American genera are endemic to the neotropics. These exceptions are *Ceiba* and

Pachira, each with one species possibly native to the Eastern Hemisphere (*Ceiba pentandra* and *Pachira glabra*), though the economic nature of these plants complicates their biogeographic history.

Species within the Bombacoideae clade are found in a range of forest types, but are most common at low or middle elevations (only a few species are found above 2,000 meters elevation). Some species inhabit wet *terra firme* forests or periodically inundated river and stream banks.

Family classification. The Bombacaceae are placed in the Malvales by Cronquist; however, recent molecular and morphological studies have shown that the family is an artificial group. Molecular studies also indicate that traditional tribal boundaries of "Bombacaceae" need to be completely reworked, suggesting that the evolutionary lineage comprising the durian group of the Paleotropics (e.g., *Coelostegia*, *Cullenia*, *Durio*, *Kostermansia*, *Neesia*) is not closely related to other "Bombacaceae" but, instead, is part of an evolutionary branch along with several genera traditionally placed in the Sterculiaceae. Two other Southeast Asian genera traditionally placed with the durian group, *Camptostemon* and *Papuodendron*, appear to be closely related to traditional members of the Malvaceae. Molecular studies also indicate that the Matisieae clade, composed of the genera *Matisia*, *Phragmotheca*, and *Quararibea*, appears to form one of the bottom-most branches of the Malvoideae clade (which includes all species traditionally assigned to the Malvaceae).

Features of the Bombacoideae and Matisieae Clades. **Habit:** usually medium to large trees, rarely hemiepiphytic (*Spirotheca*). **Trunks** swollen and bottle-shaped in some genera (e.g., *Cavanillesia*, *Eriotheca*, and *Pseudobombax*), frequently buttressed, or with straight and vertical central trunk, with branches often whorled and horizontal; spines sometimes present (*Ceiba*, *Pachira*, and *Spirotheca*). **Stipules** present, sometimes caducous. **Leaves** alternate, often palmately compound, less frequently unifoliolate or simple; petioles with swollen pulvinus at each end; venation usually palmate the veins often arising from base of blades. **Inflorescences** ramiflorous or cauliflorous, sometimes appearing terminal, the flowers solitary or in cymose clusters; epicalyx often present. **Flowers** medium to large (35 cm long in *Pachira insignis*), sometimes showy, actinomorphic or slightly zygomorphic, bisexual; sepals 5, usually valvate, often fused (for at least part of length); petals 5–7, contorted or imbricate, white, pink, red, yellow, pale orange, purple, green, or blue-green, sometimes colors contrasting, the base connate; androecium of few to many (>1,000) stamens, the filaments fused into tube, sometimes free or coalescing into bundles above tube, the anthers appearing polysporangiate (with several pollen sacs clustered together in the basal Bombacoideae clade), the thecae usually 1 or less often 2; gynoecium syncarpous, the ovary superior (subinferior in *Quararibea*), locules 2–5; placentation axile, the ovules 2–many per locule. **Fruits (Bombacoideae clade)** usually capsules or modified capsules, rarely samaras (*Cavanillesia*), the capsules usually dehiscent, the modified capsules sometimes semidehiscent (some *Catostemma*) or indehiscent (e.g., *Patinoa*, *Scleronema*), the exocarp usually woody or coriaceous. **Fruits (Matisieae clade)** drupaceous, indehiscent, fibrous-fleshy. **Seeds (Bombacoideae clade)** 1 (*Catostemma*) to many, relatively small and surrounded by dense nonwettable hairs ("kapok," growing from inner surface of fruit wall) in dehiscent fruits (e.g., *Ceiba*, *Pseudobombax*, and *Pachira* species), or the hairs reduced, velutinous, covering inner surface of fruit (e.g., larger-seeded species of *Pachira*), surrounded by radially symmetric, broad wings in species with samaras (mucilage cavities present in these species), the seed coat sometimes densely covered with wooly hairs (in *Patinoa*). **Seeds (Matisieae clade)** 1–5 (at maturity), the endocarp bony-fibrous.

Many of the moist- or wet-forest species are evergreen, but some of the wet rain-forest interior species are seasonally deciduous. Species of drier forests are typically deciduous.

Seedlings of the Bombacoideae clade are mostly epigeal and phanerocotylar, but some variation occurs, especially in the larger-seeded species. There is also considerable variability of seedling types in the Matisieae clade.

Species of *Catostemma*, *Cavanillesia*, *Ceiba*, and *Scleronema* often reach 45–50 m in height (reportedly to 70 m in *Ceiba*) with their crowns projecting above the canopy. Many genera have at least one species less than 10 m tall at maturity, including some that begin flowering when only 1–2 m in height. Likewise, *Matisia*, *Quararibea*, and *Phragmotheca*, (Matisieae clade), range in size from rain-forest understory dwarfs 2 m tall to canopy trees 40 m or more in height.

The Bombacoideae clade also includes two of the lightest of woods, the balsa (*Ochroma pyramidale*) and *bongo*, *quipo*, or *macondo* (*Cavanillesia platanifolia*), both fast-growing, pioneer trees.

The likely "basal" members of the Bombacoideae clade—namely *Ochroma*, *Patinoa*, and presumably *Septotheca*—all have simple leaves with conspicuously palmate basal venation, as do "basal" members of the Malvoideae clade (e.g., *Matisia*, *Phragmotheca*, and *Quararibea*). In contrast, the derived members of the Bombacoideae clade are characterized by palmately compound leaves, sometimes with only a single leaflet (unifoliolate), except for *Cavanillesia*, which appears to have reverted to simple leaves with palmate venation. *Pseudobombax* species are characterized by "inarticulate" leaflets, which show no zone of demarcation between the petiolules and leaflets.

Capsules of the Bombacoideae clade range from small (3 cm long by 1 cm in diameter in some *Eriotheca*) to large (30 cm long by 12 cm diameter in some *Gyranthera* and *Pachira*).

Natural history. Species that grow in dry forests and savannas have several means of conserving water, such as seasonally deciduous leaves, mucilage in tissues, and spongy wood. Some species are pioneers with seeds that are stimulated to germinate by fire (e.g., *Ochroma*), and others are found in undisturbed primary forests.

Pollinators are extremely diverse, sometimes even within genera, and include bats, bees, hawkmoths, hummingbirds, and nonflying mammals.

Fruit and seed dispersal is by wind; water, gravity, and animals (agoutis, bats, monkeys, squirrels, and birds). The nonwettable hairs ("kapok") surrounding the small seeds of some species (e.g., *Ceiba pentandra* and *Pseudobombax munguba*) help them to be dispersed primarily by wind and subsequently by water when the seeds land on the surface of rivers and streams.

Economic uses. Several genera provide commercially valuable wood (e.g., *Catostemma*, *Ceiba*, and *Scleronema*) and the wood or bark of most genera have several to many local uses. For example, large branches of *Pachira quinata* are cut and planted as living fence posts in Central and northern South America. The wood of this species is also used as siding boards on houses because mucilage in the wood keeps it from expanding and contracting throughout the wet and dry seasons. The ultralight balsa wood (*Ochroma pyramidale*) has been used historically for the construction of rafts, airplanes (model and otherwise), and even as supertanker hull insulation. Some species have been overharvested for plywood and core veneers (e.g., *Ceiba pentandra* in parts of western Amazonia).

The fruits of *Ceiba* and several other genera produce kapok, a fibrous material surrounding the seeds that has been used commercially for life preservers, cushions, and insulation. The fruits of at least one species of *Patinoa* have an edible, very tasty pulp, whereas the pulp and seeds of another species are spread onto ponds as a fish poison. The seeds of several species of *Pachira* are used widely as food, either raw or roasted. Several species of *Matisia* and *Quararibea* have brightly colored, fragrant, edible pulp, and the fruits of one species, *Matisia cordata*, has long been wild-harvested for sale in Latin American markets. This species is locally cultivated. The flowers of a Mexican-Central American species, *Quararibea funebris*, are mixed with chocolate and other ingredients to concoct *tejate*, a spicy beverage with medicinal and religious significance. The chemicals responsible for the spicy odor are now under investigation as antitumor agents. Many species are planted as ornamentals (*Ceiba* and *Pachira*) or are revered as sacred plants and play a role in Mayan folklore (e.g., *Ceiba pentandra*, and *Quararibea funebris*, so named because of funerals performed beneath its long, drooping branches).

References. ALVERSON, W. S., B. A. WHITLOCK, R. NYFFELER, C. BAYER, AND D. A. BAUM. 1999. Phylogeny of the core Malvales: evidence from *ndh*F sequence data. *Amer. J. Bot.* 86(10):1474–86. BAUM, D. A., W. S. ALVERSON, AND R. NYFFELER R. 1998. A durian by any other name: taxonomy and nomenclature of the core Malvales. *Harvard Pap. Bot.* 3(2):315–30. BAYER, C., M. F. FAY, A. Y. DE BRUIJN,

V. Savolainen, C. M. Morton, et al. 1999. Support for an expanded family concept of Malvaceae within a recircumscribed order Malvales: a combined analysis of plastid *atp*B and *rbc*L DNA sequences. *Bot. J. Linn. Soc.* 129:267–303. Bayer, C., and K. Kubitzki. 2003. Malvaceae. In *The Families and Genera of Vascular Plants*, eds. K. Kubitzki and C. Bayer. 5:225–311. Berlin: Springer-Verlag. Bernal, H. Y., and J. E. Correra Q. 1989. Bombacaceae. In *Especies vegetales promisorias de los países del Convenio Andrés Bello*, Tomo II. Bogotá, D. E., Colombia: Secretaria Ejecutiva del Convenio Andrés Bello.

BONNETIACEAE (Bonnetia Family)

Dennis Wm. Stevenson

Figure 29, Plate 7

- *trees or shrubs*

- *resinous sap white to yellow*

- *leaves alternate, simple, crowded at branch tips*

- *lateral veins closely spaced and ascending*

- *petals 5, contorted, red to pink*

- *fruits septicidal capsules, the central column persistent*

Numbers of genera and species. Worldwide, the Bonnetiaceae comprise three genera and approximately 35 species. In tropical America, there are two genera, *Archytaea* with three species and *Bonnetia* (including *Neblinaria*, *Neogleasonia*, and probably also *Acopanea*) with approximately 29 species.

Distribution and habitat. The Bonnetiaceae occur in Southeast Asia, west Malesia, the Moluccas, New Guinea (*Ploiarium*), and parts of the neotropics. Within the neotropics *Archytaea* and *Bonnetia* are found in Colombia, Venezuela, Bolivia, and Brazil, with *Bonnetia* also being known from Peru and Cuba.

Species of these genera are most commonly found in sandy savannas, in open rocky areas, and in forests at both high and low elevations; e.g., in *cerrados* of Brazil and on the *tepuis* of the Guayana highlands. The tepuis of Venezuelan Guayana are especially rich in species of Bonnetiaceae, where 26 of the 29 species of *Bonnetia*, 23 which are endemic, can be found. In forests growing in sheltered areas on *tepuis*, species of Bonnetia may dominate the vegetation.

Family classification. Cronquist treated the Bonnetiaceae as subfamily Bonnetioideae in the Theaceae (Theales). In contrast, Takhtajan recognized the family and placed it near the Clusiaceae. Recognition of the Bonnetiaceae as a family separate from the Theaceae and sister to the Clusiaceae is supported by recent molecular studies.

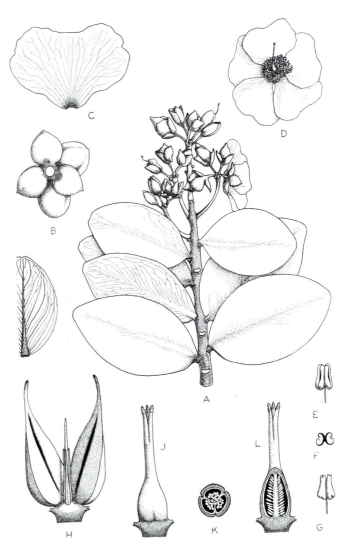

Figure 29. BONNETIACEAE. *Bonnetia celiae.* **A.** Stem with leaves, inflorescence, and detail of leaf venation (left) (x½). **B.** Basal view of flower showing calyx (x1). **C.** Adaxial view of petal (x1). **D.** Apical view of flower (x½). **E.** Adaxial view of stamen (x6). **F.** Transverse section of anther (x6). **G.** Abaxial view of stamen (x6). **H.** Fruit with one valve removed; showing septacidal dehiscence (x7½). **I.** Missing in original plate. **J.** Lateral view of gynoecium (x7½). **K.** Transverse section of ovary (x7½). **L.** Partial medial section of gynoecium (x7½). Reprinted with permission from Maguire (1972). Artist: Mary Benson.

Features of the family. Habit: small trees or shrubs, infrequently pachycaulous and candelabriform, with secretory canals producing resinous white to yellow sap. **Stipules** absent. **Leaves** alternate, crowded at branch tips, simple; blade margins entire; lateral veins closely spaced and steeply ascending, the midrib red in *Archytaea*. **Inflorescences** terminal or axillary, cymose. **Flowers** actinomorphic, bisexual; sepals 5, imbricate, distinct, unequal, persistent; petals 5, contorted, distinct, equal, red to pink; androecium of numerous stamens, distinct to basally connate or in fascicles of 5, the fascicles epipetalous in *Archytaea*, the filaments slender, glabrous, the connective sometimes with an apical gland (*Bonnetia*), the anthers short, dorsifixed, introrse; gynoecium syncarpous, the ovary superior, the carpels and locules 3 in *Bonnetia* and 5 in *Archytaea*, the styles connate, the stigmas distinct; placentation axile, the ovules many per locule. **Fruits** septicidal capsules, the central column persistent, glabrous. **Seeds** many per fruit, glabrous, smooth, dark brown; endosperm absent, the embryo linear, the cotyledons short, the radicle long.

Natural history. *Neblinaria celiae* (probably a species of *Bonnetia*), an endemic to the rainy summit of Cerro de la Nelbina in southern Venezuela, is fire resistant. Individuals of this species had a survival rate of 93 percent compared to no survival in seven co-occurring woody species after an intense fire. This rosette shrub has sparse branching, massive terminal rosettes of leaves, and thick bark. Survival was greatest in taller individuals because their terminal buds were the farthest from the thin fuel layer on the ground. The showy flowers of most species of this family suggest that they are pollinated by insects.

Economic uses. No uses are known for this family.

References. GIVINISH, T. J., R. W. MCDIARMID, AND W. R. BUCK. 1986. Fire adaptation in *Neblinaria celiae* (Theaceae), a high-elevation rosette shrub endemic to a wet equatorial tepui. *Oecologia* 70(4):481–85. GUSTAFSSON, M.H.G., V. BITTRICH, AND P. F. STEVENS. 2002. Phylogeny of Clusiaceae based on rbcL sequences. Int. J. Pl. Sci. 163(6):1045–54. HUBER, O. 1988. Guayana highlands versus Guayana lowlands, a reappraisal. Taxon 37(3):595–614. MAGUIRE, B. 1972. Bonnetiaceae. In The Botany of the Guayana Highland-Part IX., Maguire et al. *Mem. New York Bot. Gard.* 23:131–65. WEITZMAN, A. L., AND P. STEVENS. 1997. Notes on the circumscription of the Bonnetiaceae and Clusiaceae, with taxa and new combinations. *BioLlania, Ed. Especie.* 6: 551–64.

BORAGINACEAE (Borage Family)

HARTMUT H. HILGER AND HARALD FÖRTHER

Figure 30, Plate 7

- *herbs, shrubs, occasionally trees, rarely lianas*

- *indument of coarse hairs, occasionally with cystoliths*

- *leaves usually alternate, simple*

- *flowers with 5 sepals; corolla sympetalous, the petals 5; stamens 5, epipetalous; ovary superior, bicarpellate, ovules 1 per "locule"*

- *fruits indehiscent, fleshy or dry, 4-seeded; diaspores often 1-seeded nutlets*

Numbers of genera and species. Worldwide, the Boraginaceae comprise approximately 200 genera and more than 2,600 species. A few of the larger genera account for more than half of all known species: *Cordia* (± 300 species), *Heliotropium* (± 300), *Tournefortia* (± 150), *Cryptantha* (± 150), *Onosma* (± 150), *Plagiobothrys* (± 100), *Myosotis* (± 100), *Ehretia* (± 75), *Paracaryum* (including *Mattiastrum*, ± 75), *Echium* (± 70), and *Cynoglossum* (± 75). Many genera have 20–50 species and about 50 genera are monotypic.

In tropical America, there are 23 native genera (*Auxemma*, *Cordia sensu lato* (including *Varronia*, *Gerascanthus*), *Patagonula*, *Saccellium* [Cordioideae]; *Bourreria*, *Ehretia*, *Lepidocordia*, *Rochefortia*, *Tiquilia* [Ehretioideae]; *Heliotropium sensu lato* (including *Euploca* and *Schleidenia*), *Tournefortia* (including *Myriopus*) [Heliotropioideae]; *Amsinckia*, *Antiphytum*, *Cryptantha*, *Cynoglossum*, *Hackelia*, *Lasiarrhenum*, *Lithospermum*, *Macromeria*, *Moritzia*, *Pectocarya*, *Plagiobothrys*, *Thaumatocaryum* [Boraginoideae]) and approximately 500 species. The tribe Boragineae is not native to the Western Hemisphere, but many species have been introduced as ornamental plants or weeds (e.g., species of *Anchusa* and *Borago*).

Distribution and habitat. The Boraginaceae are found throughout temperate, subtropical, and tropical areas of the world. The main centers of diversity are between the Mediterranean and the Irano-Turanian region in the Eastern Hemisphere and from Central America to temperate South America in the Western Hemisphere. Species of Boraginaceae prefer temperate to warm and seasonally dry habitats and are infre-

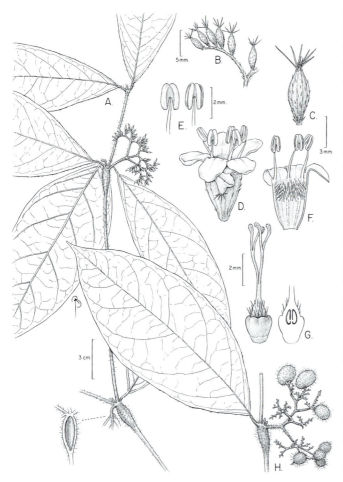

Figure 30. BORAGINACEAE. *Cordia nodosa*. **A.** Stem with immature inflorescence (right) and medial section of swollen node (left). **B.** Lateral view of part of inflorescence. **C.** Lateral view of flower bud. **D.** Lateral view of flower. **E.** Abaxial (left) and adaxial (right) views of stamens. **F.** Longitudinal section of corolla showing adnate stamens. **G.** Lateral view (left) and medial section (right) of gynoecium and subtending nectary. **H.** Stem with swollen node, leaf, and infructescence. Reprinted with permission from Mori et al. (2002). Artist: Bobbi Angell.

quent in very cold or humid tropical climates. Some weedy species, such as *Echium plantagineum*, *E. vulgare*, and *Heliotropium europaeum*, are widely naturalized.

In tropical America, the Boraginaceae are generally present in all habitats from sea level to elevations of 4,000 meters and higher in the Andes. The members of the Cordioideae have a center of distribution in lowland and humid, at least seasonally, areas of the neotropics. Many species of *Cordia* are an important component of dry and often disturbed shrub vegetation types from lowland to montane regions. The Ehretioideae generally prefer more arid regions but are also found in lower elevation forest habitats. An exception is *Tiquilia* which usually occurs in sandy or gravelly desertic habitats of Pacific America. The Heliotropioideae are found in such diverse habitats as lowland tropical rain forest and higher elevation open habitats of the Andes. Spe-

cies of *Heliotropium* are best adapted to semiarid tropical savannas and dry forest regions, whereas *Tournefortia* prefers more humid forests. The Boraginoideae are mostly restricted to open areas in Mediterranean, montane, and Andean habitats.

Family classification. The Boraginaceae are placed in the Lamiales by Cronquist. Molecular data suggest that the Hydrophyllaceae and the parasitic Lennoaceae should be incorporated into Boraginaceae *sensu lato*. Therefore, a strong argument can be made for treating the present subfamilies as families of their own: i.e., the Cordiaceae, Ehretiaceae, Heliotropiaceae, and Boraginaceae *sensu stricto*. Together with the Hydrophyllaceae and Lennoaceae, they form the order Boraginales, which is still an order of *incerta sedis* that is most probably related to the Solanales. This treatment, however, adheres to the traditional view of a widely circumscribed Boraginaceae divided into subfamilies and the recognition of the Hydrophyllaceae and Lennoaceae as separate families. Molecular data have also contributed to a new placement of genera in subfamilies and have shown that some large genera like *Heliotropium*, *Tournefortia*, and *Anchusa* are paraphyletic.

The Hydrophyllaceae resemble the Boraginaceae in habit, but often have pinnate leaves, capsular fruits, and numerous seeds. The Lennoaceae are root parasites lacking chlorophyll and possess seeds arranged in a ring.

The family is divided into five subfamilies: Cordioideae (3 genera), Ehretioideae (10–15), Heliotropioideae (5–10), Boraginoideae (4 tribes with ca. 110 genera), and the enigmatic, capsule-bearing Wellstedioideae (monogeneric) from South Africa. This classification is based primarily on the attachment of the style to the ovary, the number of stylar branches, and the type of fruit. The Boraginoideae fall into four tribes based on the type of nutlet attachment to the gynobase, the form and position of the nutlet attachment scars, and anatomical differences in the pericarp. These tribes are the Lithospermeae (e.g., *Echium* and *Lithospermum*), the Boragineae (= Anchuseae; e.g., *Anchusa* and *Borago*, *Symphytum*), the Eritrichieae (e.g., *Cryptantha* and *Eritrichium*), and the Cynoglosseae (e.g., *Cynoglossum* and *Omphalodes*). Some genera do not group with any of the above tribes, but it is too early to draw nomenclatural conclusions from results based on molecular analysis, and the creation of more tribes does not seem to be justified at this time.

Features of the family. Habit: herbs, subshrubs, shrubs, occasionally trees, or rarely lianas, the herbs annual or perennial; taproots or creeping rhizomes sometimes present, tubers rarely present (in *Lithospermum* and species of *Heliotropium*). Indument of distinctive hairs usually on all vegetative above-ground parts, usually strigose to hirsute, rarely glabrous, the hairs coarse, occasionally containing cystoliths, simple or consisting of simple and glandular hairs of different length and size, mostly stout, with calcified or silicified walls and bases, uni- or multicellular, malpighiaceous or dolabriform hairs known only from a few species of *Cordia* section *Myxa* (e.g., *C. collococca*) and *Heliotropium* section *Coeloma*). **Stipules** absent. **Leaves** usually alternate, sometimes the lower ones opposite, rarely all opposite to pseudo-opposite (*Tournefortia*), sometimes basal (especially in annual, biannual, and monocarpic species; e.g., *Plagiobothrys*), simple; petioles absent or short; blades linear to elliptic/ovate to orbicular, usually firm, sometimes soft or rarely slightly succulent (*Heliotropium curassavicum*), the margins generally entire, inconspicuously dentate, or rarely lobed (*Coldenia procumbens*). **Inflorescences** of one or more terminal or lateral helicoid or scorpioid cymes, sometimes reduced to one (pseudo-)solitary flower, or often, in *Cordia* section *Varronia*, contracted into globose or club-shaped heads, the cymes progressively unrolling during anthesis, opening acropetally (basipetally in *Cordia* section *Varronia*), elongating into spike-like or racemelike infructescence at maturity, bracts sometimes present. **Flowers** actinomorphic or less often slightly zygomorphic, usually bisexual; calyx slightly zygomorphic in *Heliotropium* and *Asperugo*, the sepals 5, distinct or connate from base to middle or above; corolla sympetalous, salverform in most genera, sometimes tubular or funnel shaped, ranging from a few millimeters to 2–3 cm long, the lobes 5, with faucal appendages ("fornices") present in Boraginoideae inside corolla tube, the appendages scale-shaped, often hairy, arising by centripetal invagination of corolla-tube; androecium of 5 stamens, epipetalous, the stamens alternate with corolla lobes, the filaments short to long, rarely appendiculate, the anthers distinct or rarely coherent by apical hairs (*Heliotropium* section *Orthostachys*), dehiscing longitudinally; annular nectary disc often present around base of ovary, in many species covered by basal appendages formed by corolla-tube; gynoecium syncarpous, the ovary superior, undivided in Cordioideae, entire or 4-lobed in Ehretioideae and Heliotropioideae, or deeply 4-lobed in Boraginoideae, the carpels 2, the locules falsely 2 per carpel (separated by false septum), the style terminal, twice 2-cleft in Cordioideae, simple, bifid, or 2 and distinct in Ehretioideae, a terminal stigmatic head in Heliotropioideae, or simple or bifid and arising from center in a seemingly sunken position (gynobasic) in Boraginoideae; placentation axile, the ovules 1 per locule, erect, ascending, horizontal, or pendulous. **Fruits** fleshy or dry drupes in Cordioideae and Ehretioideae, or mericarps (nutlets) in Heliotropioideae and Boraginoideae, the mericarps 2 (2-seeded) or 4 (1-seeded) in Heliotropioideae and in Boraginoideae, variously ornamented or glochidiate. **Seeds** 4 per fruit (sometimes less by abortion); cotyledons entire and flat, rarely bifid (*Amsinckia*) or plicate (*Cordia, Patagonula*).

The Cordioideae and Ehretioideae (with exception of *Coldenia, Tiquilia*) are shrubs or trees, the Heliotropioideae are herbs and shrubs, and the Boraginoideae are primarily herbs, sometimes subshrubs. Although the stems are usually erect, lianas (e.g., *Tournefortia volubilis* and *T. maculata*) or procumbent or creeping plants with radicant roots arising from the nodes (e.g., *Heliotropium antillanum, H. hypogaeum*, and *H. veronicifolium*) are found in the family.

Chromosome numbers vary from $2n = 8$ to $2n = 144$, but basal chromosome numbers seem to be 8 or 12.

Natural history. *Heliotropium* is one of the few flowering plant genera in which both C3 and C4 pathways of photosynthesis occur.

Pollination is accomplished primarily by insects, but hummingbird pollination (*Bourreria rubra* and *Macromeria* species) and bat pollination (*Cordia*) have been reported. Heterostyly is found in the Cordioideae (*Cordia*) and the Boraginoideae (e.g., *Anchusa, Arnebia, Cryptantha, Lithospermum*, and *Pulmonaria*). Dioecy (some *Cordia*) and gynodioecy (e.g., *Echium* and *Heliotropium*) are known in the family. Many species, especially annuals, are autogamous. Color changes of the corolla from bud through anthesis and postfertilization occur in species of *Mertensia, Myosotis*, and *Pulmonaria*.

Because the seeds of American Boraginaceae are always retained in the fruit, dispersal is related to adaptations of the fruit. Usually, the 4 seeds are dispersed separately, either as nutlets in the Boraginoideae or as separate stones (seeds surrounded by hard endocarp) in the Cordioideae and Ehretioideae (except *Tiquilia*). Sometimes 2 or 4 seeds remain united by a common endocarp (e.g., in some *Ehretia*) or 2 nutlets cling together as in *Cerinthe, Rochelia* (Boraginoideae), or some *Heliotropium*. The fleshy fruits of Cordioideae and Ehretioideae are usually eaten by animals that excrete and disperse the seeds. Dispersed by attaching to animal bodies is predominant in the Boraginoideae-Eritrichieae and Cynoglosseae (via numerous barbed prickles on the nutlets of *Hackelia* and *Cynoglossum* or the hooked-haired calyces of some *Myosotis* and *Cryptantha*). In the Boragineae and some species of *Myosotis*, elaiosomes at the base of the nutlets serve as food bodies for ants that collect the nutlets and transport them to safe sites. Wind dispersal is facilitated by a winged calyx (e.g., *Patagonula americana*), corolla (e.g., *Cordia trichotoma*), or winged nutlets (*Omphalodes*). Water dispersal, although rare, occurs in some species of *Heliotropium* (e.g., *H. gnaphalodes*) and the coastal *Mertensia maritima*.

A few species of *Cryptantha, Tiquilia*, and *Plagiobothrys* are present in both southwestern North America and southern South America, which indicates long-distance dispersal by migrating birds.

Some species of *Cordia* have modifications for harboring ants; e.g., the swollen nodes of *C. alliodora* and *C. nodosa*. Species of Heliotropioideae and Boraginoideae possess pyrrolizidine alkaloids that protect them from many plant-eating insects. Some insects are able to transform these alkaloids into pheromones that attract sexual partners.

Economic uses. The economic value of Boraginaceae is restricted to relatively few genera and species, and many are used only locally. Trees of *Cordia sebestena, C. trichotoma*,

C. myxa, species of *Saccellium*, the shrub species of *Heliotropium* (heliotropes) with fragrant flowers (e.g., *H. arborescens*), and the attractive flowering herbs of *Myosotis* (forget-me-nots) are cultivated as ornamentals.

Timber from species of *Cordia*, *Ehretia*, *Patagonula*, and *Saccellium* is used for house construction and furniture production. The edible fruits of *Bourreria succulenta*, *Cordia sebestena*, *Ehretia elliptica*, and other species are of local interest only.

The roots and rhizomes of some Lithospermeae (e.g, *Alkanna tinctoria* [alkannin], *Lithospermum erythrorrhizon* [shikonin], and *Onosma echioides* are sources of dark red and purple dyes used to color textiles, wood, and foodstuffs and as a body paint. Essential oil is extracted from *Heliotropium arborescens* and relatives for use in perfumes.

Few medical applications are known for Boraginaceae. *Cordia myxa*, *Ehretia microphylla*, *Tournefortia argentea*, and some herbaceous species of *Heliotropium*, *Amsinckia*, and *Symphytum* have been used to treat abscesses, but today this practice has nearly disappeared. *Lithospermum ruderale* was employed by Indians as a contraceptive but this may cause sterility when used in excess.

Poisonous alkaloids and pyrrolizidine alkaloids of Boraginaceae are possible causes of cancer. The unintentional ingestion of these alkaloids (e.g., in weed-contaminated flour) causes serious poisoning of humans, and livestock have been poisoned by feeding on contaminated hay. The pyrrolizidines of Boraginaceae can also be transferred by foraging bees to honey. Contact with various species is known to cause dermatitis.

Some species of *Amsinckia*, *Echium*, and *Heliotropium* have become serious cosmopolitan weeds.

References. AL-SHEHBAZ, I. A. 1991. The genera of Boraginaceae in the southeastern United States. *J. Arnold Arbor., Suppl. Ser.* 1:1–169. BERNAL, H. Y., AND J. E. CORRERA Q. 1989. Boraginaceae. In *Especies vegetales promisorias de los países del Convenio Andrés Bello*, Tomo II. Bogotá, D. E., Colombia: Secretaria Ejecutiva del Convenio Andrés Bello. BÖHLE, U.-R., AND H. H. HILGER. 1997. Chloroplast DNA systematics of "Boraginaceae" and related families—a goodbye to the old and familiar concept of five subfamilies. In Smets, E., Ronse Decraene L.P., Robbrecht E., eds. 13th Symposium Morphology, Anatomy und Systematics, Leuven. Programme & Abstracts. *Scripta Bot. Belg.* 15:30. DIANE, N., H. FÖRTHER, AND H. H. HILGER. 2002. A systematic analysis of *Heliotropium*, *Tournefortia*, and allied taxa of the Heliotropiaceae (Boraginales) based on ITS1 sequences and morphological Data. *Amer. J. Bot.* 89:287–95. FERGUSON, D. M. 1997. Phylogenetic systematics of Hydrophyllaceae, as inferred from the chloroplast gene ndhF and the nuclear rDNA ITS region. *Amer. J. Bot.* 84(Suppl. 6):192. FÖRTHER, H. 1998. Die infragenerische Gliederung der Gattung *Heliotropium* L. und ihre Stellung innerhalb der subfam. Heliotropioideae (Schrad.) Arn. (Boraginaceae). *Sendtnera* 5:35–241. GAVIRIA, J. 1987. Die Gattung *Cordia* in Venezuela. Mitt. Bot. Staatssamml. München 23:1–279. JOHNSTON, I. M. 1927. Studies in the Boraginaceae.—VI. A revision of the South American Boraginoideae. *Contr. Gray Herb.* 78:1–118. JOHNSTON, I. M. 1928. Studies in the Boraginaceae.—VII 1. The South American species of *Heliotropium*. *Contr. Gray Herb.* 81:3–73. JOHNSTON, I. M. 1930. Studies in the Boraginaceae.—VIII 1. Observations on the species of *Cordia* and *Tournefortia* known from Brazil, Paraguay, Uruguay and Argentina 1. *Contr. Gray Herb.* 92:3–89. JOHNSTON, I. M. 1935. Studies in the Boraginaceae.—X. The Boraginaceae of northeastern South America. *J. Arnold Arbor.* 16:1–64. RICHARDSON, A. T. 1977. Monograph of the genus *Tiquilia* (*Coldenia, sensu lato*), Boraginaceae: Ehretioideae. *Rhodora* 79:467–572.

BRASSICACEAE (Mustard Family)

IHSAN A. AL-SHEHBAZ

Figure 31

- *usually herbaceous*
- *leaves usually alterate, sometimes basal*
- *flowers with cross-shaped (cruciform) corolla; stamens often tetradymanous (4 long, 2 short)*
- *fruits usually 2-valved capsules*

Numbers of genera and species. Worldwide, the Brassicaceae comprise about 330 genera and 3,400 species. In tropical America, there are 34 genera, of which about 22 are native (six endemic), and approximately 200 species, of which about 175 are native. The remaining naturalized species occur in 16 genera, only *Cardamine*, *Lepidium*, *Rorippa*, and *Sisymbrium* have both native and naturalized species.

There are 105 genera (43 endemic) and about 790 species (690 native and 100 introduced) in North America, and 70 genera (30 endemic) and about 470 species (400 native and 70 introduced) in South America. The mustard genera that dominate the neotropics include *Draba* (60 of the world's

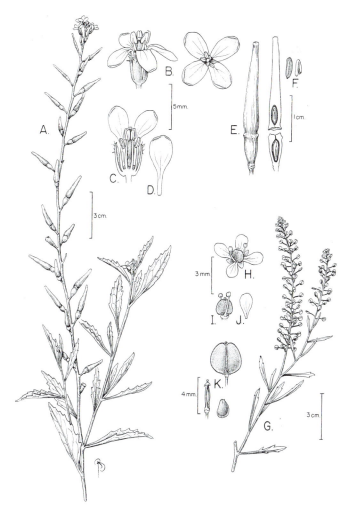

Figure 31. BRASSICACEAE. *Cakile lanceolata* (A–F) and *Lepidium virginicum* (G–K). **A.** Stem with leaves and infructescence and a few flowers at apex. **B.** Lateral (left) and apical (right) views of flowers. **C.** Lateral view of flower with two petals removed. **D.** Adaxial view of petal. **E.** Lateral view of fruit (right) and medial section of fruit showing seeds (right). **F.** Seed (left) and embryo (right). **G.** Stem with leaves and infructescences. **H.** Oblique apical view of flower. **I.** Lateral view of flower with petals removed to show gynoecium and two stamens. **J.** Adaxial view of petal. **K.** Lateral view of fruit (above), replum (left below), and seed (right below). Reprinted with permission from Acevedo-Rodríguez (1996). Artist: Bobbi Angell.

ca. 350 species), *Sisymbrium sensu lato* (21 of the world's ca. 90 species), *Lepidium* (20 of the world's ca. 180 species), and *Cardamine* (11 of the world's ca. 180 species).

Distribution and habitat. The Brassicaceae are cosmopolitan, and especially common in temperate areas. Many are successful in alpine and subalpine habitats. The centers of diversity are the Irano-Turanian region (Asia), western North America, and the Mediterranean region. Secondary centers are found along the Himalayas, the Andes south into Patagonia, and South Africa. The genera *Cardamine*, *Lepidium*,

and *Rorippa* are represented by native species on all continents except Antarctica.

Most Brassicaceae in the Western Hemisphere are found along the Rockies of the United States, the arid areas of northern Mexico, the high Andes (usually above 3,000 m elevation), and the arid regions of northern Argentina, and Chile. Tropical areas with the lowest diversity include the Caribbean, lowland Central America, and Venezuela (excluding *páramo*), Brazil, and the Guianas.

The Brassicaceae occupy various habitats, but the majority of taxa grow in the arid or semiarid areas of the temperate regions of both hemispheres. Native species that grow in the Tropics are found primarily at high elevation. Many species, especially the cushion-forming members of *Draba*, are dominant members of alpine, subalpine, arctic, and subarctic regions, and some species of *Draba* and *Lepidostemon* have been reported to grow at elevations above 6,000 meters in Kashmir and Tibet. Species of a few genera, such as *Subularia* and *Nasturtium*, are successful submersed aquatics, and those of three genera, including the sea rocket (*Cakile*), tolerate sea water and grow along sandy beaches.

Family classification. The Brassicaceae are placed in the Capparales by Cronquist. Recent morphological and molecular analyses support the monophyly of the Brassicaceae plus Capparaceae (excluding *Forchhameria*) and suggest the recognition of the following clades in the expanded family: subfamily Capparoideae, subfamily Cleomoideae, and Brassicaceae *sensu stricto*.

The number of recognized tribes in the Brassicaceae ranges from two to 19, including as many as 30 subtribes. All proposed systems are artificial because they are based on the utilization of a few characters (e.g., ratio of fruit length to width, fruit compression, cotyledonary position, type of indumentum, and nectar glands), as well as the assumption that most, if not all, characters have evolved only once. Because of convergence in almost every morphological character, it is almost impossible to construct phylogenies based solely on morphology. Of all subdivisions of the family, only the primarily Mediterranean tribe Brassiceae (ca. 50 genera and 230 species) and the South African tribe Heliophileae (six genera and ca. 80 species) are monophyletic. The Brassiceae is represented in the neotropics by some of the cultivated vegetable mustards (species of *Brassica* and *Raphanus*) and the sea rockets (*Cakile*), and are characterized by usually having conduplicate cotyledons and/or segmented fruits.

Features of the family. Habit: usually herbs or, less frequently, subshrubs, shrubs (e.g., *Romanschulzia apetala*) or lianas, often perennial (>60% of family), often with woody caudices, rhizomes, or tubers. **Stems** usually erect, sometimes creeping. **Stipules** absent. **Leaves** alternate, rarely opposite or whorled (*Cardamine*), sometimes basal, simple or compound (*Nasturtium* and many *Cardamine*), rarely dimorphic (most aquatic species of *Cardamine*, *Nasturtium*, and *Rorippa*); blades sometimes divided (*Cardamine*). **Inflores-**

cences terminal, rarely axillary (e.g., *Coronopus* or when leaves basal and flowers solitary, e.g., in *Brayopsis*), often with corymbose racemes (elongating in fruit), corymbs (*Iberis*), or solitary flowers; bracts sometimes present; pedicels long when flowers single. **Flowers** usually actinomorphic, less often zygomorphic (*Iberis*), bisexual, rarely unisexual (the plants monoecious, dioecious, or gynodioecious); calyx with 4 sepals, these usually distinct, rarely united into tube, the interior pair lateral; corolla cross-shaped (cruciform), the petals 4, rarely 0 or vestigial (*Lepidium*), alternate with sepals; androecium usually of 6 (2, 4, or 6 in *Lepidium*) stamens, often tetradynamous (outer 2 shorter than inner 4), the filaments sometimes equal in length (*Romanschulzia*); nectar glands present; gynoecium syncarpous, the ovary superior, the carpels 2, the locules 1–2, the style 1, the stigma 1, entire or with 2 lobes; placentation parietal, rarely apical, the ovules 1–numerous, usually anatropous. **Fruits** usually capsules, rarely samaroid (*Isatis*), the capsules dry, 2-valved. **Seeds** 1–numerous, variously sculptured, mucilaginous or not mucilaginous when wetted.

The smallest plants in the family only reach 1 centimeter in height. The woody habit evolved independently in several unrelated lineages, and only about 2 percent of the total number of species in the family (belonging to 16 genera) are typical shrubs. Woody climbers, which may reach 5 m in height, evolved independently in at least three unrelated genera from South America (*Cremolobus*), South Africa (*Heliophila*), and Australia (*Lepidium*). One Afro-Asian genus, *Farsetia*, includes small herbs, shrubs, or even small trees.

Cardamine shows more variation in leaf type than any other genus in the family, and includes simple, pinnately or palmately divided, pinnately or palmately compound, or bipinnately compound leaves. Some of the aquatic species of *Cardamine* and *Nasturtium* produce pinnate leaves on emergent stems and simple ones on submersed stems.

The fruits vary considerably in size, shape, and presence or absence of appendages and/or septa. In the majority of species, the fruit length does not exceed 5 centimeters. Fruits can be as small as 2–3 millimeters, but in some forms of radish, which are cultivated in India and Malaysia for their fruits, which are eaten like green beans, the fruit is said to be at least 30 cm long. The fruit is usually called a silique when it is more than three times longer than broad and a silicle when it is clearly shorter than three times the width. Numerous genera (even rarely the same species) have both silique and silicle fruit types.

Natural history. Self-pollination is common in weedy species and in those that produce cleistogamous flowers. Almost all other species are pollinated by insects, especially bees, flies, butterflies, moths, and occasionally beetles. Wind pollination has been reported only in *Pringlea antiscorbutica*, a species endemic to some subantarctic islands of the Indian Ocean.

In plants with dehiscent fruits, initial seed dispersal is limited to short distances, but because of their small size, the seeds are carried easily by rainwater or wind. Indehiscent fruits may be dispersed by wind, water, or animals. Each of these dispersal mechanisms evolved independently several times within the family.

In many genera with one- or few-seeded indehiscent fruits, the seeds are released after the disintegration of the fruit wall or they germinate within the fruit. Seed germination is epigeal throughout the family.

Economic uses. The Brassicaceae include many species grown as vegetables, sources of edible and industrial oils, condiments, and ornamentals. The family also includes more than 120 weedy species of local or cosmopolitan distribution. *Brassica* contains some of most important and nutritious vegetable and salad plants, including broccoli, brussels sprouts, cabbage, cauliflower, kale, and kohlrabi (all varieties of *Brassica oleracea*). Radish (*Raphanus sativus*), rape (*Brassica napus*), turnip (*B. rapa*), watercress (*Nasturtium officinale*), and various Chinese cabbages or mustards (varieties of *Brassica rapa* and *B. juncea*) are other important vegetables. Vegetable (e.g., canola) and industrial oils are extracted from the seeds of some *Brassica* and rank fourth in terms of tonnage of world production of plant oils. Table mustard is made from the seeds of species of *Brassica* and *Sinapis*, whereas horseradish and wasabi are the ground rhizomes of *Armoracia rusticana* and *Eutrema wasabi*, respectively. The most important ornamental mustards include aubrietia (*Aubrieta*), candytuft (*Iberis*), dame's violet (*Hesperis*), honesty or money plant (*Lunaria*), rock cress (*Arabis*), stock (*Matthiola*), sweet alyssum (*Lobularia*), and wallflower (*Erysimum*).

Arabidopsis thaliana has become the model organism in thousands of laboratories throughout the world for studies of molecular genetics, physiology, pathology, phylogeny, horticulture, and crop improvement.

References. AL-SHEHBAZ, I. A. 1977. Protogyny in the Cruciferae. *Syst. Bot.* 2:327–33. AL-SHEHBAZ, I. A. 1984. The tribes of Cruciferae (Brassicaceae) in the southeastern United States. *J. Arnold Arbor.* 65:343–73. APPEL, O., AND I. A. AL-SHEHBAZ. 2003. Cruciferae. In *The Families and Genera of Vascular Plants*, eds. K. Kubitzki and C. Bayer. 5:75–174. Berlin: Springer-Verlag. HALL, J. C., K. J. SYTSMA, AND H. H. ILTIS. 2002. Phylogeny of Capparaceae and Brassicaceae based on chloroplast sequence data. *Amer. J. Bot.* 89(1):1826–42. KOCH, M., B. HAUBOLD, AND T. MITCHELL-OLDS. 2001. Molecular systematics of the Brassicaceae: evidence from coding plastidic *mat*K and nuclear *Chs* sequences. *Amer. J. Bot.* 88(2):534–44. MEYEROWITZ, E. M., AND C. R. SOMERVILLE, eds. 1994. *Arabidopsis*. Plainview, NY: Cold Spring Harbor Laboratory Press. ROLLINS, R. C. 1993. *The Cruciferae of Continental North America*. Stanford, CA: Stanford University Press. SCHULZ, O. E. 1936. Cruciferae. *Die Natürlichen Pflanzenfamilien*, 2nd ed. 17B:227–658. VAUGHAN, J. G., A. J. MACLEOD, AND B. M. G. JONES, eds. 1976. *The Biology and Chemistry of the Cruciferae*. New York: Academic Press.

BRUNELLIACEAE (Brunellia Family)

Thomas A. Zanoni

Figure 32, Plate 8

- *trees*

- *stipules present*

- *leaves opposite or 3 per node, simple or compound*

- *flowers with petals absent; intrastaminal disc present; gynoecium apocarpous, the ovary apparently superior, but carpel bases immersed in disc*

- *fruits follicles*

Numbers of genera and species. Restricted to tropical America, the Brunelliaceae comprise a single genus, *Brunellia*, with about 65 species.

Distribution and habitat. *Brunellia* is found from Veracruz and Puebla, Mexico, southward through Central America to the Andes in Bolivia and Venezuela.

The family is usually found in humid montane forests, from 600 to 3,800 meters.

Family classification. The Brunelliaceae are placed in the Rosales by Cronquist. Recent molecular analyses place *Brunellia* in the Oxalidales. The family is considered to be close to the Cunoniaceae and possibly sister to the Cephalotaceae (see Cunoniaceae).

Features of the family. Habit: small to large trees, evergreen. Stems with broad pith when young. Stipules present, usually in pairs, sometimes 4–6 at each side of node, often small. Leaves opposite or 3 per node, simple or imparipinnately compound (simple and compound leaves may occur in same species), coriaceous; leaflets opposite, in 1–9 pairs, the terminal leaflet sometimes absent; leaflet blades with margins denticulate, serrate, or crenate. Inflorescences axillary, from young growth, dichasial. Flowers actinomorphic or nearly so, often unisexual (the plants dioecious or gynodioecious); sepals (4)5–6(8), thick, united at base, persistent in fruit; petals absent; androecium with twice as many stamens as sepals, the outer whorl alternating with sepals, the inner whorl opposite sepals; intrastaminal disc present; gynoecium apocarpous, the ovary apparently superior, but carpel bases immersed in disc, the carpels equaling number of sepals; placentation marginal, the ovules (1)2 per carpel. Fruits follicles, the follicles arranged in starlike clusters. Seeds 1–2 per follicle, small, brown or red; ariloid tissue often present along raphe and around micropyle, spongy; endosperm fleshy, the cotyledons 2.

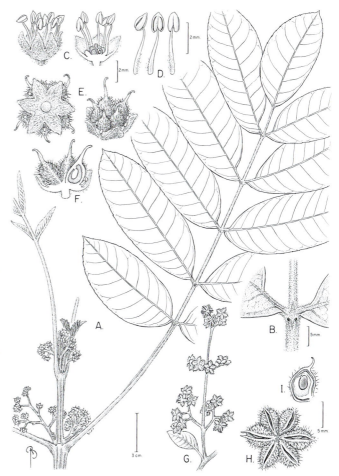

Figure 32. BRUNELLIACEAE. *Brunellia integrifolia* (A, B, E, F, Prance and Steyermark 16551; C, D, Romero-Castañeda 7553; G–I, Fendler 168). **A.** Stem with leaves and inflorescences. **B.** Detail of node. **C.** Lateral view (left) and medial section (right) of flowers. **D.** Lateral (left), adaxial (center), and abaxial (right) views of stamens. **E.** Basal (left) and apical-lateral (right) views of fruits. **F.** Lateral view of two intact carpels (left) and medial section of one carpel (right). **G.** Axillary infructescence. **H.** Apical view of dehisced fruits. **I.** Medial section of fruit. Original. Artist: Bobbi Angell.

Natural history. No information is available about pollination biology. The fruits of *Brunellia* either fall intact, often with the whole inflorescence, or the follicles open while still on the tree, exposing brightly colored seeds, at least in some species, that attract birds. The seeds have hard coats, and some probably are still viable after passing through the bird's digestive system.

Economic uses. The leaves of some species of *Brunellia* have been used in traditional medicine.

References. CUATRECASAS, J. 1970. Brunellaceae. *Fl. Neotrop. Monogr.* 2:1–189. CUATRECASAS, J. 1985. Brunelliaceae. *Fl. Neotrop. Monogr.* Suppl. 2:28–103.

BUDDLEJACEAE (Butterfly-bush Family)

ELIANE M. NORMAN

Figure 33, Plate 8

- *shrubs, trees, rarely herbs*
- *leaves opposite, decussate, simple*
- *flowers with perianth often tubular, lobed; stamens epipetalous*
- *fruits capsules*

Numbers of genera and species. Worldwide, Buddlejaceae comprise eight genera and about 125 species. In tropical America, there are four genera and 67 species. The largest genus, *Buddleja* (100 species worldwide), has 63 species. *Emorya*, found just north of the Tropics, contains two species, and *Polypremum* and *Peltanthera* are monotypic. *Sanango*, formerly included in this family, has been placed in the Gesneriaceae.

Distribution and habitat. The Buddlejaceae inhabit subtropical and tropical areas of the Americas, Asia, and Africa. In the Western Hemisphere, *Buddleja* is concentrated in southeastern Brazil, the Andes, Central America, Mexico, and the southwestern United States. *Peltanthera* inhabits lowland rain forests from Costa Rica to Bolivia and *Polypremum*, the only herbaceous member, is found in Central America, northern South America, Paraguay, and the eastern United States as far as 40°N.

The Buddlejaceae are heliophiles (except for *Peltanthera*) growing in open and disturbed habitats, often on calcareous or alkaline soils. Approximately 20 species grow in arid regions. Most of the taxa grow at 1,000–3,000 meters, but some reach 3,500–4,000 meters, especially in the mountains of Central America and the Andes.

Family classification. The Buddlejaceae are placed in the Scrophulariales by Cronquist. Traditionally, the family has been treated as a tribe in the Loganiaceae, but chemistry, molecular data, embryology, anatomy, and shared pathogens indicate a close relationship to the Scrophulariaceae.

Features of the family (for Western Hemisphere taxa). **Habit:** shrubs, trees, rarely herbs (*Polypremum*). **Stems** with glandular and stellate/candelabra (except *Peltanthera* and *Polypremum*) hairs when young. **Stipules** often represented only by an interpetiolar line (*Buddleja* and *Emorya*). **Leaves** opposite, decussate, simple. **Inflorescences** axillary or terminal, cymes, globose heads, verticels, or panicles; subtended by bracts or bracteoles. **Flowers** actinomorphic, unisexual (the plants dioecious or polygamous in *Buddleja*) or bisexual; calyx tubular or campanulate, deeply divided (*Polypre-*

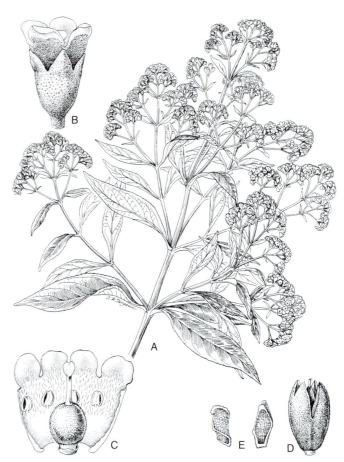

Figure 33. BUDDLEJACEAE. *Buddleja lojensis.* **A.** Stem with leaves and inflorescences. **B.** Lateral view of flower. **C.** Flower opened to show details. **D.** Lateral view of fruit. **E.** Seeds. Reprinted with permission from Norman (1982). Artist: Alice Tangerini.

mum), the lobes 4(5), ⅓–½ length of tube (*Buddleja, Emorya*); corolla tubular, funnelform, salverform, campanulate, rarely swollen (*Peltanthera*) or short and rotate (*Polypremum*), white, cream-colored, yellowish green, yellow, orange, or crimson-orange, the lobes 4(5), usually ⅓–½ length of tube, rarely longer, the lobes and inner surface of tube (in tube only in *Polypremum*) often covered with papillose or moniliform hairs; androecium of 4(5) stamens, the stamens sessile or subsessile (*Buddleja*), filamentous (*Emorya*), epipetalous, alternate with petal lobes; nectary at ovary base, often shiny; gynoecium syncarpous, the ovary usually superior, rarely subinferior (*Polypremum*), often stellate tomentose above nectary (*Buddleja* and *Emorya*), the carpels 2, the locules 2, the style 1; placentation axile, placentae 1 per locule, convoluted, adherent to septum at base (in *Polypremum*), the ovules many, anatropous. **Fruits** capsules, ovoid, oblong, or subglobular, dehiscing at septum and apex of locules, or loculical (*Pelanthera* and *Polypremum*). **Seeds** small (dust seeds), cuboidal (*Poly-*

premum), often with anterior and posterior wings (the wings 5 in *Peltanthera*, 3 in *Emorya*), the wings parallel to seed body (*Peltanthera*); seed coat often reticulate.

Species of *Buddleja* and *Emorya* in desert or semidesert habitats are small shrubs 0.5–1.5 meters tall. In more mesic habitats, the species of *Buddleja* are shrubs or trees 10–15 meters tall. Species of *Peltanthera* are trees 5–20 meters tall, and *Polypremum* is a perennial mat-forming herb.

Leaves of highland species tend to be coriaceous and entire. The leaves of species from drier areas are often small, very pubescent, and have indented margins. *Polypremum* has narrow needlelike leaves united at their bases.

Natural history. In the Western Hemisphere, most of the species are pollinated by bees, flies, wasps, butterflies, or, more rarely, hummingbirds. In the Eastern Hemisphere, butterflies are the primary pollinators. Seeds are dispersed by wind and water.

Economic uses. Many species of *Buddleja* have been used in folk medicine and are said to be effective against infections, digestive problems, and cancer. They are reported to have diuretic properties, to alleviate arthritis, and to control hemorrhaging. Wood of *Buddleja* is used in construction and for making charcoal. *Buddleja globosa* (orange ball tree) and *B. coriacea* (butterfly bush) are cultivated as ornamentals. In the Andes, *B. coriacea* and *B. incana* are used in reforestation.

References. LEEUWENBERG, A.J.M. 1979. The Loganiaceae of Africa XVIII. *Buddleja* II, Revision of the African and Asiatic species. *Meded. Landbouwhoogeschool* 79:1–163. LEEUWENBERG, A.J.M., AND P. W. LEENHOUTS. 1980. Taxonomy. *Die Natülichen Pflanzenfamilien*, A. Engler and K. Prantl, 2nd ed., Angiospermae: Ordnung Gentianales, Fam. Loganiaceae 28b(1):8–96. NORMAN, E. M. 2000. Buddlejaceae. *Fl. Neotrop. Monogr.* 81:1–225.

BURSERACEAE (Frankincense and Myrrh Family)

DOUGLAS C. DALY

Figure 34, Plate 8

- *trees and shrubs*

- *resin present, often aromatic and smelling like turpentine*

- *leaves alternate, imparipinnately compound, less often unifoliolate*

- *flowers actinomorphic, usually unisexual, small*

- *fruits with 1 seed per locule*

Numbers of genera and species. Worldwide, the Burseraceae comprise 18 genera and around 650 species. The four largest genera account for three-quarters of the diversity of the family: *Protium* (ca. 147 taxa), *Commiphora* (ca. 165), *Bursera* (ca. 100), and *Canarium* (ca. 95). The remaining genera are considerably smaller, and three are monotypic and unusual morphologically. One of the latter, *Beiselia mexicana*, is known from only one location in Michoacán, Mexico. In tropical America, there are eight genera and about 295 species.

Current work in the Protieae is focusing on generic limits in the tribe and the natural groups that can be defined within *Protium*. Phylogenetic analyses may require that the genus be divided into seven genera, which would increase the total number of genera in the family to 24.

Distribution and habitat. The Burseraceae are found in the tropical regions of America, Africa, Asia, and Australia. In the Americas, the family ranges beyond the Tropics into subtropical southern Florida, the arid regions of southern Texas and Arizona, and south into Paraguay and southern Brazil.

Within their range, the Burseraceae form an important part of the flora in a remarkable variety of habitats, from thornscrubs and deserts where total rainfall is a few hundred millimeters per year, to rain forests such as the Chocó region of Colombia, where more than 8,000 millimeters of rain fall each year. The family is of particular importance in Mexico, where the genus *Bursera* dominates many dry forests in terms of both diversity and abundance, and in Amazonia.

The family can be found in floodplain forests, and a small number of species thrive in montane forests above 2,000 meters, but the Burseraceae prefer non-inundated sites at low to middle elevations. Species can be rooted in clay, sandy, or rocky soils.

The vast majority of diversity in the Burseraceae is divided rather evenly among the tropical regions of Africa, Asia, and the Americas. In each region, all three tribes of the family occur, but one of the three—and one large genus in each tribe—predominates: Protieae (*Protium*) in the Americas, Bursereae (*Commiphora*) in Africa, and Canarieae (*Canarium*) in Asia.

While the Protieae and Canarieae are usually found in moist to wet forests, the two centers of diversity of the Bursereae are the drier parts of tropical east Africa and the dry forests and other arid formations of Mexico where 90 of the approximately 100 species of *Bursera* are endemic.

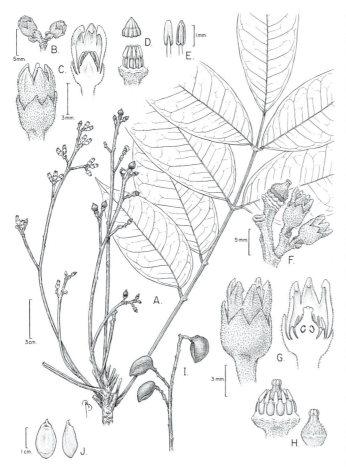

Figure 34. BURSERACEAE. *Tetragastris altissima.* **A.** Stem apex with leaf and inflorescence with flowers and young fruits. **B.** Detail of staminate inflorescence with two flower buds showing semiclasping bracts and their scars. **C.** Lateral view (left) and medial section (right) of staminate flower. **D.** Staminate flower with perianth removed (below) and ovariodisc (above). **E.** Abaxial (left) and adaxial (right) views of anthers. **F.** Detail of pistillate inflorescence with two flowers at anthesis and young fruit. **G.** Lateral view (left) and medial section (right) of pistillate flower. **H.** Pistillate flower with perianth removed (left) and gynoecium (right). **I.** Part of infructescence. **J.** Ventral (left) and lateral (right) views of pyrenes. Reprinted with permission from Mori et al. (2002). Artist: Bobbi Angell.

Other centers of diversity and endemism in the Americas are Amazonia in the broader sense (with subcenters in central Amazonia and the Guianas); the Chocó biogeographic province, which comprises the Pacific coastal forests ranging from southern Panama through Colombia to northern Ecuador; and, to a lesser degree, the West Indies and Brazil's Atlantic coastal forest complex.

Family classification. The Burseraceae are placed in the Sapindales by Cronquist. The family has long been divided into three tribes. The Canarieae comprise a more distinctive morphological group than do the Bursereae and Protieae.

In the tribe Bursereae there are no pulvinuli on the leaves.

The flowers are unisexual or perfect, 3–5(6)-merous, and hypogynous to perigynous. The ovary is usually meiomerous (fewer parts) or pleiomerous (more parts) relative to the perianth. The fruit is a dehiscent (except *Garuga*) drupe or a pseudocapsule with 1 or more unilocular pyrenes (instead of seeds as in a true capsule); in taxa in which more than 1 pyrene develops, the pyrenes are separate or separable. The cotyledons are folded and entire or palmatifid.

The tribe Bursereae subtribe Burseriinae has a 2–3-locular ovary; the fruit is a dehiscent drupe in which the locules are connivent or connate but only 1 pyrene (rarely 2 or 3) develops. The pyrene is attached basally to the receptacle. When the valves fall away, the pyrene persists for a time. The pyrene is enveloped in various patterns and degrees by an acropetally developing pseudaril that is fleshy, lipid-rich, and red or yellow. The subtribe includes the American genus *Bursera* and the pantropical genus *Commiphora*.

The tribe Bursereae subtribe Boswelliinae has dry, pseudocapsular fruits; the valves fall away to release 3–12 flattened, usually winged pyrenes that are separated by a columellate fruit axis. The subtribe includes the Neotropical genus *Beiselia* and the Paleotropical *Aucoumea* and *Boswellia* (the genus of frankincense).

In the tribe Protieae, a pulvinulus is almost always present distally on the petiolule of the terminal leaflet and is usually present distally on the petiolules of the lateral leaflets. The flowers are unisexual, hypogynous, and 4–5-merous. The ovary is isomerous relative to the perianth. The fruit is a dehiscent drupe with 1 or more unilocular pyrenes separated by a columellate structure. The pyrenes are attached apically to the columella by an inverted V-shaped structure and are suspended from it after the valves fall away. They are enveloped to various degrees by a pseudaril, which is spongy, sweet, and usually white. The pyrene is (thinly) cartilaginous to bony. The cotyledons are lobed and contortuplicate or entire and plano-convex. This tribe includes *Protium*, *Tetragastris*, and *Crepidospermum*.

In the tribe Canarieae, inverted vascular bundles are often present in the medulla of the petiole. Pulvinuli occur as in tribe Protieae. The flowers are 3-merous (except *Scutinanthe* with a 5-merous perianth), and the ovary is isomerous relative to the perianth. The fruit is an indehiscent, 2–3-locular compound drupe with a thin exocarp and a oily-resinous mesocarp (in many cases edible when ripe) enveloping a single plurilocular pyrene (1–2 pyrenes developing). The endocarp is cartilaginous to bony. The cotyledons are palmatifid to trifoliolate, and contortuplicate or folded. This tribe includes the pantropical genus *Dacryodes* and Neotropical genus *Trattinnickia*.

Recent molecular systematic research on the family has confirmed the close relationship between the Burseraceae and Anacardiaceae, the basal position of the Burseraceae in the Sapindales, the integrity of tribe Protieae and several natural groups within *Protium*, and the division of tribe Bursereae into two groups, while nesting *Commiphora* within one of two *Bursera* groups, suggesting that *Beiselia* is an outlier in the Bursereae, and calling into question tribal boundaries between Canarieae and Bursereae.

Features of the family. Habit: trees, less often shrubs, rarely epiphytes; resin present, often aromatic and smelling like turpentine. **Bark** thin and smooth to thick and fissured, shedding as flakes, variously sized plates, or papery sheets (some *Bursera*), often lenticellate, sometimes hooped, sometimes red or yellowish (some *Bursera*). **Stipules** absent. **Leaves** alternate, imparipinnately compound, less often unifoliolate; pulvinulus present (most Protieae and Canarieae) at distal end of terminal petiolule and often lateral petiolules; rachis winged (some *Bursera* and *Commiphora*); lateral leaflets opposite. **Inflorescences** axillary to subterminal, indeterminate panicles of racemes, laxly branched or variously reduced, sometimes short and fasciculate; secondary axes can be pseudospicate (some *Protium*). **Flowers** actinomorphic, 3–5(6)-parted, unisexual (the plants dioecious, or polygamodioecious in some *Bursera* and *Commiphora*) or bisexual (e.g., some *Dacryodes*), small; calyx valvate, synsepalous, usually lobed, sometimes irregulary split at anthesis (*Tetragastris* and some *Dacryodes*); corolla induplicate-valvate, apopetalous to partly sympetalous, usually pale green to greenish yellow, sometimes wine red (some *Dacryodes* and *Trattinnickia*). **Staminate flowers:** androecium diplostemonous or rarely isostemonous, sometimes didynamous, often the two series difficult to distinguish, the filaments distinct, less often connate basally, inserted at base of disc; disc intrastaminal, annular, nectariferous; reduced pistillode usually present, sometimes ontogenetically fused with disc to form conical or discoid "ovariodisc," sometimes reduced locules and ovules present, the stigmas absent. **Pistillate flowers:** staminodes present, reduced, the anthers devoid of pollen; gynoecium syncarpous, the ovary superior, the carpels and locules 2–5, the style solitary, apical, sometimes with as many short branches as locules, the stigma(s) 1 or as many as locules, capitate to discoid; placentation axile, the ovules 2 per locule, collateral, pendulous, epitropous. **Fruits** compound drupes or pseudocapsules, the pyrenes dehiscent or remaining fused together. **Seeds** 1 per locule (or aborted), usually fewer than locules, exalbuminous, the testa thin or, in some *Protium*, irregularly thickened and infolded with cotyledons; embryo minute, straight.

Virtually all vascularized tissues of Burseraceae contain resin canals. The resin may be clear, drying as a white to yellow or blackish crystalline powder or mass, or milky and drying in yellowish globules. The resin of some taxa is flammable.

All of the Protieae and the vast majority of species in the other two tribes are hypogynous. Perigynous flowers, with the disc adnate to the receptacle, occur in some species of *Bursera* and *Commiphora*.

There are five fruit types, three dehiscent and two indehiscent. In all of them, at most one fertilized ovule develops per locule. The dehiscent fruits have as many valves as developed locules; the valves fall away via acropetal septicidal dehiscence, leaving a columellate structure in the taxa in which more than pyrene develops.

In the fleshy dehiscent fruits the exposed pyrenes (stones) are partially to almost completely covered by a pseudaril. In the Protieae, the pyrenes are attached apically to the columella and suspended from it after dehiscence; the pseudaril is spongy, sweet, and usually white; and the pyrene is (thinly) cartilaginous to bony. In the Bursereae-Burseriinae, when the valves fall away, the pyrene remains attached basally, and the pseudaril is fleshy, lipid-rich, and red or yellow. The Bursereae-Boswelliinae have dry, pseudocapsular fruits and flattened, usually winged pyrenes.

The indehiscent fruit of the Canarieae consists of a single 2–3-locular compound drupe with a thin exocarp, oily mesocarp (in many cases edible when ripe), and cartilaginous to bony endocarp.

In the tribe Protieae the cotyledons are entire and planoconvex (these sometimes uncinately curved) or lobed and contortuplicate, less often transversely twice-folded (*Protium* section *Icicopsis*). The Tribe Bursereae have palmatifid cotyledons. Those of tribe Canarieae may be palmatifid or trifoliolate, and contortuplicate or folded.

Germination is epigeal or hypogeal, cryptocotylar or phanerocotylar, the eophylls opposite or alternate, simple, trifoliate, or pinnately compound.

Natural history. The remarkable degree of sympatry shown within the Burseraceae, particularly in central Amazonia, can be explained largely by niche partitioning via different microhabitats, strata, pollinators, and dispersers; however, some regions are crossroads where various species reach distribution limits that reflect past climate-mediated disturbances.

Pollination in the Burseraceae is very poorly studied, and the few published observations cite small bees as the principal visitors to flowers. One might expect a family of trees characterized by small, usually greenish flowers to have a rather limited range of pollinators. However, enough variation occurs in the flowers with respect to relative size, color (in *Trattinnickia* and *Dacryodes*), shape, sexuality, and the types and distribution and orientation of trichomes to predict diverse pollination syndromes.

The dispersal of Burseraceae fruits is somewhat better understood. The dry and flattened or winged pyrenes of the Bursereae subtribe Boswelliinae are adapted for wind dispersal. Birds are attracted to the bright red or yellow, fleshy pseudaril on the pyrenes of the Bursereae subtribe Burseriinae.

Fruits of the Protieae offer several visual signals for attracting animal dispersers. In the vast majority of the fruits, the exocarp is red or sometimes orange. Most, including some green-fruited species, have a pink columella and interior of the valves. The usually black pyrene contrasts with the sweet, spongy, white pseudaril that partly or mostly covers it. This abundant but nutritionally poor food reward usually attracts generalist birds and monkeys. However, a few species, such as the floodplain forest species *Protium krukovii*, have pale green fruits that open at night and are dispersed by bats. Pyrenes that are not dispersed right away eventually fall to the ground, where they may be dispersed or perhaps only fed upon by terrestrial animals.

The oil-rich mesocarp and often bony endocarp of the indehiscent fruits of tribe Canarieae represent a greater energy investment. The majority of these fruits apparently are dispersed by bats, birds, and primates. In the moist forests of Trinidad and northern Venezuela, *Dacryodes trinitensis* is the most important food plant of the oilbird (*Steatornis caripensis*).

The Burseraceae have two interesting relationships with bees. First, what appears to be a mature and normal fruit may have a nearly mature bee occupying the space where the seed should be. This occurs when the female oviposits in the developing fruit locule. Second, at least some species of bees in Amazonia use Burseraceae resin to seal the burrowed nests that they build in tree trunks. Beetle larvae are also commonly associated with the resin of Burseraceae.

Economic uses. The Burseraceae are best known for their resins. Two of the three Gifts of the Magi mentioned in the New Testament were Burseraceae—frankincense (*Boswellia sacra*) and myrrh (*Commiphora myrrha*)—but the diverse uses of these exudates far predate Christianity. Throughout the Tropics, and wherever tropical products have been traded, the resins have been valued for numerous cultural and practical purposes, e.g., as sealants (especially for caulking boats), in rituals as incense or fumigants, as diverse medicinals, and as fire-starters and illuminants.

The wood of Burseraceae is used principally as a fuel; in Amazonia it is prized for smoking Pará rubber (*Hevea guianensis*). With the notable exception of *Aucoumea klaineana*, the major timber tree in western Africa, the timber of Burseraceae is of minor importance. The Mexican species *Bursera aloexylon*, formerly the source of the essential oil linaloe, has an easily worked balsalike wood that is carved into intricate sculptures.

The fruits of all the Protieae have a sweet arillate structure, but this is considered only a snack or starvation food for humans and is valued more as an attractant for game. In contrast, the olivelike fruits of *Dacryodes* are appreciated throughout the Tropics, although only a few species are semidomesticated in Amazonia, and one species, *D. edulis*, is commercialized in Africa.

References. BECERRA, J. X., AND D. L. VENABLE. 1999. Nuclear ribosomal DNA phylogeny and its implications for evolutionary trends in Mexican *Bursera* (Burseraceae). *Am. J. Bot.* 86:1047–57. CLARKSON, J. J., M. W. CHASE AND M. M. HARLEY. 2002. Phylogenetic relationships in *Burseraceae* based on plastid *rps16* intron sequences. *Kew Bull.* 57: 183–93. DALY, D. C. 1989. Studies in Neotropical Burseraceae II. Generic limits in Neotropical Protieae and Canarieae. *Brittonia* 41:17–27. ENGLER, A. 1883. Burseraceae. In *Monographiae Phanerogamarum*, eds. A. L P. P. de Candolle and A. C. P. de Candolle, 4:1–169. Paris: G. Masson. FORMAN, L. L., P. E. BRANDHAM, M. M. HARLEY, AND T. J. LAWRENCE. 1989. *Beiselia mexicana* (Burseraceae) and its affinities. *Kew Bull.* 44:1–31. GAUTIER-HION, A., J.-M. DUPLANTIER, R. QURIS, F. FEER, C. SOURD, ET AL. 1985. Fruit characters as a basis of fruit choice and seed dispersal in a tropical forest vertebrate community. *Oecologia (Berlin)* 65: 324–37. GUILLAUMIN, A. 1909. Recherches sur la structure et le développement des Burseracées. Applications à la systématique. *Ann. Sci. Nat. Bot.* Série 9, 10(4):201–301. HARLEY, M. M., AND D. C. DALY. 1996. Burseraceae-Protieae. *World Pollen Spore Fl.* 20:1–44. LAM, H. J. 1932. The Burseraceae of the Malay Archipelago and Peninsula. *Bull. Jard. Bot. Buitenzorg* Série 3, 12:281–561. LEENHOUTS, P. W. 1956. Burseraceae. *Flora Malesiana*, ed. C. G. G. J. Van Steenis, Series 1, 5(2):209–96. Alphen Aan Den Rijn, The Netherlands: Sijthoff and Noordhoff International Publishers. MARCHAND, N. L. 1867–68. Recherches sur l'organisation des Burseracées. *Adansonia* 8:17–71. SWART, J. J. 1942. *A Monograph of the Genus Protium and Some Allied Genera (Burseraceae)*. Gouda: Drukkerij Koch en Knuttel.

BUXACEAE (Boxwood Family)

EGON KÖHLER

Figure 35

- *shrubs or trees*
- *leaves alternate or decussate, simple, entire*
- *flowers small, actinomorphic, unisexual; petals absent; stamens opposite sepals; ovary with 3 locules, the styles distinct; ovules 2 per locule*
- *fruits loculicidal capsules or drupelike*
- *seeds black, carunculate*

Numbers of genera and species. Worldwide, the Buxaceae comprise five genera and about 110 species. In tropical America, there are three genera, *Buxus* with about 50 species, *Styloceras* with five species, and *Sarcococca* with one species.

Distribution habitats. The Buxaceae have a disjunct distribution with centers of diversity in tropical and temperate

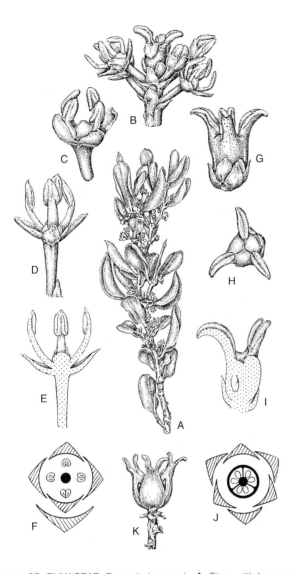

Figure 35. BUXACEAE. *Buxus bahamensis*. **A.** Stem with leaves and inflorescences (x¾). **B.** Inflorescence (x5). **C.** Lateral view of staminate flower at early anthesis (x10). **D.** Lateral view of staminate flower at later anthesis (x10). **E.** Medial section of staminate flower (x10). **F.** Floral diagram of staminate flower. **G.** Lateral view of pistillate flower (x10). **H.** Apical view of pistillate flower (x10). **I.** Medial section of pistillate flower (x10). **J.** Floral diagram of pistillate flower. **K.** Fruit (x2½). Reprinted with permission from Correll and Correll (1982). Artist: Priscilla Fawcett.

East Asia and in the Caribbean. In the Western Hemisphere, the family is distributed from southeastern United States (one species of *Pachysandra*) to Andean South America (four species of *Styloceras*) and the Caribbean coast of northern South America. In tropical America, the largest and most widespread genus, *Buxus*, has a center of diversity in Cuba. There are separate groups of *Buxus* in Eurasia and Africa.

The Buxaceae occupy a variety of habitats, from dry scrub forests and limestone cliffs to the understory of montane rain forests, and occasionally cloud forests. Most species occur on mountains, and a few reach elevations above 3,000 meters on Andean slopes. *Buxus* is frequently found on serpentine soils.

Family classification. The Buxaceae are placed in the Euphorbiales by Cronquist. Takhtajan recognizes the Buxaceae and Didymelaceae as a separate order, the Buxales.

The family comprises two subfamilies, the Buxoideae and Styloceratoideae (Takhtajan), though the Styloceratoideae is sometimes regarded as a separate family (Stylocerataceae). Current research centers on the differentiation of *Buxus* and the phylogenetic position of the family, which seem to find a better place near the base of the nonmagnoliid dicots, between hamamelid and dilleniid groups.

The rank of *Notobuxus* is still in discussion. It was recently treated as a subgenus of *Buxus*, but deviates in the number of stamens, the chromosome number, and features of the exine.

Features of the family. Habit: shrubs or trees (to 15 m tall), evergreen. Stipules absent. Leaves alternate (*Styloceras* and *Sarcococca*) or decussate (*Buxus*), simple; blades with base decurrent onto stem (*Buxus*), the margins entire; venation pinnate, less often tripliveined. Inflorescences axillary, less frequent terminal, racemes, clusters, spikes, or of solitary flowers (pistillate *Styloceras*), the racemes loose to densely glomerate, with single apical female flower (*Buxus*), the clusters or spikes often erect, with apical staminate flowers (*Sarcococca*), sometimes pendent (staminate *Styloceras*), the flowers subtended by bracts and bracteoles (*Sarcococca*). Flowers actinomorphic, unisexual (the plants monoecious or dioecious in some *Styloceras*), small. Staminate flowers: sepals 4, inconspicuous, bract-like, sometimes petal-like, or wanting (*Styloceras*); petals absent; androecium usually with 4 stamens, then stamens opposite sepals, or stamens numerous in *Styloceras*, the stamens usually inserted around pistillode; pistillode present, nectariferous (lacking in *Styloceras*). Pistillate flowers: sepals 4–6, bractlike; petals absent; gynoecium syncarpous, the ovary superior, the carpels (2)3(4), the locules (2)3(4), the styles distinct, persistent on fruit (*Buxus*), the stigma long, decurrent; nectariferous protuberances occuring between styles (*Buxus*, possibly of androecial origin); placentation axile, the ovules 2 per locule. Fruits capsules (*Buxus*), drupelike (*Sarcococca* and *Styloceras*), the capsules dehiscing loculicidally into 3 2-horned valves, the exocarp chartaceous, the detaching endocarp cartilaginous, the drupelike fruits with thin crustaceous or cartilaginous endocarp. Seeds usually, 4–6 black; caruncle usually present; endosperm fleshy, oily, the cotyledons thin, flat.

Natural history. The flowers of Buxaceae are visited by beetles (Coleoptera), bees, and other small Hymenoptera. Long exserted stamens and strong fragrances attract the insects to a nectar reward.

The seeds of *Buxus* are dispersed a short distance when the cartilaginous layer of the fruit, which partly encloses the seeds, contracts during desiccation and ejects them forcibly. The presence of caruncles suggests ant dispersal, and the occurrence of drupelike fruits in some species indicates bird dispersal.

Economic uses. The genus *Buxus* (boxwood) has more than 150 registered cultivars, mainly of *B. sempervirens* and *B. microphylla*. These species are grown as hedges and used in topiary. The closely grained wood is used to manufacture musical instruments and accessories, such as drumsticks.

References. BATDORF, L. R. 1995. *Boxwood Handbook.* Boyce, VA: American Boxwood Society. DAUMANN, E. 1974. Zur Frage nach dem Vorkommen eines Septal-nektariums bei Dikotyledonen. Zugleich ein Beitrag zur Blütenmorphologie und Bestäubungsökologie von *Buxus* L. und *Cneorum* L. *Preslia* 46:97–109. KÖHLER, E. 1985. Vorstellungen zur Evolution und Chorogenese der neotropischen *Buxus*-Arten. *Feddes Repert.* 96:663–75. KÖHLER, E. 1993. Blattnervatur-Muster der Buxaceae Dumortier und Simmondsiaceae Van Tieghem. *Feddes. Repert.* 104:145–67. KÖHLER, E., and P. BRÜCKNER. 1990. Considerations on the evolution and chorogenesis of the genus *Buxus* (Buxaceae). *Mem. New York Bot. Gard.* 55:153–68 TAKHTAJAN, A. L. 1980. Outline of the classification of flowering plants (Magnoliophyta). *Bot. Rev.* 46:225–359.

CABOMBACEAE (Fanwort Family)

DONALD H. LES

Figure 36, Plate 8

- *aquatic herbs*
- *shoots and leaves often covered by mucilaginous layer*
- *floating leaves peltate*
- *flowers usually with 3-merous perianth*

Numbers of genera and species. Worldwide, the Cabombaceae comprise two genera and six species. In tropical America, there are two genera and five species: *Brasenia* (*B. schreberi*) is monotypic, and *Cabomba* includes *C. aquatica*, *C. furcata*, *C. palaeformis*, and *C. haynesii*.

Distribution and habitat. The Cabombaceae are cosmopolitan. *Brasenia* occurs in Africa, eastern Asia, eastern Australia, North America, Mexico, Cuba, Hispaniola, Jamaica, Belize, Guatemala, and southeastern Venezuela. *Cabomba* is native to and widespread in temperate and tropical regions of the Western Hemisphere, but has become naturalized in Asia, Australia, and Europe.

Cabombaceae occur in the freshwater of ponds, small lakes, and sluggish rivers.

Family classification. The Cabombaceae are placed in the Nymphaeales by Cronquist. Takhtajan subdivided the family, placing *Brasenia* in the Hydropeltidaceae, and included this family with Cabombaceae in the order Hydropeltidales. The monophyly of Cabombaceae and its sister group relationship to Nymphaeaceae are supported by molecular and nonmolecular data. The Cabombaceae have been subdivided into two subfamilies: Cabomboideae and Hydropeltoideae, which correspond to the familial subdivisions used by Takhtajan.

Features of the family. Habit: perennial aquatic herbs, the shoots and leaves often covered by mucilaginous layer (especially *Brasenia*). Roots nodal, adventitious. Rhizomes simple or branched. Leaves alternate (floating leaves) or opposite (submersed leaves). Floating leaves peltate; blades large (up to 14×8 cm in *Brasenia*) or small (4×3.5 cm in *Cabomba*), broadly elliptic (*Brasenia*) to narrowly elliptic, sagittate, or hastate (*Cabomba*). Submersed leaves (in *Cabomba*) palmately divided, the ultimate divisions dichotomous to trichotomous, capillary. Inflorescences axillary, of solitary flowers. Flowers actinomorphic, bisexual; perianth usually 3-merous, rarely 2-merous (*Cabomba aquatica*), white, yellow, violet (*Cabomba*), or maroon to dull purple (*Brasenia*); sepals 3, petal-like (*Cabomba*), linear to narrowly ovate (*Brasenia*); petals 3, clawed (*Cabomba*), nectariferous auricles present (*Cabomba*); androecium of 3–6 (*Cabomba*) or 18–51 (*Brasenia*) stamens; gynoecium apocarpous, the ovary superior, the carpels 1–4 (*Cabomba*) or 4–18 (*Brasenia*), the stigmas capitate (*Cabomba*) or linear and decurrent (*Brasenia*); placentation dorsal/ventral, approaching laminar in *Brasenia*, the ovules 1 or 2 (*Brasenia*) or 1–5 (*Cabomba*). Fruits follicle-like (*Cabomba*) or achene-like (*Brasenia*), elongated and tapered (*Cabomba*), fusiform (*Brasenia*). Seeds globose (*Cabomba*) or ovoid (*Brasenia*), tuberculate (*Cabomba*) or smooth (*Brasenia*).

Natural history. Although both genera of Cabombaceae tolerate a fairly wide range in pH, *Brasenia* (water shield) occupies more acidic water and *Cabomba* (fanwort) more alkaline

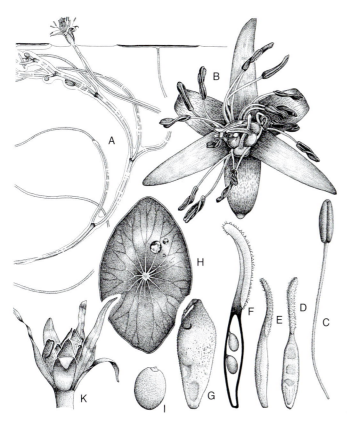

Figure 36. CABOMBACEAE. *Brasenia schreberi*. **A.** Stem with submersed and floating leaves and a flower (x½). **B.** Apical view of flower (x4). **C.** Adaxial view of stamen (x4). **D.** View of carpel (x4). **E.** Lateral view of carpel (x4). **F.** Carpel showing medial section of ovary (x6). **G.** Lateral view of fruit (x4). **H.** Leaf (x1). **I.** Seed (x4). **J.** Missing in original plate. **K.** Lateral view of fruits surrounded by persistent perianth (x2). Reprinted with permission from Cronquist (1981). Artist: William S. Moye.

zomes. Compared to *Cabomba*, *Brasenia* grows in slightly shallower waters.

Pollination is by insects in *Cabomba* and wind in *Brasenia*. The wind-pollinated flowers of *Brasenia* are pistillate the first day and staminate the next (protogynous). *Brasenia* is self-compatible, but protogyny promotes outcrossing. Flies of the genus *Notaphila* are the primary pollinators of *Cabomba*, which is also protogynous. Occasional pollination of *Brasenia* by *Notaphila* may occur, but this is insignificant.

No information is available about dispersal biology.

Economic uses. Both *Cabomba* and *Brasenia* are grown as aquarium plants, and *Brasenia* is also used as an ornamental in water gardens. The tender mucilaginous shoots of *Brasenia* are cultivated as a food in eastern Asia and its shoots and seeds are also eaten by waterfowl. Both genera are assumed to have been introduced to various parts of the world as escapes from cultivation.

References. BEAL, E. 1977. A manual of marsh and aquatic vascular plants of North Carolina with habitat data. *North Carolina Agric. Exp. Sta. Techn. Publ.* no. 247. FASSETT, N. 1951. A monograph of *Cabomba*. *Castanea* 13:116–28. HOYER, M., D. CANFIELD JR., C. HORSBURGH, AND K. BROWN. 1996. *Florida Freshwater Plants*. Gainesville, FL: University of Florida, Institute of Food and Agricultural Sciences. LES, D. H., E. L. SCHNEIDER, D. J. PADGETT, P. S. SOLTIS, D. E. SOLTIS, AND M. ZANIS. 1999. Phylogeny, classification and floral evolution of water lilies (Nymphaeaceae; Nymphaeales); a synthesis of non-molecular, *rbc*L, *mat*K, and 18S rDNA data. *Syst. Bot.* 24:28–46. ØRGAARD, M. 1991. The genus *Cabomba* (Cabombaceae)—a taxonomic study. *Nordic J. Bot.* 11:179–203. OSBORN, J., AND E. SCHNEIDER. 1988. Morphological studies of the Nymphaeaceae *sensu lato*. XVI. The floral biology of *Brasenia schreberi*. *Ann. Missouri Bot. Gard.* 75:778–94. WIERSEMA, J. 1997. Cabombaceae. In *Flora of North America North of Mexico*, ed. N. R. Morin, 3:78–80. New York: Oxford University Press. WILLIAMSON, P., AND E. SCHNEIDER. 1993. Cabombaceae. In *The Families and Genera of Vascular Plants*, eds. K. Kubitzki et al. 2:157–61. New York: Springer-Verlag.

water. In cultivation, *Cabomba* species thrive in bright sunlight and water with temperatures from 18° to 28°C. Water temperatures below 18°C may initiate dormancy in *Brasenia*, which overwinters by rhizomes and gelatinous, apical, winter buds that sink to the bottom. *Cabomba* overwinters by rhi-

CACTACEAE (Prickly Pear Family)

ALBERTO ARECES

Figure 37, Plate 9

- *trees, shrubs, or vines*
- *habitat usually dry and warm (except epiphytes)*
- *stem mostly succulent, photosynthetic*
- *areoles always present, usually with spines*

- *leaves usually not visible*
- *flowers with tepals usually numerous, white or brightly colored; ovary usually inferior, surrounded by stem tissue of pericarpel*

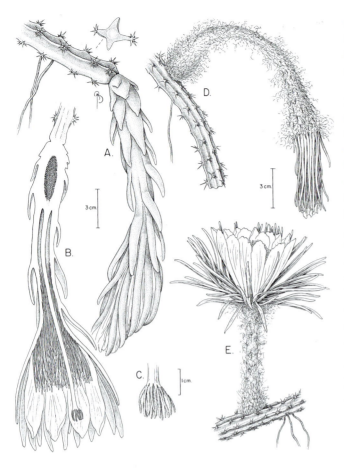

Figure 37. CACTACEAE. *Hylocereus trigonus* (A–C) and *Selenicereus grandiflorus* (D, E). **A.** Stem with flower and transverse section of stem (above). **B.** Submedial section of flower. **C.** Apex of branched style showing stigma. **D.** Stem with senescent flower. **E.** Stem with flower at anthesis. Reprinted with permission from Acevedo-Rodríguez (1996). Artist: Bobbi Angell.

Numbers of genera and species. The Cactaceae comprise circa 125 genera and 1,900 species, all of which, except for one species of *Rhipsalis*, are native to the Western Hemisphere. In tropical America, there are 100 genera and circa 1,300 species. The largest genera are *Opuntia* (190 species), *Mammillaria* (175), and *Echinopsis* (130). Twenty-eight genera have only one species.

Distribution and habitat. Except for one species, *Rhipsalis baccifera*, found in the neotropics as well as in the Eastern Hemisphere (from tropical Africa east to Sri Lanka), the Cactaceae are confined to the Western Hemisphere. In North America, *Opuntia fragilis* extends to 56°N into British Columbia and Alberta, Canada, while the South American genera *Maihuenia*, *Maihueniopsis*, and *Pterocactus* reach 50°S in Patagonia, Argentina. The greatest diversity of cacti is found in dry climatic zones between 35°N and 35°S of the equator. The desert areas of Mexico and adjacent southwestern United States are very rich in cacti, especially in the

columnar genera *Pachycereus*, *Stenocereus*, *Carnegiea*, *Myrtillocactus*, *Cephalocereus*, *Neobuxbaumia*, and *Polaskia*, and low-growing forms such as *Mammillaria*, *Echinocereus*, and *Coryphanta*.

In South America, the central Andean region (Peru, Bolivia, and northern Argentina) constitutes another center of diversity. Columnar or treelike forms are present, but the area is especially rich in taxa with a globose habit—e.g., species of *Gymnocalycium*, *Echinopsis*, *Parodia*, and *Rebutia*. Other centers of diversity are northeastern Brazil where *Pereskia*, *Tacinga*, *Facheiroa*, *Stephanocereus*, *Espostoopsis*, and other columnar and shrublike cereoids play an important role; central-western and southern Brazil, Paraguay, Uruguay, and northeastern Argentina, a region rich in species of *Frailea*, *Harrisia*, *Opuntia*, *Cereus*, *Gymnocalycium*, and *Parodia*; central to northwestern Chile with many endemic species of *Copiapoa* and *Eriosyce*; and the West Indies with the endemic genera *Consolea*, *Leptocereus*, and *Dendrocereus*. The Galápagos Islands, with the monotypic and endemic *Jasminocereus* and *Brachycereus*, as well as species of *Opuntia*, constitute a small but important center.

Cacti have a wide ecological amplitude, occupying diverse habitats from almost rainless, open deserts, to dense tropical rain forests from sea level to 5,000 meters on Andean slopes, but they are most abundant in deserts. Some narrowly endemic species are restricted to isolated outcrops of limestone, gypsum, and serpentine.

Family classification. The Cactaceae are placed in the Caryophyllales by Cronquist. Molecular studies have shown that the Cactaceae are phylogenetically closer to the Portulacaceae than to any other family of this order. The family is divided into four subfamilies: the primitive Pereskioideae, the cushion-forming Maihuenioideae, the highly derived Opuntioideae, and the large and morphologically complex Cactoideae. The Cactoideae are divided into nine tribes, each with a precise geographical range.

Features of the family. Habit: perennial trees, shrubs, or vines, often globose or short-cylindrical, sometimes columnar, spines usually present, the shrubs erect or scandent. Roots often highly developed, sometimes tuberous (used for water storage) or adventitious (epiphytes and climbers). Stems photosynthetic, usually thick and succulent (nonsucculent in *Pereskia*), simple or ramified (branched), often segmented, the joints cylindroid or flattened (e.g., *Opuntia*), the surface smooth, or more commonly ribbed or tuberculate (Cactoideae), the tubercles (succulent projections) nipplelike (e.g., *Mammillaria*), elongated (e.g., *Leuchtenbergia*), or triangular (*Ariocarpus*), often arranged in intricate helical patterns. Areoles always present, usually producing spines and trichomes, sometimes leaves (*Pereskia*) or flowers, the flowering areoles not essentially different from vegetative areoles, to very different (e.g., *Melocactus*), when different, the flowering areoles with more bristles and longer wooly hair than vegetative areoles; spines straight, curved, or twisted, stiff to bristly or sometimes very flexible, acicular, subulate, capillary, or ribbonlike, translucent to white, yellow, orange, brown, pink, red, gray, or black, usually darker at apex, the central spines (to areole) often stiff, erect, the radial spines produced at areole margins usually shorter and lacking strength of centrals. **Leaves** usually not visible (Cactoideae), sometimes reduced or small, flattened, or cylindrical to awl-shaped projections on growing point of stem (Opuntioideae), ephemeral (except *Pereskiopsis*, *Austrocylindropuntia*, and *Quiabentia*), rarely leaflike (*Pereskia*). **Inflorescences** often solitary, multiple flowers per areole rare (e.g., *Myrtillocactus* and *Lepismium*), paniculate, cymose, paniculate-cymose, or subcorymbose only in *Pereskia*. **Flowers** usually actinomorphic, sometimes zygomorphic (e.g., *Schlumbergera*), bisexual, rarely imperfectly unisexual (plants functionally dioecious or gynodioecious), 0.5–40 cm diam., basally sunken into modified stem; floral tube often present, sometimes elongate (to 30 cm long in *Hylocereus undatus* and *Selenicereus grandiflorus*), the abaxial surface often bearing scales, the scales wider and longer at apex of floral tube, merging into outer sepal-like tepals (the separation between scales and tepals clear in Pereskiodeae, Maihuenioideae, and Opuntioideae); tepals usually numerous, often brightly colored (day-blooming species), green, white, yellow, orange, red to purple, violet, rarely brown, never pure blue (found only at apex of inner tepals in *Disocactus*); androecium of numerous stamens (except Rhipsalideae), these often adnate to inner wall of floral tube, free on upper rim of receptacle (Pereskioideae), the anthers basifixed or versatile, dehiscing longitudinally; nectarial tissue present between inner stamens and style, nectar furrows, discs, or chambers located at ovary base; gynoecium syncarpous, the ovary usually inferior, rarely superior (e.g., *Pereskia lychnidiflora*), surrounded by modified stem tissue called pericarpel, the pericarpel often bearing scales, trichomes, or spines, the carpels 2–20 or more, the locules most often 1 (10–18 locules in *P. lychnidiflora*), the style columnar, frequently hollow, the stigma rays 2–20 or more, sometimes cleft at middle (e.g., *Hylocereus*). **Fruits** indehiscent or dehiscent, sometimes including receptacle-tube (some Opuntioideae), the surface often with spines, glochids, hairs, tubercles, or scales (pericarpel participates in formation); pericarpel and pericarp wall usually fleshy, vividly colored, less often somewhat dry or dry at maturity; funicles often deliquescent, forming juicy, brightly colored pulp; areoles of pericarpel sometimes developing secondary spines (as fruit becomes ripe), or areoles and spines caducous (at maturity). **Seeds** ovate, circular, elliptic, or oblong, sometimes irregular in shape, 0.5–10 mm diam., the surface pattern of testa characteristic (used in classification); embryo nonsucculent (*Pereskia*) to markedly succulent (advanced Cactoideae), usually curved, the cotyledons large (*Pereskia*) or reduced (advanced Cactoideae); perisperm present or absent in Cactoideae.

Cacti usually have a highly developed root system, which enables them to absorb the smallest amounts of moisture. *Pereskia weberiana* has globular to fusiform tuberous roots,

while *Opuntia macrorrhiza* possesses thick, fleshy root tubers that may grow at the apex into many-branched, thin, feeder roots. Epiphytic and climbing cacti develop adventitious roots that serve to absorb water and nutrients and aid in climbing.

Stems of the largest arborescent cacti may reach more than 20 meters tall with trunks more than 1 meter in diameter. In contrast, those of *Blossfeldia liliputana* are commonly less than 1 centimeter in diameter (or height) at maturity.

Cactaceae spines are extraordinarily varied in size, shape, and color. Some are no longer than a few millimeters in length, while *Cereus jamacaru* is reported to have spines to 30 centimeters long. The silky, woolly hair of *Cephalocereus senilis* is made of hair-spines, which are soft, very thin, long, and twisted structures seemingly without lignin. Plumose spines (e.g., in *Mammillaria plumosa*) have featherlike lateral projections resembling the pinnae of a feather. In contrast to these weak spines, others are hard and stiff enough to pierce the thickest leather. Spines may be needle-shaped, awl-shaped, or flattened (ribbonlike) and may have distinct margins, barbed hooks, or papery sheaths covering them. Glochids are very thin, short and brittle, specialized spines with characteristically barbed surfaces, occurring, mostly in fascicles, in the areoles of the Opuntioideae.

A unique kind of nitrogen-containing pigment called betalains typically produce the colors of flowers of Cactaceae.

Natural history. Although Cactaceae are generally self-incompatible and their flowers are mostly bisexual, other less common breeding systems, such as autogamy, cleistogamy, vivipary, functional dioecy, and gynodioecy, have been reported. Facultative asexual reproduction is also frequent and might represent an advantage in colonizing new habitats.

Bee pollination is the most common pollination system and seems to be the primitive condition, but bird, bat, and hawkmoth pollination also occur. Beetles are common visitors to cactus blossoms because larval development of many species takes place in the floral parts; however, they are not known to be effective pollinators of Cactaceae.

Cacti usually produce many seeds, but the seedling establishment is low. Seedlings often require nurse plants or the occurrence of special events; e.g., hurricanes play a major role in the establishment of cactus seedlings in the West Indies. A wide variety of animals and other agents, including bats, rodents, other mammals, birds, lizards, fish, crabs, insects, wind, and water, disperse the seeds of Cactaceae. Cacti are important in providing shelter and especially food for wildlife in arid regions. The fleshy fruits of *Carnegiea gigantea*, for example, provide food for at least 20 species of birds.

Economic uses. *Opuntia ficus-indica* is widely cultivated for its edible fruits in many tropical and subtropical areas. Fruits of other genera (e.g., *Hylocereus*, *Myrtillocactus*, *Echinocereus*, and *Pereskia*) are important in local markets. The fruits of *Pereskia portulacifolia* are marketed as Barbados gooseberries. The young stems of various species of

Opuntia are eaten cooked, and sometimes used as cattle fodder. Some species of *Ferocactus* have aromatic, sweet-sour–flavored stems, and Mexicans consume them stewed or candied. Columnar cacti, such as, *Pachycereus* and *Stenocereus*, are frequently planted to build impenetrable hedges and enclosures. The wood of many large columnar cacti is used even today for fuel and for construction in areas without trees.

Other products derived from Cactaceae were used by pre-Columbian cultures of dry regions. The Indians of Mexico, for example, obtained a red dye from the cochineal insect (*Dactylopius coccus*) that parasitizes some species of *Opuntia*. Although synthetic pigments have largely substituted the cochineal dye, it is still produced in Mexico, Peru, the Canary Islands, Chile, and some African countries, mainly for the food and cosmetic industries. The Aztecs and other Mexican Indian tribes also used *Lophophora williamsii* (peyote) for both therapeutic and religious ceremonies because of its hallucinogenic properties. Another well-known hallucinogenic species is the South American *Echinopsis pachanoi* (San Pedro). The Cactaceae are valued as ornamental plants with millions of cultivated specimens traded within North America and across international borders each year.

References. ANDERSON, E. F. 2001. *The Cactus Family.* Portland, OR: Timber Press. BENSON, L. 1982. *The Cacti of the United States and Canada.* Stanford, CA: Stanford University Press. CULLMANN, W., E. GÖTZ, AND G. GRÖNER. 1986. *The Encyclopedia of Cacti.* Portland, OR: Timber Press. GIBSON, A. C., AND P. S. NOBEL. 1986. *The Cactus Primer.* Cambridge, MA: Harvard University Press. INNES, C., AND C. GLASS. 1991. *Cacti.* New York: Portland House. LAMB, B. M. 1991. *A Guide to Cacti of the World.* Australia: HarperCollins. LEUENBERGER, B. E. 1986. Pereskia (Cactaceae). *Mem. New York Bot. Gard.* 41:1–141. SCHUSTER, D. 1990. *The World of Cacti.* New York: Facts on File, Inc.

CALLITRICHACEAE (Water Starwort Family)

C. THOMAS PHILBRICK

- *herbs*
- *often aquatic or amphibious*
- *leaves opposite, simple*
- *flowers unisexual; perianth absent*

Number of genera and species. Worldwide, the Callitrichaceae comprise a single genus, *Callitriche*, with circa 50 species. In the Western Hemisphere, there are approximately 20 species, 10 of which occur in tropical America.

Distribution and habitat. The Callitrichaceae are nearly cosmopolitan, occurring throughout the Americas, Europe, northern Africa, central and southern Asia, eastern and western Australia, New Guinea, and southern Africa. In the Western Hemisphere, the family ranges from northern Canada through Central America, and along the Andes from Colombia through central Chile and southern South America. More species occur in temperate than tropical latitudes.

Terrestrial species (e.g., *Callitriche deflexa*) occur in seasonally wet areas, such as stream banks and floodplains, often forming small dense mats on sandy soil. Amphibious species grow submerged, with floating leaves, or as a terrestrial form and can produce dense mats of highly branched stems.

Family classification. The Callitrichaceae are placed in the Callitrichales by Cronquist. It has been proposed that the Callitrichales (Callitrichaceae, Hippuridaceae, and Hydrostachyaceae) are related to the Scrophulariaceae. Embryological features suggest that the Callitrichaceae have an affinity with the Lamiaceae and Verbenaceae. Analyses of molecular data indicate that the Hippuridaceae is sister to Callitrichaceae and that these families are most closely related to taxa of the Scrophulariaceae *sensu* Cronquist.

The most widely used classification divides *Callitriche* into three sections. Section *Microcallitriche*, composed largely of terrestrial species, has leaves fairly uniform in shape and lacks floral bracts; section *Callitriche* (=*Eucallitriche*), the largest section, is made up of amphibious species with polymorphic leaves, and inflated whitish floral bracts; and section *Pseudocallitriche* includes two obligately submerged species that lack floral bracts.

Species boundaries are based largely on features of mature fruits. Chromosome number has been used as a distinguishing feature for some European taxa.

Features of the family. Habit: slender, terrestrial, amphibious, or aquatic herbs, annual or perennial. **Stems** highly branched, upright or prostrate (terrestrial plants), or lax and supported by water (aquatic plants). **Stipules** absent. **Leaves** opposite, simple, peltate scales present (terrestrial and amphibious species), linear scales present (submerged species), a narrow membranous wing connecting adjacent leaf bases at node in terrestrial species, lacking in submerged species; blades spatulate to oblong (aerial and floating leaves) or linear to oblong (submerged leaves), sometimes highly variable (amphibious species), the margins entire, the apex sometimes slightly notched; veins 1–several, the central vein most prominent. **Inflorescences** axillary, of 1–3 flowers; bracts 2 (many amphibious species), subtending flower, inflated, whitish. **Flowers** unisexual (plants monoecious), protogynous (when both sexes occur together), reduced (on submerged stems of some species); perianth absent. **Staminate flowers:** androecium of 1 stamen, the anther dehiscing by 2 lateral slits, the slits apically confluent; pollen inaperturate (submerged flowering species), or apertures (colpi) 3–4, poorly defined. **Pistillate flowers:** gynoecium syncarpous, the ovary with 4 lobes, the carpels 2, the locules 4, flattened, the styles linear, the stigmatic surface along styles; placentation axile, the ovules 2 per carpel, pendulous, anatropous. **Fruits** dry, typically splitting into 4 single-seeded units (sometimes referred to as nutlets). **Seeds** 4, the seed coat green, brownish, or black.

Stems of terrestrial species (or terrestrial forms of amphibious species) are usually less than a few centimeters long, while those of aquatic species can be up to 1 meter long.

Chromosome numbers in *Callitriche* range from $2n = 6$ to $2n = 40$ ($x = 5$). Aneuploidy and polyploidy occur. Aneuploid reduction from x = 5 is associated with obligately submersed species and underwater flowering. Amphibious and obligately terrestrial species have diploid and polyploid chromosome numbers.

Natural history. *Callitriche* is the only genus in which both aerial pollination and underwater pollination co-occur. Structural diversity of pollen is associated with growth form and pollination type. The pollen walls are thickest in terrestrial species, somewhat thinner in amphibious species, and thinnest in obligately submersed species (e.g., *C. hermaphroditica*).

In the Western Hemisphere, seven species of *Callitriche* (including *C. heterophylla* and *C. rimosa*) have a form of self-fertilization (internal geitonogamy) not known elsewhere in angiosperms. Only the anthers that occur in the axils of floating leaves reach full maturity; anthers on submerged stems develop to only a fraction of the mature size. Pistillate flowers exhibit a similar level of development (mature styles in aerial flowers, highly reduced styles in submerged flowers). Pollen grains germinate within both the mature (prior to dehiscence) and underdeveloped anthers. The resulting pollen tubes grow out of the anther, through the filament, into the vegetative tissues of the stem, and finally enter the ovary of a pistillate flower at the same or adjacent node, thereby effecting fertilization.

No information is available about dispersal biology.

Economic uses. Species of *Callitriche* are of little economic value. *Callitriche stagnalis* is used occasionally as a water-garden plant. This species is also introduced widely in the eastern and northwestern United States and New Zealand and can be a troublesome aquatic weed.

References. BACIGALUPO, N. M. 1979. El genero *Callitriche* en la Flora argentina. *Darwiniana* 22:377–96. COOPER, R. L., J. M. OSBORN, C. T. PHILBRICK. 2000. Comparative pollen morphology and ultrastructure of the Callitrichaceae. *Amer. J. Bot.* 87:161–75. FASSETT N. C. 1951. *Callitriche* in the New World. *Rhodora* 53:137–55; 161–82; 185–94; 209–22. PHILBRICK C. T., AND ANDERSON G. J. 1992. Pollination biology in the Callitrichaceae. *Syst. Bot.* 17:282–92. PHILBRICK, C. T., AND LES D. H. 2000. Phylogenetic studies in *Callitriche*: implications for interpretation of ecological, karyological and pollination system evolution. *Aquatic Bot.* 68:123–41. SCHOTSMAN, H. D. 1954. A taxonomic spectrum of the section *Eu-callitriche* in the Netherlands. *Acta Bot. Neerl.* 3:313–85. SCHOTSMAN, H. D. 1982. Biologie Florale des *Callitriche*: étude sur quelques espèces d'Espagne meridionale. *Adansonia* 3–4:111–60. SCULTHORPE, C. D. 1967. *The Biology of Aquatic Vascular Plants*. London: Edward Arnold Publishers.

CALYCERACEAE (Calycera Family)

SCOTT V. HEALD

- *herbs, resembling Asteraceae*

- *leaves alternate, often in basal rosettes, simple*

- *inflorescences capitulate; subtended by involucral bracts*

- *flowers sympetalous; stamens adnate to corolla, the filaments with glandlike bodies; ovary inferior*

- *fruits achenes with persistent calyx*

Numbers of genera and species. The Calyceraceae comprise six genera and circa 60 species restricted to South America. In tropical South America, there are two genera, *Acicarpha* (five species) and *Boopis* (13). *Calycera* (circa 15), *Moschopsis* (8), *Gamocarpha* (6), and *Acarpha* (1) are extratropical.

Distribution and habitat. Most species of Calyceraceae are found in dry, open scrub habitats of the southern Andes and Patagonia. A few species grow in coastal sand dunes. In the neotropics, *Acicarpha* grows in tropical South America; *Boopis* in the Andes, Argentina, and southern Brazil; and *Calycera* in temperate South America. *Acarpha* and *Gamocarpha* are found in temperate South America and *Moschopsis* in Patagonia, Chile.

Reports of Calyceraceae in Central America appear to be mistaken.

Family classification. Cronquist placed the Calyceraceae in their own order, the Calycerales. He attributed similarities to the Asteraceae (pollen presentation, presence of inulins, pollen wall structure) to parallelisms, stressing instead the differences in ovule placentation and putative plesiomorphic character states (habit, leaf arrangement). Consequently, he considered them derived from the Dipsacales (similar inflorescences and pendulous ovules), and more distantly related to the Asterales. Other systematists closely ally the Calyceraceae and Asteraceae. The family differs from the Asteraceae in having an entire stigma and in lacking a pappus and/or ray flowers. While debate as to the sister group of the Asteraceae continues, cladistic analyses of morphological and molecular data have reduced the list of candidates to Calyceraceae and Goodeniaceae (or the two groups combined). Wood anatomy offers one line of evidence suggesting a sister relationship between Calyceraceae and Asteraceae (libriform fibers with simple pits, vasicentric axial parenchyma), with Goodeniaceae perhaps sister to them. Moreover, these three families, together with the Brunoniaceae, form a well-supported clade sharing pollen wall and stamen filament characters. This hypothesis suggests that connate anthers, secondary pollen presentation on the style, and late style elongation are parallelisms with the Campanulaceae *sensu lato*.

Features of the family. Habit: annual, biennial, or perennial herbs (resembling Asteraceae), rarely suffructescent (typically forming only 1–2 mm thick of secondary xylem at stem base and adjacent root area), rarely pubescent. **Stipules** absent. **Leaves** alternate, often in basal rosettes, simple; blades with entire or pinnately lobed margins. **Inflorescences** terminal on scapes or axillary, capitulate, these solitary or in cymose panicles, the capitula subtended by involucral bracts; flowers numerous, opening centripetally (*Acicarpha*) or in a more complex manner; peduncles short or absent (*Acicarpha* and some species of *Boopis*); pedicels absent. **Flowers** actinomorphic or rarely slightly zygomorphic, bisexual (in *Acicarpha* peripheral flowers fertile, central flowers sterile or female-sterile); calyx with (4)5(6) small lobes; corolla sympetalous, the lobes (4)5(6), valvate; androecium with stamens equal in number and alternate with corolla lobes, adnate near summit of corolla tube, the filaments connate, at least toward base, provided with glandlike bodies adaxially toward base, the glandlike bodies alternate with filaments, ± salient, the anthers ± connate, introrse, dehiscing by longitudinal slits, secondarily presenting pollen by depositing it on extending style; gynoecium syncarpous, the ovary inferior, the carpels 2, the locule 1, the style terminal, glabrous (unlike pubescent style in Asteraceae), the stigma capitate; ovule 1, apical (unlike basal ovule in Asteraceae), pendulous. **Fruits** achenes, with persistent calyx (this lignescent and spiny in *Acicarpha* and *Calycera*), ribbed and receptacle small in *Boopis*, dispersed singly or together with entire head. **Seeds** with endosperm in various amounts, oily, the embryo straight.

The Calyceraceae store carbohydrates as inulin, possess iridoid compounds, and lack tannins, ellagic acid, and latex. The family lacks the more sophisticated chemical arsenal of the Asteraceae (polyacetylenes and sesquiterpenes, etc.).

Natural history. No information is available about pollination biology. Fruit dispersal is by attachment to animals' bodies. This is especially well developed in *Acicarpha* and *Calycera*, which possess fruits enclosed by adherent, spiny calyces. Detached capitula may also be windblown.

Economic uses. No uses are known for this family.

References. BREMER, K. 1994. *Asteraceae: Cladistics and Classification.* Portland, OR: Timber Press. CARLQUIST, S., AND M. L. DEVORE. 1998. Wood anatomy of Calyceraceae with reference to ecology, habit, and systematic relationships. *Aliso* 17(1):63–76. GUSTAFSSON, M.H.G., AND K. BREMER. 1995. Morphology and phylogenetic relationships of the Asteraceae, Calyceraceae, Campanulaceae, Goodeniaceae, and related families (Asterales). *Amer. J. Bot.* 82(2): 250–65. HANSEN, H. V. 1992. Studies in the Calyceraceae with a discussion of its relationship to Compositae. *Nordic J. Bot.* 12:63–75. PONTIROLI, A. 1963. Flora Argentina: Calyceraceae. *Revista Mus. La Plata, Secc. Bot.* 9(41):175–241.

CAMPANULACEAE (Bellflower Family)

THOMAS G. LAMMERS

Figure 38, Plate 10

- *herbs, shrubs, treelets, trees, or lianas*

- *plants with milky latex*

- *leaves usually alternate, simple*

- *flowers zygomorphic, often showy, resupinate; corolla often tubular; stamens 5, connate into column; hairs or scales often present at apex of lower anthers*

- *ovary usually inferior; stigma subtended by ring of hairs*

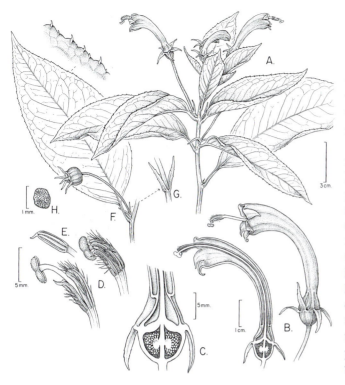

Figure 38. CAMPANULACEAE. *Centropogon cornutus*. **A.** Stem with leaves and flowers. **B.** Lateral (right) and medial section (left) of flowers. **C.** Medial section of base of flower. **D.** Two views of apical portion of androecium with style exserted to different degrees. **E.** Adaxial view of lower anther. **F.** Fruit and leaf with detail of margin (above). **G.** Detail of floral bracts. **H.** Seed. Reprinted with permission from Mori et al. (2002). Artist: Bobbi Angell.

Numbers of genera and species. Worldwide, the Campanulaceae comprise 84 genera and approximately 2,400 species. In tropical America, there are eight genera and nearly 700 species, all belonging to subfamily Lobelioideae. After cosmopolitan *Lobelia*, with more than 400 species (more than one-fourth of which are Neotropical), the largest genera are the Neotropical endemics *Siphocampylus* (229 species), *Centropogon* (217), and *Burmeistera* (96). Also found in the neotropics are the endemics *Lysipomia* (27), *Diastatea* (5), and *Heterotoma* and *Hippobroma* (both monotypic).

Distribution and habitat. The Campanulaceae are represented on all continents save Antarctica, and range from as far north as the Arctic Circle to as far south as Cape Horn. Only the Lobelioideae are found in tropical America, where 60 percent of that subfamily occurs. The three largest Neotropical genera collectively are found from southern Mexico to Bolivia and Argentina, with a few species in the Greater and Lesser Antilles.

The Campanulaceae occupy a wide range of habitats, from shallow water to sclerophyllous deserts. Species of *Burmeistera*, *Centropogon*, and *Siphocampylus* are especially abundant in mid- to high-elevation mesic to wet forests of the Andes from Colombia to Bolivia, while species of *Lysipomia* are found in *páramos* of the same region.

Family classification. The Campanulaceae are placed in the Campanulales by Cronquist. Molecular analyses suggest that the Campanulaceae form a clade with the families of this order (except Sphenocleaceae), as well as with other families such as Asteraceae and Calyceraceae.

Currently, the Campanulaceae are divided into five subfamilies: Campanuloideae, Cyphioideae, Cyphocarpoideae, Lobelioideae, and Nemacladoideae. The more temperate Campanuloideae differ from the Lobelioideae primarily in their actinomorphic flowers, nonconnate stamens, and 3–5-celled ovaries. The other three subfamilies have zygomorphic flowers and 2-celled ovaries, but the anthers (and sometimes the filaments) are distinct. The Lobelioideae traditionally have been divided into two tribes based on fruit type: dehiscent in Lobelieae, indehiscent in Delisseeae. However, current opinion considers this distinction highly artificial and seed-coat morphology seems to be a better indicator of relationships. Generic circumscription of the Lobelioideae is as problematic as the tribal classification, and it is quite likely that only a few of the genera are monophyletic.

Features of the family. Habit: herbs, shrubs, treelets, trees, lianas, sometimes cushion plants or in giant monocarpic or polycarpic rosettes, epiphytic in some *Burmeistera* and *Lysipomia*, plants ranging from a few centimeters tall to 10+ m tall. **Latex** present, milky, usually white. **Indument** of unicellular or uniseriate hairs, arbusculiform hairs in many species of *Centropogon*, a few *Siphocampylus*, and one *Burmeistera*. **Stipules** absent. **Leaves** alternate, rarely opposite or whorled, usually simple; blades sometimes deeply pinnatifid in some *Burmeistera* and *Centropogon*, the margins entire or toothed, sometimes deeply or sharply so. **Inflorescences** terminal or axillary, of solitary flowers in upper leaf axils, or if leaves subtending flowers conspicuously and abruptly smaller than foliage leaves (i.e., bracts), then racemes, sometimes transitional between these extremes, with first flowers opening in axils of normal foliage leaves and last flowers subtended by highly reduced bracts, the racemes usually terminal (sometimes branched at base); bracts resembling foliage leaves only smaller; pedicels usually present; bracteoles often present, paired, sometimes large and foliaceous. **Flowers** zygomorphic, bisexual, resupinate, rather large (avg. 30–60+ mm long), often showy; hypanthium present, often elongate and pedicel-like in species with sessile flowers; calyx adnate to ovary, 5-lobed; corolla often tubular, the tube straight or curved, sometimes slit along top or open along sides (i.e., fenestrate), the lobes 5, unilabiate (lobes deflexed in a single plane), bilabiate (with a pair of upper lobes and 3 lower lobes), tubular (lobes very short relative to tube), or rarely salverform (*Hippobroma*); nectar spurs present in *Heterotoma* and a few species of *Lobelia*; androecium of 5 stamens, the stamens connate into column, portion of column formed by anthers typically oblique, the 3 upper anthers overhang 2 lower ones, thus occluding anther tube mouth, the lower 2 anthers often with tufts of stiff hairs or scales at apex; gynoecium syncarpous, the ovary usually inferior (nearly superior in *Diastatea* and a few *Lobelia*), the carpels 2, the locules (1)2, the style 1, surrounded by connate stamens, the stigma 2-lobed, surrounded basally by a ring of hairs; placentation axile (parietal in 1-locular ovaries), the ovules usually numerous, small. **Fruits** capsules or berries (*Burmeistera*, *Centropogon*, and a few *Lobelia*), the capsules opening via two triangular apical valves (circumscissile in *Lysipomia*). **Seeds** numerous, small.

Though production of a terminal raceme typically halts further growth of that shoot, some species of *Centropogon* have the ability to resume vegetative growth from the raceme apex.

In large-flowered species of Lobelioideae, red, orange, or yellow floral pigments predominate, but greenish and maroon hues are also common. The lobes and tube of the corolla often are contrasting colors. In small-flowered species, the corolla is typically blue, purplish, or white. In many species of *Lobelia*, the lower lobes are distinctly larger than the upper, while the reverse is true in *Burmeistera* and many species of *Centropogon* and *Siphocampylus*.

Natural history. Flowers of subfamily Lobelioideae exhibit a highly specialized cross-pollination mechanism that is exclusively animal-mediated. Individual flowers are protandrous; i.e., shedding pollen before the stigma is receptive. In the staminate phase, the anthers dehisce introrsely, shedding their pollen into a tube formed by the anthers. As the style (with its ring of sweeping hairs and its as-yet-unreceptive stigma) grows up through the staminal column, it places pressure on this pollen load. The pollen usually cannot be dispersed because the overhang of the three upper anthers effectively closes the mouth of the tube. However, the mouth is forced open when a foraging pollinator brushes against the stiff hairs or scales at the apex of the two lower anthers. When this happens, an ample load of pollen is deposited on the pollinator. The style continues to elongate and sometime later, its apex emerges from the mouth of the anther tube, thus beginning the flower's pistillate phase. The stigmatic lobes unfurl, becoming receptive to pollen, and they are placed at exactly the right position to pick up pollen deposited on a pollinator by other flowers of the same species. Pollination in smaller flowers is mediated by a variety of insects, including bees, wasps, flies, butterflies, and moths; and by hummingbirds (rarely bats and hawkmoths) in larger flowers. Interestingly, the yellow-flowered *Siphocampylus sulphureus* was recently shown to be pollinated by hummingbirds by day and bats by night. Mites dwelling in the flowers are dispersed among plants from the bills and nasal cavities of visiting hummingbirds.

Birds and bats that feed on fruit are important as seed dispersers in the species that produce berries. Other species are presumably wind-dispersed and in fact, some Neotropical *Lobelia* have winged seeds. Several species of *Centropogon*

and one of *Siphocampylus*, which grow in the foothills of the Andes, bear nectaries on the outer surface of the calyx. Their sugar-rich secretions attract ants, which presumably defend the flowers against insect predators.

Economic uses. Subfamily Lobelioideae are of only minor economic importance. A few species with colorful flowers (most notably *Lobelia erinus* of South Africa) are used as ornamentals. The potential of the group for gardening certainly seems greater than its current level of usage.

The latex of species contains various alkaloids that are highly irritating to the eyes and mucous membranes and may be toxic if ingested. The alkaloid lobeline is extracted commercially from *L. inflata* (Indian tobacco) of North America, but occurs in many members of the family. It is used in certain over-the-counter preparations to help overcome nicotine addiction and formerly was much used in relieving symptoms of bronchial asthma and other respiratory disorders. In some areas of the neotropics, fresh berries and cooked leaves of various *Centropogon* species are minor foodstuffs, whereas other species are used medicinally in the treatment of wounds, flatulence, and infections of the genitourinary tract.

References. JEPPESEN, S. 1981. Lobeliaceae. In *Flora of Ecuador*, eds. G. Harling and B. Sparre, no. 14:9–170. Göteborg, Sweden: Department of Systematic Botany, University of Göteborg. LAMMERS, T. G. 1993. Chromosome numbers of Campanulaceae. III. Review and integration of data for subfamily Lobelioideae. *Amer. J. Bot.* 80:660–75. LAMMERS, T. G. 1998. Review of the Neotropical endemics *Burmeistera*, *Centropogon*, and *Siphocampylus* (Campanulaceae: Lobelioideae), with description of 18 new species and a new section. *Brittonia* 50:233–62. LAMMERS, T. G. 1998. Nemacladoideae, a new subfamily of Campanulaceae. *Novon* 6: 36–37. LAMMERS, T. G. 2002. Seventeen new species of Lobelioideae (Campanulaceae) from South America *Novon* 12: 206–33. MCVAUGH, R. 1943. Campanulaceae (Lobelioideae). N. Amer. Fl. 32A:1–134. MCVAUGH, R. 1949. Studies in South American Lobelioideae (Campanulaceae) with special reference to Colombian species. *Brittonia* 6: 450–93. MURATA, J. 1995. A revision of infrageneric classification of *Lobelia* (Campanulaceae-Lobelioideae) with special reference to seed coat morphology. *J. Fac. Sci. Univ. Tokyo*, sect. 3, 15:349–71. SAZIMA, M., I. SAZIMA, AND S. BUZATO. 1994. Nectar by day and night: *Siphocampylus sulphureus* (Lobeliaceae) pollinated by hummingbirds and bats. *Pl. Syst. Evol.* 191:237–46. STEIN, B. A. 1992. Sicklebill hummingbirds, ants, and flowers. *BioScience* 42:27–33. WIMMER, F. E. 1943. Campanulaceae-Lobelioideae, I. Teil. In *Das Pflanzenreich*, IV.276b, ed. R. Mansfeld, heft 106: i–viii, 1–260. Berlin: Wilhelm Engelmann. WIMMER, F. E. 1953. Campanulaceae-Lobelioideae, II. Teil. In *Das Pflanzenreich*, IV.276b, ed. R. Mansfeld, heft 107:i–viii, 261–814. Berlin: Wilhelm Engelmann.

CANELLACEAE (Canella Family)

Thomas A. Zanoni

Figure 39

- *trees*

- *plants aromatic*

- *leaves alternate, simple, pellucid dots often present*

- *flowers actinomorphic, bisexual; filaments fused into tube, the anthers on outside*

- *fruits berries*

Numbers of genera and species. Worldwide, the Canellaceae comprise six genera and circa 15 species. In tropical America, there are four genera: *Canella* (1 species), *Capsicodendron* (2), *Cinnamodendron* (6), and *Pleodendron* (1).

Distribution and habitat. Species of Canellaceae are found in the Americas, tropical Africa, and Madagascar. In the Western Hemisphere, the family occurs in southern Florida (*Canella*), the West Indies (*Canella, Cinnamodendron, Pleodendron*), Venezuela (*Cinnamodendron*), and Brazil (*Capsicodendron, Cinnamodendron*). Most species of the Western Hemisphere are of very local distribution, and except for the widespread West Indian *Canella winterana*, most are restricted to single islands or a few states within a country.

The family is found mostly at low elevations in mixed semievergreen to evergreen forests, often on limestone and sometimes as part of the forest canopy.

Family classification. The Canellaceae are placed in the Magnoliales by Cronquist. Other authors suggest that the family belongs near the Winteraceae, and this is supported by recent molecular studies. There is no subdivision below the family level.

Features of the family. Habit: trees, aromatic, ethereal oil cells in parenchyma of bark and leaves. Stems with nonseptate pith. Stipules absent. Leaves alternate, simple; blades often thick and coriaceous, pellucid dots often present; venation pinnate, the pattern conspicuous on dried leaves. Inflorescences terminal or axillary, cymes, racemes, or of solitary flowers in leaf axils. Flowers actinomorphic, bisexual; sepals 3; petals (4)5–12 in 1–2(4) whorls, imbricate, usually distinct or slightly connate (*Canella*); androecium usually of 6–12 (40 in *Cinnamodendron*) stamens, the filaments connate, forming tube around ovary, the anthers on outside of tube; gynoecium syncarpous, the ovary superior, the carpels 2–6, the locule 1, the stigma lobes 2–6; placentation parietal, the ovules 2–many, in 1 or 2 rows on each placenta. Fruits berries. Seeds 2–many, hard; endocarp abundant, oily.

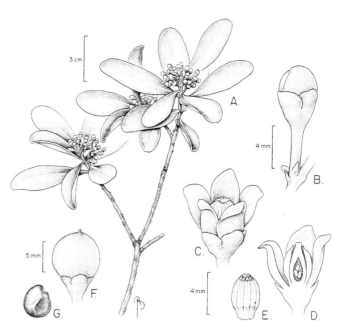

Figure 39. CANELLACEAE. *Canella winterana.* **A.** Stems with leaves and inflorescences. **B.** Lateral view of flower bud. **C.** Lateral view of flower. **D.** Medial section of flower. **E.** Lateral view of androecium with connate filaments. **F.** Lateral view of fruit. **G.** Seed. Reprinted with permission from Acevedo-Rodríguez (1996). Artist: Bobbi Angell.

Natural history. No information is available about pollination biology. The berries are eaten by birds.

Economic uses. The aromatic leaves and bark are used to make tea and traditional medicine. *Canella winterana* can serve as a substitute for cinnamon (*Cinnamomum*, Lauraceae) in flavoring foods; however, commercial use apparently has ceased.

References. Bhandari, N. N. 1971. Embryology of the Magnoliales and comments on their relationships. *J. Arnold Arbor.* 52:285–304. Ehrendorfer, F., and M. Lambrou. 2000. Chromosomes of *Takhatajania*, other Winteraceae, and Canellaceae: phylogenetic implications. *Ann. Missouri Bot. Gard.* 87:407–13. Kubitzki, K. Canellaceae. 1993. In *The Families and Genera of Vascular Plants*, eds. K. Kubitzki, J. G. Rohwer, and V. Bittrich, 2:200–03. Berlin: Springer-Verlag. Suh, Y., L. B. Thien, H. E. Reeve, and E. A. Zimmer. 1993. Molecular evolution and phylogenetic implications of internal transcribed spacer sequences of ribosomal DNA in Winteraceae. *Amer. J. Bot.* 80:1042–55. Wood, C. E., Jr. 1958. The genera of the woody Ranales in the southeastern United States. *J. Arnold Arbor.* 39:320–22.

CAPPARACEAE (Caper Family)

MICHAEL NEE

Figure 40, Plate 10

- *small trees, shrubs, sometimes vines or herbs*
- *mustard-oil glucosides present (often giving the plant a cabbagelike odor)*
- *leaves usually alternate*
- *flowers with a gynophore; placentation parietal*

Numbers of genera and species. Worldwide, the Capparaceae comprise circa 36 genera and 600 species. In tropical America, there are eight genera and circa 145 species. Several genera of the Cleomoideae are found in the deserts of northwestern Mexico, just outside the neotropics. The largest Neotropical genera are *Capparis* (circa 50 species, widespread), *Cleome* (40 species, widespread), *Forchhammeria* (10 species, centered in Mexico), and *Podandrogyne* (25 species, Central America to Andes); the rest of the genera have six or fewer species.

Distribution and habitat. The family is widespread in the Tropics and subtropics. Both *Koeberlinia spinosa* and *Capparis atamisquea* are disjunct between arid areas of Bolivia and Argentina and the Sonoran Desert region of the southwestern United States and northwestern Mexico.

Shrubs of the Capparoideae are most common in semiarid habitats and tropical deciduous forests, but are sometimes present in rain forests. The shrub species of Capparaceae growing in semiarid habitats often remain in leaf during the long, hot, dry season, whereas species of other families of tropical thorn-scrub vegetation are deciduous. *Koeberlinia spinosa* is a nearly leafless shrub with spiny branchlets. The Cleomoideae often grow in disturbed habitats. The Cleomoideae range from herbaceous desert annuals to short-lived, perennial, soft-wooded shrubs in humid areas.

Family classification. The Capparaceae are placed in the Capparales by Cronquist who recognized two subfamilies: the mainly woody and evidently more primitive Capparoideae, with affinities with the Flacourtiaceae and allied families of the Violales, and the mainly herbaceous Cleomoideae, with affinities with the Brassicaceae. Recent morphological and molecular studies suggest that this family is paraphyletic and may be better placed within a more broadly defined Brassicaceae.

Features of the family. Habit: small trees, shrubs, sometimes vines or herbs, annuals, mustard-oil glucosides present, often giving plant a cabbagelike odor. **Stipules** small or absent. **Leaves** usually alternate, rarely opposite, often simple,

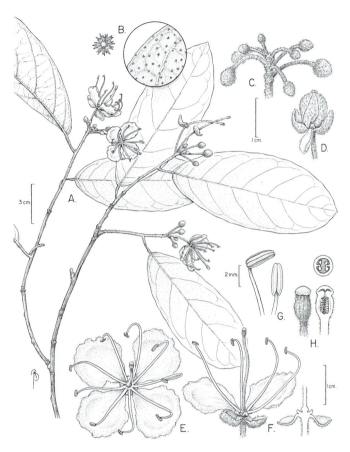

Figure 40. CAPPARACEAE. *Capparis leprieurii*. **A.** Stem with leaves, buds, and flowers. **B.** Detail of abaxial surface of nearly fully expanded leaf (right) and enlargement of stellate-echinate hair (left). **C.** Inflorescence with flowers in bud. **D.** Lateral view of mature bud with inner sepal pulled down to show nectar scale. **E.** Apical view of flower. **F.** Lateral view of flower with two petals and five stamens removed (left) and medial section of base of flower (right); both show nectar scales. **G.** Lateral (left) and abaxial (right) views of anthers. **H.** Lateral view of gynoecium at apex of gynophore (left), medial section of gynoecium (right), and transverse section of ovary (above). Reprinted with permission from Mori et al. (2002). Artist: Bobbi Angell.

sometimes compound (palmate in most Clemoideae, rarely trifoliate; e.g., *Crataeva*); blade margins entire. **Inflorescences** axillary or terminal, bracteate racemes (especially Cleomoideae). **Flowers** actinomorphic or zygomorphic, usually bisexual, often showy; sepals 2, 4, or 6, distinct or joined at base; petals 2, 4, or 6, distinct; stamens 2, 4, or 6–many, sometimes fused to gynophore forming an androgynophore; gynophore present; ovary superior; carpels 2(12), fused, the locule 1, the style 1; placentation parietal, the ovules usually numerous. **Fruits** berrylike or capsules, stipitate, the berrylike fruits coriaceous, the capsules dry or fleshy. **Seeds** large (in berrylike fruits), or small (in capsules), fleshy (in berrylike fruits), or hard (in capsules).

Natural history. The long stamens and style of most tropical species of Cleomoideae are adapted to butterfly pollination, but some of the zygomorphic flowers are pollinated by hummingbirds (*Podandrogyne* and *Steriphoma*) or bees (mostly several small genera in the western United States outside the Neotropical region).

No information is available about dispersal biology.

Economic uses. The caper, *Capparis spinosa* of the Mediterranean region, is used as a condiment, but species of Neotropical Capparaceae are seldom used for food. The sweet fruit pulp of *C. prisca* of Peru and Bolivia is edible, whereas the fruits of *C. speciosa* are so strongly scented that even swine will not eat them. The spider plant, *Cleome hasslerana* (formerly known as *C. spinosa*), originally from the Paraguay region, is grown widely as an ornamental for its showy flowers. A number of medicinal uses have been reported for species of *Capparis* and *Cleome* in Colombia.

References. BERNAL, H. Y., AND J. E. CORRERA Q. 1990. Capparaceae. In *Especies vegetales promisorias de los países del Convenio Andrés Bello*, Tomo IV. Bogotá, D. E., Colombia: Secretaria Ejecutiva del Convenio Andrés Bello. HALL, J. C., K. J. SYTSMA, AND H. H. ILTIS. 2002. Phylogeny of Capparaceae and Brassicaceae based on chloroplast sequence data. *Amer. J. Bot.* 89(1):1826–42. KERS, L. E. 2003. Capparaceae. In *The Families and Genera of Vascular Plants*, eds. K. Kubitzki and C. Bayer. 5:36–56. Berlin: Springer-Verlag. KUBITZKI, K. 2003. Koeberliniaceae. In *The Families and Genera of Vascular Plants*, eds. K. Kubitzki and C. Bayer. 5:218–219. Berlin: Springer-Verlag. RODMAN, J. E., K. G. KAROL, R. A. PRICE, AND K. J. SYTSMA. 1996. Molecules, morphology, and Dahlgren's expanded order Capparales. *Syst. Bot.* 21(3):289–307.

CAPRIFOLIACEAE (Honeysuckle Family)

PIERO G. DELPRETE

Figure 41

- *shrubs, vines, lianas, or rarely trees*
- *leaves usually opposite, decussate, simple or compound*
- *flowers sympetalous; ovary inferior or rarely subinferior*
- *fruits berries*

Numbers of genera and species. Worldwide, the Caprifoliaceae (*sensu* Cronquist) comprise 17 genera and circa 445 species. In tropical America, there are four native genera: *Lonicera* (circa 15 species), *Sambucus* (circa 10), *Symphoricarpos* (seven), and *Viburnum* (circa 60). There are no genera endemic to the neotropics.

Distribution and habitat. All genera of the Caprifoliaceae are endemic or at least occur in Eurasia and North America, and species of all of them have been introduced into cultivation.

Neotropical Caprifoliaceae are found in subtropical and tropical areas in Central and South America Species of *Symphoricarpos* are native to Mexico and Central America (common species are *S. microphyllus* and *S. rotundifolius*) and species of *Lonicera* are native to Mexico and Central America. In addition, several species of *Lonicera* native to the Eastern Hemisphere are cultivated and naturalized in Central and

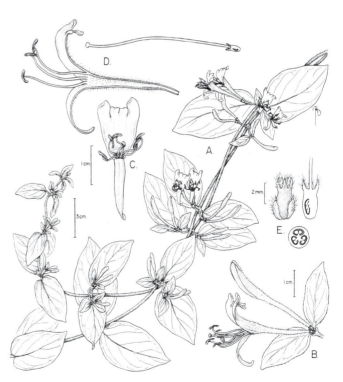

Figure 41. CAPRIFOLIACEAE. *Lonicera japonica*. **A.** Stem with leaves and inflorescences. **B.** Flower bud and flower in leaf axil. **C.** Apical view of flower. **D.** Medial section of corolla showing adnate stamens (below) and medial section of gynoecium (above). **E.** Lateral view of young fruit (left), medial section of young fruit (right), and transverse section of ovary (below). Reprinted with permission from Acevedo-Rodríguez (2003). Artist: Bobbi Angell.

South America. *Sambucus* has six species native to Mexico and Central America, two species (*S. peruviana*, *S. simpsonii*) range from Central to South America, and one species (*S. australis*) is endemic to southern Brazil, Uruguay, and Argentina. *Sambucus canadensis*, a native of North America, and *S. nigra*, a native of Eurasia, are naturalized in the neotropics. *Viburnum* is the most speciose genus of Caprifoliaceae in the neotropics, with 30 species in Mexico and Central America and 29 species in South America. Several species of *Viburnum* native to the Eastern Hemisphere have also been introduced into tropical America. *Abelia* has two species endemic to subtropical Mexico (*A. floribunda* and *A. coriacea*).

Neotropical Caprifoliaceae are present in a variety of habitats. *Sambucus* and *Viburnum* have many species endemic to semiarid and subtropical areas of Mexico and Central America, where they occur as shrubs or small trees. *Sambucus peruviana* is endemic to the rain forests of Central and South America, while *S. australis* is restricted to the subtropical forests of southern Brazil, Uruguay, and northern Argentina.

Family classification. The definition and position of the Caprifoliaceae is still debated. Cronquist placed Caprifoliaceae in the Dipsacales, along with the Adoxaceae, Valerianaceae, and Dipsacaceae. Several authors have placed *Sambucus* and *Viburnum* in the Adoxaceae, and several others have separated *Sambucus* into a monotypic family, the Sambucaceae. Recent phylogenetic analyses using morphological and molecular data support placing *Sambucus* and *Viburnum* in a monophyletic clade with *Adoxa*. The same analyses also demonstrated that the Caprifoliaceae *sensu stricto* are paraphyletic and form a monophyletic group with the Valerianaceae and Dipsacaceae, resulting in a wide delimitation of the Caprifoliaceae. The Caprifoliaceae are treated herein as defined by Cronquist.

Features of the family. Habit: shrubs, vines, lianas, or rarely trees. **Indument** extremely variable, the hairs glandular, unicellular or multicellular. **Stipules** absent, vestigial, or small, interpetiolar, sometimes transformed into extrafloral nectaries (*Sambucus* and *Viburnum*). **Leaves** opposite (decussate), rarely ternate in some *Viburnum*, simple, or pinnately compound in *Sambucus*; petioles absent in some species of several genera (e.g., *Lonicera*); blades (and leaflets of *Sambucus*) commonly elliptic, the margins dentate, serrate, or rarely entire. **Inflorescences** terminal or axillary, cymose, or of paired or solitary flowers. **Flowers** zygomorphic or actinomorphic in *Sambucus* and *Viburnum*, bisexual; calyx (4)5-merous, commonly small; corolla sympetalous, tubular, campanulate, funnel-shaped and bilabiate or rotate in *Sambucus* and *Viburnum*, the lobes imbricate or rarely valvate; androecium with stamens equal in number to calyx lobes, the filaments adnate to corolla, the anthers dorsifixed, versatile, dehiscing by longitudinal slits; gynoecium syncarpous, the ovary inferior or rarely subinferior, the carpels 2–3(5–8), the locules 2–3(5–8), 1–several often aborting, the style 1, the stigma capitate or lobed; placentation usually axile, sometimes parietal, the ovules 1–many per locule, pendulous. **Fruits** berries. **Seeds** 1–many.

Sambucus has stipules that range in shape from leaflike to glandlike. These are usually in pairs at the leaf bases and are interpreted by some authors as "pseudostipules" or "stipular appendages." These stipules have extrafloral nectaries. In *Viburnum*, the stipules are reduced to interpetiolar scars with minute extrafloral nectaries.

Most Caprifoliaceae produce iridoid compounds, saponins, proanthocyanins, tannins, and rarely alkaloids.

Calcium oxalate crystals are present in all taxa in the form of raphids, styloids, and crystal sands.

Natural history. The extrafloral nectaries on the stipules of *Sambucus* produce nectar that attracts ants. The ants apparently patrol the plants and protect them against parasitic insects, such as gall-wasps. In some species of *Viburnum*, the minute stipules have extrafloral nectaries that suggest the same ant/plant association, but this has not been documented.

Caprifoliaceae are pollinated by bees, wasps, moths, and hummingbirds. Different pollination strategies have evolved within the same genus; e.g., white-flowered species of *Lonicera* are pollinated by moths and red-flowered species are pollinated by hummingbirds. *Sambucus* and *Viburnum* are visited and most likely pollinated by Diptera, Coleoptera, Homoptera, and Hymenoptera.

The fleshy berries of species of *Lonicera*, *Viburnum*, and *Sambucus* are mostly bird dispersed.

Economic uses. Many species of Caprifoliaceae are cultivated as ornamentals. Most of these species have common names related to their ornamental features, for example, bush honeysuckle (*Diervilla*), honeysuckle (*Lonicera*), beauty bush (*Kolkwitzia*), twinflower (*Linnaea*), and coralberry or snowberry (*Symphoricarpos*). Many Paleotropical taxa have been introduced into cultivation in the Western Hemisphere as ornamentals, and several of them are naturalized. *Lonicera japonica* (Japanese honeysuckle) and *L. caprifolium* are aggressive weeds throughout the Americas.

The leaves of *Sambucus peruviana* and *S. australis* are used by indigenous people of South America as diuretics and to reduce fevers. The fruits of several species of *Sambucus* (elder) are used in Europe for flavoring liqueur (e.g., sambuca in Italy) and for making wine and in North and Central America for making jellies and pies.

References. BACKLUND, A. 1996. Phylogeny of the Dipsacales. Ph.D. dissertation, Uppsala University. BERNAL, H. Y., AND J. E. CORRERA Q. 1990. Caprifoliaceae. In *Especies vegetales promisorias de los países del Convenio Andrés Bello*, Tomo IV. Bogotá, D. E., Colombia: Secretaria Ejecutiva del Convenio Andrés Bello. BOLLI, R. 1994. Revision of the genus *Sambucus*. Dissertationes Botanicae, band 223. CANDOLLE, A. DE. 1839. Note sur le genre *Weigela*. [tiré de la Bibliothèque Universelle de Genève]. DONOGUE, M. J. 1983. The phylogenetic relationships of *Viburnum*. In N. I. Platnick and V. A. Funk (eds.), Advances in cladistics 2:143–66. DONOGUE, M. J., R. G. OLMSTEAD, J. F. SMITH, AND J. D. PALMER. 1992. Phylogenetic relationships of Dipsacales based on *rbc*L sequences. Ann. Missouri Bot. Gard. 79:333–45. FERGUSON, I. K. 1966. The genera of Caprifoliaceae in the southeastern United States. *J. Arnold Arbor.* 47:33–59. JONES, T. H. 1983. A revision of the genus *Viburnum* section *Lentago* (Caprifoliaceae). Ph.D. dissertation, North Carolina State University. JUDD, W. S., ET AL. 1994. Angiosperms family pairs: preliminary phylogenetic analyses. Harvard Pap. Bot: 5:1–51. KILLIP, E. P., AND A. C. SMITH. 1929. The genus *Viburnum* in northwestern South America *Bull. Torrey Bot. Club* 56:265–74. 1929. KILLIP, E. P., AND A. C. SMITH. 1930. The South American species of *Viburnum. Bull. Torrey Bot. Club.* 57:245–58. LIOGIER, A. 1963. Caprifoliaceae. *Flora de Cuba* 5:146–48. LIOGIER, A. 1995. Ca-

prifoliaceae. Flora de la Española 7:195–202. MORTON, C. V. 1933. The Mexican and Central American species of *Viburnum. Contrib. U. S. Natl. Herb.* 26:339–66. MÜLLER-ARGOVIENSIS, C. 1885. Caprifoliaceae. In: *Martius, Fl. Bras.* 6(4):334–338. OLMSTEAD, R. G., B. BREMER, K. M. SCOTT, AND J. D. PALMER. 1993. A parsimony analysis of the Asteridae sensu lato based on *rbc*L sequences. *Ann. Missouri Bot. Gard.* 80:700–22. REHDER, A. 1903. Synopsis of the genus *Lonicera.* Ann. Rep. Missouri Bot. Gard. 14:27–232, 20 plates. STANDLEY, P. C. 1924. Caprifoliaceae. Trees and shrubs of Mexico. Contrib. U. S. Natl. Herb. 23(4):1394–1400. THORNE, R. F. 1983. Proposed new realignments in the angiosperms. *Nordic J. Bot.* 3:85–117. WILKINSON, A. M. 1949. Floral anatomy and morphology of *Triosteum* and of the Caprifoliaceae in general. *Amer. J. Bot.* 36:481–89.

CARICACEAE (Papaya Family)

BENJAMIN M. TORKE

Figure 42, Plate 11

- *soft-wooded trees*
- *plants with milky latex*
- *leaves alternate, simple, trifoliate, or palmately compound*
- *flowers unisexual; placentation parietal*
- *fruits berries*
- *seeds numerous*

Numbers of genera and species. Worldwide, the Caricaceae comprise four genera and circa 33 species. In tropical America, there are three genera and 31 species. The largest genera are *Jacaratia* and *Carica*, with seven and 23 species, respectively. *Jarilla* is monotypic. There are two species in the African genus *Cylicomorpha*.

Distribution and habitat. The family is concentrated in the neotropics, particularly in the Andes. *Jarilla heterophylla* is found from northern Mexico and southern Baja California to northern Guatemala. *Carica* and *Jacaratia* are distributed from Mexico to central South America, with a few species, such as *J. chilensis* of northern Chile, occurring in subtropical regions.

The family is most prevalent in humid to seasonally dry tropical and subtropical forests, but some species occupy exposed or xerophytic habitats. Most species occur below 2,500 meters elevation, but several species of *Carica* reach higher

elevations, including *C. quercifolia* which has been recorded from nearly 3,500 meters.

Family classification. The Caricaceae have traditionally been placed in the Violales (i.e., *sensu* Cronquist), but recent findings place them close to the Moringaceae in an expanded Brassicales.

Relationships within the Caricaceae are poorly known. *Jarilla* possesses several unusual features of the androecium that are apparently ancestral within the family. *Jarilla* differs from *Carica* most obviously in its fruit with five basal horn-like appendages. *Jacaratia* is unique in its palmately compound leaves and in the positioning of the calyx lobes opposite the corolla lobes.

Features of the family. Habit: small trees, sparsely branched; milky latex present. Stems soft-wooded, a single layer of fiber-rich secondary phloem present (this accounts for most structural rigidity of stems), secondary xylem generally not lignified (functions in water and starch storage), the pith well developed. Stipules absent. Leaves alternate, distally clustered, simple (*Carica* and *Jarilla*), trifoliate or palmately compound (*Jacaratia*); petioles generally elongate; venation palmate, rarely more or less pinnate; blade margins entire, dentate, palmately lobed, or deeply incised. Inflorescences axillary, cymose, sparsely to much branched. Flowers actinomorphic, unisexual (plants usually dioecious, occasionally monoecious or polygamous), rarely bisexual; sepals 5, basally connate; petals 5, aestivation contorted or valvate, the

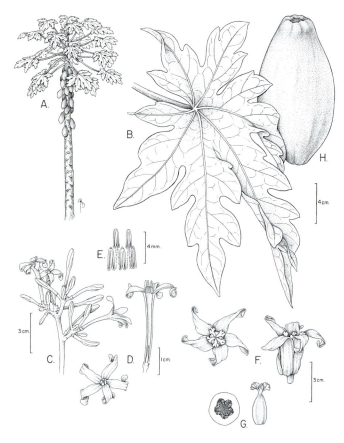

Figure 42. CARICACEAE. *Carica papaya*. **A.** Pistillate plant with upper part of stem, leaves, and fruits. **B.** Leaf. **C.** Part of staminate inflorescence. **D.** Apical view (left) and medial section (right) of staminate flower. **E.** Adaxial view of part of androecium. **F.** Apical (left) and lateral (right) views of pistillate flower. **G.** Transverse section of ovary (left) and lateral view (right) of gynoecium. **H.** Lateral view of fruit. Reprinted with permission from Mori et al. (2002). Artist: Bobbi Angell.

petals connate in elongate tube in staminate flowers, or tube short to scarcely distinct in pistillate and bisexual flowers, usually white, yellow, or green; androecium of 10 stamens, the stamens epipetalous, in 2 series, the outer series alternate petals, the filaments longer (except in *Jarilla*, with stamens of both series slightly offset petals), the inner series opposite petals, the filaments short or anthers sessile, the anther dehiscence introrse, the slits longitudinal, the thecae 2 or rarely 1 (outer series of *Jarilla*); gynoecium syncarpous, the ovary superior, the carpels 5, the locule 1, rarely 5, the style short, the stigmas 5, variously lobed; placentation parietal, the ovules numerous, anatropous. **Fruits** berries. **Seeds** numerous; endosperm oily, the embryo straight.

Natural history. The cultivated papaya is pollinated by hawkmoths and skipper butterflies, but other animals and in-sects, such as, hummingbirds, bees, and flies, frequently visit the flowers. The sweet-scented, nectar-bearing, tubular flowers of other species, often with white to yellow corollas, suggest that moths are important pollinators for the family as a whole, but there have been few observations to verify this. Dispersal probably is effected by a variety of animals, including mammals and birds that feed on the fleshy fruits.

Economic uses. The papaya (*Carica papaya*) is a major fruit crop in tropical America and elsewhere. Most commonly, the fruits are consumed raw but they also can be candied; cooked; or incorporated into beverages, preserves, pies, sherbets, and salads. Green fruits can be served as a vegetable or in salads and soups, but only after removal of skins and seeds and boiling to remove the latex.

Unripe fruits are tapped for their latex, which contains the commercially important enzyme papain. Papain readily digests protein and is the basis for commercial meat tenderizers. The enzyme has other applications in medicine, leather tanning, chewing gum, and cosmetics. A related enzyme in the latex, chymopapain, exhibits selective digestive properties that are useful in the treatment of persons with slipped spinal discs. In Panama, the ground seeds are added to honey and taken to treat intestinal parasites.

The papaya probably was domesticated in Central America in ancient times and may have arisen through hybridization, though it is believed that the species does not occur naturally outside of cultivation. Its affinities to other species of *Carica* are not well understood. The mountain papaya, *C. pubescens*, is cultivated in South America for its edible fruit at elevations above those of the common papaya. Locally, the fruits of other species, including *C. goudotiana*, *C. parviflora*, *Jacaratia mexicana*, and *Jarilla heterophylla*, are eaten or are made into beverages.

References. BADILLO, V. M. 1971. *Monografía de la Familia Caricaceae*. Maracay: Publicada por la Asociacion de profesores. BERNAL, H. Y., AND J. E. CORRERA Q. 1990. Caricaceae. In *Especies vegetales promisorias de los países del Convenio Andrés Bello*, Tomo IV. Bogotá, D. E., Colombia: Secretaria Ejecutiva del Convenio Andrés Bello. CARLQUIST, S. 1998. Wood and bark anatomy of Caricaceae: correlations with systematics and habit. *IAWA Journal* 19(2): 191–206. FREE, J. B. 1993. *Insect Pollination of Crops*. 2nd ed. London: Academic Press. KUBITZKI, K. 2003. Caricaceae In *The Families and Genera of Vascular Plants*, eds. K. Kubitzki and C. Bayer. 5:57–61. Berlin: Springer-Verlag. MORTON, J. F. 1987. *Fruits of Warm Climates*. Miami, FL: J. F. Morton. RODMAN, J. E., K. G. KAROL, R. A. PRICE, AND K. J. SYTSMA. 1996. Molecules, morphology, and Dahlgren's expanded order Capparales. *Syst. Bot.* 21:289–307.

CARYOCARACEAE (Souari Family)

SCOTT A. MORI

Figure 43, Plate 11

- *large trees, less frequently shrubs*

- *leaves opposite in* Caryocar, *alternate in* Anthodiscus, *usually palmate (mostly trifoliolate)*

- *flowers actinomorphic, nocturnal in* Caryocar, *diurnal in* Anthodiscus; *stamens numerous, the filaments often fused at base; ovary superior, with 1 ovule per locule*

- *fruits drupelike but separating into one-seeded pyrenes at maturity*

Numbers of genera and species. The Caryocaraceae comprise two genera, *Anthodiscus* (9 species) and *Caryocar* (16), restricted to tropical America.

Distribution and habitat. Species of Caryocaraceae range from Costa Rica to Paraguay and Paraná, Brazil, but are most common in Amazonia. Only a few species are found west of the Andes and in the coastal forests of eastern, extra-Amazonian Brazil. Amazonian species are found in *terra firme* forest, floodplain forests, and in forests on white sand. *Caryocar brasiliense* is a common species of savannas (*cerrado*) in the Planalto of Brazil.

Family classification. The Caryocaraceae are placed in the Theales by Cronquist, but some authors combine this family with the Theaceae and others have placed both the Caryocaraceae and the Theaceae in the Ternstroemiaceae. Molecular studies place the family in the Malpighiales among the Eurosids I. This new alignment no longer recognizes the Theales as an order and places erstwhile members of Theales *sensu* Cronquist in different clades.

Features of the family. Habit: mostly small to very large trees (some individuals of *Caryocar brasiliense* shrublike), the boles of some large *Caryocar* have conspicuous running buttresses. **Stipules** usually present, mostly caducous, leaving distinct scar, the scar crossing node in *Caryocar*, sometimes encircling stem in *Anthodiscus*; stipels present at base of leaflets in some *Caryocar*. **Leaves** opposite in *Caryocar*, alternate in *Anthodiscus*, usually palmate (mostly trifoliolate), simple leaves intermixed with palmate leaves in *Anthodiscus*; leaflet blades usually serrulate or serrate in *Caryocar*, crenulate or crenate in *Anthodiscus*. **Inflorescences** terminal, racemes. **Flowers** actinomorphic, bisexual, large and showy (especially in *Caryocar*); calyx 5(6)-lobed in *Caryocar*, cuplike with scarcely developed lobes in *Anthodiscus*; corolla with 5(6) petals, the petals slightly fused at base in *Caryo-*

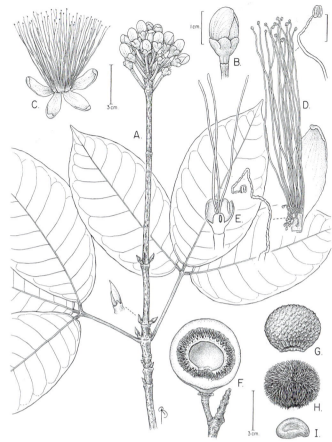

Figure 43. CARYOCARACEAE. *Caryocar glabrum* subsp. *glabrum*. **A.** Stem with leaves and inflorescence in bud and detail of axillary bud (below). **B.** Lateral view of flower bud. **C.** Lateral view of corolla and stamens as they fall from the tree. **D.** Lateral view of petal and part of the androecium (left) with detail of shorter, inner stamen (below left) and apex of longer, outer stamen (above). **E.** Medial section of gynoecium and calyx. **F.** Medial section of fruit with seed removed; note spiny endocarp. **G.** Lateral view of thin skin that covers spiny endocarp. **H.** Lateral view of endocarp. **I.** Seed. Reprinted with permission from Mori et al. (2002). Artist: Bobbi Angell.

car, fused at apices (calyptrate) in *Anthodiscus*, the petals and stamens fall together in *Caryocar* after anthesis, the petals fall as unit in *Anthodiscus* at anthesis; androecium of 55–750 stamens, the innermost stamens shorter and staminodial, the filaments often fused at base, often covered with minute, glandlike tubercules toward apex, the anthers dorsifixed or basifixed, dehiscing longitudinally; gynoecium syncarpous, the ovary superior, the carpels 4–20, the locules 4(6) in *Caryocar*, 8–20 in *Anthodiscus*, the styles distinct; placentation axile, the ovules 1 per locule. **Fruits** drupelike, separating into one-seeded pyrenes at maturity, the "endocarps" smooth or often possessing (especially in *Caryocar*) muricate, tuberculate, or spinulose surfaces. **Seeds** 1–4 in *Caryocar*, 8–20 in *Anthodiscus*; embryos with straight (*Caryocar*) or spirally twisted radicle (*Anthodiscus*), the hypocotyl fleshy, the cotyledons 2, small.

Natural history. Species of *Caryocar* flower nocturnally and are pollinated by bats. The flowers open in the early evening, the inflorescences project above the crown, and the innermost staminodes produce nectar. The petals and stamens fall as a single unit between 0600 and 0700 h. Species of *Anthodiscus* flower diurnally, and this pattern, along with its yellow flower color, suggest that insects, especially bees, are the pollinators.

Rodents eat the fruit pulp and the seeds of *Caryocar*, and presumably disperse the seeds. No information on dispersal is available for *Anthodiscus*.

Economic uses. The fruit of most species of *Caryocar* possesses an edible mesocarp and a seed that can be eaten like a nut. The common name of the family, *souari*, is derived from the name of *Caryocar nuciferum*, a species sometimes cultivated in the tropics for its edible seed. Extracts from the fruit have been used as a fish poison, and the mesocarp is employed, especially in the Planalto of Brazil, to prepare a liqueur. The bark of *Anthodiscus obovatus* is used as an ingredient of the *Strychnos*-based arrow poison of the Tukanos Indians. The wood of Caryocaraceae is durable, finishes well, is extremely resistant to insect attack, and is much used in boat building.

References. BENTHAM, G., AND J. D. HOOKER. 1862. Ternstroemiaceae tribus Rhizoboleae. *Genera Plantarum* 1: 180–81. BERNAL, H. Y., AND J. E. CORRERA Q. 1990. Caryocaraceae. In *Especies vegetales promisorias de los países del Convenio Andrés Bello*, Tomo IV. Bogotá, D. E., Colombia: Secretaria Ejecutiva del Convenio Andrés Bello. PRANCE, G. T. 1990. The genus *Caryocar* L. (Caryocaraceae): An underexploited tropical resource. *Advances Econ. Bot.* 8:177–88. PRANCE, G. T., AND M. FREITAS DA SILVA. 1973. Caryocaraceae. *Fl. Neotrop. Monogr.* 12:1–75. VOGEL, S. 1968. Chiropterophilie in der neotropischen flora. *Flora, B* 157: 565–69.

CARYOPHYLLACEAE (Pink Family)

RICHARD RABELER

Figure 44

- *herbs, shrubs, or subshrubs*
- *leaves usually opposite, sometimes in basal rosettes, whorled, or rarely alternate*
- *flowers actinomorphic; ovary superior; placentation free-central or basal*

Numbers of genera and species. Worldwide, the Caryophyllaceae comprise 82 or 88 genera and almost 3,000 species; the number of genera depends on the acceptance of a broad or narrow concept of *Silene*. In tropical America, there are 24–26 genera and about 210 species. About one-half of the species in the family are placed in the subfamily Caryophylloideae, most of these belong to the two largest genera, *Silene* (about 800 species) and *Dianthus* (over 320 species). Fifty-four of the 88 genera are endemics while 46 genera have one to three species.

Distribution and habitat. The Caryophyllaceae occur throughout the world, most commonly in north temperate areas and least so in the lowland tropics. The primary center of diversity is the Mediterranean region and adjacent southwestern Asia east to Afghanistan and south to the Arabian Peninsula, both for endemic genera (34) and large genera (e.g., *Dianthus*, *Gypsophila*, *Silene*). Within tropical regions, the family is mainly represented by species of largely north-temperate genera found mostly at higher elevations, as weeds in open areas, or as species limited to xeric areas. Within the neotropics, only 10 species are widespread, and four of these have been introduced from Eurasia. The family has few pantropic species and tropical endemics. *Drymaria* and *Polycarpaea* each have one pantropical species. These genera are the largest chiefly tropical genera in the family; *Drymaria* is most diverse in Mexico (20 endemic taxa) and the Andes (13 endemic taxa) while *Polycarpaea* is most diverse in Africa. *Cerdia*, comprised of four species, is endemic to the deserts of northwestern Mexico. *Krauseola* and *Polytepalum* are African endemics of two and one species, respectively.

The Andes form a small center of diversity in the family, where 110 (52%) of the tropical American species are restricted.

The family occupies a wide variety of habitats: arctic-alpine areas to 5,500 m in the Andes, forests, meadows, and deserts, but are nearly absent from lowland tropical forests.

Family classification. The Caryophyllaceae are placed in the Caryophyllales by Cronquist. Morphological and molecular studies support this family as a monophyletic group; however, the family's position within the Caryophyllales is

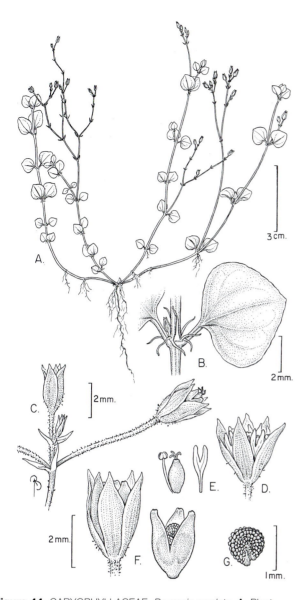

Figure 44. CARYOPHYLLACEAE. *Drymaria cordata*. **A.** Plant showing leaves and inflorescences. **B.** Detail of node showing leaf and stipules. **C.** Detail of inflorescence showing glandular pubescence. **D.** Lateral view of flower. **E.** Adaxial view of petal (right) and lateral view of gynoecium and one stamen (left). **F.** Lateral views of fruit within calyx (left) and dehisced fruit with calyx removed (right). **G.** Seed. Reprinted with permission from Mori et al. (2002). Artist: Bobbi Angell.

still under debate. In contrast to most members of the Caryophyllales, the Caryophyllaceae lack betalains.

Depending on the characters emphasized, the family can be divided into three, four, or five subfamilies. The traditional segregation is into three subfamilies; the Paronychioideae (stipules present), the Alsinoideae (stipules absent, calyx mostly free), and the Caryophylloideae (stipules absent, calyx fused). More recent segregates include, removing two genera, *Scleranthus* and *Pentasetmonodiscus*, with fused calyces and utricle fruits from the Alsinoideae to form the

Scleranthoideae, and separating species with capsules from the remainder of the Paronychioideae, which have utricle fruits, to form the Polycarpoideae. All subfamilies occur in tropical America. However, more than half of the Caryophylloideae are species that are naturalized or cultivated in tropical America.

The Alsinoideae, often considered as the basal, least specialized subfamily, may not be monophyletic, and the relationships between it and the other subfamilies are currently being investigated. Molecular studies suggest that several of the large genera (including *Minuartia* and *Silene*) are paraphyletic.

Features of the family. Habit: herbs, shrubs, or subshrubs, the herbs annual, winter annual, biennial, or perennial, sometimes with woody bases. Roots often taproots. Stems either erect or prostrate, glabrous or variously pubescent, the nodes often swollen; rhizomes sometimes present. Stipules present (Paronychioideae and Polycarpoideae), scarious. Leaves usually opposite, sometimes in basal rosettes, seldom whorled or opposite below and alternate above, or rarely alternate, simple; blade margins entire; petioles often present (usually on lower stem and rosette leaves), or leaves sessile (usually on upper stem leaves), the sessile leaves often basally connate around stem. Inflorescences terminal, less often axillary (when flowers few or singular), cymose, paniculate, less often capitate, fasciculate, or umbellate, or of one to few flowers; bracts sometimes present, leaflike or scarious; pedicel sometimes present; epicalyx sometimes present (*Dianthus*). Flowers actinomorphic, usually bisexual, less often unisexual (the plants dioecious or monoecious); sepals 4 or 5, distinct or fused (Caryophylloideae and Scleranthoideae); petals 4 or 5, sometimes fewer or absent, distinct when present, white or pink, the apex often notched; androecium with stamens equaling or twice the number of petals, sometimes fewer; gynoecium syncarpous, the ovary superior, the carpels 2–5, the locule 1, the septa rarely evident below (some *Silene*), the styles absent or 2–5, the stigmas 2–5; placentation free-central or basal, the ovules 1–numerous, usually campylotropous, bitegmic. Fruits capsules or utricles, the capsules dehiscing by teeth or valves, equal to or twice the number of styles (Alsinoideae, Caryophylloideae, and Polycarpoideae), the utricles usually indehiscent (Paronychioideae and Scleranthoideae). Seeds 1–2 or numerous, small, often kidney-shaped to circular, sometimes shield-shaped and flat, dull to shiny, often brownish or black, the surface often rough.

Anomalous secondary thickening of vascular tissue in roots and/or older stems is known in 19 genera. Flowers may exhibit additional flower parts; e.g., *Polytepalum* exhibits the extreme in having flower parts in multiples of 13.

Natural history. Two basic pollination strategies are found in the family. Many Caryophylloideae have large, brightly colored flowers with a fused calyx. These tubular flowers attract butterflies and moths. Most members of the other subfamilies have small flowers, visited mainly by flies and small bees, if at all. Reduction trends in some genera lead to apetalous flowers and self-pollination.

Dispersal is chiefly by the wind; the small seeds are blown from the open, often erect capsules. Other reported mechanisms include ant dispersal (elaiosomes are found on the seeds of two genera), water (both rain and currents), birds, and possibly other animals and humans. The small seeds of many of the weedy species often are transported as contaminates of commercial seeds.

Economic uses. The Caryophyllaceae are of minor economic importance. A number of species are weeds of cultivated and disturbed areas and some authors have listed *Spergula arvensis* (corn spurry) and *Stellaria media* (common chickweed) among the world's worst weeds. Many pinks are cultivated both in home gardens and for commercial use. The carnation (*Dianthus* species) and baby's breath (*Gypsophila* species) are the best-known trade examples; species of both genera are grown in the neotropics partly to supply much of the demand for them as cut flowers in North America. Species rich in saponin (e.g., *Saponaria* and *Gypsophila*) are commercially important in Asia, where they are used in the manufacture of beverages, halvah, soap, and shampoos. Only a few species are used medicinally, and most reports are from sources in the Eastern Hemisphere. Species of *Drymaria* are eaten in salads in French Guiana, and medicinal use of this genus is reported from Cuba, Ecuador, and Mexico.

References. Behnke, H.-D., and T. J. Mabry, eds. 1993. *Caryophyllales: Evolution and Systematics*. Berlin: Springer-Verlag. Bittrich, V. 1993. Caryophyllaceae. In *The Families and Genera of Vascular Plants*, eds. K. Kubitzki, J. G. Rohwer and V. Bittrich, 2:206–36. New York: Springer-Verlag. Chaudhri, M. N. 1968. A revision of the Paronychiinae. *Meded. Bot. Mus. Herb. Rijks Univ. Utrecht* 285:1–440. Duke, J. A. 1961. Preliminary revision of the genus *Drymaria*. *Ann. Missouri Bot. Gard.* 48:173–268. Good, D. A. 1984. A revision of the Mexican and Central American species of *Cerastium* (Caryophyllaceae). *Rhodora* 86:339–79. Greuter, W. 1995. *Silene* (Caryophyllaceae) in Greece: a subgeneric and sectional classification. *Taxon* 44:543–81. McNeill, J. 1962. Taxonomic studies in the Alsinoideae: I. Generic and infra-generic groups. *Notes Roy. Bot. Gard. Edinburgh* 24:79–155. Oxelman, B., M. Liden, R. K. Rabeler, and M. Popp. 2001. A revised generic classification of the tribe Sileneae (Caryophyllaceae). *Nordic J. Bot.* 20: 743–48. Pax, F., and K. Hoffmann. 1934. Caryophyllaceae. In *Die Natürlichen Pflanzenfamilien*, A. Engler and K. Prantl, 2nd ed. 16c:275–364. Leipzig: Wilhelm Engelmann.

CASUARINACEAE (She-oak Family)

Nathan Smith

Figure 45

- *trees*
- *branchlets equisetoid and ridged*
- *leaves whorled, reduced to scalelike teeth*
- *inflorescences spikes (staminate) or headlike (pistillate)*
- *flowers reduced, unisexual*
- *pistillate infructescences conelike; fruits samaras*

Numbers of genera and species. Worldwide, the Casuarinaceae comprise four genera and circa 90 species. In tropical America, there is a single introduced genus, *Casuarina* (17 species worldwide). *Casuarina equisetifolia* and *C. cunninghamiana* are commonly found in the neotropics, and several other species have also been introduced; however, it is not clear how many.

Distribution and habitat. The Casuarinaceae are native to Australia, Malesia, and regions of the Pacific. *Casuarina* has been introduced throughout much of tropical America.

Species of *Casuaria* are often pioneers of disturbed habitats. In tropical America, *Casuarina* is often found planted on roadsides or as a street tree.

Family classification. The Casuarinaceae are placed in the Casuarinales by Cronquist, within the Hamamelidae. Cronquist treats the family as having a single genus, *Casuarina*; however, some classifications recognize *Allocasuarina*, *Casuarina*, *Ceuthostoma*, and *Gymnostoma*. Recent molecular studies place *Casuarina* near genera of the Betulaceae, Myricaceae, Juglandaceae, and Fagaceae.

Features of the family. Habit: trees; branchlets persistent and woody or deciduous and chlorophyllous, articulate, equisetoid, often drooping, sometimes pubescent, ridged, the ridges equal to number of reduced leaves. Stipules absent. Leaves whorled, reduced to scalelike teeth. Inflorescences spikes (staminate) or headlike (pistillate) on lateral peduncles; bracts and bracteoles present, the bracts basally connate, toothlike, the flowers 1 per bract the bracteoles 2 per flower. Flowers reduced, unisexual (plants dioecious or monoecious in *C. equisetifolia*). Staminate flowers: "perianth" of 2 scales, these deciduous at anthesis; androecium of 1 stamen, the anther

Figure 45. CASUARINACEAE. *Casuarina equisetifolia.* **A.** Stem with pistillate inflorescences (x⅔). **B.** Part of needlelike stem showing scalelike leaves (x6). **C.** Whorl of fused, scalelike leaves (x24). **D.** Lateral view of pistillate inflorescence (x4). **E.** Lateral view of pistillate flower showing subtending bract and bracteole (x14). **F.** Abaxial view of pistillate flower showing bracteole (x14). **G.** Medial section of pistillate flower showing bracteole (x14). **H.** Floral diagram of pistillate flower. **I.** Lateral view of young infructescence with fruits enclosed by woody bracteoles (x2). **J.** Lateral view of mature infructescence after woody bracteoles have opened (x2). **K.** Winged fruit (x2). **L.** Lateral view of staminate inflorescence at anthesis (x4). **M.** Lateral view of young staminate inflorescence at end of photosynthetic shoot (x6). **N.** Part of staminate inflorescence showing staminate flower at anthesis (x32). **O.** Lateral view of staminate flower subtended by persistent bracteoles (x32). **P.** Lateral view of immature staminate flower showing lateral bracteoles to left and right and the lateral perianth segments above left and above right (x24). **Q.** Floral diagram of staminate flower; outermost scales are bracteoles. Reprinted with permission from Tomlinson (1980). Artist: Priscilla Fawcett.

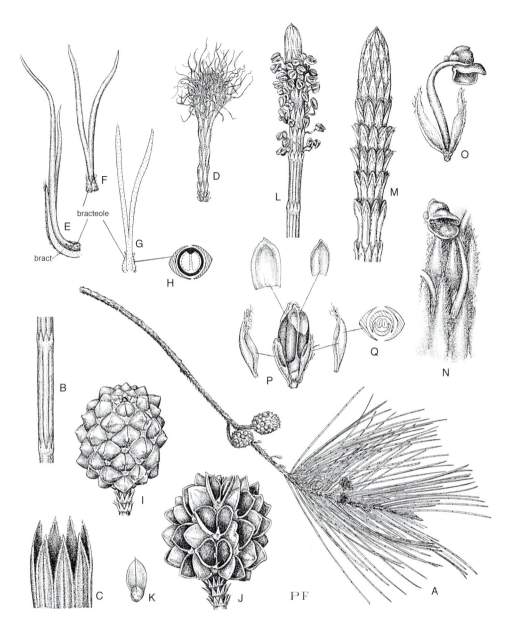

basifixed, dehiscing longitudinally. **Pistillate flowers:** perianth absent; gynoecium syncarpous, the ovary superior, the carpels 2 (only anterior locule fertile), the style 2-branched, the stigma decurrent; placentation axile, the ovules 2 per locule. **Fruits** samaras (appearing capsulelike because of subtending bracteoles). **Seeds** 1 per fruit; endosperm absent at seed maturity, the embryo large, straight, oily.

Natural history. The roots of *Casuarina* often have nodules containing the nitrogen-fixing bacterium *Frankia.*

Species of *Casuarina* are wind-pollinated. The fruits are dispersed by wind and sometimes water.

Economic uses. Species of *Casuarina* are often planted as ornamentals. In some regions, the deciduous branchlets are used as agricultural mulch as well as for fuel. The wood of *Casuarina* is used for fuel, mulch, and construction, and the plants are planted as windbreaks and as stabilizers of sandy soils. The relationship of *Casuarina* with nitrogen-fixing bacteria has made it a desirable candidate for rehabilitating soils.

References. JOHNSON, L.A.S., AND K. L. WILSON. 1989. Casuarinaceae: a synopsis. In *Evolution, Systematics, and Fossil History of the Hamamelidae,* eds. P. R. Crane and S. Blackmore. Systematics Association special volume no. 40B, 2:167–88. Oxford: Clarendon Press. JOHNSON, L.A.S., AND K. L. WILSON. 1993. Casuarinaceae. In *The Families and Genera of Vascular Plants,* eds. K. Kubitzki, J. G. Rohwer, and V. Bittrich, 2:237–42. New York: Springer-Verlag. WILSON, K. L., AND L.A.S. JOHNSON. 1989. Casuarinaceae. In *Flora of Australia,* eds. A. S. George et. al., 100–10. Canberra: Australian Government Publishing.

CECROPIACEAE (Snake Wood Family)

C. C. BERG

Figure 46, Plate 12

- *trees (or shrubs) with adventitious roots, becoming stilt-roots in terrestrial plants and long aerial roots in hemiepiphytes*

- *mucilaginous sap present, becoming black, or less frequently red, when exposed to air*

- *stipules present, usually large, fully amplexicaul (encircling twig)*

- *leaves alternate (spiral), simple; blades often palmately or radiately incised*

- *flowers unisexual; perianth uniseriate; ovary with 1 locule, the stigma 1; placentation basal, the ovule 1*

- *fruits small or large, surrounded by accrescent, fleshy perianth*

Numbers of genera and species. Worldwide, the Cecropiaceae comprise six genera and 170 species. *Cecropia* (61 species), *Coussapoa* (46), and *Pourouma* (25) are found in tropical America.

Distribution and habitat. The Cecropiaceae are pantropical with the majority of the species distributed in the neotropics. In the neotropics, the family is most common in South America, fewer species occur in Central America, and only two species of *Cecropia* are found in the West Indies.

The majority of the species are found in more or less humid lowland forests. Only *Cecropia* is well represented in humid montane and submontane habitats. Species of *Cecropia* are often dominant in secondary forests.

Family classification. The Cecropiaceae are placed in the Urticales, along with the Moraceae, Ulmaceae, and Urticaceae, by Cronquist. The family, established in 1978, consists of genera transferred from the Moraceae and one genus previously placed in the Urticaceae. Molecular studies, however, suggest placing these families in the Rosales along with the Rosaceae and Rhamnaceae, and sometimes even the Elaeagnaceae. A recent study suggests that the Cecropiaceae are polyphyletic and nested in the Urticaceae.

Cecropiaceae differ from Urticaceae in their woody habit, dioecious breeding systems, fully amplexicaul, connate stipules, alternate leaves in spirals, frequent occurrence of palmately or radiately incised blades, and the absence of conspicuous cystoliths in the epidermal cells of most genera (present only in the Asian *Poikilospermum*). Moreover, when present, the cystoliths of Cecropiaceae are composed of sil-

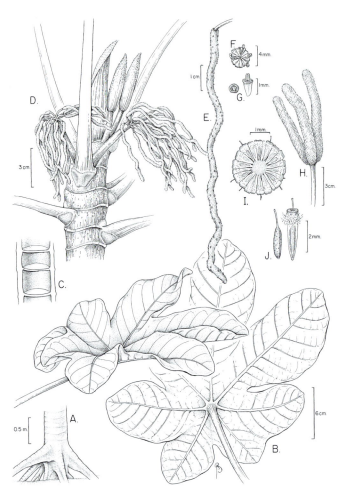

Figure 46. CECROPIACEAE. *Cecropia obtusa.* **A.** Flying buttresses at base of trunk. **B.** Oblique abaxial (right) and adaxial (left) views of peltate leaves. **C.** Medial section of stem with hollow internodes. **D.** Apex of stem with sheathing stipule, staminate inflorescences, and petioles with trichilia; note spathes covering unopened inflorescences (upper right). **E.** Lateral view of single spike of staminate inflorescence. **F.** Transverse section of staminate inflorescence. **G.** Apical (left) and lateral (right) views of staminate flowers with tubular perianths and exserted anthers. **H.** Lateral view of pistillate inflorescence. **I.** Transverse section of pistillate inflorescence. **J.** Lateral view of gynoecium (left) and entire pistillate flower with tubular perianth (right). Reprinted with permission from Mori et al. (2002). Artist: Bobbi Angell.

ica rather than calcium carbonate as in Urticaceae. None of the Cecropiaceae have the characteristic inflexed stamens found in all Urticaceae, circa 65 species of Moraceae, and some Ulmaceae.

The basal position of the ovule, the single stigma, and the absence of milky latex, are shared by Cecropiaceae and Urticaceae. Some cells and ducts in the Cecropiaceae contain a mucilaginous sap that turns black (or less frequently red) at exposure to the air. This contrasts with the milky latex of Moraceae.

A subdivision of the family has not been proposed, but the Neotropical and African genera constitute a natural entity, whereas the Asian *Poikilospermum*, with more urticaceous traits, is more distantly related.

Features of the family. Habit: trees (or shrubs), often exuding black or red mucilaginous sap when bark cut, spearmint aroma from cut bark of some species of *Pourouma*, the trees or shrubs of *Coussapoa* mostly hemiepiphytic. **Roots:** adventitious roots usually present, stilt-roots in terrestrial *Cecropia* and *Pourouma*, aerial roots in *Coussapoa*. **Stem** internodes usually hollow in *Cecropia* (sometimes entirely or largely filled with brown pith, especially in montane *Cecropia*). **Indument** often with mostly white arachnoid and/or with brown to purple, pluricellular trichomes present; trichilia at base of petiole present in most *Cecropia*, these containing Müllerian bodies (see natural history). **Stipules** present, usually large, fully amplexicaul (encircling twig), connate, often leaving conspicuous scars (as on trunk in *Cecropia*). **Leaves** alternate (spiral), simple, sometimes seemingly palmately compound (e.g., *Cecropia sciadophylla* and *Pourouma petiolulata*), basally attached (*Coussapoa* and *Pourouma*) or peltate (*Cecropia*); blades often palmately or radiately incised; venation pinnate, palmate, or radiate (in peltate blades). **Inflorescences** axillary, usually in pairs, usually ramified (simple only in some pistillate inflorescences), paniculate (pistillate inflorescences of *Pourouma* in which the infructescence resembles bunches of grapes) or rarely subumbellate, globose heads (*Coussapoa*), or bunches of spikes, enclosed by caducous spathes until anthesis (*Cecropia*). **Flowers** actinomorphic, unisexual (plants dioecious), small; perianth uniseriate; tepals 2–4 (2 in *Cecropia*), distinct or connate and forming a tube; stamens 1–4 (2 in *Cecropia*, 1, 2, or 3 in *Coussapoa*, usually 4 in *Pourouma*), antitepalous, straight in bud, the filaments distinct or fused and then the thecae 4 (when 2 stamens) or 6 (when 3 stamens) on a column (*Coussapoa*); gynoecium with ovary superior, free from perianth, carpels 2, 1-locular, the style (sub)terminal, the stigma 1, peltate to comose or penicillate; placentation basal, the ovule 1. **Fruits** achenes, small (1–3 mm long in *Cecropia* and *Coussapoa*) to large (>1 cm long in *Pourouma*), surrounded by accrescent, fleshy perianth, aggregated in heads in *Coussapoa*, spikes in *Cecropia*, panicles (or umbels) in *Pourouma*, greenish to yellowish (*Cecropia*), yellowish to orange (*Coussapoa*), or blackish (*Pourouma*). **Seeds** small (*Cecropia* and *Coussapoa*) or large (*Pourouma*).

The hemiepiphytic *Coussapoa* possesses an aerial root system consisting of at least one lead root connecting the plant with the ground and others that attach the plant to the host tree by clasping its branches and trunk. In *C. trinervia*, a species commonly found along black-water rivers in the Amazon Basin, the aerial roots produce an extensive stilt-root system, resembling that of mangrove trees.

In several, mostly montane species of *Cecropia*, the arachnoid indument is so dense on the upper surface of the leaf blade that the blade appears white, making the plants conspicuous on forested hillsides.

Many species have pearl bodies on the leaves that are commonly observed in greenhouse plants but are rarely observed in the field because they are apparently harvested by ants as soon as the young leaves open.

In *Cecropia*, the two anthers are pushed out of the flower by elongation of the filaments through a slitlike aperture in the relatively firm and fleshy apex of the tubular perianth. When the anther is pushed through the aperture, it often becomes detached from the filament.

In many species with small anthers (ca. 0.5–1.0 mm long), the anthers remain attached to the flower by sticky appendages produced at the bases of the thecae. The appendages become threadlike and the anthers remain loosely attached to the flower. In some other species with small anthers, the anthers remain loosely attached to the upper margin of the filament by filiform connections from the connective. If the anthers are long (ca. 2 mm), they remain attached to the flower by the spiral-thickenings of the vascular bundle of the filament. In all of these cases, pollen is released by wind moving past the dangling anthers. In many species in which the anthers remain attached to the filament, the spikes of the inflorescence are slender and can be easily moved by the wind, thereby releasing pollen.

Small fruits are found in the hemiepiphytic species (*Coussapoa*) and in pioneer trees (*Cecropia*) and are usually produced in larger quantities per plant than are larger seeds. In hemiepiphytic species, this increases the probability of seeds reaching and germinating at suitable sites on host trees, and, in pioneer species, it helps maintain a seed bank in the soil that facilitates colonization of gaps as they become available. In contrast, species of *Pourouma*, most of which colonize less disturbed habitats or, at least smaller gaps, have large seeds.

Natural history. The three genera of Neotropical Cecropiaceae have morphological and ecological counterparts in other parts of the world. Species of *Cecropia* share small seeds, leaves with peltate, radially incised blades, and a preference for disturbed habitats with African *Musanga* (two species); species of *Pourouma* share large seeds, frequently palmately incised leaf blades, and preference for less disturbed habitats with African *Myrianthus* (seven species); and species of *Coussapoa* share small seeds, entire leaf blades, and hemiepiphytic habit with the Malesian *Poikilospermum* (ca. 20 species).

In general, species of *Cecropia* fruit and flower year-round, a strategy ensuring the continuous "rain" of seeds needed to invade the unpredictable disturbed habitats in which they grow. Two exceptions are the riparian *C. latiloba* and *C. membranacea* which flower at high-water level along larger rivers. The seeds are dispersed by water currents and then germinate on the muddy riverbanks when the waters recede.

Species of *Cecropia* are among the most important pioneer trees of the neotropics, often occurring in extensive and dense stands along rivers, on landslides, and in human-made clearings. *Coussapoa* is second to *Ficus* (Moraceae) in the number of hemiepiphytic species in Neotropical lowlands.

The fleshy structures surrounding the seeds of Cecropiaceae are eaten and the seeds dispersed by birds, bats, monkeys, and other mammals. The pendulous infructescences of *Cecropia putumayonis* and *Pourouma ferruginea* are probably adaptations for dispersal by bats.

In central French Guiana, the two co-occurring species of *Cecropia* are dispersed primarily by bats (*C. obtusa*) or birds (*C. sciadophylla*). Most species of *Coussapoa* produce yellow or orange fruits that are eaten avidly by birds. The inner layer of the fruiting perianth of *C. asperifolia* produces a resin collected by bees for nest construction, and they may also disperse the seeds.

Most species of *Cecropia* are inhabited by aggressive, biting ants belonging to the genus *Azteca*. Three adaptations accompany this plant-animal interaction.

- Hollow internodes that provide breedings sites, protection, and space to tend scale insects, which, in turn exude sweet secretions consumed by the ants.
- A weak spot located toward the apex of the internode called a prostoma. This is perforated by ant queens, which establish colonies inside the hollow stems. The ants also perforate the solid nodes to connect the nest chambers in each internode.
- Small (1–2 mm long) whitish, ellipsoid structures called Müllerian bodies that are produced on trichilia. These food bodies contain glycogen, a common reserve carbohydrate in animals, but a rare compound in plants.

Not all *Cecropia* species have this combination of characters. For example, several species on islands and at higher elevations lack trichilia and Müllerian bodies, and some montane species lack hollow internodes. These species do not harbor ants, and insect larvae may severely damage the leaves.

The ants presumably protect many species of *Cecropia* against herbivory and remove competing plants that climb over them. Nevertheless, the leaves of *Cecropia* provide a preferred food of sloths.

Economic use. Fruits of *Pourouma* are eaten commonly, but only *P. cecropiifolia* is cultivated. Fruiting spikes of *Cecropia* are also edible. Decoctions or powder of leaves from various species of *Cecropia* are used against various diseases, and the ash of some species is mixed with coca leaves (see Erythroxylaceae) to reduce acidity when they are chewed. Wood of *Cecropia* has been used as pulp for paper fabrication. Some species introduced in other parts of the Tropics have become invasive weeds, e.g., *Cecropia peltata* in West Africa, *C. obtusifolia* in Hawaii, and *C. schreberiana* in Madagascar.

References. BERG, C. C. 1978a. Cecropiaceae, a new family of the Urticales. *Taxon* 27:39–44. BERG, C. C. 1978b. Espécies de *Cecropia* da Amazônia Brasileira. *Acta Amazon.* 8:149–82. BERG, C. C. 2000. Cecropiaceae. In *Flora de Venezuela*, ed. R. Riina, 191–249. Caracas: Fundación Instituto Botánico de Venezuela. BERG, C. C., R.W.A.P. AKKERMANS, AND E.C.H. VAN HEUSDEN. 1990. Cecropiaceae: *Coussapoa* and *Pourouma*, with an introduction to the family. *Fl. Neotrop. Monogr.* 51:1–208. BERG, C. C., AND P. FRANCO ROSSELLI. 1993. Cecropiaceae. In *Flora of Ecuador*, eds. G. Harling and L. Andersson, no. 48:1–109. Göteborg, Sweden: Department of Systematic Botany, University of Göteborg. BERNAL, H. Y., AND J. E. CORRERA Q. 1998. Moraceae (*Pourouma cecropiifolia*). In *Especies vegetales promisorias de los países del Convenio Andrés Bello*, Tomo XII. Santafé de Bogotá, D. E., Colombia: Secretaria Ejecutiva del Convenio Andrés Bello. CORRERA Q., J. E., AND H. Y. BERNAL. 1995. Moraceae. In *Especies vegetales promisorias de los países del Convenio Andrés Bello, Tomo XI*. Santafé de Bogotá, D. E., Colombia: Secretaria Ejecutiva del Convenio Andrés Bello. SYTSMA, K. J., J. MORAWETZ, J. CHRIS PIRES, M. NEPOKROEFF, E. CONTI, ET AL. 2002. Urticalean rosids: circumscription, rosid ancestry, and phylogenetics based on *rbc*L, *trn*L-F, and *ndh*F sequences. *Amer. J. Bot.* 89(9):1531–46.

CELASTRACEAE (Bittersweet Family)

JOHN D. MITCHELL

Figures 47, 48; Plate 12

- *small trees, shrubs, vines, and lianas*
- *leaves alternate or opposite, simple, rarely very reduced in size*

- *flowers actinomorphic; sepals 4–5; petals usually 4–5; intrastaminal disc usually present, usually large*
- *seeds often arillate, the aril orange, white, or red*

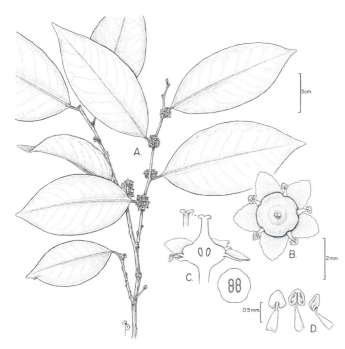

Figure 47. CELASTRACEAE. *Maytenus floribunda*. **A.** Stem with leaves and inflorescences. **B.** Apical view of flower. **C.** Medial section of flower with detail of stigma (above) and transverse section of ovary (below). **D.** Abaxial (left), adaxial (center), and lateral (right) views of stamens. Reprinted with permission from Mori et al. (2002). Artist: Bobbi Angell.

Numbers of genera and species. Worldwide, the Celastraceae comprise approximately 52 genera and about 800 species (excluding the Hippocrateaceae). In tropical America, there are between 15 and 21 genera and more than 200 species. The largest Neotropical genera are *Maytenus*, *Crossopetalum*, *Zinowiewia*, and *Schaefferia*.

Distribution and habitat. The Celastraceae are widespread, but most diverse in the Tropics and warm temperate regions of the world. In the neotropics, the primary center of generic diversity and endemism is in Mexico and Central America Extra-Amazonian Brazil is also rich in Celastraceae.

Neotropical Celastraceae grow in a wide variety of habitats including lowland tropical moist to dry forests, deserts, montane forests, and subalpine vegetation types.

Family classification. The Celastraceae are placed in the Celastrales by Cronquist. Cronquist segregated the Hippocrateaceae from the Celastraceae, but included the monotypic genus *Goupia*, which is treated by others as a separate family, the Goupiaceae. The Angiosperm Phylogeny Group places the Goupiaceae in the Malpighiales but does not assign the Celastraceae (including the Hippocrateaceae) to a specific order in the Eurosids. Judd et al. recognized the Celastrales as a distinct order and considered the Celastraceae (if Hippocrateaceae are included) to be monophyletic based on a combination of morphological and cpDNA sequence data. This treatment of the Celastraceae here follows Cronquist's classification even though valid arguments have been made for uniting the Celastraceae and Hippocrateaceae.

Features of the family. Habit: small trees, shrubs, vines, and lianas. **Stipules** often present, if present usually small (except for *Goupia* with conspicuous linear stipules on young twigs) and caducous. **Leaves** alternate or opposite, simple, rarely very reduced in size. **Inflorescences** terminal or axillary, mostly cymose, fasciculate, racemose, umbellate, or rarely of solitary flowers. **Flowers** actinomorphic, unisexual (the plants monoecious or dioecious) or bisexual, usually small,

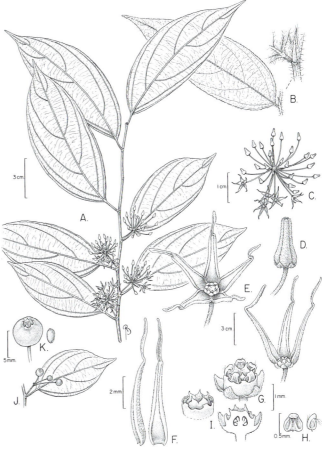

Figure 48. CELASTRACEAE. *Goupia glabra*. **A.** Stem with inflorescences. **B.** Leaf showing stipule (left) and detail of node (above). **C.** Apical view of inflorescence. **D.** Lateral view of bud. **E.** Apical-lateral view (left) and lateral view with two petals removed (below right) of flowers. **F.** Lateral (left) and adaxial (right) views of petals. **G.** Lateral view of flower with petals removed. **H.** Adaxial (left) and lateral (right) views of anthers. **I.** Apical-lateral view of gynoecium surrounded by nectary (above left) and medial section of pistillate flower with petals removed (right). **J.** Infructescence in axil of leaf. **K.** Fruit (left) and seed (right). Reprinted with permission from Mori et al. (2002). Artist: Bobbi Angell.

greenish or white, the perianth usually biseriate; sepals 4–5, usually imbricate, rarely valvate; petals (0)4–5, usually imbricate, rarely valvate (*Goupia*); androecium of 4–5 stamens, generally unicyclic, occasionally bicyclic, alternating with petals (opposite petals in similar-looking flowers of the Rhamnaceae), the filaments usually distinct, rarely basally connate, the anthers usually introrse, dehiscing longitudinally; intrastaminal disc usually present, usually large, fleshy, nectariferous; gynoecium syncarpous, the ovary usually superior, sometimes subinferior, the carpels 2–5, the locules 2–5, the style 1, or 5 (e.g., *Goupia*), terminal, simple, the stigma 2–5-lobed; placentation axile, the ovules (1)2–numerous per locule, anatropous, erect, or pendulous. **Fruits** loculicidal capsules (e.g., *Maytenus*), drupes, berries, or samaras (e.g., *Wimmeria* and *Zinowiewia*). **Seeds** (1)2–numerous, often arillate, the aril orange, white, or red; endosperm abundant to occasionally absent, the embryo large, straight, usually surrounded by endosperm.

Species of *Ilex* (Aquifoliaceae) look similar in vegetative and floral structures to species of *Maytenus* and some other species of Celastraceae, but they lack the intrastaminal disc characteristic of this family.

Natural history. Celastraceae are pollinated by bees, flies, and beetles, which are attracted to the nectar-secreting discs. Many Celastraceae (e.g., species of *Celastrus*, *Euonymus*, *Goupia*, *Gymnosporia*, and *Maytenus*), especially those associated with brightly colored arils, are dispersed by birds and monkeys that eat the fruits and excrete the seeds. *Wimmeria* and *Zinowiewia* bear samaras adapted for wind dispersal.

Economic uses. *Goupia glabra* (*cupiúba*, Portuguese) is a useful, widespread, Amazonian-Guianan tree. A decoction of its bark is used to treat toothaches by the Créoles of French Guiana, its timber is locally important, and the Piaroa Amerindians of Venezuelan Guayana make dugout canoes from its trunks. A few genera of Celastraceae are considered minor timber trees (e.g., species of *Maytenus* and *Wimmeria*). In temperate areas, some species are planted as ornamentals (e.g., *Celastrus*, bittersweet, and *Euonymous*). Species of *Maytenus* are known for their medicinal properties.

References. BERNAL, H. Y., AND J. E. CORRERA Q. 1990. Celastraceae. In *Especies vegetales promisorias de los países del Convenio Andrés Bello*, Tomo IV. Bogotá, D. E., Colombia: Secretaria Ejecutiva del Convenio Andrés Bello. BRIZICKY, G. K. 1964. The genera of Celastrales in the southeastern United States. *J. Arnold Arbor.* 45:206–34. EDWIN, G., AND DING HOU. 1975. Celastraceae. In Flora of Panama, R. E. Woodson, Jr., R. W. Schery, and collaborators. *Ann. Missouri Bot. Gard.* 62:45–56. KEARNS, D. M. 1998. Celastraceae. In *Flora of the Venezuelan Guayana*: Caesalpiniaceae—Ericaceae, eds. P. E. Berry, B. K. Holst and K. Yatskievych, 4:190–97. St. Louis, MO: Missouri Botanical Garden Press. LOESENER, T. 1942. Celastraceae. In *Die natürlichen Pflanzenfamilien*, Ed. 2, A. Engler and K. Prantl, 20b: 87–197. LOURTEIG, A., AND C. O'DONELL. 1955. Las Celastraceas de Argentina y Chile. *Natura (Buenos Aires)* 1(2): 181–233. REISSEK, S. 1861. Celastrinae, Ilicinae et Rhamneae. In *Flora Brasiliensis*, C. F. P. von Martius, XI(1):1–123. SAVOLAINEN, V., J. F. MANEN, E. DOWZERY, AND R. SPICHIGER. 1994. Molecular phylogeny of families related to Celastrales based on *rbc*L 5′ flanking regions. *Mol. Phylog. Evol.* 3:27–37. SIMMONS, M. P., C. C. CLEVINGER, V. SAVOLAINEN, R. H. ARCHER, S. MATHEWS, ET AL. 2001. Phylogeny of the Celastraceae inferred from phytochrome B gene sequence and morphology. *Amer. J. Bot.* 88(2): 313–25.

CERATOPHYLLACEAE (Hornwort Family)

LISA M. CAMPBELL

- *submersed aquatic herbs*
- *roots absent*
- *leaves whorled; blades dichotomously divided into linear segments*
- *flowers unisexual (the plants monoecious)*
- *fruits achenes, spiny*

Numbers of genera and species. Worldwide, the Ceratophyllaceae include a single genus, *Ceratophyllum*, with six species. Three species, the widespread *Ceratophyllum demersum* and the more narrowly distributed *Ceratophyllum submersum* and *C. muricatum*, are found in tropical America.

Distribution and habitat. The Ceratophyllaceae have a cosmopolitan distribution. Neotropical species occur in freshwater lakes and ponds and slow-moving waterways.

Family classification. The Ceratophyllaceae are placed in the Nymphaeales by Cronqist with other aquatic families such as the Nymphaeaceae and Nelumbonaceae. Recent molecular studies suggest these three families are not related; however, exact placement of the Ceratophyllaceae is still unresolved. Ceratophyllaceae have been treated as a separate order. *Ceratophyllum* is divided into three sections, each with two species.

Features of the family. Habit: aquatic herbs, submersed, perennial. **Roots** absent (though plants may be anchored by branchlets). **Leaves** whorled; petiole reduced or absent; blade dichotomously divided into linear, often toothed, segments. **Inflorescences** vestigial, the flowers solitary; pedicel short. **Flowers** actinomorphic, unisexual (the plants monoecious), perianth of 8–15 sepals; androecium of 3–numerous stamens, spirally arranged, the filaments short with protruding connective; gynoecium with superior ovary, the carpel 1, the style persistent, sometimes bifid, with a single stigmatic groove; placentation ventral, the ovule 1. **Fruits** achenes, variously spiny. **Seeds** minute, elliptical, the seed coat transparent; cotyledons fleshy; plumule well developed.

Natural history. Pollination is strictly by water as the pollen sinks through the water to the stigma. In some cases, the anthers break off from the plant and float to the surface before pollen is shed. The fruits bear spines that may aid in dispersal; however, the precise mechanism is not known. The plants persist by turions.

Economic uses. *Ceratophyllum* (hornwort) can rapidly choke waterways and is a breeding site for aquatic invertebrates and insects including malaria-carrying mosquitoes.

References. LES, D. 1989. The evolution of achene morphology in *Ceratophyllum* (Ceratophyllaceae). IV. *Syst. Bot.* 14:254–62. LES, D. 1993. Ceratophyllaceae. In *The Families and Genera of Vascular Plants*, eds. K. Kubitzki, J. G. Rohwer, and V. Bittrich, 2:246–50. Berlin: Springer-Verlag.

CHENOPODIACEAE (Goosefoot Family)

STEVE CLEMANTS

Figure 49

- *herbs, shrubs, or rarely trees*
- *plants often succulent*
- *leaves alternate, rarely opposite, simple*
- *flowers small; ovary superior, the locule 1*
- *fruits usually indehiscent, often subtended by persistent calyx or bracteoles*

Numbers of genera and species. Worldwide, the Chenopodiaceae comprise approximately 100 genera and 1,450 species. In tropical America, there are approximately nine genera and 75 species.

Distribution and habitat. The Chenopodiaceae are cosmopolitan, but particularly diverse in arid regions. Many species are halophytic and others are common weeds. The family is found throughout the Western Hemisphere, where species are often found in deserts, saline habitats, and weedy areas.

Family classification. Chenopodiaceae are placed in the Caryophyllales by Cronquist. The family has long been placed near the Amaranthaceae. Indeed, many botanists have commented on the close similarity of the families and the difficulty in distinguishing them and recent molecular studies indicate that the two families should be merged. The two families form a distinct group within the Caryophyllales apparently not closely related to other families in the order.

The most recent classification of the family recognizes four subfamilies and 12 tribes. However, *Sarcobatus* has subsequently been shown to be unrelated to the Chenopodiaceae and has thus been removed from the family and placed by some authors in the Bataceae.

Features of the family. Habit: annual or perennial herbs, shrubs, or rarely trees, plants often succulent, sometimes stems fleshy and nearly leafless (e.g., *Salicornia*). **Stipules** absent. **Leaves** alternate, rarely opposite, simple, reduced to sheath surrounding stem in *Salicornia* and related genera; blades often succulent, sometimes very fleshy and terete, the margins usually entire, sometimes toothed or lobed. **Inflorescences** axillary or terminal, often of congested cymes, spikes, or panicles, sometimes noncongested cymes; bract 1; bracteoles 2 or absent. **Flowers** usually actinomorphic, bisexual or less often unisexual (then plants monoecious or dioecious), small; tepals (1)5(6), sometimes absent in staminate flowers, in 1 whorl, distinct or basally connate, usually herbaceous or membranaceous, rarely scarious; androecium with stamens commonly equal in number to tepals, the stamens often opposite tepals, the filaments distinct, sometimes connate at base and inserted on disc, on calyx, or at base of ovary; gynoecium syncarpous, the ovary superior (semi-inferior in *Beta*), the carpels 2–3(5), the locule 1, the styles distinct or connate, the stigmas dry; placentation basal, the ovule 1. **Fruits** usually indehiscent utricles or sometimes a pyxis with irregular or circumscissile dehiscence, often subtended by persistent calyx or by persistent bracteoles, sometimes several fruits aggregated together by connation of somewhat

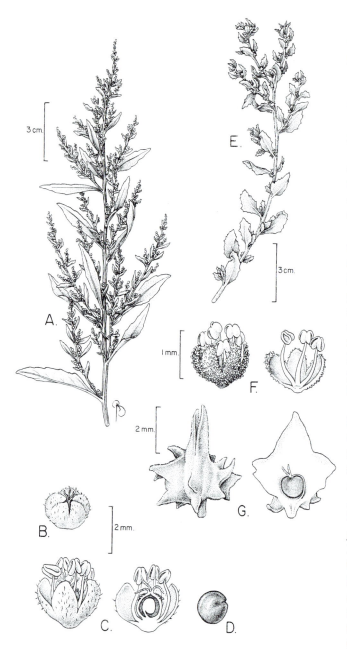

Figure 49. CHENOPODIACEAE. *Chenopodium ambrosioides* (A–D) and *Atriplex cristata* (E–G). **A.** Stem with leaves and inflorescences. **B.** Oblique-apical view of flower. **C.** Lateral view (left) and medial section (right) of flowers. **D.** Lateral view of seed. **E.** Stem with leaves and inflorescences. **F.** Lateral view (left) and medial section (right) of staminate flowers (right). **G.** Lateral view of accrescent bracteoles enclosing fruit (left) and fruit with some of bracteoles removed (right). Reprinted with permission from Acevedo-Rodríguez (1996). Artist: Bobbi Angell.

fleshy tepals. **Seeds** mostly lenticular; endosperm nearly to quite absent, the embryo annular or spirally twisted or slightly curved, the perisperm usually abundant, starchy.

Natural history. Little is known about the natural history of Neotropical Chenopodiaceae. They are often somewhat succulent, which allows them to survive in water-stressed environments. Many species have the C4 photosynthesic pathway, which is more efficient in high-light environments, such as the Tropics.

Economic uses. Spinach (*Spinacia oleracea*) is used as a salad green and a potherb. Different varieties of *Beta vulgaris* provide swiss chard, garden beets, and sugar beets.

Lambs quarters (*Chenopodium album*), one of the 18 most serious weeds in the world, was probably spread as a contaminant of crop seeds. *Chenopodium ambrosioides* (Mexican tea), a weed of gardens and fields, has long been used to treat intestinal worms.

Two species have been domesticated as grains in the neotropics. Huauzontle (*Chenopodium berlandieri* var. *nuttaliae*) was domesticated by the Aztecs and apparently used interchangeably with the domesticated amaranth grains. It probably was derived from North American varieties of the species, which were used in much the same way. Quinoa (*Chenopodium quinoa*) appears to have been domesticated in the Altiplano of Peru and Bolivia. It was a staple crop of the Inca Empire and has been used as a food for at least 5,000 years. Quinoa has 2–6 percent more protein and has a better balance of essential amino acids than wheat.

References. AELLEN, P. 1929a. Beitrag zur Systematik der *Chenopodium*-Arten Amerikas, vorwiegend auf Grund der Sammlung des United States National Museum in Washington, D. C. I. *Repert. Spec. Nov. Regni Veg.* 26:31–64. AELLEN, P. 1929b. Beitrag zur Systematik der *Chenopodium*-Arten Amerikas, vorwiegend auf Grund der Sammlung des United States National Museum in Washington, D. C. II. *Repert. Spec. Nov. Regni Veg.* 26:119–60. AELLEN, P., and T. JUST. 1943. Key and synopsis of the American species of the genus *Chenopodium* L. *Amer. Midl. Naturalist* 30:47–76. BERNAL, H. Y., AND J. E. CORRERA Q. 1991. Chenopodiaceae. In *Especies vegetales promisorias de los países del Convenio Andrés Bello*, Tomo VI. Santafé de Bogotá, D. E., Colombia: Secretaria Ejecutiva del Convenio Andrés Bello. CUSACK, D. F. 1984. Quinoa: grain of the Incas. *Ecologist* 14:21–31. DOWNIE, S. R., D. S. KATZ-DOWNIE, AND K.-Y. CHO. 1997. Relationships in the Caryophyllales as suggested by phylogenetic analyses of partial chloroplast DNA ORF2280 homolog sequences. *Amer. J. Bot.* 84(2):253–73. HUNZIKER, A. T. 1943. Las especies alimentirias de *Amaranthus* y *Chenopodium* cultivadas por los Indios de America. *Revista Argent. Agron.* 10:297–355. SIMON, L. E. 1961. Morphologia, distribucion y valor diagnostico de los pelos glandulares en especies de *Chenopodium* L. (Chenopodiaceae). *Notas Mus. La Plata, Bot.* 21(99):99–110. KÜHN, U., V. BITTRICH, R. CAROLIN, H. FREITAG, I. C. HEDGE, P. UOTILLA, AND P. G. WILSON. 1993. Chenopodiaceae. In *The Families and Genera of Flowering Plants*, eds. K. Kubitski, J. G. Rohwer, and V. Bittrich, 2:13–19. Berlin: Springer-Verlag. WILSON, H. D. 1981. Genetic variation among South American populations of tetraploid *Chenopodium* sect. *Chenopodium* subsect. *Cel-*

lulata. Syst. Bot. 6(4):380–98. WILSON, H. D. 1988a. Quinoa biosystematics. I. Domesticated populations. *Econ. Bot.* 42(4): 461–77. WILSON, H. D. 1988b. Quinoa biosystematics. II. Free-living populations. *Econ. Bot.* 42(4):478–94. WILSON, H. D., AND C. B. HEISER. 1979. The origin and evolutionary relationships of 'Hauzonthle' (*Chenopodium nuttallae* Stafford) domesticated chenopod of Mexico. *Amer. J. Bot.* 66(2): 198–206.

CHLORANTHACEAE (Chloranthus Family)

CAROL TODZIA

Figure 50, Plate 13

- *trees or shrubs*
- *prop roots often present*
- *stipules present*
- *leaves opposite, simple, aromatic; petiole bases forming distinctive sheath on stem; blade margins dentate*
- *fruits drupes*

Numbers of genera and species. Worldwide, the Chloranthaceae comprise four genera and circa 80 species. In tropical America, there is a single genus, *Hedyosmum*, with 44 species.

Distribution and habitat. The Chloranthaceae occur in tropical regions throughout the world, excluding Africa. *Hedyosmum*, the only genus in the Western Hemisphere, ranges from Veracruz, Mexico, south through Central America to Bolivia and east to Guyana (Mt. Roraima), Brazil, and the West Indies. The greatest species diversity occurs in montane regions of the neotropics. Colombia, with 17 species, harbors the greatest diversity.

The Chloranthaceae usually inhabit primary and secondary habitats in wet tropical areas. Species of *Hedyosmum* live in lowland rain forest, wet montane forest, and *subpáramo* and elfin forest. *Hedyosmum brasiliense*, occurs in gallery forest, grassy *campo*, and rocky *cerrado*. *Hedyosmum mexicanum* is present in semideciduous forest in Mexico. The majority of species are found in midelevation montane rain forest from 1,000 to 3,000 meters. *Hedyosmum cumbalense* has the highest elevational range, reaching *subpáramo* forest at 3,500 meters.

Family classification. The Chloranthaceae are placed in the Piperales by Cronquist. Recent molecular studies suggest that the Chloranthaceae form a distinct group near families such as the Piperaceae; however the family's relationship with other taxa is still unresolved.

With only four genera, there is no formal infrafamilial classification. However, *Hedyosmum* and *Ascarina*, by virtue of their unisexual flowers and woody habit, are more closely

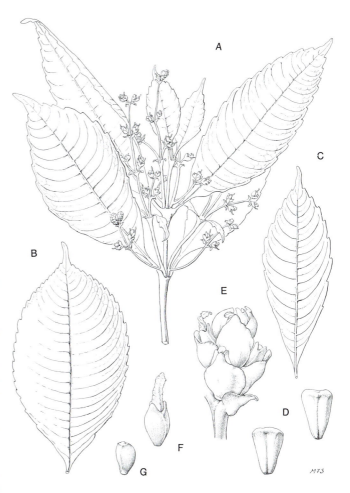

Figure 50. CHLORANTHACEAE. *Hedyosmum costaricense*. **A.** Stem with leaves and pistillate and staminate inflorescences. **B, C.** Leaves showing venation and marginal teeth. **D.** Anthers. **E.** Lateral view of pistillate inflorescence. **F.** Lateral view of pistillate flower. **G.** Lateral view of fruit. Reprinted with permission from Todzia (1988). Artist: Margaret F. Schroeder.

related to each other than to *Sarcandra* and *Chloranthus*, which have bisexual flowers and an herbaceous habit.

Features of the family. Habit: scandent (*Hedyosmum nutans* and *H. brenesii*) or erect shrubs, or large trees (to 30 m tall in *H. cuatrecazanum*), the trees often with well-developed prop roots. **Stipules** present, emerging from margin of vaginate sheath on either side of petioles. **Leaves** opposite, simple; pungently aromatic when crushed (aromas ranging from lemon to pepper and anise), sometimes glabrous (ca. half of *Hedyosmum* species, and other genera of family), pubescent in 17 species of *Hedyosmum*, the trichomes eglandular, uniseriate or multiseriate; petiole bases connate, forming distinctive sheath along stem (up to 2 centimeters), giving appearance of swollen nodes; blade margins dentate; venation pinnate. **Inflorescences** terminal or axillary, simple, rarely compound, spicate or racemose, sometimes paniculate (*Hedyosmum*); 1–3 bracts sometimes present (pistillate flowers). **Flowers** actinomorphic or zygomorphic, unisexual (the plants usually dioecious, less often monoecious), green. **Staminate flowers** without perianth; stamen 1, the anther oblong, dehiscing longitudinally. **Pistillate flowers** with perianth tissue surrounding ovary, the apex lobed, the lobes 3, small; ovary inferior or semi-inferior, sometimes nude, trigonous, carpel 1, locule 1, the styles absent or very short, the stigmas large, dry; ovule 1, pendulous from apex of locule, orthotropous. **Fruits** drupes; exocarps thin, the mesocarps fleshy. **Seeds** 1 per fruit; endosperm well developed, oily, starchy.

In most species of *Hedyosmum*, the floral bracts become fleshy and fused to various degrees. These fleshy floral bracts become succulent and white or purple at maturity forming the dispersal attractant.

Natural history. *Hedyosmum* flowers are thought to be wind-pollinated because of their long staminate inflorescences, abundant pollen, long flowering season, large dry stigmas, and green color. The white or purple fleshy fruits of *Hedyosmum* are presumed to be dispersed by birds. *Hedyosmum mexicanum*, with its large (1.5–3 cm long), light-green to yellow fruits, may be mammal dispersed.

Economic uses. The leaves of several species of *Hedyosmum* are brewed into a pleasant-tasting tea that is reputed to alleviate fever, headaches, and upset stomachs. In Ecuador, this tea is used as a substitute for black tea or coffee. The leaves of various species of *Hedyosmum* also are used externally for relieving aching joints and to reduce swelling associated with insect and snake bites. The wood of *H. scabrum* is of local economic value. The fruits of *H. mexicanum* are edible.

References. TODZIA, C. A. 1988. Chloranthaceae: *Hedyosmum. Fl. Neotrop. Monogr.* 48:1–139. TODZIA, C. A. 1993. Chloranthaceae. In *The Families and Genera of Vascular Plants*, eds. K. Kubitzki, J. G. Rohwer, and V. Bittrich, 2: 281–87. Berlin: Springer-Verlag. VERDCOURT, B. 1986. Chloranthaceae. In *Flora Malesiana*, eds. C.G.G.J. Van Steenis and W.J.J.W. De Wild, Series 1, 10(2):123–44. Alphen Aan Den Rijn, The Netherlands: Sijthoff and Noordhoff International Publishers.

CHRYSOBALANACEAE (Cocoa Plum Family)

GHILLEAN T. PRANCE

Figure 51, Plate 13

- *trees and shrubs*
- *stipules present, often small and caducous*
- *leaves alternate, simple*
- *flowers with hypanthial tube; sepals 5; petals usually 5; style gynobasic*
- *fruits drupes*

Numbers of genera and species. Worldwide, the Chrysobalanceae comprise 18 genera and circa 521 species. In tropical America, there are eight genera and 417 known species. The largest genus is *Licania* with 214 species in the neotropics and four species in the Eastern Hemisphere. *Hirtella* has 107 species in the neotropics and two species in Africa and *Couepia* has 71 species, all Neotropical. The remaining Neotropical genera are: *Acioa* with four species, *Chrysobalanus* with three species, *Exellodendron* with five species, *Maranthes* with one species in Central America (11 species in the Eastern Hemisphere), and *Parinari* with 19 Neotropical species (20 species in the Eastern Hemisphere). *Chrysobalanus icaco*, widespread in the neotropics, is the only Chrysobalanaceae to extend outside of the Tropics in the Western Hemisphere.

Distribution and habitat. Species of Chrysobalanaceae are found in Central and South America, the Caribbean, Africa, Madagascar, southern India, Southeast Asia, and on many islands of the South Pacific. Several genera occur on more than one continent and at least three are pantropical (*Licania*, *Maranthes*, and *Parinari*).

In the Western Hemisphere, the Chrysobalanaceae range from Florida, the Gulf States, and Central Mexico to Rio Grande do Sul, Brazil, where one species occurs. Several species are also found in the Caribbean.

Chrysobalanaceae are predominantly found in lowland rain forests and are often ranked among the five most important families in abundance in inventories of nonflooded forests. Many species also occur in floodplain forests. Only a few species occur above 1,000 meters elevation, but there

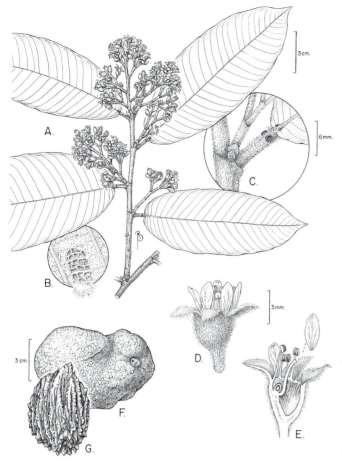

Figure 51. CHRYSOBALANACEAE. *Parinari montana*. **A.** Stem with leaves and inflorescences. **B.** Abaxial leaf surface with part of woolly pubescence removed to show detail of venation. **C.** Detail of node with stipules, base of inflorescence, and petiole with distinct glands at distal end. **D.** Lateral view of flower. **E.** Medial section of flower showing perched gynoecium, gynobasic style, cup-shaped hypanthium, and petal (above). **F.** Fruit with attachment scar (right). **G.** Seed with corrugated endocarp. Reprinted with permission from Mori et al. (2002). Artist: Bobbi Angell.

Traditionally, the family has been divided into two tribes, Chrysobalaneae and Hirtelleae. More recently it has been subdivided into four tribes: Chrysobalaneae, Parinarieae, Couepieae, and Hirtelleae, all of which occur in the Western Hemisphere and at least one other continent.

Features of the family. Habit: usually trees, less frequently shrubs. **Bark** often smooth, the outer bark thin, the inner bark often reddish and friable (see following discussion). **Stipules** present, axillary or inserted on the lower portion of petiole (*Licania*), often caducous, small to large (largest in species of *Licania* and *Parinari*). **Leaves** alternate, simple, glands often present on petioles or abaxial surface of blades. **Inflorescences** axillary, terminal, or occasionally cauliflorous, racemose, paniculate, fasciculate, spicate, or cymose; bracteoles present, sometimes enclosing small groups of flowers (*Parinari* and *Licania licaniiflora*); glands often present (*Hirtella*), stipitate or sessile. **Flowers** actinomorphic (*Chrysobalanus* and *Licania*) or zygomorphic, bisexual; hypanthial tube present; sepals 5, entire, imbricate, glands sometimes present, stipitate (*Hirtella* species) or sessile (*Couepia longipendula*); disc always present, lining receptacle or forming annular structure at mouth; petals usually 5, rarely absent (*Licania* subgenus *Moquilea* section *Leptobalanus* and subgenus *Licania*), distinct; androecium of 3–numerous (3 in *Licania* to 300 in *Couepia*) stamens, the stamens usually distinct, sometimes in complete circle or inserted unilaterally, rarely united into straplike ligule (3 species of *Acioa*), the filaments exserted (*Acioa*, *Chrysobalanus*, *Couepia*, *Hirtella*, *Maranthes*, and some *Licania*) or included (*Parinari*, *Exellodendron*, and some *Licania*), sometimes united to half length (some species of *Licania* and all *Chrysobalanus*), the anthers dorsifixed, dehiscing laterally; gynoecium with superior ovary, the ovary inserted at base, middle, or mouth of hypanthium, the carpels usually 1, rarely 3, the locules 1–2, the style filiform, arising from hypanthium at base of ovary (gynobasic); ovules 2 (in 1-locular ovaries, *Acioa*, *Chrysobalanus*, *Couepia*, *Hirtella*, *Licania*) or 1 per locule (in 2-locular ovaries, *Exellodendron*, *Maranthes*, *Parinari*), basal, erect, epitropous, the micropyle directed toward base. **Fruits** drupes, dry or fleshy, the endocarp hard and fibrous or thin and bony, indehiscent, dehiscing longitudinally (*Chrysobalanus* and most *Hirtella*), or by basal stoppers (*Parinari*). **Seeds** usually 1, sometimes 2 per fruit; endosperm absent, the cotyledons planoconvex; germination cryptocotylar or phanerocotylar.

When hit with a machete, the bark of most species chips into small fragments with a sharp metallic ring due to the presence of abundant silica grains, which also make the wood of most species exceptionally hard and difficult to saw.

Natural history. The Chrysobalanaceae have a wide range of pollinators. The smaller-flowered genera, *Chrysobalanus*, *Parinari*, *Exellodendron*, and *Licania*, usually are pollinated by small bees. Most species of *Couepia* are night-flowering

are several representations in the savannas of the Guianas, Venezuela, Amazonia, and the *cerrado* of Central Brazil, where *Licania dealbata* and *Parinari obtusifolia* are geoxylic suffrutices. Only *Licania rigida* is common in the *caatinga* of northeast Brazil. *Chrysobalanus icaco* is a shrub or small tree of coastal sand dunes in the Caribbean, South America, and West Africa, and the other two species of the genus are large rain-forest trees.

Family classification. The Chrysobalanaceae (Rosales *sensu* Cronquist) are a distinct monophyletic family previously treated as a subfamily of the Rosaceae. Recent molecular data has shown the Chrysobalanaceae to be a member of Rosidae (rosid group 1) nearest to Dichapetalaceae and Trigoniaceae, but also close to Erythroxylaceae and Violaceae. The family is now placed in the Malpighiales.

and are pollinated by hawkmoths, with the exception of two flagelliflorous species, *C. longipendula* and *C. dolichopoda*, which are pollinated by bats. *Hirtella* is pollinated mainly by butterflies. African species of *Maranthes* are bat-pollinated, but no observations have been made for the single species, *M. panamensis*, of the Western Hemisphere. The hummingbird-pollinated *Hirtella rugosa* from the mountains of Puerto Rico has bright red petals, which stay half open to form a tube in which nectar accumulates. Hummingbirds also have been observed visiting the flowers of several other species of the family, especially in *Couepia*. Experiments with *Chrysobalanus icaco* have shown it to be self-compatible.

The fruits of Chrysobalanaceae are quite uniform in structure, yet have become adapted to a wide range of dispersal agents. *Chrysobalanus icaco* produces fleshy, buoyant fruits dispersed by animals and ocean currents. Several riparian species of *Licania* drop their fruits into the water at flood time and are eaten by fish. Fruits of species of *Couepia*, *Licania*, and *Parinari* frequently are eaten by bats. Agoutis have been observed transporting the fruits of *Couepia racemosa* and *C. longipendula*, and probably disperse many other species of the family. Most species of *Hirtella*, with their small fleshy fruits, are bird-dispersed. *Parinari obtusifolia*, a low shrub of the Brazilian *cerrado*, is dispersed by rheas.

Seven species of *Hirtella* section *Myrmecophila* have domatia at the junction of the leaf lamina with the petiole. These are inhabited by ants of the genera *Allomerus*, *Azteca*, or *Solenopsis*. The leaves of most species of Chrysobalanaceae have extrafloral nectaries on the petiole or the lower surface of the leaf blades.

Economic uses. The fruits of various species are consumed frequently by local peoples. Those of *Chrysobalanus icaco* are preserved in syrup and sold in Colombia and Venezuela under the name *icacos*. Various species of *Couepia* and *Parinari* are eaten, especially *C. bracteosa* (*pajura*). Both *Acioa edulis* and *Couepia longipendula* are used locally as sources of cooking oil, which is extracted from the cotyledons. *Licania arborea* and *L. rigida* produce a fast-drying oil that is used as a substitute for tung oil in paints. *Couepia subcordata* and *Licania tomentosa* (*oiti*) are common as shade trees in towns of tropical South America.

The presence of silica grains makes the wood of Chrysobalanaceae extremely hard to work. It has many local uses, however, especially for marine and river pilings because of its resistance to marine borers. It is also resistant to termite attack. Some species are used locally for fuel and charcoal, and *Hirtella carbonaria* of Pacific coastal Colombia derives its specific name for the latter use. Throughout Amazonia, the bark of various species of *Licania* and *Couepia* is burned to form an ash full of silica grains that is mixed with clay to strengthen pottery.

References. FRITSCH, C. 1888. Ueber die Gattungen der Chrysobalanaceen. *Verh. Zool.-Bot. Ges. Wien* 38:93–95. HOOKER, J. D. 1867. Rosaceae: Chrysobalanaceae. In *Flora Brasiliensis* 14(2):5–56. Monachii: Lipsiae, Apud R. Oldenbourg in comm. PRANCE, G. T. 1972. Chrysobalanaceae. *Fl. Neotrop. Monogr.* 9:1–409. PRANCE, G. T. 1989. Chrysobalanaceae. *Fl. Neotrop. Monogr.* 9S:1–267. PRANCE, G. T. 1986. Chrysobalanaceae. In *Flora of the Guianas*, ed. Görts-Van Rijn, 85:1–146. Koenigstein: Koeltz Scientific Books. PRANCE, G. T., AND F. WHITE. 1988. The genera of Chrysobalanaceae: a study in practical and theoretical taxonomy and its relevance to evolutionary biology. *Philos. Trans., Ser. B* 320:1–184.

CISTACEAE (Rock-rose Family)

BEAT FISCHER

Figure 52

- *usually subshrubs, sometimes shrubs or herbs*
- *leaves usually alternate or whorled, often small and ericoid*
- *flowers actinomorphic, bisexual; sepals 3 or 5; petals usually 3 or 5; stamens usually numerous; ovary superior, usually 1-locular; placentation parietal, the ovules few to many*
- *fruits loculicidal capsules*

Numbers of genera and species. Worldwide, the Cistaceae comprise eight genera and circa 182 species. In the Western Hemisphere, there are three native genera, *Helianthemum* (ca. 110 species worldwide), *Lechea* (20), and *Hudsonia* (3). Only *Helianthemum* (9 species) and *Lechea* (4) occur in tropical America.

Distribution and habitat. The rock-rose family is widely but irregularly distributed in temperate or warm-temperate regions. The principal center of diversity is in the Mediterranean region, but there is a secondary center in the eastern United States. Neotropical members are found in Central America, especially in Mexico.

Neotropical species of Cistaceae usually occur at high elevations (1,500–3,000 m) in exposed areas, often on dry hills

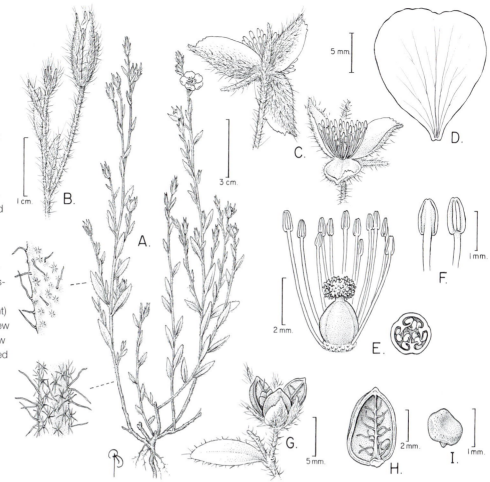

Figure 52. CISTACEAE. *Helianthemum brasiliense* (A–B, Pederson 58; C–E, Herter 257; Rambo 34692). **A.** Plant with details of stem and leaf (left) showing simple and stellate trichomes. **B.** Part of stem with flower in bud. **C.** Basal (left) and lateral (right) views of flowers. **D.** Adaxial view of petal. **E.** Flower with petals, sepals, and some stamens removed to show gynoecium (left) and transverse section of ovary (right). **F.** Abaxial (left) and adaxial (right) views of stamens. **G.** Lateral view of dehisced fruit. **H.** Adaxial view of valve of fruit with one attached seed. **I.** Seed. Original. Artist: Bobbi Angell.

and rocky slopes of alkaline or sandy soils, and in mixed forests dominated by *Pinus* and *Quercus*.

Family classification. The Cistaceae are placed in the Violales by Cronquist and the Cistales by Takhtajan and are aligned with the Bixaceae by both authors. Molecular analyses support a placement near the Bixaceae and suggest that these families belong in the Malvales with, for example, the Malvaceae, Dipterocarpaceae, Thymelaeaceae, and Sarcolaenaceae (of Madagascar). Phylogenetic relationships within the Cistaceae are poorly understood, but their monophyly is supported by the morphology of the calyx.

Features of the family. Habit: usually subshrubs, sometimes shrubs or herbs, essential oils frequently present, often resinous, hairs often present, glandular and/or nonglandular and tufted. **Stipules** sometimes present. **Leaves** usually alternate, sometimes whorled, or rarely opposite, simple; petiole vascular bundles 1–several; blades small, flat or rolled, often reduced (ericoid) or scalelike, the margins entire; venation of a single vein (as in *Lechea*), pinnate, or palmate. **Inflorescences** terminal or axillary, determinate, cymose (but often appearing racemose), or of solitary flowers. **Flowers** showy,

actinomorphic, bisexual; sepals 3 or 5, pubescent, persistent, the outer 2 (when 5) often much smaller, bracteole-like or narrower than inner 3, sometimes fused to inner 3; petals 5, sometimes 3 (e.g., *Lechea*), or absent in cleistogamous flowers of *Helianthemum*, often ephemeral, convolute, often crumpled in bud; androecium of (3–10)numerous stamens, the stamens sometimes sensitive to touch (*Helianthemum*), the filaments distinct, the anthers dehiscing longitudinally; gynoecium syncarpous, the ovary superior, the carpels 3–5(10), the locule usually 1 (or sometimes 3 incomplete locules), the style 1, undivided, sometimes very short or nearly wanting, the stigma(s) usually 1 or sometimes 3, sessile, capitate, or discoid, often lobed; placentation parietal, the ovules 2–many per placenta. **Fruits** loculicidal capsules, coriaceous or woody, the valves 3 (*Helianthemum*) or 5–10. **Seeds** 1–numerous; endosperm starchy, often hard, the embryo usually curved or coiled.

Natural history. The ephemeral flowers open only in full sunlight and usually stay open for only a few hours. The brightly colored petals and numerous stamens attract bees, flies, and beetles that collect the copious pollen. In some flowers, such as some *Helianthemum*, the stamens are sensitive, moving outward when touched by insects and powdering them with pollen. Self-pollination is distributed widely in the family because of the common occurrence of cleistogamous flowers, which often occur on the same plant as chasmogamous flowers. Self-pollination may also occur as the anthers are pressed against the stigma when the flowers close (this probably frequent in *Lechea*).

No information is available about dispersal biology.

Economic uses. The family is of limited economic importance, especially in the neotropics. The leaves of several Mediterranean *Cistus*, especially *C. ladanifer* and *C. incanus* subspecies *creticus*, produce the aromatic resin ladanum formerly used in medicine. *Cistus salviifolius* has been used in Greece as a substitute for tea. In Mexico, the shoots of *Lechea villosa* are used as a tonic and to reduce fever. Several species of *Cistus*, *Halimium*, and *Helianthemum* are grown as ornamentals.

References. ARRINGTON, J. M., AND K. KUBITZKI. 2003. Cistaceae. In *The Families and Genera of Vascular Plants*, eds. K. Kubitzki and C. Bayer. 5:62–70. Berlin: Springer-Verlag. BRIZICKY, G. K. 1964. The genera of Cistaceae in the southeastern United States. *J. Arnold Arbor.* 45:364–57. DAOUD, H. S., AND R. L. WILBUR. 1965. A revision of the North American species of *Helianthemum* (Cistaceae). *Rhodora* 67:63–82, 201–16, 255–312. HODGDON, A. R. 1938. A taxonomic study of *Lechea*. *Rhodora* 40:29–69, 87–131. JUDD, W. S., AND S. R. MANCHESTER. 1997. Circumscription of Malvaceae (Malvales) as determined by a preliminary cladistic analysis employing morphological, palynological, and chemical characters. *Brittonia* 49:384–405. WILBUR, R. L. 1966. Notes on Rafinesque's species of *Lechea* (Cistaceae). *Rhodora* 68:192–208. WILBUR, R. L., AND H. S. DAOUD. 1961. The genus *Lechea* (Cistaceae) in the southeastern United States. *Rhodora* 63:103–18.

CLETHRACEAE (Pepperbush Family)

CLAES GUSTAFSSON

Plate 13

- *trees or shrubs*

- *leaves alternate, simple*

- *inflorescences terminal, racemes*

- *flowers fragrant, white to cream; perianth 5-merous; stamens 10*

- *fruits loculicidal capsules*

Numbers of genera and species. Worldwide, the Clethraceae comprise a single genus, *Clethra*, and 73 species. In the Western Hemisphere, 47 species are recognized, 45 of which are tropical.

Distribution and habitat. The Clethraceae have a disjunct distribution with almost one third of the species in southeast Asia and Malaysia (23 species), most of the rest occur in the Americas, and one species is found on the island of Madeira. In the Americas, most species occur in mountains from Mexico to southeast Bolivia and northeast Argentina, but two species occur in southeast Brazil, two species in Jamaica and Cuba, and two species in temperate North America.

Species of *Clethra* are most diverse in tropical montane habitats and are usually found growing in acidic soils. A few of the Neotropical species reach sea level in Central America.

Family classification. The Clethraceae are placed in the Ericales by Cronquist. The latest ordinal classification placed the family in a broadly circumscribed, monophyletic Ericales. Recent molecular studies place the Clethraceae in a monophyletic group, sister to Cyrillaceae and Ericaceae *sensu lato*.

Clethra is divided into two sections, section *Clethra* and section *Cuellaria*, based mainly on seed characters. All Asian and Malesian species and the two species occurring in North America belong to section *Clethra*. The section *Cuellaria* is subdivided into two subsections of which subsection *Cuellaria* contains all South American, Central American, and Mexican species. Subsection *Pseudocuellaria* includes only the single species from Madeira.

Features of the family. Habit: trees (a few more than 20 m tall) or shrubs, usually evergreen, indument well developed on vegetative parts and inflorescences (at least when young), the hairs simple, fascicled, or stellate (placement and combination of hairs used in keys). Stems with terminal bud 1, axillary buds 1–4, the terminal bud often developing into inflorescences, the axillary buds developing vegetative shoots. Stipules absent. Leaves alternate, may appear opposite (subopposite) when crowded at stem apex, simple. Inflorescences terminal, racemes, usually several arranged in fasciculate, paniculate, or umbellate clusters, sometimes simple; bracts caducous; bracteoles absent; pedicels filiform to thick, increasing in length from flowering to fruiting. **Flowers** actinomorphic, bisexual, usually small, fragrant; sepals pubescent, the lobes 5, persistent, often slightly shorter or equal to petal length, becoming lignified during fruit development; petals 5, usually distinct, 2–6 mm. long, sometimes coherent or connate at base, often abaxially convex (spoon-shaped), glabrous or sometimes pubescent toward base, white to cream, the margins often ciliate, sometimes entire, the apex obtuse to rounded, usually erose-fimbriate, sometimes entire; androecium obdiplostemonous, of 10 stamens, the filaments slightly enlarged at base, flattened laterally, glabrous, elongating to various degrees during anthesis, the anthers becoming somewhat exserted in some species, dehiscing poricidally; disc absent; gynoecium syncarpous, the ovary superior, pubescent, the carpels 3, the locules 3(4), the styles glabrous or pubescent, the stigma lobes 3; placentation axile, the 3 pendent placentas arising from upper portion of central column, the ovules numerous per carpel, unitegmic, tenuinucellate, anatropous. **Fruits** loculicidal capsules, subglobose (3–7[–10] mm diam.). **Seeds** usually numerous, those of section *Cuellaria* flattened, winged (by the short to long, obtuse testa cells), those of section *Clethra* sometimes subtrigonous, the testa cells sometimes isodiametric, foveolate.

Chromosome numbers for the Madeiran species *Clethra arborea* ($n = 8$) and the North American species *C. alnifolia* ($n = 16$) have been reported.

Natural history. The flowers are protandrous and the pollen is shed in bud. Nothing is known about the pollinators or the dispersal biology of tropical species.

Economic uses. Several species of *Clethra*, for example the North American *C. alnifolia* (sweet pepperbush) and *C. acuminata* and the Asian *C. barbinervis*, are cultivated as ornamentals in many parts of the world and are prized for their fragrant flowers in mid- or late summer. *Clethra alnifolia* has a pink-flowered form that occurs sporadically in the wild and is also found in cultivation.

References. ANDERBERG, A. A., ET AL. 2002. Phylogenetic relationships in the order Ericales s.l.: Analyses of molecular data from five genes from the plastid and mitochondrial genomes. *Amer. J. Bot.* 89:677–87. GIEBEL, K. P., AND W. C. DICKISON. 1976. Wood anatomy of Clethraceae. *J. Elisha Mitchell Sci. Soc.* 92:17–26. GUSTAFSSON, C. 1992. Clethraceae. *Flora of Ecuador*, eds. G. Harling and L. Andersson, no. 45:1–26. Göteborg, Sweden: Department of Systematic Botany, University of Göteborg. HAGERUP, O. 1928. Morphological and cytological studies of Bicornes. *Dansk. Bot. Ark.* 6:1–27. HAMILTON, C. W. 1985. Notes and description of seven new species of mesoamerican Clethraceae. *Ann. Missouri Bot. Gard.* 72:539–43. SLEUMER, H. 1967. Monographia Clethracearum. *Bot. Jahrb. Syst.* 87:36–175.

CLUSIACEAE (Mangosteen Family)

MATS H. G. GUSTAFSSON AND MICHAEL NEE

Figure 53, Plate 14

- *trees, shrubs, or herbs*
- *stems and leaves commonly with latex*
- *leaves usually opposite, simple; blades entire*
- *flowers actinomorphic; stamens usually numerous*

Numbers of genera and species. Worldwide, the Clusiaceae comprise 36 genera and circa 1,600 species. In tropical America, there are 23 genera and circa 750 species. The exact number of species is difficult to estimate because many of the larger genera, such as *Clusia* and *Garcinia*, are poorly known. The largest genera are *Clusia* (including *Havetia*, *Havetiopsis*, *Oedematopus*, *Quapoya*, and *Renggeria*) with close to 300 Neotropical species, *Hypericum* with more than 100 Neotropical species and circa 420 species worldwide, *Chrysochlamys* (incuding *Tovomitopsis*) with circa 55 Neotropical species, *Vismia* with 52 Neotropical species, *Kiel-*

meyera with 47 Neotropical species, *Garcinia* (including *Rheedia*) with 30–40 Neotropical species and nearly 300 species worldwide, *Caraipa* with 28 Neotropical species, *Marila* with 28 Neotropical species, and *Tovomita* with 25 or more Neotropical species.

Distribution and habitat. The Clusiaceae have an almost worldwide distribution, but most genera are tropical. *Hypericum* and a few closely allied genera occur in temperate regions as well as in the montane Tropics. Tropical America is an important center of diversity.

Most of the woody genera are found in lowland humid forests, but many also occur at higher altitudes in montane forests. Species of *Hypericum*, in particular, are more common at higher altitudes. Andean species of *Clusia* can be found at above 3,000 meters in *páramo* vegetation, and some species of *Hypericum* reach elevations above 4,000 meters. Unlike most Clusiaceae, species of *Vismia* are common in early secondary vegetation.

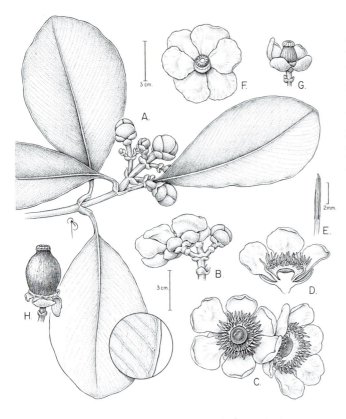

Figure 53. CLUSIACEAE. *Clusia palmicida*. **A.** Stem with leaves, buds, and detail of leaf venation (below). **B.** Lateral view of flower and buds. **C.** Apical (left) and oblique (right) views of staminate flowers. **D.** Medial section of staminate flower. **E.** Lateral view of anther. **F.** Apical view of pistillate flower. **G.** Lateral view of immature fruit. **H.** Lateral view of immature fruit. Reprinted with permission from Mori et al. (2002). Artist: Bobbi Angell.

Family classification. The Clusiaceae are placed in the Theales by Cronquist. The Bonnetiaceae have frequently been considered to be closely related to the Clusiaceae, and are similar in seed structure and secondary chemistry, although they lack the secretory organs typical of Clusiaceae. Another group that is thought to be related to the Clusiaceae is the Elatinaceae, a family of diminutive, often aquatic herbs. Molecular data indicate a close relationship to the Bonnetiaceae and perhaps also to the Malpighiaceae and Caryocaraceae.

The circumscription of the Clusiaceae has varied. *Kielmeyera* and *Neotatea*, which have alternate leaves, have been included in the Theaceae or their segregate family Bonnetiaceae. A group of genera has been segregated as the Hypericaceae, which, in the neotropics, is represented by *Hypericum*, *Santomasia*, *Thornea*, and *Vismia*. These genera are characterized by bisexual flowers with fascicled stamens and usually glandular-punctate leaves and flower parts. The group is now often treated as the subfamily Hypericoideae. Molecular data clearly show that the specialized aquatic family Podostemaceae is closely related to the Hypericoideae, and thus nested within the Clusiaceae.

Calophyllum, *Caraipa*, *Haploclathra*, *Kielmeyera*, *Mahurea*, *Mammea*, *Marila*, *Neotatea*, and three to five Paleotropical genera belong in the subfamily Kielmeyeroideae, a variable group with bisexual flowers and free, "normal" stamens with thin filaments.

The Clusioideae are a highly variable subfamily of glabrous plants, often with highly specialized androecia and very reduced cotyledons. Within this subfamily, the tribe Symphonieae (sometimes treated as a subfamily), which contains *Lorostemon*, *Moronobea*, *Platonia*, *Symphonia*, *Thysanostemon*, and the Paleotropical *Montrouziera* and *Pentadesma*, are a well-defined group with bisexual flowers and fascicled stamens. Other Clusioideae have mostly unisexual flowers. Among these, *Clusiella* and *Garcinia* (including *Rheedia*) stand somewhat apart and are sometimes placed in tribes of their own, while *Chrysochlamys*, *Clusia*, *Dystovomita*, and *Tovomita* form the strictly Neotropical tribe Clusieae, which is characterized by fleshy capsules with arillate seeds.

Features of the family. Habit: trees (some reaching 40 m high), shrubs (then often epiphytes or hemiepiphytes; (many *Clusia*), or herbs (*Hypericum* and some related genera), rarely annual, often glabrous, less frequently with hairs, the hairs stellate (*Caraipa*, *Marila*, and *Vismia*) or unicellular. **Latex** common in stems and leaves, usually yellow, sometimes orange, white, or clear, often darkening when exposed to air. **Stipules** absent, sometimes minute appendages occurring in their place. **Leaves** usually opposite, sometimes whorled, or alternate (*Caraipa*, *Kielmeyera*, *Mahurea*, and *Neotatea*), simple, often thick, coriaceous, sometimes scalelike or needlelike (*Hypericum*) and giving plants a juniper-like habit, sometimes traversed by latex ducts, or dark or transparent resin glands present (common in Hypericoideae); blade margins usually entire; petiole base sometimes with outgrowths, forming protective caplike structure over apex of stem. **Inflorescences** terminal or axillary, cymose, or rarely racemes, fascicles, or of solitary flowers; bracts and bracteoles often present. **Flowers** actinomorphic, bisexual or unisexual (plants dioecious); sepals usually 2–5 (sometimes indefinite), often appearing to intergrade with bracts on pedicel; petals (3)5(14), often yellow or white, less often pink or red; androecium usually of numerous stamens, the stamens rarely less than 10, distinct or fused into ring-shaped or massive structures, or grouped into 2–5 bundles opposite petals (Hypericoideae, Garcinieae, and Symphonieae), the anthers usually dehiscing longitudinally (several kinds of dehiscence in *Clusia* and *Garcinia*); gynoecium syncarpous, the ovary superior, the carpels 2–5 (rarely to 20), the locules equal in number to carpels, the style 1 and distally branched or 1 per carpel, or absent and stigmas sessile; placentation axile (very rarely parietal or basal), the ovules (1–) many per carpel. **Fruits** capsules or berries, the capsules dry or fleshy (*Clusia*), the dehiscence variable, the berries often large, with a coriaceous exocarp (Garcinieae and Symphonieae). **Seeds** 1–many; aril sometimes present (Clusieae), partly surrounding seed, white or orange; endosperm virtually absent, the cotyledons often much reduced (Clusioideae).

Natural history. *Symphonia globulifera* is a prominent component of swamp forests in the Amazon and develops arching roots aboveground that function as pneumatophores.

Epiphytic or primary hemiepiphytic species of *Clusia* are fairly frequent in Neotropical forests and may reach large dimensions. The primary hemiepiphytic species begins life as an epiphyte on a branch, and, as the plant develops, it sends down roots that proliferate upon reaching the ground. When these aerial roots grow down the stem of their support tree they may anastomose and thus become "stranglers."

Clusia is an extremely diverse genus in terms of flower morphology and pollination biology. The stamens are adapted differentially for different pollinators. Some species have ordinary-looking stamens, whereas others have the stamens variously united or reduced. Stamens and staminodes that are fused or have stout filaments often secrete resin. This is produced in secretory cavities in the filaments and serves as a reward for visiting bees, which pollinate the flowers and use the resin in nest construction. *Clusia columnaris* is a resin-secreting species in which the stamens are fused into a central globular structure with ring-shaped pollen sacs. In *C. schomburgkiana*, each "anther" consists of many minute, cone-shaped pollensacs. Resin is secreted around each group of pollen sacs, and these detach and are collected by bees together with the resin. An elongate mass of pollen later protrudes from each pollensac, and in this way the pollen can be deposited onto the stigma of a female flower visited by the bee. The pollinator reward in *Clusia* with more normal-looking stamens is nectar or pollen. One example is *C. criuva*, which is pollinated by nocturnal, pollen-eating beetles.

Members of the tribe Symphoniae have nectariferous flowers that are often large and reddish in color and are reported to be visited by various kinds of birds, butterflies, and monkeys. However, perching birds are probably the most effective pollinators.

Birds are attracted by the colorful arillate seeds of *Clusia* and related genera, and apparently disperse the seeds efficiently after consuming the arils. The arils of different species are quite variable morphologically and may develop either from the funicle or the micropyle of the seed.

The Paleotropical *Garcinia mangostana* (mangosteen), known to be apomictic, produces seeds via adventitious embryony. The same is true of some species of *Clusia*. No male plants of *C. rosea* seem to occur in much of its distribution area, so this species apparently relies largely on apomixis for its reproduction.

Economic uses. Several Clusiaceae are important timber trees; e.g., *Calophyllum brasiliense* (*palo maría*), which is found throughout much of tropical America. Some Clusiaceae produce edible fruits: examples are *Mammea americana* (mammee apple), the delicious fruits of various species of *Garcinia*, *Moronobea*, and *Platonia*, and the economically important *Garcinia mangostana* (mangosteen), introduced from Southeast Asia.

Clusiaceae have seeds rich in fat, and some, like those of *Platonia*, are edible. The African *Allanblackia* and *Pentadesma* are sources of a fat used in cooking.

The latex and resins of Clusiaceae have been utilized by Amerindians for glue, birdlime (a sticky substance used to capture birds), caulk for canoes, incense, and fuel to burn as a source of light.

Substances of potential or actual medicinal use are prevalent in Clusiaceae and include a drastic purgative from the Paleotropical *Garcinia gummi-gutta*, substances with anti-AIDS potential in *Calophyllum*, antidepressants in *Hypericum*, and compounds with antitumor activity found throughout the family.

Many species of *Hypericum* have showy flowers, and a number of them are grown as ornamentals in temperate areas. Some tropical taxa also are used as ornamentals; for example, *Calophyllum inophyllum* and *Clusia rosea*.

References. BITTRICH, V., AND M.C.E. AMARAL. 1996. Flower morphology and pollination biology of *Clusia* species from the Gran Sabana (Venezuela). *Kew Bull.* 51:681–94. CORRERA Q., J. E., AND H. Y. BERNAL. 1993a. Guttiferae (Clusiaceae). In *Especies vegetales promisorias de los países del Convenio Andrés Bello*, Tomo IX. Santafé de Bogotá, D. E., Colombia: Secretaria Ejecutiva del Convenio Andrés Bello. CORRERA Q., J. E., AND H. Y. BERNAL. 1993b. Hypericaceae. In *Especies vegetales promisorias de los países del Convenio Andrés Bello*, Tomo IX. Santafé de Bogotá, D. E., Colombia: Secretaria Ejecutiva del Convenio Andrés Bello. ENGLER, A. 1925. Guttiferae. In *Die Natürlichen Pflanzenfamilien*, eds. A. Engler and K. Prantl, 2nd ed. 21:154–237. Leipzig: Wilhelm Engelmann. GILL, G. E., JR., R. T. FOWLER, AND S. A. MORI. 1998. Pollination biology of *Symphonia globulifera* (Clusiaceae) in central French Guiana. *Biotropica* 30:139–44. GUSTAFSSON, M.H.G., V. BITTRICH, AND P. F. STEVENS. 2002. Phylogeny of Clusiaceae based on rbcL sequences. *Int. J. Pl. Sci.* 163(6):1045–54. KEARNS, D. M., P. E. BERRY, P. F. STEVENS, N. L. CUELLO, J. J. PIPOLY, ET AL. 1998. Clusiaceae. In *Flora of the Venezuelan Guayana: Caesalpiniaceae-Ericaceae*, eds. P. E. Berry, B. K. Holst, and K. Yatskievych, 4:248–329. St. Louis, MO: Missouri Botanical Garden Press. RODRIGUES CORREIA, M. C., W. T. ORMOND, M. C. B. PINHEIRO, AND H. A. DE LIMA. 1993. Estudo da biologia floral de *Clusia criuva* Camb. Um caso de mimetismo. *Bradea* 6:209–19.

CNEORACEAE (Cneorum Family)

ANDREW HENDERSON

- *shrubs*
- *leaves alternate, simple*
- *flowers 3-merous, yellow*
- *fruits schizocarpous, red, the mericarps 3, drupaceous*

Numbers of genera and species. Worldwide, the Cneoraceae comprise a single genus, *Cneorum*, with three species, but *C. trimerum* is the only species in tropical America.

Distribution and habitat. *Cneorum* has a highly disjunct distribution. *Cneorum tricoccon* occurs in the western Mediterranean on the coasts of Spain, France, Italy, the Balearic Islands, and Sardinia; *C. pulverulentum* occurs in the Canary Islands; and *C. trimerum* is found in Cuba.

Cneorum trimerum occurs in eastern Cuba in the Sierra Maestra at 1,300 meters in dry, rocky areas.

Family classification. The Cneoraceae are placed in the Sapindales by Cronquist, near such families as the Rutaceae, Simaroubaceae, and Zygophyllaceae, but their true affinities are still unclear. Based on molecular data, *Cneorum*, along with several other taxa, may be the sister group to the Rutaceae, and it has been suggested that it should be included within that family. It has recently been suggested that the Cuban species is not different from *C. tricoccon*, and that *C. pulverulentum* should be placed in a separate genus, *Neochamaelea*.

Features of the family. Habit: shrubs, evergreen. **Stems** glabrous or with medifixed hairs. **Stipules** absent. **Leaves** alternate, simple, small, gray-green; blades coriaceous, the margins entire. **Inflorescences** axillary, cymes or solitary flowers, the cymes with few flowers. **Flowers** actinomorphic, bisexual or unisexual (the plants andromonecious), small, yellow; sepals 3, small, persistent, distinct or connate basally; petals 3, distinct, elongate, imbricate; stamens 3, the filaments distinct, the anthers dehiscing by longitudinal slits; gynoecium syncarpous, the ovary superior, the carpels 3, the locules 3, the style terminal, the stigmas lobed; placentation axile, the ovules (1)2 per carpel, pendulous. **Fruits** schizocarpous, red, the mericarps 3, drupaceous. **Seeds** usually 2 per mericarp.

Natural history. Nothing is known about the natural history of *Cneorum trimerum*. The reproductive biology of *C. tricoccon* has been studied in the Balearic Islands where it is pollinated by bees and other insects and the seeds are dispersed by lizards.

Economic uses. No uses are recorded for this family.

References. CARLQUIST, S. 1988. Wood anatomy of Cneoraceae: ecology, relationships, and generic definition. *Aliso* 12:7–16. CHASE, M., ET AL. 1999. Phylogenetic relationships of Rutaceae: a cladistic analysis of the subfamilies using evidence from *rbc*L and *atp*B sequence variation. *Amer. J. Bot.* 86:1191–99. LOBREAU-CALLEN D., AND J. JÉRÉMIE 1986. L'espèce *Cneorum tricoccon* (Cneoraceae, Rutales) représentée à Cuba. *Grana* 25:155–58. LOBREAU-CALLEN D., S. NILSSON, F. ALBERS, AND H. STRAKA. 1978. Les Cneoraceae (Rutales): étude taxonomique, palynologique et systématique. Grana 17:125–139. TRAVEST, A. 1995a. Reproductive biology of *Cneorum tricoccon* L. (Cneoraceae) in the Balearic islands. *Bot. J. Linn. Soc.* 117:221–32. TRAVEST, A. 1995b. Seed dispersal of *Cneorum tricoccon* L. (Cneoraceae) by lizards and mammals in the Balearic islands. *Acta Oecologica* 16(2):171–78.

COLUMELLIACEAE (Columellia Family)

LENA STRUWE

Figure 54

- *shrubs or trees*
- *interpetiolar lines or stipules present*
- *leaves opposite, simple; blades with apiculate apex*
- *flowers with corolla fused at base, yellow; stamens 2, inserted in corolla tube; ovary inferior*
- *fruits capsules*

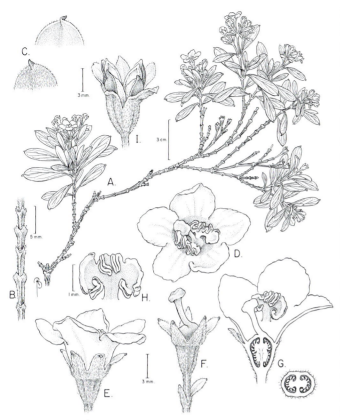

Figure 54. COLUMELLIACEAE. *Columellia oblonga* (A–H, Romoleroux 1433; I, Zak and Jaramillo 3266). **A.** Stem with leaves and inflorescences. **B.** Detail of stem showing jointed nodes. **C.** Abaxial (below) and adaxial (above) views of apices of sepals. **D.** Apical view of flower. **E.** Lateral view of flower. **F.** Lateral view of immature fruit after corolla and adnate stamens have fallen. **G.** Medial section of flower (left) and transverse section of ovary (below right). **H.** Adaxial view of stamen. **I.** Lateral view of dehisced fruit. Original. Artist: Bobbi Angell.

Numbers of genera and species. The Columelliaceae consist of only one genus, *Columellia*, with four species restricted to Andean South America.

Distribution and habitat. Species of *Columellia* are distributed from about 1,600 to 3,600 meters in the Andes of Ecuador, Peru, and western Bolivia. *Columellia oblonga* is found throughout the family's distribution, whereas the other three species are endemic to Ecuador, Bolivia, and Peru, respectively.

Family classification. Although Cronquist placed the Columelliaceae in the Rosales, the family is probably more properly positioned in the Dipsacales. The closest relative of Columelliaceae is another Andean family, the Desfontainiaceae.

Desfontainiaceae were included in Columelliaceae by Backlund, but they are kept separate here because of their distinct morphological characteristics. For example, *Desfontainia* has hypogynous flowers with tubular corollas, 5 stamens, and fleshy berries. However, the two genera are similar in having leathery, spinose leaves, distinct interpetiolar lines, and wood with many anatomical features in common. Molecular studies support the placement of *Columellia* close to Desfontainaceae and do not confirm earlier suggested relationships with such diverse families as Ericaeae, Escalloniaceae, Gentianaceae, Gesneriaceae, Ebenaceae, Hydrangeaceae, Lythraceae, Oleaceae, Onagraceae, and Saxifragaceae.

Features of the family. Habit: shrubs or trees. **Stipules** present, interpetiolar, small and distinct or represented only by lines. **Leaves** opposite, simple; blades often grayish-sericeous (at least abaxially), the apex always apiculate and often spine-tipped. **Inflorescences** terminal and/or axillary, usually dichasial cymes or panicles, rarely of solitary flowers. **Flowers** slightly zygomorphic (corolla only), bisexual; perianth usually 5-merous, but 4–8-merosity has been reported; calyx lobes gland-tipped; corolla fused at base, subrotate to subcampanulate, imbricate, yellow; androecium of 2 stamens, the stamens inserted in corolla tube, the anthers contorted, plicate; gynoecium syncarpous, the ovary inferior, the carpels 2, imperfectly 2-locular, the style 1, short, stout, the stigma depressed, capitate; placentas intruding (almost meeting at center), the ovules numerous, anatropous, unitegmic, tenuinucellate. **Fruits** imperfectly 4-locular capsules. **Seeds** numerous, minute, laterally compressed, oblong, smooth.

Natural history. No reports have been published on the pollination or dispersal of this family.

Economic uses. Decoctions, infusions, and powders of the very bitter leaves of *Columellia* are used in Peru to treat fevers and stomach disorders. The very hard wood is used for fuel and to make handles and utensils.

References. BACKLUND, A., AND B. BREMER. 1997. Phylogeny of the Asteridae s. str. Based on rbcL sequences, with particular reference to the Dipsacales. *Pl. Syst. Evol.* 207: 225–54. BRIZICKY, G. K. 1961. A synopsis of the genus *Columellia* (Columelliaceae). *J. Arnold Arbor.* 42:363–72. STEARN, W. L., G. K. BRIZICKY, AND R. H. EYDE. 1969. Comparative anatomy and relationships of Columelliaceae. *J. Arnold Arbor.* 50:36–71. STRUWE, L., AND V. A. ALBERT. 1997. Floristics, cladistics, and classification: three case studies in Gentianales. In *Plant Diversity in Malesia III*, eds. J. Dransfield, M.J.E. Coode, and D. A. Simpson, 321–52. Richmond, U.K.: Royal Botanic Gardens, Kew.

COMBRETACEAE (Indian Almond Family)

Clive Stace

Figure 55, Plate 15

- *trees, shrubs, subshrubs, and lianas*

- *combretaceous hairs present*

- *leaves opposite or alternate, simple; blade margins entire*

- *flowers with hypanthium; sepals 4–5, sometimes vestigial; petals 4–5 or absent; ovary inferior*

- *seeds 1 per fruit*

Numbers of genera and species. Worldwide, the Combretaceae comprise 13 genera and 400–500 species. In tropical America, there are five genera and circa 85 species. The two largest genera are *Combretum* (including *Thiloa*; ca. 255 species; ca. 30 species in America; center of diversity Africa) and *Terminalia* (including *Ramatuellea* and *Bucida*; circa 200; 33 in America; center of diversity Asia). *Buchenavia* contains 20 species (all American) but the other two American genera, *Conocarpus* and *Laguncularia*, have only one species each in America.

Distribution and habitat. Combretaceae occur throughout the Tropics, with extensions into warm temperate zones of Argentina, Australia, China, India, South Africa, the United States (Florida), Mexico (Baja California Sur and Bermuda). *Combretum* and *Terminalia* occur on all continents. The Neotropical mangrove genera, *Conocarpus* and *Laguncularia*, occur in both America (east and west coasts) and West Africa. *Terminalia lucida*, *Laguncularia racemosa*, and *Conocarpus erectus* are the only three species of Combretaceae indigenous to both America and Africa. In the Western Hemisphere, the majority of species are confined to tropical South America; only about 21 reach Central America and only six species extend north of the tropic of Cancer. *Terminalia australis* is the only entirely extratropical Combretaceae in the Americas.

The Combretaceae can be important constituents of forests, savannas, and mangrove swamps, and occur from sea level to above 3,000 meters.

Family classification. The Combretaceae are placed in the Myrtales by Cronquist. Morphological and molecular studies support this family as a monophyletic group, near, for example, the Lythraceae. The west African genus *Strephonema* differs from the rest of the family in several ways, notably the semi-inferior ovary and hypogeal, hemispherical cotyledons, and has been placed in a separate family, the Strephonemataceae. It possesses, however, the same almost-unique

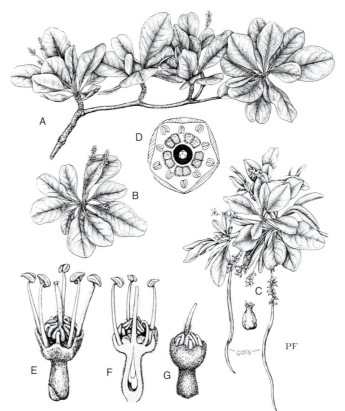

Figure 55. COMBRETACEAE. *Terminalia buceras*. **A.** Stem with leaves and inflorescences; note sympodial branching. **B.** Apical view of stem showing leaves and inflorescences. **C.** Stem with leaves, infructescences, fruit (middle), and long, tubular galls at apices of infructescences. **D.** Floral diagram. **E.** Apical-lateral view of flower. **F.** Medial section of flower. **G.** Lateral view of flower in pistillate phase. Reprinted with permission from Tomlinson (1980). Artist: Pricilla Fawcett.

diagnostic hairs as the rest of the family and is probably best treated as subfamily Strephonematoideae. Even including *Strephonema*, the Combretaceae seem very clearly defined and are easily distinguished from other families placed in the Myrtales. In the subfamily Combretoideae, four genera have a pair of bracteoles fused to the hypanthium and are recognized as tribe Laguncularieae (*Laguncularia*, one other mangrove, two Australian endemics). The remainder (tribe Combreteae) are conveniently separated into two subtribes related to *Combretum* (Combretinae) and *Terminalia* (Terminaliinae), respectively. Of the genera found in the Western Hemisphere, *Laguncularia* is the type genus of the Laguncularieae, *Combretum* (including *Thiloa* and the commonly cultivated *Quisqualis*) belong to the Combretinae, and *Terminalia* (including *Bucida* and *Ramatuellea*), *Buchenavia*, and *Conocarpus* to the Terminaliinae.

Features of the family. Habit: trees, shrubs, subshrubs (in savannas), or lianas (mostly in forests), evergreen or deciduous. Roots rarely with pneumatophores (*Laguncularia racemosa*). Stipules absent or rarely vestigial. Stems rarely with spines (several *Combretum* and *Terminalia buceras* and *T. molinetii*). Leaves opposite (e.g., *Combretum* and *Laguncularia*) or alternate (e.g., *Buchenavia*, *Conocarpus*, and *Terminalia*), simple, variously pubescent, the hairs with distinctive basal compartments, sometimes glandular (Combretinae); blade margins entire or nearly so; domatia sometimes present (common in *Terminalia*, *Buchenavia*, and *Conocarpus*), abaxial, mostly in axils of main lateral leaf veins, pocket-shaped or bowl-shaped pits; petioles sometimes with 1 or 2 glands (often in *Terminalia*, *Buchenavia*, *Laguncularia*, and *Conocarpus*). Inflorescences terminal and/or axillary, racemose, often spicate or paniculate, the flowers often greatly congested; bracteoles usually absent (2 in *Laguncularia*, fused to hypanthium). Flowers actinomorphic or sometimes slightly zygomorphic (e.g., *Combretum cacoucia*), bisexual or sometimes unisexual (the plants sometimes dioecious, e.g., *Combretum rupicola*, *Conocarpus*, and *Laguncularia*, or andromonoecious in *Terminalia*), nonfunctional sexual organs usually present in unisexual flowers; hypanthium present, often with nectar-secreting lobes or disc at base of upper section; sepals 4–5, often very small; petals often absent (e.g., *Terminalia* and *Buchenavia*), or 4–5; androecium usually of 8–10 stamens in 2 whorls, or sometimes the stamens 4–5 in 1 whorl; gynoecium syncarpous, the ovary inferior, the carpels 2–5, the locule 1, the style 1, the stigma usually punctiform, sometimes capitate, small; placentation apical, the ovules usually 2, sometimes up to 7(20), only 1 developing. Fruits indehiscent, false drupes (*Buchenavia* and many *Terminalia*), false nuts (*Laguncularia* and some *Terminalia*), or false samaras (*Combretum* and many *Terminalia*). Seeds 1 per fruit, germination epigeal or hypogeal; endosperm absent, the cotyledons variable.

The largest trees in this family are more than 50 meters tall, and the lianas often climb above 30 meters high, whereas the smallest subshrubs (not present in America) do not exceed 20 centimeters. Species of *Terminalia* are all trees or shrubs, whereas species of *Combretum* are mostly shrubs, subshrubs, or lianas, with very few trees (e.g., *C. leprosum*, up to 25 m in Brazil).

Natural history. The family displays several interesting floral adaptations, but their relationship to pollination has not been investigated sufficiently. Three floral trends are evident: loss of petals, enlargement of the hypanthium, and clustering of flowers into groups. The widely cultivated *Combretum indicum* (*Quisqualis indica*) almost uniquely has large, colored petals. The flowers are sweetly scented, especially in the evening, and the long, narrow hypanthium suggests hawkmoth pollination. In nearly all other Combretaceae, the petals are relatively small and inconspicuous or lacking. *Combretum fruticosum* and several related species exhibit the "bottle-brush" syndrome, with sessile, scentless, nectar-producing flowers crowded on an elongated axis. The flowers, of which the filaments are the most conspicuous parts, are red to yellow. These species are pollinated primarily by hummingbirds, but also by other birds, butterflies, and monkeys. *Combretum fruticosum* has been shown to be self-incompatible. Most other species of *Combretum* and the species of the other four genera have small but scented flowers, which are pollinated mainly by bees and flies.

Dispersal of the one-seeded, indehiscent false fruits depends on the modification of the surrounding receptacular tissue. In *Laguncularia*, this tissue is spongy, and the fruits presumably are dispersed by water. Many species of *Terminalia* and all those of *Buchenavia* have fruits with succulent pericarps that are eaten by animals. These species are often riparian, and their buoyant fruits may be dispersed secondarily by water. Wings aiding in wind dispersal have developed in several genera, especially *Combretum* and *Terminalia*.

Economic uses. Combretaceae are not of great economic importance. The larger species of *Terminalia* are valued as timber trees, mostly for local uses, but in some cases they reach European and American markets. In the West Indies, *Laguncularia* is valued for fence posts and *Conocarpus* for fuel. The fruits of *Terminalia catappa* (Indian almond) have edible seeds. Species of *Terminalia*, especially the Asian *T. catappa*, often are grown as shade plants. The Asian *Combretum indicum* (*Quisqualis indica*) frequently is cultivated in the tropical and warm-temperate areas of America. Other species of *Combretum* (including *Calopyxis*) also are employed as ornamentals.

References. BERNAL, H. Y., AND J. E. CORRERA Q. 1990. Combretaceae. In *Especies vegetales promisorias de los países del Convenio Andrés Bello*, Tomo IV. Bogotá, D. E., Colombia: Secretaria Ejecutiva del Convenio Andrés Bello. BERNARDELLO, L., L. GALETTO, AND I. G. RODRIGUEZ. 1994. Reproductive biology, variability of nectar features and pollination of *Combretum fruticosum* (Combretaceae) in Argentina. *Bot. J. Linn. Soc.* 114:293–308. DAHLGREN, R., AND R. F. THORNE. 1984. The order Myrtales: circumscription, variation and relationships. *Ann. Missouri Bot. Gard.* 71:633–99. DALZIEL, J. M. 1937. *The Useful Plants of West Tropical Africa*. London: Crown Agents. EXELL, A. W. 1962. Space problems arising from the conflict between two evolutionary tendencies in the Combretaceae. *Bull. Soc. Roy. Bot. Belgique* 95:41–49. EXELL, A. W., AND C. A. STACE. 1972. Patterns of distribution in the Combretaceae. In *Taxonomy, Phytogeography and Evolution*, ed. D. H. Valentine, 307–23. London: Academic Press. GRAHAM, S. A. 1964. The genera of Rhizophoraceae and Combretaceae in the southeastern United States. *J. Arnold Arbor.* 45:285–301. STACE, C. A. 1965. The significance of the leaf epidermis in the taxonomy of the Combretaceae: I. A general review of tribal, generic and specific characters. *J. Linn. Soc. Bot.* 59:229–52.

CONNARACEAE (Connarus Family)

Enrique Forero

Figure 56, Plate 15

- *trees, shrubs, or lianas*

- *leaves alternate, compound, rarely unifoliolate, imparipinnate*

- *flowers with 1 or 5, distinct carpels*

- *fruits follicles*

- *seeds arillate*

Numbers of genera and species. Worldwide, the Connaraceae comprise 16 genera and circa 300–350 species. In tropical America, there are five genera and 108 species.

The largest genus is *Connarus* with 80–100 species worldwide. In the neotropics, *Connarus* is represented by 54 species and *Rourea* by 46 species. Of the remaining Neotropical genera, *Bernardinia* is monotypic, *Cnestidium* includes two species, and *Pseudoconnarus* five species.

Distribution and habitat. The Connaraceae are pantropical. The center of distribution is Western Africa where 14 genera and 130 species occur. Connaraceae of the Western Hemisphere are found mostly within the Tropics, with only two species, *Connarus rostratus* and *Rourea gracilis*, extending past 27°S in the state of Santa Catarina, Brazil.

In tropical America, *Connarus* and *Rourea* are distributed in Mexico, Cuba, the Antilles, Central America, northern South America, Peru, Bolivia, and throughout Brazil. *Bernardinia*, *Cnestidium*, and *Pseudoconnarus* are endemic to tropical America.

Tropical American Connaraceae occupy a variety of habitats, from tropical rain forest to open vegetation types, such as the *cerrado* of Central Brazil. Most species occur below 1,000 meters elevation, but there are a few records of species reaching 1,500 meters.

Family classification. The Connaraceae are placed in the Rosales by Cronquist. Traditionally, the family has been divided into two subfamilies: Jollyodoroideae, characterized by having 2-seeded fruits, and Connaroideae, with 1-seeded fruits. Jollyodoroideae is a monotypic subfamily native to tropical Africa. All other genera, including the five found in the Western Hemisphere, belong to the Connaroideae. No other family classification, on a worldwide basis, has been proposed.

Features of the family. Habit: small trees, shrubs, or lianas. **Stipules** absent. **Leaves** alternate, compound, rarely unifoliolate, imparipinnate; blades sometimes with papillae present

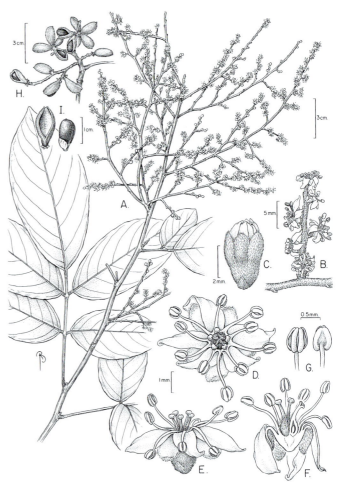

Figure 56. CONNARACEAE. *Cnestidium guianense.* **A.** Stem with leaves and inflorescences. **B.** Detail of part of inflorescence. **C.** Lateral view of flower bud. **D.** Apical view of flower. **E.** Lateral view of flower. **F.** Medial section of flower. **G.** Adaxial (left) and abaxial (right) views of anthers. **H.** Part of infructescence. **I.** Lateral views of empty fruit (left) and seed with aril (right). Reprinted with permission from Mori et al. (2002). Artist: Bobbi Angell.

on abaxial surface (*Pseudoconnarus* and some *Rourea*); hairs unicellular (most species), dendroid (many *Connarus*), or sometimes glandular. **Inflorescences** axillary, pseudoterminal or terminal, paniculate, racemose, or spicate. **Flowers** actinomorphic, bisexual, usually <1 centimeter long, dark punctations sometimes present (most *Connarus*) on petals, sepals, stamens, and styles; sepals 5, distinct or partially fused, imbricate or valvate, often pubescent, persistent in fruit; petals 5, distinct, sometimes appearing fused just above base, white, light yellow, or light pink, usually glabrous, sometimes pubescent (*Connarus*), the hairs sometimes glandular; androecium of 10 stamens, the stamens forming tube at base, 5 long, episepalous, 5 short, epipetalous, the filaments glabrous, sometimes glandular hairs present (*Connarus*), the anthers dorsifixed, glandular hairs sometimes present at top of connective (*Connarus*); gynoecium apocarpous, the ovaries superior, glabrous or pubescent, the carpels 1 (*Connarus*) or 5, the styles 1 per carpel, the stigmas capitate or 2-lobed; ovules 2 per carpel (1 aborting), nearly basal, collateral, orthotropous. **Fruits** follicles, often red, the sepals covering base, usually ascending or reflexed (*Bernardinia* and some *Rourea*). **Seeds** 1, black; aril bright red, yellow, white, or orange; endosperm abundant (*Pseudoconnarus*), poorly developed (*Cnestidium*), or absent.

In the Western Hemisphere, the presence of 1 carpel constitutes the most distinctive feature in species of *Connarus*, making it extremely easy to separate from the remaining four Neotropical genera.

In general, only 1 carpel develops into fruit in *Rourea* and *Cnestidium*, while it is common for more than 1 mature carpel per flower to develop in *Bernardinia* and *Pseudoconnarus*. In a few species of *Connarus*, the fruit looks very much like a legume.

Natural history. Pollination is poorly understood in Connaraceae but is thought to be predominantly undertaken by in-sects. Given the attractive colors of the fruit, seed, and aril, dispersal may be carried out by birds.

Economic uses. *Connarus patrisii* is believed to possess magical properties in Suriname, and *C. punctatus* is used for similar purposes in Brazil where it is known as *árvore dos feitiçeiros*. The fruit of *C. lambertii* is used as dog poison in Guatemala. Similar properties are recognized for the fruits of *Rourea glabra* in Central America and other species of *Bernardinia*, *Connarus*, and *Rourea* in Brazil, hence the common name *mata cachorro*. Medicinal properties have been reported for *Connarus schultesii* (Mexico), *Rourea glabra* (Mexico), and *R. induta* (Brazil).

References. CROAT, T. B. 1978. *Flora of Barro Colorado Island*, 421–23. Stanford, CA: Stanford University Press. FORERO, E. 1976. A revision of the American species of *Rourea* subgenus *Rourea* (Connaraceae). *Mem. New York Bot. Gard.* 26(1):1–119. FORERO, E. 1983. Connaraceae. *Fl. Neotrop. Monogr.* 36:1–207. SCHELLENBERG, G. 1938. Connaraceae. In *Das Pflanzenreich*, A. Engler, Series 4, 127(Heft 103):1–326. Leipzig: Wilhelm Engelmann.

CONVOLVULACEAE (Morning Glory Family)

DANIEL F. AUSTIN

Figure 57, Plate 15

- *herbs, shrubs, lianas, vines, rarely trees*
- *plants with milky latex, sometimes inconspicuous*
- *leaves alternate, mostly simple*
- *flowers sympetalous; filaments adnate to corolla; disc often present; ovary superior*
- *fruits often capsular*

Numbers of genera and species. Worldwide, the Convolvulaceae comprise 55 genera and 1,600–1,700 species. Twenty-two genera and at least 750 species are native to the Western Hemisphere. The largest genera of this region are *Ipomoea* (ca. 600 species), *Jacquemontia* (circa 115 species), and *Evolvulus* (ca. 98 species). Thirteen genera have a single species; those in the Americas are *Iseia*, *Itzaea*, *Lysiostyles*, *Petrogenia*, and *Tetralocularia*. In tropical America, there are 20 genera and circa 740 species.

Distribution and habitat. The Convolvulaceae mostly occur in the Tropics of the world, but some species also reach temperate zones. The greatest species diversity occurs in the Americas and Africa. *Bonamia*, *Ipomoea*, *Merremia*, and *Operculina* are pantropical. *Aniseia*, *Dicranostyles*, *Evolvulus*, *Iseia*, *Itzaea*, *Lysiostyles*, *Maripa*, *Odonellia*, *Petrogenia*, *Stylisma*, and *Tetralocularia* are endemic in the Americas.

The Convolvulaceae range from tropical rain forest to savannas, prairies, and deserts. Species often grow at low elevations, but some reach circa 3,000 meters. The family is dominated by heliophiles. Some species are halophytic (e.g., *Cressa*, *Ipomoea pescaprae*) or aquatic (*I. aquatica*).

Family classification. The Convolvulaceae are placed in the Solanales by Cronquist. Molecular data suggest that the Cuscutaceae should be included in the Convolvulaceae; however, the Convolvulaceae and Cuscutaceae are treated as separate families in this book. Several authors have suggested that the family most closely related to Convolvulaceae is the Solanaceae, while others have suggested the Polemoniaceae or Boraginaceae. A new morphological study suggests that the Hydrophyllaceae may be closer to the Convolvulaceae than any of these. However, since few species have been examined with molecular techniques, the relationships remain controversial.

Hallier divided the family into the groups Echinoconiae

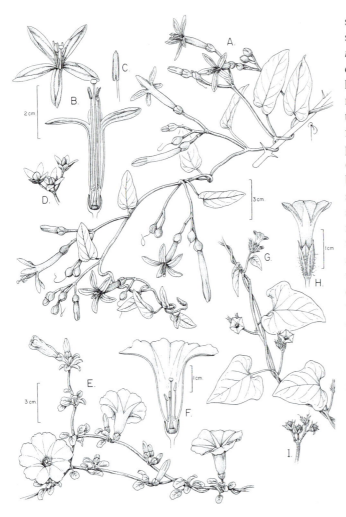

Figure 57. CONVOLVULACEAE. *Ipomoea repanda* (A–D), *I. eggersii* (E, F), and *I. triloba* (G–I). **A.** Stem with leaves and inflorescences. **B.** Apical view (above) and longitudinal section (below) of flowers. **D.** Dehisced capsules. **E.** Stem with leaves and inflorescences. **F.** Longitudinal section of flower. **G.** Stem with leaves and inflorescences. **H.** Lateral view of flower. **I.** Infructescence. Reprinted with permission from Acevedo-Rodríguez (1996). Artist: Bobbi Angell.

(spiny pollen) and Psiloconiae (comparatively smooth pollen). Recent phylogenetic evidence supports the conclusion that the Echinoconiae are monophyletic. These groups are subdivided into several tribes. Since the 1890s most people have recognized the tribes Argyreieae, Convolvuleae, Cresseae, Dichondreae, Erycibeae, Hildebrandtieae, Ipomoeeae, and Poraneae. The placement of genera in tribes, however, has changed considerably in the past 30 years as morphology of the species has become better known.

Features of the family. Habit: herbs, shrubs, lianas, vines, rarely trees (*Ipomoea*); milky latex present, sometimes inconspicuous. **Stems** climbing, prostrate (some only 10 cm long; e.g., *Dichondra*), or erect (e.g., 2 m in *Ipomoea carnea* subspecies *fistulosa* or 5–15 meters tall in *I. arborescens*). **Stipules** absent. **Leaves** alternate, mostly simple (reduced to

scales in *Merremia aturensis*); pubescence usually 2-branched, sometimes glandular or stellate (e.g., *Ipomoea, Jacquemontia*, and *Merremia*); petioles absent to longer than blade, channeled on adaxial surface; blades often cordate, less often hastate, oblong, or linear, the margins entire or divided (palmate or pinnate). **Inflorescences** terminal, axillary, sometimes both, flowers solitary or in complex clusters (derived from dichasia or less often monochasia); bracts or bracteoles present, paired, sometimes enlarged to form involucre (e.g., *Odonellia* and some *Jacquemontia*). **Flowers** actinomorphic, bisexual; calyx with 5 sepals, distinct, overlapping; corolla sympetalous (5 fused petals), rotate, bell-shaped, funnel-shaped, or salver-shaped; androecium of 5 stamens, the stamens alternating with petals, the filaments fused to corolla, the anthers dehiscing longitudinally, sometimes twisting into a spiral (*Merremia, Operculina*, and their relatives); disc often present; gynoecium syncarpous, the ovary superior, the carpels 2 (3–5 in *Ipomoea* series *Pharbitis*), the locules equal to carpel number, the styles terminal, single or divided apically for full length, producing 2 distinct stylar branches (e.g., *Bonamia* and *Evolvulus*); placentation basal or basal-axile, the ovules 4(6–10), 2 per carpel, erect, anatropous or apotropous. **Fruits** often capsular, sometimes utricular or berries, or fruits indehiscent (tribes Erycibeae and Poraneae) or spliting irregularly (*Merremia discoidesperma, M. tuberosa*, and *Operculina*), the capsular fruits dehiscing longitudinally into 4 (8–12 in some *Itzaea* and *Jacquemontia*) segments. **Seeds** 1–4 (rarely more); endosperm homogeneous, cartilaginous, the embryo large, curved or folded, the cotyledons often bifid.

The smallest flowers in the neotropics are less than 10 millimeters in diameter (*Dichondra*) and the largest are 8–12 centimeters long (*Ipomoea alba*).

Fruit size ranges from 2–3 millimeters long (*Dichondra, Evolvulus*) to 30–40 millimeters long (*Maripa panamensis* and *Merremia discoidesperma*).

Cotyledons emerge directly from the broken seed coat and are produced above-ground (epigeous) except in *Merremia discoidesperma* and *M. tuberosa*, which are hypogeous.

Natural history. Pollination frequently is accomplished by bees, and records exist for visits by 19 genera in four families (Andrenidae, Anthophoridae, Apidae, Halictidae). Bees of the Anthophoridae are particularly frequent visitors. Anthophorid bee genera *Ancyloscelis, Cemolobus*, and *Melitoma* use only pollen from *Ipomoea* to provision their nests. Some *Diadasia* use only pollen from *Calystegia* and *Convolvulus*. Moths, birds, and bats also pollinate flowers.

The nocturnally flowering *Ipomoea alba*, with long-tubular, white flowers is pollinated by moths, and at least three species of *Ipomoea* are reported to be pollinated by glossophagine bats.

One genus of beetles (*Megacerus*, family Bruchidae) is a specialist whose larvae feed on the seeds of the family. Often a single species of beetle occurs on one plant species; e.g., *Megacerus capreolus* on *Merremia tuberosa*.

Mode of dispersal is comparatively poorly known, but animals, wind, and water are vectors. Fleshy fruits are dispersed by birds and other vertebrates; *Maripa* is known as "monkey syrup" in the Guianas and is spread by monkeys. Fruits of the tribe Poraneae (e.g., *Calycobolus*) are dispersed by wind. Water and perhaps wind spread the woolly seeds of many species. In addition, many seeds have cavities within the embryo and endosperm. A number of these "labyrinth seeds" are associated with water dispersal (e.g., *Ipomoea alba, I. pescaprae,* and *Merremia discoidesperma*).

Economic uses. Various species provide medicines, vegetables, root crops, ornamentals, lawn-grass substitutes, and materials for florists. Perhaps the oldest use for the family that still persists in many places is as a purgative. Numerous American species are called *quiebra platos* or *tumba vaqueros,* in reference to their laxative nature. Chemicals involved with digestive stimulation and other actions include coumarins and several alkaloids.

Several species are used as ornamentals, usually because of their showy flowers. Europeans introduced some species into Asia by the 1500s. By the early 1600s, American *Ipomoea* introduced to Japan (later dubbed Japanese morning glory) had become the "most honorable flower." In 1979, the South American "blue daze" (*Evolvulus glomeratus*), named for its "dazing" blue flowers, was introduced into cultivation in Florida. By 1989, it had reached Australia, Asia, Europe, and Hawaii.

The best known ornamentals are the native American *Ipomoea tricolor, I. purpurea,* and *I. nil. Ipomoea tricolor* has been marketed for decades under the cultivar names Heavenly Blue and Pearly Gates. These names were applied before it was known that the seeds contained small amounts of hallucinogenic ergoline alkaloids. This physiological effect was discovered by the native Americans of Mexico before Europeans arrived but was not rediscovered until the 1940s by R. E. Schultes of Harvard. This led to a surge of recreational seed consumption by North Americans in the 1960s and 1970s. *Ipomoea tricolor* and *Turbina corymbosa* were the species most frequently used for this purpose.

Ipomoea batatas (sweet potato or yam) is the world's seventh largest food crop. Although the origin of this species is from the Western Hemisphere, it is now cultivated throughout the world, with China growing circa 80 percent of the crop. In tropical America, sweet potato generally is displaced as a staple food by manioc (*Manihot esculenta,* Euphorbiaceae). Instead, it is used as a holiday plant, an emergency food, or, in Amazonian South America, to provide red coloring for *masato* (a mild alcoholic beverage inoculated for fermenting by women chewing cooked manioc roots).

Some species, notably *Convolvulus arvensis* (field bindweed), are aggressive and persistent invaders of crops.

References. AUSTIN, D. F. 1973. The American Erycibeae (Convolvulaceae). *Maripa, Dicranostyles & Lysiostyles*—I. Systematics. *Ann. Missouri Bot. Gard.* 60:306–412. AUSTIN, D. F. 1998. Parallel and Convergent Evolution in the Convolvulaceae. *Biodiversity and Taxonomy of Flowering Plants,* eds. P. Mathews and M. Sivadasan, 201–34. Calicut, India: Mentor Books. AUSTIN, D. F., AND P. B. CAVALCANTE. 1982. *Convolvuláceas de Amazônia.* Publicacoes Avulsas No. 36. Belém: Museo Paraense Emilio Goeldi. AUSTIN, D. F., AND Z. HUÁMAN. 1996. A synopsis of *Ipomoea* (Convolvulaceae) in the Americas. *Taxon* 45:3–38. AUSTIN, D. F., AND R. A. PEDRAZA. 1983. Los géneros de Convolvulaceae en México. *Bol. Sóc. Bot. México* 44:3–16. BERNAL, H. Y., AND J. E. CORRERA Q. 1991. Convululaceae. In *Especies vegetales promisorias de los países del Convenio Andrés Bello,* Tomo VI. Santafé de Bogotá, D. E., Colombia: Secretaria Ejecutiva del Convenio Andrés Bello. CONTRERAS, J., D. F. AUSTIN, F. DE LA PUENTE, AND J. DÍAZ. 1995. Biodiversity of sweetpotato (*Ipomoea batatas,* Convolvulaceae) in southern Mexico. *Econ. Bot.* 49:286–96. HALLIER, H. 1893. Versuch einer natürlichen Gliederung der Convolulaceen auf morphologischer und anatomischer Grundlage. *Bot. Jahrb. Syst.* 16:453–591. JENETT-SIEMS, K., M. KALOGA, AND E. EICH. 1993. Ipangulines, the first pyrrolizidine alkaloids from the Convolvulaceae. *Phytochemistry* 34(2):437–40. McDONALD, J. A. 1991. Origin and diversity of Mexican Convolvulaceae. *Anal. Inst. Biol. Univ. Nac. Autón. México, Bot.* 62:65–82. McDONALD, J. A., AND T. J. MABRY. 1992. Phylogenetic systematics of New World *Ipomoea* (Convolvulaceae) based on chloroplast DNA restriction site variation. *Pl. Syst. Evol.* 180:243–59.

CORIARIACEAE (Coriaria Family)

FAVIO GONZÁLEZ

Figure 58, Plate 15

- *erect or often scandent shrubs*
- *stems angular, with distinctive, compound-like branching corky lenticels present*
- *leaves usually opposite, simple, small; venation palmate*
- *inflorescences racemes, often pendent under leaves*
- *flowers with carpels distinct or slightly fused at base*
- *fruits achenes, enclosed by fleshy petals*

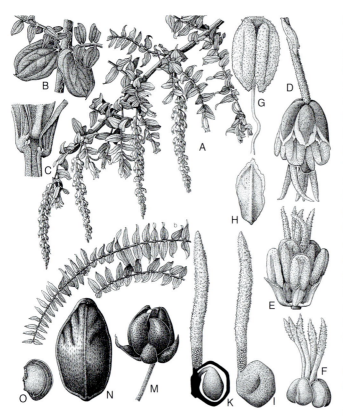

Figure 58. CORIARIACEAE. *Coriaria microphylla*. **A.** Stem with leaves and pendent inflorescences (x½). **B.** Detail of part of stem (x½). **C.** Leaf bases showing stipules (x8). **D.** Lateral view of pendent flower (x8). **E.** Flower with sepals removed to show stamens in two series (x8). **F.** Lateral view of gynoecium (x8). **G.** Adaxial view of stamen (x16). **H.** Abaxial view of petal at flowering (x16). **I.** Intact view of carpel (x16). **K.** Medial section of carpel (x16). **M.** Lateral fruit subtended by persistent sepals and accrescent petals (x4). **N.** Adaxial surface of petal at fruiting (x8). **O.** Medial section of fruit (x8). Reprinted with permission from Cronquist (1981). Artist: William S. Moye.

Numbers of genera and species. Worldwide, the Coriariaceae comprise a single genus, *Coriaria*, and five to 20 species. In the Western Hemisphere, Skog recognized only *C. ruscifolia*, but Oginuma et al. restricted this species to Chile and considered the Neotropical species as *C. microphylla* (= *C. thymifolia*)

Distribution and habitat. The Coriariaceae are most common in warm temperate areas worldwide. The distribution of *Coriaria* is disjunct, growing in the Mediterranean region, continental and insular eastern Asia, Papua New Guinea to New Zealand including the Pacific Islands, and in the Western Hemisphere from Mexico to Chile.

The Neotropical species usually grow at elevations between 600 and 3,800 meters in premontane or montane forests from Mexico to Peru. In Colombia, Venezuela, and Ecuador, *Coriaria* reaches *subpáramo* or *páramo* vegetation.

Family classification. The systematic placement of the Coriariaceae is unsettled. Traditionally, the family has been placed in either the Ranunculales (*sensu* Cronquist), the Sapindales, or the Rutales. The inclusion within the order Ranunculales, mainly based on floral characters and stem and seed-coat anatomy, is disputable. Karyomorphological, embryological, palynological, and chemical studies have found evidence of a closer relationship with a rutalean-sapindalean group rather than with the Ranunculales. Wood anatomy provides no support for a closer relationship with primitive angiosperms or with members of the order Sapindales. Molecular studies of *rbc*L, 18S rDNA, and *atpB* data show an unexpected relationship of the Coriariaceae with members of the order Cucurbitales, which includes also Anisophylleaceae, Begoniaceae, Corynocarpaceae, Cucurbitaceae, Datiscaceae, and Tetramelaceae. These analyses indicate a sister group relationship to the Corynocarpaceae, a monogeneric southwestern Pacific family, with which the Coriariaceae share several morphological traits, such as the pentamerous flowers, the presence of one pendulous, anatropous ovule per locule, and an oily embryo.

Recent molecular data indicate that the Chile-Papua New Guinea-New Zealand-Pacific Islands species group is sister to the Central American-northern South American species.

Features of the family. Habit: shrubs, erect or scandent. **Roots** often with nitrogen-fixing nodules. **Stems** angular, long and short, resulting in distinctive compoundlike branching; corky lenticels present. **Stipules** present, small, caducous. **Leaves** usually opposite, or rarely whorled, simple, small, subsessile; blades ovate to lanceolate, the margins entire; venation palmate, the veins 3(5). **Inflorescences** terminal or from previous season's stems, racemes, pendent, often hidden under densely leafy stems, the flowers numerous. **Flowers** actinomorphic, mostly bisexual (unisexual in some extra-Neotropical species), small (2–3 mm diameter); sepals 5, imbricate; petals 5, distinct, smaller than sepals, often purplish, keeled, becoming fleshy and persistent; androecium of 10 stamens, the stamens in 2 whorls, the anthers dehiscing longitudinally; gynoecium with superior ovary, the carpels 5–10, distinct or slightly fused at base, the locules 5–10, the styles long, stigmatic for much of length; ovules one per locule, pendulous, anatropous, bitegmic, the micropyle directed upward. **Fruits** achenes, small, separate, purple to black, enclosed by petals, the petals fleshy, persistent. **Seeds** slightly compressed; endosperm scanty or absent, the embryo straight, oily.

Natural history. *Coriaria microphylla* has been observed as a pioneer shrub on volcanic soils in the highlands of Central America and the Andes. Flowers of this species are bisexual and protogynous. Wind pollination and self-compatibility occur in the genus. No information is available about dispersal biology.

Economic uses. Fruits of *Coriaria microphylla* are reputed to be hallucinogenic and so toxic that deaths of cattle and children caused by their consumption have been registered. Some extra-Neotropical species are sources of dyes, and the leaves and bark are employed in tanning. The Asian *C. terminalis* is used as an ornamental. Crushed fruits from *C. myrtifolia*, a Mediterranean species, are used as a fly poison.

References. BERNAL, H. Y., AND J. E. CORRERA Q. 1991. Coriariaceae. In *Especies vegetales promisorias de los países del Convenio Andrés Bello*, Tomo VI. Santafé de Bogotá, D. E., Colombia: Secretaria Ejecutiva del Convenio Andrés Bello. CARLQUIST, S. 1985. Wood anatomy of Coriariaceae: phylogenetic and ecological implications. *Syst. Bot.* 10:174–83. GARG, M. 1980. Pollen morphology and systematic position of *Coriaria*. *Phytomorphology* 30:5–10. GOOD, R. 1930. The geography of the genus *Coriaria*. *New Phytol.* 29:170–98. OGINUMA, K., M. NAKATA, M. SUZUKI, AND H. TOBE. 1991. Karyomorphology of *Coriaria* (Coriariaceae): Taxonomic implications. *Bot. Mag. Tokyo* 103:297–308. SHARMA, V. K. 1968. Floral morphology, anatomy, and embryology of *Coriaria nepalensis* Wall. with a discussion on the interrelationships of the family Coriariaceae. *Phytomorphology* 18: 143–53. SKOG, L. 1972. The genus *Coriaria* (Coriariaceae) in the Western Hemisphere. *Rhodora* 74:242–53. SUZUKI, M., AND K. YODA. 1986a. Comparative wood anatomy of *Coriaria* of East Asia. *J. Jap. Bot.* 61:289–96 & 333–42. THOMPSON, P. N., AND R. J. GORNALL. 1995. Breeding systems in *Coriaria*. *Bot. J. Linnean Soc.* 117:293–304. TOBE, H., M. SUZUKI, AND T. FUKUHARA. 1992. Pericarp anatomy and evolution in *Coriaria* (Coriariaceae). *Bot. Mag. Tokyo.* 105:289–302. YOKOYAMA, J., M. SUZUKI, K. IWATSUKI, AND M. HASEBE. 2000. Molecular phylogeny of *Coriaria*, with special emphasis on the disjunct distribution. *Molecular Phylogenetics and Evolution* 14:11–19.

CORNACEAE (Dogwood Family)

DAVID L. LENTZ

- *trees or shrubs*

- *leaves opposite or alternate, simple*

- *inflorescences subtended by involucre of petallike bracts*

- *flowers actinomorphic, usually bisexual, small; ovary inferior*

- *fruits drupes*

Numbers of genera and species. Worldwide, the Cornaceae comprise 11 genera and circa 100 species. In tropical America, there is a single genus, *Cornus*, with four species (*C. disciflora*, *C. excelsa*, *C. florida*, and *C. peruviana*).

Distribution and habitat. The Cornaceae are predominantly distributed in the Northern Hemisphere. The family is found in Asia, Europe, Africa, and the Americas. In the neotropics, species of *Cornus* inhabit the mountains of Central and South America, where they range from the Sierra Madre Oriental in Mexico to the Bolivian Andes. Species of *Cornus* are understory plants found in humid to semihumid montane forests from 1,400 to 3,000 meters elevation.

Family classification. The Cornaceae are placed in the Cornales by Cronquist. The familial boundaries are not distinct, and some authors have suggested that the family should be separated into a number of monotypic families. Other authors suggest that the Nyssaceae and Alangiaceae should be placed within the Cornaceae. Some systematic treatments align the Cornaceae with the Grossulariaceae or the Garryaceae. Recent studies based on molecular data, however, reveal a close relationship with Hydrangeaceae and Loasaceae.

Features of the family. Habit: trees or shrubs. **Stipules** rarely present. **Leaves** opposite or alternate, simple; blade margins entire or denticulate. **Inflorescences** terminal, cymose, racemose, umbellate, or capitate, subtended by involucre of petal-like bracts. **Flowers** actinomorphic, usually bisexual, sometimes unisexual (then plants dioecious), small; sepals connate, 4-parted, adnate to ovary; petals 4, valvate; androecium of 4 stamens, the stamens alternate with petals, the filaments subulate or filiform, the anthers dorsifixed, versatile; gynoecium syncarpous, the ovary inferior, the carpels 2, the locules 2, the style columnar, the stigmas capitate or truncate; placentation axile, the ovules 1 per locule, apical, pendulous. **Fruits** drupes, globose or ovoid, the stones 2-seeded, bony or crustaceous. **Seeds** 2, flat, oblong, the testa membranaceous; endosperm abundant.

Natural history. Bees, flies, and beetles are attracted to the floral nectar by the showy bracts that often subtend the tiny flowers. The colorful drupes are sought by birds and mammals.

Economic uses. Species of *Cornus*, especially *C. florida*, are planted as ornamentals. The wood of several species is used for making furniture, guitars, stirrups, and tool handles.

References. CARRANZA, E. G. 1992. *Flora del Bajío y de Regiones Adyacentes*, fasc. 8:1–11. Pátzcuaro, México: Instituto de Ecología, A.C. Dudley, T. R., and F. S. Santamour Jr. 1992. *Cornus florida* subsp. *urbiniana*, (Rose) Rickett from México: The correct name for "*C. florida* var. *pringlei*." *Phytologia* 73(3):169–79. González Villarreal, L. M. 1996. *La familia Cornaceae en el estado de Jalisco, México*. México: Universidad de Guadalajara. Killeen, T. J., Emilia García E., and S. G. Beck, eds. 1993. *Guía de Arboles de Bolivia*. St. Louis, MO: Missouri Botanical Garden. Macbride, J. F. 1959. Flora of Peru. *Fieldiana, Bot.* 13:44–45. Savolainen, V. R., Spichiger, and J. F. Manen. 1997. Polyphyletism of Celastrales deduced from a chloroplast noncoding DNA region. *Molecular Phylogenetics and Evolution.* 7(2):145–57. Standley, P. C. 1966. Flora of Guatemala. *Fieldiana, Bot.* vol. 24, pt. 8(1, 2):67–69.

CRASSULACEAE (Stonecrop Family)

Mark E. Mort and Scott A. Mori

Figure 59

- *leaf-succulent herbs, subshrubs, or shrubs*

- *vegetative parts often with red color*

- *flowers actinomorphic; androecium typically with two whorls of stamens (one whorl in some introduced species); gynoecium apocarpous or carpels partially fused*

- *fruits usually separate follicles, rarely capsules*

Numbers of genera and species. Crassulaceae are a medium-sized family of flowering plants. Estimates of the number of species range from 900 to 1,500, placed within 30 to 35 genera. It is important to note that no two students of Crassulaceae are likely to be in complete agreement regarding the number of genera or the taxonomic composition of the genera. This fact was best emphasized by Moran, who stated that, if too much emphasis were placed on any technical feature, then the "frequent exceptions and intergradations would necessitate combination of genera until but six or a single genus remained." Several very large genera have been recognized within the family. The largest, *Sedum*, comprises as many as 500 widely distributed species. This genus has been referred to as a "dustbin taxon," and recent studies agree that *Sedum* is artificial and in need of taxonomic revision. Other large genera include *Crassula* (about 250 species, including *Tillaea*) and *Kalanchoe* (125 species, including *Bryophyllum*). The largest genera in the Western Hemisphere are *Echeveria* (with as many as 150 species in the neotropics), *Sedum* (circa 110 species, mostly found at higher elevations in central Mexico), and *Dudleya* (with approximately 40 species in southwestern North America and as a many as 20 entering the Tropics). Less speciose genera in the New World are *Crassula* (11 in the neotropics), *Graptopetalum* (12 species in southwestern North America, with perhaps half of them entering the Tropics), *Pachyphytum* (12 species in Mexico), and *Villadia* (with perhaps as many as 20 species in the Tropics, including 10 in Peru).

Distribution and habitat. Crassulaceae are nearly cosmopolitan in distribution, due in part to several widespread,

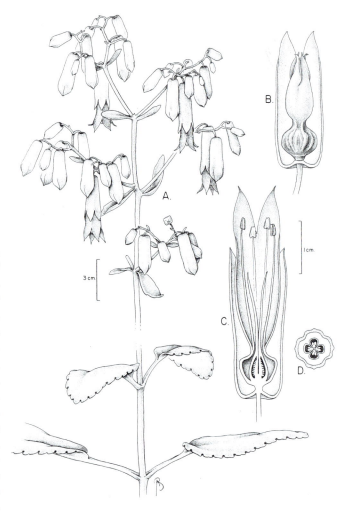

Figure 59. CRASSULACEAE. *Kalanchoe pinnata*. **A.** Stem with leaves and inflorescence. **B.** Medial section of calyx showing unopened corolla. **C.** Medial section of flower. **D.** Transverse section of ovary. Reprinted with permission from Acevedo-Rodríguez (1996). Artist: Bobbi Angell.

"weedy" genera (e.g., *Crassula* section *Tillaeoideae*). There are, however, distinct geographic regions that harbor a high diversity of Crassulaceae. These regions include southern Africa, Madagascar, Macaronesia, and Mexico.

In tropical America, Crassulaceae are most speciose in

Mexico (including Baja California), but are present, especially at elevations of 1,500 meters or more, throughout central America, the northern Andes, and southeastern Brazil. The trans-Mexican volcanic belt harbors a particularly high diversity of Crassulaceae, but the lowlands of Central and South America are devoid of species, with the exception of several alien taxa that have escaped cultivation. For example, species of *Kalanchoe* are widely cultivated and have occasionally escaped and colonized the lowlands of tropical America.

Crassulaceae are mostly plants of rocky, dry habitats. Members of the family are typically terrestrial, but several species (especially of *Sedum* in Mexico) are epiphytes, and at least one species of *Crassula* is aquatic.

Family classification. The Crassulaceae are placed in the Rosales by Cronquist and in the Saxifragales by Judd et al. The number of genera and species that should be recognized in the Crassulaceae is a topic of much debate. Likewise, the number of larger groups (i.e., subfamilies) that should be recognized has not been established. The most comprehensive morphological treatment of the family recognizes six subfamilies (Crassuloideae, Cotyledonoideae, Kalanchoideae, Sempervivoideae, Echeverioideae, and Sedoideae). These subfamilies are now considered by most to represent nonmonophyletic taxa. Recent classifications of the family have recognized two major lineages, the *Sedum*-lineage and the *Crassula*-lineage. Several authors suggest recognition of these two lineages at the subfamilial level whereas others recognize three subfamilies (Crassuloideae, Cotyledonoideae, and Sedoideae). Analyses of DNA sequence data strongly support recognizing two major lineages of Crassulaceae, but these analyses are consistent with recognizing either two or three subfamilies within the family. Thus, additional studies are required to address the question of how many subfamilies comprise Crassulaceae.

Features of the family. Habit: leaf-succulent herbs, subshrubs, or shrubs, usually perennial, rarely annual or biennial, often with localized or pervasive red coloration, especially in the root tips. **Stipules** absent. **Leaves** alternate, opposite, whorled, or basal rosettes (e.g., species of *Echeveria*), mostly simple, often thick and succulent. **Inflorescences** terminal or axillary, usually cymose, rarely in panicles or of a solitary flower. **Flowers** actinomorphic, usually bisexual, rarely unisexual (plants dioecious); calyx with 4–5(6), distinct or fused sepals; corolla with 4–5(6) distinct or fused petals; androecium with stamens mostly twice as many as petals, the stamens in a single whorl (*Crassula*-lineage) or in two whorls (*Sedum*-lineage), when in two whorls, the outer whorl sometimes alternate and free from petals, the inner whorl adnate to petals, the anthers with longitudinal dehiscence; gynoecium apocarpous or carpels slightly fused at bases, the ovary superior, the carpels (4)5(6), the number of carpels usually equal to number of petals; nectaries present at base of carpels; placentation submarginal or proxi-

mally axile, the ovules few to many in each carpel. **Fruits** usually separate follicles, rarely capsules. **Seeds** usually numerous, small; endosperm sparse.

Natural history. Most species of Crassulaceae conserve water by keeping their stomates closed during the day and open at night. During the night, atmospheric carbon dioxide is taken in and fixed for subsequent use in photosynthesis during the day. This photosynthetic strategy, called crassulacean acid metabolism, is named for the family. However, not all members of the family use this type of photosynthesis, and some are able to switch between physiological strategies. The Crassulaceae of tropical America have yet to be investigated in detail physiologically. Additional adaptations to life in stressful, low-water environments include succulent, water-holding leaf tissues; congested, often overlapping leaves; sunken stomates; and surfaces with waxes and/or trichomes.

Crassulaceae also exhibit a high degree and wide diversity of mechanisms for asexual reproduction, which make them easy to propagate in cultivation. For example, in *Kalanchoe*, conspicuous adventitious buds form along the leaf margins and drop to the ground to form new plants. In addition, some species of *Crassula* form propagules within their inflorescences, which also drop to form new plants.

Crassulaceae flowers are protandrous and presumably pollinated by insects; however, little pollination work has been conducted within the family. Seeds are very small and readily dispersed by the wind.

Economic uses. Crassulaceae are of very limited economic importance. Most economic uses involve species that are cultivated for horticultural purposes. Members of the family are common rock garden plants (e.g., species of *Sedum* and *Echeveria*) and often are grown for their colorful flowers and/or foliage. Others, such as *Crassula ovata* (jade plant) and *Kalanchoe*, are popular houseplants. The family appears to be of limited ethnobotanical importance, although some extracts, especially from species of *Kalanchoe*, are used in folk medicines.

References. BERGER, A. 1930. Crassulaceae. In *Die Natürlichen Pflanzenfamilien*, A. Engler and K. Prantl, 2nd ed., 18A:352–483. Leipzig: Wilhelm Engelmann. BERNAL, H. Y., AND J. E. CORRERA Q. 1991. Crassulaceae. In *Especies vegetales promisorias de los países del Convenio Andrés Bello*, Tomo VI. Santafé de Bogotá, D. E., Colombia: Secretaria Ejecutiva del Convenio Andrés Bello. CLAUSEN, R. T. 1975. *Sedum of North America North of the Mexican Plateau*. Ithaca, NY: Cornell University Press. HAM, R.C.H.J. VAN, AND H.'T HART. 1998. Phylogenetic relationships in the Crassulaceae inferred from chloroplast DNA restriction-site variation. *Amer. J. Bot.* 85:123–34. MORAN, R. V. 1942. The status of *Dudleya* and *Stylophylum*. *Desert Plant Life* 14:149–57. MORT, M. E., D. E. SOLTIS, P. S. SOLTIS, J. FRANCISCO-

ORTEGA, AND A. SANTOS-GUERRA. 2001. Phylogenetic relationships and evolution of Crassulaceae inferred from *matK* sequence data. *Amer. J. Bot.* 88:76–91. PILON-SMITS, E. A. H., H. 'T HART, AND J. VAN BREDERODE. 1996. Evolutionary aspects of crassulacean acid metabolism in the Crassulaceae. *In* K. Winter and J. A. C. Smith, eds. *Crassulacean Acid Metabolism*. Berlin: Springer-Verlag. SPONGBERG, S. A. 1978. The genera of Crassulaceae in the southeastern United States. *J. Arnold Arbor.* 59:198–248. STEPHENSON, R. 1994. *Sedum, cultivated stonecrops*. Portland, OR: Timber Press. WALTHER, E. 1972. *Echveria*, San Francisco: California Academy of Sciences.

CUCURBITACEAE (Squash Family)

MICHAEL NEE

Figure 60, Plate 16

- *vines*

- *tendrils present, coiling, subopposite to leaf at node*

- *leaves alternate, simple or palmately compound*

- *flowers unisexual*

Numbers of genera and species. Worldwide, the Cucurbitaceae comprise 130 genera and 900 species. In tropical America, there are 53 native genera and about 325 species, with only a few more genera and species found in extratropical areas. The largest genera *Cayaponia* (circa 60 species) and *Gurania* (circa 40) are in need of revision and thus the total number of species is uncertain. Only a few native Neotropical genera, *Lagenaria*, *Luffa*, and *Sicyos* also include species native to the Eastern Hemisphere.

Distribution and habitat. The Cucurbitaceae are found nearly worldwide except in cold-temperate and arctic regions. The great majority of the species grow in the Tropics and subtropics, mostly in humid forests but also in arid areas where they are usually only visible during the rainy season.

Family classification. The Cucurbitaceae are placed in the Violales by Cronquist. Morphological and molecular studies suggest that the family is monophyletic and closely aligned with families such as the Begoniaceae and Datiscaceae (extra-Neotropical).

The family is divided into two subfamilies, the Cucurbitoideae and Zanonioideae. In the Western Hemisphere, the bulk of the Cucurbitaceae belong to the subfamily Cucurbitoideae with tendrils that coil above the branching point and stamens that are fused in various complex ways. The more primitive Zanonioideae have tendrils that coil both above and below the branching point and stamens that are relatively unfused. (In the neotropics this includes *Fevillea* and a few small realted genera.)

The relative fusion of the flower parts and their relation to one another and the variation in fruit structure facilitate the delimitation of genera.

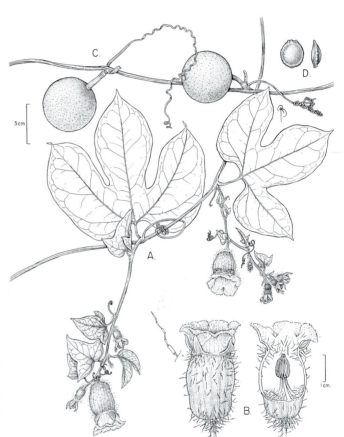

Figure 60. CUCURBITACEAE. *Cayaponia jenmanii.* **A.** Stem with leaves, tendrils, and staminate and pistillate flowers. **B.** Lateral views of staminate flowers, intact (left), detail of trichome (above left), and with perianth cut away to show connivant anthers (right). **C.** Part of stem with tendrils and fruits. **D.** Views of seed. Reprinted with permission from Mori et al. (2002). Artist: Bobbi Angell.

Features of the family. Habit: vines; stems and foliage somewhat succulent, the stems soft. **Tendrils** present, coiling, subopposite to leaf at node. **Stipules** absent. **Leaves** alternate, simple or palmately compound; blades often palmately lobed, with hairs often present on adaxial surface, often mineralized at base or with shiny "mineral plaques"; venation usually palmate. **Inflorescences** axillary, the males and females often differing, of solitary flowers (these often pistillate flowers) or variously in cymes, racemes, panicles or fascicles. **Flowers** actinomorphic (except androecium often zygomorphic), unisexual (plants usually monecious); hypanthium present; sepals (3)5(6), fused at base into hypanthium; petals equal in number, born on hypanthium, distinct or fused; androecium with basically 5 stamens, the stamens often reduced to 3, 2 with double thecae and 1 with single theca, the filaments distinct or connate, the anthers straight to highly convoluted, distinct to connate into head or ring; gynoecium syncarpous, the ovary inferior, the carpels 3 or 2 in *Gurania*, *Psiguria*, and allied genera, the locules 1 or 3, the styles equal to number of carpels, distinct or united, the stigmas usually 2-lobed; placentation parietal or axillary, the ovules one to very numerous, apical or basal. **Fruits** berries (if large and with leathery rind called a pepo) or capsules, fruits extremely bitter when unripe (and sometimes when ripe). **Seeds** 1–numerous.

The pollen is sometimes very large, and the individual grains may be easily visible to the naked eye (*Cucurbita*).

Natural history. Species of Cucurbitaceae quickly wilt and die when exposed to subfreezing temperatures. The temperate species survive the cold season either as seeds or as rootstocks, as do the ones from arid areas during the dry season.

The family is characterized by the presence of the extremely bitter substances known as cucurbitacins (tetracyclic triterpenoids), which are poisonous to most vertebrates and invertebrates. A small group of beetles not only has evolved a resistance to the deleterious effects of the cucurbitacins, but has come to depend upon them. These insects, which include the thirteen-striped cucumber beetle (*Diabrotica* species), are very serious pests of indigenous cucurbitaceous crops and also of the cucumbers (*Cucumis sativus*), melons (*C. melo*), and other species introduced from the Eastern Hemisphere.

Most Neotropical species are known or suspected to be monoecious, but field observation is needed in many species to establish this fact. Serial monoecy, in which a single plant usually produces male flowers before female flowers as growth proceeds, is apparently common.

Pollination is effected by nearly all major types of pollinators; e.g., hummingbirds, bees, bats, and moths. The male and female flowers may be quite different in appearance and size. In some species of *Cayaponia*, the males may be four times as large as the females and very different in shape, although pollinating bees appear to visit both indiscriminately.

Economic uses. The family produces a number of very important food crops, including some of the first and most important domesticated plants. The fruits of a number of species in the neotropics are eaten locally and could merit attention in future attempts to widen our stock of domesticated food plants. In the neotropics, the "squashes" of the genus *Cucurbita* are outstanding for both the quality and quantity of food provided by both the flesh and by the nutritious seeds. Remarkably, of the approximately thirteen wild species of the genus, five were domesticated independently, although the wild ancestors of two of the five are yet unknown. The *chayote* (*Sechium edule*), a species native to the mountains of eastern Mexico and best known for its edible fruits, is now widespread. Several other species of *Sechium* are used on a local scale in Central America. The genus *Cylcanthera* contains several species with edible fruits, notably *C. pedata*, originally of the Andes. A number of Cucurbitaceae have medicinal properties, one of which is the use of an extract from the seeds of *Fevillea cordifolia* to neutralize snake venom. The vascular skeleton of the fruit of *Luffa aegyptiaca* is the source of the loofah or vegetable sponge of bathrooms.

References. BERNAL, H. Y., AND J. E. CORRERA Q. 1991. Cucurbitaceae. In *Especies vegetales promisorias de los países del Convenio Andrés Bello*, Tomo VI. Santafé de Bogotá, D. E., Colombia: Secretaria Ejecutiva del Convenio Andrés Bello. CONDON, M., AND L. E. GILBERT. 1988. Sex expression of *Gurania* and *Psiguria* (Cucurbitaceae): Neotropical vines that change sex. *Amer. J. Bot.* 75: 875–84. JEFFREY, C. 1990. Appendix: An outline classification of the Cucurbitaceae. In *Biology and Utilization of the Cucurbitaceae*, eds. D. M. Bates, R. W. Robinson, and C. Jeffrey, 449–63. Ithaca, NY: Comstock Publishing Associates. LIRA, S. R. 1997. *Estudios Taxonómicos y Ecogeográficos de las Cucurbitaceae Latinoamericanas de Importancia Económica*. Mexico: Instituto de Biología, UNAM. NEE, M. 1990. The domestication of *Cucurbita* (Cucurbitaceae). *Econ. Bot.* 44(Suppl 3):56–68.

CUNONIACEAE (Cunonia Family)

JASON BRADFORD

Figure 61

- *trees or shrubs*

- *stipules usually conspicuous*

- *leaves opposite (decussate), compound or unifoliolate; petioles and rachises usually winged; blades and leaflets with margins usually toothed*

- *flowers usually diplostemonous, or sometimes stamens numerous; styles distinct, often diverging*

- *fruits follicles or septicidal capsules*

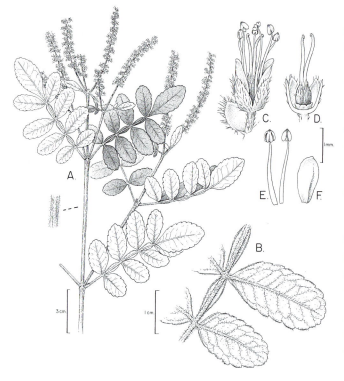

Figure 61. CUNONIACEAE. *Weinmannia neblinensis*. **A.** Stem with leaves and inflorescences and detail of part of stem (left). **B.** Upper part of pinnate leaf. **C.** Lateral view of intact flower. **D.** Lateral view of flower with stamens and part of perianth removed to show gynoecium. **E.** Adaxial (left) and abaxial (right) views of stamens. **F.** Abaxial view of petal. Reprinted with permission from Maguire and Steyermark (1989). Artist: Bobbi Angell.

Numbers of genera and species. Worldwide, the Cunoniaceae comprise 26 genera and circa 300 species, with about half the species in *Weinmannia*. Four genera and about 80 species occur in the Americas. In tropical America, there are two genera, *Lamanonia*, with about five species, and *Weinmannia*, with about 70 species; the latter is especially diverse in tropical montane forests.

Distribution and habitat. The Cunoniaceae are found in the Tropics of the Americas, Madagascar, Malesia, Australia, the South Pacific, and the western Indian Ocean (especially *Weinmannia*). The family is also found in the temperate zones of South America, South Africa, Australia, and New Zealand. Generic diversity is concentrated in New Guinea, eastern Australia, and New Caledonia, and the greatest concentration of species is found in New Caledonia.

Only four genera occur in the Americas. *Weinmannia* is distributed from Mexico and the Caribbean to Chile and Argentina. American species of *Weinmannia* are in section *Weinmannia*, which, with the exception of two species restricted to the Mascarene Islands of the Indian Ocean, is nearly endemic to the Americas. *Lamanonia* is restricted to southern Brazil, Paraguay, and Argentina. *Eucryphia* has seven species, five from Australia and Tasmania, and two species restricted to temperate South America.

Eucryphia glutinosa grows along water courses in the Mediterranean climate of Chile, and is the only deciduous-leaved species of the family. The monotypic *Caldcluvia*, an American endemic, occurs only in temperate zones of Chile and Argentina.

Most species of Cunoniaceae inhabit montane moist forests. In the Americas, *Weinmannia* is a species rich and common group of trees and shrubs of cloud forests and *subpáramo* vegetation. Species of *Lamanonia* inhabit seasonally dry forest, although plants are commonly found near creeks and other water sources, as well as at the border between riparian forests and woodlands.

Family classification. Cladistic analyses of DNA sequences place the Cunoniaceae in the Oxalidales along with Elaeocarpaceae, Cephalotaceae, Brunelliaceae, Connaraceae, and Oxalidaceae. This new classification differs from the Cronquist system by grouping families from his Rosales (Brunelliaceae, Cunoniaceae, Cephalotaceae, and Connaraceae) with families from his Geraniales (Oxalidaceae) and Malvales (Elaeocarpaceae).

Further analyses focusing within Oxalidales, and especially Cunoniaceae, reveal that Tremandraceae (Polygalales *sensu* Cronquist) are nested within Elaeocarpaceae, and that Cunoniaceae includes Eucryphiaceae, Davidsoniaceae, and Baueraceae, but not Brunelliaceae. Eucryphiaceae, Davidsoniaceae, and Baueraceae each have one or two unusual features that have kept them separate from Cunoniaceae in some classification systems; however, they have generally been regarded as satellite families of Cunoniaceae. Brunelliaceae has sometimes been considered part of Cunoniaceae but is now viewed as a close relative with a possible sister relationship to Cephalotaceae. *Cephalotus* is a pitcher plant from southwest Australia with below ground woody tissue and carpels very similar to those of *Brunellia*. The Tremandraceae share poricidal, basifixed anthers, fused styles, and loculicidally dehiscent carpels with the Eleaocarpaceae.

Despite progress toward refined family circumscription and relationships within Oxalidales, a morphological diagnosis of Oxalidales remains elusive. Although families within the order do share many obvious characters, these may be ancestral within the rosids. Interestingly, paleobotanists have long recognized the similarities of the leaves and pollen of the Elaeocarpaceae and Cunoniaceae.

The intrafamilial classification of Cunoniaceae has been revised based on phylogenetic studies. Twenty genera are placed among six tribes, Cunonieae, Codieae, Geissoieae, Caldcluvieae, Schizomerieae, and Spiraeanthemeae. The relationships of six genera are not resolved. Spiraeanthemeae is a sister clade to the rest of the family, and Schizomerieae is relatively basal. The remaining four tribes are clearly part of a large clade at the core of the family. American genera are phylogenetically divergent. *Weinmannia* is in the Cunonieae, *Lamanonia* is in the Geissoieae, *Caldcluvia* is in the Caldcluvieae, and *Eucryphia* is unplaced but nested among the core group of tribes. Each American genus has its closest relatives in the Australasian-Pacific region.

Features of the family. Habit: trees or shrubs, occasionally hemiepiphytic or strangling (some *Weinmannia*), evergreen. Bark usually gray to light brown, the fissures longitudinal. Stems commonly with lenticels. Stipules present, often conspicuous, arising from 1 (*Weinmannia*) or 2 (*Lamanonia*) primordia in a line medial from petioles. Leaves opposite (decussate), imparipinnate or unifoliolate in *Weinmannia*, trifoliolate or palmately compound in *Lamanonia*; stipels often present in *Lamanonia*; petioles and rachis often winged; blades firm, the margins (also of leaflets) usually toothed, often glandular-serrate; hairs present, generally simple; venation pinnate, craspedodromous, or semicraspedodromous; domatia of small tufts or pockets sometimes present along midvein. Inflorescences axillary, racemose; bracteoles often subtending flowers; pedicels present. Flowers actinomorphic, bisexual, small; sepals 4 in *Weinmannia* or 5–7 in *Lamanonia*, imbricate in *Weinmannia* or valvate in *Lamanonia*, distinct; petals equal to number of sepals in *Weinmannia* or absent in *Lamanonia*, when present alternate with sepals; androecium of 8 stamens in *Weinmannia* or stamens ca. 20–60 in *Lamanonia*, usually diplostemonous, the filaments slender, exceeding petals, the anthers dehiscing longitudinally; floral disc usually present, the disc free and annular in *Weinmannia* or much reduced and adnate to ovary in *Lamanonia*; gynoecium with superior ovary, the carpels 2, less often 3–5, united or less often ± distinct, the locules 4, the styles distinct, often diverging, the stigmas terminal; placentation axile, the ovules 2–many per locule, in two rows, sometimes pendulous, bitegmic, anatropous, apotropous. Fruits septicidal capsules. Seeds 2–many per fruit, small, pubescent and without wings in *Weinmannia* or winged and glabrous in *Lamanonia*; endosperm oily.

Although most species and individuals of Cunoniaceae are terrestrial trees, in some places, individuals of *Weinmannia* species may be hemiepiphytic, and even stranglers have been reported. Epiphytism in *Weinmannia* occurs in very humid, mossy, cloud forests, where little difference exists between the canopy and terrestrial soils.

Natural history. The flowers of Cunoniaceae are unrestrictive, probably produce nectar, and are known to attract various insects, birds, bats, and geckos. Many are sweetly scented, but some flowers have a slightly fetid aroma or no odor at all. Floral colors are typically white, cream, pink, or pale orange, but some possibly bird-specialized flowers are bright pink, red, or bright green. Although a variety of visitors has been documented, no detailed pollination biology has been done. However, bees are likely the predominant pollinators of the family, certainly within the neotropics.

Most genera have dry, dehiscent fruits that remain attached to the plant, and this is true for all American species. Seeds usually are dispersed by wind and have either winglike appendages or long hairs that catch the breeze. Outside the neotropics, a few genera have dry, indehiscent fruits that are dispersed intact. These may be covered by hairs, have winged-outgrowths of the carpel walls or the sepals, or be bladder-like and dispersed by water. Three genera have drupelike fruits that are dispersed by cassowaries, bats, and arboreal marsupials.

Economic uses. The wood is used in general construction. The most important, commercial, timber regions for the family are Malesia, Australia, and the western Pacific. In the Americas, species of *Weinmannia* are used mostly in local construction and cabinetry. Where the human population relies on wood for fuel, especially in the Andes and Madagascar, *Weinmannia*-dominated forests are often chopped down, and the wood is burned to make charcoal.

Most species are rich in tannins (e.g., *W. tinctoria*), and those historically prized by leather workers may be locally rare because of overexploitation.

Bee keepers depend on nectar gathered by bees from *Weinmannia* for the commercial production of honey in Madagascar and New Zealand, and *Eucryphia*-dominated forests are honey resources in Tasmania and Chile. An infusion of the leaves of *Caldcluvia paniculata* is reported to be used against bronchial and intestinal infections.

Horticultural use of species of Cunoniaceae is limited mostly to the Tropics or to temperate regions with maritime climates. Botanical gardens in California and eastern Australia, for example, grow many Cunoniaceae outdoors. Species of *Ceratopetalum*, *Cunonia*, *Davidsonia*, *Eucryphia*, *Geissois*, *Bauera*, *Weinmannia*, and *Lamanonia* are sometimes available commercially. Cultivars of *Eucryphia*, including described hybrids, have been developed for the horticultural trade. The South African *Cunonia capensis*, and several Australian species are attractive and used in native plantings. Although unavailable commercially, Pacific species of *Geissois* are perhaps the most visually striking with large, palmately compound leaves and bright red flowers. Some species of Cunoniaceae invade disturbed areas, and horticultural introductions of nonnative species should be done cautiously.

References. BERNARDI, L. 1961. Revisio generis Weinmanniae. Pars I: Sectio Weinmanniae. *Candollea* 17:123–89. BERNARDI, L. 1963. Revisio generis Weinmanniae. Pars II: Sectio Simplicifoliae. *Candollea* 18:285–334. BILONI, J. S. 1965. Notas preliminares a una revisión de las Cunoniáceas Argentinas. *Boletin de la Sociedad Argentina de Botanica* X: 292–301. BRADFORD, J. C. 1998. A cladistic analysis of species-groups in *Weinmannia* (Cunoniaceae) based on morphology and inflorescence architecture. *Ann. Missouri Bot. Gard.* 85:565–93. BRADFORD, J. C., AND R. W. BARNES. 2001. Phylogenetics and classification of Cunoniaceae (Oxalidales) using chloroplast DNA sequences and morphology. *Syst. Bot.* 26(2):354–85. BRADFORD, J. C., AND P. E. BERRY. 1998. Cunoniaceae. In *Flora of the Venezuelan Guayana*, eds. J. A. Steyermark, P. E. Berry and B. K. Holst, 4:462–69. St. Louis: Missouri Botanical Garden Press. HARLING,

G. 1999. Cunoniaceae. In *Flora of Ecuador*, eds. G. Harling and L. Andersson, no. 61:1–74. Göteborg, Sweden: Department of Systematic Botany, University of Göteborg. PEREZ-ARBELAEZ, E. 1990. *Plantas Utiles de Colombia*. Medellín: Editorial Victor Hugo. RODRIGUEZ, R. R., S. O. MATTEI, AND M. M. QUEZADA. 1983. Flora Arborea de Chile. Concepción, Chile: Editorial de la Universidad de Concepción. ZICKEL, C. S., AND H. F. LEITAO FILHO. 1993. Taxonomic revision of *Lamanonia* Vell. (Cunoniaceae). *Revista Brasil. Bot.* 16:73–91.

CUSCUTACEAE (Dodder Family)

LYTTON JOHN MUSSELMAN

Figure 62, Plate 16

- *vines*
- *plants parasitic*
- *stems yellow, orange, or red*
- *leaves reduced to scales*
- *fruits capsules*

Numbers of genera and species. Worldwide, the Cuscutaceae comprise a single genus, *Cuscuta*, and 150 species. In tropical America, there are circa 50 species of *Cuscuta*.

Distribution and habitat. The Cuscutaceae are found throughout the world but are most diverse in north temperate and Mediterranean regions. The most widely distributed species, *Cuscuta campestris* (including *C. pentagona*), is found on every continent except Antarctica.

Species of *Cuscuta* grow along streams, in fire-maintained communities, agroecosystems, and disturbed areas.

Family classification. The Cuscutaceae are placed in the Solanales by Cronquist. Traditionally, *Cuscuta* has been treated as a subfamily of the Convolvulaceae or as a separate family. *Cuscuta* shares the following features with the Convolvulaceae: scales at the base of the stamens, a trend from two styles to one style, and the presence of laticifers. Molecular work supports the inclusion of *Cuscuta* in the Convolvulaceae.

Cuscuta has traditionally been divided into three subgenera primarily based on style number. Subgenus *Monogyna* has a single style, a spicate inflorescence, and 4 or less seeds. The other subgenera have 2 styles and usually more than 4 seeds with subgenus *Grammica* distinguished by a capitate stigma and subgenus *Cuscuta* by a linear stigma. Species of the subgenus *Monogyna* (ca. 12 species) are characteristically thick and often high climbing, sometimes nearly completely covering their hosts, which are often trees and shrubs. Species of subgenus *Cuscuta* (ca. 16 species) are widespread and include several important weeds. Some of these lack

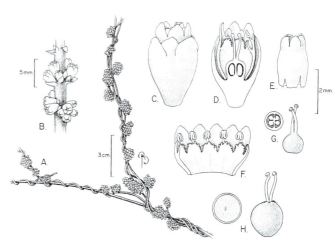

Figure 62. CUSCUTACEAE. *Cuscuta americana*. **A.** Stem with leaves and inflorescences; note twining growth form. **B.** Part of inflorescence. **C.** Lateral view of flower. **D.** Medial section of flower. **E.** Lateral view of corolla. **F.** Corolla opened to show adnate stamens and fringed scales at base of filaments. **G.** Lateral view of gynoecium (right) and transverse section of ovary (left). **H.** Lateral view of fruit with persistent styles (right) and transverse section of fruit (left). Reprinted with permission from Acevedo-Rodríguez (1996). Artist: Bobbi Angell.

chlorophyll. The largest subgenus is *Grammica* with more than 100 species. In the only worldwide monograph of the genus, Yuncker recognized 27 species of subgenus *Cuscuta* and 121 species of subgenus *Grammica*, but these numbers are generally considered to be inflated.

Features of the family. Habit: vines, scant chlorophyll usually present (in most species of subgenera *Cuscuta* and *Grammica*), masked by pigments, glabrous, extrafloral nectaries sometimes present, laticifers sometimes present. **Stems** yellow, orange, or red. **Leaves** reduced to scales. **Inflorescences** axillary, cymose or spicate (subgenus *Monogyna*). **Flowers** actinomorphic, bisexual, often small, 4 or 5-merous, reddish, white, or green; sepals 4 or 5; petals 4 or 5; infrastaminal scales present; stamens 4 or 5; gynoecium syncarpous, the ovary superior, the carpels 2(3), the locules equal to number of carpels, the styles 1 (subgenus *Monogyna*) or 2, the stigmas capitate (subgenus *Grammica*) or linear (subgenus *Cuscuta*); placentation basal-axile (or intruded-parietal), the ovules 2 per locule. **Fruits** capsules, circumscissle (subgenus *Monogyna*) or dehiscence irregular. **Seeds** 1–6, the seed coat rough, hard, requiring scarification to germinate.

The main stem of subgenus *Cuscuta* twines about its host while species of subgenus *Grammica* produce lateral branches that coil, allowing the terminal branch to continue growing.

Taxonomic features of the flowers include petal and sepal shape as well as color. A roughened seed surface characterizes dodder seeds, a character that is used when removing the parasite seed from crop plant seeds.

The only plants with which *Cuscuta* can be confused are species of *Cassytha*. This pantropical genus of the Lauraceae, a family of otherwise autotrophic plants, is remarkably similar vegetatively to *Cuscuta*.

Natural history. Species of *Cuscuta* are unique in their nastic growth, which allows them to twine around suitable hosts. Several species appear to be autogamous, but others are visited by insects. No information is available about dispersal biology.

Economic uses. Species of *Cuscuta* (dodder) are ranked as some of the worst weeds and *C. campestris* is perhaps the most widely distributed parasitic weed in the world. It often is found as a contaminant in commercial seed shipments, especially of alfalfa (*Medicago sativa*) and niger seed (*Guizotia abyssinica*). Other species of agricultural weeds include *C. indecora*, *C. monogyna*, and *C. pedicellata*.

References. DAWSON, J. H., L. J. MUSSELMAN, P. WOLSWINKEL, AND I. DOERR. 1994. Biology and control of *Cuscuta*. *Rev. Weed Sci.* 6:265–317. KELLY, C. K. 1992. Resource choice in *Cuscuta europaea*. *Proc. Natl. Acad. U.S.A.* 89:12194–197. MUSSELMAN, L. J. Parasitic weeds in the Southern United States. *Castanea* 61(3):271–92. YUNCKER, T. G. 1932. The genus *Cuscuta*. *Mem. Torrey Bot. Club* 18: 113–331.

CYRILLACEAE (Cyrilla Family)

BERTIL STÅHL

Figure 63

- *shrubs or trees*

- *leaves alternate, simple*

- *inflorescences racemes*

- *flower perianth in 5s; sepals unequal, enlarged (Purdiaea); stamens 5 or 10*

Numbers of genera and species. The Cyrillaceae comprise three genera and 14 species. In tropical America, there are two genera, *Purdiaea* with 12 species and the monotypic *Cyrilla*.

Distribution and habitat. *Purdiaea* has one species with a wide but patchy distribution in the northern Andes and the Guayana Highlands, one species in Guatemala and Belize, and 10 species in Cuba, chiefly in the eastern part of that island. *Cliftonia* and *Cyrilla* both occur in southeast United States, but *Cyrilla* also occurs throughout the West Indies, Mexico, Belize, and northern South America (except the Andes).

Cyrilla racemiflora is unusual in being distributed in temperate forest in the southeastern United States, dry forest in the Caribbean, and lowland rain forest in Venezuela and Brazil. Other members of the family are found in dry to wet montane forests.

Family classification. The Cyrillaceae have traditionally been placed in the Ericales (e.g., *sensu* Cronquist), usually close to the Ericaceae and Clethraceae, positions supported by analyses of DNA sequence data.

Features of the family. Habit: shrubs or small trees (*Cyrilla racemiflora* may reach 25 m), often branched at base (*Cyrilla*). Stipules absent. Leaves alternate, simple, sometimes crowded at stem apex (many *Purdiaea*); petioles short or nearly absent; blades often coriaceous, the margins entire. Inflorescences terminal, sometimes axillary, racemes, often with numerous flowers; bract present, inserted at base of pedicel; bracteoles 2 (*Cyrilla*) or absent (*Purdiaea*). Flowers actinomorphic or subzygomorphic with sepals of different sizes, bisexual; sepals 5, enlarging during fruit maturation in *Purdiaea*, then outer two larger, enclosing all or most of inner three; petals 5, white, pinkish, or violet; nectaries present (*Cyrilla*) on inner or basal part of petals (petals distinctly thickened in this region); androecium of 5 (*Cyrilla*) or 10 (*Purdiaea*) stamens, whorls 1 (*Cyrilla*, considered outer whorl) or 2, the outer whorl opposite sepals, the anthers narrow (*Purdiaea*) or short, caudate at base (*Purdiaea*), dehiscing by apical pores (*Purdiaea*) or by longitudinal slits; gynoecium syncarpous, the ovary superior, the carpels 2–5, the locules 3–5 (*Purdiaea*) or 2–4, the style short, entire, or 2–4 lobed (*Cyrilla*); placentation axile, the ovules 1 (*Purdiaea*) or 3 per locule. **Fruits** berries, dry, covered by enlarged sepals (*Purdiaea*). **Seeds** 1–few; endosperm copious.

In bud, the stamens are inverted and, as the filaments straighten at anthesis, the anthers, which are versatile, rotate 180°.

Natural history. *Cliftonia* and *Cyrilla* reproduce vegetatively by means of sprouts from underground roots, thus forming large and sometimes extensive clones. *Purdiaea* is pollinated by pollen-collecting bees, whereas *Cyrilla* and *Cliftonia* are pollinated by bees and possibly other insects foraging for nectar. There are no obvious adaptations for seed dispersal. Although the winged fruits of *Cliftonia* and the enlarged calyx lobes in *Purdiaea* might be seen as adaptations for wind dispersal, they also attach easily to wet surfaces like birds' feet.

Economic uses. The Cyrillaceae are of little economic importance. *Cyrilla* and *Cliftonia* are planted occasionally as ornamentals in the United States. Because of their showy inflorescences, species of *Purdiaea* also merit cultivation as ornamentals, but the area in which they could grow probably is restricted. In the United States and the West Indies, *Cyrilla racemiflora* is a highly esteemed plant among honey producers. Bees are attracted to the plants because of their large number of nectar-rich flowers, which are present over an extended period of time. In addition, hollow trunks of the species often function as beehives.

References. ANDERBERG, A. A., C. RYDIN, AND M. KÄLLERSJÖ. 2002. Phylogenetic relationships in the order Ericales s.l.: analyses of molecular data from five genes from the plastid and mitochondrial genomes. *Amer. J. Bot.* 89: 677–87. THOMAS, J. L. 1960. A monographic study of the

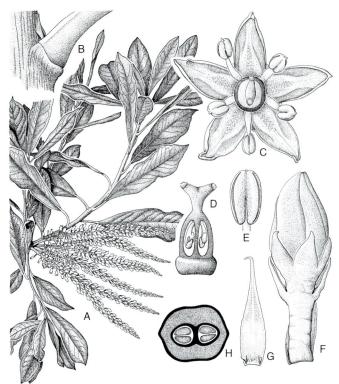

Figure 63. CYRILLACEAE. *Cyrilla racemiflora.* **A.** Stem with leaves and inflorescences (x½). **B.** Node showing stipules (x6). **C.** Apical view of flower (x12). **D.** Partial medial section of gynoecium (x12). **E.** Adaxial view of anther (x32). **F.** Lateral view of flower bud (x12). **G.** Adaxial view of bract (x12). **H.** Schematic transverse section of ovary (x20). Reprinted with permission from Cronquist (1981). Artist: William S. Moye.

Cyrillaceae. *Contr. Gray Herb.* 186:1–114. THOMAS, J. L. 1961. *Schizocardia belizensis*: a species of *Purdiaea* (Cyrillaceae) from Central America. *J. Arnold Arbor.* 42:110–11.

DESFONTAINIACEAE (Desfontainia Family)

LENA STRUWE

Plate 17

- *shrubs, rarely small trees*
- *leaves opposite, simple; interpetiolar lines present; blades with spinelike teeth*
- *inflorescences terminal, of solitary flowers*
- *flower with long, narrowly funnel-shaped corolla tube*
- *fruits white berries*

Numbers of genera and species. The Desfontainiaceae comprise a single genus, *Desfontainia*, restricted to the West-

ern Hemisphere. *Desfontainia* is sometimes considered to contain a single species, *D. spinosa*; however, some botanists recognize at least three species distinguished by variations in leaf, calyx, and corolla shape and size.

Distribution and habitat. *Desfontainia spinosa sensu lato* is distributed from Patagonia (0–1200 m) northward along the Andes (2,000–4,000 m) to Colombia and Costa Rica.

Desfontainia spinosa sensu lato grows on foggy, rainy mountain slopes in open areas as well as in cloud forests, often in association with *Sphagnum* moss. It is absent from dry and seasonally dry areas. *Desfontainia* is sensitive to habitat destruction and is now absent from many places where it has been previously collected in the high Andes of Peru.

Family classification. Although Cronquist placed the Desfontainiaceae within the Loganiaceae in the Gentianales, recent evidence puts it closer to the Dipsacales. *Desfontainia* appears to be the closest relative of the family Columelliaceae, which is also placed in the Dipsacales. This genus was earlier associated with many different families, and was considered a monotypic tribe in the Loganiaceae by Leeuwenberg.

Features of the family. Habit: shrubs, rarely small trees, much-branched and erect, or rarely decumbent. **Stipules** represented by interpetiolar line. **Leaves** opposite, simple; blades coriaceous, dark green, the margins nearly always with spinelike teeth. **Inflorescences** terminal, of solitary flowers. **Flowers** actinomorphic, bisexual, pendent or horizontally oriented, 5-merous; calyx connate at base, persistent in fruit, the lobes 5; corolla fleshy, sympetalous, the corolla tube long, narrowly funnel-shaped, bright red, distal portion of limb yellow, at least on inside, the lobes 5, short, red or yellow, contorted or imbricate in bud; androecium of 5 stamens, the stamens inserted in upper part of corolla tube, the filaments short, introrse, the anthers linear; gynoecium syncarpous, the ovary superior, the carpels 5, the locules incomplete, 5 at base, 1 at apex, the style 1, long, the stigma slender; placentation basal-axile, the placentas 5, the ovules many. **Fruits** berries, globose to ovoid, white (green when immature). **Seeds** many.

Natural history. The flowers with their tubular, red to yellow corollas probably are pollinated by hummingbirds. The berries are extremely bitter, probably because of their iridoid content, but are likely to be bird-dispersed.

Economic uses. The hallucinatory and narcotic properties of *Desfontainia* are well known among the natives of Colombia and Chile, where shamans drink a tea of the leaves to dream, see visions, and diagnose illnesses. The plants also yield a tonic for the stomach and a yellow dye that is used for coloring textiles in Chile. *Desfontainia* is cultivated occasionally and grows best in cold, wet climates.

References. BACKLUND, A., AND B. BREMER. 1997. Phylogeny of the Asteridae s. str. Based on rbcL sequences, with particular reference to the Dipsacales. *Pl. Syst. Evol.* 207: 225–54. BISSET, N. G. 1980. Useful plants. *Die Natürlichen Pflanzenfamilien*, 2nd ed., Angiospermae: ordnung Gentianales, fam. Loganiaceae, ed. A. J. M. Leeuwenberg, 28b(1): 238–44. BREMER, B., R. G. OLMSTEAD, L. STRUWE, AND J. A. SWEERE. 1994. *rbc*L sequences support exclusion of *Retzia*, *Desfontainia*, and *Nicodemia* from the Gentianales. *Pl. Syst. Evol.* 190:213–30. LEEUWENBERG, A.J.M. 1969. Notes on American Loganiaceae IV. Revision of *Desfontainia* Ruiz et Pav. *Acta Bot. Neerl.* 18:669–79. LEEUWENBERG, A.J.M. 1980. *Die Natürlichen Pflanzenfamilien*, 2nd ed., Angiospermae: Ordnung Gentianales, Fam. Loganiaceae 28b(1):1–255. SCHULTES, R. E. 1989. De speciebus varietatibusque *Desfontainia* colombianae notae. *Revista Acad. Colomb. Ci. Exact. Fis.* 17:313–19. WEIGEND, M. 2001. *Desfontainia* Ruiz and Pav. (Desfontainiaceae) revisited: A first step towards alpha-diversity. *Bot. Jahrb.* 123:281–310.

DICHAPETALACEAE (Dichapetalum Family)

GHILLEAN T. PRANCE

Figure 64, Plate 17

- *trees, shrubs, or lianas*

- *leaves alternate, simple*

- *inflorescences sometimes arising from petioles*

- *flower petals 5, the base sometimes connate into tube, the apices bifid*

- *fruits drupes, dry or fleshy*

Numbers of genera and species. Worldwide, the Dichapetalaceae comprise three genera and about 220 species. In tropical America, there are three genera and 55 species. *Stephanopodium* (12 species) is endemic to the Western Hemisphere; *Tapura* occurs in the neotropics (21 species) and in Africa; and, the largest genus, *Dichapetalum*, is pantropical (22 species in neotropics).

Distribution and habitat. Species of Dichapetalaceae are found in Central and South America, Cuba, Hispaniola, the Lesser Antilles, Africa, and tropical Asia. In the Western Hemisphere, they range from Central Mexico to São Paulo, Brazil.

The Dichapetalaceae are often found in lowland and submontane forests, usually occurring in nonflooded areas.

Family classification. The Dichapetalaceae have been placed near many families, often close to the Euphorbiaceae. More recently it has been suggested that the family should be placed in the Celastrales (*sensu* Cronquist), Rosales, or Thymelaeales. Recent molecular data indicates a relationship to the Chrysobalanaceae and Trigoniaceae, a placement suggested as early as 1921 by *H. Hallier*. Because the family consists of only three closely related genera, it has not been divided into tribes or subfamilies.

Features of the family. Habit: trees (*Dichapetalum, Stephanopodium,* and *Tapura*), shrubs (some *Tapura* and *Dichapetalum*), or lianas (most *Dichapetalum*), the trees usually understory, sometimes reaching canopy (a few *Tapura* and *Stephanopodium*). **Bark** of lianas often smooth, pale, with scattered, dark, lenticellate pustules. **Stipules** present, often caducous, the margins sometimes fimbriate (*Dichapetalum*). **Leaves** alternate, simple; blade margins entire. **Inflorescences** axillary (a few *Dichapetalum*), born on petiole or midrib (a few *Tapura*), fasciculate (*Tapura* and *Stephanopodum*), corymbose or cymose panicles (*Dichapetalum*). **Flowers** actinomorphic (*Dichapetalum* and *Stephanopodum*) or slightly zygomorphic (*Tapura*), bisexual, rarely unisexual (the plants monoecious), small; sepals 5, imbricate, often unequal in size; petals 5, imbricate, nearly equal (*Dichapetalum*), distinct or connate into tube, when tubular, the lobes equal (*Stephanopodium*) or markedly unequal (*Tapura*), the apex usually bifid or bicucullate (hence the name *Dichapetalum*); androecium with 3 or 5 stamens, the stamens distinct or adnate to corolla tube, the anthers dehiscing longitudinally; glands 5, hypogynous, equal or unequal, alternating with stamens or united into disc; gynoecium syncarpous, the ovary superior, the carpels 2 or 3, the locules 2 or 3, the styles 2 or 3, the stigmas capitate or simple; placentation apical, the ovules 2, anatropous, pendulous at apex of each locule. **Fruits** drupes, dry or fleshy, small, the epicarp frequently pubescent. **Seeds** 1 per locule, pendulous; endosperm absent, the embryo large and erect.

Natural history. Little is known about the pollination and dispersal of the family, but the flowers of *Dichapetalum* are visited by small bees.

Economic uses. No uses are recorded other than for a few local medicines. Some African species of *Dichapetalum* are poisonous, particularly to cattle.

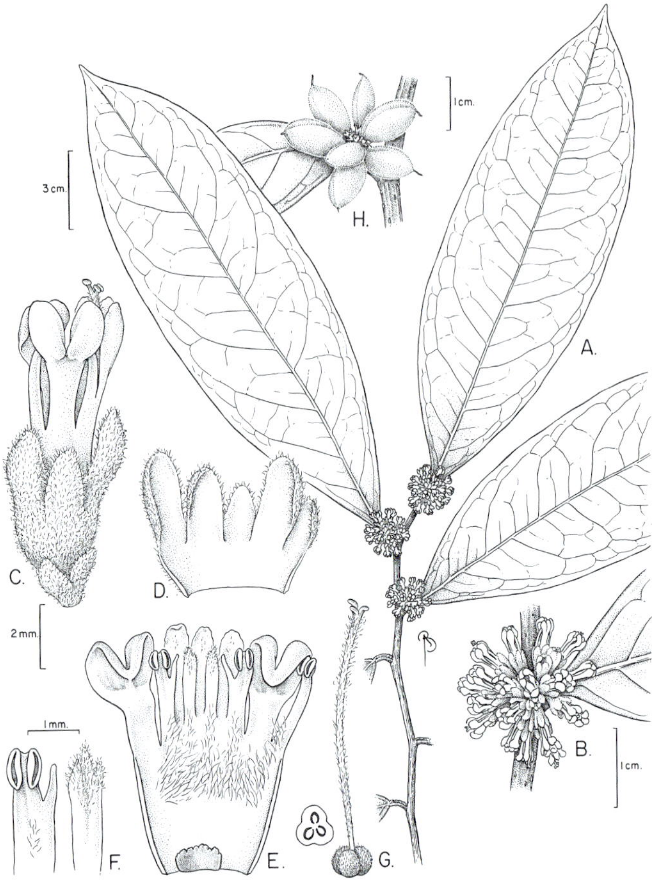

References. BAILLON, H. 1886. Dichapetalae. In *Flora Brasiliensis,* ed. C.F.P. von Martius. 12(1):365–78. ENGLER,

Figure 64. DICHAPETALACEAE. *Tapura guianensis.* **A.** Part of stem with leaves and inflorescences. **B.** Inflorescence on petiole of leaf. **C.** Lateral view of flower. **D.** Adaxial view of opened calyx. **E.** Adaxial view of opened corolla to show stamens, staminodes, and gland at base. **F.** Adaxial views of stamen (left) and staminode (right). **G.** Lateral view of gynoecium (right) and transverse section of ovary (left). **H.** Cluster of fruits on petiole of leaf. Reprinted with permission from Mori et al. (2002). Artist: Bobbi Angell.

A., AND K. KRAUSE. 1931. Dichapetalaceae. In *Die Natürlichen Pflanzenfamilien,* A. Engler and K. Prantl, 2nd ed. 19c:I–II. Leipzig: Wilhelm Engelmann. HALLIER, H. 1921. Beitrage zur Kentnis der Linaceen (DC. 1819) Dumort. *Beih. Bot. Centralbl.* 21:1–178. PRANCE, G. T. 1972. Dichapetalaceae. *Fl. Neotrop. Monogr.* 10:1–84.

DILLENIACEAE (Dillenia Family)

KLAUS KUBITZKI

Figure 65

- *Mostly lianas and scandent shrubs*
- *Leaves alternate, simple; blades often scabrous*

- *Flowers with 3–5 petals; stamens numerous; ovary superior*

Numbers of genera and species. Worldwide, the Dilleniaceae comprise 11 genera and approximately 335 species. In tropical America, there are five genera and about 70 species. *Davilla* and *Doliocarpus* comprise 20 and about 30 species, respectively, *Tetracera* possesses approximately 15 species; and *Pinzona* and *Curatella* are monotypic.

Distribution and habitat. Dilleniaceae have a pantropical distribution. *Curatella*, *Davilla*, *Doliocarpus* (including *Neodillenia*), and *Pinzona* are endemic to the neotropics, and the other Neotropical genus, *Tetracera*, is pantropical.

All species are limited to tropical lowlands. The Neotropical genera are found in humid or seasonal but mostly evergreen forests, woodlands, or savannas. Various species of *Davilla* are adapted to the sand-dune scrub (*restinga*) of eastern Brazil. *Curatella americana*, a plant characteristic of Neotropical savannas extends from southern Mexico to Bolivia and São Paulo, Brazil.

Family classification. The Dilleniaceae, placed in the Dilleniales by Cronquist, have been suggested to be related to many angiosperm families. Molecular analyses place the family at the base of the "Core Eudicots," often in association with the Vitaceae.

Various subdivisions of the family have been proposed, but none has been completely satisfactory. The four exclusively Neotropical genera, *Curatella*, *Davilla*, *Doliocarpus* (including *Neodillenia*), and *Pinzona*, have distinctly peltate stigmas and form a monophyletic group.

Features of the family. Habit: lianas, scandent shrubs, shrubs (some *Davilla*), or infrequently trees (*Curatella americana*), the trees medium-sized, tortuous. **Stipules** absent. **Leaves** alternate, simple; petiolar wings often present, persistent or caducous; blades often scabrous (due to presence of silica). **Inflorescences** terminal or axillary, panicles, ramiflorous fascicles, or thyrses (*Tetracera*). **Flowers** actinomorphic, usually bisexual, sometimes unisexual (the plants functionally dioecious in Neotropical *Tetracera*); sepals 3–5(13); petals 3–5; androecium of numerous stamens, the anthers with parallel thecae (*Curatella*, *Davilla*, *Pinzona*, and some *Doliocarpus*), or thecae arranged at obtuse angle (*Tetracera* and some *Doliocarpus*); gynoecium with superior ovary, the carpels 1–5, distinct or sometimes compound (*Curatella* and *Pinzona*), the locules 1–5, the styles distinct, the stigma prominent, peltate, or punctiform (*Tetracera* and all Eastern Hemisphere genera); placentation marginal, the ovules 1–numerous per carpel. **Fruits** indehiscent or dehiscent, the indehiscent fruits berries, dry or fleshy, the dehiscent fruits dehiscing along ventral and/or dorsal sutures. **Seeds** 1 or several (*Tetracera*) per carpel; arils often present, sometimes reduced in species with indehiscent fruits, the margins entire or lacinate (*Tetracera*); endosperm copious, oily, sometimes containing starch, the embryo small.

All Neotropical species except *Curatella americana* are shrubs or lianas. The lianas, with their scabrid young stems,

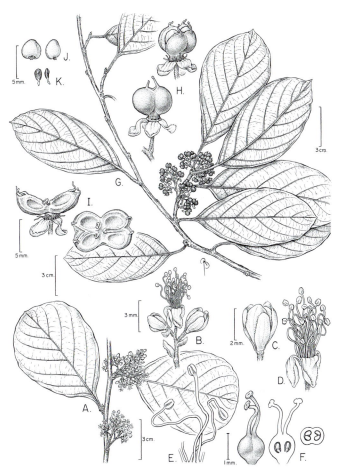

Figure 65. DILLENIACEAE. *Pinzona coriacea*. **A.** Stem with leaves and inflorescences. **B.** Detail of inflorescence. **C.** Lateral view of floral bud. **D.** Lateral view of flower. **E.** Stamens. **F.** Lateral view (left), medial section (center), and transverse section (right) of gynoecium. **G.** Stem with leaves and infructescences. **H.** Lateral views of intact fruit (below) and newly dehisced fruit (above). **I.** Lateral (left) and apical (below) views of dehisced fruit. **J.** Views of arillate seeds. **K.** Views of seeds with arils removed; note funicles. Reprinted with permission from Mori et al. (2002). Artist: Bobbi Angell.

often burn the skin when touched and are hence called *cipó de fogo* (fire liana) in Brazil. The lianas can reach the thickness of a human thigh and, in cross section, the stems of *Doliocarpus* and *Tetracera* show concentric rings.

Petiolar wings, functioning similarly to stipules in the developing terminal bud, are present in several *Davilla*.

The flowers of Dilleniaceae are usually multistaminate with centrifugal stamen development. In the Neotropical species, the stamens are arranged more or less evenly around the gynoecium or in indistinct fascicles, and the anthers are never poricidal.

Natural history. Neotropical species of *Tetracera* are functionally dioecious. The male flowers produce viable and tricolpate pollen and the gynoecium is rudimentary. In the female flowers, the numerous stamens produce empty, polyporate pollen grains.

In many members of the family, anthesis lasts for only one day. Pollination is by insects, probably solitary bees and small beetles, which visit the flowers frequently to gather pollen. In the Eastern Hemisphere, buzz pollination has been observed in species of *Dillenia* and *Hibbertia* with poricidal anthers, and buzz pollination is also known in the Neotropical *Davilla kunthii*, but this species has anthers that open by slits.

Dispersal by birds is frequent in the Dilleniaceae.

Economic uses. Dilleniaceae have limited economic uses. Pieces of cut stems of lianas yield great quantities of water used to quench the thirst of tropical travelers. *Dillenia indica* is often grown as an ornamental, and many other species of this genus, because of their beautiful flowers, are potential ornamentals. Local people use the leaves of *Curatella americana* like sandpaper.

References. AYMARD-C., G. A. 1997. Dilleniaceae novae neotropicae IX: *Neodillenia*, a new genus from the Amazon basin. *Harvard Pap. Bot.* 10:121–31. DICKISON, W. C. 1967–79. Comparative morphological studies in Dilleniaceae I–VII. *J. Arnold Arbor.* 48–52. DICKISON, W. C., J. W. NOWICKE, AND J. J. SKVARLA. 1982. Pollen morphology of the Dilleniaceae and Actinidiaceae. *Amer. J. Bot.* 69:1055–73. HOOGLAND, R. D. 1953. The genus *Tetracera* (Dilleniaceae) in the eastern Old World. *Reinwardtia* 2:185–224. KUBITZKI, K. 1970. Die Gattung *Tetracera* (Dilleniaceae). *Mitt. Bot. Staatssamml. München* 8:1–98. KUBITZKI, K. 1971. *Doliocarpus*, *Davilla* und verwandte Gattungen (Dilleniaceae). *Mitt. Bot. Staatssamml. München* 9:1–105. KUBITZKI, K. 1973. Neue und bemerkenswerte neotropische Dilleniaceen. *Mitt. Bot. Staatssamml. München* 9:707–20.

DIPTEROCARPACEAE (Meranti Family)

CYNTHIA MORTON

Figure 66

- *trees or rarely shrubs*

- *leaves alternate, simple*

- *flower perianth 5-merous; sepals often persistent, winglike*

- *seeds 1 per fruit*

Numbers of genera and species. Worldwide, the Dipterocarpaceae comprise 17 genera and more than 500 species. In tropical America there are two monotypic genera, *Pseudomonotes* (*P. tropenbosii*) and *Pakaraimaea* (*P. dipterocarpacea*).

Distribution and habitat. The Dipterocarpaceae are pantropical. Most genera are endemic to major continental areas, and none are pantropical. The largest subfamily Dipterocarpoideae contains 13 genera and 478 species and is restricted to tropical Asia and Malaysia. Monotoideae, is comprised of three genera with 34 species and is found in tropical Africa, Madagascar, and South America where the subfamily is represented by *Pseudomonotes*, known only from Araracuara, Colombia. The Parkaraimoideae, containing only *Pakaraimaea*, is restricted to the Guyana highlands of South America.

The family is frequently found in primary rain forest, savannas, and savanna woodlands.

Family classification. Although Cronquist placed the Dipterocarpaceae in the Theales, it is more appropriately aligned with the Malvales. The family is divided into three subfamilies: Dipterocarpoideae, Monotoideae, and Pakaraimoideae. Molecular studies using *rbc*L chloroplast data indicate that all three subfamilies are monophyletic and suggest that members of the Sarcolaenaceae are the closest relatives of the Dipterocarpaceae.

Features of the family. Habit: trees, rarely shrubs, indument abundant or sometimes scarce, unicellular or multicellular, waxy secretions sometimes present, often scale shaped. **Stipules** usually small or sometimes large and caducous, leaving persistent scar. **Leaves** alternate, simple; blade margins entire. **Inflorescences** terminal or axillary, racemes, panicles, or rarely cymes; bracts and bracteoles present, usually small, caducous. **Flowers** actinomorphic, bisexual; sepals 5, accrescent, usually winglike, chartaceous at maturity, distinct or connate at base, forming a cupule or cup, the cup shallow; petals 5, contorted in bud, usually longer than sepals; androecium of 5–numerous stamens, the stamens usually distinct, basifixed, the connective appendaged, sometimes strongly extended, dehiscing by longitudinal slits; gynoecium syncarpous, the ovary superior or semi-inferior, the carpels 3–4(5), the style small, terminal, entire or shortly lobed; placentation midaxial, apical, or basal (*Pseudomonotes*), the ovules 1 (*Pseudomonotes*) or 2–4 per locule. **Fruits** capsules, dry, with persistent, usually winglike sepals, the wings sometimes short (*Pakaraimaea*), the pericarp usually woody, splitting along three sutures at germination. **Seeds** 1 per fruit; endosperm usually absent.

Wood anatomy provides synapomorphies at the subfamilial level. Both Monotoideae and Pakaraimoideae share the presence of distinctive secretory cavities in the pith and lack resin canals in the wood. The Monotoideae differ from the Pakaraimoideae by containing mostly uniseriate rays whereas Pakaraimoideae consists of mainly biseriate rays. The Dipterocarpoideae, however, have resin canals in the wood, multiseriate rays, and lack secretory cavities in the pith.

The development of the calyx lobes into winglike sepals is one of the main features separating genera of Dipterocarpaceae. Aliform sepals, which may or may not be present in the Dipterocarpoideae, are universal in the Monotoideae, and are present but short in the Pakaraimoideae.

Natural history. Pollinators of Asian Dipterocarpaceae are bees, moths, butterflies, beetles, and thrips. Typically the fruits of Dipterocarpaceae fall to the ground in the immediate vicinity of the parent trees, but the winged fruits also aid in dispersal by the wind. The few wingless fruits and some of the winged fruits are dispersed by water.

Economic uses. The Asian genera *Dipterocarpus*, *Hopea*, *Shorea*, and *Vitica* are major sources of hardwood timber. Lesser known products from Asian taxa are resins used for varnishes. Substitutes for cocoa butter are derived from the fats within the seeds of some species of *Shorea*. No economic uses have been reported for either *Pseudomonotes* or *Pakaraimaea*.

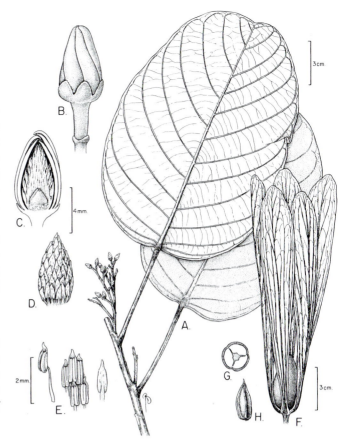

Figure 66. DIPTEROCARPACEAE. *Pseudomonotes tropenbosi*. **A.** Stem with leaves and inflorescence. **B.** Lateral view of flower bud. **C.** Medial section of flower bud. **D.** Lateral view of androecium. **E.** Lateral (left), adaxial (center), and abaxial (right) views of stamens. **F.** Lateral view of immature fruit subtended by enlarged sepals. **G.** Transverse section of ovary. **H.** Seed. Reprinted with permission from Londoño et al. (1995). Artist: Bobbi Angell.

References. ASHTON, P. S. 1982. Dipterocarpaceae. In *Flora Malesiana*, ed. C.G.G.J. Van Steenis, Series I, 9:237–552. The Netherlands: Sijthoff and Noordhoff International Publishers. ASHTON, P. S. 2003. Dipterocarpaceae. In *The Families and Genera of Vascular Plants*, eds. K. Kubitzki and C. Bayer. 5:182–97. Berlin: Springer-Verlag. BANCROFT, H. 1935. The wood anatomy of representative members of the Monotoideae. *Amer. J. Bot.* 22:717–39. DAYANANDAN, S., P. S. ASHTON, S. M. WILLIAMS, AND R. B. PRIMACK. 1999. Phylogeny of the tropical tree family Dipterocarpaceae based on nucleotide sequences of the chloroplast *rbc*L gene. *Amer. J. Bot.* 86:1182–90. DE ZEEUW, C. 1977. Pakaraimoideae, Dipterocarpaceae of the Western Hemisphere. III. Stem Anatomy. *Taxon* 26:368–80. GIANNASI, D. E., AND K. J. NIKLAS. 1977. Pakaraimoideae, Dipterocarpaceae of the Western Hemisphere. IV. Phytochemistry. *Taxon* 26:380–85. GOTTWALD, H., AND N. PARAMESWARAN. 1966. Das se- kundare Xylem der Familie Dipterocarpaceae. *Bot. Jahrb. Syst.* 85:410–508. LONDOÑO, A. C., ET AL. 1995. A new genus and species of Dipterocarpaceae from the Neotropics. I. Introduction, taxonomy, ecology, and distribution. *Brittonia* 47:225–36. MAGUIRE, B. 1977. Pakaraimoideae, Dipterocarpaceae of the Western Hemisphere. I. Introduction. *Taxon* 26:341–42. MAGUIRE, B., AND P. S. ASHTON. 1977. Pakaraimoideae, Dipterocarpaceae of the Western Hemisphere. II. Systematic, geographic and phyletic considerations. *Taxon* 26:341–85. MORTON, C. M. 1995. A new genus and species of Dipterocarpaceae from the Neotropics. II. Stem anatomy. *Brittonia* 47:237–47. MORTON, C. M., D. M. DEEPTHI DISSANAYAKE, AND S. DAYANANDAN. 1999. Phylogeny and biosystematics of *Pseudomonotes* (Dipterocarpaceae) based on molecular and morphological data. *Pl. Syst. Evol.* 216:197–205.

DROSERACEAE (Sundew Family)

Mireya D. Correa A.

Figure 67

- *small herbs*
- *leaves usually alternate, often in basal rosettes, simple; sticky glandular hairs present*
- *flowers actinomorphic, bisexual*
- *fruits loculicidal capsules*

Numbers of genera and species. Worldwide, the Droseraceae comprise four genera and about 124 species. In tropical America, there is only *Drosera* with about 20 species. With the exception of *Drosera* (ca. 120 species worldwide), all genera in the family are monotypic.

Distribution and habitat. *Drosera* is distributed in the Tropics and in temperate regions. The Neotropical species are found: 1) from southern North America to South America; 2) the Guayana-Pakaraima Region (Venezuela and Guyana) but reaching the Amazon Basin; 3) southern Brazil, northern Uruguay, Paraguay, and Argentina; and 4) southern Argentina and Chile, where only a single species, *D. uniflora*, is found.

Species of *Drosera* range from sea level to 3,000 meters and are frequently found in bogs, swamps and, wet sand on soils low in nitrogen.

Family classification. Droseraceae, Nepenthaceae, and Sarraceniaceae have often been placed in the Nepenthales (sensu Cronquist, mostly because their mutual carnivory). Recent molecular studies suggest that Droseraceae and Nepenthaceae, with Polygonaceae and Plumbaginaceae, should be placed in the Polygonales. The Polygonales have two clades. One contains Polygonaceae and Plumbaginaceae based upon ovaries with one basal ovule and indehiscent fruits and the other is formed by Droseraceae and Nepenthaceae based on molecular evidence and carnivorous habit.

The family is not divided into subfamilies.

Features of the family. Habit: small herbs. **Stems** often absent, if present then short. **Stipules** present or absent. **Leaves** usually alternate, often in basal rosettes, simple, circinate in bud, sticky glandular hairs present. **Inflorescences** terminal, 1–2 per plant, usually circinate cymes or racemes, sometimes of a solitary flower (*D. meristocaulis*), sometimes appearing scorpioid. **Flowers** actinomorphic, bisexual; sepals 4–8, imbricate, remaining attached even when petals wither; petals 4–8, morning ephemeral; androecium with 4–20 stamens, the filaments usually distinct, filiform, the anthers extrorse, dehiscing longitudinally; gynoecium syncarpous, the ovary superior, the carpels 2–5, the locule 1, the styles 3–5, distinct, simple or divided (sometime divided to base, then appearing as 6–10); placentation parietal or subbasal, the ovules numerous. **Fruits** loculicidal capsules. **Seeds** numerous, usually minute, dark, variously reticulate and ornamented.

Natural history. The carnivorous behavior of these plants is related to growing on soils low in nutrients. The glandular hairs on the leaves secrete enzymes, which form dewlike droplets that trap and digest small insects. The nutrients released by these insects allow the plant to increase the number of flowers and total weight of the seeds and tubers, thereby enhancing overall fitness.

Very little is known about pollination; however, if cross-pollination is not achieved at anthesis, the closing and withering of the petals over the gynoecium guarantees self-pollination. No information is available on dispersal biology.

Economic uses. Species of *Drosera* (sundew) have been used as homeopathic remedies for cough, corns, warts, eye and ear inflammations, rheumatic joint pain, morning sickness, and liver ailments. Ingested as tea, they were considered diuretics and aphrodisiacs.

Studies suggest that naphthoquinone extracted from *D. rotundifolia* suppresses cough and that alcohol extracts from *D. ramentacea* induce production of histamine, a substance released during allergic reactions, and acetylcholine, a substance promoting the transmission of nerve impulses in experimental animals. Because drying the plant reduces its volume by as much as 90 percent, pharmacological tinctures of *Drosera* are quite expensive.

Overdoses of *Drosera* extracts can cause irritation of skin and mucous membranes, intestinal spasms and irritation, severe cough, and bloody diarrhea. Nonetheless, *Drosera* preparations have been used in Brazil, France, Germany, India, Indochina, Madagascar, Mexico, Nepal, and the United States.

References. Albert, V. A., S. E. Williams, and M. W. Chase. 1992. Carnivorous plants: phylogeny and structural evolution. *Science* 257:1491–95. Correra Q., J. E., and H. Y. Bernal. 1992. Droseraceae. In *Especies vegetales promisorias de los países del Convenio Andrés Bello*, Tomo VII. Santafé de Bogotá, D. E., Colombia: Secretaria Ejecutiva del Convenio Andrés Bello. Dixon, K. W., and J. S. Pate. 1978. Phenology, morphology and reproductive biology of the tuberous sundew, *Drosera erythrorhiza* Lindl. *Austral. J. Bot.* 26(4):441–54. Duno De Stefano, R. 1995. El Género *Drosera* (Droseraceae) en Venezuela. *Acta Bot. Venez.* 18(1–2):67–95. Kubitzki, K. 2003. Droseraceae. In *The Families and Genera of Vascular Plants*, eds. K. Kubitzki and C. Bayer. 5:198–202. Berlin: Springer-Verlag. Seine,

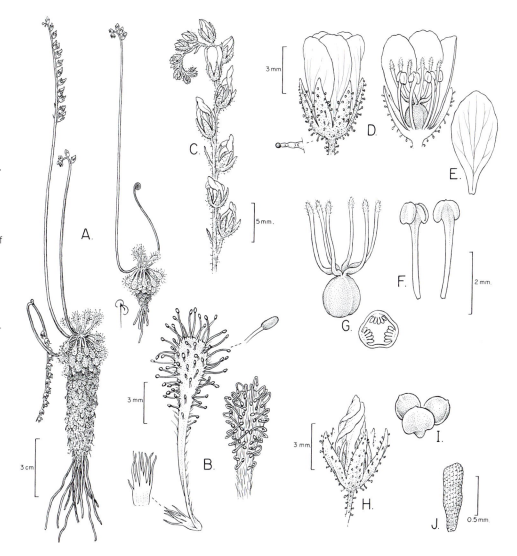

Figure 67. DROSERACEAE. *Drosera roraimae* (A, Huber 11565; B, Huber 10986; C–G, Huber 8250; H–J, Huber 11545). **A.** Plants showing roots, leaves, and inflorescences. **B.** Leaf (center), detail of stipule (left), glandular trichome (above right), and apex of leaf (right). **C.** Part of inflorescence. **D.** Lateral view of flower (left), detail of glandular trichome (below left), and lateral view of flower with some of sepals and petals removed (right). **E.** Adaxial view of petal. **F.** Adaxial (right) and abaxial (left) views of stamens. **G.** Lateral view of gynoecium (above) and transverse section of ovary (below). **H.** Lateral view of postanthesis flower. **I.** Oblique view of dehisced fruit. **J.** Seed. Original. Artist: Bobbi Angell.

R., AND W. BARTHLOTT. 1993. On the morphology of trichomes and tentacles of Droseraceae Salisb. *Beitr. Biol. Pflanzen* 67:345–66. VERHOEK-WILLIAMS, S. 1976. Healing (and poisoning) with *Drosera. Carniv. Pl. Newslett.* 5(1):12–15. WILLIAMS, S. E., V. A. ALBERT, AND M. W. CHASE. 1994. Relationships of Droseraceae: a cladistic analysis of rbcL sequence and morphological data. *Amer. J. Bot.* 81(8): 1027–37.

DUCKEODENDRACEAE (Duckeodendron Family)

MICHAEL NEE

Plate 17

- *trees*
- *leaves alternate, simple*
- *inflorescences terminal, cymes*
- *flowers synsepalous and sympetalous*
- *fruits drupes, bright orange, the mesocarp fibrous*

Numbers of genera and species. The Duckeodendraceae are comprised of a single species, *Duckeodendron cestroides*, restricted to the central Amazon basin.

Distribution and habitat. *Duckeodendron cestroides* is found only in primary Amazon rain forests.

Family classification. The Duckeodendraceae are placed in the Solanales by Cronquist. The species epithet refers to the similarity of the tubular flower and simple, entire leaves with those of *Cestrum* in the Solanaceae. Despite the admittedly close similarity of leaf venation to Solanaceae, *Duckeodendron* presents a number of differences from that family, including being a large primary forest tree with hard wood, possessing imbricate calyx lobes, and having large drupaceous fruits with bony endocarps.

Features of the family. Habit: tall trees. **Stipules** absent. **Leaves** alternate, simple; blades chartaceous, somewhat shiny adaxially, the margins entire; venation pinnate. **Inflorescences** terminal, cymes, small. **Flowers** nearly actinomorphic, bisexual; calyx synsepalous, the lobes 5, imbricate; corolla sympetalous, tubular, yellowish, the lobes 5; androecium of 5 stamens, the filaments attached to lower part of corolla tube, the anthers exserted; nectar disc at base of ovary; gynoecium syncarpous, the ovary superior, the carpels 2, the locules 2, the style 1, the stigma with 2 lobes; ovule 1 per locule (only one developing), anatropous. **Fruits** drupes, large, oblong, bright orange, the mesocarp fibrous. **Seeds** 1 per fruit.

The outer fruit wall rots quickly, leaving a thick hard endocarp surrounded by a tough persistent fibrous mesocarp.

Natural history. *Duckeodendron cestroides* apparently blooms at night, because freshly fallen flowers can be found on the forest floor in the early morning. The size, shape, and fragrance of the flowers suggest pollination by moths. The fruits fall to the forest floor, where the pericarps are probably eaten by rodents.

Economic uses. *Duckeodendron cestroides* may be used occasionally for timber.

References. CARLQUIST, S. 1988. Wood anatomy and relationships of Duckeodendraceae and Goetzeaceae. *I.A.W.A. Bull., N.S.* 9:3–12. KUHLMANN, J. G. 1950. Duckeodendraceae Kuhlmann (Nova familia). *Arq. Serv. Florest.* 3:7–8.

EBENACEAE (Ebony or Persimmon Family)

CYNTHIA SOTHERS

Figure 68, Plate 17

- *trees and shrubs*
- *bark slash exposing a black ring of inner bark*
- *leaves alternate, simple*
- *flowers actinomorphic, unisexual (plants dioecious), sympetalous; calyx persistent and often enlarged in fruit*
- *fruits berries*

Numbers of genera and species. Worldwide, the Ebenaceae comprise two genera and more than 500 species. In tropical America, there is a single genus, *Diospyros*, with about 100 species (ca. 500 worldwide).

Distribution and habitat. The Ebenaceae have a worldwide distribution, occurring primarily in the tropical and subtropical regions of Asia, Africa (including Madagascar and other Indian Ocean islands), and the Americas. Few species occur in temperate climates. *Diospyros*, has a pantropical distribution, whereas *Euclea* is restricted to Africa, Arabia, the Comoro Islands, and Socotra. The center of distribution for the family is in the Indo-Pacific region.

In tropical America, species of *Diospyros* occur mainly in lowland forests, but a few species occur at higher elevations on *tepuis* in southern Venezuela and in the Andes. The greatest number of species is found in the Amazon. There are approximately 15 species in Central America, the southern United States, and the West Indies. Species occur as far north as the southern United States (*D. texana* and *D. virginiana*) and as far south as Argentina and Paraguay (*D. hassleri*). Most species have restricted distributions and only a few, such as *D. artanthifolia*, *D. capreifolia*, *D. inconstans*, and *D. poeppigiana*, occur over extensive areas.

Family classification. The Ebenaceae are placed in the Ebenales by Cronquist, together with Lissocarpaceae, Sapotaceae, Styracaceae, and Symplocaceae. Ebenaceae differ from these families by having a strictly superior ovary (vs. inferior in Lissocarpaceae and inferior or half-inferior in Symplocaceae), no milky latex (as in Sapotaceae), and a persistent, accrescent fruiting calyx and absence of stellate hairs (as in Styracaceae). Recent molecular work has placed the Ebenaceae in the order Ericales (Asterids), next to Myrsinaceae and Polemoniaceae. *Lissocarpa* has been found to be sister to *Diospyros*. These studies indicate that the generic relationships between Ebenaceae and Lissocarpaceae have not been resolved.

Diospyros is subdivided into poorly defined sections that are based on the morphology of the calyx and corolla (number of lobes and shape) and number and pubescence of stamens. The number of floral parts are, however, variable

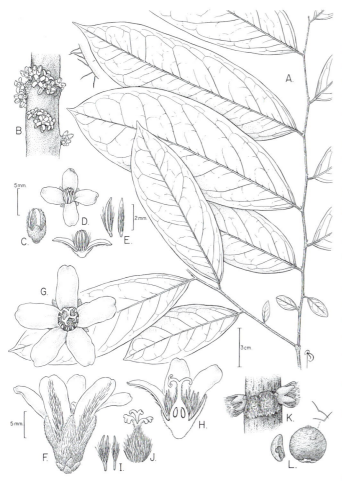

entire, truncate to deeply lobed, persistent in fruit, usually accrescent; corolla sympetalous, campanulate, urceolate, tubular, or ovate, sometimes constricted at throat, white or cream-colored, less often greenish or light pink, shortly to deeply lobed, the lobes contorted, overlapping. **Staminate flowers**: stamens 4–60(100), sometimes unequal in size, epipetalous or borne on receptacle, exserted or included, pubescent or glabrous, the filaments usually short, united at base, the anthers basifixed, usually apiculate, setulose, ocasionally 2 per filament, dehiscing longitudinally; pistillode usually present. **Pistillate flowers**: usually 2–3 times larger than staminate flowers; staminodes sometimes present; gynoecium syncarpous, the ovary superior, glabrous or hairy, carpels 2–8, the locules 2–16, the styles equal to number of carpels, distinct or joined at base, rarely completely fused; placentation axile, the ovules 2 per carpel, pendulous, anatropous, the integuments 2. **Fruits** berries, globose to subglobose, black, greenish, yellow or orange when ripe, enlarged calyx present in many species, the exocarp usually firm, the pulp soft, gelatinous, sweet-tasting. **Seeds** up to 16, rarely 1, large, often ellipsoid or segment-shaped, the testa coriaceous; endosperm abundant, smooth or ruminate.

The habit of species of *Diospyros* ranges from rare canopy trees (*D. vestita*) to more commonly understory trees and shrubs. The bark, when cut, exposes a black ring of inner bark diagnostic of Neotropical *Diospyros*. The inner wood is often yellowish. A gelatinous exudate that becomes black when the bark is cut can also be observed.

Natural history. The extrafloral glands found on the leaf blades produce a sugary exudate that may attract ants.

Pollination is mainly by insects, although few species have been studied. The flowers of cultivated species are visited by bees, wasps, and flies, and honeybees have been seen collecting nectar and pollen. At least three species in central Amazonia and French Guiana have flowers that open at night. These observations, together with the wide variation in corolla shapes and colors, indicate a more diverse set of pollinators than is known currently.

Dispersal is mainly by mammals. In the Amazon, capuchin monkeys (*Cebus apella*) have been observed eating fruit of at least one species (*Diospyros cavalcantei*). Fruits that have fallen to the ground probably are eaten by turtles, deer, tapirs, and other mammals. Common names for *Diospyros* often allude to these animals.

Economic uses. Several species of Ebenaceae from Africa and Asia are famous for their beautiful wood, generically called ebony. Because of overharvesting, some of these species, such as *Diospyros quaesita*, are nearly extinct in Sri Lanka. This species produces variegated wood, while the higher quality, evenly pitch-black wood comes from species such as *D. ebenum*.

Another important economic product is the edible fruit of *D. kaki* (persimmon), native to eastern Asia. This persimmon has extensively been cultivated throughout the world and

Figure 68. EBENACEAE. *Diospyros ropourea*. **A.** Stem with leaves and detail of ciliate margin (upper left). **B.** Part of trunk with cauliflorous flowers. **C.** Lateral view of flower bud. **D.** Apical view (above) and medial section with intact androecium (below) of staminate flower. **E.** Adaxial (left) and abaxial (right) views of stamens. **F.** Lateral view of flower showing trichomes in middle of petals. **G.** Apical view of pistillate flower. **H.** Medial section of pistillate flower. **I.** Lateral (right) and abaxial (left) views of staminodes. **J.** Lateral view of gynoecium. **K.** Immature fruits on tree trunk. **L.** Lateral view of fruit (right) with enlargement of hairs (above) and seed (left). Reprinted with permission from Mori et al. (2002). Artist: Bobbi Angell.

within species, and this has created some confusion in establishing species limits.

Features of the family. Habit: trees and shrubs, the heartwood often black, the bark slash exposing a black ring of inner bark; hairs simple or glandular when present. **Stipules** absent. **Leaves** alternate, simple; blades with distinct glands abaxially, most apparent on young growth (sometimes drying black in herbarium specimens), often occurring at base or along midrib, the margins entire. **Inflorescences** axillary, ramiflorous, or cauliflorous, cymes, fascicles, or flowers solitary. **Pistillate inflorescences** often with fewer flowers than staminate ones. **Flowers** actinomorphic, unisexual (the plants dioecious), medium-sized, 3–6-merous; calyx synsepalous, yields a fruit that is sweet tasting and very high in vitamin C. Other species less commonly cultivated for their edible fruit are *D. virginiana* (persimmon, North America) and *D. lotus* (date plum, Eurasia). Species known to be edible but not cultivated are *D. digyna* (Mexico, the West Indies), *D. ierensis* (Brazil, the Guianas, Trinidad), and *D. coccolobifolia* (northeast Brazil).

None of the Neotropical species have great commercial value. However, species such as *D. kaki* and *D. discolor* from the Philippines have been introduced in the neotropics and *D. digyna* (black sapote), native to the West Indies, is cultivated in other parts of the world.

In Africa and Malaysia, several species are used as fish poisons, but the only known Neotropical species used in this manner is *D. guianensis* in French Guiana.

Other worldwide uses include the manufacture of tools from the wood, production of black dyes from the fruit and seeds, and medicinal applications derived from several parts of the plant (mostly in China).

References. BERRY, P. E., V. SAVOLAINEN, K. J. SYTSMA, J. C. HALL, AND M. CHASE. 2001. *Lissocarpa* is sister to *Diospyros* (Ebenaceae). *Kew Bull.* 56(3):725–29. CAVALCANTE, P. B. 1963. Contribuição ao conhecimento do gênero *Diospyros* Dalech.(Ebenaceae) na Amazônia. *Bol. Mus. Par. Emilio Goeldi, N.S., Bot.* 20:1–53. CORRERA Q., J. E., AND H. Y. BERNAL. 1992. Ebenaceae. In *Especies vegetales promisorias de los países del Convenio Andrés Bello*, Tomo VII. Santafé de Bogotá, D. E., Colombia: Secretaria Ejecutiva del Convenio Andrés Bello. MORTON, C. M., M. W. CHASE, K. A. KRON, AND S. M. SWENSEN. 1996. A molecular evaluation of the monophyly of the order Ebenales based upon *rbc*L sequence data. *Syst. Bot.* 21(4):567–86. SAVOLAINEN, V. ET AL. 2000. Phylogeny of the eudicots: a nearly complete familial analysis based on *rbc*L gene sequences. *Kew Bull.* 55:257–309. WHITE, F., AND B. MAGUIRE. 1981. Ebenaceae. In Botany of the Guayana Highland. *Mem. New York Bot. Gard.* 32(11):323–29.

ELAEOCARPACEAE (Elaeocarp Family)

JERALD S. BRICKER

Figure 69, Plate 18

- *trees or shrubs*

- *trunks often irregular, buttresses often present*

- *flower perianth sometimes uniseriate, the apex of petals often fringed; stamens inserted on surface of disc*

- *seeds often arillate*

Numbers of genera and species. Worldwide, the Elaeocarpaceae comprise nine genera and about 500 species. *Elaeocarpus* (300 species of the Eastern Hemisphere, excluding Africa) and *Sloanea* (100, pantropical) comprise 90 percent of the taxa within the family. Other genera include: *Aceratium* (20, Eastern Hemisphere), *Sericolea* (15, Malesia), *Dubouzetia* (10, Moluccas to New Caledonia), *Aristotelia* (5, Peru to Chile), *Crinodendron* (4, temperate South America), *Peripentadenia* (2, Australia), and *Vallea* (1, Colombia to Bolivia). In tropical America, there are four genera (*Aristotelia*, *Crinodendron*, *Sloanea*, and *Vallea*) and 98 species.

Petenaea (1, Mexico and Guatemala), a genus traditionally placed in the Tiliaceae, may also be a member of the family, but additional research is needed before assigning it to the Elaeocarpaceae.

Distribution and habitat. Elaeocarpaceae are found in Central and South America, the Lesser and Greater Antilles, New Caledonia, New Zealand, New Guinea, Australia, Indonesia, Malaysia, Japan, Hawaii, China, Nepal, India, Ceylon, and Madagascar. There are no species native to continental Africa, although *Elaeocarpus* has been introduced to tropical west Africa.

Most genera are distributed exclusively in the Western or the Eastern Hemisphere. There are two exceptions, *Sloanea* and *Aristotelia*. Species of *Sloanea* are found in the Bahamas, the Caribbean, Central and South America, New Caledonia, Australia, China, Vietnam, Malaysia, and Madagascar (one endemic species). *Aristotelia* is represented by a single species in Chile and four species in Australia, New Zealand, and Tasmania.

In tropical America, the Elaeocarpaceae are most often found as understory trees in nonflooded rain forests and in riparian zones. Species of *Sloanea* are often found on river banks in lowland tropical rain forest. In Chile, *Crinodendron pataqua* is found in dry woodland riparian zones and *C. hookerianum*, is found in dense woods and swamps of the southern provinces of Chiloé, Llanquihue, and Valdivia, Chile.

Family classification. The Elaeocarpaceae have traditionally been placed in the Malvales (e.g., *sensu* Cronquist). The family is most closely related to the Tiliaceae but also shows

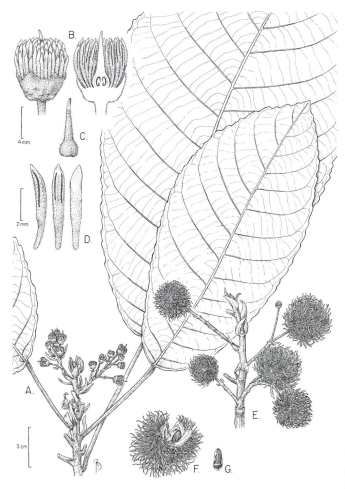

Figure 69. ELAEOCARPACEAE. *Sloanea grandiflora*. **A.** Stem with leaves and inflorescences. **B.** Lateral view (left) and medial section (right) of flower. **C.** Lateral view of gynoecium. **D.** Lateral (left), adaxial (center), and abaxial (right) views of stamens. **E.** Part of infructescence with immature fruits. **F.** Dehisced fruit. **G.** Seed with aril. Reprinted with permission from Mori et al. (2002). Artist: Bobbi Angell.

an affinity to the Flacourtiaceae of the Violales sensu Cronquist. The exact relationship of the three families is still in question. A recent molecular study of the "core families" of the Malvales (i.e., Bombacaceae, Malvaceae, Sterculiaceae, and Tiliaceae) indicate that the Elaeocarpaceae are not closely related to the four core Malvalean families and are most closely related to members of the Cunoniaceae.

Four groups of genera are recognized. *Aristotelia* and *Vallea* are closely related; *Sericolea*, *Aceratium*, and *Elaeocarpus* are grouped together; *Crinodendron*, *Dubouzetia*, and *Peripentadenia* have been treated as the tribe Tricuspidarieae; and *Sloanea* is distinct from the other eight genera.

The monotypic genus *Muntingia* has been included within the Elaeocarpaceae, although it has recently been placed in the family Muntingiaceae (as treated here), a clade within the Malvales.

Features of the family. Habit: trees (species reaching 40 m) or shrubs. Trunks often irregular, buttresses (to 6 m high)

present in species of *Dubouzetia*, *Elaeocarpus*, *Peripentadenia*, and *Sloanea*. Bark usually gray, smooth, thin. Stipules present. Leaves alternate or opposite, simple. Inflorescences axillary or terminal, racemes or panicles, occasionally of solitary flowers. Flowers actinomorphic, bisexual, rarely unisexual; perianth sometimes uniseriate (e.g., species of *Sloanea*); sepals 4 or 5, distinct; petals 4 or 5, distinct, rarely connate at base, the apex often fringed; disc present, flat or toothed (like a cogwheel, e.g., *Crinodendron*, *Dubouzetia*, *Peripentadenia*); androecium with 4–5-numerous stamens, the stamens inserted on surface of disc; gynoecium syncarpous, the ovary superior, the carpels 2–4, the locules 2–many, the style 1, sometimes grooved, tapering, the stigma not distinct; placentation axile, the ovules 2–20 per locule. Fruits capsules, berries, or drupes; exocarp smooth (i.e., *Crinodendron*, *Dubouzetia*, *Elaeocarpus*, and some *Sloanea*) or with coarse bristles (e.g., some *Sloanea*). Seeds 0–4 per locule, often arillate; endosperm copious, the embryo straight.

Natural history. One study of *Crinodendron patagua* showed that the pollinators were bees (*Bombus*, *Apis mellifera*, and several small bees, including species of Halictidae). One bug (Hemiptera: Pentatomidae) was found foraging on the flowers of *Crinodendron patagua*, presumably using the nectar or the sap of the fleshy petals characteristic of the genus as a food source.

The sugar composition of the floral nectar has been used to predict that the pollinators of *Crinodendron tucumanum* are long- and short-tongued bees similar to those visiting *C. pataqua*. *Crinodendron hookerianum*, however, was found to have a floral-nectar composition consistent with Lepidoptera and hummingbird-pollinated flowers. Other species with tube-shaped flowers are also probably butterfly- and/or hummingbird-pollinated, whereas white-flowered species are moth/bee-pollinated.

Economic uses. *Aristotelia chilensis* produces *maqui* berries that are used in Chile for medicinal purposes and to produce a local wine. Several species of *Aristotelia* and *Crinodendron* are cultivated as ornamentals in California and Great Britain. The wood of *Crinodendron*, *Aristotelia*, *Elaeocarpus*, and *Sloanea* is harvested for commercial uses, and the seeds of *E. sphaericus* are made into buttons and beads. *Sloanea* is known as *Sha yau te* by the Mayans of Belize, who boil the bark and use it to treat fever and diabetes.

References. ALVERSON, W. S., K. G. KAROL, D. A. BAUM, M. W. CHASE, S. M. SWENSEN, ET AL. 1998. Circumscription of the Malvales and relationships to other Rosidae: evidence from *rcb*L sequence data. *Amer. J. Bot.* 85:876–87. BAILEY, L. H., AND E. Z. BAILEY. 1976. *Hortus Third: A Concise Dictionary of Plants Cultivated in the United States and Canada.* New York: Macmillan. BAYER, C., M. W. CHASE, AND M. F. FAY. 1998. Muntingiaceae, a new family of dicotyledons with malvalean affinities. *Taxon* 47:37–42. BRICKER,

J. S. 1992. Pollination biology of the genus *Crinodendron* (Elaeocarpaceae). *J. Arizona-Nevada Acad. Sci.* 24–25:51–54. Coc, I. June 24, 1999. Interview by J. S. Bricker. Interview with Ignazio Coc, manager of Blue Creek Rain Forest Station. Blue Creek Village, Belize. Coode, M.J.E. 1978. A conspectus of Elaeocarpaceae in Papuasia. *Brunonia* 1(2):131–297. Coode, M.J.E. 1984. A conspectus of *Sloanea* (Elaeocarpaceae) in the Old World. *Kew Bull.* 38(3):347–427. Coode, M.J.E. 1986. *Aristotelia* and *Vallea*, closely re-lated in Elaeocarpaceae. *Kew Bull.* 40(3):479–507. Coode, M.J.E. 1988. *Crinodendron, Dubouzetia* and *Peripentadenia*, closely related in Elaeocarpaceae. *Kew Bull.* 42(4):777–814. Correra Q., J. E., and H. Y. Bernal. 1992. Elaeocarpaceae. In *Especies vegetales promisorias de los países del Convenio Andrés Bello*, Tomo VII. Santafé de Bogotá, D. E., Colombia: Secretaria Ejecutiva del Convenio Andrés Bello. Miers, J. 1886. On the Tricuspidarieae. *Ann. Mag. Nat Hist.*, 4th ser., 2:39–54.

ELATINACEAE (Waterwort Family)

Gordon C. Tucker

- *aquatic or wetland herbs*

- *stipules present, paired, interpetiolar*

- *leaves opposite or whorled, simple; venation pinnate*

- *flowers actinomorphic, bisexual, small, usually 2–5-merous; ovary superior*

- *fruits septifragal capsules*

Numbers of genera and species. Worldwide, the Elatinaceae comprise two genera, *Bergia* and *Elatine*, each with about 25 species. Both genera occur in tropical America where *Elatine* has seven and *Bergia* three species.

Distribution and habitat. The Elatinaceae are worldwide in distribution. *Elatine* is interruptedly cosmopolitan in distribution, with species occurring on all continents except Antarctica. Ten species are native to North America and about 12 to Eurasia. There are about seven species in Central America, South America, and the West Indies, mostly in temperate and Andean regions. No more than six species occur in the Paleotropics. Two species of *Elatine* are found as far north as 67° in Europe.

Species of *Bergia* are primarily found in the Paleotropics. The genus has two centers of diversity, southern Africa and Australia, each with 10 species. *Bergia capensis*, which ranges from southern Africa to India and Indonesia, is the most widely distributed species in the genus. Only three species of *Bergia* occur in the Western Hemisphere: *B. arenarioides* in Brazil; *B. capensis*, native to Africa and southern Asia, collected as an adventive on the Pacific coast of Central and South America; and *B. texana* of the central and western United States and northern Mexico.

In the neotropics, species occur in wet places from near sea level to about 4,300 meters in the Andean *páramos*.

Family classification. In the eighteenth century, Adanson noted that *Elatine* shared opposite leaves, small flowers, and tiny seeds with the Caryophyllaceae. As early as 1827, however, Cambessèdes noted similarities between the Elatinaceae and the Guttiferae (now Clusiaceae *sensu lato*, including the Hypericaceae). Recent authors have concurred in the placement of the Elatinaceae in the Theales and agreed that its affinities lie with the Clusiaceae. The reticulate sculpturing of the seed coat in the Elatinaceae is very much like that of some Clusiaceae, particularly the genus *Ploiarium*. The Angiosperm Phylogeny Group treated Elatinaceae as an unplaced family at the highest taxonomic levels, but ongoing molecular studies by D. Les (pers. comm.) support a relationship with Hypericaceae.

The anatomy of *Bergia suffruticosa* also suggests a relationship with the Clusiaceae. Similarities include presence of druses and solitary crystals, simple perforation plates, vasicentric tracheids, fibriform vessel elements, predominance of uniseriate rays, and vertical orientation of scalariform vessel-ray pitting.

Features of the family. Habit: herbaceous or woody-based annuals or short-lived perennials, aquatic or terrestrial and growing near water, small, sometimes with glandular pubescence (many *Bergia*). **Stipules** present, paired, interpetiolar. **Leaves** opposite or whorled, simple; blades ± elliptic, the margins entire, serrate, or pinnatifid; venation pinnate. **Inflorescences** axillary, flowers solitary or in small dichasial axillary clusters. **Flowers** actinomorphic, bisexual, small; sepals 2–5(6), distinct or partly connate, membranous (*Elatine*); petals 2–5, distinct, membranous; androecium of 2 or 3–6(10) stamens, the stamens in 1–2 whorls, the outer whorl alternate with petals, the anthers broadly ovoid, dehiscing by longitudinal slits; gynoecium syncarpous, the ovary superior, ovoid to depressed-ovoid, the carpels (2)3–5, the locules (2)3–5, the styles equal in number to carpels, short, the stigmas capitate; placentation axile or basal, the ovules numerous, anatropous, bitegmic, tenuinucellar, the embryo sac development of Polygonum type. **Fruits** septifragal capsules, membranous (*Elatine*) or crustacious (*Bergia*). **Seeds** numerous, ellipsoid to oblong, 0.5–1.5 mm long, the surface finely reticulate (or smooth); endosperm little or none, the embryo straight, filling nearly entire seed.

Germination is epigeal. Base chromosome numbers are 6 and 9.

Natural history. Little is known about the pollination of waterworts. Submersed plants of some species of *Elatine* set abundant seed and appear to be cleistogamous. Plants of *Elatine* growing in wet soil reportedly shed pollen directly onto their own stigmas, and some species of *Bergia* have anthers adhering to their own stigmas. In several species of *Bergia*, open flowers have never been observed. The foliage and seeds of *Elatine* are eaten by waterfowl and this, presumably, provides a means of dispersal. Similar to many aquatics, *E. triandra* and other members of the genus have different growth forms in and out of water.

Economic uses. The family is of slight economic importance. No species is recorded as being gathered for use as food or condiments, nor is any reported to be poisonous to humans or livestock. *Bergia suffruticosa* is used in Pakistan as folk medicine and in Sudan as a poultice for broken bones. Several species of *Bergia* are weeds in rice fields in the Eastern Hemisphere, as are species of *Elatine* in California, Japan, and Java. The seeds and foliage of *Elatine* are eaten by ducks, and the plants are beneficial because they consolidate mud and provide cover for small fish. Several species (e.g.,

E. hydropiper and *E. triandra*) are cultivated as "turf-forming" foliage plants in aquaria and are easy to propagate from either cuttings or seed.

References. ADANSON, M. 1763–64. *Familles des plantes*. 2 vols. Paris: Vincent. CARLQUIST, S. 1984. Wood and stem anatomy of *Bergia suffruticosa*: relationships of Elatinaceae and broader significance of vascular tracheids, vasicentric tracheids and fibriform vessel elements. *Ann. Missouri Bot. Gard.* 71:232–42. DUMORTIER, B. C. 1872. Examen critique des Élatinacées. *Bull. Soc. Roy. Bot. Belg.* 11:254–74. HUNZIKER, A. T. 1970. Sobre una nueva hidrofita argentina: *Elatine lorentziana* nov. sp. *Lorentziana* 1:5–10. LEACH, G. J. 1989. Taxonomic revision of *Bergia* (Elatinaceae) in Australia. *J. Adelaide Bot. Gard.* 11(2):75–100. MOLAU, U. 1983. Elatinaceae. In *Flora of Ecuador*, eds. G. Harling and B. Sparre, 20:19–23. Göteborg, Sweden: Department of Systematic Botany, University of Göteborg. NIEDENZU, F. 1925. Elatinaceae. In *Die Natürlichen Pflanzenfamilien*, 2nd ed. 21:270–76. Leipzig: Wilhelm Engelmann. SCHMIDT MUMM, U., AND H. Y. BERNAL. 1995. A new species of *Elatine* (Elatinaceae) from the Colombian *páramos* in the northern Andes. *Brittonia* 47:27–30. SCULTHORPE, C. D. 1967. *The Biology of Aquatic Vascular Plants*. London: Edward Arnold. TUCKER, G. C. 1986. The genera of Elatinaceae in the southeastern United States. *J. Arnold Arbor.* 67:471–83. TUCKER, G. C. 1991. Elatinaceae. In *The Jepson Manual: Higher Plants of California*, ed. J. C. Hickman, 542–44. Berkeley, CA: University of California Press.

EREMOLEPIDACEAE (Catkin-Mistletoe Family)

JOB KUIJT AND CAROL GRACIE

- *hemiparasites on woody dicots*
- *leaves foliaceous or scalelike, usually alternate, simple*
- *flowers unisexual; petals absent, 3, or 4*
- *fruits 1-"seeded" berries*
- *"seeds" with abundant viscin*

Numbers of genera and species. The Eremolepidaceae comprise three genera and 12 species. *Eremolepis* and *Ixidium* are now included within *Antidaphne*, the largest genus with nine species, followed by *Eubrachion* with two and *Lepidoceras* with one. The 10 tropical species of Eremolepidaceae are relatively rare and inconspicuous hemiparasites.

Distribution and habitat. Restricted mostly to the neotropics, the Eremolepidaceae are distributed from southern Mexico and the larger Caribbean islands throughout tropical South America and into southern Chile. With few exceptions, species of Eremolepidaceae are found at high elevations.

Family classification. The Eremolepidaceae are placed in the Santalales by Cronquist. It has been suggested that Eremolepidaceae are related to the basal Loranthaceae; however, recent molecular studies suggest an affinity with Santalaceae. Familial status for the Eremolepidaceae was first proposed in 1910, but not widely accepted until after 1968.

Features of the family. Habit: small shrubs, hemiparasitic on branches of woody dicots; plants with or without basal epicortical roots. Haustoria attachment single or multiple from epicortical roots. Stipules absent. Leaves alternate (*Antidaphne* and mature *Eubrachion*) or opposite (*Lepidoceras* and juvenile *Eubrachion*), simple, the alternate leaves scalelike (on mature *Eubrachion*), peltately attached, the margins brownish black or transparent, contrasting with blade. **Inflorescences** axillary at leafless nodes or terminal in two species, spike- or catkinlike, rarely compound. **Flowers** actinomorphic, unisexual (plants monoecious or dioecious), small, vestigial organs of opposite sex absent. **Staminate flowers:** sepals absent; petals absent, 3, or 4, in 1 whorl; androecium of 3 or 4 stamens, the stamens equal to number of petals or (3)4 when petals absent, the filaments free. **Pistillate flowers:** sepals absent; petals 2, 3, or 4, sometimes persistent in fruit; gynoecium with inferior or subinferior ovary, with a single locule, the style short, thick, the stigma small, indistinctly lobed; true ovules absent, the embryo sacs developing in a basal emergence (ovarian papilla). **Fruits** berries, black, green, ocher, or reddish. **"Seeds"** 1 per fruit, with abundant viscin, the testa absent (as in other mistletoes); endosperm present, usually white (light green in *Antidaphne viscoidea*), or absent (*Lepidoceras*), the cotyledons generally 2.

Eubrachion and *Lepidoceras* attach to their hosts by a single, simple haustorium. In contrast, most species of *Antidaphne* produce multiple epicortical roots that form secondary haustoria. This condition is also found in many species of Loranthaceae and is thought to be more primitive.

In some species of *Lepidoceras*, the sharp-tipped bud scales enclosing young shoots (and perhaps the female inflorescence shoots as well) are persistent and grow into leaves after the buds have expanded. This type of leaf development is unique among the angiosperms. The resultant leaf retains the original bud scale as a prominent tooth at its apex. Young shoots of some species of *Antidaphne* may also develop from meristematic tissue at the base of the bud scales.

Natural history. The species of *Antidaphne* show no host preference; however, those of *Eubrachion* and *Lepidoceras* are found almost exclusively on species of Myrtaceae. Nothing is known about the pollination of the small flowers, and few observations of seed dispersal have been recorded. In one case, birds were seen to eat the fruits of *A. viscoidea* and later regurgitate the "seeds."

Economic uses. No uses are known for this family.

References. KUIJT, J. 1988. Monograph of the Eremolepidaceae. *Syst. Bot. Monogr.* 18:1–60.

ERICACEAE (Heath Family)

JIM LUTEYN

Figure 70, Plate 18

- *usually subshrubs or shrubs, evergreen*

- *leaves, usually alternate, simple, coriaceous, often plinerved, often conspicuously red when young*

- *flowers usually sympetalous; corolla urceolate to tubular, often brightly colored (red to orangish); anthers often with 2 distal tubules or 2–4 awns; pollen usually borne in tetrahedral tetrads; ovary superior or inferior*

Numbers of genera and species. Worldwide, the Ericaceae comprise approximately 123 genera and 4,000 species. The largest genera are *Rhododendron* (ca. 1,000 species), *Erica* (ca. 860), and *Vaccinium* (ca. 450). In tropical America, there are 46 genera and about 900 species, with the largest genera *Cavendishia* (ca. 130 species), *Thibaudia* (60), *Psammisia* (70), *Vaccinium* (ca. 40), *Macleania* (40), *Disterigma* (ca. 40), *Gaylussacia* (42), *Gaultheria* (37), and *Ceratostema* (35).

Distribution and habitat. The Ericaceae are a diverse and geographically widespread family, occurring in temperate and cool tropical regions of all continents except Antarctica. Their greatest generic diversity occurs in the montane Andes of the neotropics. On a worldwide basis, many of the subgroupings within the family have radiated in distinct continental areas. For example, the rhododendrids have about 900 species in temperate and tropical Asia; the ericids more than 860 species in southern Africa; the epacrids about 400 species in Australia and New Zealand; the vacciniids more than 1,000 species split between the Paleotropics and the Neotropics; and the pyrolids, including the achlorophyllous monotropids, about 60 species, mostly in north temperate and boreal regions of the Northern Hemisphere, but with one species ranging south nearly to the Equator in Colombia and another species nearing the same latitude in the Malay Peninsula. In the neotropics, the Ericaceae are concentrated in northwestern South America, primarily Colombia, Ecuador, Peru, and Venezuela, where approximately 94 percent of the species are endemic.

Ericalean plants prefer partially exposed, moist, cool habitats and acid soils. In tropical America, the Ericaceae are most abundant in cooler, moist, montane forest habitats from 1,500 to 3,000 meters. In general, whenever the habitat becomes dry (e.g., on the lee side of a mountain), more sea-

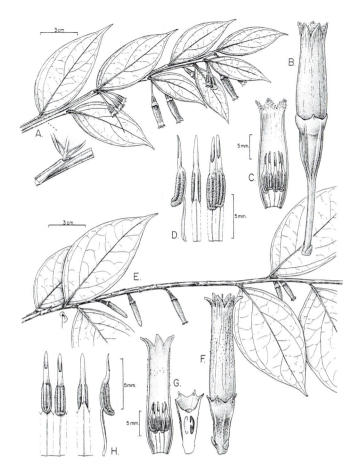

Figure 70. ERICACEAE. *Macleania alata* (A–D) and *M. subsessilis* (E–H). **A.** Stem with leaves and inflorescences and detail of winged stem (below). **B.** Lateral view of flower. **C.** Medial section of corolla showing adnate stamens. **D.** Lateral (left), abaxial (center), and adaxial (right) views of stamens. **E.** Stem with leaves and inflorescences. **F.** Lateral view of flower. **G.** Medial section of corolla showing adnate stamens (left) and medial section of calyx and ovary (right). **H.** Adaxial (left), abaxial (center), and lateral (right) views of stamens. Reprinted with permission from Luteyn (1996). Artist: Bobbi Angell.

sonal, or overly warm (tropical rain forest), Ericaceae diminish in number or disappear.

Family classification. The Ericaceae are placed in the Ericales by Cronquist. The classification systems of Ericalean families have undergone many changes over the years. For example, within Ericales, the close relationships among the families Clethraceae, Ericaceae, and Epacridaceae have been evident for many years, with these three core families making up more than 99 percent of the species of the order. In recent years, however, there has been almost universal acceptance of the inclusion of Empetraceae and Cyrillaceae in the order, based especially on similarities of embryological and palynological features with those of the Ericaceae. Inclusion of the families Grubbiaceae and Actinidiaceae have been fairly recent, and there is still some question as to these exact relationships. Within the "traditional" Ericaceae

(*sensu* Stevens), subfamily Vaccinioideae (those Ericaceae with inferior ovaries) has sometimes been recognized as a distinct family (Vacciniaceae). Furthermore, the Monotropoideae and Pyroloideae are often treated as Monotropaceae and Pyrolaceae (e.g., *sensu* Cronquist), respectively, or sometimes Monotropaceae is combined with Pyrolaceae, these relationships representing progressive stages in dependence on mycorrhizal fungi for nutrition.

Most recently, new molecular and morphological data have brought to light the need for major realignments at familial, subfamilial, tribal, and generic levels within Ericaceae, and a new, higher-level classification of Ericaceae is currently being developed. These recent analyses have resulted in the conclusion that Ericaceae, as currently recognized, are paraphyletic and that Empetraceae, Epacridaceae, Monotropaceae, and Pyrolaceae are derivative lineages out of Ericaceae. The exact relationships of Cyrillaceae, Clethraceae, and Actinidiaceae to Ericaceae are not certain at this time.

At the generic and specific levels, morphological features of taxonomic importance include, leaf size and shape, pubescence patterns, general inflorescence type, gland types and their distribution, floral color patterns, corolla type and shape, stamen type, ovary position, and fruit type.

Features of the family. Habit: usually subshrubs or shrubs (the stems to 3 m long, sometimes becoming lianoid to 10 m) or rarely small trees, evergreen to rarely deciduous, often rhizomatous, strongly mycotrophic, rarely achlorophyllous (*Monotropa* and *Pterospora*), commonly producing tannins, the shrubs terrestrial or epiphytic; pubescence usually consisting of uni- to multicellular hairs, these sometimes glandular. **Stipules** absent, the bud scales sometimes elongate and appearing pseudostipular. **Leaves** usually alternate (very rarely subopposite, subverticellate, or reduced to scales in *Monotropa*), simple, newly unfolding leaves often conspicuously red; blades coriaceous, the margins usually entire, sometimes serrulate-crenate; venation pinnate or plinerved (several strong nerves arising from at or near base and running more or less parallel toward apex); leaf scars usually with a single vascular bundle scar, the nodes usually with one trace and one gap. **Inflorescences** axillary or rarely terminal, racemose, paniculate, fasciculate, or of solitary flowers; pedicels usually present, in axils of small or large, deciduous or persistent, sometimes showy, floral bracts, normally bibracteolate. **Flowers** actinomorphic, bisexual, 4–5-merous, typically obdiplostemonous, protandrous, typically lacking odors; perianth typically biseriate, valvate, imbricate or reduplicate; calyx continuous or articulate with pedicel, synsepalous or the sepals occasionally distinct, sometimes grading into bractlike scales, rarely fleshy and accrescent to fruit; hypanthium sometimes present, terete or angled to winged, the wings alternate with calyx lobes; corolla membranous to thick-carnose, polypetalous or more commonly sympetalous, cylindric, campanulate, or urceolate, terete or angled to winged, the wings opposite lobes; androecium usually with 8–10 equal or unequal stamens, the stamens in 2 whorls, usually twice as many or rarely equal to petals, equalling or ½–⅓ corolla length, equal with each other or alternately unequal, borne on edge of obscure to prominent nectariferous disc, the filaments equal or unequal, usually straight or rarely S-shaped (geniculate), ligulate but sometimes basally dilated, sometimes also basally papillose, distinct or connate, with or without spurs, shorter or longer than anther, the anthers commonly inverted in early development, 2-celled, equal or unequal, often distally with 2 distinct or connate tubules or 2–4 terminal awns, sometimes provided with abaxial spurs, white, powdery, disintegration tissue sometimes present, the thecae smooth to coarsely granular, the base rounded to appendiculate, the tubules when present conical and rigid, or cylindric and flexible, of equal or ca. ½ of diameter of thecae, longer to shorter than thecae, the dehiscence normally introrse, rarely extrorse or latrorse, by longitudinal or more typically apical to subapical clefts or pores; pollen borne in tetrahedral tetrads or rarely monads (*Monotropa* and *Pterospora*), sometimes with viscin threads linking tetrads; gynoecium syncarpous, the ovary superior or inferior, the carpels 4–5(10), the locules usually as many as carpels, less frequently twice as many, the style 1, fluted, hollow, the stigma simple, occasionally weakly lobed; placentation usually axile, rarely intruded parietal, the ovules numerous per locule or rarely solitary, anatropous to campylotropous, with a single integument. **Fruits** loculicidal or septicidal capsules, berries, or drupes. **Seeds** usually numerous (1 per locule in *Gaylussacia*), small, somewhat short-tailed in *Bejaria*, sometimes enclosed in mucilaginous sheath, the seed coat thin, of elongated or isodiametric cells; endosperm fleshy, the embryo straight, usually white or sometimes green.

Most members of the Ericales have a long series of embryological features in common, although the only characteristics shared by all ericalean species are an ovule with one integument and a nucellus composed of a single cell layer.

Frequently the hypocotyl matures into a lignotuber that may range in size from a few centimeters to more than 1 meter in diameter.

Natural history. Species of Ericaceae often are associated with mycorrhizae. Ecologically, ericads often dominate a major vegetation type of tropical montane regions known as the "ericaceous belt," and because of their sun-loving ecology, they frequently are found as pioneers near the craters of volcanoes or in recent landslide areas.

In the neotropics, nearly 50 percent of the species of Ericaceae are epiphytes. *Pernettya prostrata* forms terrestrial carpets or creeping mats over many acres in the mountains of Mexico and Guatemala, as well as in the *superpáramo* at Nevado del Cocuy, Colombia. In the high-elevation *páramo*, *Pernettya* resists trampling by cattle and is a successional species in areas subject to grazing. It is frequently a pioneer species in new habitats created by road building, landslides, human-made fires, or volcanic activity. *Pernettya* invades the *páramo* when the vegetation is low and open, but may then

remain when vegetation recovers. Fire does not affect species of *Pernettya* directly, but helps spread them indirectly because it opens the vegetation to their colonization. In Colombia, several ericads are found as epiphytes in the Pacific-coast mangroves. In Venezuelan Guayana, *Notopora schomburgkiana* and species of *Vaccinium* are typical elements of sandy savannas.

Pollination of Ericaceae in temperate and subtropical latitudes is primarily by bees, but in the neotropics, bird pollination is the rule, with hummingbirds acting as the main vectors. With few exceptions, the genera with superior ovaries are pollinated by bees and those with inferior ovaries by hummingbirds. Many tropical American Ericaceae display the following features associated with pollination by hummingbirds: flowers odorless and relatively showy; flowers and their associated bracts often of contrasting colors in some shade of red, violet, or orange; flowers pendent or arching in habit and arranged in open, elongate, or few-flowered clusters; corollas actinomorphic and tubular in shape, with a constricted throat and spreading lobes; corolla tubes thick and fleshy; nectar-secreting disc located on top of the ovary at the base of the corolla; corolla sizes corresponding well to the size and proportions of the bills of visiting hummingbirds; sugar concentrations in the nectar falling into the range preferred by hummingbirds.

Nectar-thieving mites (*Rhinoseius* species) spend virtually their entire life cycle within the flowers of certain ericaceous hummingbird plants and depend upon the birds as well as the flowers for their survival. Their primary means of dispersal is on the bill or in the nasal cavities of hummingbirds.

Dispersal of the small, light seeds in genera such as *Bejaria*, *Lyonia*, and *Agarista*, which have capsular fruits, is by wind; however, most of the Neotropical genera possess berries, so birds or small mammals probably act as agents of dispersal.

Economic uses. The number of ericad species used as ornamentals is inordinately large when compared with other plant groups of similar size. Many of the most beautiful and prized horticultural plants throughout the temperate regions of the world are found in the Ericaceae, notable examples being azaleas and rhododendrons (both *Rhododendron*), heaths (*Erica*), and heathers (*Calluna*).

Blueberries and cranberries (both *Vaccinium*) are among the economically important members of the family, being in constant demand throughout the world. Several genera of Ericaceae are poisonous, and the major toxic substance seems to be andromedotoxin. This compound is known to occur in temperate species of *Rhododendron*, *Leucothoe*, *Menziesia*, *Ledum*, and *Kalmia*, and is probably more widespread in the order than is now known.

Very few published accounts exist of uses of native Ericaceae in the neotropics. *Vaccinium floribundum* is perhaps the most used native species, especially in Ecuador and Colombia, where its fruits are made into jams, drinks, and occasionally pies. One species of *Rhododendron* is cultivated in South America.

References. ANDERBERG, A. A. 1993. Cladistic interrelationships and major clades of the Ericales. *Pl. Syst. Evol.* 184:207–31. CORRERA Q., J. E., AND H. Y. BERNAL. 1992. Ericaceae. In *Especies vegetales promisorias de los países del Convenio Andrés Bello*, Tomo VII. Santafé de Bogotá, D. E., Colombia: Secretaria Ejecutiva del Convenio Andrés Bello. DRUDE, C.G.O. 1897. *Ericaceae*. In *Die Natürlichen Pflanzenfamilien*, A. Engler and K. Prantl, 4(1):15–65. Leipzig: Wilhelm Engelmann. KRON, K. A., W. S. JUDD, P. F. STEVENS, D. M. CRAYN, A. A. ANDERBERG, ET AL. 2002. A phylogenetic classification of Ericaceae: molecular and morphological evidence. *Bot. Rev.* 68(2):335–423. LUTEYN, J. L. 1983. Ericaceae—Part I. *Cavendishia. Fl. Neotrop. Monogr.* 35:1–290. LUTEYN, J. L. (ed.). 1995. Ericaceae—Part II. The superior-ovaried genera (Monotropoideae, Pyroloideae, Rhododendroideae, Vaccinioideae p.p.). *Fl. Neotrop. Monogr.* 67:1–560. LUTEYN, J. L. 2000. Neotropical blueberries: The Plant Family Ericaceae. http://www.nybg.org/bsci/res/lut2. LUTEYN, J. L. 2002. Diversity, adaptation, and endemism in Neotropical Ericaceae: biogeographical patterns in the Vaccinieae. *Bot. Rev.* 68(1):55–87. STEVENS, P. F. 1971. A classification of the Ericaceae: Subfamilies and tribes. *J. Linn. Soc., Bot.* 64:1–53.

ERYTHROXYLACEAE (Coca Family)

DOUGLAS C. DALY

Figure 71, Plate 18

- *shrubs or small trees*

- *stems usually with cataphylls; intrapetiolar stipules present*

- *leaves alternate (usually distichous), simple; leaf vernation involute*

- *flowers actinomorphic; petals appendaged; stamens with filaments basally connate; styles 3, distinct or basally connate*

- *fruits drupes, small, red or purplish*

Numbers of genera and species. Worldwide, the Erythroxylaceae comprise four genera and approximately 250 species, all but 10–20 of them in *Erythroxylum*. *Erythroxylum* is the only genus in tropical America, where it is represented by about 180 species.

Distribution and habitat. Although pantropical, the Erythroxylaceae are very unevenly distributed. The majority of species are Neotropical, while very few are found in Asia. *Erythroxylum* occurs on all four tropical continents, whereas the other three genera, *Aneulophus*, *Nectaropetalum*, and *Pinacopodium*, are restricted to Africa. The family has centers of diversity and endemism in Venezuela, eastern and northeastern Brazil, and Madagascar. At least 40 species of *Erythroxylum* have been recorded in Venezuela (30 of them in the Guayana region), while in northeastern Brazil the state of Bahia alone contains at least 45 species.

Species of *Erythroxlyum* seldom achieve high densities, but the genus is ecologically versatile, with species occurring as understory trees in low elevation rain forests, thick-barked shrubs or trees in savanna woodlands, microphyllous shrubs in arid thorn-scrubs, and membranous-leaved shrubs in montane habitats.

Family classification. Most recent classifications have placed the Erythroxylaceae in the Linales (e.g., *sensu* Cronquist), which includes the Hugoniaceae, Humiriaceae, Ixonanthaceae, and Linaceae. The Erythroxylaceae are distinguished from the remainder of the order by the petals having a ligular appendage toward the base adaxially, usually possessing only one locule of the ovary ovuliferous, lacking disc and nectary glands, and the presence of alkaloids.

Recent studies emphasizing molecular data have placed the Erythroxylaceae in an expanded Malpighiales that includes elements of the Linales with the Euphorbiaceae, Flacourtiaceae, Malpighiaceae, Chrysobalanaceae, Passifloraceae, Turneraceae, Violaceae, and other families.

Features of the family. Habit: shrubs or small trees, evergreen or deciduous, glabrous, the wood hard; short shoots sometimes present, these sometimes spiny (e.g., *Erythroxylum spinescens* of the Greater Antilles); cataphylls often present, imbricate, persistent. **Stipules** present, intrapetiolar, united, abaxially bicostate, leaving an obliquely transverse scar when caducous. **Leaves** alternate (usually distichous), simple; blade margins entire; venation pinnate; vernation involute, sometimes imprinting 2 parallel lines and/or a distinct central panel on abaxial surface. **Inflorescences** axillary, sometimes short-pedunculate, few-to-many flowered fasci-

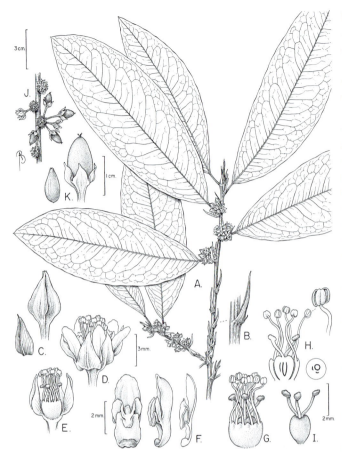

Figure 71. ERYTHROXYLACEAE. *Erythroxylum macrophyllum.*
A. Stem with leaves, stipules, cataphylls, and inflorescences. **B.** Detail of cataphyll. **C.** Lateral view of bud (above) and abaxial view of floral bract (below). **D.** Lateral view of intact flower. **E.** Lateral view of flower with petals and two sepals removed. **F.** Adaxial view (left), lateral view (center), and medial section (right) of petal. **G.** Lateral view of androecium and gynoecium. **H.** Medial section of androecium and pistil (left), transverse section of ovary (right), and detail of anther (above). **I.** Lateral view of pistil. **J.** Part of stem with infructescences. **K.** Lateral views of fruit (right) and seed (left). Reprinted with permission from Mori et al. (2002). Artist: Bobbi Angell.

cles or flowers solitary; bracteoles small, scarious. **Flowers** actinomorphic, bisexual or seldom unisexual (plants dioecious), 5-merous, usually distylous; calyx persistent, the sepals 5, basally connate, valvate; corolla with 5 petals, the petals distinct, imbricate, caducous, usually with a bilobed ligular appendage toward narrowed base adaxially; androecium usually of 10 stamens, the stamens in 2 whorls of 5, the outer whorl alternate with petals, the filaments basally connate, usually forming short tube, the anthers longitudinally dehiscent; gynoecium syncarpous, the ovary superior, the carpels and locules 3, the styles 3, distinct or basally connate, the stigmas capitellate, rarely sessile; placentation axile, ovules 1 per locule but usually only 1 ovule developing, pendulous, epitropous. **Fruits** drupes, small, red or purplish, only 1 locule fertile. **Seeds** 1 per fruit; endosperm copious, rarely absent, starchy, the embryo straight.

Natural history. *Erythroxylum* is typically distylous, i.e., some individuals have flowers with relatively short styles and long stamens, whereas others have long styles and short stamens. Distyly is seen as part of a mechanism for ensuring outcrossing and is a possible evolutionary transition to dioecy.

One of the more striking features of the family is the frequency with which up to five similar, sympatric species of *Erythroxylum* occur in the same habitat and same locality. In open vegetation of the *cerrado* region of Brazil, three sympatric species with similar flower morphology were found flowering synchronously for three months. Two were self-incompatible and the third partly so. The three species were visited by 14 species of wasps, 14 species of bees, and two species of flies. At least one of each group of insects was considered an effective pollinator.

The red or purple drupes are most likely dispersed by animals, especially birds.

Economic uses. By far the most economically important species of the family is the coca plant, *Erythroxylum coca*, which has been utilized for millennia. The leaves of this Andean shrub are masticated (formed into a wad with an alkaline admixture) to be used as a tonic and stimulant to allay hunger and altitude sickness and for many other medicinal and ritual purposes. A lowland Amazonian cultivar, *Erythroxylum coca* var. *ipadu*, has figured prominently in some indigenous cultures of western Amazonia for similar purposes.

Erythroxylum coca also is the source of cocaine, which was long used as a local anesthetic, including in ophthalmic surgery, and served as the template compound for the development of numerous invaluable, synthetic anesthestics including lidocaine, novocaine, and xylocaine. An extract of coca leaves was a primary ingredient in Coca-Cola® and still is, minus the cocaine. Coca-Cola syrup still is sold in pharmacies to calm upset stomach. Unfortunately, the coca plant is now regarded widely as a bane to society, because the therapeutic value of purified and semipurified cocaine has been distorted for recreational purposes on a massive scale. The plant is now associated with causing rather than alleviating human suffering.

In the thorn-scrub of Piauí and other parts of arid northeastern Brazil, *Erythroxylum citrifolia* is one of the plants most prominently referred to as *catuaba*, a Tupi name applied in Brazil to a number of species used for tonics and aphrodisiacs. Near human settlements, the bark is stripped from most individuals of this species. Alkaloids called catuabine A, B, and C have been isolated from *Erythroxylum vaccinifolium*. Elsewhere, other species of the genus have additional medicinal uses.

The wood of some species of *Erythroxylum* is hard, strong, and durable and is valued locally for making telephone poles, supports, and furniture.

References. BERRY, P. E. 1991. Agamospermy and the loss of distyly in *Erythroxylum undulatum* (Erythroxylaceae) from northern Venezuela. *Amer. J. Bot.* 78:595–600. CHUNG, R. C. K. 1996. Taxonomic notes on *Erythroxylum* (Erythroxylaceae) in Malesia. *Sandakania* 7:67–80. EMPÉRAIRE, L. 1983. *La caatinga du sud-este du Piauí (Brésil): etude ethnobotanique*, Mémoire 21. Paris: Éditions Recherche sur les Civilisations. GRAF, E., AND W. LUDE 1977. Alkaloids from *Erythroxylum vacciniifolium*, Part I. Isolation of catuabine A, B, and C. *Arch. Pharm. (Weinheim)* 310:1005–10. GRANJA E BARROS, M. 1998. Sistemas reprodutivas e polinização em espécies simpátricas de *Erythroxylum* P. Br. (Erythroxylaceae) do Brasil. *Revista Brasil. Bot.* 21:159–66. PLOWMAN, T. 1981. Amazonian coca. *J. Ethno-Pharmacol.* 3:195–225.

PLOWMAN, T. 1991. Erythroxylaceae Kunth. In Flora Costaricensis. *Fieldiana, Bot.*, n.s., 30–36. PLOWMAN, T., AND P. E. BERRY. 1999. Erythroxylaceae. In *Flora of the Venezuelan Guayana*, eds. J. Steyermark, P. E. Berry, and B. Holst, and K. Yatskeivych, 5:59–71. St. Louis, MO: Missouri Botanical Garden Press. SOLTIS, D. E., P. S. SOLTIS, D. R. MORGAN, S. M. SWENSEN, B. C. MULLIN, ET AL. 1995. Chloroplast gene sequence data suggest a single origin of the predisposition for symbiotic nitrogen fixation in angiosperms. *Proc. Natl. Acad. U.S.A.* 92:2647–51. THULIN, M. 1995. *Erythroxylon* [sic] (Erythroxylaceae) on Socotra. *Nord. J. Bot.* 16:301–02.

ESCALLONIACEAE (Escallonia Family)

SCOTT A. MORI

Figure 72

- *trees or shrubs, often common at higher elevations*

- *leaves alternate, simple, the margins frequently serrate or glandular*

- *flowers with nectariferous disc; ovary inferior, the styles erect, conspicuous, the stigmas capitate or peltate*

- *fruits capsules*

Numbers of genera and species. Worldwide, the Escalloniaceae comprise seven genera and 129 species. In the Western Hemisphere, there are two genera, *Escallonia* (39 species overall and approximately 22 species in the Tropics) and the extratropical *Valdivia* (1 species in central Chile).

Distribution and habitat. Species of *Escallonia* occur in the mountains of Costa Rica and Panama, in the Andes from Colombia to Tierra del Fuego, in the Andes of Venezuela, and in Uruguay and southeastern Brazil. High species diversity is found in Chile and Argentina.

Species of Escalloniaceae, often dominant in high Andean forests, are associated with species of *Buddleja*, *Hesperomeles*, *Podocarpus*, *Polylepis*, *Quercus*, and *Weinmannia*. Although most species are terrestrial, a few may be epiphytic. Some species grow to near sea level in temperate Brazil, Chile, and Uruguay.

Family classification. Although Cronquist treats this family as part of the Grossulariaceae in his order Rosales, molecular evidence supports its recognition as a separate family as has been done by Takhtajan.

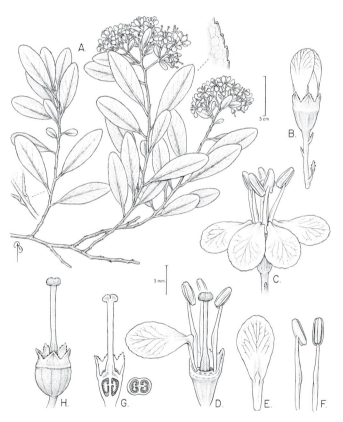

Figure 72. ESCALLONIACEAE. *Escallonia bifida* (A–G, Wasum 423; H, Rossato and Wasum 10). **A.** Stems with leaves and inflorescences, detail of blade margin (upper right) and detail of blade base (lower left). **B.** Lateral view of flower bud near anthesis. **C.** Lateral view of flower. **D.** Lateral view of flower with part of calyx, four petals, and two stamens removed. **E.** Adaxial view of petal. **F.** Lateral (left) and adaxial (right) views of stamens. **G.** Medial section of gynoecium (left) and transverse section of ovary (right). **H.** Lateral view of immature fruit. Original. Artist: Bobbi Angell.

The extra-Neotropical *Itea*, with 15 species, one in eastern North America and the others in the Eastern Hemisphere, is considered by some as part of the Escalloniaceae, by others as a member of the Grossulariaceae, and by others as a separate family, the Iteaceae.

Features of the family. Habit: trees or shrubs, usually terrestrial, rarely epiphytic; stems often with exfoliating bark. **Stipules** usually absent. **Leaves** alternate, simple; blades sometimes glandular or resinous, the margins frequently serrate or with caducous glands. **Inflorescences** terminal or axillary, racemes, panicles, or, less frequently, of solitary flowers. **Flowers** actinomorphic, bisexual; sepals 5, often fused at bases to form shallow tube; petals 5, distinct, linear, spatulate, or obovate, erect or spreading; androecium of 5 stamens, the stamens alternate with petals, the anthers dehiscing by longitudinal slits; disc epigynous, surrounding base of style; gynoecium syncarpous, the ovary inferior, the carpels 2–3, the locules 2–3, the styles well developed, simple or rarely bifid at apex, the stigmas capitate or peltate; placentation axile, the ovules numerous per locule. **Fruits** capsules. **Seeds** numerous, small; endosperm present.

Some species of *Escallonia*, especially those with smaller leaves, possess conspicuous short shoots.

Even leaves appearing at first glance to be entire reveal minute teeth or glandlike teeth at 10x magnification.

Natural history. Nothing is known about the pollination and dispersal biology of *Escallonia*. However, the presence of a nectary suggests insect pollination. Bees and butterflies have been observed visiting cultivated species outside of the native range of the genus.

Economic uses. The wood of species of *Escallonia* is used for fuel, to make charcoal, for fence posts, and in local construction. A red dye is extracted from the heartwood of *E. resinosa*. Species of *Escallonia* are well-known ornamentals in Europe, California, and New Zealand. Numerous hybrids have been produced for ornamental purposes, and hybridization also occurs between species in natural populations. *Escallonia rubra* is employed as a hedge plant in southwestern England and Ireland.

References. SLEUMER, H. 1968. Die gattung *Escallonia* (Saxifragaceae). *Verh. Kon. Ned. Akad. Wetensch., Afd. Natuurk., Tweede Sect.* 58(2):1–146.

EUPHORBIACEAE (Euphorb Family)

GRADY WEBSTER

Figures 73, 74, 75; Plate 19

- *plants usually woody*

- *plants often with white or colored latex*

- *leaves usually alternate, simple*

- *flowers unisexual; pistillate ones with superior, usually 3-carpellate ovary*

- *fruits often explosively dehiscing schizocarps*

- *seeds often carunculate*

Numbers of genera and species. Worldwide, the Euphorbiaceae comprise approximately 300 genera with about 9,000 species. In tropical America, there are 105 genera (65 endemic) and about 1,800 species. The Euphorbiaceae are divided into the following subfamilies: Phyllanthoideae, 275 species; Oldfieldioideae, 20 species; Acalyphoideae, 400 species; Crotonoideae, 700 species; and Euphorbioideae, 400 species. The genera with the most Neotropical species are *Croton* (450), *Phyllanthus* (200), *Acalypha* (225), *Chamaesyce* (175), *Euphorbia* (200), *Dalechampia* (90), *Jatropha* (100), *Manihot* (100), *Tragia* (70), and *Cnidoscolus* (65).

Distribution and habitat. The five subfamilies of Euphorbiaceae—Phyllanthoideae, Oldfieldioideae, Acalyphoideae, Crotonoideae, and Euphorbioideae—are all well represented in America. Subfamily Oldfieldioideae appears to be South American in origin (including Panama), where its two most primitive genera, *Croizatia* and *Podocalyx*, are rain-forest endemics. Prominent taxa endemic to the Western Hemisphere include tribes Adelieae, Manihoteae, Micrandreae, and Pereae. There are some striking vicarious relationships between South American or West Indian and African/Madagascan taxa: at the species level in *Amanoa, Maprounea, Pogonophora, Savia,* and *Tetrorchidium*; and at the generic level (American taxa listed first) in the vicariant generic pairs *Discocarpus/Lachnostylis, Antidesma/Hyeronima, Alchorneopsis/Discoglypremna, Joannesia/Leeuwenbergia,* and *Nealchornea/Hamilcoa*.

Although the Euphorbiaceae occur worldwide, members of the family are far more diverse in the Tropics, where they are prominent in rain forests but even more abundant in seasonal forests and deserts. In the deserts of the Western Hemisphere and thorn-scrub of Mexico and Argentina, species of *Cnidoscolus, Croton,* and *Jatropha* are especially common, along with taxa of subfamily Oldfieldioideae such as *Piran-*

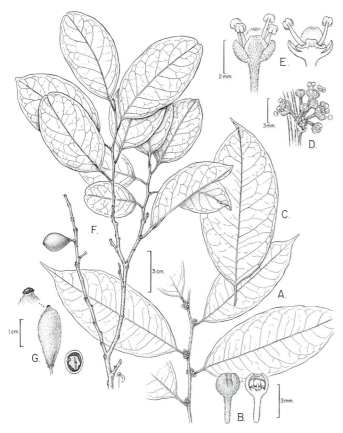

Figure 73. EUPHORBIACEAE. *Drypetes variabilis*. **A.** Stem with leaves and staminate inflorescences. **B.** Lateral view (left) and medial section (right) of staminate flower buds. **C.** Leaf. **D.** Staminate inflorescence on stem. **E.** Lateral view (left) and medial section (right) of staminate flower. **F.** Stem with leaves and fruit. **G.** Lateral view of immature fruit (left) with detail of remnant of stigma (above) and transverse section of fruit (right). Reprinted with permission from Mori et al. (2002). Artist: Bobbi Angell.

hea and *Tetracoccus* (Mexico) and *Parodiodendron* (Argentina). In lowland rain forests, there are a considerable number of species of *Acalypha*, *Alchornea*, and other genera of Alchornieae (*Amanoa*, *Croton*, *Drypetes*, *Pera*, and *Phyllanthus*). Montane rain forests also have many species of *Acalypha*, *Croton*, and *Phyllanthus*, but also *Hyeronima*, *Tetrorchidium*, and different species of *Alchornea*. The greatest generic diversity in Neotropical Euphorbiaceae is in the lowland Amazonian rain forests, where there are a number of endemic genera (i.e., *Anomalocalyx*, *Astrococcus*, *Caryodendron*, *Dodecastigma*, *Hevea*, *Micrandra*, *Micrandropsis*, *Nealchornea*, *Sagotia*, and *Sandwithia*).

Euphorbiaceae tend to be opportunistic pioneer plants, especially in tropical rain forests. Secondary successions often have a number of weedy species of various genera, especially *Acalypha*, *Croton*, and *Sapium*. A notable feature in the Amazon basin is the presence of genera adapted to inundation, including species of *Amanoa*, *Alchornea*, *Hevea*, *Micrandra*, and *Richeria*. Species of *Caperonia* and *Phyllanthus* are common in swamps; the most extreme example is

P. fluitans, a free-floating aquatic and unique in the family. A significant number of Euphorbiaceae occur in thorn forests or deserts, especially in subfamilies Oldfieldioideae, Crotonoideae (*Cnidoscolus*, *Croton*, *Jatropha*, and *Manihot*), and Euphorbioideae (*Euphorbia*, *Sapium*, and *Sebastiania*).

Family classification. The affinities of the Euphorbiaceae with other families are still not resolved, although it can be confidently placed within the Eurosidae. Earlier, as in Cronquist, the order Euphorbiales was circumscribed to include Buxaceae and Simmondsiaceae, but both of those families are now considered unrelated and not members of the Eurosidae. Recent morphological and molecular studies support a position within the core rosid clade. Suggestions of affinities with Celastrales and Malvales appear to be based on perceptions of similarities within more distant clades in the Rosidae. Some workers have regarded the Euphorbiaceae as a polyphyletic family, but if certain extra-American taxa (Pandaceae) are excluded, the family appears to be monophyletic.

Features of the family. Habit: herbs, shrubs, trees, vines, and lianas, generally woody arborescent genera display many different architectural patterns of growth; plants often contain single or multicellular laticifers bearing milky or colored latex, the latex often poisonous. **Indumentum** of simple hairs in most genera, but branched hairs (stellate or lepidote) widespread in genera of Acalyphoideae, Crotonoideae, and a few Euphorbioideae (mainly *Mabea*). **Stipules** usually prominent (although sometimes caducous), but may be secondarily lost, especially in species of *Croton* and *Euphorbia*. **Leaves** usually alternate, rarely opposite, simple, entire to palmately lobed (pinnately lobed leaves rare except in *Cnidoscolus*), or, if compound, then palmate; glands common on leaves (especially at petiole junction) in species of Acalyphoideae, Crotonoideae, and Euphorbioideae. **Inflorescences** terminal or axillary, sometimes cauliflorous or ramiflorous (*Phyllanthus*), the ultimate units cymose (these often condensed into axillary glomerules and additionally sometimes arranged in spikelike thyrses), sometimes reduced to bisexual pseudanthia, often with receptacular nectary discs. **Flowers** usually actinomorphic, unisexual (plants monoecious or dioecious); sepals (3)5–6; petals 5 or 6, or lacking (always absent in Euphorbioideae), not very showy except in some Crotonoideae (e.g. *Aleurites* and *Jatropha*). **Staminate flowers:** sepals usually imbricate in Phyllanthoideae, Oldfieldioideae, and Crotonoideae, but often valvate in Acalyphoideae; androecium usually of 5–15 stamens (the stamens reduced to 1 in *Dalembertia* or the Euphorbieae and increased to 200 or more in some Acalyphoideae and Crotonoideae), the filaments commonly connate; pistillode present in various genera (except Euphorbioideae). **Pistillate flowers:** sepals generally imbricate, often larger compared to those of staminate flowers, sometimes even foliose; petals often reduced compared to those of staminate flowers; gynoecium syncarpous, the ovary superior, the carpels (1)3(20), the locules 3, the styles usually 3, each entire (in most Euphorbioideae except in *Chamaesyce* and *Euphorbia*), bifid, or multifid (some Acalyphoideae and Crotonoideae), obturator (an extension of stylar conducting tissue) usually present and sometimes in contact with prolonged nucellar beak; placentation axile, the ovules 1 (Acalyphoideae, Crotonoideae, and Euphorbioideae) or 2 (Phyllanthoideae and Oldfieldioideae, but sometimes only one develops into seed) per locule, attached above or near middle of placenta, usually anatropous. **Fruits** usually schizocarps, with mericarps elastically dehiscing from a persistent column, the mericarps dehiscing adaxially to release 1 or 2 seeds, sometimes berries (some Phyllantheae) or drupes (Antidesmeae, *Picrodendron*, *Aleurites*, and *Hippomane*). **Seeds** often conspicuously carunculate (extension of micropyle to form caruncle common in seeds with dry testa, though absent in Phyllanthoideae); testa bitegmic, usually thin and dry (fleshy seed coats have evolved independently in various

genera, except in Oldfieldioideae); endosperm copious, oily (in many Crotonoideae and a few Acalyphoideae) and often containing poisonous proteins; embryo straight to curved.

The Euphorbiaceae are morphologically one of the most diverse families of angiosperms. There are scandent species in all subfamilies except Oldfieldioideae, with the large tribe Plukenetieae comprising mainly climbing or twining species. A remarkable feature in tribe Phyllantheae (*Phyllanthus*) is the reduction of leaves on the principal axes and restriction of flowering to specialized deciduous branchlets that mimic pinnate or bipinnate leaves of Fabaceae (subfamily Mimosoideae). In species of the West Indies and eastern Brazil, these branchlets have become modified into phylloclades; this evolution appears to have occurred independently in the two areas.

In the inflorescences of Crotonoideae, especially in the tribes Manihoteae and Jatropheae, the cymes may be developed as elaborately branched dichasia. In many Euphorbieae, the cyathia (pseudanthia) are arranged in dichotomizing inflorescences analagous to the crotonoid dichasia. Bracts may be conspicuously colored, and sometimes have conspicuous glands; in *Dalechampia* the flowers of most species are subtended by a pair of showy involucral bracts. Pseudanthia of very different morphological structure have independently evolved in *Pera*, *Dalechampia*, and the Euphorbieae; in *Euphorbia* subgenus *Poinsettia* the pseudanthia may be aggregated into a higher-order pseudanthium.

Flowers of Euphorbiaceae are extremely variable in size and degree of reduction or amplification of parts. In general, the perianth parts are discrete and 5- or 6-merous, but there are many exceptions. The flowers of *Cnidoscolus* and *Manihot*, although apetalous, have a relatively showy calyx. A floral disc is prevalent in most genera (but lacking in Euphorbioideae); it is absent in wind-pollinated taxa, but is also missing in some insect-pollinated taxa. The floral disc varies greatly in size and shape; it may be dissected, annular, or cupular. The pollen grains are highly variable in size and shape and exine ornamentation.

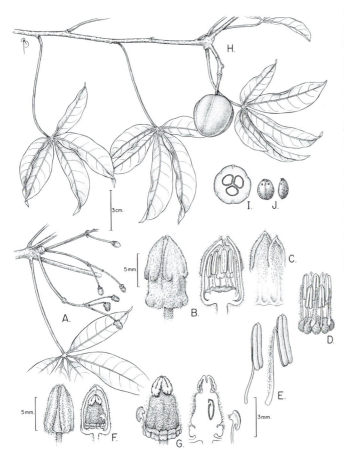

Figure 74. EUPHORBIACEAE. *Manihot* aff. *quinquepartita*. **A.** Stem with inflorescence. **B.** Lateral view (left) and medial section (right) of staminate buds. **C.** Detail of adaxial surface of imbricate sepal lobes. **D.** Lateral view of androecium and lobed disc. **E.** Views of stamens. **F.** Lateral view of intact pistillate bud (left) and lateral view with some petals and staminodes removed (right). **G.** Lateral view of ovary with one staminode (left), medial section of ovary (center), and lateral view of staminode (right). **H.** Stem, leaves, and fruit. **I.** Transverse section of fruit. **J.** Adaxial (left) and lateral (right) views of seeds. Reprinted with permission from Mori et al. (2002). Artist: Bobbi Angell.

Natural history. Most taxa of Euphorbiaceae appear to be insect pollinated, but a number are wind pollinated (*Acalypha*, *Adelia*, *Alchornea*, *Ricinus*), and some are pollinated by birds (*Cnidoscolus urnigerus* in Brazil and species of *Pedilanthus*). Genera such as *Chamaesyce*, *Croton*, and *Phyllanthus* appear to be visited by a variety of small solitary bees and wasps, but other genera are more specialized. *Hevea* seems to be pollinated effectively only by ceratopogonid midges and *Dalechampia* mostly by perfume- or resin-gathering bees. Particularly interesting situations have been reported in genera such as *Croton*, where a shift from insect pollination to wind pollination appears to be taking place, and in *Pedilanthus*, where most species are pollinated by hummingbirds, but a few (in eastern Mexico) by bees. In *Dalechampia*, pollination by pollen-collecting bees appears to be primitive and, in the course of speciation, has been replaced by pollination by bees collecting perfume (male eu-

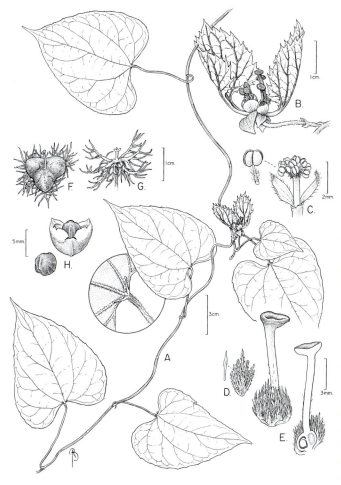

Figure 75. EUPHORBIACEAE. *Dalechampia dioscoreifolia*. **A.** Stem and inflorescence (right) and detail of leaf blade base showing gland (left). **B.** Lateral view of inflorescence. **C.** Staminate flower (right) and stamen (left). **D.** Sepal (right) and trichome from sepal (left). **E.** Lateral view (above) and medial section (right) of pistillate flower. **F.** Oblique-apical view of fruit. **G.** Lateral view of sepals after fruit has dehisced and fallen. **H.** Dehisced fruit segment (above right) and apical view of seed (below left). Reprinted with permission from Mori et al. (2002). Artist: Bobbi Angell.

glossines) or resins (mostly megachilids and euglossines). Pollination by bats has been reported for *Hura* and by opossums as well as bats in *Mabea*.

Seed dispersal in Euphorbiaceae is mainly by spreading of seeds as the result of explosive dehiscence of the fruit. For example, seeds from the large woody capsules in *Hevea* and *Hura* may be thrown over 25 meters from the plant. The common feature of a caruncle on the seed appears to be related to dispersal by ants. However, in some genera, notably *Euphorbia*, caruncles are present in some species and absent in others. Birds presumably disperse berrylike and drupelike fruits (these are especially prevalent in the Phyllanthoideae), as well as seeds with fleshy coats (e.g., *Margaritaria* and *Tetrorchidium*). Fruits and seeds of Euphorbiaceae do not have highly developed wings, and wind dispersal is rare or absent in the family.

Many Euphorbiaceae are protected from herbivores by leaf toxins, mainly alkaloids and terpenoids. A revealing example is provided by the two closely related genera of Manihoteae: the more primitive genus *Manihot* is spineless but has cyanogenic compounds, whereas the apparently derived genus *Cnidoscolus* lacks them but is armed with stinging spinelike hairs that inject histones. In the Euphorbioideae, the latex is often dangerously toxic, especially in some succulent species of *Euphorbia* and in *Hippomane* and Hureae. An extremely toxic protein, ricin, protects *Ricinus* seeds (perhaps against weevils).

Economic uses. The most important euphorbiaceous crop plant is cassava (*Manihot esculenta*), which is grown widely for the starchy tuberous roots. Some varieties contain toxic cyanogenics that have to be removed in a special process to produce the staple carbohydrate food called *farinha* throughout Brazilian Amazonia. A by-product of this process yields tapioca. The tubers of nontoxic varieties are eaten without processing in the same way as potatoes. Few other Neotropical Euphorbiaceae are used as food, although the leaves of a cultivar of *Cnidoscolus aconitifolius*, consumed as a green vegetable, are an excellent source of vitamin C. The leaves of *Manihot esculenta*, after the toxic compounds are removed, are eaten as a spinachlike vegetable in the Brazilian Amazon. A number of genera in the Acalyphoideae and Crotonoideae (especially *Caryodendron* and *Ricinus*) are cultivated for the seed oils. A minor product, wax, still is obtained from wild plants of *Euphorbia antisiphylitica* gathered in northern Mexico. Much more significant, although far less commercially valuable than it was in the late 19th and early 20th centuries, is the rubber produced from the latex of *Hevea*, especially *H. brasiliensis*. A limited plantation industry is found in various Neotropical countries, even though the major production is now in Asia. A number of compounds produced by Euphorbiaceae have medicinal properties. Extracts of herbaceous species of *Phyllanthus* are currently being investigated for activity against hepatitis virus and the reddish exudate of species of *Croton* section *Cyclostigma* (*sangre de drago*) is under study for possible value in cancer therapy.

In many genera of Crotonoideae and Euphorbioideae (plus *Omphalea* in the Acalyphoideae), the stems produce exudates rich in terpenoid compounds. The exudates of Crotonoideae are clear to whitish, yellowish, or reddish and often resinous; those in the Euphorbioideae are usually whitish and generally described as "milky latex." This latex contains rubber in the Micrandreae, Manihoteae, and Euphorbieae, and in the last, it is often toxic (dangerously so in *Hippomane*, *Ophthalmoblapton*, and some succulent *Euphorbia*).

The caustic sap found in the trunk of *Hura crepitans* renders the wood resistant to rot. Hence, this species provides most of the logs used for making floating houses along the Amazon.

Many genera of Euphorbiaceae are cultivated as garden or house plants, notably *Euphorbia pulcherrima* (poinsettia), a native of Mexico and Central America.

References. Armbruster, W. S. 1994. Early evolution of *Dalechampia* (Euphorbiaceae): insights from phylogeny, biogeography, and comparative morphology. *Ann. Missouri Bot. Gard.* 81:302–16. Correra Q., J. E., and H. Y. Bernal. 1992. Euphorbiaceae. In *Especies vegetales promisorias de los países del Convenio Andrés Bello*, Tomo VII. Santafé de Bogotá, D. E., Colombia: Secretaria Ejecutiva del Convenio Andrés Bello. Dehgan, B., and G. L. Webster. 1979. Morphology and infrageneric relationships of the genus *Jatropha* (Euphorbiaceae). *Univ. Calif. Publ. Bot.* 74: 1–73. Govaerts, R., D. G. Frodin, and A. Radcliffe-Smith. 2000. *World Checklist and Bibliography of Euphorbiaceae (with Pandaceae)*. Richmond, Surrey: Royal Botanic Gardens, Kew. Jablonski, E. 1967. Euphorbiaceae, *In* Botany of the Guayana Highland, ed. B. Maguire. *Mem. New York Bot. Gard.* Part 7, 17:80–190. Jury, S. L., T. Reynolds, D. F. Cutler, and F. J. Evans, eds. 1987. The Euphorbiales: chemistry, taxonomic and economic botany. *Bot. J. Linn. Soc.* 94:1–326. Mennega, A.M.W. 1987. Wood anatomy of the Euphorbiaceae, in particular of the subfamily Phyllanthoideae. *Bot. J. Linn. Soc.* 94:111–26. Radcliffe-Smith, A. 2001. *Genera Euphorbiaceae*. Richmond, Surrey: Royal Botanic Gardens, Kew. Rogers, D. J., and S. G. Appan. 1973. *Manihot*, Manihotoides. (Euphorbiaceae). *Fl. Neotrop. Monogr.* 13:1–272. Schultes, R. 1990. A brief taxonomic view of the genus *Hevea*. *Malaysian Rubber Research & Development Board Monograph* 14:1–57. Webster, G. L. 1987. The saga of the spurges: a review of classification and relationships in the Euphorbiales. *Bot. J. Linn. Soc.* 94:3–46. Webster, G. L. 1994a. Classification of the Euphorbiaceae. *Ann. Missouri Bot. Gard.* 81:3–32. Webster, G. L. 1994b. Synopsis of the genera and suprageneric taxa of Euphorbiaceae. *Ann. Missouri Bot. Gard.* 81:33–144. Webster, G. L., P. E. Berry, W. S. Armbruster, H.-J. Esser, L. J. Gillespie, W. J. Hayden, G. A. Levin, R. Secco, and S. V. Heald. 1999. Euphorbiaceae. In *Flora of the Venezuelan Guayana*, eds. J. A. Steyermark, P. E. Berry, K. Yatskievych, and B. K. Holst, 5:72–228. St. Louis, MO: Missouri Botanical Garden Press.

EUPHRONIACEAE (Euphronia Family)

Amy Litt

Plate 19

- *shrubs or trees*

- *stipules present, small*

- *leaves alternate, simple; blades densely pubescent abaxially*

- *flowers zygomorphic; petals 3, spatulate, clawed, purplish; androecium with 4 stamens and generally 1 staminode, these united into split tube*

- *fruits capsules, with 1 slightly winged seed per locule*

Numbers of genera and species. The Euphroniaceae comprise one genus, *Euphronia*, with three species restricted to tropical America.

Distribution and habitat. The Euphroniaceae are restricted to the Guayana Shield of southern Venezuela and bordering countries. The family is currently known from southeastern Venezuela and adjacent Guyana (*Euphronia guianensis*) and southwestern Venezuela along the border with Colombia (*E. acuminatissima*). There are also scattered collections from southern Venezuela, Colombia, and northwestern Brazil (*E. hirtelloides*).

Euphronia acuminatissima and *E. guianensis* are represented by multiple collections from relatively narrow geographic regions, whereas *E. hirtelloides*, the type species, is represented by scattered collections from a much broader geographic range.

Species of *Euphronia* are found exclusively in savannas on white sand, in rocky areas, or on exposed sandstone outcrops.

Family classification. Historically, *Euphronia* had been included in Trigoniaceae, but Cronquist and most other authors followed Lleras in placing *Euphronia* in the Vochysiaceae (Polygalales). An exception was Marcano-Berti, who placed *Euphronia* in its own family, the Euphroniaceae. Recent analyses show that *Euphronia* is not related to Vochysiaceae, but instead place it next to Chrysobalanaceae and Trigoniaceae; however, there are no apparent morphological features that relate *Euphronia* with Chrysobalanaceae. These studies also support recognition of this distinctive genus as a separate family.

Features of the family. Habit: shrubs or trees, young growth densely covered with white or gray pubescence, the branchlets, petioles, and blades may become glabrous with age. **Stipules** present, small. **Leaves** alternate, simple; blades densely pubescent, the conspicuous white or gray color contrasts with the dark glossy green of adaxial surface, the margins revolute. **Inflorescences** terminal or axillary, racemes, pubescent on most parts; bracts subtending flowers pubescent, deciduous. **Flowers** zygomorphic, bisexual, perigynous; calyx pubescent abaxially, fused at base, the lobes 5, unequal; petals 3, spatulate, clawed, 10–25 mm long, purplish, generally silky-pubescent; androecium with 4 stamens and generally 1 staminode, the stamens and staminode united at base into tube, the split opposite staminode, the fertile stamens glabrous, the anthers reddish brown, basifixed, with introrse dehiscence along a single central slit, the staminode pilose; gynoecium syncarpous, the ovary superior, subglobose, pubescent, the carpels 3, the locules 3, the style geniculate near apex, pilose, persistent in fruit, the stigma trilobed; placentation axile, the ovules 2 per locule, anatropous. **Fruits** capsules, cylindric, trivalvate, dehiscence basipetal, the exocarp thin, fleshy, pubescent. **Seeds** 1 per locule, slightly winged, glabrous, reddish brown.

Most *Euphronia* are medium-sized shrubs, but some *E. acuminatissima* are described as subshrubs (0.2 m tall),

whereas individuals of *E. hirtelloides* and *E. guianensis* are described as trees up to 10 m tall.

Natural history. No information is available about pollination and dispersal biology, but the showy flowers are most likely visited by insects.

Economic uses. No economic uses are recorded for this family.

References. LITT, A., AND M. W. CHASE. 1999. The systematic position of *Euphronia*, with comments on the position of *Balanops*: an analysis based on *rbc*L sequence data. *Syst. Bot.* 23:401–09. LLERAS, E. 1976. Revision and taxonomic position of the genus *Euphronia* Martius ex Martius & Zuccarini (Vochysiaceae). *Acta Amazon.* 6:43–7. MARCANO-BERTI, L. 1989. Euphroniaceae: una nueva familia. *Pittieria* 18:15–19. STEYERMARK, J. 1987. Flora of the Venezuelan Guyana II. *Ann. Missouri Bot. Gard.* 74:89–94.

FABACEAE (Pea or Bean Family)

DAVID S. SEIGLER

Figures 76, 77, 78, 79; Plates 20, 21

Caesalpinioideae

- *usually trees or shrubs, sometimes scandent, rarely herbs*
- *leaves usually pinnate, a few species bipinnate*
- *flowers slightly zygomorphic; wing petals covering standard in bud; stamens 10 (or 5), usually not long exserted*

Mimosoideae

- *trees, shrubs, and lianas, uncommonly herbs*
- *leaves often bipinnate*
- *inflorescences often spikes or capitate*
- *flowers often small and usually actinomorphic; stamens (5)10 to more than 100; usually exserted*

Papilionoideae (Faboideae)

- *usually herbs or vines, sometimes shrubs, trees, or lianas*
- *leaves pinnate, trifoliolate, or palmate, occasionally simple*
- *flowers zygomorphic; lateral petals enclosed by standard in bud; stamens 10, united into tube, or 9 united and one distinct*

Numbers of genera and species. Worldwide, the Fabaceae comprise 650–700 genera and about 18,000 species. Almost one-third of the species of the family belong to six genera: *Astragalus* (about 2,000 species), *Acacia* (about 1,200 species), *Crotalaria* (about 600 species), *Cassia sensu lato* (535 species, including *Chamaecrista* and *Senna*), *Indigofera* (500 species), and *Mimosa* (450–500 species). Several of these large genera appear to be heterogenous and taxonomists will undoubtedly subdivide these into a number of segregate genera. At the same time, a large number of genera are represented by relatively few species or are monotypic.

In the Western Hemisphere, there are about 272 native genera and 6,700 species. Of the three subfamilies, the Caesalpinioideae comprise approximately 61 genera (160 worldwide) and 1,205 species (about 2,000 worldwide), the Mimosoideae comprise approximately 45 genera (58 worldwide) and 1,442 species (perhaps 3,200 worldwide), and the Papilionoideae approximately 272 genera (450 worldwide) and 4,050 species (more than 11,500 worldwide).

Distribution and habitat. The Fabaceae are of cosmopolitan distribution. Many species are found in the neotropics, but others are extratropical in both the Northern and Southern Hemispheres. Some genera and occasional species are found in both South America and in Africa. The more evolutionarily advanced groups occur in South America and Af-

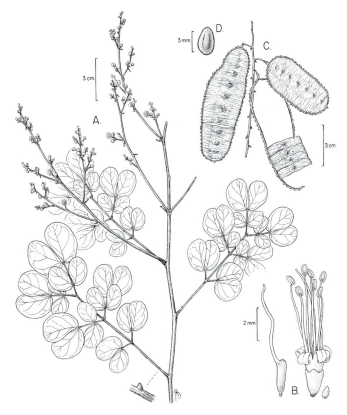

Figure 76. FABACEAE (MIMOSOIDEAE). *Mimosa guilandinae* var. *guilandinae*. **A.** Stem with bipinnately compound leaves and inflorescences. **B.** Lateral views of flower (right) and gynoecium showing subapical attachment of style (left). **C.** Lateral view of fruits showing partial dispersal of articles; note marginal prickles. **D.** Seed. Illustration prepared for *Flora of the Guianas* (in preparation). Artist: Bobbi Angell.

rica and are poorly represented in Asia. The Caesalpinioideae and Mimosoideae are mostly subtropical and tropical, but the Papilionoideae are widespread in boreal, temperate, and tropical zones.

The Fabaceae are found in almost every habitat, and often are dominant in the communities in which they occur.

Family classification. The Fabaceae *sensu lato* (as treated here) are placed as three separate families, the Mimosaceae, Caesalpiniaceae, and Fabaceae *sensu stricto*, in the Fabales by Cronquist. The most closely related families to the Fabaceae have traditionally been viewed as members of the rosaceous alliance. Some have seen a close relationship between the subfamily Caesalpinioideae and the Rosaceae and Chrysobalanaceae, whereas others have suggested that the closest relationships lie with the Connaraceae or Krameriaceae. Members of the order Sapindales also have been considered as possible relatives.

In this treatment, the Fabaceae are divided into three subfamilies: Caesalpinioideae, Mimosoideae, and Papilionoideae. The three subfamilies appear to form a monophyletic group. The results of cladistic analysis of data from *rbc*L chloroplast gene sequences confirm that the Caesalpinioideae is

basal and that the Mimosoideae appear to be derived from elements of that subfamily. Papilionoid species are relatively advanced within the group. The most archaic genera of the family appear to be the extratropical woody Caesalpinioideae, such as *Gleditsia, Gymnocladus, Ceratonia, Zenia,* and *Cercis.* The Swartzieae, a tropical South American and African group, traditionally grouped with the Caesalpinioideae but now placed in the Papilionoideae, may serve as a possible bridge between the Caesalpinioideae and the Papilionoideae. Although the Fabaceae are part of a large "Rosid I Group," the closest relatives are the Polygalaceae, the Surianaceae, and *Quillaja,* a disparate element of the Rosaceae. The Krameriaceae are basal to both the clade containing the Fabaceae and that containing the Rosaceae and a number of other families.

Although the Caesalpinioideae can be separated into seven to nine groups, these may be unnatural. Characters often used include the nature of the leaves, the irregularity of the flowers, the degree of fusion of the petals, and the mode of dehiscence of the anthers.

The Mimosoideae can be separated into tribes, largely based on the nature of the leaves, and number and degree of fusion of the filaments of the stamens. Many species are armed with spines, thorns, or prickles.

The Papilionoideae consist of from 10 or 11 to 31 tribes, based on features of habit, leaf form, and degree of fusion of stamens. Among those tribes usually recognized are: Sophoreae, Podalyrieae, Genisteae, Trifolieae, Loteae, Galegeae, Hedysareae, Vicieae, Phaseoleae, and Dalbergieae.

Features of the family. Habit: herbs, shrubs, vines, lianas, and trees, sometimes aquatic (Mimosoideae and Papilionoideae), the vines and lianas often with tendrils or hooks. **Stipules** present, often small and leaflike, large and leafy in *Pisum*, sometimes modified into spines (*Acacia*). **Leaves** usually alternate, often pinnately or bipinnately compound, the petioles and leaflets often with basal pulvini (that govern orientation). **Inflorescences** axillary or terminal, racemes, spikes, heads, or of solitary flowers. **Flowers** zygomorphic or actinomorphic in the Mimosoideae, bisexual or unisexual in some Mimosoideae (plants monoecious); sepals 5, ± fused, zygomorpic flowers sometimes with 2 or 4 lobes; petals typically 4 or 5 (sometimes fewer or absent), small and equal (the Mimosoideae), varying somewhat in size (the Caesalpinioideae), or organized into a butterfly shape with one upstanding dorsal petal (the standard), two lateral petals (the wings), and two lower ventral petals, ± fused along their margins to form a keel (the Papilionoideae); androecium usually of 10 stamens or 50–100+ stamens (in tribes Acacieae and Ingeae), the filaments, when stamens 50–100+, distinct or fused into tube or, when stamens 10, distinct or fused (monadelphous), or 9 fused with dorsal stamen distinct (diadelphus); nectary often surrounding ovary, ring-shaped; gynoecium with superior ovary, the carpel 1; placentation marginal, the ovules 2–many, arranged in two alternating rows on a single placenta. **Fruits** typically one-chambered legumes, dehiscent or indehiscent, dry or fleshy, inflated or compressed, sometimes winged, greenish or brightly colored, ranging from a few mm to 300+ mm, sometimes breaking into one-seeded segments (loments). **Seeds** 1–many, the seed coat often tough, a colored caruncle present in some genera; endosperm little or absent, the embryo large, the cotyledons conspicuous.

Seedlings are typically trifoliate or 3-lobed, but sometimes phyllodic (*Acacia, Lathyrus, Phylloxylon*).

The roots of many species of the subfamilies Mimosoideae and Papilionoideae have nodules that contain bacteria (mostly species of *Rhizobium*) that are involved in nitrogen fixation.

Several plants have apparent simple leaves, such as gorse (*Ulex*); others, such as certain species of *Acacia*, have flattened leaflike structures called phyllodes.

The leaves of many species can reorient themselves, and some are sensitive to touch.

Caesalpinioideae: Habit: trees, shrubs, sometimes scandent, rarely herbs. **Leaves** usually pinnate, a few species bipinnate. **Flowers** slightly zygomorphic, the wings covering the standard in bud; stamens 10 (or 5), distinct or monodelphous, usually not long exserted; pollen occurring in monads.

Species of this subfamily are often rich in tannins, and a

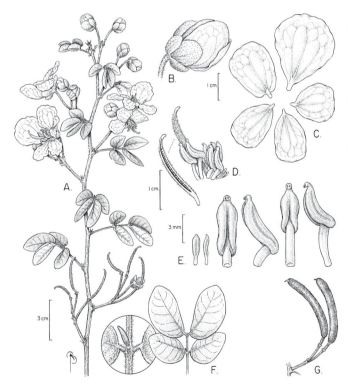

Figure 77. FABACEAE (CAESALPINIOIDEAE). *Cassia chrysocarpa.* **A.** Stem with leaves and inflorescences. **B.** Lateral view of flower bud. **C.** Adaxial views of five petals of a flower. **D.** Lateral view of androecium and gynoecium (right) and medial section of pistil (left). **E.** From left to right: adaxial and lateral views of staminodes, adaxial and lateral views of shorter stamens, and adaxial and lateral views of longer stamens. **F.** Leaf with detail of glands between leaflets. **G.** Lateral views of fruits. Reprinted with permission from Mori et al. (2002). Artist: Bobbi Angell.

number of species contain resins produced by secretory cells. Members of this subfamily normally do not fix nitrogen but obtain it via the intermediacy of ectomycorrhizae.

Mimosoideae: trees, shrubs, lianas, uncommonly herbs. **Leaves** often bipinnate, sometimes pinnate, the leaflets often numerous and small (although many *Acacia* have leaves modified into phyllodes); extrafloral nectaries often present. **Inflorescences** often spikes or capitate, showy in many species. **Flowers** usually actinomorphic, often small; stamens 5–10 to as many as 100, colored, usually exserted, usually forming conspicuous part of flower, the anthers often small; pollen usually occurring in diads and polyads; funicules often elongate.

Seed pleurograms are common in this subfamily. Plants often are rich in tannins, many species are capable of nitrogen fixation, and endomycorrhizal associations are frequent.

Extrafloral nectaries are common; these "glands" are often associated with ants. Some of the mutualistic relationships with ants are quite complex; probably the best known are the interactions of ants and certain species of *Acacia*.

Papilionoideae (Faboideae): usually herbs, occasionally vines, sometimes trees, shrubs, or lianas. **Leaves** usually pinnate, or sometimes palmate or trifoliolate, occasionally simple. **Flowers** zygomorphic, the lateral petals enclosed by the standard in bud; stamens 10, usually diadelphous but sometimes monadelphous or distinct; pollen usually occurring in monads.

Plants of this subfamily often have nitrogen-fixing microbial associates and often interact with endomycorrhizal fungi.

The Papilionoideae have the most advanced chemistry of the three subfamilies, and they are chemically diverse: isoflavonoids, alkaloids, and cyanogenic glycosides are common, canavanine occurs in large numbers of species, and nonprotein amino acids are found in the seeds of many species. The seeds often contain poisonous substances such as nonprotein amino acids, cyanogenic glycosides, trypsin inhibitors, or lectins.

Natural history. Legumes play important roles in many communities because they fix nitrogen and produce seeds rich in protein.

Insect pollination in legumes is predominant, especially in the subfamily Papilionoideae, although cleistogamy is frequent. The pollinators of the most primitive members of the family seem to be relatively general-pollinating insects, especially bees. The flowers of many species have a circular nectary surrounding the ovary that produces small quantities of nectar. A few members of subfamily Caesalpinioideae, however, have modifications for bird and bat pollination. Some members of the genera *Elisabetha, Eperua, Jacqueshuberia*, and *Hymenaea* have pendent flowers and copious nectar production that suggest bat pollination. Others have coloration that indicate bird pollination (e.g., *Bauhinia macranthera* and most species of the genus *Brownea*).

In the subfamily Mimosoideae, most plants appear to be pollinated by bees, and despite the relatively small flowers, large numbers of them often visit the flowers of many species. Some individuals of *Prosopis velutina* may produce more than 1 million flowers per year. The development of stamen tubes appears to be an adaptation for pollination by moths, birds, or bats. Visitation by sphingid moths in many taxa (especially in the tribe Ingeae) suggests that moth pollination was an intermediate stage that lead to pollination by birds and bats. The color and overall shape of the inflorescence suggest that birds and bats are pollinators of many taxa. Most *Parkia* and several *Inga* species are known to be bat pollinated.

Members of the Papilionoideae are overwhelmingly bee pollinated. The strongly zygomorphic flowers, coloration, and the special "trip mechanism" that ensures pollen-body contact are correlated strongly with bee pollination. However, some papilionoid legumes are known to be pollinated by birds (many *Erythrina*) and bats (*Alexa* and *Mucuna*). A few species (such as *Ateleia herbert-smithii*) are at least partly wind pollinated. On the whole, pollination of legumes by lepidopterans, flies, ants, beetles, and other organisms is relatively uncommon.

The earliest legume fruits were probably dehiscent and few-seeded. Specialization along several lines has occurred. Many legumes appear to be dispersed by gravity; those with wings may be aided by wind or movement in the air. In other instances, the fruits are dehiscent, and winged seeds are produced. Accessory structures may be involved in the dispersal of seeds on the ground or in the attachment of fruits to animals (*Desmodium*). Some legumes articulate and produce segments that are, of themselves, indehiscent (loments). Many legume seeds are dispersed by animals (birds, bats, and mammals). Arils or similar structures that are sweet, odoriferous, or highly colored (such as those in *Pithecellobium* and related genera) may serve as rewards for dispersing animals. In other instances, the seeds or pods are brightly colored, usually with red, red and white, or red and black patterns that mimic arils and appear to attract birds as dispersers without providing actual rewards. This is common in Neotropical genera such as *Erythrina*, *Ormosia*, and *Rhynchosia*.

The seeds and pods of a large percentage of legume species are parasitized by bruchid beetles.

The extrafloral glands that are common on many legumes of the subfamilies Caesalpinioideae and Mimosoideae often are associated with ants. The interaction between specific ants and about 12 *Acacia* species, primarily in Mexico and Central America, is highly coevolved. The plants produce special glands called Beltian bodies on the tips of the leaflets and have enlarged petiolar nectaries. These provide food for the ants, and the ants, in turn, patrol and protect the plants, largely from fungal attack and competing vegetation, but, as most botanists can attest, also from herbivores.

Economic uses. Many major food plants belong to the Fabaceae. Among these crops are soybeans, peanuts, peas, garbanzos, pigeon peas, lentils, broad beans, lima beans, lablab, jack beans, mung beans, adjuki beans, scarlet runner beans, winged beans, tamarind, and carob. The seeds of these plants are particularly important because they serve as rich sources of protein and balance the deficiency of the amino acid lysine of cereal grains. The peanut (*Arachis hypogaea*), common bean (*Phaseolus vulgaris*), lima bean (*P. lunatus*), scarlet runner bean (*P. coccineus*), and jack bean (*Canavalia ensiformis*) have origins in the Western Hemisphere. The seeds of several species of *Phaseolus* were major pre-Columbian food plants of Indians in North and South America. The common bean and the scarlet runner bean probably were domesticated in Mexico and northern Central America, whereas the lima bean appears to be derived from ancestors found in northern South America. Certainly, these beans were traded

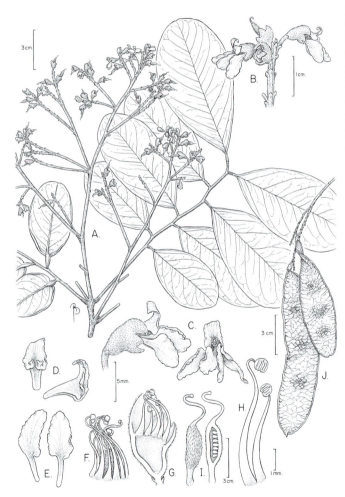

Figure 78. FABACEAE (PAPILIONOIDEAE). *Diplotropis purpurea*. **A.** Stem with leaves, flowers, and very immature fruits. **B.** Part of inflorescence. **C.** Lateral (left) and apical (right) views of flowers. **D.** Adaxial (left) and lateral (right) views of standard petal. **E.** Adaxial views of keel (left) and wing (right) petals. **F.** Androecium and upper part of gynoecium. **G.** Medial section of perianth with adnate stamens. **H.** Views of stamens. **I.** Gynoecium (left) and medial section of gynoecium (right). **J.** Lateral views of fruits. Reprinted with permission from Mori et al. (2002). Artist: Bobbi Angell.

and cultivated widely. Today, these species collectively are second only to the soybean in importance as legume crops. They are challenged for this rank by another pre-Columbian legume, the peanut or groundnut. This species is important not only as a source of protein, oil, and carbohydrate of the seeds, but as an oilseed crop. The fruits and seeds of other legumes, including a number of *Prosopis* species, were formerly important as human foods in widespread areas of North and South America.

The seeds of most legumes must be cooked before consumption to break down inhibitors of digestive enzymes and lectins. In addition, many others contain poisonous materials that are not broken down by cooking.

The seeds of the tonka bean or cumaru, *Dipteryx odorata*, are used widely for flavoring food and tobacco products and in perfume. As the seeds are dried, they undergo enzymatic changes that liberate coumarin, the major flavoring compound.

Many American legumes are valuable as forage crops, but, because few animals were domesticated in the Western Hemisphere, few of them have been cultivated for this purpose. An exception is *Leucaena leucocephala*, a Mexican mimosoid legume that is already an important forage crop in many areas of the Tropics. A number of other legumes are significant sources of livestock poisoning. These include species of *Crotalaria* (pyrrolizidine alkaloids), *Acacia* (cyanogenic glycosides); *Lupinus*, *Baptisia*, *Sophora*, and related taxa (quinolizidine alkaloids); *Astragalus* (selenium, indolizidine alkaloids, organic nitro compounds); and *Erythrina* and *Ormosia* (special types of benzylisoquinoline alkaloids).

Species of some mimosoid legumes have hallucinogenic properties that have been used by peoples of northern South America. The seeds of *Anadenanthera peregrina* (*yopo*) are the basis for an intoxicating snuff; the active components are bufotenin and N,N-dimethyltryptamine.

The wood of a number of American legumes is valuable. Among the genera and species used are: *Andira inermis*, *Dalbergia* species (*cocobolo* and rosewood), *Hymenaea courbaril* (coubaril), *Peltogyne paniculata* (purpleheart) and related species, *Platymiscium* species, *Samanea saman*, and *Vouacapoua americana* (*acapu*). *Acacia visco* is an important timber tree in southern South America.

A few species of American legumes are cultivated as ornamentals. Among these are species of *Acacia*, *Albizia*, *Calliandra*, *Caesalpinia*, *Geoffrea*, *Gleditsia*, *Gymnocladus*, *Glyricidia*, *Hymenaea*, *Pithecellobium*, *Prosopis*, *Tipuana*, *Samanea*, and *Sophora*.

Commercial tannins often are derived from the Australian *Acacia mearnsii*, and species of *Pithecellobium* are sometimes used for this purpose; e.g., *P. dulce* (*guamúchil*) in Mexico. The bark of *Stryphnodendron barbatimao* is used in Brazil in a similar manner.

The insecticide rotenone is derived from American species of *Lonchocarpus* and from Asian species of *Derris*. Roots of native *Lonchocarpus* are harvested in a number of areas in Latin America, but the plant seldom is cultivated. The roots also are used to poison fish in some areas of the Tropics.

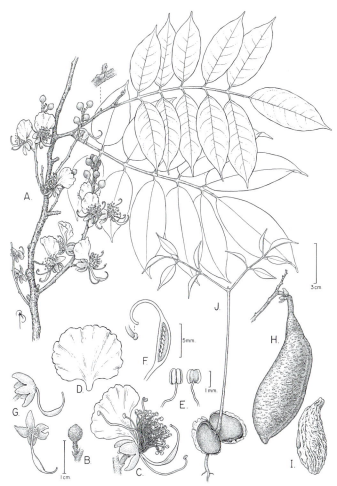

Figure 79. FABACEAE (PAPILIONOIDEAE). *Swartzia polyphylla.* **A.** Stem with leaves and cauliflorous inflorescences and detail of lateral bud showing stipule (above). **B.** Lateral view of flower bud. **C.** Lateral view of flower. **D.** Adaxial view of single petal. **E.** Adaxial (left) and abaxial (right) views of stamens. **F.** Medial section of gynoecium with detail of tip of style and stigma (above left). **G.** Lateral (above) and oblique (below) views of calyx and ovary. **H.** Lateral view of fruit. **I.** Lateral view of seed. **J.** Seedling. Reprinted with permission from Mori et al. (2002). Artist: Bobbi Angell.

Although legumes are used in folk medicine in many areas of Latin America, few of these plants have major economic importance. Previously, balsam of Peru, from species of *Myroxylon*, was used as an antiseptic for wounds and in laboratory procedures. A resinous material from species of *Copaifera* used for similar purposes is marketed locally in Brazil. Although some commercial gums, such as gum arabic or gum acacia, are isolated from *Acacia senegal* and related species, no Neotropical species seem to be exploited in this manner.

Plants of the Fabaceae have long been known to yield dyestuffs. Indigo, a blue dye prepared from isolates of certain species of *Indigofera*, was once a major item of commerce in the Eastern Hemisphere. However, a chemically identical dyestuff also was isolated from Western Hemisphere species of this genus by inhabitants of Mexico. Among other legume species in the Western Hemisphere, *Haematoxylum campechianum* (logwood) was used by pre-Columbian Americans and later in Europe as the source of a black dye. Today, haematoxylin from this species is used in laboratories as a stain for blood analysis.

The family also includes numerous weeds of local or widespread distribution. One of the most aggressive is the Asian *Pueraria montana* (kudzu vine), which has smothered native vegetation throughout the southeastern United States.

References. ARROYO, M.T.K. 1981. Breeding systems and pollination biology in Leguminosae. In *Advances in Legume Systematics*, Parts 1 and 2, eds. R. M. Polhill and P. H. Raven, 723–70. Richmond, Surrey: Royal Botanic Gardens, Kew. AUGSPURGER, C. A. 1989. Morphology and aerodynamics of wind-dispersed legumes in Advances in legume biology, eds. C. H. Stirton and J. L. Zarucchi. *Monogr. Syst. Bot. Missouri Bot. Gard.* 29:451–66. BERNAL, H. Y., AND J. E. CORRERA Q. 1990. *Habra criolla, Canavalia ensiformis (L.) DC (Fabaceae–Faboideae).* In *Especies vegetales promisorias de los países del Convenio Andrés Bello*, Monograph No. 2. Bogotá, D. E., Colombia: Secretaria Ejecutiva del Convenio Andrés Bello. BERNAL, H. Y., AND J. E. CORRERA Q. 1992. Fabaceae. In *Especies vegetales promisorias de los países del Convenio Andrés Bello*, Tomo VIII. Santafé de Bogotá, D. E., Colombia: Secretaria Ejecutiva del Convenio Andrés Bello. CORRERA Q., J. E., AND H. Y. BERNAL. 1995. Mimosaceae. In *Especies vegetales promisorias de los países del Convenio Andrés Bello*, Tomo XI. Santafé de Bogotá, D. E., Colombia: Secretaria Ejecutiva del Convenio Andrés Bello. COWAN R. S. 1967. *Swartzia (Leguminosae, Caesalpinioideae Swartzieae). Fl. Neotrop. Monogr.* 1:1–228. DICKISON, W. C. 1981. Evolutionary relationship of the Legumino-sae. In *Advances in Legume Systematics*, Parts 1 and 2, eds. R. M. Polhill and P. H. Raven, 35–54. Richmond, Surrey: Royal Botanic Gardens, Kew. ELIAS, T. S. 1981. *Mimosoideae in Advances in Legume Systematics*, eds. R. M. Polhill and P. H. Raven, 143–51, Parts 1 and 2. Richmond, Surrey: Royal Botanic Gardens, Kew. JANZEN, D. H. 1989. Natural history of a wind-pollinated Central American dry forest legume tree (*Ateleia herbert-smithii Pittier*). In Advances in legume biology, eds. C. H. Stirton and J. L. Zarucchi. *Monogr. Syst. Bot. Missouri Bot. Gard.* 29:293–376. JOHNSON, C. D. 1981. Seed beetle host specificity and the systematics of the Leguminosae. In *Advances in Legume Systematics*, Parts 1 and 2, eds. R. M. Polhill and P. H. Raven, 995–1027. Richmond, Surrey: Royal Botanic Gardens, Kew. MCKEY, D. 1989. Interactions between ants and leguminous plants in Advances in legume biology, eds. C. H. Stirton and J. L. Zarucchi. *Monogr. Syst. Bot. Missouri Bot. Gard.* 29: 673–718. MORGAN, D. R., AND D. E. SOLTIS. 1993. Phylogenetic relationships among members of Saxifragaceae *sensu lato* based on *rbc*L sequence data. *Ann. Missouri Bot. Gard.* 80:631–60. MORGAN, D. R., D. E. SOLTIS, AND K. R. ROBERTSON. Systematic and evolutionary implications of *rbc*L sequence variation in Rosaceae. *Amer. J. Bot.* 81:890–903. MORS, W. B., AND C. T. RIZZINI. 1966. *Useful Plants of Brazil.* San Francisco: Holden-Day. POLHILL, R. M., AND P. H. RAVEN. 1981. *Advances in Legume Systematics*, Parts 1 and 2. Richmond, Surrey: Royal Botanic Gardens, Kew. POLHILL, R. M., P. H. RAVEN, AND C. H. STIRTON. 1981. Evolution and systematics of the Leguminosae. In *Advances in Legume Systematics*, Parts 1 and 2, eds. R. M. Polhill and P. H. Raven, 1–26. Richmond, Surrey: Royal Botanic Gardens, Kew. SCHULTES, R. E., AND R. F. RAFFAUF. 1990. *The Healing Forest.* Portland, OR: Dioscorides Press.

FAGACEAE (Beech Family)

KEVIN C. NIXON

Figure 80, Plate 21

- *trees and shrubs*

- *leaves alternate, simple*

- *staminate inflorescences usually lax catkins*

- *flowers small, unisexual; perianth inconspicuous*

- *fruits nuts or large triangular achenes, subtended by a cupule, the rounded nut and cupule together referred to as an "acorn" in Quercus.*

Numbers of genera and species. Worldwide, the Fagaceae comprise nine genera and approximately 600–800 species. In tropical America, there are three genera, *Colomboba-lanus*, with two species; *Fagus*, with one species; and *Quercus*, with about 150 species.

Distribution and habitat. The Fagaceae (excluding *Nothofagus*) are mostly found in the Northern Hemisphere with a few species crossing the equator in Southeast Asia. They are well represented in temperate, subtropical, and tropical areas of North America and Eurasia, and are absent from sub-Saharan Africa. The greatest diversity is in Mexico and in southern China and adjacent southeast Asia.

In the neotropics, where the family is represented mostly by *Quercus*, species are concentrated in mid- to high-elevation forests, although a few species of *Quercus* are found in

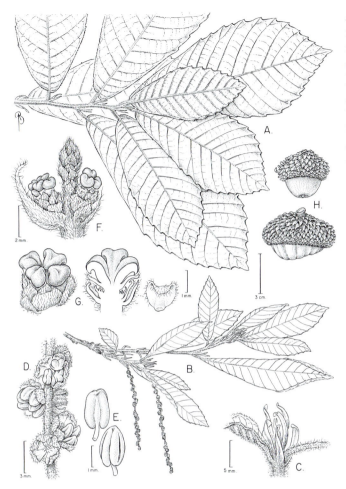

Figure 80. FAGACEAE. *Quercus insignis* (A, Purpus 7386; B–F, Jimenez 478; H, Herrera 4138 (above); Purpus 7386 (below). **A.** Stem with mature leaves. **B.** Stem with immature leaves and staminate inflorescences. **C.** Lateral view of node showing leaf base and stipules. **D.** Part of staminate inflorescence. **E.** Abaxial (above) and adaxial (below) views of stamens. **F.** Pistillate inflorescences. **G.** Intact pistillate flower (left), medial section of pistillate flower (center), and adaxial view of bracteole (right). **H.** Lateral views of fruits. Original. Artist: Bobbi Angell.

lowland wet or dry forest, to near sea level in a few cases. Diversity decreases from the highest level in montane southern Mexico, through Central America, to a single species of *Quercus* and the monotypic *Colombobalanus* found at mid-elevations in the Andes of Colombia. *Fagus* is the only other genus of Fagaceae in the neotropics, with a single species (*F. mexicana*) restricted to a few isolated populations in cloud forests of eastern Mexico in the states of Puebla, Hidalgo, and Tamaulipas.

Family classification. The Fagaceae are placed in the Fagales by Cronquist. Traditionally, the family included the Northern Hemisphere *Castanea*, *Castanopsis*, *Chrysolepis*, *Fagus*, *Lithocarpus*, and *Quercus* as well as the strictly Southern Hemisphere *Nothofagus*. During the past 20 years, however, a consensus has developed that the extratropical

Nothofagus should be treated as separate family, the Nothofagaceae. This was initially based on cladistic analysis of morphological evidence but has since been verified by several molecular studies. The family as treated here excludes Nothofagaceae. The broader relationships of the family Fagaceae remain with families traditionally placed in the Amentiferae, or more recently referred to as the Higher Hamamelididae, including Nothofagaceae, Betulaceae, Myricaeae, Juglandaceae, Casuarinaceae, and the recently described Ticodendraceae. This "higher hamamelid" clade is monophyletic on the basis of both morphological and molecular studies, and is nested among families traditionally placed in Subclass Rosidae. The higher Hamamelididae has recently been subsumed into the order Fagales (*sensu* Angiosperm Phylogeny Group classification) on the basis of molecular studies.

Subfamilial treatments of Fagaceae have varied considerably. Removal of *Nothofagus* from the family leaves at least two alternative classifications. Based on molecular evidence (but not yet supported by morphological analyses), the genus *Fagus* appears to be the sister taxon of the remainder of the family, and thus the Fagoideae should be treated as including only *Fagus*. The pattern of relationships among the remaining genera remains uncertain, although the traditional Castaneoideae (*Castanea*, *Lithocarpus*, *Castanopsis*, and *Chrysolepis*) seem to hold together well on the basis of shared morphological features. The problematic genera are the remaining three "trigonobalanoid" genera, *Colombobalanus*, *Formanodendron*, and *Trigonobalanus*, which tentatively can be placed in the Quercoideae with the genus *Quercus* (including *Cyclobalanopsis*). Currently, such a three-subfamily classification seems the best treatment, but may change as our understanding of the relationships of the trigonobalanoids become more clear.

Features of the family. Habit: trees and shrubs, the shrubs sometimes rhizomatous, evergreen or deciduous. **Stipules** distinct, scarious, usually deciduous. **Leaves** alternate, simple; blade margins entire, toothed, or lobed. **Inflorescences** axillary or at base of new growth, rarely terminal, unisexual or androgynous, catkins, spicate or capitate, rigid, flexuous, or lax (some staminate catkins); pistillate flowers subtended by or within cupule, the cupules 1–several, spicately arranged or solitary, bearing 1–3(15 or more) pistillate flowers. **Flowers** actinomorphic, unisexual (plants monecious), inconspicuous (except in mass). **Staminate flowers:** tepals about 6, typically connate with 4–6 lobes; androecium of (3)6–12(18+) stamens; pistillode often present, indurate or vestigial as central tuft of trichomes. **Pistillate flowers:** tepals about 6, distinct, in 2 whorls of 3 or connate with (3)4–6 lobes, or irregularly cleft; gynoecium syncarpous, the ovary inferior, the carpels 3–4(6 in *Castanea*), the locules initially 3 or 6, but becoming one in fruit, the styles distinct, equal to number of carpels, the stigmas decurrent or capitate; placentation axile, pendulous, the ovules 2 per locule, anatropous, bitegmic (inner integument somewhat reduced in *Fagus*). **Fruits** rounded nuts or large triangular achenes, the fruits subtended or enveloped by scaly or spiny cupule (resembling an involucre), 1–3(15 or more) nuts per cupule (1 nut per cupule in *Quercus*, the nut and cup together called an "acorn" or "bellota"); endocarp silky-tomentose or, in some *Quercus*, glabrous. **Seed** 1, filling the nut, the seed coat membranous; endosperm unnoticeable at maturity.

Chromosomes numbers are $n = 12$ (22 only in *Trigonobalanus*).

Some of the largest trees in Central America are species of *Quercus*. Oak trees have been measured at greater than 50 meters tall, and some unconfirmed reports exist of heights of 70 meters or more. These large oaks, particularly at lower elevations on deeper wet soils, exhibit buttresses typical of lowland forest trees.

Natural history. The genera *Quercus* and *Fagus* are wind-pollinated, producing vast quantities of pollen. In temperate regions, *Quercus* exhibits highly synchronized flowering within species, with virtually all species flowering in spring. In many species of the red oak group, there is a one-year lag between pollination and fertilization resulting in fruit maturation requiring approximately 18–20 months. The fruit of these species generally matures in the fall of the year following flowering, and the fruits are referred to as "biennial" in the literature. In Central America and the lowland west of Mexico, flowering typically occurs earlier in the year, during the dry season from December to March, and fruit maturation for most of these tropical species occurs between June and August, probably due to maximal availability of moisture for the short-lived seeds to germinate. There is no carryover of ungerminated seeds from year to year. Virtually all Fagaceae have fruits that are animal-dispersed, particularly by squirrels and various species of large birds such as turkeys, jays, and guans. Ripe acorns are heavy and do not float; therefore, water dispersal is unlikely.

Economic uses. The Fagaceae often are used as lumber for general construction, fence posts and railroad ties (especially members of the white oak group), flooring, trim, and furniture. Charcoal is an important product throughout the range of *Quercus*, and overproduction threatens many populations.

Large oaks, particularly *Q. corrugata* and *Q. insignis*, often are left for shade trees in coffee plantations; however, this practice is diminishing because of increased planting of sun-tolerant varieties of coffee. The leaves and bark are still used in Mexico and Central America as sources of tannins for treating leather. *Quercus* acorns provide a major food source for wildlife and are used extensively in some areas as fodder for animals, particularly pigs. Acorns are consumed by humans in some areas, but this practice is disappearing because of the time-consuming preparation needed to leach tannins from the nuts. Oaks typically harbor an extensive arthropod fauna and, because of their dominance over large areas, are likely key species in maintaining overall biodiversity throughout tropical montane South and Central America and large parts of temperate North America. Thus, the economic impact of destruction of oak forests is undoubtedly great but immeasurable.

References: ELIAS, T. S. 1971. The genera of Fagaceae in the southeastern United States. *J. Arnold Arbor.* 52:159–95. FEY, B. S., AND P. K. ENDRESS. 1983. Development and morphological interpretation of the cupule in Fagaceae. *Flora* 173:451–68. HJELMQVIST, H. 1948. Studies on the floral morphology and phylogeny of the Amentiferae. *Bot. Not. Suppl.* 2(1):1–171. NIXON, K. C. 1989. Origins of Fagaceae. In *Syst. Assoc. Spec. Vol. 40B. Evolution, Systematics, and Fossil History of the Hamamelididae*, eds. P. R. Crane and S. Blackmore, 2:23–43. Oxford: Clarendon Press. NIXON, K. C. 1993a. Infrageneric classification of *Quercus* (Fagaceae) and typification of sectional names. *Annales des Sciences Forestieres* 50(suppl. 1):25s–34s. NIXON, K. C. 1993b. The genus *Quercus* in Mexico. In *Biological Diversity of Mexico: Origins and Distribution*, eds. T. P. Ramamoorthy, R. Bye, A. Lot, and J. Fa, 447–58. Oxford: Oxford University Press. NIXON, K. C. 1997. Fagaceae. In *Flora of North America North of Mexico*. 3:436–47. New York: Oxford University Press. NIXON, K. C., AND W. L. CREPET. 1989. *Trigonobalanus* (Fagaceae): Taxonomic status and phylogenetic relationships. *Amer. J. Bot.* 76:828–41. SOEPADMO, E. 1972. Fagaceae. In *Flora Malesiana*, ed. C.G.G.J. Van Steenis, ser. 1, vol. 7, pt. 2:265–403.

FLACOURTIACEAE (Flacourtia Family)

DOUGLAS C. DALY

Figure 81, Plate 21

- *trees or shrubs*
- *stipules usually present*
- *leaves usually alternate (rarely opposite), simple; tertiary venation often scalariform or percurrent*
- *flowers actinomorphic; petals often absent; stamens often many, often in fascicles; ovary usually superior, 2–10-carpellate, usually unilocular; placentation parietal, the placentas often 3*
- *fruits berries, loculicidal capsules, or drupes*
- *seeds often with sarcotesta or aril*

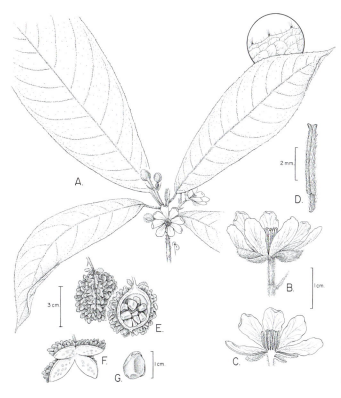

Figure 81. FLACOURTIACEAE. *Carpotroche crispidentata*. **A.** Stem with leaves and inflorescences and detail of leaf margin (upper right). **B.** Lateral view of staminate flower. **C.** Medial section of staminate flower. **D.** Adaxial view of stamen covered by trichomes. **E.** Lateral view of intact fruit (left), medial section (right) of fruit with seeds. **F.** Fruit after dehiscence. **G.** Seed. Reprinted with permission from Mori et al. (2002). Artist: Bobbi Angell.

Numbers of genera and species. Excluding the tribes Lacistemeae (as Lacistemataceae), as well as the Paropsieae and Abatieae (both now in Passifloraceae), the Flacourtiaceae comprise approximately 81 genera and 900 species worldwide. In tropical America, there are 28 genera and approximately 275 species. *Homalium*, a pantropical genus and the largest in the family with some 200 species, is represented in the neotropics by only three species. *Casearia*, with approximately 75 of its 180 species occurring in tropical America, is the largest genus in the neotropics. One classification of the family in the late 1980s recognized 29 monotypic genera worldwide, but subsequently there has been a tendency to sink some of these into other genera.

Distribution and habitat. The Flacourtiaceae are principally tropical but extend into temperate areas in Chile and Japan; only *Xylosma* and the introduced *Flacourtia* are represented in the continental United States. Several genera are both Neo- and Paleotropical, including *Casearia*, *Homalium*, *Lindackeria*, and *Xylosma*.

Most of the Neotropical genera of Flacourtiaceae display some ecological flexibility, and most tend to occur in moist lowland vegetation. With some exceptions, the family is a consistent but not generally conspicuous component of the humid Neotropical lowlands. It is one of the most species-rich families in the lowland humid forests of the Sierra Nevada de Santa Marta in Colombia, and *Laetia corymbulosa* attains high densities in the *várzea* (floodplain) forests of the lower Rio Solimões in Amazonian Brazil. Similarly, in an Amazonian floodplain forest in the Manu National Park in Peru, *Casearia decandra* reaches high densities, principally at early and middle successional stages.

There are higher-elevation habitat specialists in the family, especially among the more isolated monotypic genera. *Pineda* is endemic to montane habitats in the northern Andes; *Olmediella* is found in montane cloud forests of southern Mexico and Central America, while *Hasseltiopsis* has a similar range but is more common in pine forests; *Priamosia* is a montane taxon endemic to the Dominican Republic. *Xylosma*, with perhaps 50 species in the neotropics (and another 50 in Asia), shows a distinct preference for dry areas.

Family classification. Most of the major classifications prior to the 1990s placed the Flacourtiaceae in the Violales (i.e., *sensu* Cronquist), variously defined but often including the Passifloraceae, Lacistemaceae, Violaceae, Turneraceae, Caricaceae, Cistaceae, and Bixaceae. Unfortunately, the family has been notoriously polyphyletic or, in less technical terms, a "garbage can" for diverse genera with uncertain affinities, thereby leaving family limits blurred. Historically, the family was crocheted together by a process now called "chaining," in which divergent groups were seen as linked by apparently intermediate taxa as well as making links to various outside taxa. The result was a family defined by homoplasies, or shared non-unique archaic/basal characteristics, the limits of which are variable and arbitrary, leading one of the family's principal specialists, Hermann Sleumer, to write in 1954, "No single character exists wherewith to distinguish Flacourtiaceae from other families or to recognize them in the field."

Many characters have been examined in attempts to define and delimit the family, including anatomy, pollen, seeds, chemistry, and karyology. Principally during the 1960s and 1970s, various genera were pruned from the Flacourtiaceae and placed in such divergent families as the Euphorbiaceae, Portulacaceae, Turneraceae, Theaceae, Tiliaceae, and Myrtaceae, or into segregate families. There is a consensus that Lacistemataceae should be recognized as a distinct family and that the arborescent tribes Abatieae and Paropsieae, based on chemistry, pollen morphology, the presence of an extrastaminal corona, and other characters, belong in the Passifloraceae.

Attempts at a reorganization of angiosperm phylogeny, emphasizing molecular data, have aligned members of Cronquist's polyphyletic Flacourtiaceae with numerous other families. Recent molecular studies show that many of the non-cyanogenic taxa of Flacourtiaceae are nested within the Salicaceae, with the remainder aligning with the South African Achariaceae. Hence, the Flacourtiaceae of Cronquist no longer exist. The genera and tribes of the Flacourtiaceae as circumscribed in the twenty-first century will bear little resemblance to the family's twentieth-century counterpart. The tribes of the family fall into two distinct groups distinguished by rather fundamental chemical, anatomical, and developmental characters, and each of these groups can be further divided into tribes or clusters of tribes based on these as well as nontrivial morphological and palynological characters.

Features of the family. **Habit:** trees or shrubs, evergreen or deciduous; simple or branched axillary thorns sometimes present (e.g., *Xylosma*); trichomes usually present, simple, rarely stellate (*Macrohasseltia, Pineda, Ryania*), 2-branched, or of peltate scales. **Stipules** usually present. **Leaves** usually alternate (spiral or more often distichous), rarely opposite (*Abatia*), simple; petioles in some genera pulvinate at the base and/or apex; blades often pellucid-punctate or pellucid-lineate (Casearieae), the margins entire or often glandular-crenate (*Banara*) or -serrate, sometimes spinose-serrate; glands present at blade base in numerous taxa, these toward apex of petiole (and raised), on or between basal veins, or on margins; venation pinnate to palmate (leaves sometimes pliveined from base), usually semicraspedodromous, less often brochidodromous or eucamptodromous, the tertiary venation often scalariform or percurrent. **Inflorescences** (sub)terminal or mostly axillary, racemes, panicles, corymbs, or short cymes, often condensed to fascicles or glomerules, or reduced to solitary flowers; pedicels often articulate. **Flowers** actinomorphic, bisexual or less often unisexual (plants usually dioecious, sometimes andromonoecious), perianth 1–2-seriate; sepals (3)4–7(8+), imbricate or less often valvate, distinct or usually connate at base, rarely accrescent in fruit; petals 3–8 or absent (some *Prockia*, most Flacourtieae, all Casearieae), distinct, imbricate or valvate, usually alternate with sepals and caducous, sometimes with adaxial basal appendage, often inserted on margin of receptacle (Casearieae); nectar sometimes produced by a basal staminode-like scale on each petal; disc sometimes present, usually extrastaminal (sometimes intrastaminal), entire or usually lobed (the lobes free or adnate to filaments), or forming a ring of nectar glands; androecium of 4–many stamens, the stamens hypogynous or almost perigynous, sometimes in epipetalous bundles and alternating with nectar glands (Homalieae), the outer series of stamens sometimes sterile (Flacourtieae), the filaments distinct or rarely united into short tube, the connective sometimes elongated and glandular, the anthers dehiscing by long slits or rarely by pores; gynoecium syncarpous, the ovary superior (semi-inferior in Homalieae), the carpels 2–10, the locules sometimes 2–9 and incomplete or rarely 2(3) and complete via lamellar intrusions of parietal placentas (*Hasseltia*), the styles (0)1–many, usually ± distinct and as many as carpels, less often variously connate; placentation parietal, the ovules 2+ per placenta, anatropous or less often amphitropous or orthotropous. **Fruits** berries, loculicidal capsules partly or completely dehiscent by valves, or drupes with 1–

several endocarps; the surface sometimes winged, horned, or prickly. **Seeds** 1–many, sarcotesta (fleshy testa) present in some genera or the seed often arilloid (derived from fleshy outer layer of integument; e.g., Casearieae), rarely with cottony hairs or winged; endosperm fleshy, abundant, oily, proteinaceous, the embryo straight, the cotyledons mostly broad and cordate-foliaceous.

Germination is epigeal. During germination, the seedling usually becomes free from the fruit and seed coat and leaflike cotyledons are borne aloft by the hypocotyl. Less often, the seedling testa is persistent around the cotyledons and shed with them.

Natural history. Little documentation exists on the pollinators in Flacourtiaceae. The presence of various types of floral nectaries (discs, glands, petal appendages), plus the exposed androecium and gynoecium, suggest unspecialized insect pollinators for most taxa. In *Prockia crucis*, pollen is the only reward, and in the Mexican state of Jalisco, this species is pollinated mostly by solitary species of medium-sized bees.

Fleshy drupes or berries and capsules that reveal arillate seeds likely are dispersed by mammals and/or birds, although some appear to be adapted for wind dispersal via enlarged and winged or plumose perianth parts (*Homalium*). The fruits of *Casearia, Laetia,* and *Hasseltia* are dispersed by fruit-eating birds, specialists in the case of the latter genus. *Casearia* produces capsules that dehisce to present seeds enveloped in an oil-rich aril. A study of *C. corymbosa* in Costa Rica found that its seeds are dispersed by an assemblage of birds that strip off the oily arils in their crops and regurgitate viable seeds from perches in the surrounding forest; the yellow-green vireo (*Vireo flavoviridis*) accounts for 65 percent of the seeds removed; other important dispersers are the streaked flycatcher (*Myiodynastes maculatus*), the golden-fronted woodpecker (*Melanerpes aurifrons*), and Nutting's flycatcher (*Myiarchus nuttingi*). In the humid forests of La Selva in Costa Rica, the arillate seeds of *Casearia nitida* are dispersed by a number of birds, including obligate fruit eaters such as the keel-billed toucan (*Ramphastos sulfuratus*) and the Chestnut-mandibled toucan (*R. swainsonii*), as well as by opportunistic fruit eaters such as the social flycatcher (*Myozetetes similis*) and the gray-capped flycatcher (*M. granadensis*).

Economic uses. The Flacourtiaceae are not important economically, but several taxa have been put to some interesting uses. Paleotropical *Flacourtia indica* is cultivated widely as an ornamental and for its edible fruits. The arils of some *Casearia* and *Mayna* species are eaten, and some *Homalium* and *Prockia* also have edible fruits.

The chaulmoogra oils, originally from the Paleotropical genus *Hydnocarpus* but also derived from Neotropical *Carpotroche* (including *C. brasiliensis*) and *Casearia sylvestris* contain cyclopentenyl fatty acids and have been used to treat leprosy and skin disorders.

The chemical constituents of some Flacourtiaceae have been investigated as sources of new medicines; e.g., the casearins found in *Casearia sylvestris* have shown preliminary antitumor activity *in vitro*. Indigenous groups in the Colombian Amazon have harnessed the biological activity of several species of *Mayna*: a medicinal bath is made from the wood and leaves of *M. amazonica*, and the seed oil is used to treat skin disorders. The crushed and boiled leaves of *M. longifolia* are consumed as a toxic and therefore risky emetic, and the seeds and bark are mixed with foods to poison dogs and other animals.

Ryania, containing the potent alkaloid ryanodine, has been used as an insecticide. In parts of Amazonian Brazil, the leaves of *R. speciosa* (*capança*) are mixed with maize or other bait to kill birds that are agricultural pests.

The Flacourtiaceae yield a few woods with commercial value. One of them is *Homalium racemosum*, a primarily West Indian species, whose hard, durable wood has been used for cabinetry, flooring, furniture, boat frames, and other construction.

References. BERNHARD, A., AND P. K. ENDRESS. 1999. Androecial development and systematics in Flacourtiaceae s.l. *Pl. Syst. Evol.* 215:141–55. CHASE, M. W., S. ZMARZTY, M. D. LLEDO, K. J. WURDACK, S. M. SWENSEN, AND M. F. FAY. 2002. When in doubt, put it in *Flacourtiaceae*: a molecular phylogenetic analysis based on plastid *rbcL* DNA sequences. *Kew Bull.* 57:141–81. HOWE, H. F., AND R. B. PRIMACK. 1975. Differential seed dispersal by birds of the tree *Casearia nitida* (Flacourtiaceae). *Biotropica* 7:278–83. JUDD, W. S. 1997. The Flacourtiaceae in the Southeastern United States. *Harv. Pap. Bot.* 10:65–79. KLUCKING, E. P. 1992. *Leaf venation patterns*. Volume 6: Flacourtiaceae. Berlin: J. Cramer. LEMKE, D. E. 1988. A synopsis of Flacourtiaceae. *Aliso* 12:29–43. LOSOS, E. C. 1993. The influence of seed dispersal on primary forest succession in an Amazonian floodplain forest. Ph.D. dissertation, Princeton University. SCHULTES, R. E. 1977. De plantis toxicariis e mundo novo tropicale commentationes XVI. *Bot. Mus. Leafl.* 25:109–30. SLEUMER, H. 1980. Flacourtiaceae. *Fl. Neotrop. Monogr.* 22: 1–499. SOLTIS, D. E., P. S. SOLTIS, D. R. MORGAN, S. M. SWENSEN, B. C. MULLIN, ET AL. 1995. Chloroplast gene sequence data suggest a single origin of the predisposition for symbiotic nitrogen fixation in angiosperms. *Proc. Natl. Acad. Sci. U.S.A.* 92:2647–51. SNOW, D. W. 1981. Tropical frugivorous birds and their food plants: A survey. *Biotropica* 13:1–14. VAN DER PIJL, L. 1982. *Principles of Dispersal in Higher Plants*. 3rd ed. Heidelberg: Springer-Verlag.

FOUQUIERIACEAE (Ocotillo Family)

NATHAN SMITH

Figure 82

- *xerophytic shrubs or small trees, deciduous*

- *stems with petiolar spines; axillary short shoots often present*

- *leaves alternate, simple*

- *flowers sympetalous; corolla lobes 5, imbricate; stamens exserted*

- *fruits loculicidal capsules*

Numbers of genera and species. Worldwide, the Fouquieriaceae comprise a single genus, *Fouquieria*, and 11 species. In tropical America, there are eight species of *Fouquieria*.

Distribution and habitat. The Fouquieriaceae occur from the southwestern United States to southeastern Oaxaca, Mexico (*F. formosa*).

In tropical America, five species of *Fouquieria* occur in southern Mexico. *Fouquieria splendens* has the widest range in the family, growing from the southwestern United States to the Central Mexican Plateau where it just reaches the northern tropical limit. The remaining species are restricted to northwestern Mexico. Of the eight species found in tropical American, four species are considered narrow endemics.

Species of *Fouquieria* often grow in arid environments, from desert in the southwestern United States and northern Mexico to tropical deciduous forests and arid scrub of southeastern Mexico.

Family classification. The Fouquieriaceae are placed in the Violales by Cronquist. Some authors (e.g., Thorne and Dahlgren et al.) have suggested an affiliation with the Ericales

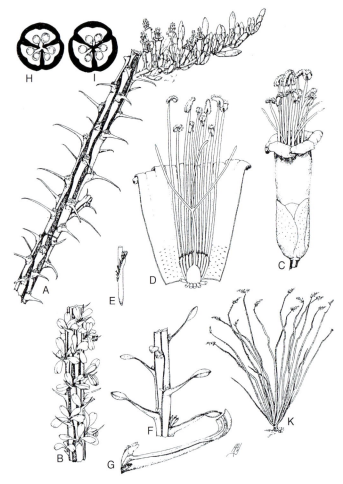

Figure 82. FOUQUIERIACEAE. *Fouquieria splendens*. **A.** Stem with spines and inflorescence (x½). **B.** Part of stem with short-shoot leaves (x½). **C.** Lateral view of flower (x2½). **D.** Flower opened to show stamens and gynoecium (x2½). **E.** Base of filament (x5). **F.** Stem with primary leaves, the petioles of which become spines (x½). **G.** Petiole of primary leaf (x1½). **H.** Schematic transverse section through upper part of ovary (x18). **I.** Schematic transverse section through lower part of ovary (x18). **K.** Plant showing habit (x¹⁄₆₀). Reprinted with permission from Cronquist (1981). Artist: Robin Jess.

quieria into subgenera *Fouquieria*, *Idria*, and *Bronnia*, a classification supported by recent molecular work.

Features of the family. Habit: xerophytic shrubs or small trees, deciduous, the base of trunk sometimes succulent, the stems often ridged, often containing chlorophyll; long or short shoots present, the long shoots with petiolar spines, the short shoots axillary. **Stipules** absent. **Leaves** alternate, simple, small, in fascicles on short shoots; petioles long on leaves of long shoots, the abaxial side developing into spine, the petioles short on leaves of short shoots; blade margins entire. **Inflorescences** terminal or subterminal, corymbosely paniculate, paniculate, racemose, or spicate; rachis often reddish pink, maroon, to dark purple, rarely green. **Flowers** actinomorphic, bisexual; calyx with 5 sepals, these distinct, imbricate, the outer 2 smaller than inner 3, thickened basally; corolla sympetalous, forming tube, the lobes 5, imbricate; androecium of 10–16(20) stamens, the stamens exserted, the filaments often pubescent above base, the anthers dorsifixed; gynoecium syncarpous, the ovary superior, basally nectariferous, the carpels 3, the locule 1 (often appearing as 3 because of parietal placentae extending nearly to center of ovary), the style 1, 3-branched, the stigmas terminal; placentation parietal for most of ovary, axile basally, the ovules 6–16(20). **Fruits** loculicidal capsules, subtended by persistent sepals. **Seeds** 3–13(18) per fruit, winged.

Natural history. Pollinators of *Fouquieria* range from hummingbirds and pearching birds to insects. Hummingbirds are the most likely pollinators of red-flowered species. Bees have been observed visiting the flowers of many species, and carpenter bees and bumblebees have been seen robbing nectar.

No information is available about dispersal; however, the winged seeds suggest dispersal by wind.

Economic uses The habit of *Fouquieria splendens* and the presence of spines and colorful red flowers has made this species desirable for hedges, fences, and general landscaping. The stems of some species (e.g., *F. splendens*) are used locally to make wax.

References. HENRICKSON, J. 1972. A taxonomic revision of the Fouquieriaceae. *Aliso* 7(4):439–537. NEDOFF, J. A., I. P. TING, AND E. M. LORD. 1985. Structure and function of the green stem tissue in ocotillo (*Fouquieria splendens*). *Amer. J. Bot.* 72(1):143–51. SCHULTHEIS, L. M., AND B. G. BALDWIN. 1999. Molecular phylogenetics of Fouquieriaceae: evidence from nuclear *r*DNA its studies. *Amer. J. Bot.* 86(4): 578–89. ZAMUDIO, P. S. 1995. Fouquieriaceae. In *Flora del Bajio y de Regiones Adyacentes*, eds. J. Rzedowski and G. C. de Rzedowski, fasc. 36:1–7. Pátzcuaro, México: Instituto de Ecología, A.C.

because of similarities in anther connectives, endosperm, connate petals, and the presence of iridoid compounds. Based on differences in wood anatomy, number of ovule integuments, and quantity of endosperm, Takhtajan places the Fouquieriaceae close to the Ericales in its own order, the Fouquieriales. Recent molecular studies have suggested the Fouquieriaceae are a sister family to the Polemoniaceae, within or near the Ericales.

Traditionally, some authors have divided the family into two genera, *Fouquieria* and the extratropical monotypic genus, *Idria* (=*F. columnaria*). Other authors have split *Fou-*

FRANKENIACEAE (Frankenia Family)

NATHAN SMITH

- *shrubs or subshrubs, usually halophytic*

- *salt glands present on stems, leaves, and calyces*

- *leaves opposite, decussate, simple, small; blade margins revolute*

- *flowers actinomorphic, usually bisexual; petals clawed*

- *fruits loculicidal capsules, surrounded by persistent calyx*

Numbers of genera and species. Worldwide, the Frankeniaceae comprise two genera and approximately 70 species. In the Western Hemisphere, there is a single genus, *Frankenia*, with 14 species. Four species of *Frankenia* occur in tropical America.

Distribution and habitat. The Frankeniaceae are discontinuously cosmopolitan. The family is most diverse in the Mediterranean region, but also occurs in Africa, Australia, Eurasia, and the Americas. *Hypericopis* is endemic to southern Iran.

In tropical America, species of *Frankenia* are found in arid, semiarid, and marine shore habitats. *Frankenia chilensis* is a more or less coastal species, occurring in southern Peru and northern Chile; *F. triandra*, an inland species, is also found in southern Peru and northern Chile, as well as northwestern Argentina and the *puna* of Bolivia, where it grows between 3,350 and 4,800 meters elevation; *F. gypsophila* is restricted to the southeastern Chihuahuan Desert in sections of Nuevo León, San Luis Potosí, and Zacatecas, Mexico, between 1,600 and 2,200 meters elevation; and *F. margaritae* is endemic to Nuevo León, where it occurs at around 1,900 meters.

Frankenia gypsophila is thought to be restricted to gypseous soils. The remaining species in tropical American are commonly found on saline soils.

Family classification. The Frankeniaceae are placed in the Violales by Cronquist, near the Tamaricaceae. Takhtajan aligns these two families in his Tamaricales. Recent molecular studies support the Tamaricaceae as the sister family to the Frankeniaceae and place these families within the Caryophyllales.

Cronquist recognized a third genus in the family, *Anthobryum*; however, some authors consider *Anthobryum* to be synonymous with *Frankenia triandra*, a classification accepted here.

Features of the family. Habit: shrubs or subshrubs, usually halophytic (gypsophilous in *Frankenia gypsophila*), the shrubs sprawling or upright, sometimes caespitose, the subshrubs cushion plants in *F. triandra*; short shoots sometimes present; salt glands present on stems, leaves, and calyces. **Indument** often present on stems and leaves; trichomes simple, unicellular. **Stipules** absent. **Leaves** opposite, decussate, simple, small, the leaf pairs united by sheathing membranous petioles or blades; petioles absent in *F. gypsophila* and *F. margaritae*; leaf sheath extending along petiole margins in petiolate species, sometimes ciliolate; blades usually sclerophyllous, decurrent in expetiolate species, the base lobed in *F. gypsophila*, the margins entire, revolute, often ciliolate (at least at apices). **Inflorescences** terminal or axillary, solitary or in few- to many-flowered dichasia; bracts 2 and distinct (*F. triandra*) or 4 and basally connate, subtending flowers, leaflike; peduncles absent except in *F. chilensis*; pedicels absent. **Flowers** actinomorphic, bisexual or unisexual in *F. triandra* (plants gynodioecious); calyx synsepalous, tubular or campanulate to urceolate in *F. triandra*, the lobes 4–5(6); corolla with 4–5(6) petals, the petals distinct, imbricate, clawed, usually white, sometimes pink or purple-pink (often only basally); ligule or scalelike appendage present adaxially at petal base; androecium with 3–6(8) stamens, the anthers dorsifixed, often orange-red; staminodes 3–5 in pistillate flowers of *F. triandra*; gynoecium with superior ovary, the ovary usually trigonous, the carpels 1 in *F. margaritae* or 3 and united, the locule 1, the style filiform, unbranched in *F. margaritae* or the branches 3; placentation basal-parietal, the ovules 1 in *F. margaritae* or 3–ca. 100. **Fruits** loculicidal capsules, surrounded by persistent calyx. **Seeds** 1–8(40) per fruit, brown to golden brown in *F. chilensis*, white, or yellow; endosperm starchy, the embryo straight.

Natural history. Salt glands often cause a conspicuous layer of salt crystals to form on the stems and leaves of Frankeniaceae. These glands probably help reduce transpiration rates, absorb water vapor, and increase the reflection of light.

Little is known about the pollination and dispersal biology of tropical American *Frankenia*.

Economic uses. In Chile, *Frankenia salina* is used as a source of salt. In Macaronesia, *F. ericifolia* has been used as a fish poison. *Frankenia laevis* (sea-heath) is occasionally used as an ornamental.

References. KUBITZKI, K. 2003. Frankeniaceae. In *The Families and Genera of Vascular Plants*, eds. K Kubitzki and C. Bayer. 5:209–12. Berlin: Springer-Verlag. WHALEN, M. A. 1987a. Wood anatomy of the American frankenias (Frankeniaceae): systematic and evolutionary implications. *Amer. J. Bot.* 74:1211–23. WHALEN, M. A. 1987b. Systematics of *Frankenia* (Frankeniaceae) in North and South America. *Syst. Bot. Mongr.* 17:1–93.

GARRYACEAE (Silk Tassel or Garrya Family)

THOMAS A. ZANONI

- *trees and shrubs*

- *leaves opposite, decussate, simple; petiole bases connate*

- *inflorescences catkinlike or racemose*

- *flowers unisexual (the plants dioecious)*

- *fruits berries*

Numbers of genera and species. The Garryaceae include *Garrya* with 14 species. In tropical America, there are 12 species of *Garrya*.

Distribution and habitat. The Garryaceae are restricted to the Western Hemisphere. The eight species of *Garrya* subgenus *Fadyenia* are found from Mexico to Guatemala, Costa Rica, Panama, and the Greater Antilles (Cuba, Jamaica, and Hispaniola), where they occur in semiarid highlands, often in the understory of pine forests, and in damp or humid habitats, up to 3,800 meters. Species of *Garrya* subgenus *Garrya* (six species) are found in western North America, from Washington to Baja California and eastward to Texas, *including* one outlier species in the mountains of Guatemala. They occur in semiarid highlands in chaparral and conifer forests.

Family classification. The Garryaceae are placed in the Cornales by Cronquist. *Garrya* is subdivided into subgenus *Garrya* and subgenus *Fadyenia*. Recent molecular studies indicate that the Garryaceae are related to *Aucuba* (Aucubaceae or within Cornaceae *sensu* Cronquist) and are among the basal families of the "Euasterids I."

Features of the family. Habit: trees or shrubs, evergreen. Trunks often several, arising from base. Stipules absent. Leaves opposite, decussate, simple, coriaceous, often pubescent, the trichomes simple; petiole bases connate; blade margins entire to subentire. Inflorescences terminal, sometimes axillary (subgenus *Garrya*), catkinlike or racemose, pendulous (subgenus *Fadyenia*), branched (subgenus *Fadyenia*); bracts present (in catkinlike inflorescences), opposite, decussate; flowers axile to bracts, (1)2 or 3(4) per cluster. Flowers inconspicuous, unisexual (the plants dioecious), green. Staminate flowers: tepals 4, apically connate, arched over stamens; stamens 4. Pistillate flowers: appendages 2 (=reduced perianth), basal to styles, vestigial or absent, the styles 2(3); ovary inferior, compound, the carpels 2(3), the locule 1; placentation parietal, the ovules 2(3), pendulous, anatropous. Fruits berries, persistent on plant, subglobose, fleshy or dry and brittle (at and after maturation), often with persistent perianth. Seeds (1)2(3), hard; endosperm abundant, the cotyledons 2.

Natural history. Species of Garryaceae are wind-pollinated. Wood rats have been observed eating the fruits of species in the southwestern United States.

Economic uses. Several North American species are used as ornamental shrubs (e.g., *Garrya elliptica*, *G. fremontii*, and *G. veatchii*). The bark has been used in traditional medicine; e.g., as an antidiarrhetic in Mexico.

References. DAHLING, G. V. 1978. Systematics and evolution of *Garrya*. *Contr. Gray Herb.* 209:1–104. DANIEL, T. F. 1993. Garryaceae. In *The Jepson Manual: Higher Plants of California*, ed. J. S. Hickman, 664, 666. Berkeley, CA: University of California Press. EYDE, R. H. 1964. Inferior ovary and genetic affinities of *Garrya*. *Amer. J. Bot.* 51:1083–92. MOSELY JR., M. F., AND R. M. BEEKS. 1955. Studies of the Garryaceae I. The comparative morphology and phylogeny. *Phytomorphology* 5:314–46. MULLIGAN, B. O. 1980. A revision of the genus Garrya. *Arbor. Bull., Washington* 43:39. NOSHIRO, S., AND P. BAAS. 1998. Systematic wood anatomy of Cornaceae and allies. *IAWA J.* 19:43–97.

GELSEMIACEAE (Carolina Jessamine Family)

LENA STRUWE AND VICTOR A. ALBERT

Figure 83

- *shrubs, small trees, or twining vines*

- *leaves opposite, simple*

- *flowers usually heterostylous, the stigmas twice dichotomously divided; corolla funnel-shaped, usually yellow or white*

- *fruits capsules*

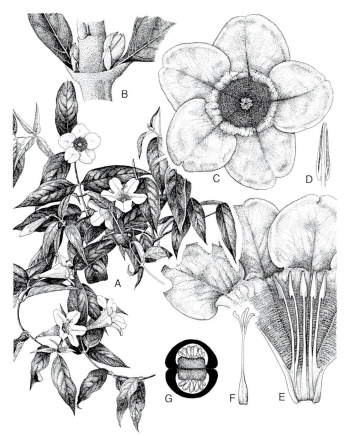

Figure 83. GELSEMIACEAE. *Gelsemium sempervirens* **A.** Stems with leaves and inflorescences (x½). **B.** Detail of node showing stipules (x8). **C.** Apical view of flower (x2). **D.** Abaxial view of anther (x4). **E.** Corolla opened to show adnate stamens (x2). **F.** Lateral view of gynoecium (x2). **G.** Schematic transverse section of ovary (x16). Reprinted with permission from Cronquist (1981). Artist: William S. Moye.

Numbers of genera and species. Worldwide, the Gelsemiaceae comprise two genera and 11 species, *Gelsemium* with three species and *Mostuea* with eight species. In tropical America, there are two species of *Gelsemium* and a single species of *Mostuea*.

Distribution and habitat. *Mostuea surinamensis* occurs in rain forests in the Guianas. The remaining species of *Mostuea* occur in tropical Africa and Madagascar. *Gelsemium* has a primarily subtropical distribution with *G. sempervirens* and *G. rankinii* present in mainly wet forests and scrub in southernmost United States, Mexico, and Guatemala. The remaining species of *Gelsemium* occurs in tropical southeast Asia.

Family classification. The Gelsemiaceae are placed in the Gentianales. The family had earlier been included in Loganiaceae (Gentianales *sensu* Cronquist) as tribe Gelsemieae, but its position as a separate family in the order Gentianales is supported by molecular and morphological phylogenetic

analyses. The relationships of Gelsemiaceae to other families in the Gentianales are still unclear, but the family appears close to the Apocynaceae in some studies.

Features of the family. Habit: shrubs, small trees, or twining vines, glabrous or pubescent; colleters (fingerlike glands) are common in leaf axils and inner base of the calyx. **Stipules** present and small or represented only by lines, interpetiolar. **Leaves** opposite, simple; blade margins entire or slightly dentate. **Inflorescences** usually axillary and 1–few-flowered. **Flowers** actinomorphic, bisexual, heterostylous; sepals 5, distinct or fused at base, often with colleters at adaxial base, persistent in fruit; corolla sympetalous, funnel-shaped, yellow or white, rarely orange, red, or lilac, the lobes 5, short, rounded, imbricate; androecium of 5 stamens, the stamens inserted in corolla tube, the anthers latrorse; gynoecium syncarpous, the ovary superior, glabrous or pubescent, the carpels 2, the locules 2, the style long, the stigma twice dichotomously divided, the lobes narrow; placentation axile, the ovules 1–many. **Fruits** dry capsules, usually bilobed and flattened in *Mostuea*. **Seeds** 1–many, often flattened, pubescent (*Mostuea*), sometimes winged (*Gelsemium sempervirens*); endosperm starchy or bony, the embryo small.

Natural history. No information is available about pollination and dispersal biology.

Economic uses. Species of *Gelsemium* are poisonous and deadly if consumed in high doses, causing paralysis and respiratory failure. The dried rhizome of *G. sempervirens* has been used in pharmacology for the last few centuries in the Americas, mainly to reduce fevers and as a sedative. In Mexico and China, species of *Gelsemium* have been used to combat fevers and spasms and as a sedative, an analgesic, and a "criminal poison." *Mostuea* has been used in Africa as a stimulant; to expel parasitic worms; for healing wounds; and to treat toothaches, colds, and stomach upsets. Both *Gelsemium* and *Mostuea* contain indole alkaloids of the C-17-type (e.g., gelsemine and sempervirine), which are similar to those found in Apocynaceae and Rubiaceae.

References. BACKLUND, M., B. OXELMAN, AND B. BREMER. 2000. Phylogenetic relationships within the Gentianales base on *ndh*F and *rbc*L sequences, with particular reference to the Loganiaceae. *Am. J. Bot.* 87:1029–43. BISSET, N. G. 1980a. Phytochemistry. In *Die Natürlichen Pflanzenfamilien*, 2nd ed., Angiospermae: Ordnung Gentianales, Fam. Loganiaceae, A. Engler and K. Prantl, 28b(1):211–33. Berlin: Duncker and Humblot. BISSET, N. G. 1980b. Useful plants. In *Die Natürlichen Pflanzenfamilien*, 2nd ed., Angiospermae: Ordnung Gentianales, Fam. Loganiaceae, A. Engler and K. Prantl, 28b(1):238–44. Berlin: Duncker and Humblot. GRIEVE, M. 1931. *A Modern Herbal*. Vol. 1. London: J. Cape. LEEUWENBERG, A.J.M. 1961. The Loganiaceae of Africa II. A revision of *Mostuea. Meded. Landbouwhogeschool* 61:1–31. LEEUWENBERG, A.J.M., ed. 1980. *Die Natürlichen Pflanzenfamilien*, 2nd ed., Angiospermae: Ordnung Gentianales, Fam. Loganiaceae 28b(1). Berlin: Duncker and Humblot. STRUWE, L., AND V. A. ALBERT. 1997. Floristics, cladistics, and classification: three case studies in Gentianales. In *Plant diversity in Malesia III*, eds. J. Dransfield, M.J.E. Coode, and D. A. Simpson, 321–52. Richmond, Surrey, U.K.: Royal Botanic Gardens, Kew. STRUWE, L., V. A. AL-

BERT, AND B. BREMER. 1994 [1995]. Cladistics and family level classification of the Gentianales. *Cladistics* 10:175–206. WYATT, R., S. B. BROYLES, J. L. HAMRICK, AND A. STONEBURNER. 1993. Systematic relationships within *Gelsemium* (Loganiaceae): evidence from isozymes and cladistics. *Syst. Bot.* 18:345–55.

GENTIANACEAE (Gentian Family)

LENA STRUWE AND VICTOR A. ALBERT

Figure 84, Plate 22

- *usually herbs, sometimes shrubs or small trees*

- *leaves usually opposite, simple; blade margins entire*

- *colleters present in leaf axils and adaxial base of calyx*

- *flower corolla sympetalous, commonly with contort aestivation; stamens inserted in corolla; ovary superior*

- *fruits usually capsules*

Numbers of genera and species. Worldwide, the Gentianaceae comprise at least 87 genera and about 1,650 species. In tropical America, there are about 45 genera and about 450 species. Generic circumscriptions, especially in the *Centaurium*, *Gentiana*, *Gentianella*, and *Irlbachia* complexes, are still being debated.

Distribution and habitat. Species of Gentianaceae are present on all continents except Antarctica; they are, however, present on the subantarctic islands. The majority of the herbaceous species are present in temperate and mountainous areas such as the Andes and the Himalayas, while the woody taxa are tropical. In the Western Hemisphere, the highest generic diversity is found on the Guayana Shield in northern South America, but species are also abundant in the Andes, the West Indies, the Brazilian Highlands, and Central America (including Mexico).

The Neotropical species of Gentianaceae can be divided into three informal groups: (1) the montane and alpine herbs of the Andes and Central America, (2) the lowland herbs (widespread or restricted to specific habitats such as white-sand savannas), and (3) a mostly (semi-) woody species group with distributions usually restricted to highland and tropical montane areas or islands in the Caribbean. Species of the first group are present in temperate areas of southernmost South America and along the Andes through Central America into North America. This group includes *Gentiana*, *Gentianella*, and *Halenia* (tribe Gentianeae), which are related to

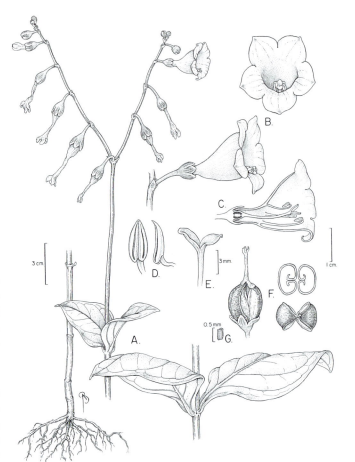

Figure 84. GENTIANACEAE. *Chelonanthus alatus*. **A.** Apex of stem with leaves and terminal inflorescence (center), base of plant showing leaf scars and roots (left), and paired leaves from midsection of stem (lower right). **B.** Apical (above) and lateral (below) views of flower. **C.** Medial section of flower. **D.** Adaxial (left) and lateral (right) views of anthers. **E.** Apex of style with bilobed stigma. **F.** Lateral view of fruit with persistent style (left); transverse section of ovary (above right) and apical view (below right) of fruit. **G.** Seed. Reprinted with permission from Mori et al. (2002). Artist: Bobbi Angell.

genera from other temperate and montane areas (Himalayas, North America, Europe, etc.). The second group contains many lowland tropical herbs; e.g., species of *Centaurium*, *Coutoubea*, *Sabatia*, and *Eustoma* (tribe Chironieae) and *Curtia* (tribe Saccifolieae), which are related to species of other tropical and subtropical regions. The third group consists of two phylogenetically distinct woody or subwoody elements, the tribe Helieae (*Chelonanthus, Irlbachia, Macrocarpaea, Symbolanthus*, etc.), endemic to the neotropics, and tribe Potalieae (*Potalia, Lisianthius*, and some additional Paleotropical genera). The herbaceous genera *Enicostema* and *Neurotheca* also belong to the Potalieae.

The gentians of the neotropics show a high degree of endemicity, especially those species restricted to *tepuis* (flat-topped mountains on the Guayana Shield), the Brazilian highland, lowland white-sand savannas, and the Andes.

Family classification. The Gentianaceae are placed in the Gentianales by Cronquist. A comprehensive tribal and subtribal classification of Gentianaceae was published by Gilg in 1895, and was based on pollen characters. Gilg classified the family into six tribes: Exaceae (Paleotropical), Helieae (Neotropical), Voyrieae and Leiphameae (Neotropical saprophytes), Rusbyantheae (monotypic, Neotropical), and Gentianeae (the largest, cosmopolitan). The tribe Gentianeae was further subdivided into several subtribes, Erythraeinae (cosmopolitan), Gentianinae (many montane species), and Tachiinae (mainly Neotropical). This classification has been considered unnatural for a long time and is inconsistent with recent phylogenetic results.

A new classification, primarily based on molecular studies, indicates that six major clades are present in the Gentianaceae and that the Neotropical taxa are dispersed among at least five of these. In this system, six tribes are accepted: Chironieae, Exaceae, Gentianeae, Helieae, Potalieae, and Saccifolieae. Compared to Gilg's classification, this new system identifies more natural groups in the family. The tribe Potalieae (three woody pantropical genera) has been moved back and forth between the Loganiaceae and Gentianaceae, but is now confidently included in Gentianaceae.

The Menyanthaceae have been included in Gentianaceae but have been shown to be more closely related to Campanulaceae and associated families. Finally, *Saccifolium bandeirae*, the only species of the Neotropical Saccifoliaceae and an endemic to Sierra de la Neblina, at the border of Amazonian Brazil and Venezuela, is now included in the tribe Saccifolieae, which is considered the most basal group in Gentianaceae.

Features of the family. Habit: small annual herbs (*Curtia* and *Coutoubea*), achlorophyllous, saprophytic herbs (*Voyria* and *Voyriella*), perennial herbs (*Chelonanthus*, many *Gentiana* and *Gentianella*, and *Lisianthius*), shrubs or small understory rain-forest or cloud-forest trees (*Macrocarpaea, Potalia,* and *Symbolanthus*); colleters (small fingerlike, multicellular glands) present in leaf axils and adaxial base of calyx, the colleters secrete a resin that protects the developing buds and stem apices. **Stipules** absent but most genera with an interpetiolar line or low ocrea connecting leaf bases. **Leaves** usually opposite, alternate in *Saccifolium, Voyria,* and *Voyriella*, simple, scalelike (*Voyria* and *Voyriella*); blades often

coriaceous, flat (saccate in *Saccifolium*), the margins entire or rarely dentate. **Inflorescences** usually terminal or axillary, dichotomously branched cymes (sometimes with partly monochasial branches), spikes (*Coutoubea*), more rarely racemes, or of solitary flowers (*Saccifolium* and most *Tachia*). **Flowers** usually actinomorphic, bisexual, 4–5-merous (rarely 6–8-merous in *Chorisepalum*, some *Gentiana*, and some *Sabatia*, or 8–10-merous in *Potalia*); calyx tubular, short or long, fused at base (rarely distinct; e.g., *Chorisepalum* and *Potalia*), often with glandular ridges or wings, persistent or deciduous in fruit; corollas sympetalous, often showy and brightly colored, tubular, salverform, funnelform, or rotate, the lobes contort to the right (partly valvate in *Aripuana*, imbricate in *Bartonia, Obolaria,* and *Saccifolium*); androecium with stamens equal to corolla lobes, the stamens usually distinct (filaments united in *Potalia*), inserted in corolla tube or in sinuses of corolla lobes, the anthers introrse, rarely latrorse or extrorse, distinct (connate in *Hockinia* and some species of *Curtia, Gentiana,* and *Tapeinostemon*), sometimes versatile (*Gentianella* and *Coutoubea*), helically curved (*Centaurium*), or recurved backward (e.g., *Chelonanthus, Symbolanthus*) after anthesis; gynoecium syncarpous, the ovary superior, often with glandular disc at base, the carpels 2, the locules 1–2, the stigma capitate, simple, or bilamellate; placentation parietal and axile (often transformations between both types in same individuals), the ovules usually numerous. **Fruits** capsules, berries (*Anthocleista, Fagraea, Potalia,* and some species of *Chironia,* and *Tripterospermum*), or indehiscent and dry, the capsules usually dry, dehiscing along the sutures apically or medially, rarely 4-valvate (*Chorisepalum*), or coriaceous-fleshy (*Symbolanthus*). **Seeds** usually numerous, angular to rounded, sometimes winged, usually very small; endosperm present, the embryo small.

The family contains seco-iridoids and xanthones as secondary phytochemical compounds.

Voyria and *Voyriella*, are white, bluish, pink, or yellow achlorophyllous saprophytes. They are small herbs with scale-like leaves that grow on the rain-forest floor.

Natural history. Insects pollinate most Gentianaceae, but few detailed pollination studies have addressed the Neotropical gentians. The flowers of *Macrocarpaea, Rogersonanthus,* and *Symbolanthus* may be bat-pollinated (large corolla tube openings, greenish color, and a floral nectary); this has been reported for *Chelonanthus alatus*. Other species have flowers that could be hummingbird-pollinated (e.g., species of *Lagenanthus* and *Lehmanniella*). The long, narrow, tubular flowers of *Aripuana* could be hawkmoth-pollinated.

Wind or rainwash probably spreads the seeds of the capsular species, whereas animals presumably disperse the seeds of species with berries.

The hollow stems of *Tachia* often are inhabited by ants. Many species of Gentianaceae have mycorrhizae.

Economic uses. A few species of Gentianaceae are used in commercial horticulture; e.g., *Eustoma grandiflorum* (prairie gentian or lisianthus) as a cut flower, *Exacum affine* (Persian violet) as a pot plant, and many species of *Gentiana* (gentian) as rock-garden ornamentals. The family has important pharmacological uses in traditional medicine worldwide. Extracts are used to combat inflammations, fevers (e.g., malaria), fungal diseases, and gastrointestinal problems. The active compounds are the very bitter seco-iridoids and xanthones, most of which are unique to the family. Pharmacologically, the most commonly used genera are *Centaurium*, *Gentiana*, *Gentianella*, and *Swertia*, which are found mostly in the northern temperate regions. *Potalia* is the most widely used gentian in the neotropics, where it provides treatments for snake bites, poisonings, inflammations, fevers, and syphilis. *Tachia* is used to treat malaria.

References. BACKLUND, M., B. OXELMAN, AND B. BREMER. 2000. Phylogenetic relationships within the Gentianales base on *ndh*F and *rbc*L sequences, with particular reference to the Loganiaceae. *Amer. J. Bot.* 87:1029–43. BISSET, N. G. 1980. Useful plants. Pp. 238–244 in A. Engler and K. Prantl's *Die Natürlichen Pflanzenfamilien*, Angiospermae: Ordnung Gentianales, Fam. Loganiaceae, 28b(1):238–44. Berlin: Duncker and Humblot. CORRERA Q., J. E., AND H. Y. BERNAL. 1993. Gentianceae. In *Especies vegetales promisorias de los países del Convenio Andrés Bello*, Tomo IX. Santafé de Bogotá, D. E., Colombia: Secretaria Ejecutiva del Convenio Andrés Bello. GILG, E. 1895. Gentianaceae. In *Die Natürlichen Pflanzenfamilien*, eds. A. Engler and K. Prantl, vol. 4(2):50–108. Leipzig: Verlag von Wilhelm Engelmann. JENSEN, S. R., AND J. SHRIPSEMA. 2002. Chemotaxonomy and pharmacology of Gentianaceae. In *Gentianaceae—Systematics and Natural History*, eds. L. Struwe and V. A. Albert, 573–631. Cambridge, U.K.: Cambridge University Press. MACHADO, I.C.S., I. SAZIMA, AND M. SAZIMA. 1998. Bat pollination of the terrestrial herb *Irlbachia alata* (Gentianaceae) in northeastern Brazil. *Pl. Syst. Evol.* 209:231–37. MAGUIRE, B. 1981. Gentianaceae. In The Botany of the Guayana Highland—Part XI, eds. B. Maguire and collaborators. *Mem. New York Bot. Gard.* 32:330–88. MAGUIRE, B., AND J. M. PIRES. 1978. Saccifoliaceae—a new monotypic family of the Gentianales. In The Botany of the Guayana Highland—Part X, eds. B. Maguire and collaborators. *Mem. New York Bot. Gard.* 29:230–45. PRINGLE, J. S. 1995. Gentianaceae. In *Flora of Ecuador*, eds. G. Harling and L. Andersson, no. 53:1–131. Göteborg: Department of Systematic Botany, Göteborg University. STRUWE, L. 1999. *Morphological and Molecular Phylogenetic Studies in Neotropical Gentianaceae*. Stockholm, Sweden: Stockholm University. STRUWE, L., V. A. ALBERT, AND B. BREMER. 1994 [1995]. Cladistics and family level classification of the Gentianales. *Cladistics* 10:175–206. STRUWE, L., J. KADEREIT, J. KLACKENBERG, S. NILSSON, M. THIV, K. B. VON HAGEN, AND V. A. ALBERT. 2002. Systematics, character evolution, and biogeography of Gentianaceae, including a new tribal and subtribal classification. In *Gentianaceae—Systematics and Natural History*, eds. L. Struwe and V. A. Albert, 21–309. Cambridge, U.K.: Cambridge University Press. STRUWE, L., P.J.M. MAAS, O. PIHLAR, AND V. A. ALBERT. 1999. Gentianaceae. In *Flora of the Venezuelan Guayana*, eds. P. E. Berry, K. Yatskievych, and B. K. Holst, 5:474–542. St. Louis, MO: Missouri Botanical Garden Press. THIV, M., L. STRUWE, V. A. ALBERT, AND J. W. KADEREIT. 1999. The phylogenetic relationships of *Saccifolium bandeirae* Maguire & Pires (Gentianaceae) reconsidered. *Harvard Pap. Bot.* 4:519–26.

GERANIACEAE (Geranium Family)

ERNEST T. DeMARIE

Figure 85

- *usually herbs, sometimes woody*

- *plants often producing aromatic oils*

- *stipules usually present*

- *leaves alternate or occasionally opposite, simple, often palmately lobed or trifid*

- *flowers actinomorphic or zygomorphic in* Erodium; *ovary superior, often lobed or grooved; placentation axile*

- *fruits usually schizocarps composed of 5 mericarps, sometimes capsules*

Number of genera and species. Worldwide, the Geraniaceae comprise as many as 14 genera and 700 species. In the Western Hemisphere, there are at least five genera with the vast majority of species (about 100) belonging to *Geranium*. *Erodium* contains few Neotropical species, but several adventive species of the Eastern Hemisphere are naturalized in the region. Other genera of the Western Hemisphere are *Balbisia* (8 species, at least 2 Neotropical), *Rhynchotheca* (1 species endemic to tropical South America), *Viviania* (6), and *Wendtia* (3). In tropical America, there are five genera (*Balbisia*, *Erodium*, *Geranium*, *Hypseocharis*, and *Rynchotheca*) and 75–125 species.

African Geraniaceae have been well studied, but in the

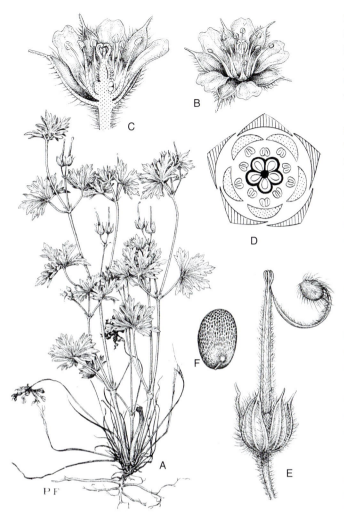

Figure 85. GERANIACEAE. *Geraniuim carolinianum*. **A.** Plant showing roots, leaves, and fruits (x⅔). **B.** Apical view of flower (x4). **C.** Medial section of flower (x6). **D.** Floral diagram. **E.** Lateral view of fruit (x4). **F.** Seed (x8). Reprinted with permission from Correll and Correll (1982). Artist: Priscilla Fawcett.

Western Hemisphere further work is needed on all of the taxa south of the United States in order to clarify species limits and to develop a consensus for the familial placement of all genera other than *Geranium* and *Erodium*.

Distribution and habitat. The Geraniaceae are most numerous in temperate and subtropical areas of the world, with a major concentration of genera and species in southern Africa. Species of *Geranium* are found on all continents except Antarctica, but are most common in temperate regions. Nevertheless, subtropical and tropical species occur on oceanic islands (Hawaii, New Zealand) and in tropical montains. *Pelargonium* is primarily African, but some adventive species may have become naturalized in the neotropics. *Erodium*, like *Geranium*, is cosmopolitan, but has few species in the Western Hemisphere. Most species of *Erodium* encountered

in the neotropics appear to be naturalized adventives. Several smaller, and often controversial, genera are often included in the Geraniaceae, such as *Rhynchotheca* (Andean South America), *Balbisia* (Andean South America from Peru to Chile), *Hypseocharis* (Peru to Chile), *Viviania* (southern Brazil to Chile), and *Wendtia* (Chile and Argentina).

Geraniaceae are found in many habitats, but rarely occur in hot and humid lowlands or very dense forest. Some Neotropical species of *Erodium*, *Balbisia*, and *Geranium* occur in seasonally arid areas. Most species of *Geranium* occur as montane plants; e.g., many of the Central American species inhabit oak/pine forests while others are found in *páramo*. Neotropical Geraniaceae usually occur at high altitudes, and include a number of cushion-forming species of *Geranium* on the Andean plateau and in the *páramos* of Central and South America. *Rhynchotheca* occurs in the *altiplano* and *páramo* areas of Peru and Ecuador; *Balbisia* is usually found in sclerophyllous vegetation from Peru through Chile; and *Hypseocharis* is found in open montane areas.

Family classification. The Geraniaceae are placed in the order Geraniales by Cronquist. *Erodium*, *Geranium*, *Monsonia*, *Pelargonium*, and *Sarcocaulon* comprise the subfamily Geranieae and represent a natural group. The subfamily Wendtiae includes the Western Hemisphere genera *Wendtia*, *Rynchotheca*, and *Balbisia*. The remaining genera are not closely related to each other. Further study may demonstrate that most of these, as well as the genera of Wendtiae, *Dirachma*, and *Viviania*, should be excluded from the Geraniaceae. Molecular studies of the chloroplast gene *rbc*L indicate that the Geraniaceae should exclude the problematic genera of the Western Hemisphere, and include *Hypseocharis*, a genus traditionally placed in the Oxalidaceae (*sensu* Cronquist).

Molecular data suggest that Geraniales should include only Geraniaceae *sensu stricto* (*Erodium*, *Geranium*, *Pelargonium*, *Sarcocaulon*, *Hypseocharis*, and *Bieberstinia* of the Eastern Hemisphere). For the most, data from the study of seed structure supports this classification.

Features of the family. Habit: small to midsized herbs (*Geranium*, *Erodium*, and *Hypseocharis*) or sometimes woody shrubs (*Rhynchotheca* and *Balbisia*), erect or creeping, solitary or colonial, sometimes forming dense cushions (many *Geranium*), often with thickened roots; lateral branchlet apices forming spines in *Rhynchotheca*. Indumentum: multicellular, capitate-glandular trichomes often present, these often producing aromatic oils. Stipules present except in *Hypseocharis*. Leaves alternate, occasionally opposite (*Rhynchotheca*, *Balbisia*), simple; blades usually palmately lobed, occasionally pinnatifid (*Erodium*, *Hypseocharis*), typically trifid in *Rhynchotheca* and *Balbisia*, rarely unlobed in some *Rhynchotheca*, the margins incised or serrate. Inflorescences axillary, cymes or occasionally of solitary flowers, rarely terminal fascicles (*Rhynchotheca*). Flowers actinomorphic, sometimes zygomorphic (*Erodium*), bisexual or rarely unisexual (staminate and bisexual in *Rhynchotheca*), often showy; epicalyx present in *Balbisia*; sepals 5, usually connate; petals 5 (0 in *Rhynchotheca*), distinct, often shades of blue or purple, sometimes red or yellow; nectaries alternate with petals (absent in *Rhynchotheca* and *Balbisia*); androecium usually with 10 (15 in *Hypseocharis*) stamens, the stamens in 2–3 whorls (1 in *Balbisia*), the outer whorl sometimes reduced to staminodes (*Erodium*), the filaments usually basally connate, the anthers dehiscing longitudinally; gynoecium syncarpous, the ovary superior, often lobed or grooved, the carpels 5 (3 in *Balbisia)*, the locules 5 or 3 (*Balbisia*), the style solitary, the stigmas distinct, usually 5; placentation axile, the ovules 2 (2 rows of many in *Balbisia* and *Hypseocharis*) per carpel (1 sometimes not functional). **Fruits** schizocarps or loculicidal capsules in *Balbisia* and *Hypseocharis*, a beaked dehiscent capsule in *Rhynchotheca*, the schizocarps with 5 mericarps, the mericarps separate from persistent elongate column in *Geranium* and *Erodium*. **Seeds** 1 per mericarp or many per capsule (*Balbisia*); endosperm usually absent.

Some Andean *altiplano* and *páramo* species of *Geranium* form dense, often colonial cushions, and other species of *Geranium* spread by means of above-ground runners, which readily form adventitious roots. Species of *Hypseocharis* are acaulescent herbs with leaves displayed in a rosette and thickened roots; species of *Rhynchotheca* are small to large, usually spiny, shrubs or small trees; and species of *Balbisia* are small shrubs with small, densely pubescent, dissected foliage, and large showy yellow flowers.

Natural history. Most species of Geraniaceae are self-fertile, but this is not always the case. Little research has been done on the pollination of the family, but bees are known to pollinate some species of *Geranium*. No information is available about dispersal biology.

Economic uses. *Pelargonium* (geranium), *Geranium* (crane's bill, geranium), and, to a lesser extent, *Erodium* (stork's bill),

have contributed numerous ornamental species and hybrids to horticulture. *Sarcocaulon* is increasingly popular among succulent enthusiasts, and some species of *Monsonia* are in limited cultivation among collectors of Geraniaceae in North America, Europe, and South Africa.

The Geraniaceae of Neotropical America are barely known in horticulture, but many species of *Geranium* from this area are very attractive and merit consideration for use as ornamentals. Occasionally, some of the smaller South American species of *Geranium*, along with species of *Wendtia* and *Viviania*, are grown in alpine houses by rock gardeners.

Some species of *Erodium*, *Geranium*, and sometimes *Pelargonium* (e.g., *P. grossularoides*), usually annuals or poorly developed perennials from seasonally arid regions with abundant seeds, are weedy and have become pests.

Species of *Pelargonium* and its hybrids (principally in section *Pelargonium*) are grown commercially for geranium oil, which is extracted from the leaves and used in fragrances. Species of *Geranium* also produce volatile oils, but no commercial use is known for Neotropical species. In the Eastern Hemisphere, species of *Sarcocaulon* are covered with a thick waxy substance, which burns slowly; hence, they have been used at times as torches.

References. BECKETT, K., AND C. GREY-WILSON. 1993. *Encyclopedia of Alpines*. Worcestershire: Alpine Garden Society Publications Ltd. BOESWINKEL, F. D. 1997 Seed structure and phylogenetic relationships of the Geraniales. *Bot. Jahrb. Syst.* 119:2:277–331. BOESEWINKEL, F. D. 1988. The seed structure and taxonomic relationships of *Hypseocharis* Remy. *Acta Bot. Neerl.* 37:111–20. KNUTH, K. 1931. Geraniaceae. In *Die Natürlichen Pflanzenfamilien*, eds. A. Engler and K. Prantl, 2nd ed. 19a:43–66. Leipzig: Wilhelm Engelmann. PRICE, R., AND J. PALMER. 1993. Phylogenetic relationships of the Geraniaceae and Gerianales from *rbc*L sequence comparisons. *Ann. Missouri Bot. Gard.* 80: 661–71.

GESNERIACEAE (African Violet Family)

MIRIAM L. DENHAM

Figure 86, Plate 22

- *herbs, subshrubs, occasionally lianas, rarely shrubs or small trees*

- *indumentum of tapered, uniseriate, and glandular trichomes*

- *flowers zygomorphic; corolla sympetalous, often bilabiate; stamens 4 or 5, often didynamous, the fifth stamen often represented by a staminode; disc usually present; ovary usually unilocular; placentation parietal*

- *fruits usually loculicidal capsules, occasionally berries, or seldom berrylike capsules*

- *seeds numerous, small*

Numbers of genera and species. Worldwide, the Gesneriaceae comprise 133–150 genera and 2,500–3,700 species. In the Western Hemisphere, the estimated number of genera is 50 or more, and the number of species from 1,600 to 1,800. In the Gesnerioideae, *Besleria*, with more than 200 species, vies with *Columnea sensu lato* as the largest Neotropical genus. In the Cyrtandroideae (mostly Eastern Hemisphere), *Cyrtandra*, with more than 500 species, is the largest genus. According to Burtt and Wiehler, there are eight monotypic genera in the neotropics.

Distribution and habitats. With the exception of one pantropical species, all Gesneriaceae native to the Western Hemisphere are members of the Gesnerioideae. The Gesnerioideae are Neotropical except for the tribe Coronanthereae, which includes a few genera from Australia, New Zealand, the South Pacific, and temperate South America. The Gesnerioideae are distributed from the Caribbean and the tropic of Cancer in Mexico south to Argentina and Chile. *Koellikeria erinoides* (Gesnerioideae) is one of the more widespread monotypic species, ranging from southern Mexico through Bolivia to Argentina. The southernmost species, *Mitraria coccinea* (Coronanthereae), is found on the island of Chiloé at 40°S latitude.

Figure 86. GESNERIACEAE. *Drymonia coccinea.* **A.** Stem with leaves and inflorescences subtended by bracts. **B.** Lateral view of flower. **C.** Medial section of flower with corolla and androecium removed to show superior ovary and adaxial nectary. **D.** Medial section of the corolla and androecium; note short spur on corolla, small, reduced staminode at base, and paired, but not connivent, fertile stamens. **E.** Abaxial (left) and adaxial (right) views of stamens showing basal dehiscence. Reprinted with permission from Mori et al. (2002). Artist: Bobbi Angell.

The Cyrtandroideae are primarily Paleotropical in distribution, with only *Rhynchoglossum azureum* (Klugieae, Cyrtandroideae) found in the neotropics. The type genus of this subfamily, *Cyrtandra*, has numerous species, many of which are endemic to the Hawaiian Islands.

Gesneriaceae are found primarily in moist environments from tropical rain forests of the lowlands to temperate forests of the mountains. A number are adapted, often through dormancy, to withstand a dry season. While a few are widely distributed weedy plants sometimes found along roadsides and in other disturbed places, many are of limited distributions.

Thin-leaved species of *Gesneria* often grow on mossy rocks along shady waterways, frequently in the spray of waterfalls. Other gesneriads are found in drier habitats and may have thick leaves (e.g., the epiphytic *Codonanthe*) or very pubescent leaves (*Sinningia hirsuta*). *Sinningia leucotricha* has very silvery-sericeous leaves and a tuber, both adaptations that permit it to grow in full sun and to survive dry periods. Some species, such as *Kohleria spicata*, are pioneers in newly exposed soil.

Family classification. Cronquist included the Gesneriaceae within the Scrophulariales of the Asteridae. Recent molecular studies place the family in the Lamiales *sensu lato*.

The Gesneriaceae are divided into two subfamilies, the Gesnerioideae with six tribes and the Cyrtandroideae with five tribes. The Gesnerioideae include the Gloxinieae, Episcieae, Beslerieae, Napeantheae, Gesnerieae, and Coronanthereae and comprise species with isocotylous seedlings and usually half-inferior to inferior ovaries. The Cyrtandroideae include the Klugieae, Didymocarpeae, Trichosporeae, Cyrtandreae, and Titanotricheae and comprise species with anisocotylous seedlings and superior ovaries; however, Western Hemisphere plants with superior ovaries (Episcieae, Beslerieae, and Coronanthereae) are placed in the Gesnerioideae.

Burtt and Wiehler have published a revised classification utilizing cotyledon growth, ovary position, nectiferous disc position, nodal anatomy, chromosome number, and chemistry. This new system elevates the tribe Coronanthereae to a new subfamily, Coronantheroideae, to encompass those members of the Gesneriaceae ranging from southern Chile through the South Pacific islands to Australia.

Features of the family. Habit: herbs or subshrubs, occasionally lianas, rarely shrubs or small trees, terrestrial or epiphytic (ca. 25% of Gesnerioideae), polycarpic or sometimes monocarpic, evergreen, deciduous, or marcescent. **Roots** fibrous, adventitious roots often present at nodes (in humid conditions). **Stems** sometimes erect when young and sprawling with age, the internodes usually well developed, sometimes very short, the plants then appearing acaulescent and producing a tight rosette of leaves. **Indumentum** of young stems, leaves, pedicels and calyces often with living, tapered, uniseriate, and glandular trichomes. **Stipules** essentially absent (pseudostipules present in a few species; e.g., *Rhytido-phyllum auriculatum* as basal auricles of leaf). **Leaves** usually opposite, equal to strongly unequal or one of pair absent, sometimes alternate, rarely whorled, simple; blades rarely deeply divided, the margins entire to toothed, the teeth often crenate. **Inflorescences** axillary or terminal, cymes, racemes, or of solitary flowers; bracts conspicuous, inconspicuous, or absent; bracteoles sometimes present in compound inflorescences. **Flowers** zygomorphic, bisexual, often protandrous, inconspicuous to large and showy, the larger flowers yellow, red, orange, or greenish to white; calyx clasping base of corolla or widely spread (especially in fruit), the sepals 5, essentially distinct or ± united into short tube with well-developed lobes or the tube longer and often with small lobes; corolla sympetalous, composed of 5 petals, the petals partially or nearly completely united, the corolla usually tubular with bilabiate limb, or rotate (can be nearly actinomorphic), campanulate, salverform, infundibuliform, to almost cylindrical, the tube short or long, gibbous to spurred at base, erect in calyx or placed at angle with calyx; androecium with 4–5 stamens, the stamens epipetalous, often didynamous, the missing stamen reduced to a staminode or lacking, the filaments sometimes coiled or turned downward as stigma becomes receptive (effectively moving anthers away from stigma), the anthers dehiscing by pores or slits, when four separate or connivent and joined by sides or apices; nectiferous disc usually present, annular, lobed, or divided, distinct from ovary (except in Coronanthereae); gynoecium syncarpous, the ovary superior, half inferior, or inferior, the carpels 2, the locules 1(2), the style 1, terminal, slender, the stigma capitate, mouth-shaped, or 2-branched; placentation parietal, the placentae 2, sometimes fleshy, occasionally fusing to create 2 locules, the ovules numerous, anatropous, tenuinucellar, unitegumentic or bitegumentic. **Fruits** commonly loculicidal capsules (sometimes septicidal or both loculicidal and septicidal), occasionally berries, or seldom berrylike capsules with fleshy walls that eventually dehisce. **Seeds** numerous, small, 0.2–0.4 mm long without appendages; endosperm cellular.

The Neotropical species range widely in size. Some species are inconspicuous herbs with miniature flowers. The smallest is *Sinningia pusilla* with blooms about 2 centimeters long on a 2.5-centimeters-wide plant. Other species are large bushes or vines with large, brilliantly colored flowers; for example, *Solenophora calycosa* reaches 8 meters in height and has scarlet-orange, tubular flowers 6–8 centimeters long. Some of the epiphytic vines, such as *Columnea crassifolia*, are large and sprawling with bright-red, about 8-centimeter-long flowers.

After germination, the seedlings of the Gesnerioideae are isocotylous and those of the Cyrtandroideae are anisocotylous.

Chromosome numbers in the Gesnerioideae are reported as $n = 8$, 9, 10, 11, 12, 13, 14, or 16, with 9 being almost constant in the Episcieae and $n = 13$ characteristic of many Gloxinieae. Chromosome numbers have been used, along with morphological characters, to unite some genera (*Hypocyrta* with *Nematanthus*) and to split others (*Moussonia* from *Kohleria*).

The Gesneriaceae are not known to have iridoid, cyanogenic, or saponiferous compounds or the common leaf phenolics. They are reported to have orobanchine and several caffeoyl esters; sanangoside appears to be restricted to the Gesnerioideae, as are the anthocyanins gesnerin, found in flowers, and columnin, found in leaves and stems.

The Gesneriaceae have a great diversity of uniseriate tapered and glandular trichomes on their stems and leaves. Sometimes several different types of hairs are found on the same plant. Multiseriate trichomes of Neotropical Gesneriaceae have been observed only inside corollas and on the leaves of *Rhynchoglossum azureum* (Cyrtandroideae). Many of the trichomes in the Gesneriaceae have living cells, in contrast with the trichomes of related plants, which are dead when the leaf reaches maturity.

Natural history. Many gesneriads reproduce vegetatively by forming offsets of various kinds, which sometimes results in the formation of large cloned populations.

Reproductive and vegetative cycles of Gesneriaceae are often seasonal, and many of their adaptations are for surviving dry periods. Polycarpic species may have perennial stems that are woody at the base and produce new growth, or annual stems that grow from an annual or a perennial tuber, or commonly from "scaly rhizomes" after flowering or fruiting.

Some species possess succulent stems that allow them to lose leaves in adverse conditions and then initiate new growth when moisture returns. Only *Neomortonia nummularia* and *Alsobia punctata* are known to be regularly deciduous. The former produces swollen areas at or between the nodes of older stems from which roots readily develop.

Certain Neotropical Gesneriaceae have striking foliage patterns, such as species of *Episcia* and *Corytoplectus*.

Many species of Gesneriaceae are protandrous; however, those with short-lived flowers may have mature pollen and receptive stigmas at the same time. Therefore, they can be self-pollinated if they are not cross-pollinated. A strong correlation exists between the color of the flower (and sometimes of the calyx) and the type of pollinator. Many percent Gesnerioideae are pollinated by hummingbirds attracted either to brightly colored flowers, often red, orange, or yellow, or to dark red spots or patterns on the abaxial leaf blade surfaces (e.g., some species of *Columnea*). A significant number of the Gesnerioideae are pollinated by Neotropical euglossine bees. In addition to nectar, the males also collect fragrances, possibly to use directly or indirectly in the attraction of mates. A few Gesneriaceae with drab, white, cream to green, or purple flowers are pollinated by bat of the genera *Glossophaga* and *Brachyphylla*. Other gesneriads are pollinated by butterflies (purple flowers), moths (white flowers), flies, and non-native honeybees.

The small seeds of some Gesnerioideae are thought to have been wind-dispersed from one island to another in the Caribbean by tropical storms. Many of the Gesnerioideae (e.g., *Kohleria*) have dry capsules that dehisce into two apical valves with openings partially restricted by stiff hairs. These fruits act like a pepper-shaker, releasing the seeds over a longer period of time. Some capsules in *Gesneria* (Gesnerioideae) dehisce so that the open fruit becomes a splash cup, which allows the seeds (or sometimes the newly germinated seedlings) to be washed away by rain or by the spray from waterfalls.

Birds, which often are attracted by brightly colored calyces, and bats eat the fruits of some Gesneriaceae and then excrete the seeds. *Drymonia* has some species in which the inside of the fruit walls contrast in color with the rounded mass of seeds when the capsule opens and the valves spread. These are possibly adaptations to an unknown vertebrate disperser. Ants carry away the seeds of some species of Gesneriaceae, and species of *Codonanthe* grow only in epiphytic ant gardens.

Economic uses. Many gesneriads and their hybrids are grown as ornamentals. The most commonly grown genus is *Saintpaulia* (Cyrtandroideae), the African violet from Kenya and Tanzania. *Sinningia speciosa* (Gesnerioideae) and its many hybrids, species of *Streptocarpus* (Cyrtandroideae), hybrids of *Columnea* (Gesnerioideae), species of *Episcia* (Gesnerioideae), and other Gesneriaceae also are cultivated ornamentals.

A report in 1995 indicated that 122 species of Neotropical gesneriads were utilized medicinally by the indigenous populations of South America in 50 different ways; among them are snakebite treatment, contraception, and analgesics. Only a few of these plants have been investigated to determine the presence of active compounds. A few gesneriads have been reported to cause dermatitis (e.g., *Achimenes grandiflora*, *Columnea pilossisima*, *Nautilocalyx melittifolus*, *Primulina tabacum*, *Saintpaulia ionantha*, *Sinningia speciosa*, and *Streptocarpus* hybrids).

References. BEAUFORT-MURPHY, H. 1983. The seed surface morphology of the Gesneriaceae utilizing the scanning electron microscope and a new system for diagnosing seed morphology. *Selbyana* 6(1–4):220–422. BURTT, B. L. AND H. J. WIEHLER. 1995. Classification of the family Gesneriaceae. *Gesneriana* 1(1):1–4. FRITSCH, K. 1893, 1894. Gesneriaceae. *Die Natürlichen Pflanzenfamilien*, eds. A. Engler and K. Prantl, 4(3b):133–85. Leipzig: Wilhelm Engelmann. HARBORNE, J. B. 1967. *Comparative Biochemistry of the Flavonoids*. New York: Academic Press. MITCHELL, J., AND A. ROOK. 1979. Botanical Dermatology. Vancouver: Greengrass. RUSSO, E. B. 1992. Headache treatments by native peoples of the Ecuadorian Amazon: a preliminary cross-disciplinary assessment. *J. Ethno-Pharmacol.* 36:193–206. SKOG, L. E., AND J. K. BOGGAN. 2000. Bibliography of the Gesneriaceae, 2nd ed. Washington, D.C.: Department of Botany, Smithsonian Institution. SMITH, J. F. 2000. Phylogenetic resolution within the tribe Episcieae (Gesneriaceae): congruence of ITS and *ndh*F sequences from parsimony and maximum likelihood analyses. *Amer. J. Bot.* 87(6):883–97. WIEHLER, H. 1983. A Synopsis of the Neotropical Gesneriaceae. *Selbyana* 6(1–4):1–219. WIEHLER, H. 1995. 122 species of the rain forests plant family Gesneriaceae used medicinally in the neotropics. *Gesneriana* 1(1):98–120. WILLIAMS, N. H. 1978. Pollen structure and the systematics of the Neotropical Gesneriaceae. *Selbyana* 2(2–3):310–22.

GOODENIACEAE (Goodenia Family)

MATS H. G. GUSTAFSSON

Figure 87, Plate 22

- *shrubs*
- *leaves alternate, simple*
- *inflorescences axillary, dichasia*
- *flowers zygomorphic, the corolla fanlike; specialized stylar outgrowth called an "indusium" present*

Numbers of genera and species. Worldwide, the Goodeniaceae comprise 12 genera and about 410 species. The largest genera are *Goodenia* with 180 species and *Scaevola* with about 100 species. In tropical America, there is a single genus, *Scaevola*, with three species.

Distribution and habitat. The majority of the Goodeniaceae are restricted to Australia, where they can be found in practically all vegetation types. Only *Scaevola* occurs to any extent outside Australia, with a number of species in Malesia and on Pacific islands. *Scaevola plumieri* and *S. taccada* (=*S. sericea*) are widespread on tropical seashores; *S. plumieri* occurs throughout the neotropics and the Paleotropical *S. taccada* is naturalized in the Bahamas.

Only two additional species of Goodeniaceae occur in the Western Hemisphere: *Scaevola wrigtii* is endemic to eastern Cuba and *Selliera radicans* occurs in central Chile.

Family classification. The Goodeniaceae are placed in the Campanulales by Cronquist, however, recent molecular data indicate that the closest relatives are the Asteraceae and Calyceraceae. The genera form four distinct groups, supported by both morphological and molecular characters. *Lechenaul-*

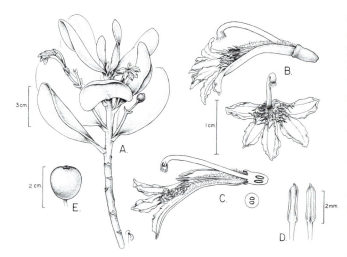

Figure 87. GOODENIACEAE. *Scaevola plumieri.* **A.** Stem with leaves and inflorescences. **B.** Oblique-apical (below) and lateral (above) views of flowers. **C.** Medial section of flower (above) and transverse section of ovary (below). **D.** Abaxial (left) and adaxial (right) views of anthers. **E.** Lateral view of fruit. Reprinted with permission from Acevedo-Rodríguez (1996). Artist: Bobbi Angell.

tia and *Brunonia* constitute a group of their own; *Dampiera* and *Anthotium* another; and the remaining genera, including *Goodenia* and *Scaevola*, form a fourth group. These groups differ markedly in characters such as habit, inflorescence type, floral symmetry, pollen morphology, ovary position, and fruit type.

Features of the family. Habit: shrubs. **Stipules** absent. **Leaves** alternate, simple. **Inflorescences** axillary, dichasia. **Flowers** zygomorphic, bisexual; calyx synsepalous, the lobes 5; corolla sympetalous, with deep adaxial slit, the lobes 5, often pointing down, fanlike in appearance, or 2 lobes shaped slightly different, directed upward, the margins of the lobes

sometimes winged, thin, fringed, folded inwards in bud; androecium of 5 stamens; gynoecium syncarpous, the ovary inferior, the carpels 2, the locules 2, the style bearing a cuplike, apical indusium, the stigma developing as outgrowth of indusium; placentation axile, the ovules 1 per locule. **Fruits** indehiscent, the outer mesocarp fleshy, the inner mesocarp corky, the endocarp hard. **Seed** 1 per locule; endosperm abundant.

The presence of an indusium is unique to the Goodeniaceae. It is a cuplike or bilabiate structure at the apex of the style. Pollen is deposited into the indusium from the anthers in bud. When the flower opens, the pollen is removed from the indusium by visiting insects. Later, the stigma develops, usually as an outgrowth from the indusium.

Natural history. Insects are the most common pollinators; e.g., various Hymenoptera are reported to pollinate *Scaevola plumieri*. The corky mesocarps of *S. plumieri* and *S. taccada* facilitate dispersal by sea currents, which may explain the very wide, coastal distribution of these species.

Economic uses. Species of several genera are grown as ornamentals because of their abundant and colorful flowers. *Scaevola plumieri* and *S. taccada* have various uses in traditional medicine, particularly in southern Asia and Australia. The fleshy exocarp of *S. plumieri* is reported to be edible.

References. CAROLIN, R. C., M.T.M. RAJPUT, AND D. A. MORRISON. 1992. Goodeniaceae. In *Flora of Australia* 35: 4–300. Canberra: Australian Government Publishing Service. GUSTAFSSON, M.H.G., A. BACKLUND, AND B. BREMER. 1996. Phylogeny of the Asterales sensu lato based on *rbc*L sequences with particular reference to the Goodeniaceae. *Pl. Syst. Evol.* 199:217–42. KRAUSE, K. 1912. Goodeniaceae. In *Das Pflanzenreich,* ed. A. Engler, 4(277):1–207. Leipzig: Wilhelm Engelmann.

GROSSULARIACEAE (Gooseberry or Currant Family)

MAXIMILIAN WEIGEND

Figure 88

- *shrubs with distinct long- and short-shoots*

- *stipules always present, but often reduced to fimbriate wings along petiole base*

- *leaves alternate, simple*

- *flowers with hypanthium; petals typically included in calyx lobes; ovary inferior, the style bifid*

- *fruits berries*

Numbers of genera and species. Worldwide, the Grossulariaceae comprise a single genus, *Ribes,* and 150–200 species. In tropical America, there are at least 40 species of *Ribes.*

Distribution and habitat. *Ribes* has three centers of diversity: Asia, North America (including Mexico), and South America. In tropical America, *Ribes* is restricted to montane and alpine habitats, mostly above 2,500 meters and reaching elevations of more than 4,000 meters. The genus is extremely diverse in the Andes, especially in moister regions such as the eastern slope of the Central Andes. The species are found in cloud forest, open *páramos*, and especially on and at the base of rocks and in fragmented high-altitude forests with genera such as *Gynoxys* and *Polylepis*. In Peru, some species (e.g., *R. viscosum* and *R. cuneifolium*) form nearly exclusive stands of scrub forest up to 4 meters tall.

Family classification. The Grossulariaceae are placed in the Rosales by Cronquist. Cronquist included many genera in the Grossulariaceae, including *Brexia*, *Itea*, *Pterostemon* (see Pterostemonaceae), and *Tetracarpaea*. However, recent molecular and morphological analyses suggest that Cronquist's Grossulariaceae is unnatural and that the family is best restricted to *Ribes*. It is further suggested that Grossulariaceae *sensu stricto* is best placed within the order Saxifragales and is probably the sister taxon to Saxifragaceae *sensu stricto*. Similarity between Grossulariaceae and Saxifragaceae is striking in floral characters, but Grossulariaceae are easily distinguished on the basis of their inferior ovaries that mature into berries, whereas Saxifragaceae have superior ovaries and dry fruits. The genus *Ribes* is divided into six subgenera; *Grossularia* is nested in *Ribes* and represents one of the subgenera. Three of the subgenera are found in the neotropics: the largely North American subgenera *Calobotrya* and *Grossularia* enter the neotropics from the north and reach their southern limit in northern Guatemala (*R. ciliatum* and *R. microphyllum*). The dioecious South American species of *Ribes* belong to the monophyletic subgenus *Parilla*, with two sections: extratropical section *Parilla* (Argentina and Chile) and the tropical Andean section *Andina* (one species in northern Argentina, most restricted to tropical Andes, and a single species in Costa Rica and Panama).

Features of the family. Habit: Shrubs (sometimes with dwarf habit <10 cm tall) or lianescent shrubs >5 m long, rarely deciduous, mostly evergreen or facultatively deciduous in drought conditions, usually densely glandular and/or covered with simple hairs, sometimes strongly resinous. **Stipules** present, adnate to petiole, the margins typically fimbriate, sometimes reduced to fimbriate wings along petiole base. **Leaves** alternate, sometimes in clusters on short-shoots, simple; blades variously lobed, rarely undivided, the margins serrate or serrulate; venation often palmate. **Inflorescences** subterminal, always racemose, with typically more than 20 flowers (rarely reduced to 1–3 flowers); bracts and bracteoles typically present, sessile, ovate, usually densely pubescent and/or glandular, the margins often fimbriate. **Flowers** actinomorphic, usually unisexual (plants dioecious in South America and southern Central America: subgenus *Parilla*), rarely bisexual (northern Central America: subgenera *Calobotrya* and *Grossularia*), often small; hypanthium present; calyx tube campanulate to nearly rotate, the lobes 5, ovate-acuminate; petals 5, small, typically included in calyx, obovate or oblanceolate; androecium of (4)5 stamens, the filaments short (stamens included or shortly exserted), the anthers apically and basally emarginate; gynoecium syncarpous, the ovary inferior, the carpels 2, the locule 1, the style 1, apically bifid, the stigmas 2; apical disc often surrounding style; placentation parietal, the ovules few to many, anatropous. **Fruits** berries, globose, yellow, red, or black, often densely glandular, insipid, crowned with persistent perianth. **Seeds** few to many, brown, oblique ovoidal, the testa smooth; endosperm copious, oily.

Natural history. The flowers of *Ribes* are probably pollinated by insects (dioecy, small flowers, nectar secretion), but direct observations on pollination are not available, apart from the observation of hummingbird pollination of the relatively large, red-flowered *R. macrobotrys* (Th. Franke, Munich, pers. comm.). The berries are avidly eaten by Andean birds, and the seeds are undoubtedly bird dispersed; however, dispersal seems to relatively inefficient because many taxa are narrowly endemic. A few species produce underground xylopodia and form clonal stands.

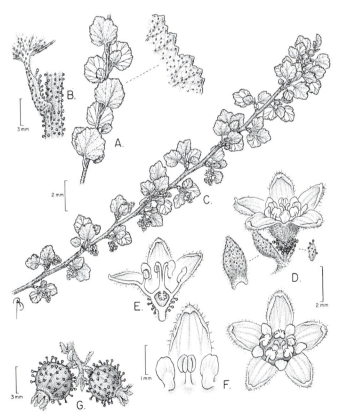

Figure 88. GROSSULARIACEAE. *Ribes pentlandii.* **A.** Stem with leaves and detail of margin (above right). **B.** Detail of part of stem and leaf base showing glandular trichomes. **C.** Stem with leaves and inflorescences. **D.** Lateral view of flower (above), details of bract (left), bracteole (right), and apical view of flower (below). **E.** Medial section of flower. **F.** Adaxial view of adnate stamen with a staminode on each side. **G.** Lateral views of fruits. Reprinted with permission from Weigend and Binder (2001). Artist: Bobbi Angell.

Economic uses. Many species of *Ribes* are cultivated for their fruits; e.g., *R. grossularia* (gooseberries), *R. nigrum* (black currants), and *R. rubrum* (red currants) and its hybrids. Several additional species are grown as garden ornamentals, including the Chilean *R. gayanum*. The South American species are locally used as hedge plants, for wind breaks, and as a source of firewood.

References. FREIRE, F. A. 1998. New species of *Ribes* (Grossulariaceae) from South America. *Novon* 8:354–58. FREIRE, F. A. 2002. A new species of *Ribes* (Grossulariaceae), along with notes and a key to the Ecuadorian species. *Syst. Bot.* 27(1):14–18. JANCZEWSKI, E. 1907. Monographie des groseilliers, *Ribes*, L. *Mem. Soc. Phys. Genève* 35:199–517. SOLTIS, D. E., R. K. KUZOFF, E. CONTI, R. GORNALL, AND K. FERGUSON. 1996. *Mat*K and *rbc*L gene sequence data indicate that Saxifraga (Saxifragaceae) is polyphyletic. *Amer. J. Bot.* 83:371–82. SOLTIS, D. E., D. R. MORGAN, A. GRABLE, P. S. SOLTIS, AND R. K. KUZOFF. 1993. Molecular systematics of Saxifragaceae sensu stricto. *Amer. J. Bot.* 80:1056–81. SPONGBERG, S. A. 1972. Genera of Saxifragaceae. *J. Arnold Arbor.* 53:466–77. WEIGEND, M., AND M. BINDER. 2001. A revision of the genus *Ribes* (Grossulariaceae) in Bolivia. *Bot. Jahrb. Syst.* 123/1:111–34. WEIGEND, M., AND M. BINDER. 2001. Three new species of *Ribes* (Grossulariaceae) from Central and South America. *Syst. Bot.* 26(4):727–37. WEIGEND, M., O. MOHR, AND T. J. MOTLEY. 2002. Phylogeny and classification of the genus *Ribes* (Grossulariaceae) based on 5S-NTS sequences and morphological and anatomical data. *Bot. Jahrb. Syst.* 124(2):163–83.

GUNNERACEAE (Gunnera Family)

LUIS EDUARDO MORA-OSEJO

Figure 89, Plate 23

- *herbs*
- *rhizome parenchyma with symbiotic blue-green algae*
- *apical meristem and distal sector of rhizome protected by scalelike leaves (lepidophylls)*
- *leaves alternate, in rosettes, simple, often large; petioles often long; venation palmate*
- *flowers very small; stamens usually 2, sometimes 1; styles 2*

Number of genera and species. Worldwide, the Gunneraceae comprise a single genus, *Gunnera* with six subgenera and 68 species. The subgenera *Misandra* (South America), *Ostenigunnera* (extratropical in Uruguay and southern Brazil), and *Panke* (Central and South America and Hawaii) are present in the Western Hemisphere. The largest subgenus, *Panke*, has 53 species worldwide and 37 species in the neotropics. The other subgenus in tropical America, *Misandra*, has only a single species in the neotropics.

Distribution and habitat. *Gunnera* is an austral-antarctic genus widely distributed in the mountains of Africa, southeast Asia, Tasmania, New Zealand, Hawaii, and South and Central America. During the Upper Cretaceous and the Early Tertiary, the genus was more widely distributed than it is today.

Species of Gunneraceae grow in bogs, permanently flooded sites, ravine banks, shaded rocky cliffs, on volcanic soils and rocks, along roadsides, and on sand dunes.

Gunnera magellanica and *G. lobata* grow in the most southern regions of South America. However, the distribution of *G. magellanica* extends northward through the Andes to the Páramo de Ruiz in Colombia, where it grows at elevations of 3,200–4,000 meters.

Family classification. The Gunneraceae are placed in the Haloragales with the Haloragaceae by Cronquist. In the past, *Gunnera* has been placed in the Haloragaceae as a monotypic genus of subfamily Gunneroideae.

Gunnera is placed in a monotypic family because of its tetrasporic embryo, pseudomonomerous gynoecium, unilocular ovary with two distinct terminal styles, cellular endosperm development, and polystelic rhizomes. A symbiotic relationship with *Nostoc* in all species of *Gunnera* supports the recognition of the Gunneraceae as a distinct family.

Phylogenetic analyses based on the chloroplast gene *rbc*L do not support a relationship of *Gunnera* with the Haloragaceae or with the Saxifragaceae. Analyses based on *rbc*L, *atp*B, and 18S support a sister group relationship between the African *Myrothamnus flabellifolis* (Myothamnaceae) and *Gunnera*, in spite of their pronounced morphological differences. Based on a morphological analysis, the South American species *G. herteri* has been established as sister to all other *Gunnera*.

Features of the family. Habit: herbs, perennial; rhizomes present, usually creeping or decumbent, sometimes suberect (*Gunnera colombiana*) with symbiotic blue-green algae, the apical meristem and distal sector protected by scalelike leaves (lepidophylls). **Stipules** absent or median axillary scale (considered stipular by some authors) often present. **Leaves** alternate, in rosettes, simple, small to large; petioles present, often long; blades sometimes peltate, glabrous or pubescent, the adaxial surface sometimes areolate and strongly scabrous (some species of subgenus *Panke*), the base sometimes cordate, the margins regular or irregularly toothed, crenate, or lobulate, the apex acute, round, or obtuse; venation palmate. **Inflorescences** axillary or terminal, commonly erect panicles, usually of many flowers. **Flowers** zygomorphic, bisexual in subgenus *Panke* or unisexual in subgenus *Misandra* (plants monoecius or dioecious), very small; sepals 2(3), valvate, often fleshy, with scalelike caducous, elongate, apices; petals frequently 2, sometimes absent; androecium usually of 2 stamens or sometimes 1 in unisexual flowers, the filaments short, the anthers apiculate or nonapiculate; gynoecium syncarpous, the ovary inferior, the carpels 2, the locule 1, the styles 2, the stigmas papillate; placentation apical, the ovule 1, pendulous. **Fruits** drupaceous or dehiscent, the pericarp frequently fleshy (drupaceous fruits) or sometimes membranaceous or coriaceous (dehiscent fruits). **Seeds** with copious, oily endosperm, the embryo small.

The species with the largest leaves and rhizomes are *G. insignis* and *G. magnifica*. The leaves of these species have petioles to 2.5 meters long and leaf blades to 2.2 meters wide.

Scalelike leaves, called lepidophylls, protect the apical and distal region of the rhizome where dense aggregations of glands are located.

Species with unisexual flowers are sometimes monoecious, with the proximal flowers female and the distal flowers male. But several species, such as *G. lobata, G. magellanica,* and *G. macrophylla* with unisexual flowers, are dioecious.

Natural history. When populations of closely related species establish contact along roadsides, they often interbreed. The resulting hybrids are easily recognized because they possess characters intermediate to those of both parents.

Species of *Gunnera* grow in habitats poor in nitrogen and have coevolved a symbiotic relationship with the blue-green alga *Nostoc punctiforme*, which fixes nitrogen. Dense populations of *G. pilosa, G. brephogea,* and *G. atropurpurea* in nitrogen-poor habitats in the mountains of Colombia are probably the result of the competitive advantage provided by this symbiotic relationship.

Very little information is available on pollination and dispersal biology. The seeds of *Gunnera* germinate readily. *Gunnera colombiana*, for example, has dehiscent fruits and seeds that germinate soon after dispersal. The seedlings have mucilage nodules and channels on the hypocotyls that facilitate the penetration of *Nostoc* into the parenchyma cells of the rhizome.

Economic uses. In Chile, the petioles of *Gunnera tinctorea* are used as ingredients in sweet meats and for making preserves, and in Colombia, the leaves of *G. manicata* and *G. brephogea* are utilized for wrapping meats as a means of preserving them. Natives of Java used the fruits of *G. macrophylla* as a stimulant. The fruits and the vegetative parts of *Gunnera* are used as astringents.

Several species of *Gunnera* are cultivated in North American and European gardens.

Species of *Gunnera* are canidates for recovering degra-

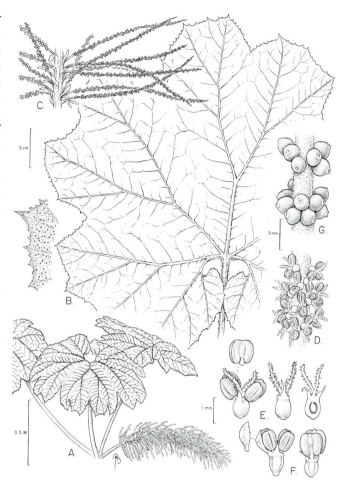

Figure 89. GUNNERACEAE. *Gunnera insignis* (A, D, G, photos by Carol Gracie; B, Lent 277; C, Lepiz and Ramirez 394; E, Hill 17747; F, Burger 3923B). **A.** Plant showing leaves and inflorescences. **B.** Part of leaf (right) and detail of margin (left) showing abaxial punctations. **C.** Inflorescences. **D.** Detail of inflorescence. **E.** Lateral view of bisexual flower (left), adaxial view of stamen (above left), lateral view of pistillate flower (center), and medial section of pistillate flower (right). **F.** Lateral views of staminate flowers with detail of petal (above left). **G.** Part of infructescence. Original. Artist: Bobbi Angell.

dated mountainous tropical landscapes because of their ability to colonize pioneer habitats and to fix nitrogen.

References. Bader, F. J. 1961. Das Areal der Gattung *Gunnera L. Bot. Jahrb. Syst.* 80(3):281–93. Brown, R. 1814. Halorragaceae. In *A voyage to Terra australis*, M. Flinders, 2:549. London: G. & W. Nicol. Correra Q., J. E., and H. Y. Bernal. 1993. Haloragaceae. In *Especies vegetales promisorias de los países del Convenio Andrés Bello*, Tomo IX. Santafé de Bogotá, D. E., Colombia: Secretaria Ejecutiva del Convenio Andrés Bello. Jartzen, M. 1980. The occurrence of *Gunnera* pollen in the fossil record. *Biotropica* 12(2):117–23. Mora-Osejo, L. E. 1978. Nuevas especies de *Gunnera L. Del Neotrópico-I. Caldasia* 12(57): 171–79. Mora-Osejo, L. E. 1984. Haloragaceas. In *Flora de*

Colombia, 3:1–178. Bogotá, Colombia: Imprenta Nacional. PRAGLOSKI, J. 1970. The pollen morphology of the Haloragaceae with reference to taxonomy. *Grana* 10:159–239. SCHINDLER, A. K. 1905. Halorrhagaceae. In *Das Pflanzenreich*, ed. A. Engler, series 4, 225(heft 23):1–133. SOLTIS, D. E., A. E. SENTERS, M. J. ZANIS, S. KIM, J. D. THOMPSON, ET AL. 2003. Gunnerales are sister to other core Eudicots: implications for the evolution of pentamery. *Amer. J. Bot.* 90(3):461–70. SILVESTER, W. B. 1976. Endophyte adaptation in *Gunnera-Nostoc*-symbiosis. In *Nitrogen Fixation in Plants*, ed. P. S. Nutman, 521–38. New York: Cambridge University Press. WANNTORP L., H.-E. WANNTORP, B. OXELMAN, AND M. KÄLLERSJÖ. 2001. Phylogeny of *Gunnera*. *Plant Syst. Evol.* 226:85–107. WEBER, H., AND L. E. MORA. 1958. Zur Kenntnis der Gattung *Gunnera* L. in Costa Rica. *Beitr. Biol. Pflanzen* 34:467–77. (Festschrift W. Troll).

HALORAGACEAE (Water Milfoil Family)

NATHAN SMITH AND DENNIS WM. STEVENSON

Figure 90

- *aquatic or wetland herbs*
- *leaves simple, the margins entire to pinnately divided, often dimorphic on same plant*
- *flowers small, often unisexual, often 4-merous; ovary inferior*
- *fruits drupelike or nutlets*

Numbers of genera and species. Worldwide, the Haloragaceae comprise eight genera and approximately 145 species. In tropical America, there are three genera: *Myriophyllum* with three species, *Laurembergia* with one species, and *Proserpinaca* with one species.

Distribution and habitat. The Haloragaceae are cosmopolitan. The family is primarily found in the Southern Hemisphere with the majority of species in Australia. In tropical America, species of *Myriophyllum* are found in the West Indies, Central America, and South America. In South America, species have been most commonly collected throughout the Andes and in the lowlands of southeastern Brazil. Some species occur at elevations greater than 3,000 meters. *Laurembergia* is widespread in tropical South America, and *Proserpinaca* is found from Mexico to Guatemala and in the West Indies.

Neotropical Haloragaceae grow in slow-moving water or in wetland habitats.

Family classification. The Haloragaceae and Gunneraceae are placed in the Haloragales by Cronquist. Past classifications have placed *Gunnera* within the Haloragaceae as a monotypic genus of subfamily Gunneroideae (see Gunneraceae). Recent molecular studies by the Angiosperm Phylogeny Group suggest that *Myriophyllum* (Haloragaceae) and *Gunnera* are not closely related.

Features of the family. Habit: herbs, aquatic. Stipules absent. Leaves whorled (*Myriophyllum*), subwhorled, opposite

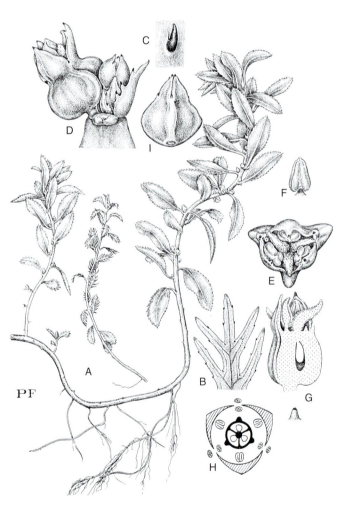

Figure 90. HALORAGACEAE. *Proserpinaca palustris*. **A.** Stems with roots, leaves, and axillary inflorescences (left and right) and young plant (center) (x⅔). **B.** Apical part of pectinate leaf (x6). **C.** Abaxial view of gland, typical of those found on most parts of plant (x60). **D.** Detail of inflorescence (x16). **E.** Apical view of flower (x16). **F.** Adaxial view of stamen (x16). **G.** Medial section of flower (above; x16) and lateral view of gland that displaces petals (below; x60). **H.** Floral diagram. **I.** Lateral view of fruit (x6). Reprinted with permission from Correll and Correll (1982). Artist: Priscilla Fawcett.

or alternate (*Laurembergia*), or alternate (*Proserpinaca*), simple to pinnately divided, the leaf position and leaf type sometimes variable on same plant; blades finely divided (often in submersed portion) to ovate to lanceolate, the margins entire, sparsely toothed, or serrate. **Inflorescences** axillary, often of solitary flowers or in spikes. **Flowers** actinomorphic, unisexual (plants usually monoecious) or less often bisexual, small; sepals 3–4 or absent in pistillate *Myriophyllum*, valvate when present; petals 4, sometimes rudimentary (*Proserpinaca*) or absent (pistillate *Laurembergia* and *Myriophyllum*), when present imbricate, yellow, blue-green, or red-purple; androecium of 4, or more commonly 8 stamens, then the stamens in 2 whorls, the outer whorl opposite sepals, the filaments short, the anthers basifixed, dehiscing by longitudinal slits; gynoecium syncarpous, the ovary inferior, the carpels (2)4, the locules 1–4, the styles 4 or absent, distinct; ovules 1–2 per locule, pendulous. **Fruits** drupelike or splitting into mericarps (nutlets). **Seeds** 1–4 per fruit.

Natural history. Flowers of Halaragaceae are mostly wind-pollinated; however, bees have been observed visiting the flowers of some species. No information is available on dispersal biology.

Economic uses. Species of water-milfoil (e.g., *Myriophyllum aquaticum* and *M. spicatum*) are invasive weeds in lakes. Other species of *Myriophyllum* are used to poison animals. Some of *Myriophyllum* and *Proserpinaca* are grown ornamentally, for example, in fish aquaria.

References. AIKEN, S. G. 1981. A conspectus of *Myriophyllum* (Haloragaceae) in North America. *Brittonia* 33:57–69. CORRERA Q., J. E., AND H. Y. BERNAL. 1993. Haloragaceae. In *Especies vegetales promisorias de los países del Convenio Andrés Bello*, Tomo IX. Santafé de Bogotá, D. E., Colombia: Secretaria Ejecutiva del Convenio Andrés Bello. MORA-OSEJO, L. E. 1984. Haloragaceas. In *Flora de Colombia*, 3:1–178. Bogotá, Colombia: Imprenta Nacional. ORCHARD, A. E. 1981. A revision of South American *Myriophyllum* (Haloragaceae), and its repercussions on some Australian and North American species. *Brunonia* 4:27–65. PRAGLOSKI, J. 1970. The pollen morphology of the Haloragaceae with reference to taxonomy. *Grana* 10:159–239. SCHINDLER, A. K. 1905. Halorrhagaceae. In *Das Pflanzenreich*, ed. A. Engler, IV. 225 (Heft 23):1–133. Leipzig: Wihelm Engelmann. WANNTORP L., H.-E. WANNTORP, B. OXELMAN, AND M. KÄLLERSJÖ. 2001. Phylogeny of *Gunnera*. *Plant Syst. Evol.* 226:85–107.

HAMAMELIDACEAE (Witch-hazel Family)

DENNIS WM. STEVENSON

- *shrubs or trees*

- *leaves alternate, simple*

- *flowers with the stamen connective often ± prolonged; gynoecium syncarpous, the styles distinct, the stigmas decurrent*

- *fruits capsules, somewhat woody*

Numbers of genera and species. Worldwide, the Hamamelidaceae comprise 30 genera and approximately 100 species. In tropical America, there are three genera: *Liquidambar* (one species), *Matudaea* (two), and *Molinadendron* (three).

Distribution and habitat. The Hamamelidaceae have a widely scattered relictual distribution, but are most diverse in eastern Asia. In the neotropics, *Liquidambar* is distributed from southern Mexico to Nicaragua, *Matudaea* from Mexico to Honduras, and *Molinadendron* from Sinaloa, Mexico to Costa Rica.

Neotropical species generally prefer the cool upland regions of Central American mountains. For example, *Liquidambar* is associated with pine-oak forests at 800–1,400 meters.

Family classification. The Hamamelidaceae are placed in the Hamamelidales by Cronquist. However, molecular studies suggest the Hamamelidaceae are better placed with families such as the Saxifragaceae. The family is divided into four subfamilies, two of which, the Hamamelidoideae and the Altingioideae, are found in the neotropics. The Hamamelidoideae is further divided into four tribes, one of which, the Fothergilleae, with *Matudaea* and *Molinadendron*, is Neotropical. The Altingioideae, has no infrasubfamilial classification and contains only three genera, one of which, *Liquidambar*, is found in the neotropics. Some authors suggest that the Altingioideae is better recognized as a separate family, the Altingiaceae.

Features of the family. Habit: shrubs or trees. **Stipules** present, distinct, scarious, deciduous (*Liquidambar*) or evergreen. **Leaves** alternate (distichous or rarely spiral; e.g., *Liquidambar*), simple; blade margins entire, toothed, or lobed. **Inflorescences** axillary, spikes, heads, condensed thyrses or panicles. **Flowers** actinomorphic or rarely slightly zygomorphic, bisexual or unisexual in *Liquidambar* (plants andromonoecious), generally small, yellow, reddish, white, or green; perianth absent (*Liquidambar* and *Matudaea*) or present, when present of 4 or 5 imbricate, generally persistent sepals (*Moli-*

nadendron); petals absent; androecium of 4–20 stamens, the connective often ± prolonged, the anthers basifixed, dehiscing by 1 or 2 valves; gynoecium syncarpous, the ovary superior (*Matudaea*), subinferior (*Molinadendron*), or inferior (*Liquidambar*), the carpels 2, the locules 2, the styles distinct, the stigmas decurrent; placentation axile, the ovules usually 1 or up to 40 per carpel in *Liquidambar*. **Fruits** capsules, somewhat woody, the infructescence ripening together as one unit in *Liquidambar*. **Seeds** 1 per locule, ovoid or winged (*Liquidambar*).

Natural history. The available data indicate insect pollination to be most common. The woody capsular fruits of the subfamily Hamamelidoideae have an ovoid seed that is forcibly ejected up to several meters from the parent plant when the fruit dehisces. In contrast, the seeds of *Liquidambar* are winged and most likely dispersed by wind.

Economic uses. Extracts from species of *Hamamelis* are used widely in lotions for treating muscular aches and as an astringent. *Liquidambar* is the source of wood that is valued for furniture and window frames. Storax, an aromatic balsam used medicinally, as an ingredient for perfuming powders and soaps, and as incense, is derived from the bark of the Asiatic *Liquidambar orientalis* and, to a less extent, the eastern North American *L. styraciflua*. In the Eastern Hemisphere, several genera, such as *Corylopsis* and *Parrotia*, are cultivated widely as ornamentals.

References. Endress, P. 1977. Evolutionary trends in the Hamamelidales-Fagales. *Plant. Syst. Evol., Suppl.* 1:321–47. Endress, P. 1993. Hamamelidaceae. In *The Families and Genera of Vascular Plants*, ed. K. Kubitzki, 2:322–31. New York: Springer-Verlag. Ernst, W. 1993. The genera of Hamamelidaceae and Platanaceae in the southeastern United States. *J. Arnold Arbor.* 44:193–210.

HERNANDIACEAE (Hernandia Family)

Klaus Kubitzki

Figure 91, Plate 23

- *trees, shrubs, or lianas*

- *leaves alternate, usually simple; ethereal oil cells present*

- *flowers with anthers dehiscing by valves; ovary inferior, the ovule 1, pendulous*

- *fruits nuts*

Number of genera and species. Worldwide, the Hernandiaceae comprise four genera and about 60 species: *Hernandia* (ca. 22 species), *Illigera* (19), *Gyrocarpus* (three), and *Sparatthanthelium* (ca. 13). In tropical America, there are three genera (*Hernandia*, *Gyrocarpus*, and *Sparatthanthelium*) and 23 species.

Distribution and habitat. The largest genus, *Hernandia*, has a pantropical distribution with a center of diversity in the Indo-Pacific region, where it extends to coastal East Africa in the west and far into the Pacific, Central and northern South America, and the Caribbean. *Illigera* extends from western Africa to Indochina and Malesia. One species of *Gyrocarpus* is found in all continents, mainly along tropical shores, but also in the interior of the continents with many outliers that have acquired subspecific status. *Sparattanthelium* is found in the Guayanan region, Amazonia, and the drier regions of northeastern and eastern/central Brazil.

Members of the family occupy a diverse range of habitats, from the seashore to inland forests and semiarid woodlands.

Family classification. The Hernandiaceae are placed in the Laurales by Cronquist. Two subfamilies, Hernandioideae (*Hernandia* and *Illigera*) and Gyrocarpoideae (*Gyrocarpus* and *Sparatthanthelium*), are distinguished. These are well characterized and sometimes have been considered to represent two unrelated lineages. Molecular studies indicate that the Lauraceae and Monimiaceae are the closest relatives of the Hernandiaceae.

Features of the family. **Habit:** trees, shrubs, or lianas, often evergreen. **Stipules** absent. **Leaves** alternate, usually simple, ethereal oil cells present, cystoliths present (Gyrocarpoideae); blade margins entire (sometimes shallowly palmately lobed in *Gyrocarpus*); venation pinnate or with 3 veins arising from the base. **Inflorescences** terminal, thyrses (*Hernandia*) or dichasia (*Gyrocarpus* and *Sparattanthelium*), the thyrses of 3-flowered cymes of 2 staminate flowers and 1 pistillate flower, the dichasia repeatedly ramified, in a single plane; bracteoles accrescent in pistillate flowers of *Hernandia*, absent in *Gyrocarpus* and *Sparattanhelium*. **Flowers** actinomorphic or zygomorphic, bisexual (*Gyrocarpus* and *Sparattanhelium*) or unisexual (plants monoecious in *Hernandia*); tepals 4–8; androecium of 3–7 stamens, the filaments sometimes with 1–2 nectariferous glands, the anthers dehiscing by valves; gynoecium with inferior ovary, the carpel 1; pla-

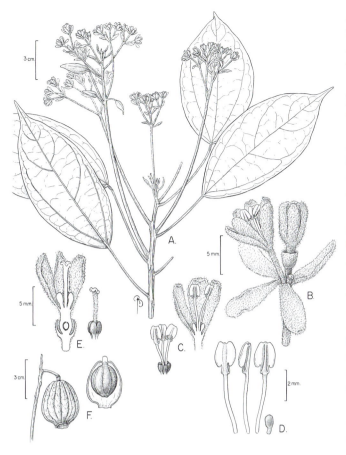

Figure 91. HERNANDIACEAE. *Hernandia guianensis*. **A.** Stem with leaves and inflorescences. **B.** Part of inflorescence subtended by four bracts; note open staminate flower. **C.** Medial section of staminate flower (right) and lateral view of androecium surrounded by glands (left). **D.** Abaxial (left), lateral (center), and adaxial (right) views of stamens, and lateral view of gland (far right). **E.** Medial section of pistillate flower (left) and lateral view of gynoecium surrounded by glands (right). **F.** Lateral view of bracteole-enclosed fruit (left) and fruit with front half of fused bracteoles removed (right). Reprinted with permission from Mori et al. (2002). Artist: Bobbi Angell.

centation apical, the ovule 1, pendulous. **Fruits** nuts (often referred to as drupes), dry, sometimes enclosed by bracteoles (*Hernandia*), sometimes with 2 wings (*Gyrocarpus*), the wings long, spatulate, erect. **Seeds** 1; endosperm absent.

In the Hernandioideae, most flowers and young fruits are shed during fruit development and only a few fruits per infructescence reach maturity. In contrast, in *Gyrocarpus* and *Sparattanthelium* (Gyrocarpoideae) many fruits per infructescence mature. In these genera, the axes of the dichasia become robust and woody and in *Sparattanthelium*, together with the fruits, assume a silvery or cream-colored surface that appears varnished.

Just as in the related Lauraceae, pollen in Hernandiaceae is remarkable because of the near absence of an exine, which is represented only by a thin layer and small spines of sporopollenin. Part of the intine, consisting of cellulose and polyglucanes, is radially channeled throughout; these channels

may act as repositories for substances involved in fertilization. Pollen grains lacking nearly all sporopollenin are so delicate that they do not fossilize and, therefore, pollen of the Hernandiaceae is not present in the fossil record.

In fruits of *Hernandia* the two bracteoles subtending the pistillate flowers are accrescent and form a bivalvate, red-colored envelope (*Hernandia bivalvis*), or fuse to form a bell-shaped or cupulate envelope enclosing the fruit (*H. guianensis*). The fruit wings of *Gyrocarpus* resemble those of the Dipterocarpaceae; but, in contrast to this family, they are not accrescent perianth lobes but arise from two independent meristems situated on the ovary wall below the perianth.

Natural history. No information is available on pollination biology. Hernandiaceae are most interesting because of their dispersal mechanisms, which provide clues for understanding the distribution of the family. Although several species of *Hernandia* grow in forests and are dispersed by wind or animals, an early switch to dispersal by water apparently occurred. This is suggested by the disjunct distributions in the Pacific, in Central and northern South America, and in the Caribbean of various species or species groups whose fruits have retained the capacity to float. *Hernandia nymphaeifolia* has the widest distribution, extending from Malesia to East Africa/Madagascar, Australia, and Polynesia. The spongy mesocarp of this species has been shown to permit drifting in the sea for up to 82 days. The tender cupule that surrounds the fruit and forms an air space in some species is quickly rubbed off, but it may permit short-distance dispersal of the fruits by allowing them to float in still water, as in *Hernandia guianensis*, a species of the flooded forests of coastal Guyana.

The fruits of *Gyrocarpus* are equipped with large wings, but dispersal by wind seems to be efficient only over short distances. As in *Hernandia*, the mesocarp of *G. americanus* fruits is spongy and the endocarp very resistent, so the fruits are capable of drifting in the sea for at least two months. *Gyrocarpus americanus* is a strand tree whose distribution extends from East Africa over South and Southeast Asia, Malesia, Australia to Polynesia, and Central and northern South America. The presence of this species in the Magdalena Valley of Colombia may be related to former marine transgressions. *Gyrocarpus jatrophifolius*, a deciduous tree distributed in Mexico and Central America, has seeds with a papery coat that is not adapted for water dispersal.

Sparattanthelium has no obvious adaptations for specialized dispersal. The hard nuts may be scattered by animals such as rodents.

Economic uses. Some species of Hernandiaceae are utilized for their timber.

References. HESSE, M., AND K. KUBITZKI. 1983. The sporoderm ultrastructure in *Persea*, *Nectandra*, *Hernandia*, *Gomortega* and some other lauralean genera. *Pl. Syst. Evol.*

141:299–311. KRESS, J., AND D. E. STONE. 1982. Nature of sporoderm in monocotyledons, with special reference to the pollen grains of *Canna* and *Heliconia*. *Grana* 21:129–48. KUBITZKI, K. 1969. Monographie der Hernandiaceen. *Bot.* *Jahrb. Syst.* 89:78–209. KUBITZKI, K. 1993. Hernandiaceae. In *The Families and Genera of Vascular Plants*, eds. K. Kubitzki, J. G. Rohwer, and V. Bittrich, 2:334–38. Berlin: Springer-Verlag.

HIPPOCASTANACEAE (Horse-Chestnut Family)

NATHAN SMITH

Plate 23

- *trees*

- *leaves opposite, palmately compound; leaflets 3*

- *flowers zygomorphic; petals 4–5, clawed, red or mostly white, stamens 6–8; ovary superior; placentation axile*

- *fruits loculicidal capsules*

Number of genera and species. Worldwide, the Hippocastanaceae comprise two genera and 15 species. In tropical America, there is a single genus, *Billia*, and two species.

Distribution and habitat. *Billia hippocastanum* is found in Costa Rica, Guatemala, and Mexico and *B. rosea* (=*B. columbiana*) grows in Costa Rica, Panama, Colombia, Venezuela, and Ecuador. The extratropical genus *Aesculus* grows in the United States, Baja California, Europe, and eastern Asia.

Species of *Billia* are found in mixed forests, often on slopes or along rivers between 100 and 3,000 meters.

Family classification. The Hippocastinaceae are placed in the Sapindales by Cronquist. Molecular analyses have shown that *Aesculus* and *Billia* are a monophyletic group. Many authors, however, treat *Aesculus* and *Billia* as a derived subfamily (the Hippocastanoideae) within the Sapindaceae *sensu lato* (see Sapindaceae).

Features of the family. Habit: trees; branches often with yellowish lenticels. **Stipules** absent. **Leaves** opposite, palmately compound; leaflets 3 per leaf, coriaceous, the margins entire. **Inflorescences** terminal, panicles, glabrous (*B. rosea*) or golden tomentose (*B. hippocastanum*); bracts present (*B. hippocastanum*) or inflorescence subtended by normal leaves (*B. rosea*). **Flowers** zygomorphic, bisexual or functionally unisexual (then plants andromonoecious, the unisexual flowers often at inflorescence apices); calyx with 5 sepals, the sepals distinct or slightly basally connate, usually unequal in size, red, purple, white, or green; corolla with 4–5

petals, the petals distinct, clawed, red, purple, or rarely pink in *B. hippocastanum*, or mostly white, sometimes pink abaxially, and the base often yellow in *B. rosea*, the upper 2 petals often longer and more narrow than 2 lateral petals, the lower or fifth petal equal or vestigial to lateral petals, or absent; disc present, extrastaminal, usually unilateral, rarely annular; androecium of 6–8 stamens, the stamens distinct, ascending, often differing in length, included or the longer stamens exserted (common in staminate flowers), the filaments red or white; gynoecium syncarpous, the ovary superior, glabrous, red, the carpels 3, the locules usually 3, the style simple, often pubescent, the stigma undivided to inconspicuously 3-lobed; placentation axile, the ovules 2 per locule. **Fruits** loculicidal capsules, the pericarp smooth, thick. **Seeds** 1–3 per fruit, 3–5 cm diameter.

The leaves of *Billia* are similar to those of *Caryocar* (Caryocaraceae), however, the petioles of *Billa* lack stipels and the blade margins are entire whereas the petioles of *Caryocar* have stipels and the blade margins are usually serrulate or serrate.

Natural history. No information is available on pollination and dispersal.

Economic uses. No uses are known for the Neotropical species. Species of *Aesculus*, such as *A. hippocastanum* (horse chestnut), are widely cultivated as ornamental trees.

References. FOREST, F., J. N. DROUIN, R. CHAREST, L. BROUILLET, AND A. BRUNEAU. 2001. A morphological phylogenetic analysis of *Aesculus* L. and *Billia* Peyr. (Sapindaceae). *Can. J. Bot.* 79:154–69. GADEK, P. A., E. S. FERNANDO, C. J. QUIM, S. B. HOOT, T. TERRAZAS, ET AL. 1996. Sapindales: Molecular delimitation and infraordinal groups. *Amer. J. Bot.* 83(6):802–11. HARDIN, J. W. 1957a. A revision of the American Hippocastanaceae. *Brittonia* 9(3):145–71. HARDIN, J. W. 1957b. A revision of the American Hippocastanaceae—II. *Brittonia* 9(4):173–95. ULLOA, C. U., AND JØRGENSEN, P. M. 2001. *Billia rosea*: the correct name for *Billia columbiana* (Hippocastanaceae). *Novon* 11(2):287.

HIPPOCRATEACEAE (Hippocratea Family)

JULIO ANTONIO LOMBARDI AND CAROL GRACIE

Figure 92, Plate 23

- *lianas, scandent shrubs, shrubs, or trees*

- *stipules minute*

- *leaves usually opposite or subopposite, simple*

- *flower perianth 5 merous; extrastaminal nectiferous disc usually present; stamens usually 3*

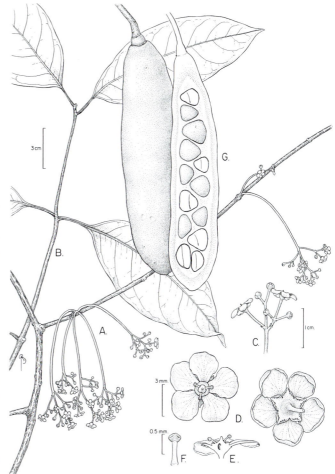

Numbers of genera and species. Worldwide, the Hippocrateaceae comprise 24 genera and more than 300 species. In tropical America, there are 12 genera and about 130 species. The largest genera in the Neotropics are *Salacia* (ca. 25 species), *Tontelea* (ca. 21), and *Cheiloclinium* (ca.13).

Distribution and habitat. The Hippocrateaceae are pantropical, with the number of species in the Eastern and the Western Hemisphere about equal. One of the largest genera, *Salacia*, is found in both hemispheres as are *Cuervea*, *Elachyptera*, *Hippocratea*, *Prionostemma*, and *Pristimera*.

The family is primarily found in lowland moist forest. In the neotropics, the centers of distribution are in the Amazon basin and the rain forests of Atlantic coastal Brazil. *Hippocratea volubilis* is a liana which inhabits both wet and dry forests. Some species of *Pristimera* are found in seasonally inundated forest, *Cuervea kappleriana* occurs along coastal areas and rivers, *Peritassa campestris*, *Salacia crassifolia*, and *Tontelea micrantha* are shrubs with underground xylopodia found in the *cerrados* of Brazil and Paraguay. Species of *Hylenaea* are lianas found along rivers in the Amazon Basin.

Family classification. The Hippocrateaceae are placed in the Celastrales by Cronquist. Although the Hippocrateaceae were first proposed as a separate family almost 200 years ago by Jussieau, many taxonomists include them in the Celastraceae. Modern cladistic and molecular studies support the recognition of the Hippocrateaceae as a monophyletic group nested inside the Celastraceae as, alternatively, one subfamily, the Hippocrateoideae, or two subfamilies, the Hippocrateoideae and Salacioideae.

The most obvious features that distinguish the Hippocrateaceae from the Celastraceae occur in the androecium. Flowers of Hippocrateaceae have only three stamens (with the exception of a few species of *Cheiloclinium*, which have five) rather than four or five, and the stamens are located within the nectiferous disc at the base of the ovary rather than outside of the disc or fused with it as in Celastraceae. The anthers of Celastraceae generally dehisce introrsely, while those of Hippocrateaceae dehisce in various ways, but almost never

Figure 92. HIPPOCRATEACEAE. *Tontelea cylindrocarpa.* **A.** Stem with inflorescences. **B.** Apex of stem with leaves. **C.** Part of inflorescence. **D.** Apical (left) and basal (right) views of flower. **E.** Medial section of flower. **F.** Adaxial view of stamen. **G.** Lateral view (left) and medial section of fruit (right) showing embedded seeds. Reprinted with permission from Mori et al. (2002). Artist: Bobbi Angell.

introrsely. Anther dehiscence is often by transverse slits in the Hippocrateaceae instead of by longitudinal slits in Celastraceae. Unlike many Celastraceae, the seeds of Hippocrateaceae do not have an aril or endosperm.

Features of the family. Habit: mostly lianas, scandent shrubs, shrubs, or trees, the trees sometimes small and slender with upper branches ± scandent. **Stipules** minute, usually caducous, sometimes forming interstipular scar. **Leaves** usually opposite or subopposite, rarely alternate, simple; blade margins often crenulate, serrate, or entire in *Salacia* and most species of *Tontelea*. **Inflorescences** axillary or on short branches beneath leaves (some may falsely appear to be terminal), paniculate, corymbose, pseudocymose, dichotomously branched, or fasciculate; bracts, and sometimes bracteoles, present, small. **Flowers** actinomorphic, bisexual, small; perianth usually persistent; sepals 5, connate at very base, not enclosing petals in bud; petals 5, distinct, alternate to sepals, usually yellow-green to white; extrastaminal nectiferous disc usually present, usually well developed; androecium usually of 3 stamens (5 in some *Cheiloclinium*), the stamens reflexed outward after anthesis, the filaments broadly expanded in most genera (wider than long), sometimes connate to inner disc wall, the anthers dehiscing by transverse or oblique slits; gynoecium syncarpous, the ovary superior, often triangular in shape, the carpels usually 3 (5 in some *Cheiloclinium*), the locules equal to number of carpels, the style short, awl-shaped, sometimes absent, the stigmas usually 3, entire, bilobed, or obscure; placentation axillary or subapical, the ovules 1–10 per locule, patent or somewhat pendulous. **Fruits** drupes, berries, woody capsules, or schizocarps, the drupes may be 3-locular, the capsules commonly 3-lobed, the schizocarps with three strongly divergent dehiscent mericarps on swollen receptacle in *Hippocratea* and *Pristimera*. **Seeds** usually 3–6 (in drupes), 6 to ± 30 (in capsules), often three-sided (in drupes), sometimes winged at base (in capsules) or embedded in mucilaginous pulp (in drupes); endosperm absent.

Lianas of the genus *Salacia* often have dimorphic branching with one type of branch having recurved branchlets modified for climbing. Other genera climb by twining. The cross section of the stem of some species of liana (e.g., *Tontelea nectandrifolia*) have alternating red and yellow-tan, more or less concentric rings. *Prionostemma aspera* has reddish sap.

The discs of *Peritassa* and some species of *Tontelea* are distinctively cylindrical and free from the ovaries. In most species of *Tontelea*, however, the inner disc wall is connate to the ovary. The disc of *Prionostemma aspera* is expanded and covered with short hairs, and that of species of *Cheiloclinium* covers all of the pistil except the stigmas and the base of the stamens. In this genus, the free portion of the stamens emerges from three or five small pockets on the lateral surface of the disc.

Natural history. Many of the lianas climb high into the canopy of the forest. No information is available on pollination. The seeds of species with capsular fruits are adapted for dispersal by wind or by water (*Cuervea kappleriana* and species of *Hylenaea*). The drupes of other species are consumed and dispersed by several species of monkeys.

Economic uses. No significant uses are known for species of Hippocrateaceae. Fruits of some species of *Peritassa* and *Salacia* are eaten locally. The seeds of *Hippocratea volubilis* are reported to be edible and to provide a source of oil. In Africa, twining lianas of the family are used in building rope bridges.

References: GÖRTS-VAN RIJN, A.R.A., AND M. W. MENNEGA. 1994. Hippocrateaceae. *Flora of the Guianas*, ser. A, 16:3–81. Koenigstein: Koeltz Scientific Books. MENNEGA, A.M.W. 1997. Wood anatomy of the Hippocrateoideae (Celastraceae). *IAWAJ*, 18:331–68. ROOSMALEN, M.G.M. VAN. 1985. *Fruits of the Guianan Flora*. Utrecht, Netherlands: Institute of Systematic Botany, Utrecht University. SIMMONS, M. P., AND J. P. HEDIN. 1999. Relationships and morphological character change among genera of Celastraceae *sensu lato* (including Hippocrateaceae). *Ann. Missouri Bot. Gard.* 86:723–57. SMITH, A. C. 1940. The American species of Hippocrateaceae. *Brittonia* 3:341–555.

HUGONIACEAE (Hugonia Family)

CAROL ANN KEARNS

Figure 93, Plate 24

- *medium to large trees of lowland forests*
- *leaves alternate, simple*
- *flower petals 5, irregular; stamens 10 or 15, unequal*
- *fruits drupelike*

Numbers of genera and species. Worldwide, the Hugoniaceae comprise about six genera and 40 species. Genera include *Hugonia, Durandea, Hebepetalum, Indorouchera, Philbornea, Roucheria*, and sometimes *Ctenolophon*. Takhatajan places *Ctenolophon* in its own monogeneric, Paleotropical family Ctenolophonaceae. In tropical America, the Hugoniaceae are represented by about 10 species in the two closely related genera, *Hebepetalum* (treated as *Roucheria* in some floras) and *Roucheria*.

Distribution and habitat. The family is represented in Africa, Madagascar, Indomalaysia, and New Caledonia, as well as in the neotropics. *Hebepetalum* and *Roucheria* are South American trees of wet lowland forests, occasionally reaching montane areas up to 2,000 meters.

Family classification. The Hugoniaceae are placed in the Linales by Cronquist. The family is closely allied with the Linaceae and included within the Linaceae by some authors.

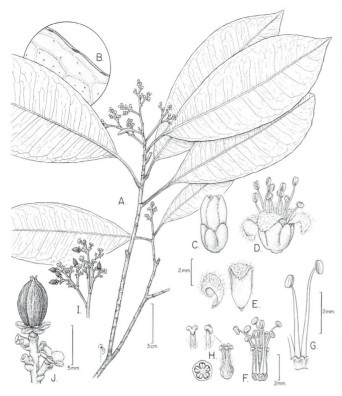

Features of the family. Habit: medium to large trees. **Stipules** present, deciduous. **Leaves** alternate, simple, the epidermis mucilaginous. **Inflorescences** terminal, racemes, spikes, or panicles. **Flowers** somewhat zygomorphic (with asymmetrical calyx and sometimes asymmetrical androecium), bisexual, small, yellow, white, or green; calyx with 5 imbricate sepals, the sepals more or less unequal ; corolla with 5 petals, the petals irregular, convolute; androecium with 10 or 15 stamens, the stamens alternate or opposite petals, unequal in length, the filaments united at base, often forming a tube, the anthers dehiscing by slits; staminodes sometimes present; gynoecium syncarpous, the ovary superior, lacking false septa, the locules 2–5, the styles 1–5, often partially fused at base; placentation apical-axile, the ovules 2 per locule, pendulous. **Fruits** drupelike. **Seeds** with or without endosperm, the embryo straight to slightly curved.

Natural history. No information is available on pollination. The drupelike fruits of at least some species are dispersed by fruit-eating birds, such as trogons and toucans.

Economic uses. The African species *Hugonia* produce edible fruits that are consumed by humans.

Figure 93. HUGONIACEAE. *Hebepetalum humiriifolium*. **A.** Stem with leaves and inflorescences in bud. **B.** Abaxial leaf surface showing inconspicuous punctations. **C.** Lateral view of bud just before anthesis. **D.** Lateral view of flower at anthesis. **E.** Lateral (left) and abaxial (right) views of petals. **F.** Lateral view of flower with perianth removed. **G.** Views of stamens with basal nectaries. **H.** Lateral view of gynoecium (right), detail of stigmas (above left), and transverse section of ovary (below left). **I.** Part of infructescence. **J.** Detail of infructescence with fruit. Reprinted with permission from Mori et al. (2002). Artist: Bobbi Angell.

References. JARDIM, A. G. 1999. A Revision of *Roucheria* Planch. and *Hebepetalum* Benth. (Hugoniaceae). M.S. thesis. University of Missouri, St. Louis. Dissertation Abstracts: Accession number: AAG1395639. PARRADO-ROSSELLI, A., AND J. CAVELIER. 1998. Fruit size and primary seed dispersal of five canopy plant species of the Colombian Amazon. *Abstracts From Forest Canopies 1998: Global Perspectives*. November 4–8, 1998. Sarasota, FL: Marie Selby Botanical Gardens. http://www.selby.org/research/cano/conf.htm.

HUMIRIACEAE (Humiria Family)

DANIEL SABATIER

Figure 94, Plate 24

- *trees and shrubs*

- *leaves alternate, simple; dotlike glands often present*

- *flowers actinomorphic, bisexual; anther connectives thick; stamens often numerous; intrastaminal disc present*

- *Fruit endocarp woody, valvately dehiscent*

Numbers of genera and species. Worldwide, the Humiriaceae comprise eight genera and about 65 species, all of which except one are native to tropical America. The largest genera are *Vantanea* (20 species), *Humiriastrum* (17 species), and *Sacoglottis* (11 species). *Humiria balsamifera* is a widely distributed complex of 15 varieties.

Distribution and habitat. The Humiriaceae occur throughout tropical America. The greatest number of species are

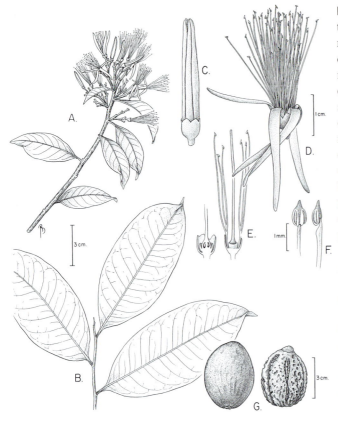

Figure 94. HUMIRIACEAE. *Vantanea guianensis.* **A.** Stem with leaves and inflorescences. **B.** Stem with leaves. **C.** Lateral view of flower bud. **D.** Lateral view of open flower showing numerous stamens. **E.** Medial section of base of flower (left) with corolla, androecium, and upper part of gynoecium removed (note axile placentation of ovules), and longitudinal section of flower (right) with corolla removed (note connate filament bases and cupular disc). **F.** Adaxial (left) and lateral (right) views of stamens showing the expanded and prolonged connective. **G.** Lateral views of intact fruit (left) and endocarp (right). Reprinted with permission from Mori et al. (2002). Artist: Bobbi Angell.

found in the Amazon basin where several monotypic genera (*Duckesia*, *Endopleura*, and *Hylocarpa*) are endemic. A single species, *Sacoglottis gabonensis*, is found in forested areas of western tropical Africa.

The family occurs in a variety of habitats from mountain scrub vegetation to swamp forests. Species may grow at elevations up to 2,000 meters in the Guayana Highlands, but most species occur at low elevations in tropical rain forests and savanna woodlands. While *Humiria balsamifera* is often dominant in forests that grow on leached sands, most species of the family are usually found as scattered individuals.

Family classification. The Humiriaceae are placed in the Linales by Cronquist near the Ixonanthaceae and Hugoniaceae. Recent molecular studies place *Humiria* in an expanded Malpighiales among the Eurosids I.

Based on floral and fruit features, two tribes are recognized: Humirioideae and Vantaneoideae. The latter, with only one genus, *Vantanea*, is the most primitive.

Features of the family. Habit: trees or shrubs, evergreen, the shrubs sometimes prostrate in open areas. **Wood** usually red-brown. **Bark** smooth and lenticellate, irregularly peeling, deeply longitudinally fissured or reticulately cracked, the inner bark usually fibrous, reddish. **Buttresses** sometimes present, small, thick. **Stems** sometimes angled or winged. **Stipules** small and geminate or absent. **Leaves** alternate, simple; petioles often swollen at base; blades sometimes with striations running lengthwise, often dotlike glands present, the margins entire, crenate, or serrate, rolled inward when young, the apex often retuse (species of *Humiria* and *Vantanea*); venation brochidrodromous. **Inflorescences** axillary, rarely terminal, paniculate, equal to or larger than leaves, often well developed and conspicuous, the axis often ending in dichasial or pleiochasial cymes; bracts small. **Flowers** actinomorphic, bisexual, usually inconspicuously colored (except *Vantanea guianensis* with relatively large, bright red flowers); sepals 5, quincuncial or imbricate, connate at base, forming a cupule or small tube, sometimes bearing marginal or dorsal glands; petals 5, distinct, contorted, cochlear or quincuncial, linear, oblong, or elliptic; androecium of numerous (*Vantanea*) or 10–30 stamens, the stamens definite or indefinite in number, the filaments connate at base, the anthers usually with strongly developed connective, the thecae 2 or 2–4; intrastaminal disc present, ringlike or formed by free scales; gynoecium syncarpous, the ovary superior, the carpels (4)5(8), the locule 1, the style simple, cylindrical, more or less elongate, the stigma indistinctly divided; placentation axile, the ovules 1–2 (*Humiria* and *Vantanea*) per carpel, anatropous, pendulous, with a ventral raphe, the integuments 2. **Fruits** drupaceous, small (<1 cm diameter in some *Humiria*) to relatively large (to 10 cm long in some *Vantanea*), globose or ovoid to oblong-elliptic, often yellow, orange, brown, or black (most *Humiria* and some *Humiriastrum*) when ripe, the exocarp usually thin, the mesocarp usually fleshy, firm, or coriaceous, rarely juicy or compact fibrous, rich in oil, the endocarp woody, compact, spongious or cavernous, valvately dehiscent. **Seeds** few; endosperm homogenous, the embryo large, the cotyledons foliaceous.

Distinctions between genera are based on variations in androecium structure. In *Vantanea* (Tribe Vantaneoideae), the stamens are monotypic, numerous (40–200 or more; rarely 15–18), pluriseriate, and indefinite in number. The filaments are flexuous, and each connective bears 2 bilocular anthers at the base. In the other genera (tribe Humirioideae), the stamens usually appear in one or infrequently two whorls (*Hylocarpa*), their number is reduced (10–30) and definite, the filaments are rigid and compressed, and the 2–4 thecae are always unilocular. In *Hylocarpa* the stamens are identical, they are of two different sizes in *Duckesia*, *Endopleura*, *Humiria*, *Humiriastrum*, and *Sacoglottis*, and of three types in *Schistostemon*. The latter genus is characterized by its 5 3-parted, 3 antheriferous, larger stamens resulting from the fusion of 3 stamens.

The endocarp of the fruit provides very distinctive generic characters. In *Humiria* and *Humiriastrum*, 5 conspicuous apical apertures (foramina) alternate with 5 longitudinal or sub-apical valves. In *Duckesia, Endopleura, Hylocarpa,* and *Vantanea,* the valves occupy most of the length of the fruit and alternate with the more or less developed ribs. In *Endopleura,* the ribs are well developed and deeply longitudinally grooved. In *Sacoglottis* and *Schistostemon,* the valves are very well developed, covering most of endocarp surface. The latter two genera are also similar in having their endocarps filled with conspicuous, bubblelike, resinous cavities. Such cavities occur in *Duckesia* and are present but inconspicuous in some *Humiriastrum.*

Natural history. Little is known about the pollination biology of the family, but the red flowers of *Vantanea guianensis* are likely visited and pollinated by hummingbirds. Dispersal is by fruit-eating or seed-eating animals, including birds, bats, rodents, monkeys, or large terrestrial mammals like tapirs. The woody endocarps float, so secondary dispersal by water is possible. The presence of *Sacoglottis gabonensis* in West Africa is probably the result of water dispersal.

Economic uses. Although there are no true crop plants among Humiriaceae, many of them are exploited locally. *Humiria balsamifera* produces the *umiri*-balsam used in folk medicine. Fruits of several species are edible, and those of *Endopleura uchi* often are sold in Amazonian markets. Wood is used locally for heavy construction.

References. CAVALCANTE, P. B. 1974. *Frutas comestíveis da Amazônia* 1:1–83. Belém, Pará: Conselho Nacional de Pesquisas, Instituto Nacional de Pesquisas da Amazonia, Museu Paraense Emilio Goeldi. CAVALCANTE, P. B. 1979. *Frutas comestíveis da Amazônia* 3:1–61. Belém, Pará: Conselho Nacional de Pesquisas, Instituto Nacional de Pesquisas da Amazonia, Museu Paraense Emilio Goeldi. CUATRECASAS, J. 1961. A taxonomic revision of the Humiriaceae. *Contr. U.S. Natl. Herb.* 35(2):25–214. DUCKE, A. 1922. Plantes nouvelles ou peu connues de la région amazonienne IIéme partie Humiriaceae. *Arch. Jard. Bot. Rio de Janeiro* 3:175–80, 271.

HYDNORACEAE (Hydnora Family)

LYTTON JOHN MUSSELMAN

Plate 24

- *subterranean holoparasites, chlorophyll absent*
- *roots fleshy*
- *leaves absent*
- *flowers with hypanthial tube; tepals 3–4; ovary inferior*

Numbers of genera and species. Worldwide, the Hydnoraceae comprise two genera, *Hydnora* and *Prosopanche,* and six species. In tropical America, there is a single genus, *Prosopanche,* and two species.

Distribution and habitat. The Hydnoraceae occur in Central and South America, Africa, and contiguous regions of the Arabian Peninsula. *Prosopanche americana* is known from many sites in Argentina and by a single collection from Costa Rica (as *P. costaricensis*). *Prosopanche bonacinae* occurs in Argentina, Paraguay, and Brazil. The family is usually found in semiarid regions.

Family classification. The Hydnoraceae are placed by Chronquist in the Rafflesiales, an order dominated by parasitic plants. Recent molecular data suggest that Hydnoraceae are related to genera of the Aristolochiaceae.

Features of the family. Habit: herbs, subterranean holoparasites, scales and nodes absent, chlorophyll absent. **Roots** adventitious, short, fleshy, succulent, sharply angled in cross section, mucilage and tannin canals prominent, root hairs absent. **Haustoria** present. **Leaves** absent. **Inflorescences** of solitary flowers, arising from roots. **Flowers** actinomorphic, bisexual; buds tubular, opening after breaking through soil; hypanthium prolonged above ovary into tube; tepals 3 or 4; androecium complex, forming dome or cap with a small central opening, the stamens as many as tepals, fused together, sessile; staminodes 3, inserted below orifice to chamber; ovary inferior, compound, the carpels 3(4), the locule 1; placentation parietal, the ovules in 3 groups. **Fruits** opening circumscissilely, the interior fleshy, the placentae edible. **Seeds** numerous, small; endosperm well developed, the embryo minute, undifferentiated.

The pollen of *Hydnora* is monosulcate and that of *Prosopanche* is mainly disulcate.

Natural history. *Prosopanche americana* is parasitic on species of *Prosopis* (Fabaceae), and *Prosopanche bonacinae* parasitizes species of many dicot families.

The flowers of *P. americana* last between 48 and 72 hours. When they open at dusk, a very strong fruity odor is produced. At this time, the temperature inside the flower rises above ambient temperature. The stigma is receptive only during the first night, when beetles (weevils and sap beetles) first arrive. The flowers become functionally male on the second day, and by the third night, pollen is released in copious amounts. As the beetles leave the flowers, they are dusted with pollen; they then move to first-day flowers with receptive stigmas.

Seed dispersal may be by nocturnal mammals, such as foxes or armadillos, that ingest the fruit for its aromatic and pleasant-flavored pulp.

Economic uses. The roots of *Prosopanche americana* are harvested on a large scale, dried, and sold as *guaycuru* in the markets of many Argentine cities. More than three tons per year are sold in La Paz, a center of commerce in herbal medicine in central Argentina. *Guaycuru* is used as a cure for diarrhea and is employed in a remarkably similar way as the dried rhizomes of *Hydnora* in Sudan. *Guaycuru* is also burned for inhalation by asthmatics. It is harvested from both living and dead plants, especially in arroyos where water has exposed the roots of the host, *Prosopis*. The fruits of *Prosopanche* have been used for food, eaten either raw or fried.

References. Cocucci, A. E., and A. A. Cocucci. 1996. *Prosopanche* (Hydnoraceae): somatic and reproductive structures, biology, systematics, phylogeny and potentialities as a parasitic weed. In *Advances in Parasitic Plant Research*, eds. M. T. Moreno, J. I. Cubero, D. Berner, D. Joel, L. J. Musselman, and C. Parker, 179–93. Cordoba, Spain: Junta de Andalucia, Dirección General de Investigación Agraria. Musselman, L. J., and J. H. Visser. 1989. Taxonomy and natural history of *Hydnora* (Hydnoraceae). *Aliso* 12(2):317–26. Musselman, L. J., and P. Vorster. 2000. Finding furtive flowers. *Plant Talk* 21:38–39. Nickrent, D. L., A. Blarer, Y.-L. Qiu, D. E. Soltis, P. S. Soltis, and M. Zanis. 2002. Molecular data place Hydnoraceae with Aristolochiaceae. *Amer. J. Bot.* 89(11):1809–17.

HYDRANGEACEAE (Hydrangea Family)

Larry Hufford

Figure 95

- *shrubs or lianas*

- *leaves opposite, simple*

- *flowers with 4–many stamens; ovary inferior or subinferior; placentation axile and/or parietal*

- *fruits capsules*

Numbers of genera and species. Worldwide, the Hydrangeaceae comprise 15 genera and approximately 220 species. The most species-rich genera are *Philadelphus* (71 species), *Deutzia* (62 species), and *Hydrangea*. (The traditionally circumscribed paraphyletic genus has 29 species, whereas the monophyletic *Hydrangea* clade has approximately 59 species.)

In tropical America, there are three genera: *Deutzia*, *Hydrangea*, and *Philadelphus*. The monophyletic *Hydrangea* section *Cornidia* has been circumscribed to include two subsections: *Monosegia* (eight species, including *H. integrifolia* of the paleotropics) and *Polysegia* (four species). Fourteen species of *Philadelphus* subgenus *Gemmatus* are largely Neotropical. *Deutzia* subgenus *Neodeutzia* (four species) is restricted to the neotropics.

Distribution and habitat. Most Hydrangeaceae occur in the subtropical Northern Hemisphere, especially in North America and Asia. The larger genera of the family, including *Deutzia*, *Hydrangea*, and *Philadelphus*, as well as *Decumaria*, which has only two species, are disjunct between Asia and North America.

Deutzia, *Hydrangea*, and *Philadelphus*, with numerous species in both the Western and Eastern Hemispheres, include taxa that are found in the tropics. *Deutzia* includes a few species in Neotropical Mexico; *Philadelphus* subgenus *Gemmatus* is distributed from central Mexico to Costa Rica; and Neotropical species of *Hydrangea* section *Cornidia* extend from northern Mexico to central Chile and Argentina, where they are found in wet montane forests.

Family classification. The Hydrangeaceae are placed in the Rosales by Cronquist; however, recent studies indicate that the family is sister to the Loasaceae and close to the Cornaceae, and together these families are well supported as members of the Cornales. *Fendlera* and *Jamesia* comprise subfamily Jamesioideae, the sister group to the rest of the Hydrangeaceae of subfamily Hydrangeoideae. Hydrangeoideae consist of the tribes Philadelpheae and Hydrangeeae. In the Philadelpheae, *Deutzia* and *Kirengeshoma* are sister taxa to *Carpenteria* and *Philadelphus*. In the Hydrangeeae, *Cardiandra* and *Deinanthe* form a monophyletic group that appears to be the sister to the *Hydrangea* clade. Relationships in the *Hydrangea* clade, which includes *Hydrangea*, *Broussaisia*, *Dichroa*, *Decumaria*, *Pileostegia*, *Schizophragma*, and *Platycrater* are uncer-

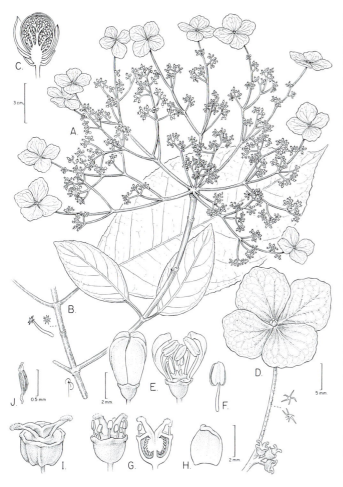

distinct; androecium of 4–10 or >15 stamens, diplostemonous to polystemonous (including Neotropical *Philadelphus* and *Deutzia*); gynoecium syncarpous, the ovary inferior or subinferior, the carpels 2–4, the locules 2 at base, 1 distally, the styles synstylous in *Philadelphus*, separate in *Deutzia* and *Hydrangea*; placentation axile and/or parietal, the ovules many. **Fruits** capsules, variously dehiscent. **Seeds** small, the seed coat reticulate.

The plesiomorphic condition for fruit dehiscence in the family is septicidal and dehiscence extends basipetally from the apex of the ovary. Fruit dehiscence in *Philadelphus* is similar except that it is loculicidal. Although *Deutzia* has septicidal dehiscence, it is distinctive in extending acropetally from the base of the ovary to form valves (corresponding to individual carpels) that spread outward from the base. *Deutzia* also has interstylar dehiscence, creating a gap at the apex of the fruit. *Hydrangea* is similar to *Deutzia* in having a dehiscence zone between the separate styles to create an opening at the fruit apex.

Natural history. Little is known about pollination and dispersal biology of Hydrangeaceae, particularly the tropical species. The sterile, showy flowers, however, probably attract pollinators.

Economic uses. Many members of the family are used as ornamentals, especially species of *Deutzia*, *Hydrangea*, *Kirengeshoma*, *Philadelphus* (mock orange), and *Schizophragma* from the Eastern Hemisphere. Roots and leaves of several *Hydrangea* contain alkaloids with poisonous and medicinal properties.

References. Hu, S.-Y. 1954. A monograph of the genus *Philadelphus*. *J. Arnold Arbor.* 35:275–333. Hufford, L. 1997. A phylogenetic analysis of Hydrangeaceae based on morphological data. *Int. J. Pl. Sci.* 158(5):652–72. Hufford, L., M. L. Moody, and D. E. Soltis. 2001. A phylogenetic analysis of Hydrangeaceae based on sequences of the plastid gene *matK* and their combination with *rbcL* and morphological data. *Int. J. Pl. Sci.* 162:835–46. Lawson-Hall, T., and B. Rothera. 1995. *Hydrangeas: A gardeners' guide.* Portland: Timber Press. McClintock, E. 1957. A monograph of the genus *Hydrangea*. *Proc. Calif. Acad. Sci.* 29: 147–256. Nevling, L. I. 1964. Climbing hydrangeas and their relatives. *Arnoldia (Jamaica Plain)* 24:17–39. Soltis, D. E., Q.-Y. Xiang, and L. Hufford. 1995. Relationships and evolution of Hydrangeaceae based on *rbc*L sequence data. *Amer. J. Bot.* 82:504–14. Stern, W. L. 1978. Comparative anatomy and systematics of woody Saxifragaceae. *Hydrangea*. *Bot. J. Linn. Soc.* 76:83–113. Styer, C. H., and W. L. Stern. 1979. Comparative anatomy and systematics of woody Saxifragaceae. *Deutzia*. *Bot. J. Linn. Soc.* 79:291–319. Styer, C. H., and W. L. Stern. 1979. Comparative anatomy and systematics of woody Saxifragaceae. *Philadelphus*. *Bot. J. Linn. Soc.* 79:267–89. Zaïkonnikova, T. I. 1975. A key to the species of the genus *Deutzia* Thunberg (Saxifragaceae). *Baileya* 19:133–44.

Figure 95. HYDRANGEACEAE. *Hydrangea peruviana* (A, E, F, MacBryde and Simmons 851; B, I, J, Delprete 6108; C, D, G, H, Holm-Nielsen 6935). **A.** Stem with leaves and inflorescence. **B.** Details of trichomes on stem. **C.** Medial section of flower bud. **D.** Part of inflorescence showing sterile flower, stellate trichomes, and young fruits. **E.** Lateral views of staminate flowers intact (left) and with several petals and stamens removed (right). **F.** Adaxial view of stamen. **G.** Lateral view of pistillate flower with petals removed (left) and medial section of same (right). **H.** Adaxial view of petal. **I.** Oblique-apical view of immature fruit. **J.** Seed. Original. Artist: Bobbi Angell.

tain. It is clear, however, that *Hydrangea* as circumscribed traditionally is not monophyletic.

Features of the family. Habit: shrubs or lianas (*Hydrangea* section *Cornidia*), the shrubs with strong basitonic branching; trichomes present, stellate in *Hydrangea* section, *Cornidia* and *Deutzia*. **Stipules** absent. **Leaves** opposite, simple. **Inflorescences** terminal or axillary, cymose. **Flowers** actinomorphic, bisexual or some sterile (most *Hydrangea*), the sterile flowers showy, on periphery of inflorescences; sepals usually 4–5, valvate, enlarged on sterile flowers; corolla usually with 4–5 petals, sometimes more varying even within inflorescences, valvate (most species of *Hydrangea* clade, some species of *Deutzia*) or imbricate (in more basal clades, including Neotropical *Philadelphus* and *Deutzia*), the petals

HYDROPHYLLACEAE (Waterleaf Family)

Maria Hofmann

Figure 96, Plate 24

- *herbs, subshrubs, shrubs, rarely small trees*
- *plants often covered with eglandular and/or glandular hairs*
- *leaves usually alternate, simple*
- *inflorescences often scorpioid*
- *fruits capsules*

Numbers of genera and species. Worldwide, the Hydrophyllaceae comprise 17 genera and approximately 300 species. The largest genera are *Phacelia* (±200 species), *Nama* (±40 species), and *Hydrolea* (±11 species). Five genera have only one species. In tropical America, there are four genera (*Hydrolea, Nama, Phacelia, Wigandia*) and about 20 species.

Distribution and habitat. Hydrophyllaceae are distributed throughout most of the temperate and tropical regions of the world, except Australia, where *Hydrolea zeylanica* and *Phacelia tanacetifolia* have been introduced. The family has a center of diversity in western North America. *Phacelia* and *Nama* have a few species that reach South America; *Wigandia* is an essentially tropical genus restricted to Central and South America; and *Hydrolea*, the only pantropical genus, is distributed in Central and South America, the West Indies, Central Africa, and tropical Asia. The South African *Codon* (two species), is the only genus that does not occur naturally in the Western Hemisphere.

The Hydrophyllaceae are a common element in a wide variety of habitats. In Central and South America, species are present from sea level to above 4,000 meters in the Andes. Species of *Hydrolea* prefer marshes, wet thickets, meadows, or sand along streams, rivers, and lakes and those of *Nama* occupy diverse habitats ranging from arid, alkaline-gypseous flats to more mesic, but seasonally dry slopes at higher elevations, especially preferring disturbed areas. *Nama dichotomum* and *N. jamaicense* are common weeds in gardens, fields, and dry hillsides. *Phacelia* is well represented in Mexico and in the Andes as a common herb in fields, along roadsides, on dry or moist meadows, or on gravelly soil of rocky slopes and *P. cumingii* is remarkable for its range in elevation, occurring from near sea level to 4,000 meters in the Andes of Chile and Argentina. *Wigandia* is a weedy genus reaching more than 3,000 meters in the Andes; it frequently grows in waste places, dry slopes, and oak-pine forests, and its species are often among the first plants to invade the sides of new roads.

Family classification. The Hydrophyllaceae are placed in the Solanales by Cronquist and the Boraginales by Takhtajan. Systematic placement of the family has traditionally been based on flower and fruit characters. As inferred by molecular analysis, the family seems to have its closest relatives within the "ehretioid" members (woody and tropical) of Boraginaceae and, with the exceptions of *Hydrolea* and *Codon*, seems to form a monophyletic group. Within the Hydrophyllaceae, four tribes are recognized: Hydroleae (*Hydrolea*), Hydrophylleae (five genera), Nameae (four genera), and Phacelieae (seven genera).

Features of the family. Habit: herbs, subshrubs, shrubs (to 2 m in *Hydrolea spinosa*), sometimes armed with thorns, rarely small trees (to 5 m in *Wigandia*), decumbent, ascending, or erect, unbranched or highly branched, the herbs annual or perennial, the subshrubs robust; stems, leaves, and flowers often variously pubescent, the hairs unicellular-eglandular, pluricellular-eglandular, pluricellular-glandular, sometimes stinging in *Wigandia*. **Roots** slender or stout taproots, fibrous, or tuberous. **Rhizomes** sometimes present. **Stipules** absent. **Leaves** alternate, rarely opposite, the basal leaves sometimes in rosettes, simple (the simple leaves sometimes pinnatifid) or compound (bi- or tripinnate in *Phacelia*); blades oblong, lanceolate, sometimes deeply divided, the margins entire or lobed. **Inflorescences** terminal or axillary, scorpioid cymes (unrolling during anthesis, then inflorescences raceme-like), or flowers solitary or paired in axils (e.g., *Nama*); peduncles sometimes absent. **Flowers** actinomorphic, bisexual; sepals fused at base, the lobes 5, ovate or lanceolate, similar or unequal, persistent until fruit has ripened; corolla sympetalous, rotate, campanulate, or funnelform, white, rarely yellow or bluish to violet, the lobes 5; stamens 5, epipetalous, equally or unequally inserted on corolla tube near base, included or exserted, a pair of corolla scales sometimes present near base of each filament, the filaments glabrous or pubescent, the anthers dehiscing longitudinally; nectary present at base of ovary; gynoecium syncarpous, the ovary superior or subinferior, pubescent, usually glandular, the carpels 2, the

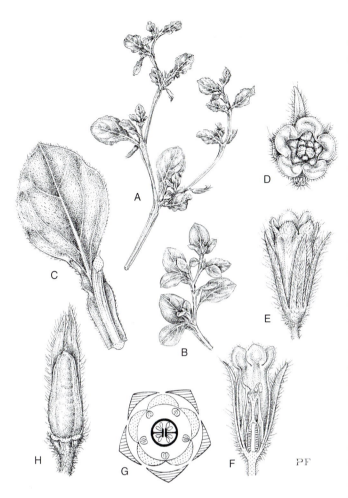

Figure 96. HYDROPHYLLACEAE. *Nama jamaicense.* **A.** Stems with leaves, flowers, and fruits (x⅔). **B.** Stem with leaves (x⅔). **C.** Leaf showing winged petiole (x2). **D.** Apical view of flower (x8). **E.** Lateral view of flower (x6). **F.** Medial section of flower (x6). **G.** Floral diagram. **H.** Lateral view of fruit with three sepals removed (x6). Reprinted with permission from Correll and Correll (1982). Artist: Priscilla Fawcett.

locules 1 or 2(*Hydrolea*), the style 1 (bifid or deeply bifurcate in *Phacelia*) or 2 (rarely 3–5 in *Hydrolea*), slender, pubescent to hispid at base (*Nama*, *Phacelia*, and *Wigandia*), glandular-pubescent (*Hydrolea*), or rarely glabrous (*N. dichotomum*), the stigmas capitate (paddlelike in *Wigandia*); placentation parietal (with 2 placentae) or axile (*Hydrolea*), the ovules few to numerous (usually 4, sometimes less, to >400 in *Hydrolea*), anatropous, unitegmic, tenuinucellate. **Fruits** capsules, ovoid, 2–4 valved, dehiscing loculicidally or septicidally, the apex obtuse or subacute. **Seeds** few to numerous, ovoid to cylindrical, varying in shape and ornamentation (the ornamentation important in defining genera); endosperm oily, the embryo small, straight, the cotyledons entire.

Chromosome numbers vary from $n = 5$ (*Phacelia* subgenus *Cosmanthus*) to $n = 38$ (*Wigandia kunthii*). No basic chromosome number is discernible.

Natural history. Pollination is accomplishs primarily by nectar- or pollen-collecting bees and wasps, but flies, butterflies, and pollen-eating beetles have been reported as possible pollinators. Although protandry and flower structure favor cross-pollination, some species (e.g., *Phacelia*) are self-compatible. Heterostyly is known in *Eriodictyon*, *Nama*, and *Phacelia* and gynodioecy occurs in *Phacelia* (e.g., *P. linearis*).

Dispersal is primarily by ejection of seeds out of the dehiscing capsules. In *Hydrolea spinosa*, the seeds remain afloat for several days and can be dispersed by water currents or waterfowl. The seeds of *Nemophila* possess a elaiosome, which suggests ant dispersal.

Economic uses. Some Hydrophyllaceae with showy flowers have been introduced into the neotropics as ornamentals and some of these have become weeds (e.g., species of *Nemophila* and *Phacelia*). Some species are used locally in folk medicine, but members of the family are of little economic importance as medicinals. *Nama jamaicense* (*Sacha tabaco*) is cultivated as tobacco in parts of northeast Argentina, and the leaves are used in Mexico to treat gastric ulcers. In Honduras, extracts from the cut rhizomes and roots of *Wigandia caracasana* are used to cure venereal diseases, and an infusion of the leaves is a remedy for rheumatism in both Honduras and Costa Rica. In Guatemala, the leaves of *W. kunthii* are sometimes used to impart aroma to tamales, and the larger stems are used as firewood.

The trichomes of species of *Wigandia*, *Turricula parryi*, and species of *Phacelia* inflict an unpleasant sting that causes contact dermatitis. The chemical components responsible for this reaction are phenolics exuded from the heads of the glandular trichomes. When the leaves or stalks of *Wigandia caracasana*, *Hydrolea spinosa*, and some *Phacelia* are crushed, a persistent brownish exudate discolors whatever it comes in contact with.

References. BORSINI, O. E. 1946. Contribución a las "Hydrophyllaceae" argentinas I. El género "Nama." *Lilloa* 12: 9–21. BRAND, A. 1913. Hydrophyllaceae. In *Das Pflanzenreich*, ed., A. Engler, series 4, 251(heft 59):1–210. Leipzig: Wilhelm Engelmann. CONSTANCE, L. 1963. Chromosome number and classification in Hydrophyllaceae. *Brittonia* 15: 273–85. DAVENPORT, L. J. 1988. A monograph of Hydrolea (Hydrophyllaceae). *Rhodora* 90:169–208. DEGINANI, N. B. 1982. Revisión de las especies argentinas del género *Phacelia* (Hydrophyllaceae). *Darwiniana* 24:405–35. DI FULVIO, T. E. 1989a. Embriologia de *Nama jamaicense* (Phacelieae, Hydrophyllaceae). *Kurtziana* 20:9–31. DI FULVIO, T. E. 1989b. Observaciones embriológicas en especies Argentinas de *Hydrolea* (Hydrophyllaceae) con especial referéncia a la endospermogénesis. *Kurtziana* 20:33–64. FERGUSON, D. M. 1999. Phylogenetic analysis and relationships in Hydorphyllaceae based on *ndh*F sequence data. *Syst. Bot.* 23(3): 253–68. HOFMANN, M. 1999. Flower and fruit development in the genus *Phacelia* (Phacelieae, Hydrophyllaceae): characters of systematic value. *Syst. & Geogr. Pl.* 68:203–12. REYNOLDS, G. W., W. EPSTEIN, AND E. RODRIGUEZ 1986. Unusual contact allergens from plants in the family Hydrophyllaceae. *Contact Dermatitis* 14:39–44.

ICACINACEAE (Icacina Family)

Rodrigo Duno de Stefano

Figure 97, Plate 25

- *trees, lianas, or sometimes scandent shrubs*
- *leaves alternate, simple*
- *flowers with stamens equal to number of petals; ovary usually with 1 locule, the ovules 2, pendent from apex*
- *fruits drupes*

Numbers of genera and species. Worldwide, the Icacinaceae comprise approximately 52 genera and 400 species. In tropical America, there are 12 genera and 54–57 species. The largest Neotropical genus is *Emmotum* with 10 species. The Neotropical *Calatola*, *Casimirella*, *Citronella*, and *Pleurisanthes* have six or seven species each, and *Dendrobangia*, *Discophora*, *Leretia*, *Mappia*, *Oecopetalum*, *Ottoschulzia*, and *Poraqueiba* have fewer than three species each. The taxonomy of some Neotropical genera is not very well known, especially of climbing genera such as *Pleurisanthes*.

Distribution and habitat. Icacinaceae occur predominantly in the Tropics, rapidly decreasing in number of species toward the subtropics. Genera of the family are mostly endemic to major phytogeographical realms, an exception is *Citronella*, which is found in America, Asia, and Oceania.

Only a few species in the Western Hemisphere occur in subtropical regions, and *Citronella mucronata* is found outside of the Tropics and subtropics. Most tropical American genera are widespread, but three genera, *Mappia*, *Oecopetalum*, and *Ottoschultzia* are mostly confined to the Caribbean.

The Icacinaceae occupy a variety of habitats excluding desert, swamp forests (at least in the neotropics), and very cold areas at high elevations. They are most abundant in tropical lowland rain forests. No species is reported to be dominant in any vegetation type.

Family classification. The Icacinaceae are closely related to the Aquifoliaceae. Cronquist placed these families in the Celastrales, but Savolainen et. al., using molecular data, have demonstrated that the Celastrales *sensu* Cronquist is polyphyletic and can be divided into two main clades. The first clade includes *Icacina* (Icacinaceae), Aquifoliaceae, and *Camellia* (Theaceae), and the second clade includes *Euonymus* (Celastraceae), *Hippocratea*, and *Salacia* (Hippocrateaceae).

A study employing molecular and morphological data of a large number of taxa found that Icacinaceae as previously circumscribed do not have a common origin. These genera are euasterids but segregate into the Garryales, Aquifoliales, and Apiales. *Icacina* and related genera (including most

Figure 97. ICACINACEAE. *Dendrobangia boliviana*. **A.** Stem with leaves and inflorescences and detail of adaxial surface of young leaf showing stellate hairs (upper left). **B.** Detail of inflorescence. **C.** Oblique-apical (left) and lateral (right) views of flower. **D.** Opened corolla and gynoecium. **E.** Lateral (left) and adaxial (right) views of stamen. **F.** Part of stem with leaf and fruit. **G.** Medial section of fruit with intact seed. Reprinted with permission from Mori et al. (2002). Artist: Bobbi Angell.

Neotropical genera but not *Dendrobangia* and *Discophora*) are found in the Garryales. *Dendrobangia* may belong in the Cardiopteridaceae (Celastrales *sensu* Cronquist) and *Discophora* may be best placed in the new family Stemonuraceae; both families now are placed in the Aquifoliales. Nevertheless, until more data accumulates, the family is herein treated in the traditional sense.

At present, there is no satisfactory classification of the Icacinaceae. Engler's wood-anatomical characterizations of the tribes Icacineae, Iodeae, Sarcostigmateae, and Phytocreneae were based on insufficient material and have not held up. Bayle and Howard did not propose a new familial classification, but they recognized three groups based on a combination of nodal anatomy and type of vessel perforations. The first group, with trilacunar nodes and scalariform vessel perforation, includes the Neotropical *Citronella*, *Dendrobangia*, *Emmotum*, *Oecopetalum*, *Ottoschultzia*, and *Poraqueiba*. The second group, with trilacunar nodes and mixture of simple and scalariform vessel perforations, includes only one Neotropical genus, *Discophora*. The third group, with unilacunar nodes and simple vessel perforations, includes the Neotropical *Casimirella*, *Leretia*, *Mappia*, and *Pleurisanthes*.

Features of the family. Habit: trees, lianas, sometimes scandent shrubs. **Stipules** absent. **Leaves** alternate, simple; blades sometimes with small domatia abaxially (*Citronella* and *Mappia*); venation pinnate. **Inflorescences** axillary, sometimes terminal, or opposite leaves (*Citronella*), racemes, thyrsoids, cymes, pseudospikes (pistillate plants of *Calatola*), or of one or two flowers (*Ottoschulzia*); pedicels generally articulated at base of flowers (not so in *Pleurisanthes*). **Flowers** actinomorphic or rarely zygomorphic, bisexual, sometimes unisexual in *Calatola* and *Citronella* (plants polygamous in some *Citronella*, the flowers functionally unisexual), small; sepals usually (3)5(6), small, nearly distinct to variously connate into tube (*Dendrobangia*), rarely accrescent (*Oecopetalum*), the lobes imbricate, rarely valvate; petals (3)5(6), distinct or connate, the apex inflexed; androecium with stamens equal to number of petals, the stamens alternate petals, distinct; gynoecium syncarpous, the ovary superior, the carpels 1(2–3), the locules 1(2), the style 1, sometimes short, the stigma punctiform, subcapitate, or capitate; placentation apical, the ovules 2, pendent, anatropous, unitegmic. **Fruits** drupes, usually subglobose or globose, sometimes laterally compressed (*Discophora*), the epicarp usually thin, often colored, the mesocarp variably fleshy, sometimes rich in oils, the endocarp hard. **Seed** 1; endosperm generally abundant, the embryo straight, the cotyledons sometimes foliaceous.

Natural history. Nothing is known about the pollination of Icacinaceae. The fleshy fruits may be dispersed by animals.

Economic uses. In tropical America, only two species are of economic importance. *Poraqueiba sericea* has an edible fleshy fruit rich in oil, and flour is produced from its seeds. The fruit, known as *umari*, is sold in Amazonian markets. *Casimirella ampla* has a large starch-rich tuber that is edible after the bitter-tasting compounds are washed out. In Africa, the seeds and tubers of *Icacina oliviformis* and *I. senegalensis* are processed into a starchy flour.

References: BAYLE, I. W., AND R. A. HOWARD. 1941a. The comparative morphology of the Icacinaceae. I. Anatomy of the node and internode. *J. Arnold Arbor.* 22(1):125–31. BAYLE, I. W., AND R. A. HOWARD. 1941b. The Comparative Morphology of the Icacinaceae. II. Vessel. *J. Arnold Arbor.* 22(2):171–87. BAYLE, I. W., AND R. A. HOWARD. 1941c. The comparative morphology of the Icacinaceae. III. Imperforate tracheary elements and xylem parenchyma. *J. Arnold Arbor.* 22(3):432–42. BAYLE, I. W., AND R. A. HOWARD. 1941d. The comparative morphology of the Icacinaceae. IV. Rays of the secondary xylem. *J. Arnold Arbor.* 22(4):556–68. HEINTZELMANN C. E., AND R. A. HOWARD. 1948. The comparative morphology of the Icacinaceae. V. The pubescence and the crystal. *Amer. J. Bot.* 35:42–52. KAREHED, J. 2001. Multiple origins of the tropical forest tree family Icacinaceae. *Amer. J. Bot.* 88(12):2259–74. SAVOLAINENE, V., J. F. MANENE, E. DOUZARY, AND R. SPICHIGER. 1994. Molecular phylogeny of families related to Celastrales based on rbc 5' flaking sequences. *Mol. Phylogenetics and Evolution* 3(1):27–37. SLEUMER, H. 1971. Icacinaceae. In *Flora Malesiana*, ed. C.G.G.J. Van Steenis, Series 1, 7(1):1–87. Alphen Aan Den Rijn, Netherlands: Sijthoff and Noordhoff International Publishers.

ILLICIACEAE (Star-anise Family)

NATHAN SMITH AND QI LIN

Figure 98

- *shrubs or small trees*
- *plants aromatic*
- *leaves alternate (spiral), simple; blade margins entire*
- *flowers with numerous tepals; gynoecium apocarpous*
- *fruits aggregates of follicles, often appearing stellate*

Numbers of genera and species. Worldwide, the Illiciaceae comprise a single genus, *Illicium*, and 34 species. In tropical America, there are three species.

Distribution and habitat. The Illiciaceae have a disjunct distribution. Species of *Illicium* are native to Cuba (*I. cubense*); Haiti and the Dominican Republic (*I. parviflorum*); Veracruz, Mexico (*I. floridanum*); the southeastern United States (*I. floridanum* and *I. parviflorum*); and Southeast Asia.

Neotropical species of *Illicium* are often found in moist broadleaf or pine forests.

Family classification. *Illicium* was originally placed in the Magnoliaceae, and later segregated into its own family in the Magnoliales. Cronquist placed the family next to the Magnoliales, in the Illiciales, along with the Schisandraceae. Recent analyses suggest the Illiciaceae hold a basal position in an-

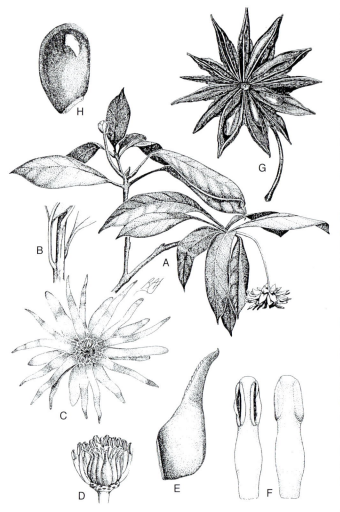

mens; androecium of 4–8 or numerous stamens, the stamens spirally arranged, the filaments thick, short, the anthers basifixed, dehiscing by longitudinal slits; gynoecium apocarpous, the ovary superior, the carpels 8–21, sometimes appearing whorled, the styles short, partially fused, the stigmas ventrally decurrent along upper half of each carpel; placentation ventral, nearly basal, the ovules 1 per carpel, anatropous. **Fruits** follicles, these in aggregates of 1–13, the aggregates often appearing stellate, the follicles splitting along adaxial suture. **Seeds** ellipsoid, smooth, laterally flattened; endosperm abundant, oily, the embryo small, straight.

Natural history. Insects are presumed to be the pollinators of species of *Illicium*. The flowers of *I. floridanum* smell like fish and attract many insects, especially flies (Diptera). Ballistic seed dispersal occurs throughout the family and is well documented in *I. floridanum*.

Economic uses. Oil extracted from the seeds of *Illicium verum* (Chinese star anise), a native of southern China and Indochina, is used in anise-flavored liqueurs and to produce anethole (anise oil). Anethole has many medicinal uses; e.g., as an antiseptic, a stimulant, and a carminative. The unripe fruits are chewed to relieve bad breath and aid digestion, and the dried fruits are used as a condiment in Asia. The toxic seeds of *Illicium anisatum* (Japanese star anise), a species native to Asia, have been used to poison fish. In China, the seeds of this species also have been used medicinally; e.g., for treating toothaches.

Illicium anisatum, *I. floridanum* (purple anise), *I. parviflorum*, and *I. verum* are planted as ornamentals.

Figure 98. ILLICIACEAE. *Illicium floridanum*. **A.** Stem with leaves, erect floral bud, and pendent flower (x¼). **B.** Part of stem showing leaf bases (x1). **C.** Apical view of flower (x1½). **D.** Lateral view of flower with perianth and some stamens removed (x3). **E.** Lateral view of carpel (x12). **F.** Adaxial (left) and abaxial (right) views of stamens (x14). **G.** Apical view of fruit showing dehisced follicles (x1½). **H.** Seed (x5). Reprinted with permission from Cronquist (1981). Artist: William S. Moye.

giosperm evolution along with families such as the Amborellaceae, Nymphaeaceae, and Schisandraceae.

Features of the family. Habit: shrubs or small trees, aromatic (ethereal oil cells present), evergreen, glabrous. **Stipules** absent. **Leaves** alternate (spiral), sometimes appearing whorled when congested at stem apices, simple; blades coriaceous, the margins entire. **Inflorescences** axillary, supra-axillary, or subterminal, of 1(2–3) flowers. **Flowers** actinomorphic, bisexual; perianth with 12–33 tepals, the tepals distinct, spirally arranged, red or yellow, the outermost usually small, sometimes appearing like bracts or sepals, the middle often petal-like, the inner sometimes reduced or transitional to sta-

References. HAO, G., R.M.K. SAUNDERS, AND M.-L. CHYE. 2000. A phylogenetic analysis of the Illiciaceae based on sequences of internal transcribed spacers (ITS) of nuclear ribosomal DNA. *Plant Syst. Evol.* 223:81–90. KENG, H. 1993. Illiciaceae. In *The Families and Genera of Vascular Plants*, eds. K. Kubitzki, J. G. Rohwer, and V. Bittrich, 2: 344–47. New York: Springer-Verlag. LIN, Q. 1989. Systematics and evolution of the family Illiciaceae. Ph.D. thesis [in Chinese]. Forestry college, South China Agric. Univ., Guangzhou, China. LIN, Q. 1999. The geographical distribution of the family Illiciaceae. In *The Geography of Spermatophytic Families and Genera*, ed. Lu Anming, 75–85. Beijing, Science Press. LIN, Q. 2000. Taxonomic notes on the genus *Illicium* Linn. *Acta Phytotax. Sin.* 38(2):167–81. LIN, Q. 2001. Taxonomy of the genus *Illicium* Linn. *Bull. Bot. Res.* 21(2):161–74. SAUNDERS, R.M.K. 1995. Systematics of the genus *Illicium* L. (Illiciaceae) in Malesia. *Bot. J. Linn. Soc.* 117:333–52. SMITH, A. C. 1947. The families Illiciaceae and Schisandraceae. *Sargentia* no. 7:1–224. SMALL, E. 1996. Confusion of common names for toxic and "star anise" (*Illicium*) species. *Econ. Bot.* 50(3):337–39.

IXONANTHACEAE (Ixonanthes Family)

NELSON RAMÍREZ

Figure 99

- *trees or shrubs*
- *leaves alternate, simple*
- *flowers 5-merous; intrastaminal disc present*
- *fruits capsules*
- *seeds winged or arillate*

Numbers of genera and species. Worldwide, the Ixonanthaceae comprise five genera and about 22 species. In tropical America, there are two genera, *Cyrillopsis* (2 species) and *Ochthocosmus* (7).

Distribution and habitat. The Ixonanthaceae are found in tropical regions of the world. *Cyrillopsis* and *Ochthcosmus* are from South America, *Ixonanthes* from Asia, *Phyllocosmus* from Africa, and *Allantospermum* from Asia and Africa.

The species of Ixonanthaceae occur in tropical forests, shrublands, and savannas. Most Neotropical species grow between 100 and 1,200 meters.

Family classification. The Ixonanthacee are placed in the Linales by Cronquist. The family was traditionally part of the Linaceae, but recent studies support its recognition as a family as well as the segregation of several other families from the Linaceae. The absence of secretory canals, the presence of imbricate petals persistent in fruit, and an intrastaminal disc are features that separate the Ixonanthaceae from the Linaceae and its relatives.

Features of the family. Habit: trees (to 30 m tall) or shrubs, the shrub stems sometimes slender, wiry, wandlike, with sparse leaves. **Stipules** small or wanting. **Leaves** alternate, simple; blade margins entire or toothed. **Inflorescences** axillary or terminal, cymes, thyrses, or racemes; peduncles long or short. **Flowers** actinomorphic or nearly so, small, bisexual; sepals 5, imbricate, distinct or connate at base; corolla frequently reflexed; the petals 5, imbricate or involute, distinct, persistent in fruit; androecium with 5 stamens, sometimes versatile, the filaments folded in bud, distinct or basely adnate to intrastaminal nectary disc, expanded at base, the anthers short, dehiscing by longitudinal slits; intrastaminal nectary disc present, annular to cupular, well developed; gynoecium syncarpous, the ovary superior or subinferior, plurilocular, divided into locelli (as in Linaceae), the partitions sometimes not developed toward apex, the carpels (2)5, the style folded in bud, terminal, the stigma ± capitate; placentation axile-

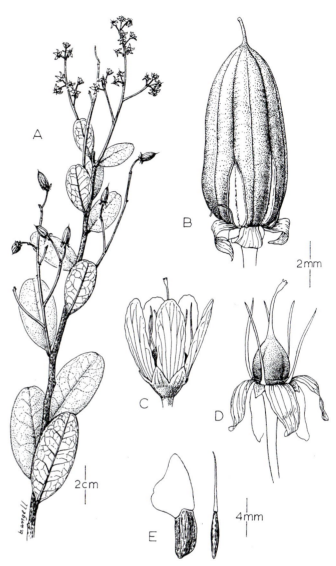

Figure 99. IXONANTHACEAE. *Ochthocosmus longipedicellatus* (A–D) and *O. roraimae* var. *parvifolius* (E). **A.** Stem with leaves, inflorescences, and infructescences. **B.** Lateral view of fruit. **C.** Lateral view of flower. **D.** Lateral view of flower shortly after anthesis. **E.** Views of winged seeds. Reprinted with permission from Steyermark and Luteyn (1980). Artist: Bobbi Angell.

apical, the ovules 1–2 per locule, pendulous, epitropous, with ventral raphe, the micropyle directed upward and outward. **Fruits** septicidal or sometimes loculicidal capsules. **Seeds** 2–9, winged or arillate; endosperm little or absent.

The pollen of the Ixonanthacee is binucleate and tricolporate.

Natural history. The flowers of *Ochthocosmus attenuatus* and *O. longipedicellatus* live more than two days and are protandrous. The pollinators of *O. attenuatus* and *O. longipedicellatus* are small bees and flies, which are attracted by both nectar and pollen. Species with winged seeds are dispersed by the wind, and those with arils by birds.

Economic uses. Species of the Ixonanthaceae are of little economic importance. The bark of *Ixonanthes icosandra* is used for tanning fishing nets in the Malay Peninsula.

References. FORMAN, L. L. 1965. A new genus of Ixonanthaceae with notes on the family. *Kew Bull.* 19:517–26. HALLIER, H. F. 1923. Bietrage zur Kenntnis der Linaceae

(DC. 1819) Dumort. *Beih. Bot. Centralbl.* 39(2):1–19. BHOJ RAJ AND SURYAKANTA. 1968. Pollen morphology of some genera of Linaceae. *J. Palynol.* 4(2):73–6. RAMIREZ, N. S., AND P. E. BERRY. 1999. Ixonanthaceae. In *Flora of the Venezuelan Guayana*, eds. J. S. Steyermark, P. E. Berry, K. Yatskievych, and B. K. Holst, 5:664–71. St. Louis, MO: Missouri Botanical Garden Press. STEYERMARK, J. A., AND J. L. LUTEYN. 1980. Revision of the genus *Ochthocosmus* (Linaceae) *Brittonia* 32:128–43. VAN HOOREN, A.M.N., AND H. P. NOOTEBOOM. 1984. Linaceae and Ctenolophonaceae especially of Malesia, with notes on their demarcation and the relationships with Ixonanthaceae. *Blumea* 29:547–63.

JUGLANDACEAE (Walnut Family)

FAVIO GONZÁLEZ

Figure 100

- *trees, usually aromatic*

- *leaves alternate (Carya and Juglans) or opposite (Alfaroa and Oreomunnea), pinnately compound*

- *flowers unisexual, often in separate inflorescences; perianth uniseriate; staminate flowers usually catkins; pistillate flowers with inferior ovary, the ovary usually 2-locular below (4–8 in Alfaroa and Oreomunnea) and 1-locular above, the ovule 1*

- *fruits drupaceous nuts or 3-winged and samaroid*

Numbers of genera and species. Worldwide, the Juglandaceae comprise nine genera and about 61 species. The largest genera are *Carya* (ca. 14 species) and *Juglans* (ca. 21; ca. 10 Neotropical). The other genera are *Alfaroa* (ca. 7), *Annamocarya* (2), *Cyclocarya* (1), *Engelhardia* (6, including the newly described monotypic *Alfaropsis*), *Oreomunnea* (3), *Platycarya* (1), and *Pterocarya* (6). In tropical America, there are four genera (*Alfaroa*, *Carya*, *Juglans*, and *Oreomunnea*) and approximately 20–22 species.

Distribution and habitat. The Juglandaceae are well represented in temperate and subtropical regions of the Northern Hemisphere and fewer species reach the Tropics of Asia and America. *Annamocarya*, *Cyclocarya*, *Engelhardia*, *Platycarya*, and *Pterocarya* are found only in the Eastern Hemisphere. *Carya* and *Juglans* grow in both the Western and Eastern Hemispheres. *Carya* is found from eastern North America to Mexico and in East Asia. Most species of *Juglans* are found in southeast Europe to East Asia and Japan; in the Western Hemisphere, the genus extends from North America and the West Indies into the Southern Hemisphere. *Alfaroa* and *Oreomunnea* range from Mexico to Colombia.

Neotropical Juglandaceae inhabit montane or premontane forests.

Family classification. The Juglandaceae have been included either in the subclass Rosidae, as a member of the Rutales close to Anacardiaceae, or in the subclass Hamamelidae, as a member of the Juglandales (*sensu* Cronquist) or the Fagales. Thorne placed the order Juglandales along with the Myricaceae and the order Fagales, within his superorder Rosanae. Most authors have proposed a close relationship with the Asiatic family Rhoipteleaceae because both families have pinnately compound leaves and bicarpellate, 1-seeded ovaries. Molecular data show that Juglandaceae are part of the order Fagales, along with the Betulaceae, Casuarinaceae, Fagaceae, Myricaceae, Nothofagaceae, Rhoipteleaceae, and Ticodendraceae. These families are currently included in the Fagales. Molecular data also confirm that Juglandaceae is sister to Rhoipteleaceae.

Three family classification systems have been proposed based primarily on differences in fruit morphology. Leroy proposed subfamilies Oreomunneoideae, including all genera having winged fruits plus *Alfaroa*, and the Juglandoideae, including genera with drupes (i.e., *Carya* and *Juglans*). Manning placed *Platycarya* into its own subfamily, Platycaryoideae, and all other genera in the Juglandioideae. *Juglans* is placed, along with the extra-Neotropical *Cyclocarya* and *Pterocarya*, in the tribe Juglandeae; the extratropical *Carya* into the tribe Hicorieae; and *Alfaroa*, *Oreomunnea*, and the Asiatic *Engelhardia* in the Engelhardieae. Based on living and fossil material, Manchester suggested that the family is better

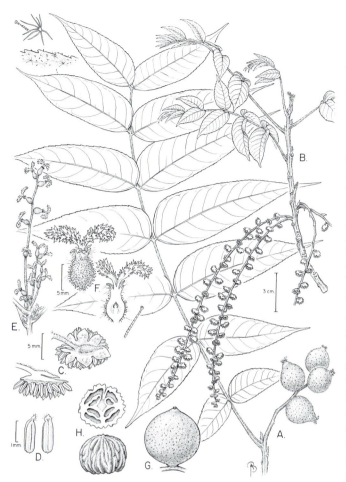

Figure 100. JUGLANDACEAE. *Juglans neotropica* (A, Wurdack 1535; B–D, Mena 1007; E, F, Rose 22332; G, Vásquez 7; H, Garcia-Barriga 17314). **A.** Stem with pinnate leaf, infructescence, and details of leaflet margin and stellate trichomes (upper left). **B.** Stem with immature leaves and staminate inflorescences. **C.** Basal view (above) and medial section (below) of staminate flowers. **D.** Lateral (left) and adaxial (right) views of stamens. **E.** Pistillate inflorescences. **F.** Lateral view (left) and medial section (right) of pistillate flowers with detail of trichome (below). **G.** Lateral view of fruit. **H.** Lateral view of intact endocarp (below) and transverse section of endocarp (above). Original. Artist: Bobbi Angell.

grouped into two clades, the Platycaryoideae (*Alfaroa, Engelhardia, Oreomunnea,* and *Platycarya*) and Juglandoideae (*Carya, Cyclocarya, Juglans,* and *Pterocarya*).

Although incongruent with fossil evidence, a cladistic analysis based upon *cp*DNA data shows two major clades in the family, one with *Juglans, Pterocarya, Carya,* and *Platycarya,* and the other with *Oreomunnea, Alfaroa,* and *Engelhardia.*

Features of the family. Habit: trees, resinous, usually aromatic, evergreen (*Alfaroa* and *Oreomunnea*) or deciduous (*Carya* and *Juglans*), trichomes often present on stems, flowers, and fruits, the indument stellate (mainly in *Juglans*)

or of peltate scales, usually on young buds or leaflets. **Pith** chambered (in *Juglans*) or solid (in *Alfaroa, Carya,* and *Oreomunnea*). **Stipules** absent. **Leaves** alternate (*Carya* and *Juglans*) or opposite (*Alfaroa* and *Oreomunnea*), pinnately compound; leaflets (3)5–31, the terminal leaflet often present in *Juglans,* absent, or vestigial and forming a small claw in other genera, the petiolules short, increasing in size toward apex of rachis, the leaflet margins serrate or entire (or nearly so in *Oreomunnea* and old trees of *Alfaroa*). **Inflorescences** terminal (pistillate catkins of *Carya* and *Juglans*) or lateral (staminate catkins of *Carya* and *Juglans*), terminal or lateral in *Alfaroa* and *Oreomunnea,* catkins, panicles, or of solitary flowers, the panicles androgynous in *Alfaroa* and *Oreomunnea,* the pistillate flowers in spikes (*Alfaroa* and *Oreomunnea*). **Staminate catkins** usually pendulous; flowers surrounded by bract and 2 bracteoles, fused to receptacle, appearing as part of calyx. **Pistillate catkins** usually erect, solitary (*Juglans*); flowers subtended by an abaxial, 3-lobed, accrescent bract with 1 (*Juglans*) or 3 vascular bundles, in *Carya* with 4–6-lobed involucre fused to ovary; bracteoles 2–3 (absent in pistillate flowers of *Alfaroa*), lateral, adaxial, or both, accrescent. **Flowers** reduced, actinomorphic or slightly zygomorphic (androecium of *Juglans* and *Oreomunnea*), unisexual (the plants monoecious) or bisexual; sepals 4 in Juglans, 2 in *Alfaroa* and *Oreomunnea,* lacking in *Carya*; petals absent. **Staminate flowers:** androecium of 4 stamens (*Carya*), 6–12 (*Alfaroa*), 7–ca.100 (*Juglans*), 8–25 (*Oreomunnea*), the stamens in 1 or more series, the anthers sessile or subsessile, basifixed, erect, dehiscing longitudinally; pistillode sometimes present. **Pistillate flowers:** sepals fused to ovary; staminodes sometimes present; gynoecium syncarpous, the ovary inferior, the carpels 2, the locules usually 2 below (sometimes 4–8 in *Alfaroa* and *Oreomunnea* because of development of additional septa), usually 1 above, the styles 2, the stigmas usually 2, papillose; placentation at apex of incomplete septum, the ovule 1, orthotropous, unitegmic. **Fruits** drupaceous nuts or 3-winged and samaroid (*Oreomunnea*), tightly enclosed by coriaceous or fibrous husk derived from perianth, bracts, and bracteoles, the husk dehiscent in most *Carya* and *Juglans.* **Seeds** 1 per fruit, the embryo oily, the cotyledons corrugate, with 4 lobes when expanded; endosperm absent.

The coriaceous or fibrous husk surrounding the fruit is formed by the fusion of the fleshy perianth and the usually accrescent and expanded bract and bracteoles. These form the outer part of the fruit of *Carya* and *Juglans* and form the wings of the fruit of *Oreomunnea.* The bracts are scalelike and much smaller in the wingless nut of *Alfaroa.*

Natural history. The inflorescence morphology, floral reductions, and small pollen of Juglandaceae are typical of wind-pollinated plants. The occurrence of self-fertilization in *Oreomunnea* is suspected and supported by the production of viable seeds from isolated trees in both Central and South American species.

Animal dispersal is common for the relatively large fruits of *Carya* and *Juglans* and perhaps *Alfaroa*, which has seeds that are rich in fats. Wind dispersal is facilitated by the winged, relatively small fruits of *Oreomunnea*.

Economic uses. Some species, particularly of *Carya* and *Juglans*, are a sources of fine timber. Along with members of some other genera, several species of *Juglans* (e.g., *J. neotropica*) produce edible nuts (walnuts). The oil of the nuts also is used in the cosmetic and painting industries. Several species of *Carya* and *Juglans* are planted as ornamentals.

References. GUNTHER, L. E., G. KOCHERT, AND D. E. GIANNASI. 1994. Phylogenetic relationships of the Juglandaceae. *Pl. Syst. Evol.* 192:11–29. HJELMQVIST, H. 1948. Studies on the floral morphology and phylogeny of the Amentiferae. *Bot. Not.* (Suppl.) 2:1–171. LEROY, J. F. 1955. Étude sur les Juglandaceae. *Mém. Mus. Natl. Hist. Nat., Sér. B, Bot.* 6:1–246. MANCHESTER, S. R. 1987. The fossil history of the Juglandaceae. *Monogr. Syst. Bot. Missouri Bot. Gard.* 21:1–137. MANNING, W. E. 1938. The morphology of the flower of the Juglandaceae. I. The inflorescence. *Amer. J. Bot.* 25:407–19. MANNING, W. E. 1940. The morphology of the flower of the Juglandaceae. II. The pistillate flowers and fruit. *Amer. J. Bot.* 27:839–52. MANNING, W. E. 1948. The morphology of the flower of the Juglandaceae. II. The staminate flowers. *Amer. J. Bot.* 35:606–21. MANNING, W. E. 1949. The genus *Carya* in Mexico. *J. Arnold Arbor.* 30:425–32. MANNING, W. E. 1957. The genus *Juglans* in Mexico and Central America. *J. Arnold Arbor.* 38(2):121–50. MANNING, W. E. 1960. The genus *Juglans* in South America and the West Indies. *Brittonia* 12:1–25. MANNING, W. E. 1978. The classification within the Juglandaceae. *Ann. Missouri Bot. Gard.* 65:1058–87. MANOS, P., AND D. E. STONE. 2001. Evolution, phylogeny, and systematics of the Juglandaceae. *Ann. Missouri Bot. Gard.* 88: 231–269. SMITH, J. F., AND J. J. DOYLE. 1995. A cladistic analysis of chloroplast DNA restriction site variation and morphology for the genera of the Juglandaceae. *Amer. J. Bot.* 82(9):1163–72. STONE, D. E. 1972. New World Juglandaceae, III. A new perspective of the tropical members with winged fruits. *Ann. Missouri Bot. Gard.* 59:297–321.

KRAMERIACEAE (Rhatany Family)

BERYL B. SIMPSON

Figure 101

- *sprawling herbs to large shrubs (to 2 m tall)*

- *plants hemiparasitic; haustoria present*

- *leaves alternate, usually simple*

- *flowers zygomorphic; petals relatively small, with 2, one on each side of ovary, modified into oil-secreting structures*

- *fruits capsules, variously covered with barbs*

- *seeds 1 per fruit*

Numbers of genera and species. Confined to the Western Hemisphere, the Krameriaceae comprise a single genus, *Krameria*, and 18 species. In tropical America, there are 12 species.

Distribution and habitat. Species of Krameriaceae occur from Kansas in the United States into Mexico, through Central America, and into South America, where they reach their southern limit in northern Chile and Argentina. One species also occurs sporadically in the West Indies. Mexico has the highest diversity with 11 species, the United States has three species, and Brazil has five species.

Species of *Krameria* grow in deserts, grasslands, savannas, or scrub vegetation. *Krameria cytisoides*, however, is found primarily in the oak or oak-pine shrublands in the Sierra Madre Oriental of Mexico and *K. sonorae* grows in the Sonoran thorn-scrub. Most species occur below 1,500 meters, but *K. lappacea* reaches 3,600 meters in the Peruvian and Bolivian Andes.

Family classification. The Krameriaceae are placed in the Polygalales by Cronquist. Shared ancestry with the Fabaceae subfamily Papilionoideae and Polygalaceae have been proposed, but recent molecular work consistently suggests a relationship with the Zygophyllaceae. *Krameria* has never been formally divided into subgeneric groups although the species fall naturally into three clades based on both morphological and molecular evidence. All species of Krameriaceae share similar floral and fruit features that differentiate them from other flowering plant families.

Features of the family. Habit: sprawling herbs to large shrubs (to 2 m tall), perennial, hemiparasitic. **Haustoria** present, penetrating host roots. **Stipules** absent. **Leaves** alternate, simple, or trifoliolate in *Krameria cytisoides*. **Inflorescences** of solitary flowers in leaf axils or in terminal racemes or open panicles. **Flowers** zygomorphic, bisexual, showy; sepals 4–5, distinct, pink, purple, yellow, or rose; petals 4–5,

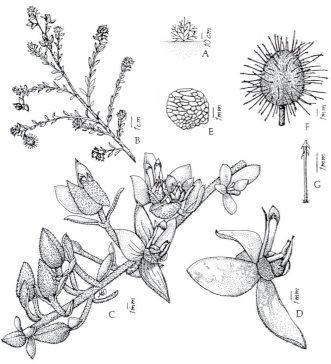

Figure 101. KRAMERIACEAE. *Krameria lappacea.* **A.** Schematic sketch of growth habit. **B.** Stem with leaves and inflorescences. **C.** Detail of stem with inflorescences. **D.** Lateral view of flower. **E.** Elaiophore, which surrounds ovary. **F.** Lateral view of fruit. **G.** Lateral view of spinelike trichome taken from fruit. Reprinted with permission from Simpson (1989). Artist: M. C. Ogotzaly.

comparatively small, (2)3 petals distinct or partially fused and forming a "flag," 2 petals, one on each side of ovary, fleshy, circular or wedge-shaped, modified into oil-secreting structures; androecium of 3–4 stamens, if 4 stamens then paired and sometimes didynamous, if 3 with 2 below other, curving over ovary, protruding at almost right angles from flower, the anthers with terminal pores; gynoecium pseudo-monomerous, the ovary superior, pear-shaped, the carpels 2 (appearing as 1), the locule 1, the style curved, slightly longer than stamens, protruding from flower; placentation parietal, the ovules 2, pendulous near apex of locule. **Fruits** capsules, round, variously covered with barbs. **Seeds** 1 per fruit, large; endosperm absent, the embryo small, the cotyledons fleshy.

The seeds germinate readily and produce seedlings with two large cotyledons and a root lacking root hairs. The absence of root hairs means that the seedling is unable take in water from the soil. Seedlings can live for several weeks on the stored reserves of the cotyledons, but they will eventually die if they do not attach to the root of a host plant.

The pollen of *Krameria* is unique in having a striate exine that makes it look like a ball of string. The pollen germinates through one of 3 pores, slits, or combination of pores and slits situated around the equatorial axis.

Natural history. All species of *Krameria* are pollinated by solitary female bees of the genus *Centris* (Apidae). Species of *Krameria* do not produce nectar, but these bees visit the flowers to collect oils secreted by the glandular petals. These are fatty oils that are not volatile or fragrant. When collecting oil, a female bee orients her body with the main axis of the flower, grasps the flag with her mandibles, straddles the stigma and anthers, and scrapes her fore- and midlegs over the outer surface of the glandular petals to rupture the cuticle. While in flight, after she leaves the flower, the bee transfers the oils to the densely branched scopal hairs of her hind legs for transport to the nest. When landing on another flower, the bee first contacts the slightly exserted stigma, thereby pollinating the flower if she is carrying pollen. She then immediately contacts the terminal anther pores and receives pollen on the ventral side of her head and at the juncture of the first pair of legs. Some *Centris* females may actively collect *Krameria* pollen, but most do not. They may carry scopal loads of oil or pollen alone, combined pollen and oil, or oil mixed with soil.

The oils are used with nectar and pollen as part of the larval food. They also may be used by some species of *Centris* for lining the walls of the nest cells. Sixteen species of *Centris* have been recorded visiting *Krameria*, but a one-to-one species correlation does not exist other than that resulting from the limited geographical distributions of either partner. *Centris* females visiting *Krameria* also visit other plant taxa for oil, nectar, and/or pollen. Non-oil-collecting species of bees have also been recorded visiting *Krameria* for pollen and to collect trichomes for nest materials.

Dispersal of *Krameria* fruits is by animals. The fruits of most species have spines with retrorse barbs that catch on feathers, fur, or human clothing. If fruits are not pulled from a plant by a passing animal, they eventually fall to the ground. Over time, the pericarp splits and releases the seed, which then can be carried farther by rain or wind.

Economic uses. Roots of species of *Krameria* have been used by indigenous people of both North and South America, primarily for their styptic properties and as a dye source. Noting its use by Andean Indians, H. Ruiz, an influential eighteenth-century Spanish botanist, experimented with root extracts and proclaimed *Krameria* one of the two most important medicinal herbs in the world, exceeded only by *Cinchona*. Ruiz claimed that *K. lappacea* was effective for a variety of ailments, such as menstrual disorders, hemorrhaging and intestinal problems. As a result of Ruiz's proselytizing, the species was incorporated into most European pharmacopoeias, and from the end of the eighteenth century until the beginning of the twentieth century, *Krameria* root extract was used medicinally in Europe and North America as an astringent, eye wash, and oral styptic. Taken internally as a tea or decoction, it was used to induce menstruation and abortion, to cure excessive menstrual bleeding, and to treat kidney problems and various cancers. Several other species of *Krameria* were used as substitutes for *K. lappacea*, the "true rhatany." During the 1970s, *Krameria* tea was suspected of causing esophageal cancer in the West Indies and as a result, the genus became the object of a series of studies by the United States National Institutes of Health. Both its purported beneficial qualities and its presumed carcinogenic properties are now discounted. Its sole remaining uses are as a dye plant, as an ingredient in toothpaste because of its styptic qualities, and in some cosmetics for its astringent properties.

References. CANNON, W. A. 1910. The root habits and parasitism of *Krameria canescens* Gray. In The conditions of parasitism in plants, eds. D. T. Macdougal and W. A. Cannon. *Publ. Carnegie Inst. Wash.* 129:5–24. CORRERA Q., J. E., AND H. Y. BERNAL. 1993. Krameriaceae. In *Especies vegetales promisorias de los países del Convenio Andrés Bello*, Tomo IX. Santafé de Bogotá, D. E., Colombia: Secretaria Ejecutiva del Convenio Andrés Bello. GADEK, P. A., E. S. FERNANDO, C. J. QUINN, S. B. HOOT, T. TERRAZAS, ET AL. 1996. Sapindales: molecular delimitation and infraordinal groups. *Amer. J. Bot.* 83:802–11. MILBY, T. H. 1971. Floral anatomy of *Krameria lanceolata*. *Amer. J. Bot.* 58:569–76. MUSSELMAN, L. J. 1975. Parasitism and haustorial structure in *Krameria lanceolata* (Krameriaceae). A preliminary study. *Phytomorphology* 25:416–22. RUIZ, H. 1797. Memoria sobre la ratanhia. Acad. Nac. Medicina (Madrid) 1:349–66. SIMPSON, B. B. 1982. *Krameria* (Krameriaceae) flowers: orientation and elaiophore morphology. *Taxon* 31:517–28. SIMPSON, B. B. 1989. Krameriaceae. *Fl. Neotrop. Monogr.* 49: 1–109. SIMPSON, B. B. 1991. The past and present uses of rhatany (*Krameria*, Krameriaceae). *Econ. Bot.* 45:397–409. SIMPSON, B. B., J. L. NEFF, AND D. SEIGLER. 1977. *Krameria*, free fatty acids and oil-collecting bees. *Nature* 267: 150–51. SIMPSON, B. B., AND J. J. SKVARLA. 1981. Pollen morphology and ultrastructure of *Krameria* (Krameriaceae): utility in questions of intrafamilial and interfamilial classification. *Amer. J. Bot.* 68:277–94. TURNER, B. L. 1958. Chromosome numbers in the genus *Krameria*: evidence for familial status. *Rhodora* 60:101–06.

LACISTEMATACEAE (Lacistema Family)

DOUGLAS C. DALY

Figure 102, Plate 25

- *shrubs or small trees*

- *leaves alternate, simple*

- *inflorescences axillary, often catkinlike spikes*

- *flowers small; petals absent; stamen 1; placentation parietal*

- *fruits capsules*

- *seeds with brightly colored sarcotesta*

Numbers of genera and species. The Lacistemataceae comprise two genera and about 14 species restricted to tropical and subtropical America. *Lacistema* has approximately 11 species, while *Lozania* has 3 or 4 species.

Distribution and habitat. The Lacistemataceae are mostly Neotropical, with some species extending into the subtropics of the Western Hemisphere. *Lacistema* ranges from Mexico, Central America, and the West Indies to Argentina, while *Lozania* occurs from Costa Rica through Panama into northern South America. *Lacistema* has a minor center of diversity in Brazil's Atlantic coastal forests.

Lozania occurs in lowland humid forests as well as cloud forests and other montane forests. *Lacistema* is most common in low elevation rain forests, but several species are found in dry forests.

Few of the species of Lacistemataceae are common where they occur, with the major exception of *Lacistema aggregatum*, an ecologically flexible species that can be found throughout much of the ecological and geographic range of the family.

Family classification. Most of the major classifications prior to the 1990s placed the Lacistemataceae in the Violales (e.g., *sensu* Cronquist), variously defined but including the Passifloraceae, Flacourtiaceae, Violaceae, Turneraceae, Caricaceae, and Bixaceae. During the 1990s, one of the earlier attempts at a preliminary reorganization of angiosperm phylogeny, incorporating and emphasizing molecular data, placed the Lacistemataceae in an expanded Malpighiales that includes the first four of these families but also accommodates the Erythroxylaceae, Euphorbiaceae, Linaceae, Malpighiaceae, Ochnaceae, and others. Similar morphology has led some authors to suggest that the Lacistemataceae may be closely related to Flacourtiaceae and Salicaceae, however, recent molecular analyses do not confirm this relationship.

The family has long been allied with the Flacourtiaceae, and even placed by some within that family. Both groups have stipulate leaves, a unilocular ovary (sometimes second-

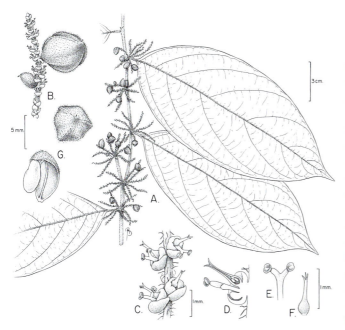

Figure 102. LACISTEMATACEAE. *Lacistema grandifolium.* **A.** Stem with leaves and axillary infructescences. **B.** Part of infructescence showing developing fruit amidst flowers. **C.** Part of inflorescence showing much reduced flowers and bifid stamens. **D.** Medial section of flower. **E.** Adaxial view of bifid stamen. **F.** Lateral view of gynoecium. **G.** Apical view of fruit (above) and fruit valve with single seed (below). Reprinted with permission from Mori et al. (2002). Artist: Bobbi Angell.

connective or with each theca stipitate; and inflorescences in catkinlike spikes or racemes.

Features of the family. Habit: shrubs or small trees. **Stipules** present, deciduous. **Leaves** alternate, simple; blade margins entire or toothed (*Lozania*). **Inflorescences** axillary, slender, spiciform racemes or more often catkinlike spikes; bracteoles 2. **Flowers** zygomorphic, usually bisexual, sometimes unisexual (species andromonoecious or monecious), small; sepals absent or (1)2–6, unequal; petals absent; androecium of 1 stamen, the stamen inserted on or within disc, the anther thecae separated by an expanded connective or sometimes individually stipitate, opening by longitudinal slits; disc annular to semilunate, sometimes cupular, fleshy; gynoecium syncarpous, the ovary superior, the carpels 2–3, the locule 1, the style 1, the stigmas 2–3, distinct; placentation parietal, the ovules 1–2 on each placenta, pendulous. **Fruits** capsules. **Seeds** 1–2; sarcotesta brightly colored, oil-rich; endosperm copious, oily, the embryo straight, the cotyledons broad and foliar.

Natural history. No information is available on pollination. The fruits of *Lacistema* are dispersed by both specialist and nonspecialist, fruit-eating birds.

Economic uses. No economic uses are known for this family.

References. CHASE, M. W., S. ZMARZTY, M. D. LLEDO, K. J. WURDACK, S. M. SWENSEN, AND M. F. FAY. 2002. When in doubt, put it in Flacourtiaceae: A molecular phylogenetic analysis based on plastid *rbcL* DNA sequences. *Kew Bull.* 57:141–81. SNOW, D. W. 1981. Tropical frugivorous birds and their food plants: a survey. *Biotropica* 13:1–14. SOLTIS, D. E., P. S. SOLTIS, D. R. MORGAN, S. M. SWENSEN, B. C. MULLIN, ET AL. 1995. Chloroplast gene sequence data suggest a single origin of the predisposition for symbiotic nitrogen fixation in angiosperms. *Proc. Natl. Acad. Sci. U.S.A.* 92:2647–51.

arily so in Flacourtiaceae), parietal placentation, and a straight embryo with oily, copious endosperm. Like some Flacourtiaceae, the Lacistemataceae have a (2)3-locular capsular fruit that opens to reveal seeds enveloped in a fleshy, brightly colored, arillate sarcotesta.

The Lacistemataceae can be distinguished from the Flacourtiaceae by its single stamen (vs. usually 10+ stamens) with the anther thecae either well separated by an expanded

LAMIACEAE (Mint Family)

ROGIER DE KOK

Figure 103, Plate 25

- *herbs or subshrubs, occasionally shrubs or small trees*
- *stems usually quadrangular*
- *leaves usually decussate or whorled, usually simple, aromatic*
- *flowers usually zygomorphic; corolla often bilabiate*
- *fruits usually consisting of 4 mericarps (nutlets)*

Numbers of genera and species. Worldwide, the Lamiaceae comprise about 190 genera and 5,500 species. More than half of the species belong to eight genera: *Salvia* (900 species), *Scutellaria* (360), *Plectranthus* (300), *Stachys* (300), *Hyptis* (280), *Teucrium* (250), *Thymus* (220), and *Nepeta* (200). In Central America and southern Mexico, there are about 15 native genera and 140–150 species, 10 genera and 90–100 species in the West Indies, and about 27 genera and 680 species in South America.

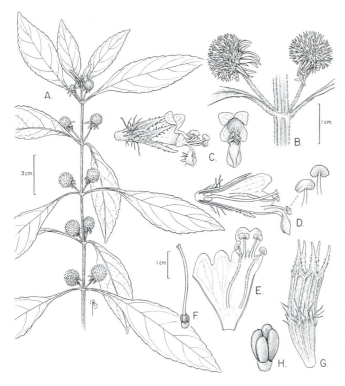

Figure 103. LAMIACEAE. *Hyptis lanceolata*. **A.** Stem with leaves and inflorescences. **B.** Detail of node with inflorescences and petioles. **C.** Lateral (left) and apical (right) views of flower. **D.** Medial section of flower (left) and detail of anthers (right). **E.** Corolla opened to show arrangement of stamens. **F.** Lateral view of gynoecium. **G.** Lateral view of calyx. **H.** Oblique-apical view of fruit comprised of four nutlets. Reprinted with permission from Mori et al. (2002). Artist: Bobbi Angell.

Distribution and habitat. The Lamiaceae have a cosmopolitan distribution but are especially abundant in the Mediterranean and eastward into central Asia. Other species-rich areas are China, Africa, and South America. In South and Central America, the family is dominated by two cosmopolitan genera, *Hyptis* and *Salvia*, which comprise about 60 percent of the total number of species. The rest of the family in South and Central America mainly consist of genera endemic to the Western Hemisphere. In Mexico, the Lamiaceae are dominated by *Salvia*, which is particularly rich in species (ca. 280 for the country); the number of species of Lamiaceae decreases as one goes north into the United States and Canada.

The Lamiaceae are typically found in regions subject to a warm, seasonal climate, especially in open, rocky areas, in thickets, along riverbanks and ponds, dry riverbeds and in tropical or subtropical regions in montane habitats. In north temperate regions they can also be found in forest. While many herbaceous species occur in damp habitats, others are typically found in semiarid areas. Several herbaceous or annual species are very common along paths and roadsides and in pastures and in cultivated or disturbed areas. Only a few genera are found in tropical rain forests.

Family classification. The Lamiaceae are placed in the Lamiales by Cronquist. The family is closely related to the Ver-

benaceae and was considered by Cronquist to be more distantly related to the Boraginaceae and Lennoaceae on the basis of leaf orientation, chemical features of the former, and the parasitic habit of the later, although today this is disputed. Molecular evidence suggests close relationships among the Lamiaceae and the Verbenaceae, Orobanchaceae, Acanthaceae, Bignoniaceae, Scrophulariaceae, and Stilbaceae.

Traditionally, division of Lamiaceae and the Verbenaceae was based on whether the taxa were mostly woody with a terminal or subterminal style (Verbenaceae) or mainly herbaceous with a gynobasic style (Lamiaceae). Until recently, the most widely accepted subfamily classification was that of Briquet, who classified the Lamiaceae *sensu stricto* into nine subfamilies and 14 tribes.

The limitations of this classification were early pointed out by Junell and later elaborated upon by Cantino. A proposed new classification of the families (now in press) gives groups that are both more easily communicable and apparently monophyletic. The Verbenaceae in this new concept is restricted to subfamily Verbenoideae, characterized by a racemose inflorescence and a salverform corolla, whereas in the newly defined Lamiaceae the inflorescence is cymose and the corollas are tubular and usually bilabiate. These morphological differences are supported by chemical, anatomical, embryological, and pollen characters. In this new classification, such genera as *Vitex*, *Clerodendrum*, *Aegiphila*, and the commercially important *Tectona*, are now included within the Lamiaceae.

For this publication, however, the authors of the Lamiaceae and Verbenaceae have decided to treat them in the traditional sense. This is not because they do not agree with the modern concept, but because the most modern classification of these families is still not generally available.

Features of the family. Habit: herbs, sometimes shrubs, rarely trees or vines, the herbs annual or perennial, often aromatic. **Stems** often quadrangular, well-developed collenchyma present in angles; nodes unilacunar. **Indument** often present, the hairs frequently multicellular (uniseriate) and commonly with short-stalked epidermal glands containing characteristic ethereal oils (these chemically very diverse, but most often monoterpenoids, sesquiterpenoids, or diterpenoids). **Stipules** absent. **Leaves** opposite (decussate) or in whorls of three or more per node, usually simple or rarely compound; petioles with a ± arcuate vascular strand or vascular bundles in a ring (in cross section); leaflets, when present, opposite or alternate along axis. **Inflorescences** axillary or terminal, variable, flowers solitary or in dense clusters; bracts leaflike to greatly reduced, usually persistent; bracteoles often present. **Flowers** usually zygomorphic or very rarely almost actinomorphic, bisexual or sometimes functionally unisexual (plants gynodioecious or rarely dioecious); calyx actinomorphic or zygomorphic (often bilabiate), persistent during fruit development, the sepals connate, tubular, the tube often ribbed, the lobes usually 5, sometimes more or 0 or 2; corolla often bilabiate, the petals connate into tube, the lobes 4–5, the upper lip usually with 2 lobes, these often united and forming a hood, which may be entire, or upper lip absent in *Teucrium*, the lower lip usually with 3 lobes, the middle lobe usually broader or longer; androecium often didynamous, the stamens 4 or 2, if the latter then one pair absent or staminodal, attached to or inserted on corolla, the anthers usually with 2 thecae, these often divergent, sometimes widely so with the connective much developed; disc usually present below ovary, often with a nectariferous lobe; gynoecium syncarpous, the ovary superior, usually deeply 4-lobed, the carpels 2, each usually deeply lobed, giving appearance of 4-locular ovary (due to intrusion or constriction of ovary wall resulting in a false partition), the style 1, usually gynobasic, rarely terminal, the stigma bifid; placentation basal to axile, the ovules 2 per carpel (4 locules each with 1 ovule), sometimes aborting. **Fruits** consisting of 1–4 mericarps (or nutlets), the pericarp hard or rarely fleshy, the mericarps distinct or rarely weakly adherent to form globose, weakly lobed structure; myxocarpy (the production of mucilage by fruits, when they become wet) in many genera. **Seeds** 1 per mericarp (ovule sometimes aborted); endosperm usually absent or scanty, oily when present, the embryo straight, or rarely bent, axially attached; germination usually epigeous.

The Lamiaceae produce a great variety of secondary compounds and are known for their essential oils, especially a wide range of monoterpenoids and sesquiterpenoids, particularly in subfamily Nepetoideae. Other subfamilies are usually poor in such compounds, producing instead various iridoid compounds. A wide range of phenolic compounds, especially flavonoids and caffeic acid esters, such as rosmarinic acid are also common. Some species of Lamiaceae are reported to contain alkaloids and cyanogenic glycosides, but these are not common. Fatty acids, such as linolenic acid or laballenic acid are widely reported from seed oils. Lamiaceae often accumulate potassium nitrate, and commonly store carbohydrate as stachyose and/or oligogalactosides.

Natural history. The Lamiaceae are mostly cross-pollinated, and the intricate methods by which cross-pollination is accomplished reflect a long history of coevolution between plants and pollinators. Within the family, bees and birds (mainly hummingbirds in the neotropics) are the most common pollinators, and flies, wasps, butterflies, hawkmoths, and beetles are less common.

Seed dispersal is accomplished by gravity, wind, water, mammals, birds, ants, and possibly even snails. In many species, the calyx enlarges and plays an important role in dispersal, restricting the release of the mericarps. In some examples, the calyx becomes detached with the mericarps still inside. The calyx lobes may be hooked, aiding dispersal by animals, or the calyx may become fleshy and cause the fruit to resemble a berry or drupe. In other species, the calyx becomes dry and papery and then is shed with the mericarps to aid in wind dispersal. Some species have winged mericarps to aid dispersal by wind, and others have air-filled cavities that may assist in dispersal by water. Many species of Lamiaceae have become widely dispersed by human activity either through cultivation or as weeds. Vegetative propagation, such as via underground rhizomes, is found in many Lamiaceae, while a few species produce underground tubers.

Economic uses. Many species of Lamiaceae are of economic importance as ornamentals, spices, perfumes, religious objects, or medicines. Illnesses as varied as fever, psychosomatic disorders, respiratory ailments, and ulcers are regularly treated by application of various species as infusions (either as teas or washes) or as inhalants. In the neotropics, species of Lamiaceae are particularly important at the local community level by providing inexpensive medicines. Many herbs are also grown in backyard gardens for personal consumption. A few are grown commercially on a large scale such as *Mentha arvensis* subspecies *haplocalyx* variety *piperascens*, which produces peppermint oil for flavoring, and various *Lavandula* species, from which lavender oil, much prized in the perfumery trade, is distilled. Many Lamiaceae of economic importance were originally imported from the Eastern Hemisphere, for example basil (*Ocimum basilicum*), and especially from the Mediterranean region, such as mint (*Mentha* species), oregano or marjoram (*Origanum* species) rosemary (*Rosmarinus officinalis*), thyme (*Thymus* species), and sage (*Salvia offinalis*). Outside this area, *Pogostemon cablin*, from India, produces the patchouli oil used in perfume, while various *Salvia* and *Hyptis* species are sold as spices under the name 'Chia' in Mexico.

References. BAKER, J. G., AND O. STAPF. 1900. Verbenaceae & Labiatae. In *Flora of Tropical Africa*, ed. W. T. Thistleton-Dyer, 5:273–502. London: Reeve & Co. BENTHAM, G., AND J. D. HOOKER. Verbenaceae & Labiatae. In *Genera Plantarum*, Linnaeus, 2:1131–1223. London: Reeve & Co. BERNAL, H. Y., AND J. E. CORRERA Q. 1994. Labiatae (Lamiaceae). In *Especies vegetales promisorias de los países del Convenio Andrés Bello*, Tomo X. Santafé de Bogotá, D. E., Colombia: Secretaria Ejecutiva del Convenio Andrés Bello. BOUMAN, F., AND A.D.J. MEEUSE 1992. Dispersal in Labiatae. In *Advances in Labiate Science*, eds. R. M. Harley and T. Reynolds, 193–202. Richmond, U.K.: Royal Botanic Gardens, Kew. BRIQUET, J. 1895. Labiatae. In *Die Natürlichen Pflanzenfamilien*, eds. A. Engler and K. Prantl, div. 4(3a, 3b):183–374. Leipzig: Wilhelm Engelmann. CANTINO, P. D. 1992. Evidence for a polyphyletic origin of the Labiatae. *Ann. Missouri Bot. Gard.* 79:361–79. CANTINO, P. D. 1992. Towards a phylogenetic classification of the Labiate. In *Advances in Labiate Science*, eds. R. M. Harley and T. Reynolds, 27–37. Richmond, U.K.: Royal Botanic Gardens, Kew. CANTINO, P. D., R. M. HARLEY, AND S. J. WAGSTAFF. 1992. Genera of Labiatae: status and classification. In *Advances in Labiate science*, eds. R. M. Harley and T. Reynolds, 511–22. Richmond, U.K.: Royal Botanic Gardens, Kew. HARLEY, R. M., S. ATKINS, A. BUDANTSEV, P. D. CANTINO, B. CONN, ET AL. Lamiaceae, in ed. J. W. Kadereit, The Families and Genera of Vascular Plants (K. Kubitzki, ed. in chief) vol. VI, in press. HEDGE, I. C. 1992. A global survey of the biogeography of the Labiatae. In *Advances in Labiate Science*, eds. R. M. Harley and T. Reynolds, 7–17. Richmond, U.K.: Royal Botanic Gardens, Kew. HEINRICH, M. 1992. Economic botany of American Labiatae. In *Advances in Labiate Science*, eds. R. M. Harley and T. Reynolds, 475–88. Richmond, U.K.: Royal Botanic Gardens, Kew. HUCK, R. B. 1992. Overview of pollination biology in the Lamiaceae. In *Advances in Labiate Science*, eds. R. M. Harley and T. Reynolds, 167–81. Richmond, Surrey, U.K.: Royal Botanic Gardens, Kew. JUNELL, S. 1934. Zur gynäceummmorphologie und Systematik der Verbenaceen und Labiate. *Symb. Bot. Upsal.* 4:1–219. OLMSTEAD, R. O., C. W. DEPAMPHILIS, A. D. WOLFE, N. D. YOUNG, W. J. ELISONS, AND P. A. REEVES. 2001. Disintegration of the Scrophulariaceae. *Amer. J. Bot.* 88:348–61.

LAURACEAE (Avocado Family)

SANTIAGO MADRIÑÁN

Figure 104, Plate 25

- *trees or sometimes shrubs (except* Cassytha, *a parasitic twining vine)*

- *plants often emanating odor of essential oils from cut bark and crushed leaves*

- *leaves usually alternate, simple; blade margins entire*

- *flowers with anthers dehiscing by hinged flaps*

- *fruits drupes, 1-seeded, often subtended by thickened receptacle (cupule)*

Numbers of genera and species. Worldwide, the Lauracae comprise 52 genera and ca. 2,750 species, however, the total number of both species and genera are far from accurately known. Approximately 80 percent of the known species are included in large genera with 100–400 species each, and ca. 50 percent of the genera possess only one to three species. In tropical America, there are 27 genera and about 1,000 species. The neotropics harbor most of the Perseeae while the Laureae occur primarily in the paleotropics and subtropical/temperate regions.

The Neotropical genera are: *Anaueria* (endemic; monotypic), *Gamanthera* (endemic; monotypic), *Paraia* (endemic; monotypic), *Phyllostemonodaphne* (endemic; monotypic), *Povedadaphne* (endemic; monotypic), *Systemonodaphne* (endemic; monotypic; the generic synonym *Kubitzkia* still in use), *Chlorocardium* (endemic; two species), *Dicypellium* (endemic; two), *Urbanodendron* (endemic; three), *Williamodendron* (endemic; three), *Caryodaphnopsis* (endemic; 15), *Aiouea* (endemic; 20), *Cassytha* (ca. 20; 1 pantropical), *Mezilaurus* (endemic; 20), *Rhodostemonodaphne* (endemic; 38), *Aniba* (endemic; 40), *Endlicheria* (endemic; 40), *Licaria* (endemic; 40), *Pleurothyrium* (endemic; 45), *Cinnamomum* (including American *Phoebe*; ca. 60 worldwide), *Nectandra* (endemic; 120), *Persea* (including Asian *Machilus*; ca. 200 worldwide), *Beilschmiedia* (ca. 250 worldwide), *Cryptocarya* (ca. 350 worldwide, the

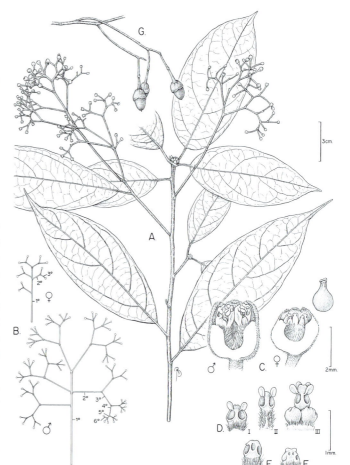

Figure 104. LAURACEAE. *Rhodostemonodaphne morii.* **A.** Stem with leaves and inflorescences. **B.** Diagram of branching patterns of inflorescences. **C.** Medial sections of staminate (left) and pistillate (right) flowers with gynoecium removed, fertile gynoecium shown above. **D.** Adaxial views of fertile stamens of different series showing valvate dehiscence of anthers and appendages at base of stamen at right. **E.** Staminode of one series. **F.** Staminode of another series. **G.** Stem with three fruits. Reprinted with permission from Mori et al. (2002). Artist: Bobbi Angell.

great majority Southeast Asia); *Ocotea* (ca. 350, mostly Neo-tropical, with about 60 species in Madagascar, Africa, and the Canary Islands), and *Litsea* (ca. 400, the great majority in the Eastern Hemisphere).

Distribution and habitat. The Lauraceae inhabit the Tropics worldwide, with centers of high species diversity in northern South America, Southeast Asia, and Madagascar. Some species occur in the subtropics and a few reach temperate zones (to ca. 45°N latitude) in eastern North America, Japan, Mediterranean Europe, New Zealand, and Chile. Most genera are endemic to a major biogeographic region, with only a few reputedly having disjunct distributions. Distribution patterns, however, depend on the extent to which the genera currently recognized represent natural groups, and generic limits (particularly in the larger genera) are still under debate. Thus, genera like *Persea*, currently with species from Asia and America, might well be split into the earlier recognized Asian *Machilus*, leaving only the American species in *Persea*. Recently, a large number of American species of the primarily Asian genus *Phoebe* have been transferred to *Cinnamomum*, leaving *Phoebe* restricted to Asia, but keeping *Cinnamomum* as an Asian/American disjunct.

Species of Lauraceae are an important element of both Neotropical and Paleotropical floras, with species in almost every ecosystem, except deserts and *páramos*. The Lauraceae are mainly found in lowland to montane forests, where they can be among the most common families. Nevertheless, individuals of given species are often rare.

Family classification. The Lauraceae (Laurales *sensu* Cronquist) together with Atherospermataceae, Calycanthaceae *sensu lato*, Gomortegaceae, Hernandiaceae, Monimiaceae *sensu stricto*, and Siparunaceae, form a well-supported clade (the Laurales) on the basis of molecular characters, perigynous flowers, and carpel(s) embedded in a fleshy receptacle.

The family has traditionally been divided into two tribes, the Perseeae and the Laureae, although various subfamilial and differing tribal classifications have been proposed; these, however, are all very similar in their grouping of taxa, notwithstanding their differences in ranks. A notable exception is *Cassytha*, which differs from all other Lauraceae in its parasitic climbing habit, and because of this has been segregated into a separate tribe, subfamily, or even family, the Cassythaceae. Its anomalous vegetative morphology should not be misleading as to its true relationships, as is often the case with parasitic members of other families. *Cassytha* bears various floral and fruiting characters that suggest a close relationship with members of the *Cryptocarya*-group currently placed in the Perseeae. Molecular analyses have placed *Cassytha* as sister to the family as a whole, or near the *Cryptocarya*-group, the former most likely due to long branch attraction caused by limited molecular data. The two-tribe classification, based primarily on inflorescence and floral characters, is still not strictly phylogenetic. Information from wood anatomy has suggested maintaining the two-tribe scheme

while also highlighting the distinct anatomical characters of the *Cryptocarya*-group.

Most species of Lauraceae are included in large genera with 100+ species, and these apparently include members of separate evolutionary lineages. On the other hand, the high number of very small genera, with one to three species each, may represent separate evolutionary lineages.

Features of the family. Habit: trees, sometimes shrubs, rarely parasitic vines (*Cassytha*), the trees often large, sometimes with small buttresses; bark usually smooth, the slash often emanating strong odor of essential oils, which range from sweet to fetid depending on species; wood white to yellow. **Stipules** absent. **Leaves** usually alternate (spiral), sometimes pseudo-opposite, or opposite (e.g., *Cinnamomum* and *Caryodaphnopsis*), simple, often aromatic when crushed; blade margins entire; transluscent gland dots often present (visible with hand lens); secondary venation typically running parallel to primary vein for short distance, brochidodromous to eucamptodromous, sometimes acrodromous, the leaves often bearing strong basal secondaries (e.g., most *Cinnamomum*). **Inflorescences** axillary (may appear terminal, the vegetative apical bud hidden), usually compound, sometimes of 1–few flowers, the subfamilies defined in general (but not exclusively) by presence of different inflorescence types, the Laureae involucrate and racemose or umbellate, the Perseeae not involucrate, mostly thyrsoid. **Flowers** actinomorphic, bisexual or unisexual (plants sometimes functionally unisexual, dioecious or monoecious), usually (2)3(4)-merous; receptacle generally well developed and fleshy; perianth parts (4)6(8), generally distinguishable only by position (thus tepalar); androecium most often with 9 stamens, generally in 4 alternating whorls, the third whorl often with paired basal glands, the fourth whorl generally staminodial, sessile or shortly filamentous, the anthers introrse or extrorse (this orientation often constant and depending on whorl), bearing 1–2 pairs of locelli, dehiscing by hinged flaps; gynoecium with superior ovary, often enclosed in receptacle, the carpel 1, the locule 1, the style short, the stigma discoid or inconspicuous; placentation apical, the ovule 1. **Fruits** drupes, the pericarp fleshy, the endocarp forming distinct membrane, often seated on, or partially to almost completely enclosed by, swollen receptacle, the receptacle (cupule) often red and contrasting with green to black ripe fruit at maturity. **Seeds** 1 per fruit, large.

Generally no exudate is produced from the slash of the bark, but in a few species ample liquid or mucilage is sometimes present (e.g., *Ocotea caparrapi*). When growing in forests, trees of Lauraceae are generally unbranched for most of their length, bearing a crown with horizontal pseudo-verticillate branches.

Various genera have been segregated on the basis of their reproductive systems (e.g., the dioecious *Endlicheria* and *Rhodostemonodaphne*), but others, such as *Ocotea*, include both dioecious and monoecious species.

Androecial characters, such as the number of staminal

whorls, the number of locelli in the anther, anther dehiscence, and presence of paired basal glands, have been the basis of generic delimitation. However, though generally constant within the groups they define, some variation in these features occur, thus the elevated number of genera, and, in particular, the high number of monotypic genera.

Natural history. The flowers of the bisexual species are protogynous, and synchronized dichogamy has been reported in several. These include two classes of individuals with complementary phenologies. In one class, the stigmas are receptive in the morning and the anthers dehisce in the afternoon. In the other class, the stigmas are receptive in the afternoon, and the anthers dehisce on the following morning. Thus, the classes interbreed. Some species have scented flowers, whereas others have odorless flowers. The staminal glands and staminodes produce nectar in a number of species, but in others they swell and shrink, generating movement of the staminal whorls. Bees, wasps, flies, and moths have been reported to visit flowers of Lauraceae.

Sex change has been reported in the gynodioecious *Ocotea tenera* in Costa Rica. Spatial patterns of sex distribution in natural and experimental plots have been described as nonrandom, suggesting labile sex expression of individuals that is influenced by the presence of neighboring trees.

A long-term study of fruiting phenology of laurels in a lower montane forest in Costa Rica found that species produced fruits in different seasons, fruit production varied from year to year, and this variation was not related to meteorological factors. The fruits of the Lauraceae accounted for 60–80 percent of all the fruits eaten by birds in the locality. Fruits of this family are important in the diets of oilbirds (*Steatornis caripensis*). They are also consumed by monkeys, bats, and many other mammals. The fruits are rich in lipids, nitrogen, and nonstructural carbohydrates.

Economic uses. Important economic products obtained from the Lauraceae are avocados (*Persea americana*), cinnamon (*Cinnamomum zeylanicum*), and bay leaf (*Laurus nobilis*), which are exploited sustainably from plantations. The leaves of various species of Lauraceae are used locally as bay substitutes. Avocado production is a vast industry worldwide, and many varieties and cultivars have been selected. The Lauraceae also are used for timber production, although this is done in a nonsustainable manner from naturally occuring trees. The wood of Lauraceae is valued for its fine grain and aromatic odor. Examples of exploitation of species of Lauraceae to near extinction are the Brazilian rosewood (*Aniba roseodora*), a source of essential oils used to make perfumes; the *laurel comíno* (*Aniba perutilis*), a precious timber from northwestern Colombia; and greenheart (*Chlorocardium rodiei*), a valuable timber from the Guianas.

References. BERNAL, H. Y., AND J. E. CORRERA Q. 1994. Lauraceae. In *Especies vegetales promisorias de los países del Convenio Andrés Bello*, Tomo X. Santafé de Bogotá, D. E., Colombia: Secretaria Ejecutiva del Convenio Andrés Bello. KOSTERMANS, A.J.G.H. 1957. Lauraceae. *Commun. Forest Res. Inst.* 57:1–64. KUBITZKI, K. AND H. KURZ. 1984. Syncronyzed dichogamy and dioecy in Neotropical Lauraceae. *Pl. Syst. Evol* 147:253–66. KUBITZKI K., AND S. RENNER. 1982. Lauraceae I (*Aniba* and *Aiouea*). *Fl. Neotrop. Monogr.* 31:1–125. MEZ, C. 1889. Lauraceae Americanae. *Jahrb. Königl. Bot. Gart. Berlin* 5:1–556. RENNER, S. S. 1999. Circumscription and phylogeny of the Laurales: evidence from molecular and morphological data. *Amer. J. Bot.* 86: 1301–15. RICHTER, H. G. 1981. Anatomie des sekundären Xylems und der Rinde der Lauraceae. *Naturwiss. Vereins in Hamburg* 5:1–148. ROHWER, J. G. 1993. Lauraceae. In *The families and genera of vascular plants*, eds. K. Kubitzki, J. G. Rohwer, and V. Bittrich, 2:426–437. New York: Springer-Verlag. ROHWER, J. G. 1994. A note on the evolution of the stamens in the Laurales, with emphasis on the Lauraceae. *Bot. Acta* 107:103–10. ROHWER, J. G. 2000. Toward a phylogenetic classification of the Lauraceae. Evidence from *mat*K sequences. *Syst. Bot.* 25:60–71. ROHWER, J. G., H. G. RICHTER, AND H. VAN DER WERFF. 1991. Two new genera of Neotropical Lauraceae and critical remarks on the generic delimitation. *Ann. Missouri Bot. Gard.* 78:388–400. WERFF, H. VAN DER. 1991. A key to the genera of Lauraceae in the New World. *Ann. Missouri Bot. Gard.* 78:377–87. WERFF, H. VAN DER, AND H. G. RICHTER. 1996. Toward an improved classification of the Lauraceae. *Ann. Missouri Bot. Gard.* 83: 409–18. WHEELWRIGHT, N. T., AND A. BRUNEAU. 1992. Population sex ratios and spatial distribution of *Ocotea tenera* (Lauraceae) trees in a tropical forest. *J. Ecol.* 80:425–32.

LECYTHIDACEAE (Brazil Nut Family)

SCOTT A. MORI

Figures 105, 106; Plate 26

- *trees, infrequently shrubs*

- *stems with fibrous bark*

- *leaves alternate, simple*

- *flowers actinomorphic or zygomorphic; filament bases always fused into a ring; ovary usually inferior*

- *fruits most frequently woody, circumscissile capsules, less frequently somewhat fleshy and berrylike or indehiscent with thin, woody walls*

Numbers of genera and species. Worldwide, the Lecythidaceae comprise approximately 20 genera and 292 species. In tropical America, there are 10 genera and 204 known species. The largest genus is *Eschweilera*, with 85 species. *Allantoma* (*A. lineata*), *Asteranthos* (*A. brasiliensis*) and *Bertholletia* (*B. excelsa*) are monotypic. The other Neotropical genera are *Cariniana* (15), *Couratari* (19), *Couroupita* (3), *Grias* (7), *Gustavia* (40), and *Lecythis* (26).

Distribution and habitat. Species of Lecythidaceae are found in tropical forests of Central and South America, Africa, and Asia. In the Western Hemisphere, the Lecythidaceae range from southern Mexico where one species, *Eschweilera mexicana*, occurs to Paraguay, which marks the southern limit of *Cariniana estrellensis*. A single species, *Grias cauliflora*, is found in Jamaica.

Lecythidaceae are predominantly trees of lowland forests where they are most speciose and abundant in nonflooded forests (*terra firme*) of the Amazon Basin and the Guianas. For example, a single 100-hectare plot on *terra firme* in central Amazonian Brazil possesses 38 different species with 11–24 species in each hectare. In the Western Hemisphere, less than 10 percent of the species are found above 1,000 meters elevation and relatively few species occur in periodically flooded forests. Dry habitats such as the *llanos* of Colombia and Venezuela, the *caatinga* of Brazil, and the *chacó* of Paraguay are especially poor in species of Lecythidaceae. They are also infrequent in heavily disturbed habitats.

Family classification. Traditionally, the Lecythidaceae were placed in the Myrtales, but Cronquist treats the family as a monofamilial order, the Lecythidales in his Dilleniidae. Molecular data align the Lecythidaceae in the enlarged order Ericales as sister to the Sapotaceae, a position supported by a few embryological (shared nuclear endosperm formation) and anatomical (shared trilacunar nodes) features. There are

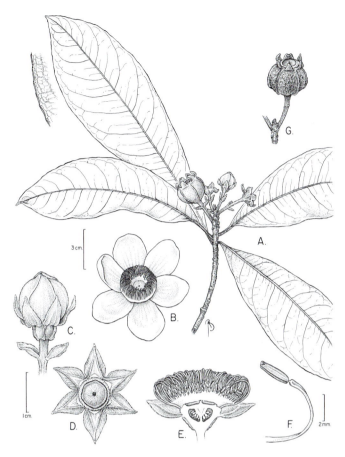

Figure 105. LECYTHIDACEAE. *Gustavia hexapetala.* **A.** Stem with leaves, flower bud, and immature fruits. **B.** Apical view of flower. **C.** Lateral view of flower bud. **D.** Apical view of flower after corolla and stamens have fallen. **E.** Medial section of flower. **F.** Lateral view of stamen showing poricidal dehiscence. **G.** Lateral view of fruit. Reprinted with permission from Mori et al. (2002). Artist: Bobbi Angell.

no apparent morphological characters, however, that support this placement.

The family is divided into five subfamilies, the Planchonioideae, with six genera and 59 species in tropical Asia, Malaysia, northern Australia, the Pacific Islands, and Madagascar; the Foetidioideae, with a single genus and 17 species in Madagascar, Mauritius, and East Africa; the Napoleonaeoideae, with two genera and 11 species in West Africa; the Scytopetaloideae, with a single species (*Asteranthos brasiliensis*) in the Negro and Orinoco river basins of Brazil and Venezuela and three to six genera and as many as 21 species in Africa; and the Lecythidoideae of the Western Hemisphere.

Features of the family. Habit: understory to emergent trees, infrequently shrubs. **Bark** fibrous, often can be peeled in long strips from trunk and stems. **Indument** mostly absent, the hairs, when present, usually unicellular and simple, stellate in some species of *Couratari*. **Stipules** absent or very small

and caducous. **Leaves** alternate, simple, medium-sized, sometimes large and clustered at branch apices (e.g., *Grias* and
some *Gustavia*). **Inflorescences** usually terminal or axillary,
sometimes ramiflorous or cauliflorous, fasciculate, spicate, racemose, or paniculate. **Flowers** actinomorphic (*Allantoma,
Asteranthos, Grias, Gustavia*) or zygomorphic, intermediate in
Cariniana, bisexual, often large and showy; calyx cuplike,
2–6-lobed, or in some *Grias*, completely enclosing bud; corolla with 4–8(18) distinct petals; androecium with staminal
bases fused into ring (actinomorphic genera), the ring sometimes expanded on one side into a hood unique to this family
(zygomorphic genera), the stamens usually numerous, sometimes as few as 10 in *Couratari*, the anthers usually dehiscing laterally or opening by apical pores in *Gustavia*; gynoecium syncarpous, the ovary half (e.g., *Asteranthos*) to usually
completely inferior, the carpels 2–6(10), the locules equal in
number to carpels, the style nearly absent to well developed,
straight or obliquely oriented; placentation axile, the ovules
sometimes appearing basal (some *Eschweilera*), 2–115 per
locule, anatropous. **Fruits** somewhat fleshy and berrylike (*Grias*
and *Gustavia*), indehiscent with thin, woody walls (*Asteranthos, Couroupita*, and a few *Lecythis*), or, most frequently,
circumscissile capsules. **Seeds** 1–50 per fruit, winged in
Cariniana and *Couratari*, in species without wings, an aril
present or absent, if present, the aril lateral, basal, or rarely
surrounding seed; endosperm usually lacking or well developed and ruminate in *Asteranthos*, the cotyledons leaflike (*Cariniana, Couratari, Couroupita*), plano-convex (*Gustavia*), or
absent.

The smallest Lecythidaceae is *Eschweilera nana* of the
Brazilian *cerrado* which is a shrub or small tree, and the
largest are *Bertholletia excelsa* and species of *Cariniana,
Couratari*, and *Lecythis*, which may attain 55 meters in height.

The cut wood of a number of species of Lecythidaceae,
especially of *Couratari* and *Gustavia*, is characterized by fetid
aromas probably caused by the presence of relatively high
concentrations of sulfur compounds in the volatiles.

The flowers of *Asteranthos* differ from other Lecythidaceae of the Western Hemisphere in the possession of a corona that is probably of petalar origin but is thought by some
to be staminal in origin.

The fruits of *Bertholletia* are essentially indehiscent; i.e.,
they possess lids but the openings are smaller in diameter
than the diameter of the seeds. Dehiscent fruits usually remain in the tree at maturity, whereas indehiscent or secondarily indehiscent ones fall to the ground with the seeds inside.

Chromosome numbers are $x = 17$ for the Lecythidoideae,
$x = 16$ for the Napoleonaeoideae, and $x = 13$ for the Planchonioideae. *Asteranthos brasiliensis* is $x = 21$ and there are
no available counts for the Foetidioideae.

Natural history. The most important pollinators of Lecythidaceae are bees. However, at least two species (*Lecythis bar-
nebyi* and *L. poiteaui*) and perhaps a third (*L. brancoensis*)
are pollinated by bats, and some species of *Grias* now are
suspected to be pollinated by beetles. Different species of

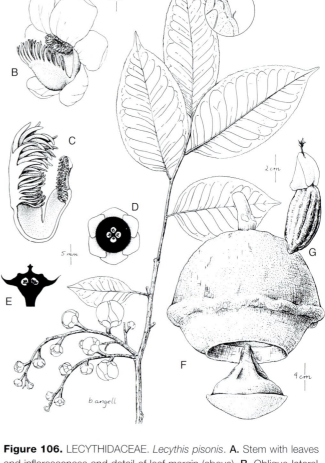

Figure 106. LECYTHIDACEAE. *Lecythis pisonis*. **A.** Stem with leaves
and inflorescences and detail of leaf margin (above). **B.** Oblique-lateral
view of flower. **C.** Medial section of androecium. **D.** Transverse section
of ovary. **E.** Medial section of ovary. **F.** Lateral view of fruit with operculum. **G.** Seed with funicle surrounded by aril. Reprinted with permission from Mori and Prance (1990). Artist: Bobbi Angell.

Lecythidaceae offer nondifferentiated pollen, differentiated
or fodder pollen, and nectar as rewards to pollinators.

Species with winged seeds (*Cariniana* and *Couratari*) are
dispersed by the wind. The seeds of *Lecythis pisonis* are dispersed by bats, which eat the aril and discard the seeds. The
pulp of *Couroupita guianensis* is eaten by peccaries, and the
seeds, which are embedded in the pulp, presumably pass
through their digestive tracts and are thereby dispersed. The
fruits of at least some species of *Gustavia* are eaten by mammals, which then disperse the seeds. The seeds of *Bertholletia
excelsa*, which fall to the ground inside the mature fruits, are
consumed by agoutis and squirrels, which also cache some
of them for future consumption. Forgotten seeds germinate
a year later after the bony seed coat has softened.

Primates often open unripe fruits of Lecythidaceae and
consume the seeds. For example, one study revealed that
about 70 percent of the winged seeds of *Cariniana micrantha*
were destroyed and almost 30 percent of the remaining seeds
became inviable as a result of predation by capuchin monkeys

(*Cebus apella*) in a central Amazonian forest, thereby greatly reducing seed production from that tree in that year.

Economic uses. Economically, the Brazil nut (*Bertholletia excelsa*) is the most important species of Lecythidaceae. Seeds are still gathered almost exclusively from wild trees. Other species, such as *Lecythis pisonis* of Brazil, have equally delicious seeds, but because the fruits are dehiscent and the seeds are carried away by bats, they are much more difficult to harvest than the Brazil nut is. Some species (e.g., *Lecythis minor* and *L. ollaria*), are slightly toxic if grown on selenium-rich soils. The consumption of too many of their seeds is accompanied by dizziness and loss of hair and fingernails. The mesocarps of *Grias haughtii*, *G. neuberthii*, *G. peruviana*, and some species of *Gustavia* (e.g., *G. speciosa*) are edible. Extracts of the bark of *Cariniana domestica* possess anticoagulants, which have been used by Amerindians as arrow and spear poisons. There are few medicinal uses of Lecythidaceae. The timber of some species, especially *Cariniana pyriformis*, *C. estrellenis*, and *C. legalis*, is exploited commercially, but the wood of most species possesses too much silica to be worked easily.

References. ANDERBERG, A., C. RYDIN, AND M. KÄLLERSJÖ. 2002. Phylogenetic relationships in the order Ericales *s. l.*: analyses of molecular data from five genes from the plastid and mitochondrial genomes. *Amer. J. Bot.* 89(4):677–87. BERKOV, A., B. MEURER-GRIMES, AND K. L. PURZYCKI. 2000. Do Lecythidaceae specialists (Coleoptera, Cerambycidae) shun fetid tree species? *Biotropica* 32(3):440–51. BERNAL, H. Y., AND J. E. CORRERA Q. 1994. Lecythidaceae. In *Especies vegetales promisorias de los países del Convenio Andrés Bello*, Tomo X. Santafé de Bogotá, D. E., Colombia: Secretaria Ejecutiva del Convenio Andrés Bello. JACOBS, J. W., C. PETROSKI, P. A. FRIEDMAN, AND E. SIMPSON. 1990. Characterization of the anticoagulant activities from a Brazilian arrow poison. *Thrombosis and Haemostasis* 63(1):31–35. MORI, S. A. 1992. The Brazil nut industry—past, present, and future. In *Sustainable Harvest and Marketing of Rain Forest Products*, eds. M. Plotkin and L. Famolare, 241–51. Washington, D.C.: Island Press. MORI, S. A., AND G. T. PRANCE. 1990a. Lecythidaceae—Part II. The zygomorphic-flowered New World Lecythidaceae (*Couroupita, Corythophora, Bertholletia, Couratari, Eschweilera, & Lecythis*). *Fl. Neotrop. Monogr.* 21(II):1–373. MORI, S. A., AND G. T. PRANCE. 1990b. Taxonomy, ecology, and economic botany of the Brazil nut (*Bertholletia excelsa* Humb. & Bonpl.: Lecythidaceae). *Advances Econ. Bot.* 8:130–50. MORTON, C. M., S. A. MORI, G. T. PRANCE, K. G. KAROL, AND M. W. CHASE. 1997. Phylogenetic relationships of Lecythidaceae: A cladistic analysis using *rbc*L sequence and morphological data. *Amer. J. Bot.* 84:530–40. MORTON, C. M., G. T. PRANCE, S. A. MORI, AND L. G. THORBURN. 1998. Recircumscription of the Lecythidaceae. *Taxon* 47:817–27. PERES, C. A. 1991. Seed predation of *Cariniana micrantha* (Lecythidaceae) by brown Capuchin monkeys in central Amazonia. *Biotropica* 23(3):262–70. PRANCE, G. T., AND S. A. MORI. 1979. Lecythidaceae—Part I. The actinomorphic-flowered New World Lecythidaceae (*Asteranthos, Gustavia, Grias, Allantoma, & Cariniana*). *Fl. Neotrop. Monogr.* 21: 1–270. TSOU, C.-H. 1994. The embryology, reproductive morphology, and systematics of Lecythidaceae. *Mem. New York Bot. Gard.* 71:1–110. TSOU, C.-H., AND S. A. MORI. 2002. Seed coat anatomy and its relationship to seed dispersal in subfamily Lecythidoideae of the Lecythidaceae (Brazil nut family). *Bot. Bull. Acad. Sin.* 43:37–56. ZEEUW, C. H. DE. 1990. Secondary xylem of neotropical Lecythidaceae. Pp. 4–59 in Lecythidaceae—Part II. The zygomorphic-flowered New World Lecythidaceae (*Couroupita, Corythophora, Bertholletia, Couratari, Eschweilera, & Lecythis*), S. A. Mori and G. T. Prance *Fl. Neotrop. Monogr.* 21(II): 1–373.

LENNOACEAE (Lennoa Family)

GEORGE YATSKIEVYCH

Figure 107, Plate 26

- *herbs*
- *plants obligate root parasites; chlorophyll absent*
- *stems fleshy*
- *leaves reduced to scales*
- *fruits capsules*

Numbers of genera and species. The Lennoaceae comprise two genera, *Lennoa* (monotypic) and *Pholisma* (three species). In tropical America, there is a single species, *Lennoa madreporoides*.

Distribution and habitat. The Lennoaceae are restricted to tropical and subtropical America. The distribution of *Lennoa* extends through most of Mexico with sporadic occurrences in Guatemala, Nicaragua, and northern Colombia and Venezuela. The genus *Pholisma* is endemic to the southwestern United States and northwestern Mexico.

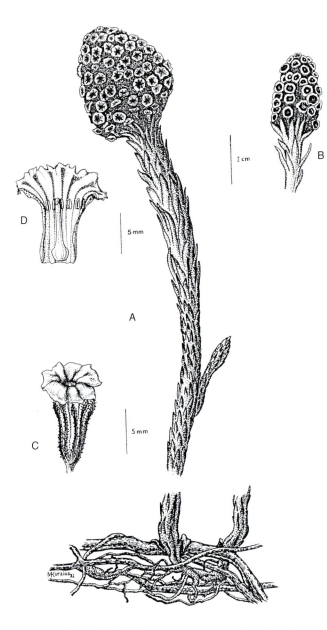

Figure 107. LENNOACEAE. *Pholisma arenarium* (species extra-Neotropical). **A.** Plant with roots, leaves, and inflorescence. **B.** Inflorescence. **C.** Lateral view of flower. **D.** Corolla opened to show gynoecium and adnate stamens. Reprinted with permission from Yatskievych and Mason (1986). Artist: Margaret Kurzius.

Members of the Lennoaceae occur most frequently in arid or seasonally dry climates. *Lennoa madreporoides* occurs in a variety of habitats ranging from coastal sand dunes to oak forests and margins of agricultural fields.

Family classification. The Lennoaceae are placed in the Lamiales by Cronquist. The unusual morphology of Lennoaceae, including the subterranean parasitic habit and the unusual number of parts in the flowers and fruits, has led to disagreement about the affinities of the Lennoaceae. Most early authors accepted a relationship with saprophytic members of Ericaceae (i.e., Monotropoideae). Other alignments have been with Primulaceae, *Cuscuta* (Cuscutaceae), Hydrophyllaceae, and Verbenaceae. Molecular studies support a relationship with the Boraginaceae, and in particular, the relatively primitive subfamily Ehretioideae.

Features of the family. Habit: herbs, obligate root parasites, chlorophyll absent, vegetative parts white to brown. **Roots** fleshy, branched, often coralloid, usually associated with haustorial masses, frequently forming connections to host roots. **Stems** fleshy, usually subterranean, originating from haustoria. **Stipules** absent. **Leaves** reduced to scales, in dense spiral series, small. **Inflorescences** terminal, dense cymose panicles (sometimes spikes or concave heads in *Pholisma*), sometimes so congested to appear capitate. **Flowers** actinomorphic or slightly zygomorphic, bisexual, the perianth persistent; sepals deeply 8-lobed (4–10 in *Pholisma*); corolla sympetalous, shallowly 8-lobed (4–10 in *Pholisma*); androecium of 8(4–10 in *Pholisma*) stamens, the stamens in 2 rows (1 in *Pholisma*), adnate to corolla tube, the filaments short, the anthers dehiscing by longitudinal slits; gynoecium syncarpous, the ovary superior, the carpels usually 8 (5–9 in *Pholisma*), the locules twice as many as carpels, the styles stout, terminal, the stigmas capitate or slightly lobed; placentation axile, the ovules 2 per carpel but 1 per apparent locule, anatropous. **Fruits** capsules, fleshy, irregularly circumscissile, the perianth persisting (even after dehiscence). **Seeds** 2 per carpel, wedge-shaped, arranged like segments of an orange around a central axis; endosperm present, the embryo small, undifferentiated.

Natural history. As obligate parasites devoid of chlorophyll, these plants are limited in distributions by the availability of suitable host species. *Lennoa madreporoides* parasitizes mostly selected members of Asteraceae tribe Heliantheae but occasionally may be found on roots of *Okenia* (Nyctaginaceae) and *Tribulus* (Zygophyllaceae). *Pholisma arenarium* parasitizes various shrubby Asteraceae, as well as a few species of *Croton* (Euphorbiaceae) and *Eriodictyon* (Hydrophyllaceae). *Pholisma culiacanum* thus far has been found only on woody species of Euphorbiaceae (*Croton, Euphorbia, Jatropha*), and *P. sonorae* occurs on roots of *Tiquilia* (Boraginaceae), *Ambrosia* and *Pluchea* (Asteraceae), and the shrubby *Eriogonum deserticola* (Polygonaceae), whose range is almost exactly the same as that of its parasite.

The relationships between species of Lennoaceae and their host plants are perplexing and fascinating. Although these parasites often occur in arid regions, including the driest portions of the North American continent, they produce fleshy stems that in extreme situations can outweigh host plants by a factor of more than 30 without apparent damage to the host. This has led to the suggestion that in times of stress, host plants are able to reabsorb moisture from their parasites, but further study is needed.

Flowers of Lennoaceae produce nectar and apparently are insect-pollinated. Seed dispersal is accomplished by a variety of means, including ants and mammals, but primarily by water and wind. Sometimes whole inflorescences may be dispersed by wind and presumably shed seeds as they break apart. For species present in disturbed habitats, human activities (mostly agricultural) also account for some dispersal of seeds.

Economic uses. Species of Lennoaceae are not known to parasitize crop plants and thus have no direct economic importance as weeds. *Lennoa* has a history of use as a minor potherb in Mexico. Its mention in the literature extends back to the reports of Francisco Hernandez, an eighteenth-century physician-explorer in Mexico. Perhaps the best documented ethnobotanical use of the family, however, is for *Pholisma sonorae*, which has stems that may grow to more than a meter in length. Known as sandfood, it was once a major element in the diets of several groups of Native Americans residing in and around the mouth of the Colorado River. Plants were eaten raw, boiled, or roasted or dried for grinding into flour and were valued as much for their water content as for their nutritive properties.

References. NABHAN, G. 1980. *Ammobroma sonorae*, an endangered parasitic plant in extremely arid North America. *Desert Pl.* 2:188–96. SMITH, R. A., AND C. W. DE PAMPHILIS. 1998. Phylogenetic placement of the holoparasitic family Lennoaceae: preliminary molecular evidence. *Amer. J. Bot.* 85(suppl. 6):157. SMITH, R. A., D. M. FERGUSON, T. J. BARKMAN, AND C. W. DE PAMPHILIS. 2000. Molecular phylogenetic evidence for the origin of Lennoaceae: a case of adelphoparasitism in the angiosperms? *Amer. J. Bot.* 87(suppl. 6):158. YATSKIEVYCH, G. 1985. Notes on the biology of the Lennoaceae. *Cactus and Succulent Journal (U.S.)* 57:73–79. YATSKIEVYCH, G., AND C. T. MASON, JR. 1986. A revision of the Lennoaceae. *Syst. Bot.* 11:531–48.

LENTIBULARIACEAE (Bladderwort Family)

GARRETT E. CROW

Figure 108, Plate 26

- *herbs, carnivorous*

- *leaves alternate, sometimes whorled or in rosettes, simple, bearing bladders or traps; blades entire to highly dissected*

- *flowers zygomorphic, bisexual; placentation free-central*

- *fruits usually capsules*

Numbers of genera and species. Worldwide, the Lentibulariaceae comprise three genera and approximately 280 species. In tropical America, there are three genera. *Utricularia* accounts for most of the diversity, with about 83 Neotropical species (215 worldwide), *Genlisea* has about 11 species (20 worldwide) and *Pinguicula* about 35 species (50 worldwide).

Distribution and habitat. The Lentibulariaceae are nearly cosmopolitan in distribution, ranging from the subarctic to tropical savannas and forests. The largest genus, *Utricularia*, is widely distributed, occurring as submerged aquatics, semiterrestrials in wetlands and seasonally wet habitats, or epiphytes in montane tropical rain forests and cloud forests. The epiphytic species of *Utricularia* (section *Orchidoides*), a Neotropical group consisting of nine species, are centered primarily in the Andes but also range into the mountains of Central America. *Pinguicula* is primarily a warm-temperate genus that extends into the Andes, with *P. antarctica* reaching Tierra del Fuego. A few species, such as *P. vulgaris*, have a boreal distribution. *Genlisea* is a tropical genus, occurring in the neotropics, from Belize to Bolivia and Brazil, and Africa.

Family classification. The Lentibulariaceae are placed in the Scrophulariales by Cronquist. The family appears to be derived from the closely related Scrophulariaceae and molecular analyses place *Utricularia* and *Pinguicula* near taxa of the Scrophulariaceae and Lamiaceae. The genus *Utricularia* has been subdivided into subgenus *Utricularia* and subgenus *Polypompholyx*. The latter subgenus, consisting of three Australian species characterized by a four- rather than two-parted calyx, is sometimes treated as a segregate genus. The extremely diverse subgenus *Utricularia* is further subdivided into 33 sections.

Features of the family. Habit: carnivorous herbs, annual or perennial, free-floating aquatics (species of *Utricularia* and *Genlisea*), semiterrestrial, or epiphytic, the semiterrestrial species often with rhizoids or stolons; tubers sometimes present. **Roots** absent. **Stipules** absent. **Leaves** alternate, sometimes whorled or in rosettes (*Genlisea*, *Pinguicula*, and some *Utricularia*), bearing carnivorous bladders or traps; blades of *Utricularia* usually small, narrowly linear to somewhat obovate, thin, the margins entire or of highly dissected capillary segments in submersed species. **Inflorescences** of solitary flowers on scapes (*Pinguicula*) or in few- to many-flowered scapose racemes; bracts and bracteoles present, basifixed or peltate. **Flowers** zygomorphic, bisexual; calyx 2(4),

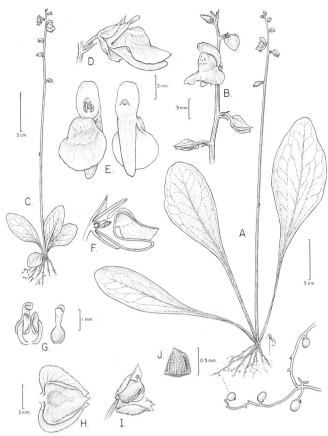

Figure 108. LENTIBULARIACEAE. *Utricularia calycifida* (A, B, Mori and Smith 25105; C, Mutchnick P.60; D–H, Tillet et al. 45205, I, J, Hahn 4640). **A.** Plant showing basal leaves, inflorescence, and detail of bladders (below). **B.** Apex of inflorescence. **C.** Plant of another individual showing roots, basal leaves, and inflorescence. **D.** Lateral view of flower. **E.** Apical (left) and basal (right) views of flowers. **F.** Medial section of flower. **G.** Lateral views of stamens and gynoecium (left) and gynoecium (right). **H.** Lateral view of bracteoles subtending immature fruit. **I.** Apical view of dehisced fruit subtended by bracteoles. **J.** Seed. Original. Artist: Bobbi Angell.

or 5 lobed; corolla sympetalous, often with conspicuous palate at throat, 5-lobed, 2-lipped, the lower lip spurred, the spur sometimes short and saccate; androecium with 2 stamens, the stamens epipetalous, the anthers dehiscing longitudinally; staminodes 2 when present; gynoecium syncarpous, the ovary superior, the carpels 2, the locule 1, the style 1 or absent, the stigma 2-lobed; placentation free-central, the ovules 1–numerous. **Fruits** usually capsules, rarely indehiscent, the capsules dehiscing circumscissiley by 2–4 valves or irregularly. **Seeds** numerous, minute.

At first glance, the epiphytic species of *Utricularia* in Neotropical rain- and cloud-forest habitats are likely to be mistaken for orchids, with which they may grow. The 2-lipped, zygomorphic flowers tend to be quite showy; the leaves can be fairly large and somewhat leathery; and the tubers are similar to orchid pseudobulbs.

Natural history. Semiterrestrial species of the Lentibulariaceae often are anchored in wet, sandy, or peaty substrates by rhizoids or stolons. Tubers are sometimes present, and these are important for allowing plants to survive dessication during the dry season. Epiphytes are found commonly anchored in mossy substrates. Aquatic species are free-floating, but sometimes become anchored or stranded as water level subsides.

The family is especially interesting because of the presence of carnivorous traps. In *Pinguicula* (butterworts), the trap mechanism is passive and consists of a rosette of leaves covered with stalked glandular hairs that trap insects and sessile glands that secrete digestive enzymes. In *Utricularia* (bladderworts), the plants bear numerous bladders in which the digestive processes occur. The trap usually is a stalked, globose, saclike structure with a door. Around the trap door are bristles that function as trigger hairs. Absorptive hairs within the bladder create a vacuum, and, if the trigger hairs are touched, an extremely rapid rush of water into the trap sucks microscopic animals inside. Considerable variation occurs in trap morphology, and this variation reflects the taxonomic sections. In *Genlisea*, the trap is a complex tubular structure consisting of a footstalk, a hollow bladder, a tubular neck, and two twisted arms; the inner epidermis of the trap is coated with hairs and glands. It is not clear whether this trap functions as a passive organ with unidirectional movement like an eel trap or lobster pot, but the traps have recently been shown to lure protozoans by secreting a chemical attractant.

No information is available on pollination and dispersal, but the zygomorphic, showy flowers point to insects as pollinators.

Economic uses. Because of the enormous interest in carnivorous plants as novelties, a number of plant societies in various countries cultivate several species of Lentibulariaceae.

References. BARTHLOTT, W., S. POREMBSKI, E. FISCHER, AND B. GEMMEL. 1998. First protozoa-trapping plant found. *Nature* 392:447. CROW, G. E. 1992. The genus *Utricularia* (Lentibulariaceae) in Costa Rica. *Brenesia* 38:1–18. FROMM-TRINTA, E. 1979. Revisão das espécies do gênero *Genlisea* St.-Hil. (Lentibulariaceae) das regiões sudeste e sul do Brasil. *Rodriguésia* 31(49):17–139. GODFREY, R. K., AND H. L. STRIPLING. 1961. A synopsis of *Pinguicula* (Lentibulariaceae) in the southeastern United States. *Amer. Midl. Naturalist* 66:395–409. HESLOP-HARRISON, Y. 1978. Carnivorous plants. *Sci. Amer.* 238(2):104–15. LLOYD, F. E. 1976. *The carnivorous plants.* Waltham, MA: Chronica Botanica Company. REUT, M. S. 1993. Trap structure of the carnivorous plant *Genlisea* (Lentibulariaceae). *Bot. Helv.* 103(1):101–11. RITTER, N. P., AND G. E. CROW. 2000. Notes on the Lentibulariaceae in Bolivia: a new genus record (*Genlisea*) for the country, with two additional species records in the genus *Utricularia*. *Rhodora* 102:217–24. TAYLOR, P. 1989. The genus *Utricularia*—a taxonomic monograph. *Kew Bull., Addit. Ser.* 14:1–724. TAYLOR, P. 1991. The genus *Genlisea*. *Carniv. Pl. Newslett.* 20:20–35.

LEPIDOBOTRYACEAE

Barry E. Hammel and Nathan Smith

Figure 109

- *trees*

- *leaves alternate, unifoliolate; petiole and petiolule pulvinate, the petiolule/petiole juncture articulate*

- *inflorescences usually leaf-opposed*

- *flowers with stamen filaments fused (at least basally) into tube; locules 2, ovules 2 per locule, pendulous*

- *seeds 1(2) per fruit, black, surrounded by red-orange aril*

Numbers of genera and species. Worldwide, the Lepidobotryaceae comprise two genera, *Ruptiliocarpon* and *Lepidobotrys*, each with a single species. Only *Ruptiliocarpon* occurs in tropical America.

Distribution and habitat. *Ruptiliocarpon caracolito* occurs in Costa Rica, Panama, Colombia, Ecuador, Peru, and Suriname. In Costa Rica the species is most common on the southern Pacific slope, in the Golfo Dulce region (Osa Peninsula to Golfito), and the hills above Quepos. It is rare on the Atlantic slope where it is known from the vicinity of Barbilla and from the Llanuras de San Carlos. *Ruptiliocarpon* grows on well-drained soils in primary forest from sea level to 400 meters. *Lepidobotrys* is restricted to tropical Africa.

Family classification. Although Cronquist did not account for *Ruptiliocarpon*, he placed *Lepidobotrys* in the Oxalidaceae (Geraniales). Other classifications have placed this genus in the Sapindales, Linaceae, Erythroxylaceae, or its own family. Morphologically, *Ruptiliocarpon* and *Lepidobotrys* share similarities in wood, leaves, inflorescence position, flowers, fruits, and seeds.

It has been suggested that *Ruptiliocarpon* belongs in the Sapindales because it resembles *Trichilia* (Meliaceae) in wood anatomy and flower morphology, especially in the presence of a staminal tube. However, the position of the floral nectary (i.e., never part of the staminal tube in the Meliaceae), as well as differences in vessel pits and pollen, suggest that *Ruptiliocarpon* does not belong in the Sapindales. It has also been suggested the *Ruptiliocarpon* belongs in or near the Fabaceae, but flower and fruit morphology indicate that these taxa are not closely related. Thus, *Ruptiliocarpon* and *Lepidobotrys* are here treated as a separate family.

Features of the family. Habit: trees (to 40 m tall), evergreen. Indument: trichomes often present on leaves and re-

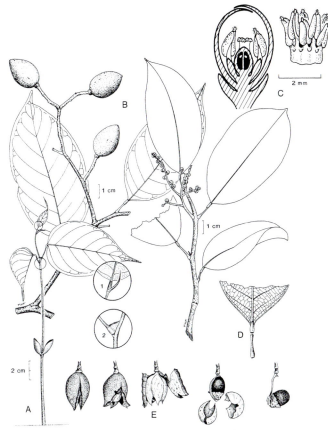

Figure 109. LEPIDOBOTRYACEAE. *Ruptiliocarpon caracolito*. **A.** Seedling with details of circled nodes (1, stipel; 2, stipule). **B.** Stems with leaves and infructescences (left) and leaves and inflorescences (right). **C.** Medial section of flower (left) and lateral view of androecium (right). **D.** Base of leaf showing articulation of petiole. **E.** Lateral views of fruits showing different stages of dehiscence and seeds subtended by aril (right) Reprinted with permission from Hammel and Zamora (1993). Artist: Francisco Hodgson.

productive structures. **Stipules** present, deciduous. **Leaves** alternate (spiral), unifoliolate; petiole pulvinate at base; petiolule pulvinate, subtended by single stiple, articulate at petiole juncture; leaflet elliptic, the base obtuse, the margins entire, the apex acute to acuminate; venation reticulate, the veins conspicuous abaxially. **Inflorescences** usually leaf-opposed, rarely terminal, panicle of spikes; bract present; flowers subtended by 3 bracteoles. **Flowers** actinomorphic, unisexual (plants dioecious), inconspicuous, greenish; calyx with 5 sepals, the sepals imbricate, distinct; corolla with 5 petals, the petals imbricate, distinct; staminodes and pistillodes present; androecium of 10 stamens, the stamens in 2 whorls, the filaments fused at least basally into tube, the tube more conspicuous in staminate flowers, the antipetalous anthers sessile, the antisepalous filaments distinct beyond tube, the tube nectariferous in staminate flowers (this unknown for female flowers); gynoecium syncarpous, the ovary superior, the carpels 2, the locules 2, the style ± absent, the stigma ± 2-lobed; placentation near locular apices, the ovules 2 per locule, pendulous. **Fruits** capsules, the exocarp irregular rupturing. **Seeds** 1(2) per fruit, pendulous, globose, black, partially (1/3) surrounded by red-orange aril.

Natural history. Pollination and dispersal biology are unknown; however, seedlings often are found below parent trees.

Economic uses. In Costa Rica, *Ruptiliocarpon* is used locally for lumber in the construction of boxes and cabinets.

References. HAMMEL, B. E., AND N. A. ZAMORA. 1993. *Ruptiliocarpon* (Lepidobotryaceae): a new arborescent genus and tropical American link to Africa, with reconsideration of the family. *Novon* 3:408–17. MENNEGA, A.M.W. 1993. Comparative wood anatomy of *Ruptiliocarpon caracolito* (Lepidobotryaceae). *Novon* 3:418–22. TOBE, H. AND B. HAMMEL. 1993. Floral morphology, embryology, and seed anatomy of *Ruptiliocarpon caracolito* (Lepidobotryaceae). *Novon* 3:423–28.

LEPUROPETALACEAE (Lepuropetalon Family)

AMY BERKOV

- *herbs, in small hemispherical tufts*
- *leaf blades spatulate, usually with lines of reddish glands*
- *flower petals irregular in size, scalelike or absent*
- *fruits capsules, opening at apices*

Numbers of genera and species. The Lepuropetalaceae include a single species, *Lepuropetalon spathulatum*.

Distribution and habitat. *Lepuropetalon spathulatum* is known from the southern United States, Mexico, Ecuador, Brazil, Argentina, Uruguay, and Chile.

The Lepuropetalaceae are found in disturbed areas, growing amidst grasses and other small annual herbs, sometimes in damp and often sandy soil. *Lepuropetalon spathulatum* is not very common. The species forms diminutive, often rather dense tufts, and is among the smallest terrestrial herbs, growing in patches less than 2 centimeters broad.

Family classification. The placement of the Lepuropetalaceae is not fully resolved. Cronquist retains *Lepuropetalon* within the Saxifragaceae, in the Rosales. Takhtajan segregates numerous small families from this diverse assemblage, including the Lepuropetalaceae, and maintains that Lepuropetalaceae are distinct from Saxifragaceae on the basis of flavonoid profile and *rbc*L sequence data. Both *rbc*L and 18S rDNA sequence data support *Lepuropetalon* and *Parnassia* (traditionally placed in the Saxifragaceae) as sister groups, and Takhtajan places the Lepuropetalaceae in the Order Parnassiales. A recent ordinal level classification includes both *Lepuropetalon* and *Parnassia* in the Celastrales.

Features of the family. Habit: herbs, annual, in small hemispherical tufts. **Stipules** absent. **Leaves** alternate and/or basal, simple, glabrous; blades spatulate, generally 2–6 mm long, the margins entire; glands present, in many short lines, reddish. **Infloresecences** terminal, of solitary flowers. **Flowers** actinomorphic (although calyx lobes and petals may be irregular in size), bisexual, small; sepals 5, connate at base, forming cup, the lobes spreading, oval; petals (0)5, scalelike when present, alternate with sepals, inserted on rim of cup, irregular in size, white; androecium with 5 stamens, the stamens opposite sepals, the anthers dehiscing longitudinally; staminodes (0)5, opposite petals; gynoecium syncarpous, the ovary subinferior, the carpels 3–4, the locule 1, the styles 3–4, short, slightly fused at base, the stigmas capitate; placentation parietal, the ovules numerous. **Fruits** capsules (about 2 mm long), opening at apices. **Seeds** numerous, minute, oval, the surface pitted; endosperm scant.

Natural history. Nothing is known about the pollination or seed dispersal of *Lepuropetalon spathulatum*.

Economic uses. The family has no known economic uses.

References. CORRELL, D. S., M. C. JOHNSON, AND COLLABORATORS. 1970. Manual of the vascular plants of Texas. Renner, TX: Texas Research Foundation. GAY, C. 1847. *Historia física y política de Chile*. 3:1–484. Santiago, Chile: Museo de Historia Natural de Chile. SAVOLAINEN, V., et al. 2000. Phylogeny of the eudicots: a nearly complete familial analysis based on *rbc*L sequences. *Kew Bull.* 55:257–309. SMALL, J. K. 1933. *Manual of the Southeastern Flora*. New York: J. K. Small. SOLTIS, D. E., AND P. S. SOLTIS. 1997. Phylogenetic relationships in Saxifragaceae *sensu lato*: a comparison of topologies based on 18S *rDNA* and *rbc*L sequences. *Amer. J. Bot.* 84(4):504–22. ZULOAGA F., AND O. MORRONE, eds. 1999. *Catálogo de las plantas vasculares de la Republic Argentina*, II. St. Louis, MO: Missouri Botanical Garden Press.

LINACEAE (Flax Family)

CAROL ANN KEARNS

- *herbs*

- *leaves alternate or opposite, simple*

- *flowers actinomorphic; sepals and petals 5; filaments connate at base; ovary superior*

- *fruits septicidal capsules*

Numbers of genera and species. Worldwide, the Linaceae comprise six (to 33) genera and 220–300 species. *Linum* is the largest genus, containing more than 200 species of herbs and small shrubs. Only *Linum* occurs in the Western Hemisphere, with about 45 species in the Tropics and subtropics.

Distribution and habitat. The Linaceae are found throughout the world. *Linum* is widespread, with more than 200 species worldwide. Species richness is greatest in the Mediterranean, but many species of *Linum* also occur in the neotropics, including the cultivated flax. Native species tend to be small herbs of upland dry areas.

Family classification. The Linaceae are placed in the Linales by Cronquist. The family is closely allied with the Hugoniaceae. Both Cronquist and Takhtajan consider the Hugoniaceae as a separate family, although many authors maintain the woody, tropical genera of Hugoniaceae within the Linaceae. Recent molecular studies by the Angiosperm Phylogeny Group place the family within an expanded Malpighiales of the Eurosids I.

The genera generally recognized as belonging to the family include: *Linum, Radiola, Anisadenia, Tirpitzia, Reinwardtia,* and several genera that were at one time lumped under *Linum* (e.g., *Adenolinum, Cliococca, Mesyniopsis*).

Features of the family. Habit: herbs, annual or perennial. **Stipules** sometimes present, small or modified into glands. **Leaves** alternate or opposite, simple, often sessile; blades often narrow. **Inflorescences** terminal, cymose or racemose. **Flowers** actinomorphic, bisexual, often showy; sepals 5; petals 5, distinct or fused at base, sometimes clawed, imbricate or convolute, ephemeral, generally yellow (native tropical and subtropical species), often reddish in bud; androecium with 5 stamens, the stamens alternate to petals, the filaments connate at base, the anthers introrse; staminodes sometimes present; nectaries often present at base of petals, or external to filaments; gynoecium syncarpous, the ovary superior, the carpels 2–5, incomplete septa often present and giving appearance of twice as many locules, the styles equal in number to locules, filiform, distyly present in some species of *Linum*, the stigmas capitate; placentation axile, the ovules 2 per locule. **Fruits** septicidal capsules. **Seeds** with endosperm present, scanty or absent, the embryo straight, chlorophyllous, oily.

Natural history. The flowers of the extratropical *Linum lewisii*, though self-compatible, are dependent on insects for pollen transfer. Flowers are visited by more than 45 insect species that differ significantly in their ability to transport and deposit pollen. The abundance of small bee pollinators decreases with altitude and muscoid flies are the dominant pollinators at higher elevations. Populations at all elevations produce abundant seed.

Heterostyly in the Linaceae is accompanied by a sporophytic incompatibility system in which incompatible pollen is inhibited on the stigma. Distyly is present in *Linum* and the Old World *Reinwardtia*. Heterostylous plants have two or three different mating types differing in style and stamen lengths, size and sculpturing of pollen grains, and structure of the stigmatic papillae. Crossings within mating types are unsuccessful, whereas cross-fertilization between types produces fertile seeds.

No information is available on dispersal biology.

Economic uses. The most economically important species is *Linum usitatissimum* the source of flax. Because cultivation is worldwide, and flax tends to become naturalized, its origin is somewhat unclear. Many varieties are cultivated, some for their fibers and others for linseed oil. In India alone, 26 varieties and 123 races of linseed flax have been identified.

Fiber flax is grown in cool, humid, northern climates. The fibers are used to produce linen, which is very durable and conducts heat well, making it an excellent fabric for hot climates. Depending on the cultivar and method of production, flax fibers are suitable for anything from coarse, strong rope to the highest quality damask, cambric, and fine lace. Coarser fibers sometimes are used for making fire hoses, fishing lines and nets, and for sewing shoes.

Flax is possibly the oldest textile plant in cultivation. A *Linum* species was cultivated and its fibers woven by Neolithic Lake Dwellers in eastern Switzerland. Flax is depicted in ancient Egyptian tomb paintings from about 3000 B.C. The paintings show both the plant and the process of making linen. Egyptian mummies are wrapped in linen, and remains of linen cloth have been dated at about 6,000 years old. In Teutonic mythology, flax plants are under the protection of Hulda, the goddess who taught humans the art of cultivating and weaving the fibers.

A major region of flax fiber cultivation is the former Soviet Union. Commercial production also is carried out in Belgium, the Netherlands, and France. Ireland is a center of linen production, although most of the fibers used are imported from France.

Several species other than *Linum usitatissimum* have been used in fiber production on a smaller scale. For example, some Native Americans used fibers from *L. lewissi* to produce fishing nets and fabric. Aboriginal Australians ate the seeds of *L. marginale* and used its fibers for fishing net and cord. Several native European species have been cultivated in localized regions.

The flax grown for linseed oil is a bushier variety that favors drier climates. The plants are cultivated in the United States (the Dakotas, Wyoming, Montana), Argentina, Canada, India, and parts of the former Soviet Union. These oil cultivars have seeds that are larger than those of fiber cultivars and contain 32–43 percent oil. Linseed oil readily absorbs oxygen and dries to a thin elastic film. This makes it valuable for use in the manufacture of paint, varnish, putty, and linoleum, as well as for sealing porous stone and concrete. The seed residue after oil expression is a nutritious feed for livestock. In addition to these uses, most cigarette papers are made from the coarse fibers of linseed oil plants because the fibers burn evenly and do not have a strong taste.

Other Linaceae of economic value include several showy species of *Linum* cultivated as garden perennials (*L. arboreum*, *L. flavum*, *L. grandiflorum*) and an attractive flowering shrub, *Reinwardtia indica*, commonly cultivated in temperate greenhouses.

References. MILDNER, R. A., AND C. M. ROGERS. 1978. Revision of the native South American species of *Linum* (Linaceae). *Phytologia* 39(5):343–90. ROGERS, C. M. 1968. Yellow-flowered species of *Linum* in Central America and Western North America. *Brittonia* 20:107–35.

LISSOCARPACEAE (Lissocarpa Family)

CAROL GRACIE

- *shrubs or small trees*
- *leaves alternate, simple*
- *flower corona present; stamens 8, adnate to corolla tube; ovary inferior*
- *fruits drupes*

Numbers of genera and species. The Lissocarpaceae comprise a single genus, *Lissocarpa*, and five species.

Distribution and habitat. The Lissocarpaceae are endemic to tropical South America. Species are found in seasonally flooded areas of the upper Rio Negro basin; in lowland regions of Brazil, Colombia, and Venezuela, and Guyana; and, in montane regions of southern Venezulela, Bolivia, and Peru. Some species are commonly associated with white sand and others with clay soils.

Family classification. The Lissocarpaceae are placed in the Ebenales by Cronquist. Molecular analyses indicate that *Lissocarpa* is sister to *Diospyros* (Ebenaceae).

The family has been segregated out of the Ebenaceae on the basis of having an inferior versus superior ovary; more or less ovoid rather than spherical fruits; a fruiting calyx not conspicuously expanded; glabrous stems and leaves; bisexual versus unisexual flowers; staminal filaments that are connate in their bases; and a corona in the throat of the corolla.

Features of the family. Habit: shrubs or small trees, stems and leaves glabrous. **Stipules** absent. **Leaves** alternate, simple; blades somewhat coriaceous, the margins entire; venation pinnate. **Inflorescences** axillary, small cymes or racemes; bracts 2. **Flowers** actinomorphic, bisexual; calyx 4-lobed; corolla tube present, 4-lobed, yellowish; corona present in throat of corolla, 8-lobed; androecium of 8 stamens, the stamens about equal in length to corolla, the filaments connate at base, adnate to lower corolla tube, the connective prolonged and extending beyond anthers, the anthers linear, dehiscing longitudinally; gynoecium syncarpous, the ovary inferior, plurilocular, the carpels 4, the style terminal, the stigma capitate, four-lobed; placentation axile, the ovules 2 per placenta, pendulous. **Fruits** drupes, ± ovoid, smooth (the generic name means smooth fruit), fleshy. **Seeds** 1–2 per fruit.

Natural history. No information is availailable on pollination biology. The seeds of *Lissocarpa benthamii* and *L. guianensis* are dispersed by animals that eat the fruits.

Economic uses. On the upper Rio Negro of Brazil, the leaves of *Lissocarpa benthamii* are boiled in water to prepare a bath for cleansing skin ulcers. The leaves are of minor use in the preparation of a fish poison.

References. BERRY, P. E. 1999. A synopsis of the family Lissocarpaceae. *Brittonia* 51(2):214–16. BERRY, P. E., V. SAVOLAINEN, K. J. SYTSMA, J. C. HALL, AND M. CHASE. 2001. *Lissocarpa* is sister to *Diospyros* (Ebenaceae). *Kew Bull.* 56(3):725–29. ROOSMALEN, M.G.M. VAN. 1985. *Fruits of the Guianan Flora*. Utrecht: Institute of Systematic Botany.

LOASACEAE (Rock Nettle Family)

MAXIMILIAN WEIGEND

Figure 110, Plate 27

- *usually herbs or subshrubs*

- *plants usually with stinging and/or scabrid and glochidiate hairs*

- *flowers with well developed, mostly cymbiform petals; androecium 5- or 10-merous to polymerous; staminodia often present; placentation parietal, the ovules usually numerous*

- *fruits cypselas or capsules*

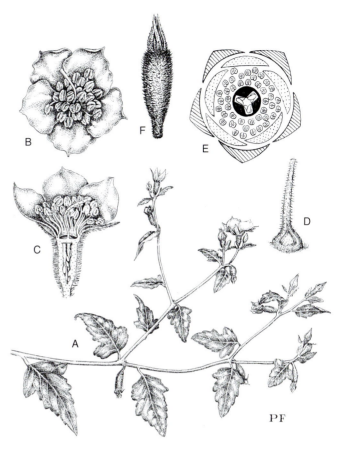

Numbers of genera and species. Worldwide, the Loasaceae comprise 20 genera and approximately 330 species. Currently 13 genera are accepted in subfamily Loasoideae (>200 species). The two largest genera are *Nasa* (>100 species) and *Caiophora* (ca. 60 species). Six genera have only one or two species. Three genera are accepted in subfamily Mentzelioideae (ca. 90 species) with *Mentzelia* by far the largest with ca. 75 species. Subfamily Gronovioideae has three genera, all of which have only 1–2 species. Subfamily Petalonychoideae consists of a single, extratropical genus. In tropical America, there are 15 genera and ca. 180 species.

Distribution and habitat. The Loasaceae are mostly restricted to the tropical and subtropical regions of the Americas. Overall diversity of the family is highest in Andean South America (Loasoideae) with a second, smaller center of diversity in subtropical Mexico (Mentzelioideae, Gronovioideae). A few species reach temperate zones, both in the Southern and Northern Hemispheres (to southern Argentina and Canada).

Mentzelioideae have their center of diversity in Mexico and the southwestern United States where all three genera are distributed, but only *Mentzelia* is found in South America. *Mentzelia* is poorly represented in the American Tropics with one weedy species (*M. aspera*) and a group of poorly understood species of the dry western slopes of the Andes and the semidesert of the inner-Andean valleys found there. The other two tropical genera of Mentzelioideae are herbs or shrubs of semideserts, with the largest number of species in Mexico. *Eucnide* reaches south into Guatemala while *Schismocarpus* is endemic to Oaxaca, Mexico.

Loasoideae are almost exclusively South American, with only three of the 200 species found in Central America. Two small extra-American groups occur in Polynesia, southwest Africa, and southern Arabia. *Blumenbachia* is found in the south temperate and subtropical zone of South America and barely enters the Tropics in Brazil (Minas Gerais, São Paulo). The tropical genera of Loasoideae are geographically and ecologically segregated. *Nasa* is North and Central Andean

Figure 110. LOASACEAE. *Mentzelia floridana*. Fawcett. **A.** Stem with leaves, flowers, and fruits (x⅔). **B.** Apical view of flower (x2). **C.** Medial section of flower (x2). **D.** Trichome from calyx (x40). **E.** Floral diagram. **F.** Lateral view of fruit (x2). Reprinted with permission from Correll and Correll (1982). Artist: Priscilla Fawcett.

with most species at low and intermediate elevations (1,000–2,500 meters) and a few representatives in the higher zones (*puna*) at up to 4,600 meters. Most species are found in cloud forests, but some occur in tropical rain forest, tropical dry forest, coastal *loma* vegetation, Andean grasslands, and on scree slopes. *Aosa* is Brazilian and Hispaniolan and is found primarily in *caatinga*, on rock outcrops, and in mesic forests. *Caiophora* is found mostly above 2,500 meters in the Central and Southern Andes and prefers open vegetation (scree slopes) or the base of rocks in *puna*. *Chichicaste* occurs below 1,000 meters in the rain forests of southern Central America and *Loasa* is restricted to Chile with only one species in the *loma* vegetation of coastal Peru.

Gronovioideae are represented by two genera in the Tropics, both of which are climbing plants of tropical dry forests. *Gronovia* has one endemic species in Mexico and another species ranging from Mexico to northern Peru and *Fuertesia* is endemic to Hispaniola.

Most Loasaceae are found in dry habitats (semideserts,

deserts, or rocky habitats on steep slopes (all Mentzelioideae and some Loasoideae). One of the two species of *Klaprothia* is found in cloud forest and about 90 species of *Nasa* occur in cloud forest, *subpáramo* forest, and *puna*.

Family classification. The Loasaceae are placed in the Violales by Cronquist. They have now been shown to be closely allied to the Cornaceae by Hempel et al. Loasaceae show remarkable morphological similarities in placentation, fruit shape, trichome characters, dilated filaments, and stem structure with *Philadelphus*, *Deutzia*, *Fendlera* and *Jamesia*, all considered members of the Hydrangeaceae of the Cornales.

Loasaceae are characterized by the presence of urticant and/or scabrid/glochidiate hairs, iridoid compounds, hydathode teeth on the leaves, and thyrsoids, bracteate inflorescences.

The family is divided into four subfamilies, the polyandric (rarely obdiplostemonous) Loasoideae and Mentzelioideae and the haplostemonous Gronovioideae and Petalonychoideae. Other features uniting the Loasoideae and Mentzelioideae are the showy petals with numerous parallel veins, the frequent but not universal occurrence of ring-shaped nectaries fused to the ovary wall, the usually numerous ovules on parietal placentae, and the capsular fruits. Morphologically, the Loasoideae differ from Mentzelioideae in a typically reticulate (vs. polyhedral to striate) testa, the presence of antesepalous staminodia in groups of five or more (vs. no or a single antesepalous staminodium), and deeply cymbiform, clawed petals (vs. flat, unclawed petals). Further evidence of a relationship between the Gronovoideaeae and Petalonychoideae are the common occurrences of inconspicuous petals with only one principal vein that branches in the upper half of the petal, well-developed, cup-shaped nectaries free from the ovary wall, a single pendulous ovule per ovary, and cypselas as fruits. The Gronovioideae are distinguished from the Petalonychoideae by persistent versus caducous sepals and thrysoid versus racemose inflorescences. Separate treatment of the Gronovioideae and the Petalonychoideae as the family Gronoviaceae, however, is not justified.

Generic and tribal limits in Mentzelioideae are still problematic, but the Loasoideae fall into two morphologically distinct tribes, the tetramerous Klaprothieae and the penta-to octamerous Loaseae.

Features of the family. Habit: herbs, subshrubs, rarely shrubs, trees, or lianas, the herbs annual or perennial, sometimes rosulate (some *Caiophora*), sometimes with horizontal, lignescent rhizomes (some *Nasa*), plants usually branched from base, the stems stout and erect or weak and scandent with long internodes (*Caiophora*, *Gronovia*), nonscandent species rarely exceeding 2 m in height (only *Mentzelia arborescens* is a small tree to 7 m). **Bark** of woody species often whitish and exfoliating. **Indument:** glochidiate or scabrid hairs always present, the trichomes covering entire plant except roots, stinging hairs (setae) found in most genera, glandular hairs occasionally present (especially in *Nasa*). **Stipules** absent, pseudostipules present in a few *Nasa*. **Leaves**

opposite below (sometimes first foliage leaves only, and these lost in mature plants), alternate above, rarely opposite throughout (e.g., *Caiophora*), simple or compound; petioles present; leaflets (when present) petiolate or sessile, ovate; simple blades ovate or orbiculate, rarely linear, mostly deeply lobed (entire in *Fuertesia*), sometimes pinnatisect to pinnatifid, the margins irregularly lobed to regularly once- or twice serrate or with hydathode teeth and mucronate apices; venation semicraspedodromous. **Inflorescences** terminal, frondose or bracteose thyrsoids, these usually dichasial, very rarely racemose (*Petalonyx*); bracts usually 2 per flower, sometimes 1 (*Nasa*) or absent (*Aosa*). **Flowers** actinomorphic, bisexual, showy, usually erect but sometimes pendent (e.g., *Caiophora*, *Nasa*, *Xylopodia*), (4–)5 (6–8)-merous; sepals distinct nearly to base, rarely united nearly to apex (*Gronovia longiflora*), with 3 veins, the margins entire, rarely serrate (*Caiophora*); petals well developed, usually distinct, with 1–numerous principal veins, white, yellow, or red, spreading or erect, membranous, slightly (*Mentzelia*) to very profoundly (most Loasoideae) cymbiform, rarely flat (*Petalonyx*, Gronovioideae, *Eucnide*), apiculate, the base sometimes clawed (Loasoideae), the margins entire or serrate (many *Caiophora*) or laciniate (*Fuertesia*); androecium usually 5-merous, 10-merous, or polymerous, the filaments long and filiform, rarely short (Gronovioideae), white, the anthers basifixed, the connective usually undifferentiated, with longitudinal dehiscence; staminodia often present (absent in Gronovioideae), these filiform (*Petalonyx*), apically forked, or lanceolate, sometimes petal-like, sometimes in two-tiered antesepalous groups (in Loasoideae), the outer tier usually united to form floral scales, the inner tier distinct to base, the floral scales poorly differentiated and pale yellow to green (e.g., *Chichicaste*, *Presliophytum*, *Xylopodia*) or morphologically elaborate and brightly colored (*Aosa*, *Caiophora*, *Nasa*); nectary disc present on ovary summit, usually well developed (at least in Loasoideae), sometimes cup-shaped (Gronovioideae, *Petalonyx*), rarely absent (some Mentzelioideae); gynoecium syncarpous, the ovary inferior to largely superior (position variable even in closely related groups), the carpels 3–5, the locule 1, the style 1, approximately as long as filaments, the stigma punctiform (*Mentzelia*), dome-shaped (*Schismocarpus*), slightly widened (*Eucnide*), or of 3–5 parallel or divergent lobes (Loasoideae, Gronovioideae); placentation parietal, the placentae variable in structure (this important in defining genera), the ovules usually numerous (sometimes reduced to 2–3, e.g., *Loasa* series *Macrospermae*), rarely a single pendulous ovule (Gronovioideae, *Petalonyx*). **Fruits** cypselas (Gronovioideae, *Petalonyx*) or capsules, straight or twisted antidromously (*Caiophora*), the capsules dehiscing by apical valves, or apical valves plus 1 loculicidal, longitudinal slit (some *Nasa*), or apically closed and open only with 3–5 longitudinal, septicidal slits (*Cajophora*), the calyx persistent or rarely (*Petalonyx*) caducous. **Seeds** numerous, rarely few or 1, the testa usually brown or black, reticulate or striate, rarely poorly differentiated and colorless (Gronoviodieae, *Petalonyx*); endosperm oily, copious, the embryo small, straight, the cotyledons ± ovate, often apically emarginate, an apical hydathode always present.

Iridoid compounds are generally found in all Loasaceae.

The base chromosome numbers for the family are $x = 6$ (Loasoideae) and $x = 7$ (Mentzelioideae).

Species of Loasoideae have a wide range of leaf shapes. For example, peltate, trifoliolate, palmate, or bipinnate leaves are widespread in *Nasa* and very rare in the other genera. In *Caiophora* and allied groups and in *Loasa*, the blades are usually pinnatisect to pinnatifid with decurrent leaf bases. The leaves of *Fuertesia* are coriaceous, deeply cordate, and possess entire margins, a feature found only in this genus.

Natural history. Some species of Loasaceae are attacked frequently by insects, especially by pyralid and geometrid larvae (Lepidoptera), but mammalian herbivores are deterred effectively by the stinging hairs. Thus, Loasaceae are pre-adapted to grazed environments and are often locally abundant in high Andean pastures.

Pollination is by insects. Gronovioideae and Mentzelioideae are believed to have a relatively unspecialized pollination biology and are known to be visited by a wide range of insects, but most frequently by Hymenoptera. Pollination is accomplished by flies (Diptera) in *Klaprothia*. In some Loasoideae, stamen movement is triggered by twisting of the floral scales, and these species are visited by colletid bees (Colletidae, Hymenoptera). Some of the most advanced species of Loasoideae do not display that mechanism and are either pollinated by bumblebees or hummingbirds. In *Nasa* and *Caiophora*, the very large, tubular, red flowers with copious nectar are adapted for pollination by hummingbirds.

Seed dispersal in many taxa (e.g., species of *Nasa*) is inefficient, and this has led to narrowly endemic species. The deeply pitted seeds of *Caiophora* and the small, dustlike seeds of *Presliophytum* and *Eucnide* are adaptations for wind dispersal. A few species of Loasaceae (e.g., *Aosa plumierii*, species of *Blumenbachia*, and *Klaprothia mentzelioides*) have indehiscent fruits (burs with barbed trichomes) that attach to animals. In the Gronovioideae and *Petalonyx*, the entire indehiscent, one-seeded fruit is dispersed by the wind.

Economic uses. Tropical Loasaceae include no commercially important plants; however, they are used extensively in folk medicine, especially in the Andes. Species of *Caiophora* and *Nasa* are used to treat colds, respiratory problems, liver conditions, and other ailments and are sold regularly in Andean markets. Some species of *Mentzelia* are used to treat gastric ulcers in Peru.

A few species of Loasaceae are agricultural and roadside weeds, and many species cause discomfort to humans because of their irritating hairs.

References. DARLINGTON, J. 1934. A monograph of *Mentzelia. Ann. Missouri Bot. Gard.* 21:103–226. DOSTERT, N., AND WEIGEND, M. 1999: A synopsis of the *Nasa triphylla* complex (Loasaceae), including some new species and subspecies. *Harvard. Pap. Bot.* 4(2):439–67. HEMPEL, A. L., P. A. REEVES, R. G. OLMSTEAD, AND R. K. JANSEN. 1995. Implications of rbcl sequence data for higher order relationships of the Loasaceae and the anomalous aquatic plant *Hydrostachys* (Hydrostachyaceae). *Plant Syst. Evol.* 194:25–37. MOODY, M. L., L. HUFFORD, D. E. SOLTIS, AND P. S. SOLTIS. 2001: Phylogenetic relationships of Loasaceae subfamily Gronovioideae inferred from *mat*K and ITS sequence data. *Amer. J. Bot.* 88:326–36. POSTON, M. E., AND J. W. NOWICKE. 1990. A reevaluation of *Klaprothia* and *Sclerothrix* (Loasaceae, Klaprothieae). *Syst. Bot.* 15(4):671–77. POSTON, M. E., AND J. W. NOWICKE. 1993. Pollen morphology, trichome types, and relationships of the Gronovioideae (Loasaceae). *Amer. J. Bot.* 80(6):689–704. SCHLINDWEIN, C., AND D. WITTMANN. 1997. Microforaging routes of *Bicolletes pampeana* (Colletidae) and bee-induced pollen presentation in *Cajophora arechavaletae* (Loasaceae). *Bot. Acta* 109:1–7. WEIGEND, M. 1997. Loasoideae in Eastern South America and on Hispaniola: Names, types and a key. *Sendtnera* 4: 202–20. WEIGEND, M. 2000. Loasaceae. In *Flora of Ecuador*, eds. L. Andersson and G. Harling, no. 162, 64: 1–92. Göteborg, Sweden: Department of Systematic Botany, University of Göteborg. WEIGEND, M. 2001. Loasaceae. In *Flora de Colombia*, eds. R. Bernal and E. Forero, no. 22: Bogotá, D.C., Colombia: Instituto de Ciencias Naturales, Universidad Nacional de Colombia. WEIGEND, M., J. KUFER, AND A. A. MUELLER. 2000. Phytochemistry and the systematics and Ecology of Loasaceae & Gronoviaceae (Loasales). *Amer. J. Bot.* 87:1002–11.

LOGANIACEAE (Logania or Strychnine Family)

LENA STRUWE

Figure 111, Plate 27

- *herbs, shrubs, lianas, or trees*

- *tendrils often present in* Strychnos

- *leaves opposite, simple; interpetiolar lines often present*

- *flowers sympetalous; ovary superior or semi-inferior*

- *fruits capsules or berries*

Numbers of genera and species. Worldwide, the Loganiaceae comprise 10 genera and about 400 species. In tropical America, there are five genera and about 90 species. The most species-rich genus is *Strychnos* with nearly 200 species. The remaining genera in the Western Hemisphere are *Spigelia* (ca. 50 species), *Antonia* (1), *Bonyunia* (4), and *Mitreola* (ca. 6 species, 1 species in neotropics).

Distribution and habitat. The Loganiacae are mainly tropical and subtropical in distribution. *Antonia* and *Bonyunia* are restricted to tropical South America, whereas *Strychnos* is more widespread and occurs also in Central America (as well as in other tropical areas around the world). *Spigelia* is distributed in tropical and subtropical areas in the Americas (*S. anthelmia* has become naturalized in Asia and Africa) and *Mitreola* has one widespread species (*M. petiolata*) in the Tropics as well as a few endemic species in America, Madagascar, Southeast Asia, and Malesia. Most woody species are grow in tropical forests, and some shrubby or herbaceous species occur in open or disturbed areas such as roadsides, savannas, and grasslands.

Family classification. The Loganiaceae were placed in the Gentianales by Cronquist. The circumscription of Loganiaceae has varied from one to 29 genera over time. Recent studies have shown that the family (in the largest circumscription *sensu* Leeuwenberg) are highly poly- and paraphyletic. Genera and families that have been excluded from Loganiaceae are Buddlejaceae, Desfontainiaceae, Gelsemiaceae, *Polypremum*, *Plocosperma*, tribe Potalieae (Gentianaceae), *Retzia*, and *Sanango* (Gesneriaceae). Recent molecular analyses have shown that the previously segregated families Geniostomaceae and Strychnaceae should be included in Loganiaceae.

The Loganiaceae can be divided into four tribes. Tribe Loganieae contains the mainly Asian, Australian, and Pacific *Geniostoma*, *Labordia*, *Logania*, *Mitrasacme*, and *Mitreola*, with dry-walled fruits and mostly imbricate corolla aestivation. Tribes Antonieae, Spigelieae, and Strychneae have valvate corolla aestivation. The Antonieae are pantropical (*Antonia*, *Bonyunia*, *Norrisia*, and *Usteria*) and are characterized by being shrubs or trees with dry capsules and flattened seeds. Species of the monotypic tribe Spigelieae are herbaceous and possess capsular fruits with circumscissile dehiscence. The most species-rich tribe is Strychneae with three genera, *Gardneria*, *Neuburgia*, and *Strychnos*, all with fleshy fruits, but the monophyly of this tribe is questionable.

Recently, two new genera, *Phyllangium* and *Schizacme*, were segregated from *Mitrasacme*, but they are not accepted here since they may be derived inside *Mitrasacme*. Further phylogenetic studies are needed to clarify this.

Features of the family. Habit: herbs, shrubs, lianas, or small to rather large trees, the herbs ephemeral or annual, sometimes aquatic; colleters (fingerlike multicellular glands) usually present in leaf axils and inner base of calyces; ten-

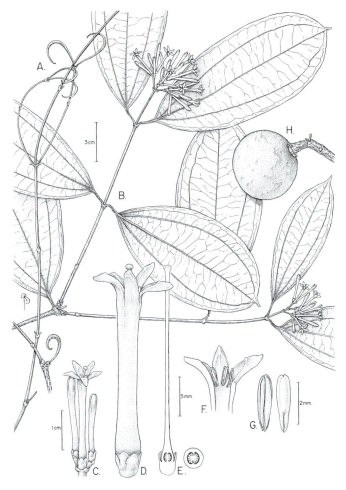

Figure 111. LOGANIACEAE. *Strychnos melinoniana.* **A.** Apical part of stem showing recurved tendrils. **B.** Stem with leaves and inflorescence. **C.** Part of inflorescence with central flower and two lateral buds. **D.** Lateral view of flower. **E.** Medial section of gynoecium (left) and transverse section of ovary (right). **F.** Medial section of apical part of corolla showing adnate stamens. **G.** Adaxial (left) and abaxial (right) views of anthers. **H.** Lateral view of fruit. Reprinted with permission from Mori et al. (2002). Artist: Bobbi Angell.

drils (of leaf origin) often present in *Strychnos*, the tendrils axillary, coiled in a single plane, thick. **Stipules** only present as interpetiolar lines or ocreas. **Leaves** opposite, simple; blade margins entire; venation in most *Strychnos* acrodromous, with three parallel, curved veins. **Inflorescences** axillary or terminal, usually cymose. **Flowers** actinomorphic, bisexual; calyx connate at base, the lobes 4–5; corolla sympetalous, the lobes 4–5, imbricate or valvate; androecium of 4–5 stamens, the stamens isomerous, inserted in corolla tube; gynoecium syncarpous, the ovary superior or semi-inferior, the carpels 2, the locules 2, the styles usually fused, the stigmas of various shapes; placentation axile, the ovules usually numerous. **Fruits** capsules or berries, the capsules dry and apically dehiscent (*Antonia*, *Bonyunia*, some *Mitreola*), mitra-shaped with persistent styles in *Mitreola* or rounded and basally dehiscent (*Spigelia*), the berries fleshy or coriaceous (*Strych-*

nos). **Seeds** 2–numerous, flattened or angular, sometimes winged (*Antonia* and *Bonyunia*).

Seco-iridoids and complex indole alkaloids are present in tribe Strychneae but absent from tribes Antonieae and Spigelieae.

Natural history. The sympetalous, tubular flowers of Loganiaceae suggest animal pollination. A number of species of *Strychnos* have white flowers and at least some species of *Spigelia* have red flowers and this suggests moth and hummingbird pollination, respectively. The pulp surrounding the seeds of at least some species of *Strychnos* is known to be eaten by monkeys even though the seeds are poisonous. The capsular fruits of *Antonia ovata* release winged seeds carried away by the wind.

Economic uses. *Strychnos* is well known and well studied as the source of several poisonous, complex, indole alkaloids such as strychnine and brucine, which are similar to those occurring in Apocynaceae. The most commonly used is the *nux vomica*, or poison nut from the Asian species *S. nux-vomica*. In South America, species of *Strychnos* provide arrow (curare) and fish poisons and possess many pharmacological properties. Extracts from this genus have been used to treat fevers, gastrointestinal problems, malaria, rheumatism, venereal disease, and lung infections. The fruits of some species of *Strychnos* are edible. *Geniostoma* is used in the Pacific to treat gastrointestinal and skin problems. *Antonia ovata* has been reported to be the source of a fish poison in Guyana and Brazil, the wood of *Norrisia* is used for carpentry and tools, and extracts from *Usteria* are used locally to treat fe-

vers. The rhizome of *Spigelia marylandica* is a traditional Native American herbal medicine of the southern United States; it has been used commonly as an effective means of expelling tapeworms and round worms (thus, the vernacular names wormwood and wormgrass). However, large doses are deadly. Other species of *Spigelia* are used for similar purposes throughout the Western Hemisphere.

References. BACKLUND, M., B. OXELMAN, AND B. BREMER. 2000. Phylogenetic relationships within the Gentianales based on *ndh*F and *rbc*L sequences, with particular reference to the Loganiaceae. *Amer. J. Bot.* 87:1029–43. BISSET, N. G. 1980. Phytochemistry. In A. Engler and K. Prantl's *Die natürlichen Pflanzenfamilien*, Angiospermae: Ordnung Gentianales, Fam. Loganiaceae, 28b(1):211–333. Berlin: Duncker and Humblot. BREMER, B., R. G. OLMSTEAD, L. STRUWE, AND J. A. SWEERE. 1994. *rbc*L sequences support exclusion of *Retzia*, *Desfontainia*, and *Nicodemia* from the Gentianales. *Pl. Syst. Evol.* 190:213–30. CONN, B. J., E. A. BROWN, AND C. R. DUNLOP. 1996. Loganiaceae. In *Flora Australia*, eds. A. E. Orchard and A. Wilson, 28:1–72. Melbourne: CSIRO Australia. LEEUWENBERG, A.J.M. 1980. In *Die Natürlichen Pflanzenfamilien*, 2nd ed., Angiospermae: ordnung Gentianales, fam. Loganiaceae, vol. 28b(1):1–255. Berlin: Duncker and Humblot. STRUWE, L., AND V. A. ALBERT. 1997. Floristics, cladistics, and classification: three case studies in Gentianales. In *Plant Diversity in Malesia III*, eds. J. Dransfield, M.J.E. Coode, and D. A. Simpson, 321–52. Richmond, Surrey: Royal Botanic Gardens, Kew. STRUWE, L., V. A. ALBERT, AND B. BREMER, 1994 [1995]. Cladistics and family level classification of the Gentianales. *Cladistics* 10:175–206.

LORANTHACEAE (Mistletoe Family)

JOB KUIJT AND CAROL GRACIE

Figure 112, Plate 27

- *usually shrubs, hemiparasitic; rarely terrestrial and parasitic on roots*
- *stipules absent*
- *leaves opposite, or more rarely alternate or whorled, simple*
- *flowers with sepals reduced to inconspicuous rim (calyculus); stamens opposite petals; ovary inferior*
- *fruits 1-"seeded" berries or drupes*

Numbers of genera and species. Worldwide, the Loranthaceae comprise about 70 genera and perhaps more than 900 species, making it the most species-rich of the three mis-

tletoe families. In tropical America, there are 14–15 genera and about 230 species. The largest genera are *Psittacanthus*, *Struthanthus*, *Cladocolea*, *Phthirusa*, and *Dendropemon*.

Distribution and habitat. With few exceptions, the Loranthaceae occur in tropical and subtropical regions where species are found in both lowlands and highlands. One genus, *Dendropemon*, is endemic to the Caribbean. *Cladocolea* is found in Central America. The largest genus, *Psittacanthus* ranges from Argentina to Baja California, with very slight representation in the southern Caribbean. *Struthanthus* and *Phthirusa* range from central Mexico far into South America but do not occur in the Caribbean except for Jamaican *Phthirusa*. *Psittacanthus* shows distinct low-elevation preferences while its taxonomically closest genus, *Aetanthus*, is strictly high-elevation Andean. Many species of *Phthirusa* and *Struthanthus* also prefer low-elevation habitats.

Family classification. The Loranthaceae are placed in the Santalales by Cronquist. For many years botanists aligned all parasitic plants of similar habit into one broadly defined family, the Loranthaceae. A closer look at the evidence has resulted in the division of the Loranthaceae into three separate families, Viscaceae, Eremolepidaceae, and a more strictly defined Loranthaceae. Molecular studies confirm at least the status and affinities of Loranthaceae and Viscaceae. The principal criteria used to define the Loranthaceae are the presence of a rim (calyculus) on the ovary; usually bisexual flowers (plants dioecious if flowers unisexual); endosperm usually without chlorophyll; and differences in the embryology and pollen. Although many species of Loranthaceae have large, brightly colored flowers with four or more petals, an almost equal number have small inconspicuous flowers. The differences between genera in Loranthaceae are not always clear.

Features of the family. Habit: usually shrubs, sometimes small trees, occasionally sprawling vines, hemiparasitic on woody dicots, rarely terrestrial and parasitic on roots (only *Gaiadendron*), evergreen. **Haustoria** attachment single (then often very large) or multiple; epicortical roots absent or formed from base of plant, from stems, or from both. **Stems** often green and somewhat brittle when young; sometimes dichotomously branched. **Stipules** absent. **Leaves** frequently opposite, more rarely alternate or whorled, simple, scalelike in two rare species; blades frequently ± coriaceous or fleshy, the margins entire; venation pinnate, palmate, or obscure. **Inflorescences** axillary and/or terminal, indeterminate or determinate spikes, racemes, or umbels, the lateral units (e)bracteolate monads, dyads, or triads, or of solitary flowers in leaf axils (*Ixocactus*). **Flowers** actinomorphic, sessile or pedicellate, usually bisexual, or unisexual (then plants dioecious); calyx reduced to a rim (calyculus), usually inserted near apex of ovary beneath petals; corolla usually tubular, splitting into individual petals, the petals (4)6(7), sometimes large and brightly colored; androecium with stamens equal in number, the stamens adnate, opposite petals, mostly dimorphic; staminodes present in pistillate flowers; gynoecium with inferior ovary, the style short (in small-flowered species) or long and slender (in large-flowered species), the stigma a small inconspicuous button; placentation anomalous, in inconspicuous central cavity of ovary, the ovules often replaced by a basal central body, the papilla or mamelon. **Fruits** berries or drupes, often colorful, 2–14 mm. **"Seeds"** 1 per fruit, surrounded by or capped by viscid material; endosperm usually present at maturity, the embryo green, the cotyledons sometimes more than 2 (*Psittacanthus*).

The genus *Psittacanthus* (meaning "parrot flowers") includes some spectacularly colorful species; in contrast the flowers of *Struthanthus* are generally small and greenish white, and those of *Phthirusa* are often tiny and deep red-violet.

The calyculus is very difficult to discern in flowers of *Oryctanthus*. Its variable prominence in different genera is thought to represent the calyx at various stages of phylogenetic disappearance.

With the exception of *Psittacanthus* and *Aetanthus*, the "seeds" contain endosperm at maturity. In *Psittacanthus*, the endosperm has been replaced by the developing embryo. Exceptional in the family, the endosperm of *Phthirusa pyrifolia* contains chlorophyll, which is the normal condition in the closely related family Viscaceae.

The "seeds" of tropical Loranthaceae germinate quickly, producing erect seedlings within two weeks after the "seeds" reach a host. The radicle forms a strongly adhesive haustorial disc on the host. The cotyledons of Neotropical Loranthaceae initially supply the seedling with stored nutrients but later

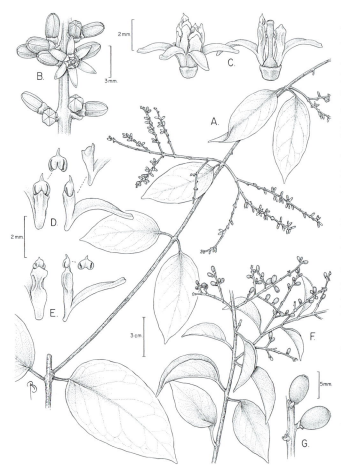

Figure 112. LORANTHACEAE. *Phthirusa stelis*. **A.** Stem with leaves and staminate inflorescences. **B.** Detail of staminate inflorescence with open flower and buds. **C.** Lateral views of staminate flowers intact (left) and with two petals removed (right). **D.** Adaxial (left) and lateral (right) views of short stamens with details of anther (above left) and attachment of filament to base of tepal (above right). **E.** Adaxial (left) and lateral (right) views of long stamen with detail of anther (above right). **F.** Stem with leaves and infructescences. **G.** Detail of infructescence with immature fruits. Reprinted with permission from Mori et al. (2002). Artist: Bobbi Angell.

become photosynthetic. *Psittacanthus* has many species with more than 2 cotyledons; *P. schiedeanus*, for example, may have up to 12 fleshy cotyledons.

Natural history. Loranthaceae are hemiparasites that generally attach to the aerial portions of their hosts, but one species (*Gaiadendron punctatum*) is probably a terrestrial root parasite. Although species are generally leafy and photosynthetic, they also parasitize their hosts by taking water and nutrients through haustoria in contact with the host's vascular tissue. Most tropical mistletoes attack a wide variety of host species. Some species of *Struthanthus* grow as scandent shrubs, using their recurved leaves and epicortical roots to anchor themselves to the branches of the host. These roots grow along the branches of the host plant and develop secondary haustoria at intervals, thereby permitting the parasite to obtain a greater flow of nutrients from the host. The production of epicortical roots also allows those seedlings that have germinated upon the leaf of a host to secure their hold to a branch and, hence, avoid being shed with the leaf. Not all Loranthaceae form epicortical roots; e.g., both *Tristerix* and *Psittacanthus* are attached to their hosts exclusively at the sites of their primary haustoria.

Most of the showy mistletoes possess the tubular, brightly colored (often red), scentless, and abundant nectar-producing flowers typical of bird pollination. In the neotropics, most of these species, especially of *Psittacanthus*, are pollinated by hummingbirds. Species with small, inconspicuous flowers (e.g., *Struthanthus*, *Oryctanthus*, *Phthirusa*, and *Ixocactus*) are most likely insect-pollinated.

Birds are attracted by the often colorful fruits and eat their flesh; the "seeds" rapidly pass through their digestive tracts. The sticky "seeds," still surrounded by viscid material, sometimes are rubbed onto the branches of the host by the birds in an effort to remove them from their bodies.

Economic uses. In Mexico and Central America, curiosities called *rosas de palo* (woodroses) are derived from the hosts of Loranthaceae. They consist of the woody outgrowths of a host plant that develop an enlargement around the haustorium of a species of *Psittacanthus*. Once the parasite dies and decays, the convoluted impression of its haustorium on the host tree's branch remains. The branches are cut, sometimes polished, and sold to tourists. Some species of Loranthaceae, especially *Phthirusa*, are considered pests of plantation-grown plants in South America.

References. KUIJT, J. 1976. Revision of the genus *Oryctanthus* (Loranthaceae). Bot. Jahrb. Syst. 95:478–534. KUIJT, J. 1986. Loranthaceae. *Flora of Ecuador*, eds. G. Harling, and B. Sparre, no. 24:113–94. Göteborg, Sweden: Department of Systematic Botany, University of Göteborg. KUIJT, J. 1992. Nomenclatural changes, new species, and a revised key for the genus *Oryctanthus* (Loranthaceae). Bot. Jahrb. Syst. 114:173–83.

LYTHRACEAE (Loosestrife Family)

SHIRLEY A. GRAHAM

Figure 113, Plate 27

- *herbs, subshrubs, or trees*

- *leaves usually opposite, decussate, simple; blade margins entire*

- *flowers perigynous, the floral tube surrounding ovary; petals crinkled, crepelike, at rim of floral tube*

- *fruits typically capsular*

Numbers of genera and species. Worldwide, 31 genera and about 600 species are recognized. The tropical American *Cuphea* is the largest (ca. 260 species), followed by the Brazilian *Diplusodon* (ca. 70). Nineteen genera possess three or fewer species.

The family is represented in tropical America by 16 native and three cultivated genera (ca. 384 species). Other genera found in this region are: the Caribbean endemic *Ginoria* (14 species); *Pleurophora* (ca. 11); *Lafoensia* (5); *Heimia* (3), *Crenea* and *Haitia* (2 each); and *Adenaria*, *Lourtella*, *Pehria*, and *Physocalymma* (1 each). A few species of predominantly Asian genera of Lythraceae are present in tropical America: *Ammannia* (4 species in the neotropics), *Lythrum* (1), *Nesaea* (3), and *Rotala* (2). Several species of *Lagerstroemia* (crape-myrtle), *Lawsonia inermis* (henna), and *Punica granatum* (pomegranate, Punicaceae *sensu* Cronquist) are Asian species commonly cultivated in warm regions of the Americas.

Distribution and habitat. The genera of the Lythraceae are evenly distributed between the Tropics and subtropics of the Eastern and Western Hemispheres. Fourteen genera are endemic to the Western Hemisphere, mostly to South America. *Decodon*, *Didiplis*, *Lythrum*, and *Peplis* are northern temperate genera. The remainder of the family are of African and Asian distribution.

In the Western Hemisphere, the family occurs from eastern

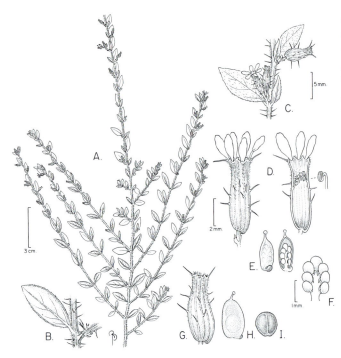

Figure 113. LYTHRACEAE. *Cuphea carthagenensis*. **A.** Stems with leaves, flowers, and fruits. **B.** Detail of stem with leaf and branch at node. **C.** Detail of stem with flower and fruits enclosed in calyces. **D.** Lateral view (left) and medial section of flower with enlargement of stamen (right). **E.** Lateral views of intact gynoecium with nectary disc at base (left) and medial section of gynoecium (right). **F.** Detail of ovules on placenta. **G.** Lateral view of fruit enclosed in calyx. **H.** Lateral view of fruit. **I.** Seed. Reprinted with permission from Mori et al. (2002). Artist: Bobbi Angell.

Canada to southern Argentina. The large genera *Cuphea* and *Diplusodon* have diversified extensively in the eastern Brazilian highlands. *Cuphea* has a secondary center of speciation in the mountains of western Mexico. The monotypic *Lourtella*, described from Peru in 1987, has recently been discovered in arid land to the west of Santa Cruz, Bolivia, a disjunction of nearly 2,000 kilometers. The cultivated *Lawsonia* and *Lagerstroemia* are occasionally naturalized in tropical America. *Nesaea* poses one of the family's most perplexing biogeographic questions because three endemic species occur in north-central Mexico and adjacent Texas, isolated from the remaining species of the genus in Africa, India, and Australia.

The Lythraceae occupy diverse habitats, including montane forests, low tropical rain forests, deserts, white-sand savannas, and fresh- and saltwater shores; some are amphibious or aquatic. Several herbaceous genera are associated with aquatic or marsh habitats; in tropical America these are *Ammannia*, *Lythrum*, and *Rotala*.

Family classification. The Lythraceae are placed in the Myrtales by Cronquist. Molecular and morphological information aligns the Lythraceae, its sister family the Onagraceae, and the Combretaceae (sister to the lythracean-onagra-

cean lineage) together in one of the two large clades of the order. Cladistic analyses support a broader, more natural interpretation of the family than has traditionally been accepted. Three monogeneric satellite families, Sonneratiaceae, Trapaceae, and Punicaceae, are now included in the Lythraceae as subfamilies Sonneratioideae, Duabangoideae, and Punicoideae, along with the Lythroideae (Lythraceae *sensu stricto*). The subfamily Lythroideae comprises two highly artificial tribes: Lythreae, with incomplete septa in the upper part of the ovary, and Nesaeeae, with complete septa. The division fails because all genera are now known to have incomplete septa. Relationships among genera cross current tribal assignments.

Major evolutionary lines in the family are uncertain, although a repeating pattern of Afro-Asian to American relationships is apparent. Cladistic analyses of *rbc*L and *trn*L-F sequences support the sister relationship of the endemic tropical American genera *Adenaria* and *Pehria* which, in turn, are sister to the Afro-Asian genera *Koehneria* and *Woodfordia*. *Lafoensia*, another South American endemic, consistently occurs within an African clade with *Capuronia*, *Galpinia*, and *Punica*. *Ginoria* and *Crenea* are related to the Mauritian *Tetrataxis*. The lack of resolution and absence of well-supported relationships in phylogenetic analyses is probably due in part to a rapid expansion of early lythraceous stock in Gondwana followed by extinction in many lines. Additional gene sequences are needed to clarify relationships that are currently intractable.

The genera are distinctive and well separated. The only exceptions are possible congenerics *Ammannia-Nesaea* and *Lythrum-Peplis*.

Features of the family. Habit: herbs, subshrubs, shrubs, or trees. Stems often four-angled or narrowly 4-winged when young. Stipules commonly absent from flanks of petioles, fleshy stipular processes present in leaf axils. Leaves usually opposite, rarely subalternate, generally decussate, simple, rarely dimorphic in amphibious species; blade margins entire, the subapex rarely with porate or nonporate nectar-secreting chambers (*Lafoensia* in tropical America); intramarginal vein present. Inflorescences axillary or terminal, thyrses, cymes, umbelliform clusters, or flowers solitary; epicalyx of small teeth often present, the teeth alternating with calyx lobes. Flowers actinomorphic or weakly to strongly zygomorphic, bisexual in American genera, perigynous; calyx lobes 4–6; floral tube persistent, surrounding ovary; petals 4–many, crinkled, with a central vein inserted immediately below rim of floral tube, rose, purple, white, or yellow, caducous; androecium of 4–many stamens, the stamens in 2 whorls, the filaments alternating in length, the anthers dorsifixed, versatile, introrse, basifixed in *Crenea* and *Pleurophora*; nectary often present, annular or unilateral (*Cuphea*); gynoecium syncarpous, the ovary superior (Lythroideae), semi- to fully inferior (other subfamilies), the locules 2–4, the style 1, the stigma wet or dry; placentation axile, the septa incomplete near apex, the ovules numerous, crassinucellate, bitegmic.

Fruits typically capsular, rarely berrylike. **Seeds** numerous, small, morphologically diverse; endosperm lacking. A few genera have tree species that reach 30 meters in height. These include *Ginoria*, *Lafoensia*, and *Physocalymma* in the neotropics.

Most genera are glabrous, or at most pubescent. Exceptions in tropical America are *Cuphea* with cystolitic, malpighiaceous, or glandular hairs; *Diplusodon*, which can have long simple hairs or stellatelike clusters of hairs; and a closely related group of genera with globose, multicellular glands that includes the Neotropical genera *Adenaria*, *Cuphea*, *Lourtella*, *Pehria*, and *Pleurophora*.

Wood anatomy has been extensively surveyed at the generic level in the Lythraceae. The family is characterized by vestured pits in the secondary xylem and internal phloem in the secondary tissues, a combination diagnostic of Myrtales. The generalized anatomical condition for the family is solitary or short radial multiple vessels, heterogeneous type I rays, septate fibers, and scanty paratracheal parenchyma. Specialized features of some genera include gelatinous and/or chambered crystalliferous fibers, spiral vessel wall thickenings, vascular tracheids, and in the perennial herbs, juvenilistic homogeneous rays. Wood anatomical features are widely shared among the genera and with other families of the order, restricting the contribution of wood anatomy to the understanding of natural relationships among the genera.

An unusual feature of the seed coat in 17 genera is the occurrence of inverted epidermal hairs. These evert from the epidermal cells when seeds become wet. The hairs are mucilaginous and possibly serve to osmotically draw water into the seed coat to soften it and facilitate germination. In the tropical American *Cuphea*, *Pleurophora*, and *Lafoensia*, the hairs are spirally formed.

The base number of the Sonneratioideae and Duabangoideae is 12; in Punicoideae and Lythroideae it is 8. The base of 8 may have been derived through aneuploid reduction from $x = 12$, which is the base number for the order Myrtales. Diverse, wide-ranging aneuploid and polyploid numbers appear in *Ammannia*, *Cuphea*, *Lythrum*, and *Rotala*. In *Cuphea*, where 127 species have been counted, 22 different chromosome numbers have been reported.

Natural history. Flowers of most species are odorless and are visited promiscuously for nectar or pollen by bees, butterflies, moths, hummingbirds, or bats (larger flowers). Bat pollination occurs in *Lafoensia* and the Old World *Sonneratia*. Although outcrossing predominates, self-compatibility is the rule in all genera tested. The Lythraceae are among about 25 families that have developed a distylous breeding system and one of only five families with tristylous species. *Adenaria* is incipiently tristylous. Although many *Lythrum* are di- or tristylous, the tropical American *L. maritimum* is monomorphic.

No information is available on dispersal biology.

Economic uses. *Lawsonia*, native to the Eastern Hemisphere, is the source of the cosmetic dye henna. The genus is also cultivated in warm regions throughout the world for its fragrant flowers. *Lagerstroemia indica*, crape myrtle or reseda, is an ornamental small tree or shrub popular in urban landscapes of the Tropics because of its showy, terminal inflorescences of rose to white flowers and its long flowering period. The Eurasian species *Lythrum salicaria* (purple loosestrife) has become an invasive weed in many temperate areas of North America.

In the Western Hemisphere, alkaloids in *Heimia* produce auditory hallucinogenic effects. The genus is also of pharmacological interest for its strong anti-inflammatory properties. Teas prepared from *Heimia*, from the eastern Asian *Woodfordia fruticosa*, and from some species of *Cuphea*, especially *C. carthagenensis*, are folk medicines taken for a wide variety of medical problems. Seeds of *Cuphea* contain significant amounts of short- to medium-chain fatty acids, such as caprylic, capric, and especially lauric acid, that are used in the food and chemical industries. Attempts to domesticate selected species as a source of speciality oils continue to be made in spite of the advances in genetic engineering that have led to lauric acid production in rapeseed (*Brassica*).

A genetically altered strain of *Cuphea* with elevated levels of short- and medium-chain triglycerides is under study as a source of nongumming diesel fuel. In South America, the extremely hard wood of *Lafoensia* is used in construction, and a yellow fabric dye is obtained from the wood and leaves.

References. BAAS, P. 1986. Wood anatomy of Lythraceae—additional genera (*Capuronia*, *Galpinia*, *Haitia*, *Orias*, and *Pleurophora*). *Ann. Missouri Bot. Gard.* 73:810–19. CAVALCANTI, T. B. 1995. Revisão de *Diplusodon* Pohl (Lythraceae). Ph.D. dissertation, *Univ. São Paulo*, São Paulo, Brazil. CONTI, E., A. LITT, P. G. WILSON, S. A. GRAHAM, B. G. BRIGGS, ET AL. Interfamilial relationships in Myrtales: Molecular phylogeny and patterns of morphological evolution. *Syst. Bot.* 22:629–47. GRAHAM, A., J. NOWICKE, J. SKVARLA, S. GRAHAM, V. PATEL, AND S. LEE. 1985–1990. Palynology and systematics of the Lythraceae. I–III. *Amer. J. Bot.* 72:1012–31; 74:829–50; 77:159–77. GRAHAM, S. 1989. *Cuphea*: a new plant source of medium-chain fatty acids. *CRC Crit. Rev. Food Sci. Nutri.* 28:139–73. GRAHAM, S. A., P. BAAS, AND H. TOBE. 1987. *Lourtella*, a new genus of Lythraceae from Peru. *Syst. Bot.* 12:519–33. GRAHAM, S. A., AND T. B. CAVALCANTI. 2000. New chromosome counts in the Lythraceae and a review of chromosome numbers in the family. *Syst. Bot.* 26: 445–58. KOEHNE, E. 1903. Lythraceae. In *Das Pflanzenreich*, A. Engler, Series 4, 216 (Heft 17):1–366. Leipzig: Wilhelm Engelmann. LOURTEIG, A. 1986a. Revisión del genero *Crenea* Aublet (Litraceas). *Caldasia* 15:121–42. LOURTEIG, A. 1986b. Revision del genero *Lafoensia* Vandelli (Litraceas). *Mem. Soc. Cienc. Nat. La Salle* 45:115–57.

MAGNOLIACEAE (Magnolia Family)

MARIA LÚCIA KAWASAKI

Figure 114, Plate 27

- *shrubs or trees*
- *stipules often large, deciduous, leaving conspicuous scars around stems*
- *leaves alternate, simple*
- *flowers usually showy, solitary, stamens and carpels numerous*
- *fruits follicles*

Numbers of genera and species. Worldwide, the Magnoliaceae comprise about ten (or 2 when considering *Magnolia sensu lato*) genera and about 220 species. The family is especially diverse in Southeast Asia. In tropical America, there are about 60 species. Depending on generic concepts, there are either three genera: *Magnolia* (ca. 15 species), *Talauma* (ca. 30 species), and *Dugandiodendron* (ca. 15 species); two genera: *Magnolia* and *Talauma* (including *Dugandiodendron*); or a single genus, *Magnolia* (including *Talauma* and *Dugandiodendron*).

Distribution and habitat. Most species of Magnoliaceae are found in temperate eastern and tropical southeastern Asia. In the Western Hemisphere, the species are distributed from temperate eastern North America to tropical and subtropical South America. The Neotropical species are found from Mexico to Brazil, and in the West Indies. Introduced species of *Liriodendron*, *Magnolia*, and *Michelia*, are often cultivated as ornamentals.

Most Neotropical Magnoliaceae are found in Colombia. The number of species decreases toward the south, with only four species of *Talauma* found in Brazil. *Magnolia* and *Talauma* include both Eastern and Western Hemisphere species; the controversially segregated genus *Dugandiodendron* is found mostly in Colombia.

Tropical American species occur mostly at middle elevations in northern Andean cloud forests, where they are often locally endemic. A few species are also found in lowland moist forests.

Family classification. The Magnoliaceae are placed in the Magnoliales by Cronquist, with families such as the Annonaceae and Myristicaceae. Recent molecular studies suggest that the Magnoliaceae and other families within the Magnoliales may not be among the most primitive families of flowering plants. Molecular and morphological analyses also indicate that the Magnoliaceae are monophyletic and make

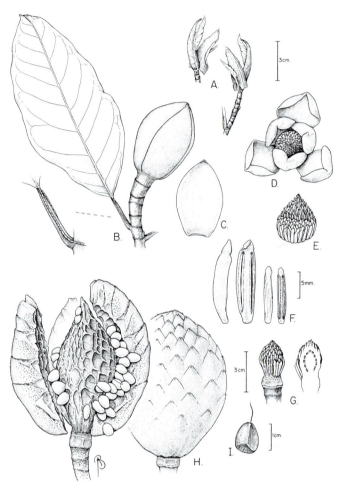

Figure 114. MAGNOLIACEAE. *Talauma boliviana.* **A.** Two views of young stems showing vegetative buds and stipules. **B.** Stem with leaf and flower bud; note stipule scars (right) and detail of petiole (left). **C.** Adaxial view of sepal. **D.** Apical view of flower. **E.** Androecium (outer whorls) and gynoecium (inner whorls). **F.** From left to right: lateral and adaxial views of larger stamens and lateral and adaxial views of smaller stamens. **G.** Lateral view of gynoecium after some stamens have fallen (left) and medial section of gynoecium (right). **H.** Lateral view of intact (right) and dehisced (left) fruits. **I.** Seed. Reprinted with permission from Nee (1994). Artist: Bobbi Angell.

up two groups, one represented by *Liriodendron* and another composed of a broadly defined *Magnolia*. Two subfamilies are traditionally recognized. The first is the Liriodendroideae (recognized by some authors as the Liriodendraceae) with two species of *Liriodendron* (the tulip tree, *L. tulipifera* from eastern North America and *L. chinense* from China). This subfamily is characterized by lobed leaves, samaroid fruits, and a testa adnate to the endocarp. The second is the Magnolioideae. This subfamily includes all other genera and is characterized by entire leaves, follicular fruits, and a thick and fleshy testa free from the endocarp. The Neotropical genera are distinguished mostly by their fruit characters.

Features of the family. Habit: shrubs or trees (often reaching 40 m), producing alkaloids, cell walls with high silica content, ethereal oil cells present in parenchyma. **Indument** (when present) composed of simple hairs. **Stipules** often large, covering apical bud, deciduous, leaving conspicuous scars around stems. **Leaves** alternate, simple, usually large; petioles long, often conspicuously grooved; blade margins entire (lobed in *Liriodendron*); venation finely reticulate. **Inflorescences** terminal, of solitary flowers; bracts present. **Flowers** actinomorphic, bisexual, usually showy; tepals usually 9–21, petal-like or sometimes differentiated into sepals and petals, distinct, often in sets of three, in several whorls, white; androecium of numerous stamens, the stamens distinct, spirally arranged, the filaments very short, the connective usually prolonged, forming an appendage, the anthers linear, dehiscing by longitudinal slits; gynoecium apocarpous, the ovaries superior, the carpels often numerous, spirally arranged, often nectariferous; placentation marginal, the ovules usually 2 per carpel. **Fruits** follicles (samaroid in *Liriodendron*), woody, dehiscing longitudinally (*Magnolia sensu stricto*) or partially fused and circumscissile (*Talauma* and *Dugandiodendron*). **Seeds** 1–2 per follicle, usually large, connected to slender funicules; endosperm abundant, oily, the embryo very small.

The family's vascular structure is characterized by multilacunar nodes and vessel segments with scalariform perforations.

Natural history. The flowers of the Magnoliaceae are commonly fruity scented and pollinated by beetles. The seeds are dispersed by birds and small mammals that feed on the fleshy, red/orange seed-coat.

Economic uses. Many species, are hybrids, and cultivars commonly grown as ornamentals around the world, notably species of *Magnolia*. The bark of the Chinese species *M. officinalis* is used medicinally to make a tonic.

Although the tulip tree (*Liriodendron tulipifera*) produces timber of economic importance, the wood of Neotropical species generally has only local uses in furniture making.

References. DOYLE, J. A., ET AL. 1994. Integration of morphological and ribosomal RNA data on the origin of angiosperms. *Ann. Missouri Bot. Gard.* 81:419–50. FRODIN, D., AND R. GOVAERTS. 1996. *World checklist and bibliography of Magnoliaceae.* Richmond Surrey, U.K.: Royal Botanic Gardens, Kew. LOCONTE, H., AND D. W. STEVENSON. 1991. Cladistics of the Magnoliidae. *Cladistics* 7:267–96. LOZANO-C., G. 1983. Magnoliaceae. In *Flora de Colombia*, ed. P. Pinto, 1–120. Bogotá: Universidad Nacional de Colombia. LOZANO-C., G. 1994. Dugandiodendron y Talauma *(Magnoliaceae) en el Neotrópico*. Bogotá: Instituto de Ciencias Naturales. NOOTEBOOM, H. P. 1985. Notes on Magnoliaceae with a revision of *Pachylarnax* and *Elmerrillia* and the Malesian species of *Manglietia* and *Michelia*. *Blumea* 31(1):65–121. NOOTEBOOM, H. P. 1993. Magnoliaceae. In *The Families and Genera of Vascular Plants*, eds. K. Kubitzki, J. G. Rohwer, and V. Bittrich, 2:391–401. Berlin: Springer-Verlag. QIU, Y. L., M. W. CHASE, D. H. LES, AND C. R. PARKS. 1993. Molecular phylogenetics of the Magnoliidae: cladistic analyses of nucleotide sequences of the plastid gene *rbc*L. *Ann. Missouri Bot. Gard.* 80:587–606. THIEN, L. B. 1974. Floral biology of *Magnolia. Amer. J. Bot.* 61:1037–45. VÁZQUEZ-G., J. A. 1994. Magnolia (Magnoliaceae) in Mexico and Central America: a synopsis. *Brittonia* 46(1):1–23.

MALESHERBIACEAE (Malesherbia Family)

KARLA GENGLER-NOWAK

Plate 27

- *xerophytic shrubs and subshrubs*
- *plants usually densely pubescent, the hairs multicellular glandular and simple*
- *stipules usually lobed*
- *leaves alternate, simple*
- *flowers with floral tube, corona, and androgynophore*
- *fruits loculicidal capsules*

Numbers of genera and species. The Malesherbiaceae comprise a single genus, *Malesherbia*, with 24 species and five varieties. In tropical America, there are 13 species of *Malesherbia*. The family is restricted to South America.

Distribution and habitat. The Malesherbiaceae are dry habitat plants endemic to the Pacific coastal desert and adjacent arid Andes of Chile, Peru, and Argentina. Their distribution includes all of the arid regions of Chile, with the notable exception of the hyperarid Atacama Desert. North of the Atacama Desert, the family extends to the inter-Andean valleys east of Lima, Peru and to the central Peruvian Andes. Species of *Malesherbia* are found from the coast to 3,750 meters in the Andes.

The Malesherbiaceae grow in mediterranean, desert, and

dry montane habitats of varying degrees of aridity. Most prefer rocky, sunny locations inhabited by few other plants. Road cuts and gullies are favorite habitats.

Family classification. The Malesherbiaceae are placed in the Violales by Cronquist. Recent molecular studies suggest that the family should be placed in an expanded Malpighiales. The family is closely related to Turneraceae and Passifloraceae. Because the species north of the Atacama Desert are morphologically quite different from those south of the desert in Chile and Argentina, two genera, the more southern *Gynopleura* and the more northern *Malesherbia*, were once recognized. However, molecular analysis supports the recognition of only *Malesherbia*. The Peruvian species form a monophyletic group that evolved from the more primitive Chilean/Argentine species south of the Atacama Desert.

Features of the family. Habit: xerophytic shrubs and sub-shrubs (from 2 m in some Peruvian species to 3.5 cm *M. humilis*, a Chilean species), semidecumbent in several species. Indument: dense (all but one species), usually with both multicellular glandular and simple hairs. Stipules usually present, often 1–5-lobed. Leaves alternate, simple, sessile, some species with long, narrow leaf bases resembling petioles, the lower leaves often withering during flowering; blades lanceolate, ovate, obovate, spatulate, or pinnatisect, the margins entire, serrate, or lobed, sometimes revolute, ciliate with glandular hairs in most species. Inflorescences terminal, indeterminate, usually racemes or panicles. Flowers actinomorphic, bisexual, blue, purple, white, yellow, red, pink-orange, or light green, dense hairs sometimes causing white or yellow cast; floral tube present, tubular or funnelform, 10-nerved, densely pubescent abaxially, usually sparsely pubescent adaxially; sepals and petals emerging from apex of floral tube; sepals 5, often perpendicular to floral tube at anthesis, the margins lined with glandular hairs in many species; petals 5, often perpendicular to floral tube at anthesis, the apex with 1–5 glandular hairs in some species; corona present, inserted inside floral tube just below sepals and petals, reduced to ridge in some Chilean species or larger and more colorful than perianth and floral tube in some Peruvian species; androgynophore prominent, elevating ovary above nectaries at base of floral tube, formed by fusion of lower parts of five filaments around gynophore, or by ovary stalk; androecium of 5 stamens, the anthers longitudinally dehiscent; gynoecium syncarpous, the ovary superior, the carpels 3, the locule 1, the styles 3, distinct, emerging near apex of ovary, generally extending stigmas beyond anthers; placentation parietal, the ovules numerous. Fruits loculicidal capsules, the dried perianth persistent, the capsule elongating upon maturity, the 3 valves split, bending back to release seeds, the valves rupturing corona in those species in which corona restricts floral opening. Seeds 1–many, elliptical, 1.2–3.1 mm long, the seed coat dark brown to black, sculpted with many ± regular rows of rectangular pits.

In most Neotropical species, the juncture of the androgynophore and the base of the ovary is marked by a ring of thickened tissue. The filaments separate at the base of the ovary and usually are long enough to project the anthers beyond the floral tube. In most Chilean/Argentine species, the stiff filaments widely separate the anthers, whereas in the Peruvian species, the stamens are often closely crowded and somewhat pendent. In the Peruvian species, the corona generally presses inward on the filaments and styles.

Natural history. The larger Peruvian shrubs with their brightly colored, candelabra-like inflorescences are impressive sights growing out of cracks in the vertical cliffs of road cuts or canyons. The pollinators of Malesherbiaceae are mostly unknown, although large bees have been seen visiting Chilean species. One species, *Malesherbia humilis*, is the exclusive pollen source for an endemic long-tongued bee, which presumably also pollinates the plant. Most Neotropical species have very long, showy flowers that may be hummingbird-pollinated. Although self-pollination has not yet been shown, the withering perianth and corona do press the stamens and styles of unfertilized flowers together, making stigma-pollen contact possible. Three species, *Malesherbia fasciculata*, *M. linearifolia*, and *M. paniculata*, are geitonogamous.

The mature fruit is dislodged easily from the pedicel by wind or passing animals and the seeds are likely dispersed when the capsules are rolled along the ground by wind and water.

Heliconiid larvae, which are noted for their herbivory of Passifloraceae, are known to feed on the ovules of Peruvian Malesherbiaceae.

Economic uses. In Peru, *Malesherbia scarlatiflora* (veronica) is a popular cure-all herb sold in Lima. A tea made from *M. ardens* (lampaya) has been used to treat influenza and *M. tubulosa* is sometimes used to treat bruises. Malesherbiaceae, like Turneraceae and Passifloraceae, possess poisonous cyanogenic glycosides. Several montane Chilean/Argentine species reportedly are fatal to goats.

References. FAY, M. F., S. M. SWENSEN, AND M. W. CHASE. 1997. Taxonomic affinities of *Medusagyne oppositifolia* (Medusagynaceae). *Kew Bull.* 52:111–20. GENGLER, K. M. 2000. Evolution and biogeography of the Malesherbiaceae, an endemic family of western South America. Dissertation, Columbus, OH: Ohio State University. RICARDI, M. 1967. Revisión taxonómica de las Malesherbiaceas. *Gayana, Bot.* no. 16:3–139. ROZEN, J. G., JR., AND L. RUZ. 1995. South American panurgine bees (Andrenidae: Panurginae), Part II. Adults, immature stages, and biology of *Neffapis longilingua*, a new genus and species with an elongate glossa. *Amer. Mus. Novit.* 3136:1–15. SPENCER, K. C., AND D. S. SEIGLER. 1985. Cyanogenic glycosides of *Malesherbia*. *Biochem. Syst. & Ecol.* 13:23–24.

MALPIGHIACEAE (Malpighia Family)

Wᴵʟʟᴵᴀᴍ R. Aɴᴅᴇʀsᴏɴ

Figures 115, 116; Plate 28

- *trees, shrubs, vines, and a few perennial herbs*

- *indument of unicellular hairs, usually 2-branched*

- *leaves usually opposite, simple, many with large multicellular glands on petiole, abaxial surface, or margins*

- *flowers mostly bilaterally symmetrical; 4 or all 5 sepals usually bearing 2 large abaxial glands; petals 5, mostly clawed; stamens mostly 10; ovary superior, mostly tricarpellate with the styles distinct; ovules 1 per locule*

- *fruits mostly schizocarpic and winged in vines, mostly unwinged and dry or fleshy in shrubs and trees*

Numbers of genera and species. Currently approximately 65 genera and 1,260 species of Malpighiaceae are recognized worldwide. Fifty genera and approximately 1,110 species occur only in the Western Hemisphere, except for two species found also in western Africa (*Heteropterys leona* and *Stigmaphyllon bannisterioides*). The largest genera, all of them mostly or entirely Neotropical, are *Banisteriopsis* (94 species), *Bunchosia* (68), *Byrsonima* (127), *Heteropterys* (136), *Stigmaphyllon* (92), and *Tetrapterys* (70). Sixteen genera have only one species.

Distribution and habitat. The Malpighiaceae have little tolerance for extreme cold and, therefore, show a typically tropical distribution. In the Western Hemisphere, a few species reach southern Florida, Texas, New Mexico, and Arizona, and in the south the family is moderately well represented to 35°S, the latitude of Buenos Aires; only a few species occur farther south, to about 39°S. A similar pattern exists in the paleotropics, but it is much less dramatic there because there are only about 150 species in the Eastern Hemisphere.

The great center of diversity of Malpighiaceae is South America north of the tropic of Capricorn. Except for Chile, which has only two species, all the countries in tropical South America have substantial numbers of species, Brazil having far more than any other. In the *cerrados* of Minas Gerais, Brazil, for example, there is an astonishing diversity of Malpighiaceae. Some species have extensive distributions (e.g., *Banisteriopsis muricata*, from Mexico to Argentina); but many more species are restricted to much smaller regions, and narrow local endemism is fairly common. Patterns of species richness differ from genus to genus; for example,

Figure 115. MALPIGHIACEAE. *Byrsonima aerugo.* **A.** Stem with leaves and inflorescences. **B.** Node showing petiole bases and connate intrapetiolar stipules. **C.** Lateral view of flower bud with sessile pedicel subtended by two short bracteoles and one long, reflexed bract; note oil glands on calyx. **D.** Lateral (left) and apical (right) views of flowers. **E.** Adaxial (left) and lateral (right) views of stamens. **F.** Lateral view of gynoecium. **G.** Part of infructescence with one fruit removed (center) and transverse section of fruit (left), showing three seeds in a common stony endocarp surrounded by fleshy mesocarp; detail of sericeous apex of fruit (above right). Reprinted with permission from Mori et al. (2002). Artist: Bobbi Angell.

Byrsonima has many species in southern Venezuela and the Guianas and rather few in Ecuador, while the reverse is true for *Stigmaphyllon*. The family is well represented in the tropical West Indies, but not in the extratropical Bahamas.

The Malpighiaceae have adapted to diverse habitats in the neotropics, including wet, mesic, and seasonally dry forests, shrubby savannas, and grasslands. Few grow high in the Andes because few can tolerate the temperatures at higher elevations, and few have succeeded in extreme deserts. Although they are not rare in wet forests like those of Amazonia, Malpighiaceae are more numerous in well-drained savannas like those of the Brazilian Planalto, and in the shrubby associations found in upland habitats of the Venezuelan Guayana.

Family classification. Cronquist followed earlier workers and put the Malpighiaceae in his order Polygalales, on the basis of morphological similarities. That placement is not supported by molecular data, and recent authors have recognized the morphologically diverse order Malpighiales, comprising Malpighiaceae, Euphorbiaceae, Passifloraceae, Violaceae, and other families. Both morphological and molecular data agree that the family is monophyletic, but so isolated that one still cannot say which families are closest to it.

The infrafamilial classification of the Malpighiaceae is in a state of flux. Earlier authors divided the family on the basis of fruits: two subfamilies with the fruits unwinged versus winged or bristly, with each subfamily then divided into tribes defined principally by details of the fruits. Some of these groupings have been supported by later studies that incorporated other aspects of the morphology and molecular data, but in many cases the family is proving to be much more complicated. William R. Anderson asserted many years ago that the three genera with similar fleshy fruits (*Bunchosia*, *Byrsonima*, and *Malpighia*) were quite unrelated to each other, and chloroplast DNA supports that conclusion. Bristly fruits like those found in *Echinopterys*, *Henleophytum*, *Lasiocarpus*, *Ptilochaeta*, and *Tricomaria*, rather than marking a natural and convenient tribe, clearly evolved independently at least three times in the family. While it does seem likely that the relative development of the lateral and dorsal wings on the samaras will continue to be useful in grouping many genera of wing-fruited vines, those "rules" have been violated a number of times. For example, *Heteropterys*, with a large dorsal wing, belongs in a clade of lateral-winged genera (a molecular result supported by the nonfruit morphology); on the other hand, *Diplopterys* and *Cordobia*, both with the lateral wing dominant, are sisters to genera with a dominant dorsal wing, and this result is supported by nonfruit morphology. A number of genera that are morphologically isolated are still not satisfactorily placed by molecules or morphology, and the large wing-fruited clade that comprises the vast majority of the family's genera and species is still poorly resolved. Nevertheless, certain things can now be stated with some confidence: 1) The Malpighiaceae probably originated in the Western Hemisphere and the Malpighiaceae of the Eastern Hemisphere are probably derived from at least eight independent dispersal events. 2) The original Malpighiaceae were very likely shrubs or trees, with the habit of woody vines evolving between one and four times. 3) The earliest Malpighiaceae probably produced fruits that lacked flesh, wings, or bristles; dispersal by water may have been ancestral. 4) The base chromosome number in the family was probably $x = 6$; however, all but the lowest branches of the family tree seem to have numbers based on $x = 10$, and that shift (perhaps by aneuploidy from an ancestor with $n = 12$) probably occurred at about the time of the origin of winged fruits. 5) The pollen was originally radially symmetrical, probably tricolporate, and the shift to globally symmetrical pollen happened once, at the base of the clade containing most of the wing-fruited genera. 6) Winged fruits may have evolved several times or once; but if only once, the wings were ± completely lost in several descendant clades. 7) There is a strong correlation between the vining habit and winged fruits versus the shrubby or arborescent habit and unwinged fruits, but the phylogenetic path to that correlation is probably not simple, suggesting repeated evolutionary convergence on an adaptive association of habit and method of dispersal.

As morphological data are combined with more and better molecular data, the resolution of the phylogeny of the Malpighiaceae should improve enough to allow the proposal of a new infrafamilial classification that will be both useful and phylogenetically accurate.

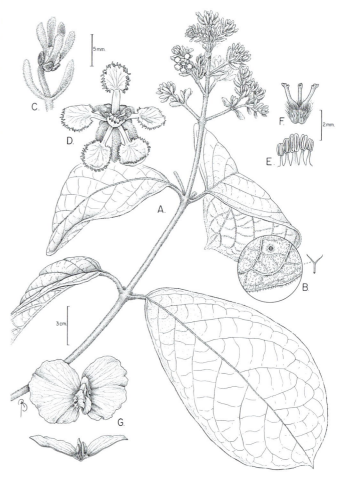

Figure 116. MALPIGHIACEAE. *Jubelina rosea.* **A.** Stem with leaves and inflorescence. **B.** Detail of abaxial leaf surface showing gland and stalked, bifurcate hair. **C.** Oblique-apical view of flower bud showing spatulate bracteoles and sepals, each lateral sepal bearing one large abaxial gland. **D.** Oblique-apical view of flower, the posterior petal uppermost. **E.** Adaxial view of part of the androecium; the central stamen would be opposite one of the posterior-lateral petals. **F.** Lateral view of gynoecium with anterior style in center. **G.** Abaxial view (above) and medial section of fruit (below). Reprinted with permission from Mori et al. (2002). Artist: Bobbi Angell.

Features of the family. Habit: Trees, shrubs, erect or trailing subshrubs or herbs with perennial underground stems, and woody to herbaceous, perennial vines that climb by twining stems. **Latex** rarely present (*Galphimia, Lophanthera, Spachea,* and *Verrucularia*). **Indument:** hairs always unicellular, usually 2-branched and medifixed or submedifixed, basifixed or stellate in a few genera. **Stipules** usually present beside or on the petiole or axillary to it, distinct or variously connate, minute to more than 14 cm long, absent in some genera or species. **Leaves** usually opposite and decussate, sometimes whorled, subopposite or alternate in a few genera or species, often bearing large multicellular glands on the petiole or blade (usually the abaxial surface or margin) or both; blade simple, mostly entire, rarely lobed, the margins never truly toothed but sometimes pseudodentate or ciliate at the location of marginal glands or stout bristlelike hairs. **Inflorescences** terminal or axillary, very diverse, most often racemose or paniculate but with the flowers often ultimately borne in umbels or corymbs of 4 or more. **Flowers** subtly to strongly bilaterally symmetrical in most Neotropical species with the plane of symmetry passing through the anterior (often eglandular) sepal and the posterior (often erect and differentiated) "flag" petal, a few radially symmetrical or nearly so, mostly bisexual, a few genera dioecious or functionally dioecious, hypogynous except perigynous in *Barnebya*, small (about 6 mm in diameter) to fairly large (about 4 cm diam.); sepals 5, mostly imbricate in bud, the great majority of Neotropical species bearing 2 (rarely only 1) large, multicellular, abaxial glands on all 5 sepals or on lateral 4 (most Paleotropical species with calyx glands much reduced in number and size or absent); petals 5, distinct, mostly clawed, alternating with sepals, imbricate, the posterior innermost and 1 of anterior-lateral pair outermost, most often yellow, pink, or white, sometimes other colors but very rarely blue; androecium usually of 10 stamens in a single whorl, the stamens sometimes fewer, up to 15 in *Lasiocarpus*, borne on receptacle between perianth and gynoecium, the filaments always present, short to long, alike or heteromorphic, distinct or partially connate, the anthers alike or heteromorphic, 4-locular, mostly longitudinally dehiscent along inner edge of each locule, with apical or subapical pores or very short slits in a few genera; gynoecium superior, usually comprising 3 distinct to connate carpels, mostly 1 anterior on plane of symmetry and 2 posterior on each side of plane of symmetry, the carpels only 2 in several genera and very rarely 4, mostly all fertile, each fertile locule containing 1 pendent anatropous ovule, the styles mostly as many as carpels and distinct, but connate or reduced in number in a few genera. **Fruits** fleshy or dry; fleshy fruits mostly an indehiscent drupe or berry, yellow, red, blue, or black; dry fruits indehiscent in a few genera, but schizocarpic in most, splitting apart into mericarps (typically up to 3); dry fruits or mericarps of some genera nutlets with smooth walls, those of some genera or species containing aerenchyma, but most bearing wings or bristles. **Seeds** 1 per locule or mericarp, never released (i.e., dehiscence never loculicidal, or at least not sufficiently so to allow the seed to escape); endosperm absent.

The family is easier to recognize in flower than in fruit because the flowers are so uniform, but once one has placed a plant in the Malpighiaceae, it is much easier to identify it to genus with fruits than with flowers because the genera are defined primarily by characters of the fruits.

Natural history. As noted above, most Neotropical Malpighiaceae are recognized easily by the large paired glands on the abaxial surface of the sepals and by the clawed petals. Stefan Vogel has shown that these structures are adaptations for pollination by oil-collecting bees, which land on the flower, reach between the petals (hence the importance of the space left by the claws), and collect the oil produced by the glands. They mix this oil with pollen and pack it into brood cells with one egg each, and the mixture eventually is consumed by the growing larvae. The flower produces no sugary nectar so, except for the oil, pollen is the only reward for pollinators. Malpighiaceae that have lost the calyx glands must rely on pollen to attract pollinators, and in some such groups (e.g., *Galphimia*) the anthers are enlarged. Almost nothing has been published on the pollination of these eglandular species. William R. Anderson has postulated that the Malpighiaceae now in the Eastern Hemisphere descended from several species that emigrated from South America to Africa after the separation of the continents. The oil-bees that pollinate Neotropical Malpighiaceae did not reach the Eastern Hemisphere, so it is not surprising that the calyx glands of Eastern Hemisphere species are mostly reduced or absent.

The majority of Malpighiaceae in the Western Hemisphere have winged or bristly fruits adapted for dispersal by wind. Three Neotropical genera (*Bunchosia, Byrsonima,* and *Malpighia*) produce edible, fleshy fruits that presumably are bird-dispersed. Several genera, mostly trees that grow along Amazonian rivers, have smooth aerenchymatous fruits that surely are dispersed by water, and scattered species in genera with winged fruits have more or less completely lost their wings and become adapted secondarily for water dispersal. Finally, a number of genera, most relatively near the base of the phylogenetic tree, produce small, smooth, dry fruits without any obvious adaptation for dispersal. These fruits, generally 1 to several millimeters in diameter, presumably are dispersed by wind or rainwater. It is difficult to understand how some of those groups (e.g., *Pterandra*) have achieved their extensive present-day distributions.

Economic uses. The Malpighiaceae are of modest economic importance. One of the species with fleshy fruits, *Malpighia emarginata* (often erroneously called *M. punicifolia*), has long been cultivated for the red cherrylike fruits, which are rich in vitamin C. It bears many common names, of which the ones most frequently encountered are *acerola* and Barbados cherry. In recent years, manufacturers of vitamins have taken to adding vitamin C from *M. emarginata* to their concoctions in order to make them more "natural" (and correspondingly more expensive), and commercial plantations for the cultivation of the species exist in Mexico and probably elsewhere. The fruits of *Byrsonima crassifolia*, which look like yellow cherries, are consumed commonly in Mexico, Central America, and northern South America. In Spanish-speaking areas, the common name is usually *nance* or *nanche*, whereas in Brazil it is *muricí* or *murucí*. *Bunchosia glandulifera* has a pleasant-tasting fruit the size of a small plum and surely has been cultivated by indigenous peoples in South America for a very long time; it is not known from unequivocally wild populations. Fruits of various other species of *Bunchosia*, *Byrsonima*, and *Malpighia* are consumed from Mexico to Brazil, and the plants (all shrubs or small trees) often are grown in dooryards, both as ornamentals and for the fruits.

A number of other Malpighiaceae are planted as ornamentals, and some are available in warm regions from nurseries. The commonest of these is *Galphimia gracilis* (often misidentified as *G. glauca*), a shrub with bright yellow flowers that give it common names like *lluvia de oro*, *ramito de oro*, and *spray of gold*. Other Neotropical species popular in warm gardens and greenhouses are *Malpighia coccigera* (Singapore holly), *Stigmaphyllon ciliatum* (Brazilian gold vine), and *S. floribundum* (orchid vine). *Lophanthera lactescens*, a handsome tree with long inflorescences of yellow flowers, is known in the wild from only one small area in eastern Amazonia, but it thrives when planted along busy, polluted streets and is now popular in towns and cities throughout Brazil. Two species native to the Eastern Hemisphere are cultivated occasionally in the neotropics, *Hiptage benghalensis* and *Tristellateia australasiae* (*bagnit*). Many other members of the family are very showy and, hence, are also candidates for cultivation.

At least one member of the family, *Banisteriopsis caapi*, is a potent hallucinogen and has become famous among those interested in drug plants under its scientific name and such vernacular names as *ayahuasca*, *caapi*, and *yagé*. It is cultivated widely in Amazonian South America, where it is used by native populations as one ingredient in the preparation of a beverage that is said to produce spectacular multicolored visions after some hours of preliminary vomiting.

References. ANDERSON, C. 1997. Monograph of *Stigmaphyllon* (Malpighiaceae). *Syst. Bot. Monogr.* 51:1–313. ANDERSON, C. 1997. Revision of Pterandra (Malpighiaceae). *Contr. Univ. Michigan Herb.* 21:1–27. ANDERSON, W. R. 1978 ["1977"]. Byrsonimoideae, a new subfamily of the Malpighiaceae. *Leandra* 7:5–18. ANDERSON, W. R. 1979. Floral conservatism in neotropical Malpighiaceae. *Biotropica* 11:219–23. ANDERSON, W. R. 1981. Malpighiaceae. In The botany of the Guayana Highland—Part XI. *Mem. New York Bot. Gard.* 32:21–305. ANDERSON, W. R. 1990. The origin of the Malpighiaceae—The evidence from morphology. *Mem. New York Bot. Gard.* 64:210–24. ANDERSON, W. R. 1993. Chromosome numbers of neotropical Malpighiaceae. *Contr. Univ. Michigan Herb.* 19:341–54. ANDERSON, W. R. 2001. Malpighiaceae. In *Flora of the Venezuelan Guayana*, eds. P. E. Berry, K. Yatskievych, and B. K. Holst, 6:82–185. Missouri Botanical Garden Press, St. Louis. BERNAL, H. Y., AND J. E. CORRERA Q. 1994. Malpighiaceae. In *Especies vegetales promisorias de los países del Convenio Andrés Bello*, Tomo X. Santafé de Bogotá, D. E., Colombia: Secretaria Ejecutiva del Convenio Andrés Bello. CAMERON, K. M., M. W. CHASE, W. R. ANDERSON, AND H. G. HILLS. 2001. Molecular systematics of Malpighiaceae: Evidence from plastid *rbcL* and *matK* sequences. *Amer. J. Bot.* 88:1847–62. CHASE, M. W., ET AL. 1993. Phylogenetics of seed plants: an analysis of nucleotide sequences from the plastid gene *rbcl*. *Ann. Missouri Bot. Gard.* 80:528–80. DAVIS, C. C., W. R. ANDERSON, AND M. J. DONOGHUE. 2001. Phylogeny of Malpighiaceae: Evidence from chloroplast *ndhF* and *trnL-F* nucleotide sequences. *Amer. J. Bot.* 88:1830–1846. GATES, B. 1982. *Banisteriopsis, Diplopterys* (Malpighiaceae). *Fl. Neotrop. Monogr.* 30:1–237. JUDD, W. S., C. S. CAMPBELL, E. A. KELLOGG, AND P. F. STEVENS. 1999. Plant Systematics: A Phylogenetic Approach. [i]–xvi, 1–464. Sutherland, MA: Sinauer Associates, Inc. NIEDENZU, F. 1928. Malpighiaceae. In *Das Pflanzenreich*, Series IV, 141(Hefte 91, 93, 94):1–870. Leipzig: Wilhelm Engelmann. VEGA, A. S., M. A. CASTRO, AND W. R. ANDERSON. 2002. Occurrence and phylogenetic significance of latex in the Malpighiaceae. *Amer. J. Bot.* 89(11):1725–29. VOGEL, S. 1974. Ölblumen und ölsammelnde Bienen. *Tropische und subtropische Pflanzenwelt* 7:[1]–267. Mainz: Akademie der Wissenschaften und der Literatur.

MALVACEAE (Mallow Family)

PAUL A. FRYXELL

Figure 117, Plate 28

- *usually shrubs or subshrubs, less frequently herbs, rarely trees*

- *leaves alternate, usually simple, often with stellate hairs*

- *flowers often subtended by epicalyx; stamens monadelphous; pollen spiny*

- *fruits capsules or schizocarps*

Numbers of genera and species. Worldwide, the Malvaceae comprise about 110 genera and about 1,800 species. Seventy-eight genera occur in the Western Hemisphere (roughly 70% of the family) including an estimated 1,375 species. The largest genera are *Pavonia* (ca. 250 species), *Hibiscus* (ca. 180 species), *Abutilon* (ca. 160 species), *Sida* (ca. 100 species), *Nototriche* (100+ species), and *Cristaria* (ca. 75 species). In tropical America, there are 61 genera and about 1,000 species. Nine Neotropical genera have only one species each, and a few others have only two.

Distribution and habitat. The Malvaceae have a wide distribution in the Americas, Africa, Europe, Asia, Australia, and Oceania. Species in the Western Hemisphere range from central Argentina to the United States, and a few species occur slightly north of the Canadian border. The southernmost species is *Neobaclea crispifolia*, from central Argentina, and the northernmost species is probably *Sphaeralcea coccinea* from the southern prairie provinces of Canada.

Most of the Malvaceae are found in drier habitats, ranging from severe deserts to more mesic environments. Wet habitats, such as the Amazon Basin, are relatively species-poor in Malvaceae, supporting primarily river-bank plants like *Hibiscus peruvianus* and *H. sororius*, and a few cosmopolitan weeds. *Malvella* occurs in saline microhabitats such as desert mudflats and irrigation-ditch banks. A few species of *Hibiscus*, *Malachra*, and *Pavonia* are found in swampy habitats on lake shores and river banks, usually in stagnant water. *Talipariti tiliaceum* variety *pernambucense* and a few species of *Pavonia* (e.g., *P. paludicola* and *P. kearneyi*) are confined to brackish-water mangrove habitats. Two genera, *Acaulimalva* and *Nototriche*, occur above treeline in the Andean *páramos* and *punas*. Three genera are characteristically acaulescent, forming perennial "cushion plants" in the high elevation South American *páramo* and *puna* habitats (*Acaulimalva* and *Nototriche*) and the lower-elevation North American desert habitats of northern Mexico and western Texas (*Fryxellia*).

Family classification. The Malvaceae are placed in the Malvales by Cronquist. Recent analyses suggest that the Malvaceae should be defined more broadly to include taxa from the Bombacaceae, Sterculiaceae, and Tiliaceae, families that are not considered monphyletic as defined by Cronquist (see discussion of Malvales).

Five tribes are recognized. The Decaschistieae, including only *Decaschistia* (18–20 species), are found primarily in southern Asia and northern Australia. The remaining four tribes all have Neotropical representatives. The Gossypieae comprise eight genera and about 100 species, including four relatively large Neotropical genera (*Gossypium*, *Thespesia*, *Cienfuegosia*, and *Hampea*) and four small, non-Neotropical genera (*Kokia*, *Cephalohibiscus*, *Lebronnecia*, and *Gossypioides*). The Hibisceae include the large and polymorphic genus *Hibiscus* and other genera such as *Abelmoschus*, *Alyo-*

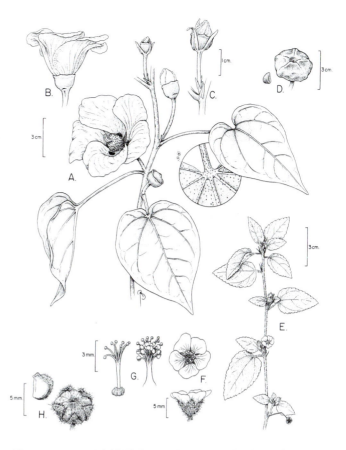

Figure 117. MALVACEAE. *Thespesia populnea* (A–D) and *Sidastrum multiflorum* (E–H). **A.** Stem with leaves and inflorescences, insert shows detail of abaxial base of leaf with indument. **B.** Lateral view of flower. **C.** Lateral view of flower bud showing epicalyx and subtending bracteoles. **D.** Oblique-apical view of fruit (right) and seed (left). **E.** Stem with leaves and inflorescences. **F.** Lateral (below) and apical (above) views of flowers. **G.** Lateral view of gynoecium (left) and androecium (right). **H.** Oblique-apical view of fruit (schizocarp; right) and fruit segment (mericarp; left). Reprinted with permission from Acevedo-Rodríguez (1996). Artist: Bobbi Angell.

gyne, *Fioria*, *Kosteletzkya*, *Talipariti*, and *Wercklea*, as well as a number of distinctive genera from Madagascar. The taxonomy of *Hibiscus* is as yet unresolved, and the number of genera in the tribe Hibisceae cannot be stated with assurance. The Malvavisceae comprise eight Neotropical genera as well as some species native to the Eastern Hemisphere. The largest and most diverse genus in the Malvavisceae is *Pavonia*, with 224 species in the Western Hemisphere (and perhaps 250 species worldwide). Other genera in the Malvavisceae are *Peltaea* (16 species), *Malachra* (8–10 species), *Urena* (6–8 species), *Malvaviscus* (5–10 species), and the monotypic *Phragmocarpidium* (Brazil), *Rojasimalva* (Venezuela), and *Anotea* (Mexico). The Malveae are the largest and most diverse tribe, including about 60 genera and more than 800 species, such as the large genera *Abutilon*, *Sida*, *Nototriche*, and *Cristaria*. This tribe is predominantly Neotropical but is also represented in Africa, Europe, Asia, and Australia.

The Matisieae clade, composed of *Matisia*, *Phragmotheca*, and *Quararibea*, are here treated within the Bombacaceae; however, these genera appear to be allied more closely with the traditional Malvaceae.

Features of the family. Habit: shrubs or subshrubs, rarely trees (e.g., *Robinsonella* and *Bastardiopsis*), sometimes herbs, perennial or less often annual, sometimes prostrate. **Stipules** usually present. **Leaves** alternate, simple or rarely palmately compound, often with stellate hairs or sometimes with simple, glandular, or lepidote hairs, prickles sometimes present; blades often ovate, variously lobed or parted, the margins entire or crenate to dentate; venation usually palmate or sometimes pinnate; abaxial nectaries sometimes present on principal veins (in Gossypieae, some Hibisceae, and *Urena*). **Inflorescences** axillary or terminal, panicles, racemes, or flowers often solitary, less often in spikes, umbels, or heads; epicalyx (or involucel) often present, the bractlets of epicalyx 3–many, distinct or fused, often narrowly linear to lanceolate, sometimes bifurcate or foliaceous, usually whorled directly below calyx or rarely inserted on calyx or on pedicel below calyx in a spiral pattern. **Flowers** actinomorphic or rarely somewhat zygomorphic, usually bisexual, rarely unisexual (then plants dioecious or gynodioecious); calyx ± synsepalous, sepals usually 5, imbricate; petals 5, distinct, fused at base to staminal column, caducous with staminal column following anthesis; stamens numerous, monadelphous (the vasculature of the staminal column commonly pentamerous), the filaments inserted along length of column, sometimes in several whorls at discrete levels along column or at apex (Malveae), the apex often with a crown of 5 sterile teeth (except Malveae), the teeth usually triangular; pollen spiny, often large; gynoecium syncarpous, the ovary superior, the carpels, locules, styles, and stigmas 3–many; placentation axile. **Fruits** capsules (Hibisceae, Gossypieae) or schizocarps (Malveae, Malvavisceae), sometimes fleshy (*Anotea*, *Malvaviscus*). **Seeds** solitary or numerous, pubescent (e.g., *Gossypium*), glabrous, or scaly, sometimes arillate (*Hampea*).

The flowers vary widely in size, ranging from large and showy (e.g., *Hibiscus*, *Wercklea*) to small and inconspicuous (e.g., *Sidastrum*, *Kearnemalvastrum*).

The presence of an involucel is characteristic of nearly all members (rarely suppressed in individual species) of the tribes Gossypieae, Hibisceae, and Malvavisceae, but of only about half of the genera of the Malveae.

The gynoecium and fruits of the Malvaceae are useful for the classification of tribes and genera. In the tribe Malvavisceae, the flower has 10 styles and stigmas and the fruit only 5 carpels. Developmental studies have shown that this pattern results from an initially 10-carpelled ovary, alternate carpels of which do not develop. The styles and stigmas, however, persist through flower development. In the other tribes, the number of styles and stigmas in the flower and the number of carpels in the fruit are the same, from as few as 3 to more than 40.

Natural history. The spiny pollen of the Malvaceae is typically large and heavy (sometimes sticky), and is thus not adapted to wind pollination. Pollinators include bees, moths, hummingbirds, and less often bats. Adaptations for attracting pollinators include prominently exserted anthers and stigmas (e.g., *Malvaviscus*, *Periptera*, *Anotea*, some species of *Hibiscus*, *Pavonia*), coupled with corolla colors appropriate to specific pollinators, including dark spots (nectar guides) at the base of the petals. In some species, the flowers are sometimes cleistogamous.

The succulent arils of *Hampea* aid in bird dispersal. Although the mechanisms are not always clear, seed pubescence probably has implications for seed dispersal by wind, especially in the capsular-fruited Gossypieae and Hibisceae. In the schizocarpic-fruited Malvavisceae and Malveae, dispersal is more clearly related to characteristics of the mericarps than of the seeds contained in them. Some of these features are obvious, such as barbed spines that facilitate animal dispersal in *Pavonia* section *Typhalea* and in the Neotropical species of *Urena*, or wings that aid in wind dispersal in *Horsfordia* or *Lecanophora*. Often these dispersal adaptations are coupled with seed dormancy that is broken down by weathering or bacterial action (sometimes over a period of many years) or passage through the digestive tract of a bird or mammal, and the inherent delays permit dispersal to be amplified both in time and in space. In *Abutilon theophrasti* such seed-coat dormancy enables seeds to lie in the soil and germinate sporadically for as long as 20 years, a characteristic that renders this species one of the most pernicious weeds in North America.

Economic uses. The overriding economic importance of the family Malvaceae derives from the world's cotton crop, and it is based on four domesticated species of *Gossypium*. These four species were evidently domesticated independently in different parts of the world. Two species from the Eastern Hemisphere, *Gossypium arboreum* and *G. herbaceum*, are both diploids, and the other two species from the Western Hemisphere, *G. barbadense* and *G. hirsutum*, are both tetraploids. All have been of major economic importance since before recorded history, but in modern times, the more productive *G. hirsutum* (upland cotton) is gradually replacing the others. *Gossypium barbadense* (pima cotton or Egyptian cotton) maintains a smaller-scale hold on the market because of its longer and higher-quality fiber. In addition to the fiber (seed hairs) they produce, cotton plants are also of economic value for the edible oil that is expressed from their seeds. The protein-rich meal that remains after oil extraction is used for livestock feed or can be processed into a protein-rich flour for human consumption.

Many species are prized as ornamental shrubs, notably *Hibiscus rosa-sinensis*, *H. syriacus*, *Malvaviscus penduliflorus*, and *Alcea rosea*. *Hibiscus cannabinus* (kenaf) has commercial value as a source of bast fibers for making cordage or paper pulp. *Hibiscus sabdariffa* (roselle or flor de Jamaica) is commonly used, especially in the Tropics, for making beverages or condiments from the fleshy calyces, and in the temperate zone it is the principal ingredient in "Red Zinger" tea. The immature fruits of *Abelmoschus esculentus* (okra) are widely used as a vegetable. Other Malvaceae have economically more marginal uses; e.g., species of *Sida* as medicinals and species of *Sida*, *Anoda*, *Herissantia*, *Malva*, and *Malvastrum* as agricultural weeds.

References. Bayer, C., and K. Kubitzki. 2003. Malvaceae. In *The Families and Genera of Vascular Plants*, eds. K. Kubitzki and C. Bayer. 5:225–311. Berlin: Springer-Verlag. Bernal, H. Y., and J. E. Correra Q. 1994. Malvaceae. In *Especies vegetales promisorias de los países del Convenio Andrés Bello*, Tomo X. Santafé de Bogotá, D. E., Colombia: Secretaria Ejecutiva del Convenio Andrés Bello. Fryxell, P. A. 1988. Malvaceae of Mexico. *Syst. Bot. Monogr.* 25:1–522. Fryxell, P. A. 1989. Malvaceae. In *Flora of the Lesser Antilles: Leeward and Windward Islands*, ed. R. Howard, 5:199–263. Jamaica Plain, MA: Arnold Arboretum, Harvard University. Fryxell, P. A. 1992. Malvaceae. In *Flora of Ecuador*, eds. G. Harling and L. Andersson, 44 (118):1–141. Göteborg, Sweden: Department of Systematic Botany, University of Göteborg. Fryxell, P. A. 1997. The American genera of Malvaceae II. *Brittonia* 49:204–69. Fryxell, P. A. 1999. *Pavonia cavanilles* (Malvaceae). *Fl. Neotrop. Monogr.* 76:1–284. Gürke, M. 1892. Malvaceae II. In *Flora Brasiliensis*, ed. C.F.P. von Martius, 12(3):457–586, plates 81–114. Kearney. T. H. 1951. The American genera of Malvaceae. *Amer. Midl. Naturalist* 46:93–131. Robyns, A. 1966. Family 115, Malvaceae, in Flora of Panama. *Ann. Missouri Bot. Gard.* 52:497–578. Schumann, K. 1891. Malvaceae I. In *Flora Brasiliensis*, ed. C.F.P. von Martius, 12(3):253–456, plates 51–80. Wiggins, I. L. 1964. Flora of the Sonoran Desert. In *Vegetation and Flora of the Sonoran Desert*, F. Shreve and I. L. Wiggins, 2:875–917. Stanford, CA: Stanford University Press.

MALVALES

William Surprison Alverson

Recent molecular and morphological studies have shown that three of the four traditional families at the core of the order Malvales—Bombacaceae, Sterculiaceae, and Tiliaceae—are artificial and that the Elaeocarpaceae, based on molecular data, are not related to these families. Only the traditional Malvaceae appears to be a monophyletic group. Despite the familiarity of the names Bombacaceae, Sterculiaceae, and Tiliaceae, the results of these recent phylogenetic studies present us with a difficult choice. Use of these traditional names could continue in the future, but they would refer to groups with a different and very reduced content, since many of the genera and species we have traditionally associated with these names are now known not to be closely related. As an alternative, recent publications have placed virtually all of the genera belonging to the traditional families Bombacaceae, Malvaceae, Sterculiaceae, and Tiliaceae into a single group, called either the family Malvaceae or the Malvaceae clade (also written as "/Malvaceae"). Within this Malvaceae clade, major groups have been given names with subfamily endings, such as Bombacoideae (or /Bombacoideae). Two sets of names have emerged from these recent studies, one adhering to traditional rules of nomenclature and a second following the rules of phylogenetic nomenclature. Fortunately, the content and names of these malvalean groups are nearly identical in either system.

The Matisieae clade, which falls within the Malvoideae clade but is not included in the treatment of the traditional family Malvaceae, is included in the Bombacaceae treatment in this book.

In summary, the families placed by Cronquist in the Malvales (Elaeocarpaceae, Tiliaceae, Sterculiaceae, Bombacaceae, and Malvaceae) are undergoing considerable revision in overall relationships and family circumscriptions. Because a universally accepted system for these taxa has not yet been established, the five traditional families are recognized as such in this book.

In addition, the genera *Muntingia*, *Dicraspidia*, and *Neotessmannia*, variously placed in the Elaeocarpaceae, Flacourtiaceae, and Tiliaceae, are herein considered a separate family, the Muntingiaceae.

Proposed changes in family circumscription and relationships, supported for the most part by evidence from molecular studies, are presented in the discussion of each family.

MARCGRAVIACEAE (Shingle Plant Family)

STEFAN DRESSLER

Figures 118, 119; Plate 29

- *lianas, scandent shrubs, or treelets*

- *plants often hemiepiphytic*

- *leaves alternate, simple, dimorphic in* Marcgravia; *glands present abaxially*

- *extrafloral bracteal nectaries present*

- *flowers actinomorphic; petals distinct to somewhat connate, fully fused in* Marcgravia; *ovary superior*

- *fruits capsular*

Numbers of genera and species. The Marcgraviaceae comprise seven genera and approximately 130 species restricted to tropical America. The largest genus is *Marcgravia* (ca. 60 species), followed by *Souroubea* (19), *Marcgraviastrum* (15), *Schwartzia* (14), *Sarcopera* (ca. 10), *Ruyschia* (7), and *Norantea* (2).

Distribution and habitat. The Marcgraviaceae, endemic to the neotropics, range from southern Mexico to northern Bolivia. Species of Marcgraviaceae are also found at higher elevations in the West Indies. The center of diversity of the family is northern South American.

Marcgravia is found in Central and South America, including the West Indies, with species occurring as far north as the tropic of Cancer in western Cuba. *Souroubea* ranges from Mexico to Bolivia, but is absent from the West Indies. *Marcgraviastrum* ranges from southern Nicaragua along the Andes to Peru and east into Suriname with two species found in the eastern part of the Brazilian Shield. *Schwartzia* is distributed from Costa Rica through the Andes south to Bolivia, in the Caribbean Basin, and in eastern Brazil. *Sarcopera* ranges from Honduras through the Andes to northern Bolivia and the Guayana Highlands. *Ruyschia* usually occurs at higher altitudes in Central America (3 species), the northern Andes (three species), and the Lesser Antilles (1 species). *Norantea* is distributed in the Caribbean and Amazonian drainage of northern South America, south to Brazil and Bolivia.

Species of the family are mostly found in primary humid tropical lowland forests, montane rain forests, and cloud forests. They often prefer higher altitudes, but only *Ruyschia* is restricted to them. Altitudinal vicariance among species occurs; for example, on Trinidad, *Marcgravia hartii* is found between 200 and 250 meters, *M. tobagensis* between 170 and 600 meters, and *M. elegans* is found only above 900 meters.

Figure 118. MARCGRAVIACEAE. *Marcgravia rectiflora* (A–G) and *M. sintenisii* (H–K). **A.** Stem with leaves and inflorescence showing bracteal nectaries in center. **B.** Inflorescence (right) and apical view of flower (left). **C.** Lateral view (right) and medial section (left) of bracteal nectary. **D.** Medial section (left) and lateral view (right) of calyptrate corollas. **E.** Lateral view of flower with corolla and part of stamens removed. **F.** Infructescence. **G.** Stem with juvenile leaves. **H.** Stem with adult leaves and detail of margin and abaxial surface showing punctuations (lower left). **I.** Stem with inflorescence showing bracteal nectaries in center. **J.** Medial section (below) and lateral view (above) of bracteal nectary. **K.** Lateral (above) and apical (below) views of flowers after corolla has fallen. Reprinted with permission from Acevedo-Rodríguez (2003). Artist: Bobbi Angell.

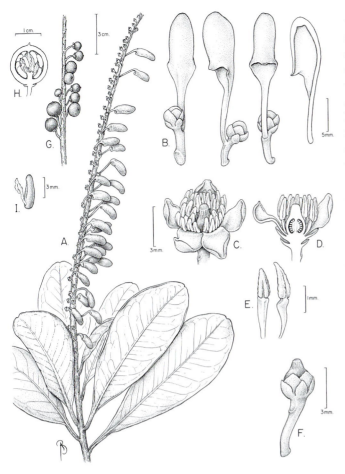

Figure 119. MARCGRAVIACEAE. *Norantea guianensis*. **A.** Stem with leaves and inflorescence. **B.** Three views of flower buds with associated bracteal nectaries and lateral section of bracteal nectary (far right). **C.** Oblique-apical view of flower. **D.** Medial section of flower. **E.** Adaxial (left) and lateral (right) views of stamens. **F.** Lateral view of immature fruit partially enclosed by calyx. **G.** Part of infructescence. **H.** Medial section of fruit. **I.** Seed with funicle. Reprinted with permission from Mori et al. (2002). Artist: Bobbi Angell.

Family classification. The Marcgraviaceae are placed in the Theales by Cronquist. Many characteristics such as external morphology, polymorphic sclereids, pollen morphology, and epicuticular waxes are also found in Theaceae. Seed structure resembles that of the tribe Adinandreae of Ternstroemiaceae. There are strong anatomical affinities (e.g., raphide bundles) with Tetrameristaceae and Pellicieraceae, two other families long regarded as close relatives of Theaceae. Molecular analyses place the Marcgraviaceae in an expanded Ericales, sister to the Tetrameristaceae and Pellicieraceae, but somewhat distant from Theaceae and Ternstroemiaceae.

The only existing infrafamilial classification recognizes two subfamilies: Noranteoideae (all genera except *Marcgravia*) and Marcgravioideae (only *Marcgravia*). Inflorescence morphology and the proposed pollination system of *Ruyschia* and *Souroubea* indicate that they might be basal within the Marcgraviaceae. *Norantea sensu lato* shows considerable morphological diversity in, for example, inflorescence structure and pollen morphology and Roon and Bedell consider it to be a heterogeneous assemblage of species. Hence, the genus has been divided into *Norantea stricto sensu*, *Schwartzia*, *Sarcopera*, and *Marcgraviastrum* by Roon and Dressler. The presence of heterophylly, contraction of the inflorescence axis, differentiation of sterile and fertile flowers, increase in number of stamens and ovary locules, reduction in corolla merosity, pollination system, and more highly specialized wood anatomy suggest that *Marcgravia* is the most advanced genus.

Features of the family. Habit: lianas or shrubs, terrestrial or hemiepiphytic. **Stems** often slender, ± scrambling, dimorphic in *Marcgravia* (the sterile stems creeping or root-climbing, mostly angled, bearing two rows of small, juvenile, cordate leaves, the fertile stems free and pendulous, usually rootless, terete, bearing adult leaves). **Stipules** absent. **Leaves** alternate (distichous in *Marcgravia*, spiral in remaining genera), simple, dimorphic in *Marcgravia*, petiolate to subsessile, the developing leaves convolutely enclosing shoot-tip (rather characteristic of family, similar to some Theaceae); blades usually thick, the margins entire or slightly crenate (some *Marcgravia*), the apex forming a drip-tip (some *Marcgravia*), an apical mucro present in all genera, the mucro often caducous when leaf fully expanded; glands present abaxially, the glands solid or poriform, often in specific patterns, sometimes grading into marginal glands, sometimes secreting a sweetish liquid in early stages of leaf development; venation pinnate (brochidodromous), the secondary veins ascending. **Inflorescences** terminal, sometimes cauliflorous on short lateral shoots, racemose, forming pseudospikes in *Sarcopera* or pseudoumbels in *Marcgraviastrum* and *Marcgravia*; extrafloral bracteal nectaries present, often conspicuously colored, these secreting sweetish liquid, the bracteal nectaries consisting of a bract fused to petiole in all but *Marcgravia*, in *Marcgravia*, the apical (central) flowers sterile and provided with nectaries, the nectary fused to abortive pedicel, tubular-clavate to pitcher- or boat-shaped, the fertile flowers lacking nectaries, the bracteal nectaries foliaceous to gibbose in *Ruyschia*, cup- or spur-shaped and often auriculate in *Souroubea*, and sac- or pitcher-shaped in *Norantea*, *Sarcopera*, *Schwartzia*, and *Marcgraviastrum*; bracteoles 2, generally sepal-like. **Flowers** actinomorphic, bisexual; calyx persistent, the sepals 4 in *Marcgravia*, 5 in other genera, thick, imbricate, quincuncial or, in *Marcgravia*, decussate; petals 5, or in *Marcgravia* 4, rarely 3 or 6 (*Souroubea*), distinct to somewhat connate, or in *Marcgravia*, completely fused into a calyptra, imbricate, and reflexed or, in *Marcgravia*, caducous at anthesis; androecium with stamens in 1 or 2 series, the stamens 3 or 5 in *Ruyschia* and *Souroubea*, 6–12(25) in *Sarcopera*, 20–35 in *Norantea*, (5)7–100 in *Marcgraviastrum*, *Marcgravia*, and *Schwartzia*, the filaments distinct or basally connate; gynoecium syncarpous, the ovary superior, the carpels 2–20, completely or incompletely 2–20-locular, the style 1, the stigma lobed or umbonate; placentation axile, the placentae intruding into locules, the ovules 10–20 to numerous in *Marcgravia*. **Fruits** capsular, globose, the calyx persistent, the pericarp rather coriaceous, splitting to expose seeds embedded in pulplike placentae. **Seeds** few to numerous, the testa shiny, reticulate.

The leaves of *Marcgravia* are distinctly dimorphic. The juvenile leaves are relatively small, have cordate blade bases, grow tightly appressed to tree trunks, and sometimes markedly overlap one another. These kinds of leaves are called shingle leaves, hence the common English name of the family. In contrast, the adult leaves of *Marcgravia* and all other genera are larger, often petiolate, do not have markedly cordate blade bases, are not appressed to tree trunks, and do not overlap one another.

Natural history. In the early literature on pollination biology, the inflorescence of *Marcgravia* was interpreted as an adaptation for bird pollination; however, bird pollination is not universal in the family, or even in *Marcgravia*.

The glands of the bracteal nectaries secrete nectar into the modified bracts that often form cuplike structures from which pollinators drink. These glands are apparently homologous with those found on normal leaves.

Ruyschia and *Souroubea* have small flowers, and the bracteal nectary is merely gibbous in the former genus. Species of both genera seem to be better adapted to insect pollination. The flowers of some species emit a very strong, sweet smell, a feature not typical of bird-pollinated plants. In *Souroubea*, butterfly pollination has been observed, and moth pollination is likely; however, the flowers and nectaries of some species of *Souroubea* reach dimensions that also suggest hummingbird pollination. Inflorescences of *Norantea*, *Sarcopera*, and *Schwartzia* mostly have brightly colored nectaries and robust inflorescences, and bird pollination has been reported for a few species. Species of *Marcgraviastrum* and *Marcgravia* have been reported as bat pollinated, and bat pollination may also occur in *Schwartzia*. The presence of dull, green to brownish nectaries and nocturnal flowering, features of bat-pollinated plants, are frequent in *Marcgravia*. Nevertheless, a few species of *Marcgravia* have brightly colored nectaries, and some species of this genus have been observed to be visited by hummingbirds; in addition, opossums have been recorded taking nectar from species of Marcgravia.

Despite their elaborate inflorescences, many Marcgraviaceae are probably autogamous and even cleistogamous, as has been shown for *Marcgravia coriacea* (syn. *M. cuyuniensis*).

Field observations are rather scarce, but the brightly colored pulp with the small seeds exposed when the fruits split open suggests that animal dispersal is probable; toucans and aracaris, for example, have been reported to consume the fruits of Marcgraviaceae.

Exudates from glands on the leaves may attract and feed ants during early leaf development, and this has been observed in *Norantea guianensis*. The ants presumably protect the leaves from phytophagous insects when the leaves lack sclereids and are prone to insect attack.

Economic uses. Apart from occasional horticultural use in the Tropics, the family has no significant economic value. Extracts from species of *Marcgravia*, *Norantea*, *Sarcopera*, and *Souroubea* have been reported to be used to treat headaches, toothaches, centipede stings, diarrhea, and syphilis. Local tribes apparently eat the fruits of some species of *Marcgravia*.

References. BAILEY, I. W. 1922. The pollination of *Marcgravia*: a classical case of ornithophily? *Amer. J. Bot.* 9:370–84. BEDELL, H. G. 1985. A generic revision of Marcgraviaceae I. The *Norantea* complex. Ph.D. dissertation (ined.), College Park, MD: University of Maryland. DRESSLER, S. 1997. 321. *Marcgravia umbellata.* [*Curtis's*] *Bot. Mag.*, ser. 6, 14:130–36. DRESSLER, S. 2000. A new species of *Marcgravia* (Marcgraviaceae) from Amazonia with some notes on the *Galeatae* group including a key. *Willdenowia* 30:369–74. DRESSLER, S. 2001. Marcgraviaceae. In *Flora of the Venezuelan Guayana*, eds. J. A. Steyermark, P. E. Berry, and B. K. Holst, 6:248–60. St. Louis, MO: Missouri Botanical Garden Press. DRESSLER, S., AND M. TSCHAPKA. 2002: Bird versus bat pollination in the genus *Marcgravia* and the description of a new species. *Bot. Mag.*, ser. 6, 19(2):104–14. JOLIVET, P. 1996. *Ants and Plants. An Example of Coevolution.* Leiden: Backhuys Publishers. MACHADO, I. C., AND A. V. LOPES. 2000. *Souroubea guianensis* Aubl.: Quest for its legitimate pollinator and the first record of tapetal oil in the Marcgraviaceae. *Ann. Bot. (London)* 85:705–11. PUTZ, F. E., AND H. A. MOONEY, eds. 1991. *The Biology of Vines.* Cambridge, MA: Cambridge University Press. ROON, A. C. DE. 1967. Foliar sclereids in the Marcgraviaceae. *Acta Bot. Neerl.* 15:585–628. ROON, A. C. DE 1975. Contributions towards a monograph of the Marcgraviaceae. Thesis. Utrecht. ROON, A. C. DE, AND S. DRESSLER. 1997. New taxa of *Norantea* Aubl. s.l. (Marcgraviaceae) from Central America and adjacent South America. *Bot. Jahrb. Syst.* 119:327–35. SAZIMA, I., S. BUZATO, AND M. SAZIMA. 1993. The bizarre inflorescence of *Norantea brasiliensis* (Marcgraviaceae): Visits of hovering and perching birds. *Bot. Acta* 106:507–13. SAZIMA, M., AND I. SAZIMA. 1980. Bat visits to *Marcgravia myriostigma* TR. et PL. (Marcgraviaceae) in southeastern Brazil. *Flora* 169:84–88. TSCHAPKA, M., AND O. VON HELVERSEN. 1999. Pollinators of syntopic *Marcgravia* species in Costa Rican lowland rain forest: Bats and opossums. *Plant Biol.* 1:382–88. VOGEL, S. 1958. Fledermausblumen in Südamerika. *Oesterr. Bot. Z.* 104:491–530.

MARTYNIACEAE (Unicorn Plant Family)

Thomas A. Zanoni

Figure 120

- *herbs*

- *leaves opposite or alternate, simple, sticky, emitting disagreeable odor when damaged*

- *flowers zygomorphic, bisexual; petals connate into tube, the lobes 5*

- *fruits with 2 projections, the projections sharp*

Numbers of genera and species. Endemic to the Western Hemisphere, the Martyniaceae include *Craniolaria* with two species, *Martynia* with one species, and *Proboscidea* (including *Ibicella*) with about 14 species. All species of Martyniaceae occur in tropical America, however, some reach extratropical regions of arid Mexico and the southern United States.

Distribution and habitat. *Craniolaria* is found in the Greater Antilles, Venezuela, Colombia, Paraguay, Argentina, Brazil, and Bolivia; *Martynia* ranges from Mexico to Costa Rica, Venezuela, and the West Indies; and *Proboscidea* is found in temperate and warm temperate United States, Mexico, Brazil, Paraguay, and Argentina. The family has been cultivated and naturalized outside its natural range.

Species are often found in arid and disturbed habitats such as cultivated and abandoned fields and pastures and on the sides of roads.

Family classification. The Martyniaceae are considered to be closely allied to the Pedaliaceae (Scrophulariales *sensu* Cronquist) and were placed within this family by Cronquist. Olmstead et al. maintain the family as distinct from Pedaliaceae and other families related to the Scrophulariaceae. The family is not subdivided above the generic level.

Features of the family. Habit: herbs, annual or perennial, the perennial herbs dying down to ground, the aerial parts (except corolla) covered with glandular trichomes, the trichomes completely uniseriate or the stalk cells uniseriate and the apical cells 4–8, forming broad head, secretory, filled with mucilage, the foliage emitting a disagreeable odor when damaged. **Roots** of perennial herbs thickened. **Stipules** absent. **Leaves** opposite or alternate, simple, sticky; blade margins entire to sinuate or almost lobed. **Inflorescences** terminal (subsequent growth of stems from nodes below inflorescence may make them appear lateral); bracts 1–22 centimeters long; bracteoles 2. **Flowers** zygomorphic, bisexual; calyx unequal, 5-lobed, sometimes split down one side; corolla some-

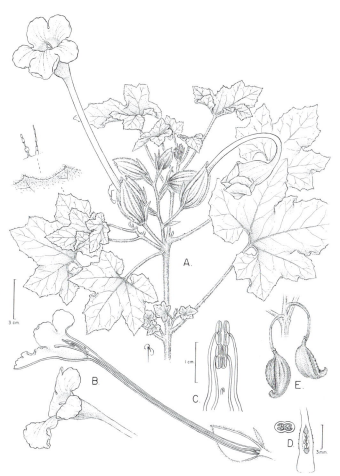

Figure 120. MARTYNIACEAE. *Craniolaria annua* (A, Bunting 5379; B, Mostacedo 274; C, D, Zanoni 26048; E, Romero-Castañeda 10543). **A.** Stem with leaves, inflorescences, and details of leaf blade margin and trichomes (left). **B.** Medial section of flower (above) and lateral view of corolla apex (below). **C.** Adaxial view of stamens and staminode (center below). **D.** Transverse (left) and medial (right) sections of ovary. **E.** Fruits. Original. Artist: Bobbi Angell.

what bilabiate, the petals connate into tube, the lobes 5, flared at mouth of tube, sometimes bearing bright colored spots; androecium with 2 or 4 stamens, the stamens in 2 pairs if 4, alternating with petal lobes, adnate to corolla; staminodes 1 or 3, sometimes as small knobs at corolla throat; gynoecium syncarpous, the ovary superior, the carpels 2, the locule 1, the style 1, the stigma 2-lobed; placentation parietal, the placentae 2, protruding into locule, the ovules few to many, anatropous. **Fruits** capsules, partially or completely dehiscent, the valves 2, the exocarp thin, fleshy, greenish, sometimes detaching from endocarp when dry, the endocarp hard, elliptic, flattened, dehiscing longitudinally, sculpted with ridges, with projections (cat's claws or unicorn's horns), the projections 2, short or long, sharp. **Seeds** with sparse endosperm; cotyledons 2, fleshy.

Natural history. Species of bees of the genera *Anthophora*, *Augochlorella*, *Bombus*, *Centris*, *Lasioglossum*, *Megachile*, and *Mellisodes* have been reported to pollinate species of *Proboscidea*. The flowers of *Craniolaria*, characterized by long corolla tubes and late afternoon/early evening anthesis, are probably pollinated by moths.

Fruit dispersal is facilitated by short or long clawlike hooks on the endocarp that attach to the bodies of animals.

Economic uses. Species of Martyniaceae are considered agricultural weeds, and evidence indicates that some of them produce allelopathic compounds that suppress the growth of other plants. The endocarps sometimes get caught in the feet, mouths, and eyes of livestock and cause considerable damage.

The unusual flowers and fruits of species of Martyniaceae have led to their cultivation as ornamentals. The clawed fruits have been used for handicrafts on a minor scale, but only one species, *Proboscidea louisianica*, has been grown for commercial use. In the southern United States, the tender, immature fruits of this species have been processed as pickles, and the cooked leaves and roasted seeds are eaten. The roots of *Craniolaria annua* have been reported to be cooked and eaten by native people of the Americas.

Some species also have been used in traditional medicine. For example, Native American Indians used the roots of *Proboscidea* to treat arthritis.

References. BRETTING, P. K., AND S. NILSSON. 1988. Pollen morphology of the Martyniaceae and its systematic implications. *Syst. Bot.* 13:51–59. CARLQUIST, S. 1987. Wood anatomy of Martyniaceae and Pedaliaceae. *Aliso* 11:473–83. HEATHERLY, A. N. 1998. Healing Plants: A Medicinal Guide to Native North American Plants and Herbs. New York: Lyons Press. HURD, P. D., JR., AND E. G. LINLEY. 1963. Pollination of the unicorn plant (Martyniaceae) by an oligolectic corolla-cutting bee (Hymenoptera: Apoidea). *J. Kansas Entomol. Soc.* 36:248–52. MERCER, K. L., D. S. MURRAY, AND L. M. VERHALEN. 1987. Interference of unicorn-plant (*Proboscidea louisianica*) with cotton (*Gossypium hirsutm*). *Weed Sci.* 35:807–12. OLMSTEAD, R. G., C. W. DE PAMPHILIS, A. D. WOLFE, N. D. YOUNG, W. J. ELISONS, AND P. A. REEVES. 2001. Disintegration of the Scrophulariaceae. *Amer. J. Bot.* 88(2):348–61. PHILIPPI, A., AND R. J. TYRL. 1979. The reproductive biology of *Proboscidea louisianica* (Martyniaceae). *Rhodora* 81:345–61. THIERET, J. W. 1976. Floral biology of *Proboscidea louisianica* (Martyniaceae). *Rhodora* 78:169–79. THIERET, J. W. 1977. The Martyniaceae in the southeastern United States. *J. Arnold Arbor.* 58:25–39. VAN ESELTINE, G. P. 1929. A preliminary study of the unicorn plants (Martyniaceae). *New York Agric. Exp. Sta. Bull.* 149: 1–41.

MELASTOMATACEAE (Black Mouth Family)

SUSANNE S. RENNER

Figure 121, Plate 30

- *usually shrubs, treelets, herbs, or rarely tall trees*

- *leaves usually opposite, simple; blades with 3 or more primary veins ascending from at or near base, the tertiary veins conspicuous and running at right angles to midrib*

- *flowers actinomorphic except for androecium, which can be secondarily zygomorphic through uneven growth of filaments; petals either large, purplish red or pink, or rarely yellow or small and white; anthers apically dehiscent*

- *fruits capsules or berries with numerous small seeds per locule*

Numbers of genera and species. Worldwide, the Melastomataceae comprise some 155 genera and about 4,500 species (ca. 1,000 species in tropical Asia, 240 in Africa, 225 in Madagascar, 50 in India, and seven in tropical Australia). In tropical America, there are 100 genera and about 3,000 species. The largest genus in the family and in tropical America is *Miconia*, with about 1,000 species.

Distribution and habitat. Except for *Rhexia* (endemic to North America), the Melastomataceae are distributed in tropical regions of the world. During the Tertiary, when climates in the Northern Hemisphere were tropical to subtropical, Melastomataceae were widespread in Eurasia and North America.

The centers of diversity of the Melastomataceae are the Andes, Guayana, and the Brazilian coastal rain forests. In terms of morphological diversity, the family's primary center lies in Malesia and Indochina.

The Melastomataceae are found in dry to moist habitats from sea level to high elevations. Species of the family are

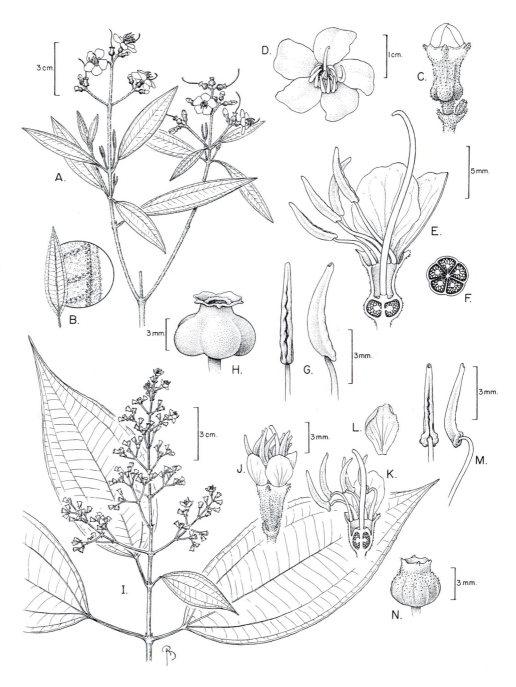

Figure 121. MELASTOMATA-
CEAE. *Tetrazygia elaeagnoides*
(A–H) and *Miconia laevigata*
(I–N). **A.** Stems with leaves and
inflorescences. **B.** Leaf and inset
showing detail of abaxial surface
showing indument. **C.** Lateral
view of flower bud. **D.** Apical
view of flower. **E.** Medial section
of flower. **F.** Transverse section
of ovary. **G.** Lateral (right) and
adaxial (left) views of stamens.
H. Lateral view of fruit. **I.** Stem
with leaves and inflorescence.
J. Lateral view of flower. **K.** Medial section of flower. **L.** Adaxial
view of petal. **M.** Lateral (right)
and adaxial (left) views of stamens. **N.** Lateral view of fruit.
Reprinted with permission from
Acevedo-Rodríguez (1996).
Artist: Bobbi Angell.

predominantly understory shrubs and herbs of tropical montane forests, although a few genera have radiated into lowland forests and many also occur in seasonally inundated
grasslands. In the neotropics, the typical habitat of *Blakea,
Brachyotum, Graffenrieda, Merania, Miconia,* and *Topobea*
is montane moist forest. *Miconia* is most diverse in the Andes of Colombia and Ecuador. Certain genera, such as *Aci-
santhera, Macairea, Pterolepis, Rhynchanthera,* and *Tibouchina,* occur only in savannas and white-sand areas. Finally,
there are many small genera, such as *Comoliopsis, Mallophy-
ton, Neblinanthera, Ochthephilus, Phainantha, Tateanthus,*
and *Tryssophyton,* that are more or less restricted to the
slopes or plateaus of tabletop mountains in Guayana.

Family classification. The Melastomataceae have always
been considered a core family of the Myrtales (e.g., *sensu*
Cronquist), and this is supported by molecular phylogenetic
analyses. Capsular or baccate fruit with numerous small
seeds per locule distinguish the Melastomataceae from their
sister family, the Memecylaceae. Other differences between
the families include the presence of an elliptic terpenoid-
producing gland on the stamens of Memecylaceae but not
Melastomataceae and leaf venation. Leaves of Melastomataceae have three or more primary veins ascending from at or
near the base, with the tertiary veins conspicuous and running at right angles to the midrib. Memecylaceae leaves, by
contrast, lack conspicuous tertiary veins (three thick primary

veins may sometimes be present, although this is rarer in the Neotropical *Mouriri* and *Votomita* than in the Paleotropical *Memecylon* and its satellite genera).

The family has traditionally been divided into 13 tribes and three subfamilies, of which Memecylaceae were one (as Memecyloideae). Whether Memecylaceae are included in Melastomataceae as a subfamily or ranked as a family depends on one's taste (both groups are monophyletic); however, the 13 traditional tribes clearly were not all monophyletic, and based on modern morphological and molecular analyses several have recently been recircumscribed. As currently understood, the monophyletic tribes of Melastomataceae are the following nine: the Astronieae, with four genera and 150 species in Southeast Asia; the Bertolonieae, a Neotropical group with 13 genera and 90 species of mostly understory shrubs and herbs; the Blakeeae, a Neotropical group of two very similar genera, *Blakea* and *Topobea*, and 160 species of terrestrial and epiphytic shrubs, most of them in the Andes; the Dissochaeteae, a Paleotropical group with numerous poorly circumscribed genera (based on several sets of molecular data, Dissochaeteae must include the Eastern Hemisphere tribes Sonerileae and Oxysporeae in order to be monophyletic); the Kibessieae, with one genus (*Pternandra*) and 15 species in tropical Southeast Asia; the pantropical Melastomeae (including the Neotropical Tibouchineae, the Paleotropical Osbeckieae, and the North American Rhexieae with the single genus *Rhexia*), with about 550 species in 48 genera, 30 of them in the neotropics; the Merianieae, a Neotropical group with 16 genera and 220 species of mostly shrubs or treelets in the Andes; the Miconieae with 30 genera and approximately 1,800 species; and the Microlicieae, a Neotropical group of 11 genera and 210 species of mostly shrubs and herbs found on sandy soil in temporarily inundated grasslands.

Features of the family. Habit: shrubs, treelets, herbs, or rarely tall trees (some species of *Loreya*, *Miconia*, and *Tessmannianthus* reach 45 m in height), less frequently scandent shrubs or lianas, sometimes facultative or obligate epiphytes (especially in Eastern Hemisphere). **Stipules** absent. **Leaves** opposite, simple; blades with 3 or more primary veins ascending from at or near base, the tertiary veins conspicuous and running at right angles to midrib. **Inflorescences** terminal and/or axillary, paniculate cymes, umbels, or rarely of solitary flowers. **Flowers** actinomorphic (androecium sometimes secondarily zygomorphic), bisexual, small to large, all flower parts distinct from each other except for ovary and hypanthium, these ± fused; hypanthium present; perianth usually biseriate; sepals commonly (3)4–5(6 or 8), usually imbricate, rarely valvate in bud, usually basally connate, the lobes distinct; petals equal to number of sepals, imbricate in bud, white, pink to deep reddish purple to bluish purple, rarely yellow or yellow and orange; androecium sometimes secondarily zygomorphic through uneven growth of filaments, diplo- or haplostemonous, the stamens 5–10(16), rarely to 96 in *Conostegia*, the anthers basifixed, apically

dehiscent by 1, 2, or 4 pores; gynoecium syncarpous, the ovary superior to ± completely inferior, the carpels equal to number of locules, the locules 3–6, the style elongate, the stigma punctate to capitate; placentation axile, the ovules numerous per locule, anatropous. **Fruits** capsules or berries (depending on degree of lignification or fleshiness of the receptacle and ovary wall, and on whether fruit splits open at maturity). **Seeds** numerous per locule, embedded in pulp in berries, straight, cuneate, or curved; endosperm absent, the embryos minute; germination phanerocotylar.

Fleshy capsules and berries have evolved repeatedly in the family. This transition usually goes along with a change from more open habitats, where wind dispersal of seeds is advantageous, to more closed habitats, where animal dispersal is favored.

Natural history. Most Melastomataceae have nectarless flowers adapted for pollination by pollen-collecting female bees. The bees cause the pollen to be expelled through the apical anther pores by buzz pollination. The stamens of many Melastomataceae bear conspicuous yellow appendages that enhance their visual attractiveness and make them easier for bees to grasp. Close contact between bees and stamens is essential for buzz pollination to be effective. Some 80 species in 11 genera offer nectar as a reward for pollinators, which include hummingbirds, bats, rodents, and wasps.

Melastomataceae berries are usually relatively small (0.5–3 cm in diameter) and blue, black, or red. They are very attractive to birds and provide the major part of the diets for some groups of Neotropical birds. The seeds are viable after passage through the gut. The berries of a few melastomes are large and yellow and taken by marsupials, monkeys, and bats.

Leaves of some Melastomataceae (e.g., *Maieta*, *Tococa*, and certain *Clidemia*), have saclike outgrowths at their leaf bases serving as shelters for ants that enter them through two small holes on the lower surface. The ants protect the leaves from herbivores, such as caterpillars, which they kill or drive away. In some cases, the ants also inject a herbicide into the growing tissues of other plants growing nearby, thereby creating a competitor-free space for the ant-housing melastome.

Economic uses. Although many Melastomataceae have beautiful foliage and flowers, few are in cultivation in greenhouses, probably because they require the presence of certain fungi in their roots in addition to tropical light and humidity regimes. A few species of glory bushes (*Tibouchina* species) occasionally are cultivated outdoors in the southeastern United States and elsewhere in the warm Tropics.

Introduced melastomes can become aggressive weeds, and one species, *Miconia calvescens*, is on the list of the world's 100 most noxious weeds because it forms large monospecific stands in Hawaii and Tahiti. Scientists estimate that a quarter of the Tahitian flora currently is threatened by this weed.

Native people worldwide extract bluish dyes from the

leaves, bark, or fruits of species of Melastomataceae. The family name comes from the Greek words "*mela*," meaning "black" and *stoma*, meaning "mouth," because eating the purple-blue succulent berries will dye the mouth black.

References. BERRY, P., A. GRÖGER, B. K. HOLST, T. MORLEY, F. A. MICHELANGELI, ET AL. 2001. Melastomataceae. In *Flora of the Venezuelan Guayana*, eds. P. Berry, B. Holst, and K. Yatskievych, 263–528. Portland, OR: Timber Press. CLAUSING, G., AND S. S. RENNER. 2001. Molecular phylogenetics of Melastomataceae and Memecylaceae: implications for character evolution. *Amer. J. Bot.* 88:486–98. RENNER, S. S. 1989. A survey of reproductive biology in neotropical Melastomataceae and Memecylaceae. *Ann. Missouri Bot. Gard.* 76:496–518. RENNER, S. S. 1993. Phylogeny and classification of the Melastomataceae and Memecylaceae. *Nordic J. Bot.* 13:519–40. RENNER, S. S., G. CLAUSING, AND K. MEYER. 2001. Historical biogeography of Melastomataceae: the roles of Tertiary migration and long-distance dispersal. *Amer. J. Bot.* 88:1290–1300. WURDACK, J. 1980. *Melastomataceae*. In *Flora of Ecuador*, eds. G. Harling, and B. Sparre, no. 13:1–405. Göteborg, Sweden: Department of Systematic Botany, University of Göteborg. WURDACK, J. J., AND R. KRAL. 1982. The genera of Melastomataceae in the southeastern United States. *J. Arnold Arbor.* 63:429–39. WURDACK, J., T. MORLEY, S. RENNER. 1993. Melastomataceae. In *Flora of the Guianas*, eds. A.R.A. Görts-Van Rijn, ser. A:1–725. Koenigstein, Germany: Koeltz Scientific Books.

MELIACEAE (Mahogany Family)

TERENCE D. PENNINGTON

Figures 122, 123; Plate 30

- *trees, occasionally shrubs*
- *leaves alternate (spiral), usually pinnate*
- *flowers actinomorphic; stamens partially or completely united into a tube; intrastaminal nectary-disc usually present*
- *fruits capsules, berries, or drupaceous*
- *seeds dry and winged or fleshy and arillate*

Numbers of genera and species. Worldwide, the Meliaceae comprise approximately 50 genera and 550 species. In tropical America, there are eight genera and about 130 species. Two other genera, *Melia* and *Azadirachta*, which are native to Asia, are now widely cultivated in the neotropics for their timber and as ornamentals.

Distribution and habitat. The Meliaceae are mostly pantropical with only *Toona sinensis* in China and *Melia azedarach* now widely cultivated outside the Tropics. In the neotropics, the family is most diverse in the Guianas and in the Brazilian Amazon to Amazonian Peru and Ecuador. Other centers of diversity occur in the Petén of southern Mexico and Guatemala, the Greater Antilles, and southeastern Brazil.

The majority of species of the largest genera, *Trichilia* and *Guarea*, are trees of lowland rain forest. Some species of *Guarea* extend into montane and cloud forest up to 2,500 meters (e.g., *G. kunthiana*) and all species of *Ruagea* and the monotypic *Schmardaea* are restricted to between 1,500 and 3,200 meters in the Andes and mountains of southern Central America. A few species of *Trichilia* are adapted to dry scrub in the Greater Antilles, and these have small, spiny, coriaceous leaves. The important timber producing genera, *Swietenia* and *Cedrela*, occur in wet evergreen rain forest and in deciduous forests with well-defined dry seasons.

Family classification. The Meliaceae are placed in the Sapindales by Cronquist. Recent molecular studies by the Angiosperm Phylogeny Group support the Meliaceae as being close to the Simaroubaceae and Rutaceae.

The family falls naturally into two large subfamilies, Melioideae and Swietenioideae, which are clearly distinguished by several well-correlated floral, fruit, wood anatomical, and molecular characters. The distinction between these two groups, however, is obscured by the Malagasy *Capurionianthus* and *Quivisianthe*. These genera share some of the characteristics of both Melioideae and Swietenioideae but are sufficiently isolated from them and from each other to be treated as separate subfamilies, the Capurionianthoideae and Quivisianthoideae.

The Melioideae have naked buds, 1–2-ovulate locules, fleshy or leathery loculicidal capsules, berries, or drupes, and usually arillate seeds. The Melioideae comprise about 35 genera and 500 species, the most important genera in the neotropics are *Trichilia* (ca. 70 species) and *Guarea* (ca. 35). Two other small American genera (*Ruagea* and *Cabralea*) and two introduced genera (*Azadirachta* and *Melia*) are also in this subfamily. The Swietenioideae have buds protected by scales, multiovulate locules, woody septifragal capsules, and usually winged seeds. This subfamily is represented in the

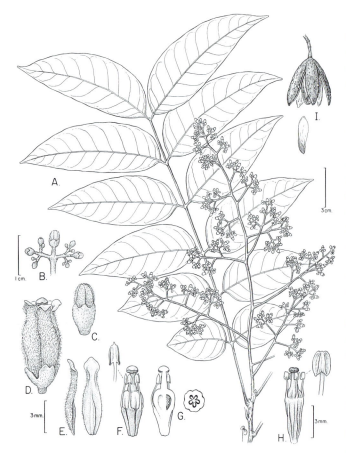

Figure 122. MELIACEAE. *Cedrela odorata*. **A.** Stem with one leaf and terminal inflorescence. **B.** Part of inflorescence with buds at different stages. **C.** Lateral view of flower bud showing cup-shaped calyx. **D.** Lateral view of flower. **E.** Lateral (left) and adaxial (right) views of petals. **F.** Lateral view of pistillate flower with petals removed to show staminodes and gynoecium and detail of staminode (above). **G.** Medial section of gynoecium (left) and transverse section of ovary (right). **H.** Lateral view of staminate flower with petals removed to show stamens and pistillode and detail of anther (above right). **I.** Lateral view of open fruit (above) and winged seed (below). Reprinted with permission from Mori et al. (2002). Artist: Bobbi Angell.

neotropics by *Carapa* (3 species), *Cedrela* (ca. 10), *Schmardaea* (1), and *Swietenia* (3).

Features of the family. Habit: small or large trees, occasionally shrubs. **Bark** with spicy scent when cut (useful for separating family from Burseraceae, Anacardiaceae, and Sapindaceae). **Indument** of unicellular or multicellular hairs, the hairs usually simple, less often stellate, malpighiaceous, or with lepidote scales. **Stipules** absent. **Leaves** alternate (spiral), pinnate, rarely trifoliolate or unifoliolate; blades often with transparent glandular lines or dots. **Inflorescences** axillary or terminal, panicles or thyrses. **Flowers** actinomorphic, functionally unisexual (plants monoecious, dioecious, or polygamous, both staminate and pistillate flowers with well-developed rudiments of opposite sex); sepals 4–5, usu-

ally distinct or partially united, in 1 whorl; petals 3–7, distinct or partially united; androecium usually with 5–10 stamens, the filaments partially or completely fused into tube, rarely distinct (as in *Trichilia lepidota*); intrastaminal nectary-disc usually present, annular to cup-shaped; gynoecium syncarpous, the ovary superior, the carpels 2–13, the locules 2–13, the style 1, the stigma usually capitate or discoid; placentation axile, the ovules 1–2 or many per locule, collateral, superposed, or biseriate. **Fruits** capsules, berries, or drupaceous (*Azadirachta* and *Melia*), the capsules loculicidal, septicidal, or septifragal. **Seeds** 1–many, dry and winged or fleshy and unwinged, the dry and winged seeds usually attached to a large woody columella (*Cedrela*, *Schmardaea*, and *Swietenia*), the unwinged and fleshy seeds usually with an arillode or sarcotesta (*Cabralea*, *Guarea*, *Ruagea*, and *Trichilia*), rarely with a corky or woody sarcotesta (*Carapa*); endosperm usually absent (except in a few species of *Trichilia*).

The two largest American genera, *Guarea* and *Trichilia*, have different branching patterns. *Guarea* tends to be pachycaulous with relatively thick branches, while *Trichilia* is leptocaulous with finer branches.

The shoot apex of most species in the subfamily Swietenioideae is protected by small bud scales (perulae), which are generally absent in the Melioideae.

Many Asian species produce white exudate from the cut bark, but in the Americas this is restricted to a few species of *Trichilia* (e.g., *T. havanensis*). However, white exudate is found in the cut pericarp of some fruit; e.g., *Cabralea canjerana*.

The genus *Guarea* is unusual in having pinnate leaves with a terminal bud. The growth characteristics of the bud vary from species to species; in some it is dormant and inactive, while in the majority of species it has intermittent growth. One or two pairs of new leaflets are produced at each flush of growth, with growth taking place over several years, and, as the leaf gets older, the lowermost leaflets begin to fall. The leaf, therefore, has some of the characteristics of a branch, with the petiole becoming woody.

The leaflets of many *Trichilia* are heteromorphic with the basal one or more pairs greatly reduced in size and resembling stipules. These vestigial leaflets are commonly referred to as "pseudostipules" and are highly characteristic of certain species. They may be foliaceous or reduced to minute scales.

The inflorescence of some species of *Guarea* has intermittent growth over a period of many months. This can result in ripe fruit and open flowers on the same inflorescence at the same time (e.g., *Guarea pubescens*).

All genera of the subfamily Swietenioideae (*Carapa*, *Cedrela*, *Schmardaea*, and *Swietenia*) are monoecious, whereas genera of the subfamily Melioideae are more varied, but with the majority of species dioecious. In dioecious plants, the male inflorescence is often much larger and floriferous than the female inflorescence. In the inflorescence of monoecious plants, the male flowers usually outnumber the female flowers.

Natural history. The small flowers of the majority of Meliaceae are thought to be pollinated by small Hymenoptera and thrips (Thysanonptera). Nectar is secreted by a nectary at the base of the staminal tube, which is often bright orange or yellow and strongly scented. Nocturnal bees have been implicated in the pollination of some small-flowered species, and thrips are often present in the flowers of American *Trichilia* and *Swietenia*. Access to nectar is restricted by the small space between the style-head and the stamens, and, therefore, is available only to very small insects or those with slender proboscises.

The impressive variation of fruit and seed morphology is linked to different modes of seed dispersal. All genera of the Swietenioideae (*Cedrela*, *Schmardaea*, and *Swietenia*) possess dry capsular fruits and winged seeds and are wind-dispersed. Most species of *Trichilia* have reddish or yellowish capsules that open to expose bright-orange, fleshy arillodes partially or completely surrounding black seeds. These arillodes, which are rich in lipids, attract birds. In *Guarea*, the seed is surrounded by a fleshy orange sarcotesta that contrasts with the white inner pericarp of the dehiscing capsule, but in some species (e.g., *G. cristata*) the attraction is provided by the pericarp itself. In these species, the fruit is tardily dehiscent or indehiscent, but the pericarp becomes fleshy, often with brilliant red-colored ridges and folds. Primates (e.g., *Cebus apella*) eat the fleshy pericarp and discard the central part of the fruit containing the seeds. Some riparian species (e.g., *G. guidonia*) have leathery brown capsules that open to release fleshy seeds into the water, where they are consumed and dispersed by fish.

The genera of the subfamily Swietenioideae are attacked by the shoot borer *Hypsipyla* (Lepidoptera, Pyralidae), which burrows into and destroys the shoot apex of seedlings and young trees. This has prevented the successful cultivation of commercially important timber such as species of *Cedrela* and *Swietenia* in Latin America.

Economic uses. The family provides all of the true mahogany on the commercial timber market. *Swietenia mahagoni* (native to the West Indies and Florida) was introduced to the European market in the late seventeenth century, but stands of native trees now have been exhausted. Species of *Swietenia* provide the most attractive of all cabinet timber, which is easy to work and has a beautiful luster, color, and grain. Today all mahogany on the commercial market comes from *S. macrophylla*, a widespread species distributed from southern Mexico to Bolivia. In the eighteenth century, shipments of this species came from Honduras and Nicaragua, but today most come from Brazil and Bolivia. It is now grown widely in plantations in Asia and the Pacific.

Another very important joinery timber known as Spanish cedar, because of its fragrance, is provided by *Cedrela odorata*, a major plantation species grown throughout the Tropics. The genus *Cabralea* also produces a fine timber similar in appearance to that of *Cedrela*, and several species of *Guarea* also have entered the commercial timber market as sources of plywood and veneer. An oil is extracted from the seeds of *Carapa guianensis* that is used to make soap, for burning in lamps, and as a repellent of blood-sucking insects. Other important products from the family are restricted to Asia; species of *Lansium* and *Sandoricum* provide edible fruits and *Azadirachta indica* (neem) produces a powerful insecticide.

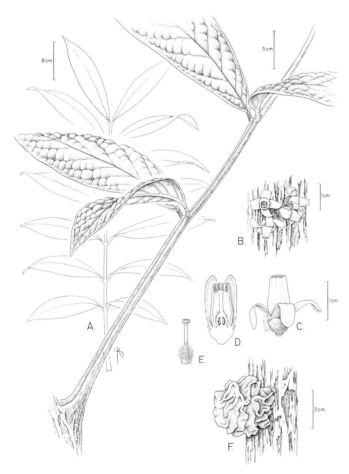

Figure 123. MELIACEAE. *Guarea michel-moddei.* **A.** Stem and base of pinnately compound leaf with a diagram of the whole leaf in background. **B.** Cauliflorous flowers. **C.** Lateral view of flower showing spreading petals and erect staminal tube. **D.** Medial section of flower showing anthers inserted within the staminal tube and ovary with axile placentation. **E.** Lateral view of gynoecium. **F.** Oblique-apical view of fruit. Reprinted with permission from Mori et al. (2002). Artist: Bobbi Angell.

References. CORRERA Q., J. E., AND H. Y. BERNAL. 1995. Meliaceae. In *Especies vegetales promisorias de los países del Convenio Andrés Bello*, Tomo XI. Santafé de Bogotá, D. E., Colombia: Secretaría Ejecutiva del Convenio Andrés Bello. GRIJPMA, P., AND B. T. STYLES. 1973. *Bibliografía Selectiva sobre Meliáceas.* Centro Interamericano de Documentacion e Informacion Agricola IICA-CIDIA. 1–143. How-ARD, F. W., S. NAKAHARA, AND D. S. WILLIAM. 1995. Thy-sanoptera as apparent pollinators of West Indian mahogany, *Swietenia mahogoni* (Meliaceae). *Ann. Sci. For.* 52:283–86. MÜLLNER, A. N., R. SAMUEL, S. A. JOHNSON, M. CHEEK, T. D. PENNINGTON, AND M. W. CHASE. 2003. Molecular phylogenetics of Meliaceae based on nuclear and plastid DNA sequences. *Amer. J. Bot.* 90(3):471–80. PENNINGTON, T. D., AND B. T. STYLES. 1975 A generic monograph of the Meliaceae. *Blumea* 22:419–540. PENNINGTON, T. D., B. T. STYLES, AND D.A.H. TAYLOR. 1981. Meliaceae. *Fl. Neotrop. Monogr.* 28:1–470.

MEMECYLACEAE (Memecylon Family)

SUSANNE S. RENNER

Figure 124, Plate 30

- *trees or shrubs; nodes swollen*

- *leaves opposite, simple; venation usually pinnate*

- *flowers actinomorphic, white, yellow, pink, or blue; anther connective usually bearing gland*

- *fruits berries*

- *seeds usually 1–2 per locule; germination cryptocotylar*

Numbers of genera and species. Worldwide, the Memecylaceae comprise six genera and approximately 350 species. In tropical America, there are two genera, *Mouriri*, with 81 species, and *Votomita*, with 10 species. Genera of the Eastern Hemisphere are *Memecylon*, *Warneckea*, *Spathandra*, and *Lijndenia*.

Distribution and habitat. Memecylaceae occur in tropical forests throughout the world. In tropical America, *Mouriri* occurs from Mexico to Bolivia as well as in the West Indies and *Votomita* is found from Panama to northern South America and in Cuba.

The family's only fossil record is *Memecylon* wood from northern Germany from the Oligocene (40 Ma). The presence of *Memecylon* in the Northern Hemisphere, the family's modern pantropical distribution, and its morphological diversity in the Paleotropics, suggest that Neotropical Memecylaceae are derived from ancestors that entered South America from North America.

Memecylaceae are mainly found in moist lowland forest.

Family classification. Cronquist placed the Memecylaceae in the Melastomataceae as part of his Myrtales. The close relationship between Memecylaceae and Melastomataceae and their placement in Myrtales is strongly supported by molecular data. Differences between Memecylaceae and Melastomataceae include the leaf venation, the number and size of the seeds, and the presence of an elliptic terpenoid-producing gland on the staminal connectives of Memecylaceae, but not Melastomataceae. Melastomataceae have berries or capsules

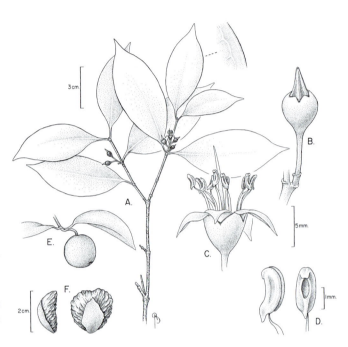

Figure 124. MEMYCYLACEAE. *Mouriri collocarpa*. **A.** Stem with leaves, inflorescences, and detail of leaf margin (above right). **B.** Part of inflorescence with flower bud. **C.** Lateral view of flower. **D.** Lateral (left) and adaxial (right) views of stamens; note the elliptical concave gland on anther. **E.** Lateral view of fruit on leafy stem tip. **F.** Lateral (left) and front (right) views of seeds. Reprinted with permission from Mori et al. (2002). Artist: Bobbi Angell.

with numerous small seeds, Memecylaceae have berries with one or two large mature seed. Leaves of Memecylaceae also lack the densely spaced parallel tertiary veins characteristic of Melastomataceae. The wider family concept favored by Cronquist, uniting Melastomataceae and Memecylaceae into a single family, while perfectly justified since they are sister groups, creates a rather heterogeneous family.

Modern classifications have never subdivided the Memecylaceae into subfamilies or tribes, which attests to the morphological cohesiveness of the six genera.

Features of the family. Habit: trees or shrubs; nodes swollen. **Stipules** absent. **Leaves** opposite, simple; venation pinnate or rarely subtrinerved (this more common in the Eastern Hemisphere). **Inflorescences** at nodes of young wood, sometimes cauliflorous, cymose, umbelloid, fasciculate, or sometimes solitary at nodes of older wood. **Flowers** actinomorphic, bisexual, biseriate, all flower parts distinct except for fused ovary and hypanthium; hypanthium present; perianth present; sepals (4)5, minute, imbricate in bud; petals equal to number of sepals, imbricate in bud, yellow, pink, or bluish; androecium diplostemonous, the stamens (8)10, the anthers basifixed, apically dehiscent by 2 short slits, these functioning as pores, the anther connectives dorsally bearing concave gland, 0.3–0.8 mm long, covered by terpenoid exudate; gynoecium syncarpous, the ovary inferior, the carpels equal to number of locules, the locules 1–5, the style elongate, the stigma punctate; placentation free central (1-locular), central-basal (2–5-locular), basal, or axile (in 10 species of *Mouriri* and 4 species of *Votomita*), the ovules up to 16 per locule in *Mouriri trunciflora*, anatropous. **Fruits** berries. **Seeds** 1–2 per locule; cotyledons well developed, thick, fleshy; germination cryptocotylar.

The Memecylaceae are often tall trees that can reach 35 m in height and 60 cm in diameter. Canopy trees of species of Memecylaceae are unbuttressed, but have basally swollen trunks and small, round crowns.

Natural history. The short slits in the anthers of Memecylaceae function as pores through which the pollen grains must be expelled before they are placed on a pollinator. Several species of *Mouriri* are buzz pollinated by female pollen-collecting bees. The pollen then adheres to the bee's body by electrostatic attraction. The ecological role of the terpenoid glandular exudate produced by the dorsal anther glands of all Memecylaceae is still unclear because none of the pollinating bees observed so far showed any interest in it. Perhaps the glands play a role in odor production or visual orientation to the pollen source.

All Memecylaceae have berries, ranging in diameter from 0.5 to 10 centimeters. Their color at maturity is commonly yellow to red, less often purple-black or black. The smaller-fruited species are bird-dispersed, and some of the larger-fruited species are monkey-dispersed. Fish eat the fruits of at least one riparian species of *Mouriri*.

Economic uses. Memecylaceae wood sometimes is used for general construction but is only moderately resistant to decay.

References. CLAUSING, G., AND S. S. RENNER. 2001. Molecular phylogenetics of Melastomataceae and Memecylaceae: implications for character evolution. *Amer. J. Bot.* 88: 486–98. MORLEY, T. 1976. Memecyleae (Melastomataceae). *Fl. Neotrop. Monogr.* 15:1–295. MORLEY, T. 1993. Mememcyloideae. In *Flora of the Guianas*, ed. A.R.A. Görts-Van Rijn, ser. A:302–63. Koenigstein, Germany: Koeltz Scientific Books. MORLEY, T. 1999. A new species of *Votomita* (Melastomataceae) from Venezuela, with thoughts on ovule and seed number and seed size. *Novon* 9:241–44. RENNER, S. S. 1989. A survey of reproductive biology in neotropical Melastomataceae and Memecylaceae. *Ann. Missouri Bot. Gard.* 76:496–518. RENNER, S. S. 1993. Phylogeny and classification of the Melastomataceae and Memecylaceae. *Nordic J. Bot.* 13:519–40.

MENISPERMACEAE (Moonseed Family)

RUPERT BARNEBY† AND PAM WHITE

Figure 125, Plate 31

- *vines or lianas, less frequently small trees, subshrubs, or herbs*
- *leaves alternate, usually simple*
- *flowers unisexual (plants dioecious); perianth commonly in cycles of 3, often minute, greenish white or dull reddish; gynoecium apocarpous*
- *fruits monocarps, the monocarps drupelike, 1-seeded, the endocarps bony or woody, often ornamented*

Numbers of genera and species. Worldwide, the Menispermaceae comprise approximately 70 genera and more than 500 species. In tropical America, there are 17 genera and about 166 species; the largest genera are *Abuta* (ca. 32 species) and *Odontocarya* (ca. 30).

Distribution and habitats. The Menispermaceae are pantropical and most diverse and numerous in humid lowland forest. A few genera are adapted to monsoon climates and deserts and yet fewer species are found in temperate woodlands (some *Menispermum* and *Calycocarpum*). In the Southern Hemisphere, a few species extend south into Argentina and Chile and through Southeast Asia into Polynesia and Australia. In the Northern Hemisphere, species of Menispermaceae are rare outside tropical latitudes.

Family classification. The Menispermaceae are placed in the Ranunculales by Cronquist. The placement of the Menispermacae near families such as the Berberidacae, Ranunculaceae, and Papaveraceae is supported by recent phylogenetic analyses of molecular and morphological data. Tribes and genera are distinguished principally by characters of the en-

Figure 125. MENISPERMACEAE. *Abuta grandifolia*. **A.** Stem with leaves and pistillate inflorescence. **B.** Staminate inflorescence. **C.** Detail of staminate inflorescence. **D.** Apical view of staminate flower. **E.** Adaxial view of inner sepal. **F.** Lateral views of androecium (left) and single stamen (right). **G.** Detail of pistillate inflorescence. **H.** Apical view of pistillate flower. **I.** Lateral view of pistillate flower with sepals removed (above) and medial section of carpel (below). **J.** Infructescence with two fruits. **K.** Lateral view of seed (right) and medial section of seed (above left). Reprinted with permission from Mori et al. (2002). Artist: Bobbi Angell.

docarp, the endosperm, and the embryo, but not, or only incidentally, by characters of the staminate flower. The Menispermaceae known at the beginning of the twentieth century were classified by Diels into eight tribes, and recently consolidated by Kessler into five.

Features of the family. Habit: vines or lianas, less frequently small trees, subshrubs, or herbs. **Stems** either cylindric or, when woody, sometimes anomalously thickened on two sides and becoming ribbonlike, the young stems with a ring of vascular bundles separated by broad medullary rays. **Indumentum** of simple, basifixed trichomes or absent. **Stipules** absent. **Leaves** alternate, usually simple, rarely palmately lobed or (in *Disciphania*) decompound; petioles often pulvinate at each end, providing vertical and horizontal adjustment of blade, the pulvinules sometimes inert or subobsolete; blades usually basifixed, sometimes peltate, the margins entire or denticulate; venation palmate or pinnate. **Inflorescences** of both sexes either serially supra-axillary or cauliflorous, either spiciform or racemose-paniculate, foliate or not; bracteoles present. **Flowers** usually actinomorphic (zygomorphic in *Cissampelos*), unisexual (plants dioecious), often minute,

greenish white or dull reddish; perianth commonly imbricate, in cycles of three, the sepals 6–many, distinct or partly united, the petals 6 or absent (the pistillate sepal and the petal 1 each and the staminate perianth 4-merous in *Cissampelos*). **Staminate flowers** with stamens 6-, 3-, seldom 12-merous upward, or reduced to 1 stamen, the filaments either distinct or united into a column, the anthers dehiscing by slits, these most commonly vertical but often tilted by dilation or twisting of either filament or connective and appearing obliquely extrorse, obliquely introrse, or horizontal. **Pistillate flowers** with androecium either represented by staminodes or suppressed; gynoecium apocarpous, the ovary superior, the carpels 3, 6 or more in *Sciadotenia*, or 1 in *Cissampelos*, either sessile on a dilated torus or rarely either stipitate or elevated on a stipelike gynophore, the stigma often linguiform, sometimes lobed; placentation submarginal, the ovules 2 per carpel (only 1 maturing). **Fruits** monocarps, the monocarps drupelike, the exocarp membranous or coriaceous, red, yellow, the mesocarp often mucilaginous, the endocarp crustaceous, bony, or woody, either smooth externally or often engraved or ornamented with papillae or processes, the adaxial face often produced from various directions into cavity as a septum, or an externally concave condyle. **Seeds** 1 per monocarp; endosperm continuous, ruminate, or absent, when absent the bony cotyledons assuming storage function, the embryo conforming to seed-cavity and to condyles when present, the radicle very short, the cotyledons either linear-vermiform, or thick and horny, then pressed face to face, or foliaceous and then divaricate in one plane.

Natural history. Very little is known or published about pollination and dispersal of the Menispermaceae. Insect pollination has been reported in species bearing flowers on stems. The fruits of *Abuta grandifolia* are consumed by large birds, monkeys, and rodents. Bird-dispersed fruits occur in *Cissampelos.*

Economic uses. Menispermaceae are rich in alkaloids that are important ingredients of the arrow poison curare, which has been used for selective paralysis in clinical surgery. The use of decoctions from the bark and leaves of Menispermaceae as arrow and dart poisons and the power of crushed stems and herbage to stun fish were discovered by hunter-gatherers independently in Asia, Africa, and America. Bark of false *pareira brava* (*Cissampelos pareira*), which furnished a drug used in treatment of diseases of the urinary tract, formerly was exported in quantity from Brazil. Contributions of Menispermaceae to folk medicine are many and various, entering into therapy for fevers, stomach complaints, snakebites, and skin disorders.

References. BARNEBY, R. C. 1970. Revision of Neotropical Menispermaceae tribe Tinosporeae. *Mem. New York Bot. Gard.* 20(2):81–158. BARNEBY, R. C., AND B. A. KRUKOFF. 1971. Supplementary notes on American Menispermaceae VIII. A generic survey of the American Triclisieae and Anomospermeae. *Mem. New York Bot. Gard.* 22(2):1–89 Diels, L. 1910. Menispermaceae In *Das Pflanzenreich*, A. Engler, ser. IV, 94:1–345. Leipzig: Wilhelm Engelmann. Forman, L. L. 1992. The correct names for the tribes of Menispermaceae. *Kew Bull.* 37:367–68. Hoot, S. B., S. Magallon, and P. R. Crane. 1999. Phylogeny of basal eudicots based on three molecular data sets: *atp*B, *rbc*L, and 18S nuclear ribosomal DNA sequences. *Ann. Missouri Bot. Gard.* 86:1–32. Kessler, P.J.A. 1993. Menispermaceae. In *The Families and Genera of Vascular Plants*, eds. K. Kubitzki, J. G.

Rohwer, and V. Bittrich, 2:402–15. Berlin: Springer-Verlag. Krukoff, B. A., and R. C. Barneby. 1970. Supplementary notes on American Menispermaceae VII. *Mem. New York Bot. Gard.* 20(2):71–8. Loconte, H., L. M. Campbell, and D. W. Stevenson. 1995. Ordinal and familial relationships of Ranunculid genera. *Pl. Syst. Evol.* [Suppl] 9:99–118. Miers, J. 1871. A complete monograph of the Menispermaceae. *Contributions to Botany* 3:1–385. Thanikaimoni, G. 1984. Ménispermacées: palynologie et systématique. *Trav. Sect. Sci. Tech. Inst. Franc. Pondichéry* 18:1–128.

MENYANTHACEAE (Bogbean Family)

Robert Ornduff†

Figure 126, Plate 31

- *aquatic or wetland herbs*

- *leaves alternate, simple; petiole bases sheathing; blades cordate to reniform*

- *flowers actinomorphic; petals crested medially, fringed marginally; stamens epipetalous*

- *fruits capsules, usually dehiscing by apical valves*

- *seeds flattened or lenticular*

Numbers of genera and species. Worldwide, the Menyanthaceae comprise five genera and about 53 species. In tropical America, there is a single genus, *Nymphoides*, and four species (40 species worldwide).

Distribution and habitat. The Menyanthaceae are of nearly cosmopolitan distribution. *Nymphoides* is especially well represented in Australia and Africa. In tropical America, *Nymphoides fallax* ranges from central Mexico into Guatemala and *N. grayana* occurs in western Cuba and the central Bahamas. Specimens from the Western Hemisphere conventionally referred to *N. humboldtiana* are better included in *N. indica*, which thus becomes a circumtropical species. In the Americas, this species ranges from central Mexico and Cuba southward to Argentina (but not Chile). The Colombian *Nymphoides flaccida* is a distinctive member of the *indica* group, but the status of other taxa described from South America, particularly Brazil, is unclear.

Fauria (*Nephrophyllidium*), *Liparophyllum*, *Menyanthes*, and *Villarsia* occur outside tropical America.

Many Menyanthaceae grow in bodies of water in which the water level fluctuates significantly throughout the year. Some species occur in ephemeral pools.

Family classification. For much of their taxonomic history, the Menyanthaceae were included as a tribe or subfamily of the Gentianaceae. More recently, its familial status generally has not been questioned, but its relationships remain uncertain. In 1981, Cronquist asserted that the family "obviously" belongs to the Asteridae, and that it possesses no "significant characters that are not well known in one or another of the two orders Solanales and Gentianales. . . . It seems clear that [it] should be referred to one of these orders." In 1988, he indicated that "the weight of the evidence favors a position in the Solanales." Recent molecular and cladistic studies confirm the inclusion of the family in the Asteridae and suggest that the family belongs in the Asterales along with the Calyceraceae, Goodeniaceae, and Asteraceae.

Features of the family. Habit: aquatic or wetland herbs, perennial. **Stipules** absent. **Leaves** alternate, simple; petiole bases sheathing; blades cordate to reniform, aerial, emergent, floating, or rarely submerged. **Inflorescences** terminal, aerial, in heads, fasicles, panicles, or of solitary flowers. **Flowers** actinomorphic, usually bisexual, sometimes functionally unisexual, often distylous; sepals 5, basally connate; petals 5, basally connate, white, yellow, or bicolored, crested medi-

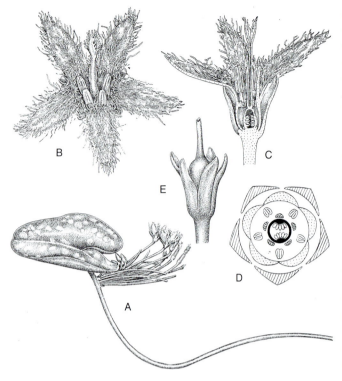

Figure 126. MENYANTHACEAE. *Nymphoides grayanum.* **A.** Stem with floating leaf and inflorescence (x½). **B.** Apical view of flower (x3). **C.** Medial section of flower (x3). **D.** Floral diagram. **E.** Lateral view of fruit subtended by calyx. Reprinted with permission from Correll and Correll (1982). Artist: Priscilla Fawcett.

Natural history. In aquatic species of *Nymphoides*, rapid curvature of the pedicel causes the submerged flower bud to rise above the water level, after which the flower opens; in a few hours, the pedicel recurves, the flower is submerged, and the fruit develops underwater. Individual flowers of *Nymphoides* last only a few hours. Distyly is often, but not always, accompanied by an incompatibility system that favors intermorph fertilizations.

Pollination is accomplished usually by insects, rarely by wind or via autogamy. When fruit maturation occurs underwater, seed release results from irregular breakdown of the fleshy fruit walls. Seed coats of aquatic species often are water resistant, so the seeds float after release from the fruits and, thus, are dispersed via water.

Economic uses. Several species of *Nymphoides* are grown as aquarium or pond plants and bear names such as water fringe or water snowflake, referring to features of the corollas, or floating hearts, referring to the leaf shape. Banana plant is a name used for *N. aquatica* of the southeastern United States because of the clusters of adventitious fleshy roots of plantlets produced at the submerged junction of petioles and stems. The Eurasian *N. peltata* has become naturalized in various places of the United States. It is likely that commonly cultivated species have become established locally elsewhere, and some have become noxious weeds (e.g., *N. indica* and *N. peltata*). In India, species of *Nymphoides* provide treatments for ulcers, bites, and intestinal worms. Leaves of *Menyanthes* have been substituted for hops in brewing, and the sap has been used as a remedy for dyspepsia and bowel trouble or, in large doses, as a purgative and emetic. This species also has been effective as a tonic and astringent, for treating rheumatism, and to expel parasitic worms. It is used as a cure for arthritis in Germany and as food in Eurasia and boreal America.

anly, the margins fringed, sometimes with long crisped hairs; androecium with 5 stamens, the stamens epipetalous, the anthers dehiscing by longitudinal slits; 5 staminode-like structures present, alternating with filaments; nectaries usually present; gynoecium syncarpous, the ovary half-inferior, the carpels 2, the locule 1, the style terminal, the stigma simple to broadly 2-lobed; placentation parietal, the placentas 2, the ovules 2–numerous. **Fruits** capsules, aerial, usually dehiscing by apical valves. **Seeds** 1–2(-numerous), flattened or lenticular, glabrous or ornamented with trichomes.

In some species of *Nymphoides*, adventitious roots are produced from what appears to be the submerged petiole, but the site of development usually is interpreted as the junction of the petiole and a petiole-like stem below it. The flowers also are produced at this site. A few species of *Nymphoides* bear submerged leaves during the dormant season and early in the growing season and floating leaves thereafter. The Colombian *N. flaccida* is unusual in growing in swiftly flowing rivers and is the only known member of the family with exclusively submerged leaves.

References. BOHM, B. A., K. W. NICHOLLS, AND R. ORNDUFF. Flavonoids of the Menyanthaceae: intra- and interfamilial relationships. *Amer. J. Bot.* 73:204–13. CHUANG T. I., AND R. ORNDUFF. 1992. Seed morphology and systematics of Menyanthaceae. *Amer. J. Bot.* 79:1396–1406. DOWNIE, S. R., AND J. D. PALMER. 1992. Restriction site mapping of the chloroplast DNA inverted repeat: a molecular phylogeny of the Asteridae. *Ann. Missouri Bot. Gard.* 79:266–83. OLMSTEAD, R. G., B. BREMER, K. M. SCOTT, AND J. D. PALMER. 1993. A parsimony analysis of the Asteridae *sensu lato* based on *rbc*L sequences. *Ann. Missouri Bot. Gard.* 890:700–22. ORNDUFF, R. 1969. Neotropical *Nymphoides* (Menyanthaceae): Meso-American and west Indian species. *Brittonia* 21: 346–52. WOOD, C. E. 1983. The genera of Menyanthaceae in the southeastern United States. *J. Arnold Arbor.* 64:431–45.

MOLLUGINACEAE (Carpet-weed Family)

Michael Nee

Figure 127, Plate 31

- *herbs, usually short-lived annuals*
- *leaves opposite, alternate, or whorled, simple*
- *flower petals absent or small if present*
- *fruits capsules*

Numbers of genera and species. Worldwide, the Molluginaceae comprise 13 genera and 100 species. In tropical America, there are two genera, *Glinus* with two species and *Mollugo* with about eight species.

Distribution and habitat. The family is widespread in tropical, subtropical, and temperate parts of the world, partly because of the spread of a few weedy members such as *Mollugo verticillata*, which is found from southern Canada to Argentina. Most of the genera and species are found in Africa and other parts of the Eastern Hemisphere.

Neotropical species are adapted to seasonally bare soil where there is little competition from other plants. *Glinus* is mainly confined to sandbars and banks of streams.

Family classification. The Molluginaceae are placed in the Caryophyllales by Cronquist and the family has often been included in the Aizoaceae. Morphological and molecular analyses place the Molluginaceae near families such as the Portulacaceae, Cactaceae, Nyctaginaceae, Aizoaceae, Phytolaccaceae, Amaranthacae, and Caryophyllaceae.

Features of the family. Habit: herbs, low, often mat-forming, usually short-lived annuals. **Stipules** sometimes present, then conspicuous. **Leaves** opposite, alternate, or whorled, simple; blades sometimes slightly succulent, the margins entire. **Inflorescences** axillary, open cymose or of solitary flowers. **Flowers** actinomorphic, usually bisexual; sepals (4)5, persistent; petals absent or small if present; androecium usually of 5–10 stamens; gynoecium syncarpous, the ovary superior, multilocular below, often unilocular above the carpels 2–5, the styles distinct; placentation axile, the ovules usually numerous. **Fruits** capsules. **Seeds** usually numerous, small, sometimes arillate.

Natural history. No information is available on pollination biology. *Glinus* and *Mollugo* are capable of germinating from seed, flowering, and producing seeds in just a few

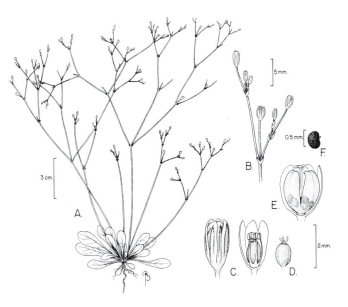

Figure 127. MOLLUGINACEAE. *Mollugo nudicaulis.* **A.** Plant showing roots, basal leaves, and inflorescences. **B.** Detail of inflorescence. **C.** Lateral views of flower (left) and flower with part of perianth removed (right). **D.** Lateral view of gynoecium. **E.** Lateral view of dehisced fruit. **F.** Seed. Reprinted with permission from Acevedo-Rodríguez (1996). Artist: Bobbi Angell.

weeks. The minute seeds are produced in great abundance and are dispersed easily by water and by the muddy feet of passing animals.

Economic uses. *Mollugo verticillata* is often a weed of gardens and cultivated fields.

References. Bogle, A. L. 1970. The genera of Molluginaceae and Aizoaceae in the South-Eastern United States. *J. Arnold Arbor.* 51:431–62. Nee, M. 1985. Molluginaceae. In *Flora de Veracruz,* eds. A. Gómez-Pompa and V. Sosa, fasc. 43:1–8. Xalapa, Mexico: INIREB.

MONIMIACEAE (Monimia Family)

Susanne S. Renner

Figure 128

- *shrubs or treelets*

- *leaves usually opposite, simple; blades conspicuously toothed, at least apically and in young leaves*

- *flowers unisexual, usually small*

- *fruits drupes on recurved fleshy or woody receptacles, often striking in color and size*

- *seed 1 per carpel*

Numbers of genera and species. Worldwide, the Monimiaceae comprise 25 poorly understood genera and 200 species. In tropical America, there are four genera, *Mollinedia* (ca. 20 species) and *Hennecartia*, *Macropeplus*, and *Macrotorus* (each with a single species).

Distribution and habitat. The Monimiaceae are pantropically distributed, occurring in the neotropics from Mexico to Chile, equatorial Africa, Madagascar, Sri Lanka, Malesia, and Australasia. The family is found in moist, mostly lowland habitats. The five genera of the Western Hemisphere, *Hennecartia*, *Macropeplus*, *Macrotorus*, *Mollinedia*, and *Peumus* are distantly related and are found in widely different habitats. *Mollinedia* occurs in understory of lowland moist forest from Central America to the Amazon basin and in gallery forests in Brazil, Paraguay, and Argentina. Its close relatives are found in gallery forests in southern Brazil and Paraguay (*Macropeplus* and *Macrotorus*) and Argentina (*Hennecartia*). *Peumus* is found in sclerophyllous Chilean forests between 30° and 41° latitude from sea level to 1,500 meters.

Family classification. The placement of the Monimiaceae in the Laurales by Cronquist is supported by molecular data.

Monimiaceae are closely related to Lauraceae and Hernandiaceae, but the relationships among these families are not yet clear. An indeterminate and often high number of floral parts distinguishes the Monimiaceae from the Lauraceae, which usually have trimerous flowers with a single carpel, and Hernandiaceae, which usually have 4- or 5-merous flowers and a single carpel.

Before the availability of molecular data, Monimiaceae included three divergent elements, the Siparunaceae, the Atherospermataceae, and the Monimiaceae in the strict sense. However, Siparunaceae and Atherospermataceae are only distantly related to Monimiaceae and to each other.

Monimiaceae are usually subdivided into the Hortonioideae, with the single species *Hortonia floribunda* of Sri Lanka; the pantropical Mollinedioideae, with 21 genera and about 180 species; and the Monimioideae, with three genera,

Figure 128. MONIMIACEAE. *Mollinedia ovata*. **A.** Stem with leaves and staminate inflorescences. **B.** Detail of staminate inflorescence. **C.** Medial section of staminate flower. **D.** Views of stamens. **E.** Stem with leaf and pistillate inflorescences. **F.** Detail of pistillate inflorescence. **G.** Medial section of pistillate flower. **H.** Lateral view of receptacle with immature fruits. **I.** Immature monocarps (left and center) with remnant stigmas and medial section of fruit (right). **J.** Stem with leaves and infructescences and detail of leaf margin showing tooth (upper left). **K.** Monocarp. Reprinted with permission from Mori et al. (2002). Artist: Bobbi Angell.

the monotypic *Peumus* of Chile, *Palmeria*, with 14 species in New Guinea and tropical Australia, and *Monimia*, with three species in Mauritius and Réunion. A phylogenetic analysis based on DNA sequences supports recognizing these three major groups.

Features of the family. Habit: shrubs or treelets; exudates generally absent (lacticiferous cells present in some species). **Stipules** absent. **Leaves** opposite or rarely whorled, simple; blades conspicuously toothed, at least apically and in young leaves. **Inflorescences** axillary or borne on leafless nodes of older wood, cymes. **Flowers** actinomorphic, usually unisexual (plants monoecious, dioecious, or polygamous) or with rudiments of opposite sex in *Peumus boldus*, perigynous, usually small; perigon usually present, sepal-like or petal-like, medium-sized, the tepals 3–many, distinct or reduced; androecium of 8–1,800 stamens, the stamens arranged irregularly inside receptacle, gradually becoming exposed on recurved receptacle, the filaments distinct, with basal nectary glands in *Peumus* and *Monimia*, the anthers longitudinally or transversely dehiscent (e.g., *Hennecartia*), the slits sometimes apically confluent; gynoecium apocarpous, the ovaries superior, the carpels 1–1,000 or more, often deeply embedded in receptacle tissue, ± enclosed in receptacle throughout anthesis, the styles prominent to very short, distinct, terminal, the stigmas terminal or decurrent; placentation apical, the ovules 1 per carpel, anatropous. **Fruits** drupes, stalked or sessile, the receptacle fleshy or woody, often striking in color and size. **Seeds** 1 per carpel.

After anthesis, the tepals of the female flowers fall off individually or as a calyptra and the receptacle becomes woody and disclike. The juicy, dark blue or red drupes that develop from the carpels are borne on this receptacle, much as in some Annonaceae. Because of this similarity, some species of Monimiaceae were originally described as species of Annonaceae. In a few species, the drupes are dark blue and are subtended by a long red stalk.

Natural history. *Peumus* is pollinated by nectar-feeding flies or bees, and *Mollinedia* by small thrips (*Lenkothrips sensitivius*) that enter the flask-shaped female flowers through the small hole at the flower apex to lay eggs. The same thrips visit the male flowers to feed on pollen. The pollination of *Hennecartia* needs to be studied in the field. The male flowers do not seem to offer a reward for pollinators because the tightly packed stamens, whose anthers open by horizontal slits,

literally hide the pollen. In female flowers, the one or two carpels are enclosed completely in the receptacles, and a secondary receptive surface is formed by the papillose tepals that surround the top of the receptacles, rather than by the tip of the style as in other flowering plants. Pollen grains presumably are transported there by insects and then germinate to grow down the stylar canals to the ovules. The drupes of *Mollinedia*, *Macrotorus*, *Macropeplus*, and *Hennecartia* are animal-dispersed, probably mainly by birds.

Economic uses. Of the Neotropical Monimiaceae, only *Peumus* has economic value. A medicinal tea is prepared from the leaves of *boldo* (*P. boldus*) and into the 1900s this was available in pharmacies under the name *Folia Boldo* or *Boldo* Leaf Oil.

References. ENDRESS, P. K. 1992. Protogynous flowers in Monimiaceae. *Pl. Syst. Evol.* 181:227–32. LORENCE, D. H. 1985. A monograph of the Monimiaceae (Laurales) of the Malagasy region (Southwest Indian Ocean). *Ann. Missouri Bot. Gard.* 72:1–165. RENNER, S. S. 1998. Phylogenetic affinities of Monimiaceae based on cpDNA gene and spacer sequences. *Persp. Plant Ecol. Evol. Syst.* 1:61–77. RENNER, S. S., AND A. CHANDERBALI. 2000. What is the relationship among Hernandiaceae, Lauraceae, and Monimiaceae, and why is this question so difficult to answer? *Intern. J. Plant Science* 161:S109–S119. RENNER, S. S., AND G. HAUSNER. 1997. Siparunaceae and Monimiaceae. In *Flora of Ecuador*, eds. G. Harling and L. Andersson, no. 59:1–125. Göteborg, Sweden: Department of Systematic Botany, University of Göteborg. WILLIAMS, G., P. ADAMS, AND L. A. MOUNDS. 2001. Thrips (Thysanoptera) pollination in Australian subtropical rain forest, with particular reference to pollination of *Wilkiea huegeliana* (Monimiaceae). *J. Nat. Hist.* 35:1–21.

MORACEAE (Mulberry Family)

C. C. BERG

Figure 129, Plate 31

- *plants usually woody, less often herbaceous; milky latex present*

- *stipules present, often conspicuous and/or fully encircling the twig*

- *leaves alternate (spiral or distichous), rarely opposite, simple*

- *flowers unisexual; perianth uniseriate or absent; stamens 1–4; gynoecium with 1 locule; placentation apical, the ovule 1*

- *fruits often enclosed by accrescent fleshy perianth or receptacle*

Numbers of genera and species. Worldwide, the Moraceae comprise 37 genera and approximately 1,050 species. In tropical America, there are 19 genera and approximately 270 species. The largest are *Ficus* with approximately 120 species in the neotropics (ca. 750 worldwide) and *Dorstenia* with 46 species (105 worldwide). Another large genus, *Artocarpus*, with more than 50 species, is confined to the Asian-Australasian region. The other genera have at most 25 species, and often have only one to three species.

Distribution and habitat. The Moraceae occur throughout the Tropics, with some taxa (*Morus*) extending to subtropical or northern warm temperate regions. In the neotropics, most tribes and genera are distinctly associated with the South American continent. There is less diversity in Central America and the Caribbean. Many Neotropical genera have distinct relationships with African Moraceae, e.g., *Dorstenia* is unique in showing two widely separated centers of diversity, eastern Brazil/the Greater Antilles/Central America and Africa. The tribe Moreae is largely concentrated in Central America and the northern Andes, an area that also shows a center of diversity for the tribe Ficeae (the genus *Ficus*). Both Neotropical Moreae and Ficeae show distinct relationships with Asian Moraceae.

Along with *Ficus*, many other woody Neotropical Moraceae (in total about 100 species) are important components of lowland rain forests, consequently, this family often ranks among the top tree families in species diversity and abundance of individuals in ecological studies, especially in western Amazonia.

Family classification. The Moraceae are placed in the Urticales by Cronquist, along with the Cecropiaceae, Ulmaceae, and Urticaceae. Molecular studies, however, suggest placing these families in the Rosales along with the Rosaceae and Rhamnaceae, and sometimes even the Elaeagnaceae. The family is characterized by the presence of milky latex and the apical position of the ovule.

The Moraceae are divided into five tribes: the Moreae, largely woody and characterized by staminate flowers with urticaceous features; the Dorstenieae, with *Dorstenia* largely herbaceous and characterized by basically bisexual inflorescences; the Castilleae, woody and characterized by unisexual involucrate inflorescences and self-pruning branches; the Ficeae, woody and characterized by urceolate to spherical inflorescences enclosing the flowers; and the Artocarpeae, woody and usually characterized by unisexual and structurally diverse inflorescences (in the neotropics, the staminate inflorescences are spicate to racemose with flowers that lack urticaceous features). All the tribes are pantropical, but Artocarpeae, Ficeae, and Moreae are most speciose and diverse in Asia-Australasia, the Castilleae are concentrated in the neotropics, and the Dorstenieae are about equally distributed in Africa and the neotropics.

The Cannabaceae (the hemp family) with two small genera, *Cannabis* (hemp) and *Humulus* (hop), were once regarded as a subfamily of Moraceae, but are now recognized as a distinct family that also may not belong to the Urticales.

Features of the family. Habit: trees, shrubs, subshrubs, less often lianas or herbs, the trees and shrubs terrestrial or hemiepiphytic; branches sometimes abscising (Castilleae), sometimes armed with thorns (*Maclura*) or prickles (*Poulsenia armata*). **Latex** present, milky, sometimes watery, often turning brownish when exposed to air (in Castilleae). **Stipules** present, often conspicuous (to 10 cm long in some *Ficus*), the bases often encircling stems, leaving circular scars, caducous, persistent (*Dorstenia*) or subpersistent. **Leaves** alter-

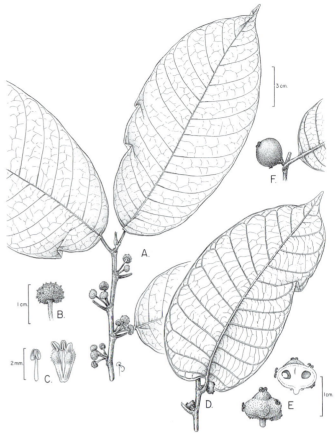

Figure 129. MORACEAE. *Maquira sclerophylla*. **A.** Stem with leaves and staminate inflorescences. **B.** Staminate inflorescence. **C.** Lateral views of staminate flower (right) and stamen (left). **D.** Stem with leaf and pistillate inflorescences. **E.** Lateral view (below) and medial section (above) of pistillate inflorescences. **F.** Lateral view of fruit on stem. Reprinted with permission from Mori et al. (2002). Artist: Bobbi Angell.

nate (spiral or distichous), rarely opposite (*Bagassa*), simple; blade margins usually entire, rarely spinose-dentate (species of *Sorocea* and *Clarisia ilicifolia*); venation usually pinnate, the lateral veins usually distinctly loop-connected near margin, sometimes (as in Moreae and Ficeae) the relatively well-developed basal lateral veins may depart at more acute angles than other veins (tending to tripliveined). **Inflorescences** usually axillary, sometimes ramiflorous or cauliflorous, often in pairs, unisexual or bisexual, racemes (e.g., *Sorocea*), spikes (e.g., staminate *Bagassa*), globose heads (e.g., pistillate *Bagassa*), capitate with a discoid receptacle, the receptacle sometimes convex, cup-shaped, bivalvate (*Castilla*), or urceolate to spherical with enclosed flowers (*Ficus*), involucral bracts sometimes present, the pistillate flowers free or fused with surrounding flowers and/or receptacle. **Flowers** actinomorphic, unisexual (plants monoecious, dioecious, or polygamous), usually 4-merous; perianth uniseriate or absent. **Staminate flowers:** tepals (0)4 or more (as in *Naucleopsis*), distinct or connate; stamens (1)4, antitepalous, straight or inflexed in bud, bending outward suddenly at anthesis; pistillodes sometimes present (as in genera with urticaceous flowers). **Pistillate flowers**: tepals (3)4, mostly connate; gynoecium with ovary free or fused to perianth, the carpels 2, the locule 1, the stigmas 1–2, usually elongate or filiform to band-shaped; placentation apical, the ovule 1. **Fruits** achenes (*Ficus*, but achenes inside fleshy spherical to urceolate receptacle, which serves as functional fruit), drupes (*Trophis involucrata*), or drupaceous (e.g., *Sorocea* and *Pseudolmedia*), enclosed in enlarged fleshy perianth or fleshy receptacle, often many-seeded fleshy structures (infructescences), the achenes often with sticky surface, the drupaceous structures often yellow to orange, less often blackish (as in *Sorocea*) or whitish (when dehiscent, *Dorstenia*), the dehiscent fruits with 2 valves, the exocarp turgid-fleshy, ejecting the kernels (endocarps). **Seeds** large or small; endosperm absent in large seeds (e.g., *Brosimum*) or present when seeds small (e.g., *Ficus*), the cotyledons sometimes unequal, 1 of the 2 strongly reduced in *Sorocea*.

Worldwide, about 50 percent of all *Ficus* (and thus about ⅓ of all woody Moraceae) are hemiepiphytic. The other 50 percent of the species of *Ficus* (and ⅔ of all woody Moraceae) are terrestrial trees, shrubs, or climbers.

Nearly 100 species, most belonging to *Dorstenia*, are herbaceous. In the neotropics, some nonforest species of *Dorstenia* are geophytic.

Species of the tribe Castilleae, common in various types of lowland forest, have a characteristic architecture. Typically, the leaves are spirally arranged on the trunk and erect branches, but the horizontal branches bear distichous leaves. These branches fall from the tree, sometimes still bearing green leaves, and leave concave abscission scars on the stem.

Inflorescences are diverse and can be very complex in structure. The staminate and pistillate inflorescences can be similar or very different in structure. In the bisexual inflorescences of the tribe Dorstenieae, the pistillate flower(s) is (are) immersed in the receptacle and the staminate ones are superficial. The number of flowers per inflorescence varies from thousands (in several species of *Ficus*) to just one. Uniflorous pistillate inflorescences are not uncommon, but uniflorous staminate ones are only found in species of *Perebea*.

Fruits enclosed by an enlarged fleshy perianth form, together with the fruit, a drupaceous structure or pseudodrupe. Pseudodrupes may be fused to form many seeded drupaceous structures (*Maquira pro parte*). The many-seeded infructescences of *Naucleopsis* are often spinose because of hardened tepals. If the pistillate flowers are fused with the receptacle, the receptacle may form the fleshy layer of a 1–many-seeded drupaceous structure (e.g., *Brosimum*), thus forming a pseudofruit composed of the true fruit(s), the perianth(s), the receptacle, and sometimes the bracts.

Natural history. Hemiepiphytic species of *Ficus* (approximately 100 in the neotropics) usually start their lives on the main branches or stems of trees. The young plant uses most of its resources to send an aerial root down to the forest floor, and, as soon as that has been achieved, the treelet receives the water and nutrients needed for more rapid growth. Additional aerial roots are produced; some grow down to the forest floor and others embrace the branches and/or trunk of the host tree for support. The aerial roots of some species of *Ficus* may form a network around the trunk of the host tree, sometimes forming a cylinder strong enough to support the tree when the host tree dies. This network of aerial roots may inhibit flow of water and nutrients to the host tree. Moreover, the crown of the fig competes with the host tree for light. Such competition is probably more important in killing the host tree than "strangulation," and, therefore, calling these plants "strangler figs" is more romantic than realistic. Many hemiepiphytic *Ficus* do not overcome their hosts, and only a few species (e.g., *F. gomelleira*, *F. nymphaeifolia*, and *F. schultesii*) are vigorous enough to overpower the host tree and survive as free-standing trees.

In a small number of species, pollination is carried out by the wind. The staminate flowers release their pollen explosively so it is exposed to weak air currents such as those found above the running water of forest streams. Wind pollination has been demonstrated in *Brosimum alicastrum* and may be expected in other species with catkinlike staminate inflorescences.

For species that lack morphological adaptations for wind pollination, occur in dense forest, and have condensed staminate inflorescences, some evidence indicates that pollination is carried out by small beetles and flies that use the inflorescences as breeding sites for their larvae. In many other cases, the pollination mechanism is not known.

The unique and complex pollination system in *Ficus* is well known. The urceolate to spherical inflorescences of *Ficus* have an apical opening (ostiole) more or less tightly closed by stiff bracts. The staminate and pistillate flowers are packed tightly on the inner surface of the inflorescence (syconium). The pistillate flowers have different style lengths, but due to compensating differences in the lengths of the pedicels, the stigmas are arranged at the same level and are coherent. In dioecious species of the Eastern Hemisphere (such as *Ficus carica*, the edible fig), the trees (and figs) with only long-styled pistillate flowers produce the seed, whereas those with short-styled pistillate flowers and staminate flowers are used as breeding sites for the fig wasp larvae and produce the pollen needed to pollinate the long-styled flowers.

In the neotropics, the pollinators are species of several genera of fig wasps (Agaonidae, Chalcidoidea, Hymenoptera) who grow and mate only within the fig. The winged females transport the pollen from an inflorescence that is releasing pollen to another with receptive stigmas. One or a few of these specialized insects usually manage to get through the barrier of bracts around the ostiole but lose their wings and parts of their antennae on the way in. When they reach the central cavity of the inflorescence, they lay eggs in the ovaries of flowers with short styles. Their ovipositors penetrate the style to reach the ovule. While they are laying eggs, pollen is deposited on the stigmas, either actively from pockets in the wasp's thorax in which pollen is stored or passively from the wasp's body (if pockets are lacking). The wasps die inside the fig, and the developing larvae consume the seed tissue of the short-styled flowers, which develop into gall fruits.

When seeds developing in the ovaries with long styles are nearly mature, the wasp larvae hatch into adults. The wingless and blind male wasps with well-developed mouth parts leave the gall fruits first. They bite an opening in the walls of the (gall) fruits containing the female insects and copulate with them while inside the fruit. The female insects either actively collect pollen from the staminate flowers and store it in pollen pockets or otherwise become dusted by pollen. The female wasps leave the inflorescences usually through tunnels made by the male fig wasps in the wall of the syconium or through the ostiole. After the pollinators have left, the wall of the syconium becomes softer, loses latex, and may change color, thus becoming attractive to animal dispersers.

In principle, each *Ficus* species has its own species of pollinator. The life span of the tiny female fig wasps is only a few days. After leaving a mature syconium, the female wasps are guided by chemical attractants to trees with receptive syconia. In order to sustain pollinators, species of *Ficus* provide syconia at all stages of development throughout the year. Individuals of Neotropical species generally flower simultaneously, each individual species with its own rhythm; consequently, individuals of different species are in flower and fruit throughout the year. Production of figs year-round provides an essential food source for many arboreal animals, and, therefore, figs are considered keystone food sources in Neotropical forests.

Most Moraceae produce fruits that are surrounded by a fleshy external layer. The fruit plus the surrounding tissue is consumed by birds, bats, and monkeys, the fruits are excreted, and the seeds are thus dispersed. In the neotropics, only the ballistically dispersed propagules of *Dorstenia* are dry.

Economic uses. Several tree species, such as *Brosimum guianense* and *B. rubescens*, provide timber for building furniture and making tools. *Bagassa guianensis* also provides good, durable timber.

Two species of *Castilla*, one occurring in Central America and the other in the Amazon Basin, yield a rubber that was economically important around the turn of the twentieth century. In northernmost Amazonian Brazil and the Pacific coastal region of Colombia and Ecuador, the latex of some species of *Naucleopsis* is used to prepare an arrow poison that affects the cardiac system and not the nervous system, as does the far more commonly used arrow poison curare of the Menispermaceae. A cardiac glycoside obtained from the related Paleotropical genus *Antiaris* also is used as an arrow poison in Asia.

The latex of some species of *Ficus* is used to treat intestinal worm infections; the latex of *Maclura tinctoria* is used to treat toothaches; and various species of *Dorstenia*, in particular *D. cayapia* and *D. contrajerva*, have broad medicinal applications.

A proteolytic enzyme called ficin is derived from the latex of *Ficus carica* and *F. glabrata*. Such enzymes are used in the food industry as ingredients in tenderizers and to produce protein hydrosylates. Some species of *Brosimum*, such as *B. potabile* and *B. utile* (cow tree), yield an abundant latex consumed by humans.

Bark fibers of *Poulsenia* are used to prepare bark cloth, and those of some species of *Ficus* are used to make *amate* paper in Mexico.

The seeds of *Brosimum alicastrum* (breadnut) are eaten, boiled, roasted, or ground into a flour to make bread or tortillas that provided an important food source for Maya Indians. Several Paleotropical Moraceae have been introduced into the neotropics as fruit trees. The seedless variety of *Artocarpus altilis* (breadfruit) is baked, boiled, or fried and eaten in much the same way as potatoes are. The seed-containing variety of the same species is prized for its edible seeds. Both the aril and seeds of *Artocarpus heterophyllus* (jak or jackfruit) are eaten.

Species of *Ficus* are grown widely as ornamentals and houseplants. Because of the absence of their pollinators, introduced species of *Ficus* generally cannot reproduce. However, pollinators that recently arrived have become established, and some of the introduced figs have become naturalized (as in Florida) and, therefore, have the potential of becoming pests.

References. BERG, C. C. 1972. Olmedieae and Brosimeae (Moraceae). *Fl. Neotrop. Monogr.* 7:1–228. BERG, C. C. 1989. Systematics and phylogeny of the Urticales. In *Evolution, Systematics, and Fossil History of the Hamamelidae*, 'Higher' Hamamelidae, eds. P.R. Crane and S. Blackmore, 2:193–220. Oxford, U.K.: Clarendon Press. BERG, C. C. 1992. Moraceae. In *Flora of the Guianas*, ed. A.R.A. Görts-van Rijn, ser. A, fasc. 11:10–92. Koenigstein, Germany: Koeltz Scientific Books. BERG, C. C. 2001. Moreae, Artocarpeae, *Dorstenia* (Moraceae). With introductions to the family and *Ficus* and with additions and corrections to Flora Neotropica Monograph 7. *Fl. Neotrop. Mongr.* 83:1–346. BERG, C. C., AND J. E. SIMONIS. 2000. Moraceae. In *Flora de Venezuela*, ed. R. Riina, 5–189. Caracas: Fundación Instituto Botánico de Venezuela. BURGER, W. C. 1977. Flora Costaricensis: Moraceae. *Fieldiana Bot.* 40:95–215. CORRERA Q., J. E., AND H. Y. BERNAL. 1995. Moraceae. In *Especies vegetales promisorias de los países del Convenio Andrés Bello*, Tomo XI. Santafé de Bogotá, D. E., Colombia: Secretaria Ejecutiva del Convenio Andrés Bello.

MUNTINGIACEAE

Nᴀᴛʜᴀɴ Sᴍɪᴛʜ

Figure 130

- *trees or shrubs*

- *stellate trichomes often present*

- *stipules usually present, peltate in* Dicraspidia

- *leaves alternate (distichous), simple; blade base asymmetrical, cordate; venation palmate*

- *flowers actinomorphic; stamens numerous; locules usually 5–many*

- *fruits indehiscent, berrylike*

Numbers of genera and species. Restricted to tropical America, the Muntingiaceae comprise two or three genera, each with a single species.

Distribution and habitat. *Muntingia calabura* has a wide distribution in tropical America and has been introduced to the paleotropics; *Dicraspidia donnell-smithii* is known from Colombia, Panama, Costa Rica, and Honduras; and *Neotessmannia uniflora* is known from one location in eastern Peru.

The Muntingiaceae are found in a variety of habitats. *Muntingia* is found in dry, semideciduous, and evergreen forests. Both *Muntingia* and *Dicraspidia* can be found along rivers and in other disturbed areas such as roadsides.

Family classification. Although the Muntingiaceae are a recently recognized clade within the Malvales, further investigation of this group is still needed. Based on the absence of data, the placement of *Neotessmannia* within the Muntingiaceae remains suspect. Traditionally, *Muntingia* was placed within families such as the Elaeocarpacae and Flacourtiaceae (*sensu* Cronquist), and all three genera have been placed in the Tiliacae (*sensu* Takhtajan). Morphological and molecular data do not support the Elaeocarpaceae and Flacourtiaceae as being close to the Muntingiaceae. Although some authors suggest that the Muntingiaceae appear similar to the Tiliaceae, the two families differ in, for example, indument, stipules, leaves, inflorescence, and flower morphology, and the Muntingiaceae lack the mucilage canals or cavities common to the Tiliaceae. Instead, these morphological and molecular studies propose that the Muntingiaceae are near the Cistaceae, Dipterocarpaceae, and Sarcolaenaceae, and more distantly related to the traditional Malvales.

Features of the family. Habit: trees or shrubs. **Indument** of simple, stellate, and glandular trichomes. **Stipules** present (unknown for *Neotessmannia*), often solitary (*Muntingia*) or

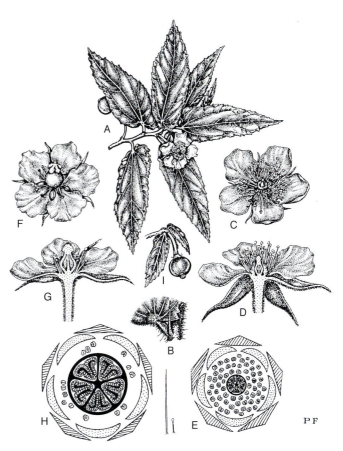

Figure 130. MUNTINGIACEAE. *Muntingia calabura*. **A.** Stem with leaves and flower (x½). **B.** Node showing stipule and trichomes (above, x1½) and trichomes from stem (below, x10). **C.** Apical view of staminate flower (x1½). **D.** Medial section of staminate flower (x1½). **E.** Floral diagram of staminate flower. **F.** Apical view of bisexual flower (x1½). **G.** Medial section of bisexual flower (x1½). **H.** Floral diagram of bisexual flower. **I.** Stem with leaves and fruit (x1½). Reprinted with permission from Correll and Correll (1982). Artist: Priscilla Fawcett.

2 in dimorphic pairs (1 stipule peltate and often leaflike) in *Dicraspidia*. **Leaves** alternate, distichous, simple; blade base asymmetrical, cordate, the margins serrate; venation palmate. **Inflorescences** supra-axillary, solitary or few-flowered. **Flowers** actinomorphic, usually bisexual; calyx of (4)5(7) sepals, the sepals valvate, basally connate, forming broad cuplike tube; corolla ± crumpled in bud, the petals (4)5(7), imbricate, distinct, longer than sepals, white to pink (*Muntingia*) or yellow; androecium usually of numerous stamens, the filaments filiform, distinct or nearly so, the anthers dehiscing by longitudinal slits (sometimes only apically in *Dicraspidia*); disclike structure (receptacle) surrounding gynoecium in *Muntingia*, nectariferous; gynoecium syncarpous, the ovary superior (*Muntingia*), subinferior (*Dicraspidia*), or inferior (*Neotessmannia*), the carpels 5(6–7), the locules 5–many,

sometimes apically unilocular, the style thick, the stigma lobed to decurrent; ovules numerous, pendulous (unknown for *Neotessmannia*). **Fruits** indehiscent (unknown for *Neotessmannia*), berrylike, often reddish at maturity. **Seeds** numerous per fruit.

Natural history. Reports suggest that *Muntingia calabura* usually is pollinated by bees, but many other insects, including moths and butterflies, visit the flowers. *Muntingia* is thought to produce flowers and fruits simultaneously on the same individual throughout the year. One study proposed that the genus has evolved to display its flowers above the branches. However, within days of anthesis, the pollinated flowers move below the branches and leaves, so the fruits are displayed in a different position.

In Costa Rica, the fruits of *Muntingia* are known to be dispersed by at least six species of birds, including the orange-chinned parakeet (*Brotogeris jugularis*) and the scrub euphonia (*Euphonia affinis*); six species of bat, including the short-tailed leaf-nosed bat (*Carollia perspicillata*) and the common long-tongued bat (*Glossophaga soricina*); white-throated capuchin (*Cebus capuchinus*) and spider monkies (*Ateles geoffroyi*); the white-nosed coati (*Nasua narica*); and the variegated squirrel (*Sciurus variegatoides*).

Economic uses. *Muntingia calabura* is used ornamentally. The fruits of this species are edible, and the species has been introduced into the paleotropics for this reason.

References. BAYER, C. 2003. Muntingiaceae. In *The Families and Genera of Vascular Plants*, eds. K. Kubitzki and C. Bayer. 5:315–19. Berlin: Springer-Verlag. BAYER, C., M. W. CHASE, AND M. F. FAY. 1998. Muntingiaceae, a new family of dicotyledons with malvalean affinities. *Taxon* 47:37–42. BAYER, C, M. F. FAY, A. Y. DE BRUIJN, V. SAVOLAINEN, C. M. MORTON, ET AL. 1999. Support for an expanded family concept of Malvaceae within a recircumscribed order Malvales: a combined analysis of plastid *atp*B and *rbc*L DNA sequences. *Bot. J. Linn. Soc.* 129:267–303. CORRERA Q., J. E., AND H. Y. BERNAL. 1992. Elaeocarpaceae. In *Especies vegetales promisorias de los países del Convenio Andrés Bello*, Tomo VII. Santafé de Bogotá, D. E., Colombia: Secretaria Ejecutiva del Convenio Andrés Bello. FLEMING, T. H., C. F. WILLIAMS, F. J. BONACCORSO, AND L. H. HERBST. 1985. Phenology, seed dispersal, and colonization in *Muntingia calabura*, a Neotropical pioneer tree. *Amer. J. Bot.* 72(3): 383–91. WEBB, C. J. 1984. Flower and fruit movements in *Muntingia calabura*: a possible mechanism for avoidance of pollinator-disperser interference. *Biotropica* 16(1):37–42.

MYOPORACEAE (Myoporum Family)

THOMAS A. ZANONI

Figure 131

- *trees*
- *leaves alternate, simple; blades pellucid punctate*
- *flowers zygomorphic; staminode 1, adnate to upper corolla lip, bearded*
- *fruits drupaceous*

Numbers of genera and species. Worldwide, the Myoporaceae comprise three genera and about 120 species. Only *Bontia daphnoides* is found in tropical America. In the Eastern Hemisphere, *Myoporum* has about 30 species and *Eremophilia* has about 90 species.

Distribution and habitat. The Myoporaceae are pantropical. *Bontia daphnoides* is found on the West Indian Islands from the Cayman Islands to the Netherlands Antilles and is possibly also native to Guyana and Venezuela.

Bontia daphnoides is a coastal species often growing in sand on saline soils, and on limestone rock with little soil.

Family classification. The Myoporaceae are placed in the Scrophulariales by Cronquist. Molecular analyses place *Myoporum* within an unresolved Lamiales. No formal subdivisions of the family are recognized.

Features of the family. Habit: small trees, usually branching just above ground; hairs often present, simple; secretory cavities scattered on herbaceous stems and leaves. **Stipules** absent. **Leaves** alternate, simple; blades pellucid punctate, the margins entire or toothed. **Inflorescences** axillary, cymes, or of solitary flowers. **Flowers** zygomorphic, bisexual; calyx synsepalous, the sepal lobes 5, imbricate or open; corolla bilabiate, fused into tube yellow, the lobes 5; androecium of 4 stamens, the stamens adnate to corolla tube, alternating with petal lobes; staminode 1 (sometimes present), adnate to

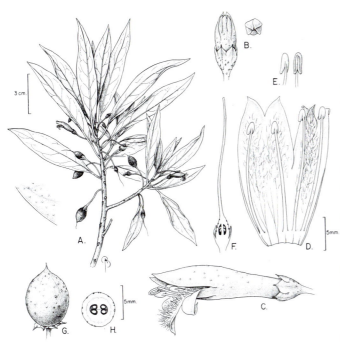

Figure 131. MYOPORACEAE. *Bontia daphnoides*. **A.** Stem with leaves, flowers, developing fruits, and detail of abaxial leaf surface showing punctations. **B.** Lateral (left) and apical (right) views of flower buds. **C.** Lateral view of flower. **D.** Corolla opened to show adnate stamens. **F.** Medial section of pistil subtended by calyx. **G.** Lateral view of fruit. **H.** Transverse section of fruit. Reprinted with permission from Acevedo-Rodríguez (1996). Artist: Bobbi Angell.

upper corolla lip, bearded; gynoecium syncarpous, the ovary superior, the carpels 2, the locules 2, sometimes appearing as 4–10 because of supernumerary partitions, the style 1, the stigma simple; placentation apical, the ovules 1–8 per locule, pendulous, anatropous. **Fruits** drupaceous, pulp surrounding stone thin, fleshy to dry, the stone 2 or 4 celled, or sometimes separating into 1-seeded drupelike segments. **Seeds** 1–4 per cell, small; endosperm absent or nearly absent.

Natural history. Hummingbirds have been observed visiting the flowers of cultivated plants in Florida. The bright-yellow, fleshy fruit suggests that dispersal may be by birds, but many fruits fall directly below the plants and may be transported by water when high or storm tides reach them.

Economic uses. Members of the family are cultivated occasionally as ornamental plants in the subtropics; e.g., *Bontia daphnoides* in the Western Hemisphere.

References. CARLQUIST, S., AND D. A HOEKMAN. 1986. Wood anatomy of Myoporaceae: ecological and systematic considerations. *Aliso* 11(3):317–34. OLMSTEAD, R. G., AND P. A. REEVES. 1995. Evidence for the polyphyly of the Scrophulariaceae based on chloroplast *rbc*L and *ndh*F sequences. *Ann. Missouri Bot. Gard.* 82:176–93. ZONA, S. 1998. The Myoporaceae in the southeastern United States. *Harvard Pap. Bot.* 3:171–79.

MYRICACEAE (Bayberry Family)

ANDREW S. ROBERTS

Figure 132

- *small trees and shrubs, often aromatic*
- *leaves alternate, simple*
- *inflorescences catkins*
- *flowers unisexual; perianth absent*
- *fruits drupes or nutlets, sometimes enveloped by accrescent bracts, sometimes covered by waxy layer*

Number of genera and species. Worldwide, the Myricaceae comprise three genera and 40–55 species. In tropical America, there is a single genus, *Myrica*, and about 12 species.

Distribution and habitat. The Myricaceae are found on all of the major land masses except Australia and New Zealand.

The majority of species occur in temperate and subtropical regions, and the family is most diverse in southern Africa.

In the neotropics, the Myricaceae are most often found in montane forests, cloud forests, and *páramos*. They are seldom found in lowland forests. Species of Myricaceae often occur in disturbed habitats.

Family classification. The Myricaceae are placed in the monofamilial order Myricales by Cronquist. Morphological and molecular analyses place the family near the Juglandaceae.

There are two natural groups within the genus *Myrica* that are distinguished by bud and leaf characters, inflorescence insertion, stamen number, and the structure of the ovaries and fruit. Some authors have argued that these groups should be recognized as individual genera, and others have considered them as subgenera or sections. Subsequent to the prepa-

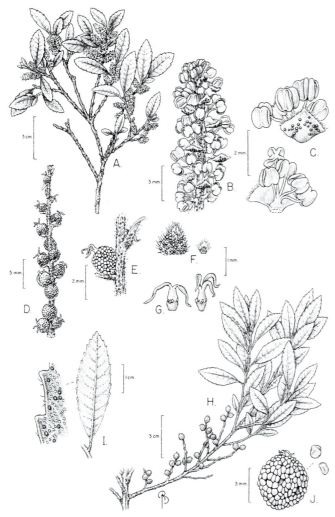

staminate flowers or single bract subtending pistillate flowers; bracteoles sometimes present in pairs subtending staminate flowers or often 2 or more subtending pistillate flowers. **Flowers** unisexual (plants monoecious or dioecious), small; perianth absent. **Staminate flowers:** androecium of 2–8(20) stamens, the stamens usually 4, in a single whorl, the anthers extrorse, dehiscing by longitudinal slits. **Pistillate flowers:** gynoecium syncarpous, the ovary superior, the carpels 2, the locule 1, the styles distinct or connate near base; placentation basal, the ovule 1, orthotropous. **Fruits** drupes or nutlets, sometimes enveloped by accrescent bracteoles, sometimes covered by waxy layer. **Seeds** with minimal endosperm, if any, the embryo straight.

Natural history. Many Myricaceae form relationships with the nitrogen-fixing bacterium *Frankia*. This gives them a competitive advantage in nutrient-poor habitats, such as sand dunes and boggy areas. Some species of *Myrica* have developed anti-geotrophism at the tips of root nodule lobes and branch roots, extensive internal air spaces, and large bracts that adhere to the fruit and facilitate flotation as adaptations for growing in poorly drained areas. Like other families in the Hamamelidae, the Myricaceae are wind-pollinated. The seeds are dispersed by fruit-eating birds or some fruits float and are dispersed by water.

Economic uses. In the neotropics, the waxy vegetable tallow that coats the fruits of some species of *Myrica* was a source of wax for candle production. To collect the wax, the fruits were gathered and boiled, and the wax then was skimmed off the top of the boiling water. Candles made of bayberry wax (also called myrtle wax or *cera de laurel*) were important sources of illumination in colonial North and South America. As recently as the beginning of the twentieth century, bayberry wax was imported regularly from South America and southern Africa to be traded in New England.

In northern Europe, *Myrica gale* has a long history of use, serving as a flavoring for beer, a source of yellow dye for wool, and as protection against witches. Currently, researchers in Scotland are exploring the prospects of large-scale cultivation of *M. gale* to produce steam-distilled volatile oil for use as an insect repellent. Some species of *Myrica* have minor medicinal uses.

References. BAIRD, J. R. 1969. A taxonomic revision of the plant family Myricaceae of North America, north of Mexico. Unpublished thesis, University of North Carolina, Chapel Hill. BERNAL, H. Y., AND J. E. CORRERA Q. 1998. Myricaceae (*Myrica pubescens*). In *Especies vegetales promisorias de los países del Convenio Andrés Bello*, Tomo XII. Santafé de Bogotá, D. E., Colombia: Secretaria Ejecutiva del Convenio Andrés Bello. CHEVALIER, A. 1901. Monographie des Myricacées. *Mem. Soc. Nat. Cherbourg* 32:85–340. GOLDBERG, A. 1986. *Classification, Evolution and Phylogeny of the Families of Dicotyledons*. Washington, D.C.: Smithsonian Institution Press. MACDONALD, A. D. 1989. The morphology and rela-

Figure 132. MYRICACEAE. *Morella chevalieri* (= *Myrica* species in this book). **A.** Stem with leaves and staminate inflorescences. **B.** Staminate inflorescence. **C.** Adaxial (below) and abaxial (above) views of staminate flowers. **D.** Pistillate inflorescence. **E.** Part of inflorescence with immature fruit and pistillate flower. **F.** Primary (left) and secondary (right) bracts. **G.** Gynoecium with two styles, the normal condition for family (left) and gynoecium with three styles (right). **H.** Stem with leaves and infructescences. **I.** Leaf and detail of margin and abaxial surface showing peltate scales (far left). **J.** Lateral view of fruit and detail of warty protuberances (above). Reprinted with permission from Parra-O. (2000). Artist: Bobbi Angell.

ration of this treatment, Parra-O transferred some tropical American species of *Myrica* into the genus *Morella*.

Features of the family. Habit: small trees and shrubs, often evergreen, often aromatic. **Indument:** trichomes often present, distinctive and of two forms: one elongate, colorless and unicellular, the other peltate and glandular, often with a multicellular head and multicellular, basally embedded stalk. **Stipules** absent. **Leaves** alternate, simple; blades with margins entire, serrate, irregularly dentate, or lobed; venation pinnate. **Inflorescences** axillary, catkins; bracts subtending tionships of the Myricaceae. In *Evolution, Systematics and Fossil History of the Hamamelidae: Higher Hamamelidae*, eds. P. R. Crane and S. Blackmore, 2:147–65. Oxford: Systematics Association Special Volume no. 40B, Clarendon Press. PARRA-O, C. 2002 (issued 2003). New combinations in South American Myricaceae. *Brittonia* 54(4):322–26. SIMPSON, M.J.A., D. F. MACINTOSH, J. B. CLOUGHLEY, AND A. E. STUART. 1996. Past, present and future utilization of *Myrica gale* (Myricaceae). *Econ. Bot.* 50(1):122–29. SUD-BERG, M. D. 1985. Pollen of the Myricaceae. *Pollen & Spores* 27(1):15–28. WEBSTER, G. L. 1995. Panorama of tropical cloud forests. In *Biodiversity and Conservation of Neotropical Montane Forests*, eds. S. P. Churchill, H. Balslev, E. Forero, and J. L. Luteyn, 53–77. Bronx, NY: New York Botanical Garden. WILBUR, R. L. 1994. The Myricaceae of the United States and Canada: Genera, subgenera and series. *Sida* 16(1):93–107. WILLIAMS, L. O. 1957. Bayberry wax and bayberries. *Econ. Bot.* 12(1):103–07.

MYRISTICACEAE (Nutmeg Family)

THOMAS K. WILSON

Figure 133, Plate 32

- *trees, sometimes shrubs*

- *plants usually with reddish exudate in trunk*

- *myristicaceous branching present*

- *leaves alternate (distichous), simple*

- *flowers unisexual (plants usually dioecious); androphore usually present*

- *fruits usually dehiscent, 1-seeded, the seeds usually arillate*

Numbers of genera and species. Worldwide, the Myristicaceae comprise 19 genera and about 400 species. In tropical America, there are five genera and 84 species. *Compsoneura* has 12 species, *Iryanthera* 24 species, *Osteophloeum* one species, *Otoba* six species, and *Virola* 45 species. A sixth monotypic genus, *Bicuiba*, is segregated from *Virola* by some authors.

Distribution and habitat. The Myristicaceae are a large pantropical family. *Compsoneura* is found in Central and northern South America; *Iryanthera* in northern South America and Panama; *Osteophloeum* in northern South America; *Otoba* in Central and northern South America; and *Virola*, in tropical South and Central America.

The family is found mainly in low-elevation rain forests and is an important component of Amazonian forests.

Family classification. The Myristicaceae are placed in the Magnoliales by Cronquist. There is little doubt that this family is in the magnolialean complex, but beyond that there is little uniformity of opinion. The family shares some characters with the Canellaceae (androphore and some similarity in seed structure), but if the Myristicaceae are related to the Canellaceae it is not a close relationship. The Myristicaceae

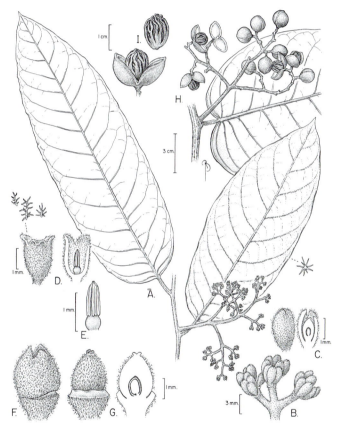

Figure 133. MYRISTICACEAE. *Virola sebifera*. **A.** Stem with leaves and inflorescence and enlargement of stellate hair from abaxial leaf surface (right). **B.** Part of inflorescence. **C.** Lateral view (left) and medial section of pistillate flower (right). **D.** Lateral view (left) showing enlargement of dendritic hairs on perianth and medial section (right) of staminate flower. **E.** Lateral view of staminate flower with perianth removed. **F.** Lateral view of developing fruit with perianth beginning to abscise. **G.** Lateral view of fruit after perianth has fallen (left) and medial section of immature fruit (right). **H.** Stem with base of leaf and infructescence. **I.** Lateral view of dehisced fruit with seed (below) and seed covered with laciniate aril (above). Reprinted with permission from Mori et al. (2002). Artist: Bobbi Angell.

and Annonaceae also share some characters, but again the relationship is not close. Recent molecular studies suggest that the Myristicaceae may be part of a clade consisting of Eupomatiaceae-Himantandraceae and Annonaceae-Degeneriaceae. These molecular studies, while suggesting some very interesting associations, are based on a very limited number of samples; for example, molecular data from the Myristicaceae was obtained from one sample of *Knema latericia*.

At one time, all species were classified in *Myristica*, an indication of the close uniformity of both floral and vegetative structure throughout the family. Since the early 1900s, the family has been divided into many genera, based mainly on the structure of the male flower, aril, and inflorescence. Of particular importance is the number and arrangement of the stamens. The androecium in flowers of *Compsoneura* varies from a short androphore and four distinct anthers to an elongate androphore with ten connate anthers; *Osteophloeum* has filaments fused into an elongate androphore and 12–20 anthers; *Otoba* has filaments fused to an elongate androphore and 3(4) apically distinct anthers; *Virola* has filaments fused into a androphore and 4–6 anthers, which are sometimes apically distinct; and *Iryanthera* has fused filaments and 3 or 4 anthers.

Features of the family. Habit: trees, sometimes shrubs, usually evergreen; ethereal oil cells present, emitting ranalean odor (perfumy and/or turpentiney) when leaves and twigs crushed; myristicaceous branching present. **Exudate** present, usually reddish in trunk, translucent to pink in stems. **Indument**: vegetative and reproductive parts glabrous or commonly with 2-5-branched, translucent to reddish-brown trichomes, the trichomes sometimes glandular within flowers. **Stipules** absent. **Leaves** alternate (distichous), regularly spaced, simple; blade margins entire. **Inflorescences** usually terminal, sometimes cauliflorous, racemes, corymbs, or very complex. **Flowers** actinomorphic, unisexual (plants usually dioecious), small (usually <5 mm); perianth uniseriate, urceolate, in 1 whorl; tepals 3 (not easily distinguished prior to flowering) small, thick, fleshy, valvate, white to creamy-green to yellow, sometimes greenish, connate to varying degrees, the apex distinct, reflexed when open; androphore usually present, the anthers 4–20, sometimes distinct at apex, dehiscing longitudinally (extrorse); gynoecium flask-shaped, the ovary superior, the locule 1, the style short or absent, the stigma 2-lobed; placentation subbasal to basal, the ovule 1, anatropous. **Fruits** dehiscent (often referred to as a capsule or dehiscent berry) or rarely indehiscent, large (4–5 cm diameter), the outer husk thick, 2–4 valved. **Seeds** 1 per fruit, large, usually enveloped by aril, the aril a fingerlike network of red to crimson, pink, or sometimes white tissue.

The "Ranalean odor" of Myristicaceae is produced by ethereal oil cells in the leaves and twigs. The odor is quite perfumy and or turpentiney. Canals in the bark produce a reddish, sometimes clear exudate, called "kino," which is one of the diagnostic characters of the family.

Natural history. Pollination of some species has been found to be accomplished by small, diverse insects. The lipid rich arils are favorite foods of many birds, including toucans and trogons, which presumable disperse the seeds. Monkeys have been observed feeding on the arils of *Virola*.

Economic uses. The name "nutmeg," applied to the spice as well as to the plant that produces it, is derived from the Latin *meg* for musk, referring to the musky aroma of the seeds.

The most important products of the family are the spices nutmeg (the whole or grated seed) and mace (the ground aril). The original home of the nutmeg of commerce, *Myristica fragrans*, is the Moluccas Islands. It was cultivated there by the Portuguese as early as 1512. When the Dutch drove the Portuguese out in the early 1600s, they tried to maintain a nutmeg trade monopoly, but fruit pigeons carried the seeds to neighboring islands, and the monopoly dissolved. By the middle 1800s, nutmeg seeds had been introduced into the West Indies. Today, most of the world's supplies of nutmegs and mace come from this region, chiefly Grenada. The seeds are rich in fat (24–30%), are used in making perfume and candles, and are often eaten.

Many Myristicaceae produce indole alkaloids of the beta-carboline and tryptamine subgroups. The exudate obtained from the bark of several species of *Virola* is reported to be hallucinogenic. A snuff is made from this material by some South American Indians. *Myristica fragrans* is also supposed to have hallucinogenic properties, however, this has been subsequently debated by Gils and Cox. Several medical reports exist of people who have "overdosed" on ground nutmeg.

Generally, the wood of the Myristicaceae is of little value because it has a high moisture content and is mostly sapwood. However, the wood of *Virola surinamensis* is used widely in plywood construction, and blow guns are crafted from some species of *Iryanthera*. In some regions, such as Amazonian Peru, species of *Iryanthera*, *Otoba*, and *Virola* have become part of the timber trade.

References. BERNAL, H. Y., AND J. E. CORRERA Q. 1998. Myristicaceae (*Iryanthera laevis*). In *Especies vegetales promisorias de los países del Convenio Andrés Bello*, Tomo XII. Santafé de Bogotá, D. E., Colombia: Secretaria Ejecutiva del Convenio Andrés Bello. GILS, C. G., AND P. A. COX. 1994. Ethnobotany of nutmeg in the Spice Islands. *J. Ethno-Pharmacol.* 42:117–24. IGERSHEIM, A., AND ENDRESS, P. K. 1997. Gynoecium diversity and systematics of the Magnoliales and winteroids. *Bot. J. Linn. Soc.* 124:213–71. KÜHN, U., AND K. KUBITZKI. 1993. Myristicaceae. In *The Families and Genera of Vascular Plants*, eds. K. Kubitzki, J. G. Rohwer, and V. Bittrich, 2:457–67. New York: Springer-Verlag. QIU, Y.-L., M. CHASE, D. H. LES, AND C. R. PARKS. 1993. Molecular phylogenetics of the Magnoliidae: cladistic analyses of nucleotide sequences of the plastid gene rbcL. *Ann. Missouri Bot. Gard.* 80:587–606.

MYRSINACEAE (Myrsine Family)

Bertil Ståhl

Figure 134, Plate 32

- *shrubs, trees, sometimes subshrubs, sometimes epiphytes*
- *leaves alternate, sometimes pseudoverticillate, simple*
- *leaves, flowers, and fruits with secretory cavities, these appearing as dark dots or lines*
- *flowers with free-central placentation*
- *fruits drupes*

Numbers of genera and species. Worldwide, the Myrsinaceae comprise 30–50 genera and an estimated 1,250 species. In tropical America, there are about 15 genera and 400 species. The largest genera are *Ardisia* (also in the Eastern Hemisphere), *Cybianthus* (including *Conomorpha*, *Grammadenia*, and *Weigeltia*), *Geissanthus*, *Myrsine* (also in the Eastern Hemisphere; including *Rapanea*), *Parathesis*, *Stylogyne*, and *Wallenia*. The largest genus, *Ardisia*, has been split into a dozen segregate genera, few of which have been accepted.

Distribution and habitat. The Myrsinaceae occur throughout the Tropics and subtropics of the world and have a few representatives in warm temperate areas. Most large genera have a wide Neotropical distribution, but some are more restricted, such as *Wallenia* (Caribbean), *Geissanthus* (Andean), and *Parathesis* (mainly Mesoamerican). In the neotropics, the family is found primarily in humid and wet areas.

The Myrsinaceae are most diversified in montane forests, where species are found at elevations up to 4,000 meters. They often constitute an important element of the tree and shrub flora in montane forests, whereas in low-elevation forests they grow mostly as understory shrubs.

Family classification. The Myrsinaceae are placed in the Primulales by Cronquist. The family is usually considered closely related to the Theophrastaceae, but recent phylogenetic studies suggest that they are more closely related to groups within the Primulaceae.

Traditionally, the Myrsinaceae are divided into two subfamilies, the Maesoideae, including the genus *Maesa* (Eastern Hemisphere), and the Myrsinoideae, including the rest of the family. Myrsinoideae are further divided into two tribes, the Ardisieae, with many ovules arranged in two or more series on the placenta, and Myrsineae, with a single series of ovules on the placenta. It is evident, however, that this classification is largely artificial. *Maesa* is only distantly related to other Myrsinaceae and has recently been placed in

Figure 134. MYRSINACEAE. *Ardisia guianensis*. **A.** Stem with leaves and inflorescences and detail of abaxial surface of leaf showing secretory cavities (above). **B.** Detail of inflorescence showing flowers in various stages with secretory cavities. **C.** Lateral view of corolla opened to show adnation of stamens. **D.** Lateral view of gynoecium in persistent calyx with two sepals removed. **E.** Abaxial (left) and adaxial (right) views of anthers. **F.** Placenta with ovules (left) and lateral view of gynoecium with medial section of ovary (right). **G.** Infructescence (left) and lateral view of fruit showing secretory cavityies (right). Reprinted with permission from Mori et al. (2002). Artist: Bobbi Angell.

its own family (Maesaceae), and some genera placed in the Myrsineae are certainly most closely related to groups in the Ardisieae.

Features of the family. Habit: subshrubs, shrubs, or small to medium-sized trees, evergreen, sometimes epiphytes (e.g., *Cybianthus* subg. *Grammadenia*); secretory cavities present, the cavities appearing as dark dots or lines on leaves, flowers, and fruits. Stipules absent. Leaves alternate or sometimes pseudoverticillate, simple; petioles usually short, occasionally absent; blades often coriaceous, the margins entire or variously serrate. Inflorescences terminal or axillary, panicles (*Ardisia* and *Geissanthus*), racemes (some *Cybianthus* and *Wallenia*), or fascicles (*Myrsine*); bract 1, subtending flowers. Flowers actinomorphic, bisexual or unisexual (the plants dioecious or gynodioecious), usually small, usually 4- or 5-merous; sepals (3)4–5; corolla usually sympetalous the petals (3)4–5, often white, pink, or greenish, the surfaces sometimes ± granular (caused by minute trichomes; *Parathesis* and many *Cybianthus*), the lobes contorted or imbricate in bud, often strongly recurved at anthesis; stamens equal in number and opposite petals, the filaments often more or less adnate to corolla tube, frequently short, but in some genera (e.g., *Geissanthus*) long, the anthers included or sometimes exserted and versatile, dehiscing longitudinally with introrse slits or by apical pores; gynoecium syncarpous, the ovary superior, the carpels probably 5, the locule 1, the style short or long, the stigma ± truncate; placentation free-central, the ovules few to many. **Fruits** drupes, globose, small, the mesocarp variously thick, juicy, usually turning red or black at maturity, the endocarp woody. **Seeds** 1, globose or slightly ovoid, smooth or rugose (ruminate), usually with an immersed hilum.

Some species of *Cybianthus* are monocaulous, with the leaves clustered at the top of the stem.

Natural history. Very little is known about the reproductive biology of the family. Most species seem to be pollinated by insects, and the fruits are usually dispersed by birds. Autogamy has been documented in *Ardisia* and may occur in other genera as well.

Economic use. The family is of little economic importance. Locally, the wood of several species is used for construction, and fruits with thick mesocarps are often eaten. Species of *Ardisia* are cultivated as ornamentals.

References. ANDERBERG, A. A., AND B. STÅHL 1995. Phylogenetic interrelationships in the order Primulales, with special emphasis on the family circumscriptions. *Canad. J. Bot.* 73:1699–730. AGOSTINI, G. 1980. Una nueva clasificación del genero *Cybianthus* (Myrsinaceae). *Acta Bot. Venez.* 10: 129–85. LUNDELL, C. L. 1966. Myrsinaceae. In Flora of Guatemala, eds. P. C. Standley and L. O. Williams, *Fieldiana Bot.* 24(8):135–200. LUNDELL, C. L. 1966. The genus *Parathesis* of the Myrsinaceae. *Contr. Texas Res. Found., Bot. Stud.* 5:1–206. LUNDELL, C. L. 1971. Myrsinaceae. In Flora of Panama, ed. R. E. Woodson. *Ann. Missouri Bot. Gard.* 58:285–353. PASCARELLA, J. B. 1997. Breeding systems of *Ardisia* Sw. (Myrsinaceae). *Brittonia* 49:45–53. PIPOLY, J. J. 1987. A systematic revision of the genus *Cybianthus* subgenus *Grammadenia* (Myrsinaceae). *Mem. New York Bot. Gard.* 43:1–76. PIPOLY, J. J. 1992a. The genus *Geissanthus* (Myrsinaceae) in the Chocó floristic province. *Novon* 3:463–74. PIPOLY, J. J. 1992b. The genus *Cybianthus* subgenus *Conomorpha* (Myrsinaceae) in Guayana. *Ann. Missouri Bot. Gard.* 79:908–57. PIPOLY, J. J. 1998. The genus *Cybianthus* (Myrsinaceae) in Ecuador and Peru. *Sida* 18:1–160. STEARN, W. T. 1969. A synopsis of Jamaican Myrsinaceae. *Bull. Brit. Mus (Nat. Hist.) Bot.* 4:145–78.

MYRTACEAE (Myrtle Family)

MARIA LÚCIA KAWASAKI AND BRUCE K. HOLST

Figures 135, 136; Plate 32

- *trees and shrubs*

- *leaves usually opposite, simple; blades typically glandular-punctate, often emitting spicy aroma when crushed*

- *flowers usually with white petals; stamens often many; ovary inferior*

- *fruits usually berries*

Numbers of genera and species. Worldwide, the Myrtaceae comprise approximately 100 genera and 3,000–3,500 species. In the Western Hemisphere, there are about 30 genera and 1,500 or more species. The largest genera in the Western Hemisphere are *Eugenia* (ca. 500 species), *Myrcia* (ca. 400), *Calyptranthes* (ca. 100), and *Psidium* (ca. 100). Three genera in the Western Hemisphere are monotypic: *Accara elegans*, *Myrrhinium atropurpureum*, and *Tepualia stipularis*.

Distribution and habitat. The Myrtaceae are found throughout tropical and subtropical regions of the world, with most species concentrated in tropical America and Australia. The large native genera are widespread in the neotropics. The two Neotropical genera with the most restricted geographical distribution are *Accara*, endemic to high-montane habitats of southeastern Brazil, and *Tepualia*, found in similar habitats in Chile and Argentina. *Myrcianthes fragrans* occurs farther

Figure 135. MYRTACEAE. *Calyptranthes thomasianum* (A–E), *Eugenia biflora* (F–J), and *E. earhartii* (K–M). **A.** Inflorescence. **B.** Flower showing calyptrate calyx (above right) and medial section of flower (below left). **C.** View of anther. **D.** Stems with leaves and infructescences. **E.** Infructescence. **F.** Stems with leaves and inflorescences. **G.** Lateral view of flower bud. **H.** Medial section of flower. **I.** Adaxial view of petal. **J.** Lateral view of fruit (above) and seed (below). **K.** Stems with leaves. **L.** Cauliflorous inflorescence. **M.** Oblique-apical view of immature fruit. Reprinted with permission from Acevedo-Rodríguez (1996). Artist: Bobbi Angell.

north than any native Myrtaceae species in the Western Hemisphere, reaching central-eastern Florida in the United States. Several Australian and Asian species are often found in cultivation in the neotropics, especially those of the genera *Eucalyptus* and *Syzygium*. A single species, *Myrtus communis*, is native to Europe.

Species of Myrtaceae are found in practically all terrestrial habitats except arid or semiarid regions. They occur mostly at low elevations but can be found in highland areas of the Andes, the Guayana Shield, and Brazil. In highland habitats, the species are often locally endemic.

Family classification. The Myrtaceae are placed in the Myrtales by Cronquist. Molecular studies, supported by the common occurrence of internal phloem and a hypanthiuim,

suggest a heretofore-unsuspected relationship with the Vochysiaceae.

The Myrtaceae are traditionally divided into two subfamilies, each with approximately the same number of species: Myrtoideae, concentrated in tropical America but also found in Africa, southern Asia, and Australia; and Leptospermoideae, concentrated in tropical Asia and Australia, with a single native Neotropical genus, *Tepualia*, found in Chile and adjacent Argentina. In the Myrtoideae, which includes the single tribe Myrteae, the main taxonomic problem is the delimitation of genera.

Features of the family (mostly referring to the Myrtoideae). **Habit:** subshrubs to large trees, internal phloem present, oleiferous glands often present, the glands often causing spicy aroma when crushed. **Bark** fairly smooth or rough and fissured, sometimes peeling in large plates (e.g., *Psidium guajava*). **Indumentum** usually of unicellular, simple hairs or T-shaped hairs (e.g., *Calyptranthes*, *Myrceugenia*). **Stipules** absent. **Leaves** opposite (alternate only in cultivated species of Lepstospermoideae), simple; blades typically glandular-punctate, the margins entire; venation with regular marginal vein often present (absent in a few *Campomanesia*). **Inflorescences** axillary or terminal, panicles, dichasia, racemes, or of solitary flowers, the main axis or racemes often reduced and inflorescences then appearing fasciculate or glomerate; bracteoles often 2, subtending flower. **Flowers** actinomorphic, bisexual; hypanthium present, fused to ovary, occasionally prolonged above ovary apex; sepals open in bud or closed and opening by regular or irregular tears, or forming caplike structure (calyptra), when present, the lobes 4–5, distinct; petals usually 4–5, rarely absent (some *Calyptranthes*), distinct, usually white, rarely reddish (*Acca*, *Myrrhinium*) or pink or bluish (*Eugenia*); androecium often of numerous stamens (4–8 in *Myrrhinium*), the filaments usually whitish, the anthers, usually with terminal gland, often dehiscing longitudinally by slits, sometimes by apical pores; gynoecium syncarpous, the ovary inferior, the carpels 2–18, the locules equal to number of carpels, the style typically filiform, the stigma punctiform or capitate; placentation axile, the ovules 2–many per locule. **Fruits** berries, rarely capsules (*Tepualia*), crowned by persistent sepal-lobes or scars. **Seeds** 1–many, the seed coat usually membranous or chartaceous, sometimes hard and bony (e.g., *Psidium*); endosperm absent, the embryo distinct.

In the neotropics, trees usually reach 15–20(30) meters high, but some Australian species of *Eucalyptus* are among the tallest trees in the world, reaching more than 100 meters.

Among the native Neotropical genera, the largest flowers are usually found in *Psidium* and *Campomanesia*.

Generic distinctions have been traditionally and disproportionately based on the morphology of the calyx and prolongation of the hypanthium, both of which are variable and probably more useful at the specific level.

There are three main types of embryo, each characterizing the three traditional subtribes of the American Myrteae: Myrciinae, with membranous, folded cotyledons, and a well-developed and elongate hypocotyl; Eugeniinae, with thick, separate or fused, fleshy cotyledons, and a very short or indistinct hypocotyl; and Myrtinae, with very small and membranous cotyledons, and a well-developed, elongate or spiraled hypocotyl.

Natural history. Flowers of Myrtaceae last for a brief time, and the petals and stamens fall off almost immediately after the flowers open. Pollination is predominantly by insects, especially bees, but reddish-flowered species are pollinated by birds. In *Acca sellowiana* and *Myrrhinium atropurpureum*, birds are attracted by, and feed on, the reddish petals that become sweet as the anthers release pollen grains. Self-pollination is observed commonly and hybridization is frequent. Fruits are dispersed mostly by birds and small mammals.

Economic uses. The introduced and largely cultivated species are economically important for timber and medicinal properties (*Eucalyptus* species); as ornamentals (myrtle, *Myrtus communis*; bottlebrushes, *Callistemon* and *Melaleuca*; tea tree, *Leptospermum scoparium*); as spice (clove, *Syzygium aromaticum*); and for the edible fruits (water rose-apple, *S. aqueum*; rose apple, *S. jambos*; Malay apple, *S. malaccense*). The fruits of most native, Neotropical species are edible. The guava (*Psidium guajava*) is probably the species of Myrtaceae best known around the world. Other native species commonly cultivated for their edible fruits are *jabuticaba* (*Myrciaria cauliflora*), *pitanga* or Suriname cherry (*Eugenia uniflora*), and Brazil cherry (*E. brasiliensis*). Many other species in several genera often are known locally and have potential economic value: *araçá-boi* (*E. stipitata*) and *camu-camu* (*Myrciaria dubia*) in the Amazon region; *uñi* (*Ugni molinae*) in Chile; and *cambuci* (*Campomanesia phaea*) in southeastern Brazil and *guaviroba* (*Campomanesia* species) in central and southeastern Brazil. A few species, including the guava, have medicinal uses; two species of *Pimenta* from the Caribbean region (allspice, *P. dioica*, and bay tree, *P. racemosa*) are important sources of spice, and other species are occasionally cultivated in gardens as ornamentals, for example, *feijoa* or pineapple guava (*Acca sellowiana*) and *Myrrhinium atropurpureum*.

Psidium cattleyanum (strawberry guava) and *P. guajava* are serious weeds in the Hawaiian and Galápagos islands.

References. BERNAL, H. Y., AND J. E. CORRERA Q. 1998. Myrtaceae. In *Especies vegetales promisorias de los países del Convenio Andrés Bello*, Tomo XII. Santafé de Bogotá, D. E., Colombia: Secretaria Ejecutiva del Convenio Andrés Bello. BRIGGS, B. G., AND L. A. S. JOHNSON. 1979. Evolution in the Myrtaceae—evidence from inflorescence structure. *Proc. Linn. Soc. New South Wales* 102:157–256. CONTI,

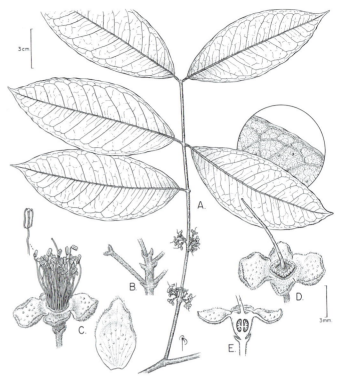

Figure 136. MYRTACEAE. *Eugenia argyrophylla.* **A.** Stem with leaves and inflorescences and detail of abaxial surface of leaf with punctations. **B.** Detail of part of inflorescence showing bracts. **C.** Lateral view of flower with detail of stamen (above left) and adaxial view of petal (below right). **D.** Oblique-apical view of flower after stamens have fallen. **E.** Medial section of flower. Reprinted with permission from Mori et al. (2002). Artist: Bobbi Angell.

E., A. LITT, AND K. J. SYTSMA. 1996. Circumscription of Myrtales and their relationships to other rosids: evidence from rbcL sequence data. *Amer. J. Bot.* 83(2):221–33. LANDRUM, L. R. 1981. A monograph of the genus *Myrceugenia* (Myrtaceae). *Fl. Neotrop. Monogr.* 29:1–137. LANDRUM, L. R. 1986. *Campomanesia, Pimenta, Blepharocalyx, Legrandia, Acca, Myrrhinium,* and *Luma* (Myrtaceae). *Fl. Neotrop. Monogr.* 45:1–179. LANDRUM, L. R., AND M. L. KAWASAKI. 1997. The genera of Myrtaceae in Brazil: an illustrated synoptic treatment and identification keys. *Brittonia* 49:508–36. MCVAUGH, R. 1956. Tropical American Myrtaceae. *Fieldiana, Bot.* 29(3):145–228. MCVAUGH, R. 1963. Tropical American Myrtaceae, II. *Fieldiana, Bot.* 29(8):391–532. MCVAUGH, R. 1968. The genera of American Myrtaceae—an interim report. *Taxon* 17:354–418. MORI, S., B. BOOM, A. M. DE CARVALHO, AND T. S. DOS SANTOS. 1983. Ecological importance of Myrtaceae in an eastern Brazilian wet forest. *Biotropica* 15(1):68–70. NIC LUGHADHA, E., AND C. PROENÇA. 1996. A survey of reproductive biology of the Myrtoideae (Myrtaceae). *Ann. Missouri Bot. Gard.* 83:480–503.

NELUMBONACEAE (Lotus-lily Family)

LISA M. CAMPBELL

- *aquatic herbs*
- *leaves usually floating or emergent, large, peltate*
- *flowers large, showy; carpels embedded in receptacle*
- *fruits achenes*

Numbers of genera and species. Worldwide, the Nelumbonaceae comprise one genus and two species. Only the naturalized *Nelumbo nucifera* is found in tropical America.

Distribution and habitat. Nelumbonaceae are aquatic plants native to North America, Asia, and Australia. The sacred-lotus, *Nelumbo nucifera*, is native to subtropical and tropical Asia and Australia and is locally naturalized in the neotropics. The smaller-flowered *Nelumbo lutea* is found in North America. *Nelumbo* is usually found in lakes and slow-moving, shallow water.

Family classification. The Nelumbonaceae are placed in the Nymphaeales by Cronquist. Traditionally *Nelumbo* has been considered related to other waterlilies, either as part of Nymphaeaceae or as a separate family. The family has also been placed near the aquatic Ceratophyllaceae. Molecular analyses place the Nelumbonaceae near the Platanaceae and Proteaceae.

Features of the family. Habit: aquatic herbs, perennial, producing benzyl isoquinoline and other alkaloids. **Rhizomes** fleshy, with swollen tubers, the nodes distinct, adventitous roots present, the aerenchyma well developed. **Leaves** arising from rhizomes, alternate (distichous), in sympodial unit composed of 2 scale leaves and 1 foliage leaf, simple, the large leaves floating or emergent, peltate; blades orbicular, the upper surface covered with epicuticlar wax, the small leaves fewer, submerged; blades lanceolate. **Inflorescences** of solitary flowers; peduncles long, emerging above water. **Flowers** large, showy, actinomorphic, bisexual; perianth caducous; sepals 2–5; petals 20–30, spirally arranged, larger than sepallike members, yellow, pink, or red; androecium of numerous stamens (200–400), the stamens spirally arranged, the filaments long, continuing into connective, the connective laminar, protroding, the anthers introrse-latrorse; gynoecium apocarpous, the ovaries superior, the carpels 8–30, embedded in receptacle; receptacle turbinate, spongy, accrescent; placentation parietal, the ovules 1, apical. **Fruits** achenes. **Seeds** large, ovoid, the seed coat thin.

Natural history. Increased temperature in the flower enhances the volatility of compounds that attract a variety of insect pollinators, usually beetles (Coleoptera), flies (Diptera), and bees (Hymenoptera). The enlarged, dried receptacle and the fruits float, and the seeds have great longevity; features facilitate water dispersal and seed germination and seedling establishment, respectively.

Economic uses. *Nelumbo nucifera* is cultivated in Asia for its edible storage tubers, rhizomes, embryos, and receptacles. In most of the world, including the neotropics, it is cultivated as an ornamental, both for the flowers and foliage. The common name, sacred lotus, refers to the special importance placed on the flowers by ancient Egyptian and some Asian cultures. The dried receptacles are used in flower arrangements.

References. LOCONTE, H. 1995. Comparison of alternative hypotheses for the origin of the angiosperms. In *Flowering Plant Origin, Evolution & Phylogeny*, eds. D. W. Taylor and L. J. Hickey, 267–85. New York: Chapman & Hall. SCHNEIDER, E. L., AND J. D. BUCHANAN. 1980. Morphological studies of Nymphaeaceae. XI. The floral biology of *Nelumbo pentapetala*. *Amer. J. Bot.* 67:182–93. SKUBATZ, H., P. S. WILLIAMSON, E. L. SCHNEIDER, AND B.J.D. MEEUSE. 1990. Cyanide-insensitive respiration in thermogenic flowers of *Victoria* and *Nelumbo*. *J. Exp. Bot.* 41(231):1335–39. SOHMER, S. H., AND D. F. SEFTON. 1978. The reproductive biology of *Nelumbo pentapetala* (Nelumbonaceae) on the Upper Mississippi River: II. The insects associated with the transfer of pollen. *Brittonia* 30:355–64. WILLIAMSON, P. S., AND E. L. SCHNEIDER. 1993. Nelumbonaceae. In *The Families and Genera of Vascular Plants*, eds. K. Kubitzki, J. G. Rohwer, and V. Bittrich, 2:470–73. Berlin: Springer-Verlag.

NOLANACEAE (Nolana Family)

Michael Nee

Plate 32

- *herbs or shrublets*

- *leaves alternate, sometimes in pairs, simple*

- *flower corolla campanulate or funnelform, 5-lobed; stamens 5, the filaments adnate to corolla tube*

- *fruits schizocarps*

Numbers of genera and species. The Nolanaceae, a family endemic to the Western Hemisphere, comprise, according to Mesa, a single genus, *Nolana*, and 18 species, of which 15 are in tropical America. Other modern authors have suggested that there may be as many as 83 American species of *Nolana*.

Distribution and habitat. *Nolana* is almost entirely confined to Peru and Chile from 8° to 33°S latitude, but one species reaches 43°S and another is found on the Galápagos Islands.

Species of Nolanaceae are adapted to the *loma* vegetation of the arid regions of the Pacific Coast of South America, the climate of which is influenced by the cold Humboldt Current. Rainfall is rare and unpredictable, but atmospheric fog and drizzle may be a nearly daily occurrence during part of the year. A few species are found at up to 4,000 meters.

Family classification. The Nolanaceae are placed in the Solanales by Cronquist. The family is evidently close to the Solanaceae and sometimes even united with that family, which recent molecular studies support. The ovary and fruit provide technical characters for separating the two families. The Solanaceae are almost entirely uniform in having two united carpels with a terminal style. Schizocarpous fruits are almost unknown in the Solanaceae, and their evolution in the Nolanaceae has apparently led to carpellary arrangements unique in the Angiosperms, with up to 27 "carpels," sometimes arranged in concentric ranks.

The species with five carpels united in a five-loculate ovary and with a terminal style seem to be closest to the Solanaceae, and have been segregated by some authors as the genus *Alona*. Other authors recognize a single genus, *Nolana*, with two subgenera *Nolana* and *Alona*. Variation in the carpels has led to the creation of several other genera, but the family is usually considered as consisting only of the single genus *Nolana*.

Features of the family. Habit: herbs or subshrubs. **Stipules** absent. **Leaves** alternate, sometimes in pairs, simple, usually anisophyllous, sometimes very succulent, sometimes much reduced. **Inflorescences** axillary, usually of solitary flowers. **Flowers** actinomorphic or somewhat zygomorphic, bisexual; calyx (2)5-lobed; corolla campanulate or funnelform, 5-lobed; androecium of 5 stamens, the filaments adnate to corolla tube, the anthers longitudinally dehiscent; gynoecium with superior ovary, the carpels 5(or 3, or perhaps up to 27 in some species), the number and arrangement variable within species, united at base, the style from apex of ovary or from between carpels; placentation axile or basal, the ovules several. **Fruits** schizocarps, the endocarp stony. **Seeds** 1–7 per mericarp.

Natural history. Little is known about the pollination and dispersal biology of this family.

Economic uses. The Nolanaceae, which look like miniature petunias, have minor use as ornamentals.

References. Ferreyra, R. 1961. Revisión de las especies peruanas del género *Nolana*. *Mem. Mus. Hist. Nat. "Javier Prado"* 12:1–71. Johnston, I. M. 1936. A study of the Nolanaceae. *Contr. Gray Herb.* 112:1–83. Mesa, A. 1981. Nolanaceae. *Fl. Neotrop. Monogr.* 26:1–197. Tago-Nakazawa, M., and M. O. Dillon. 1999. Biogeografía y evolución del Clado *Nolana* (Nolaneae-Solanaceae). *Arnaldoa* 6(2):81–116.

NYCTAGINACEAE (Four-O'Clocks or Bougainvillea Family)

DOUGLAS C. DALY AND ANDREW S. ROBERTS

Figure 137, Plate 33

- *herbs, shrubs, or trees*

- *leaves usually opposite or subopposite, simple*

- *inflorescences often subtended by conspicuous involucre, or flowers sometimes subtended by sepal-like bracts;*

- *sepals united to form a tube; corolla absent; stamens connate at base to form short tube; ovary superior; the ovule 1, placentation basal, stipitate*

- *fruits often surrounded by accrescent perianth tube, with a single seed (anthocarps)*

Numbers of genera and species. Worldwide, the Nyctaginaceae comprise approximately 32 genera and 400 species. In tropical America, there are 23 genera and approximately 180 species. Most of the Neotropical taxa are in the tribe Pisonieae, consisting of *Guapira*, *Neea*, and *Pisonia*. The first two of these are exclusively Neotropical; *Guapira* contains some 55 species and *Neea* has some 130 taxa described but perhaps 50 species. *Pisonia* has been poorly defined and consists of up to 75 species with about 25 of them Neotropical. *Mirabilis*, the Four O'Clocks genus, has some 15 species in the neotropics out of a total of approximately 60 species.

Distribution and habitat. The Nyctaginaceae, better represented in the neotropics than in the paleotropics, are mostly tropical and subtropical, with a strong presence in some arid, warm-temperate regions. The principal Neotropical genera are endemic to the Western Hemisphere. *Guapira* ranges from southern North America to Brazil, Paraguay, and Bolivia; *Neea*, with a center of diversity in Amazonia, ranges from Florida and central Mexico through Central America and the West Indies to Bolivia; *Mirabilis* and *Pisonia* are pantropical; and *Boerhavia* occurs in the neotropics. *Boerhavia* and *Mirabilis* have centers of diversity in the southwestern United States. The Nyctaginaceae are relatively diverse in Venezuelan Guayana, where *Guapira* is represented by 15 species and *Neea* by 25 species.

The Nyctaginaceae figure prominently in several rather diverse environments. Some are at least partially C4 plants and adapted to conditions of arid habitats. A number of taxa are well adapted to dry, disturbed conditions, such as most species of *Reichenbachia*, *Salpianthus*, and *Boerhavia*.

Some species of *Pisonia* occur on tropical islands; *P. aculeata* is a pantropical weed found principally of sea beaches. In contrast, species of *Guapira* and *Neea* are frequent understory trees and shrubs in nonflooded Amazonian forests.

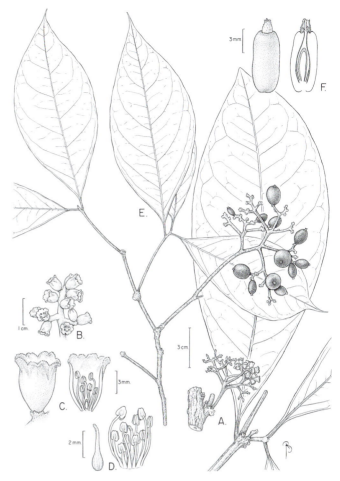

Figure 137. NYCTAGINACEAE. *Neea floribunda*. **A.** Stem with leaves (right) and part of stem with inflorescence (left). **B.** Detail of inflorescence. **C.** Lateral view of flower (left) and medial section of flower (right). **D.** Lateral views of gynoecium (left) and androecium surrounding gynoecium (right). **E.** Stem with leaves and infructescence. **F.** Lateral view of fruit (left) and medial section of fruit (right). Reprinted with permission from Mori et al. (2002). Artist: Bobbi Angell.

Guapira opposita is an ecologically important tree in hillside forests of Brazil's Atlantic forest complex in the state of Paraná.

Several members of the family are pantropical weeds, including the variable *Boerhavia diffusa* and *B. erecta*, but several genera have somewhat restricted distributions. *Colignonia* is a small genus of Andean herbs, ranging from Colombia to Argentina at elevations between 1,500–4,500 meters. The monotypic *Leucaster* (*L. caniflorus*) as well as *Ramisia*, with 1–2 species, are restricted to eastern and southeastern Brazil. The two species of *Reichenbachia* occur in the drier lowlands of Bolivia, Paraguay, and Argentina. *Salpianthus ovatifolia* has a broader distribution and ranges from Mexico through Central America into Venezuela and Colombia, plus Cuba.

Family classification. The Nyctaginaceae are most closely related to the Phytolaccaceae, especially *Petiveria*, which is sometimes segregated as a distinct family, the Petiveriaceae. Nyctaginaceae and Phytolaccaceae are generally considered to be primitive members of the Caryophyllales (e.g., *sensu* Cronquist), formerly known as the Centrospermae, and both have been linked to *Sarcobatus* of the Chenopodiaceae by molecular studies. The Caryophyllales are usually characterized by the presence of betalains rather than anthocyanins, anomalous secondary growth, stipitate ovules, free-central or basal placentation, and a strongly curved or folded embryo.

Both the Nyctaginaceae and Phytolaccaceae lack petals and have uniovulate locules, but the Nyctaginaceae are distinguished by their exstipulate, usually opposite leaves; sepals united to form a tube often resembling a tubular corolla (this sometimes subtended by sepal-like bracteoles); a solitary carpel; and mostly cymose or capitate (vs. racemose or spicate or less often paniculate or cymose) inflorescence often subtended by a conspicuous involucre.

In contrast to the position of the family, there has been no consensus as to subdivision of the Nyctaginaceae or even delimitation of some of the larger genera. One of the more comprehensive treatments of the family recognizes five tribes. The Pisonieae, which accounts for most Neotropical taxa, are comprised of trees and shrubs with mostly imperfect flowers and straight embryos (unlike classic Caryophyllales). The Nyctagineae are characterized by a generally herbaceous to shrubby habit, mostly perfect flowers, the fruit enclosed in the persistent base of the calyx tube, and the embryo more or less folded or hooked. The Colignonieae includes only *Colignonia*, an Andean genus of about 11 species. The Boldoeae are also monogeneric, with *Boldoa* restricted to Mexico and Central America, and the Leucastereae consist of four monotypic South American genera: *Andradea*, *Leucaster*, *Ramisia*, and *Reichenbachia* (the latter sometimes considered to have two species).

Some genera are difficult to circumscribe, and this taxonomy is confused to the point where the approximate number of species is uncertain. *Neea* is variable in habit and in morphology of leaves, pubescence, inflorescences, flowers, and fruit. It is also dioecious, so plants with male flowers are hard to match with those having female flowers or fruits. Even when herbarium specimens are prepared with care, the leaves tend to dry black and brittle, often abscising from the stem and/or disintegrating, thereby making them difficult to study.

Features of the family. Habit: herbs, shrubs, or trees, erect or less often scandent (e.g., *Bougainvillea*), sometimes armed with axillary thorns (e.g., *Pisonia*); trichomes (when present) sometimes stipitate and viscid-glandular; betalains present; woody taxa showing anomalous secondary growth, with consecutive concentric rings of vascular bundles. Stipules absent. Leaves opposite, subopposite, rarely whorled (opposing leaves sometimes unequal) or alternate (e.g., *Salpianthus* and *Bougainvillea*), simple, often drying black; blades usually entire. Inflorescences terminal or axillary, variously branched but usually the ultimate branches cymose; the flowers often in cymose or sometimes capitate pseudanthia; involucre often present, calyxlike and subtending a single corollalike calyx (*Mirabilis* and *Okenia*) or corolloid and subtending a cluster of flowers (*Bougainvillea*); bracteoles 1–3. Flowers usually actinomorphic or rarely the perianth lobes irregular, bisexual or seldom unisexual (plants dioecious), usually 5-merous; calyx synsepalous, commonly corolloid, forming a well-developed, often slender, elongate tube, the lobes (3)5(8), induplicate-valvate, plicate, or contorted in bud; corolla absent; androecium usually with stamens as many as calyx lobes, the stamens sometimes fewer or more numerous (1–30), alternating with calyx lobes, sometimes exserted (*Guapira*), the filaments usually unequal in length, distinct or more often connate at base to form short tube; intrastaminal annular disc often present around ovary; gynoecium with superior ovary, the carpel 1, the style long, slender, the stigma capitate, penicillate, or fimbriate; placentation basal, the ovule 1 per carpel, basal, stipitate. Fruits diclesia (a type of indehiscent anthocarp in which the perianth encloses or is accrescent around the pericarp and aids in dispersal), also often called an achene, maturing fleshy, coriaceous, or woody, sometimes (e.g., some *Pisonia*) provided with one or more vertical series of stipitate glands. Seeds 1 per fruit; endosperm absent; perisperm abundant or scanty, starchy; embryo large, peripheral, straight or more often curved around perisperm.

Natural history. The pollination biology of the Nyctaginaceae is poorly known. Nectar is produced at the filament bases in at least some genera. Hawkmoths have been observed pollinating *Mirabilis*.

In the Nyctaginaceae, the calyx encloses the pericarp, and it displays a remarkable number of adaptations to aid in dispersal. An unusual mechanism occurs in *Okenia*, which includes two species of glandular-pubescent annual herbs occurring on sandy soils in the Florida Keys and coastal and inland areas of Mexico. After pollination, the pedicel elongates, and the young fruit (enclosed in the oblong, thickened, corky base of the calyx tube) is pushed into the soil, where it matures.

The anthocarps of many species of *Pisonia*, *Commicarpus*, and *Boerhavia* have longitudinal ranks of stalked glands that make the fruit adhere to the bodies of birds and other passing animals. Not surprisingly, these taxa are widespread in the Tropics.

Neea and some species of *Pisonia*, both with fleshy anthocarps, are dispersed by both specialist and nonspecialist, fruit eating birds. At La Selva, Costa Rica, fruits of *N. psychotrioides* are pendent on long pedicels and are thus accessible to aerial feeders such as manakins, which swallow them whole and later pass the seeds.

Economic uses. The Nyctaginaceae are economically important only as ornamentals (mostly species of *Bougainvillea* and *Mirabilis*). The well-known four-o'clocks, which have escaped from cultivation in parts of the Tropics, are cultivars of *M. jalapa*. This species also yields a dye that has been used in China to color jellies.

Most other uses are local and usually medicinal. Several sources report that the leaves of *Boerhavia hirsuta* have been used in the Tocantins region of Amazonia to treat malaria. A decoction from the leaves of *Pisonia aculeata* has provided treatments for rheumatism and venereal disease in Jamaica and on the Yucatán Peninsula of Mexico, and an extract of the fruits of *Pisonia capitata* has been utilized in Mexico to reduce fevers. *Neea parviflora* has been used in Peru to prevent tooth decay. The roots of *Boerhavia tuberosa* have been consumed as a vegetable in parts of Peru.

References. BURGER, W. C. 1983. Nyctaginaceae. In Flora costaricensis, ed. W. Burger. *Fieldiana, Bot.*, n.s., no. 13:180–

89. HEIMERL, A. 1934. Nyctaginaceae. In *Die Natürlichen Pflanzenfamilien*, 2nd ed. 16c:86–134. Leipzig: Wilhelm Engelmann. MOERMOND, T. C., J. S. DENSLOW, D. J. LEVEY, AND E. SANTANA-C. 1986. The influence of morphology on fruit choice in Neotropical birds. In *Frugivores and seed dispersal*, eds. A. Estrada and T. H. Fleming, 137–46. Dordrecht: W. Junk. SNOW, D. W. 1981. Tropical frugivorous birds and their food plants: a survey. *Biotropica* 13:1–14. STANDLEY, P. C. 1946. Nyctaginaceae. In Flora of Peru. *Fieldiana, Bot.* 13(part 2):518–46. STEYERMARK, J. A. 1987. Flora of the Venezuelan Guayana-III. *Ann. Missouri Bot. Gard.* 74:609–58. WOODSON, R. E., JR., R. W. SCHERY, AND H. J. KIDD. 1961. Nyctaginaceae. In Flora of Panama, eds. R. E. Woodson, R. W. Schery, et al., *Ann. Missouri Bot. Gard.* 48:51–65.

NYMPHAEACEAE (Water Lily Family)

DONALD J. PADGETT AND DONALD H. LES

Figure 138, Plate 33

- *aquatic freshwater herbs*
- *leaves alternate, simple; blades usually floating*
- *inflorescences of solitary flowers*
- *flowers usually showy, petals and stamens usually numerous; styles united, forming an expanded disc*

Numbers of genera and species. Worldwide, the Nymphaeaceae comprise six genera and approximately 55 species. In tropical America, there are three genera and 21 native species. In the neotropics, the mainly temperate genus, *Nuphar*, has one species (*N. advena*); *Victoria* has two species (*V. cruziana*, and *V. amazonica*); and the largest genus, *Nymphaea*, has about 18 species (ca. 40 species worldwide). A number of nonindigenous species and cultivars have been introduced as ornamentals, and several African species (*N. caerulea*, *N. lotus*, and *N. capensis*) are naturalized in the neotropics.

Distribution and habitat. Water lilies are distributed throughout the world. *Nymphaea* is the most widespread genus, with species in both temperate and tropical regions, *Victoria* occurs exclusively in tropical/subtropical South America, and *Nuphar* occurs mainly in the north-temperate zone but extends into Cuba and Mexico in the Western Hemisphere.

Nymphaeaceae occur in freshwater pools and sluggish rivers. They usually grow in shallow waters on rich organic substrates that may be seasonally dry.

Family classification. The Nymphaeaceae are placed in the Nymphaeales by Cronquist and are thought to hold a pivotal position in early angiosperm evolution. At the family level, current studies of morphological and molecular data have centered on intergeneric relationships and on the affinities of the water lilies to the Cabombaceae. Although Nymphaeaceae and Cabombaceae are clearly sister groups and are sometimes combined into a single family, the nearest relatives of these two groups remain uncertain. Although *Nelumbo* was traditionally placed in this family, it is now considered to be a separate family, the Nelumbonaceae.

The family is subdivided into three subfamilies: Barclayoideae, Nupharoideae, and Nymphaeoideae. All except Barclayoideae have members in the Western Hemisphere.

Features of the family. Habit: freshwater aquatic, usually perennial herbs. **Rhizomes** elongate and horizontal, often tuberous, or short and erect. **Stems** on or just below substrate, sometimes cormlike (when rhizome short and erect), anchored by adventitious roots. **Stipules** present in *Nymphaea* and *Victoria*. **Leaves** alternate, simple, armed with sharp spines on petioles and leaf surfaces (*Victoria*); blades often with upturned margins in *Victoria*; petioles elongate when blades exposed to air, or often short when blades submersed; exposed blades usually floating, sometimes emergent, peltate or lobed at base, ovate to orbicular (from less than 6 cm in some *Nymphaea* to >2 m in *Victoria amazonica*), the margins entire or dentate, the submersed blades (*Nuphar* and *Nymphaea*) usually translucent, delicate. **Inflorescences** axillary, of solitary flowers, the flowers born above water; pe-

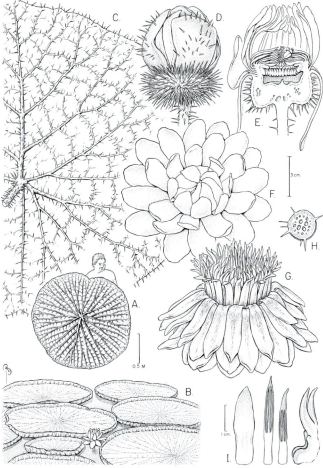

Figure 138. NYMPHAEACEAE. *Victoria amazonica* (A, B, D, F–H, unvouchered photos by C. Gracie and S. Mori; C, I, Prance 22745; E. unvouchered photo by C. Gracie). **A.** Moacir Fortes showing underside of leaf. **B.** Flower surrounded by leaf blades floating on water. **C.** Abaxial view of part of leaf. **D.** Lateral view of bud. **E.** Medial section of flower. **F.** Apical view of flower. **G.** Apical-lateral view of flower. **H.** Transverse section of pedicel. **I.** Abaxial view of stamen (left), adaxial view of outer stamen (middle left), adaxial view of inner stamen (middle right), and lateral view of staminode (right). Original. Artist: Bobbi Angell.

duncles stout. **Flowers** actinomorphic, bisexual, often showy, fragrant; sepals 4–9, usually green (petal-like and yellow in *Nuphar*); petals usually numerous, scalelike (*Nuphar*), often grading into stamens, white, pink, yellow, blue, red, or purple; androecium of numerous stamens, the stamens straplike, usually distinct; gynoecium with inferior (*Nymphaea* and *Victoria*) or superior (*Nuphar*) ovary, the carpels 3–40, completely to incompletely fused, the styles united to form an expanded disc; placentation laminar, the ovules numerous, anatropous. **Fruits** berrylike capsules, usually ovoid, dehiscence irregular, sometimes with prickles (*Victoria*). **Seeds** numerous, ovoid, sometimes arillate, the aril pulpy.

With the exception of species of *Victoria*, Neotropical species are long-lived perennials. Cultivated *Victoria* usually behave as annuals and must be grown from seeds each year.

Natural history. The Nymphaeoideae, includes both day- and night-flowering species. Anthesis usually lasts for 2–3 days, and the perianth color changes over this period in *Victoria* and some *Nymphaea*. Diurnal flower closure often occurs and imprisons visiting insects overnight. In *Victoria*, the internal temperature of the flowers rises to nearly 10°C above the ambient temperate on the first evening of anthesis, presumably to dissipate odors and attract pollinators. In most species, the flowers are pistillate on the first and staminate on the next evenings of anthesis. Water lilies flower and fruit during wet periods in tropical regions or during warm summer months in temperate areas.

Most water lilies are adapted for insect pollination. For many *Nymphaea*, bees (Hymenoptera, Halictidae) are the principal pollinators along with beetles (Coleoptera) and flies (Diptera). *Nuphar* is pollinated by beetles of the genus *Donacia* and scarab beetles (*Cyclocephala*) are important pollinators of *Victoria* and *Nymphaea* subgenus *Hydrocallis*. Some Neotropical species of *Nymphaea* are self-compatible and autogamous.

Fruits of all water-lily genera but *Nuphar* develop underwater. In *Nuphar*, seeds are dispersed in floating, aerenchymatous masses. The seeds of *Nymphaea* and *Victoria* are provided with arils that enable them to float and disperse on the water surface. Short-range dispersal of seeds and fruits is primarily by water, but long-distance dispersal probably occurs through transport by waterfowl, which are known to consume the seeds. Rootstocks and tubers of *Nymphaea mexicana* are also consumed by waterfowl, but it is uncertain whether they are dispersed in this fashion.

Economic uses. Water-lily species and hybrids are cultivated widely as ornamental aquatics. The seeds and rhizomes of most genera contain starch and protein and frequently are used as food by humans, waterfowl, and other animals. Water-lily seeds are consumed in Central America, and *Victoria cruziana* is known in Paraguay as *mais del aqua* because of its large, edible seeds.

The Maya used *Nymphaea* flowers to induce narcotic trances in religious rituals. The water lily was an important symbol that appeared in many of the paintings, decorations, and sculptures of the Maya. The ancient Maya capital of Copan (in modern Honduras) was governed from about 504–544 A.D. by a ruler known as the Waterlily Jaguar.

References. CONARD, H. S. 1905. The waterlilies: a monograph of the genus *Nymphaea*. *Publ. Carnegie Inst. Wash.* 4: 1–272. COOK, C.D.K. 1990. *Aquatic Plant Book.* The Hague, The Netherlands: SPB Academic Publishing. KAHN, F., B. LEÓN, AND K. R. YOUNG. 1993. *Las plantas vasculares en las aguas continentales del Perú.* Lima, Perú: IFEA. LES, D. H., E. L. SCHNEIDER, D. J. PADGETT, P. S. SOLTIS, D. E. SOLTIS, AND M. ZANIS. 1999. Phylogeny, classification and floral evolution of water lilies (Nymphaeaceae; Nymphaeales): a synthesis of non-molecular, *rbc*L, *mat*K, and 18S rDNA data. *Syst. Bot.* 24:28–46. PRANCE, G. T., AND J. R. ARIAS. 1975. A study of the floral biology of *Victoria amazonica* (Poepp.) Sowerby (Nymphaeaceae). *Acta Amazon.* 5:109–39. SCHNEIDER, E. L., AND P. S. WILLIAMSON. 1993. Nymphaeaceae. In *The Families and Genera of Vascular Plants*, eds. K. Kubitzki, J. G. Rohwer, and V. Bittrich, 3:486–93. New York: Springer-Verlag. VELÁSQUEZ, J. 1990. *Semillas de plantas acuaticas vasculares del sur del estado Anzoátegui.* Caracas, Venezuela: CORPOVEN. VELÁSQUEZ, J. 1994.

Plantas acuáticas vasculares de Venezuela. Caracas, Venezuela: Universidad Central de Venezuela. WERKHOVEN, M.C.M., AND G.M.T. PEETERS. 1993. Aquatic macrophytes. In *The freshwater ecosystems of Suriname*, ed. P. E. Ouboter, 99–112. Boston: Kluwer Academic Publishers. WIERSEMA, J. H. 1987. A monograph of *Nymphaea* subgenus *Hydrocallis* (Nymphaeaceae). *Syst. Bot. Monogr.* 16:1–112. WIERSEMA, J. H. 1988. Reproductive biology of *Nymphaea* (Nymphaeaceae). *Ann. Missouri Bot. Gard.* 75:195–804.

NYSSACEAE (Sour Gum Family)

NATHAN SMITH

Figure 139

- *trees*

- *leaves alternate, simple, often clustered at branch apices; blades usually entire*

- *flowers usually unisexual; stamens 8–15, staminodes 8-15 in pistillate flowers; disc present; ovary inferior; ovules 1 per locule, pendulous*

- *fruits drupaceous*

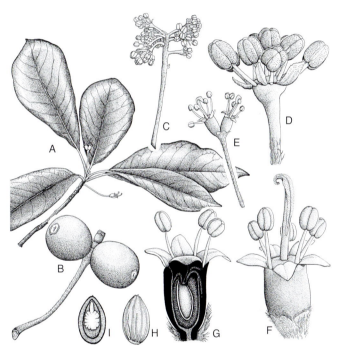

Figure 139. NYSSACEAE. *Nyssa sylvatica.* **A.** Stem with inflorescence (x½). **B.** Infructescence (x2). **C.** Staminate inflorescence (x2). **D.** Lateral view of staminate flower (x8). **E.** Pair of perfect flowers (x2). **F.** Lateral view of perfect flower. **G.** Perfect flower with medial section of ovary (x8). **H.** Lateral view of endocarp (x2). **I.** Medial section of endocarp (x2). Reprinted with permission from Cronquist (1981). Artist: William S. Moye.

Numbers of genera and species. Worldwide, the Nyssaceae comprise three genera and about eight species. In tropical America, there is a single genus, *Nyssa*, and two species.

Distribution and habitat. The Nyssaceae occur in Asia, the eastern United States, Mexico, Costa Rica, and Panama. The cultivated *Camptotheca acuminata* and *Davidia involucrata* are native to China.

In tropical America, *Nyssa sylvatica* is found in eastern Mexico in Chiapas, Hidalgo, and Puebla. This species is most common between 1,100 and 1,650 meters, and is often found growing in forests with *Liquidambar*, *Pinus*, *Platanus*, and *Quercus*. *Nyssa talamancana* is found in wet, midelevation forests between circa 700 and 1,000 meters in Costa Rica and Panama.

Family classification. The Nyssaceae are placed in the Cornales by Cronquist. Most studies suggest that the Nyssaceae are closely related to the Cornaceae and some authors place it within this family. Cronquist includes *Davidia* within the family (as treated here), however, this monotypic genus is often included in its own family, the Davidiaceae.

Recent molecular analyses place the Nyssaceae in a more expanded monophylectic Cornaceae. These studies, based on *rbc*L and *mat*K genes, have shown that two clades exist

within the Nyssaceae, one with *Nyssa*, *Camptotheca*, *Davidia*, and a few other genera, and another with *Alangium* and *Cornus*.

Features of the family. Habit: trees to 40 m tall. **Indument:** trichomes often present on petioles, blade margins, and peduncles. **Stipules** absent. **Leaves** alternate, simple, often clustered at branch apices, deciduous; blades entire or rarely with few teeth. **Inflorescences** axillary, umbels, umbel-like racemes, sometimes globose, sometimes of solitary flowers in pistillate plants; bracts often present. **Flowers** ± actinomorphic, usually unisexual (plants polygamous or dioecious); sepals 5, small; petals 5(6), imbricate; androecium with 8–15 stamens; staminodes 8–15 in pistillate flowers; nectary disc present; gynoecium syncarpous, the ovary inferior, the carpels 1–2, the locules 1–2, the stigma 2–3 lobed, sometimes papillate; ovules 1 per locule, pendulous. **Fruits** drupaceous, blue-black or red, the endocarps hard, these usually with locule(s) opening apically by triangular valves. **Seeds** 1 per locule (usually 1 per fruit); endosperm copious, the embryo straight.

Natural history. In the northeastern United States, *Nyssa sylvatica* is pollinated mostly by bees and other insects, and seeds are often dispersed by birds and possibly rodents.

Economic uses. *Camptotheca acuminata*, *Davidia involucrata*, and species of *Nyssa* (e.g., *N. aquatica*, water tupelo,

and *N. sylvatica*, black tupelo), are grown as ornamentals. Some species of *Nyssa* provide timber and edible fruits, and the nectar from the flowers is collected by bees to produce honey. *Captotheca acuminata* is the source of camptothecin, an alkaloid that has been shown to have antitumor activity.

References. EYDE, R. H. 1963. Morphological and paleobotanical studies of the Nyssaceae, I. A survey of the modern species and their fruits. *J. Arnold Arbor.* 44(1):1–59. HAMMEL, B. E., AND N. A. ZAMORA. 1990. *Nyssa talamancana* (Cornaceae), an addition to the remnant Laurasion tertiary flora of southern Central America. *Brittonia* 42(3):165–70. NEE, M. 1986. Nyssaceae. In *Flora de Veracruz*, eds. A. Gómez-Pompa and V. Sosa, fasc. 52:1–6. XIANG, Q.-Y., D. E. SOLTIS, AND P. S. SOLTIS. 1998. Phylogenetic relationships of Cornaceae and close relatives inferred from *mat*K and *rbc*L sequences. *Amer. J. Bot.* 85(2):285–97.

OCHNACEAE (Ochna Family)

CLAUDE SASTRE

Figure 140, Plate 33

- *usually shrubs or trees*
- *stipules present, caducous in* Ouratea
- *leaves alternate, usually simple; secondary venation parallel or subparallel*
- *flowers with sepals, petals, and stamens usually distinct; petals often yellow; gynoecium borne on gynophore*
- *fruits many-seeded capsules (Sauvagesioideae), indehiscent and single-seeded (Elvasia), or black monocarps on red torus (Ouratea)*

Numbers of genera and species. Worldwide, the Ochnaceae comprise 30 genera and approximately 500 species. There are 16 genera and more than 300 species native to tropical America. The largest Neotropical genus is *Ouratea* (200 species), followed by *Sauvagesia* (35), *Luxemburgia* (17), *Tyleria* (12), and *Elvasia* (11). Nine Neotropical genera have only one or two species.

Distribution and habitat. Ochnaceae occur throughout tropical regions of the world except in the Pacific islands. Genera of Ochnaceae are endemic to major continental areas, except for *Sauvagesia*, which has a number of species in both the Western and Eastern Hemispheres. Only one species, *Sauvagesia erecta*, occurs both in the neotropics (the Antilles and Central and South America) and the paleotropics (tropical Africa and Madagascar). *Tyleria* and *Philacra*

are endemic to the Guayana Highlands and *Luxemburgia* is endemic to eastern Brazil. Many species of *Sauvagesia* have wide distributions while the majority of the species of *Ouratea* are restricted endemics, especially in the Guayana Highlands, where they are well represented.

The Ochnaceae occupy diverse habitats in rain forests, savannas, and vegetation associated with isolated outcrops, such as inselbergs. Most species occur at low elevations, but a few reach the summits of Mt. Roraima (2,600 m), Sierra de la Neblina (2,800 m), and mountains near Medellín, Colombia (2,800 m).

Family classification. The Ochnaceae are placed in the Theales by Cronquist. Because of similar fruit morphology, Casimir de Candolle placed *Ochna* and *Ouratea* near the Annonaceae and *Sauvagesia*, because of its capsular fruits, has been included in the Violaceae and even treated as a separate family, the Sauvagesiaceae. Recent molecular studies suggest that the Ochnaceae belong in an expanded Malpighiales near the Medusagynaceae (Theales *sensu* Cronquist) and Quiinaceae.

The Ochnaceae are divided into two subfamilies: the Ochnoideae, with a 1-seeded carpel and exalbuminate seeds, and the Sauvagesioideae, with a two or more seeded carpel and albuminate seeds. The Ochnoideae are divided into three tribes: the Ochneae (including *Ouratea*), with fruits with one to ten distinct carpels situated on a torus; the entirely Neotropical Elvasiae, with the carpels united in fruit; and the African Lophireae, with pluri-ovulate carpels and winged

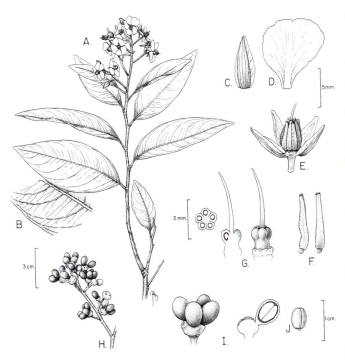

Figure 140. OCHNACEAE. *Ouratea litoralis*. **A.** Stem with leaves and inflorescence. **B.** Detail of abaxial surface of leaf. **C.** Adaxial view of sepal. **D.** Adaxial view of petal. **E.** Lateral view of flower with petals removed. **F.** Adaxial (left) and abaxial (right) views of stamens. **G.** Lateral (right) and medial section (left) of gynoecium and transverse section of ovary (above left). **H.** Infructescence. **I.** Fruit monocarps on enlarged receptacle (left) and medial section of receptacle and a monocarp (right). **J.** Embryo. Reprinted with permission from Acevedo-Rodríguez (1996). Artist: Bobbi Angell.

fruits. The Sauvagesioideae is divided into two tribes: the Indo-Malaysian Euthemideae with bi-ovulate carpels and the Sauvagesieae with carpels more than two ovulate. The mostly Neotropical Sauvagesioideae is further divided into two subtribes: the Sauvagesineae, with actinomorphic flowers and the Luxemburgineae, with zygomorphic flowers.

Features of the family. Habit: shrubs and trees, sometimes herbs (most *Sauvagesia*), or rarely vines (monospecific *Krukoviella*). Stipules present, triangular and mostly caducous in *Ouratea*, persistent and glanduloso-ciliate in *Sauvagesia*. Leaves alternate, simple or imparipinnate in monospecific *Rhytidanthera*; blades sessile or shortly petiolate, rarely long (*Luxemburgia* section *Luxemburgia*), the margins generally toothed; secondary venation parallel or subparallel (at least in proximal half), straight in many genera (e.g., *Blastemanthus* and *Elvasia*) or curved (e.g., *Ouratea*). Inflorescences usually terminal, axillary in some species of *Ouratea* and *Sauvagesia*, generally compound spikes or large panicles, sometimes in bostryches, rarely reduced to solitary flowers (*S. tenella*); bracts present, caducous or persistent; peduncles articulate. Flowers actinomorphic or less frequently zygomorphic (Luxemburginae) bisexual; sepals 5, generally dis-

tinct (except for *Ouratea* section *Kaieteuria*), coriaceous, green; petals 3–5 (5–10 in *Blastemanthus*), distinct, often yellow (*Ouratea*), sometimes rose to white (*Sauvagesia* and *Wallacea*); androecium with 5–many stamens, the stamens distinct, the filaments short (except in *Elvasia*), the anthers dehiscing longitudinally or poricidally; staminodes sometimes present in Sauvagesineae; gynoecium borne on gynophore, the ovary superior, the carpels 2–10, distinct or united, the locules equal to carpel number or 1 in Sauvagesioideae, the styles and stigmas united; placentation parietal to axile, the ovules 1–many. **Fruits** many-seeded capsules in Sauvagesioideae, single-seeded, dry and indehiscent in most *Elvasia*, or single-seeded monocarps, the monocarps fleshy, black, on red torus in *Ouratea*. **Seeds** 1–many, albuminous (Sauvagesioideae) or exalbuminous (Ochnoideae), usually not winged, less frequently winged in some genera (e.g., *Tyleria*).

Habit is variable in the Ochnaceae; e.g., *Cespedesia spathulata* is a tree 25–30 meters tall, while *Sauvagesia tenella* is a small herb 3–5 centimeters tall.

The veins of the leaves and often the bark of the stems have files of cells called "cristarque" cells. Cristarque cells have sclerified walls and contain spherical oxalate crystals greater than 20 microns in diameter.

Natural history. Pollination is by bees in *Ouratea*. Self-pollination may occur in *Sauvagesia* and related genera. The fleshy, black monocarps of species of *Ouratea* attract birds and most likely are dispersed by them. Riparian species often are dispersed by water and species with winged seeds (e.g., *Cespedesia*) are dispersed by the wind. Some species (e.g., *Elvasia elvasioides*) may be dispersed by gravity.

Economic uses. The large leaves of *Cespedesia spathulata*, ranging from Costa Rica to central Brazil, are used for roofing and in basketry by Amerindians. *Sauvagesia erecta* is the source of a herbal medicine used for treating eye disorders. Species of some Ochnaceae, such as the African *Lophira alata*, are harvested for their timber.

References. CANDOLLE, C. DE 1811. Monographie des Ochnacées et des Simaroubacées. *Ann. Mus. Natl. Hist. Nat.* 17:398–425. EICHLER, A. 1871. Sauvagesiaceae. In *Flora Brasiliensis*, Martius. 13(1):398–419. ENGLER, A. 1876. *Ochnaceae*. In *Flora Brasiliensis*, Martius. 12(2):301–66. FARRON, C. 1963. Contribution à la taxonomie des Ourateae Engler. *Ber. Schweiz. Bot. Ges.* 73:196–217. KANIS, A. 1968. A revision of the Ochnaceae of the Indo-Pacific area. *Blumea* 16(1):1–82. SASTRE, C. 1975. L'importance des caractères anatomiques dans la systématique des Ochnacées. C. R. 100° Congrès Nat. Soc. Sav. 2185–196. TIEGHEM (VAN), P. 1902. La cristarque dans la tige et la feuille des Ochnacées. *Bull. Mus. Hist. Nat. (Paris)* 8:266–73. TIEGHEM (VAN), P. 1902. Sur les Ochnacées. *Ann. Sc. Nat. (Paris)*, sér. 8, 16:161–416. TIEGHEM (VAN), P. 1904. Sur les Luxemburgiacées. *Ann. Sc. Nat. (Paris)*, sér. 8, 19:1–96.

OLACACEAE (Olax Family)

TERENCE D. PENNINGTON

Figures 141, 142; Plate 34

- *trees, sometimes shrubs, or rarely lianas*

- *stipules absent*

- *leaves alternate, simple; blade margins usually entire; venation usually pinnate*

- *flowers actinomorphic, usually bisexual; stamens often equal in number and opposite petals; ovules pendulous*

- *fruits drupes, often subtended or enclosed by accrescent calyx*

- *seed 1 per fruit*

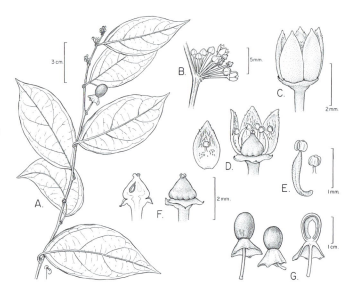

Figure 141. OLACACEAE. *Heisteria scandens.* **A.** Stem with leaves, inflorescences, and a fruit. **B.** Inflorescence. **C.** Lateral view of flower. **D.** Lateral view of flower with two petals removed (right) and adaxial view of petal with adnate stamen (left). **E.** Lateral (left) and adaxial (right) views of stamens. **F.** Lateral view (right) and medial section (left) of gynoecium. **G.** Lateral views of two fruits (left) and medial section of fruit with undeveloped seed (right). Reprinted with permission from Mori et al. (2002). Artist: Bobbi Angell.

Numbers of genera and species. Worldwide, the Olacaceae comprise approximately 27 genera and about 180 species. In tropical America, there are 14 genera and about 90 species, of which *Heisteria* (33 species) and *Schoepfia* (23) are the largest.

Distribution and habitat. The Olacaceae are found throughout the Tropics of America, Africa, and Asia. In the Western Hemisphere, the family extends from the southern United States (*Ximenia*) and Baja California throughout Central and South America to Bolivia, Paraguay, and Argentina. Species also occur in the Greater and Lesser Antilles.

The Olacaceae are primarily a family of lowland rain-forest trees, common in the understory but sometimes reaching the canopy. A few genera (*Schoepfia* and *Ximenia*) extend into dry deciduous forest, savanna scrub, and seashore beaches.

Family classification. The Olacaceae are placed in the Santalales by Cronquist and related to the Opiliaceae, Santalaceae, and Loranthaceae. Recent molecular studies support the placement of the Olacaceae near these families.

The family has been divided into three subfamilies, largely on the basis of the number of ovule integuments. Recent research on leaf and wood anatomy, however, has shown that these subfamily divisions are untenable and that some of the tribes are heterogeneous; therefore, it is probably best to treat the Olacaceae without subfamilial divisions.

Features of the family. Habit: small to medium sized trees, sometimes shrubs (*Ximenia*), rarely lianas, sometimes root parasites (*Schoepfia* and *Ximenia*), evergreen. **Latex** sometimes present (*Chaunochiton, Heisteria,* and *Minquartia*), then apparent as white exudate when petiole or small branch is cut. **Stipules** absent. **Leaves** alternate (spiral or distichous), simple; blade margins usually entire, sinuate-dentate in *Brachy-*

nema; venation usually pinnate. **Inflorescences** axillary, racemes, panicles, umbels, spikes, or fascicles, usually (shorter than leaves except *Minquartia*). **Flowers** actinomorphic, usually bisexual, rarely unisexual (occasionally in *Ximenia*), sometimes heterostylous (*Schoepfia*), usually small, greenish yellow; sepals 4–5-lobed, cupular, or reduced to a small ridge, often accrescent in fruit; petals 4 or 5, distinct or partially united, occasionally forming long tube (*Brachynema* and *Schoepfia*), valvate; androecium with stamens equal to or up to twice as many as petals, the stamens opposite petals, episepalous or epipetalous, in 1 whorl, distinct, the anthers generally dehiscing lengthwise; intra- or extra-staminal nectary disc sometimes present, annular or of distinct glands; gynoecium syncarpous, the ovary superior to sub- or completely inferior (*Schoepfia*), the locules 1–3(7), the stigmas 3–5-lobed; placentation free-central if ovary 1-locular or axile if more than 1-locular, the ovules pendulous, 2–3(7) if 1-locular or 1 per locule if more than 1-locular. **Fruits** drupes, often subtended or enclosed by accrescent and colorful calyx, the pericarp fleshy, thin, the endocarp woody. **Seeds** 1 per fruit; endosperm copious, oily, the embryo small.

Species of *Ximenia* are mostly shrubby and sometimes characterized by axillary spines and short and long shoots.

A few genera (e.g., *Minquartia*) have closely parallel tertiary venation oriented at right angles to the secondary veins, but in the majority of the species the higher order venation

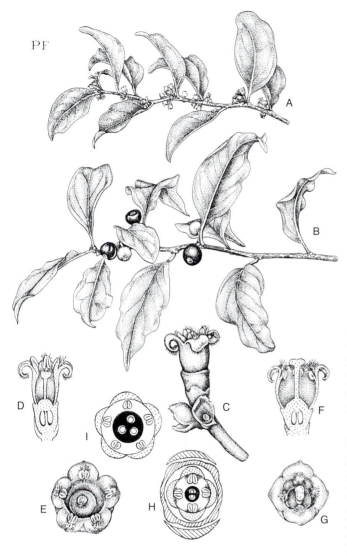

PF

is obscure. Species of *Maburea* and *Curupira* are unusual in having leaves 3-nerved from the base.

The accrescent calyx is fleshy and red in *Heisteria*, and, in *Chaunochiton*, it is large, chartaceous and brown. In *Aptandra*, the calyx is thick, cupular, and green and encloses the lower half of the fruit. In *Cathedra*, the nectary-disc is accrescent and forms a cupule enclosing the fruit.

Natural history. There are few observations on the pollination of Olacaceae, but the small flowers are sweet-scented, so insects are probably the pollinators. The fleshy fruits are yellow, red, or black and often animal-dispersed. The fruits of *Minquartia guianensis* are taken by primates (spider and howler monkeys). The inflated calyx of species of *Chaunochiton* facilitates wind dispersal.

Economic uses. A few species of Olacaceae provide useful timber. *Minquartia guianensis*, which is widespread throughout tropical America, furnishes a hard, durable wood that is used widely for construction. The fluted trunks often are employed as telephone poles and in the construction of rustic restaurants and tourist lodges. *Ximenia americana* has a pale, yellow-brown wood used as a substitute for sandalwood because of its fragrance. The fruit of *X. americana* (hog plum) is edible, and the seed is a purgative.

References. BAAS, P., E. VAN OOSTERHOUD, AND C.J.L. SCHOLTES. 1982. Leaf anatomy and classification of the Olacaceae, *Octoknema* and *Erythropalum*. *Allertonia* 3:155–210. DEFILIPS, R. 1969. Parasitism in *Ximenia* (Olacaceae). *Rhodora* 71:439–43. MAAS, P.J.M., F. D. BOESEWINKEL, P. HIEPKO, D. LOBREAU-CALLEN, L. VAN DER OEVER, AND B.J.H. TER WELLE. 1992. The identity of 'Unknown Z': *Maburea* Maas, a new genus of Olacaceae in Guyana. *Bot. Jahrb. Syst.* 114(2):275. SLEUMER, H. O. 1935. Olacaceae. In *Die Natürlichen Pflanzenfamilien*, A. Engler and K. Prantl, 2nd ed., 16b:5–32. Leipzig: Wilhelm Engelmann. SLEUMER, H. O. 1983. Olacaceae. *Fl. Neotrop. Monogr.* 38:1–159. WERTH, C. R., W. V. BAIRD, AND L. J. MUSSELMAN. 1979. Root parasitism in *Schoepfia* Schreb. *Biotropica* 11:140–43.

Figure 142. OLACACEAE. *Schoepfia chrysophylloides*. **A.** Stem with leaves and inflorescences (x⅔). **B.** Stem with leaves and infructescences (x⅔). **C.** Part of inflorescence with one open flower (x6). **D.** Medial section of short-styled flower (x4). **E.** Apical view of short-styled flower (x4). **F.** Medial section of long-styled flower (x4). **G.** Apical view of long-styled flower (x4). **H.** Floral diagram of long-styled flower. **I.** Floral diagram of short-styled flower, showing inner parts only. Reprinted with permission from Correll and Correll (1982). Artist: Priscilla Fawcett.

OLEACEAE (Olive Family)

PETER GREEN

Figure 143

- *trees, shrubs, and lianas*

- *leaves opposite, simple or pinnately compound*

- *flowers actinomorphic, usually bisexual; corolla usually sympetalous, 4-lobed; stamens usually 2, epipetalous*

- *fruit type variable, usually drupaceous*

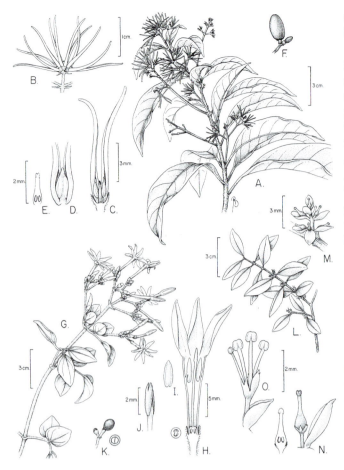

Figure 143. OLEACEAE. *Chionanthus compactus* (A–F), *Jasminum fluminense* (G–K), and *Forestiera eggersiana* (L–O). **A.** Stem with leaves and inflorescences. **B.** Part of inflorescence. **C.** Medial section of flower. **D.** Detail of base of petals showing one adnate stamen. **E.** Medial section of gynoecium. **F.** Lateral view of fruit. **G.** Stem with leaves and inflorescences. **H.** Medial section of flower. **I.** Detail of anther. **J.** Detail of stigma. **K.** Fruit (left) and transverse section of fruit (right). **L.** Stem with leaves and inflorescences. **M.** Pistillate inflorescences. **N.** Lateral view (right) and medial section (left) of pistillate flowers. **O.** Lateral view of staminate flower with subtending bracteole. Reprinted with permission from Acevedo-Rodríguez (1996). Artist: Bobbi Angell.

Numbers of genera and species. Worldwide, the Oleaceae comprise 22–23 genera and more than 400 species. In tropical America, there are eight genera, of which seven are native. The largest *Jasminum* has more than 200 species in the Eastern Hemisphere, some of which are cultivated as ornamentals or found as escapes in the neotropics. *Chionanthus* (including *Linociera* and *Tessaranda*) is the second largest genus and is represented by some 24 American species. *Forestiera* has about five species; *Menodora* seven species; *Fraxinus* three species; *Priogymnanthus*, a recently recognized Neotropical genus, two species; and *Osmanthus* and *Schrebera* each one species in tropical America.

Although not strictly tropical, the monotypic genus *Hesperelaea* (closely related to *Chionanthus*) from the Mexi-

can island of Guadalupe, appears to have been exterminated by goats.

Distribution and habitat. Species of Oleaceae are found throughout the tropical world with a center of diversity in southeastern Asia. The largest Neotropical genus, *Chionanthus*, is recorded from Central and South America and the West Indies; *Forestiera* is found in Central America and the West Indies; *Fraxinus* is predominantly a temperate genus of trees but species are also found in Central America, usually above 1,000 meters; *Osmanthus americanus* reaches the Tropics in Mexico; and *Schrebera*, which is found in Peru, provides an interesting example of disjunct distributions. The type species, *Schrebera swietenioides* (and one other little-known species), occurs in southeastern Asia; three are found in tropical Africa, and *S. americana* is Neotropical. The main distribution for *Menodora* is outside the Tropics, both to the north in California and Mexico and to the south in Argentina but species occur in southern Mexico, Bolivia, and northern Paraguay.

Although the *Jasminum* is not native to the Western Hemisphere, species have become naturalized. For example, *Jasminum fluminense* was first described from Brazil in 1825 and named after Rio de Janeiro. It was, however, an early introduction by the Portuguese from East Africa into Brazil and, having escaped from cultivation, was mistakenly believed to be a native Brazilian plant.

Species of Neotropical Oleaceae are often found in savanna and forest habitats.

Family classification. Although Cronquist placed the Oleaceae in the Scrophulariales, the family is sometimes placed in the Oleales (e.g., Takhtajan). Recent molecular analyses place the Oleaceae in an unresolved Lamiales with many members of Scrophulariales as defined by Cronquist. The family is currently divided into two subfamilies, the Jasminoideae and the Oleoideae. In the Western Hemisphere, most of the representatives belong to the Oleoideae, tribe Oleeae. *Menodora* is the only genus of Jasminoideae in the Western Hemisphere. The familial classification of Oleaceae needs amending in light of more recent observations.

Features of the family. Habit: trees, shrubs, and lianas, sometimes suffrutescent (*Menodora*). Stipules absent. Leaves opposite (alternate in some *Jasminum*), simple or pinnately compound. Inflorescences terminal or axillary, basically cymose, ranging from paniculate to racemose-decussate, subumbellate, or fasciculate. Flowers actinomorphic, usually bisexual, sometimes unisexual (plants dioecious), small; calyx usually small, 4-toothed; corolla early caducous (*Priogymnanthus*), sometimes absent (*Forestiera* and some species of *Fraxinus*), typically sympetalous, the lobes 4; androecium of 2 (4 in some *Chionanthus* and *Priogymnanthus*) stamens, the stamens epipetalous; gynoecium syncarpous, the ovary superior, the carpels 2, the locules 2, the stigma ± bilobed; placentation axile, the ovule usually 1, pendulous, ascending.

Fruits usually drupes, sometimes samaras (*Fraxinus*) or woody capsules (*Schrebera* and *Menodora*), the capsules circumscissile (*Menodora*). **Seeds** usually 1 per fruit.

Natural history. In the Oleoideae, several genera are noted for their sweet fragrance. Although observations have not been recorded for Neotropical species of *Fraxinus*, in the Eastern Hemisphere, a plant's sexuality can vary from male in one year to female and seed-producing the next.

Economic uses. In temperate regions, the Oleaceae are best known for the economically important olive (*Olea europaea*), for decorative garden plants (e.g., *Forsythia* and *Syringa*, lilac), and for timber trees (*Fraxinus*, ash). In the neotropics, however, the Oleaceae are of minor economic importance; e.g., species of *Jasminum* are cultivated widely as ornamentals.

References. GREEN, P. S. 1969. Studies in the genus *Jasminum* IV: the so-called New World species. *Kew Bull.* 23: 273–75. GREEN, P. S. 1994. A revision of *Chionanthus* (Oleaceae) in S. America and the description of *Priogymnanthus*, gen. nov. *Kew Bull.* 49:261–86. JOHNSON, L.A.S. 1957. A review of the family Oleaceae. *Contr. New South Wales Natl. Herb.* 2:395–418. MELCHIOR, H. 1964. Oleaceae. In *Syllabus Der Pflanzenfamilien*, ed. A. Engler, 2:403–05. Berlin: Gebrüder Borntraeger. STEYERMARK, J. A. 1932. A revision of the genus *Menodora*. *Ann. Missouri Bot. Gard.* 19:87–177. WILSON, K. A., AND C. E. WOOD. 1959. The genera of Oleaceae in the southeastern United States. *J. Arnold Arbor.* 40:369–84. ZONA, S. 1991. A morphometric and taxonomic reevaluation of *Haenianthus* (Oleaceae). *Canad. J. Bot.* 69:489–93.

ONAGRACEAE (Evening Primrose Family)

PAUL E. BERRY AND PETER C. HOCH

Figure 144, Plate 34

- *usually herbs or shrubs*

- *leaves alternate, opposite, or whorled, simple*

- *flowers often 4-merous; hypanthium present; stamens usually twice as many as sepals; ovary inferior*

- *fruits loculicidal capsules, sometimes nutlike or berries*

Numbers of genera and species. Worldwide, the Onagraceae comprise 17 genera and approximately 656 species. The largest genera are *Epilobium* (164 species), *Oenothera* (119), *Fuchsia* (108), *Ludwigia* (82), and *Camissonia* (61). In the Western Hemisphere, there are 17 genera and about 517 species. In tropical America, there are 12 genera, and about 240 species, with *Fuchsia*, *Oenothera*, and *Ludwigia* the most speciose.

Distribution and habitat. The Onagraceae are cosmopolitan, but the family is most diverse in western North America, with a secondary center of speciation in tropical and Andean South America. Species of the family grow in lowland swamps to high montane meadows and scree slopes, tropical cloud forests, deserts, and boreal forests.

In the neotropics, *Fuchsia* is largely confined to montane cloud forests, *Oenothera* is widespread in open and generally drier montane habitats, and *Epilobium* occurs in high montane areas generally above tree line. *Ludwigia* is most common in lowland swamps.

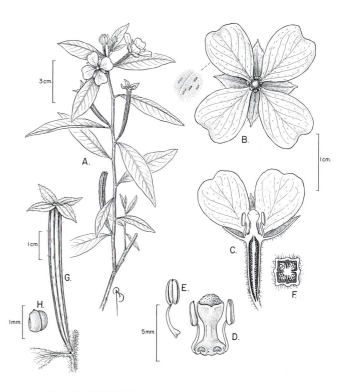

Figure 144. ONAGRACEAE. *Ludwigia octovalvis.* **A.** Stem with leaves, flowers, and fruits. **B.** Apical view of flower with detail of petal surface showing punctations (left). **C.** Medial section of flower. **D.** Detail of stamens and gynoecium. **E.** Abaxial view of stamen. **F.** Transverse section of ovary. **G.** Lateral view of fruit. **H.** Seed. Reprinted with permission from Mori et al. (2002). Artist: Bobbi Angell.

Family classification. The Onagraceae are placed by Cronquist in the Myrtales near families such as the Lythraceae and Combretaceae. Recent molecular studies by the Angiosperm Phylogeny Group also place the Onagraceae within the Myrtales, at the base of the rosid clade. The family forms a well-defined, monophyletic group, based on a suite of shared derived characters, such as a four-nucleate embryo sac, presence of abundant raphides in vegetative cells, septa dividing the sporogenous tissue, and pollen with paracrystalline beaded ektexine and viscin threads on the proximal wall.

The family has been divided into seven tribes, all of which occur in the Western Hemisphere. Five of the tribes, based on the genera *Ludwigia*, *Fuchsia*, *Circaea*, *Lopezia*, and *Hauya*, are monogeneric. As currently circumscribed, Epilobieae includes *Epilobium* and *Chamerion*, and the Onagreae comprises nine genera centered in western North America. *Ludwigia* is clearly the sister group to the rest of the family, which divides into two loosely defined clades, one consisting of *Circaea*, *Fuchsia*, *Hauya*, *Lopezia*, and *Megacorax*, and the other comprising the tribes Epilobieae and Onagreae.

Features of the family. Habit: herbs, shrubs, lianas (*Fuchsia*), or trees (*Hauya*, some *Fuchsia*), the herbs annual or perennial. **Stipules** sometimes present. **Leaves** alternate, opposite, or whorled, simple; blade margins entire or lobed. **Inflorescences** usually axillary, spicate, paniculate, or of solitary flowers. **Flowers** actinomorphic or zygomorphic, usually bisexual or sometimes unisexual (species of *Fuchsia*, then plants dioecious or gynodioecious), typically 4-merous, sometimes 2-merous (*Circaea*) or 5- to 7-merous (some *Ludwigia*); hypanthium present, extending beyond ovary (except in *Chamerion* and *Ludwigia*); sepals 2–7, distinct, valvate; petals 2–7, sometimes absent (some species of *Fuchsia* and *Ludwigia*); nectary often near base of tube; androecium usually with twice as many stamens as sepals, equal to number of sepals, or rarely 1 or 2 (*Lopezia*), the stamens in two sets (when twice as many as sepals) or in one set (*Circaea* and some *Ludwigia*); pollen shed as monads, tetrads, or polyads (species of *Ludwigia*), loosely held together by slender viscin threads; staminodes sometimes present in *Lopezia* and *Fuchsia*; gynoecium with inferior or rarely semi-inferior ovary, the carpels 2 or 4–7, the locules 2 or 4–7, the style 1, the stigma capitate, cylindrical, clavate, or strongly lobed; placentation axile, the ovules 1–many, anatropous. **Fruits** loculicidal capsules, sometimes nutlike, or berries. **Seeds** 1–many, small, naked or sometimes with wings or tufts of hairs; endosperm absent.

Natural history. About half the species in the family are autogamous. Some species promote outcrossing through protandry (*Epilobium*, *Chamerion*, *Clarkia*, and *Lopezia*) or protogyny (*Fuchsia*). Male sterility and gynodioecy have evolved in several lineages of *Fuchsia*, and dioecy occurs in two different sections of this genus. Most outcrossing members of the family are pollinated by bees, with some very specialized interactions known to occur in the Onagreae. Hawkmoths, sphinx moths, noctuids, and other small moths also pollinate a suite of other species in the Onagreae, whereas birds are the main pollinators of *Fuchsia* (hummingbirds in the neotropics and honeyeaters in New Zealand) and of some *Lopezia*, *Epilobium*, and *Xylonagra*. Flies pollinate some species of *Lopezia* and *Fuchsia*.

The fleshy fruits of *Fuchsia* are bird-dispersed. Most other genera have capsular fruit; some of these have seeds with a tuft of hairs (*Epilobium* and *Chamerion*) and are wind-dispersed, while others have seeds that are water- or ant-dispersed. The indehiscent fruits of *Circaea* are covered with hooked hairs that stick to the bodies of passing animals.

Economic uses. Many Onagraceae are cultivated as ornamentals, especially species of *Clarkia*, *Epilobium* (willow herb), *Fuchsia*, and *Oenothera* (evening primrose). Evening primrose oil, derived from seeds of *Oenothera biennis* and related species, is now used extensively as a dietary supplement to treat afflictions such as dermatitis, premenstrual syndrome, and high cholesterol levels. Some Epilobieae at higher latitudes, such as fireweeds (*Chamerion angustifolium*), can be weedy. *Ludwigia* has some weedy species in wet areas of the Tropics. Species of *Oenothera* are reported to have minor medicinal uses.

References. BERNAL, H. Y., AND J. E. CORRERA Q. 1998. Oenotheraceae (Onagraceae) (*Oenothera multicaulis*). In *Especies vegetales promisorias de los países del Convenio Andrés Bello*, Tomo XII. Santafé de Bogotá, D. E., Colombia: Secretaria Ejecutiva del Convenio Andrés Bello. GODLEY, E. J., AND P. E. BERRY. 1995. The biology and systematics of *Fuchsia* in the South Pacific. *Ann. Missouri Bot. Gard.* 82:473–516. HOCH, P. C., J. V. CRISCI, H. TOBE, AND P. E. BERRY. 1993. A cladistic analysis of the plant family Onagraceae. *Syst. Bot.* 18:31–47. LEVIN, R. A., W. L. WAGNER, P. C. HOCH, M. NEPOKROEFF, J. C. PIRES, ET AL., 2003. Family-level relationships of Onagraceae based on chloroplast *rbc*L and *ndh*F data. *Amer. J. Bot.* 90: 107–15. RAVEN, P. H. 1979. A survey of reproductive biology in Onagraceae. *New Zealand J. Bot.* 17:575–93. RAVEN, P. H. 1988. Onagraceae as a model of plant evolution. In *Plant Evolutionary Biology*, eds. L. D. Gottlieb and S. K. Jain, 85–107. London: Chapman and Hall.

OPILIACEAE (Opilia Family)

PAUL HIEPKO AND CAROL GRACIE

Figure 145

- *trees, shrubs, or lianas, hemiparasitic*
- *leaves alternate (distichous), simple*
- *flower perianth uniseriate*
- *fruits drupes*
- *seeds 1 per fruit*

Numbers of genera and species. Worldwide, the Opiliaceae comprise 10 genera and 33 species. In tropical America, there is one genus, *Agonandra*, with 10 species. *Agonandra* is the largest genus in the family and endemic to the Western Hemisphere.

Distribution and habitat. Opiliaceae are widespread in tropical and subtropical regions of both the Western and Eastern Hemispheres, but the greatest diversity is found in Africa and Asia). *Agonandra* is found from northern Mexico, through Central America, and into South America. In South America, species are found almost exclusively east of the Andes with only *A. excelsa* known from the Pacific slopes.

Most Neotropical species are native to seasonally dry forests. However some, such as *Agonandra silvatica*, are trees inhabiting the rain forests of the Guianas, Peru, Brazil, and northern Bolivia.

Family classification. The Opiliaceae are placed in the Santalales by Cronquist. The family was formerly included in the closely related Olacaceae or sometimes in the Santalaceae, both of which are also hemiparasitic. However, the Opiliaceae have been segregated from the Olacaceae based on differences in the structure of the disc, the reduction (rather than enlargement) of the calyx to a merely cupuliform torus, and the strictly unilocular ovary. According to molecular studies, Opiliaceae are distinct from and more derived than Olacaceae.

Features of the family. Habit: trees, shrubs, or lianas, hemiparasitic. **Bark** of trunk and older stems usually fissured or furrowed, corky in *Agonandra brasiliensis*. **Stipules** absent. **Leaves** alternate (distichous), simple; blades vary in form and size within species, coriaceous, smooth, usually decurrent on petiole, the margins entire. **Inflorescences** mostly axillary, sometimes terminal in *Agonandra racemosa*), racemes; bracts present, subtending groups of 1–3(4) flowers. **Flowers** actinomorphic, unisexual (plants dioecious), small, greenish; perianth uniseriate. **Staminate flowers:** tepals (3)4–5;

Figure 145. OPILIACEAE. *Agonandra brasiliensis* (A–E, Richards 6583; F, G, Heringer 10571; H, Evans et al. 2636; I, Nee 37864). **A.** Stem with leaves and inflorescences. **B.** Part of inflorescence. **C.** Lateral views of staminate flower just beginning to open (left) and opened staminate flower (right). **D.** Lateral view of staminate flower with petal removed to show nectaries and pistillode. **E.** Nectary. **F.** Lateral view of bud of pistillate flower. **G.** Lateral view (left) and medial section (right) of pistillate flower with petals removed. **H.** Stem with leaves and infructescences. **I.** Medial section of fruit (right) and seed (left). Original. Artist: Bobbi Angell.

disc present, the lobes conspicuous, sometimes fused, alternating with tepals; androecium with stamens equal in number to tepals; rudimentary gynoecium present. **Pistillate flowers:** tepals caducous; staminodes lacking; disc annular or cupular; gynoecium syncarpous, the ovary superior, unilocular, the carpels 2–5, the stigma sessile; placentation basal, the ovule 1, erect. **Fruits** drupes, globular (1–2.5 cm diam.), the pericarp thin, usually yellow to orange, the mesocarp fleshy, the endocarp woody or crustaceous. **Seeds** 1 per fruit, large; endosperm oily, the embryo long, narrow, the cotyledons 3 or 4, linear.

The members of the family always have an underground

attachment by haustoria to the roots of other plants from which they derive water and nutrients.

Dried leaves are often finely tuberclulate, which is caused by cystoliths located in the mesophyll.

Natural history. The small, inconspicuous flowers of *Agonandra* are probably pollinated by wind or small insects. The fruits of *Agonandra silvatica*, *A. brasiliensis*, and *A. macrocarpa* are eaten by deer and monkeys and the fruits of *A. racemosa* are consumed by birds.

Economic uses. Young leaves and inflorescences of *Champereia* and *Melientha* are frequently used as vegetables in Southeast Asia. People eat the fruits of *Agonandra brasiliensis* in Venezuela, and a rubber substitute is made of the partially hydrogenated oil from the seeds. The wood of the same species is used for furniture and carving in Brazil and Bolivia.

References. HIEPKO, P. 1984. Opiliaceae. In *Flora Malesiana*, ed. C.G.G.J. Van Steenis, ser. 1, 10:31–52. Alphen Aan Den Rijn, Netherlands: Sijthoff and Noordhoff International Publishers. HIEPKO, P. 1993. Opiliaceae. In *Flora of the Guianas*, ed. Görts-Van Rijn, ser. A, 14:36–39. Koenigstein: Koeltz Scientific Books. HIEPKO, P. 2000. Opiliaceae. *Fl. Neotrop. Monogr.* 82:1–53.

OROBANCHACEAE (Broom-rape Family)

JOHN L. BROWN

Plate 34

- *herbaceous root parasites*
- *plants often fleshy; glandular hairs present; chlorophyll absent*
- *leaves scales, brownish*
- *flowers zygomorphic, bisexual; ovary superior*
- *fruits bivalvate capsules*

Numbers of genera and species. Worldwide, the Orobanchaceae comprise 17 genera and 150 species. In tropical America, there are two genera, *Orobanche* (7 species) and *Conopholis* (2 species).

Distribution and habitat. The family is chiefly north temperate Eurasian. The largest genus, *Orobanche*, is quite common throughout temperate Eurasia. The Neotropical species are found in Central America and Andean South America at higher elevations.

Family classification. The Orobanchaceae are placed in the Scrophulariales by Cronquist, and are most closely related to members of the Scrophulariaceae, a family that possesses species of hemiparasites. Recent morphological and molecular analyses suggest that the family is monophyletic; however, these studies further suggest that the Orobanchaceae belong to a larger monophylectic group that includes other parasitic Scrophulariaceae.

Features of the family. Habit: herbaceous root parasites, often fleshy, usually annual, chlorophyll absent; glandular hairs present on stems, leaf scales, and flowers. Roots rarely extensive. Haustoria present. Stems usually 1 per plant. Stipules absent. Leaves scales, alternate, crowded, brownish. Inflorescences terminal, racemes or spikes. Flowers zygomorphic, bisexual; calyx tubular, the sepals connate, the lobes 2–5; corolla 2-lipped, the petals 5, connate; androecium with 4 stamens, the stamens in 2 groups, inserted below middle of corolla tube, alternating with lobes, a single stamen sometimes lost, the anthers dehiscing by longitudinal slits; staminode sometimes present; gynoecium syncarpous, the ovary superior, the carpels 2–3, the locule 1, the style 1, the stigma 2–4-lobed; placentation parietal, the placentas 4, the ovules numerous. Fruits bivalvate capsules. Seeds numerous.

Natural history. Pollination for species of the family has been reported to be by insects and birds. The seeds are light and probably wind-dispersed.

Economic uses. The family has no economic value. Species are occasionally serious pests of the plants they parasitize.

References. YOUNG, N. D., K. E. STEINER, AND DEPAMPHILIS C. W. 1999. The evolution of parasitism in Scrophulariaceae/Orobanchaceae: Plastid gene sequences refute an evolutionary transition series. *Ann. Missouri Bot. Gard.* 86(4): 876–93.

OXALIDACEAE (Wood-sorrel Family)

JOHN D. MITCHELL

Figure 146, Plate 35

- *generally herbs or subshrubs*

- *leaves alternate, compound, sometimes unifoliolate; pulvini prominent*

- *flowers actinomorphic; stamens usually 10, obdiplostemonous, the antepetalous ones shorter; heterostylous*

- *fruits usually loculicidal capsules*

- *seeds elastically ejected by sarcotesta*

Numbers of genera and species. Worldwide, the Oxalidaceae comprise five genera and more than 900 species (excluding *Hypseocharis* and the Lepidobotryaceae). In tropical America, there are two native genera, *Oxalis* and *Biophytum*, and more than 200 species. The tropical Asian *Averrhoa* includes two species that are widely cultivated in the neotropics.

Distribution and habitat. The Oxalidaceae are widespread, but most abundant in the Tropics and temperate zones of the Southern Hemisphere. The largest genus, *Oxalis*, is cosmopolitan and particularly diverse in the Andes. Chile, which is mostly extratropical, includes approximately 115 species of *Oxalis*. *Biophytum* is a pantropical genus with about 75 species worldwide.

The Oxalidaceae occur in both dry and moist habitats from the lowlands to alpine areas. Species of *Oxalis* occupy habitats ranging from lowland dry or moist forests up to the snow line in mountains. Some species are found in disturbed areas such as roadsides and cultivated land; and few species of *Oxalis* are weeds introduced from areas outside the neotropics (e.g., *Oxalis corniculata* from the Mediterranean region). Species of *Biophytum* typically grow in open to shaded sites in tropical moist to wet forest.

Family classification. Cronquist included the Oxalidaceae in the Geraniales. The Angiosperm Phylogeny Group, however, placed the Oxalidaceae in its own order along with the Elaeocarpaceae, Connaraceae, and Cunoniaceae, and excluded the Geraniaceae from this grouping. Cronquist included the Lepidobotryaceae in the Oxalidaceae, but that family is treated separately in this book.

The genus *Averrhoa* is treated by most authors, including Cronquist, as being a member of the Oxalidaceae. However, Hutchinson segregated it from the Oxalidaceae into its own family, the Averrhoaceae. The Andean genus *Hypseocharis* has been transferred into the Geraniaceae by Boesewinkel.

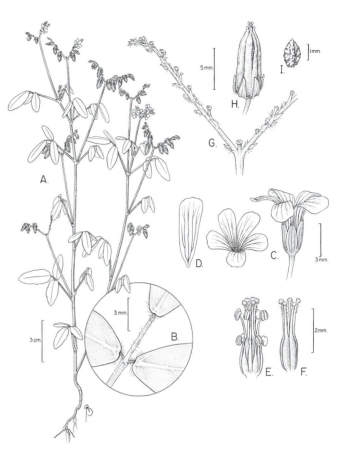

Figure 146. OXALIDACEAE. *Oxalis barrelieri*. **A.** Plant with roots, leaves, flowers, and fruits. **B.** Detail of rachis and bases of leaflets showing trichomes. **C.** Oblique-apical (left) and lateral (right) views of flower. **D.** Adaxial view of petal. **E.** Lateral view of flower with calyx and corolla removed to show dimorphic stamens. **F.** Lateral view of gynoecium. **G.** Infructescence after fruits have dehisced and fallen. **H.** Lateral view of fruit. **I.** Seed. Reprinted with permission from Mori et al. (2002). Artist: Bobbi Angell.

Judd et al., and Price and Palmer have concluded that both morphological and DNA characters support the monophyly of the Oxalidaceae as here circumscribed.

Features of the family. Habit: usually herbs or subshrubs, rarely shrubs, trees, vines, or lianas, often with bulbs, tubers, or fleshy rhizomes, soluble and crystalline oxalates often present. **Stipules** sometimes present, adnate to petioles. **Leaves** alternate, sometimes basal (some *Oxalis*), 1–3(4)-foliolate (*Oxalis*) or pinnate (*Biophytum* and *Averrhoa*); petioles often with prominent pulvini responsible for "sleep" movements of leaflets. **Inflorescences** axillary or occasionally cauliflorous, usually cymose, umbelliform, racemiform, or of solitary flowers. **Flowers** actinomorphic, bisexual, small and inconspicuous to somewhat large and showy; sepals 5, usually imbricate; petals 5, convolute or imbricate in bud, clawed, often white, yellow, orange, pink, red, lavender, or purple; androecium usually of 10 stamens, obdiplostemonous, the antepetalous stamens shorter, the filaments usually basally connate, the anthers dehiscing longitudinally; gynoecium heterostylous, bi- or trimorphic, syncarpous, the ovary superior, the carpels 5, the locules 5, the styles 5, distinct, the stigma capitate, often bifid; placentation axile, the ovules 1–5(15) per locule, pendulous, epitropous. **Fruits** usually loculicidal capsules, or berries in *Averrhoa*, usually 5-locular. **Seeds** 1–15 per carpel, bitegmic; sarcotesta present, basal, breaking elastically to eject seed; endosperm usually present, the embryo straight.

The only trees in the Neotropics of Oxalidaceae are the two introduced species of *Averrhoa*. Species of *Biophytum* often resemble miniature tree ferns.

Natural history. Flowers of *Oxalis* are visited by bees, butterflies, and other insects attracted to nectar secreted at the filament bases. Many species display nectar guides on their petals. The Oxalidaceae are characterized by heterostyly, which ensures a high degree of outcrossing. Self-pollination also occurs in the family, as shown by the presence of cleistogamous flowers in several weedy species of *Oxalis*.

Seeds of species of *Oxalis* are ejected from the dehiscent capsules. The fleshy berries of the two introduced species of *Averrhoa* are apparently dispersed by vertebrates.

Economic uses. Some species of *Oxalis*, especially *oca* (*O. tuberosa*), which is indigenous to the Andes, produce locally utilized edible tubers. Two species of *Averrhoa* yield edible fruits; *A. carambola* (*carambola* or star fruit) is cultivated widely in the neotropics for its delicious fruits and *Averrhoa bilimbi* (*belimbing asam* or cucumber fruit) bears a fruit that looks like a small pickle. This juicy and fairly acidic berry is pickled, used in curries, and stewed as a vegetable. Some Neotropical species of *Oxalis* are grown as ornamentals and other widespread species are persistent weeds, such as *O. corniculata*, which is often found in greenhouses.

References. BERNAL, H. Y., AND J. E. CORRERA Q. 1998. Oxalidaceae (*Oxalis tuberosa*). In *Especies vegetales promisorias de los países del Convenio Andrés Bello*, Tomo XII. Santafé de Bogotá, D. E., Colombia: Secretaria Ejecutiva del Convenio Andrés Bello. BOESEWINKEL, F. D. 1988. The seed structure and taxonomic relationships of *Hypseocharis* Remy. *Acta Bot. Neerl.* 37:111–20. BURGER, W. 1991. Oxalidaceae. In Flora Costaricensis, ed. W. Burger. *Fieldiana, Bot.*, n.s., 28:2–16. EMSHWILLER, E. 2002. Biogeography of the *Oxalis tuberosa* alliance. *Bot. Rev.* 68(1):128–52. KNUTH, R. 1930. Oxalidaceae. In *Das Pflanzenreich IV; Regni vegetabilis conspectus*, ed. A. Engler, heft 95:1–481. Leipzig: Wilhelm Engelmann. KNUTH, R. 1931. Oxalidaceae. In *Die Natürlichen Pflanzenfamilien*, A. Engler and K. Prantl, 2nd ed. 19a:11–42. Leipzig: Wilhelm Engelmann. LOURTEIG, A. 1980. Oxalidaceae. In Flora of Panama, eds. R. E. Woodson, R. W. Schery, and collaborators, *Ann. Missouri Bot. Gard.* 67:823–50. LOURTEIG, A. 1994. *Oxalis* L. subgénero *Thamnoxys* (Endl.) Reiche emend. Lourt. *Bradea* 7(1):1–199. LOURTEIG, A. 2000. *Oxalis* L. subgéneros *Monoxalis* (Small) Lourt., *Oxalis* y *Trifidus* Lourt. *Bradea* 7(2):201–629. PRICE, R. A., AND J. O. PALMER. 1993. Phylogenetic relationships of Geraniaceae and Geraniales from *rbcL* sequences. *Ann. Missouri Bot. Gard.* 80:661–71.

PAPAVERACEAE (Poppy Family)

LISA M. CAMPBELL

Figure 147, Plate 35

- *herbs or pachycaulous treelets*
- *plants with latex, the latex often orange or yellow*
- *leaves usually alternate, simple*
- *flowers usually showy, actinomorphic, bisexual*
- *fruits capsules*

Numbers of genera and species. Worldwide, the Papaveraceae comprise 23 genera and about 220 species. Three genera contain the majority of species; *Papaver* has 80 mostly north temperate species; *Meconopsis* has 48 species with a center of diversity in south-central Asia; and *Argemone* has 32 species in the Western Hemisphere. In tropical America, there are three native genera, *Argemone* with approximately eight species, *Bocconia* with about nine species, and *Hunnemannia* with one species. Some species of *Papaver* have been introduced.

Distribution and habitat. Papaveraceae are predominantly north-temperate herbs, and there are several endemic genera in eastern and western North America and eastern Asia. Of the three genera found in tropical America, *Argemone* and *Bocconia* have centers of diversity in North and Central America, respectively, but also occur in the West Indies and South America. *Hunnemannia*, with two species and one Neotropical, is endemic to the highlands of eastern Mexico.

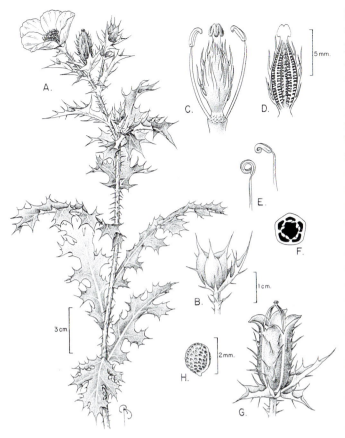

Figure 147. PAPAVERACEAE. *Argemone mexicana.* **A.** Stem with leaves, flower, and immature fruit. **B.** Lateral view of immature fruit. **C.** Lateral view of flower with perianth removed. **D.** Medial section of gynoecium. **E.** Lateral views of stamens. **F.** Transverse section of ovary. **G.** Lateral view of dehisced fruit. **H.** Seed. Reprinted with permission from Acevedo-Rodríguez (1996). Artist: Bobbi Angell.

In the neotropics, Papaveraceae occur in dry to moist lowlands and in the highlands of Central America.

Family classification. The Papaveraceae and the extra-Neotropical Fumariaceae are placed in the Paparverales by Cronquist. Other systems of classification include the 16 genera and more than 500 species of Fumariaceae in Papaveraceae and recent morphological and molecular studies place the members of these two families in the Ranunculales near families such as the Menispermaceae, Berberidaceace, and Ranunculaceae.

Excluding Fumariaceae, the Papaveraceae are divided into five subfamilies: Platystemonoideae (4 genera); Papaveroideae (7, including *Argemone*); Escholzioideae (3 genera); Glaucioideae (2); and the bicarpellate Chelidonioideae with orange latex and arillate seeds (7, including *Bocconia*). Kadereit recognized four subfamilies, placing Glaucioideae in the Chelidonoideae and *Canyba* in Papaveroideae rather than the Platystemonoideae. Based on molecular data, the Platystemonoideae belong within the Papaveroideae.

Features of the family. Habit: herbs or pachycaulous treelets (*Bocconia*), sometimes subshrubs, annual or perennial; latex present, often orange or yellow, sometimes white, watery in *Hunnemannia*; trichomes (branched in *Bocconia*) or prickles sometimes present. **Stipules** absent. **Leaves** usually alternate, sometimes subopposite, simple, often glaucous; blade margins entire to deeply incised. **Inflorescences** axillary or terminal, of solitary flowers, racemose, or paniculate (highly branched in *Bocconia*). **Flowers** actinomorphic, bisexual, usually showy; buds nodding or erect; sepals 2 or 3, caducous; petals often 4 or 6, absent in *Bocconia*, in 2 whorls when present, imbricate and crumpled in bud; androecium of many stamens, the stamens pendulous in *Bocconia*; gynoecium syncarpous, the ovary superior, the carpels (2 in *Bocconia*) 3–7, the locule 1, the style sometimes short or absent (*Hunnemannia*), the stigmas fused, usually discoid, persistent in fruit; placentation parietal, the ovules usually numerous, rarely 1 (*Bocconia*). **Fruits** capsules, variously shaped, glabrous or hairs and prickles present, the dehiscence basipetal or acropetal. **Seeds** many (1 in *Bocconia*), small (the largest in *Bocconia*), often arillate.

Natural history. Most species are insect-pollinated. An exception is *Bocconia*, in which the apetalous flowers with pendulous stamens are wind-pollinated. The seeds of some Papavaraceae are ballistically dispersed or released by shaking of the capsules; but the orange or red arillate seeds of some *Bocconia* remain attached to the dehisced fruit and are probably bird-dispersed, although ants may also aid in dispersal.

Economic uses. Papaveraceae are rich in isoquinoline alkaloids. The latex of various species of *Papaver* contains pharmaceutically useful alkaloids, including opium, codeine, and morphine, from which heroine is derived. The latex is collected from incisions made in the immature capsules. *Argemone* is used as a purgative, and *Bocconia* is used to treat warts. The latex of both genera is used as a dye. Species of several genera, including *Papaver* and *Argemone*, are cultivated ornamentals, and *A. mexicana* is now a weed in lowland sites in the Tropics.

References. HOOT, S. B., J. W. KADEREIT, F. R. BLATTNER, K. B. JORK, A. E. SCHWARZBACH, AND P. R. CRANE. 1997. Data congruence and phylogeny of the Papaveraceae s.l. based on four data sets: *atp*B and *rbc*L sequences, and *trn*K and restriction sites, and morphological characters. *Syst. Bot.* 22:575–90. HUTCHINSON, J. 1920. *Bocconia* and *Maclaeya*. *Kew Bull.* 1902:275–82. KADEREIT, J. W. 1993. Papaveraceae. In *The Families and Genera of Vascular Plants*, eds. K. Kubitzki, J. G. Rohwer, and V. Bittrich, 2:494–506. Berlin: Springer-Verlag. LOCONTE, H., L. M. CAMPBELL, AND D. WM. STEVENSON. 1995. Ordinal and familial relationships of Ranunculid genera. *Pl. Syst. Evol.*, suppl., 9:99–118. OWNBY, G. B. 1958. Monograph of the genus *Argemone* for North America and the West Indies. *Mem. Torrey Bot. Club* 21:1–159.

PASSIFLORACEAE (Passion Flower Family)

CHRISTIAN FEUILLET

Figure 148, Plate 36

- *vines or lianas, sometimes herbs, shrubs, or small trees*

- *plants often with axillary tendrils; extrafloral glands or nectaries often present*

- *leaves alternate, usually simple*

- *flowers with extrastaminal corona; gynoecium and androecium usually on common stalk (androgynophore)*

- *seeds arillate*

Numbers of genera and species. Worldwide, the Passifloraceae comprise approximately 18 genera and 700 species. The largest are *Adenia* (100 species), *Basananthe* (25), and *Passiflora* (500+). Six genera have only one species. In tropical America, there are four genera (*Ancistrothyrsus, Dilkea, Mitostemma,* and *Passiflora*) and somewhere around 500 species. *Ancistrothyrsus* has two, *Mitostemma* has three, and *Dilkea* has five species; however, the latter genus is in need of revision and there are probably many more.

Distribution and habitat. The Passifloraceae occur throughout tropical areas of the world. A few species reach northern subtropical areas in the United States and other areas in Asia. In the Southern Hemisphere, the Passifloraceae are found in northern Argentina, southern Africa, Australia, and New Zealand. Most genera are endemic to the Western or Eastern Hemisphere. The exception is the predominantly American *Passiflora*, with an additional 20 species ranging from southern Asia to New Zealand. In the Western Hemisphere, most Passifloraceae are found within the Tropics, but a few species are extratropical. For example, *Passiflora incarnata* and *P. lutea* reach 39°N in the eastern United States and *P. caerulea* reaches 34°S in Argentina. Except for *Passiflora*, the genera of the Western Hemisphere are mostly limited to tropical South America east of the Andes: *Ancistrothyrsus* and *Dilkea* are found in the Amazonian rain forest, and *Mitostemma* in the southern Guianas and southeastern Brazil.

Passifloraceae occupy a variety of habitats, from savannas to *várzea*, but are most abundant in tropical rain forests on *terra firme*. Many species are found in secondary vegetation along disturbed roadsides. Most species occur at low and middle elevations, but some grow above tree line on Andean slopes.

Family classification. The Passifloraceae are placed in the Violales by Cronquist. Recent studies suggest that the Pas-

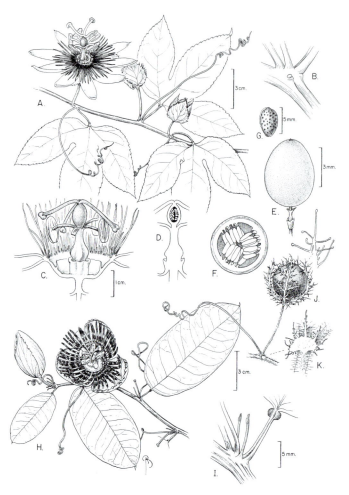

Figure 148. PASSIFLORACEAE. *Passiflora edulis* (A–G), *P. laurifolia* (H, I), and *P. foetida* (J, K). **A.** Stem with leaves, a solitary flower, buds, and axillary tendrils. **B.** Detail of node. **C.** Longitudinal section of flower. **D.** Medial section of androgynophore and gynoecium. **E.** Lateral view of fruit. **F.** Transverse section of fruit. **G.** Seed. **H.** Stem with leaves, a solitary flower, and axillary tendrils. **I.** Detail of node showing elongated stipules. **J.** Lateral view of fruit showing subtending bracteoles and axillary tendril. **K.** Detail of stipule. Reprinted with permission from Acevedo-Rodríguez (1996). Artist: Bobbi Angell.

sifloraceae belong in an expanded Malpighiales near families such as the Turneraceae and Achariaceae. The Passifloraceae are divided into two tribes: Paropsieae and Passifloreae. Other authors include Flacourtiaceae tribe Abatieae in the Passifloraceae, hence this tribe has not been properly considered in either the Passifloraceae or Flacourtiaceae. The Paropsieae are endemic to the Eastern Hemisphere. The axillary bud of the Paropsieae develops into a vegetative branch or into a fertile short stem. Unpublished molecular data (Chase, pers. comm.) suggest that the Paropsieae may be sister to both Passifloreae and Turneraceae. The Passifloreae includes most of the taxa in the family. In the Passifloreae, the axillary bud grows into a commonly epedunculate inflorescence that is often reduced to a terminal tendril, and vegetative branching is produced by additional buds.

Features of the family. Habit: vines or lianas, sometimes perennial herbs, shrubs, or trees; extrafloral glands or nectaries often present. Stems sometimes from a perennial root stock or fleshy caudex. Tendrils (modified inflorescences) often present, axillary, sometimes early deciduous above base, then leaving blunt spine. Stipules usually present, often small, sometimes foliose, then to 7 cm long, often deciduous. Leaves alternate, simple or rarely compound; petiolar and/or laminar nectaries present; blade margins unlobed or lobed; venation pinnate, palmate, or pedate. Inflorescences mostly axillary and sessile, less frequently terminal or cauliflorous, cymose, rarely racemose or fasciculate, 1–several-flowered, sometimes reduced to tendril, the tendril a modified pedicel of central flower; peduncle often lacking (*Passiflora*). Flowers actinomorphic, bisexual; hypanthium present, small to large, flat or campanulate to cylindric; sepals (3)5(8); petals as many as sepals, rarely absent, alternating with sepals; extrastaminal corona of filaments present, the filaments in 1 to many rows; operculum usually present, membranous; nectar ring present; limen usually present, membranous; androecium with (4)5 or 8(10) stamens, the stamens borne on androgynophore (*Passiflora*) or at bottom of hypanthium, the filaments usually distinct, the anthers dorsifixed, versatile; gynoecium syncarpous, the ovary superior, borne on androgynophore (*Ancistrothyrsus* and *Passiflora*) or gynophore, the carpels 3–4(5), the locule 1, the styles as many as carpels, the stigmas clavate; placentation parietal, the ovules numerous. Fruits berries, fleshy and irregularly dehiscent, or capsules, the berries ranging from 0.5–ca. 15 cm diameter, globose and black when small or obovoid and thick-walled when large, the pericarp thick and rindlike to chartaceous. Seeds few to many, arillate; endosperm oily, fleshy, the embryo large, straight.

Germination, when known (*Adenia* and *Passiflora*), is almost always epigeal. Chromosome number (when known): $x = 6$–12.

Natural history. The poisonous leaves of Passifloraceae are adaptations to protect the plants against insect herbivory. Few groups of insects have broken this line of defense, and some, e.g., heliconid butterflies, sequester cyanogenic compounds that make them unpalatable to birds.

Other features of *Passiflora* are also believed to be linked to the evolutionary pressure of herbivory. The most obvious are nectaries on leaf petioles and blades, bracts, and stipules that attract ants or serve as egg mimics. The ants protect passion-flower plants from predation, and the mimic eggs dissuade plant-eating insects from laying their eggs on the plants. Furthermore, plants of the same species of passion flower look different because of the wide variety of leaf shapes, sometimes on the same plant, and the diversity of color and habit of growing-stem apices. Because of this variation, it has been hypothesized that herbivorous insects are not able to easily develop search images for species of *Passiflora*.

Pollination mechanisms are diverse. The most important pollinators are hummingbirds, wasps, various bees, moths, and even bats. Many species cannot self-pollinate because of chemical barriers, whereas others are capable of limited self-pollination. Some species make their pollen available before their stigmas are receptive (protandrous) as a means of ensuring cross pollination. A wide variety of animals disperse the seeds of Passifloraceae, including birds, bats, and monkeys. Many birds and mammals are attracted by the fleshy or juicy arils. A few species possess such hard-shelled fruits that only rodents are able to open them.

Economic uses. Several Neotropical species of *Passiflora* are grown for their edible fruits or juice and are internationally (*P. edulis*) or locally important crop plants. A few species are used in folk medicine (*P. mexicana* and *P. incarnata*) and *P. incarnata* is employed in herbal and homeopathic medicines, especially in Europe. Medicinal extracts of Passifloraceae are used mostly for sedation, relieving anxiety, and treating muscular spasms. The seeds of *Passiflora coriacea* furnish an insecticide. Several American species are naturalized in the Eastern Hemisphere, but one, *P. tarminiana* (not *P. mollissima* as previously reported), is invasive and has become a particular threat to tree fern forests in Hawaii.

References. CERVI, A. C. 1997. Passifloraceae do Brasil. Estudo do gênero *Passiflora* L., subgênero *Passiflora*. *Fontqueria* 45:1–92. ESCOBAR, L. K. 1988. Passifloraceae In *Flora de Colombia*, eds. P. Pinto and G. Lozano, 10:1–138. Bogotá: Universidad Nacional de Colombia. HOLM-NIELSEN L. B., P. M. JØRGENSEN, AND J. E. LAWESSON. 1988. Passifloraceae. In *Flora of Ecuador*, eds. G. Harling and L. Andersson. no. 31:1–130. Göteborg, Sweden: Department of Systematic Botany, University of Göteborg. KILLIP, E. P. 1938. The American species of Passifloraceae. *Publ. Field Mus. Nat. Hist., Bot. Ser.* 19:1–613. MACDOUGAL, J. M. 1994. Revision of Passiflora subgenus Decaloba section Pseudodysosmia (Passifloraceae). *Syst. Bot. Monogr.* 41:1–146. WILDE, W.J.J.O. DE. 1971. The systematic position of tribe Paropsieae, in particular the genus *Ancistrothyrsus*, and a key of the genera of Passifloraceae. *Blumea* 19:99–104. WILDE, W.J.J.O. DE. 1974. The genera of tribe Passifloreae (Passifloraceae) with special reference to flower morphology. *Blumea* 22:37–50.

PEDALIACEAE (Sesame Family)

Thomas A. Zanoni

Figure 149, Plate 36

- *herbs*
- *glandular trichomes present, plants sometimes viscid*
- *leaves opposite, subopposite, or alternate, simple*
- *flowers zygomorphic, sympetalous; ovary superior*
- *fruits loculicidal capsules*

Numbers of genera and species. Worldwide, the Pedaliaceae comprise 13 genera and about 60 species. In tropical America, there is a single genus, *Sesamum*, and one naturalized species.

Distribution and habitat. *Sesamum orientale* and *Ceratotheca triloba* are cultivated in the Western Hemisphere where they are found in weedy habitats outside cultivation. Only *S. orientale* occurs in the neotropics.

Family classification. The Pedaliaceae are placed in the Scrophulariales by Cronquist. In the most recent analyses by Olmstead et al., the Pedaliaceae and Martyniaceae are among the families closely related to the Scrophulariaceae.

The family is divided into three tribes: Sesamothamneae (*Sesamothamnus*), Sesameae (*Ceratotheca, Dicerocaryum, Josephina, Linariopsis,* and *Sesamum*), and Pedalieae (*Harpagophytum, Holubia, Pedalium, Pterodiscus, Rogeria,* and *Uncarina*). Traditionally, the Pedaliaceae included *Trapella,* an aquatic plant found in eastern Asia and now placed in the Trapellaceae, and the American genera *Craniolaria, Martynia,* and *Proboscidea,* now placed in the Martyniaceae.

Features of the family. Habit: herbs, annual or perennial; aerial parts (except corolla) with distinct trichomes, the trichomes uniseriate or the stalk cells uniseriate and the apex cells 4–8, glandular, the plants sometimes viscid. **Stipules** absent. **Leaves** opposite, subopposite, or alternate, simple; blade margins entire or lobed. **Inflorescences** axillary, of solitary flowers, or cymose with few flowers; bracts present, small, deciduous. **Flowers** zygomorphic, bisexual; calyx 5-lobed, slightly unequal; corolla sympetalous, forming a tube usually bilabiate, the lobes 5, imbricate; androecium usually of 4 stamens, the stamens paired, adnate to corolla tube, alternating with petal lobes; staminode 1 or absent; nectary disc present at base of ovary; gynoecium syncarpous, the ovary superior, the carpels 2, the locules 1–2 (sometimes appearing as 4), the style terminal, the stigma lobes 2; placentation axile (locules 2) or parietal (locule 1, appearing as 4 because of intruded placenta), the ovules 1–numerous, anatropous.

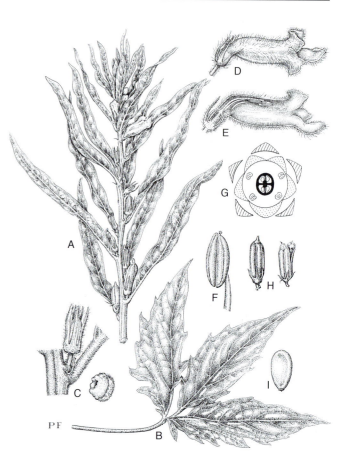

Figure 149. PEDALIACEAE. *Sesamum orientale.* **A.** Stem with leaves, fruits below, and flowers above (x½). **B.** Leaf from lower part of stem (x⅜). **C.** Node with axillary flower bud (left, x2¼) and detail of gland from below flower (right, x12). **D.** Lateral view of flower (x1½). **E.** Medial section of flower (x1½). **F.** Adaxial view of anther (x7). **G.** Floral diagram. **H.** Lateral views of intact (left) and dehisced (right) fruits (x¾). **I.** Seed (x7). Reprinted with permission from Correll and Correll (1982). Artist: Priscilla Fawcett.

Fruits loculicidal capsules, nonfleshy, often covered by spines, hooks, ridges, or other projections. **Seeds** many per fruit, smooth to rough; endosperm mostly lacking, oily.

Natural history. Flowers of Pedaliaceae are visited by bees and moths. The cultivated sesame is usually self-pollinated, but is nonetheless visited by bees. The spines or other projections on the fruit attach to passing animals, thereby facilitating dispersal. The mucilage-bearing hairs of the vegetative parts may be an adaptation for conserving water or for protecting plants against insect predation.

Economic uses. *Sesamum orientale* (=*S. indicum*) may be the oldest crop used for the production of oil. The earliest evidence of cultivated sesame comes from India and the Middle East. Although the place of origin of sesame cultivation is not known, Ethiopia may have been the center of diversity for the genus: however, no wild species closely related to *Sesamum orientale* are known. Ground sesame seeds are used to produce halva (a confection) and tahini (a paste), both popular in Middle Eastern cuisine, and whole seeds are used for baked goods. The edible oil of sesame seeds, the principal commercial product of the Pedaliaceae is very stable, and foods cooked in it keep longer than those cooked in other vegetable oils. Sesame oil also is used in the manufacture of soap, medicine, and cosmetics. The meal obtained from the expressed seeds contains 34–50 percent protein and is used as animal feed and as a protein-rich additive to some flours consumed by humans. Burma, China, India, Nigeria, Sudan, and Mexico are the major producers of sesame seeds.

References. ASHRI, A. 1989. Sesame. In *Oil Crops of the World*, eds., G. Röbbelen, R. K. Downey, and A. Ashri, 375–87. New York: McGraw-Hill Publishing Company. BEDIGIAN, D. 1984. Sesmum indicum L.: Crop Origin, Diversity, Chemistry and Ethnobotany. Ph.D. diss., University of Illinois at Urbana-Champaign. IHLENFELDT, H.-D. 1967. Über die Abgrenzung und die natürliche Gliederung der Pedaliaceae R. Br. *Mitt. Staatsinst. Allg. Bot. Hamburg* 12:43–128, Taf. IV–XII. MANNING, S. D. 1991. The genera of Pedaliaceae in the southeastern United States. *J. Arnold Arbor.*, suppl. ser., 1:313–47. OLMSTEAD, R. G., C. W. DE PAMPHILIS, A. D. WOLFE, N. D. YOUNG, W. J. ELISONS, AND P. A. REEVES. 2001. Disintegration of the Scrophulariaceae. *Amer. J. Bot.* 88(2):348–61.

PELLICIERACEAE (Panama Mangrove Family)

DAWN FRAME

Plate 36

- *mangrove trees*

- *trunks with fluted buttresses*

- *leaves spiral, simple, often with extrafloral nectaries*

- *flowers showy (starlike); petals and stamens 5*

- *fruits indehiscent, turbinate, woody*

Numbers of genera and species. The Pellicieraceae consist of a singe genus and species, *Pelliciera rhizophorae*.

Distribution and habitat. *Pelliciera* is mostly restricted to the Pacific coast of Central America and northern South America, from the Gulf of Nicoya, Costa Rica, to the Esmeraldas River, Ecuador. A few scattered populations are known from the Caribbean coasts of Nicaragua, Panama, and Colombia.

Pelliciera grows only in mangrove habitats. Fossil pollen attributable to *Pelliciera* has been found in Tertiary sediments in Mexico, Panama, the Caribbean, northern South America, and Nigeria. Among Neotropical mangroves, *Pelliciera* appears to be comparatively sensitive to soil salinity and cannot grow in soils with a salt concentration greater than about 37 percent. It also has a preference for slightly elevated places. These observations have led to the hypothesis that climatic changes at the end of the Tertiary, resulting in progressive aridity, sea-level changes, and more seasonality of the climate over much of its range, caused increased soil salinity and, thus, the gradual elimination of this genus from many regions by the early Pliocene.

Family classification. The Pellicieraceae are placed in the Theales by Cronquist. Traditionally, *Pelliciera rhizophorae* has been treated as an unusual member of the Theaceae or Ternstroemiaceae and placed in its own tribe; however, it is now commonly recognized as a distinct family. While a number of plants of theaceous affinities grow in moist, swampy places, *Pelliciera* is the sole taxon to be a true mangrove. Recent studies have revealed a heretofore unsuspected link to another isolated family of theaceous affinity, the Tetrameristaceae, through the recently described genus *Pentamerista*, a small tree of the savannas of the Alto Orinoco-Casiquiare drainages of Venezuela.

Features of the family. Habit: mangrove trees. **Trunks** with fluted, almost obconical, base, the buttresses formed by the emergence of shoot-born roots. **Stipules** absent. **Leaves** spiral, simple, sessile, aggregated at ends of branches; blades coriaceous, asymmetric, the margins, except for deciduous glandular teeth, entire, with pair of extrafloral nectaries often present near base; venation impressed, except for midrib, obscure. **Inflorescences** axillary, of solitary flowers; bracts 2, subtending and enveloping flower bud, pink. **Flowers** actinomorphic, bisexual, large, showy (starlike); sepals 5, distinct, ovate, adaxially concave, proximal half of adaxial surface covered with glands; petals 5, distinct, white to pinkish red, approximately 6 centimeters long, somewhat resembling a tapering candle in outline; androecium of 5 distinct stamens, the stamens just surpassing style, appressed to longitudinal grooves of ovary, the anthers basally sagittate, long, narrow; pistil conic-cylindrical, similar in length to stamens and petals; gynoecium syncarpous, the ovary superior, the carpels

2, the locules 2 (sometimes 1 by abortion), the style long, narrow, the stigma barely bifid; placentation axile, the ovules 1 per locule. **Fruits** indehisent, woody, turbinate, corrugated, strongly beaked, reddish brown, covered with resinous pustules; pericarp corky. **Seed** 1; endosperm absent, the embryo large, well developed.

Natural history. Commonly, *Pelliciera* has three sets of glands: on the long margin of the asymmetric leaves, on the adaxial surface of the sepals, and a paired set at the site of leaf insertion (but in some parts of its range, these may be absent). Observational evidence suggests that the first are salt glands and the latter two are floral and extrafloral nectaries, respectively. Polybiine wasps and *Trigona* bees have been observed foraging on the floral nectaries.

Although the fruit is woody, the wall is readily susceptible to mechanical damage, so the seeds are injured easily. When ripe, fruits drop directly into the soil near the mother plant or float for a short time and at low tide settle into the soil, where the seeds rapidly germinate. Seed viability apparently lasts only a short time, and, thus, the plant cannot be dispersed over long distances.

A study conducted in Rincón, Península de Osa, Costa Rica, disclosed a nonobligatory association between *Pelliciera* and *Azteca* ants. The ants prefer *Pelliciera* to other mangroves and nest in damaged places above high tide mark on the tree. Once installed, they aggressively defend the tree against all invaders, killing and carrying off to their nest any intruders. The ants living on *Pelliciera* display a diverse range of food-gathering tactics. They forage among the root crevices or may go farther afield and visit other plants during low tide. The ants may feed on the floral and extrafloral nectaries of *Pelliciera*, and, finally, they tend scale insects (Homoptera). They may eat the scale insects or collect their "honeydew." The ants are believed to select trees that have been partially damaged by either storms or wood-boring insects (e.g., *Sphaeroma destructor*). The generality of the *Pelliciera*/ant association is not known, but a positive correlation appears to exist between the presence of extrafloral nectaries and ants.

Economic uses. No uses are recorded for this family.

References. COLLINS, J. P., R. C. BERKELHAMER, AND M. MESLER. 1977. Notes of the natural history of the mangrove *Pelliciera rhizophorae* Tr. & Pl., (Theaceae). *Brenesia* 10/11:17–29. FUCHS, H. P. 1970. Ecological and palynological notes on *Pelliciera rhizophorae*. *Acta Bot. Neerl.* 19:884–94. HOWE, M. A. 1911. A little-known mangrove of Panama. *J. New York Bot. Gard.* 12:61–72. JIMÉNEZ, J. A. 1984. A hypothesis to explain the reduced distribution of the mangrove *Pelliciera rhizophorae* Tr. & Pl. *Biotropica* 16:304–08. MAGUIRE, B., C. DE ZEEUW, Y.-C. HUANG, AND C. C. CLARE, JR. 1972. Botany of the Guayana Highland—Part IX. Tetrameristaceae. *Mem. New York Bot. Gard.* 23:165–92. TOMLINSON, P. B. 1986. The Botany of Mangroves. Cambridge, U.K.: Cambridge University Press.

PERIDISCACEAE (Pau Santo Family)

DOUGLAS C. DALY

Plate 37

- *trees*
- *stipules present, stipular scars conspicuous*
- *leaves alternate, simple; petioles pulvinate at both ends; triveined*
- *flowers without petals; disc present; ovary superior*
- *seeds 1 per fruit*

Numbers of genera and species. The Peridiscaceae comprise two monotypic genera, *Peridiscus* and *Whittonia*, restricted to northern South America.

Distribution and habitat. The Peridiscaceae are found in a limited area in the northwestern and central part of the Amazon Basin and the northeastern Guayana Shield in Guyana and Brazil. *Peridiscus lucidus* was collected originally by Richard Spruce on the Uaupés and Pacimoni Rivers, and it is primarily a Rio Negro species, but more recent work has produced collections from the lower Rio Negro as well as from a surprising disjunct population in Amapá, Brazil. *Whittonia guianensis* is represented by very few collections and appears to be endemic to the Potaro River valley of Guyana.

Whittonia is known only from riverine forests, while *Peridiscus* has been found in black-water floodplain forests, river islands, stream margins, moist cliff faces, and at least once in *terra firme* forest.

Family classification. Most of the major classifications prior to the 1990s placed the Peridiscaceae in the Violales (e.g., *sensu* Cronquist), variously defined but including the Flacourtiaceae, Bixaceae, Lacistemataceae, Violaceae, Turneraceae, Caricaceae, and Passifloraceae. A recent attempt at a reorganization of angiosperm phylogeny, incorporating and emphasizing molecular data, was unable to place the Peridiscaceae in any order with confidence.

For some time, *Peridiscus* was placed with various families of the order Violales, mostly because of scant material and errors in early descriptions. It was initially placed in the Bixaceae, then the Capparaceae, and later the Flacourtiaceae.

The Brazilian botanist J. G. Kuhlmann cited the presence of stipules, apetaly, imbricate sepals, many stamens with monothecal anthers, a conspicuous disc surrounding the unilocular ovary, 3–4 styles, ovules pendulous from the ovary apex, seeds solitary, horny endosperm, and a minute, straight embryo located laterally in a shallow cavity near the seed apex as justification for segregating the Peridiscaceae as a distinct family. Subsequent authors have circumscribed the family to include *Peridiscus* and a second genus, *Whittonia*. C. R. Metcalfe commented that, based on its midrib and petiole anatomy and the presence of crystal idioblasts in the leaf epidermis, the family resembles *Soyauxia* (now Passifloraceae, but formerly placed in the Flacourtiaceae).

A number of features recall some Flacourtiaceae, including the presence of stipules, the pulvinate petiole, triplivenation, numerous stamens, distinct styles, and oily endosperm. The family can be distinguished from the Flacourtiaceae (as well as the Bixaceae and Capparaceae) because it has apetalous flowers, monothecal anthers, the ovary clearly unilocular, and apical placentation.

The Peridiscaceae is probably not close to the Capparaceae because the latter has no endosperm, the ovary is septate, and the embryo is large and curved.

Features of the family. Habit: trees, deciduous. **Bark** fissured, rough, dark brown. **Wood** with dark brown sapwood, the heartwood dull sulfur yellow. **Stipules** present, intrapetiolar, the stipular scars conspicuous. **Leaves** alternate, simple; petioles pulvinate at both ends; blades large, coriaceous, glossy, the margins entire; venation of 3 principal veins from base with large abaxial pit in axil of each of basal lateral veins. **Inflorescences** axillary, in clusters of small racemes (*Peridiscus*) or fascicles (*Whittonia*); bracteoles large, persis-

tent. **Flowers** actinomorphic, bisexual, small, fragrant, pale yellow, apparently perigynous in *Peridiscus*; sepals 4–5(6) in *Peridiscus* or 7 in *Whittonia*, (sub)equal, imbricate, the inner ones sometimes petallike (*Whittonia*), reflexed at anthesis; petals absent; androecium of numerous stamens, the stamens seated around (*Peridiscus*) or on disc, the filaments distinct or irregularly connate toward base, flexuous (versus incurved) in *Whittonia*, the anthers small, dehiscing by longitudinal slits, the theca 1; disc fleshy, cupulate or annular, multilobate, pulviniform in *Whittonia*, surmounted by ovary and stamens in *Whittonia*; gynoecium syncarpous, the ovary superior (half immersed in disc in *Peridiscus*), glabrous (*Peridiscus*) or lanate (*Whittonia*), the carpels 3–4, the locule 1, the styles 3(4), distinct, distally subulate; placentation apical, the ovules 6–8, pendulous. **Fruits** (known only from *Peridiscus*) drupaceous. **Seeds** 1 per fruit; endosperm abundant, corneous, the embryo small, lying alongside endosperm, straight, the radicle thick, cylindric, the cotyledons ovate-lanceolate, membranous.

Natural history. No information is available on pollination or dispersal biology.

Economic uses. Despite its noble name (*pau santo* or *palo santo*, sainted tree) in the upper Rio Negro, there are no published uses for *Peridiscus*.

References. KUHLMANN, J. G. 1947. Peridiscaceae (Kuhlmann). *Arq. Serv. Florest.* 3:3–5. METCALFE, C. R. 1962. Notes on the systematic anatomy of *Whittonia* and *Peridiscus*. *Kew Bull.* 15(3):471–75. SANDWITH, N. Y. 1962. Contributions to the flora of tropical America: LXIX. A new genus of Peridiscaceae. *Kew Bull.* 15(3):467–71. SOLTIS, D. E., P. S. SOLTIS, D. R. MORGAN, S. M. SWENSEN, B. C. MULLIN, ET AL. 1995. Chloroplast gene sequence data suggest a single origin of the predisposition for symbiotic nitrogen fixation in angiosperms. *Proc. Natl. Acad. Sci. USA* 92: 2647–51.

PHYLLONOMACEAE (Phyllonoma Family)

SCOTT A. MORI

Figure 150

- *shrubs or small trees, terrestrial or epiphytic*
- *stipules with glandular hairs on adaxial surface*
- *leaves alternate, simple*
- *inflorescences borne on adaxial leaf blade surface*
- *flowers with inferior ovary; placentation parietal*
- *fruits berries, turning white at maturity*
- *seed coat tuberculate*

Numbers of genera and species. The Phyllonomaceae comprise a single genus *Phyllonoma* with four species endemic to the neotropics.

Distribution and habitat. Species of Phyllonomaceae are found in the mountains of Mexico and Central America and in the Andes of South America from Colombia to northwestern Bolivia where they occur in cloud forests between 1,000 and 3,000 meters.

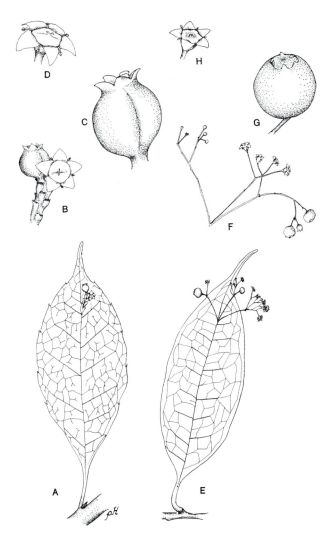

Family classification. Although Cronquist treats this family as part of the Grossulariaceae (Rosales), molecular work supports its segregation as a separate family.

Features of the family. Habit: shrubs or small trees, terrestrial or epiphytic. **Stipules** small, ovate to triangular, with glandular hairs on adaxial surface. **Leaves** alternate, simple. **Inflorescences** borne on adaxial leaf blade surface, cymose and branched or racemose and essentially unbranched. **Flowers** actinomorphic, bisexual, small (2–4 mm diameter); sepals 5, distinct; petals 5, distinct, greenish, greenish yellow, or red or purple tinged; androecium with 5 stamens, the stamens alternate with petals, the anthers dehiscing by longitudinal slits; gynoecium syncarpous, the ovary inferior, the carpels 2, the locule 1, the style usually bifid; placentation parietal, the ovules usually 2–3 per locule. **Fruits** berries, globose or subglobose, turning white at maturity. **Seeds** to 6 per fruit, oblong, the seed coat tuberculate; endosperm present.

The presence of axillary buds, stipules, a normal leaf anatomy of palisade and spongy mesophyll, and an identical morphology of sterile and fertile leaves support the view that the inflorescence-bearing structure is a true leaf and not a phyllode. Consequently, the inflorescences of *Phyllonoma* arise from the adaxial surface of a true leaf, and not from the fusion of an inflorescence axis with a leaf. This feature alone serves to distinguish Phyllonomaceae from all other Neotropical families of plants.

Natural history. Nothing is known about the pollination and dispersal biology of the family.

Economic uses. No economic uses of Phyllonomaceae are known. The curious epiphyllous inflorescences make species of this family candidates for growing in greenhouses.

References. Mori, S. A., and J. A. Kallunki. 1977. A revision of the genus *Phyllonoma* (Grossulariaceae). *Brittonia* 29:69–84.

Figure 150. PHYLLONOMACEAE. *Phyllonoma tenuidens* (A–D) and *P. ruscifolia* (E–H). **A.** Leaf with inflorescence (ca. x3). **B.** Inflorescence (ca. x10). **C.** Lateral view of fruit (ca. x10). **D.** Oblique-apical view of flower (ca. x15). **E.** Leaf with inflorescence (ca. x2). **F.** Inflorescence (ca. x2). **G.** Lateral view of fruit (ca. x8). **H.** Oblique-apical view of flower (ca. x10). Reprinted with permission from Mori and Kallunki (1977). Artist: Phoebe Hunter.

PHYTOLACCACEAE (Pokeweed Family)

Daniel Atha

Figure 151, Plate 37

- *herbs, shrubs, lianas, or trees*
- *stems mostly with successive lateral cambiums (anomalous secondary growth)*

- *leaves alternate, simple; blade margins entire*
- *flowers with calyx often corollalike; corolla absent; placentation basal, the ovule 1 per locule*

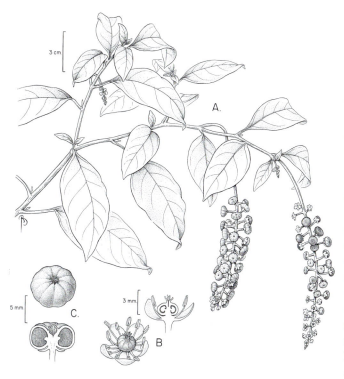

Figure 151. PHYTOLACCACEAE. *Phytolacca rivinoides*. **A.** Stems with leaves and inflorescences. **B.** Oblique-apical view (left) and medial section (right) of flowers. **C.** Oblique-apical view (above) and medial section (below) of fruits. Reprinted with permission from Mori et al. (2002). Artist: Bobbi Angell.

Number of genera and species. Worldwide, the Phytolaccaceae *sensu lato* comprises 17 genera and 72 species. In tropical America, there are 14 genera and approximately 64 species. *Phytolacca* is the largest genus with approximately 20 species worldwide, followed by the Neotropical genus, *Seguieria* with 16 species. *Agdestis*, *Gallesia*, and *Petiveria* are monotypic. The remaining genera have two or three species each.

Distribution and habitat. The Phytolaccaceae are found in the Tropics and subtropics of the world, but are most diverse and numerous in the neotropics. The family probably evolved in the lowland Tropics and subtropics of South America, as suggested by the number of genera that are endemic or native there and in adjacent Argentina and Chile (e.g., *Anisomeria*, *Ercilla*, *Gallesia*, *Hilleria*, *Schindleria*, and *Sequieria*). *Phytolacca* is cosmopolitan. Several genera such as *Hilleria*, *Petiveria*, *Phytolacca*, and *Rivina* are native to the Americas, but species of these genera have been introduced and have become widespread in warmer parts of the world. *Trichostigma*, *Ledenbergia*, and *Microtea* are widespread in the neotropics, though not common. *Stegnosperma* and *Agdestis* are found in Mexico and Central America, with *Agdestis* also occurring in the Greater Antilles.

In the Tropics and subtropics, *Hilleria*, *Petiveria*, *Phytolacca*, *Rivina*, and *Schindleria* are most often found in disturbed sites.

Family classification. The Phytolaccaceae are placed in the Caryophyllales by Cronquist. Despite the application of such modern techniques as chemotaxonomy and gene-sequence analysis, there remain several problematic genera which are only weakly supported as belonging to the Phytolaccaceae *sensu lato*. The most recent monograph of the family recognizes six subfamilies and all are mono-tribic except the Rivinoideae, which is divided into two tribes. Nowicke's classification of the family is based on carpel number, ovary position, pollen morphology, and fruit type. By all accounts, the Phytolaccoideae (*Anisomeria*, *Ercilla* and *Phytolacca*) remain together and sometimes its genera are the only genera that remain in the Phytolaccaceae *sensu stricto*. The Rivinoideae (*Gallesia*, *Hilleria*, *Ledenbergia*, *Monococcus*, *Petiveria*, *Rivina*, *Schindleria*, *Sequieria*, and *Trichostigma*) are retained as a subfamily by some authors, though more commonly elevated to the rank of family (Petiveriaceae). The Microteoideae consist of *Microtea* and *Lophiocarpus*, and are characterized by uni-carpellate ovaries, 2–4 stigmas, one-seeded carpels, and achenes. Cronquist and most other workers recognize the phyletic affinity of these two genera but exclude them from the Phytolaccaceae, often placing them in the Chenopodiaceae. The remaining subfamilies (Agdestioideae, Barbeuioideae, and Stegnospermoideae) are often segregated as families. *Achatocarpus* and *Phaulothamnus* are small American genera, sometimes included in the Phytolaccaceae, but often placed in the Achatocarpaceae (as treated in this book). Until the phylogeny of the family is better understood, it seems prudent to consider the core species as a single family, divided into the subfamilies Phytolaccoideae, Rivinoideae, and Microteoideae, as done in this treatment, or as two separate families, Phytolaccaceae and Petiveriaceae.

Features of the family. Habit: suffrutescent herbs, shrubs, lianas, or trees; raphides of calcium oxalate crystals often present. **Stems** with successive lateral cambiums (anomalous secondary growth). **Stipules** sometimes present, often thorny. **Leaves** alternate, simple; petioles absent in *Lophiocarpus* and *Microtea*; blade margins entire. **Inflorescences** axillary, leaf opposed, or rarely terminal, spicate, racemose, or paniculate. **Flowers** actinomorphic or slightly zygomorphic, bisexual or rarely unisexual (plants dioecious), small; calyx often corollalike, the sepals 4 or 5, in 1 whorl, distinct or slightly connate, mostly equal; corolla absent; staminodes petallike in *Stegnosperma* and *Agdestis*; androecium of 3–many stamens, the stamens in 1–2 whorls, sometimes arising from hypogynous disc, the filaments distinct or basally connate; gynoecium apocarpous or syncarpous, the ovaries superior (subinferior in *Agdestis*), the carpels 1–16, the locules 1–16, the styles none or short, the stigmas as many as styles; placentation basal or axile, the ovules 1 per carpel. **Fruits** berries, drupes, drupelets, or capsules, the exocarp dry or fleshy, smooth or ornamented, spinulose, hooked or samaroid. **Seeds** often arillate; endosperm absent, perisperm present, the embryo curved.

Natural history. Very little is known about the pollination biology of this family. The presence of floral nectaries in *Phytolacca* suggests pollination by insects, and the fetid flowers of *Agdestis* indicate pollination by flies. The brightly colored berries or drupes of *Phytolacca* and *Rivina* indicate bird dispersal and the winged fruits of *Seguieria* and *Gallesia* are dispersed by the wind.

Economic uses. Phytolaccaceae are not economically important, though some species are exploited widely for their medicinal properties. *Phytolacca* and *Rivina* are reported to be toxic and are used medicinally throughout the Americas and both have been used for the preparation of dyes and as ornamentals. The fruits of *Phytolacca* have a high saponin content and occasionally are used to launder clothes or to kill mollusks, especially in Africa, where schistosomiasis is prevalent. Paradoxically, young *Phytolacca* leaves, known as poke salet, are eaten, though only after boiling in several changes of water. *Petiveria* and *Gallesia* smell strongly of garlic and are used medicinally, as are *Microtea* and *Trichostigma*.

References. BEHNKE, H. D. 1994. Sieve element plastids: their significance for the evolution and systematics of the order. In *Caryophyllales: Evolution and Systematics*, eds. H. D. Behnke and T. J. Mabry, 87–121. Berlin: Springer-Verlag. BROWN, G. K., AND G. S. VARADARAJAN. 1985. Studies in Caryophyllales I: re-evaluation of classification of Phytolaccaceae s.l. *Syst. Bot.* 10:49–63. HEIMERL, A. 1934. Phytolaccaceae. In *Die natürlichen Pflanzenfamilien*, A. Engler and K. Prantl, 2nd ed., 16c:135–64. MANHART, J. R., AND J. H. RETTIG. 1994. Gene sequence data. In *Caryophyllales: Evolution and Systematics*, eds. H. D. Behnke and T. J. Mabry, 235–46. Berlin: Springer-Verlag. MIKESELL, J. E. 1979. Anomalous secondary thickening in *Phytolacca americana* L. (Phytolaccaceae). *Amer. J. Bot.* 66:997–1005. NOWICKE, J. W. 1969. Palynotaxonomic study of the Phytolaccaceae. *Ann. Missouri Bot. Gard.* 55:294–363. RETTIG, J. H., H. D. WILSON, AND J. R. MANHART. 1992. Phylogeny of the Caryophyllales- gene sequence data. *Taxon* 41:201–09. ROHWER, J. G. Phytolaccaceae. 1993. In *The Families and Genera of Vascular Plants*, eds. K. Kubitzki, J. G. Rohwer, and V. Bittrich, 2:506–15. Berlin: Springer-Verlag. WALTER, H. 1909. Phytolaccaceae. In *Das Pflanzenreich*, A. Engler, Series 4, 83(heft 39):1–154. Leipzig: Wilhelm Engelmann. WHEAT, D. 1977. Successive cambia in the stem of *Phytolacca dioica*. *Amer. J. Bot.* 64: 1209–17.

PICRAMNIACEAE (Picramnia Family)

WM. WAYT THOMAS

Figure 152, Plate 37

- *shrubs or small trees*

- *leaves alternate, compound; leaflets alternate*

- *inflorescences usually pendent or arching*

- *flowers actinomorphic, unisexual (plants dioecious); gynophore present*

- *fruits berries (Picramnia) or samaras (Alvaradoa)*

Numbers of genera and species. The Picramniaceae comprise two genera and 46 species endemic to the neotropics. *Picramnia* contains 41 species, and *Alvaradoa* has five species.

Distribution and habitat. The Picramniaceae are restricted to the American Tropics. The largest genus, *Picramnia*, is usually found in rain forests, although a few species are adapted to the drier *cerrado* and *campo rupestre* habitats of the Brazilian Planalto. *Alvaradoa* is typically found in arid areas. A third, as yet undescribed genus, is found in western Amazonian from Peru to Panama in lowland rain forests.

While few species are characteristic of wet areas, *Picramnia* is often on forested stream banks. Some species are apparently restricted to certain soil types; e.g., *Picramnia polyantha* is found in forests over limestone in southern Mexico and Guatemala and *P. ferrea* is restricted to an area in Brazil where the soils are very high in iron. The rare, prostrate, *Picramnia campestris*, the smallest species of the genus, is found in the Brazilian *campo rupestre*.

Family classification. Although anomalous when compared to other Simaroubaceae, *Picramnia* and *Alvaradoa* have generally been treated as separate, monotypic subfamilies of the Simaroubaceae of the Sapindales (e.g., Cronquist). Molecular analyses, however, demonstrate that *Picramnia* and *Alvaradoa* are best treated as a separate family of uncertain placement within the Rosidae. See the discussion under Simaroubaceae for an explanation of the realignment of that family.

Features of the family. Habit: small trees or shrubs. Stipules absent. Leaves alternate, compound (imparipinnate); leaflets alternate, shiny (many *Picramnia*), mimosoidlike (*Alvaradoa*), the margins wavy (many *Picramnia*). Inflorescences axillary, racemose or paniculate, usually pendent or arching. Flowers actinomorphic, unisexual (plants dioecious), small (several millimeters long at most); perianth 3–5-merous; calyx persistent; petals short-lived, usually maroon, pale yellow, or greenish; androecium of 3–5 stamens, the stamens opposite petals, sometimes borne on a column; gynoecium borne on small disc or gynophore, syncarpous, the carpels 2 or 3 (2 carpels sterile in *Alvaradoa*, but all potentially fertile in *Picramnia*), the locules 1–3, the style virtually absent, the stigmas 2(3), divergent, persistent; placentation apical, the ovules then pendulous, or basal, the ovules then erect, the ovules 2 per locule, epitropous or apotropous. Fruits berries (*Picramnia*) or samaras (*Alvaradoa*). Seeds plano-convex to narrowly ellipsoid.

Natural history. Individuals of a population of *Picramnia* are characteristically widely scattered, raising questions as to how pollination is effected in these dioecious forest plants with such inconspicuous flowers. Studies suggest that *Alvaradoa* is wind-pollinated.

The flattened samaras of *Alvaradoa* suggest that the fruits are wind-dispersed. Although little documentation is available, all species of *Picramnia* probably are bird-dispersed. Most species bear pendent infructescences of conspicuous red or orange berries that turn black one by one as they ripen. This conforms to the syndrome of bicolored fruit display described by Willson and Thompson in which birds selectively consume the few dark fruits in an otherwise red infructescence. Emerald toucanets have been observed eating the berries of *P. antidesma* in Costa Rica.

Treelets of *Picramnia magnifolia* usually have hollow stems inhabited by ants.

Economic uses. The wood of *Alvaradoa amorphoides* is strong and used for carpentry and fuel. Fruits of *Picramnia latifolia* are edible, and the fruiting branches of *P. antidesma*, with their deep green leaves and red fruits, are used to decorate homes and altars.

The bark, leaves, and roots of several species of *Picramnia* are said to be very bitter and provide treatments for a variety of maladies including malaria, intestinal and stomach ailments, and venereal disease. Decoctions of *Alvaradoa* are used in the Yucatán to treat digestive problems, skin diseases, urinary complaints, and rheumatism.

References. CRONQUIST, A. 1944. Studies in the Simaroubaceae—IV. Resume of the American genera. *Brittonia* 5: 128–47. ENGLER, A. 1931. Simarubaceae. In *Die Natürlichen Pflantzenfamilien*, A. Engler and K. Prantl, 2nd ed., 19a:359–405. Leipzig: Wilhelm Engelmann. FERNANDO,

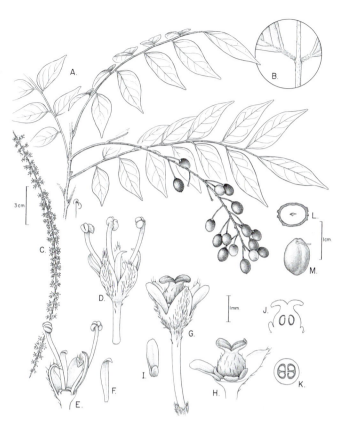

Figure 152. PICRAMNIACEAE. *Picramnia antidesma* subsp. *fessonia* (A, B, Tonduz 9082 and Williams 24544; C–K, Vásquez 1258; L, M, Tonduz 9082). **A.** Stem with leaves and infructescence. **B.** Detail of part of leaf rachis and bases of leaflets. **C.** Inflorescence. **D.** Lateral view of staminate flower. **E.** Medial section of staminate flower. **F.** Adaxial view of petal from staminate flower. **G.** Lateral view of pistillate flower. **H.** Lateral view of pistillate flower with most of petals and sepals removed. **I.** Petal with nectary of pistillate flower. **J.** Medial section of gynoecium and nectaries. **K.** Transverse section of ovary. **L.** Transverse section of seed. **M.** Lateral view of seed. Original. Printed with permission from W. Thomas of The New York Botanical Garden. Artist: Bobbi Angell.

E. S., AND C. J. QUINN. Picramniaceae, a new family, and a recircumscription of Simaroubaceae. *Taxon* 44:177–81. MORTON, J. F. 1981. *Atlas of Medicinal Plants of Middle America*. Springfield, IL: C.C. Thomas. PIRANI, J. R. 1990. As espécies de *Picramnia* Sw. (Simaroubaceae) do Brasil: Uma sinopse. *Bol. Bot. Univ. São Paulo* 12:115–80. THOMAS, W. W. 1988. A conspectus of Mexican and Central American *Picramnia* (Simaroubaceae). *Brittonia* 40(1):89–105. THOMAS, W. W. 1990. The American genera of Simaroubaceae and their distribution. *Acta Bot. Brasil.* 4:11–18. TOMLINSON, P. B. 1980. *The Biology of Trees Native to Tropical Florida*. Allston, MA: Harvard University Printing Office. WILLSON, M. F., AND J. N. THOMPSON. 1982. Phenology and ecology of color in bird-dispersed fruits, or why some fruits are red when they are "green." *Canad. J. Bot.* 60:701–13.

PIPERACEAE (Pepper Family)

Michael Nee

Figure 153, Plate 37

- *herbs (less often vines), shrubs, subshrubs, small trees; aromatic*

- *nodes prominently swollen*

- *leaves alternate, sometimes opposite or whorled, simple*

- *inflorescences dense spikes or racemes of tiny flowers*

- *sepals and petals absent*

- *seeds 1 per fruit*

Numbers of genera and species. Worldwide, the Piperaceae comprise about 10 genera and 1,500–2,000 species. In tropical America, there are four genera, *Peperomia*, *Piper*, *Pothomorphe*, and *Sarcorhachis* and perhaps 1,000 species.

Piper and *Peperomia* are in need of so much critical study that estimates of the number of species are uncertain and likely inflated. In the late nineteenth and early twentieth centuries, specialists on the American species were notorious splitters, and careful work on local floras has greatly reduced the number recognized species, while at the same time continuing to uncover undescribed species.

Distribution and habitat. The Piperaceae are pantropical, mostly occurring in moist areas. The family is especially well represented in the neotropics in moist mid- to low-elevation Andean forests and is uncommon in central Amazon rain forest. Most species of *Piper* and *Pothomorphe* prefer the disturbed habitats of small to large gaps and many species of *Peperomia* are epiphytes. While almost all species of *Piper* are adapted to fairly humid, often forested areas, a few species of *Peperomia* are found in areas with a long and severe dry season. The family scarcely extends outside of the Tropics.

Species of *Piper* and allied genera are terrestrial, although a few are lianas. *Peperomia* consists of herbaceous plants, varying from moderately to strongly succulent, that often are small vines, and epiphytes in the canopy. Some species grow upon rocks, usually in mossy mats; a few are terrestrial, and a few are associated with epiphytic ant nests.

Family classification. The Piperaceae are placed by Cronquist near the Saururaceae in the Piperales. Recent molecular and morphological analyses support the Piperaceae and Saururaceae as sister groups and suggest that they are related to families such as the Aristolochiaceae and Hydnoraceae. The family consists essentially of two genera, *Peperomia* and *Piper*,

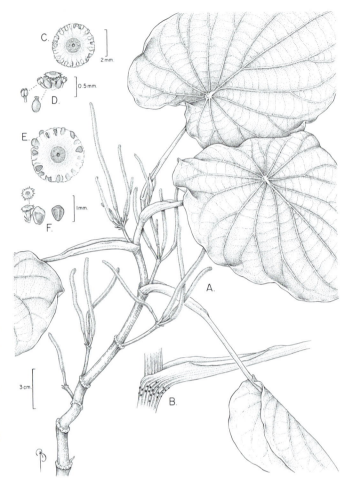

Figure 153. PIPERACEAE. *Pothomorphe peltata.* **A.** Stem with leaves and inflorescences. **B.** Detail of petiole clasping the stem; note glands. **C.** Transverse section of inflorescence. **D.** Lateral view of floral unit with peltate bract flanked by a flower on each side (above), details of gynoecium (below center), and stamen (left). **E.** Transverse section of infructescence. **F.** Peltate bract (left) with apical view of bract (above), fruit (center), and seed (right). Reprinted with permission from Mori et al. (2002). Artist: Bobbi Angell.

with a few satellite genera sometimes segregated from them, notably *Pothomorphe* which differs from *Piper* mainly by the axillary inflorescences of umbellate spikes. Based on recent molecular studies, *Pothomorphe* will probably be merged with *Piper*. There are sufficient differences between *Piper* and *Peperomia* to sometimes lead to segregation of *Peperomia* and *Sarcorhachis* as a separate family, the Peperomiaceae.

Features of the family. Habit: herbs, shrubs, subshrubs, small trees, less often vines. **Wood** weak, prominent rays present. **Nodes** prominently swollen. **Stipules** united with petiole, forming ± sheathing base (*Piper*) or absent (*Peperomia*). **Leaves** alternate, sometimes opposite or whorled in

Peperomia, simple; blade margins entire. **Inflorescences** opposite leaves (*Piper*), or variously terminal or clustered in leaf axils (*Peperomia*), dense spikes or racemes, the flowers aggregated; bracts present, subtending flowers. **Flowers** bisexual, small; sepals absent; petals absent; androecium of 2 stamens in *Peperomia* or stamens (1)6(10), often in 2 groups of 3, the anthers dehiscing by 1 slit in *Peperomia* or 2 slits in *Piper*, the thecae 1 (*Peperomia*) or 2 (*Piper*); gynoecium with superior ovary, syncarpous in *Piper*, the carpels 1 in *Peperomia* or 3–4 in *Piper*, the locule 1 in *Piper*, the styles nearly obsolete, the stigmas 3–4; ovules 1. **Fruits** berrylike or drupes, small. **Seeds** 1.

Natural history. The dense spicate inflorescence is usually pollinated by small bees, which scrape pollen from the surface. The fruits are very small, and the whole infructescence is usually the dispersal unit. Fruit-eating bats are the primary dispersal agents of *Piper*.

Economic uses. Black pepper is produced from the fruits of *Piper nigrum*, a climbing species originally from southern India and Ceylon, but now cultivated worldwide, including the neotropics, where plantations in the Amazon have had varying success. Several other species of the Eastern Hemisphere are used widely as spices or to make drinks or are chewed to increase saliva, but the species of the Western Hemisphere are of little commercial value. The plants of Piperaceae produce ethereal oils; some of these are aromatic but not particularly pleasant, but others are delightfully fragrant. Because of these aromatic properties, many species of *Piper* and some of *Peperomia* have been used in folk medicine. The rhizomes of *Piper methysticum* (native to the islands of the South Pacific) are used to make a beverage called kava. This beverage acts as a mild anesthetic and tranquilizer and is consumed socially by Polynesians; however, because of the psychoactive properties of kava, its use has spread throughout the world. Recent reports of liver damage caused by the consumption of kava have resulted in its being banned by some European countries. Species of *Peperomia* are commonly grown as houseplants.

References. Burger, W. 1971. Piperaceae. In Flora Costaricensis, ed. W. Burger. *Fieldiana, Bot.* 35:5–227. Jaramillo, M. A., and P. S. Manos. 2001. Phylogeny and patterns of floral diversity in the genus *Piper* (Piperaceae). *Amer. J. Bot.* 88(4):706–16. Semple, K. S. 1974. Pollination in Piperaceae. *Ann. Missouri Bot. Gard.* 61:868–71. Yuncker, T. G. 1958. The Piperaceae—a family profile. *Brittonia* 10:1–7.

PLANTAGINACEAE (Plantain Family)

Flor Chavez

Figure 154

- *usually herbs*
- *leaves alternate, often in basal rosettes*
- *inflorescences spikes or appearing headlike*
- *flowers small, perianth usually 4-merous; corolla sympetalous, scarious*
- *fruits usually circumscissile capsules*

Numbers of genera and species. Worldwide, the Plantaginaceae comprise three genera (*sensu* Cronquist) and between 213 and 265 species. In tropical America, there are two genera, *Plantago* and the monotypic *Bougueria*, and about 25–30 species.

Distribution and habitat. The Plantaginaceae are a cosmopolitan family. Species of *Plantago* are most diverse in temperate regions of the world. In the Western Hemisphere, many species occur in tropical montane habitats, but are more or less absent from tropical lowlands. Many species also occur in temperate regions of North America, Chile, and Argentina. *Bougueria* is native to the Andes of Peru, Bolivia, and northern Argentina. Three species of *Littorella* are found in Europe, and temperate North and South America. One species of *Plantago* is endemic to the island of Trinidad and another to the Galápagos Islands.

In tropical America, species of *Plantago* occupy a wide variety of habitats from sea level to high-altitude *páramos*. They are often found as weeds along roadsides, trails, and in pastures, grasslands, and forest gaps. Although species are often habitat specific, *Plantago* can be found in both wet and

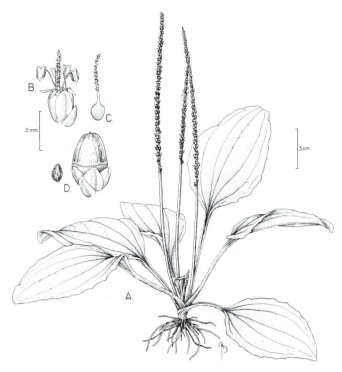

Figure 154. PLANTAGINACEAE. *Plantago major.* **A.** Plant with roots, basal leaves, and inflorescences. **B.** Lateral view of flower. **C.** Lateral view of gynoecium. **D.** Lateral views of fruit (right) and seed (left). Reprinted with permission from Acevedo-Rodríguez (1996). Artist: Bobbi Angell.

dry climates, and on clay, sand, or rocky substrates. *Bougueria* grows at high elevations in *puna*.

Family classification. The Plantaginaceae are placed in the Plantaginales by Cronquist. Traditionally, there has been a wide consensus that the family is monophyletic and closely related to the Scrophulariaceae. Preliminary molecular studies place Plantaginaceae close to *Veronica* (Scrophulariaceae *sensu* Cronquist). These studies suggest that rearrangements of taxa in the traditional Plantaginaceae, Scrophulariaceae, Buddlejaceae, Myoporaceae, Callitrichaceae, Hippuridaceae, and Orobanchaceae are needed. In an attempt to create a monophyletic Scrophulariaceae, some authors have suggested that many taxa of Scrophulariaceae, Callitrichaceae, and Hippuridaceae should be included in the Plantaginaceae.

In a recent phylogeny of the Plantaginaceae *sensu stricto* based on chemical, morphological, and embryological data, Rahn recognized a single genus, *Plantago*, and six subgenera, including *P.* subgenus *Bougueria* and *P.* subgenus *Littorella*. In this study, more than half of the species in tropical America occur in the monophyletic subgenus *Plantago* section *Virginica*. The remaining Neotropical species are placed in three subgenera and four sections that are predominant in the Eastern Hemisphere.

Features of the family. Habit: usually herbs, sometimes small shrubs, sometimes forming cushions, the herbs annual or perennial. Stipules absent. Leaves alternate, often in a basal rosette, simple; petiole base often sheathing; blades elliptic, narrowly elliptic, or linear, often pubescent (at least abaxially), the margins often with conspicuous or inconspicuous teeth and hairs; venation parallel, the veins sometimes slightly curved. Inflorescences axillary, spikes or appearing headlike; scape often present; bracts present. Flowers appearing actinomorphic (calyx asymmetric), usually bisexual (*Bougueria* often reported to be gynomonoecious), protogynous, small; calyx with 4 sepals, the sepals asymmetric, in pairs, the anterior pair often more narrow, basally connate; corolla sympetalous, scarious, the lobes usually 4 (rarely absent), imbricate; androecium of 1 (*Bougueria*) or 4 stamens, the stamens alternate with corolla lobes, the filaments adnate to corolla, the anthers dehiscing by longitudinal slits; gynoecium syncarpous, the ovary superior, the carpels 2, the locules usually 2 (1 in *Bougueria*), the style terminal, the stigma often 2-lobed; placentation axile, the ovules 1–4(many) per ovary (*Plantago*) or basal, the ovule 1 per ovary (*Bougueria*). Fruits circumscissile capsules in *Plantago* or nuts in *Bougueria*. Seeds usually (1)2–3(4–many) per capsule; embryo straight, or curved in *Bougueria*.

Natural history. The small flowers often are wind-pollinated; however, some species are known to be cleistogamous and others have been reported to be pollinated by insects.

Economic uses. Psyllium, composed of the seeds and sometimes the seed coats of some species of *Plantago* (e.g., *P. ovata*), is high in fiber and mucilage and is used to treat constipation, atherosclerosis, and other ailments.

Many species of *Plantago* (plantain) are weeds; e.g., *P. major*, *P. virginica*, and *P. rugelii*. The leaves and seed coats of some species (e.g., *P. lanceolata*) are used as animal fodder.

References. LÓPEZ-TÉLLEZ, A., AND S. A. REYES. 1999. Plantaginaceae. In *Flora de Veracruz*, eds. V. Sosa et. al., fasc. 108:1–20. Xalapa, Veracruz, Mexico: Instituto de Ecología, A. C. MOSTACERO, J., AND F. MEJIA. 1993. *Taxonomia de Fanerogamas Peruanas*. Trujillo, Peru: Editorial Libertad. OLMSTEAD, R. G., C. W. DE PAMPHILIS, A. D. WOLFE, N. D. YOUNG, W. J. ELISONS, AND P. A. REEVES. 2001. Disintegration of the Scrophulariaceae. *Amer. J. Bot.* 88(2):348–61. RAHN, K. 1996. A phylogenetic study of the Plantaginaceae. *Bot. J. Linn. Soc.* 120(2):145–98. RAHN, K. 1975. Plantaginaceae. In *Flora of Ecuador*, eds. G. Harling and B. Sparre, Opera Botanica ser. B, no. 4:25–38. Göteborg, Sweden: Department of Systematic Botany, University of Göteborg. RAHN, K. 1974. *Plantago* section *Virginica*: a taxonomic revision of a group of American plantains, using experimental, taximetric and classical methods. *Dansk Botanisk Arkiv*. Bind 30, nr. 2:11–178.

PLATANACEAE (the Plane-tree Family)

Michael Nee

- *trees*

- *leaves alternate, simple; petioles expanded at base, covering axillary buds*

- *inflorescences aggregated into dense ball-like heads*

- *flowers unisexual; perianth uniseriate*

- *fruits achenes or nutlets with long hairs*

Numbers of genera and species. Worldwide, the Platanaceae comprise a single genus, *Platanus*, and about six species. In tropical America, there are two species of *Platanus*, although several temperate species are commonly cultivated in tropical montane areas.

Distribution and habitat. The Platanaceae mostly occur in northern temperate and subtropical regions, only reaching as far south as Guatemala in the neotropics.

Species of *Platanus* often grow along rivers or even along seasonal watercourses in arid regions. The main species in tropical America, *P. mexicana*, is a member of the temperate deciduous forest zone of Mexico and Guatemala, where it occurs with other genera characteristic of north-temperate deciduous forests.

Family classification. The Platanaceae are placed in the Hamamelidales by Cronquist. Recent morphology and molecular analyses suggest that the Platanaceae are better placed with families such as the Proteaceae and Nelumbonaceae.

Features of the family. Habit: trees, slightly aromatic; vegetative buds covered by petiole base. **Bark** characteristically smooth, light colored, sometimes white on upper portion of tree, often flaking off in large plates, the lower bark thick, dark, furrowed. **Stipules** leaflike, prominent. **Leaves** alternate, simple; petioles expanded at base, covering axillary buds; blades usually with 3 or more lobes, often densely covered with branched hairs (at least when young) abaxially, the margins coarsely dentate; venation generally strongly 3-nerved, pinnate in seedlings. **Inflorescences** terminal, pedunculate, the flowers aggregated into 1–several dense, ball-like heads. **Flowers** actinomorphic, unisexual (plants monoecious), small. **Staminate flowers:** sepals 3–4(7), short; petals vestigial; androecium with stamens equal to number of sepals, the filaments very short, the anthers long, linear. **Pistillate flowers:** sepals 3–4(7), short; petals absent; gynoecium apocarpous, the ovary superior, the carpels generally 5–8, the stigmas elongate; placentation apical, the ovules 1 per carpel, pendulous. **Fruits** elongate achenes or nutlets, long hairs present. **Seeds** oily; endosperm scanty, the embryo straight.

Natural history. Species of *Platanus* produce copious pollen and are wind-pollinated. The fruiting heads eventually begin disintegrating, releasing the fruits, which can be dispersed by the wind for short distances because of the long hairs. The main dispersal method, however, is floating in the water of the streams along which the plants grow.

Economic uses. The wood of the larger species is used as lumber for various kinds of construction. The interesting bark, quick growth, and resistance to city pollution make them suitable for use as street trees.

References. Nee, M. 1981. Platanaceae. *Flora de Veracruz*, eds. A. Gómez-Pompa, V. Sosa et al., fasc. 19:1–9. Xalapa, Mexico: INIREB.

PLOCOSPERMATACEAE (Plocosperma Family)

Lena Struwe

- *shrubs*

- *leaves (sub)opposite, simple*

- *flowers with corolla slightly zygomorphic, widely funnel-shaped, blue-violet to purple; stamens 5, versatile; ovary superior, stipitate, the stigma twice dichotomously divided*

- *fruits capsules*

Numbers of genera and species. The Plocospermataceae comprise a single species, *Plocosperma buxifolium*, restricted to Mexico and Guatemala. Earlier authors have recognized three species characterized by variations in size differences of the leaves and fruits and the density of the indumentum.

Distribution and habitat. *Plocosperma* occurs on shrub dominated hillsides at 200–700 meters in southern Mexico and Guatemala.

Family classification. *Plocosperma* was placed in the Gentianales by Cronquist, within the Apocynaceae. The name *Plocosperma* refers to the seeds, which possess a tuft of hairs at one end, a seed type found in many species of Apocynaceae. *Plocosperma* has also been classified it as a member of the Loganiaceae tribe Gelsemieae (now segregated as Gelsemiaceae), based on the presence of imbricate corolla aestivation and twice dichotomously divided stigmas. In Leeuwenberg's treatment of the Loganiaceae, *Plocosperma* was placed in its own tribe, the Plocospermeae. Recent phylogenetic and phytochemical analyses have shown that *Plocosperma* does not belong in the Gentianales but instead probably belongs in the Lamiales. Cornosides and verbascosides, compounds found in the Lamiales, have been found in *Plocosperma* but are absent from Gentianales. Moreover, the hairs on the seeds are not homologous to those found in Apocynaceae.

Lithophytum was considered a monotypic genus hesitantly assigned to the Solanaceae. It was subsequently transferred to the Verbenaceae by D'Arcy and Keating, and later to the Hydrophyllaceae by Cronquist. This confusion ended when Chiang and Frame showed that *Lithophytum* is synonymous with *Plocosperma*. It is interesting that the placement of *Lithophytum* in the vicinity of Verbenaceae was phylogenetically more correct than the long-time inclusion of *Plocosperma* in the Gentianales.

Features of the family. Habit: shrubs or small treelets, glabrous or hairy, the hairs normal or glandular. **Stipules** absent. **Leaves** (sub)opposite, simple, small; blades coriaceous, ovate to oblong, the apex obtuse. **Inflorescences** axillary, dichasia; peduncles and pedicels short, the flowers positioned 1–7 together. **Flowers** slightly zygomorphic (corolla only), functionally unisexual (plants dioecious), the functionally male flowers with non-functional ovary and no style or stigma, the functionally female flowers with stamens but without viable pollen; calyx rather small, fused at base, lacking colleters, the lobes 5; corolla sympetalous, broadly funnel-shaped, blue-violet to purple, the lobes 5, rounded, imbricate; androecium of 5 stamens, the stamens inserted in lower part of corolla tube, the filaments long, the anthers versatile, oblong; gynoecium with superior ovary, stipitate, nectariferous tissue at base, the carpels presumably 4, the locule 1, the style short, the stigma slender, twice dichotomously divided; placentation parietal, the placentas 2, the ovules 4, erect, at base (2 on each side). **Fruits** 2-valved capsules, very narrow, long. **Seeds** 1–4, long, narrow, the apices with tufts of hairs.

Natural history. The pollinators of *Plocosperma* are unknown. The tufted seeds are presumed to be wind-dispersed, but no observations of this have been reported.

Economic uses. No uses for *Plocosperma* are known.

References. CHIANG, F., AND D. FRAME. 1987. The identity of *Lithophytum* (Loganiaceae, Plocospermeae). *Brittonia* 39: 260–62. D'ARCY, W. G., AND R. C. KEATING. 1973. The affinities of *Lithophytum*: a transfer from Solanaceae to Verbenaceae. *Brittonia* 25:213–25. ENDRESS, M. E., B. SENNBLAD, S. NILSSON, L. CIVEYREL, M. W. CHASE, ET AL. 1996. A phylogenetic analysis of Apocynaceae s. str. and some related taxa in Gentianales: a multidisciplinary approach. *Opera Bot. Belg.* 7:59–102. JENSEN, S. R. 1992. Systematic implications of the distribution of iridoids and other chemical compounds in the Loganiaceae and other families of the Asteridae. *Ann. Missouri Bot. Gard.* 79:284–302. LEEUWENBERG, A.J.M. 1967. Notes on American Loganiaceae I. Revision of *Plocosperma* Benth. *Acta Bot. Neerl.* 16:56–61. LEEUWENBERG, A.J.M. 1980. Angiospermae: Ordnung Gentianales, Fam. Loganiaceae. In *Die Natürlichen Pflanzenfamilien*, 2nd ed., A. Engler and K. Prantl, 28b(1):1–255. Berlin: Duncker and Humblot. STRUWE, L., V. A. ALBERT, AND B. BREMER. 1994. Cladistics and family level classification of the Gentianales, *Cladistics* 10(2):175–206.

PLUMBAGINACEAE (Leadwort Family)

MARK TEBBITT

Figure 155

- *mostly perennial herbs and shrubs*

- *leaves alternate, sometimes in basal rosettes, simple*

- *inflorescences bracteate; bracts often sheathing, dry, membranous*

- *flowers 5-merous; stamens opposite petals; placentation basal, the ovule 1*

- *fruits achenes or capsules*

Numbers of genera and species. Worldwide, the Plumbaginaceae comprise 27 genera and about 1,000 species. The largest genera are *Limonium* (300+ species), *Acantholimon* (120+), and *Armeria* (ca. 80). In tropical America, there are two genera: *Limonium* with two species and *Plumbago* with three species (about 15 worldwide). Two species native to the Eastern Hemisphere, *Plumbago auriculata* and *P. indica*, are also commonly naturalized in the neotropics.

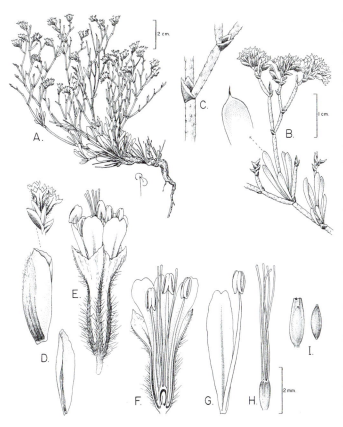

Figure 155. PLUMBAGINACEAE. *Limonium bahamense* (Zanoni 25446). **A.** Plant with root, leaves, and inflorescences. **B.** Stem with leaves and inflorescence and detail of leaf apex (left). **C.** Detail of rachises of inflorescence. **D.** Outer bract with position in inflorescence shown (above) and floral bract (below). **E.** Lateral view of flower. **F.** Medial section of flower. **G.** Adaxial view of stamen adnate to petal. **H.** Lateral view of gynoecium. **I.** Lateral views of fruit (left) and seed (right). Original. Printed with permission from James Luteyn. Artist: Bobbi Angell.

Distribution and habitat. The Plumbaginaceae have a worldwide distribution, but many genera are restricted to the arid mountains of Central Asia.

Plumbago is distributed throughout the tropical, subtropical, and warm temperate regions of the world. In the neotropics, *Plumbago scandens* is found in dry scrubland from Mexico to South America, *P. pulchella* in tropical forest in Mexico, and *P. caeruela* in the Peruvian Andes. *Limonium* is found worldwide in coastal and mountainous areas. Both Neotropical species of *Limonium* occur in coastal areas of the West Indies. The widespread *Armeria* is also represented in the Western Hemisphere, but it is restricted to temperate regions of North and South America.

Several taxa show adaptations to life in dry or saline habitats, including a cushion habit, linear to subulate, fleshy or scleromorphous leaves, glandular mechanisms of salt secretion, and the ability to accumulate chemicals that regulate the volume and concentration of the fluid within the cells.

Family classification. The Plumbaginaceae are placed in the monofamilial Plumbaginales by Cronquist. Currently, Plumbaginaceae are thought to be closely related to Polygonaceae rather than with Primulaceae as previously held. Similarities in floral morphology and placentation traditionally thought to support a close affinity between Plumbaginaceae and Primulaceae probably evolved independently.

Plumbaginaceae are split into two distinct tribes, Plumbaginoideae (including *Plumbago*) and Staticoideae (including *Limonium*), which some authors have treated as subfamilies. Secondary chemistry, pollen type, and DNA sequence data, as well as geographical distribution support the monophyly of the two taxa and of the Plumbaginaceae as a whole. In fact, the taxonomic differences between the Plumbaginoideae and Staticoideae are more extensive than found between many family pairs in the Caryophyllales, and several authors have recognized them as separate families.

Plumbaginoideae possess leafy stems; usually simple inflorescences; almost fused, five-valved capsular fruits; and are distributed throughout the Tropics and warm temperate regions. Staticoideae usually have basal rosettes; thyrsic inflorescences; utriculate or pyxidiate fruits; and are mostly distributed in the Mediterranean and central Asia. The circumscription of several genera, especially *Limonium* and segregate genera, is still debated. Many segregate genera are not distinguishable from *Limonium*, in which they were included previously. The widespread occurrence of hybridization and apomixis are causes of taxonomic confusion.

Features of the family. Habit: mostly perennial herbs and shrubs, self-supporting or twining. **Stipules** absent. **Leaves** alternate, sometimes in basal rosettes, simple; blade margins entire or lobed. **Inflorescences** terminal, determinate racemes or in broadly paniculate, racemose, or capitulate structures; bracts often present, sheathing, dry, membranous. **Flowers** actinomorphic, bisexual, often heterostylous; sepals 5, fused to form tube, the tube 5- or 10-ribbed, often dry and membranous; petals 5, distinct or fused into long tube; androecium of 5 stamens, the stamens opposite petals, the filaments mostly free in Plumbaginoideae, basally fused to petals in Staticoideae, the anthers dorsifixed, dehiscing by longitudinal slits; gynoecium syncarpous, the ovary superior, the carpels 5, the locule 1, the styles 5, distinct or connate, the stigmas dry, papillate, capitate to cylindric; placentation basal, the ovule 1. **Fruits** achenes or capsules, the achenes dry, membranous, at least partly enclosed within persistent calyx, the capsules 5-valved. **Seeds** small; endosperm starchy, the embryo straight, the perisperm absent.

Studies have shown that the petals of Plumbaginaceae represent dorsal outgrowths of the stamens, which explains the alternation between calyx and stamen whorls in the flower.

Natural history. Many Plumbaginaceae possess a heteromorphic, self-incompatible, breeding system; however, this mechanism appears to be absent in the genera endemic to the Southern Hemisphere. Pollinators include bees, flies, and small beetles. In the majority of species, the fruits possess persistent calyces and scarious bracts and bracteoles, which assist in wind dispersal.

Economic uses. The family includes species of ornamental value. Many species of *Armeria* and its cultivars are grown commonly as rock garden or border plants, the dried flowers of several species of *Limonium*, particularly *L. sinuatum* (perennial sea lavender), are important in the cut flower trade, and species of *Ceratostigma* and *Plumbago* are popular greenhouse and garden plants.

Species of *Plumbago* and *Limonium* are used medicinally throughout the world in the local treatment of a variety of ailments. The active ingredient, plumbagin, appears to stimulate the central nervous and muscular systems and helps promote secretions of sweat, urine, and bile. The leaves of a few species also are eaten locally or used as animal forage.

References. HARBORNE, J. B. 1967. Comparitive biochemistry of the flavonoids—IV. Correlations between chemistry, pollen morphology and systematics in the family Plumbaginaceae. *Phytochemistry.* 6:1415–28. KUBITZKI, K. 1993. Plumbaginaceae. In *The Families and Genera of Vascular Plants*, eds. K. Kubitzki, J. G. Rohwer, and V. Bittrich, 2: 523–30. Berlin: Springer-Verlag. LLEDÓ, M. D., M. B. CRESPO, K. M. CAMERON, M. F. FAY, AND M. W. CHASE. 1989. Systematics of Plumbaginaceae based upon cladistic analysis of *rbc*L. *Syst. Bot.* 23(1):21–29. PAX, F. 1889. Plumbaginaceae. In *Die Natürlichen Pflanzenfamilien*, A. Engler and K. Prantl, IV.1:116–25. Leipzig: Wilhelm Engelmann.

PODOSTEMACEAE (River-Weed family)

C. THOMAS PHILBRICK

Figure 156, Plate 38

- *aquatic herbs*

- *holdfasts present*

- *leaves alternate, distichous or tristichous*

- *flowers bisexual, small; tepals present*

- *fruits capsules, often with prominent ribs*

Numbers of genera and species. Worldwide, the Podostemaceae comprise 48 genera and about 270 species. In tropical America, there are 19 genera and 165 species. The largest Neotropical genera are *Apinagia* (ca. 50 species), *Marathrum* (25), and *Rhyncholacis* (25).

Distribution and habitat. The Podostemaceae are pantropical with a wide distribution in the neotropics, where they range from central Mexico, through Central America, northeast South America, much of the Amazon Basin, and into eastern Argentina and Uruguay. *Tristicha* is the only genus occurring in both the paleotropics and neotropics. A single species, *Podostemum ceratophyllum*, is temperate; occurring in eastern North America as far north as New Brunswick, Canada.

Podostemaceae are restricted to rivers that exhibit distinct high-low water seasonality. Most species are found attached to rocks in river rapids and waterfalls and usually occur only in open, high light areas, although some (e.g., *Tristicha trifaria*) can grow under considerable shading by riverine forest.

Family classification. The Podostemaceae are placed in the Podostemales by Cronquist. The combination of unconventional morphology, unusual embryology, and reduced anatomy has led to vast differences of opinion regarding systematic relationships of the Podostemaceae. Studies of embryological features suggest the Saxifragaceae and Crassulaceae as possible close relatives and recent analyses of *rbc*L sequence data lends support to this, and also suggests an affinity of Podostemaceae with Hydrostachyaceae. Gustafsson et al., based on molecular data, have demonstrated that the Podostemaceae are nested inside Clusiaceae as sister of subfamily Hypericoideae or tribe Hypericeae. Hence, the Clusiaceae are paraphyletic if the Podostemaceae are not included. Sinking the Podostemaceae in the Clusiaceae, however, would create a heterogenous family not easily identified morphologically. It has been proposed that the Podostemopsida be considered a class of angiosperms equivalent in rank to monocotyledons and dicotyledons.

The most widely used classification of the family recognizes two subfamilies, the Tristichoideae and Podostemoideae, each of which is further divided into two tribes. Tristichoideae have a distinct 3–5–lobed perianth and leaves surrounding the young flowers. In the neotropics, the tribe Tristicheae (3-lobed perianth, 1–3 stamens, ovary 3-locular) is represented by *Tristicha*, and the tribe Weddellineae (5-lobed perianth, 5–25 stamens, ovary 2-locular) by *Weddellina*. Podostemoideae have scalelike tepals and flowers enclosed within a sacklike spathella. The tribe Mourereae (2-sided, spikelike monochasial inflorescence) is composed of *Lonchostephus*, *Mourera*, and *Tulasneantha*. The largest tribe

Eupodostemeae (flowers solitary, in fascicles, or extra-axillary inflorescences) encompasses the remaining 14 Neotropical genera. Some taxonomists treat Podostemaceae as a single family (Podostemaceae *sensu lato*) while others recognize two families, Tristichaceae and Podostemaceae *sensu stricto*.

Features of the family. Habit: aquatic herbs, annual or perennial, rhizoids sometimes present on lower surface of roots and holfasts, polysaccharide "glue" secreted, the glue aids in attachment to substrate. **Roots** with holdfasts (haptera), the holdfasts disk- or fingerlike, branched or flattened, attaching to rocks. **Shoots** typically derived from lateral region of roots, thin and elongate (e.g., *Oserya* and *Podostemum*) to crustaceous and thalloid (e.g., *Marathrum*), sometimes dimorphic (e.g, *Weddellina*), unbranched (fertile stems) or

branched (vegetative stems), sometimes with holdfasts. **Stipules** present or absent. **Leaves** alternate, distichous or tristichous (*Tristicha*), dichotomously forked (e.g., *Oserya* and *Podostemum*), variously lobed (e.g., *Marathrum* and *Mourera*), to compound (e.g., *Marathrum*, *Rhyncholacis* and *Weddellina*), prickles, tubercles, or fine, threadlike filaments sometimes present (e.g., *Apinagia* and *Mourera*), silica cells sometimes present; blade divisions or lobes flattened, cylindrical, or threadlike, the threadlike divisions lacking vascular tissue (e.g., *Marathrum rubrum* and *Vanroyenella plumosa*). **Inflorescences** of Podostemoideae axillary to leaves or bracts, solitary flowers (e.g., *Oserya*), fascicles (e.g., *Marathrum* and *Vanroyenella*), or spikelike monochasia (*Mourera*), 2-sided (up to 60 cm long) or Tristichoideae terminal, flowers solitary; pedicels of central cylinder surrounded by parenchymatous tissue, elongating considerably after anthesis, hardened (the parenchymatous tissue shed) at fruit maturity, the flowers enclosed in sacklike spathella. **Flowers** bisexual, small; tepals in Podostemoideae 1–25 (sometimes referred to as staminodes), scalelike , linear, spatulate, or toothlike, arranged in complete whorl (or whorls) around ovary (e.g., *Apinagia*, *Marathrum*, and *Mourera*), or incomplete (e.g., *Apinagia* and *Marathrum*), or arising on one side (e.g., *Marathrum*, *Oserya*, and *Podostemum*); tepals in Tristichoideae 3–6, flattened, greenish brown, pink, or white; androecium of 1 (e.g, *Oserya* and *Tristicha*) to 35 (*Mourera*) stamens, the filaments usually distinct, sometimes fused into andropodium for over ½ length (*Podostemum*), 1 tepal-like appendage arising from apex of fused filaments (*Podostemum*), the anthers dehiscing introrsely or extrorsely; gynoecium syncarpous, the ovary superior, the carpels 2 or 3, the locules 2 (Podostemoideae and *Weddellina*) or 3 (*Tristicha*), the styles usually equal to number of locules, the stigma rarely 1 (*Weddellina*), globular and papillose (*Weddellina*); placentation axile, the placenta expanded and fleshy (Podostemoideae and *Weddellina*), the ovules numerous. **Fruits** capsules, often with prominent ribs when mature, dehiscing by longitudinal slits, the valves sometimes persistent. **Seeds** circa 35 (*Oserya* and *Podostemum*) to 2,400 (*Mourera fluviatilis*).

The lack of double fertilization and endosperm, the reduced embryo-sac development, and the presence of a nucellar plasmodium make the Podostemaceae unique among angiosperms. Podostemaceae are the largest family of strictly aquatic plants. The high number of species, lack of vegetative propagules of dispersal and reproduction, high incidence of sexual reproduction, and lack of aerenchyma set the Podostemaceae apart from most other groups of aquatic angiosperms.

The plant body is composed of a prostrate or disclike axis, from which stems arise. This axis can be of root (as in most species) or shoot origin, is green and presumed photosynethic, and exhibits a bewildering array of forms ranging from cylindrical to dorsoventrally flattened, ribbonlike, to crustaceous. The plant can be creeping or attached basally with the proximal regions floating in the current.

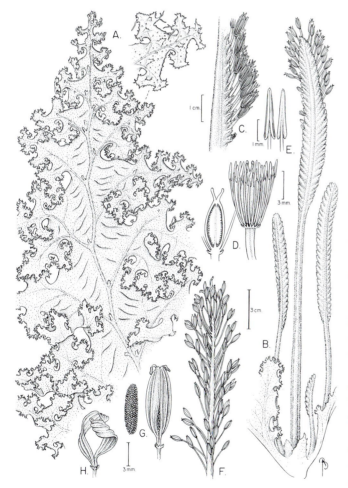

Figure 156. PODOSTEMACEAE. *Mourera fluviatilis* (A, D, E, Irwin 55346; B, Irwin 47135; C, Mori photo, without voucher; F–H, Irwin 48177). **A.** Aquatic leaf with detail of one lobe (upper right). **B.** Inflorescences. **C.** Part of inflorescence. **D.** Lateral view of flower (right) and medial section of gynoecium (left). **E.** Adaxial (left) and abaxial (right) views of stamens. **F.** Part of infructescence. **G.** Lateral views of fruit (right) and seeds on central column (left). **H.** Twisted valves of dehisced fruit. Original. Artist: Bobbi Angell.

Plants vary in size from the tiny mosslike *Tristicha trifaria* with leaves ca. 1 mm long, to the large, course leaved *Mourera fluviatilis* with leaves to 2 m long.

Mourera fluviatilis exhibits a course, thickened stem that creeps tightly appressed to rocks. *Tristicha trifaria* possesses complex photosynthetic appendages (ramuli), which are arranged variously along the shoot axis. Leaflike scales occur on these ramuli.

In *Mourera* dehiscence in the outer whorl of stamens is introrse, while the inner whorl is extrorse.

Natural history. Vegetative growth takes place during periods of high water when the plants are submerged. As the water level drops and plants are exposed, the leaves typically die back and flowering occurs.

Anecdotal accounts implicate both wind and insect pollination in various species, although detailed studies are lacking. For some species, the lack of a perianth and production of large amounts of dry, readily wind-borne pollen suggest wind pollination; however, the large number of ovules is in marked contrast to the typical situation in wind-pollinated plants. The presence of distinctly colored stamen filaments and tepals and observations of insects visiting flowers support the occurrence of insect pollination in some species. Experimental evidence indicates that self-pollination is common in species of *Marathrum* and *Podostemum*.

Studies of species in Mexico indicated that perennial species produced far fewer seeds than annual species. The outer seed coat is composed of mucilaginous cells that collapse when dry but absorb water quickly when wet. These cells play a central role in the attachment of seeds to substrates. After germination, the radicular end of the seedling emerges from the seed coat and then bends toward and contacts the substrate.

Most Podostemaceae grow in largely oligotrophic mountainous rivers. Anecdotal accounts suggest that many species are sensitive to pollution, although a detailed study is lacking. Siltation (e.g., as a result of agriculture or deforestation) is predictably detrimental because it covers plants and disrupts the surfaces of solid substrates on which seeds and seed-lings attach. Recent studies indicate that cyanobacteria and biofilms play a central role in the attachment of Podostemaceae to rocks.

The ecological value of Podostemaceae in tropical rivers is poorly known. River weeds are often the sole macrophytes that occur in abundance in tropical rivers. The dense beds of river weeds likely provide habitat and food for river biota and may be important sources of primary productivity.

Economic uses. Some species are used as forage for cattle during the dry season. Leaves of a species of *Rhyncholacis* are dried, pulverized, and used as a pepperlike seasoning, and the ashes of burned leaves are utilized as a salt substitute by native peoples in the Amazon. In parts of Mexico, species of *Marathrum* are reported to be used as a liver treatment, although this remains unconfirmed.

References. Cook, C. D. K. 1990. *Aquatic Plant Book*. The Hague: SPB Academic Publishing. Cusset, C., and G. Cusset. 1988. Étude sur les Podostemales. 9. Délimitations taxinomiques dans les Tristichaceae. *Adansonia* 10:149–77. Graham, S. A., and C. E. Wood, Jr. 1975. The Podostemaceae in the southeastern United States. *J. Arnold Arbor.* 56: 456–65. Gustafsson, M. H. G., V. Bittrich, and P. F. Stevens. 2002. Phylogeny of Clusiaceae based on rbcL sequences. *Int. J. Pl. Sci.* 163(6):1045–54. Jäger-Zürn, I., and M. Grubert. 2000. Podostemaceae depend on sticky biofilms with respect to attachment to rocks in waterfalls. *Int. J. Plant Sci.* 161:599–607. Philbrick, C. T., and A. Novelo R. 1995. New World Podostemaceae: ecological and evolutionary enigmas. Brittonia 47:210–22. Philbrick, C. T., and A. Novelo R. 1994. Seed germination of Mexican Podostemaceae. *Aquatic Bot.* 48:145–51. Sculthorpe, C. D. 1967. *The Biology of Aquatic Vascular Plants*. New York: St. Martin's Press. Van Royen, P. 1951. The Podostemaceae of the New World. Part I. *Meded. Bot. Mus. Herb. Rijks Univ. Utrecht.* 107:1–151. Van Royen, P. 1953. The Podostemaceae of the New World. II. *Acta Bot. Neerl.* 2: 1–20. Van Royen, P. 1954. The Podostemaceae of the New World. III. *Acta Bot. Neerl.* 3:215–63.

POLEMONIACEAE (Phlox Family)

Dieter Wilken

Figure 157, Plate 38

- *herbs, sometimes shrubs or lianas*
- *leaves usually alternate, opposite only in* Loeselia, *simple or compound*
- *flower sepals, petals, and stamens 5, the sepals and petals connate, the stamens adnate to corolla; ovary superior, the locules 3, the style with 3 stigmatic branches*
- *fruits capsules*

Numbers of genera and species. Worldwide, the Polemoniaceae comprise about 20 genera and 350 species. The largest genera have temperate distributions, and include *Gilia* (60 species), *Phlox* (60), *Linanthus* (35), and *Navarettia* (30). In tropical America, there are seven genera and 40 species: *Bonplandia* (1 species), *Cantua* (5), *Cobaea* (20), *Gilia* (1), *Huthia* (2), *Loeselia* (10), and *Polemonium* (1).

Distribution and habitat. Most species of Polemoniaceae are found in temperate western North America. Several North American genera (*Collomia*, *Gilia*, *Linanthus*, *Ipomopsis*, *Navarettia*, *Phlox*, and *Polemonium*) are each represented by one or two species in temperate South America. At least two, *Phlox gracilis* and *Polemonium micranthum*, occur as far south as Tierra del Fuego. Most species of *Polemonium* are found in temperate North America, but a few occur in Eurasia, including the northern slopes of the Himalayas. The almost exclusively tropical genera, *Cantua*, *Huthia*, *Cobaea*, and *Loeselia*, are found primarily in southern Mexico, Central America, and South America as far south as Bolivia and Peru. However, a few species have their northern limits in the dry subtropical deserts of North America. For example, *Loeselia glandulosa*, a relatively common plant of Central America, Ecuador, and Venezuela, occurs as far north as southern Arizona and Texas. Major centers of endemism in the family include Central America and northwestern South America, the Andean highlands, and California.

Species with a tropical distribution generally occur in the understory of drier upland forests, in pine-oak woodlands, and cloud forests at higher elevations. Species of *Cobaea* can be found climbing over shrubs at forest margins or well into the canopy of cloud forests.

Family classification. The Polemoniaceae are placed in the Solanales by Cronquist. The family has traditionally been placed close to Boraginaceae, Convolvulaceae, and Hydrophyllaceae, but recent evidence from molecular studies suggests that they may have shared a common ancestor with Ericaceae and Fouquieriaceae.

The family is divided into three major groups or subfamilies: Acanthogilioideae, Cobaeoideae, and Polemonioideae. *Cobaea*, the sole member of the Cobaeoideae, has sometimes been treated as a separate family. With the exception of *Cobaea* and the Cantueae, relationships among remaining genera are unclear.

Features of the family. Habit: herbs, sometimes shrubs (*Huthia*) or lianas (*Cobaea*), the herbs usually perennial, sometimes annual; stems and leaves glandular and viscid, often with skunklike odor. **Stipules** absent. **Leaves** usually alternate or opposite in *Loeselia*, simple or, in *Cobaea*, pinnate, with the terminal leaflet modified into tendril; blade margins entire to pinnately lobed (*Bonplandia*, *Cantua*, and *Huthia*), serrate or spinulose (*Loeselia*). **Inflorescences** axillary or terminal, cymose racemes or panicles, sometimes of

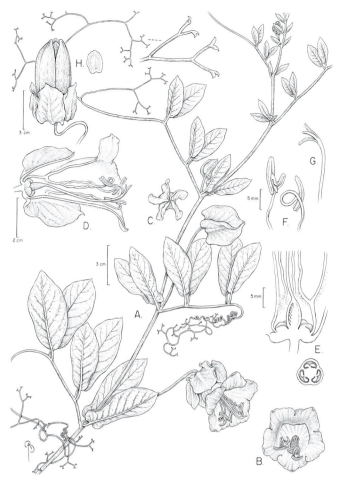

Figure 157. POLEMONIACEAE. *Cobaea scandens* (A–G, drawn from life, not vouchered; H, Callejas 10183). **A.** Stem with leaves, flowers, tendrils, and detail of tendril (above). **B.** Apical view of flower. **C.** Basal view of calyx. **D.** Longitudinal section of flower. **E.** Medial section of base of flower (above) and transverse section of ovary (below). **F.** Stamens. **G.** Apex of style showing stigma. Original. Artist: Bobbi Angell.

solitary flowers (in *Cobaea* and a few annual species). **Flowers** usually actinomorphic, or zygomorphic in some *Loeselia*, bisexual; calyx of 5 connate sepals; corolla of 5 connate petals; androecium of 5 stamens, the stamens adnate to corolla, the anthers dehiscing by longitudinal slits; gynoecium syncarpous, the ovary superior, the carpels 3, the locules 3, the style 1, with 3 stigmatic branches; placentation axile, the ovules 1–many per locule. **Fruits** capsules. **Seeds** 1–many, often mucilaginous when wet, typically small and ovoid to ellipsoid, with smooth to sculptured surfaces, or large and flat, with conspicuous marginal wings in *Cantua*, *Cobaea*, and *Huthia*.

Woodiness is considered derived in the temperate genera, but some species of tropical *Cantua* and *Huthia* are woody, suggesting that the common ancestor to all Polemoniaceae may have been a shrub. Most other tropical species are herbaceous perennials (e.g., *Loeselia* and *Polemonium*). Some, like *Loeselia glandulosa* and *Gilia incisa*, can be either annual or perennial, depending on local climate.

Natural history. A remarkable diversity of floral morphology in the Polemoniaceae is associated with an array of pollinators that include beetles, flies, hawkmoths, butterflies, bees, hummingbirds, and bats. Most temperate species are pollinated by relatively small bees, flies, and beetles while the large, bell-shaped flowers of tropical *Cobaea* typically are pollinated by bats and hawkmoths. The brightly colored, red, tubular flowers in *Cantua* and *Loeselia mexicana* are visited by hummingbirds. The Aztec name *huizitzil-xochitl* for the latter species refers to its attractiveness to hummingbirds. Smaller flowers in some species of *Loeselia* and *Bonplandia geminiflora* are pollinated primarily by bees. Although a few temperate genera have explosive capsules, the seeds of most species are dispersed by gravity when the capsule dehisces.

The odor-producing compounds produced from glands on the stems and leaves are derived from coumarins and are considered to be herbivore deterrents.

Economic uses. *Cobaea scandens* (cup and saucer vine) is widely cultivated throughout the world as an ornamental vine and *Cantua buxifolia*, the national flower of Peru, was cultivated first by the Incas as a decoration around temples. Other species are used in herbal medicine; e.g., the leaves and shoots of *Loeselia mexicana* reportedly are used as a purgative and to induce vomiting, and a tea made from the flowers of *Cobaea scandens* in Mexico and Central America has served as a cough remedy. The leaves and stems of some species of *Loeselia*, *Cantua*, and *Ipomopsis* produce a soapy solution used for washing.

References. GRANT, V. 1959. *Natural History of the Phlox Family*. The Hague, Netherlands: Martinus Nijhoff. GRANT, V., AND K. GRANT. 1965. *Flower Pollination in the Phlox Family*. New York: Columbia University Press.

POLYGALACEAE (Milkwort Family)

CLAES PERSSON

Figure 158, Plate 38

- *herbs, subshrubs, shrubs, trees, lianas*

- *leaves usually alternate, rarely opposite or verticillate, simple*

- *flowers usually zygomorphic; sepals often petal-like; stamens with filaments forming cleft sheath or tube; ovary with 1 ovule per locule*

Numbers of genera and species. Worldwide, there are approximately 22 genera and 950–1,000 species. The four largest genera are *Polygala* (300–350 species; ca. 100 Neotropical), *Monnina* (ca. 140 Neotropical), *Muraltia* (115; Africa), and *Securidaca* (ca. 80; ca. 75 Neotropical). Six genera have only one or two species. In tropical America, there are 11 genera and about 400 species.

Distribution and habitat. The Polygalaceae are a widespread family absent only in New Zealand, many southern Pacific islands, and the northern parts of the Northern Hemisphere. Most genera are restricted to major continental regions. However, the genus *Polygala* is nearly cosmopolitan, and *Securidaca*, which has its center of distribution in the neotropics, also has a few species in Africa and Southeast Asia. In the Western Hemisphere, the family is mostly tropical, but *Hualania* is restricted to central Argentina and *Ptero-*

monnina has members in extratropical areas. The distribution of *Polygala* ranges from southern Argentina to northern Ontario in Canada.

The Polygalaceae occur in a variety of habitats, from semi-arid regions and savannas to humid rain forests. Most genera are confined to low elevations, but species of a few occur above 2,000 meters (e.g., *Monnina* and *Pteromonnina*).

Family classification. Traditionally, the Polygalaceae were included in Polygalales (e.g., *sensu* Cronquist). However, recent cladistic analyses suggest that the Polygalaceae should be placed in the Fabales together with Fabaceae, Surianaceae, and Quillajaceae.

The family is here divided into three tribes: Polygaleae, Moutabeae, and Carpolobieae. Polygaleae and Moutabeae have representatives in the Western Hemisphere, whereas Carpolobieae is strictly African. Chloroplast DNA sequences support the monophyly of Polygaleae and Carpolobieae, whereas the monophyly of Moutabeae could not be confirmed. Although most traditional genera are corroborated as monophyletic, DNA data indicate that both *Polygala* and *Bredemeyera* are polyphyletic. *Acanthocladus* and *Badiera*, taxa often assigned to *Polygala*, are more closely related to *Bredemeyera*, and *Hualania*, which is often included in *Bredemeyera*, has its closest relatives elsewhere.

Features of the family. Habit: herbs, subshrubs, shrubs, trees, or lianas, the herbs annual or perennial; anomalous growth of stem typical in Moutabeae and some Polygaleae, especially among lianas; rarely with short spines on stems (*Moutabea*) or with stems ending in a spine (one species of *Bredemeyera*, and several species of *Acanthocladus*). **Stems** sometimes with stalked or sessile glands (extrafloral nectaries) at leaf and inflorescence nodes (sometimes incorrectly called stipules). **Stipules** absent. **Leaves** usually alternate, rarely opposite or verticillate (as in some *Polygala*), simple, sometimes scalelike or needlelike, sometimes with glands; blade margins entire. **Inflorescences** terminal or axillary, usually racemes or variously elaborated panicles, rarely spikes, heads, or of solitary flowers; bracts often present, persistent or caducous; bracteoles usually subtending flowers, paired, usually caducous. **Flowers** usually zygomorphic, rarely actinomorphic (*Diclidanthera*), bisexual; sepals usually 5, often caducous, usually distinct or rarely ± united, usually quincuncial, the two inner sepals usually larger and petal-like (the flag) but sometimes almost similar to outer sepals (as in species of *Moutabea*); petals 5 (Carpolobieae and Moutabeae), 4 (rarely in Moutabeae), or 3 (Polygaleae); androecium usually of (4–7)8 stamens, or the stamens 10, the filaments generally connate, at least in lower half, forming a cleft sheath or tube, usually adnate to petals, the anthers basifixed, bi- to tetrasporangiate, usually with a falcate slit forming two apical or subapical pores, or less often forming a marginal or ventral, longitudinal slit; annular nectary often present (possessing or lacking a process) at base of ovary, or on staminal sheath (as in *Bredemeyera*); gynoecium syncarpous, the ovary superior, the carpels 2–8, the locules 2 or pseudomonomerous in Polygaleae, 2–8 in Moutabeae; the placentation (sub)apical, ovules 1 per locule, pendulous, anatropous, bitegmic. **Fruits** usually capsules, sometimes berries (Moutabeae), drupes (e.g., *Monnina*), dry and indehiscent (sometimes referred to as wingless samaras), or samaras, the samaras single-winged (*Securidaca*) or double-winged (*Pteromonnina* and *Ancylotropis*), the capsules often with a ± pronounced wing (e.g., *Bredemeyera* and some *Polygala*). **Seeds** 1 per locule, glabrous or pilose, sometimes villous or with a comb of long hairs (e.g., *Bredemeyera*); aril sometimes present; endosperm typically abundant.

In Polygaleae, the corolla is zygomorphic with three petals, the upper two are united at the base to the lower petal but distinct and overlapping above. The lower petal is carinate (boat-shaped) and sometimes apically crested with fringes,

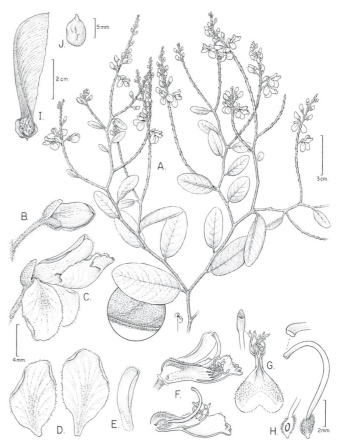

Figure 158. POLYGALACEAE. *Securidaca volubilis.* **A.** Stems with leaves and inflorescences and detail of pubescence on abaxial surface of leaf (lower left). **B.** Lateral view of flower bud. **C.** Lateral view of flower. **D.** Adaxial views of two petaloid sepal wings. **E.** Adaxial view of an upper petal. **F.** Lateral views of flower with one upper petal and two wings removed (above) and with two upper petals, two wings, and part of staminal sheath removed (below). **G.** Adaxial view of staminal sheath with detail of anther (above). **H.** Medial section of ovary (left) and lateral view of gynoecium (right) with detail of stigma (above). **I.** Lateral view of fruit. **J.** Seed. Reprinted with permission from Mori et al. (2002). Artist: Bobbi Angell.

a closed beak, or two open bilobed lobes. In the Moutabeae, the corolla is typically 5-merous, with a transition from zygomorphic (e.g., *Moutabea*) to actinomorphic (as in *Diclidanthera*) flowers.

Some species of *Moutabea, Polygala* and *Bredemeyera* have variously elaborated arils, caruncles, or chalazal outgrowths.

Natural history. Most Polygalaceae are bee pollinated but a few cases of butterfly and bird pollination have also been recorded. Secondary pollen presentation has been recorded in two Brazilian species, *Polygala vauthieri* and *P. monticola*. In these species, a basketlike structure on the style apex serves as the pollen presenter. Pollen from the basket is deposited onto bees during their visits to the flowers. Tertiary pollen presentation has been observed in bee pollinated *Polygala* from South Africa. In this process, pollen masses are deposited on the end of the style, the style springs out when the keel is pressed down by flower visitors, and pollen is placed dorsally on the visitors. The keel then returns to its original position, and the remaining pollen is moved onto the tip of the keel (the rostrum). On subsequent visits by pollinators, pollen on the rostrum dusts the visitors ventrally.

Several different dispersal agents occur in Polygalaceae, including birds (e.g., *Diclidanthera* and *Polygala*), ants (e.g., *Polygala*), and mammals (e.g., spider monkeys eat the fruits of *Moutabea*). The animals eat the fruits and defecate the seeds. In addition, wind and water play an important role in dispersing winged fruits (e.g., *Securidaca*).

Economic uses. The Polygalaceae are of little economic importance. However, the North American species *Polygala senega* (snakeroot) was used as a pharmaceutical drug for treatment of bronchitis and asthma. It was also employed by the Seneca Indians for treating snakebites, hence its common name. In the neotropics, some species are used locally in herbal medicine. A decoction of *Securidaca diversifolia* is taken as a treatment for venereal diseases in Panama and Venezuela. In Alta Verapaz, Guatemala, the roots of *Polygala floribunda* are chewed to cleanse teeth and harden the gums, and shaved roots produce a fine lather that is utilized to treat dandruff and eczema. A root decoction of *P. paniculata* is taken as a diuretic, and the mashed roots are made

into a poultice that is used for treating rheumatism. In El Salvador and Guatemala, an infusion of the crushed root of *P. angustifolia* is used in small doses as a pectoral or in large doses as an emetic. An infusion of root extracts of *Bredemeyera floribunda* sometimes is taken as an diuretic. The Central American *Polygala costaricensis* is sometimes utilized as a substitute for *ipecacuanha* (*Caropichea ipecacuanha*, Rubiaceae) as an expectorant. The fruits of *Monnina salicifolia* are used to produce a blue dye.

References. BERNARDI, L. 2000. Consideraciones taxonómicas y fitogeográficas acerca de 101 Polygalae Americanas. *Cavanillesia Altera*, ser. 1:1–456. BLAKE, S. 1916. *A revision of the genus* Polygala *in Mexico, Central America and the West Indies*. Cambridge, MA: Harvard University Press. ERIKSEN, B. 1993. A revision of *Monnina* subg. *Pterocarya* (Polygalaceae) in Northwestern South America. *Ann. Missouri Bot. Gard.* 80:191–201. ERIKSEN, B. 1993. Phylogeny of the Polygalaceae and its taxonomic implications. *Pl. Syst. Evol.* 186:33–55. MENDES MARQUES, M. DO C. 1980. Revisão das espécies do gênero *Bredemeyera* Willd. (Polygalaceae) do Brasil. *Rodriguésia* 67:3–33. MENDES MARQUES, M. DO C. 1996. *Securidaca* L. (Polygalaceae) do Brasil. *Arch. Jar. Bot. Rio de Janeiro* 34(1):7–144. PERSSON, C. 2001. Phylogenetic relationships in Polygalaceae based on plastid DNA sequences from the trnL-F region. *Taxon* 50:763–79. VERKERKE, W. 1985. Ovules and seeds of Polygalaceae. *J. Arnold Arbor.* 66:353–94.

POLYGONACEAE (Buckwheat or Knotweed Family)

DANIEL ATHA

Figure 159

- *herbs, shrubs, vines, lianas, or trees*

- *stems often with conspicuous swollen nodes; ocrea present*

- *leaves usually alternate, simple*

- *flower tepals 3–6; ovary unilocular, with a single, basal ovule*

- *fruits achenes, often enclosed in persistent, expanded perianth*

Numbers of genera and species. Worldwide, the Polygonaceae comprise 45 genera and approximately 1,100 species. In tropical America, there are 13 genera and about 250 species. The largest genus in the neotropics is *Coccoloba* with between 120 and 200 species, followed by *Ruprechtia*

(19 or 20 species), *Triplaris* (18), and the weedy *Rumex* (ca. 20) and *Persicaria* (ca. 20).

Distribution and habitat. The Polygonaceae are cosmopolitan, with most genera and species occurring in northern temperate regions. Thirty-one genera are found in the Western Hemisphere: 16 of these genera are restricted to western North America, with three disjunct to Chile and Argentina. Of the 13 tropical and subtropical American genera, *Ruprechtia*, *Triplaris*, *Coccoloba* are fairly widespread in the Neotropics; *Neomillspaughia*, *Podopterus*, *Gymnopodium*, *Antigonon* (except for the widely cultivated *Antigonon leptopus*) are restricted to Central America; the monotypic *Leptogonum* is endemic to Hispaniola; *Symmeria* is amphiatlantic; *Muehlenbeckia* is amphipacific; and *Polygonum*, *Rumex*, *Persicaria* are cosmopolitan, generally weedy, and prefer the temperate-like climates above 2,000 m in the tropics. Most of the shrubs and trees of the Triplarideae and Coccolobeae are found at low to midelevations in open forest. Some species are widespread weeds (e.g., *Polygonum aviculare*, *Rumex obtusifolius*, and *Persicaria hydropiperoides*) in midmontane habitats, while *Polygonum punctatum* is widespread throughout lowland to midmontane habitats.

Family classification. The Polygonaceae are placed in the monotypic Polygonales by Cronquist. Traditionally, the Polygonaceae were placed near various families in the Caryophyllales on the basis of the unilocular ovary and single, basal ovule. However, studies have revealed that the family lacks P-type sieve-tube plastids, anatropous ovules, betalain pigments, and perisperm-characters uniting the well-defined Caryophyllales. Recent publications define the order more broadly, including families such as the Plumbaginaceae, Droseraceae, and Nepenthaceae. It is believed that taxa of the Polygonales are closely related to the Caryophyllales and, in a recent study by the Angiosperm Phylogeny Group, the Polygonaceae and other taxa of the Polygonales were included within this order.

All of the Neotropical genera belong to the subfamily Polygonoideae, distinguished from the other subfamily, Eriogonoideae, by the presence of well-defined stipules (ocrea). The Eriogonoideae, with 2 tribes and 17 genera (about 325 species), is entirely temperate Western Hemisphere and does not reach the Tropics.

Most of the Neotropical genera are in the two predominately Neotropical tribes: Triplarideae (*Gymnopodium* [3 species], *Leptogonum* [1], *Ruprechtia* [20], *Symmeria* [1], *Triplaris* [18]) and the Coccolobeae (*Antigonon* [3–6], *Coccoloba* [120], *Muehlenbeckia* [9], *Neomillspaughia* [2] and *Podopterus* [3]). The remaining genera fall into the predominantly Eastern Hemisphere tribes: Rumicieae (*Rumex*) and Polygoneae (*Persicaria* and *Polygonum*).

Features of the family. Habit: herbs, shrubs, trees, lianas (e.g., some *Coccoloba*) or vines (*Antigonon*). Stems sometimes hollow (*Ruprechtia* and *Triplaris*), often with conspicuous swollen nodes. Stipules present, membranaceous or scarious, bilobed or fringed, connate to form an ocrea sheathing stem, the ocrea persistent or deciduous, leaving distinctive annular scar when deciduous. Leaves alternate, occasionally whorled or opposite, simple; petioles often flattened; extrafloral nectaries sometimes present at petiole base; blade margins entire; venation pinnate. Inflorescences axillary or terminal, cymose, often arranged in spikes, panicles, racemes, or heads; flowers single or fascicled, often subtended by bract(s). Flowers actinomorphic, bisexual or unisexual (then plants generally dioecious, sometimes monoecious), relatively small; tepals 3–6, in 1–2 whorls (1 when 5 tepals), sometimes petallike, ± connate into short tube, sometimes brightly colored, sometimes persistent and accrescent in fruit, the inner whorl sometimes enlarged or modified with hooks, spines, wings, or tubercles; annular-nectary disc often present around base of ovary, or nectaries several, placed

between bases of stamens; androecium of 2–9 stamens (usually 6 in two cycles of 3), the filaments distinct or connate at base, often of two lengths, those of inner series often dilated, the anthers dehiscing longitudinally by slits; gynoecium syncarpous, the ovary superior, the carpels (2)3, the locule 1, the style(s) 1–3, the stigmas capitate or feathery; placentation basal, the ovule 1, orthotropous. **Fruits** achenes, lenticular or trigonous, sometimes closely subtended and/or enclosed by persistent, expanded, membranaceous tepals or enclosed in fleshy perianth (e.g. *Coccoloba*). **Seeds** with copious endosperm, the embryo curved or straight.

Natural history. Some members of the family have large lax inflorescences and plumose stigmas that facilitate wind pollination. However, most species are pollinated by bees and wasps seeking nectar secreted at the base of the stamens (e.g., *Polygonum*). Species in which the perianth segments expand in fruit to form wings are wind-dispersed (e.g.,

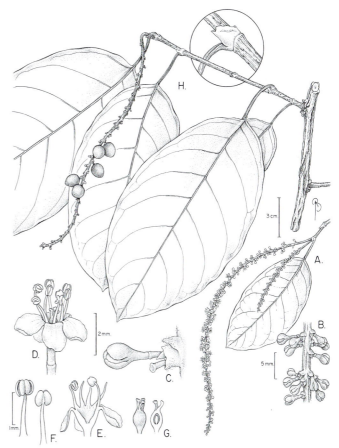

Figure 159. POLYGONACEAE. *Coccoloba parimensis*. **A.** Stem with leaf and inflorescence. **B.** Detail of inflorescence with buds. **C.** Lateral view of bud in sheathing bract. **D.** Lateral view of flower. **E.** Medial section of flower with gynoecium removed. **F.** Adaxial (left) and abaxial (right) views of anthers. **G.** Lateral view (left) and medial section (right) of gynoecium. **H.** Stem with leaves and infructescence and detail of ocrea at leaf node (above). Reprinted with permission from Mori et al. (2002). Artist: Bobbi Angell.

Triplaris, *Neomillspaughia* and *Gymnopodium*), while *Coccoloba* and *Muehlenbeckia* have fleshy perianths surrounding the fruits, thereby suggesting animal dispersal.

The hollow stems of *Triplaris* and occasionally *Ruprechtia* harbor vicious stinging ants of the genus *Pseudomyrmex*; the ants swarm out of small holes in the stems upon the slightest disturbance of their host to protect the hosts from phytophagous insects; e.g., leaf-cutting ants (*Atta*).

Economic uses. Few Polygonaceae have economic value. Cultivated ornamentals include *Antigonon leptopus* (coral vine), *Coccoloba uvifera* (sea grape), and *Muehlenbeckia platyclada* (solitaria). *Rheum rhaponticum* (rhubarb) and *Fagopyrum esculentum* (buckwheat) are of minor importance

as food crops in temperate zones. Some species of *Coccoloba* (e.g., *C. uvifera*) have edible fruit.

References. BRANDBYGE, J. AND B. ØLLGAARD. 1984. Inflorescence structure and generic delimitation of *Triplaris* and *Ruprechtia* (Polygonaceae). *Nordic J. Bot.* 4:765–69. GRAHAM, S., AND C. WOOD. 1965. The genera of Polygonaceae in the south eastern United States. *J. Arnold Arbor.* 46: 91–121. LAUBENGAYER, R. 1937. Studies in the anatomy and morphology of the polygonaceous flower. *Amer. J. Bot.* 22:460–73. NOWICKE, J., AND J. SKVARLA. 1977. Pollen morphology and the relationship of the Plumbaginaceae, Polygonaceae and Primulaceae to the order Centrospermae. *Smithsonian Contr. Bot.* 37:1–64.

PORTULACACEAE (Purslane Family)

UNO ELIASSON

Figure 160, Plate 39

- *herbs, low shrubs or subshrubs, often succulent*

- *leaves alternate or apparently opposite, simple*

- *flowers usually with 2 sepals; petals usually 5; locule 1; placentation basal or free-central*

- *fruits capsules, dehiscing circumscissilely or by longitudinal valves*

- *seeds often distinctly sculptured; endosperm absent or nearly absent; perisperm often abundant*

Numbers of genera and species. Worldwide, the Portulacaceae comprise 25-30 genera and 450-500 species. *Portulaca* is the largest genus, but specific delimitations are difficult and the estimates of the number of species range from about 40 to near 150. *Calandrinia* in the wide sense comprises some 50–100 species, but has been demonstrated to consist of several lineages that are likely to be formally recognized as different genera in the future. In addition, the borderline between some of the segregates of *Calandrinia* and *Talinum* requires further study. *Montia* appears to be a fairly natural genus of less than a dozen species of cool climates and some segregates have sometimes been referred to separate genera. Eleven of the 29 genera (including segregates from *Calandrinia*) are monospecific. In tropical America and bordering regions there are about 10 genera and probably less than 30 species.

Distribution and habitat. The Portulacaceae are more or less cosmopolitan, but are most speciose in the Southern

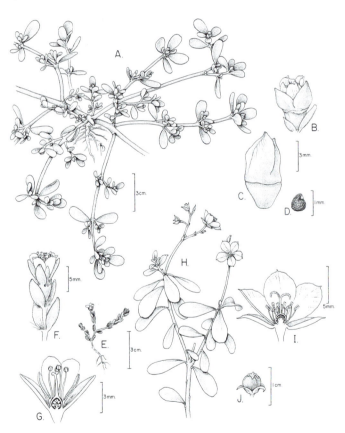

Figure 160. PORTULACACEAE. *Portulaca oleracea* (A–D), *P. quadrifida* (E–G), and *Talinum fruticosum* (H–J). **A.** Stems with leaves and flowers. **B.** Lateral view of flower. **C.** Lateral view of fruit. **D.** Seed. **E.** Plant with roots, leaves, and flowers. **F.** Stem with leaves and flower. **G.** Medial section of flower. **H.** Stems with leaves and flowers. **I.** Medial section of flower. **J.** Lateral view of fruit. Reprinted with permission from Acevedo-Rodríguez (1996). Artist: Bobbi Angell.

Hemisphere. Many species are concentrated in western North America, Andean South America, and South Africa. The family is absent or poorly represented in the Arctic, the Amazon basin, and deserts of Africa and Australia. Of the genera found in tropical America and bordering regions, *Calandrinia sensu lato* is found throughout the Andes, *Lenzia* occurs in Chile, *Mona* in Colombia and Venezuela, *Monocosmia* in Chile and Argentina, *Montia* is widespread in temperate to tropical regions, *Portulaca* is widespread in tropical and subtropical regions, *Schreiteria* grows in Argentina but probably not north of the tropic of Capricorn, *Talinaria* occurs in Mexico, *Talinopsis* in Mexico and farther north, and *Talinum sensu lato* is found throughout tropical America.

Many Portulacaceae are lowland species adapted to arid or semiarid conditions through various degrees of succulence. Among these are species of *Anacampseros*, *Talinum*, *Portulaca*, and *Calandrinia sensu stricto*. A few species occur in disturbed habitats.

Some species of Portulacaceae are adapted to high elevations. Among the extremes is *Lenzia chamaepitys*, which grows between 4,000 and 4,500 meters in Chile. These are some of the highest elevations known for vascular plants in the world. The plant reaches only 2 centimeters in height and possesses stiff, linear, densely arranged leaves.

Family classification. The Portulacaceae are placed in the Caryophyllales by Cronquist. The family is one of the families strongly nested among the other betalain-producing families of the Caryophyllideae, and, as currently circumscribed, are closely allied with the Cactaceae, Basellaceae, and Didiereaceae. The close alliance of Cactaceae with the Portulacaceae has been demonstrated with molecular data.

The subfamilial classification is a matter of controversy. Seven tribes were recognized by McNeill whereas the number was reduced to four by Carolin. Among the tribes recognized by Carolin, the Portulaceae and Talineae comprise the vast majority of genera whereas the Portulacarieae and Calyptrotheceae have only 1–3 genera each. This classification, however, should be regarded as tentative.

Features of the family. Habit: herbs, low shrubs, or subshrubs, the herbs annual or perennial, ± succulent; roots swollen and tuberous in several species; stems prostrate to erect. **Stipules** absent but hairs, bristles, or scales present in leaf-axils of many species, these generally interpreted as reduced stipules, the axillary pubescence copious in some species. **Leaves** alternate (spiral) or apparently opposite, simple; petioles poorly defined; blades flattened to terete, normally glabrous, ± succulent, the base usually narrow, the margins entire. **Inflorescences** of solitary flowers or paniculate, but commonly described as dichasia converting distally into monochasia, the monochasia frequently straightened to resemble racemes or spikes, the axes sometimes reduced, resulting in condensed headlike inflorescences. **Flowers** actinomorphic or slightly zygomorphic, bisexual; sepals usually 2 (5 or more in *Lewisia*), mostly unequal in size when 2, cadu-

cous in *Talinum*; petals (2)5(12 or rarely more), sometimes connate at base; androecium of (1 in *Monocosmia*)5(numerous) stamens, the stamens opposite petals, often grouped in bundles when numerous, the filaments usually free, sometimes fused basally to perianth base, the anthers dehiscing introrsely by longitudinal slit; pollen spinose, the endexine poorly developed; gynoecium syncarpous, the ovary superior or in *Portulaca* inferior or subinferior, the carpels (2)3(ca. 8), the locules as many as carpels in young ovary, 1 in mature ovary, the style cleft to various lengths, the branches and/or stigmas as many as carpels; placentation basal or free-central, the ovules few to numerous, mostly campylotropous. **Fruits** capsules, dehiscing circumscissilely or by longitudinal valves, the valves in some genera longitudinally involute. **Seeds** (1)3–numerous, cochleate-reniform to angular or rounded, the testa often distinctly sculptured; sarcotesta present, surrounding seed; endosperm absent or almost absent; perisperm often abundant.

In contrast to related families, the secondary xylem of Portulacaceae is produced from a normal cambium and there is no anomalous secondary growth. Like in all members of the Caryophyllales sieve-element plastids are of the P-type, with a broad ring of peripheral filaments.

Copious pubescence and imbricate leaves or scales are adaptations of many Portulacaceae to dry or cold environments; however, apart from axillary pubescence, trichomes are scarce in the family. Simple as well as multicellular trichomes occur in certain species of *Calandrinia sensu lato* and glandular trichomes are known in some species segregated from *Calandrinia* and in *Lenzia*, a monospecific genus at high altitudes in Chile.

Based on developmental evidence, the sepals of Portulacaceae should probably be interpreted as bracteoles and the petals as modified petallike sepals.

Chromosome counts based on about 80 species in 19 genera show several base numbers ranging from six to 12. Counts in genera that, from a morphological point of view, are regarded as phylogenetically primitive, suggest a base number of six.

Natural history. In the arid coastal areas of the Galápagos Islands, the endemic *Portulaca howellii* develops leaves and flowers during the rainy season and endures the dry season as fleshy leafless stems. *Talinum guadalupense*, in contrast to the mainly herbaceous species of the genus, is a shrub with thick, water-storing stems and branches. The plant flowers and bears rosettes of large, succulent leaves during moist conditions, but only groups of smaller leaves remain during the dry season.

Flowers of Portulacaceae are normally insect-pollinated, although species that have small flowers and grow in inhospitable environments probably are self-compatible and self-pollinated, at least to some extent. Some infraspecific entities within the polymorphic pantropical species *Portulaca oleracea* produce cleistogamous as well as chasmogamic flowers.

Birds probably play a role in the dispersal of several species. The fruit valves of some genera are longitudinally involute, which may be an adaptation for ejecting seeds. The sarcotesta or aril-like structure of some species may be an adaptation to dispersal by ants, but studies are lacking. Vegetative parts of several species of *Portulaca* are buoyant and may be dispersed by sea water. This probably explains the relatively wide distribution of *P. lutea* on islands in the Pacific. The seeds of the Argentine monospecific genus *Grahamia* possess a membranous wing, but its efficiency as an aid in wind dispersal is not documented.

Economic uses. The family is of limited economic importance. Some species with large flowers are grown as ornamentals; e.g., *Portulaca grandiflora* (moss rose) and certain species of *Calandrinia sensu lato*, *Lewisia*, and *Talinum* (fame-flower). The true *Portulaca grandiflora*, indigenous to Argentina, has many cultivars bred for a wide range of flower colors. Rootstocks of *Lewisia rediviva* are rich in starch that served as a food source for American Indians. The weedy species *Portulaca oleracea* (purslane) sometimes is cooked as a vegetable or eaten raw in salad.

References. CAROLIN, R. C. 1987. A review of the family Portulacaceae. *Austral. J. Bot.* 35:383–412. CAROLIN, R. C. 1993. Portulacaceae. In *The Families and Genera of Vascular Plants*, eds. K. Kubitzki, J. G. Rohwer and V. Bittrich, 2: 544–55. New York: Springer-Verlag. ELIASSON, U. H. 1996. Portulacaceae. In *Flora of Ecuador*, eds. G. Harling and L. Andersson, 55:29–53. Göteborg, Sweden: Department of Systematic Botany, University of Göteborg. HERSHKOVITZ, M. A. 1991. Taxonomic notes on *Cistanthe, Calandrinia*, and *Talinum* (Portulacaceae). *Phytologia* 70:209–25. HERSHKOVITZ, M. A. 1993. Revised circumscriptions and subgeneric taxonomies of *Calandrinia* and *Montiopsis* (Portulacaceae) with notes on phylogeny of the portulacaceous alliance. *Ann. Missouri Bot. Gard.* 80:333–65. HERSHKOVITZ, M. A., AND E. A. ZIMMER. 1997. On the evolutionary origins of the cacti. *Taxon* 46:217–32. MCNEILL, J. 1975. A generic revision of Portulacaceae tribe Montieae using techniques of numerical taxonomy. *Canad. J. Bot.* 53:789–809. NOWICKE, J. W. 1994. Pollen morphology and exine ultrastructure. In *Caryophyllales: Evolution and Systematics*, eds. H.-D. Behnke and T. J. Mabry, 167–221. Berlin: Springer-Verlag. PAX, F., AND K. HOFFMANN. 1934. Portulacaceae. In *Die Natürlichen Pflanzenfamilien*, A. Engler and K. Prantl, 2nd ed., 16c:234–62. Leipzig: Wilhelm Engelmann. RODMAN, J. E., M. K. OLIVER, R. R. NAKAMURA, J. U. MCCLAMMER JR., AND A. H. BLEDSOE. 1984. A taxonomic analysis and revised classification of Centrospermae. *Syst. Bot.* 9:297–323. TURNER, B. L. 1994. Chromosome numbers and their phyletic interpretation. In *Caryophyllales: Evolution and Systematics*, eds. H.-D. Behnke and T. J. Mabry, 27–43. Berlin: Springer-Verlag.

PRIMULACEAE (Primrose Family)

BERTIL STÅHL

Figure 161

- *herbs, sometimes subshrubs*

- *leaves alternate or opposite (some* Anagallis*), sometimes basal* (Samolus), *simple*

- *flowers actinomorphic, sympetalous; ovary usually superior; placentation free-central*

- *fruits capsules*

Numbers of genera and species. Worldwide, the Primulaceae comprise about 20 genera and 800 species. In tropical America, there are four genera, *Anagallis* (including *Centunculus*), *Lysimachia* (subgenus *Theopyxis*), *Pelletiera*, and *Samolus*, and 10 species. Two additional genera, *Primula* and *Androsace* (with one species each) occur in Patagonia.

Distribution and habitat. The Primulaceae have a worldwide distribution but are poorly represented in the Tropics, and only one genus, *Samolus*, is centered in the Southern Hemisphere. Most species in tropical America have wide distributions and only a few are restricted to this area.

Tropical American species of Primulaceae are found both in the lowland and in mountains with temperate climates. They grow in open, nonforested habitats.

Family classification. The Primulaceae are placed in the Primulales by Cronquist. The family is usually divided into five tribes of which the Samoleae, containing only *Samolus*, and the Lysimachieae occur in the neotropics.

Recent phylogenetic studies have shown that the Primulaceae are an unnatural group. All genera which occur in tropical America, except *Samolus*, are more correctly placed in

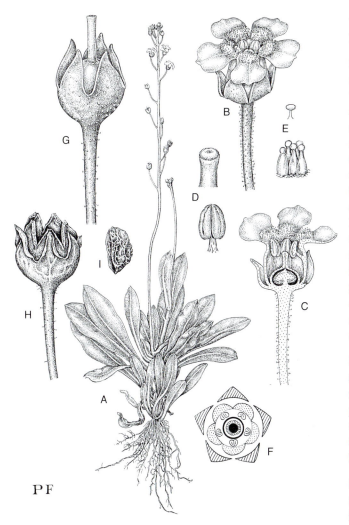

the Myrsinaceae. *Samolus* is more closely related to Theophrastaceae.

Features of the family. Habit: herbs, sometimes subshrubs, the herbs annual or perennial, the vegetative and floral parts with secretory cavities appearing as red or brownish lines or dots, sometimes with glandular hairs. **Stipules** absent. **Leaves** alternate or opposite (some *Anagallis*), sometimes basal (*Samolus*), simple. **Inflorescences** axillary, often of solitary flowers, sometimes racemes, umbels, or panicles, the racemes, umbels, and panicles lax. **Flowers** actinomorphic, bisexual, typically 5-merous; sepals 5; corolla sympetalous, rotate, urceolate or campanulate in *Samolus*, white or blue, the petals 3 (*Pelletiera*) or 5; androecium of 5 stamens, the stamens opposite petals, the anthers dehiscing by inward-facing slits; gynoecium syncarpous, the ovary superior, or semi-inferior in *Samolus*, the carpels probably 5, the locule 1, the style 1; placentation free-central, the ovules usually numerous (2 in *Pelletiera*). **Fruits** capsules, dehiscing by valves or lids (*Anagallis*). **Seeds** few to many, small, dark brown, winged (*Lysimachia*).

Natural history. Although poorly studied, tropical American Primulaceae are probably autogamous or insect-pollinated. *Primula*, has heterostylous flowers. The seeds are probably mostly dispersed by gravity; however, the winged seeds of species of *Lysimachia* that grow in *páramo* bogs may be dispersed by the wind or even by adhering to the wet feet of birds.

Economic use. Besides some species of *Primula* (primrose) and *Cyclamen*, which are grown as ornamentals, the family is of no economic use. Some species of *Anagallis* are introduced weeds.

References. LOURTEIG, A. 1942. Primulaceae argentinae. *Lilloa* 8:231–67. LOURTEIG, A. 1967. Primuláceas. Pp. 1–17 in P. R. Reitz, *Flora ilustrada Catarinense.* Itajai, Brasil: Herbario "Barbosa Rodrigues." STÅHL, B. 1990. Primulaceae. In *Flora of Ecuador*, eds. G. Harling and L. Andersson, 39:23–35. Göteborg, Sweden: Department of Systematic Botany, University of Göteborg.

Figure 161. PRIMULACEAE. *Samolus ebracteatus.* **A.** Plant with roots, leaves and inflorescences (x⅔). **B.** Lateral view of flower (x6). **C.** Medial section of flower (x6). **D.** Apex of style and stigma (above) and adaxial view of anther (below; both x12). **E.** Trichome from pedicel (above) and trichomes from throat of corolla (below; both x65). **F.** Floral diagram. **G.** Lateral view of undehisced fruit (x6). **H.** Lateral view of dehisced fruit (x6). **I.** Seed (x40). Reprinted with permission from Correll and Correll (1982). Artist: Priscilla Fawcett.

PROTEACEAE (Protea Family)

PETER H. WESTON

Figure 162, Plate 39

- *shrubs or trees*

- *leaves usually alternate, less frequently opposite or whorled, compound or simple*

- *flowers with uniseriate perianth; tepals and stamens 4;*

stamens adnate to tepals; carpel 1; style serves as "pollen presenter"

- *fruits follicular with winged seeds or indehiscent with wingless seeds*

Numbers of genera and species. Worldwide, the Proteaceae comprise 79 genera and about 1,700 species. In the Western Hemisphere, there are eight genera and 91 native species. The largest American genera are *Roupala* (51 species), *Euplassa* (20), and *Panopsis* (11) but recent, partly published revisionary work for *Flora Neotropica*, recognizes fewer species of *Roupala* and 20 species of *Panopsis*. In tropical America, there are six genera and 86 species.

Distribution and habitat. The Proteaceae are mostly confined to the Southern Hemisphere. The center of diversity of the Proteaceae at all taxonomic levels is Australia, followed by southern Africa, temperate to tropical South and Central America, New Caledonia, Southeast Asia from India and Japan to Indonesia, New Guinea, Madagascar, Fiji, New Zealand, and Vanuatu.

Perhaps the most interesting aspect of the family's distribution is the pattern of repeated disjunctions, linking isolated Gondwanic land masses, shown by at least 12 different taxa. For example, two of the eight South American genera (*Lomatia* and *Orites*) also occur in Australia and the other six are all closely related to genera that occur elsewhere in the Southern Hemisphere (*Embothrium* and *Oreocallis* to *Telopea* and *Alloxylon* in Australia; *Euplassa* and *Gevuina* to *Hicksbeachia* and *Bleasdalea* in Australia; *Kermadecia* and *Sleumerodendron* in New Caledonia, and *Turrillia* in Vanuatu and Fiji; *Roupala* to *Floydia* and *Darlingia* in Australia; and *Panopsis* to *Macadamia* in Australia and *Brabejum* in South Africa).

Species of Proteaceae tend to have relatively narrow distributions, and none occurs on more than one continent. However, an American species, *Roupala montana*, is the most widely distributed species, stretching from southern Mexico into southern Brazil and Bolivia. The highest diversity of species in the Western Hemisphere occurs in southeastern Brazil and in the northern Andes from Peru to Venezuela.

The distribution of the Proteaceae in South America shows a clear disjunction between the temperate southwest and the neotropics. Only one species, *Lomatia hirsuta*, occurs in both tropical and temperate South America.

Most species of Proteaceae prefer acidic, moderately watered but well-drained soils that tend to be nutrient-deficient. Many of the species in the Western Hemisphere are rainforest trees on *terra firme*, but others grow in seasonally inundated Amazonian forests (e.g., *Panopsis rubescens*), shrublands, and savannas from low elevations to above 3,800 meters in the northern Andes. Some populations of *Embothrium coccineum* thrive at high elevations in Chile, where they are buried under snow for considerable periods during the winter.

Family classification. The Proteaceae are placed in the Proteales along with the Elaeagnaceae by Cronquist. Morphology gives few clues as to the sister group of the Proteaceae, but molecular data from a combination of chloro-

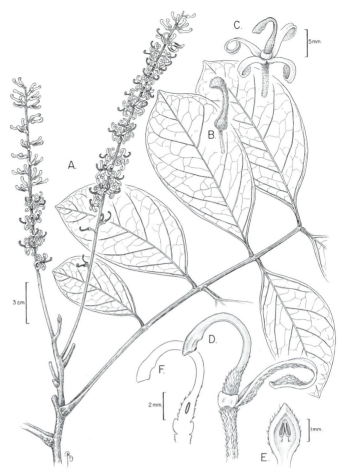

Figure 162. PROTEACEAE. *Euplassa pinnata*. **A.** Stem with leaf and inflorescences. **B.** Lateral view of flower bud; note valvate aestivation of calyx. **C.** Oblique-apical view of flower. **D.** Lateral view of flower with one sepal attached. **E.** Stamen adnate to adaxial surface of sepal. **F.** Medial section of gynoecium. Reprinted with permission from Mori et al. (2002). Artist: Bobbi Angell.

plast and nuclear loci suggest that it is the Platanaceae. According to molecular evidence, the Nelumbonaceae are also closely related to the Proteaceae.

The Proteaceae are currently divided into seven subfamilies: Bellendenoideae, Eidotheoideae, Sphalmioideae, Carnarvonioideae, Persoonioideae, Proteoideae, and Grevilleoideae, the first four of which are monotypic. Only the largest subfamily, Grevilleoideae, is represented in South America. The Grevilleoideae, Sphalmioideae, and Carnarvonioideae form a well-supported clade but the relationships between them and the other subfamilies are still poorly understood. The monophyly of at least the Proteoideae is suspect.

Features of the family. Habit: prostrate shrubs (0.1 m) to large rain-forest trees (40 m); proteoid roots present (see discussion below). **Stipules** absent. **Leaves** usually alternate, less frequently opposite or whorled (some *Panopsis*), compound or simple, sometimes varying throughout development (see discussion below); blades coriaceous, the margins entire, toothed, deeply dissected, or lobed; venation usually reticulate. **Inflorescences** (in Grevilleoideae) terminal or lateral, racemelike, the axis bearing lateral flower pairs, each pair sessile or with a common stalk. **Flowers** actinomorphic (e.g., *Orites, Panopsis, Roupala*) or zygomorphic (e.g., *Embothrium, Euplassa, Gevuina, Lomatia, Oreocallis*), bisexual, seldom unisexual (plants then monoecious or dioecious); perianth uniseriate; tepals 4, sometimes slightly or strongly curved; androecium with 4 stamens, the stamens opposite tepals, the filaments adnate to tepals for part or all of length, the anthers dehiscing by slits; nectary glands often present, intrastaminal, the glands often in whorl of 4 (e.g., *Euplassa, Orites, Roupala*), alternating with tepals or variously reduced and/or fused; gynoecium with superior ovary, sessile (e.g., *Euplassa, Gevuina, Orites, Panopsis, Roupala*) or borne on gynophore (e.g., *Embothrium, Lomatia, Oreocallis*), the gynophore sometimes elongated, the carpel 1, straight or slightly or strongly curved, the style usually well developed, the apex modified as a "pollen-presenter" (see below), the "pollen-presenter" below or surrounding stigma, the stigma terminal, but sometimes appearing lateral, minute; placentation marginal, the ovules usually 2–many. **Fruits** (of the Grevilleoideae) follicles (e.g., *Embothrium, Lomatia, Oreocallis, Orites, Roupala*) or indehiscent and evolved from follicles, the indehiscent fruits of *Panopsis* thick and coriacious, or drupelike in *Euplassa* and *Gevuina*. **Seeds** 1–many per fruit, flat and winged in follicular fruits or wingless in indehiscent fruits.

A feature characteristic of most genera, and all genera of the Western Hemisphere, is the production of proteoid roots. These are small, lateral roots of limited growth that form dense clusters on "ordinary" roots. They are produced in seasonal flushes and possibly enhance the rate at which the root system acquires nutrients. Clusters of proteoid roots often form on the outside of the root ball in potted proteaceous plants.

Some species (e.g., *Roupala montana*) produce simple, entire leaves as seedlings, compound or lobed leaves as juveniles, and then revert to simple, entire leaves as adults. Many other species show a reduced version of this developmental transition (e.g., *Gevuina avellana*, in which the leaves do not revert to a simple form in the adults) and others produce only simple, entire leaves (e.g., *Oreocallis*) at all stages of their life cycles.

Natural history. The Proteaceae are primitively insect-pollinated, but pollination by birds, and, in some cases, other vertebrates, has evolved repeatedly in different lineages. Most American taxa probably are bee-pollinated, but species of *Embothrium* and *Oreocallis* are pollinated by hummingbirds.

In the bud, the apex of the style or "pollen-presenter" is adjacent to, and inside, the anthers, which shed their pollen onto it before the flower opens. The style instead of the anthers, therefore, "presents" the pollen to pollinators, hence the name "pollen-presenter." The "pollen-presenter" may be more or less radially symmetrical (e.g., *Embothrium, Panopsis, Roupala*) or oblique and flattened (e.g., *Euplassa, Gevuina, Lomatia, Oreocallis*). In a few genera (e.g., *Orites*), pollen is taken directly from the anthers by the pollinators. Although the stigma is always terminal on the style, in some taxa it appears to be lateral because of the extremely asymmetrical morphology of the "pollen-presenter."

The winged seeds of follicular-fruited taxa are dispersed by wind, often rotating like helicopter propellers as they fall. Dispersal of the heavy, globose fruits of most species of *Panopsis* is probably by gravity, whereas the elongated fruits of *P. rubescens* probably are dispersed by flowing water. The succulent fruits of *Euplassa* and *Gevuina* probably are dispersed by large vertebrates; and the similar fruits of their close relatives across the Pacific are eaten by cassowaries, fruit bats, and possibly also other large mammals.

Economic uses. The most important crop plants in the Proteaceae are the Australian macadamias (*Macadamia integrifolia, M. tetraphylla,* and their hybrids) that produce edible nuts. These are grown commercially in parts of the Western Hemisphere, most significantly in Costa Rica. The American endemic *Panopsis* is closely related to *Macadamia*, and at least some of its species are likely to have edible nuts that perhaps have commercial potential. *Gevuina avellana* is used as a nut crop in Chile, and the closely related *Euplassa* also may include some species with edible seeds.

Many genera native to Australia and South Africa, especially *Protea*, include species that are economically important as cut flowers, and an even greater range of taxa are grown as ornamentals. The American *Embothrium, Lomatia,* and *Gevuina* include species that have been used successfully as garden plants and street trees in Chile and Europe. All of the American genera, especially *Embothrium* and *Oreocallis*, include beautiful species that are underutilized horticulturally.

The wood of most species of Proteaceae is durable and attractively figured, resembling that of *Platanus*. It is suitable for fine woodwork, furniture manufacturing, and for construction when the trees are large enough. The timber of the larger Chilean species, such as *Gevuina avellana*, is exploited commercially, and many other Neotropical species undoubtedly have potential as timber.

The bark and leaves of many species of Proteaceae are used locally for their medicinal properties. For example, the bark of *Lomatia hirsuta* is used as a purgative.

References. Douglas, A. W. 1995a. Affinities. In *Flora of Australia*, eds. A. E. Orchard and P. McCarthy, 16:6–14. Canberra: Australian Government Publishing Service. Douglas, A. W. 1995b. Morphological features. In *Flora of Australia*, eds. A. E. Orchard and P. McCarthy, 16:14–20. Canberra: Australian Government Publishing Service. Drinnan,

A. N., P. R. Crane, and S. B. Hoot. 1994. Patterns of floral evolution in the early diversification of non-magnoliid dicotyledons (eudicots). *Pl. Syst. Evol., Suppl.* 8:93–122. Edwards, K. S., and G. T. Prance. 1993. New species of *Panopsis* (Proteaceae) from South America. *Kew Bull.* 48: 637–662. Hoffmann, A. E. 1994. *Flora silvestre de Chile, zona araucana*, 3d ed. Santiago: Ediciones Fundacion Claudio Gay. Hoot, S. B., and A. W. Douglas. 1998. Phylogeny of the Proteaceae based on *atp*B and *atp*B-*rbc*L intergenic spacer region sequences. *Austral. Syst. Bot.* 11: 301–20. Johnson, L.A.S., and B. G. Briggs. 1975. On the Proteaceae—the evolution and classification of a southern family. *Bot. J. Linn. Soc.* 70:83–182. Orchard, A. E. 1995. Utilisation. In *Flora of Australia*, eds. A. E. Orchard and P. McCarthy, 16: 37–41. Canberra: Australian Government Publishing Service. Prance, G. T., and V. Plana. 1998. The American Proteaceae. *Austral. Syst. Bot.* 11(3):287–99. Sleumer, H. 1954. Proteaceae americanae. *Bot. Jahrb. Syst.* 76:139–211. Weston, P. H., and M. D. Crisp. 1996. Trans-Pacific biogeographic patterns in the Proteaceae. In *The Origin and Evolution of Pacific Island Biotas, New Guinea to Eastern Polynesia: Patterns and Processes*, eds. A. Keast and S. E. Miller, 215–32. Amsterdam: SPB Academic Publishing.

PTEROSTEMONACEAE (Pterostemon Family)

Amy Berkov

- *shrubs*
- *leaves alternate, simple; blades glossy adaxially, pubescent abaxially, the margins toothed*
- *flowers with 5 stamens and 5 staminodes, the filaments toothed near apex*
- *fruits woody capsules, the sepals and petals persistent*

Numbers of genera and species. Endemic to tropical America, the Pterostemonaceae include a single genus, *Pterostemon*, and two species, *Pterostemon mexicanus* and *P. rotundifolius*.

Distribution and habitat. Species of Pterostemonaceae are endemic to central and southern Mexico in the states of Querétero, Hidalgo, Puebla, Oaxaca, and Guerrero.

The two species of *Pterostemon* are found in arid, hilly regions where they are sometimes locally abundant on chalky limestone soils between 1,400 and 2,650 meters.

Family classification. Pterostemon is placed by Cronquist within the Grossulariaceae in the Rosales. Takhtajan considers the Pterostemonaceae as a separate family near the Iteaceae and belonging to the Saxifragales. Molecular analyses indicate that *Pterostemon* and *Itea* are sister groups, but Takhtajan points out morphological differences, including the number of locules, the number of stamens, and the number of pores in the pollen grains, that separate the two. According to *rbc*L data, both *Pterostemon* and the Iteaceae are nested within the Saxifragales.

Features of the family. Habit: shrubs. Stipules present, minute, caducous. Leaves alternate, simple; blades oval to almost circular, the adaxial surface glossy, the abaxial surface pubescent, the margins toothed; veins usually prominent abaxially; hydathodes present; hairs present, simple, unicellular; glands present, multicellular, conical or peltate. Inflorescences subterminal, cymes, relatively few flowered. Flowers actinomorphic, bisexual, showy, aromatic, white to pink; calyx connate into tube, the tube pubescent, fused to ovary, the lobes 5, erect, triangular; petals 5, imbricate, reflexed, pubescent; stamens 5, opposite sepals, the filaments broad, coarsely toothed near apex, the anthers dehiscing longitudinally; staminodes 5, opposite petals, lacking anthers, coarsely toothed near apex; gynoecium syncarpous, the ovary inferior, the carpels 5, the locules 5, the style 1, the stigmas 5, radiate; placentation axile, the ovules 4–6 per locule. Fruits septicidal capsules, woody, crowned by persistent sepals and petals. Seeds few, elongate.

The glands apparently secrete a resinous exudate that is responsible for the shiny adaxial surface of the leaves.

Natural history. Nothing is known about the pollination or dispersal biology of the family.

Economic uses. No economic uses of this family are known.

References. Rzedowski, J. 1978. *Vegetación de México*. Mexico: Editorial Limusa. Savolainen, V., M. F. Fay, D. C. Albach, A. Backlund, M. van der Bank, et al. 2000. Phylogeny of the eudicots: a nearly complete familial analysis based on *rbc*L sequences. *Kew Bull.* 55:257–309. Soltis, D. E., and P. S. Soltis. 1997. Phylogenetic relationships in Saxifragaceae *sensu lato*: a comparison of topologies based on 18S *r*DNA and *rbc*L sequences. *Amer. J. Bot.* 84(4):504–22. Wilkinson, H. P. 1994. Leaf and twig anatomy of the Pterostemonaceae (Engl.) Small: ecological and systematic features. *Bot. J. Linn. Soc.* 115:115–31.

QUIINACEAE (Quiina Family)

GEORG ZIZKA AND JULIO SCHNEIDER

Figure 163, Plate 39

- *shrubs or medium-sized trees*
- *stipules interpetiolar, usually conspicuous*
- *leaves opposite or whorled, simple or pinnate; venation craspedodromous, the tertiary veins parallel and closely spaced (except in* Quiina*)*
- *flowers actinomorphic; stamens usually numerous*
- *fruits berrylike or follicles*

Numbers of genera and species. The Quiinaceae, a family restricted to the neotropics, include *Froesia* (5 species), *Lacunaria* (10), *Quiina* (34), and *Touroulia* (2).

Distribution and habitat. The Quiinaceae are restricted to tropical America from northern Belize and the West Indies south to Bolivia and southern Brazil. Most of the species occur in northern South America. *Quiina* has a wide distribution, similar to that of the family and species of *Lacunaria*, as well as *Froesia* and *Touroulia*, occur principally in northern South America and the Amazonian lowlands, but at least *Lacunaria panamensis* is found in Panama.

The Quiinaceae occur principally in primary, lowland, nonflooded rain forests, but some species occur in seasonally flooded forests. One species of *Froesia* grows in premontane and cloud forests in northern Venezuela at about 1,500 meters.

Family classification. The Quiinaceae were placed in the Theales by Cronquist; however, modern treatments based on molecular analyses align the family in the Malpighiales. An important anatomical feature of *Froesia* and *Touroulia* is the possession of cristarque cells (U-shaped cristalliferous sclereids), which are shared with Ochnaceae and Scytopetalaceae, the former is usually regarded as closely related to Quiinaceae. *Lacunaria* and *Quiina* both have mucilaginous cavities, particularly in the petioles, leaves, and pericarps.

The Quiinaceae are considered monophyletic, being well characterized by anatomical features of the wood and by leaf venation.

Features of the family. **Habit:** shrubs or medium-sized trees (to 30 m), evergreen. **Stipules** present, interpetiolar, usually conspicuous, foliaceous or setose, entire or divided into several setose parts (*Froesia*). **Leaves** opposite (*Quiina* [except *Q. pteridophylla*], *Froesia*, *Touroulia*) or in whorls of 4 (*Lacunaria* [except *L. oppositifolia*]), crowded at apex of stem (in *Touroulia* and *Froesia*), simple, or pinnately compound in *Touroulia* and *Froesia*; venation craspedodromous,

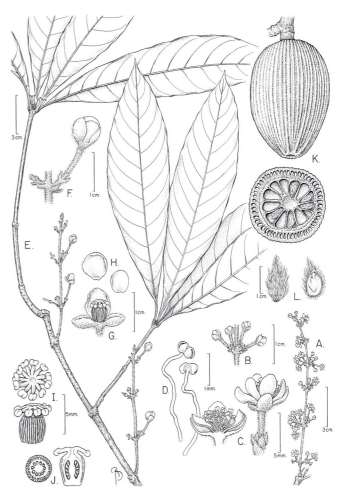

Figure 163. QUIINACEAE. *Lacunaria jenmanii.* **A.** Part of staminate inflorescence. **B.** Detail of staminate inflorescence. **C.** Medial section (left) and lateral view (right) of staminate flower. **D.** Adaxial (left) and abaxial (right) views of stamens. **E.** Stem with leaves and pistillate inflorescences. **F.** Detail of pistillate inflorescence. **G.** Lateral view of pistillate flower with three petals and one sepal removed. **H.** Adaxial views of two petals. **I.** Apical view of stigma (above) and lateral view of gynoecium (below). **J.** Transverse (left) and medial sections (right) of gynoecium. **K.** Lateral view (above) and transverse section (below) of fruit; note cavities in pericarp. **L.** Lateral view (left) and medial section (right) of seed. Reprinted with permission from Mori et al. (2002). Artist: Bobbi Angell.

the tertiary veins parallel and closely spaced (except in *Quiina*), intersecondary veins present in *Quiina*, absent in *Lacunaria*. **Inflorescences** terminal (*Froesia*, *Touroulia*, rarely *Lacunaria*) or axillary (*Quiina*, *Lacunaria*), thyrsoid or bostryxlike; pedicels present. **Flowers** actinomorphic, bisexual (*Froesia*) or unisexual (plants androdioecious in *Quiina* and *Touroulia* or dioecious in *Lacunaria*), 4–25 mm diameter; sepals (3)4–5(6), imbricate; petals (3)4–8, variable in shape; androecium of 9 to >90 stamens in *Lacunaria*, *Quiina*, and

Touroulia, to >300 stamens in *Froesia*, the filaments fili-form, free or adnate to petals in some *Quiina*; gynoecium usually syncarpous (3 distinct carpels in *Froesia*), the ovary superior, the carpels 2–14, the locules and styles equal in number to carpels; placentation axile, the ovules (1)2(4) per locule. **Fruits** berrylike or 1–3 follicles in *Froesia*. **Seeds** 1 to more than 20 in berrylike fruits or 1 per follicle, glabrous in *Froesia* or densely villous in remaining genera.

Some species with entire leaves as adults produce pinnati-fid leaves as juveniles. Pollen dimorphism occurs in *Quiina*.

Delimitation of species is especially difficult in *Quiina* and *Lacunaria* because the species display variability in morpho-logical features. Species of *Froesia* form a close-knit, mor-phologically similar group and are best separated by vegeta-tive characters. In *Touroulia*, the two species of similar habit differ conspicuously in leaf venation and size of floral parts.

Natural history. There are no observations on pollination and few reports of dispersal, but insect pollination and ani-mal dispersal are most likely. Monkeys have been reported to eat the fruits of some species.

Economic uses. No economic uses have been reported, but the fruits of some species of *Lacunaria* and *Quiina* are known to be edible.

References. AMARAL, M.C.E. 1991. Phylogenetische Sys-tematik der Ochnaceae. *Bot. Jahrb. Syst.* 113:105–96. FOS-TER, A. S. 1950a. Morphology and venation of the leaf of *Quiina acutangula* Ducke. *Amer. J. Bot.* 37:159–71. FOSTER, A. S. 1950b. Venation and histology of the leaflets of *Tour-oulia guianensis* Aubl. and *Froesia tricarpa* Pires. *Amer. J. Bot.* 37:848–62. FOSTER, A. S. 1951. Heterophylly and foliar venation in *Lacunaria*. *Bull. Torrey Bot. Club* 78:382–400. GOTTWALD, H., AND N. PARAMESWARAN. 1967. Beitrage zur Anatomie und Systematik der Quiinaceae. *Bot. Jahrb. Syst.* 87(3):361–81. PIRES, J. M. 1948. Notas sobre a Flora Neo-tropica. 1: *Froesia*. *Bol. Técn. Inst. Agron. N.* 15:22–25. PIRES, J. M. 1950. Contribuição para a Flóra Amazônica. *Bol. Técn. Inst. Agron. N.* 20:41–51. SCHNEIDER, J., U. SWENSON, AND G. ZIZKA. 2002. Phylogenetic reconstruction of the neotropi-cal family Quiinaceae (Malpighiales) based on morphology with remarks on the evolution of an androdioecious sex dis-tribution. *Ann. Missouri Bot. Gard.* 89(1):64–76. SCHNEID-ER, J., AND G. ZIZKA. In press. Quiinaceae. In: *Flora of the Venezuelan Guayana*, eds. J. A. Steyermark, P. E. Berry and B. K. Holst. Timber Press; Miss. Bot. Garden. STEYERMARK, J. A., AND G. S. BUNTING. 1975. Revision of the genus *Froesia* (Quiinaceae). *Brittonia* 27:172–78. ZIZKA, G., AND J. SCHNEIDER. 1999. The genus *Toroulia* Aubl. (Quiinaceae). *Willdenowia* 29:1–8.

RAFFLESIACEAE (Rafflesia Family)

JOHN D. MITCHELL

- *herbs*
- *plants holoparasitic; chlorophyll absent*
- *leaves reduced, scalelike*
- *flowers with 4–10 tepals; filaments united in tube or central column*
- *fruits berries*

Numbers of genera and species. Worldwide, the Raffle-siaceae comprise nine genera and about 55 species. In tropi-cal America, there are four genera, *Apodanthes*, *Bdallophy-ton*, *Mitrastema*, and *Pilostyles*, and approximately 13 species.

Distribution and habitat. The Rafflesiaceae have a pan-tropical to marginally temperate distribution. *Apodanthes* and *Bdallophyton* are endemic to the neotropics; *Apodanthes* is distributed from Mexico to northern South America; and *Bdal-lophyton* is found from Mexico to Costa Rica. Three genera, *Rafflesia*, *Rhizanthes*, and *Sapria*, are restricted to southern Asia and Malesia and *Berlinianche* is endemic to Africa. The remaining genera are widely distributed, including *Mitra-* *stema* found from Mexico to Guatemala and northwestern Colombia and *Pilostyles*, ranging from California south to Chile and Argentina.

Neotropical Rafflesiaceae occur in a wide range of habi-tats, including tropical moist forests, montane forests, tropi-cal dry forests, and deserts.

Family classification. The Rafflesiaceae are placed in the Rafflesiales by Cronquist. The family is divided into two subfamilies by Meijer, the Mitrastemoideae, with only *Mi-trastema* (= *Mitrastemon*), and the Rafflesioideae, which consists of the tribes Rafflesieae, Apodantheae, and Cyti-neae. Cronquist segregates the Mitrastemoidae as a separate family, the Mitrastemonaceae and Takhtajan divides the Raf-flesiaceae into the Apodanthaceae, Mitrastemonaceae, Raf-flesiaceae, and Cytinaceae. Traditionally, most authors have agreed that the Rafflesiaceae and Hydnoraceae are closely related. An affinity between the Rafflesiaceae and the Aristo-lochiaceae has also been proposed by several individuals. However, to date, the family's alignment is still unresolved.

Features of the family. Habit: holoparasitic herbs, chloro-phyll absent. **Stipules** absent. **Leaves** reduced, scalelike, whorled around base of solitary flower or on flowering stem. **Inflorescences** terminal or axillary, racemes, spikes, or of solitary flowers, very short to 25 cm long as in *Bdallophyton*; fleshy scales (leaves) sometimes subtending flowers. **Flowers** actinomorphic, unisexual (plants monoecious or dioecious) or rarely bisexual, sometimes putrid smelling; tepals 4–10, imbricate; androecium of 5–numerous stamens, the filaments united into tube or central column, the anthers dehiscing longitudinally, transversely, or poricidally; gynoecium syncarpous, the ovary usually inferior or semi-inferior, rarely superior (*Mitrastema*), the carpels 4–10, rarely fewer, the locule 1, sometimes variously divided into numerous interconnected ovule-bearing chambers, the style short or absent, the stigma capitate, discoid, or multilobed; placentation parietal, the ovules numerous, anatropous or orthotropous (e.g., *Bdallophyton*). **Fruits** berries, indehiscent to irregularly dehiscent. **Seeds** numerous, the testa hard; endosperm 1–3 layered, the embryo undifferentiated.

In the neotropics, the flowers are small to medium-sized and inconspicuous (e.g., *Apodanthes* and *Pilostyles*). In contrast, the world's largest flowers, nearly 1 m in diameter, are found in Southeast Asian species of *Rafflesia*.

Natural history. The Rafflesiaceae are found on roots, stems, and branches of various trees, shrubs, and vines. Species of this family derive their nutrition by penetrating the tissues of roots or stems of woody host plants via hyphaelike strands or filaments. This myceliumlike endophytic system usually is implanted close to the host's cambium, however, much deeper penetration of the host via the rays into the xylem also occurs.

The widespread *Apodanthes* parasitizes mostly the branches of various species of Flacourtiaceae; *Bdallophyton* is parasitic on the roots of *Bursera simaruba* and possibly other *Bursera*; *Mitrastema* is a root parasite of *Quercus*; and species of *Pilostyles* are stem parasites of various legumes.

The Rafflesiaceae are pollinated mainly by flies (Diptera), bees, and wasps (Hymenoptera). Some genera produce the smell of rotting flesh. The flowers of *Bdallophyton bambusarum* (= *B. americanum*) are pollinated by flies of the genera *Perckiamya* and *Peckia* (Sarcophagidae); the flowers of *Apodanthes* are visited by *Trigona* bees, and the flowers of *Pilostyles* are visited by flies and bees.

The seeds of *B. bambusarum* are dispersed by the mouse *Peromyscus mexicanus*, and the berries of *Apodanthes* are eaten by tanagers of the genus *Thraupis*. The reproductive biology of the Neotropical genera has been studied only in *Bdallophyton*.

Economic uses. No economic uses are known for Neotropical Rafflesiaceae. In southeast Asia, the giant flowers of *Rafflesia*, among the largest known in the world, are major ecotourist attractions.

References GARCÍA-FRANCO, J. G., AND V. RICO-GRAY. 1996a. Dispersión, viabilidad, germinación y banco de semillas de *Bdallophyton bambusarum* (Rafflesiaceae) en la costa de Veracruz, México. *Revista Biol. Trop.* 44:87–94. GARCÍA-FRANCO, J. G., AND V. RICO-GRAY. 1996b. Distribution and host specificity in the holoparasite *Bdallophyton bambusarum* (Rafflesiaceae) in a tropical deciduous forest in Veracruz, Mexico. *Biotropica* 28:759–62. GARCÍA-FRANCO, J. G., AND V. RICO-GRAY. 1997. Reproductive biology of the holoparasitic endophyte *Bdallophyton bambusarum* (Rafflesiaceae). *Bot. J. Linn. Soc.* 123:237–47. GÓMEZ, L. D. 1983. Rafflesiaceae. In *Flora Costaricensis*, ed. W. Burger. *Fieldiana Bot.*, n.s., 13:89–93. IGERSHEIM, A., AND P. K. ENDRESS. 1998. Gynoecium diversity and systematics of the paleoherbs. *Bot. J. Linn. Soc.* 127:(4)289–370. KUIJT, J., D. BRAY, AND A. R. OLSON. 1985. Anatomy and ultrastructure of the endophytic system of *Pilostyles thurberi* (Rafflesiaceae). Canad. J. Bot. 63:1231–40. MATUDA, E. 1947. On the genus *Mitrastemon*. *Bull. Torrey Bot. Club* 74:133–141. MEIJER, W. 1993. Rafflesiaceae In *The Families and Genera of Vascular Plants*, eds. K. Kubitzki, J. G. Rohwer, and V. Bittrich, 2:557–63. Berlin: Springer-Verlag. NICKRENT, D. L., R. J. DUFF, AND D.A.M. KONINGS. 1997. Structural analyses of plastid-derived 16S rRNAs in holoparasitic angiosperms. *Pl. Molec. Biol.* 34(5):731–43. VATTIMO, I. 1971. Contribuição ao conhecimento da tribu Apodanthea R. Br. Parte I, conspecto das especies. Rodriguezia 26, no. 38:37–62.

RANUNCULACEAE (Buttercup Family)

DENNIS WM. STEVENSON

Figure 164

- *herbs or sometimes lianas (Clematis)*

- *leaves alternate or rarely opposite (Clematis), simple to compound (often highly dissected)*

- *flowers apocarpous*

- *fruits usually achenes or follicles, sometimes berries*

- *seeds many in follicles and berries*

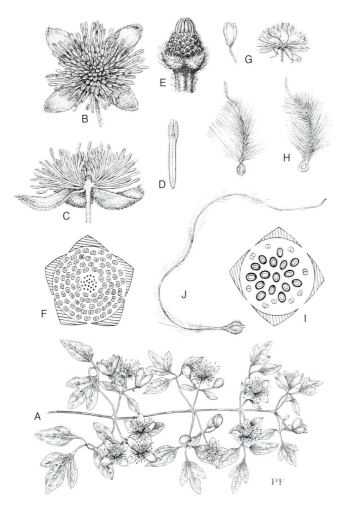

Figure 164. RANUNCULACEAE. *Clematis bahamica*. **A.** Stem with leaves and staminate flowers (x2/3). **B.** Apical view of staminate flower (x2). **C.** Medial section of staminate flower (x2). **D.** Stamen (x6). **E.** Receptacle of staminate flower showing staminodes (x14). **F.** Floral diagram of staminate flower. **G.** Lateral views of pistillate flower bud (left) and pistillate flower with only one petal remaining (both x2). **H.** Lateral view (left) and medial section (right) of gynoecium (both x6). **I.** Floral diagram of pistillate flower. **J.** Lateral view of fruit (x2). Reprinted with permission from Correll and Correll (1982). Artist: Priscilla Fawcett.

Numbers of genera and species. Worldwide, the Ranunculaceae comprise 60 genera (including *Glaucidium*) and approximately 2,500 species. In tropical America, there are 11 native genera and about 90–100 species. Many extratropical genera are cultivated as ornamentals (e.g., *Actaea* and *Delphinium*) and may, therefore, be found in the neotropics.

The 11 native genera of the neotropics represent only two of the five subfamilies, Ranunculoideae and Thalictroideae. Within the Ranunculoideae, only two of the three tribes are found: the Anemoneae with *Anemone* (5 species), *Barneoudia* (3), *Clematis* (15), and *Oreithales* (1), and the Ranunculeae with *Aphanostemma* (1), *Callianthemoides* (1), *Hamadryas* (6), *Krapfia* (8), *Laccopetalum* (1), and *Ranunculus*

(40–50). In the Thalictroideae, approximately 10 species of *Thalictrum* are known from the neotropics.

Distribution and habitat. The Ranunculaceae are one of the most cosmopolitan of the flowering plant families. The family prefers more or less wet temperate climates and relatively few are found in the Tropics, especially lowland rain forests.

The South American genera represent montane and temperate range extensions of North American taxa; e.g., *Anemone*, *Clematis*, *Ranunculus*, and *Thalictrum*. Of the seven genera endemic to Central and South America, *Barneoudia*, *Callianthemoides*, and *Hamadryas* are limited to higher elevations of Argentina and Chile. Within the Neotropics, *Laccopetalum*, *Oreithales*, and *Krapfia* are associate with alpine areas of the Andes and *Aphanostemma* is found in low, wet and sandy areas from southern Brazil to northern Argentina.

Generally, Neotropical Ranunculaceae prefer cool, wet habitats. Consequently, they are found at higher elevations in the Andes and are often a component of *páramo* vegetation. They often grow at the margins of pools, in bogs, or in other poorly drained sites.

Family classification. The Ranunculaceae are placed in the Ranunculales by Cronquist. The family is closely related to the Berberidaceae, Menispermaceae, and Papaveraceae. The most recent treatment of the Ranunculaceae by Tamura divides the family into five subfamilies: Hydrastoideae (only *Hydrastis*), Helleboroideae (with 17 genera in four tribes), Isopyroideae (with 11 genera in three tribes), Ranunculoideae (with 29 genera in three tribes), and Thalictroideae (only *Thalictrum*). Recent studies have shown that *Hydrastis* and *Glaucidium* (formerly a genus of uncertain position thought to be allied with either *Paeonia* or the Dilleniaceae) are closely related and together form a basal group in the Ranunculaceae. The Thalictroideae would appear to be part of the Isopyroideae. The large Ranunculoideae and Helleboroideae are supported by both molecular and morphological data.

Features of the family. Habit: herbs or lianas (*Clematis*), the herbs usually annual, sometimes biennial or perennial, sometimes aquatic. **Stipules** absent. **Leaves** alternate or rarely opposite (*Clematis*), simple, palmate, or pinnate (often highly dissected); petioles and petiolules generally present, becoming tendril-like in *Clematis*. **Inflorescences** terminal or occasionally axillary (*Clematis*), of solitary flowers, racemes, panicles, or occasionally cymes (*Clematis*). **Flowers** usually actinomorphic or rarely zygomorphic (e.g., *Delphinium*), bisexual or rarely unisexual (plants dioecious), generally large; calyx with 5–8+ sepals, the sepals distinct, often petal-like, particularly in species without petals (e.g., species of *Oreithales*); corolla with 0–13 petals, the petals distinct when present, white, yellow, blue, or red, often nectariferous (e.g., *Laccopetalum*) and called honey-leaves; androecium of 5–many stamens, often transitional with petals, the filament and anthers well defined; gynoecium apocarpous, the ovaries superior, the carpels 1–many, the styles short, the stigma well developed, often long (e.g., *Clematis*); placentation marginal, the ovules 1–many, sometimes basal. **Fruits** usually achenes or follicles, less frequently berries (e.g., *Actaea*). **Seeds** many in follicles and berries.

Natural history. The Ranunculaceae are primarily insect-pollinated, but a few species are wind-pollinated (e.g., some *Thalictrum*), and some are bird-pollinated (e.g., red-flowered species of *Clematis*, *Delphinium*, and *Aquilegia*). Within the neotropics, the Andean *Ranunculus gusmani* has been demonstrated to be hummingbird-pollinated, but most other species are bee-pollinated. Epithelial nectaries are found on the upper petal surfaces or, when the petals are absent, on the staminodia.

Achenes or small seeds from dehiscent follicles are most likely dispersed by gravity while plumose achenes, such as those of *Clematis*, are dispersed by the wind.

Economic uses. Species of *Actaea* (baneberry), *Adonis*, *Aquilegia* (columbine), *Clematis*, *Delphinium* (larkspur), *Helleborus* (hellebore), and *Ranunculus* (buttercup) are cultivated as ornamentals because of their showy flowers. Seeds of *Nigella sativa* (black cumin) are used for flavoring, for example, in the *nan* bread of northern India and in Armenian string cheese. *Aconitum* (monk's hood), which contains the alkaloid aconitine, and *Thalictrum* are used as stimulants and emetics, but are very toxic. *Laccopetalum* is sold in local markets as an astringent. Some Ranunculaceae (e.g., species of *Delphinium*) are considered noxious weeds because they contain isoquinoline alkaloids, glycosides, or cyanide compounds, which can poison livestock if plants are eaten.

References. Duncan, T., and C. Keener. 1991. A classification of the Ranunculaceae with special reference to the Western Hemisphere. *Phytologia* 70:24–27. Hoot, S. 1995. Phylogeny of the Ranunculaceae based on preliminary *atp*B, *rbc*L and 18S nuclear ribosomal DNA sequence data. *Pl. Syst. Evol., Suppl.* 9:241–51. Hoot, S., and P. Crane. 1995. Interfamilial relationships in the Ranunculidae based upon molecular systematics. *Pl. Syst. Evol., Suppl.* 9:119–31. Loconte, H., L. Campbell, and D. Stevenson. 1995. Ordinal and familial relationships of ranunculid genera. *Pl. Syst. Evol., Suppl.* 9:99–118. Tamura, M. 1993. Ranunculaceae. In *The Families and Genera of Vascular Plants*, ed. K. Kubitzki, 2:563–83. New York: Springer-Verlag.

RHABDODENDRACEAE (Rhabdodendron Family)

Ghillean T. Prance

Figure 165, Plate 39

- *trees or shrubs*

- *leaves alternate, simple, gland-dotted*

- *flowers with 5 petals; stamens numerous; styles gynobasic*

- *fruits drupes*

Numbers of genera and species. The Rhabdodendraceae comprise a single genus, *Rhabdodendron*, and three species, all of which are endemic to South America.

Distribution and habitat. The Rhabdodendraceae are confined to the Guianas, Amazonia, and northeastern Brazil. Only *Rhabdodendron amazonicum*, found in the rain forests on *terra firme* in the Guianas and in central and eastern Amazonian Brazil, is widespread. The other two species are local endemics: *R. macrophyllum* is a shrub confined to white sand areas between the Trombetas River and Manaus, Brazil, and *R. gardnerianum* is found only in western Bahia in northeastern Brazil, but no details about habitat are known.

Family classification. The Rhabdodendraceae are placed in the Rosales by Cronquist. Affinities of *Rhabdodendron* have been suggested with such widely separated families as Chrysobalanaceae, Phytolaccaceae, and Rutaceae. Relationship to the Chrysobalanaceae is based on similar gynobasic styles, to the Phytolaccaceae mainly on the occurrence of secondary phloem in the wood, and to the Rutaceae mainly because of lysigenous secretory cavities in the leaves, specialized "spicular" cells transversing the leaf mesophyll, and peltate hairs. Most recent molecular studies employing *rbc*L sequence data indicate a relationship with the Caryophyllidae, which includes the Phytolaccaceae, but do not support relationships to any of the other families.

pal lobes 5, small or indistinct; petals 5, distinct, imbricate, minutely punctate caducous at anthesis (at least in *R. amazonicum*); disc absent; androecium of numerous stamens (ca. 45), the filaments short, flattened, the anthers long, linear, basifixed, dehiscing longitudinally; gynoecium with superior ovary, inserted at base of concave receptacle, the carpel 1, the locule 1, the style gynobasic, the stigmatic surface thick, elongate, ascending from the base or middle; placentation basal, the ovule 1, campylotropous. **Fruits** drupes, globose, small. **Seeds** 1, reniform-globose; endosperm absent, the cotyledons thick, fleshy, the radicle small, bent inward toward hilum.

Natural history. *Rhabdodendron macrophyllum* is self-compatible but is also pollinated by small, pollen-gathering bees, especially species of *Melipona* and *Trigonia*. *Melipona* vibrates the anthers (buzz pollination) to extract pollen. No information is available on dispersal biology, but the fruits are most likely dispersed by animals, especially birds.

Economic uses. No uses are recorded for any of the species.

References. BEHNKE, H.-D. 1976. Sieve element plastids of *Fouquieria*, *Frankenia* (Tamaricales) and *Rhabdodendron* (Rutaceae), taxa sometimes allied with Centrospermae (Caryophyllales). *Taxon* 25:265–68. FAY, M. F., K. M. CAMERON, G. T. PRANCE, M. D. LLEDO, AND M. W. CHASE. 1997. Familial relationships of Rhabdodendron (Rhabodendraceae): Plastid *rbc*L sequences indicate a caryophyllid placement. *Kew Bull.* 52(4):923–32. PRANCE, G. T. 1968. The systematic position of *Rhabdodendron* Gilg. & Pilg. *Bull. Jard. Bot. Belg.* 38:127–46. PRANCE, G. T. 1972. Rhabdodendraceae. *Fl. Neotrop. Monogr.* 11:1–22. PRANCE, G. T. 2003. Rhabdodendraceae. In *The Families and Genera of Vascular Plants*, eds. K. Kubitzki and C. Bayer. 5:339–41. Berlin: Springer-Verlag. PUFF, C., AND A. WEBER. 1976. Contribution to the morphology, anatomy and karyology of *Rhabdodendron*, and a reconsideration of the systematic position of the Rhabdodendraceae. *Pl. Syst. Evol.* 125:195–222. RECORD, S. J. 1933. The woods of *Rhabodendron* and *Duckeodendron*. *Trop. Woods* 33:6–10. TOBE, H., AND P. H. RAVEN. 1989. The embryology and systematic position of *Rhabdodendron* (Rhabdodendraceae). In *Plant taxonomy, phytogeography and related subjects*, ed. K. Tan, 233–48. Edinburgh: University Press.

Figure 165. RHABDODENDRACEAE. *Rhabdodendron amazonicum*. **A.** Stem with leaves and inflorescences. **B.** Leaf with detail of abaxial surface and lepidote scale. **C.** Part of inflorescence. **D.** Lateral view of flower. **E.** Lateral view of flower with most of anthers disarticulated. **F.** Medial section of flower (left) and gynoecium with gynobasic style (right). **G.** Adaxial (right) and lateral (left) views of anther. **H.** Part of infructescence. **I.** Medial section of fruit. Reprinted with permission from Mori et al. (2002). Artist: Bobbi Angell.

Features of the family. Habit: small trees or shrubs (*Rhabdodendron macrophyllum*). **Wood** with anomalous secondary phloem (*R. gardnerianum* and *R. amazonicum*). **Stipules** minute or absent. **Leaves** alternate, simple, coriaceous, gland-dotted; blade margins entire. **Inflorescences** axillary, racemes or panicles of racemes. **Flowers** actinomorphic, bisexual; se-

RHAMNACEAE (Buckthorn Family)

Scott V. Heald

Figure 166, Plate 40

- *mostly trees and shrubs, sometimes lianas, rarely subshrubs or herbs; often with spines, hooks, or tendrils (in lianas)*
- *leaves usually alternate, occasionally opposite, simple*
- *inflorescences usually cymes*
- *flowers small; perianth valvate; petals often enveloping stamens; disc prominent*
- *fruits drupelike, capsules, or schizocarps*

Numbers of genera and species. Worldwide, the Rhamnaceae comprise about 58 genera and 900 species. Twenty-three genera and about 170 species are native to tropical America. The principal Neotropical genera are *Ziziphus* (30 species), *Rhamnus* (21), *Colubrina* (20), and *Gouania* (5).

Distribution and habitat. Rhamnaceae are a cosmopolitan family most common in tropical and subtropical regions, and absent only from the arctic and Antarctica.

Species of Rhamnaceae are most commonly found in hot tropical lowlands in all kinds of habitats, ranging from rain forest to dry forests and savannas. Some species of Rhamnaceae are found in cloud forests.

Family classification. The Rhamnaceae are placed in the Rhamnales by Cronquist. Others have suggested a relationship with the Celastraceae. The Rhamnaceae differ from the Vitaceae in the following respects: mostly trees or shrubs, less frequently lianas versus nearly always lianas; ovary ± superior versus ovary inferior; ovules mostly 1 per locule versus ovules 2 per locule; and fruits mostly drupaceous versus fruits baccate. The Rhamnaceae differ from Celastraceae in having the stamens opposite the petals rather than the sepals. Based on a number of anatomical similarities, Thorne placed the Rhamnaceae in an expanded Malvanae clade, next to Urticales. Molecular analyses support the placement of the Rhamnaceae in the Rosales along with taxa of Cronquist's Urticales and families such as the Elaeagnaceae and Rosaceae.

Features of the family. Habit: trees, shrubs, or lianas (the lianas with tendrils), rarely subshrubs or herbs (*Crumenaria*), spines often present. **Stems** often with mucilage cells, sometimes with mucilage cavities in primary cortex; nodes generally bearing multiple buds, often 1 or more develop into a thorn, short-shoot, or inflorescence axis. **Stipules** usually

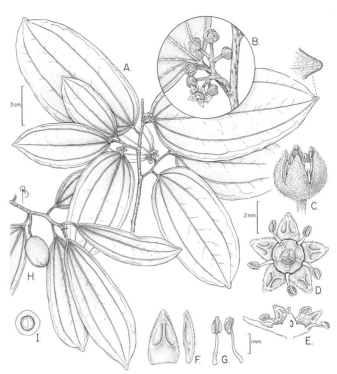

Figure 166. RHAMNACEAE. *Ziziphus cinnamomum.* **A.** Stem with leaves, inflorescences, and detail of leaf apex (right). **B.** Axillary inflorescence. **C.** Lateral view of partially opened flower. **D.** Apical view of flower. **E.** Medial section of flower. **F.** Lateral (right) and adaxial (left) views of sepals. **G.** Adaxial (left) and lateral (right) views of stamens. **H.** Stem with leaves and fruit. **I.** Transverse section of fruit. Reprinted with permission from Mori et al. (2002). Artist: Bobbi Angell.

present, small, spinelike, caducous. **Leaves** usually alternate, occasionally opposite, simple, with mucilage cells; blades with or without glands or pocket domatia at base, the margins entire or serrate; venation pinnate or with several main veins arising from base. **Inflorescences** axillary or terminal, usually cymes, less often racemes. **Flowers** actinomorphic, bisexual or rarely unisexual (then plants andromonoecious), often protandrous, small; hypanthium present; sepals 4–5, cuneate, thick, valvate, often deciduous; petals (0)4–5, clawed, often incurved and ± enveloping stamens, valvate; androecium with 4–5 stamens, the stamens opposite petals or alternate sepals when petals lacking, the filaments adnate to base of petals, the anthers generally inserted into hooded petals; intrastaminal disc present, adnate to hypanthium and sometimes also ovary; gynoecium syncarpous, the ovary superior to inferior, the carpels 2–3(5), the locules 2–3(5) or fewer, the styles 2–4, distinct or connate; placentation basal the ovules 1 per locule (2 in *Karwinskia*). **Fruits** essentially drupes with several stones or a single plurilocular stone, or dry and dehiscent capsules or schizocarps. **Seeds** few, sometimes with dorsal groove; endosperm scant or absent, the embryo usually straight, large, oily.

Natural history. Flowers are thought to be insect-pollinated. Various small bees, flies, and beetles have been observed visiting the flowers of species of *Rhamnus* in Mexico and *Trevoa quinquenervia* in central Chile. Capsular-fruited species have winged seeds borne on the wind or seeds that are dispersed by means of explosive splitting of the fruit wall. Drupelike fruits are eaten by mammals or birds. The drupes of *Ziziphus cinnamomum* are eaten by capuchin (*Cebus apella*) and spider (*Aleles paniscus*) monkeys. A few species of *Discaria* have fruits that float and are dispersed by water currents.

Economic uses. Species of Rhamnaceae are used as medicines, food (edible fruits), dyes, soaps, charcoal, cultivated ornamentals, and timber. A few species of the Eastern Hemisphere have spiritual significance; e.g., *Ziziphus spina-cristi* (Mediterranean to Arabia) is suggested to be the plant used to make Christ's crown of thorns. Many members of the family contain alkaloids and chemicals related to quinine that have medicinal applications. Species of *Rhamnus* are often sources of purgatives. The bark of *Colubrina glandulosa* is used in Brazil to prepare *saguaragy* to treat fevers, extracts from the bark of *Trevoa trinervia* (from Chile) are applied to burns, and the bark of *Gouania domingensis* is chewed as a stimulant in the West Indies. Edible fruits are produced by species of *Ziziphus* and *Colubrina*. *Ziziphus mistol* is used to prepare an alcoholic drink in the Andes. Yellow dyes are extracted from the bark, and blue and green dyes come from the fruits of several species of *Rhamnus*. The saponin-rich roots of *Colletia spinosissima* are sources of soap, and the stems of *Gouania lupuloides* create a soapy mouthwash when chewed.

Most of the cultivated ornamental Rhamnaceae are North American species of *Ceanothus* (California lilacs), but a few species of *Discaria*, *Colubrina*, and *Colletia* have caught the gardener's eye. *Ziziphus chloroxylon* (cogwood in Jamaica) and *Colubrina arborescens* (snakebark in Central America and the West Indies) are exploited for their timber.

References. ALVERSON, W. S., K. G. KAROL, D. A. BAUM, M. W. CHASE, S. M. SWENSEN, ET AL. 1998. Circumscription of the Malvales and relationships to other Rosidae: evidence from *rbc*L sequence data. *Amer. J. Bot.* 85(6):876–87. JOHNSTON, M. C., AND L. A. JOHNSTON. 1978. *Rhamnus. Fl. Neotrop. Monogr.* 20:1–96. RICHARDSON, J. E., M. F. FAY, Q.C.B. CRONK, D. BOWMAN, AND M. W. CHASE. 2000. A phylogenetic analysis of Rhamnaceae using *rbc*L and *trn*L-F plastid DNA sequences. *Amer. J. Bot.* 87(9): 1309–24.

RHIZOPHORACEAE (Red Mangrove Family)

MATS H. G. GUSTAFSSON

Figure167, Plate 40

- shrubs or trees

- aerial roots often prominent (Rhizophoreae)

- stipules interpetiolar, caducous

- leaves usually opposite, simple

- plants viviparous (Rhizophoreae)

Numbers of genera and species. Worldwide, the Rhizophoraceae comprise 14–15 genera and about 130 species. In tropical America, there are three genera and 18 species. *Rhizophora* is represented by three species, *Cassipourea* by about eight species, and *Sterigmapetalum* by seven species.

Distribution and habitat. The Rhizophoraceae occur throughout the Tropics and extend into the subtropics of North America and Asia. The greatest diversity is found in the paleotropics. The most diverse genera have wide distributions. *Rhizophora*, a mangrove, occurs in most tropical coastal areas; *Cassipourea* is distributed in tropical America, Africa, and Ceylon, and *Sterigmapetalum* is endemic to the neotropics.

In the neotropics, mangrove Rhizophoraceae grow in association with *Avicennia* (Avicenniaceae), *Conocarpus* (Combretaceae), and *Pelliciera* (Pellicieriaceae), and often play a dominant role in mangrove vegetation. Most nonmangrove Rhizophoraceae grow in wet tropical forests, but a few species of *Cassipourea* are found in dry scrub.

Family classification. Cronquist placed the Rhizophoraceae in the Rhizophorales next to the Myrtales; however, evidence from embryology and anatomy does not support this alignment. Based on a number of morphological characters, affinities with, for example, Celastraceae, Elaeocarpaceae, and Erythroxylaceae have been suggested. Recent molecular studies have indicated that the Erythroxylaceae are the closest relatives of Rhizophoraceae.

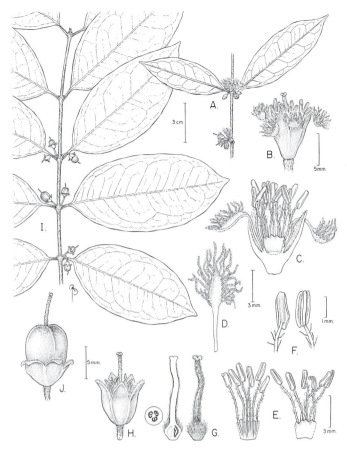

Figure 167. RHIZOPHORACEAE. *Cassipourea guianensis*. **A.** Stem with leaves and inflorescences. **B.** Lateral view of flower. **C.** Medial section of flower with gynoecium removed. **D.** Adaxial view of petal. **E.** Abaxial (left) and adaxial (right) views of part of androecium and disc. **F.** Abaxial (left) and adaxial (right) views of anthers. **G.** Lateral view of gynoecium (right), medial section of gynoecium (center), and transverse section of ovary (left). **H.** Lateral view of flower past anthesis after the petals have fallen. **I.** Stem with leaves and immature fruits. **J.** Lateral view of immature fruit. Reprinted with permission from Mori et al. (2002). Artist: Bobbi Angell.

The family can be divided into three tribes. The Macarasieae comprise six or seven genera with capsular fruit and occur throughout the family's distribution. Of these, *Cassipourea* and *Sterigmapetalum* are found in the neotropics. The Gynotrocheae comprise four genera, which occur in Asia and Madagascar. The Rhizophoreae constitute a morphologically well-defined and highly derived group comprising the mangrove genera *Bruguiera*, *Ceriops*, *Kandelia*, and *Rhizophora*, of which the latter is the only Neotropical representative.

Features of the family. Habit: shrubs or trees (to 50 m), often with prominent aerial roots (Rhizophoreae). Stipules interpetiolar, enveloping shoot apex when young, imbricate (Rhizophoreae), or valvate (Macarisieae), caducous, bearing axillary colleters that exude a gummy secretion. Leaves opposite or sometimes verticillate, simple; blade margins entire

(Rhizophoreae) or finely toothed (Macarisieae). **Inflorescences** axillary, cymose, fasciculate, or dichotomous; pedicels articulate. **Flowers** actinomorphic, usually bisexual, or unisexual (plants monoecious; e.g., *Sterigmapetalum*); sepals 4–many, fused at base; petals 4–many, fused at base, equal in number to sepal lobes, the base often narrow, the apex apically fringed, or cleft, rarely entire (as in *Rhizophora*); androecium with stamens twice as many as petals, or numerous; gynoecium syncarpous, the ovary superior (in *Cassipourea* and *Sterigmapetalum*) or inferior (in *Rhizophora*), the carpels 2–6, the locules 2–6, the style simple; placentation apical or axile, the ovules 2 per locule, pendulous. **Fruits** berrylike or capsules (in *Cassipourea* and *Sterigmapetalum*). **Seeds** 1 (Rhizophoreae) or 2–many per fruit, winged (*Sterigmapetalum*) or arillate (in *Cassipourea*), the testa fibrous (Rhizophoreae); embryo chlorophyllous, even in non-viviparous genera.

Natural history. Unrelated species of mangroves have independently evolved adaptations to high and variable salinity, waterlogged soil, and tidal currents. Salt glands occur in many mangroves, but the Rhizophoraceae seem to lack specialized salt-secreting structures and avoid excessive salt uptake by a poorly understood "ultrafiltration" mechanism in the rootlets. Mangroves have variously specialized roots that allow aeration of the tissues, which is important because the roots are surrounded by soil low in oxygen. In *Rhizophora*, numerous stilt roots develop from the trunk and sometimes enter the substrate long distances from the main stem. During submersion at high tide, oxygen inside the porous roots is depleted, but during ebb tide, oxygen is renewed through numerous lenticels on the exposed parts.

In mangrove genera of the Rhizophoreae, the seed germinates within the fruit while still attached to the mother plant (vivipary), so that a large seedling axis, up to 1 meter in *Rhizophora*, protrudes from the fruit. Detached seedlings float and are dispersed by sea currents.

Economic uses. Several Rhizophoraceae produce valuable timber, notably *Carallia*, *Cassipourea*, and the mangrove genera. The mangroves also are important as sources of charcoal and firewood. The bark of mangroves is used for tanning, and the sap yields a black dye.

Mangrove vegetation is of considerable importance to fisheries (e.g., as a provider of nutrients), and also acts as a stabilizer of shorelines.

References. DAHLGREN, R.M.T. 1988. Rhizophoraceae and Anisophylleaceae: summary statement, relationships. *Ann. Missouri Bot. Gard.* 75:1259–77. JUNCOSA, A. M., AND P. B. TOMLINSON. 1988a. A historical and taxonomic synopsis of Rhizophoraceae and Anisophylleaceae. *Ann. Missouri Bot. Gard.* 75:1278–95. JUNCOSA, A. M., AND P. B. TOMLINSON. 1988b. Systematic comparison and some biological characteristics of Rhizophoraceae and Anisophylleaceae. *Ann.*

Missouri Bot. Gard. 75:1296–1318. PRANCE, G. T., M. F. DA SILVA, B. W. ALBUQUERQUE, I. DE JESUS DA SILVA ARAÚJO, L. M. MEDEIROS CARREIRA, ET AL. 1975. Revisão taxonômica das espécies amazônicas de Rhizophoraceae. *Acta Amazon.* 5(1):5–22. SCHWARZBACH, A. E., AND R. E. RICKLEFS. 2000. Systematic affinities of Rhizophoraceae and Anisophylleaceae, and intergeneric relationships within Rhizophoraceae, based on chloroplast DNA, nuclear ribosomal DNA, and morphology. *Am. J. Bot.* 87(4):547–64. STEYERMARK, J. A., AND R. LIESNER. 1983. Revision of the genus *Sterigmapetalum* (Rhizophoraceae). *Ann. Missouri Bot. Gard.* 70:179–93. TOMLINSON, P. B. 1986. *The Botany of Mangroves.* Cambridge, U.K.: Cambridge University Press.

ROSACEAE (Rose Family)

JOHN D. MITCHELL

Figure 168, Plate 40

- *herbs, trees, or shrubs*
- *leaves usually alternate, rarely opposite, simple or compound*
- *stipules usually present*
- *flowers with hypanthium; nectariferous disc usually present; sepals 5; petals usually 5*

Numbers of genera and species. Worldwide, the Rosaceae comprise approximately 100 genera and more than 3,000 species. In tropical America, there are approximately 30 genera and 800 indigenous species and about 10 genera and perhaps less than 100 introduced species. The largest genera in the neotropics are *Lachemilla*, *Rubus*, *Prunus*, and *Acaena*.

Distribution and habitat. The primary area of diversity of the family is in temperate to subtropical regions of the Northern Hemisphere. Some genera, such as *Acaena* and *Polylepis*, are centered in the Southern Hemisphere. Rosaceae of the neotropics are most diverse and abundant in montane habitats, with Neotropical species usually occurring above 1,000 meters. Various species of *Polylepis* sometimes dominate forests and woodlands in the Andes from about 3,500 to 4,000 meters in northern Venezuela and Colombia to northern Chile and Argentina. *Polylepis* forests often occur as islands surrounded by *páramo* or *puna*. A highly threatened locally endemic avifauna is dependent on these vanishing forests.

Páramo and *puna* are the principal habitats of several genera such as *Geum*, *Lachemilla*, *Margyrricarpus*, *Acaena*, *Aphanes*, and *Potentilla*. Various North American centered genera (e.g., *Rosa*, *Amelanchier*, *Cercocarpus*, *Purshia*) extend into the neotropics only in Mexico or northern Central America. This group of genera include taxa typically associated with pine-oak forests, chapparal, piñon-pine woodland, spruce-fir forests, and temperate deciduous forests.

Prunus is one of the few genera of Rosaceae to occur in

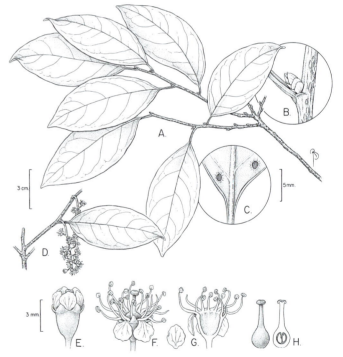

Figure 168. ROSACEAE. *Prunus accumulans*. **A.** Stem with leaves. **B.** Detail of stem with bud in leaf axil. **C.** Detail of abaxial base of leaf blade showing glands. **D.** Stem with leaf and inflorescences. **E.** Lateral view of flower bud beginning to open. **F.** Lateral view of flower (left) and adaxial view of petal (right). **G.** Medial section of flower with gynoecium removed. **H.** Lateral view (left) and medial section (right) of gynoecium. Reprinted with permission from Mori et al. (2002). Artist: Bobbi Angell.

lowland tropical rain forest. The family, however, is very poorly represented in tropical rain forest; e.g., there are only two species of Rosaceae in the Guianan flora.

Family classification. The Rosaceae are placed in the Rosales by Cronquist. Molecular data indicate that the Rosaceae are related to the Urticaceae, Moraceae, Ulmaceae, Rhamnaceae, Elaeagnaceae, etc., which have been placed together in the Rosales by the Angiosperm Phylogeny Group. The family has traditionally been divided into four subfamilies: the Spiraeoideae, with the following tribes: Gillenieae, Neillieae, Spiraeeae, and the heterogeneous assemblage of Quillajaeae (mostly Neotropical and North American); the Rosoideae, including the tribes Alchemilleae, Dryadeae, Potentilleae, Poterieae, Roseae, and Rubeae; the Maloideae (Pomoideae); and the Prunoideae (Amygdaloideae). A recent *rbc*L analysis suggests that *Quillaja* does not belong in the Rosaceae, but instead is allied with the Polygalaceae. The Maloideae and Prunoideae are considered by some authors to be the most cohesive and possibly the most natural of the subfamilies; however, a recent study suggests that the Maloideae and Rosoideae are the only monophyletic subfamilies of the Rosaceae. The Spiraeoideae generally are regarded as being polyphyletic.

Features of the family. Habit: herbs, trees, or shrubs, the herbs annual or perennial. **Stipules** usually present, adnate to petiole or distinct, persistent or caducous. **Leaves** usually alternate, rarely opposite, simple or compound (pinnate or palmate). **Inflorescences** terminal or axillary, racemose, cymose, paniculate, or of solitary flowers; epicalyx sometimes present (e.g., *Lachemilla*). **Flowers** actinomorphic, usually bisexual, sometimes unisexual (plants dioecious), small and inconspicuous or large and showy; hypanthium present, usually internally lined with a nectariferous disc; perianth usually biseriate; sepals 5, usually imbricate; petals (0)5, usually imbricate; androecium of 1–numerous stamens, the filaments distinct, the anthers typically dehiscing longitudinally; ovary superior or inferior, carpels 1 (mainly in Prunoideae) to many, distinct or ± connate, locules as many as carpels, the styles distinct, usually terminal, sometimes lateral or subbasal; placentation axile, the ovules 1–many, usually 1 or 2 per locule, apical to subbasal, usually anatropous, sometimes campylotropous or hemitropous. **Fruits** drupes (*Prunus*), pomes (*Hesperomeles* and *Crataegus*), capsules, aggregates of follicles, achenes, or drupelets (e.g., *Rubus*). **Seeds** 1–many per fruit; endosperm usually absent, rarely abundant, the cotyledons fleshy or flat.

Petals are rarely absent as in *Acaena, Lachemilla, Aphanes*, and *Polylepis*. Stamens are rarely reduced to 5 or even 1 as in *Aphanes*.

Natural history. Rosaceae are pollinated mostly by insects. No specialized associations of Rosaceae flowers with specific kinds of insects are known (but this may be due to lack of study). A few genera, e.g., *Acaena, Lachemilla*, and *Polylepis*, may be wind-pollinated.

The seeds of many Rosaceae, e.g., species of *Prunus, Hesperomeles*, and *Rubus*, are dispersed by being passed through the guts of animals. Other genera, e.g., species of *Acaena* and *Agrimonia*, bear dry fruits with barbs and/or hooks that get caught on the bodies of mammals.

Economic uses. Several introduced species of Rosaceae are cultivated in the neotropics for their edible fruits; e.g., *Eriobotrya japonica* (loquats), species of *Pyrus* (pears), and species of *Malus* (apples). In other genera, both indigenous and nonindigenous taxa often bear edible fruits, e.g., species of *Rubus* (raspberries and blackberries) and *Prunus* (cherries, apricots, almonds, and plums.

Species of *Rosa* (rose), *Cotoneaster, Rhaphiolepis, Photinia*, and *Pyracantha* (firethorn) are planted as ornamentals. Species of *Quillaja* contain saponins and can be used to make a soap substitute, and the wood of some *Prunus* is used for construction.

References. GAVIRIA, J. 1997. Sinopsis del género *Lachemilla* (Focke) Rydberg (Rosaceae) para Venezuela. *Plantula* 1:189–212. KALKMAN, C. 1993. Rosaceae. In *Flora Malesiana*, ed. C.G.G.J. Van Steenis, ser. 1, 11:227–451. Alphen Aan Den Rijn, Netherlands: Sijthoff and Noordhoff International Publishers. LEE, S., AND J. WEN. 2001. A phylogenetic analysis of *Prunus* and the Amygdaloideae (Rosaceae) using ITS sequences of nuclear ribosomal DNA. *Amer. J. Bot.* 88(1):150–60. MCVAUGH, R. 1950. Rosaceae. In Flora of Panama, eds. R. E. Woodson, Jr., and R. W. Schery. *Ann. Missouri Bot. Gard.* 37:147–78. MORGAN, D. R., D. E. SOLTIS, AND K. R. ROBERTSON. 1994. Systematics and evolutionary implications of *rbc*L sequence variation in Rosaceae. *Amer. J. Bot.* 81(7):890–903. POTTER, D. F. GAO, P. ESTEBAN BOTTIRI, S.-H. OH, AND S. BAGGETT. 2002. Phylogenetic relationships in Rosaceae inferred from chloroplast *mat*K and *trn*L-*trn*F nucleotide sequence data. *Pl. Syst. Evol.* 231:77–89. ROBERTSON, K. 1974. The genera of Rosaceae in the southeastern United States. *J. Arnold Arbor.* 55:611–62. ROMOLEROUX, K. 1995. Rosaceae in the high Andes of Ecuador. In *Biodiversity and Conservation of Neotropical Montane Forests*, eds. S. Churchill, H. Balslev, E. Forero, and J. Luteyn, 404–13. Bronx, NY: New York Botanical Garden. ROMOLEROUX, K. 1996. Rosaceae. In *Flora of Ecuador*, eds. G. Harling and L. Andersson. 56(79):1–152. Göteborg, Sweden: Department of Systematic Botany, University of Göteborg. RZEDOWSKI, J., AND G. DE RZEDOWSKI (eds.). *Flora Fanerogámica del Valle de México*. I:257–79. SIMPSON, B. 1979. A revision of the genus Polylepis (Rosaceae: Sanguisorbeae). *Smithsonian Contr. Bot.* 43:1–62.

RUBIACEAE (Coffee or Quinine Family)

PIERO G. DELPRETE

Figures 169, 170, 171; Plates 41, 42

- *stipules intrapetiolar (interpetiolar in* Elaeagia *and* Capirona*)*

- *leaves usually opposite, rarely whorled (3–6 per node), or appearing whorled because of leaflike stipules* (Galium) *or axillary short-shoots (e.g.,* Spermacoce*); blades undivided, the margins entire (never dentate)*

- *flowers commonly actinomorphic, rarely zygomorphic; corollas sympetalous (except for* Dialypetalanthus*), (3)4–5(15)-merous; stamens commonly as many as corolla lobes (except for* Dialypetalanthus*); ovary usually inferior, rarely some fruits becoming falsely half-superior (e.g.,* Gleasonia *and* Platycarpum*) or superior (*Pagamea*) at maturity*

Cinchonoideae

- *trees, shrubs, lianas*

- *stipules entire, rarely bifid (not fimbriate)*

- *calycophylls absent (present in* Kerianthera*)*

- *flowers actinomorphic (zygomorphic in* Coutarea *and* Hillia*); stamens inserted at base, of tube, or near corolla mouth*

- *calcium oxalate raphides absent (present in* Hillia *and* Hamelia*)*

Ixoroideae

- *trees, shrubs, herbs, vines*

- *stipules entire, rarely bifid (not fimbriate)*

- *calycophylls present in many genera*

- *flowers actinomorphic (zygomorphic in* Henriquezieae, Molopanthera, *and* Posoqueria*); stamens inserted at middle of tube or near corolla mouth*

- *calcium oxalate raphides absent*

Rubioideae

- *mostly herbs and shrubs, rarely trees*

- *stipules entire, bifid, or fimbriate (Spermacoceae* sensu lato*)*

- *calycophylls absent*

- *flowers actinomorphic (corolla tube basally gibbous in* Palicourea*); stamens inserted at middle of near corolla mouth*

- *calcium oxalate raphides present*

Numbers of genera and species. The Rubiaceae are the fourth largest family of flowering plants (after Asteraceae, Orchidaceae, and Fabaceae *sensu lato*), with approximately 650 genera and 13,000 species worldwide. The largest genus in the family is *Psychotria sensu lato*, with about 1,700 species worldwide. In tropical America, there are approximately 217 genera and more than 5,000 species. A recent provisional checklist was published by Andersson, but considering the vast areas still to be explored in the neotropics (especially the Amazon Basin and the Brazilian Atlantic forests), the number of taxa are likely to increase. The largest genera in the neotropics are: *Psychotria sensu lato* (ca. 600 species), *Palicourea* (ca. 230), *Rudgea* (ca. 220), *Faramea* (ca. 200), *Rondeletia* complex (ca. 200), *Guettarda* (ca. 140), *Manettia* (ca. 130), *Coussarea* (ca. 120), *Spermacoce sensu lato* (including *Borreria*, ca. 180), *Randia* (ca. 90), *Chomelia* (ca. 75), *Galium* (including *Relbunium*, ca. 60), *Ixora* (ca. 50), *Notopleura* (ca. 73), *Sabicea* (ca. 55), *Alibertia sensu lato* (including *Borojoa*, ca. 180), *Simira* (ca. 45), *Gonzalagunia* (ca. 40), and *Mitracarpus* (ca. 40). Seventy-two Neotropical genera are monospecific, and 17 have only two species.

In the Western Hemisphere, according to the most recent phylogenetic studies, the subfamily Cinchonoideae comprises about 65 genera, the Ixoroideae about 84 genera, and the Rubioideae about 68 genera.

Distribution and habitat. The Rubiaceae are of cosmopolitan distribution and predominantly pantropical. Almost one-half of the species and about one-third of the genera occur in the neotropics and have adapted to virtually every habitat: from *páramo* to arid and desertic environments. Rubiaceae are especially diverse in the Amazon Basin, Andean cloud forests, *cerrados, caatingas, restingas,* and the Atlantic forests of Brazil. Many genera are endemic to the Guayana Highlands and the Greater Antilles. Most species of *Hillia, Cosmibuena,* and several species of *Notopleura* and *Psychotria* are epiphytic shrubs adapted to live in the forest canopy. *Limnosipanea* is a short-seasonal, semiaquatic herb endemic to seasonally inundated habitats of central Brazil and the Venezuelan *llanos.* Many members of the Spermacoceae are herbs and subshrubs frequently found in disturbed habitats, such as roadsides and cow pastures.

Family classification. The Rubiaceae have traditionally been treated as a monophyletic family, and this has been confirmed by recent molecular phylogenies. Cronquist positioned this family in its own order, the Rubiales, excluding it from the Gentianales because of the absence of internal phloem. Recent phylogenetic studies have shown that the Rubiaceae is undoubtedly the basal family of the Gentianales.

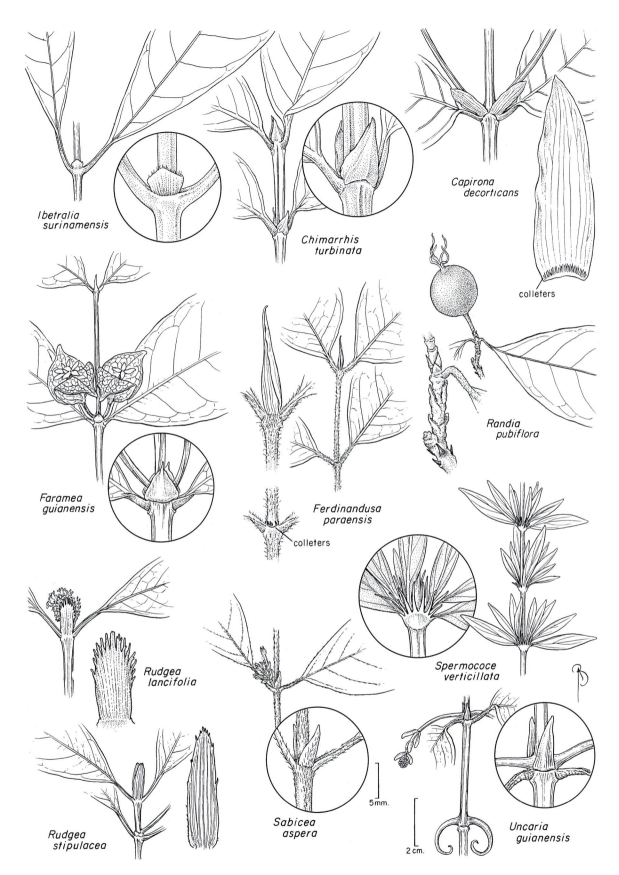

Ibetralia
surinamensis

Chimarrhis
turbinata

Capirona
decorticans

colleters

Randia
pubiflora

Faramea
guianensis

Ferdinandusa
paraensis

colleters

Spermococe
verticillata

Rudgea
lancifolia

Rudgea
stipulacea

Sabicea
aspera

5mm.

Uncaria
guianensis

2 cm.

Figure 169. RUBIACEAE. Variations in stipules of Rubiaceae. Reprinted with permission from Mori et al. (2002). Artist: Bobbi Angell.

Figure 170. RUBIACEAE. *Chimarrhis microcarpa*. **A.** Stems with leaves and inflorescences. **B.** Detail of abaxial leaf surface showing tufts of pubescence in the vein axils. **C.** Part of inflorescence. **D.** Lateral left (left) and medial section (right) of pin flowers. **E.** Lateral view (left) and medial section (right) of thrum flowers. **F.** Detail of stigma. **G.** Lateral view of stipule. Reprinted with permission from Mori et al. (2002). Artist: Bobbi Angell.

The classification of Rubiaceae is in a state of flux. Robbrecht proposed the most recent comprehensive classification, in which he recognized four subfamilies (i.e., Rubioideae, Antirrheoideae, Ixoroideae, and Cinchonoideae) and 44 tribes. Recent phylogenies using molecular and morphological data suggest that the family should be divided in three subfamilies: Rubioideae, Ixoroideae, and Cinchonoideae. In all of the phylogenetic studies, the Rubioideae are shown to be monophyletic and basal to the remaining two subfamilies.

A considerable number of tribal rearrangements have been recently proposed within the Ixoroideae and Cinchonoideae, most of them based on molecular phylogenetic analyses. Historical Rubiaceae classifications were mostly based on fruit features and, according to these recent phylogenies, seemingly similar fruit types have evolved several times. Characters such as mesocarp fleshiness, number of ovules per locule, and ovule insertion and placentation should not be dismissed, but should be carefully reanalyzed and re-evaluated in order to produce natural phylogenies.

While drastic rearrangements have been recently proposed at the subfamilial and tribal levels in the Rubiaceae, Robbrecht's classification is still the system used in floristic treatments worldwide. According to recent molecular phylogenies, 29 tribes occur in the neotropics, 14 of which are endemic: Cinchoneae, Hamelieae, Hillieae, Isertieae, Strumpfieae, Condamineeae, Henriquezieae, Hippotideae, Retiniphylleae, Rondeletieae, Sabiceae, Sipaneeae, Coussareae, and Perameae. The other 15 tribes present in the neotropics also occur in the paleotropics.

The definition and delimitation of *Psychotria*, *Cephaelis*, and *Palicourea* are also in a state of flux. Many authors have variably segregated many genera from and/or included them in *Psychotria* (i.e., *Callicocca*, *Carapichea*, *Cephaelis*, *Chytropsia*, *Evea*, *Gamotopea*, *Grumilea*, *Heteropsychotria*, *Ipecacuanha*, *Mapouria*, *Montamans*, *Myristiphyllum*, *Naletonia*, *Nonatelia*, *Notopleura*, *Palicourea*, *Petagomea*, *Psychotrophum*, *Ronabea*, and *Tapogomea*). Molecular phylogenies have shown that *Psychotria*, as currently circumscribed, is paraphyletic. Taylor recently suggested close relationships between *Heteropsychotria* and *Palicourea*, and recently separated *Notopleura* from *Psychotria* based on inflorescence position, fruit color, and flower and stipule morphology.

Phylogenetic studies have also shown that the Hedyotideae and Spermacoceae, two tribes considered distantly related by Robbrecht, represent a monophyletic group.

The monotypic Amazonian genus *Dialypetalanthus* has usually been treated as the sole member of the family Dialypetalanthaceae, which has been variably placed in the Myrtales, Rosales, Gentianales, or Rubiales. An attempt at placing *Dialypetalanthus* was published by Piesschaert et al., but it failed to reach a clear conclusion about the systematic position of the genus. Delprete aligned *Dialypetalanthus* in the Rondeletieae complex because of its interpetiolar, bifid stipules and many-seeded capsules. A recent molecular phylogenetic study by Fay et al. confirmed this placement, and *Dialypetalanthus* was tentatively positioned near *Calycophyllum*, *Capirona*, *Condaminea*, and other members of the Condamineeae *sensu* Rova et al., even though it is exceptional within the family by having flowers with distinct petals and 16–25 stamens in two whorls.

Features of the family. Habit: trees, shrubs, less frequently lianas, vines, and herbs, mostly terrestrial, rarely epiphytic or aquatic (*Limnosipanea* and species of *Spermacoce*). **Stipules** present, entire, divided, or fimbriate, and either distinct, connate, or sheathing at base, often caducous and only represented by scars, usually interpetiolar, or rarely intrapetiolar (e.g., *Capirona*, most species of *Elaeagia*, some species of *Isertia* and *Gleasonia*), rarely with 4 stipules in *Condaminea* (these partially intrapetiolar), or leaflike in *Galium*; stipular colleters present in most genera, producing resinous exudates (copious in *Elaeagia*, *Ladenbergia*, and *Retiniphyllum*), the resin probably protects terminal buds from herbivory. **Leaves** usually opposite, rarely 3–6-whorled, sometimes appearing whorled because of leaflike stipules (*Galium*) or axillary

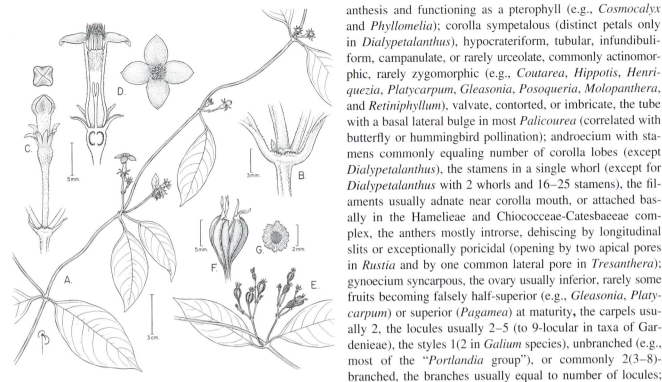

Figure 171. RUBIACEAE. *Manettia reclinata*. **A.** Stem with leaves and inflorescences. **B.** Detail of node showing stipules and axillary bud. **C.** Lateral (below) and apical views of floral buds (above). **D.** Medial section (left) and apical view (right) of flower. **E.** Stem with leaves and infructescences. **F.** Lateral view of dehiscing fruit. **G.** Seed. Reprinted with permission from Mori et al. (2002). Artist: Bobbi Angell.

short-shoots (i.e., brachyblasts in Spermacoceae), decussate, simple; blade margins entire (never dentate), rarely aniso-phyllous (e.g., *Faramea*, *Sabicea*), with deeply lobed blades in several species of *Pentagonia*; myrmecophilous pouches present at leaf base in some species of *Duroia*, *Remijia*, and *Hoffmannia*; foliar pellucid glands present only in the sister genera *Rustia* and *Tresanthera*, and in *Heterophyllaea*. **Inflorescences** terminal or axillary, cymes, panicles, umbels, racemes, spikes, heads, or uniflorous; many genera of Gardenieae dioecious, with female flowers solitary and male flowers in corymbose, fasciculate, spicate, or paniculate inflorescences; colorful extrafloral bracts sometimes present, these function as pollinator attractants (e.g., *Psychotria* section *Cephaelis*). **Flowers** commonly actinomorphic, rarely zygomorphic, commonly bisexual, less often unisexual (then plants usually dioecious), tetracyclic, (3)4–5(15)-merous (high merosity usually found in several members of tribe Gardenieae, the highest in 12–15-merous flowers of *Riodocea* and the 8–11-merous flowers of *Kutchubaea*); calyx cupular, short tubular, or reduced to a wavy line, the lobes usually minute, linear, or rarely foliose, with colleters present adaxially, in many genera with capsular fruits one lobe expanding into a foliose colorful lobe (calycophyll, e.g., *Pogonopus* and *Warszewczia*), or sometimes expanding after

anthesis and functioning as a pterophyll (e.g., *Cosmocalyx* and *Phyllomelia*); corolla sympetalous (distinct petals only in *Dialypetalanthus*), hypocrateriform, tubular, infundibuliform, campanulate, or rarely urceolate, commonly actinomorphic, rarely zygomorphic (e.g., *Coutarea*, *Hippotis*, *Henriquezia*, *Platycarpum*, *Gleasonia*, *Posoqueria*, *Molopanthera*, and *Retiniphyllum*), valvate, contorted, or imbricate, the tube with a basal lateral bulge in most *Palicourea* (correlated with butterfly or hummingbird pollination); androecium with stamens commonly equaling number of corolla lobes (except *Dialypetalanthus*), the stamens in a single whorl (except for *Dialypetalanthus* with 2 whorls and 16–25 stamens), the filaments usually adnate near corolla mouth, or attached basally in the Hamelieae and Chiococceae-Catesbaeeae complex, the anthers mostly introrse, dehiscing by longitudinal slits or exceptionally poricidal (opening by two apical pores in *Rustia* and by one common lateral pore in *Tresanthera*); gynoecium syncarpous, the ovary usually inferior, rarely some fruits becoming falsely half-superior (e.g., *Gleasonia*, *Platycarpum*) or superior (*Pagamea*) at maturity, the carpels usually 2, the locules usually 2–5 (to 9-locular in taxa of Gardenieae), the styles 1(2 in *Galium* species), unbranched (e.g., most of the "*Portlandia* group"), or commonly 2(3–8)-branched, the branches usually equal to number of locules; placentation axile, rarely parietal (e.g., *Randia*), the ovules 1–many per locule, anatropous, horizontal, erect, or pendulous. **Fruits** fleshy berries, leathery berries (Gardenieae), drupes (with woody pyrenes), loculicidal, septicidal, or transverse capsules, samaroid (e.g., *Allenanthus*), pseudosamaras (e.g., *Cosmocalyx*, and *Phyllomelia*), schizocarps (e.g., *Richardia*), or syncarps (e.g., *Morinda*). **Seeds** usually free (i.e., not directly surrounded by fruit tissue), inside of woody pyrenes (e.g., *Psychotria*), or sometimes embedded in a gelatinous pulp (Gardenieae), with smooth or sculptured exotesta, sometimes with lateral (e.g. *Simira*), bipolar (e.g. *Cinchona*), or concentric (e.g., *Coutarea*) wings, or with tuft of hairs (exotestal extensions) on one side (*Hillia*); endosperm always present, the albumen usually abundant or rarely absent, the embryo embedded in endosperm, straight or curved, the radicle superior or inferior.

The vast majority of the Rubiaceae are shrubs 2–5 meters tall, followed by trees 7–15 meters tall. In the Amazon Basin, several genera are represented by tall canopy trees to 50–55 meters tall with large buttresses (e.g., *Chimarrhis*, *Capirona*, *Calycophyllum*, and *Platycarpum*). In temperate zones, this family is encountered as herbs and small shrubs.

Rubiaceae are reported to have the highest degree of heterostyly of all angiosperms, a feature often associated with pollen dimorphism. Within the Neotropical tribes, it is more common in the Spermacoceae, Hedyotideae, and Psychotrieae, and is also present in various genera of the Cinchoneae, Rondeletieae, Guettardeae, and Hamelieae.

Stylar pollen presentation is common in members of the Gardenieae and Ixoreae. This mechanism is a complex adaptation that requires protandrous flowers, a style that elongates above the anthers while pollen is released, and style branches that open after all the pollen is released. The pollen is deposited on the distal external portion of the style, and it is transferred from the presenting style to the receptive stigma by the pollinators.

Calcium oxalate crystals are found as raphides, styloids, druses, and crystal sand, and can be stored in various plant parts. These crystals are commonly present in the hairs of members of the Guettardeae. Calcium oxalate crystals can be seen with the naked eye or at low magnifications in leaf blades and corollas.

Most Rubiaceae produce alkaloids that are stored in the bark, roots, leaves, flowers, fruits, seeds, and pollen. About 70 Neotropical genera, most of them belonging to the Cinchonoideae, produce quinine-related compounds (e.g., *Cinchona, Ladenbergia, Joosia, Pogonopus, Rustia, Coutarea, Exostema*, etc.), that are usually accumulated in the bark.

Natural history. Rubiaceae are pollinated by bees, wasps, butterflies, moths (e.g., hawkmoths), hummingbirds, and bats. Wind pollination is present only in the Paleotropical Anthospermeae and Theligonieae. *Palicourea* is pollinated mostly by butterflies and hummingbirds, whereas *Psychotria sensu lato* is pollinated mostly by bees. Species of *Rustia* are pollinated by bees, wasps, butterflies, and hummingbirds. *Posoqueria* has narrowly tubular corollas to 27 centimeters long that are visited by hawkmoths. In *Posoqueria*, a ball of pollen is deposited onto one of the five anthers while the corolla is still closed. After the corolla has opened, it is the pollen from that anther that is placed onto the pollinator when it visits the flower. A similar mechanism is also present in the small flowers of the related genus *Molopanthera*.

Because of the large variety of fruit and seed types, seed dispersal is diverse in the Rubiaceae. Berrylike and drupelike fruits are usually dispersed by birds and mammals. The fruits of some *Galium* covered by uncinate trichomes are dispersed externally by various animals. The small winged or unwinged seeds of capsular fruits and mericarps and pseudosamaras are dispersed by the wind.

Some species of *Duroia* (e.g., *D. saccifera*) have two contiguous pouches at the base of the leaf blades, which are inhabited by the ants *Solenopsis corticolis* and *Brachymyrmex heeri* that guard the plants from herbivores. Other species, such as *Remijia physophora* (Cinchoneae) and *Hoffmannia vesciculifera* (Hamelieae), also have ant-pouches at the base of their leaves. *Duroia hirsuta* has swollen terminal internodes with entrance holes for ants, which live in the stems and regularly descend to the ground to cut young seedlings competing with their host plant; *Patima guianensis* also has hollow stems inhabited by ants of the genus *Allomerus*. *Henriquezia* and *Platycarpum* (Henriquezieae) have adaxial glands at the petiole bases that produce extrafloral nectar utilized by ants. Domatia present on the abaxial side of the leaves of many species of Rubiaceae usually host a large variety of mites. Although their function has not been studied in this family, in other plants, the mites remove the spores of fungi and bryophytes.

Economic uses. Coffee is the major product of the Rubiaceae. *Coffea* is a genus of approximately 100 species native to Africa, Madagascar, and islands of the Indian Ocean; the cultivated species, e.g., *C. arabica, C. canephora*, and *C. robusta* originated in East Africa.

Because the Rubiaceae produce a myriad of different alkaloids, the family is one of the primary sources of natural medicines, hallucinogens, and poisons. Many genera of the Cinchoneae (e.g., *Cinchona* and *Ladenbergia*) are sources of quinine, the only known remedy for malaria until synthetic drugs became available. Malaria is responsible for the greatest number of deaths in the history of humankind, and it is still responsible for many deaths in most tropical countries worldwide. As new strains of malaria evolve in Africa and the Amazon Basin, natural remedies such as quinine should be re-evaluated in the fight against this deadly disease. *Carapichea ipecacuanha*, native to Brazil, is the source of the emetic ipecac and is a minor crop in several South American countries. *Pogonopus* and several other genera are the sources of active compounds with proven anticancer activity that involve inhibition of microtubule formation during cell division. *Morinda citrifolia* (*noni*) has recently received considerable attention for its many medicinal properties, ranging from reducing high blood pressure to serving as an anticancer agent. *Uncaria* (*uña de gato*, cat claws, or gambier) has numerous reputed medicinal uses and extracts from the bark of *Pausynistalia yohimbe*, a liana of African origin, is the source of a potent aphrodisiac.

Psychotria viridis and related species are used as important ingredients in the preparation of the hallucinogenic *ayahuasca* in the Amazon Basin. Several species of *Psychotria* and *Palicourea* are poisonous plants responsible for cattle paralysis and death in tropical America.

Many arboreal genera of Rubiaceae (e.g., *Simira, Chimarrhis, Calycophyllum, Parachimarrhis*, and *Capirona*) are sources of timber used for construction of furniture, houses, and boats. The buttresses of *Chimarrhis* are employed by indigenous people of the Amazon Basin to make canoe paddles, a use reflected in their common names: *pau de remo* (Brazil) and *bois pagaïe* (French Guiana).

Several genera of the Gardenieae produce large edible fruits. *Genipa* (called *genipapo* in Brazil and *caruto* in Venezuela) is cultivated for its fruits that are eaten fresh or used to prepare juices and alcoholic beverages. An extract of the green fruits of *G. americana* is used to make a black dye employed for coloring cloth and as a body paint by indigenous tribes. *Borojoa patinoi* (= *Alibertia sensu lato*) is a tree cultivated in the Chocó of Colombia for its fleshy fruits (*borojó*) that are eaten fresh or used to make juices with attributed aphrodisiac properties, and *B. sorbilis* is well known in the western Amazon for its large, delicious fruits (called *huito* in Peru and *puruí* in Brazil). *Catesbaea spinosa* (Spanish guava) is cultivated in the Greater Antilles for its fruits that are eaten fresh or used to prepare juices and jams.

Several species of *Mussaenda, Ixora*, and *Gardenia*, native to tropical Asia, and *Pentas lanceolata*, native to Africa, are common ornamentals in tropical America. Neotropical genera often cultivated as ornamentals are: *Bouvardia*, *Hamelia*, *Ixora*, *Manettia*, *Pogonopus*, *Randia*, *Rondeletia*, and *Warszewiczia*.

References. ANDERSSON, L. 1992. A provisional checklist of Neotropical Rubiaceae. *Scripta Bot. Belg.* 1:1–200. ANDERSSON, L., AND J. ROVA. 1999. The *rps*16 intron and the phylogeny of the Rubioideae (Rubiaceae). *Pl. Syst. Evol.* 214:161–86. ANDREASEN, K., B. G. BALDWIN, AND B. BREMER. 1999. Phylogenetic utility of the nuclear *r*DNA ITS region in subfamily Ixoroideae (Rubiaceae): comparisons with cpDNA *rbc*L sequence data. *Pl. Syst. Evol.* 217:119–35. BACKLUND, M., B. OXELMAN, AND B. BREMER. 2000. Phylogenetic relationships within the Gentianales based on *ndh*F and *rbc*L sequences, with particular reference to the Loganiaceae. *Amer. J. Bot.* 87:1029–43. BREMER, B., K. ANDREASEN, AND D. OLSSON. 1995. Subfamilial and tribal relationships in the Rubiaceae based on *rbc*L sequence data. *Ann. Missouri Bot. Gard.* 82:383–97. BREMER, B., AND J.-F. MANEN. 2000. Phylogeny and classification of the subfamily Rubioideae. *Pl. Syst. Evol.* 225:43–72. CARDOSO VIEIRA, R., P. G. DELPRETE, G. GUIMARÃES LEITÃO, AND S. GUIMARÃES LEITÃO. 2001. Anatomical and chemical analyses of leaf secretory cavities of *Rustia formosa* (Rubiaceae). *Amer. J. Bot.* 88:2151–56. DELPRETE, P. G. 1996. Evaluation of the tribes Chiococceae, Condamineeae, and Catesbaeeae (Rubiaceae) based on morphological characters. *Opera Bot. Belg.* 7:165–92. DELPRETE, P. G. 1999. Rondeletieae (Rubiaceae), Part I. *Fl. Neotrop. Monogr.* 77:1–226. DELPRETE, P. G., AND R. CORTÉS. 1998. Rubiaceae of the New World. http://www.nybg.org/bsci/res/delpic2.html (Dec. 15, 2002). FAY, M. F., B. BREMER, G. T. PRANCE, M. VAN DER BANK, D. BRIDSON, AND M. CHASE. 2000. Plastid sequence data show *Dialypetalanthus* to be a member of Rubiaceae. *Kew Bull.* 55:853–64. NEPOKROEFF, M., B. BREMER, AND K. SYSTMA. 1997. Reorganization of the genus *Psychotria* (Rubiaceae) inferred from ITS and *rbc*L sequence data. *Amer. J. Bot.* 84(suppl.): 219. PIESSCHAERT, F., E. ROBBRECHT, AND E. SMETS. 1997. *Dialypetalanthus fuscescens* Kuhlm. (Dialypetalanthaceae): the problematic taxonomic position of an Amazonian endemic. *Ann. Missouri Bot. Gard.* 84:201–23. ROBBRECHT, E. 1988. Tropical woody Rubiaceae. Characteristic features and progressions. Contributions to a new subfamilial classification. *Opera Bot. Belg.* 1:1–271. ROBBRECHT, E., ed. "1993" [1994]. Advances in Rubiaceae macrosystematics. *Opera Bot. Belg.* 6:1–200. ROGERS, K. G. 1984. *Gleasonia*, *Henriquezia*, and *Platycarpum* (Rubiaceae). *Fl. Neotrop. Monogr.* 39:1–135. ROVA, J.H.E., P. G. DELPRETE, L. ANDERSSON, AND V. A. ALBERT. 2002. A *trn*L-F cpDNA sequence study of the Condamineeae-Rondeletieae-Sipaneeae complex with implications on the phylogeny of the Rubiaceae. *Amer. J. Bot.* 89: 145–59. TAYLOR, C. M. 2001. Overview of the neotropical genus *Notopleura* (Rubiaceae: Psychotrieae), with the description of some new species. *Ann. Missouri Bot. Gard.* 88: 478–515.

RUTACEAE (Rue Family)

JACQUELYN KALLUNKI

Figure 172, Plate 42

- *trees, shrubs, rarely herbs*
- *leaves usually aromatic, glandular-punctate*
- *flowers usually actinomorphic; intrastaminal disc usually present; ovary superior*

Numbers of genera and species. Worldwide, the Rutaceae comprise approximately 157 genera and 1,600 species, of which 72 percent belong to the largest subfamily, the Rutoideae. The Citroideae comprise about 210 species, the Toddalioideae about 162 species, the Flindersioideae about 17 species, the Spathelioideae about 14 species, and the Dictyolomatoideae 1 or 2 species. The largest genera of the family are *Zanthoxylum* (ca. 180 species in the Eastern and Western Hemispheres) and *Melicope* (233 species in the Eastern Hemisphere). In the Western Hemisphere, there are 58 genera and 343 native species, of which the largest are *Zanthoxylum* (ca. 72 species) and *Conchocarpus* (44 species). Fifty-two genera, including 18 in the Western Hemisphere, contain only a single species. In tropical America, there are about 48 genera and about 350 species.

Distribution and habitat. The Rutaceae are primarily distributed in tropical and subtropical regions of both the Eastern and Western Hemispheres. The subfamilies Citroideae and Flindersioideae are native to the Eastern Hemisphere, the Spathelioideae and the Dictyolomatoideae to the Western Hemisphere, and the Toddalioideae and Rutoideae to both the Eastern and the Western Hemispheres. About one-quarter of all species in the family occur in the Western Hemisphere. Only *Zanthoxylum* and *Thamnosma* are native to both hemispheres. In the Western Hemisphere, most Rutaceae are tropical, with the exception of *Cneoridium* and some species of *Thamnosma*, *Zanthoxylum*, *Choisya*, and *Ptelea*, which occur in North America, and *Pitavia*, which occurs in Chile.

In tropical America, the Rutaceae are commonly found in the understory of moist forests.

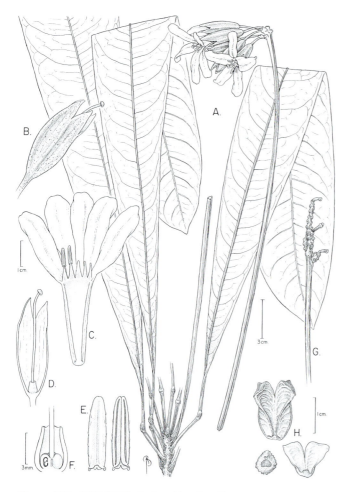

Figure 172. RUTACEAE. *Erythrochiton brasiliensis*. **A.** Apex of stem with leaves and inflorescence (broken to fit page). **B.** Lateral view of calyx with exserted style. **C.** Corolla opened to show adnate stamens (three anthers fallen). **D.** Lateral view of nectary disc and style surrounded by part of calyx. **E.** Abaxial (left) and adaxial (far right) views of anthers. **F.** Medial section of disc, ovary (with one carpel shown in medial section), and base of style. **G.** Old inflorescence. **H.** Dehisced fruit segment (above), endocarp (below right), and seed (below left). Reprinted with permission from Mori et al. (2002). Artist: Bobbi Angell.

Family classification. Cronquist's placement of the Rutaceae in the Sapindales is supported by molecular data. The common presence of bitter triterpenoids suggest relationships with the Meliaceae and Simaroubaceae. This diverse family is divided (according to Engler) into six subfamilies, eight tribes, and 28 subtribes. Engler's concepts of the subfamilies were based primarily on fruit type (e.g., indehiscent in the Toddalioideae and dehiscent in the Rutoideae). Recent phytochemical and molecular studies have indicated that the Toddalioideae and the Rutoideae are not monophyletic and should be combined and that the Dictyolomatoideae and Spathelioideae should also be combined. Fruit type does not appear to be a distinguishing character at the subfamily level as indehiscent fruits probably have evolved in the family more than once.

Features of the family. Habit: trees, shrubs, rarely herbs (e.g., *Apocaulon* and *Ertela*), the trees and shrubs usually aromatic, glandular-punctate, the glandular dots containing aromatic oils, sometimes armed in *Zanthoxylum*. **Stipules** absent. **Leaves** alternate, opposite, rarely whorled, pinnately or palmately compound, trifoliolate, unifoliolate, rarely simple; blades rarely pinnately dissected. **Inflorescences** terminal, lateral, or axillary, sometimes cauline, or rarely borne abaxially on midrib of leaf in the Colombian *Erythrochiton hypophyllanthus*, thyrses, cymes, racemes, spikes, or cincinni derived from thyrses or cymes. **Flowers** actinomorphic or sometimes zygomorphic (e.g., in many Galipeinae), the zygomorphy due to curvature or unequal lobes of corolla or to partial sterilization of androecium; bisexual or seldom unisexual (then plants dioecious); sepals (4)5, distinct or basally connate, usually quincuncial or sometimes valvate; petals (4)5, usually distinct or sometimes (most notably in some Galipeinae) united to some distance from base, usually imbricate; androecium usually with 5 or 10 stamens, the stamens sometimes more numerous, sometimes with only 2 (and 3 or 5 staminodes) or 3 (and 2 staminodes) fertile stamens (in Galipeinae), the filaments distinct or less often connate below and then sometimes adnate to corolla, the anthers introrsely dehiscent by longitudinal slits, sometimes apically apiculate or glandular, sometimes basally appendaged; intrastaminal disc usually present, the disc annular, cupular, or cylindrical, rarely unilateral, sometimes modified into gynophore, rarely obsolete; gynoecium with superior ovary, the carpels (1–2)4–5, ± connate into plurilocular ovary, the style(s) distinct or connate; placentation axile, the ovules usually (1)2 per locule, several per locule in Dictyolomatoideae. **Fruits** (4)5-locular capsules, 1–5 dehiscent mericarps (characteristic of the Rutoideae), few- to several-seeded berries or hesperidia (e.g., *Citrus*), drupes (many Toddalioideae), or less often samaras (e.g., Spathelioideae). **Seeds** 1–several per carpel; endosperm absent or present, the embryo diverse, the cotyledons either straight and sometimes embedded in endosperm or not embedded in endosperm and either unfolded and often hemispherical or folded along midnerve and often crumpled.

Natural history. The flowers are usually white, possess an intrastaminal disc, and probably are insect-pollinated. Bees have been observed visiting flowers of *Erythrochiton* in Peru and of *Conchocarpus* species in Brazil. The red flowers of *Decagonocarpus cornutus* in Colombia are visited by hummingbirds.

This family displays a diversity of fruit types. The fleshy ones may be dispersed by animals and the winged ones by wind. Many of the dry, dehiscent fruits of the Rutoideae have a separating, elastic, bony endocarp, which, upon drying, opens explosively and disperses the seeds.

Economic uses. Species of *Citrus* are the most economically important and most familiar members of the Rutaceae. Many of these species produce flavorful fruits rich in vitamin

C; e.g., lemons (*C. limon*), sweet oranges (*C. sinensis*), limes (*C. aurantifolia*), and grapefruits (*C. paradisi*). The rind of one variety of orange yields bergamot, an essential oil used in perfumery. Although all species of *Citrus* are natives of Asia, citrus plants are cultivated throughout the world in climates where soils are suitable, moisture is sufficient, and frost is insufficient to kill them. The citrus-growing regions occupy a belt that encircles the globe and extends no more than 35°N and 35°S of the equator.

The alkaloid pilocarpine, used in treatment of glaucoma, is obtained from *Pilocarpus microphyllus* and *P. pennatifolius*. Levels of the alkaloid are much higher in leaves of the former, which is cultivated in northeastern Brazil for pilocarpine extraction.

Compounds used to combat fevers have been obtained from bark of *Galipea jasminiflora* (native to southern Brazil) and *Angostura trifoliata* (the official "angostura bark," native to Venezuela).

Zanthoxylum flavum (West Indian silkwood) and *Euxylophora paraensis* (*pão amarello*, endemic to Pará, Brazil) are valued for their timber. Several genera of Rutaceae are grown as ornamentals.

References. BURKE, J. H. 1967. The commercial citrus regions of the world. In *The Citrus Industry*, eds. W. Reuther, H. J. Webber, and L. O. Batchelor. 1:40–189. University of California. ENGLER, A. 1931. Rutaceae. In *Die Natürlichen Pflanzenfamilien*, A. Engler and K. Prantl, 2nd ed., 19a:187–459. Leipzig: Wilhelm Engelmann. MORTON, C. M., J. A. KALLUNKI, AND M. W. CHASE. 1999. Phylogenetic relationships of Rutaceae: a cladistic analysis of the subfamilies using evidence from *rbc*L and *atp*B sequence variation. *Amer. J. Bot.* 86:1191–99. SILVA, M. F. DAS GRAÇAS FERNANDES DA, O. R. GOTTLIEB, AND F. EHRENDORFER. 1988. Chemosystematics of the Rutaceae: suggestions for a more natural taxonomy and evolutionary interpretation of the family. *Pl. Syst. Evol.* 161:97–134. STILES, F. G. 1996. A new species of Emerald Hummingbird (Trochilidae, *Chlorostilbon*) from the Sierra de Chiribiquete, southeastern Colombia, with a review of the *C. mellisugus* complex. *Wilson Bull.* 108:1–20.

SABIACEAE (Sabia Family)

KLAUS KUBITZKI

Figure 173

- *trees*
- *leaves alternate, simple or imparipinnate, sometimes heteromorphic*
- *flowers with stamens opposite petals; ovary superior*
- *fruits drupes*

Numbers of genera and species. Worldwide, the Sabiaceae comprise three genera and more than 50 species. In tropical America, there are two genera and about 20 species. The South American *Ophiocaryon* has about seven species, and *Meliosma* has about 15 species in Asia and more than 10 species in the Western Hemisphere. The Asian *Sabia* includes about 19 species.

Distribution and habitat. The family is represented in Mexico, Central America, the Caribbean, the Guianas, and northern Brazil (but seems to be lacking in most parts of Amazonia), in the Andes south to Peru, and in eastern/southeastern Brazil (Espírito Santo to Paraná).

Neotropical Sabiaceae are found in humid and dry forests.

Family classification. The Sabiaceae are placed in the Ranunculales by Cronquist. Recent molecular studies have placed the family among the "Lower Eudicots," where they often appear in close proximity to the Proteaceae and Buxaceae. These families, however, are considerably different morphologically.

Features of the family. Habit: trees, evergreen or rarely deciduous. Stipules absent. Leaves alternate, simple or imparipinnate, sometimes heteromorphic; petiole bases often subwoody; petiolules often with pulvini; blade margins dentate or entire; venation pinnate. Inflorescences terminal or axillary, long panicles, the lateral axes spreading, the flowers densely crowded, nearly sessile. Flowers actinomorphic or zygomorphic, bisexual, relatively small, sepals (4)5; petals (4)5; androecium of 5 stamens (2 fertile and 3 staminodial), swollen or collarlike extension formed by connective or filament present, the anther thecaeunilocellate; gynoecium with superior ovary, the carpels 2(3), the apices distinct or united to form a common style, the locules 2(3); placentation axile, the ovules usually 2 per carpel, unitegmic. Fruits drupes, the endocarp bony or crustaceous. Seeds 1 per fruit; endosperm usually reduced, the cotyledons on extended and curled hypocotyl (hence the name "snake nut" for *Ophiocaryon paradoxum*).

In *Ophiocaryon*, the leaves can be large with pinnae up to 40 centimeters long. Leaf dimorphism is found in several *Ophiocaryon* and some *Meliosma* with sterile shoots often bearing pinnate leaves while those of flowering branches are simple. In *Meliosma*, the margins of the leaves of saplings

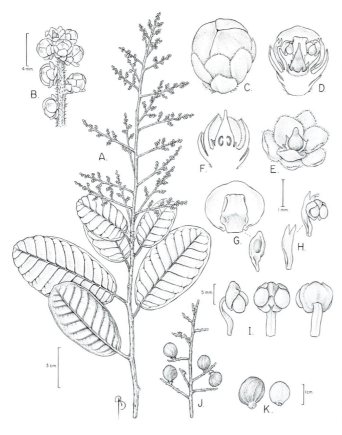

Figure 173. SABIACEAE. *Meliosma impressa* (A, Zanoni 30366; B–I, Liogier 12028; J, K, Howard 9431). **A.** Stem with leaves and inflorescence. **B.** Part of inflorescence. **C.** Apical view of flower bud. **D.** Medial section of flower bud. **E.** Oblique-apical view of gynoecium and nectary subtended by calyx and bracteoles. **F.** Medial section of flower with petals and stamens removed. **G.** Staminode subtended by sepal (above) and lateral view of staminode (below). **H.** Stamen subtended by petal (above) and petal (below). **I.** Lateral (left), adaxial (center), and abaxial (right) views of stamens. **J.** Part of infructescence. **K.** Lateral views of fruit (left) and seed (right). Original. Artist: Bobbi Angell.

and sterile shoots are more strongly serrate than those of mature or reproductive shoots.

Natural history. In *Meliosma*, flower structure is linked closely to the poorly understood, but obviously sophisticated, pollination system. The three outer petals are slightly imbricate and completely enclose the stamens, staminodes, and gynoecium. The two inner petals are strongly reduced, and the tow functional stamens are adnate to them. In bud, the anthers are sharply bent inward, and the anthers fit into cavities in adjacent staminodes. This complex of stamens and staminodes envelops the pistil, and the staminodes are often somewhat connate at the apex, to form an opening through which the style protrudes. The anthers open when the flowers are still in bud, but pollen cannot be released as long as the anthers remain locked in the cavities of the staminodes. At maturity, the stamens snap backward at the slightest touch and release pollen. This mechanism has been described for Asian *Meliosma*, but no field observations on the pollination of American Sabiaceae have yet been reported.

No information is available on dispersal biology.

Economic uses. No uses are recorded for this family.

References. BANEBY, R. C. 1972. Meliosmaceae-*Ophiocaryon*. *Mem. New York Bot. Gard.* 23:114–20. CARLQUIST, S., P. L. MORRELL, AND S. R. MANCHESTER. 1993. Wood anatomy of Sabiaceae (s.l.); ecological and systematic implications. *Aliso* 13:521–49. URBAN, I. 1895. Über die Sabiaceengattung Meliosma. *Ber. Deutsch. Bot. Ges.* 13:211–22, t. 19. URBAN, I. 1900. Sabiaceae. In *Symbolae Antillanae*, 1: 499–518. Berlin: Borntraeger. VAN BEUSEKOM, C. F. 1971. Revision of *Meliosma* (Sabiaceae), section *Lorenzanea* excepted, living and fossil, geography and pyhlogeny. *Blumea* 19:355–529. VAN DE WATER, TH. P. M. 1980. A taxonomic revision of *Sabia* (Sabiaceae). *Blumea* 26:1–64.

SALICACEAE (Willow Family)

MICHAEL NEE

Figure 174

- *trees or shrubs*

- *leaves alternate, simple*

- *inflorescences axillary, catkins*

- *flowers reduced, unisexual*

- *fruits capsules*

- *seeds small, tuft of long white hairs present*

Numbers of genera and species. Worldwide, the Salicaceae comprise four genera and about 300 species. In tropical America, there are two genera, *Populus*, with about four species (ca. 30 worldwide) and *Salix* with 10 species (ca. 275 worldwide) plus several cultivars and escaped species from the Eastern Hemisphere.

Distribution and habitat. The Salicaceae occur primarily in the temperate and arctic regions of the Northern Hemisphere, and little has been published on the few Neotropical

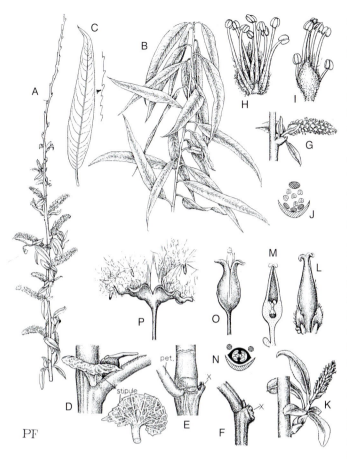

either by vegetative reproduction or by germination of the abundantly produced seeds. Some *Salix* and *Populus* also form clones from underground stems or roots.

Family classification. The Salicaceae are placed in the monofamilial Salicales by Cronquist. Recent molecular studies support the inclusion of many noncyanogenic taxa of Flacourtiaceae into a more broadly defined Saliaceae.

The monotypic *Idesia* of eastern Asia and related genera of the Flacourtiaceae are similar to the Salicaceae. Salicin, a widespread compound in the Salicaceae, also occurs in *Idesia* and four other Flacourtiaceae, but is found almost nowhere else. Moreover, *Idesia* and Salicaceae are hosts to similar rust fungi.

Features of the family. Habit: trees or shrubs; wood characteristically pale, soft, weak. Bark often smooth and light-colored to white in *Populus*, or dark and furrowed or flaky in *Salix*. Stipules present. Leaves alternate, simple, the terminal bud often resinous; blade margins glandular-toothed or entire. Inflorescences axillary, catkins; bract present, subtending each flower. Flowers reduced, unisexual (plants dioecious); calyx reduced to disc- or cup-shaped structure in *Populus* or 2–3(5) glands in *Salix*; petals absent; androecium of many stamens in *Populus*, usually only 2 stamens in *Salix*; gynoecium syncarpous, the ovary superior, the carpels 2(4), the locule 1, the style 1, the stigmas equal to number of carpels; placentation parietal, the ovules several to many. Fruits capsules, small, the valves 2–4. Seeds several per fruit, small, bearing tuft of long white hairs.

All species of *Populus* are trees, some of them large. Many species of *Salix* are single- or multistemmed shrubs, although some are erect trees.

Natural history. Although species of *Salix* are generally dioecious, in parts of lowland Amazonia, *S. humboldtiana* often has flowers of both sexes in the catkins of a single tree and occasionally possesses bisexual flowers. The extent and significance of this have not been investigated.

The flowers are wind-pollinated in *Populus* and probably mostly insect-pollinated in *Salix*. The tufts of long white hairs attached to the small seeds facilitate efficient wind dispersal.

Economic uses. The temperate and subarctic species of *Populus* are major sources of pulp for paper-making, but species of the neotropics are not abundant enough to be very important in this respect. Wood of the larger species of *Salix* and *Populus* has a number of additional minor uses. Species of *Salix* sometimes are used for erosion control along streams because of their ability to sprout readily from cuttings and quickly form dense stands that protect riversides from eroding during periodic flooding. *Salix humboldtiana* performs this role naturally along many tropical lowland rivers, including the Amazon.

The supple twigs of *Salix* have been used traditionally for weaving baskets and for making other handicrafts. Some

Figure 174. SALICACEAE. *Salix caroliniana*. **A.** Stem with leaves and male catkins (x⅓). **B.** Stem with leaves (x⅓). **C.** Leaf (x3) and detail of margin (x4). **D.** Node showing stipules (x3) and detail of stipule (below). **E.** Shoot articulation showing sympodial grow (x3); "pet." is the petiole and the "x" indicates an aborted terminal bud. **F.** Aborted terminal bud at x before lateral bud grows out. **G.** Male catkin on stem (x1⅓). **H.** Adaxial view of staminate flower (x8). **I.** Abaxial view of staminate flower (x8). **J.** Floral diagram of staminate flower. **K.** Pistillate catkin on stem (x1⅓). **L.** Adaxial view of pistillate flower (x8). **M.** Medial section of pistillate flower (x8). **N.** Floral diagram of pistillate flower; the glands are cross-hatched. **O.** Lateral view of fruit just beginning to dehisce (x4). **P.** Open fruit showing comose seeds (x4). Reprinted with permission from Tomlinson (1980). Artist: Priscilla Fawcett.

representatives. Species diversity diminishes greatly south of the tropic of Cancer, and the family does not reach New Guinea, Australia, or the Pacific Islands. In the neotropics, species of *Salix* are found both in the highlands and lowlands, usually near water, while *Populus* is mainly confined to the uplands of Mexico. Only *Salix humboldtiana* is found south of Honduras; it is a widespread riverine species ranging from northern Mexico to northern Chile, Argentina and Uruguay. The monotypic genera, *Chosenia* and *Toisusu*, are restricted to eastern Asia.

Many aspects of the biology demonstrate the adaptation of members of this family as early-successional species. Many species of *Salix* will root very readily from fallen branches or twigs and are capable of colonizing unstable riparian habitats species of both genera are cultivated as ornamental trees, and being of temperate origin, can grow in mountainous regions in the neotropics.

The leaves and bark of *Salix* had numerous medical uses. Isolation of salicin from the bark eventually led to the development of aspirin.

References. ARGUS, G. W., AND C. L. MCJANNET. 1992. A taxonomic reconsideration of *Salix taxifolia sensu lato* (Sal-

icaceae). *Brittonia* 44:461–74. CHASE M. W., S. ZMARZTY, M. D. LLEDÓ, K. J. WURDACK, S. M. SWENSEN, AND M. F. FAY. 2002. When in doubt, put it in Flacourtiaceae; a molecular phylogenetic analysis based on plastid *rbc*L DNA sequences. *Kew Bull.* 57:141–81. ECKENWALDER, J. E. 1977. North American cottonwoods (*Populus*, Salicaceae) of sections *Abaso* and *Aigeiros*. *J. Arnold Arbor.* 58:193–208. NEE, M. 1984. Salicaceae. In *Flora de Veracruz*, fasc. 34: 1–24. Xalapa, Mexico: INIREB.

SANTALACEAE (Sandalwood Family)

MICHAEL NEE

Figure 175

- *trees, shrubs, or perennial herbs, hemiparasitic*

- *leaves alternate, simple*

- *flowers with uniseriate perianth, the tepals 4–5(8); placentation free-central*

- *seeds 1 per fruit*

Numbers of genera and species. Worldwide, the Santalaceae comprise 35 genera and 400 species. In tropical America, there are six genera and 20 species. About half the species belong to the woody *Acanthosyris*, *Cervantesia*, and *Jodina* and half to the herbaceous genera *Arjona*, *Quinchamalium*, and *Thesium*.

Distribution and habitat. The Santalaceae are distributed nearly worldwide, especially in tropical and subtropical regions.

The herbaceous *Arjona* and *Quinchamalium* are found in the Andes, but most of their species are extratropical, and *Thesium* has a couple of species in the Planalto of Brazil and the *tepuis* of southern Venezuela, but more than 200 in the Eastern Hemisphere. Among the woody genera, *Jodina rhombifolia* is confined to the *chacó* and surrounding arid areas, *Cervantesia tomentosa* occupies Andean cloud forests, and species of *Acanthosyris* are mostly found in moist to semideciduous forests of South America.

Family classification. The Santalaceae are placed by Cronquist in the Santalales near families such as the Opiliaceae and Loranthaceae. Recent molecular analyses support a close relationships with these two families.

Features of the family. Habit: trees, shrubs, or perennial herbs, hemiparasitic. **Roots** attached to roots of host plant. **Stems** sometimes thorny. **Stipules** absent. **Leaves** alternate,

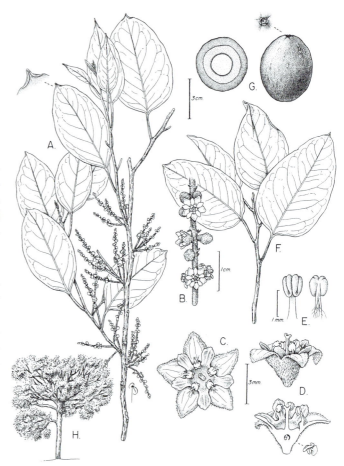

Figure 175. SANTALACEAE. *Acanthosyris asipapote.* **A.** Stem with immature leaves and inflorescences and detail of leaf blade apex (above left). **B.** Part of inflorescence. **C.** Apical view of flower; note lobed nectary between stamens. **D.** Lateral view (above) and medial section (below) of flower with detail of convoluted placental stalk (right). **E.** Adaxial (left) and abaxial (right) views of stamens. **F.** Stem with mature leaves. **G.** Lateral view with detail of apex (right) and transverse section (left) of fruits. **H.** Plant showing habit. Reprinted with permission from Nee (1996). Artist: Bobbi Angell.

simple, rarely reduced to scales; blade margins entire, or spine-tipped lobes present in *Jodina*. **Inflorescences** axillary or terminal, spikes or fascicles in panicles. **Flowers** actinomorphic, bisexual, small, greenish; perianth uniseriate, tepals united below into cup or tube, the lobes 4–5(8), rarely fewer, in a single series; androecium with stamens equal to number of tepals, the stamens opposite tepal lobes, the filaments often adnate to tepals; nectrary often present and lobed, the lobes sometimes conspicuous; gynoecium syncarpous, the ovary superior to inferior, the carpels 3, the locule 1, the style 1, the stigmas 3; placentation free-central, the ovules 1–4. **Fruits** nuts or drupes, sometimes large. **Seeds** 1 per fruit.

Natural history. All species are suspected of being hemiparasites, but only a few have been so documented. No information is available on pollination and dispersal biology.

Economic uses. Neotropical species have few economic uses, in contrast to the long-treasured sandalwood and the oil extracted from it for perfumery produced from *Santalum album* of southern India. Species sometimes can be deleterious to crops, although the plants are not visibly hemiparasitic, as is the case with Loranthaceae and Viscaceae. For example, *Acanthosyris paulo-alvinii*, kills cocoa trees in Bahia, Brazil.

References. Nee, M. 1996. A new species of *Acanthosyris* (Santalaceae) from Bolivia and a key to the woody South American Santalaceae. *Brittonia* 48:574–79. Stauffer, H. U. 1961. Südamerikanische Santalaceae I: *Acanthosyris, Cervantesia* und *Jodina* (Santalales-Studien VII). *Vierteljahrsschr. Naturf. Ges. Zürich* 106:406–12.

SAPINDACEAE (Soapwort Family)

Hans T. Beck

Figures 176, 177, 178; Plate 43

- *lianas, trees, or sometimes shrubs*

- *leaves usually alternate, usually pinnately compound*

- *tendrils derived from inflorescences present in lianas*

- *flowers with (4)5-merous perianth petals often with scaly or tufted basal appendages; extrastaminal nectary disc present; ovary superior*

- *fruits winged or dehiscent, when dehiscent the seeds with aril or sarcotesta*

Numbers of genera and species. Worldwide, the Sapindaceae comprise approximately 147 genera and 2,215 species. In the Western Hemisphere, there are 34 genera and about 968 known species. The largest are the lianas *Serjania* and *Paullinia* with 220 and 180 species, respectively, all occurring in tropical America, except *P. pinnata*, which is also found naturally in tropical Africa.

Distribution and habitat. Sapindaceae are primarily tropical and subtropical. The family has centers of diversity in tropical America and tropical Asia. In the Southern Hemisphere, some species extend into more arid, subtropical areas of South America, southern Africa, India, Australia, and the Pacific Islands. A few species reach northern subtropical areas in the United States, Africa, and Asia. *Dodonaea* and *Cardiospermum* are pantropical.

Widespread in the neotropics, Sapindaceae occur commonly in habitats composed of primary and secondary non-flooded *terra firme* forests (e.g., species of *Cupania* and *Talisia*) to inundated *várzea* (e.g., *Matayba*) and *igapó* forests (e.g., *Pseudima*). Although species of Sapindaceae range from sea level to 3,000 meters, diversity is greatest below 1,500 meters in coastal, montane, and Amazonian habitats. However, certain genera commonly occur in more arid habitats, including intermontane valleys as well as *restinga* and *cerrado* (e.g., *Serjania, Urvillea,* and *Cardiospermum*).

Family classification. The Sapindaceae are placed in the Sapindales by Cronquist, and this is supported by molecular analyses. The family in the traditional strict sense has been divided into two subfamilies, the Dodonaeoideae and Sapindoideae, with a total of 12–14 tribes. Aceraceae and Hippocastanaceae have traditionally been treated as separate families. Recent reassessments by various authors have broadly redefined the family to include seven subfamilies: the Dodonaeoideae, Koelreuterioideae, Stylobasioideae, Emblingioi-

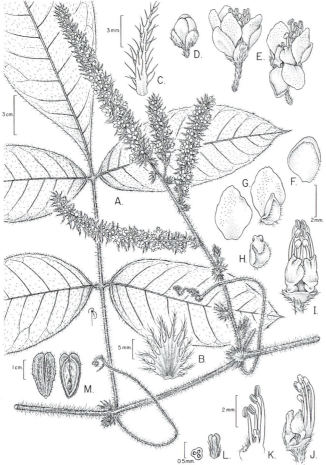

appearing paniculate, racemose, corymbose, umbellate, or fasciculate; tendrils paired at base of inflorescence in lianas. **Flowers** actinomorphic to weakly zygomorphic, bisexual or unisexual (plants monoecious, dioecious, or polygamodioecious), usually small; calyx with (4)5 sepals, the sepals distinct or basally connate; corolla with (4)5 petals, the petals distinct or sometimes basally connate, usually imbricate, often unequal, sometimes clawed, mostly with scaly or tufted basal appendages adaxially, greenish, white, or yellow; extrastaminal nectary disc present, sometimes unilateral; an-

Figure 176. SAPINDACEAE. *Paullinia rubiginosa.* **A.** Stem with leaves, tendrils, and inflorescence. **B.** Lateral view of stipule. **C.** Lateral view of bract. **D.** Lateral view of bud. **E.** Lateral views of flowers, intact (left) and with one petal removed (right). **F.** Adaxial view of sepal. **G.** Abaxial view of petal (left) and adaxial view of petal with appendage (right). **H.** Adaxial view of petal appendage. **I.** Lateral view of flower with sepals and petals removed; note petal appendages inserted on nectary disc glands. **J.** Lateral view of flower with sepals and petals removed. **K.** Medial section of flower with sepals and petals removed. **L.** Lateral view of intact gynoecium (right) and transverse section (left) of pistillode. **M.** Lateral view of intact (left) and dehisced fruits (right). Reprinted with permission from Mori et al. (2002). Artist: Bobbi Angell.

deae, Sapindoideae, Aceroideae, and Hippocastanoideae. The Aceroideae and Hippocastanoideae, derived groups within the Sapindaceae, are treated as separate families in this book for practical reasons of plant identification.

Features of the family. Habit: lianas, trees, sometimes shrubs, the liana stems often with secondary anomalous vascular bundles. **Stipules** frequently present in lianas, sometimes conspicuously large, absent in trees. **Leaves** usually alternate, very rarely opposite, usually pinnately compound (rarely unifoliolate) or sometimes palmately compound, persistent or deciduous. **Inflorescences** terminal, axillary, or sometimes cauliflorous in lianas, determinate, cymose and

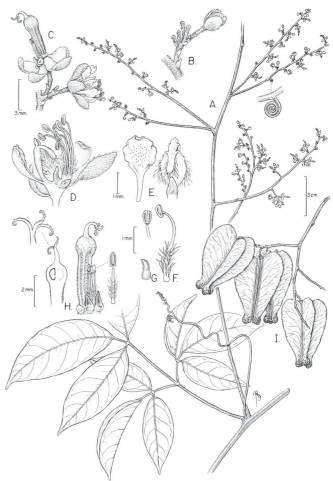

Figure 177. SAPINDACEAE. *Serjania grandifolia.* **A.** Stem with leaf, tendril, inflorescence, and detail of tendril (above). **B.** Detail of inflorescence with bud, bracts, and pedicel bases. **C.** Detail of inflorescence with one functionally pistillate flower and one functionally staminate flower. **D.** Longitudinal section of functionally staminate flower. **E.** Adaxial view of petal with appendage removed (left) and adaxial view of petal appendage and subtending gland with petal removed. **F.** Lateral view of stamen with detail of adaxial view of apical portion of stamen (upper left). **G.** Lateral view of pistillode. **H.** Medial section of gynoecium (left) with detail of stigma (above), gynoecium with a few staminodes and glands (center), and detail of staminode (right). **I.** Stem with infructescence. Reprinted with permission from Mori et al. (2002). Artist: Bobbi Angell.

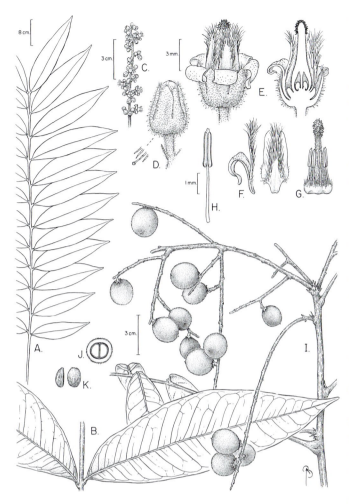

Figure 178. SAPINDACEAE. *Talisia mollis*. **A.** Leaf. **B.** Detail of leaf showing two subopposite leaflets. **C.** Part of inflorescence. **D.** Lateral view of flower bud with detail of hairs. **E.** Lateral view (left) and medial section (right) of flower. **F.** Lateral (left) and adaxial (right) views of petals with appendages. **G.** Lateral view of pistillate flower with petals and appendages removed. **H.** Adaxial view of stamen. **I.** Stem with infructescences. **J.** Transverse section of fruit. **K.** Lateral (left) and frontal (right) views of seeds. Reprinted with permission from Mori et al. (2002). Artist: Bobbi Angell.

droecium with 4–10 stamens, the stamens often 8, in a single whorl, the filaments distinct, the anthers dehiscing by longitudinal slits; pistillode vestigial in staminate flowers; gynoecium syncarpous, the ovary superior, the carpels 2–3, the locules (1)3(4), the styles 1–3, the stigmas simple or lobed; placentation usually axile, sometimes parietal, the ovules 1 per locule. **Fruits** capsules, drupes, schizocarps, or berries, often winged (*Serjania*, *Thouinia*, *Paullinia*, and *Diatenopteryx*), the capsules bladdery in *Cardiospermum* (usually septifragal), *Dodonaea* (septifragal), or leathery, woody, or chartaceous, e.g., *Paullinia* (septifragal) and *Cupania* (loculicidal). **Seeds** 1–3 per fruit, globose or flattened, frequently arillate or with sarcotesta in genera with dehiscent fruits.

Natural history. The most important pollinators of the Sapindaceae are bees; however, *Dodonaea* is wind-pollinated. Fruit dispersal in mesic habitats tends to be by water or animals. For example, in *Paullinia*, birds are attracted to the contrasting colors of red capsules with black seeds partially covered by white arils. In more xeric habitats with open canopies or in savannalike scrublands, wind dispersal tends to predominate (e.g., *Serjania*).

Economic uses. *Blighia* (akee) arils areedible when ripe, but poisonous if unripe. Another native Neotropical fruit with an edible aril comes from *Melicoccus* (genip, Spanish lime). The tropical Asian *Dimocarpus* (longan), *Litchi*, and *Nephelium* (rambutan) are encountered commonly under cultivation in the neotropics. Timber is harvested from *Cupania*, *Hypelate*, *Matayba*, and *Melicoccus*. Binding and construction materials are made from the stems of *Serjania* and *Paullinia*. *Dilodendron* provides oil from its edible seeds. Beads are made from the seeds of *Cardiospermum* and *Sapindus*. Soap substitutes are obtained from *S. saponaria*. The crushed stems of species of *Serjania* and *Paullinia* are used to poison or stun fish. A stimulating beverage very popular in Brazil is made from seeds of *P. cupana* (*guaraná*), which has the highest caffeine content of any plant.

References. ACEVEDO-RODRÍGUEZ, P. 1993. Systematics of Serjania (Sapindaceae) Part I: a revision of Serjania sect. Platycoccus. *Mem. New York Bot. Gard.* 67:1–93. BARKLEY, F. A. 1957. Sapindaceae of southern South America. *Lilloa* 28:111–79. BECK, H. T. 1991. The taxonomy and economic botany of the cultivated guaraná and its wild relatives and the generic limits within the Paullineae (Sapindaceae). Ph.D. thesis, New York: City University of New York. FERRUCCI, M. S. 1991. Sapindaceae. In *Flora del Paraguay*, eds. R. Spichiger and L. Ramella. St. Louis, MO: Editions des Conservatoire et Jardin botaniques de la Ville de Geneve/Missouri Botanical Garden. GADEK, P. A., E. S. FERNANDO, C. J. QUINN, S. B. HOOT, T. TERRAZAS, ET AL. 1996. Sapindales: molecular delimitation and infraordinal groups. *Amer. J. Bot.* 83(6):802–11. HUNZIKER, A. T. 1978. Notas criticas sobre Sapindaceas argentinas. II. Contribución al conocimiento del género Urvillea. *Bol. Acad. Nac. Ci.* 52:219–28. JOLY, C. A., G. M. FELIPPE, AND T. S. MELHEM. 1980. Taxonomic studies in *Magonia* St. Hil. (Sapindaceae). *Brittonia* 32:380–86. MULLER, J., AND P. W. LEENHOUTS. 1976. A general survey of pollen types in Sapindaceae in relation to taxonomy. In *The Evolutionary Significance of the Exine*, eds. I. K. Ferguson and J. Muller, 407–45. Linn. Soc. Symp. Ser. No. 1. London: Academic Press. RADLKOFER, L. 1931–1934. Sapindaceae. In *Das Pflanzenreich*, A. Engler. 98(IV.165):1–1539. REITZ, R. 1980. Sapindaceas. In *Flora Ilustrada Catarinense*, ed. R. Reitz. SAPI:1–156. VOTAVA, F. V. 1976. A taxonomic revision of the genus *Thouinia* (Sapindaceae). Ph.D thesis. New York: Columbia University.

SAPOTACEAE (Sapodilla Family)

TERENCE D. PENNINGTON

Figure 179, Plate 44

- *trees or rarely shrubs*

- *leaves alternate, simple; blade margins entire*

- *plants with latex, the latex usually white*

- *inflorescences fasciculate*

- *flowers actinomorphic, sympetalous; stamens opposite petal lobes; staminodes frequently present*

- *fruits usually berries; seeds with smooth, shiny testa, the hilum rough, more pale than testa*

Numbers of genera and species. Worldwide, the Sapotaceae comprise 53 genera and approximately 1,100 species. In tropical America, there are *Chromolucuma* (2 species), *Chrysophyllum* (44), *Diploon* (1), *Ecclinusa* (11), *Elaeoluma* (4), *Manilkara* (30), *Micropholis* (38), *Pouteria* (ca. 200), *Pradosia* (23), *Sarcaulus* (5), and *Sideroxylon* (50).

Distribution and habitat. The family is pantropical with species distributed more or less equally among America, Africa, and Asia. The greatest species richness is in a broad swath from the Guianas across Brazilian Amazonia to Amazonian Peru, Ecuador, and Colombia, where they are a major component of lowland rain forest. The region surrounding Manaus in the central Brazilian Amazonia contains more than 100 species, thereby making it the most species-rich family of trees in this area.

The Sapotaceae are typically species of lowland rain forest below 1,000 meters. The majority are found in undisturbed, nonflooded forest while a smaller proportion are confined to periodically or permanently flooded forest. In Amazonia, the Sapotaceae provide a spectacular example of the high diversity and low density so characteristic of South American forests. In a 25-hectare plot north of Manaus, 70 species were recorded and 87 percent of these had two individuals or fewer per hectare. Some species of *Ecclinusa* are well represented in the savannas of the Guayana Highland, and *Sideroxylon* has radiated into semiarid regions of Central America, Mexico, and the West Indies, with a few species even extending into the southern United States.

Family classification. The Sapotaceae are placed in the Ebenales by Cronquist. Recent molecular studies by the Angiosperm Phylogeny Group suggest that the Sapotaceae are within an expanded Ericales; however, further studies are needed.

The family is divided into five tribes based on calyx structure, number of stamens relative to corolla lobes, presence

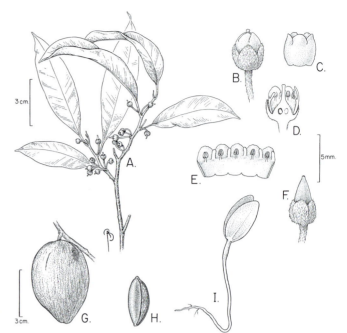

Figure 179. SAPOTACEAE. *Micropholis melinoniana*. **A.** Stem with leaves and inflorescences. **B.** Lateral view of flower; note exserted stigma. **C.** Lateral view of corolla. **D.** Medial section of flower. **E.** Adaxial view of corolla opened to show alternating stamens and staminodes. **F.** Lateral view of immature fruit. **G.** Lateral view of mature fruit. **H.** Seed; note hilar scar on right. **I.** Seedling with cotyledons. Reprinted with permission from Mori et al. (2002). Artist: Bobbi Angell.

or absence of staminodes, corolla lobe appendages, and position of the seed scar. The Mimusopeae contains 17 genera and circa 160 species. The majority of the genera are African, *Eberhardtia* is Asian, and *Manilkara* is pantropical. The Isonandreae comprise seven genera and circa 260 species confined to tropical Asia and the Pacific region. The Sideroxyleae have six genera and circa 90 species. The largest genus, *Sideroxylon* (75 species), is pantropical, and the monotypic *Diploon* is confined to South America. The Chrysophylleae are the largest tribe, with 18 genera and circa 600 species. The largest genus is the pantropical *Pouteria*, with circa 320 species. The Omphalocarpeae have four genera and circa 10 species restricted to Africa, Asia, and islands of the Pacific.

Features of the family. Habit: small or large trees, rarely shrubs (*Sideroxylon*, especially those of semiarid habitats), usually evergreen. Bark usually fissured or scaling (variation in thickness, color, texture, fissuring, and scaling provide characters for species recognition), rarely smooth (useful for distinguishing Sapotaceae from Moraceae). Latex usually present in stems, leaves, and fruit, sticky, usually white, rarely yellow (e.g., *Pouteria flavilatex*). Stipules infrequently present (*Ecclinusa*). Leaves alternate (spiral or less frequently distichous), simple; blade margins entire. **Inflorescences** axillary, ramiflorous, or cauliflorous, fasciculate, often densely clustered. **Flowers** actinomorphic, bisexual (e.g., *Manilkara*) or unisexual (plants monoecious or dioecious), small, usually 2–10 millimeter long; calyx of three types, the sepals 5, usually distinct, imbricate, in 1 whorl (most genera, especially *Pouteria*), the sepals 5–12, strongly imbricate, spirally arranged (*Pouteria* section *Aneulucuma*), or the sepals 6, biseriate, in 2 whorls of 3, valvate (*Manilkara*); corolla sympetalous, rotate, cyathiform, or tubular, the lobes 4–6(9), sometimes subdivided into 3 or more segments (*Manilkara* and many *Sideroxylon*); androecium with 4–6(12) stamens, the stamens opposite petal lobes, adnate within corolla tube or at base of lobes, exserted (*Manilkara*, *Sideroxylon*, *Pradosia*, *Diploon*, and *Elaeoluma*) or included (common in *Pouteria* and *Chrysophyllum*); staminodes often alternating with stamens, in 1 whorl, small; gynoecium syncarpous, the ovary superior, the locules 1–6(15); placentation axile, the ovules 1 per locule, rarely 2 and basal (*Diploon*). **Fruits** berries, rarely drupaceous (*Pradosia*), the berries fleshy or coriaceous, to 12 cm diam., the drupaceous fruits with cartilaginous endocarps. **Seeds** 1–several, the testa hard (in berries), smooth, shiny brown, the hilum pale, more rough than testa.

The trunks of species may be cylindrical (e.g., *Manilkara*) or fluted (many *Pouteria*) and buttressing is very common. The size, form, and branching of the buttresses is species-specific; e.g., *Micropholis obscura* has characteristic convex buttresses, while *Pouteria egregia* has buttresses spreading several meters from the trunk. Bark patterns are useful for species recognition in the field.

Leaf venation provides features useful for distinguishing genera, sections, and species. Of particular interest is the admedial venation found in *Chrysophyllum* and *Sideroxylon* in which the tertiary veins descend from the leaf margin, decreasing in size toward the midrib and running parallel to the secondary veins.

Sexual dimorphism between male and female flowers of monoecious or dioecious species may involve loss of anthers, or the complete loss of stamens in the female flowers. In some species of *Pouteria*, the male flowers are smaller than the female flowers.

The staminodes are well developed in *Manilkara* and may be variously lobed, toothed, or divided and sometimes petal-like. In *Pouteria*, they are small simple structures, and in *Chrysophyllum* they are absent.

Seed shape, position of the hilar scar, and extent of the scar relative to the shiny smooth area of the testa provide useful taxonomic characters. Many species have strongly laterally compressed seeds with a narrow adaxial scar (e.g., *Chrysophyllum*), while others are broadly ellipsoid with a broader adaxial scar, which sometimes covers most of the seed surface (e.g., *Pouteria speciosa*).

There are two basic embryo types: those with thin, flat, leafy cotyledons and an exserted radicle (usually correlated with the presence of copious endosperm) and those with thick plano-convex cotyledons with the radicle included (correlated with the absence of endosperm). The embryo type and presence or absence of endosperm are strongly correlated with other floral characters and are useful in separating genera.

Natural history. Two unrelated species, *Pradosia brevipes* and *Pouteria subcaerulea*, have a specialized subterranean habit, in which the much-branched crown of the tree is underground and only the ultimate shoot tips are above ground. This is an adaption to the periodic fires of the *cerrado* and *campo* grasslands of southeastern Brazil. Species of *Sideroxylon* are commonly thorny, especially when growing in exposed, drier places. The thorns are derived from modified axillary shoots and may protect these species from predation.

Few direct observations have been made of pollination of Sapotaceae, but some of the nocturnal-flowering species of *Manilkara* with dull-colored flowers are pollinated by bats. Although the individual flowers are small, the inflorescences are tightly clustered below the foliage and present a large, exposed floral surface with exserted stamens and staminodes. The corolla itself is slightly fleshy, tastes sweet, and is removed easily as a whole together with stamens and staminodes. The reward for pollinators, therefore, may be the corolla itself. Many of the smaller-flowered *Pouteria* species have a similar inflorescence arrangement, are nocturnal flowering, and probably are visited by moths.

The fruits vary in size from 1 to 12 centimeters in diameter and are colored yellow, purple, black, brown, or green; larger fruits often are brown and rough-skinned. Some of the smaller yellow fruits, such as those of *Micropholis venulosa* and *Pradosia schomburgkiana*, are dispersed by birds, but primates are the principal dispersers in Amazonia, where the fruit forms an important part of their diet. The seeds are either swallowed and pass through the gut or they are rejected after the pericarp has been consumed. Bats are recorded as dispersing a number of species with soft fruits, such as *Manilkara zapota* and *Pouteria psammophila*. The soft fruits of species such as *Pouteria plicata*, which inhabit permanently flooded forests, are eaten and dispersed by fish. Many of the larger-fruited *Pouteria* and *Chrysophyllum* have a hard, almost woody pericarp. In these species, the innermost layer (1–3 mm thick) surrounding the seed is composed of a succulent sweet jelly that animals eat after gnawing through the thick outer pericarp.

Economic uses. The Sapotaceae are economically important for their timber, edible fruit, seed oil, and trunk latex. In tropical America, *Manilkara* provides an important heavy-construction timber that is resistant to insect and fungal attacks. Its deep reddish-brown color makes it appreciated for parquet. In Asia, many species of Sapotaceae provide excellent, moderately hard and very heavy hardwoods for construction.

The majority of species with edible fruit are from Central America and Andean South America, where they have been major items of local commerce for centuries. *Pouteria lucuma* (*lucuma*) has a fruit with a rather dry yellow or orange pulp that weighs up to 1 kilogram. Its distinctive flavor (like maple syrup) makes it popular for drinks, puddings, and cakes. *Lucuma* is a good source of carbohydrates, iron, and vitamins, and, because of its year-round production and ease of storability, it is a valuable food source when other crops are in short supply. Other important fruits from the same region are *Pouteria sapota* (*sapote*) and *P. campechiana* (*caniste*). *Manilkara zapota* (*chicu, sapodilla*), a native of southern Mexico, is now cultivated extensively for its fruit in the Americas and tropical Asia. The wild plant is a canopy tree 30–40 meters tall, but horticultural advances have produced an orchard-sized tree that fruits after only a few years.

In several species, oil is extracted from the seeds, only one of which, *Pouteria butyrocarpa* of southeastern Brazil, occurs in tropical America.

Latex from the cut bark of *Manilkara* was formerly of great commercial importance, but its use has declined because of the availability of synthetics. Balata, obtained from *M. bidentata* (Guyana and northern Amazonian Brazil), is an isomer of rubber with the property of becoming plastic at high temperatures and then becoming hard again when cooled, features that make it suitable for the insulation of electric cables. This latex is chemically identical to the true *gutta-percha* (produced from the Asian *Palaquium*), which is still used extensively in dentistry for root-canal fillings. The latex of *Manilkara zapota* was the source of chewing gum (chicle), though this also has been replaced largely by synthetics. However, as a result of the search for sustainable, nontimber forest products, the chicle industry based on *M. zapota* is now undergoing a revival in the Petén of Guatemala and adjacent Belize.

References. ANDERBERG, A. A. 1993. Cladistic relationships and major clades of the Ericales. *Pl. Syst. Evol.* 184: 207–31. PENNINGTON, T. D. 1990. Sapotaceae. *Fl. Neotrop. Monogr.* 52:1–770. PENNINGTON, T. D. 1991. *The Genera of Sapotaceae*. Richmond, Surrey, U.K.: Royal Botanic Gardens, Kew.

SARRACENIACEAE (Pitcher Plant Family)

KENNETH M. CAMERON

Figure 180, Plate 44

- *insectivorous herbs*

- *leaves tubular, pitcherlike, with cap over "pitcher" mouth, with downward pointing hairs on inside of "pitcher"*

- *flowers actinomorphic, showy; tepals 4; anthers poricidal; ovary superior*

- *fruits capsules*

Number of genera and species. The Sarraceniaceae comprise three genera (*Darlingtonia, Heliamphora, Sarracenia*) and 14 species, all restricted to the Western Hemisphere. In tropical America, *Heliamphora* with five species is the only genus.

Distribution and habitat. Sarraceniaceae are restricted to wet, nutrient-poor soils in North and South America.

Species of *Heliamphora* are confined to the high, wet, flat-topped mountain formations (*tepuis*) of northwestern Brazil, southeastern Venezuela, and western Guyana. Many of the species are restricted to particular *tepuis*. For example, *H. ionasi* is confined to the summits of Ilu-tepui, *H. tatei* occurs exclusively on Cerro de la Neblina, and *H. minor* is found only on the summits of Ayuan-tepui and Chimanta-tepui.

Heliamphora nutans may be the most widespread species, being found in wet, open savannas of the Roraima mountain chain. *Darlingtonia* and *Sarracenia* are restricted to North America.

These pitcher plants of the Western Hemisphere are not to be confused with the Australian pitcher plant family (Cephalotaceae) or the tropical pitcher plants (Nepenthaceae) from the Eastern Hemisphere.

Family classification: The Sarraceniaceae are placed in the Nepenthales by Cronquist. The family has traditionally been recognized as closely related to other carnivorous plant families such as Droseraceae and Nepenthaceae. The greater affinities of these carnivores to other flowering plants, however, has been controversial. Current molecular studies indicate an alliance among Sarraceniaceae, Actinidiaceae, Roridulaceae, and Ericaceae, with other carnivorous families distantly related. A recent proposal to divide the family into Heliamphoraceae and Sarraceniaceae, the latter being further subdivided into subfamilies Darlingtoniodeae and Sarracenioideae, is not supported by DNA sequence data.

Features of the family. Habit: herbs, insectivorous. **Stipules** absent. **Leaves** alternate, in rosettes, attached to rhizome or upright stem, simple, tubular (forming a "pitcher"),

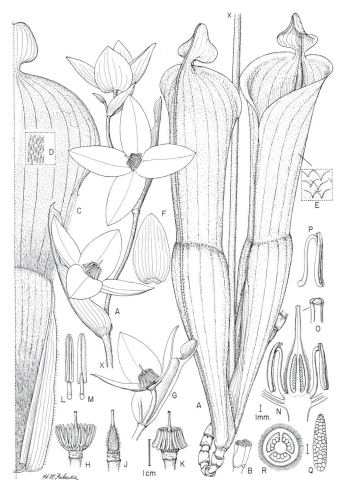

Figure 180. SARRACENIACEAE. *Heliamphora neblinae.* **A.** Basal part of plant with two pitcherlike leaves (right) and inflorescence (left) (x½). **B.** Transverse section of very base of leaves (x½). **C.** Pitcherlike leaf opened to show inner surface (x½). **D.** Detail of trichomes lining inner surface of leaf (x5). **E.** Detail of trichomes on exterior surface of leaf (x5). **F.** Perianth segment (x½). **G.** Lateral view of flower with part of perianth removed and subtending bract in medial section (x½). **H.** Young flower with perianth removed to show stamens and gynoecium; note erect anthers (x1). **J.** Lateral view of gynoecium (x1). **K.** Lateral view of flower after anthesis with perianth removed; note reflexed anthers (x1). **L.** Adaxial view of stamen (x2½). **M.** Abaxial view of stamen (x2½). **N.** Medial section of flower after anthesis; note reflexed anthers (x2½). **O.** Details of stigma (x15). **P.** Lateral view of stamen after anthesis showing reflexed anther (x2½). **Q.** Seed (x3⅓). **R.** Transverse section of ovary (x3⅓). Reprinted with permission from Maguire (1978). Artist: Haruto M. Fukuda.

internally lined with stiff downward-pointing hairs and digestive glands; blades folded lengthwise, the margins partly fused, the midrib extending over mouth of pitcher to form small cap, the cap often red and nectar-producing. **Inflorescences** terminal, arising from center of leaf rosettes, racemes, up to 60 centimeters tall. **Flowers** actinomorphic, bisexual, large, showy; tepals 4, green-white, often light pink at maturity; androecium of 10–20 stamens, the filaments distinct, the anthers basifixed, poricidal; gynoecium syncarpous,

the ovary superior, the carpels 3, the locules 3, the style simple, the stigmas subentire; placentation axile below, intruded-parietal above. **Fruits** capsules. **Seeds** numerous.

Natural history. The most noticeable feature of the family is the hollow, tubular leaf modified for pitfall carnivory. Insects are attracted to the leaves and fall into a pool of fluid containing bacteria and digestive enzymes. Their bodies are broken down and the released nutrients are absorbed by the leaf. The interior of the tubular leaves provides a unique microhabitat for other organisms. Studies of this genus indicate that a number of insects employ these leaves as incubators for their larvae. The interactions between plants and animals are complex and fascinating in this family.

The brightly colored leaves, often marked with dark red veins and producing copious nectar, frequently are mistaken for flowers and clearly serve to attract would-be pollinators and other insects to the awaiting traps; however, the large, fragrant, attractive flowers of *Sarracenia* and *Darlingtonia* are modified for bee pollination. Observations of *Heliamphora* in the field indicate that the flowers of this genus are nectarless and have poricidal anthers that are buzz-pollinated by several different species of bee. No information is available on dispersal biology.

Economic uses. Because of their fascinating insectivorous nature, many species are collected and cultivated as ornamental curiosities; however, they have specific cultural demands and rarely survive long in cultivation. The attractive green and white leaves of *Sarracenia leucophylla* often are sold fresh or dried for the florist trade. Unfortunately, these practices have led to overcollecting in the wild and present a serious threat to the survival of these unique plants.

References. ARBER, A. 1941. On the morphology of the pitcher-leaves in *Heliamphora, Sarracenia, Darlingtonia, Cephalotus,* and *Nepenthes. Ann. Bot. (Oxford)* 5:563–78. BAYER, R. J., L. HUFFORD, AND D. E. SOLTIS. 1996. Phylogenetic relationships in Sarraceniaceae based on *rbc*L and ITS sequences. *Syst. Bot.* 21:121–34. CHEERS, G. 1992. A guide to carnivorous plants of the world. New York: HarperCollins. CHRTEK, J., Z. SLAVIKOVA, AND M. STUDIEKA. 1992. Beitrag zur Morphologie und Taxonomie der Familie Sarraceniaceae. *Preslia* 64:1–10. DEBUHR, L. E. 1975. Phylogenetic relationships of the Sarraceniaceae. *Taxon* 24:297–306. JUNIPER, B. E., R. J. ROBINS, AND D. M. JOEL. 1989. The carnivorous plants. San Diego, CA: Academic Press. MAGUIRE, B. 1978. Sarraceniaceae. In The botany of the Guyana Highlands, part ten. *Mem. New York Bot. Gard.* 29:36–61. RENNER, S. S. 1989. Floral biological observations on *Heliamphora tatei* (Sarraceniaceae) and other plants from Cerro de la Neblina in Venezuela. *Pl. Syst. Evol.* 163:21–29. SCHNELL, D. E. 1976. *Carnivorous Plants of the United States and Canada.* Winston-Salem, NC: John F. Blair Publishers.

SAURURACEAE (Lizard's-tail Family)

David L. Lentz

- *aquatic or semiaquatic herbs*
- *plants aromatic*
- *leaves alternate, basal*
- *flower perianth absent*
- *fruits capsules, 4-valved*

Numbers of genera and species. Worldwide, the Saururaceae comprise five genera and seven species. Only *Anemopsis californica* is found in tropical America.

Distribution and habitat. The Saururaceae are found in North America and eastern Asia. Only two species are native to the Western Hemisphere, *Anemopsis californica* and *Saururus cernuus*. The former ranges from California and Oklahoma in the southwestern United States to Querétero, Mexico, and is found in marshes, bogs, and other moist places up to 1,900 meters. *Saururus cernuus* grows in eastern North America from Canada to Texas and Florida.

Family classification. The Saururacae are placed in the Piperales by Cronquist. Recent molecular studies and cladistic analyses based on morphological data have confirmed that the family is closely related to the Piperaceae.

Features of the family. Habit: aquatic or semiaquatic herbs, perennial; rhizomes stout; aromatic compounds from ethereal oil cells in parenchymatous tissue. **Stipules** present, fused to petioles. **Leaves** alternate, basal, arising from apical portion of rhizome, simple. **Inflorescences** terminal, spikes; bracts forming petal-like involucre subtending spikes. **Flowers** tiny, actinomorphic, bisexual; perianth absent; androecium of 6 stamens, the filaments large, swollen at base, the anthers basifixed, dehiscence longitudinal; gynoecium syncarpous, the ovary embedded in receptacle, the carpels 3–4, the locule 1, the style 3, distinct, the stigmas decurrent; placentation parietal, the ovules 6–10 per carpel. **Fruits** capsules, 4-valved. **Seeds** cylindrical, ovate, <1 mm (in greatest dimension); endosperm scanty, the embryo tiny, the perisperm substantial.

Natural history. *Anemopsis californica* flowers from August through November. Mature seeds germinate five weeks after they are exposed to water. In addition to seed propagation, this species often reproduces vegetatively from its rootstocks. It is threatened with extinction in many areas because its aquatic habitat is so vulnerable to human influences.

No information is available on pollination and dispersal biology.

Economic uses. Rhizomes of *Anemopsis californica*, also referred to as *yerba mansa*, *hierba del mansa*, and *raíz del manso*, are used in the manufacture of beads for necklaces or, when ground and infused in water, as a treatment for fever, malaria, and dysentery.

References. Calderónde Rzedowski, G. 1996. *Flora del Bajio y de Regiones Adyacentes*. Pátzcuaro, México: Instituto de Ecología, A.C. Tucker, S. C., A. W. Douglas, and L. Han-Xing. 1993. Utility of ontogenetic and conventional characters in determining phylogenetic relationships of Saururaceae and Piperaceae (Piperales). *Syst. Bot.* 18 (4): 614–41. Wu Cheng-Yih and K. Kubitzki. 1993. Saururaceae. *The Families and Genera of Vascular Plants*, eds. K. Kubitzki, J. G. Rohwer, and V. Bittrich, 2:586–88. Berlin: Springer-Verlag.

SAXIFRAGACEAE (Saxifrage Family)

Douglas E. Soltis

Figure 181

- *perennial herbs*
- *leaves alternate, primarily basal, rarely opposite, usually simple*
- *flowers usually with 5 sepals, 5 petals, and 5 or 10 stamens; ovary of 2 fused carpels, ± united*
- *fruits capsules*

Numbers of genera and species. Worldwide, the Saxifragaceae *sensu stricto* consist of about 30 genera and approximately 500 species. In tropical America, there are three genera and perhaps seven species. The largest genera of Saxifragaceae *sensu stricto* are *Saxifraga* (in its broad sense approximately 400 species), *Heuchera* (50), *Chrysosplenium* (50), *Micranthes* (70), and *Mitella* (20).

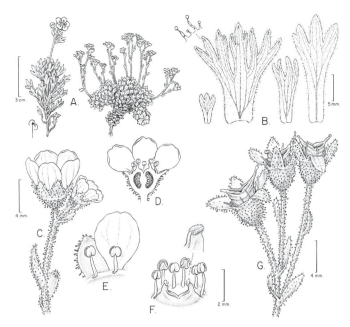

Figure 181. SAXIFRAGACEAE. *Saxifraga magellanica* (A, Dillon et al. 2988 (left) and Goodall 386 (right); B, from assorted specimens, not vouchered; C–F, Goodall 386; G. Sobel and Strudwick 2623). **A.** Plants with leaves and inflorescences. **B.** Leaves showing variation in size and detail of trichomes (above left). **C.** Part of inflorescence. **D.** Medial section of flower. **E.** Detail of stamen attachment, opposite sepal (left) and opposite petal (right). **F.** Summit of ovary showing some of stamens and detail of stigma (above). **G.** Part of infructescence. Original. Artist: Bobbi Angell.

Distribution and habitat. Saxifragaceae are nearly cosmopolitan in distribution, but most diverse in temperate, often mountainous parts of the Northern Hemisphere. The greatest number of genera occur in North America, especially the western cordillera. Very few Saxifragaceae occur in the Tropics.

In the neotropics, several species of *Saxifraga* occur in the Andes as far north as Colombia. These include *S. magellanica*, *S. pavonii*, and *S. boussingaultii*. *Hieronymusia alchemilloides* is found in the Andes of northern Argentina and *Heuchera*, a predominantly North American genus, has species in southern Mexico. *Chrysosplenium* is found in the Andes of Chile, but does not appear to reach the Tropics.

Family classification. The Saxifragaceae are placed in the Saxifragales. The family has been variously defined. In the broadest sense Saxifragaceae *sensu lato* consisted of 17 highly diverse subfamilies, and included not only herbaceous genera, but also the woody genera now segregated into other families such as Hydrangeaceae, Grossulariaceae, and Escalloniaceae. Recent authors define the family more narrowly. A series of molecular systematic studies reveal a well-defined and strongly supported Saxifragaceae *sensu stricto* corresponding to the Saxifragoideae of Engler and identical to the familial circumscriptions of Takhtajan and Thorne. These

same molecular phylogenetic studies also demonstrate that groups considered part of a broadly defined Saxifragaceae (e.g., hydrageoids, escallonoids) are only distantly related to Saxifragaceae *sensu stricto*. These studies also reveal that Cronquist's view of Saxifragaceae (placed in the Rosales) is too broad. For example, Cronquist included *Eremosyne*, *Francoa*, *Lepuropetalon* (Lepuropetalaceae), *Penthorum*, *Parnassia*, *Vahlia*, and several other genera that are clearly not part of Saxifragaceae *sensu stricto*. The Saxifragaceae *sensu stricto* are most closely related to the shruby genera *Itea* (not in neotropics), *Pterostemon* (Pterostemonaceae), and *Ribes* (Grossulariaceae).

Although previous workers have recognized tribes and subtribes within Saxifragaceae *sensu stricto*, several decades of systematic study indicate that, for the most part, these do not represent natural groups. Phylogenetic and systematic studies suggest the presence of well-marked clades that have only been recognized informally; e.g., the *Boykinia* group, *Heuchera* group, and *Darmera* group.

Even following this narrow view, Saxifragaceae remain a morphologically diverse group. For example, ovary position varies in the family from completely inferior to what has been reported as completely superior. In fact, this complete range of variation in ovary position has been reported within individual genera, including *Saxifraga* and *Lithophragma*. *Saxifraga* encompasses species with carpels nearly distinct and species with the carpels united almost up to the stigmas. Placentation within *Saxifraga* varies from essentially marginal, through axile below and marginal above, to wholly parietal. More than half of the species of Saxifragaceae *sensu stricto* belong to the highly variable *Saxifraga*, a genus that recent studies indicate is polyphyletic.

Features of the family. Habit: perennial herbs, often with multicellular hairs, root tips red (anthocyanic). **Stipules** wanting or represented by expanded margins of sheathing petiolar leaf bases. **Leaves** alternate, these primarily basal, rarely opposite, simple, or more rarely pinnately or palmately compound or decompound; venation pinnate or often palmate. **Inflorescences** axillary or terminal, cymose to racemose. **Flowers** actinomorphic or less often somewhat zygomorphic, bisexual or rarely functionally unisexual (plants polygamodioecious), sometimes perigynous; sepals typically (3)5; petals usually as many as sepals, often clawed, sometimes cleft or dissected; androecium of 3–10 stamens, the stamens usually as many as or twice as many as calyx lobes, the anthers dehiscing by longitudinal slits; intrastaminal nectary disc or annulus often present; gynoecium with superior to inferior ovary, the carpels 2(3), ± connate, at least toward base to form compound, often ± deeply lobed ovary, the lobes commonly prolonged into hollow or solid stylar beaks, terminated by a usually capitate stigma; placentation variously axile or parietal, the ovules numerous on each placenta, anatropous, bitegmic or sometimes unitegmic, crassinucellular. **Fruits** capsules, dry, most often septicidal or dehiscent along ventral sutures of carpels above level of union. **Seeds** generally numerous, small; endosperm copious, oily, the embryo small to fairly large, straight.

Natural history. No information is available on pollination and seed dispersal of this family.

Economic uses. Species of *Astilbe*, *Bergenia*, *Heuchera*, and *Tiarella* are frequently cultivated as garden-ornamentals, and species of *Saxifraga* and several other genera often are grown in rock gardens. *Tolmiea menziesii* and *Saxifraga stolonifera* are common houseplants.

References. ENGLER, S. 1890. Saxifragaceae. In *Die Natürlichen Pflanzenfamilien*, A. Engler and K. Prantl, 3:42–93. ENGLER, S. 1928. Saxifragaceae. In *Die Natürlichen Pflanzenfamilien*, A. Engler and K. Prantl, 2nd ed., 18a:74–226. Leipzig: Wilhelm Engelmann. MORGAN, D. R., AND D. E. SOLTIS. 1993. Phylogenetic relationships among Saxifragaceae *sensu lato* based on *rbc*L sequence data. *Ann. Missouri Bot. Gard.* 80:631–60. SOLTIS, D. E., R. K. KUZOFF, E. CONTI, R. GORNALL, AND K. FERGUSON. 1996. *Mat*K and *rbc*L gene sequence data indicate that Saxifraga (Saxifragaceae) is polyphyletic. *Amer. J. Bot.* 83:371–82. SOLTIS, D. E., D. R. MORGAN, A. GRABLE, P. S. SOLTIS, AND R. K. KUZOFF. 1993. Molecular systematics of Saxifragaceae *sensu stricto*. *Amer. J. Bot.* 80:1056–81. SOLTIS, D. E., AND P. S. SOLTIS. 1997. Phylogenetic relationships in Saxifragaceae *sensu lato*: a comparison of topologies based on 18S *r*DNA and *rbc*L sequences. *Amer. J. Bot.* 84:504–22. SPONGBERG, S. A. 1972. The genera of Saxifragaceae in the Southeastern United States. *J. Arnold Arbor.* 53:409–98. THORNE, R. F. 1992. An updated phylogenetic classification of the flowering plants. *Aliso* 13:365–89. WEBB, D. A., AND R. J. GORNALL. 1989. *A Manual of Saxifrages and Their Cultivation*. Portland, OR: Timber Press.

SCROPHULARIACEAE (Foxglove Family)

NOEL HOLMGREN

Figure 182, Plate 45

- *herbs, subshrubs, sometimes shrubs or vines*

- *leaves alternate, opposite, or rarely whorled, simple to pinnately dissected*

- *flowers typically zygomorphic, bisexual; ovary superior, the carpels and locules 2; placentation axile*

- *fruits typically capsules*

- *seeds usually numerous; endosperm well developed*

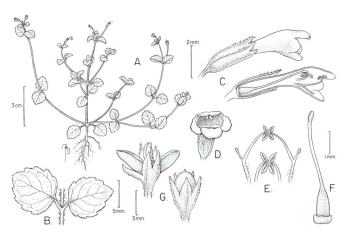

Figure 182. SCROPHULARIACEAE. *Lindernia crustacea*. **A.** Plant with roots, leaves, flowers, and fruits. **B.** Part of stem with two leaves. **C.** Lateral view (above) and longitudinal section (below) of flower. **D.** Oblique-apical view of flower. **E.** Adaxial views of stamens, the upper pair with appendages. **F.** Lateral view of gynoecium. **G.** Lateral views of intact (right) and dehisced (left) fruits. Reprinted with permission from Mori et al. (2002). Artist: Bobbi Angell.

Numbers of genera and species. Worldwide, the Scrophulariaceae comprise approximately 250 genera and about 4,000 species. In the Western Hemisphere, there are 125 genera, 85 of which are represented in the neotropics by about 750 species. Forty-one genera are endemic to the neotropics and 18 of these are monotypic. Twelve genera have been introduced since the European conquest. Several genera include attractive garden plants, which is the source of most introductions that have become established. Nearly two-thirds of the species are in *Calceolaria* (181 species), *Castilleja* (52), *Russelia* (50), *Bartsia* (45), *Bacopa* (41), *Stemodia* (28), *Angelonia* (26), *Lamourouxia* (25), *Penstemon* (25), and *Agalinis* (24).

Distribution and habitat. The Scrophulariaceae are well represented throughout the world, but are most common in temperate regions and tropical mountains. The larger Neotropical genera are concentrated in the mountains of Mexico, Central America, the West Indies, and the Andes. Scrophulariaceae are poorly represented in the Amazonian lowland and are curiously rare in the Guayana Highlands. In mountainous areas, the predominant genera are *Alonsoa*, *Bartsia*, *Calceolaria*, *Castilleja*, *Lamourouxia*, *Penstemon*, and *Russelia*. In lowland savannas, *llanos*, *caatingas*, and other open habitats, the more commonly encountered species are in *Agalinis*, *Angelonia*, *Bacopa*, *Buchnera*, *Lindernia*, *Lophospermum*, *Scoparia*, and *Stemodia*.

Species of Scrophulariaceae are found from sea level to alpine tundra. As herbs and shrubs, the Scrophulariaceae are best represented in open vegetation types and are scarce in tropical rain forests.

Family classification. The Scrophulariaceae are placed in the Scrophulariales by Cronquist. With minor modifications systematists have been using the familial classification proposed by Bentham more than 150 years ago. A recent molecular genetic study of representatives of the families and major tribes in the subclass Asteridae, using DNA sequences in the chloroplast genes *rbc*L, *rbc*2, and *ndh*F, has indicated radically different relationships and is leading to a classification resulting in considerable reshuffling of taxa. In this newly proposed classification, the Buddlejaceae, Myoporaceae, Callitrichaceae, Hippuridaceae, Plantaginaceae, and Orobanchaceae are integrated with members of the traditional Scrophulariaceae to form five presumed monophyletic families. It is premature to use this new arrangement because of an insufficient sample size, some unresolved problems, and an absence of a truly monographic attempt to test the hypotheses by using morphological evidence. The following arrangement of taxa represents the traditional familial circumscription with three subfamilies (Scrophularioideae, Antirrhinoideae, and Rhinanthoideae) and 14 Neotropical tribes. The unifying characters of the family are: a bilateral corolla, a bicarpellate ovary with axile placentation, many-seeded capsules, and seeds with well-developed endosperm.

Scrophularioideae. In the neotropics, this subfamily consists of fewer than 30 species in the tribes Verbasceae (introduced *Verbascum*), Scrophularieae, Leucophylleae, and Alonsoeae. The tribe Scrophularieae, represented in Hispaniola by four species of *Scrophularia*, is characterized by a short corolla with four fertile stamens and an adaxial scalelike staminode. The tribe Leucophylleae, consisting of *Leucophyllum*, *Eremogeton*, and *Heteranthia*, are woody shrubs. The tribe Alonsoeae, with the sole genus *Alonsoa*, is characterized by its resupinate (upsidedown) flowers.

Antirrhinoideae. The Antirrhinoideae includes 70 percent of the Neotropical Scrophulariaceae in the tribes Caprarieae, Gratioleae, Angeloneae, Cheloneae, Russelieae, Antirrhineae, Veroniceae, and Calceolarieae. The small tribe Caprarieae consists only of *Capraria*, which has alternate leaves, nearly radially symmetrical flowers, and some members with five fertile stamens. The tribe Gratioleae includes 29 genera in the neotropics, the best known of which are *Bacopa*, *Stemodia*, *Scoparia*, and *Lindernia*. Sixteen genera of Gratioleae are endemic to the neotropics, eight of which are monotypic. The tribe is difficult to characterize, but all species have opposite leaves and most species have a branched style. The tribe Angeloneae consists of the endemic *Angelonia*, *Basistemon*, and *Monopera*. Members of the tribe have a bisaccate corolla tube containing elaiophores, which secrete an oil that

is collected by the pollinating bees. The tribe Cheloneae includes *Penstemon*, *Tetranema*, and *Uroskinnera*. Some 25 species of *Penstemon* are distributed south of the tropic of Cancer, extending to Guatemala. It is the largest genus of vascular plants endemic to North America, with a total of about 300 species. *Tetranema* and *Uroskinnera* are endemic to Mexico and Central America. The tribe Russelieae, with its sole representative, *Russelia*, has diversified into about 50 species ranging from Mexico to Colombia. The tribe Antirrhineae, with its spurred or saccate corollas and capsules dehiscing by pores, is represented by 10 genera, four of which are present as single introduced species. The larger genera are *Lophospermum*, *Galvezia*, *Maurandya*, and *Gambelia*. The tribe Veroniceae has traditionally been placed in the Rhinanthoideae because of the external placement of the lower three corolla lobes in bud, but DNA evidence indicates greater affinity with members of the Antirrhinoideae. The tribe includes the four-corolla–lobed genera *Veronica* and *Aragoa*. The latter is a genus of shrubs endemic to the Andes of Colombia and adjacent Venezuela. The tribe also includes *Ourisia*, *Sibthorpia*, and the introduced *Digitalis* of the Eastern Hemisphere (with five-lobed corollas). The tribe Calceolarieae, consisting of *Calceolaria*, *Jovellana*, and *Porodittia*, are of southern origin. The tribe has no apparent evolutionary ties with any other and perhaps should be elevated to subfamilial rank. *Calceolaria*, with more than 180 species in Neotropical mountains, reaches its greatest diversity in the Peruvian Andes, where it has adapted to almost every conceivable montane habitat. The genus is readily recognized by its unique bilabiate corolla with a hooded upper lip and an inflated, pouched lower lip. Inside the pouch is an elaiophore patch that secretes an oil that is collected by bees.

Rhinanthoideae. The Rhinanthoideae are characterized by the lower corolla lip covering the upper in bud, and consists wholly of hemiparasitic species. Two tribes are represented in the Western Hemisphere: the Buchnereae and Euphrasieae. The Buchnereae corolla has a flat upper lip usually with 2 distinct lobes. It includes *Agalinis*, *Buchnera*, *Escobedia*, *Esterhazya*, *Seymeria*, and *Velloziella*. The Euphrasieae corolla has a keeled, usually entire upper lip, often forming a hood enclosing the stamens and style. The tribe includes the large and taxonomically difficult genera *Bartsia* and *Castilleja*, as well as *Lamourouxia* and *Pedicularis*.

Features of the family. Habit: herbs, subshrubs, sometimes shrubs or vines, species of Rhinanthoideae hemiparasitic. Stipules absent. Leaves alternate, opposite, or rarely whorled, simple to pinnately dissected. Inflorescences terminal and/or axillary, determinate or indeterminate, thyrses, racemes, spikes, or of solitary flowers in leaf axils or axils of leaflike bracts. Flowers typically zygomorphic, bisexual; calyx united into lobed tube or cleft to base, the lobes 4 or 5, rarely 2 or entire, imbricate; corolla sympetalous, sometimes spurred or saccate at base, weakly to usually strongly bilabiate, the lobes 4 or 5, rarely 3; androecium with 2, 4, occasionally 5, or rarely 3 stamens, the stamens fused to corolla tube, alternating with corolla lobes, the anthers sometimes unequal as in *Castilleja*, usually dehiscing by longitudinal slits; staminode(s) sometimes present; gynoecium syncarpous, the ovary superior, the carpels 2, the locules 2, the style terminal, the stigma simple or 2-lobed; placentation axile, the ovules few to usually numerous per locule. **Fruits** septicidal capsules, less often loculicidal, both septicidal and loculicidal, or opening by pores (in tribe Antirrhineae), rarely berries (*Leucocarpus*). **Seeds** usually numerous or less often few, angular or winged; endosperm oily, well developed, the embryo straight to curved.

Woodiness occurs in shrubs of *Basistemon, Calceolaria, Castilleja, Eremogeton, Galvezia, Hemichaena, Leucophyllum, Russelia,* and *Uroskinnera*. Members of the subfamilies Scrophularioideae and Antirrhinoideae are autotrophic and all members of the Rhinanthoideae are hemiparasitic with specialized roots that attach to the roots of the host plant.

Most commonly there are 4 functional stamens. In *Verbascum* and some *Capraria* there are 5 stamens; there are 4 functional stamens and one staminode in *Penstemon, Scrophularia, Tetranema,* and *Uroskinnera*; and in some *Lindernia* there are 2 functional stamens and an abaxial pair of staminodes. A complete reduction to 2 stamens is a feature of *Calceolaria, Hebe,* and *Veronica*.

Natural history. Pollination is effected by bees, wasps, flies, moths, butterflies, and birds, and, in some aquatic plants the pollen may be transferred by water. The family is noted for its high degree of diversity in floral structure and coloration. Nectar is the most common pollinator reward, but bees also collect pollen and oil from specialized flowers.

Seeds are dispersed by animals, wind, and water. Animal-dispersed seeds are most likely to be lodged in fur or feathers. The seeds of *Leucocarpus*, enclosed in a berrylike fruit, probably remain viable after passing through an animal's gut. Wind dispersal is common in genera with small, light seeds with an alveolate-reticulate coat or winged margins.

Economic uses. The drugs digitalin and lanoxin, extracted from species of *Digitalis* (mostly *D. lanata*), are commonly used in controlled doses to treat congestive heart failure by strengthening heart contractions. Larger doses are toxic and can cause death.

Alonsoa meridionalis (mask flower), *Angelonia* species, *Antirrhinum majus* (snapdragon), *Calceolaria* species (slipper worts), *Cymbalaria muralis* (Kenilworth ivy), *Digitalis purpurea* (foxglove), *Leucophyllum frutescens* (*ceniza*), *Linaria vulgaris* (butter-and-eggs), *Lophospermum erubescens* (creeping gloxinia), *Mimulus* species (monkey flower), *Ourisia* species, *Penstemon* species (beard tongues), *Russelia equisetiformis* (fountain bush), *Tetranema roseum* (Mexican foxglove), *Veronica* species (speedwells), and other species are popular as garden ornamentals. The subfamily Rhinanthoideae includes many attractive species, but they are difficult to grow because of their hemiparasitic nature.

Castilleja arvensis, Parentucellia viscosa, Scoparia dulcis, Verbascum species, and *Veronica* species are weedy, but are of minor concern.

References. KAMPNY, C. M. 1995. Pollination and flower diversity in Scrophulariaceae. *Bot. Rev.* 61:350–66. BENTHAM, G. 1846. Scrophulariaceae. In *Prodromus Systematis Naturalis Regni Vegetabilis*, ed. A. de Candolle, 10:188–586. Paris: Treuttel et Würtz. MOLAU, U. 1988. Scrophulariaceae. Part 1. Calceolarieae. *Fl. Neotrop. Monogr.* 47:1–326. OLMSTEAD, R. G., C. W. DE PAMPHILIS, A. D. WOLFE, N. D. YOUNG, W. J. ELISONS, AND P. A. REEVES. 2001. Disintegration of the Scrophulariaceae. *Amer. J. Bot.* 88(2):348–61. OLMSTEAD, R. G., H. J. MICHAELS, K. M. SCOTT, AND J. D. PALMER. 1992. Monophyly of the Asteridae and identification of their major lineages inferred from DNA sequences of rbcL. *Ann. Missouri Bot. Gard.* 79:249–65. PENNELL, F. W. 1935. The Scrophulariaceae of eastern temperate North America. *Acad. Nat. Sci. Philadelphia Monogr.* 1:1–650. THIERET, J. W. 1967. Supraspecific classification in the Scrophulariaceae: a review. *Sida* 3:87–106. WETTSTEIN, R. VON. 1891. Scrophulariaceae. In *Die Natürlichen Pflanzenfamilien*, eds. A. Engler and K. Prantl, div. 4, 3b:39–107. Leipzig: Wilhelm Engelmann.

SETCHELLANTHACEAE

NATHAN SMITH

- *shrubs of arid habitats*

- *plants pubescent, the trichomes T-shaped*

- *leaves alternate, often clustered on short-shoots, simple*

- *flowers actinomorphic, bisexual; corolla blue; androgynophore present; stamens numerous; ovary trisulcate*

- *fruits capsules, reflexed*

Numbers of genera and species. Endemic to Mexico, the Setchellanthaceae comprise the monotypic genus *Setchellanthus*.

Distribution and habitat. *Setchellanthus caeruleus* has a disjunct distribution in the Tehuacá Desert of Oaxaca and in the extratropical southern section of the Chihuahua Desert. It is usually found on limestone in cactus and scrub vegetation.

Family classification. Based on fruits and the assumed presence of musturd oils (glucosinolates), *Setchellanthus caeruleus* was placed in the Capparaceae (Capparales *sensu* Cronquist). A recent study of morphology, as well as a *rbc*L gene analysis, indicate that *Setchellanthus* belongs in its own family within Dahlgren's expanded Capparales and nearly basal to many of Cronquist's core Capparales families. A study of vegetative anatomy has also shown that *Setchellanthus* shares many characters with the Capparales *sensu lato* as well as with the Cistaceae of the Violales; however, a palynological study found that the pollen of *Setchellanthus* differs greatly from the pollen of taxa within these families.

Features of the family. Habit: shrubs; stems rigid. Indument of trichomes covering much of plant, the trichomes dense, strigose, appressed, T-shaped. Stipules absent. Leaves alternate, on long-shoots and often clustered on short-shoots on same plant, simple. Inflorescences axillary (to long-shoot leaves), of solitary flowers. Flowers actinomorphic, bisexual, showy; calyx with 5–7 sepals, the sepals connate in bud, irregularly splitting into 1–2 flaps, the flaps becoming reflexed, semipersistent; corolla with 5–7 petals, these obovate-spatulate, blue, glabrous; androecium with (40)60–76 stamens, the stamens in 5–7 groups, the anthers basifixed; androgynophore present, short (elongating in fruit); gynoecium syncarpous, the ovary superior, trisulcate, the carpels 3, the locules 3, the styles glabrous, 3-branched at apex, the branches stigmatic; placentation axile, the ovules ca. 10–14 per carpel, anatropous. Fruits capsules, linear, trisulcate, reflexed. Seeds 3–10 per carpel, the seed coat pithlike, soft, forming a thin wing proximally; endosperm nearly absent.

Natural history. Nothing is known about the pollination and dispersal biology of this family.

Economic uses. No uses are known for this family.

References. CARLQUIST, S., AND R. B. MILLER. 1999. Vegetative anatomy and relationships of *Setchellanthus caeruleus* (Setchellanthaceae). *Taxon* 48:289–302. ILTIS, H. H. 1999. Setchellanthaceae (Capparales), a new family for a relictual, glucosinolate-producing endemic of the Mexican deserts. *Taxon* 48:257–75. KAROL, K. G., J. E. RODMAN, E. CONTI, AND K. J. SYTSMA. 1999. Nucleotide sequence of *rbc*L and phylogenetic relationships of *Setchellanthus caeruleus* (Setchellanthaceae). *Taxon.* 48:303–15. KUBITZKI, K. 2003. Setchellanthaceae. In *The Families and Genera of Vascular Plants*, eds. K. Kubitzki and C. Bayer. 5:353–54. Berlin: Springer-Verlag. TOBE, H., S. CARLQUIST, AND H. H. ILTIS. 1999. Reproductive anatomy and relationships of *Setchellanthus caeruleus* (Setchellanthaceae). *Taxon* 48:277–83. TOMB, A. S. 1999. Pollen morphology and relationships of *Setchellanthus caeruleus* (Setchellanthaceae). *Taxon* 48:285–88.

SIMAROUBACEAE (Tree-of-Heaven Family)

WM. WAYT THOMAS

Figure 183, Plate 45

- *usually trees or shrubs*

- *bark often with bitter taste*

- *leaves alternate, usually compound (except for* Castela*)*

- *flowers often with appendaged stamen filaments; carpels borne on gynophore or disc, distinct or weakly united, the styles basally united*

- *fruits drupaceous*

Numbers of genera and species. Worldwide, the Simaroubaceae comprise 13 genera and about 130 species. In tropical America, six genera and 55 species are native. The largest genus is *Quassia* with 40 species, all but one of which are African or Asian. The largest American genus is *Simaba*, with 25 species. The other American genera are *Castela* (including *Holacantha*) with 15 species, *Simarouba* and *Picrasma*, each with six species (*Picrasma* also has six species in the Eastern Hemisphere), *Picrolemma* (including *Cedronia*) with two species, and *Quassia* with one. A native of China, *Ailanthus altissima* is naturalized in temperate regions of North and South America.

Distribution and habitat. The Simaroubaceae are primarily a tropical family with a main center of diversity in tropical America and a secondary center in tropical West Africa.

Although the different American genera have different distribution patterns, most are found in humid lowland forests. The genus *Simarouba* is widespread in tropical America; *Picrasma*, also known from the paleotropics, is found in lower montane forests, and *Picrolemma* is found in the Amazon Basin and lower montane forests from Colombia to Ecuador. *Quassia amara*, the only species of the genus native to the Americas, is widely scattered in lowland forests (probably

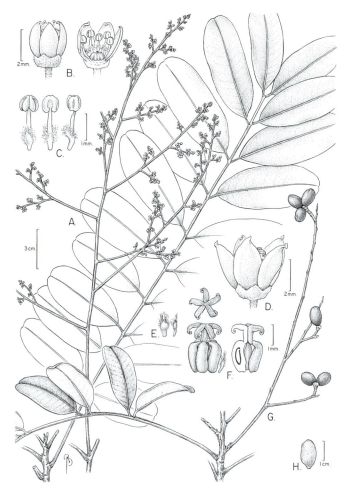

Figure 183. SIMAROUBACEAE. *Simarouba amara.* **A.** Stems with leaf and inflorescence. **B.** Staminate flowers: lateral views of intact flower (left) and flower with two petals and part of calyx removed (right). **C.** Adaxial (left), abaxial (center), and lateral (right) views of stamens showing pubescent appendages. **D.** Lateral view of pistillate flower. **E.** Adaxial (left) and lateral (right) views of staminodia. **F.** Lateral view of pistil (left) with apical view of stigmatic lobes (above); note free carpels with united style and separated stigmatic lobes; a staminode (center); and lateral view with several carpels removed and one carpel in medial section (right). **G.** Stem with infructescence and base of leaf; note multiple fruits from a single flower. **H.** Seed. Reprinted with permission from Mori et al. (2002). Artist: Bobbi Angell.

dispersed by humans because of its medicinal properties) but is most likely native to the Guianas. Although found throughout tropical South America (especially the widespread *Simaba cedron*), *Simaba* is most diverse in the Planalto of Brazil, where it is found in the drier, more open *cerrado*. *Castela* is a shrubby, thorny genus of arid areas and is most diverse in Mexico.

Family classification. The Simaroubaceae, placed in the Sapindales by Cronquist, have close affinities with the Rutaceae, Sapindaceae, Anacardiaceae, Burseraceae, Meliaceae, and Cneoraceae. Molecular data support this placement in

the Sapindales. The Rutaceae, having in common similar chemistry and wood anatomy, differ from Simaroubaceae in the presence of punctate glands and in the absence of the quassinoid compounds unique to the Simaroubaceae. The Burseraceae and Anacardiaceae, although morphologically similar, differ from the Simaroubaceae in having resinous inner bark, distinct wood anatomy, and the absence of quassinoids. Meliaceae usually differ in having connate filaments.

Engler divided the family into six subfamilies with most genera in the large Simarouboideae and the rest scattered in the remaining five subfamilies. These five subfamilies have subsequently been removed from the Simaroubaceae and placed in other families; Surianoideae as Surianaceae, Kirkioideae as the Kirkiaceae, Irvingioideae as the Irvingiaceae, and the Picramnioideae and Alvaradoideae as separate genera within the Picramniaceae. Molecular analysis confirms that the Simaroubaceae should be limited to Engler's subfamily, Simarouboideae, but that it should also include the monotypic family Leitneriaceae endemic to the southeastern United States.

Features of the family. Habit: trees or shrubs, rarely herbaceous with woody rootstocks (species of *Simaba*). Stipules absent. Leaves alternate, compound, rarely simple (*Castela*); leaflets 1–29. Inflorescences axillary or terminal, paniculate, sometimes racemose, cymose, or of solitary flowers. Flowers actinomorphic, bisexual or unisexual (plants dioecious in *Simarouba* and *Castela* and andromonoecious or functionally dioecious in *Picrasma* and *Ailanthus*); perianth 5-merous, or 4–8-merous in *Castela*; androecium usually with stamens twice as many as petals or equal to petals in *Picrasma* and *Picrolemma*, the stamens alternating with staminodia in *Picrasma* and *Picrolemma*, the filaments appendaged in *Quassia*, *Simaba*, and *Simarouba*; gynoecium with carpels borne on gynophore or disc, the ovaries superior, the carpels usually as many as petals, distinct or weakly united, the styles basally united, the stigmas divergent or capitate; ovules apical and pendulous to basal and ascending, usually solitary. Fruits drupaceous (technically each is a druparium), the druparia 1(2–5). Seeds 1 per druparium.

The largest species are rain-forest trees reaching 25 m in height (*Simarouba amara*, *S. glauca*, *Simaba guianensis*, and *Picrasma excelsa*). The smallest are fire-adapted, suffruticose species of *Simaba*, such as *S. pohliana* from the Brazilian *cerrado*, that are almost herbaceous above ground but with an enlarged, woody, underground rootstock.

Species of *Castela* have small, simple leaves that are often caducous and two species of *Simaba* (*S. obovata* and *S. monophylla*) are unifoliolate. The number of leaflets can be as many as 29 in *Simaba cedron*.

The Simaroubaceae possess a characteristic "bitter principle." This bitter taste, found in most genera, comes from the presence of a compound unique to the family, the quassinoids. More than 80 quassinoids have been isolated, and many have been found to possess potential medicinal qualities.

Natural history. Pollination is accomplished by insects, and most species possess more or less small, open flowers accessible to a variety of visitors. *Simarouba amara*, for example, has small cream-colored flowers and is pollinated by many different small insects. Some genera (e.g., *Simaba* and *Quassia*), however, have elongate flowers and staminal appendages that may restrict access by certain visitors. *Quassia amara*, with deep pink, 4-centimeter-long flowers, is pollinated by bees and hummingbirds.

Little is known about the specifics of dispersal, but it is likely carried out by animals. *Castela texana*, for instance, is dispersed by birds and small mammals in southern Texas. Ants nest in the hollow stems of both species of *Picrolemma*. The giant red-winged grasshopper (*Tropidacris cristata*, Romaleidae) often feeds on species rich in secondary compounds and has been found feeding on *Quassia amara* in Costa Rica and on *Simaba cedron* in Amazonia.

The leaves of some species of *Simaba* are infected by ascomycete fungi in the genus *Phyllachora*. In Panama, *P. concentrica* forms rings of infection that create a curious target-like pattern. The Kuna Indians of San Blas Island, Panama, call the infected plants "*sapi garda*" and believe that they have medicinal properties that can enhance intelligence.

Economic uses. In the neotropics, the Simaroubaceae are not of great economic importance. *Simarouba amara* and *S. glauca* are planted as low-grade timber and pulp trees because they are relatively fast-growing. The fruits of *S. glauca* are edible and are sold for their oil in southern Mexico. Extracts of the wood or bark of *Picrasma* and *Quassia* have been used commercially as bitter flavorings and as substitutes for hops.

Although there has been no large-scale pharmaceutical exploitation of this family, the quassinoids present in many species of Simaroubaceae have been proven clinically to be effective against amoeba infections, malaria, and some forms of cancer. The American genera are used locally against a variety of ailments including dysentery, intermittent fever, malaria, dyspepsia, anorexia, and intestinal worms.

References. Bawa, K. S., S. H. Bullock, D. R. Perry, R. E. Coville, and M. H. Grayum. 1985. Reproductive biology of tropical lowland rain forest trees. Part 2. Pollination systems. *Amer. J. Bot.* 72:346–56. Cronquist, A. 1944a. Studies in the Simaroubaceae—I. The genus *Castela*. *J. Arnold Arbor.* 25:122–28. Cronquist, A. 1944b. Studies in the Simaroubaceae—II. The genus *Simarouba*. *Bull. Torrey Bot. Club* 71:226–34. Cronquist, A. 1944c. Studies in the Simaroubaceae—III. The Genus *Simaba*. *Lloydia* 7:81–92. Cronquist, A. 1944d. Studies in the Simaroubaceae—IV. Resume of the American genera. *Brittonia* 5:128–47. Engler, A. 1931. Simarubaceae. In *Die Natürlichen Pflantzenfamilien*, A. Engler and K. Prantl, 2nd ed. 19a:359–405. Leipzig: Wilhelm Engelmann. Fernando, E. S., P. A. Gadek, and C. J. Quinn. 1995. Simaroubaceae, an artificial construct: evidence from *rbc*L sequence variation. *Amer. J. Bot.* 82: 92–103. Morton, J. F. 1981. *Atlas of Medicinal Plants of Middle America*. Springfield, IL: Charles C. Thomas Publ. Nooteboom, H. P. 1966. Simaroubaceae. *Fl. Malesiana*, ser. 1, 6:193–226. Alphen Aan Den Rijn, Netherlands: Sijthoff and Noordhoff International Publishers. Nooteboom, H. P. 1972. Simaroubaceae. *Fl. Malesiana*, ser. 1, 6: 968–72. Alphen Aan Den Rijn, Netherlands: Sijthoff and Noordhoff International Publishers. Roubik, D. W., N, M. Holbrook, and G. Parra V. 1985. Roles of nectar robbers in reproduction of the tropical treelet *Quassia amara* (Simaroubaceae). *Oecologia* 66:161–67. Rowell, H. F. 1983. *Tropidacris cristata*. In *Costa Rican Natural History*, ed. D. H. Janzen, 772–73. Chicago: Univ. of Chicago Press. Thomas, W. W. 1990. The American genera of Simaroubaceae and their distribution. *Acta Bot. Brasil.* 4:11–18.

SIPARUNACEAE (Siparuna Family)

Susanne S. Renner

Figure 184, Plate 45

- *shrubs, treelets, or trees*

- *plants with pungent, lemonlike smell present when leaves, fruits, or bark crushed/slashed*

- *leaves opposite or whorled, simple*

- *flowers unisexual, usually small and inconspicuous; stamens and carpels usually many*

- *fruits drupelets enclosed in fleshy receptacle, the drupelets usually with a reddish-orange fleshy aril*

Numbers of genera and species. Worldwide, the Siparunaceae comprise two genera, *Glossocalyx* and *Siparuna*, and about 60 species. In tropical America, there is a single genus, *Siparuna*, and at least 60 species, some yet to be described. Based on a molecular phylogenetic analysis, a second Neotropical genus, *Bracteanthus*, should be considered part of *Siparuna*.

Distribution and habitat. Species of *Siparuna* occur from tropical Mexico south through Central America, the Lesser

Antilles, Trinidad, and northern South America to Bolivia and Paraguay. The single species of *Glossocalyx* (*G. longicuspis*) consists of shrubs or treelets that occur in Cameroon, Gabon, the Congo, and Nigeria, and on the island of Bioko (Fernando Póo).

Siparunaceae are found in moist forests from the lowlands to 3,800 meters. They are most diverse in Andean midelevation forests, especially in Peru, Ecuador, and Colombia. A few species occur in gallery forests in Central and South American grasslands.

Family classification. The Siparunaceae were included in the Monimiaceae and placed in the Laurales by Cronquist; however, they are out of place in Monimiaceae as demonstrated by morphological and molecular data. Instead, they are most closely related to two extratropical Southern Hemisphere families, Gomortegaceae, with one species in Chile, and Atherospermataceae, with two species in Chile and 12 species in Australasia (a few of them in subtropical and tropical forest). A phylogenetic analysis of Siparunaceae based on DNA sequences shows that *Glossocalyx* is sister to *Siparuna* and that the morphologically unusual species *S. decipiens* is sister to all other species of *Siparuna*. Most of the circa 14 monoecious species of *Siparuna* are basal to the dioecious species, but two are nested among dioecious species, showing that dioecy evolved at least twice within the genus. There is little morphological reason, or need, to subdivide the genus.

Features of the family. Habit: shrubs, treelets, or trees (to 40 m); exudates rarely present (e.g., *Siparuna pachyantha* and *S. decipiens*). **Stipules** absent. **Leaves** opposite or in whorls of 3–6, simple; blade margins entire or denticulate. **Inflorescences** axillary or borne on leafless nodes of older wood, cymes. **Flowers** actinomorphic, unisexual (plants monoecious or dioecious), without traces of opposite sex organs; perigon of 4–6 distinct or basally connate tepals or perigon calyptrate (*S. decipiens*), the tepals cream, yellowish orange, or more rarely reddish (perhaps in early fruiting stages); androecium with 1–72 stamens, the stamens usually many, arranged irregularly inside receptacle, only upper part exposed through hole in floral roof, the filaments usually distinct, rarely laterally fused, lacking glandular appendages, dehiscing by single apically hinged valve; gynoecium apocarpous, the ovaries superior, the carpels 3–30, usually many, enclosed in receptacle throughout anthesis and early fruit development, the styles distinct, the stigmas decurrent, only upper part of styles and stigmas exposed via small central hole in floral roof; placentation basal, the ovules 1 per locule, anatropous, unitegmic, crassinucellate. **Fruits** drupelets enclosed in fleshy receptacle, the receptacle smooth or with spines or tubercles, red or rarely yellow, usually bursting open to display drupelets at maturity, the drupelets usually with an aril, the aril fleshy, red or orange. **Seeds** 1 per drupelet.

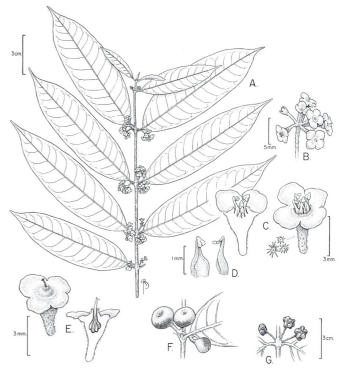

Figure 184. SIPARUNACEAE. *Siparuna poeppigii*. **A.** Stem with leaves and staminate inflorescences. **B.** Part of staminate inflorescence. **C.** Oblique-apical view (right) and medial section (left) of staminate flowers with detail of stellate-lepidote hairs (center). **D.** Adaxial (left) and lateral (right) views of stamens. **E.** Oblique-apical view (left) and medial section (right) of pistillate flowers. **F.** Fresh fruits. **G.** Dried fruits. Reprinted with permission from Mori et al. (2002). Artist: Bobbi Angell.

Siparunaceae are easily recognized in the field by the peculiar and pungent, lemonlike smell that their leaves, fruits, or bark give off when crushed or slashed.

In some species (e.g., *Siparuna decipiens*, *S. glycycarpa*), the receptacle does not burst open at maturity and these same species lack an aril around their drupelets.

Natural history. Flowers of *Siparuna* are pollinated at night by gall midges (cecidomyiids) that use the flowers as brood sites for their larvae. To lay an egg, the female midge inserts her abdomen into the central opening in the floral roof and moves it rhythmically for about one to two minutes. If the flower is male, the midge's hairy abdomen becomes covered with pollen, and pollination is accomplished when the midge visits a female flower. Male flowers apparently are better sites for egg laying or larval development; at least, female flowers and mature fruits are rarely found to contain larvae.

The arillate drupelets of *Siparuna* are bird-dispersed. The fat-rich arils are especially attractive to flycatchers, some of which are *Siparuna* specialists (e.g., the ochre-bellied flycatcher, *Mionectes oleagineus*). Other birds seen taking the fruitlets are red-legged honeycreepers (*Cyanerpes cyaneus*), blue-black grosbeaks (*Cyanocompsa cyanoides*), and red-capped manakins (*Pipra mentalis*). The large fruiting receptacles of species such as *S. cristata*, *S. decipiens*, and *S. pachyantha* are taken and eaten by bats and monkeys that feed on the receptacles.

Economic uses. Native people throughout the neotropics use extracts of leaves or "fruits" of *Siparuna* to prepare baths that are thought to help cure headaches, colds, fevers, stomachaches, diarrhea, and a range of other physical and spiritual afflictions. Snakebites, insect bites, or herpes sores are believed to heal more speedily after the application of *Siparuna* leaves. That extracts of *Siparuna* indeed have antiplasmodial activity and their effectiveness as an antimalarial remedy has been confirmed by recent pharmaceutical trials.

References. ANTONIO, T. M., WALLER, G. R., AND C. J. MUSSINAN. 1984. Composition of essential oil from the leaves of *Siparuna guianensis*. *Chemica Indigena (London)* 14:514–15. FEIL, J. P. 1992. Reproductive ecology of dioecious *Siparuna* (Monimiaceae) in Ecuador—a case of gall midge pollination. *Bot. J. Linn. Soc.* 110:171–203. LÓPEZ, J. A., Y. ALY, AND P. L. SCHIFF, JR. 1988. Alkaloids of *Siparuna pauciflora*. *Pl. Med.* 54(6):552–53. RENNER, S. S., AND G. HAUSNER. 1997. Siparunaceae and Monimiaceae. In *Flora of Ecuador*, eds. G. Harling and L. Andersson, no. 59: 1–125. Göteborg, Sweden: Department of Systematic Botany, University of Göteborg. RENNER S. S., AND G. HAUSNER. In rev. Siparunaceae. *Fl. Neotrop. Mongr.* RENNER, S. S., A. E. SCHWARZBACH, AND L. LOHMANN. 1997. Phylogenetic position and floral function of *Siparuna* (Siparunaceae: Laurales). *Intern. J. Pl. Sci.* 158(6 Suppl.):S89–S98. RENNER, S. S., AND H. WON. 2001. Repeated evolution of dioecy from monoecy in *Siparuna* (Siparunaceae, Laurales). *Syst. Biol.* 50:700–12.

SOLANACEAE (Potato Family)

MICHAEL NEE

Figures 185, 186; Plate 46

- *shrubs, trees, vines, or herbs*
- *leaves alternate, usually simple; blades never with sharp teeth*
- *flowers with base of stamen filaments adnate to corolla tube; locules 2*
- *fruits capsules or berries*

Numbers of genera and species. Worldwide, the Solanaceae comprise about 95 genera and 2,200 species, but the total for the family depends largely on the estimate of species for *Solanum*, which is estimated by different authors to have from about 1,000 to more than 2,000 species, but most likely encompasses about 1,200 species (ca. 700 Neotropical). In tropical America, there are 63 genera and approximately 1,575 species.

Distribution and habitat. The Solanaceae occur throughout the world, with the greatest representation in the Tropics and subtropics. They are absent from arctic regions. The neotropics, particularly South America, is the clear center of diversity at both the generic and specific levels. In South America, about two-thirds of the genera have native representatives and about one-third of the total genera are endemic.

Australia is home to the endemic subfamily Anthocercideae, but otherwise only the genera *Solanum* (with about 110 species including an endemic subgenus *Archaesolanum*), *Nicotiana*, and *Physalis* are native to that continent. Africa has a considerable number of species of *Solanum* (ca. 100), along with *Physalis*, *Lycium*, *Withania*, and the endemic *Discopodium* of East Africa and *Tsoala* of Madagascar. Eurasia has a relatively small number of species, but includes several endemic genera.

The family is found in nearly all habitats, from the driest to the wettest. Relatively few genera and species are found in lowland rain forests on poor soil, but the family is well represented in tropical montane rain forests and in seasonally dry forests on good soils.

Family classification. The Solanaceae are placed in the Solanales by Cronquist. The family is close to the Hydrophyllaceae and Boraginaceae, although often, including in molecular analyses, they are placed next to the Convolvulaceae, which much more nearly resemble the Gentianales. Studies suggest that the Nolanaceae should be included in the Solanaceae; however, the Nolanaceae and Solanaceae are treated as separate families in this book. The Caribbean *Goetzea* is treated by some in the Solanaceae and by others as a separate family, the Goetzeaceae.

The family has traditionally been divided into two major subfamilies, the Cestroideae and the Solanoideae (the first of which is restricted to the Western Hemisphere), and the small subfamily Anthocercideae (found only in Australia and adjacent islands). The Cestroideae are characterized by capsular fruits (except *Cestrum* with berries), angular seeds, and

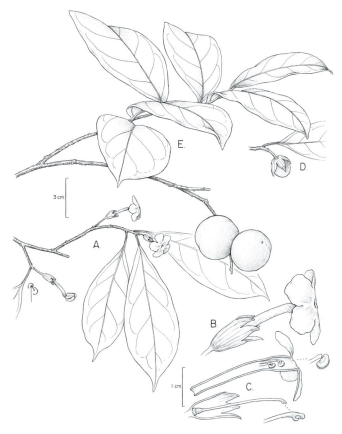

Figure 185. SOLANACEAE. *Brunfelsia guianensis*. **A.** Stem with leaves and flowers. **B.** Lateral view of flower. **C.** Medial section of corolla with detail of stamen (above) and gynoecium surrounded by one-half of calyx with detail of stigma (below). **D.** Lateral view of immature fruit on stem. **E.** Stem with leaves and two mature fruits. Reprinted with permission from Mori et al. (2002). Artist: Bobbi Angell.

straight or nearly straight embryos. The Solanoideae have baccate fruits, reniform-flattened seeds, and curved embryos. The Solanoideae are found worldwide.

Features of the family. Habit: shrubs, trees, vines, or herbs. **Wood** usually soft. **Stipules** absent, modified stipulelike leaves sometimes present. **Leaves** alternate, simple or less often pinnately compound; blades often somewhat fleshy, the margins entire or variously lobed, but without sharp teeth. **Inflorescences** terminal or axillary, or, in *Solanum*, usually emergent from stem between nodes, often cymose (the flowers in one-sided racemelike cymes), the cymose inflorescences paniculate or racemose. **Flowers** actinomorphic or zygomorphic, usually bisexual, unisexual in some *Solanum* (plants andromonoecious; i.e., inflorescence including basal bisexual flower(s) and distal male flowers; rarely dioecious); calyx usually 5-lobed, the lobes never imbricate, the tube (and sometimes the lobes) often enlarged in fruit; corolla sympetalous, usually 5-lobed; androecium of 4–5 stamens, the base of filaments adnate to corolla tube, the anthers longitudinally or poricidally dehiscent; nectary often present at ovary base;

gynoecium syncarpous, the ovary superior, the carpels usually 2, rarely 5 (*Nicandra*), the locules 2, the style 1, the stigmas sometimes 2-lobed, never split (as in the related families Hydrophyllaceae or Boraginaceae-Ehretioideae); placentation axile, the ovules few–numerous. **Fruits** capsules (most Cestroideae) or berries (Solanoideae). **Seeds** usually numerous, prismatic and sometimes winged (Cestroideae) or reniform-flattened (Solanoideae); embryo straight (Cestroideae) or curved (Solanoideae).

Many species, including cultivated potatoes, tomatoes, chilies, petunias, etc., are herbaceous. Both herbaceous and soft-woody vines occur in the family and a few species are epiphytes or hemiepiphytes. Very few species are forest trees, but some may reach 30 meters. Subgenus *Leptostemonum* of *Solanum* is characterized by sharp prickles. Species with four stamens usually have bilaterally symmetrical corollas.

Natural history. Several Amazonian species of *Markea* are epiphytes or hemiepiphytes that are associated with nests of stinging ants.

Pollination is accomplished by a great variety of insects and vertebrates, and the flowers vary in form (actinomorphic or zygomorphic) and size (very small to 30 cm long in hawkmoth-pollinated *Solandra* and *Datura*), depending on the pollinator. The flowers of *Solanum*, *Lycianthes*, and *Lycopersicon* (a total of about 950 species in the neotropics) produce no nectar. They are buzz-pollinated by bees whose reward is the pollen with which they feed their broods. This is the largest group of buzz-pollinated plants in the angiosperms. This pollination system has resulted in modification of the anthers from longitudinally dehiscent (typical of the rest of the Solanaceae) to poricidally dehiscent.

The berries are generally dispersed by birds or mammals. Fruit-eating bats, such as species of *Sturnira*, are important dispersers of the seeds of *Solanum* into disturbed areas.

Economic uses. The family is characterized by a general adaptation to disturbed and often nutrient-rich habitats. This has allowed some species to become aggressively invasive weeds of pastures or cultivated fields; e.g., jimson weed (*Datura stramonium*) and horsenettle (*Solanum carolinense*).

The potato (*Solanum tuberosum*) from the Andes of Peru and Bolivia is the fourth most important food plant by weight worldwide. Other major domesticated species include the tomato (*Lycopersicon esculentum*), eggplant (*Solanum melongena*), and chilies (*Capsicum* species). Minor crops are the tree-tomato (*Cyphomandra betacea*), pepino (*Solanum muricatum*), and uchuva (*Physalis peruviana*).

The family also is known for the large number of alkaloids of various kinds, giving it a well-deserved reputation for being poisonous. The addictive alkaloid nicotine is found in high quantities in some species of *Nicotiana*, notably *N. tabacum*. This species does not exist in the wild, but is a tetraploid hybrid derivative from two wild and very different species, *N. tomentosiformis* and *N. sylvestris*, from Bolivia and

Figure 186. SOLANACEAE. *Solanum rugosum*. **A.** Stem with leaves and inflorescence. **B.** Detail of abaxial leaf surface showing stellate pubescence and single trichome (above) with rays and midpoint. **C.** Lateral view of flower bud. **D.** Apical view of flower at anthesis. **E.** Medial section of flower. **F.** Transverse section of ovary. **G.** Adaxial (left) and lateral (right) views of stamens. **H.** Infructescence (above) and transverse section of fruit (below). Reprinted with permission from Mori et al. (2002). Artist: Bobbi Angell.

northwestern Argentina. It arose in pre-Columbian times and has been spread worldwide in cultivation to become the nearly exclusive raw material for tobacco products. Other Solanaceae, such as *Datura* (including *Brugmansia*), have been sources of steroid alkaloids in medicine and have been used widely as hallucinogens.

The family includes ornamentals, such as hybrids of *Petunia*, species of *Brunfelsia*, *Datura*, *Browallia*, *Solandra*, *Streptosolen*, and *Iochroma*. All of these are native to the Western Hemisphere.

References. BOHS, L. 1994. *Cyphomandra* (Solanaceae). *Fl. Neotrop. Monogr.* 63:1–175. D'ARCY, W. G. 1991. The Solanaceae since 1976, with a review of its biogeography. In *Solanaceae III: Taxonomy, Chemistry, Evolution*, eds. J. G. Hawkes, R. N. Lester, M. Nee, and N. Estrada-R., 75–137. Richmond, Surrey, U.K.: Royal Botanic Gardens, Kew. HUNZIKER, A. T. 1979. South American Solanaceae: a synoptic survey. In *The Biology and Taxonomy of the Solanaceae*, eds. J. G. Hawkes, R. N. Lester, and A. D. Skelding, 49–85. London: Academic Press (for Linnean Society of London, symposium series no. 7). HUNZIKER, A. T. 2001. *Genera Solanacearum: The Genera of Solanaceae Illustrated, Arranged According to a New System*. Ruggell, Lichtenstein: A.R.G. Gantner. NEE, M. 1999. A synopsis of *Solanum* in the New World. In *Solanaceae IV: Advances in Classification and Utilization*, eds. M. Nee, D. E. Symon, R. N. Lester, and J. P. Jessop, 285–333. London: Royal Botanic Gardens, Kew. OLMSTEAD, R. G., J. A. SWEERE, R. E. SPANGLER, L. BOHS, AND J. D. PALMER. 1999. Phylogeny and provisional classification of the Solanaceae based on chloroplast DNA. In *Solanaceae IV: Advances in Classification and Utilization*, eds. M. Nee, D. E. Symon, R. N. Lester, and J. P. Jessop, 111–37. London: Royal Botanic Gardens, Kew.

SPHENOCLEACEAE (Sphenoclea Family)

JOHN L. BROWN

Plate 46

- *herbs of wet places*
- *large vertical air passages present in cortex*
- *leaves alternate, simple*
- *flowers actinomorphic, bisexual; corolla sympetalous*
- *fruits capsules, membranous*

Numbers of genera and species. Worldwide, the Sphenocleaceae comprise a single genus, *Sphenoclea*, with two species.

Distribution and habitat. *Sphenoclea zeylanica* is pantropical and a second species is endemic to West Africa. It is found in wet places from the southern United States throughout South America (except Argentina and Chile).

Family classification. Based on embryological and pollen characters, the Sphenocleaceae are placed in the Campanulales by Cronquist, although habit similarities suggest a relationship to the Phytolaccaceae. Molecular studies by the Angiosperm Phylogeny Group align the Sphenocleaceae in the

Solanales of the euasterids I, near families such as the Sola-naceae and Convolvulaceae.

Features of the family. Habit: herbs, annual, somewhat suc-culent, large vertical air passages present in cortex. **Stipules** absent. **Leaves** alternate, simple; blade margins entire. **Inflo-rescences** terminal, spikes; bracts small; bracteoles 2. **Flow-ers** actinomorphic, bisexual; calyx synsepalous, 5-lobed; corolla sympetalous, 5-lobed, light green, caducous; androe-cium of 5 stamens, the stamens fused to corolla base, the filaments short, the anthers dehiscing longitudinally; gynoe-cium syncarpous, the ovary inferior or subinferior, the car-pels 2, the locules 2, the stigma short, capitiate; placentation axile, the ovules numerous, anatropous. **Fruits** capsules, mem-branous. **Seeds** numerous.

Natural history. Nothing is known about the pollination and dispersal biology of this family.

Economic uses. *Sphenoclea zeylandica* often grows as a weed in rice beds

References. WILBUR, R. L. 2001. Sphenocleaceae. In *Flora de Nicaragua*, eds. W. D. Stevens, C. Ulloa Ulloa, and O. M. Montiel, no. III: 2426–27.

STAPHYLEACEAE (Bladdernut Family)

GERARDO A. AYMARD C.

Figure 187

- *trees or shrubs*

- *leaves opposite or alternate, usually imparipinnate or trifoliolate*

- *sepals and petals (4)5; stamens 5; ovary superior; annular disc present*

- *fruits berries or membranous inflated capsules*

Numbers of genera and species. Worldwide the Staphy-leaceae comprise about five genera and 50–60 species. In tropical America, there are three genera and 17 species. *Tur-pinia* has 12 Neotropical species (30–40 worldwide); *Sta-phylea* has one Neotropical species (9 or 10 worldwide); and *Huertea*, with four species, is endemic to the neotropics.

Distribution and habitat. Staphyleaceae are distributed pri-marily in the northern regions of both the Eastern and the Western Hemispheres, but the family also extends into the Andes, the West Indies, and parts of Eastern Asia. *Staphylea* is principally temperature in both Asia and America but reaches Mexico, *Turpinia* is pantropical, and *Huertea* ranges from Honduras to the Andes of Venezuela, Colombia, Ecua-dor, and Peru and is also found in Cuba and Hispaniola. The Asian *Euscaphis* and *Taspicia* are monotypic. To date, the family is unknown from the Guayanan Shield and the Ama-zon Basin.

Species of Staphyleaceae occur in forests at low and high elevations. *Huertea* and *Turpinia* are common trees in wet forests up to 3,000 meters.

Family classification. The Staphyleaceae have been sug-gested to have phylogenetic relationships with several groups.

These conflicting points of view have centered around place-ment of the family in Celastrales, Sapindales (*sensu* Cronquist), or the Cunoniaceae/Saxifragaceae. Contemporary systematists, however, consider the Staphyleaceae to be primitive mem-bers of the Sapindales. Features such as the five-parted calyx and corolla, flowers with a disc, pinnately compound leaves, and follicular fruits support a common ancestry with the Sa-pindaceae. Other authors have emphasized similarities in flo-ral morphology and anatomy between the Staphyleaceae and Saxifragaceae *sensu lato*. Flowers in both families are typi-cally actinomorphic, have a pentamerous perianth, and fre-quently share adnation of sepal, petal, and stamen filaments into a floral cup fused basally with the gynoecium; however, *rbc*L sequence data for representatives of the families of a putative sapindalean/rutalean alliance, demonstrate that sev-eral families previously placed in the Sapindales, like Staph-yleaceae, show no affinity to core sapindalean taxa. The molecular evidence suggests affinities with *Crossosoma* (Cros-sosomataceae) and the Geraniaceae.

The Staphyleaceae are divided into two subfamilies. The Staphyleoideae, consisting of *Euscaphis*, *Staphylea*, and *Tur-pinia*, are characterized by opposite leaves, stipules, sepals always more or less separate, disc usually distinct, carpels not united their entire length, capsular fruits, and wood with

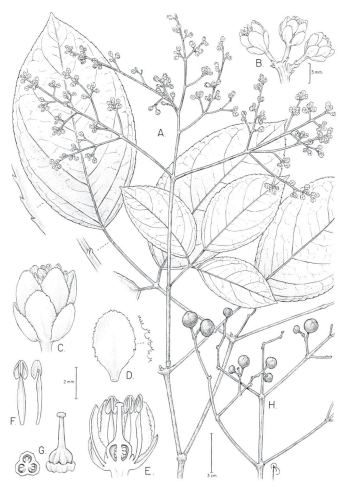

nate. **Inflorescences** terminal or axillary in upper leaves, paniculate or thyrsiform. **Flowers** actinomorphic, bisexual or sometimes unisexual (then plants monoecious); trichomes often present, unicellular or multicellular, uniseriate, nonglandular; sepals (4)5, free, variously connate, imbricate, alternate with petals; petals (4)5, distinct or fused with floral tube; androecium of 5 stamens, the stamens alternate with petals, born in a single cycle, often seated external to and below lobed, annular disc, the filaments complanate, the anthers dorsifixed, 2-lobed, dehiscing by longitudinal slits; annular disc present; gynoecium with superior ovary, the ovary entire, lobed, or 3-parted, sometimes embedded in disc, the carpels 1–3(4), distinct or united, locules 1(4), the styles 1–3, distinct to completely fused, the stigma capitate; placentation axile, basal, or near basal, the ovules 1–2–many (6–12), bitegmic, anatropous. **Fruits** berries or membranous inflated capsules. **Seeds** 1–few; endosperm fleshy, the embryo straight.

Natural history. Knowledge of pollination systems and dispersal agents of the Staphyleaceae is limited; however, insect pollination seems to be most likely. Flowers in many species are adapted to long-tongued insects. In addition, the hypogynous disc surrounding the ovary has been reported to be nectar-secreting.

Economic uses. Several species of *Staphylea* are used as ornamentals, and *Turpinia occidentalis* of the West Indies is the source of a useful wood.

References. BISSE, J. 1988. *Arboles de Cuba*. La Habana: Editorial Cientifico-Tecnica. CARLQUIST, S., AND D. A. HOEKMAN. 1985. Wood anatomy of Staphyleaceae: ecology, statistical correlations, and systematics. *Flora* 177:195–216. CROAT, T. 1976. Staphyleaceae. In Flora of Panama. *Ann. Missouri Bot. Gard.* R. E. Woodson, Jr., R. W. Schery and collaborators. 63:393–98. DICKISON, W. C. 1986. Floral morphology and anatomy of Staphyleaceae. *Bot. Gaz.* 147(3): 312–26. DICKISON, W. C. 1987. A palynological study of the Staphyleaceae. *Grana* 26:11–24. GADEK, P. A., E. S. FERNANDO, C. J. QUINN, S. H. HOOT, T. TERRAZAS, M. C. SHEAHAN, AND M. W. CHASE. 1996. Sapindales: molecular delimitation and infraordinal groups. *Amer. J. Bot.* 83(6): 802–11. SALES, F., AND I. C. HEDGE. 1996. Biogeographical aspects of selected SW Asiatic woody taxa. *Ann. Naturhist. Mus. Wien.* 98(suppl.):149–61. SOSA, V. 1988. Staphyleaceae. In *Flora de Veracruz*, eds. A. Gómez-Pompa et al., fasc. 57:1–11. Xalapa, Mexico: INIREB. SPONGBERG, S. 1971. Staphyleaceae in the southeastern United States. *J. Arnold Arbor.* 52:196–203. STANDLEY, P., AND J. STEYERMARK. 1949. Staphyleaceae. In Flora of Panama. *Fieldiana, Bot.* 24(6):223–25. UMADEVI, I., M. DANIEL, AND S. D. SABNIS. 1986. Inter-relationships among the families Aceraceae, Melianthaceae and Staphyleaceae. *J. Pl. Anat. Morphol.* 3(2): 169–72.

Figure 187. STAPHYLEACEAE. *Turpinia occidentalis* (A–G, Callejas et al. 8450; H, Zak 1221). **A.** Stem with leaves and inflorescence. **B.** Part of inflorescence. **C.** Lateral view of flower. **D.** Adaxial view of petal with detail of margin. **E.** Medial section of flower. **F.** Adaxial (left) and lateral (right) views of stamens. **G.** Lateral view of gynoecium (right) and transverse section of ovary (left). Original. Artist: Bobbi Angell.

bordered pits. The subfamily Tapiscioideae, consisting of *Huertea* and *Taspicia*, are distinguished by alternate leaves, sometimes simple leaves, stipules not always present, sepals fused, disc small or absent, carpels totally fused, drupaceous or baccate fruits, and wood with simple pits. However, results from molecular studies suggest that the subfamily Tapiscioideae (including *Huertea*) is not related to the remainder of the family. Evidently, the affinities of Staphyleaceae will not be resolved until a more intensive sampling of its putative relatives has been undertaken.

Features of the family. Habit: trees or shrubs. **Stipules** and stipels usually present, sometimes reduced to glands or absent. **Leaves** opposite or rarely alternate, imparipinnate or trifoliolate, or rarely simple; leaflets serrate; venation pin-

STERCULIACEAE (Chocolate Family)

<small>Paul A. Fryxell</small>

Figures. 188, 189; Plate 47

- *trees, shrubs, or subshrubs*

- *leaves alternate, usually simple, sometimes palmately compound; stellate hairs commonly present*

- *flowers often with staminodes; ovary superior*

Numbers of genera and species. Worldwide, the Sterculiaceae comprise 67 genera and almost 1,800 species. In tropical America, there are 16 genera and about 450 species. The Neotropical *Chiranthodendron*, *Neoregnellia*, and *Rayleya* are monotypic. The most speciose genera are *Ayenia*, *Byttneria*, *Helicteres*, *Melochia*, *Sterculia*, and *Waltheria*.

Distribution and habitat. Sterculiaceae have a wide distribution in the Americas, Africa, Asia, Australia, and Oceania. In the Western Hemisphere, species range from the southernmost United States to northern Argentina and Uruguay.

The family is found in a wide variety of habitats, including seasonally dry forests, wet forests, scrub vegetation, and along beaches.

Family classification. The Sterculiaceae are placed in the Malvales by Cronquist. However, recent molecular analyses suggest that the Sterculiaceae are an artificial group (see Malvales). Of the numerous tribes recognized, five may be found in the neotropics: the Sterculieae, including the pantropical *Sterculia* (ca. 200 species) plus several Eastern Hemisphere genera; the Hermannieae, including *Hermannia* (ca. 300 species, four from the Western Hemisphere), *Melochia* (>50 species, mostly Neotropical), *Physodium* (four Mexican species), *Waltheria* (ca. 60 species, mostly Neotropical), and *Dicarpidium* (1 Australian species); the Byttnerieae, including *Byttneria* (ca. 130 tropical species, of which ca. 80 are Neotropical), *Ayenia* (ca. 70 Neotropical and subtropical), *Rayleya* (one species from Brazil), *Herrania* (ca. 20 Neotropical), *Theobroma* (ca. 20 Neotropical species), *Guazuma* (4 Neotropical), and five or six Eastern Hemisphere genera; the Helictereae, including *Helicteres* (>60 worldwide; 38 Neotropical), *Reevesia* (ca. 20 tropical, 2 of which are Mexican, the remainder Asian), the monotypic Cuban *Neoregnellia*, plus three Eastern Hemisphere genera; and the Fremontieae, including *Fremontodendron* (1–3 species from California and northern Mexico), *Chiranthodendron* (1 from Mexico), and the hybrid between them, *Chiranthofremontia lenzii*. Arguments have been put forward that the Fremontieae are better placed in the Bombacaceae allied to the genus *Bernoullia*, rather than in the Sterculiaceae, but the matter is not yet resolved.

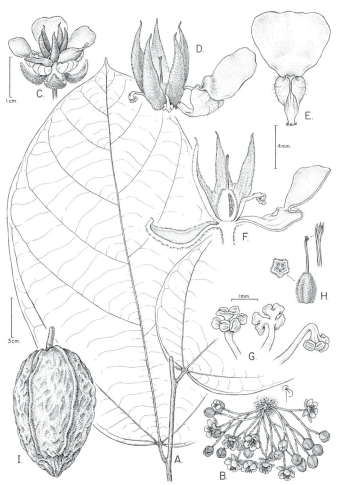

Figure 188. STERCULIACEAE. *Theobroma velutinum*. **A.** Stem with leaves. **B.** Cauliflorous inflorescence. **C.** Apical-lateral view of flower. **D.** Lateral view of flower with some petals removed to show style in center of five staminodes; note two stamens (left and center) and one petal with stamen inserted into petal (right). **E.** Adaxial view of petal showing pocket (or hood) into which the stamen is inserted. **F.** Medial section of flower; note stellate pubescence on abaxial surface of sepals. **G.** Adaxial (left), abaxial (center), and lateral (right) views of anthers. **H.** Lateral view of gynoecium with transverse section of ovary (left) and detail of style (above). **I.** Lateral view of fruit; note pubescence. Reprinted with permission from Mori et al. (2002). Artist: Bobbi Angell.

Uladendron has been assigned to the Malvaceae (tribe Hibisceae), where it evidently does not belong. It is apparently better accommodated in the Sterculiaceae; its affinities are not yet understood but are under investigation.

Features of the family. Habit: trees, shrubs, and subshrubs, less often herbs, sometimes scandent. **Stipules** present. **Leaves** alternate, usually simple, sometimes palmately compound (e.g., some *Sterculia*); stellate hairs commonly present, or hairs simple or glandular; blades usually unlobed but some-

<small>**360** • STERCULIACEAE</small>

times palmately lobed (e.g., some *Sterculia*), with nectaries sometimes present on underside of principal nerves. **Inflorescences** axillary, sometimes leaf-opposed, terminal, or cauliflorous in a few genera, often cymase. **Flowers** actinomorphic or somewhat zygomorphic, bisexual, 5-merous; sepals valvate, more or less synsepalous (inflated in *Physodium*), showy (Sterculieae and Fremontieae and *Physodium*); petals 5 (highly specialized in Byttnerieae) or absent (in Sterculieae and Fremontieae); androecium with 5–many stamens, the stamens prominent (Fremontieae), distinct or connate into tube, or on elongated androgynophore (Helictereae and Sterculieae); staminodes often present as sterile teeth alternating with stamens or groups of stamens; gynoecium apocarpous (Sterculieae) or syncarpous, the ovary superior, the carpels 1 (*Waltheria*) to 5, the locules as many as carpels; placentation axile (or marginal, or deeply intruded parietal), the ovules solitary or numerous. **Fruits** woody or chartaceous, sometimes spiny, rarely fleshy, dehiscent or indehiscent, in *Sterculia* the carpels distinct, radially divergent, with urticating hairs inside. **Seeds** 1–several per carpel.

The stamens of *Chiranthodendron* are the very distinctive "hand-flower" or "monkey's paw" flower that simulates a thumb and four fingers.

The androgynophore, which is prominently developed in *Helicteres* and less so in many of the species of *Ayenia*, is an elongated structure within the flower that elevates both the androecium and the gynoecium well above the sepals.

Natural history. The Sterculiaceae have a wide variety of pollination modes, including bird pollination in *Chiranthodendron*; insect pollination in the highly specialized flowers of *Ayenia*, *Byttneria*, *Theobroma*, and presumably *Guazuma*; and fly pollination in *Sterculia*. The genus was named after the Roman god Sterculius, the god of manure, because of the fetid odor of its flowers, which relates to its mode of pollination. Most species of *Waltheria* and many of *Melochia* have distylous flowers as a means of promoting outcrossing, presumably mediated by insects. *Waltheria* also shows an extreme form of pollen dimorphism related to distyly. Dispersal is relatively less specialized and includes passive dispersal of seeds from fruits without obvious adaptations in such genera as *Ayenia* and *Helicteres*. The more specialized fruits, such as the woody fruits of *Guazuma* and the fleshy fruits of *Theobroma*, evidently are dispersed by animals.

Economic uses. Species of Sterculiaceae are sources of cacao (chocolate, *cupuaçu*), which is obtained from the fermented seeds of *Theobroma* (principally *T. cacao*) and used in making confections and beverages. The flavoring derived from the nuts of African species of *Cola* is used in preparing beverages. Other less important uses are for stem fibers (e.g., *Helicteres*, *Guazuma*), mucilages, gums, and medicinal preparations. This family includes several ornamental trees and shrubs, many introduced from the Eastern Hemisphere, from genera such as *Brachychiton*, *Dombeya*, *Firmiana*, and *Sterculia*. The weedy tree *Guazuma ulmifolia* is often grown in living fences and as a shade tree for livestock. The mucilage of this species, usually extracted from the bark, is used to make a skin lotion and, in the past, was the major ingredient in locally produced hair and shaving creams.

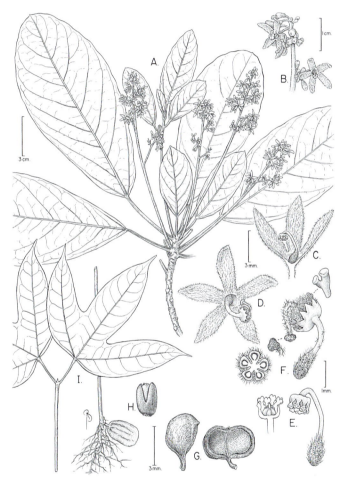

Figure 189. STERCULIACEAE. *Sterculia frondosa*. **A.** Stem with leaves and inflorescences. **B.** Detail of inflorescence. **C.** Lateral view of staminate flower with two perianth units removed. **D.** Apical view of pistillate flower. **E.** Androgynophore of staminate flower with section of apex (left) showing pistillode. **F.** Androgynophore of pistillate flower with details of staminode (above), stigma (below), and transverse section of ovary (left). **G.** Lateral view of intact segment of fruit (left) and adaxial view of dehisced fruit segment (right). **H.** Seed. **I.** Seedling showing three-lobed leaves (left) and cotyledon at base of stem (right). Reprinted with permission from Mori et al. (2002). Artist: Bobbi Angell.

References. BAYER, C., AND K. KUBITZKI. 2003. Malvaceae. In *The Families and Genera of Vascular Plants*, eds. K. Kubitzki and C. Bayer. 5:225–311. Berlin: Springer-Verlag. BERNAL, H. Y., AND J. E. CORRERA Q. 1998. Sterculiaceae (*Guazuma ulmifolia*). In *Especies vegetales promisorias de los países del Convenio Andrés Bello*, Tomo XII. Santafé de Bogotá, D. E., Colombia: Secretaria Ejecutiva del Convenio Andrés Bello. BORNSTEIN, A. J. 1989. Sterculiaceae, In *Flora of the Lesser Antilles: Leeward and Windward Is-*

lands, ed. R. Howard, 5:272–92. Jamaica Plain, MA: Arnold Arboretum, Harvard University. CRISTÓBAL, C. L. 1960. Revisión del género *Ayenia* (Sterculiaceae). *Opera Lilloana* 4: 1–230. CRISTÓBAL, C. L. 1976. Estudio taxonómico del género *Byttneria* Loefling (Sterculiaceae). *Bonplandia* 4:1–428. CRISTÓBAL, C. L. 2001. Taxonomía del género *Helicteres* (Sterculiaceae). Revisión de las especies americanas. *Bonplandia* 51(1–4):1–206. CUATRECASAS, J. 1964. Cacao and its allies: a taxonomic revision of the genus *Theobroma*. *Contr. U.S. Natl. Herb.* 35:379–614. DORR, L. J., AND L. C. BARNETT. 1989. A revision of *Melochia* sect. *Physodium* (Sterculiaceae). from Mexico. *Brittonia* 41:404–23. FREYTAG, G. F. 1951. A revision of the genus *Guazuma*.

Ceiba 1:193–225. FRYXELL, P. A. 2001. Sterculiaceae. In *Flora Novo-Galiciana*, ed. R. McVaugh, 3:110–47. GOLDBERG, A. 1967. The genus *Melochia* L. (Sterculiaceae). *Contr. U.S. Natl. Herb.* 34:191–363 + 9 plates. ROBYNS, A. 1964. Sterculiaceae, Flora of Panama. *Ann Missouri Bot. Gard.* 51:69–106. SAUNDERS, J. G. 1993. Four new distylous species of *Waltheria* (Sterculiaceae) and a key to the Mexican and Central American species and species groups. *Syst. Bot.* 18:356–76. SCHUMANN, C. 1886. Sterculiaceae. In *Flora Brasiliensis*, ed. C. F. P. von Martius, 12(3):1–114. STANDLEY, P. C. 1923. Sterculiaceae. In *Trees and Shrubs of Mexico*, vol. 23:794–814. Contributions from the United States National Herbarium.

STYRACACEAE (Styrax Family)

PETER W. FRITSCH

Figure 190, Plate 47

- *trees or occasionally shrubs*

- *stellate or scalelike hairs present*

- *leaves alternate, simple*

- *flowers typically campanulate; corolla usually white or pinkish*

- *fruits usually drupes*

Numbers of genera and species. Worldwide, the Styracaceae comprise 11 genera and approximately 160 species. In tropical America, there is a single genus, *Styrax*, and approximately 80 species. The largest genus in the family is *Styrax* with 130 species worldwide and approximately 84 species in the Western Hemisphere.

Distribution and habitat. The Styracaceae have a widespread but disjunct distribution, occurring in the Western Hemisphere, the Mediterranean region, and eastern and southeastern Asia.

All genera except *Halesia* and *Styrax* are strictly Asian. *Halesia* is disjunct between China and the United States, and the distribution of *Styrax* essentially mirrors the general distribution of the family. In the Western Hemisphere, *Styrax* occurs from the United States to Uruguay and northwestern Argentina, and is found in all countries of tropical America except Chile and some countries of the West Indies.

Styracaceae are common in upland forests of many types. They also occur in lowland rain forests, subalpine forests, pastures, plantations, and savannas. In the neotropics, *Styrax* is most commonly found between 500 and 2,500 meters.

Figure 190. STYRACACEAE. *Styrax pallidus.* **A.** Stem with leaves and inflorescences; note the valvate corollas of flower buds. **B.** Abaxial leaf surface showing stellate pubescence and stellate hair (below). **C.** Lateral view of flower. **D.** Medial section of flower with gynoecium removed to show connate filament bases adnate to corolla. **E.** Medial section of flower with the corolla and androecium removed; note axile placentation. **F.** Transverse sections of ovary through apex (above), middle (center), and base (below), showing the incomplete partitioning of locules. Reprinted with permission from Mori et al. (2002). Artist: Bobbi Angell.

Family classification. Molecular evidence suggests that the Ebenales (including Styracaceae), Ericales, Primulales, some families of the Theales, and several other families (all taxa *sensu* Cronquist) form a monophyletic group. Relationships among many of the families of this expanded order Ericales largely remain unresolved. Anatomical and morphological studies point toward a close relationship with some members of the Ericales *sensu* Cronquist, but molecular evidence suggests a sister-group relationship with Diapensiaceae. A phylogenetic analysis based on morphology and three molecular data sets strongly supports the monophyly of the family, with *Huodendron* and *Styrax* forming a well-supported clade that is sister to a clade comprising the rest of the genera.

The genus *Styrax* is divided into the primarily north-temperate section *Styrax* and the tropical evergreen section *Valvatae*. All but two of the Neotropical species of *Styrax* belong to series *Valvatae* of section *Valvatae*. Species of this series differ from all other species of *Styrax* by the combination of evergreen habit and possession of a drupe. The only other Neotropical species of *Styrax* are the Mexican and Mesoamerican *S. glabrescens* and *S. jaliscanus* in series *Cyrta* of section *Styrax*. Several South American species with five stamens per flower were previously placed in *Pamphilia*, and two others with reduced numbers of ovules were placed within *Styrax* section *Foveolaria*, but these taxa are now included within *Styrax* series *Valvatae*. Nine Mexican and Mesoamerican species have certain primitive floral features that suggest a southern North American origin for Neotropical evergreen *Styrax*.

Features of the family. Habit: trees or occasionally shrubs, usually evergreen. **Bark** gray, typically smooth, exuding resin in many species following injury to cambium. **Stems** typically grayish brown with purplish cast, an interlacing to peeling outer layer present, the vegetative buds occurring in pairs, each consisting of 1–2 outer scales, these buds developing into first leaves of season. **Indument** of stellate hairs or radiate or peltate scales always present. **Stipules** absent. **Leaves** alternate, simple; blade margins usually entire, rarely glandular-serrate or lobed; venation pinnate. **Inflorescences** axillary or terminal, usually racemose or paniculate, rarely cymose; bracteoles present. **Flowers** actinomorphic, bisexual or occasionally unisexual (then plants gynodioecious); hypanthium present, inconspicuous, adnate basally to ovary; calyx synsepalous, generally campanulate or cupuliform, usually with 5 small teeth; corolla sympetalous, campanulate, usually white, less often pink or flushed with pink, or rarely yellow, becoming lobed at same level at which corolla becomes free from androecium, the lobes usually 5 (rarely more), nearly always longer than tube, frequently recurved to strongly reflexed, valvate or rarely imbricate in bud, pubescent; androecium usually with twice as many stamens as corolla lobes, rarely more or equal in number, the stamens in 1 series, adnate to corolla proximally, free and often forming tube for some distance distally, the inner face of filaments typically pubescent, the pubescence evenly distributed along surface or aggregated into dense mass sometimes covering pair of longitudinally oriented auricles, the anthers basifixed, oblong to linear, longitudinally dehiscent; stami-

nodes present in pistillate flowers; gynoecium syncarpous, the ovary superior to subinferior, 3-carpellate, with 3 septa at base but 1-locular through distal attenuation of septa, the style 1, simple, filiform, hollow; placentation essentially axile, rarely basal, the ovules 1–circa 8 per carpel, bitegmic; placental obturators usually present. **Fruits** usually sweet-tasting drupes, rarely capsules or nutlike, the calyx and hypanthium persistent, the drupes dark purple, the capsules dehiscing by 3 valves. **Seeds** nearly always 1, completely filling fruit cavity, surrounded by usually purplish-flecked endocarp (in species with drupes), the seed coat brown, usually minutely reticulate, thick and hard; endosperm copious, the cotyledons usually flattened or rarely nearly terete.

Natural history. Pollination is effected mainly by bees and wasps. Fruit morphology suggests dispersal by animals. Phylogenetic studies suggest that gynodioecy in *Styrax* has evolved twice from full hermaphroditism, once in Cuba and Hispaniola (*S. obtusifolius*) and once in the Andes and southern Brazil (eight species).

Economic uses. The balsamic resins of the Asian *Styrax benzoin*, *S. paralleloneurus*, and *S. tonkinensis* are sources of benzoin, which is used in the pharmaceutical, confection, and fragrance industries. The resin of several Neotropical species of *Styrax* is used medicinally (e.g., *S. guyanensis* and *S. rigidifolius*) and for incense on a local scale, and the fruits of others are sometimes sold in local markets for food. Species of *Styrax* and *Halesia* occasionally are cultivated as ornamentals.

References. ANDERBERG, A. A., RYDIN, C., AND KÄLLERSJÖ, M. 2002. Phylogenetic relationships in the order Ericales s.l.: analyses of molecular data from five genes from the plastid and mitochondrial genomes. *Amer. J. Bot.* 89: 677–87. DICKISON, W. C. 1993. Floral anatomy of the Styracaceae, including observations on intra-ovarian trichomes. *Bot. J. Linn. Soc.* 112:223–55. FRITSCH, P. W. 1997. A revision of *Styrax* (Styracaceae) for western Texas, Mexico, and Mesoamerica. *Ann. Missouri Bot. Gard.* 84:705–61. FRITSCH, P. W. 1999. Phylogeny of *Styrax* based on morphological characters, with implications for biogeography and infrageneric classification. *Syst. Bot.* 24:356–78. FRITSCH, P. W. 2001. Phylogeny and biogeography of the flowering plant genus *Styrax* (Styracaceae) based on chloroplast DNA restriction sites and DNA sequences of the internal transcribed spacer region. *Molec. Phylogenet. Evol.* 19:387–408. FRITSCH, P. W., C. M. MORTON, C. T. CHEN, AND C. MELDRUM. 2001. Phylogeny and biogeography of the Styracaceae. *Int. J. Pl. Sci.* 162(S6):S95–S116. GONSOULIN, G. J. 1974. A revision of *Styrax* (Styracaceae) in North America, Central America, and the Caribbean. *Sida* 5:191–258. MORTON, C. M., M. W. CHASE, K. A. KRON, AND S. M. SWENSEN. 1996. A molecular evaluation of the monophyly of the order Ebenales based upon *rbc*L sequence data. *Syst. Bot.* 21:567–86. PERKINS, J. 1907. Styracaceae. In *Das Pflanzenreich*, ed. A. Engler, ser. 4, 241(heft 30):1–111. Leipzig: Wilhelm Engelmann.

SURIANACEAE (Bay Cedar or Suriana Family)

WM. WAYT THOMAS

Figure 191, Plate 48

- *shrubs or small trees*
- *leaves alternate, simple and fleshy, or compound with winged rachises*
- *flower gynoecium apocarpous, the styles emerging from base of carpels*
- *fruits drupaceous or nutlike*

Numbers of genera and species. Worldwide, the Surianaceae comprise five genera and nine species. In tropical America, there are two genera, *Suriana* (1 species) and *Recchia* (3).

Distribution and habitat. *Suriana* is found along seacoasts throughout the Tropics. *Recchia* is restricted to the humid forests (1 species) and dry forests (2 species) of southern Mexico. *Cadellia*, *Guilfoylia*, and *Stylobasium*, are endemic to Australia.

Family classification. The Surianaceae were described as a distinct family in 1834, but Engler subsequently treated them as a subfamily of the Simaroubaceae. Cronquist recognized the Surianaceae as a separate family of the Rosales. Fernando et al. demonstrated that *Suriana* and *Recchia* are unrelated to the Simaroubaceae and should be aligned with the Rosales in the Surianaceae. The Angiosperm Phylogeny Group places the family in the Fabales along with the Fabaceae and Polygalaceae.

Features of the family. Habit: shrubs or small trees. **Stipules** present in *Recchia*, minute. **Leaves** alternate, simple, or pinnate in two species of *Recchia*, fleshy and grouped at stem apices in *Suriana*; rachises winged when leaves compound. **Inflorescences** usually axillary and small, of 1–few flowers in *Suriana*, paniculate in *Recchia*. **Flowers** actinomorphic, bisexual; sepals 5; petals 5, distinct; androecium of 10 stamens, the stamens distinct, the anthers longitudinally dehiscent; gynoecium apocarpous, the ovaries superior, carpels 2–5, the styles distinct, emerging from base of carpel; placentation basal or marginal, the ovules 2, anatropous. **Fruits** monocarps, the monocarp drupaceous in *Recchia*, nutlike in *Suriana*, 1–5 developing per flower. **Seeds** one per fruit.

Natural history. Nothing is known about the pollination or dispersal of this family.

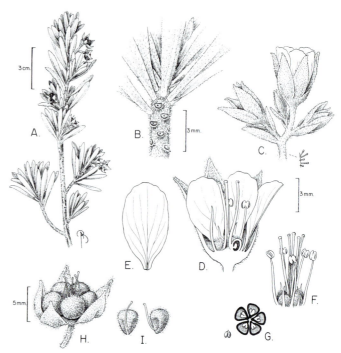

Figure 191. SURIANACEAE. *Suriana maritima.* **A.** Stems with leaves and inflorescences. **B.** Detail of stem showing petiole scars. **C.** Part of inflorescence with detail of glandular trichomes (below). **D.** Medial section of flower. **E.** Adaxial view of petal. **F.** Flower with perianth removed. **G.** Transverse section of fruit (right) and seed (left). **H.** Lateral view of fruit. **I.** Adaxial (left) and lateral (right) views of fruit segments. Reprinted with permission from Acevedo-Rodríguez (1996). Artist: Bobbi Angell.

Economic uses. The heartwood of *Suriana* is hard, polishes well, and is used to make small articles. *Suriana* is used medicinally to clean old sores, to combat rectal bleeding, to relieve rheumatism, to halt diarrhea, and to heal mouth sores and toothaches. No documented uses of *Recchia* are known.

References. DAHLGREN, R. 1977. A commentary on a diagrammatic presentation of the Angiosperms in relation to the distribution of character states. *Pl. Syst. Evol., Suppl.* 1: 253–83. ENGLER, A. 1931. Simarubaceae. In *Die Natürlichen Pflanzenfamilien*, A. Engler and K. Prantl, 2nd ed., 19a:359–405. Leipzig: Wilhelm Engelmann. FERNANDO, E. S., P. A. GADEK, AND C. J. QUINN. 1995. Simaroubaceae, an artificial construct: evidence from *rbc*L sequence variation. *Amer. J. Bot.* 82:92–103. MORTON, J. F. 1981. *Atlas of Medicinal Plants of Middle America.* Springfield, IL: Charles C. Thomas.

SYMPLOCACEAE (Sweetleaf Family)

Bertil Ståhl

Figure 192, Plate 48

- *shrubs or trees*

- *leaves alternate, simple; blade margins often glandular-denticulate*

- *flowers actinomorphic; sepals 5; petals 5–10; filaments flattened and often abruptly constricted at apex; ovary usually inferior*

- *fruits drupes*

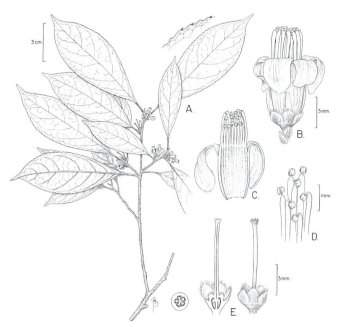

Figure 192. SYMPLOCACEAE. *Symplocos martinicensis.* **A.** Stem with leaves, inflorescences, and detail leaf margin (above). **B.** Lateral view of flower. **C.** Medial section of flower with gynoecium removed to show connate filament bases adnate to the corolla. **D.** Apices of stamens showing constricted filaments and longitudinal dehiscence of anthers. **E.** Transverse section (left), medial section (center), and lateral view (right) of flower with corolla and androecium removed. Reprinted with permission from Mori et al. (2002). Artist: Bobbi Angell.

Numbers of genera and species. Worldwide, the Symplocaceae comprise a single genus, *Symplocos*, and about 300 species. In tropical America, there are around 150 species.

Distribution and habitat. The Symplocaceae are distributed in tropical and subtropical areas of the Americas, Asia, and Australasia, with a few species extending into temperate Asia and North America. *Symplocos* occurs throughout the neotropics, being particularly diverse in the Andes. There are also a fair number of species in the Guianan Highlands, southern Brazil, Mesoamerica, and the Antilles. The family is absent from the central Amazon.

Although many species of Symplocaceae occur in the lowlands, the majority grow in wet or humid montane forests between 1,500 and 4,000 meters. A large number of the Andean species have very restricted distributions.

Family classification. The systematic position of Symplocaceae is somewhat enigmatic. The family is often placed next to the Styracaceae in the Ebenales (i.e., Cronquist), but some individuals place it in the Theales and others in the Cornales. Studies based on *rbc*L sequence data place the family as sister to either Sapotaceae or Ternstroemiaceae.

The most recent classification recognizes a single genus, *Symplocos*, divided into two subgenera, *Symplocos*, which is most abundant in the neotropics, and *Hopea*, which is dominant in the Eastern Hemisphere. Older classifications recognize a larger number of genera or subgeneric taxa.

Features of the family. Habit: shrubs or small to medium-sized trees, densely branched, dense pubescence often present on young stems and abaxial surface of leaves (many species of subgenus *Symplocos*). **Stipules** absent. **Leaves** alternate, simple; petioles short; blades usually coriaceous, the margins often revolute, usually distinctly glandular-denticulate. **Inflorescences** in axils of extant or fallen leaves, often sparsely branched panicles, few flowered fascicles, or sometimes of solitary flowers; bracts 3 (often appearing as more numerous due to reductions in adjacent flowers). **Flowers** ac-

tinomorphic, bisexual or unisexual in subgenus *Hopea* (then plants dioecious), usually less than 2 cm wide at anthesis; calyx with 5 sepals; corolla with 5 (subgenus *Hopea*) or 5–10 (subgenus *Symplocos*) petals, the petals united but with overlapping margins, white, pink, purple, or green (subgenus *Hopea*); androecium of 5 to more than 100 stamens, the stamens in 1–4 whorls, often adnate to base of corolla, the filaments curved inward, flattened and abruptly constricted at apex (subgenus *Symplocos*), or straight, filiform, and gradually tapering toward apex (subgenus *Hopea*); nectariferous disc surrounding style base; gynoecium syncarpous, the ovary inferior or less often subinferior, the carpels 3–5, the locules 3–5, the style well differentiated from ovary; placentation axile, the ovules usually 3 per locule. **Fruits** drupes, olive-shaped or subglobose, the exocarp black, juicy, the endocarp hard. **Seed** usually 1 per locule.

The leaves of many species dry yellowish due to large concentrations of aluminium.

Natural history. No studies on the reproductive biology of Neotropical species have been carried out. The flowers are often sweet-scented, which together with their morphology, suggests that they are pollinated by bees. The fruits probably are dispersed by birds.

Economic use. Besides local use of wood for construction, the leaves of some species have been used to make medicinal infusions. The Colombian *Symplocos theiformis* (*té de Bogotá*) was at one time promoted as a Latin American substitute for tea. The fragrant flowered Asian *S. paniculata*, (sapphire berry) is grown as an ornamental.

References. MAI, D. H. 1986. Über antillische Symplocaceae. *Feddes Repert.* 97:1–28. OCCHIONI, P. 1974. As espécies de Symplocaceae da flora do Parana. *Leandra* 4/5:31–52. STÅHL, B. 1991. Symplocaceae. In *Flora Ecuador*, eds. G. Harling and L. Andersson, no. 44:1–44. Göteborg, Sweden: Department of Systematic Botany, University of Göteborg. STÅHL, B. 1993. The genus *Symplocos* (Symplocaceae) in Peru. *Candollea* 48:351–82. STÅHL, B. 1994. The genus *Symplocos* (Symplocaceae) in Bolivia. *Candollea* 49:369–88. STÅHL, B. 1995. Diversity and distribution of Andean Symplocaceae. In *Biodiversity and Conservation of Neotropical Montane Forests*, eds. S. P. Churchill, H. Balslev, E. Forero, and J. L. Luteyn, 397–405. Bronx, NY: New York Botanical Garden. STÅHL, B. 1996. The genus *Symplocos* (Symplocaceae) in Colombia. *Candollea* 51:323–64.

TEPUIANTHACEAE (Tepuianthus Family)

BRIAN BOOM AND DENNIS WM. STEVENSON

Figure 193

- *trees or shrubs*

- *plants densely pubescent*

- *leaves alternate or opposite, simple*

- *flowers with extrastaminal disc; ovary superior; placentation apical, the ovules 1 per locule*

- *fruits loculicidal capsules, densely sericeous on outer surface*

Numbers of genera and species. The Tepuianthaceae comprise a single genus, *Tepuianthus*, and six species.

Distribution and habitat. The Tepuianthaceae are endemic to the Guayana region of Venezuela, Brazil, and Colombia. *Tepuianthus savannensis*, is known from lowland white-sand savannas in southwestern Venezuela, from 100 to 150 meters elevation. The other five species are each restricted to or near the summits of different elevated sandstone mountains (*tepuis*) of the Guayana region. Species of *Tepuianthus* are often dominant trees in dwarf upland woodlands.

Family classification. Various authors have suggested that the Tepuianthaceae belong in the Sapindales or Celastrales (e.g., *sensu* Cronquist). The family may be most closely related to the Simaroubaceae of the Sapindales. The equivocal position of the Tepuianthaceae is still ambiguous even with the addition of molecular data. With only six described species, the family has not been subjected to infrafamilial classification.

Features of the family. Habit: trees to 10 m or infrequently shrubs (*T. auyantepuiensis*), pubescent, the trichomes simple, dense, covering stems, petioles, lower surfaces of leaf blades, peduncles, pedicels, and outer surfaces of sepals and fruits. **Stipules** absent. **Leaves** usually alternate, sometimes oppo-

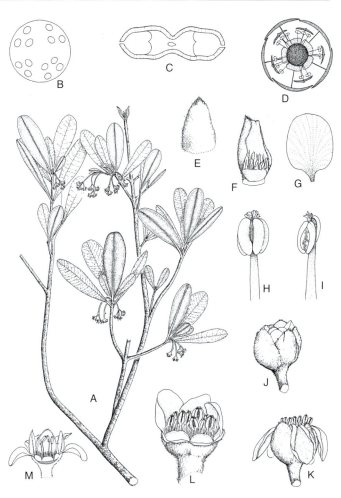

Figure 193. TEPUIANTHACEAE. *Tepuianthus colombianus*. **A.** Stems with leaves and inflorescences (x½). **B.** Diagram showing arrangement of stamens. **C.** Schematic transverse section of anther. **D.** Floral diagram. **E.** Adaxial view of sepal (x8). **F.** Abaxial view of sepal with stamen remnants (x7). **G.** Adaxial view of petal (x7). **H.** Adaxial view of stamen (x13). **I.** Lateral view of stamen (x13). **J.** Lateral view of flower bud (x3½). **K.** Lateral view of intact flower (x3½). **L.** Lateral view of flower with some sepals and petals removed (x5). **M.** Schematic lateral view of flower (x3). Reprinted with permission from Maguire and Steyermark (1981). Artist: Unknown.

site, simple, small; blade margins entire. **Inflorescences** terminal or axillary, cymose. **Flowers** actinomorphic, usually unisexual (plants androdioecious), rarely bisexual, small; receptacle thickened; sepals 5, imbricate, distinct, densely sericeous abaxially, glabrous adaxially; petals 5, imbricate, distinct, equal in length to sepals, glabrous, yellowish; extrastaminal disc present, of 5–10 fleshy glands, the glands glabrous abaxially, usually densely pubescent adaxially; androecium of 5 (*T. auyantepuiensis* and *T. aracensis*) to 12–16 stamens, the stamens in 1–3 whorls, the filaments glabrous, the anthers versatile, dorsifixed, introrse, bilocular, usually suborbicular; gynoecium syncarpous, the ovary superior, rudimentary in staminate flowers, broadest at base and gradually narrowed apically, the carpels 3, the locules usually 3, the styles absent (staminate flowers) or 3 (bisexual flowers), the stigmas forked; placentation apical, the ovules one per locule, pendulous. **Fruits** loculicidal capsules, dehiscent into 3 cells, densely sericeous on outer surface. **Seeds** 3 per fruit, glabrous, smooth, dark brown; endosperm copious, the embryo small, the cotyledons poorly differentiated.

Natural history. Extremely little is known about the biology of the Tepuianthaceae.

The complicated leaf anatomy of *Tepuianthus auyantepuiensis* seems to be an adaptation for the strong ultraviolet radiation, high winds, and temporary drought of *tepui* summits and upper slopes. The upper epidermis is multilayered, occupying up to three-quarters of the transverse leaf section and forming what is proportionally the thickest upper leaf epidermis known. Additionally, slimy cell walls in the leaf epidermis of *T. auyantepuiensis* prevent excessive transpiration, as does the presence of resin-containing cells.

Economic uses. No uses are known for the family.

References. KUBITZKI, K. 2003. Tepuianthaceae. In *The Families and Genera of Vascular Plants*, eds. K. Kubitzki and C. Bayer. 5:371–72. Berlin: Springer-Verlag. MAGUIRE, B., AND J. A. STEYERMARK. 1981. Tepuianthaceae, Sapindales. In The botany of the Guayana Highland—Part XI, B. Maguire et al. *Mem. New York Bot. Gard.* 32:4–21. ROTH, I., AND H. LINDORE. 1990. Blatt- und Rindenstruktur von *Tepuianthus auyantepuiensis*, einer neueren Familie aus Venezuela. *Bot. Jahrb. Syst.* 111:403–21. STEYERMARK, J. A. 1987. Notes of the flora of Serra Aracá. *Acta Amazon.* 16/17: 219–21.

TERNSTROEMIACEAE (Ternstroemia Family)

DENNIS WM. STEVENSON AND JANICE WASSMER STEVENSON

Figure 194, Plate 48

- *trees or shrubs*

- *leaves alternate, sometimes distichous, simple; blades coriaceous, glossy*

- *midrib depressed adaxially, raised abaxially*

- *perianth parts imbricate, distinct*

- *fruits often fleshy, indehiscent or with irregular or circumscissile, dehiscence*

Numbers of genera and species. Worldwide, the Ternstroemiaceae comprise 10 genera and approximately 300 species. In tropical America, there are four genera, *Cleyera* with 16 species, *Frezieria* with approximately 42 species, *Symplocarpon* with nine species, and *Ternstroemia* with approximately 60 species.

Distribution and habitat. The Ternstroemiaceae widespread, but mostly pantropical. *Clayera* and *Ternstroemia* extend into Japan and the Himalayas, and *Freziera* and *Symplocarpon* are endemic to the Neotropics.

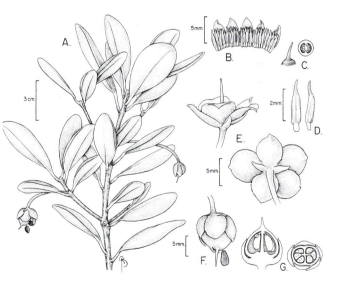

Figure 194. TERNSTROEMIACEAE. *Ternstroemia peduncularis.* **A.** Stem with leaves and fruits. **B.** Corolla spread open to show stamens. **C.** Upper part of gynoecium (left) and transverse section of ovary (above). **D.** Views of stamens. **E.** Lateral (above) and basal (below) views of flowers with petals and stamens removed. **F.** Lateral view of fruit with persistent calyx and pendulous seed. **G.** Medial (left) and transverse (right) sections of fruit. Reprinted with permission from Acevedo-Rodríguez (1996). Artist: Bobbi Angell.

Family classification. Cronquist and Takhtajan treat the Ternstroemiaceae as subfamily Ternstroemioideae of the Theaceae, although its recognition as a family began in 1813. Recent molecular studies indicate that the Ternstroemioideae is not part of the Theaceae, and, thus, should be recognized as a distinct family. On the other hand, the generic sampling for molecular data is not extensive and changes may yet be in order. The Ternstroemiaceae, whether or not treated as a subfamily of the Theaceae, are divided into two groups traditionally treated as tribes. The Ternstroemieae contains two genera, the pantropical *Ternstroemia* and the Indomalesian and Chinese *Anneslea*. The pantropical Adinandreae include 8 genera, among which *Cleyera*, *Frezieria*, and *Symplocarpon* are the Neotropical representatives.

Features of the family. Habit: trees (to 10 m high) or frequently shrubs. **Stipules** absent. **Leaves** alternate, spiral or distichous (*Cleyera* and *Frezieria*), simple; blades coriaceous, glossy, the margins entire; midrib depressed adaxially and raised abaxially. **Inflorescences** axillary, cymose, composed of 1–4 flowers or flowers solitary (*Ternstroemia*). **Flowers** actinomorphic, bisexual or unisexual (the plants dioecious in *Frezieria*); sepals 5, imbricate, distinct; petals 5, imbricate, distinct, white to pinkish, often semisucculent, conspicuous; staminodia present in female flowers; androecium of 10–30+ stamens, in 1 (*Cleyera* and *Frezieria*) or 2 to numerous series, the filaments glabrous or pubescent (*Cleyera*), the anthers basifixed, often shorter than filaments (*Cleyera* and *Frezieria*), introrse, bilocular, usually suborbicular; pistillode present in staminate flowers; gynoecium syncarpous, the ovary superior or semi-inferior (*Symplocarpon*),

broadest at base and abruptly narrowed apically, the carpels and locules mostly 3 but often 2 in *Ternstroemia* and rarely 1 (*T. parvifolia*), the styles very short, the same number as carpels, the stigmas simple; placentation axile, the ovules (1)2–20. **Fruits** fleshy or dry, indehiscent or with irregular or circumscissile dehiscence. **Seeds** 3–60 per fruit, small, glabrous, smooth, brown to black, with or without aril; endosperm copious, the embryo small, the cotyledons shorter than radicle.

Natural history. Very little is known about the biology of the Ternstroemiaceae. The nature of the flowers, however, suggests insect pollination. The fruits indicate dispersal by birds and other animals.

Economic uses. The Ternstroemiaceae have limited economic uses. *Cleyera ochnacea* (sakaki in Japanese) is the sacred tree of Shintoism and is often planted in groves around shrines. A few other species of *Cleyera*, *Eurya*, and *Ternstroemia* are planted as ornamentals, and *T. japonica* is sometimes grown as a hedge plant. Some species have limited medicinal uses, and the leaves of others are used for making mildly stimulating teas. A few species of the Indomalesian and Chinese *Anneslea* and *Eurya* provide timber.

References. Morton, C. M., M. C. Chase, K. A. Kron, and S. M. Swensen. 1996. A molecular evaluation of the monophyly of the order Ebenales based upon *rbcL* sequence data. *Syst. Bot.* 21:567–86. Prince, L. M., and C. R. Parks. 2001. Phylogenetic relationships of Theaceae inferred from chloroplast DNA sequence data. *Amer. J. Bot.* 88:2309–20.

TETRAMERISTACEAE (Punah Family)

Dennis Wm. Stevenson

Figure 195

- *trees or shrubs*

- *leaves alternate (spiral), simple, crowded at branch tips; blades coriaceous*

- *flowers with glandular pits on adaxial surface of sepals; filaments flattened, connate basally*

- *fruits berries*

Numbers of genera and species. Worldwide, the Tetrameristaceae comprise two genera and four species. In tropical America, there is one genus, *Pentamerista*, and one species.

Distribution and habitat. The genera of Tetrameristaceae are disjunct with *Tetramerista* occurring in Sumatra, the Ma-

lay Peninsula, and Borneo; and *Pentamerista* found in low-elevation savannas between the Alto Orinoco and Alto Rio Negro of Venezuela.

Family classification. Both Cronquist and Takhtajan place the Tetrameristaceae in the Theales, but historically the family was included as a subfamily of the Theaceae. Recent mo-

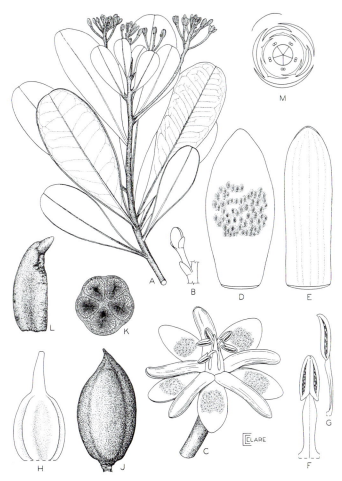

Figure 195. TETRAMERISTACEAE. *Pentamerista neotropica.* **A.** Stem with leaves and inflorescences (x½). **B.** Flower bud showing bract at base and bracteoles on pedicel (x2). **C.** Oblique-apical view of flower (x4). **D.** Adaxial view of sepal showing glandular pits (x10). **E.** Adaxial view of petal (x10). **F.** Adaxial view of stamen (x10). **G.** Lateral view of stamen (x10). **H.** Lateral view of immature fruit (x10). **J.** Lateral view of dried mature fruit (x3). **K.** Transverse section of dried mature fruit (x3). **L.** Seed (x3). **M.** Floral diagram. Reprinted with permission from Maguire et al. (1972). Artist: Charles C. Clare, Jr.

lecular studies indicate that the Tetrameristaceae does not have affinities with the Theaceae but instead is most closely related to the Marcgraviaceae. As early as 1916, Hallier had recognized this relationship. With only two genera and four species, there is no infrafamilial classification.

Features of the family. Habit: trees (to 15 m) or shrubs. Stipules absent. Leaves alternate (spiral), simple, crowded at branch tips; blades coriaceous, glossy, the margins entire, the apex rounded to emarginate; venation pinnate. Inflorescences axillary, condensed racemes. Flowers actinomorphic, bisexual, small; sepals 5, imbricate, distinct, with numerous glandular pits on middle of adaxial surface; petals 5, imbricate, distinct, sepals, greenish; androecium of 5 stamens, the stamens alternate with petals, the filaments flattened, connate basally, the anthers basifixed, introrse; gynoecium syncarpous, the ovary superior, the carpels and locules 5, the style undivided, the stigma simple to minutely lobed; placentation axile, the ovule solitary in each locule, at base of septum. Fruits berries, the pericarp firm, fleshy. Seeds 4–5 per fruit, relatively large; endosperm copious, the embryo straight, basal, the cotyledons shorter than radicle.

Natural history. Very little is known about the biology of the Tetrameristaceae. The nature of the flowers, however, indicates insect pollination. The berries suggest seed dispersal by animals.

Economic uses. No uses are known for this family.

References. HALLIER, H. 1916. Beitrage zur Flora von Borneo, Marcgraviaceae. *Bot. Centralbl. Beib.* 34:38. MORTON, C. M., M. C. CHASE, K. A. KRON, AND S. M. SWENSEN. 1996. A molecular evaluation of the monophyly of the order Ebenales based upon *rbcL* sequence data. *Syst. Bot.* 21:567–86. PRINCE, L. M., AND C. R. PARKS. 2001. Phylogenetic relationships of Theaceae inferred from chloroplast DNA sequence data. *Amer. J. Bot.* 88:2309–20.

THEACEAE (Tea Family)

DENNIS WM. STEVENSON AND JANICE WASSMER STEVENSON

- *trees or shrubs*

- *leaves alternate, simple*

- *flowers with 5 large petals; stamens numerous*

- *fruits loculicidal capsules, with persistent central column*

- *seeds with oblong apical wings*

Numbers of genera and species. Worldwide, the Theaceae comprise 15 genera and approximately 350 species. In tropical America, there is one genus, *Laplacea* (= Neotropical *Gordonia*) and three to eight species.

Distribution and habitat. The Theaceae are pantropical with some genera extending into temperate areas in eastern North America and eastern Asia (e.g., *Stewartia*). Within the neotropics, *Laplacea* is found in the West Indies, Mexico throughout Central America to Peru, southern Brazil, and Central Bolivia. Species of *Laplacea* are primarily found in cloud forests.

Family classification. The Theaceae are placed in the Theales by Cronquist, who recognized an inclusive Theaceae consisting of four subfamilies: Asteropeioideae (endemic to Madagascar), Bonnetioideae, Ternstroemioideae, and Theoideae. Takhtajan excluded the Asteropeioideae and Bonnetioideae from the Theaceae, preferring to recognize them as distinct families. This view is supported by recent molecular studies that also indicate that the Ternstroemioideae is not part of the Theaceae and should be recognized as a distinct family. This view is followed here with the Theaceae being limited to the Theoideae of Cronquist. Traditionally, the Theoideae have been divided into three tribes: Stewartieae, Theeae, and Gordonieae, the latter including *Laplacea*. This recognition of three lineages is supported by phylogenetic analyses of molecular data; however, the placement of *Laplacea* is still unclear.

Traditionally, Neotropical species of Theaceae *sensu stricto* have been placed in *Laplacea*. For the past 20 years, there has been a trend to include *Laplacea* in *Gordonia*; however, molecular studies have shown that *Laplacea* is distinct from *Gordonia*. This recognition of *Laplacea* is supported on morphological grounds in that *Laplacea* has separate styles and stigmas as compared to *Gordonia* with fused styles and stigmas. The number of recognized species of *Laplacea* in the neotropics varies with different authors, but is between three and eight. The variation has to do with species concepts being based upon leaf characters that appear not to be as well defined as originally proposed.

Features of the family. Habit: trees (to 20 m) or frequently shrubs. Stipules absent. Leaves alternate (spiral), simple, often clustered at branch apices; petioles short; blades chartaceous to coriaceous, the margins dentate to entire. Inflorescences axillary, of single flowers; bracteoles present, sepallike. Flowers actinomorphic, sometimes bisexual mostly unisexual; sepals 5, unequal; petals 5, imbricate, distinct, white to pinkish, sometimes basally connate; androecium of 30+ stamens, the stamens in numerous series, sometimes basally to fully connate into tube, free from petals, the anthers versatile, introrse; staminodia present in female flowers; gynoecium syncarpous, the ovary superior, rudimentary in staminate flowers, the carpels and locules 4–10, the styles as many as locules, as long as ovary to very short, distinct, the stigmas simple; placentation axile, the ovules 4–10 per locule.

Fruits loculucidal capsules, the calyx persistent, the central column persistent. Seeds 4–10 per fruit, flat, with oblong apical wings; endosperm copious, the embryo thick, the cotyledons fleshy.

Natural history. Little is known about the pollination and dispersal biology for Neotropical Theaceae.

Economic uses. *Camellia sinensis*, the tea plant, is a small evergreen tree usually maintained in cultivation as a shrub by constant pruning. According to Chinese folklore, its use for tea was discovered about 2500 B.C. The tannins in tea provide the astringency and caffeine provides the stimulating properties. The characteristic appearances and flavors of black, green, and semifermented teas arise more from different processing and manufacturing methods than from the type of leaf used to produce the tea. In China, the oil expressed from the fruit of *Camellia sasanqua* is said to be equal to olive oil. In Japan, the dried leaves of this species are mixed with tea to impart a characteristic aroma. *Laplacea semiserrata* is used as a diuretic and aphrodisiac in Brazil. The tropical Asian *Schima wallichii* provides timber for construction and bark used as a fish poison.

Camellia japonica is the popular ornamental camellia, and *C. sasanqua* is also cultivated for its fragrant flowers. Many species of *Stewartia* are grown for their attractive bark, simple, usually toothed leaves that color well in autumn; and cup-shaped, white flowers. *Franklinia altamaha*, the Ben Franklin tree, is an ornamental known only from cultivation. The original grove of *Franklinia* trees was last seen in 1790, and no one has found this species growing in the wild in spite of efforts to relocate during the past 200 years.

References. MORTON, C. M., M. C. CHASE, K. A. KRON, AND S. M. SWENSEN. 1996. A molecular evaluation of the monophyly of the order Ebenales based upon *rbcL* sequence data. *Syst. Bot.* 21:567–86. MORTON, C. M., K. G. KAROL, AND M. C. CHASE. 1997. Taxonomic affinities of *Physena* (Physenaceae) and *Asteropeia* (Theaceae). *Bot. Rev.* 63:231–39. POOL, A. 2001. Theaceae. *Flora de Nicaragua* 3:2443–48. PRINCE, L. M., AND C. R. PARKS. 2001. Phylogenetic relationships of Theaceae inferred from chloroplast DNA sequence data. *Amer. J. Bot.* 88:2309–20. WEITZMAN, A. 1995. Diversity of Theaceae and Bonnetiaceae in the montane neotropics. In *Biodiversity and Conservation of Neotropical Montane Forests*, eds. S. Churchill, H. Balslev, E. Forero, and J. Luteyn, 365–75. Bronx, NY: New York Botanical Garden Press.

THEOPHRASTACEAE (Theophrasta Family)

BERTIL STÅHL

Figure 196, Plate 48

- *subshrubs to small trees*
- *leaves alternate, simple, often clustered at stem apices; blades coriaceous*
- *flowers with stamens inserted on corolla tube, opposite petal lobes, the anthers partly filled with white meal of calcium oxalate crystals*
- *fruits berries*

Numbers of genera and species. The Theophrastaceae comprise six genera and about 95 species restricted to tropical America. The two largest genera are *Clavija* and *Jacquinia* with 55 and 33 species, respectively. The remaining genera contain one or two species each.

Distribution and habitat. The Theophrastaceae are distributed from northern Mexico and southern Florida to southern Brazil and Paraguay. The family has a center of diversity in and around the Caribbean, although *Clavija*, the largest genus, is most diverse in northwestern South America.

Most species of Theophrastaceae are understory shrubs growing in various types of forests, from dry, deciduous forests to rain forests. Although the family occurs mainly in lowland forest, many species of *Clavija* are found in premontane Andean forests between 1,000 and 2,000 meters. In the Amazon, a few species of *Clavija* grow in temporarily inundated forests, and, in the West Indies, many species of *Jacquinia* grow in thorn-scrub.

Family classification. The Theophrastaceae are placed in the Primulales by Cronqist next to the Myrsinaceae, within which they have sometimes been included as a subfamily. However, in most modern classifications they are given family rank, a view strongly supported by recent phylogenetic studies.

Features of the family. Habit: subshrubs to small trees. **Stems** unbranched or few-branched (e.g., *Clavija*). **Stipules** absent. **Leaves** alternate, simple, often clustered at stem apices, in 1 or several pseudowhorls; blades coriaceous, the margins sometimes spinose-dentate (*Neomezia*, *Theophrasta*, and some *Clavija* species), the apex spine-tipped (most *Jacquinia* species). **Inflorescences** borne directly on main stem (*Clavija*), terminal or subterminal (above leaves), racemes, sometimes appearing as corymbs or umbels, less often of solitary flowers (*Deherainia*). **Flowers** actinomorphic, bisexual or functionally unisexual (most *Clavija* are functionally dioecious or polygamodioecious), 5- or sometimes 4-merous, from 0.5 to 4 cm diameter at anthesis; sepals 4–5; corolla

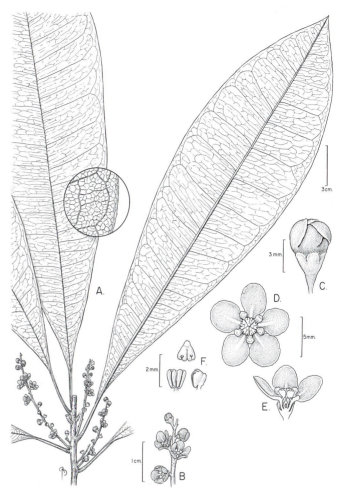

Figure 196. THEOPHRASTACEAE. *Clavija lancifolia* subsp. *chermontiana*. **A.** Stem with leaves and inflorescences and detail of leaf venation (center). **B.** Inflorescence. **C.** Lateral view of bud. **D.** Apical view of flower. **E.** Medial section of flower. **F.** Apical (above), abaxial (below left), and lateral (below right) views of anthers. Reprinted with permission from Mori et al. (2002). Artist: Bobbi Angell.

campanulate or subrotate, the petals 4–5, thick, waxy, different shades of orange, green (*Deherainia*), buff (*Theophrasta*), yellow (*Votschia*), or white (many *Jacquinia*); appendages (probably staminodes) inserted on corolla, alternating with petal lobes; androecium with stamens equal to number of petals, the stamens inserted on corolla tube, opposite corolla lobes, usually forming a cone at the onset of anthesis, later spreading, the filaments fused into tube (staminate flowers of *Clavija*), the anthers dehiscing extrorsely by slits; gynoecium syncarpous, the ovary superior, the carpels probably 5, the locule 1, the style 1; placentation free-central, the ovules few to numerous. **Fruits** berries, the pericarp dry, sometimes thick. **Seeds** few to many, large, embedded in juicy, sweet pulp.

Leaves vary in size from 1 to a few centimeters long in

Jacquinia to more than 1 meter long in several species of *Clavija*. Leaves of most Theophrastaceae have subepidermal fiber strands, which appear as fine striations running parallel to the secondary veins.

Anthers are partly filled out with a white meal of calcium oxalate crystals, a character that, together with the presence of subepidermal leaf fibers is used to diagnose the family as monophyletic.

Natural history. *Jacquinia nervosa*, which occurs in dry forests in Central America, is deciduous during the rainy season.

Pollination is carried out by insects. However, because nectar production is low or nearly nonexistent and the amount of pollen produced is low, pollination may be based largely on deceit. Flowers of most species of *Clavija* and *Jacquinia* emit a fruity or perfumed scent and probably are visited by bees, whereas the floral scents of *Deherainia*, *Neomezia*, and *Theophrasta* are fetid and seem to attract flies. In Ecuador, gall midges have been observed visiting a species of *Clavija*, but it is unclear if they are pollinators (C. Ott and S. S. Renner, pers. comm.). The seeds probably are dispersed by birds or rodents and possibly monkeys.

Economic use. The Theophrastaceae are of marginal economic value. Green parts and bark of several species of *Jacquinia* contain large amounts of saponins and have been used as a substitute for soap and as a fish poison (*barbasco*). On the Ecuadorian coast, crushed, immature fruits of *J. sprucei* are used to kill or stupefy unwanted fish in shrimp-farm baskets. The orange flowers of *Clavija* and *Jacquinia* are used by indigenous people as ornamentals and for making ephemeral, sweet-scented necklaces. The fruits of *Clavija* are edible.

References. KNUDSEN, J. T., AND B. STÅHL. 1994. Floral odours in the Theophrastaceae. *Biochem. Syst. & Ecol.* 22(3): 259–68. STÅHL, B. 1987. The genus *Theophrasta* (Theophrastaceae). Foliar structures, floral biology and taxonomy. *Nordic J. Bot.* 7:529–38. STÅHL, B. 1989. A synopsis of Central American Theophrastaceae. *Nordic J. Bot.* 9:15–30. STÅHL, B. 1991. A revision of *Clavija* (Theophrastaceae). *Opera Bot.* 107:1–77. STÅHL, B. 1993. *Votschia*, a new genus of Theophrastaceae from northeastern Panama. *Brittonia* 45:204–07. STÅHL, B. 1996. A synopsis of *Jacquinia* (Theophrastaceae) in the Antilles and South America. *Nordic J. Bot.* 15:493–511.

THYMELAEACEAE (the Daphne Family)

KERRY BARRINGER AND LORIN I. NEVLING, JR.

Figure 197, Plate 49

- *shrubs and trees, rarely lianas or herbs, poisonous*

- *leaves usually alternate, sometimes opposite, simple*

- *flowers with floral tube; ovary pseudomonomerous*

- *fruits usually drupes, sometimes nuts*

Number of genera and species. Worldwide, the Thymelaeaceae comprise about 45 genera and 450 species. In tropical America, there are seven genera and 75 species. The largest genus in the neotropics is *Daphnopsis* (about 50 species). The other genera have fewer than 10 species each.

Distribution and habitat. The Thymelaeaceae occur in tropical, subtropical, and temperate climates throughout the world. They are most diverse in Australia and tropical Africa and are also abundant in the Mediterranean and on the steppes of central Asia.

In the Western Hemisphere, species are predominantly tropical and subtropical. Two species of *Dirca* occur north of Mexico and four species of *Ovidia* grow in southern South America.

In the neotropics, species of Thymeleaceae occur in both montane and lowland regions, often in moist forest. Plants of the family are never a dominant or conspicuous part of their habitat.

Family classification. The Thymelaeaceae are placed in the Myrtales by Cronquist. Some authors feel the family may be aligned with the Elaeagnaceae, because of their internal phloem and prominent floral tube, but this placement is not supported by embryological and molecular data. The Euphorbiaceae and Flacourtiaceae have also been suggested as possible relatives based on similarities in pollen and biochemisty. Recent molecular analyses place the Thymelaeaceae with members of the Malvales.

The Thymelaeaceae have been variously divided into subfamilies, and some of these have been raised to family rank; e.g., the Gonystylaceae, Daphnaceae, and Aquilariaceae. Despite the rank at which they are recognized, these groups appear to be closely related. Only the subfamily Thymel-

Figure 197. THYMELAEACEAE. *Schoenobiblus daphnoides.* **A.** Stem with leaves and inflorescences. **B.** Detail of part of inflorescence (right) and inflorescence after flowers have fallen (left). **C.** Lateral view of staminate flower bud. **D.** Lateral view of staminate flower. **E.** Longitudinal section of staminate flower with two perianth lobes and three stamens removed; note pistillode in center of flower. **F.** Stem with leaves and infructescence. **G.** Longitudinal section of fruit with seed intact. Reprinted with permission from Mori et al. (2002). Artist: Bobbi Angell.

aeoideae is represented in the neotropics. The Neotropical members are distinguished by having three, four, five, or eight distinct stamens, a pseudomonomerous ovary, and a well-developed floral tube.

Features of the family. Habit: usually shrubs or small trees, rarely large trees, lianas, or herbs, the stems and leaves tough and flexible because of long fibers in bark and phloem. **Stipules** absent. **Leaves** alternate or sometimes opposite, sometimes with close-set internodes causing alternate leaves to appear opposite or whorled, simple; blades usually tough, the toughness due to sclerids and long fibers, the margins entire; venation pinnate, the veins often slightly impressed adaxially, prominent abaxially. **Inflorescences** axillary or at apices of short, axillary branches, often in umbellate clusters, or variously arranged clusters, of solitary flowers. **Flowers** actinomorphic or appearing so, unisexual (the plants usually dioecious in *Daphnopsis*, *Funifera*, and *Schoenobiblus*) or sometimes bisexual, a distinct floral tube present, the tube tubular or campanulate, often ribbed, usually pale green, white, or cream; sepals 4–5, borne on apex of floral tube, narrowly ovate to triangular, usually pale green, white, or cream; petals equal to or twice as many as sepals, lacking, or reduced to minute scales or slight ridge, borne at apex of floral tube; androecium with 3–5 or 8 stamens, the stamens

usually equal to or twice as many as sepals, distinct, borne at apex of floral tube or within tube, sometimes in 2 distinct whorls (when twice as many as sepals, the whorls inserted at different heights in floral tube), absent in pistillate flowers or reduced to staminodia, the filaments usually short; nectary disc usually present at base of floral tube, entire or of a few separate nectaries, sometimes conspicuously lobed and corona-like; gynoecium sometimes borne on short gynophore, the ovary superior, pseudomonomerous, the locule 1, the style usually terminal, sometimes slightly lateral, the stigma capitate; placentation apical, the ovule 1; pistillode often present in staminate flowers. **Fruits** usually drupes, sometimes nuts, often turning white, yellow, or orange when ripe. **Seeds** relatively large, fleshy caruncle or aril often present, the caruncle usually white, sometimes becoming exposed after pericarp of drupe dries and splits open; endosperm sometimes present, oily, the embryo straight.

All parts of the plants contain many poisonous and mutagenic substances, but the most common is daphnin, a type of coumarin.

Some species of *Daphnopsis* appear to have a thick, woody root or underground stem from which branches sprout. The young branches are often flexible and difficult to break because of strong fibers in the phloem and cortex and because of a poorly lignified xylem. There is often a thin cylinder of a internal phloem in the stems.

Natural history. No information is available on pollination biology. The fruits of Thymmelaceae are probably bird-dispersed.

Economic uses. Species of *Daphne*, native to the Eastern Hemisphere, often are cultivated as ornamentals in warm-temperate climates. Fruits, leaves, and bark are used as fish poisons, and, rarely, as purgatives. The tough phloem fibers often are twisted into cords. The inner bark of *Lagetta lagetto*, the West Indian lace bark or gauze tree, is stretched to form a delicate, lacelike net that is used as an ornamental textile in Jamaica. In the Eastern Hemisphere, the fibers of some species are utilized for making fine paper.

References. DOMKE, W. 1934. Untersuchungen über die systematische und geographische Gliederung der Thymelaeaceen. *Bibioth. Bot.* 27(111):1–151. GILG, E. 1894. Studien über die Verwandschaftsverhältniße der Thymelaeales und über die anatomische Methode. *Bot. Jahrb. Syst.* 18: 488–574. HEINIG, K. H. 1951. Studies of the floral morphology of the Thymelaeaceae. *Amer. J. Bot.* 38:113–32. HERBER, B. E. 2003. Thymelaeaceae. In *The Families and Genera of Vascular Plants*, eds. K. Kubitzki and C. Bayer. 5:373–96. Berlin: Springer-Verlag. NEVLING, L. I., JR. 1959. A revision of the genus *Daphnopsis*. *Ann. Missouri Bot. Gard.* 46:257–358. NEVLING, L. I., JR. 1962. The Thymelaeaceae of the southeastern United States. *J. Arnold Arbor.* 43:428–34.

NEVLING, L. I., JR. 1964. Note on the genus *Ovidia*. *Darwiniana* 13:72–86. NEVLING, L. I., JR. 1976. A new species of *Funifera*. *Phytologia* 32:480–82. PLOWMAN, T., AND L. I. NEVLING, JR. 1986. A new species of *Lasiadenia* (Thymelaeaceae) from Venezuela. *Brittonia* 38:114–18. SUPPRIAN, K. 1894. Beitrage zur Kenntnis der Thymelaeaceae und Pen-

naeaceae. Thesis, Friedrich-Wilhelm-Universität zu Berlin. Leipzig: Wilhelm Engelmann. WEBERLING, F., AND U. HERKOMMER. 1989. Untersuchungen zur Infloreszenzmorphologie der Thymelaeaceen. *Tropische und subtropische Pflanzenwelt*, ser. 68:1–124. Mainz: Akademie der Wissenschaften und der Literatur.

TICODENDRACEAE

DENNIS WM. STEVENSON

Figure 198

- *trees*

- *stipule scars encircling nodes*

- *leaves alternate, simple; blade margins toothed*

- *staminate inflorescences in spikelike clusters of thyrses*

- *flowers unisexual; perianth reduced or absent; stamens 8–10; ovary inferior*

- *fruits drupes*

Numbers of genera and species. The family Ticodendraceae comprises a single species, *Ticodendron incognitum*.

Distribution and habitat. *Ticodendron incognitum* is found in wet montane forests along the Alantic coast of Central America from Guatemala to Central Panama.

Family classification. The Ticodendraceae was discovered in Central America in 1989 and thus was not considered by Cronquist. It is generally agreed that this family is related to the Fagaceae, Betulaceae, and Nothofagaceae. Molecular analyses suggest that the Ticodendraceae and Betulaceae are sister groups.

Features of the family. Habit: trees, evergreen. **Stipules** 2, small, cauducous, leaving scar encircling nodes. **Leaves** alternate, simple; petioles short; blade margins toothed. **Staminate inflorescences** axillary, borne in spikelike clusters of thyrses, each cymule with 1–3 flowers. **Pistillate inflorescences** axillary, of solitary flowers. **Flowers** actinomorphic, unisexual (plants dioecious). **Staminate flowers:** perianth absent; androecium of 8–10 stamens, the filaments pubescent, the anthers basifixed, longitudinally dehiscent; gynoecium vestigial, rarely present. **Pistillate flowers:** perianth reduced to rim; androecium absent; gynoecium syncarpous, the ovary inferior, the carpels 2, the locules 2 per carpel, the styles 2, the stigmatic surface pubescent; placentation marginal, the

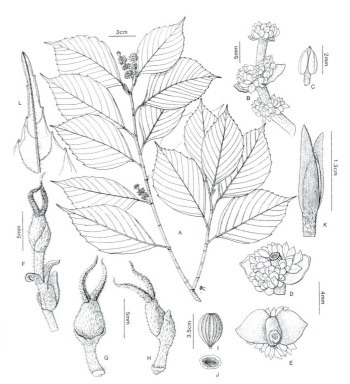

Figure 198. TICODENDRACEAE. *Ticodendron incognitum*. **A.** Stem with leaves and staminate inflorescences. **B.** Staminate inflorescence. **C.** Adaxial view of stamen. **D.** Apical view of staminate flowers. **E.** Basal view of staminate flowers showing subtending bracts. **F.** Pistillate inflorescence. **G.** Adaxial view of pistillate flower. **H.** Lateral view of pistillate flower. **I.** Lateral view of endocarp. **J.** Transverse section of endocarp. **K.** Lateral view of stipules. **L.** Detail of leaf apex. Reprinted with permission from Gómez-Laurito and Gómez P. (1989). Artist: John Myers.

ovules 1 per locule (only 1 of 4 ovules developing). **Fruits** drupes (similar to a walnut). **Seeds** with large, oily embryos.

Natural history. Very little is known about the biology of *Ticodendron*. The reduced perianth of the unisexual flowers; the rather long pubescent stigmas; and numerous, small pollen grains indicate wind pollination. The fruits, with a single large, oily embryo, suggest dispersal by animals.

Economic uses. No uses are known for this family.

References. HAMMEL, B., AND W. BURGER. 1991. Neither oak nor alder, but nearly: the history of Ticodendraceae. *Ann. Missouri Bot. Gard.* 78:89–95. KUBITZKI, K. 1993. Ticodendraceae. In *The Families and Genera of Vascular Plants*, eds. K. Kubitzki, J. G. Rohwer, and V. Bittrich, 2:594–96. New York: Springer-Verlag. TOBE, H. 1991. Reproductive morphology, anatomy, and relationships of *Ticodendron*. *Ann. Missouri Bot. Gard.* 78:135–42.

TILIACEAE (Basswood Family)

PAUL A. FRYXELL

Figure 199, Plate 49

- *usually trees or shrubs*
- *leaves usually alternate, often distichous; blade base ± asymmetrical*
- *flowers actinomorphic, usually bisexual; stamens often in fascicles*

Numbers of genera and species. Worldwide, the Tiliaceae comprise about 50 genera and more than 700 species. In tropical America, there are about 20 genera and more than 150 species. The largest genus, *Triumfetta*, has about 50 Neotropical species. Other relatively speciose Neotropical genera include *Apeiba*, *Corchorus*, *Heliocarpus*, *Luehea*, *Mortoniodendron*, and *Trichospermum*. A few Neotropical genera, *Hydrogaster*, *Pentaplaris*, and *Vasivaea*, have only one or a few species each.

Distribution and habitat. Tiliaceae occur widely in tropical parts of the Americas, and in tropical Africa, Asia, Australia, and Oceania. The genus *Tilia* is characteristically found in temperate areas in Asia, North America, and Europe and extends into the neotropics at higher elevations in Mexico. *Corchorus* is pantropical, and *Trichospermum* occurs in Malaysia and Oceania, with a few species reaching tropical America.

The family is often found as trees in forested habitats and as shrubs in weedy habitats.

Family classification. The Tiliaceae have traditionally been placed in the Malvales (i.e., *sensu* Cronquist), but recent molecular analyses suggest that the family is artificial (see Malvales). The genera *Prockia*, *Hasseltia*, and a few others are now recognized as belonging to the Flacourtiaceae, and the genera *Crinodendron*, *Elaeocarpus*, *Petenaea*, *Sloanea*, and *Vallea* are now generally transferred to the Elaeocarpaceae. Of the remaining genera, *Heliocarpus* and *Triumfetta* are clearly allied (tribe Triumfettieae) on the basis of both floral and fruit morphology. The Lueheeae include *Apeiba*, *Luehea*, *Lueheopsis*, *Mollia*, and possibly *Trichospermum*, although the latter is sometimes allied with the Paleotropical *Grewia*

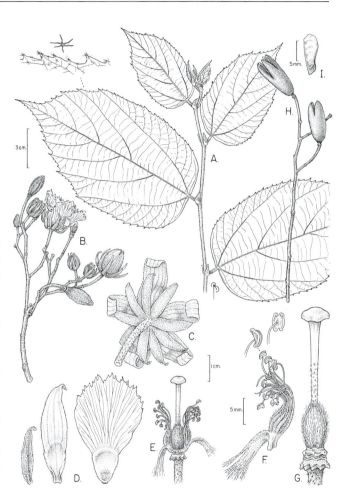

Figure 199. TILIACEAE. *Luehea speciosa*. **A.** Stem with leaves and detail of leaf margin and stellate hair (above left). **B.** Inflorescence. **C.** Basal view of flower showing epicalyx. **D.** Adaxial views of petal (right), sepal (center), and unit of epicalyx (left). **E.** Lateral view of gynoecium and two fascicles of stamens. **F.** Lateral view of fascicle of stamens with pubescent staminodes and detail of anthers (above). **G.** Lateral view of gynoecium. **H.** Part of infructescence. **I.** Winged seed. Reprinted with permission from Mori et al. (2002). Artist: Bobbi Angell.

in the tribe Grewieae. *Tilia* is relatively isolated in the Tilieae on the basis of its distinctive inflorescence and fruit structure and by its temperate distribution. *Muntingia* is sometimes placed in the Tilieae as well. Taxonomic placement of

Muntingia is uncertain, having been variously placed in the Elaeocarpaceae, Flacourtiaceae, and Tiliaceae. In this book it is treated in the Muntingiaceae and considered a separate clade within the Malvales. The Neotropical genera *Asterophorum*, *Berrya* (*Carpodiptera*), *Corchorus*, *Hydrogaster*, *Mortoniodendron*, *Pentaplaris*, and *Vasivaea* are more isolated.

Features of the family. Habit: trees or shrubs, rarely herbs (*Corchorus*); stellate or simple hairs present, sometimes peltate scales present. **Stipules** present. **Leaves** usually alternate, often distichous, simple; blades ovate or elliptic, the base ± asymmetrical, the margins usually serrate. **Inflorescences** axillary or terminal, often cymes, sometimes paniculate, or of solitary flowers. **Flowers** actinomorphic, usually bisexual, sometimes unisexual (plants polygamodioecious or dioecious); epicalyx sometimes present; sepals 3–5, valvate, distinct or connate at base; petals usually 5, sometimes absent; stamens 10–many, often in fascicles; gynoecium syncarpous, the ovary superior, the carpels 2–10, the locules 2–10, the style 1, the stigma capitate or capitellate; placentation axile (or intruded parietal), the ovules solitary or numerous. **Fruits** capsules, nuts, or berries. **Seeds** 1–many per carpel, sometimes pilose, sometimes arillate (*Mortoniodendron*).

Natural history. Insect pollination is common, especially in the showy-flowered genera such as *Luehea*. In *Tilia*, wind pollination may be operative, and as many as 32,000 pollen grains may be released from a single flower.

Several modes of seed dispersal have evolved in the Tiliaceae. In spiny-fruited genera (e.g., *Triumfetta* and *Heliocarpus*), the fruits are evidently dispersed by attachment to fur or feathers. The arillate seeds of *Mortoniodendron* are likely dispersed by birds attracted to the fleshy arils. Seeds with wings (e.g., in *Luehea*) probably are dispersed by the wind. The well-known winged infructescences of *Tilia* (functionally equal to samaras) are adaptations for wind dispersal, although the effectiveness of this mechanism has been questioned.

Economic uses. Stem fibers of economic importance (jute) are obtained primarily from *Corchorus capsularis* and secondarily from *C. olitorius*. Species of *Tilia* (basswood, linden, lime) and of *Apeiba* are sources of timber, and the former is grown as a shade tree, especially in temperate regions. The fragrant flowers of *Tilia* are sources of an excellent honey and an oil that is used in perfumery. The introduced African *Sparrmannia* is grown occasionally as an ornamental tree in Mexico.

References. BAYER, C., AND L. J. DORR. 1999. A synopsis of the Neotropical genus *Pentaplaris* with remarks on its systematic position within core Malvales. *Brittonia* 51:134–48. BAYER, C. AND K. KUBITZKI. 2003. Malvaceae. In *The Families and Genera of Vascular Plants*, eds. K. Kubitzki and C. Bayer. 5:225–311. Berlin: Springer-Verlag. BORNSTEIN, A. J. 1989. Tiliaceae. In *Flora of the Lesser Antilles: Leeward and Windward Islands*, ed. R. Howard, 5:184–99. Jamaica Plain, MA: Arnold Arboretum, Harvard University. BURRET, M. 1926. Beiträge zur Kenntniss der Tiliaceen. *Notizbl. Bot. Gart. Berlin* 9:592–880. FRYXELL, P. A. 2001. Tiliaceae. In *Flora Novo-Galiciana*, ed. R. McVaugh, 3:68–109. JONES, G. N. 1968. Taxonomy of American species of Linden (*Tilia*). *Illinois Biol. Monogr.* 39:1–156. LAY, K. K. 1949. A revision of the genus *Heliocarpus*. *Ann. Missouri Bot. Gard.* 36:507–41. LAY, K. K. 1950. The American species of *Triumfetta*. *Ann. Missouri Bot. Gard.* 37:315–95. ROBYNS, A. 1964. Flora of Panama part VI, family 114. Tiliaceae. *Ann. Missouri Bot. Gard.* 51:1–35. SCHUMANN, C. 1886. Tiliaceae. In *Flora Brasiliensis*, C. F. P. von Martius, 12(3):117–200. STANDLEY, P. C. 1923. Tiliaceae. In Trees and shrubs of Mexico. *Contr. U.S. Natl. Herb.* 23:734–46.

TOVARIACEAE (Tovaria Family)

MICHAEL NEE

Figure 200, Plate 49

- *coarse herbs or soft-woody shrubs, producing a rank odor*

- *leaves alternate, trifoliolate*

- *flowers usually with 8 sepals, petals, and stamens*

- *fruits berries*

- *seeds numerous per fruit, small*

Numbers of genera and species. The Tovariaceae are endemic to tropical America and make up a single genus, *Tovaria*, and two species.

Distribution and habitat. *Tovaria pendula* is a montane species found from Veracruz, Mexico to Bolivia, and *T. diffusa* is native to Jamaica.

Species of *Tovaria* grow in montane forests, where they

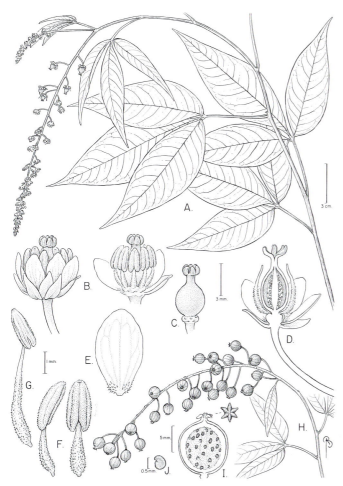

are adapted for quick growth in sunny openings caused by landslides and other disturbances.

Family classification. The Tovariaceae are placed in the Capparales by Cronquist. The family has often been included in the Capparaceae, from which it differs mainly by its 6–8 rather than two carpels and by the presence of endosperm. Vegetatively, species of *Tovaria* resemble those of Capparaceae subfamily Cleomoideae. Recent analyses also support an alignment with other members of Cronquist's Capparales; e.g., the Brassicaceae and the extra-Neotropical Resedaceae.

Features of the family. Habit: coarse herbs or soft-woody shrubs, producing a rank odor. **Stipules** absent. **Leaves** alternate, trifoliolate. **Inflorescences** terminal, elongate racemes. **Flowers** actinomorphic, bisexual; sepals (6)8(9); petals (6)8(9); androecium of (6)8(9) stamens, the stamens arising from within lobed nectary disc, the anthers dehiscing by longitudinal slits; gynoecium syncarpous, the ovary superior, the carpels 6–8, the locule 1, but appearing as more because of intruded placentas, the style short, beaklike, the stigmas spreading; placentation parietal, the ovules numerous. **Fruits** berries, soft, juicy. **Seeds** numerous per fruit, small; endosperm present.

Natural history. Nothing is known about the pollination and dispersal biology of this family.

Economic uses. The family has no known economic uses.

References. APPEL, O., AND C. BAYER. 2003. Tovariaceae. In *The Families and Genera of Vascular Plants*, eds. K. Kubitzki and C. Bayer. 5:397–99. Berlin: Springer-Verlag. CASTILLO-CAMPOS, G. 1996. Tovariaceae. In *Flora de Veracruz*, fasc. 91:1–7. Xalapa, Mexico: INIREB. D'ARCY, W. G. 1979. Capparaceae-Tovariaceae. In Flora of Panama, eds. R. E. Woodson, Jr., R. W. Schery et al. *Ann. Missouri Bot. Gard.* 66:117–22. RODMAN, J. E., K. G. KAROL, R. A. PRICE, AND K. J. SYSTMA. 1996. Molecules, morphology, and Dahlgren's expanded order Capparales. *Syst. Bot.* 21:289–307.

Figure 200. TOVARIACEAE. *Tovaria pendula* (A, Nee et al. 26377; B–G, Lert 855; H–J, Morales 1496). **A.** Stem with leaves and inflorescences. **B.** Lateral views of flower, intact (left) and with some bracts, sepals, and petals removed (right). **C.** Lateral view of gynoecium. **D.** Medial section of flower. **E.** Adaxial view of petal. **F.** Lateral (left) and adaxial (right) views of immature stamens. **G.** Lateral-adaxial view of mature stamen. **H.** Stem with leaves and infructescence. **I.** Medial section of fruit with persistent sigma (below left) and apical view of sigma (above right). **J.** Seed. Original. Artist: Bobbi Angell.

TRIGONIACEAE (Trigonia Family)

MARIA LÚCIA KAWASAKI

Figure 201, Plate 49

- *usually lianas, sometimes shrubs or trees*
- *leaves usually opposite, simple*
- *flowers zygomorphic*
- *fruits septicidal capsules, trigonous*
- *seeds pubescent*

Numbers of genera and species. Worldwide, the Trigoniaceae comprise four genera and about 35 species. In tropical America, there are two genera and about 30 species. *Trigonia*, the largest genus, includes about 27 species in the Western Hemisphere. The other three genera are represented by a single species each: *Trigoniodendron spiritusanctense* (southeastern Brazil), *Humbertiodendron saboureaui* (Madagascar), and *Trigoniastrum hypoleucum* (southeastern Asia).

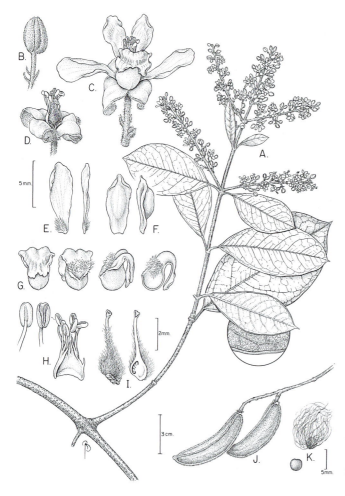

Figure 201. TRIGONIACEAE. *Trigonia villosa*. **A.** Stem with leaves and inflorescences and detail of abaxial surface of leaf showing pubescence (lower right). **B.** Lateral view of floral bud. **C.** Oblique-apical view of flower. **D.** Lateral view of flower after petals have fallen. **E.** Adaxial (left) and lateral (right) views of a lateral petal. **F.** Adaxial (left) and lateral (right) views of anterior petal. **G.** Abaxial (left), adaxial (center), and lateral (right) views and medial section (far right) of saccate posterior petal. **H.** Androecium (right) adaxial (center) and abaxial (left) views of anthers. **I.** Lateral view of intact gynoecium with basal nectary (left) and medial section (right) of gynoecium. **J.** Lateral views of fruits. **K.** Seed with hairs (above) and with hairs removed (below). Reprinted with permission from Mori et al. (2002). Artist: Bobbi Angell.

Distribution and habitat. In the neotropics, the Trigoniaceae are represented by *Trigonia*, which occurs from Mexico to Paraguay, and *Trigoniodendron*, known only from the state of Espírito Santo in southeastern Brazil.

Neotropical species of Trigoniaceae are found in lowland, periodically flooded or nonflooded moist forests, commonly in disturbed areas.

Family classification. The Trigoniaceae are traditionally placed in the Order Polygalales (i.e., *sensu* Cronquist), and related to the Vochysiaceae and Polygalaceae. Molecular studies, however, have suggested affinities with the Chrysobalanaceae and Dichapetalaceae. The two genera of Neotropical Trigoniaceae are distinguished by the arrangement of the leaves (opposite in *Trigonia* and alternate in *Trigoniodendron*).

Features of the family. Habit: lianas, sometimes shrubs or trees. **Indumentum** often present, of simple hairs. **Stipules** present, interpetiolar, often connate, often deciduous, leaving noticeable scars. **Leaves** opposite, rarely alternate (*Trigoniodendron*), simple; blades often bicolored, covered by whitish hairs abaxially, the margins entire; venation pinnate. **Inflorescences** terminal or axillary, racemes or panicles; bracteoles 2, subtending flower. **Flowers** zygomorphic, bisexual; sepals connate, the lobes 5, unequal; petals 5, unequal, white, the posterior (upper) petal largest, forming saccate standard, the two lateral petals spatulate, the anterior (lower) petals often forming a saccate keel; nectary glands 2, often present, in front of posterior petal; androecium with (5)6–7(8) stamens, the filaments united on anterior side of flower, the anthers dehiscing by longitudinal slits; staminodes 0–4; gynoecium syncarpous, the ovary superior, the carpels 3, the locules 3, rarely 1, the style simple, the stigma capitate; placentation axile, rarely parietal in 1-locular ovaries, the ovules several per locule, biseriate. **Fruits** septicidal capsules, trigonous. **Seeds** pubescent; endosperm absent, the embryo straight.

The Eastern Hemisphere genera are distinguished from the Western Hemisphere genera by the type of fruit (3-winged samaras in *Humbertiodendron* and *Trigoniastrum*) and by the number of ovules in each locule (one in *Humbertiodendron* and two in *Trigoniastrum*).

Natural history. Flowers of the Trigoniaceae are pollinated by insects, especially bees. The hairy seeds are dispersed mainly by wind, but dispersal by water has also been suggested for a few species.

Economic uses. The family is of little economic importance. The wood of some species has local uses.

References. BOESEWINKEL, F. D. 1987. Ovules and seeds of Trigoniaceae. *Acta Bot. Neerl.* 36:81–91. GUIMARÃES, E. F., AND J. R. MIGUEL. 1987. Contribuição ao conhecimento de Trigoniaceae brasileiras. VI. *Trigoniodendron* E. F. Guimarães and J. R. Miguel. *Revista. Brasil. Biol.* 47(4): 559–63. LLERAS, E. 1978. Trigoniaceae. *Fl. Neotrop. Monogr.* 19:1–73.

TROPAEOLACEAE (Nasturtium Family)

FLOR CHAVEZ

Figure 202

- *usually climbing or prostrate vines*
- *plants containing mustard oils*
- *leaves alternate, usually simple, usually peltate*
- *flowers zygomorphic, bisexual; calyx spurred; stamens 8*
- *fruits schizocarps*

Numbers of genera and species. Endemic to the Western Hemisphere, the Tropaeolaceae comprise three genera and 89 species. In tropical America, there is a single genus, *Tropaeolum*, and ca. 60 species of the total of 86 species found in the genus.

Distribution and habitat. *Tropaeolum* ranges from southern Mexico to extratropical temperate Chile. Species of this genus are mostly of Andean distribution and are rarely found in tropical lowland forests. The remaining genera in the family, *Magallana* (two species) and *Tropaeastrum* (1), are endemic to Patagonia.

Family classification. The Tropaeolaceae are placed in the Geraniales by Cronquist, near the Geraniaceae, Limnanthaceae, and Balsaminaceae. Molecular analyses place this family in a redefined Brassicales, sister to *Akania* of Australia and *Bretschneidera* of Asia.

Genera within the family can be distinguished morphologically by fruit type (schizocarps vs. winged samaras in *Magallana*), pedicels (erect in *Magallana* vs. usually pendent in *Tropaeolum*), and the perianth (e.g., calyx spur much reduced or absent in *Trophaeastrum*).

Features of the family. Habit: herbaceous, usually vines, these climbing (by twining petioles) or prostrate, annual or perennial; mustard oils present; rhizome or tuber present when plant perennial; hairs sometimes present on leaves and flowers. **Stipules** usually present, usually small and caducous. **Leaves** alternate, usually simple, rarely palmately compound, the simple leaves usually distinctly peltate or rarely subpeltate; petioles always present, rarely short, often cirrhose; blades often palmately lobed, sometimes deeply so, or unlobed, the margins entire, the apices sometimes emarginate or mucronate; venation palmate in simple leaves. **Inflorescences** axillary, of solitary flowers, the solitary flowers sometimes clustered, or rarely in umbels; pedicels usually pendent, sometimes cirrhose. **Flowers** zygomorphic, bisex-

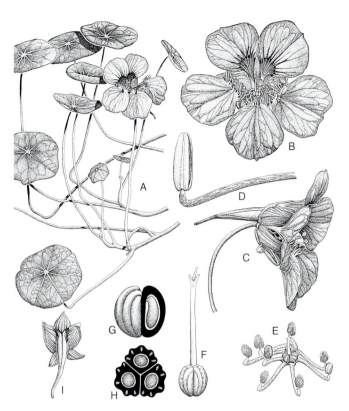

Figure 202. TROPAEOLACEAE. *Tropaeolum majus*. **A.** Stems with leaves and flower (x½). **B.** Apical view of flower (x1). **C.** Lateral view of flower (x1). **D.** Stamen (x8). **E.** Apical view of stamens and gynoecium (x2). **F.** Lateral view of gynoecium (x4). **G.** Partial medial section of ovary (x8). **H.** Schematic transverse section of ovary (x8). **I.** Basal view of calyx (x1). Reprinted with permission from Cronquist (1981). Artist: William S. Moye.

ual; calyx with 5 lobes, rarely bilabiate, spurred, variable in color (e.g., green, yellow, red, or orange); corolla with 5 or rarely 2 petals, the petals often spatulate or clawed, the upper 3 and lower 2 often contrasting in size and shape, variable in color (e.g., green, yellow, red, purple, or blackish), sometimes with spots or contrasting colors, the margins sometimes dentate and/or ciliate; androecium of 8 stamens, the filaments distinct, the anthers basifixed, dehiscing by longitudinal slits; carpophore sometimes present; gynoecium syncarpous, the ovary superior, the carpels 3, the locules 3, the style 1, the stigmas 3; placentation axile, the ovules 1 per locule, pendulous. **Fruits** schizocarps, the mericarps 3. **Seeds** 3 per fruit; endosperm absent, the embryo straight.

Natural history. *Tropaeolum* has been reported to be pollinated by bees and hummingbirds. Nectar is known to accumulate in the calyx spur of this genus. No information is available on dispersal biology.

Economic uses. Several species of *Tropaeolum* are grown as ornamentals or for food. For example, *T. majus* (nasturtium) is a common ornamental known only from cultivation and is probably of hybrid origin. Other traditional uses of this species are as a diuretic and as food (e.g., pickled flower buds or the fresh flowers as a garnish for salads). *Tropaeolum peregrinum* is another popular ornamental native to Peru. In the Andes of Venezuela and Bolivia, *T. tuberosum*, locally known as *mashua* or *añu*, is cultivated as a food crop for its edible tubers.

References. ANDERSSON, L., AND S. ANDERSSON. 2000. A molecular phylogeny of Tropaeolaceae and its systematic implications. *Taxon* 49:721–36. BAYER, C., AND O. APPEL. 2003. Tropaeolaceae. In *The Families and Genera of Vascular Plants*, eds. K. Kubitzki and C. Bayer. 5:400–04. Berlin: Springer-Verlag. FABBRI, L. T., AND J. J. VALLA. 1998. Some aspects of the reproductive biology of *Tropaeolum pentaphyllum* (Tropaeolaceae). *Darwiniana* 36:51–58. RODMAN J., R. A. PRICE, K. KAROL, E. CONTI, K. J. SYTSMA, AND J. D. PALMER. 1993. Nucleotide sequences of the *rbc*L gene indicate monophyly of mustard oil plants. *Ann. Missouri Bot. Gard.* 80:686–99. SPARRE, B. 1973. Tropaeolaceae. In *Flora of Ecuador*, eds. G. Harling and P. Sparre, *Opera Bot.* ser. B, 2:1–30. SPARRE, B., AND L. ANDERSSON. 1991. A taxonomic revision of the Tropaeolaceae. *Opera Bot.* 108:1–139.

TURNERACEAE (Turnera Family)

MARÍA MERCEDES ARBO

Figure 203, Plate 50

- *herbs, shrubs, or rarely trees*
- *leaves alternate, simple, with nectaries in many* Turnera
- *inflorescences mostly of solitary flowers, often adnate to petiole in many* Turnera
- *flowers actinomorphic; sepals 5, variously connate; petals 5, distinct; styles 3, the stigmas generally brushlike; placentation parietal*
- *fruits loculicidal capsules*
- *seeds arillate*

Numbers of genera and species. Worldwide, the Turneraceae comprise ten genera and about 190 species. In tropical America, there are four genera and about 170 species. *Turnera* (120 species) and *Piriqueta* (41 species) are the largest genera. *Erblichia* has one species in the Western Hemisphere and four species in Madagascar and *Adenoa* is monotypic.

Distribution and habitat. *Adenoa* is endemic to Cuba and *Erblichia odorata* is found in Mesoamerica. *Piriqueta* and *Turnera* are widespread in tropical America, but they also have one and two species, respectively, in Africa. Brazil harbors the highest number of species with the greatest concentration of endemism found in the mountains of the states of Bahia, Goiás, and Minas Gerais.

Although most species are found in the tropics between sea level and 2600 meters, *Piriqueta cistoides* subspecies *caroliniana* extends close to 33°N in the United States and

Figure 203. TURNERACEAE. *Turnera glaziovii*. **A.** Stem with leaves and inflorescence. **B.** Lateral (right) and adaxial (left) views of petioles showing glands. **C.** Lateral (right) and apical (left) views of flowers. **D.** Medial section of flower with gynoecium removed. **E.** Lateral (left) and abaxial (right) views of stamens. **F.** Lateral view of gynoecium (center), medial section of gynoecium (right), and transverse section of ovary (left). **G.** Lateral view of fruit on stem (right) and seed (left). Reprinted with permission from Mori et al. (2002). Artist: Bobbi Angell.

P. *taubatensis* and *Turnera sidoides* extend into temperate Argentina.

The Turneraceae occupy a variety of habitats, from grasslands to tropical rain forest. Species of the family are especially abundant in Brazilian *cerrado* and *campo rupestre* at higher elevations. Although diversity of Turneraceae is low in forest environments, *Erblichia odorata* and the Amazonian species of *Turnera* series *Salicifoliae* and *Stenodictyae* grow in lowland forests.

Family classification. The Turneraceae have long been considered close relatives of Passifloraceae, Malesherbiaceae, and Violaceae. The members of these and several other families, all three-carpellate and with parietal placentation, were traditionally placed in the order Parietales. The position of this group within the recognized orders of dicots has changed in the several decades. Turneraceae and Passifloraceae share many morphological and anatomical traits, and the presence of cyclopentenoid cyanohydrin glycosides suggest relationships with other families such as Flacourtiaceae. Cronquist places all of the aforementioned families and 20 others in the order Violales.

Recent phylogenetic analyses, based upon one or several genes, combined or not with morphology, chemistry, and other non-DNA characters, confirm the close relationships of Turneraceae with Passifloraceae, Malesherbiaceae, and Violaceae; however, the new analyses place the families in the order Malpighiales together with families such as the Euphorbiaceae (also three-carpellate) and Salicaceae.

These phylogenies were obtained by sampling only one species from each family in most cases, so, although the monophyly of the order Malpighiales is apparently well supported, additional research needs to be done to determine the relationships of Turneraceae with the other members of the order.

Features of the family. Habit: herbs, shrubs, or rarely trees, the stems erect or decumbent, frequently with serial axillary buds; trichomes usually present, stellate in *Adenoa* and *Piriqueta*, simple and unicellular in *Erblichia* and most *Turnera*, glandular hairs often present, these often long and capitate with swollen bases in *Piriqueta*, capitate and short stipitate in *Turnera* series *Papilliferae*, sessile and capitate in most *Turnera* series *Annulares* and *T.* series *Microphyllae*. **Stipules** generally small or wanting, developed in *Erblichia*, *Turnera* series *Salicifoliae*, and *T.* series *Microphyllae* and *Capitatae*. **Leaves** alternate, simple, often bearing adaxial extrafloral nectaries at apex of petiole or base of blade margin (rarely abaxial), the nectaries of *Turnera* series *Turnera* with porelike; blades with margins entire, crenate, or toothed, rarely pinnatifid. **Inflorescences** axillary or terminal, usually of solitary flowers, cymose or racemose in some *Piriqueta* and *Turnera* series *Salicifoliae*, *Capitatae*, and *Anomalae*, epiphyllous by adnation of peduncle and petiole in *Turnera* series *Turnera* and *Leiocarpae*; bracteoles 2, generally subtending flowers. **Flowers** actinomorphic, bisexual, ephemeral, frequently showy, hetero- or homostylous; sepals 5, nearly distinct in *Erblichia*, united into 10-nerved tube in *Adenoa*, *Piriqueta*, and *Turnera*, the lobes quincuncial; corona present in *Piriqueta*, narrow, fringed, inserted at bases of petal and sepal lobes; corolla commonly yellow, sometimes red, orange, pink, or white, frequently with purple spot at base of each petal, the petals 5, distinct, ligulate in *Erblichia*, clawed, the claw adnate to calyx, forming floral tube; androecium with 5 stamens, the stamens alternate with petals, the filaments inserted at base of floral tube (*Adenoa*, *Erblichia*, *Piriqueta* and several series of *Turnera*, then flowers hypogynous), or each filament with basal nectary and margins adnate to floral tube up to throat, then with 5 nectariferous pockets (*Turnera* series *Turnera* and *T.* series *Anomalae*, then flowers perigynous), the anthers commonly dorsifixed, nearly basifixed in *Erblichia* and *Turnera* series *Turnera*, dehiscing by longitudinal slits; gynoecium syncarpous, the ovary generally superior or slightly half-inferior in *Turnera* series *Turnera* and *Anomalae*), the carpels 3, the locule 1, the styles 3, distinct, erect or reflexed, glabrous or pilose, the stigmas generally brushlike; placentation parietal, the ovules 1–numerous per placenta, anatropous, bitegmic, crassinucellar. **Fruits** loculicidal capsules, smooth, verrucous, or tuberculate. **Seeds** 1–60, straight or curved, commonly reticulate, sometimes ridged, slightly pitted, with distinct exostome, sometimes with prominent, navellike chalaza; aril present, fleshy, membranous when dry, glabrous to exceptionally hairy, generally inserted around hilum.

Adenoa, *Erblichia*, and some *Piriqueta* and *Turnera* are homostylous, but many species of Turneraceae are heterostylous. Most heterostylous species have long and short styled flowers but some species (e.g., *Piriqueta morongii* and *Turnera macrophylla*) possess long, short, and homostylous flowers.

The seeds of some Turneraceae are so distinctive that they can be used to identify species. For example, the seeds with conical prominences and dotlike depressions of *Piriqueta racemosa* and the crested seeds of *Turnera sidoides* are unique in the family.

Natural history. Most species of Turneraceae flower in the morning, and the flowers last only a few hours. Pollination is accomplished mainly by bees and butterflies. *Erblichia odorata* is pollinated by hummingbirds, and probably the orange-red flowers of *Turnera* series *Stenodictyae* also are visited by hummingbirds. If insect pollination in some species with homostylous flowers does not occur, the corolla withers and pushes the anthers into full contact with the stigmas, thereby facilitating self-pollination.

Seeds of Turneraceae with oily arils are gathered by ants that carry them to their nests, where they consume the arils. The nectar secreted by extrafloral nectaries of these species attracts several species of ants, which in turn may defend the plant from predation. The butterfly *Euptoieta hegesia* (Nymphalidae), the Mexican fritillary, uses *Turnera ulmifolia* as its primary host plant in Jamaica. The ants that visit the extrafloral nectaries of *T. ulmifolia* attack the early-instar caterpillars of that butterfly, which feed on its leaves.

Economic uses. *Erblichia odorata* is a beautiful tree sometimes cultivated in Mesoamerica as an ornamental, and its wood has been used for railroad ties and for general construction. An infusion and a liquor made with the leaves of *Turnera diffusa* are said to be aphrodisiacs. *Turnera subulata*, a common tropical weed, is used as an ornamental in southern Brazil. There are several other species, such as *T. panamensis* and *T. bahiensis*, with showy, abundant flowers that merit use in tropical horticulture.

References. ARBO, M. M. 1987. Turneraceae. *Flora del Paraguay*, 1–65. St. Louis, MO: Conservatoire et jardin botaniques de la ville de Geneve & Missouri Botanical Garden. ARBO, M. M. 1995. Turneraceae. I. *Piriqueta. Fl. Neotrop. Monogr.* 67:1–156. ARBO, M. M. 1997. Estudios sistemáticos en *Turnera* (Turneraceae). I. Series Salicifoliae y Stenodictyae. *Bonplandia (Argentina)* 9(3–4):151–208. ARBO, M. M. 2000. Estudios sistemáticos en *Turnera* (Turneraceae). II. Series Annulares, Capitatae, Microphyllae y Papilliferae. *Bonplandia (Argentina)* 10:1–82. FERNÁNDEZ, A. 1987. Estudios cromosómicos en *Turnera* y *Piriqueta* (Turneraceae). *Bonplandia (Argentina)* 6:1–21. GONZÁLEZ, A. M. 1998. Colleters in *Turnera* and *Piriqueta. Bot. J. Linn. Soc.* 128(3):215–28. SCHAPPERT, P. 2000. A World for Butterflies. Toronto: Key Porter Books Limited. SHORE, J. S., AND S.C.H. BARRETT. 1987. Inheritance of floral and isozyme polymorphisms in *Turnera ulmifolia* L. *J. Heredity* 78:44–48. URBAN, I. 1883. Monograhie der familie der Turneraceen. *Jahrb. Königl. Bot. Gart. Berlin* 2:1–152. URBAN, I. 1898. Plantae novae americanae imprimis Glaziovianae. II. Turneraceae adjectis specierum nonnullarum africanarum descriptionibus. *Bot. Jahrb. Syst.* 25, Beibl. 40:2–12.

ULMACEAE (Elm Family)

C. C. BERG

Figure 204, Plate 50

- *shrubs, trees, or rarely lianas; copious sap and fusiform cystoliths absent*

- *stipules present, small*

- *leaves alternate (usually distichous), rarely opposite, simple*

- *flowers usually unisexual; perianth uniseriate; tepals 4–5; stamens usually 4–5; ovary 1-locular, the stigmas 2; the ovule 1, placentation apical*

- *fruits samaras, drupes, or drupelets*

Numbers of genera and species. Worldwide, the Ulmaceae comprise 15 genera and approximately 150 species. In tropical America, there are seven genera and about 25 species. *Ampelocera* (9 species), *Lozanella* (2), and *Phyllostylon* (2) are endemic to the neotropics. *Aphananthe* (1 species), *Celtis* (8–10), *Trema* (1 or 2), and *Ulmus* (2) also occur in the paleotropics and/or northern temperate regions.

Distribution and habitat. The Ulmaceae occur throughout the Tropics, subtropics, and temperate regions of the Northern Hemisphere. *Ampelocera*, unlike other Ulmaceae, is distinctly associated with the lowlands of South America. *Lozanella* occurs in the northern Andes and Central America, and *Phyllostylon* has one species in southern South America and another in the Greater Antilles, Central America, and northernmost South America.

The Ulmaceae are found in rain forest (*Ampelocera*), in montane forest (*Lozanella*), or in drier habitats (*Celtis*). *Trema micrantha* is a common tree of disturbed habitats.

Family classification. The Ulmaceae are placed in the Urticales, along with the Cecropiaceae, Moraceae, and Urticaceae, by Cronquist. Molecular studies, however, suggest placing these families in the Rosales along with the Rosaceae and Rhamnaceae, and sometimes even the Elaeagnaceae.

The Ulmaceae and Moraceae share 1-locular ovaries with a solitary apical ovule, but the Ulmaceae lack the latex and fruits surrounded by an accrescent calyx of the Moraceae.

The Ulmaceae are divided into two subfamilies. The Ulmoideae, with samaras as fruits and a predominantly northern temperate distribution, is represented in the neotropics by *Phyllostylon* and *Ulmus*; and the Celtoideae, with drupes

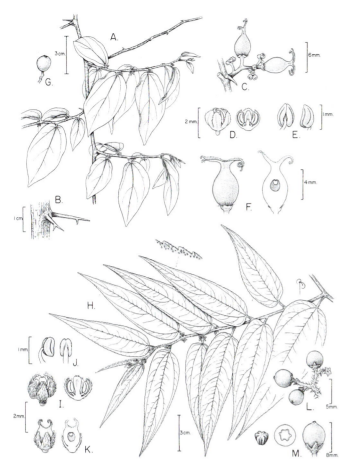

Figure 204. ULMACEAE. *Celtis iguanaea* (A–G) and *Trema micrantha* (H–M). **A.** Stems with leaves and axillary inflorescences. **B.** Detail of stem showing stipular spines. **C.** Inflorescence with immature fruits. **D.** Lateral view (left) and medial section (right) of staminate flowers. **E.** Lateral (right) and abaxial (left) views of stamens. **F.** Lateral view (left) and medial section (right) of immature fruit. **G.** Lateral view of mature fruit. **H.** Stem with leaves and axillary inflorescences and detail of leaf margin showing teeth (above). **I.** Lateral view (left) and medial section (right) of staminate flower. **J.** Lateral (left) and abaxial (right) views of stamens. **K.** Lateral view (left) and medial section (right) of pistillate flowers. **L.** Infructescence. **M.** Endocarp (left), transverse section of fruit (center), and lateral view of fruit (right). Reprinted with permission from Acevedo-Rodríguez (1996). Artist: Bobbi Angell.

as fruits and a more tropical distribution, is represented in the neotropics by *Ampelocera, Aphananthe, Celtis, Lozanella,* and *Trema.* These subfamilies are often regarded as families, the Celtidaceae and Ulmaceae, a position supported by molecular data. According to molecular data, *Ampelocera,* traditionally placed in the Celtidoideae, is more closely aligned with genera of the Ulmoideae.

Features of the family. Habit: shrubs to large trees, rarely lianas (*Celtis iguanaea*), sometimes with spines (most *Cel-*

tis); copious sap and fusiform cystoliths absent. **Stipules** present, lateral, small. **Leaves** alternate (usually distichous), rarely opposite, simple; venation often triple-nerved (e.g., *Trema*). **Inflorescences** axillary, usually in pairs, cymose or sometimes the pistillate inflorescences of solitary flowers. **Flowers** actinomorphic, functionally unisexual, clearly unisexual (plants usually monoecious), or bisexual, small; perianth uniseriate; tepals 4–5; androecium usually of 4–5 stamens, rarely more, the stamens antipetalous, the filaments straight or inflexed in bud; gynoecium syncarpous, the ovary superior, free from perianth, the carpels 2, the locule 1, the stigmas 2, mostly elongate, sometimes furcate (*Celtis*); ovule 1, apical. **Fruits** samaras, drupes, or drupelets. **Seeds** large to small.

The three endemic Neotropical genera have some special features. *Ampelocera* has coriaceous and (sub)entire leaf blades, possibly bisexual flowers, and more stamens (up to 16) than the 4 or 5 tepals, the latter unusual in the Urticales. Species of *Lozanella* resemble species of Urticaceae because of their opposite leaves and urticaceous stamens. *Phyllostylon* possesses, in contrast to the other genera of the subfamily Ulmoideae, a terminally winged fruit, which resembles half of a maple (*Acer*) fruit.

In some species of *Celtis* and *Lozanella,* the staminate flowers are almost of the urticaceous type; i.e., with inflexed stamens bending outward elastically to suddenly release pollen.

Natural history. Most Neotropical species of *Celtis* are provided with spines that may protect them from herbivory. The curved spines of *C. iguanaea* aid the species in climbing.

Transport of pollen by wind is likely for the majority of the species, but not for the arborescent *Ampelocera.* Winged fruits (*Phyllostylon* and *Ulmus*) are dispersed by wind and the fleshy fruits of the remaining genera by animals. Birds avidly seek the fruits of *Trema micrantha.*

Economic uses. The wood of some species is used for construction or tools. In Mexico, bark fibers of *Trema micrantha* are used to make amate paper. The drupaceous fruits of some species are edible.

References. BERG, C. C., AND S. DAHLBERG. 2001. A revision of *Celtis* subg. *Mertensia* (Ulmaceae). *Brittonia* 53(1): 66–81. MANCHESTER, S. R. 1989. Systematics and fossil history of the Ulmaceae. In *Evolution, Systematics, and Fossil History of the Hamamelidae*: 'Higher' Hamamelidae, eds. P. R. Crane and S. Blackmore, 2:221–51. New York: Oxford University Press. NEE, M. 1984. Ulmaceae. In *Flora de Veracruz,* no. 40:1–38. Xalapa, Mexico: INIREB. TODZIA, C. A. 1989. A revision of *Ampelocera* (Ulmaceae). *Ann. Missouri Bot. Gard.* 76:1087–1102. TODZIA, C. A. 1992. A reevaluation of the genus *Phyllostylon* (Ulmaceae). *Sida* 15: 263–70.

URTICACEAE (Nettle Family)

C. C. Berg

Figure 205, Plate 50

- *herbs, sometimes shrubs or small trees; often with conspicuous fusiform cystoliths, sometimes stinging trichomes present*

- *stipules present, mostly small*

- *leaves alternate or opposite and often anisomorphic, simple*

- *flowers unisexual; perianth uniseriate; tepals 3–5, sometimes absent; stamens 3–5, antitepalous, inflexed in bud, bending outward suddenly at anthesis; ovary 1-locular, the stigma 1; the ovule 1, placentation basal*

- *fruits achenes*

Number of species and genera. Worldwide, the Urticaceae comprise 40–52 genera and 700–2,000 species (most likely between 1,000 and 1,200 species). In tropical America, there are 13 genera and 300 or more species. Six genera are Neotropical endemics.

The largest genus in the neotropics, *Pilea*, has 250–600 species worldwide. It is likely that as many as half of the Neotropical species of *Pilea* have not yet been described, and the total number of species in the neotropics may prove to be up to 300. Excluding *Pilea*, the Neotropical urticaceous flora comprises about 60 species, of which 14 belong to *Boehmeria*, 5–10 to *Myriocarpa*, 14 to *Pouzolzia*, and 5–8 to *Urera*.

Distribution and habitat. The Urticaceae are abundantly represented in Asia and well represented in the neotropics. Relative to other regions, the family is poorly represented in tropical Africa. In the neotropics, Urticaceae are diverse in the northern Andes and adjacent lowlands, Central America, and the Greater Antilles, but poorly represented in most of the lowlands of South America. Some species extend into subtropical and temperate regions of the Northern Hemisphere. *Urera* is widespread in the neotropics. *Pilea*, a genus of both the Western and Eastern Hemispheres, is well represented in the northern part of the Andes and Central America and in Jamaica. About 50 species of *Pilea* are found in Jamaica, the majority with very restricted distributions; in Costa Rica, 26 species have been recorded, only three in common with Jamaica; and Ecuador, about 50 species are known, and only seven of these are also found in Costa Rica. In the neotropics, *Pilea* has a few widely distributed species and many species with restricted ranges.

Species of Urticaceae are most common in forests at mid-

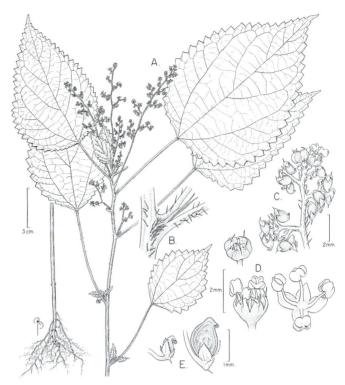

Figure 205. URTICACEAE. *Laportea aestuans*. **A.** Apex of stem with leaves and inflorescences and base of stem with roots (left). **B.** Detail of stem showing stinging hairs. **C.** Infructescence with one flower still at anthesis (above right). **D.** Apical view of flower bud (above) and lateral (below left) and apical (below right) views of staminate flowers at anthesis. **E.** Lateral views of immature (left) and mature (right) fruits subtended by perianths. Reprinted with permission from Mori et al. (2002). Artist: Bobbi Angell.

dle elevations where they are especially frequent at forest margins.

Family classification. The Urticaceae are placed in the Urticales, along with the Moraceae, Cecropiaceae, and Ulmaceae, by Cronquist. Molecular studies, however, suggest placing these families in the Rosales along with the Rosaceae and Rhamnaceae and sometimes even the Elaeagnaceae.

No matter where families of the Urticales are placed, they are so closely related that they could be considered subfamilies of the same family. The technical characters that separate them are the position of the single ovule (basal in Urticaceae and Cecropiaceae and apical in Moraceae and Ulmaceae) and the occurrence of milky latex (present in Moraceae but usually not in the other families). The herbaceous habit common in Urticaceae is also found in Moraceae but is less frequent in that family. The urticaceous stamens, characteristic for the Urticaceae, are also found in one of the tribes of the Moraceae and some Ulmaceae, but are lacking in Cecropiaceae. The unclear delimitation between Urticaceae and Moraceae, caused by a group of species possessing characters of both families, was solved by placing them in a separate family, the Cecropiaceae.

The family can be subdivided into five tribes, four of them occurring in the neotropics. The subdivision is based on several characters, such as the presence/absence of stinging hairs, and features of the perianth and pistillodes.

Features of the family. Habit: usually perennial herbs, sometimes shrubs or small trees (*Myriocarpa* and *Urera*), wood soft, sap present in mucilage-containing ducts and cells, the sap watery, rarely milky, cystoliths often present in epidermis, the cystoliths often fusiform (clearly visible in dried material), stinging (urticating) hairs or prickles present in some genera. **Stipules** present, mostly small. **Leaves** alternate or opposite, often anisomorphic (especially in *Boehmeria* and *Pilea*), simple; venation often triple-nerved, the basal lateral veins often reaching margin above middle of blade. **Inflorescences** usually axillary, often in pairs, panicles, glomerules, or spikes. **Flowers** actinomorphic or zygomorphic (in pistillate flowers of *Pilea*), unisexual (plants monoecious or dioecious), small; perianth uniseriate; tepals 3–5, absent in pistillate flowers of *Myriocarpa* and *Phenax*, well developed in staminate flowers; androecium of 3–5 stamens, the stamens antitepalous, inflexed in bud, elastically bending outward at anthesis and suddenly ejecting pollen; pistillodes often present; gynoecium syncarpous, the ovary superior, free from perianth, the carpels 2, the locule 1, the stigma 1, comose or elongate; placentation basal, the ovule 1. **Fruits** achenes, small, sometimes partially enclosed in perianth, the perianth usually dry, sometimes fleshy (e.g., *Urera*). **Seeds** small.

Species of *Pilea* are small, sometimes somewhat succulent herbs to about 1 m tall. Some, such as *P. imparifolia* are

climbers. The leaves of *Pilea* are always opposite and often dissimilar and pistillate flowers have 3 tepals, one large and two smaller lateral ones. The most common species, a pantropical weed, is *P. microphylla*.

Urticating hairs are confined to nine genera and, in the neotropics, are present in only approximately 10 species of *Urtica* in the mountains, a few species of *Urera* in the lowlands, one species of *Laportea*, and the monotypic *Discocnide*. *Urera baccifera* (with entire leaves) and *U. laciniana* (with lobe leaves) have potent ± spinose stinging hairs.

Natural history. The staminate flowers are adapted to wind pollination by explosively releasing their pollen. Species of Urticaceae are often found on the forest floor and along small streams where water currents create the weak air movements needed to carry the pollen ejected by the flowers.

The achenes, surrounded by a fleshy perianth, are probably dispersed by animals that defecate them after the perianths have been removed. In many other species, however, adaptations for dispersal are not apparent.

Economic uses. In Mexico, bark fibers of *Pouzolzia*, *Myriocarpa*, *Urera*, and *Urtica* are sometimes used to make amate paper. Some species of *Pilea*, especially those with silvery stripes on their leaves, are cultivated as houseplants.

References. BURGER, W. C. 1977. Flora Costaricensis: Utricaceae. *Fieldiana, Bot.* 40:218–83. FRIIS, I. 1989. Review of Urticaceae. In: P.R. Crane and S. Blackmore (eds.). *Evolution, Systematics, and Fossil History of the Hamamelidae*: 'Higher' Hamamelidae. 2:285–308. WILMOT-DEAR, C. M., AND I. FRIIS. 1996. The New World species of *Boehmeria* and *Pouzolzia* (Urticaceae, tribus Boehmerieae). A taxonomic revision. *Opera Bot.* no. 129:5–103.

VALERIANACEAE (Valerian Family)

FAVIO GONZÁLEZ

Figure 206

- *herbs, less often vines, subshrubs, or shrubs*
- *plants often strong-smelling*
- *leaves usually opposite and decussate, the bases clasping*
- *flowers sympetalous; sepals persistent in fruit, expanding into parachute-like pappus; ovary inferior*
- *fruits cypselas*

Numbers of genera and species. Worldwide, the Valerianaceae comprise eight–16 genera and about 400 species.

The number of genera is controversial mostly because of the uncertain circumscription of *Valeriana sensu lato*, the largest genus with about 250 species, many of which are found in the Northern Hemisphere. In tropical America, depending on the circumscription of *Valeriana*, there are one to six genera. Most authors treat *Valeriana* as a single genus, but small genera such as the Neotropical *Aretiastrum* (7 species), *Astrephia* (1), *Belonanthus* (5), *Phyllactis* (3), and *Stangea* (7), have been segregated from it. An estimated 185 species of *Valeriana sensu lato* (i.e., including these five segregate genera) are present in tropical America, most of them centered in South America.

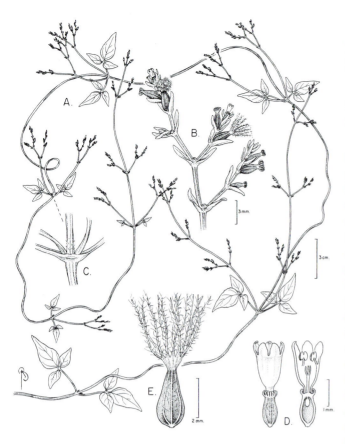

Figure 206. VALERIANACEAE. *Valeriana scandens.* **A.** Stem with leaves and inflorescences mostly in bud. **B.** Part of inflorescence with young fruits. **C.** Detail of node. **D.** Lateral view (left) and medial section (right) of flower. **E.** Lateral view of fruit. Reprinted with permission from Acevedo-Rodríguez (In press). Artist: Bobbi Angell.

Distribution and habitat. The Valerianaceae are diverse in the Mediterranean, absent in Australia, and poorly represented in Africa. In the neotropics, the Valerianaceae are well represented in Andean premontane and montane forests, *páramos*, and *punas*. *Aretiastrum* is found at high elevations in Ecuador and Peru; *Astrephia* in tropical South America; *Belonanthus* in Peru and Bolivia; *Phyllactis* in the high Andes of Colombia, Ecuador, Peru, and northern Bolivia; and *Stangea* ranges from Peru to Argentina. *Valeriana* is well diversified in tropical America, especially in the Andes. The genus is also present in Europe, Africa, and North America.

Species of *Valeriana* are important components of the *páramo*. In this ecosystem, their habit varies from long climbers, shrubs, and rosette plants with prolific and dense inflorescences to tiny cushion plants with a reduced number of flowers.

Family classification. The Valerianaceae are placed in the Dipsacales by Cronquist, close to the Caprifoliaceae and Dipsacaceae. Cladistic studies suggest that the Dipsacaceae and the Valerianaceae are sister groups that should be included within the newly reorganized Caprifoliaceae *sensu lato*. This placement is supported by molecular data.

The Old World *Triplostegia* has been segregated into its own family Triplostegiaceae (e.g., *sensu* Takhtajan), which has been suggested to be the sister group of the remaining Valerianaceae.

Delimitation of genera is usually based on differences in inflorescence morphology, the shape of the calyx, and the number of stamens.

Features of the family. Habit: herbs, less often vines, subshrubs, or shrubs, the herbs sometimes rosettelike or cushionlike, perennial or annual, plants often strong-smelling (rank), especially when dry. **Stipules** absent. **Leaves** usually opposite, rarely alternate, decussate (not appearing so in rosette plants), simple, then sometimes pinnatifid or irregularly divided, or pinnately compound; blades with bases of leaf pairs clasping, connate, the blade margins variously toothed. **Inflorescences** terminal, determinate, cymose corymbs or panicles, the panicles usually pyramidal, sometimes very compressed; bracts and bracteoles usually present. **Flowers** actinomorphic to zygomorphic, bisexual, rarely unisexual; sepals reduced or inconspicuous, accrescent to form parachute-like pappus in fruit; corolla 5-merous, sympetalous, tubular, often slightly irregular or 2-lipped, usually inflated or less often with nectariferous spur at base, the lobes imbricate; androecium of 3 stamens, the stamens adnate to corolla tube, the anthers versatile, the thecae 2, tetrasporangiate or bisporangiate (in *Aretiastrum, Belonanthus, Phyllactis,* and *Stangea*), dehiscing longitudinally; gynoecium syncarpous, the ovary inferior, the carpels 3, the locule usually appearing as 1 (2 locules failing to develop), the style single, slender, the stigma with 2 or 3 lobes; ovule 1, pendulous, anatropous, unitegmic. **Fruits** cypselas, usually ribbed, crowded by variously accrescent sepals, the sepals hairy or plumose. **Seeds** lacking endosperm when ripe, the embryo large, straight, oily.

Some species of *Aretiastrum, Belonanthus, Phyllactis, Stangea,* and *Valeriana* possess anomalous secondary growth in which the vascular bundles are arranged in a starlike stele.

Natural history. Large numbers of insects are attracted to the white flowers that often contrast to purple or reddish rachises. Wind plays an important role in dispersal of species of *Valeriana*, especially in the *páramo*.

Economic uses. The roots and leaves of many species of *Valeriana* are used in traditional medicine for their reputed tranquilizing properties. Some species of the extratropical *Centranthus* and *Patrinia* are cultivated as ornamentals. Other species yield dyes or perfumes; e.g., the aromatic oil nard or spikenard mentioned in the Bible, is extracted from *Nardostachys jatamansi*. The leaves of *Valerianella locusta* (native to Europe, northern Africa, and western Asia) are eaten in salads.

References. BACKLUND, A., AND K. BREMER. 1998. To be or not to be—principles of classification and monotypic plant families. *Taxon* 47: 391–400. Eriksen, B. 1989a. Notes on generic and infrageneric delimitation in Valerianaceae. *Nord. J. Bot.* 9(2):179–87. Eriksen, B. 1989b. Valerianaceae. In *Flora of Ecuador*, eds. G. Harling and L. Andersson, no. 34:1–60. Göteborg, Sweden: Department of Systematic Botany, University of Göteborg. Clarke, G. 1978. Pollen morphology and generic relationships in the Valerianaceae. *Grana* 17:61–75. Judd, W. S., R. W. Saunders, and M. J. Donoghue. 1994. Angiosperm family pairs: preliminary cladistic analyses. *Harvard Pap. Bot.* 5: 1–51. Larsen, B. B. 1986. A taxonomic revision of *Phyllactis* and *Valeriana* sect. *Bracteata* (Valerianaceae). *Nord. J.* *Bot.* 6(4):427–46. Lorcher, H., and F. Weberling. 1982. Zur Achsenverdickung hochandiner Valerianaceen. *Ber. Deutsch. Bot. Ges. Bd.* 95:57–74. Meyer, F. G. 1951. *Valeriana* in North America and the West Indies (Valerianaceae). *Ann. Missouri Bot. Gard.* 38:377–503. Muller, K. A. 1870. Valerianaceae, In *Fl. Brasiliensis*, C.F.P. von Martius 6(4): 339–50. Olmstead, R. G., B. Bremer, K. M. Scott, and J. D. Palmer. 1993. A parsimony analysis of the Asteridae *sensu lato* based on *rbc*L sequences. *Ann. Missouri Bot. Gard.* 80:700–22. Weberling, F. 1961. Die Infloreszenzen der Valerianaceen und ihre systematische Bedeutung. *Abh. Akad. Wiss. Lit. Mainz, math.-nat. Kl.* 5:151–281.

VERBENACEAE (Verbena Family)

Sandy Atkins

Figures 207, 208; Plate 50

The Verbenaceae are treated here in the broad sense; i.e., consisting of subfamilies Verbenoideae (true Verbenaceae) and Viticoideae (now considered part of the Lamiaceae).

- *herbs, shrubs, trees, or lianas*

- *leaves usually opposite, simple or sometimes palmately compound*

- *flowers often slightly zygomorphic; corolla tubular with spreading limb, occasionally 2-lipped; stamens usually 4, rarely 2 or 5, didynamous; ovary superior, unlobed or slightly 4-lobed, the style terminal*

- *fruits drupes or schizocarps*

Numbers of genera and species. Worldwide, the Verbenaceae *sensu lato* comprise approximately 70 genera and 2,000 species. There are 11 genera with only one species each. In the Western Hemisphere, there are 42 genera and about 1,100 native species. Worldwide, the major genera include *Clerodendrum* (400 species), *Vitex* (ca. 250), *Verbena* (250), *Lippia* (200), *Premna* (200), *Aegiphila* (150), *Lantana* (150), and *Callicarpa* (140). In tropical America, there are 24 genera and circa 700 species.

Distribution and habitat. The Verbenaceae are found throughout the world with the exception of the Arctic and Antarctic, and the driest deserts. The family is most abundant in the Tropics. One genus, *Vitex*, has a worldwide distribution, with species in Europe, Asia, Central and South America, and tropical Africa; but most genera are confined to one or two continents.

Of the 24 genera native to tropical America, 12 have an exclusively Western Hemisphere distribution. For example, *Aegiphila* occurs only in the Western Hemisphere and is almost completely tropical. It is found from Cuba and Mexico to Argentina, while its close relative *Callicarpa*, which is largely an Asian genus, has many species in the United States and also occurs in Cuba and parts of Central America. *Citharexylum*, which is found only in the Western Hemisphere, has a similar distribution to *Aegiphila*, while another, *Xolocotzia*, is confined to Mexico.

The two largest genera of the family, *Vitex* and *Clerodendrum*, are both pantropical, but have very different distribution patterns in the neotropics. *Vitex*, with about 85 Neotropical species, is found from Guatemala to Panama and in Colombia, Ecuador, the Guianas, Brazil, Venezuela, Bolivia, and Peru while *Clerodendrum* is represented by very few species in Central America and Brazil. *Amasonia*, thought to be closely related to *Clerodendrum*, has four species in tropical America.

Herbs and shrubs also display a variety of distribution patterns. *Verbena*, for example, which has many species in temperate North and South America, is not nearly so species-rich in the Tropics but does occur from Mexico to Brazil. *Lantana* and *Lippia*, both also found in Africa, are far more numerous in the American Tropics and occur from Mexico through Central America and the West Indies throughout tropical South America to Argentina. *Priva* also has this distribution, but with fewer species. *Aloysia*, which is closely related to *Lippia*, is found only in tropical and subtropical America.

Two other closely related genera, *Stachytarpheta* and *Bouchea*, are both native to the Western Hemisphere. *Stachytarpheta* is found from Mexico to Argentina and *Bouchea* has a similar distribution, but with fewer species.

Trees of the family are found at low to midelevations

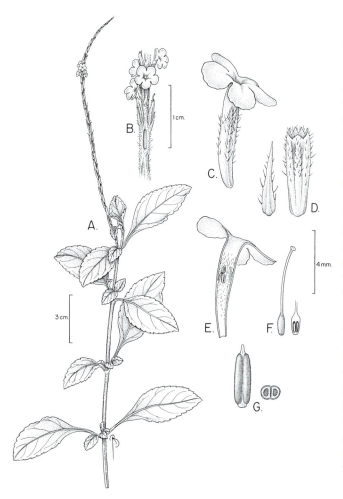

Figure 207. VERBENACEAE. *Stachytarpheta cayennensis.* **A.** Stem with leaves and inflorescence. **B.** Part of inflorescence showing flowers half-immersed in pits of rachis. **C.** Lateral view of flower. **D.** Lateral views of bract (left) and calyx (right). **E.** Medial section of corolla and stamen showing divaricate thecae on left side of corolla tube and staminode on right side. **F.** Lateral view (left) and medial section (right) of part of gynoecium. **G.** Lateral view (left) and transverse section (right) of fruit. Reprinted with permission from Mori et al. (2002). Artist: Bobbi Angell.

where they occupy areas of open forests, wooded slopes, forest margins, and thickets rather than primary rain forest. Exceptions are some species of *Citharexylum* and *Vitex*, which can be found in cloud forest at high elevations and dense rain forest, respectively. Some species of *Vitex* are characteristic sand-dune plants and others can be found at the edges of mangrove lagoons, on the edges of sandy swamps, or as dominant plants in periodically flooded forest in the Amazon (e.g., *V. cymosa*).

The shrubs and herbs are found in well-drained grassland and savannas, dry hillsides, alluvial plains, and on the banks of rivers. Some species are weeds in agricultural fields and on roadsides, and some genera, like *Stachytarpheta* in Brazil, occur in habitats such as *caatinga*, *campo rupestre*, and quartzitic outcrops.

Some races of *Phyla nodiflora* are alkali-resistant. The genera *Acantholippia, Junellia, Lampayo, Diostea, Neosparton, Dipyrena*, and *Parodianthus* are typically xerophytic and are found in desert regions or high alpine areas. Some alpine groups are found at very high altitudes in the Andes of South America; e.g., *Junellia seriphioides* is found at 4,000 meters in Peru. In Mexico *Glandularia teucriifolia* can be found at 3,650 meters, *Aegiphila bogotensis* grows at 3,650 meters in Colombia, and *Lantana haughtii* has been collected at 5,180 meters in Peru. Many species of Verbenaceae are found in weedy habitats.

Family classification. The Verbenaceae are placed in the Lamiales by Cronquist, but the classification of the family is not without problems. There have been many attempts to define it and divide it into groups. One of the earliest and virtually the only truly monographic work on the family was that of Schauer in 1847. Schauer recognized three tribes and 10 subtribes, embracing 42 genera. He included the Avicennieae and the Symphoremeae. In 1876, Bentham proposed the inclusion of the Phrymeae, Stilbeae, and the Chloantheae. Until recent times, the most widely accepted classification was that of Briquet in 1895. Although this is not strictly a monographic work as it does not attempt to list, describe, and differentiate all the species in each genus, Briquet's work represents the culmination of almost 150 years of research and investigation into the group and is a source of much systematically arranged information. He classified the family into seven subfamilies and 13 tribes thus:

Subfamily 1. Stilboideae Briq.
Subfamily 2. Verbenoideae Briq.
  Tribe 1. Euverbeneae Briq.
  Tribe 2. Lantaneae Endl.
  Tribe 3. Priveae Briq.
  Tribe 4. Monochileae (Schau.) Briq.
  Tribe 5. Petreeae Briq.
  Tribe 6. Citharexyleae Briq.
Subfamily 3. Chloanthoideae Briq.
  Tribe 7. Achariteae Briq.
  Tribe 8. Chloantheae Benth.
  Tribe 9. Physopsideae Briq.
Subfamily 4. Viticoideae Briq.
  Tribe 10. Callicarpeae Briq.
  Tribe 11. Tectoneae Briq.
  Tribe 12. Viticeae
  Tribe 13. Clerodendreae Briq.
Subfamily 5. Caryopteridoideae Briq.
Subfamily 6. Symphoremoideae Briq.
Subfamily 7. Avicennioideae Briq.

This classification is based largely on gynoecial structure and supposes that most Lamiaceae have a deeply four-lobed ovary with a gynobasic style, and that most Verbenaceae have an unlobed ovary with a terminal style. Examination of the variation within both families reveals a continuum rather than a clear distinction. It is now widely accepted that the

Figure 208. VERBENACEAE. *Vitex triflora*. **A.** Stems with leaves and inflorescences. **B.** Apex of inflorescence showing terminal flower at anthesis. **C.** Apical view of flower. **D.** Medial section of flower. **E.** Adaxial (left) and abaxial (right) views of apices of stamens. **F.** Lateral view of apex of gynoecium. **G.** Lateral view of base of gynoecium (left) and transverse section (right) of ovary. **H.** Lateral view (right) and transverse section (left) of fruit. Reprinted with permission from Mori et al. (2002). Artist: Bobbi Angell.

Lamiaceae evolved from the Verbenaceae, and the boundary between the families is somewhat arbitrary. Junell, whose work on gynoecium morphology proposed revolutionary changes in the systematics of the group, considered only Briquet's Verbenoideae to be truly verbenaceous. Modern systematists, seeking to reflect evolution in their classifications, take the view that if the circumscription of the Verbenaceae is restricted only to the 34 or so genera (1,035 species) of the traditional subfamily Verbenoideae, excluding tribe Monochileae, that this would make a monophyletic group. This is supported by the studies of the Lamiaceae-Verbenaceae by Cantino and adopted by Thorne for his phylogenetic scheme. The remaining two-thirds of the traditional family Verbenaceae have been transferred to the Lamiaceae, which now include the Caryopteridoideae, Chloanthoideae, and the Viticoideae.

The Verbenoideae, are distinguished by a racemose inflorescence and salverform or funnel-shaped corolla, whereas the inflorescence is cymose in the Lamiaceae and the corollas are tubular and usually bilabiate. These morphological differences are supported by embryological and pollen characters. Some modern floristic treatments and textbooks now treat the families according to the new practice; however, for this publication, the authors of the two families have decided to treat them in the traditional sense. This is not because they do not agree with the modern concept, but because the classification of these families is still in a state of flux.

Features of the family. Habit: herbs, shrubs, trees, or lianas, sometimes aromatic. **Stems** often square, sometimes (*Lantana* and *Duranta*) armed with prickles or thorns; **Stipules** absent. **Leaves** opposite (occasionally whorled or subopposite as in *Amasonia*), simple or sometimes palmately compound in *Vitex*; blade margins entire, serrate, or lobed. **Inflorescence** axillary and/or terminal, racemose (Verbenoideae) or cymose (Viticoideae), usually in heads, spikes, umbels, or thyrses, occasionally of solitary flowers; pedicels present or absent; involucral bracts sometimes present. **Flowers** slightly to distinctly zygomorphic, usually bisexual, sometime unisexual (plants dioecious), large and showy (e.g., some *Clerodendrum*) to very small (e.g., some *Lippia*); calyx always tubular, persistent, sometimes enlarged in fruit, the lobes 4–5, sometimes elongated or so reduced as to make calyx appear truncate; corolla sympetalous, the tube straight and narrow or funnel-shaped, with spreading limb, the limb sometimes slightly 2-lipped, the lobes (4)5; androecium usually of 4 stamens (rarely 2 or 5), didynamous, the anthers dorsifixed, dehiscing longitudinally; 2 reduced staminodes sometimes present (*Stachytarpheta*), usually attached ca. halfway up corolla tube; gynoecium syncarpous, the ovary superior, unlobed or slightly 4-lobed, the carpels 2, the locules basically 2 but typically appearing 4-locular due to false septa (8-chambered in *Duranta* and 10-chambered in *Geunsia*), the style terminal or occasionally arising from center of shallowly lobed ovary (Viticoideae), the stigma 1, lobed; placentation axile, the ovules 1 per locule, usually anatropous, erect. **Fruits** drupes or schizocarps, the drupes with 2 or 4 pyrenes, the schizocarps splitting into 2 or 4 nutlets, enclosed or subtended by persistent calyx.

Verbenaceae exhibit almost every imaginable variation. In size they vary from prostrate herbs like *Verbena supina* (in the dry areas of the Mediterranean), *V. hayekii*, and *V. weberbaueri* (of the high Andes), and *Phyla subterranea* of the Peruvian desert of Arequipa, to tall trees like *Tectona grandis* (teak), which grows to 50 m, and the Brazilian *Vitex excelsa*, which grows to 60 m. Some xerophytic species of the genus *Acantholippia* have leaves which are tiny and scalelike, while those of *Tectona* can be 91 centimeters long and 45 centimeters wide. In species of *Diostea*, the small leaves are shed in times of drought, and species of *Neosparton* have leafless branches. The leaves can be tough and leathery, as in some species of *Petrea*, or thin and fragile, as in *Aegiphila membranacea*. The surface of the leaves can be so scabrid that the surface can be very rough to the touch as in *Petrea bracteata* (the sandpaper vine). Pubescence can be densely white, silky, (*Stachytarpheta sericea*), golden stellate (*Callicarpa horsfieldii*), or shiny golden glandular (*Lippia alnifolia*).

Natural history. Pollinators of Verbenaceae appear to be small Hymenoptera, Diptera, and Lepidoptera, and there is evidence of at least one species, *Rhaphithamnus venustus*, being pollinated by hummingbirds. Some species of *Lantana* and *Stachytarpheta* are known to produce natural hybrids.

Dispersal within the family is variable. The cultivated and sometimes escaped *Tectona grandis* (teak), originally from the Old World, is chiefly dispersed by water, either by seasonal flooding of rivers or by wash-down from rain. Some *Vitex* and *Clerodendrum* are dispersed by water. The dark blue or black fruits of most *Clerodendrum* are surrounded by red calyces and dispersed by birds. The yellow fruits of *Duranta* and the black fruits of *Lantana* are also dispersed by birds. A few species, such as *Priva lappulacea*, have adapted spiny fruits or viscid hairs on the calyx that adhere to the fur of animals.

Economic uses. *Tectona grandis*, *Gmelina arborea*, and species of *Vitex* and *Citharexylum* (fiddlewood) are important timber trees. *Gmelina arborea* has been cultivated extensively in many parts of Asia, Africa, and South America as a source of pulp for paper and lumber and as a shade or ornamental tree. Many herbaceous species of Verbenaceae have medicinal properties, and infusions are made from species of *Lippia*, *Premna*, *Stachytarpheta*, and *Verbena* for treating a variety of complaints. Essential oils are obtained from *Lippia*, and *Pitraea* provides edible tubers. The family contains hundreds of ornamentals, including species of *Callicarpa* (beauty berry), *Citharexylum*, *Clerodendrum*, *Duranta*, *Glandularia*, *Holmskioldia*, *Verbena* (vervain), and *Vitex*.

References. BENTHAM, G. 1876. Verbenaceae. In *Genera Plantarum*, vol. 2. London: Reeve and Co. BRIQUET, J. 1895. Verbenaceae. In Dienatüralichen Pflanzen familien, A. Engler and K. Prantl, 4(3a): 132–82. Leipzig: Wilhelm Engelmann. CANTINO, P. D. 1992a. Evidence for a polyphyletic origin of the Labiatae. *Ann. Missouri Bot. Gard.* 79:361–79. CANTINO, P. D. 1992b. Toward a phylogenetic classification of the Labiatae. In *Advances in Labiate Science*, eds. R. M. Harley and T. Reynolds. Richmond, Surrey, U.K.: Royal Botanic Gardens, Kew. JUNELL, S. 1934. Zur Gynäceummorphologie und Systematik der Verbenaceen und Labiaten. *Symb. Bot. Upsal.* 4:1–219. SCHAUER, J. C. 1847. Verbenaceae. In Prodromus systemis naturalis regni vegetabilis, ed. A. De Candolle, 11: 522–700. Paris: Victoris Masson. WAGSTAFF, S. J., AND R. G. OLMSTEAD. 1997. Phylogeny of Labiatae and Verbenaceae inferred from *rbc*L sequences. *Syst. Bot.* 22(1):165–79.

VIOLACEAE (Violet Family)

CYNTHIA SOTHERS

Figures 209, 210; Plate 51

- *trees, shrubs, lianas, and herbs*
- *leaves alternate or opposite, rarely distichous, simple*
- *flowers actinomorphic to zygomorphic; sepals, petals, and stamens 5 (stamens rarely 3); anthers often with appendages*
- *fruits usually capsular*

Numbers of genera and species. Worldwide, the Violaceae comprise 25 genera and more than 800 species, mostly belonging to subfamily Violoideae. In tropical America, there are 15 genera and about 300 species. The largest genus is by far *Viola*, with about 400 species, about 100 of which are found in the neotropics. Other large genera are *Hybanthus* (100 species worldwide; 75 in the Western Hemisphere) and *Rinorea* (ca. 160 worldwide; 48 in the neotropics). The smaller, strictly Neotropical genera include *Amphirrhox* (1 species), *Anchietea* (8), *Corynostylis* (4), *Fusispermum* (3), *Gloeospermum* (14), *Leonia* (6), *Paypayrola* (8), *Rinoreocarpus* (1), and *Schweiggeria* (2).

Distribution and habitat. The Violaceae have a worldwide distribution, occurring in temperate as well as tropical regions, but only *Viola* occurs in both temperate and tropical America. In the neotropics, *Viola* is restricted to higher-elevation montane regions. The only pantropical genus is *Rinorea*, which has centers of distribution in America, Africa (including Madagascar), India-Southeast Asia, and the Australian-Pacific region.

Rinorea is distributed mainly in lowland forests and submontane regions, but also occurs in the Andes in cloud forests as well as in flooded forests, extending from Mexico to Paraguay but excluding the West Indies. Other tree genera, such as *Leonia*, *Paypayrola*, *Gloeospermum*, and *Rinoreocarpus*, occur mostly in lowland forests; *Fusispermum* is found in the lowlands as well as at higher altitudes, and *Anchietea* is predominantly found in cloud forest. *Amphirrhox longifolia*, a shrub or small tree, and *Corynostylis arborea*, a liana, are two widely distributed lowland species ranging from Central America to northern South America and throughout the Amazon.

Family classification. The Violaceae are placed in the Violales by Cronquist. Recent molecular data has placed the family in the large order Malpighiales (Eurosids I), close to Lacistemataceae and Goupiaceae. The family displays considerable variation in the structure of its flowers and fruit. An important character used in classification is the intergeneric gradient from actinomorphic to zygomorphic flowers. The Violaceae are divided into three subfamilies: the Violoideae (worldwide), the Leonoideae, and the Fusispermoideae (both Neotropical and monogeneric).

The Violoideae is further subdivided into two tribes: the Violeae, represented by *Viola*, *Hybanthus*, and smaller genera such as *Anchietea*, *Corynostylis*, *Mayanaea*, *Noisettia*, *Orthion*, and *Schweiggeria*; and the Rinoreeae, consisting of woody plants with actinomorphic (or slightly zygomorphic) flowers. The Rinoreeae is further subdivided into the subtribe Rinoreinae (strictly actinomorphic), which includes *Gloeospermum*, *Rinorea* and *Rinoreocarpus*, and the Paypayrolinae (slightly zygomorphic/subactinomorphic as a result of the wider and bilobed shape of the anterior petal), consisting of *Amphirrhox* and *Paypayrola*. In the tribe Violeae, zygomorphy is strongly expressed in the anterior petal and the anterior filaments, which are distinctly swollen or spurred near the base. The tribe also presents a gradual transition from a woody to an herbaceous habit.

The monogeneric subfamily Leonoideae consists of a strictly actinomorphic flowered woody genus, *Leonia*. It differs from the Violoideae in several characters such as irregular to quincuncial aestivation of petals, thecae almost horizontally oriented on the upper margin of a tube, anthers that lack dorsal connective scales, and a globose and indehiscent fruit with large muscilaginous seeds.

Fusispermum (with actinomorphic flowers) is placed in its own subfamily, the Fusispermoideae, because it differs from other genera by the convolute aestivation of its petals, the anthers apically as well as ventrally appendaged by two minute fringed scales instead of dorsally appendaged by connective scales, and the presence of two seed types.

It is believed that the family evolved from a hypothetical

Figure 209. VIOLACEAE. *Leonia glycycarpa* var. *glycycarpa*. **A.** Stem with leaves and inflorescences. **B.** Inflorescence. **C.** Detail of inflorescence. **D.** Lateral views of flower intact (right) and with two petals and half of calyx removed (left). **E.** Lateral (above), adaxial (below left), and abaxial (below right) views of stamens. **F.** Lateral view (left) and medial section (right) of gynoecium. **G.** Lateral view (left) and medial section (below) of fruit. Reprinted with permission from Mori et al. (2002). Artist: Bobbi Angell.

woody ancestor with actinomorphic flowers, five equal sepals and petals, five free stamens, and a five-merous ovary. In most *Leonia* these primitive features are still present (except for the fused filaments). A tendency toward zygomorphy then progressed as expressed in *Amphirrhox* and *Paypayrola* (both woody) toward a completely zygomorphic and predominantly herbaceous state in the tribe Violeae.

Features of the family. Habit: trees, shrubs, lianas, or herbs, the shrubs sometimes scandent. **Stipules** present, subpersistent or deciduous. **Leaves** alternate or opposite, rarely distichous (*Gloeospermum*), simple; blade margins usually crenulate, serrate, or entire; venation pinnate. **Inflorescences** axillary, or cauliflorous (*Leonia*) terminal, spicate, racemose, paniculate, sometimes cymose, or of solitary flowers; bracteoles 2, pedicels usually articulate. **Flowers** actinomorphic,

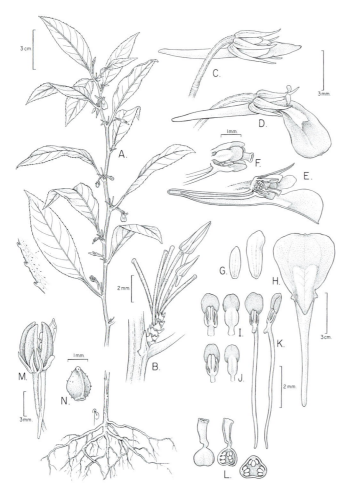

Figure 210. VIOLACEAE. *Noisettia orchidiflora*. **A.** Upper stem with leaves and inflorescences, lower stem with roots, and detail of adaxial leaf margin (far left). **B.** Node with inflorescence fascicle and stipule. **C.** Lateral view of flower bud. **D.** Lateral view of flower. **E.** Medial section of flower. **F.** Lateral view of anthers and stigma with upper part of style. **G.** Adaxial views of petals. **H.** Adaxial view of lower petal. **I.** Upper (left) and abaxial (right) views of lateral anther. **J.** Adaxial (left) and abaxial (right) views of anther of stamen associated with upper petals. **K.** Adaxial (left) and lateral (right) views of stamens associated with lower petal. **L.** Lateral view (left), medial section (center), and transverse section (right) of gynoecium. **M.** Lateral view of dehisced fruit. **N.** Lateral view of seed. Reprinted with permission from Mori et al. (2002). Artist: Bobbi Angell.

subactinomorphic, or zygomorphic, bisexual, sometimes indistinctly perigynous; sepals 5; petals 5, equal to unequal, distinct or slightly connate at base, the anterior petal often swollen, enlarged on one side, or spurred (zygomorphic flowers); androecium of 5 (3 in *Leonia triandra*) stamens, the filaments and dorsal glands distinct or fused with each other, forming a tube, the anthers usually introrse, rarely extrorse, usually dorsally appendaged by minute (*Paypayrola*) to well-developed (*Rinorea*) connective scales, the appendages of 2 ventral fringed scales or absent, usually dehiscing longitudinally; gynoecium syncarpous, the ovary superior, sessile, the carpels (2)3(5), the locule 1, the style 1, usually filiform,

often subclavate at apex, erect, curved, or sigmoid, the stigma variable, erect or curved toward anterior petal; placentation parietal, the ovules 1–several per carpel. **Fruits** capsular or baccate (*Gloeospermum*), generally small (1–5 cm long), the indehiscent fruits globose, the capsular fruits frequently 3-valved, the valves ± symmetric, usually greenish. **Seeds** 3–15 per fruit, uniform, rarely of 2 different kinds, globose to pyriform, or flat and winged (*Anchietea* and *Corynostylis*).

The flowers of the actinomorphic *Leonia* and *Rinorea* are mostly small, dull cream-colored or yellow; the subactinomorphic *Paypayrola* and *Amphirrhox* are larger and also cream-colored or yellow; and the zygomorphic *Anchietea*, *Corynostylis*, *Noisettia* have larger, more showy flowers. The well-developed connective scales in *Rinorea* are sometimes bright orange and contrast with the lighter color of the petals.

Lowland Violaceae are represented primarily as shrubs (*Amphirrhox*, *Leonia cymosa*, and *Rinorea*) or understory trees (*Rinorea*), and occasionally as larger subcanopy trees (*Leonia glycycarpa*, *Paypayrola*, and *Rinorea*). The wood is generally soft and light-colored (occasionally reddish), and the bark smooth and unfissured.

Natural history. A few species of *Rinorea* have domatia on the abaxial leaf surface that harbor mites. Whether a symbiotic relationship exists is not clear, but the mites may protect the leaves from herbivores or from fungal attack in return for shelter.

The dorsal glands and glandular tubes found in several species of *Rinorea* are functioning nectaries that attract insects, such as bees. During the flowering period, the pleasant, sweet smell of the flowers fills the forest, and bees can be heard visiting the flowers. Some *Viola* and *Hybanthus* possess cleistogamous flowers.

The bases of the seeds of *Rinorea* sometimes have a caruncle that is attractive to ants, which, in turn, may disperse the seeds. The seeds of *Paypayrola grandiflora* are enclosed in a bright orange arillike flesh that attracts birds. In addition to animals, seeds of species of Violaceae may also be dispersed by wind or water.

Economic uses. The Violaceae have little economic use. The family is best known for its cultivated species of *Viola* (violet, pansy). Some species of *Viola* (e.g., *V. odorata*) yield essential oils used in flavorings, perfumes, toiletries, and liqueurs. In Suriname, the branchlets and twigs of some species of *Rinorea* are used for making sieves, as well as for sticks used to mix drinks. The fruits of *Leonia glycycarpa* are edible, and the roots of *Anchietea*, *Corynostylis*, and *Hybanthus* are used medicinally as emetics.

References. HEKKING, W.H.A. 1988. Violaceae: part I, *Rinorea* and *Rinoreocarpus*. *Fl. Neotrop. Monogr.* 46:1–207. SAVOLAINEN, V. et al. 2000. Phylogeny of the eudicots: a nearly complete familial analysis based on *rbc*L gene sequences. *Kew Bull.* 55:257–309.

VISCACEAE (Christmas Mistletoe Family)

JOB KUIJT AND CAROL GRACIE

Figure 211, Plate 51

- *hemiparasitic subshrubs or shrubs on woody plants, primarily dicots*

- *leaves opposite; blades well-developed, scalelike, or both*

- *flowers without sepals; petals 3 or 4, in 1 whorl; stamens adnate to petals*

- *fruits one-"seeded" berries*

- *"seeds" with abundant viscin*

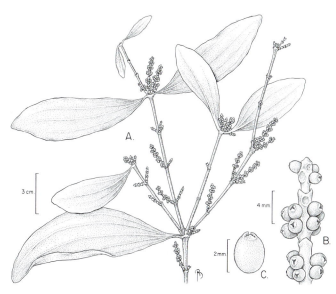

Figure 211. VISCACEAE. *Phoradendron crassifolium*. **A.** Stem with leaves and inflorescences. **B.** Detail of inflorescence. **C.** Lateral view of pistillate flower. Reprinted with permission from Mori et al. (2002). Artist: Bobbi Angell.

Numbers of genera and species. Worldwide, the Viscaceae comprise seven genera and perhaps 600 species. Three genera of Viscaceae are represented in tropical America: *Phoradendron* (ca. 234 species), *Dendrophthora* (ca. 120), and *Arceuthobium* with only a few species in the neotropics, for a total of about 360 species.

Distribution and habitat. The Viscaceae are well known in temperate regions, but are much more common in the Tropics. All genera but *Arceuthobium*, a parasite of conifers, occur exclusively in either the Eastern or the Western Hemispheres. *Phoradendron* is generally limited to lower and middle elevations in the neotropics, but reaches into the northeastern and northwestern United States. In contrast, *Dendrophthora*, at least the continental species, shows a distinct preference for high elevations; however, in the Caribbean, many species occur at or near sea level. Continental species of *Dendrophthora* are mostly Andean-Mesoamerican (reaching into southern Mexico) poorly represented east of the Andes. *Arceuthobium* is native to both the northern portions of the Eastern and Western Hemispheres, where it is largely found in temperate and dry subtropical areas; only in Kenya does it cross the equator and then only for a short distance. In the Americas, one species of *Arceuthobium* is endemic to Hispaniola, while on the continent, the genus extends south into Honduras.

Family classification. The Viscaceae are placed in the Santalales by Cronquist. The family has been segregated out of the originally broadly defined Loranthaceae based on the absence of a calyculus; very small, inconspicuous flowers; a perianth in one whorl of four or fewer petals; unisexual flowers; plants either monoecious or dioecious; simple, chlorophyllous endosperm; and differences in the embryology and pollen.

Dendrophthora is marginally distinguished from *Phora-*

dendron by the presence of one locule in the anther rather than two. The other genera of the family, including *Arceuthobium*, are more clearly defined. Molecular studies confirm the integrity of Viscaceae and the advanced position of this family in the Santalales.

Features of the family. Habit: subshrubs or shrubs, hemiparasitic on woody plants, primarily dicots. **Haustoria** attachment single, but endophyte branched, extending into host tissues, in some giving rise to additional shoots; epicortical roots absent. **Stems** brittle, round, flattened, or keeled. **Stipules** absent. **Leaves** opposite, simple, well developed or scalelike, often both on same plant in *Dendrophthora and Phoradendron*, evergreen; blade margins entire. **Inflorescences** axillary, terminal, or both, spikelike, the spike pedunculate, each rachis with 1 or more fertile internodes bearing flowers in serial groupings (*Dendrophthora and Phoradendron*). **Flowers** actinomorphic, unisexual (plants dioecious or monoecious), small, usually greenish or yellow, sessile or nearly so. **Staminate flowers**: sepals absent; petals usually 4, in 1 whorl; androecium with stamens equal to petal number, adnate to petals, surrounding small central disc or prominence, the filaments short or absent. **Pistillate flowers**: sepals absent; petals 3–4, in 1 whorl, often barely visible; staminodes absent; gynoecium with inferior ovary, the style short, the stigma small, sessile and knoblike; placenta-like body (ovarian papilla) massive, nearly filling locule, true ovules absent, the embryo sacs developing in the ovarian papilla. **Fruits** berries, usually shiny, smooth or warty, usually white, sometimes yellowish or red. "Seeds" 1 per fruit, surrounded or capped by viscid tissue; endosperm bright green (because of presence of chlorophyll).

Unlike many species in the Loranthaceae and Eremolepidaceae, plants in the Viscaceae do not produce epicortical roots and are attached to the host only through the primary haustorium that usually expands within the host.

Many species are heterophyllous in that they produce a succession of larger leaves alternating with scalelike leaves (cataphylls) along or at the base of the shoots.

Natural history. The small flowers of Viscaceae are pollinated almost exclusively by insects, especially Hymenoptera. Secretions from the glandular disc in male flowers may serve as an attractant, but pollen also serves as a pollinator reward in some genera.

Viscaceae develop on branches of trees after the sticky "seeds" have been dispersed by birds. The "seeds" germinate rapidly, at least in the Tropics, and a haustorium, which supplies the plant with water and minerals, forms and penetrates the host. Host specificity, as in most other mistletoes, is generally low. Some species of the Phoradendron, however, appear to parasitize only other mistletoes.

Economic uses. Branches of two species are collected to provide the decorative and symbolic mistletoe used at Christmas time: *Viscum album* from western Europe and *Phoradendron tomentosum* from the United States. Until early in the twentieth century, a birdlime was prepared from the viscid tissue of *Viscum album* in Europe. The berries were soaked, boiled, crushed, and kneaded to form a paste that was spread onto branches placed near food put out to attract small birds. When the birds perched on the branches, they became stuck in the sticky paste and were captured.

References. KUIJT, J. 1961. A revision of *Dendrophthora* (Loranthaceae). *Wentia* 6: 1–145. KUIJT, J. 1986. Viscaceae. *Flora of Ecuador*, eds. G. Harling and B. Sparre, no. 24: 11–112. Göteborg, Sweden: Department of Systematic Botany, University of Göteborg. KUIJT, J. 2000. An update on the genus *Dendrophthora* (Viscaceae). *Bot. Jahrb. Syst.* 122: 169–93. KUIJT, J. (In press). A monograph of *Phoradendron* (Viscaceae). *Syst. Bot. Monogr.*

VITACEAE (Grape Family)

JULIO ANTONIO LOMBARDI

Fig. 212, Plate 51

- *lianas, rarely shrubs*

- *leaves alternate, simple or compound*

- *plants usually with leaf-opposed tendrils and inflorescences*

- *fruits berries*

- *seeds 1(2–4)*

Numbers of genera and species. Worldwide, the Vitaceae comprise 13 or 14 genera and about 800 species. In the Western Hemisphere, there are five genera and about 108 native species. In tropical America, there are four genera, *Cissus* (ca. 75 species), *Vitis* (ca. 5), *Ampelocissus* (4), and *Ampelopsis* (2).

Asiatic species of *Tetrastigma* and *Parthenocissus*, Eurasian *Vitis vinifera*, and some North American *Vitis*, together with many hybrids of *Vitis* species, are cultivated in tropical America, but none has been naturalized. *Cissus quadrangularis*, originally from India and southeastern Asia, is naturalized in Jamaica.

Distribution and habitat. The Vitaceae occur in tropical and subtropical areas of the world. Regions with the greatest number of species are the neotropics, paleotropics, Australia, and subtropical North America. A few species reach Canada, Japan, and southern Chile. Some smaller genera are restricted to Africa and southeastern Asia, while others occur both in Asia and North/Middle America. *Cissus* and *Vitis* have tropical Southern and subtropical Northern Hemisphere distributions, respectively.

In the Western Hemisphere, the majority of species occur in tropical South America and subtropical North America, but *Parthenocissus quinquefolia* reaches Canada and *Cissus striata* subspecies *striata* occurs in Argentine Patagonia and central and southern Chile.

Species are found in deserts to swampy inland areas but are more abundant in tropical rain forests and subtropical and montane forests. Some species reach more than 3,000 meters on Andean and Central American mountain slopes.

Family classification. The Vitaceae are placed in the Rhamnales by Cronquist, but in the Vitales or "Core Eudicots" in recent classifications. The family is not split into subfamilies, except when it includes the genus *Leea* (Eastern Hemisphere, sometimes considered a separate family, Leeaceae), and then the family is divided in subfamilies Leeoideae and Vitoideae. The relationships among genera are unclear, and phylogenetic studies have not yet been made.

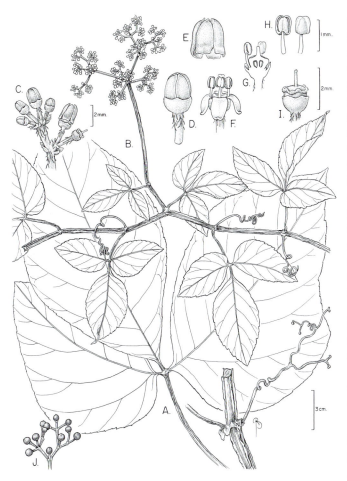

Figure 212. VITACEAE. *Cissus erosa*. **A.** Leaf (left) and part of stem with branching tendril (right). **B.** Stem with leaves and inflorescence. **C.** Detail of inflorescence. **D.** Lateral view of bud. **E.** Calyptrally dehiscent corolla. **F.** Lateral view of flower. **G.** Medial section of flower with petals removed. **H.** Abaxial (right) and adaxial (left) views of anthers. **I.** Developing ovary surrounded by calyx. **J.** Infructescence. Reprinted with permission from Mori et al. (2002). Artist: Bobbi Angell.

Features of the family. Habit: lianas or rarely shrubs (in South America in open habitats). **Roots** sometimes adventitious (many *Cissus*). **Stems** usually woody, climbing, rarely forming aerial tubers (some *Cissus*), or sometimes short, woody, and subterranean in some shrubs). **Tendrils** usually present, leaf-opposed, unbranched or with 1–2 orders of branching in some *Ampelocissus*, *Ampelopsis*, and *Vitis*. **Stipules** present, usually small, caducous, sometimes persistent, rarely transformed into spines, sometimes dilated and embracing entire node. **Leaves** alternate, simple (*Vitis* and many *Cissus*) or compound (trifoliate in many *Cissus*, palmate in some *Cissus*, pinnate, bipinnate, or tripinnate in a few South American *Cissus*). **Inflorescences** leaf-opposed or terminal, rarely axillary, cymose or racemose, sometimes with 1–2 tendril-like branches (*Ampelocissus*, *Ampelopsis*, and *Vitis*); bract and bracteoles small, sometimes nectar secreting, the bract subtending each branch. **Flowers** actinomorphic, bisexual, sometimes unisexual (plants monoecious or

polygamous), small; buds ellipsoid, oval, or conical, sometimes spherical or cylindrical; sepals 4–5, fused, inconspicuous, truncate, rounded, or rarely lobed (some *Cissus*), usually without free lobes; petals 4–5, small, valvate, distinct or connate at base, or distally coherent and calyptra-like (*Vitis*), caducous at anthesis, rarely persistent (some South American *Cissus*); androecium of 4–5 stamens, the stamens minute, distinct; intrastaminal disc present, adnate to ovary (*Cissus* and *Ampelocissus*), free and ringlike (*Ampelopsis*), of separated glands (*Vitis*), or absent (*Parthenocissus*), sometimes the outer border projected above, forming small cup (some *Cissus*); gynoecium syncarpous, the ovary superior, the carpels 2, the locules 2, the style simple, the stigma minute, entire; ovules 2 per locule. **Fruits** berries, spherical (0.5–2.0 cm diameter or larger) or ellipsoid (2.7–4.0 cm long), the epicarp thin and chartaceous or thick and crustaceous (ellipsoid fruits), the mesocarp fleshy and juicy, the endocarp adherent to seed testa, more fibrous than mesocarp. **Seeds** 1(2–4), the testa variously ribbed, grooved, with two ventral intrusions into endosperm, dorsal chalaza usually present (except in most *Cissus*); endosperm ruminate, 3-lobed, corneous, the embryo minute.

Germination of Vitaceae seeds is epigeous, and the usually carnose, apical, fingerlike lobed cotyledons are apparently opposite.

Natural history. Pollination in this family is not well documented but may be carried out by insects. Self-pollination also has been recorded. Seed dispersal by birds, mammals, and fish has been observed. In the Western Hemisphere, many species of *Cissus* are infected by a rust, *Mycosyrinx cissi*, that forms witch's brooms in the inflorescences.

Economic uses. Grapes are cultivated worldwide for the production of wine, nonalcoholic juice, table fruits, and raisins. *Vitis vinifera* (European grape), *V. labrusca* (slip skin grape), *V. rotundifolia* (muscadine grape), and hybrids of these or other species are grown widely in tropical and subtropical America. Roots of American *Vitis* species are resistant to infestation by the scale insect *Phylloxera*, which destroyed many vineyards in Europe: therefore, they are used as rootstocks for *V. vinifera* cultivars.

In Central America, species of *Ampelocissus* are grown for the edible fruits that are used in the production of vinegar and wine. Species of *Cissus* are used by indigenous people in the Americas for medicines and a few are cultivated for food. Some species are boiled, macerated, or grated and used in traditional medicines to treat rheumatic arthritis, itching, infections, inflammation, abscesses, and diabetes. *Cissus erosa* subspecies *erosa* is used by menstruating women to stop bleeding.

References. BRIZICKY, G. K. 1965. The genera of Vitaceae in the southeastern United States. *J. Arnold Arbor.* 46:48–67. LOMBARDI, J. A. 2000. Vitaceae–Gêneros *Ampelocissus*, *Am-*

pelopsis e *Cissus. Fl. Neotrop. Monogr.* 80:1–250. MOORE, M. O. 1991. Classification and systematics of eastern North American *Vitis* L. (Vitaceae) north of Mexico. *Sida* 14:339–67. MULLINS, M. G., A. BOUQUET, AND L. E. WILLIAMS.

1992. *Biology of the Grapevine.* Cambridge, U.K.: Cambridge University Press. VAUGHAN, J. G., AND C. GEISSLER. 1997. *The New Oxford Book of Food Plants.* Oxford, U.K.: Oxford University Press.

VOCHYSIACEAE (Vochysia Family)

AMY LITT

Figure 213, Plate 52

- *trees*

- *stipules present, sometimes modified into glands*

- *leaves opposite or whorled, simple*

- *flowers zygomorphic; 1 calyx often with spurred sepal; petals usually reduced to 3 or 1; fertile stamen 1; style simple*

- *fruits usually capsules with winged seeds, less frequently the fruits indehiscent and winged*

Numbers of genera and species. Worldwide, the Vochysiaceae comprise seven genera and approximately 200 species, all of which are Neotropical except for the African *Erismadelphus* (2 species) and the recently described *Korupodendron* (1 species). The largest genus is *Vochysia* (100 species). *Salvertia* has only one species, although there is morphological and molecular evidence that this genus should not be considered separate from *Vochysia.* Likewise there is some evidence that *Callisthene* (eight species) should be included in *Qualea* (50 species).

Distribution and habitat. The Vochysiaceae are predominantly Neotropical with only a few species of *Erismadelphus* and *Korupodendron* found in the forests of tropical west Africa. In the Western Hemisphere, the range of the family coincides with that of *Vochysia,* species of which are found from southern Brazil north into the Yucatán of Mexico. *Qualea* has a similar but somewhat narrower range, and *Callisthene* and *Salvertia* are restricted to savannas within this region. *Erisma* is predominantly Amazonian, but one species is found in the Atlantic coastal forest of Brazil and another occurs in Panama.

While Vochysiaceae are found in a variety of habitats from lowland rain forest, gallery forest, and montane forest at 1,100 meters, they are especially dominant in *cerrado.*

Family classification. Studies suggest that the traditional placement of the family in the Polygalales (*sensu* Cronquist) is in error and point instead to an affinity with the Myrtales.

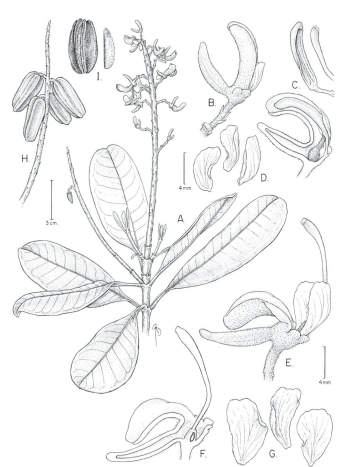

Figure 213. VOCHYSIACEAE. *Vochysia surinamensis.* **A.** Stem with leaves and inflorescence. **B.** Lateral view of flower at early anthesis. **C.** Stamen (above left), style (above right), and longitudinal section of flower with two petals removed showing base of gynoecium, stamen surrounding upper part of style, and petal surrounding base of stamen (below). **D.** Adaxial (left and middle) and lateral (right) views of petals. **E.** Lateral view of flower at later anthesis with expanded gynoecium after stamen has fallen. **F.** Medial section of flower; note spurred calyx-lobe. **G.** Adaxial views of petals. **H.** Part of infructescence with immature fruits. **I.** Lateral views of fruit (left) and winged seed (right). Reprinted with permission from Mori et al. (2002). Artist: Bobbi Angell.

Some evidence from anatomy, embryology, and floral development supports this placement.

The family is comprised of two tribes, Erismeae (*Erisma* and *Erismadelphus*) and Vochysieae (*Vochysia, Qualea, Cal-*

listhene, and *Salvertia*). Species of Erismeae have winged, indehiscent fruits (vs. capsules with winged seeds in the Vochysieae) and an inferior unilocular ovary (vs. superior and trilocular in the Vochysieae). Recent morphological, developmental, and molecular analyses support the close relationship between *Erisma* and *Erismadelphus* but question the monophyly of the Vochysieae.

An analysis of the relationships of the genera of Vochysiaceae has indicated that *Vochysia* and *Salvertia* and *Qualea* and *Callisthene* are closely related. It does not, however, indicate that these two groups are more closely related to each other than either pair is to Erismeae. Thus the analysis demonstrates that there are three groups in the family with no clear relationships among them: Erismeae (*Erisma* and *Erismadelphus*), *Vochysia/Salvertia*, and *Qualea/Callisthene*. The position of *Korupodendron* has not been determined, but it shows clear affinities to Erismeae.

A number of morphological characters have been used to characterize the Vochysieae, but a re-examination of some of these has shown that the similarities are superficial. For instance, all four genera of the Vochysieae have capsular fruits with winged seeds, in contrast to the indehiscent winged fruits of Erismeae; however, the wings of the seeds are formed by two different mechanisms: in *Vochysia* and *Salvertia*, they are composed of compressed hairs, whereas in *Qualea* and *Callisthene*, they are formed as an extrusion of the testa. Furthermore, the mode of dehiscence of the fruits is distinctly different. In *Qualea* and *Callisthene*, the three valves separate and pull apart to release the seeds. The valves remain attached only at the base and sometimes leave a central column. In *Vochysia* and *Salvertia*, the valves stay attached and the outer wall of the fruit splits to release the seeds. Thus, characters that were thought to unite the four genera of Vochysieae are not homologous. Morphological and developmental characters support recognition of the same three groups suggested by molecular evidence analysis.

Cronquist includes *Euphronia* in this family; however, molecular analyses suggest that *Euphronia* is best considered as a monotypic family allied with Chrysobalanaceae. Recognition of *Ruizterania*, a segregate of *Qualea*, as a separate genus leaves the latter paraphyletic, thus *Ruizterania* is included in *Qualea*.

Features of the family. Habit: medium-sized to very large trees, young parts often densely pubescent, the hairs simple, or stellate in *Erisma*. Stipules present, small, in pairs, generally deciduous; extrafloral nectaries present in some *Qualea* and *Callisthene*, in pairs, on stem at petiole base, associated with or formed from stipules. Leaves opposite or whorled, simple. Inflorescences terminal or axillary, usually large showy racemes, reduced in some *Qualea* and *Callisthene* to one or a few axillary flowers. Flowers zygomorphic, bisexual, perigynous (in Vochysieae, the bases of outer floral organs fused to form distinct floral cup surrounding ovary) or epigynous (in Erismeae, but ovary free on side where spur extends outward from base of flower); calyx frequently showy (particularly in yellow-flowered *Vochysia*), the sepals 5, the fourth sepal spurred, elongate relative to other four in *Vochysia*, *Callisthene*, and some *Qualea*; petals 5 in *Salvertia*, 3 in most *Vochysia*, 1 in *Callisthene*, *Erisma*, *Qualea*, and a few *Vocyhsia* (e.g., *V. pacifica*), and absent in a few *Vochysia* (e.g., *V. apopetala*), yellow (*Vochysia*), the remaining genera varying greatly in shape, size, and color, often with conspicuous nectar guides; androecium of 1 stamen, the stamen opposite a petal (except in *Callisthene* and *Qualea* in which it is slightly offset from that position), the filament often thick, the anther often large, dorsi- or basifixed, dehiscing longitudinally, the connective often broad, sometimes extending beyond tip of anther thecae; gynoecium with inferior (Erismeae) or superior (Vochysieae) ovary, the locule(s) 1 (Erismeae) or 3 (Vochysieae), the style simple, the stigma terminal or sometimes lateral (*Salvertia*, some *Vochysia*), capitate (Erismeae and some Vochysieae); placentation marginal (Erismeae) or axile, the ovules 2 (*Erisma*, *Vochysia*, *Salvertia*) to many (*Qualea*, *Callisthene*) per locule, anatropous. Fruits loculicidal capsules (Vochysieae) or indehiscent and winged (Erismeae), the wings absent in *Erisma calcaratum*. Seeds 1 (Erismeae) to numerous (Vochysieae), winged in Vochysieae, the wing circumferential in *Callisthene*, unilateral in *Qualea*, *Salvertia*, and *Vochysia*, without wings in *Erisma*; endosperm absent, the embryo straight, the cotyledons petiolate, leafy.

Natural history. Species of savannas, such as *Qualea grandiflora*, are adapted to the periodic fires of this habitat. These trees tend to have thick, corky barks; copious gums; tough or deciduous leaves; and contorted growth forms. Some, such as *Vochysia herbacea* and *V. pumila*, have underground woody stems called xylopodia that enable them to survive burning and sprout new shoots after fires. On the other hand, some species, such as *Erisma laurifolium*, are among the tallest trees of the Amazon.

Most species of Vochysiaceae are thought to be pollinated by large solitary bees, although little work has been done to verify this. *Qualea grandiflora*, *Salvertia convallariodora*, and possibly other species are hawkmoth-pollinated. Species of *Vochysia* show a distinctive secondary pollination presentation. Prior to anthesis, the anther, which in the bud flanks the style, opens and sheds pollen onto the style. The flower opens by reflexing the elongate fourth sepal, which exposes the petals and style. The tip of the anther remains caught in the sepal as it reflexes, and this action appears to pull the stamen out of the flower. The stamen drops off, leaving the style coated with pollen from where it is picked up and transferred to the stigma of another flower by pollinators.

Nearly all species of Vochysiaceae appear to be winddispersed, either by winged seeds (Vochysieae) or winged fruits (Erismeae). The only exception, *Erisma calcaratum*, is common in inundated forests. It differs from all other species in having a corky wingless fruit that is water-dispersed. Although it is not the most abundant species in the genus, it is the most widely distributed.

Economic uses. No species of this family is used extensively, and none is exploited commercially on a large scale. Many are used locally for timber, and some efforts have been made to cultivate species of *Vochysia* in plantations as quick-growing trees to provide shade for young mahogany trees and eventually to be cut for timber. Locally, several species are used for a number of medicinal purposes. Gums are used to protect cuts; teas made from leaves are used as tonics or to aid digestion; and scattered reports mention species being used as a contraceptive, as an arrow poison, to expel parasitic worms, and for oils. The seeds of *Erisma japura* and *E. splendens* are seasonally important food resources for indigenous groups in the Amazon, who value them so highly that they have been used for trade.

References. BOESEWINKEL, F. D., AND M. VENTURELLI. 1987. Ovule and seed structure in Vochysiaceae. *Bot. Jahrb. Syst. Pflanz.* 108:547–66. DUFOUR, D. A., AND J. L. ZARUCCHI. 1979. *Monopteryx angustifolia* and *Erisma japura*: their uses by indigenous peoples in the northwestern Amazon. *Bot. Mus. Leafl.* 27:69–91. FLORES, E. M. 1993. *Vochysia guatemalensis, Vochysia ferruginea. Trees and seeds from the neotropics* 2:1–52. KAWASAKI, M. L. 1998. Systematics of *Erisma* (Vochysiaceae). *Mem. New York Bot. Gard.* 81: 1–40. KEAY, R.W.J., AND F. A. STAFLEU. 1953. *Erismadelphus. Acta Bot. Neerl.* 1(4):594–99. LITT, A. 1999. Floral morphology and phylogeny of Vochysiaceae. Ph.D. dissertation, New York: City University of New York. OLIVEIRA, P. E. 1998. Reproductive biology, evolution, and taxonomy of Vochysiaceae in central Brazil. In *Reproductive Biology in Systematics, Conservation and Economic Botany*, eds. S. J. Owen and P. J. Rudall, Kew, Richmond, Surrey, U.K.: Royal Botanic Gardens, Kew. STAFLEU, F. A. 1948. A monograph of the Vochysiaceae. I. *Salvertia* and *Vochysia. Recueil Trav. Bot. Neerl.* 41:398–540. STAFLEU, F. A. 1952. A monograph of the Vochysiaceae. II. *Callisthene. Acta Bot. Neerl.* 1(2): 222–42. STAFLEU, F. A. 1953. A monograph of the Vochysiaceae. III. *Qualea. Acta Bot. Neerl.* 2(2):144–217.

WINTERACEAE (Pepper Tree or "Winter's Bark" Family)

DAWN FRAME

Figure 214, Plate 52

- *trees or shrubs*

- *wood lacking vessels*

- *fresh bark and leaves with burning, pepperlike taste*

- *leaves alternate, simple; blades with abaxial surface usually glaucous*

- *flowers apocarpous, the carpels asymmetric and saclike*

- *fruits berrylike monocarps*

Numbers of genera and species. Worldwide, the Winteraceae comprise eight genera and approximately 100 species: *Belliolum* (8 species), *Bubbia* (31), *Drimys* (4), *Exospermum* (2), *Pseudowintera* (2), *Takhtajania* (1), *Tasmannia* (40), and *Zygogynum* (6). *Drimys*, the sole and endemic American genus, is widespread and has undergone little differentiation at the species level; however, numerous varieties have been recognized.

Distribution and habitat. The Winteraceae grow from Veracruz in central-eastern Mexico to the Straits of Magellan, and the Juan Fernandez Islands, and from Luzon and Borneo, including the lesser Sunda Islands, southward through New Guinea and New Caledonia, and along the eastern edge of Australia to Tasmania and New Zealand. A disjunct genus, *Takhtajania*, grows in Madagascar.

Typically, Winteraceae favor wet tropical montane to cool temperate rain forests.

Family classification. Once thought to be closely related to the Magnoliaceae (Magnoliales *sensu* Cronquist), the Winteraceae are now placed near Illiciaceae and Schisandraceae (Illiciales *sensu* Cronquist) and Canellaceae (Magnoliales *sensu* Cronquist), sometimes in their own order, Winterales.

Like many archaic angiosperms, there is considerable variation in the number of floral organs within a species, a fact that explains the difficulty of specific, and even sometimes, generic circumscription.

Features of the family. Habit: trees or shrubs. Wood lacking vessels. Stipules absent. Leaves alternate, simple; blades often coriaceous, the abaxial surface usually glaucous (wax deposits plugging the stomata), the margins entire. Inflorescences terminal or axillary, cymose. Flowers actinomorphic, bisexual; sepals 2–3; petals 2–25; androecium of few to numerous stamens; pollen in tetrads; gynoecium apocarpous, the ovary superior, the carpels 1–24, asymmetric, distinctly saclike, stigmatic cells present on stylelike extension of carpel; placentation marginal, the ovules numerous, in two rows.

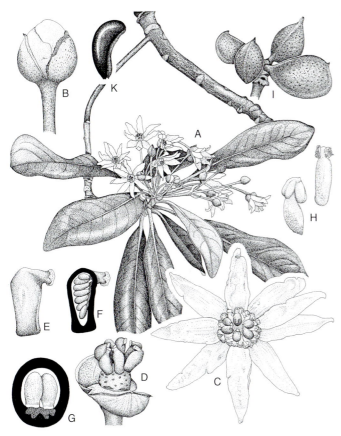

Figure 214. WINTERACEAE. *Drimys winteri*. **A.** Stem with leaves and inflorescence (x½). **B.** Lateral view of flower bud (x4). **C.** Apical view of flower (x2). **D.** Lateral view of flower with petals and stamens removed (x4). **E.** Lateral view of intact carpel (x8). **F.** Partial medial section of carpel (x8). **G.** Transverse section of carpel (x16). **H.** Abaxial (left) and adaxial (right) views of stamens (x8). **I.** Fruiting carpels (x2). **K.** Seed (x5). Reprinted with permission from Cronquist (1981). Artist: William S. Moye.

Fruits monocarps, the monocarps berrylike. **Seeds** few to many; endosperm abundant, the embryo small.

Winteraceae are one of the few angiosperm families to lack vessels in their wood. This feature is of particular evolutionary interest because it is shared with gymnosperms, and there is debate about whether vessels were secondarily lost or perhaps never existed in the family.

Although family representatives are often shrubs or small trees, individuals of *Drimys* can reach 15 meters tall and have boles more than 50 centimeters in diameter.

Natural history. A reproductive biology study of *Drimys brasiliensis* has demonstrated that visitors to the white, pleasantly scented flowers are primarily beetles, flies, and thrips, which eat pollen and lick stigmatic exudate. The species is protogynous; moreover, it is self-compatible and capable of vegetative reproduction by means of horizontal runners. The

fruits appear to be dispersed by birds belonging to the orders Thraupidae and Thyrranidae. Seed germination *in vitro* can take five or six months; however, this time might be reduced greatly after seed transit through a bird's gut.

Fossil pollen attributable to the family is among the earliest angiosperm type recorded and dates back to the Barremian-Aptian period of the lower Cretaceous, over 110 million years ago.

Economic uses. Known in trade as Winter's bark and source of the family name, the bark of *Drimys* (especially *D. winteri*) was formerly of some economic importance. It was collected first by John Winter, captain of one the vessels of Sir Francis Drake's expedition of 1577. Drake's ship and two others were damaged by a storm and forced to land at the Straits of Magellan, where the crews spent several weeks recuperating. Winter tested a plant he found growing there as a remedy for scurvy, a common complaint of sailors at the time. The plant, which we now know as *D. winteri*, was very effective and became a favorite antiscorbutic in Europe. Currently, Winter's bark is little used, except possibly locally in regions where it is native, and it is reported to be toxic when taken internally in high concentration. The wood of *Drimys* is of little commercial interest, although it may be used locally whenever neither durability nor strength are required.

References. BERNAL, H. Y., AND J. E. CORRERA Q. 1998. Winteraceae (*Drimys winteri*). In *Especies vegetales promisorias de los países del Convenio Andrés Bello*, Tomo XII. Santafé de Bogotá, D. E., Colombia: Secretaria Ejecutiva del Convenio Andrés Bello. EHRENDORFER, F., AND M. LAMBROU. 2000. Chromosomes of *Takhtajania*, other Winteraceae, and Canellaceae: phylogenetic implications. *Ann. Missouri Bot. Gard.* 87:407–13. GOTTSBERGER, G., I. SILBERBAUER-GOTTSBERGER, AND F. EHRENDORFER. 1980. Reproductive biology in the primitive relic angiosperm *Drimys brasiliensis* (Winteraceae). *Pl. Syst. Evol.* 135: 11–39. KAROL, K. G., Y. SUH, G. E. SCHATZ, AND E. A. ZIMMER. 2000. Molecular evidence for the phylogenetic position of *Takhtajania* in the Winteraceae. *Ann. Missouri Bot. Gard.* 87:414–32. MORAWETZ, W. 1984. How stable are genomes of tropical woody plants? Heterozygosity in C-banded daryotypes of *Porcelia* as compared with *Annona* (Annonaceae) and *Drimys* (Winteraceae). *Pl. Syst. Evol.* 145:29–39. RICO-GRAY, V., M. PALACIOS-RIOS, AND L. B. THIEN. 1995. Winteraceae. In *Flora de Veracruz*, eds. A. Gómez-Pompa and V. Sosa, fasc. 88:1–8. Xalapa, Mexico: INIREB. SMITH, A. C. 1943. The American species of *Drimys*. *J. Arnold Arbor.* 24:1–33. STANDLEY, P. C., AND J. A. STEYERMARK. 1946. Winteraceae. In Flora of Guatemala, eds. P. C. Standley and J. A. Steyermark. *Fieldiana, Bot.* 24(4):269–70. SUH, Y. L. B. THIEN, H. E. REEVE, AND E. A. ZIMMER. 1993. Molecular evolution and phylogenetic implications of internal transcribed spacer sequences of ribosomal DNA in Winteraceae. *Amer. J. Bot.* 80: 1042–55.

ZYGOPHYLLACEAE (Creosotebush Family)

DUNCAN M. PORTER

Figure 215, Plate 52

- *woody or herbaceous*

- *stipules usually present, sometimes spiny*

- *leaves usually opposite, compound*

- *flowers usually with 5-merous perianth; stamens usually 10*

- *fruits capsules or schizocarps, sometimes winged or spiny*

Numbers of genera and species. Worldwide, the Zygophyllaceae comprise 24 genera and approximately 234 species. The largest genera in the family are *Zygophyllum* (80 species), *Fagonia* (30), *Balanites* (25), and *Tribulus* (25). Ten genera have only one species. In the Western Hemisphere, 13 genera and 61 species are native. In tropical America, there are 10 genera and 38 species. Three species of *Tribulus* are naturalized in the neotropics.

Distribution and habitat. Species of Zygophyllaceae occur mainly in the warmer arid and semiarid areas of the world. A number grow in saline soils. They are generally thought of as desert plants, but this is by no means true for all species. A number of species have more temperate distributions, reaching the north-central United States, Spain and France, central Asia, Mongolia, Australia, Argentina, and Chile. Many species are narrow endemics, and the majority of genera naturally occur within a single continental area. Exceptions are *Balanites*, *Kelleronia*, *Seetzenia*, and *Tetradiclis* (Africa and Asia), *Tribulus* and *Zygophyllum* (Africa, Europe, Asia, and Australia), *Fagonia* (Africa, Asia, North America, and South America), and *Guaiacum*, *Kallstroemia*, and *Larrea* (North and South America). *Bulnesia*, *Guaiacum*, *Izozogia*, *Kallstroemia*, *Larrea*, *Metharme*, *Morkillia*, *Pintoa*, *Plectrocarpa*, *Porlieria*, *Sericodes*, and *Viscainoa* are endemic to the Western Hemisphere. *Tribulus terrestris* (puncture vine), native to the Mediterranean region, is an introduced weed found throughout drier temperate areas of the world, including the central and western United States and tropical South America. *Tribulus cistoides* (burrnut), from tropical Africa, is a weed in dry habitats of the tropical and subtropical Americas and the Pacific Islands; *T. longipetalus*, from the Middle East, has become established in northwestern Peru; and *Kallstroemia parviflora*, native to the United States and Mexico, has become a roadside weed in northern Peru and adjacent Ecuador.

Family classification. The Zygophyllaceae are placed in the Sapindales by Cronquist. The most recent study of the

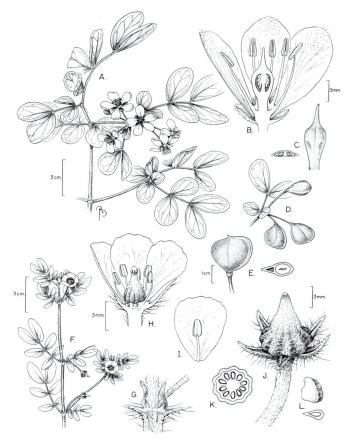

Figure 215. ZYGOPHYLLACEAE. *Guaiacum officinale* (A–E) and *Kallstroemia maxima* (F–L). **A.** Stems with leaves and inflorescence. **B.** Medial section of flower. **C.** Lateral view (right) and transverse section of gynoecium (left). **D.** Stem with leaf and fruits. **E.** Lateral view (left) and transverse section (right) of fruit. **F.** Stems with leaves and inflorescences. **G.** Detail of node showing stipules. **H.** Longitudinal section of flower. **I.** Adaxial view of petal and stamen. **J.** Fruit with persistent calyx. **K.** Transverse section of fruit. **L.** Lateral view (above) and transverse section (below) of fruit segments. Reprinted with permission from Acevedo-Rodríguez (1996). Artist: Bobbi Angell.

family recognizes five subfamilies: Morkillioideae, Tribuloideae, Seetzenioideae, Larreoideae, and Zygophylloideae. All except Seetzenioideae occur in the Western Hemisphere. *Malacocarpus*, *Peganum*, *Tetradiclis*, and *Nitraria*, native to the Eastern Hemisphere and traditionally classified as Zygophyllaceae, are better placed in the Peganaceae and Nitrariaceae, respectively, and *Balanites*, often placed in its own family, is accepted as a member of the Zygophyllaceae. The remaining Zygophyllaceae form a monophyletic group with affinities only with Krameriaceae, and even this relationship is distant as *Krameria* shares no significant characters with Zygophyllaceae.

Features of the family. Habit: shrubs, subshrubs, or perennial herbs, sometimes annual herbs (*Kallstroemia* and *Tribulus*) or trees (*Bulnesia* and *Guaiacum*). Stipules usually present, spiny in some Western Hemisphere shrubs (*Porlieria* and *Fagonia*). Leaves usually opposite, alternate in *Morkillia mexicana* and *Viscainoa geniculata*, compound (pinnate, or palmate in *Fagonia*), rarely reduced to 1 or 2 leaflets. Inflorescences axillary or terminal, of solitary flowers or in cymes (always terminal). Flowers actinomorphic to slightly zygomorphic, bisexual; sepals usually 5; petals usually 5; stamens usually 10, sometimes with appendages, distinct or fused at filament bases; nectary disc or glands often present between or around base of filaments and ovary; gynoecium syncarpous, the ovary superior, often angled or winged, the carpels usually 5, the locules usually 5(10 in *Kallstroemia*), the stigma lobed; placentation axile, the ovules 1 or more per locule. Fruits capsules or schizocarps, sometimes winged or spiny, the capsules loculicidal or septicidal. Seeds 2–25 per fruit; endosperm sometimes absent.

The leaves are reduced to a single leaflet in *Viscainoa geniculata* (guayacán) from Mexico. In several species of *Larrea*, the two leaflets are partially fused, and in the Chilean *Pintoa*, the leaflets are densely dotted with glands on their undersurfaces.

Natural history. All members of the family are insect-pollinated. Self-pollination also takes place in *Kallstroemia* by a novel method. When the flowers first open in the morning, the petals and stamens spread horizontally. By around noon, the filaments of the stamens have slowly curved upward, moving the anthers to the stigma just before the petals close around them. This clockwise twisting of the petals around the style appresses the anthers to the stigma, resulting in self-pollination in the absence of insect pollination. *Larrea tridentata* is also known to be self-compatible, but it lacks this mechanism for self-pollination.

The seeds of *Fagonia* become sticky when moistened and may be dispersed externally by animals. Most genera have hard mericarps or seeds with thick seed coats and may be dispersed internally by animals. The winged fruits of *Bulnesia* and *Morkillia* and some species of *Tribulus* and *Zygophyllum* are wind-dispersed. In some species of *Tribulus*, the mericarps bear sharp spines that may attach to birds' or mammals' feet as well as automobile or airplane tires.

Seeds of *Kallstroemia* are viable for at least three years, and they germinate intermittently at irregular intervals. The seeds of *Larrea tridentata* and *Tribulus terrestris* exhibit dormancy, and the fruit wall of *Zygophyllum dumosum* has been found to contain a water-soluble inhibitor of seed germination. Clones of *Larrea tridentata* growing in the deserts of southern California, are estimated to be more than 10,000 years old.

Economic uses. Many members of the Zygophyllaceae have local medicinal uses, probably because of the alkaloids or resins they contain. The resins of *Guaiacum officinale* (lignum vitae), a small tree that grows from the West Indies to Colombia and Venezuela, and *G. sanctum* (lignum sanctum), which is distributed from the Florida Keys to Nicaragua and Costa Rica, were previously used as a cure for syphilis. This and the value of their hard, durable wood for making marine bearings, bowling balls, mortars and pestles, brush backs, and mallet heads have made them very rare in many parts of their ranges. Species of *Bulnesia* are also used for many of the same purposes. Saponins found in *Guaiacum angustifolium* (soapbush) of Texas and northern Mexico are utilized locally in soap-making. About 25 percent of the surface area of Mexico is estimated to be covered by *Larrea tridentata* (creosote bush) and this has led to a number of studies attempting to find economic uses for this abundant plant. The most successful has been the discovery of antioxidants in the resin, which have been used to keep chocolate candies fresh and rubber from deteriorating.

References. Campos López, E., T. J. Mabry, and S. Fernández Tavizon. 1979. *Larrea*. Mexico: Consejo National de Ciencia y Tecnologia. Comas, C. I., V. A. Confalonieri, and J. H. Hunziker. 1998. The genus *Bulnesia* revisited: a cladistic analysis of seed protein data. *Biochem. Syst. Ecol.* 26(6):611–18. Navarro, G. 1997. *Izozogia nellii* (Zygophyllaceae), new genus and species from the Gran Chaco de Santa Cruz (Bolivia). Palacios, R. A., and J. H. Hunziker. 1984. Revisión taxonómica del género Bulnesia (Zygophyllaceae). *Darwiniana* 25:299–320. Porter, D. M. 1967. Another *Tribulus* adventive in the New World. *Rhodora* 69:455–56. Porter, D. M. 1969. The genus *Kallstroemia* (Zygophyllaceae). *Contr. Gray Herb.* 198:41–153. Porter, D. M. 1974. Disjunct distributions in the New World Zygophyllaceae. *Taxon* 23:339–46. Sheahan, M. C., and M. W. Chase. 1996. A phylogenetic analysis of Zygophyllaceae R. Br. based on morphological, anatomical and *rbc*L DNA sequence data. *Bot. J. Linn. Soc.* 122:279–300. Sheahan, M. C., and M. W. Chase. 2000. Phylogenetic relationships within Zygophyllaceae based on DNA sequences of three plastid regions, with special emphasis on Zygophylloideae. *Syst. Bot.* 25(2):371–84.

A. *Pachystachys coccinea* (Acanthaceae). Inflorescence with bracts subtending flowers. © Mori.

B. *Phaulothamnus spinescens* (Achatocarpaceae). Fruits; note dark seed seen through translucent berry. © Mitchell.

C. *Saurauia madrensis* (Actinidiaceae). Flowers. © Gracie.

D. *Mesembryanthemum crystallinum* (Aizoaceae). Flowers and succulent leaves. © Schmid.

Plate 2 ▪ ANACARDIACEAE

A. *Anarcardium occidentale.* **1.** Flowers, white turning red with age. © Gracie. **2.** Fruit at apex subtended by fleshy, red pedicel. © Gracie.

B. *Tapirira mexicana.* Inflorescence. © Mitchell.

C. *Schinus terebinthifolia.* Flowers. © Gracie.

A. *Fusaea longifolia.* Flower with green petals, a ring of yellow staminodes, a ring of yellowish-white anthers, and central carpels. © Gracie.

B. *Xylopia aromatica.* Flower with two whorls of petals of different sizes. © Gracie.

C. *Guatteria punctata.* Immature apocarpous fruits composed of stipitate monocarps. © Gracie.

D. *Duguetia microphylla.* Pseudosyncarpous fruit. © Mori.

Plate 4 ▪ APOCYNACEAE, AQUIFOLIACEAE

A. *Mandevilla hirsuta* (Apocynaceae). Fruits; note that carpels separate as fruits mature. © Mori.

B. *Tabernaemontana arborea* (Apocynaceae). Inflorescence. © Smith.

C. *Calotropis procera* (Apocynaceae). Flowers; note corona. © Gracie.

D. *Asclepias curassavica* (Apocynaceae). Flowers; note corona. © Gracie.

E. *Cynanchum blandum* (Apocynaceae). Flower and fruit. © Gracie.

F. *Ilex petiolaris* (Aquifoliaceae). Staminate flowers; note green pistillodes. © Gracie.

A. *Aristolochia elegans* (Aristolochiaceae). Apex of perianth on right and lower part of second perianth on left. © Mori.

B. *Barnadesia arborea* (Asteraceae). Capitula subtended by bracts. © Gracie.

C. *Espeletia pycnophylla* subsp. *angelensis* (Asteraceae). Habit of plants. © Luteyn.

D. *Oyedaea wurdackii* (Asteraceae). Capitula with central disk flowers surrounded by radiate flowers. © Gröger.

E. *Chimantaea mirabilis* (Asteraceae). Habit of plants. © Pruski.

F. *Stomatochaeta cymbifolia* (Asteraceae). Capitulum. © Pruski.

Plate 6 ▪ AVICENNIACEAE, BALANOPHORACEAE, BIGNONIACEAE, BIXACEAE

A. *Avicennia germinans* (Avicenniaceae). Inflorescence; note unequal pairs of stamens. © Mori.

B. *Helosis cayennensis* (Balanophoraceae). **1.** Inflorescence with peltate bracts. © Gracie. **2.** Close-up of inflorescence; note 3-merous perianth and fused stamens. © Gracie.

C. *Arrabidaea bilabiata* (Bignoniaceae). Flowers. © Gracie.

D. *Bixa orellana* (Bixaceae). Flower and immature fruits. © Gracie.

A. *Pachira aquatica* (Bombacaceae). Nocturnal flower; note fascicles of stamens. © Gracie.

B. *Ochroma pyramidale* (Bombacaceae). Flower and bud. © Gracie.

C. *Ceiba pentandra* (Bombacaceae). Dehisced fruit with seeds surrounded by hairs (kapok). © Mori.

D. *Bonnetia sessilis* (Bonnetiaceae). Flower. © Gracie.

E. *Cordia dentata* (Boraginaceae). Part of inflorescence. © Mori.

F. *Tournefortia bicolor* (Boraginaceae). Inflorescence. © Gracie.

Plate 8 ▪ BRUNELLIACEAE, BUDDLEJACEAE, BURSERACEAE, CABOMBACEAE

A. *Brunellia costaricensis* (Brunelliaceae). Flowers; note intrastaminal disk and apocarpous gynoecium. © Gracie.

B. *Buddleja nitida* (Buddlejaceae). Inflorescence. © Gracie.

C. *Protium cuneatum* (Burseraceae). Flower; note intrastaminal disc. © Gracie.

D. *Cabomba furcata* (Cabombaceae). Habit of plant with flowers; note filiform submersed leaves. © Gracie.

A. *Pereskia grandiflora*. Flower and leaves. © Gracie.

B. *Epiphyllum phyllanthus*. Apices of tubular flowers. © Areces.

C. *Opuntia dillenii*. **1.** Flower and bud. © Areces. **2.** Fruit; note areoles with glochids. © Areces.

D. *Pilocereus royenii*. Flower and part of stem; note spines and trichomes. © Areces.

E. *Stenocereus hystrix*. Dehisced fruit revealing small black seeds; note areoles with spines. © Areces.

Plate 10 ▪ CAMPANULACEAE, CAPPARACEAE

A. *Centropogon cornutus* (Campanulaceae). **1.** Flower. © Gracie. **2.** Close-up of flower; note stigma protruding from connate anthers. © Gracie.

B. *Capparis sola* (Capparaceae). Flower; note gynophore subtending green ovary. © Gracie.

C. *Crataeva tapia* (Capparaceae). Trifoliolate leaves and stipitate fruits. © Gracie.

D. *Steriphoma cinnabarinum* (Capparaceae). Inflorescence; note gynophores subtending whitish ovaries. © Gracie.

A. *Carica papaya* (Caricaceae). **1.** Staminate inflorescences. © Mori. **2.** Pistillate flower. © Mori. **3.** Immature fruits. © Mori.

B. *Anthodiscus amazonicus* (Caryocaraceae). Inflorescence; note flowers with calyptrate corollas. © Mori.

C. *Caryocar glabrum* subsp. *glabrum* (Caryocaraceae). Nocturnal flower. © Mori.

Plate 12 ▪ CECROPIACEAE, CELASTRACEAE

A. *Cecropia obtusa* (Cecropiaceae). **1.** Close-up of staminate spikes; note anthers. © Gracie. **2.** Muellerian bodies on trichilia. © Gracie.

B. *Cecropia latiloba* (Cecropiaceae). Habit; note palmately divided leaves. © Gracie.

C. *Maytenus octogona* (Celastraceae). **1.** Inflorescence; note stamens alternate with perianth lobes and intrastaminal disc. © Mori. **2.** Dehisced fruit revealing red aril. © Mori.

A. *Hedyosmum scabrum* (Chloranthaceae). Inflorescences; note leaves with connate petiole bases and dentate blade margins. © Todzia.

B. *Hirtella racemosa* var. *racemosa* (Chrysobalanaceae). Flowers; note gynobasic style. © Gracie.

C. *Clethra pringlei* (Clethraceae). **1.** Infructescence; note immature fruits with persistent calyces. © Mori. **2.** Inflorescence. © Mori.

Plate 14 ▪ CLUSIACEAE

A. *Clusia candelabrum.* Pistillate flower. © Gracie.

B. *Clusia microstemon.* Staminate flower; note resin covering stamens. © Gracie.

C. *Clusia nemorosa.* Fruits, one dehisced; note orange arillate seeds. © Lobova.

D. *Hypericum laricifolium.* Part of branch with flower; note reduced leaves. © Gracie.

A. *Terminalia amazonia* (Combretaceae). Infructescence of winged fruits. © Mori.

B. *Combretum rohrii* (Combretaceae). Inflorescence. © Mori.

C. *Connarus lambertii* (Connaraceae). Dehisced fruit with arillate seed. © Gracie.

D. *Ipomoea setifera* (Convolvulaceae). Flowers. © Gracie.

E. *Coriaria ruscifolia* (Coriariaceae). **1.** Close-up of flowers; note exserted stamens. © Gracie. **2.** Branch with racemes. © Gracie.

Plate 16 ▪ CUCURBITACEAE, CUSCUTACEAE

A. *Rytidostylis amazonica* (Cucurbitaceae). Flower and fruit. © Gracie.

B. *Psiguria triphylla* (Cucurbitaceae). Inflorescence. © Gracie.

C. *Gurania subumbellata* (Cucurbitaceae). **1.** Close-up of pistillate inflorescence. © Gracie. **2.** Staminate inflorescence. © Gracie. **3.** Developing infructescence. © Gracie.

D. *Cuscuta americana* (Cuscutaceae). Inflorescences. © Gracie.

A. *Desfontainia spinosa s. l.* (Desfontainiaceae). Flowers and leaves; note spiny leaf apices and marginal teeth. © Struwe.

B. *Tapura guianensis* (Dichapetalaceae). Inflorescences on petioles. © Gracie.

C. *Duckeodendron cestroides* (Duckeodendraceae). Immature fruit and leaves. © Mori.

D. *Diospyros guianensis* (Ebenaceae). Flower. © Mori.

Plate 18 ▪ ELAEOCARPACEAE, ERICACEAE, ERYTHROXYLACEAE

A. *Sloanea floribunda* (Elaeocarpaceae). Close-up of flowers; note stamens inserted on disc. © Gracie.

B. *Sloanea laxiflora* (Elaeocarpaceae). Flowers; note uniseriate perianth. © Mori.

C. *Pernettya prostrata* (Ericaceae). **1.** Flowering branches. © Gracie. **2.** Branch with fruit; note accrescent, fleshy sepals. © Gracie.

D. *Erythroxylum coca* (Erythroxylaceae). Leaf; note distinct paler central band resulting from involute vernation. © Gracie.

E. *Erythroxylum columbinum* (Erythroxylaceae). Axillary inflorescence; note basally connate filaments. © Thomas.

A. *Pera distichophylla* (Euphorbiaceae). Bisexual pseudanthium. © Gracie.

B. *Conceveiba guianensis* (Euphorbiaceae). Infructescence; note fruits with three valves and persistent styles. © Mori.

C. *Chamaesyce amplexicaulis* (Euphorbiaceae). Pseudanthia. © Mori.

D. *Euphronia guianensis* (Euphroniaceae). Flower; note three petals. © Mori.

Plate 20 ▪ FABACEAE (CAESALPINIOIDEAE, PAPILIONOIDEAE)

A. *Cassia leiandra* (Caesalpinioideae). Flower; note heteromorphic stamens and sigmoid-shaped longer stamens. © Gracie.

B. *Dicorynia guianensis* (Caesalpinioideae). Flowers; note three petals, two stamens, and pistil with dark ovary and white style. © Mori.

C. *Clitoria amazonum* (Papilionoideae). Flowers. © Gracie.

D. *Swartzia auriculata* (Papilionoideae). **1.** Flowers. © Gracie. **2.** Dehisced fruit revealing arillate seed. © Gracie.

A. *Parkia discolor* (Mimosoideae). Inflorescence; note proximal fringe of staminodial flowers. © Mori.

B. *Neptunia prostrata* (Mimosoideae). Inflorescence of dimorphic flowers. © Gracie.

C. *Pentaclethra macroloba* (Mimosoideae). Branch with inflorescences; note bipinnately compound leaves. © Mori.

D. *Pithecellobium saman* (Mimosoideae). Inflorescence. © Mori.

E. *Quercus costaricensis* (Fagaceae). Close-up of staminate flowers. © Mori.

F. *Ryania speciosa* (Flacourtiaceae). Flower. © Gracie.

Plate 22 ▪ GENTIANACEAE, GESNERIACEAE, GOODENIACEAE

A. *Voyria acuminata* (Gentianaceae). Habit of flowering plant. © Gracie.

B. *Gentianella cernua* (Gentianaceae). Flowers. © Luteyn.

C. *Chrysothemis pulchella* (Gesneriaceae). Flowers; note red-orange calyces. © Mori.

D. *Episcia sphalera* (Gesneriaceae). Flower; note spur at base of corolla. © Mori.

E. *Scaevola plumieri* (Goodeniaceae). Flower; note strongly zygomorphic corolla. © Gracie.

A. *Gunnera insignis* (Gunneraceae). **1.** Habit; note large leaves. © Gracie. **2.** Close-up of inflorescence; note red stamens and white fuzzy stigmas. © Gracie.

B. *Hernandia guianensis* (Hernandiaceae). **1.** Inflorescence with pistillate flower; note curved style with yellow glands at base. © Gracie. **2.** Fruits enclosed by inflated bracteoles. © Mori.

C. *Billia rosea* (Hippocastanaceae). Inflorescence. © Luteyn.

D. *Salacia impressifolia* (Hippocrateaceae). Flower; note 3 reflexed stamens, extrastaminal nectiferous disc, and triangular ovary. © Gracie.

Plate 24 ▪ HUGONIACEAE, HUMIRIACEAE, HYDNORACEAE, HYDROPHYLLACEAE

A. *Hebepetalum humiriifolium* (Hugoniaceae). Flowers. © Mori.

B. *Vantanea guianensis* (Humiriaceae). Inflorescence. © Sabatier.

C. *Prosopanche americana* (=*P. costaricensis*; Hydnoraceae). Subterranean flower. © Maas.

D. *Wigandia urens* var. *caracasana* (Hydrophyllaceae). Flower. © Mori.

A. *Dendrobangia boliviana* (Icacinaceae). Flowers; note attenuate petal apices. © Gracie.

B. *Lacistema grandifolium* (Lacistemataceae). Infructescences. © Mori.

C. *Scutellaria costaricana* (Lamiaceae). Inflorescence. © Gracie.

D. *Rhodostemonodaphne kunthiana* (Lauraceae). Flowers. © Gracie.

E. *Aiouea guianensis* (Lauraceae). Immature fruit; note swollen red cupule. © Gracie.

F. *Ocotea diffusa* (Lauraceae). Flower and buds. © Gracie.

A. *Lecythis pisonis* (Lecythidaceae). **1.** Flowers; note androecial hood. © Gracie. **2.** Dehisced fruit and arillate seeds. © Gracie.

B. *Gustavia longifolia* (Lecythidaceae). Flowers; note actinomorphic androecium with the stamens free at the apex and fused at the base. © Gracie.

C. *Lennoa madreporoides* (Lennoaceae). Flowers. © Yatskievych.

D. *Utricularia calycifida* (Lentibulariaceae). Inflorescence; note swollen palate in throat of flower. © Mori.

E. *Lissocarpa guianensis* (Lissocarpaceae). Flower; note 8-lobed corona in throat of corolla. © Westra.

A. *Mentzelia aspera* (Loasaceae). Flower and immature fruits; note apiculate petals, persistent sepals, and trichomes covering entire plant. © Gracie.

B. *Strychnos tomentosa* (Loganiaceae). Inflorescence and opposing tendril; note parallel curved veins in leaves. © Gracie.

C. *Psittacanthus cucullaris* (Loranthaceae). Apices of branches with flowers, developing fruits, and leaves; note opposite, coriaceous leaves and calyculus (rim) on developing fruits. © Gracie

D. *Talauma boliviana* (Magnoliaceae). Dehisced fruit; note red seeds on slender funicles. © Nee.

E. *Cuphea cyanea* (Lythraceae). Flower; note petals inserted just below floral tube, each petal with a central vein. © Smith.

F. *Malesherbia scarlatiflora* (Malesherbiaceae). Inflorescence. © Gengler-Nowak.

Plate 28 ▪ MALPIGHIACEAE, MALVACEAE

A. *Byrsonima punctulata* (Malpighiaceae). Close-up of inflorescence; note paired glands on calyces and clawed petals. © Gracie.

B. *Heteropterys orinocensis* (Malpighiaceae). Fruits; note large dorsal wings. © Gracie.

C. *Thespesia populnea* (Malvaceae). Apical view of flower; note staminal column and dark-colored pattern at base of petals. © Jansen-Jacobs.

D. *Malvaviscus arborea* (Malvaceae). Flowers; note epicalyx and exserted staminal tube. © Westra.

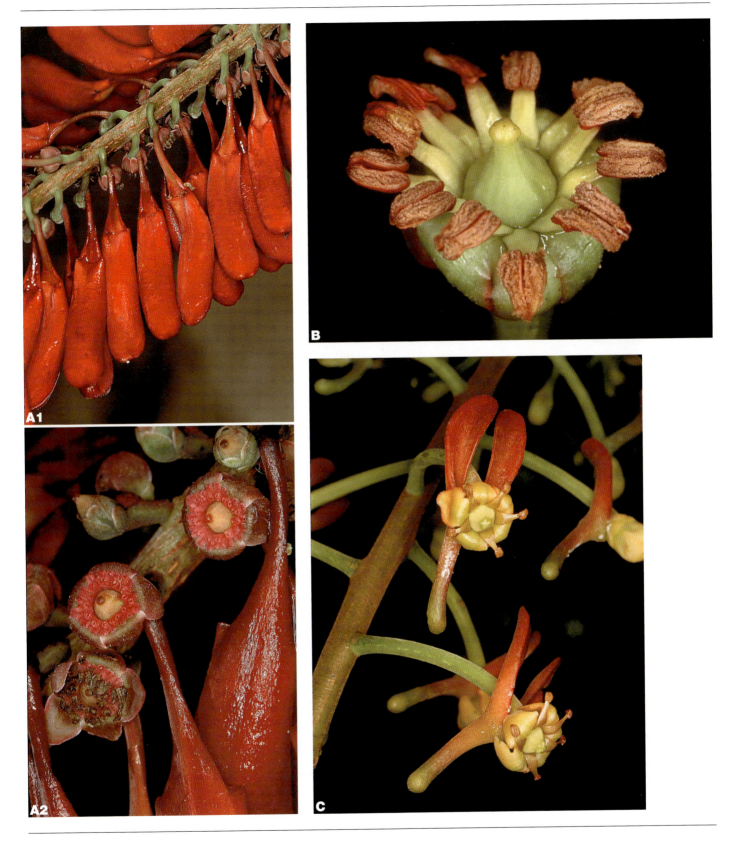

A. *Norantea guianensis*. **1.** Close-up of inflorescence; note cuplike nectaries arising from bases of flowers. © Gracie. **2.** Close-up of flowers. © Gracie.

B. *Schwartzia costaricensis*. Close-up of flower. © Mori.

C. *Souroubea guianensis*. Part of inflorescence; note bracteal nectaries subtending flowers. © Mori.

Plate 30 ▪ MELASTOMATACEAE, MELIACEAE, MEMECYLACEAE

A. *Monochaetum floribundum* (Melastomataceae). Branch with flower; note curved, parallel veins in leaves and appendages on stamens. © Gracie.

B. *Miconia ceramicarpa* var. *candolleana* (Melastomataceae). Infructescence with fruits maturing from red to bluish white. © Gracie.

C. *Maieta guianensis* (Melastomataceae). Flowers with paired anthers. © Gracie.

D. *Swietenia mahagoni* (Meliaceae). **1.** Flowers; note staminal tube and capitate stigma. © Gracie. **2.** Intact and dehisced capsules, the latter showing winged seeds. © Gracie.

E. *Mouriri crassifolia* (Memecylaceae). Flowers; note poricidal anthers. © Gracie.

A. *Orthomene prancei* (Menispermaceae). Staminate flower with six stamens. © Gracie.

B. *Abuta rufescens* (Menispermaceae). Staminate flower with six stamens. © Gracie.

C. *Nymphoides indica* (Menyanthaceae). Flowers and floating leaves; note fringed petals. © Westra.

D. *Mollugo floriana* subsp. *floriana* (Molluginaceae). Flowers. © Gracie.

E. *Ficus gomelleira* (Moraceae). Syconium in leaf axil; note stem with terminal stipule and stipule scars, and ostiole at apex of syconium. © Mori.

Plate 32 ▪ MYRISTICACEAE, MYRSINACEAE, MYRTACEAE, NOLANACEAE

A. *Virola michelii* (Myristicaceae). Flowers; note 3 tepals. © Gracie.

B. *Virola venosa* (Myristicaceae). Dehisced fruit; note red aril covering seed. © Mori.

C. *Ardisia guianensis* (Myrsinaceae). Branch with terminal infructescence. © Mori.

D. *Psidium acutangulum* (Myrtaceae). Flowers; note exserted style. © Gracie.

E. *Calyptranthes spruceana* (Myrtaceae). Inflorescence; note hypanthium. © Gracie.

F. *Nolana galapagensis* (Nolanaceae). Part of branch and flower; note succulent leaves. © Gracie.

A. *Neea floribunda* (Nyctaginaceae). Flowers; note uniseriate perianth. © Gracie.

B. *Victoria amazonica* (Nymphaeaceae). Floating leaves and first day flower. © Gracie.

C. *Ouratea poeppigi* (Ochnaceae). Flowers. © Gracie.

D. *Wallacea insignis* (Ochnaceae). Flowers. © Gracie.

Plate 34 ▪ OLACACEAE, ONAGRACEAE, OROBANCHACEAE

A. *Heisteria cauliflora* (Olacaceae). Branch with immature and mature fruits; note persistent calyces. © Gracie.

B. *Minquartia guianensis* (Olacaceae). Inflorescence. © Gracie.

C. *Fuchsia paniculata* (Onagraceae). Flowers; note lobed stigma. © Gracie.

D. *Conopholis alpina* (Orobanchaceae). Fruiting plants. © Kallunki.

A. *Averrhoa bilimbi* (Oxalidaceae). **1.** Flowers. © Gracie. **2.** Cauliflorous inflorescence and infructescence. © Gracie.

B. *Oxalis debilis* (Oxalidaceae). Flowers. © Mori.

C. *Bocconia frutescens* (Papaveraceae). Habit; note immature infructescences. © Gracie.

Plate 36 ▪ PASSIFLORACEAE, PEDALIACEAE, PELLICIERACEAE

A. *Passiflora quadriglandulosa* (Passifloraceae). Flower; note filamentous corona and androgynophore. © Gracie.

B. *Passiflora cf. costata* (Passifloraceae). Longitudinal section of flower; note corona and androgynophore. © Smith.

C. *Sesamum indicum* (Pedaliaceae). Stem with leaves and flower. © Mori.

D. *Pelliciera rhizophorae* (Pellicieraceae). **1.** Flower. © Mori. **2.** Fruits. © Mori.

A. *Peridiscus luciduas* (Peridiscaceae). Flowers. © INPA/DFID.

B. *Ledenbergia seguierioides* (Phytolaccaceae). Inflorescences. © Nee.

C. *Picramnia pentandra* (Picramniaceae). Branch with infructescence; note pinnately compound leaves. © Thomas.

D. *Piper aduncum* (Piperaceae). Branch with arched inflorescences; note swollen nodes. © Mori.

Plate 38 ▪ PODOSTEMACEAE, POLEMONIACEAE, POLYGALACEAE

A. *Mourera fluviatilis* (Podostemaceae). Habit; note flowering spikes. © Mori.

B. *Cantua quercifolia* (Polemoniaceae). Apex of plant with inflorescence. © Luteyn.

C. *Polygala spectabilis* (Polygalaceae). Inflorescence. © Mori.

D. *Securidaca diversifolia* (Polygalaceae). Flower. © Smith.

A. *Portulaca howellii* (Portulacaceae). Flowers; note succulent leaves. © Eliasson.

B. *Roupala consimilis* (Proteaceae). Inflorescence; note flower-pairs with common stalk. © Gracie.

C. *Quiina guianensis* (Quiinaceae). Inflorescence. © Gracie.

D. *Rhabdodendron amazonicum* (Rhabdodendraceae). Flowers; note numerous stamens and absence of caducous petals. © Mori.

Plate 40 ▪ RHAMNACEAE, RHIZOPHORACEAE, ROSACEAE

A. *Ziziphus mauritiana* (Rhamnaceae). Branch apex with inflorescences and one immature fruit; note intrastaminal disc. © Gracie.

B. *Rhizophora mangle* (Rhizophoraceae). **1.** Flowers. © Gracie. **2.** Viviparous fruits; note seedling axis protruding from fruit. © Gracie.

C. *Acaena elongata* (Rosaceae). Plant with infructescence. © Gracie.

A. *Warszewiczia coccinea*. Part of inflorescence; note red foliose calyx lobes (calycophylls). © Gerlach.

B. *Faramea anisocalyx*. Inflorescence; note leaflike lavender bracts. © Delprete.

C. *Hamelia axillaris*. Inflorescence; note opposite leaves, entire leaf margins, stipules, and inferior ovaries. © Delprete.

D. *Posoqueria longiflora*. Inflorescences; note long tubular corollas modified for sphinx moth pollination. © Maas.

Plate 42 ▪ RUBIACEAE, RUTACEAE

A. *Osa pulchra* (Rubiaceae). Pendent flowers. © Gilbert.

B. *Palicourea crocea* (Rubiaceae). Inflorescence; note slight bulge at base of corolla. © Gracie.

C. *Genipa americana* (Rubiaceae). Flower. © Gracie.

D. *Hortia arborea* (Rutaceae). Flowers in tightly congested inflorescence. © Mori.

A. *Paullinia pinnata.* Inflorescence; note paired, coiled tendrils at base. © Gracie.

B. *Talisia megaphylla.* Flower; note exserted, tufted petal appendages. © Gracie.

C. *Serjania grandifolia.* Two winged fruits; note that wings are at base and seeds at apex of fruit. © Gracie.

D. *Paullinia tricornis.* Infructescence; note dehised fruit with black seed subtended by white aril. © Gracie.

Plate 44 ▪ SAPOTACEAE, SARRACENIACEAE

A. *Micropholis obscura* (Sapotaceae). Inflorescence; note nectar in flowers, stamens opposite corolla lobes, and staminodes alternate with corolla lobes. © Gracie.

B. *Manilkara zapota* (Sapotaceae). Fruit. © Mori.

C. *Heliamphora tatei* var. *neblinae* (Sarraceniaceae). **1.** Habit; note pitcherlike leaves. © Beitel. **2.** Close-up of flower. © Beitel.

A. *Alonsoa meridionalis* (Scrophulariaceae). Resupinate flowers. © Gracie.

B. *Simaba trichilioides* (Simaroubaceae). Fruits; note that fruits are of separate druparia. © Thomas.

C. *Simaba pohliana* (Simaroubaceae). Flowers. © Thomas.

D. *Siparuna guianensis* (Siparunaceae). Receptacles; one dehisced and revealing drupelets surrounded by white arils. © Renner.

E. *Siparuna echinata* (Siparunaceae). Inflorescence; note styles protruding through hole in floral roof . © Mori.

Plate 46 ▪ SOLANACEAE, SPHENOCLEACEAE

A. *Witheringia maculata* (Solanaceae). Flowers and immature fruits subtended by persistent calyx. © Mori.

B. *Brugmansia aurea* (Solanaceae). Flowers. © Gracie.

C. *Solanum monachophyllum* (Solanaceae). Flower; note spines on branch. © Gracie.

D. *Sphenoclea zeylanica* (Sphenocleaceae). Inflorescences. © Mori.

A. *Theobroma cacao* (Sterculiaceae). **1.** Flower; note white sepals, dimorphic petals with basal hood and yellow expanded blades (apices of stamens inserted in hoods), and red-violet staminodes. © Mori. **2.** Cauliflorous fruits. © Mori.

B. *Herrania mariae* (Sterculiaceae). Cauliflorous flowers; note red staminodes and long white apical petal blades arising from basal petal hoods. © Gracie.

C. *Styrax pallidus* (Styracaceae). Flowers; note cupuliform calyx and strongly reflexed corolla lobes. © Gracie.

A. *Suriana maritima* (Surianaceae). **1.** Apical part of plant with flower. © Smith. **2.** Fruits. © Thomas.

B. *Symplocos martinicensis* (Symplocaceae). Inflorescences. © Mori.

C. *Ternstroemia pungens* (Ternstroemiaceae). Fruits; note persistent calyces. © Mori.

D. *Deherainia smaragdina* (Theophrastaceae). Flower; note appendages alternate with petal lobes and stamens opposite petal lobes. © Gracie.

A. *Schoenobiblus daphnoides* (Thymelaeaceae). **1.** Staminate flowers. © INPA/DFID. **2.** Pistillate flowers. © INPA/DFID.

B. *Mollia speciosa* (Tiliaceae). Flowers. © Gracie.

C. *Apeiba albiflora* (Tiliaceae). Fruit. © Gracie.

D. *Tovaria pendula* (Tovariaceae). Flowers; note superior ovaries and spreading stigmas. © Gracie.

E. *Trigonia spruceana* (Trigoniaceae). Inflorescence. © Gracie.

Plate 50 ▪ TURNERACEAE, ULMACEAE, URTICACEAE, VERBENACEAE

A. *Piriqueta cistoides* (Turneraceae). Flower. © Gracie.

B. *Trema micrantha* (Ulmaceae). Inflorescence and developing fruits. © Gracie.

C. *Urera baccifera* (Urticaceae). Apex of branch with inflorescences. © Sundue.

D. *Petrea volubilis* (Verbenaceae). Inflorescence; note lavender calyces. © Mori.

A. *Corynostylis pubescens* (Violaceae). Flowers; note spurred anterior petal and anthers surrounding the style. © Gracie.

B. *Rinorea pubiflora* (Violaceae). Flowers. © Mori.

C. *Phoradendron platycaulon* (Viscaceae). Branch with inflorescences; note flattened photosynthetic stems and the absence of leaves in this species. © Gracie.

D. *Cissus erosa* (Vitaceae). Inflorescence. © Gracie.

Plate 52 ▪ VOCHYSIACEAE, WINTERACEAE, ZYGOPHYLLACEAE

A. *Erisma calcaratum* (Vochysiaceae). Flower; note single petal, single stamen, and single style. © Gracie.

B. *Qualea (Ruizterania) retusa* (Vochysiaceae). Flower; note single petal, single stamen, and single style. © Gracie.

C. *Vochysia venezuelana* (Vochysiaceae). Flower; note three petals, single stamen, and single style. © Mori.

D. *Drimys winteri* (Winteraceae). Flower; note apocarpous gynoecium and numerous stamens with yellow anthers. © Gracie.

E. *Guaiacum sanctum* (Zygophyllaceae). **1.** Flower; note superior, angled ovary and ten stamens. © Smith. **2.** Dehisced fruit revealing red seeds. © Gracie.

A. *Yucca filifera* (Agavaceae). Habit; note persistent dead leaves. © Gracie.

B. *Echinodorus* muricatus (Alismataceae). Flowers. © Gracie.

C. *Allium ursinum* (Alliaceae). Flowers; note three-merous ovaries. © Gracie.

D. *Bomarea pardina* (Alstroemeriaceae). Flowers; note spotted inner tepals. © Luteyn.

Plate 54 ▪ AMARYLLIDACEAE, ARACEAE

A. *Worsleya rayneri* (Amaryllidaceae). Flower. © Gracie.

B. *Zephyranthes* cf. *cearensis* (Amaryllidaceae). Flower. © Thomas.

C. *Montrichardia arborescens* (Araceae). Leaves and inflorescence. © Gracie.

D. *Philodendron imbe* (Araceae). Habit; note aerial roots. © Gracie.

A. *Acrocomia intumescens* (Arecaceae). Habit; note pinnately compound leaves. © Thomas.

B. *Mauritia flexuosa* (Arecaceae). **1.** Habit; note palmately compound leaves and infructescences. © Mori. **2.** Fruits; note scales. © Bernal.

C. *Ananas ananassoides* (Bromeliaceae). Inflorescence; note tubular flowers subtended by spiny bracts. © Gracie.

D. *Aechmea huebneri* (Bromeliaceae). Plant with inflorescence; note epiphytic habit. © Gracie.

E. *Guzmania nicaraguensis* (Bromeliaceae). Close-up of inflorescence; note flowers subtended by red bracts. © Mori.

Plate 56 ▪ BURMANNIACEAE, CANNACEAE, COMMELINACEAE, COSTACEAE

A. *Burmannia bicolor* (Burmanniaceae). Inflorescence; note winged, connate tepals. © Gracie.

B. *Canna indica* (Cannaceae). Flower; note single stamen angled to left, style with white pollen, and curved staminode (labellum). © Maas.

C. *Elasis hirsuta* (Commelinaceae). Flower. © Gracie.

D. *Costus barbatus* (Costaceae). Apex of stem with inflorescence; note tubular yellow corollas subtended by showy, reflexed, red bracts. © Smith.

A. *Asplundia heteranthera* (Cyclanthaceae). Inflorescence of nocturnal flowers; note long staminodes. © Gracie.

B. *Cyclanthus bipartitus* (Cyclanthaceae). Inflorescence of spadix of alternating rings of staminate and pistillate flowers; note subtending spathes. © Gracie.

C. *Evodianthus funifer* (Cyclanthaceae). Inflorescence (note subtending spathes) and immature infructescence. © Thomas.

D. *Hypolytrum pulchrum* (Cyperaceae). Inflorescence of compound spikes. © Thomas.

E. *Dioscorea standleyi* (Dioscoreaceae). Stem with leaves and inflorescences; note arched venation in leaves. © Gracie.

F. *Paepalanthus bifidus* (Eriocaulaceae). Habit. © Gracie.

Plate 58 ▪ HAEMODORACEAE, HELICONIACEAE

A. *Xiphidium caeruleum* (Haemodoraceae). **1.** Habit; note distichous leaves and inflorescence. © Luteyn. **2.** Close-up of flowers. © Luteyn.

B. *Heliconia pendula* (Heliconiaceae). Infructescence; note immature white fruits and mature blue fruits. © Mori.

C. *Heliconia wagneriana* (Heliconiaceae). Inflorescences of colorful bracts and green flowers. © Mori.

A. *Egeria densa* (Hydrocharitaceae). Apices of plants with flowers. © Gracie.

B. *Orthrosanthus chimboracensis* (Iridaceae). Flowers. © Luteyn.

C. *Hydrocleys nymphoides* (Limnocharitaceae). Habit showing floating leaves and emergent flowers. © Mori.

D. *Maranta leuconeura* (Marantaceae). Inflorescence. © Westra.

E. *Mayaca sellowiana* (Mayacaceae). Apex of plant with flower. © Mori.

Plate 60 · ORCHIDACEAE

A. *Cattleya violacea.* Flowers. © Gracie.

B. *Acacallis cyanea.* Flowers; note highly modified labellum. © Gracie.

C. *Catasetum macrocarpum.* Flowers. © Gracie.

D. *Galeandra devoniana.* **1.** Epiphytic habit. © Gracie. **2.** Flower; note curved spur. © Gracie.

E. *Brassavola martiana.* Flower. © Gracie.

A. *Echinochloa polystachya* var. *spectabilis* (Poaceae). Inflorescences. © Gracie.

B. *Paspalum repens* (Poaceae). Close-up of flowers along axis of inflorescence; note white stamens and magenta stigmas. © Gracie.

C. *Reussia rotundifolia* (= *Pontederia rotundifolia*; Pontederiaceae). Inflorescence. © Gracie.

D. *Eichhornia crassipes* (Pontederiaceae). Habit; note inflated petioles. © Thomas.

Plate 62 ▪ RAPATEACEAE, SMILACACEAE, STRELITZIACEAE

A. *Rapatea ulei* (Rapateaceae). Flower; note copious mucilage between bracts subtending inflorescence. © Gracie.

B. *Stegolepis angustata* (Rapateaceae). Flowers. © Gracie.

C. *Smilax saülensis* (Smilacaceae). Stem with leaves; note prickles on stem and stipular tendrils. © Gracie.

D. *Phenakospermum guyannense* (Strelitziaceae). **1.** Habit; note inflorescence and boatlike bracts subtending flowers. © Gracie. **2.** Close-up of flower. © Mori.

A. *Tacca sprucei* (Taccaceae). Habit; note inflorescence. © Stevenson.

B. *Thurnia polycephala* (Thurniaceae). Inflorescences. © Campbell.

C. *Sciaphila purpurea* (Triuridaceae). Staminate flower above, pistillate flower below; note bearded apices of tepals. © Gracie.

D. *Vellozia furcata* (Velloziaceae). Flowering plant. © Thomas.

E. *Vellozia compacta* (Velloziaceae). Flower. © Thomas.

Plate 64 ▪ XYRIDACEAE, ZINGIBERACEAE

A. *Abolboda macrostachya* (Xyridaceae). Flowers. © Campbell.

B. *Xyris blepharophylla* (Xyridaceae). Flowers. © Thomas.

C. *Alpinia purpurata* (Zingiberaceae). Inflorescence; note white flowers subtended by red bracts. Species not native to the neotropics. © Gracie.

D. *Zingiber spectabile* (Zingiberaceae). Inflorescence; note spotted magenta flowers subtended by orange bracts. Species not native to the neotropics. © Gracie.

MONOCOTYLEDONS

Traditionally, the monocotyledons have been treated as plants that have 1 cotyledon (or the embryo sometimes undifferentiated with no apparent cotyledons); root systems consisting of short-lived primary roots; stems generally with scattered vascular bundles, or in 2 or more rings; leaves that are mostly parallel-veined; flower parts, when of definite number, typically borne in sets of 3, seldom 4, almost never 5 (carpels often fewer); pollen uniaperturate or of uniaperturate-derived types. These characters (taken from Cronquist 1988) broadly define the monocotyledons within the Cronquist (1981) and Dahlgren et al. (1995) systems.

Current molecular and morphological studies suggest that the monocotyledons treated in this traditional sense form a monophyletic group (Judd et al., 2002)

AGAVACEAE (Agave Family)

ANDREW HENDERSON

Figure 216, Plate 53

- *herbs or trees, mostly occurring in open, often arid habitats*
- *leaves in basal rosettes, often succulent, tough, persistent*
- *inflorescences usually large and many-flowered*
- *flowers usually bisexual; tepals and stamens 6*

Numbers of genera and species. The Agavaceae comprise eight genera and about 300 species native to the Western Hemisphere, and most of these occur in tropical America. The largest genera are *Agave* (about 200 species), *Furcraea* (20), *Manfreda* (26), and *Yucca* (35–40). Other genera are *Beschorneria* (7), *Hesperaloe* (5), *Prochynanthes* (1), and *Polianthes* (14).

Distribution and habitat. Species of Agavaceae occur throughout tropical and subtropical areas of the Western Hemisphere, but also reach temperate regions. In the north, they are widespread in the United States and just reach Canada; in the south they reach Bolivia. They are especially abundant in the southwestern United States and Mexico. Species of *Agave*, especially *A. americana*, are now widely naturalized throughout tropical and subtropical parts of the world.

The Agavaceae are particularly common in arid regions, occurring on dry, rocky slopes and in dry woodlands.

Family classification. The Agavaceae are placed in the Asparagales by Dahlgren et al. and have been suggested to be related to the Hyacinthaceae and Themidaceae. The family is divided into two subfamilies, the Yuccoideae (*Yucca* and *Hesperaloe*) and the Agavoideae (all other genera), based in part on the position of the ovary. This division, the monophyly of the family, and the basal position of *Hosta* and possibly *Xanthorrhoea* are supported by recent molecular data.

Features of the family. Habit: herbs or trees, small to very large, stout, perennial, often rhizomatous, often reproducing by lateral vegetative buds. **Leaves** alternate, simple, crowded in basal rosettes, often succulent, tough, persistent, sessile; blades often fleshy, strap-shaped, linear, or elliptic, the base nonsheathing, the margins sometimes prickly, the apex gradually tapering to a sharp point. **Inflorescences** terminal or axillary (plants monocarpic or polycarpic, respectively), racemes, panicles, or spikes, usually large, many-flowered.

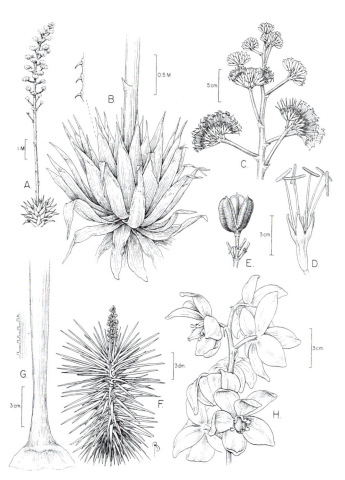

Figure 216. AGAVACEAE. *Agave missionum* (A–E), *Yucca aloifolia* (F–H). **A.** Plant showing leaves and inflorescence. **B.** Base of plant with detail of spiny leaf margin (left above). **C.** Apical part of inflorescence. **D.** Lateral view of flower. **E.** Lateral view of dehisced fruit. **F.** Plant with inflorescence. **G.** Base of leaf with detail of erose margin (left). **H.** Flowers. Reprinted with permission from Acevedo-Rodríguez (1996). Artist: Bobbi Angell.

Flowers actinomorphic or slightly zygomorphic, usually bisexual or unisexual (then plants dioecious); tepals 6, of 2 similar petallike whorls, often thick and fleshy, usually white or yellowish; androecium of 6 stamens, the stamens adnate to base of tepals, the filaments variable in length, the anthers dorsifixed; gynoecium syncarpous, the ovary superior (Yuccoideae) or inferior (Agavoideae), the carpels 3, the locules 3, the style short or long, the stigma capitate, 3-lobed or 3-branched; placentation axile, the ovules anatropous. **Fruits** capsules or berries. **Seeds** several to numerous, black, flattened.

Natural history. Pollination is known to be accomplished by moths, hummingbirds, and bats. Two features of the family have attracted much attention: semelparity in *Agave* and moth pollination in *Yucca*. Most species of *Agave* are found in xeric habitats, where plants grow vegetatively for many years. The common name of *A. americana*, the century plant, refers to this long period of vegetative growth after which plants produce a large inflorescence, set seed, and then die. Various theoretical models for the evolution of semelparity are based on *Agave*.

Species of *Yucca* are pollinated by moths of the family Prodoxidae. This association is often cited as a classic example of a co-evolved obligate mutualism, involving pollination and seed predation. Female moths collect pollen from a *Yucca* flower and place it on a stigma of another flower. At the same time, they deposit eggs in the ovary. Moth larvae then develop in the ovary and eventually eat some of the seeds. Recent studies suggest that this association has arisen several times within *Yucca*.

Vegetative reproduction by lateral budding is known to occur in all genera of Agavaceae. The seeds of capsular fruits often are dispersed by wind. The berries are known to be dispersed by gravity; however, birds have been observed dispersing the fruits of *Yucca aloifolia*.

Economic uses. Species of Agavaceae have been used extensively by humans, especially by the Aztecs. Currently, several species of *Agave* are important economic plants because their leaves are sources of strong fibers (sisal) used for cordage and twine. The thickened leaf bases of *Agave* are used to make alcoholic drinks, such as *pulque* and tequila. Several species are important horticulturally, and *Polianthes tuberosa* is grown commercially as a cut flower. Species of *Agave* are reported to possess minor medicinal properties.

References. BOGLER, D., J. NEFF, AND B. SIMPSON. 1995. Multiple origins of the yucca-yucca moth association. *Proc. Nat. Acad. Sci. USA* 92: 6864–67. BOGLER, D., AND B. SIMPSON. 1995. A chloroplast DNA study of the Agavaceae. *Syst. Bot.* 20:191–205. CORRERA Q., J. E., AND H. Y. BERNAL. 1989. Agavaceae. In *Especies vegetales promisorias de los países del Convenio Andrés Bello,* Tomo I. Santafé de Bogotá, D. E., Colombia: Secretaria Ejecutiva del Convenio Andrés Bello. EGUIARTE, L. 1995. Hutchinson (Agavales) vs. Huber y Dahlgren (Asparagales): análisis moleculares sobre la filogenia y evolución de la familia Agavaceae sensu Hutchinson dentro de las monocotiledóneas. *Bol. Soc. Bot. México* 56:45–56. GARCÍA-MENDOZA, A., AND R. GALVÁN. 1995. Riqueza de las familias Agavaceae y Nolinaceae en México. *Bol. Soc. Bot. México* 56:7–24. GENTRY, A. 1982. *Agaves of continental North America*. Tucson, AZ: University of Arizona Press. SANDOVAL, L. 1995. Análisis cladístico de la familia Agavaceae. *Bol. Soc. Bot. México* 56:57–68. SCHAFFER W., AND V. SCHAFFER. 1979. The adaptive significance of variations in reproductive habit in Agavaceae. *Ecology* 60:1051–69. VERHOEK, S. 1998. Agavaceae. In *The Families and Genera of Vascular Plants*, ed. K. Kubitzki, 3: 60–70. New York: Springer-Verlag.

ALISMATACEAE (Arrow-head Family)

ROBERT R. HAYNES

Figure 217, Plate 53

- *aquatic or wetland herbs*
- *plants with milky sap*
- *leaves alternate, basal, simple; basal sheath present*
- *inflorescences on scapes*
- *flowers with distinct parts; perianth in 3s; gynoecium apocarpous, the carpels 5–100s*
- *fruits achenes*

Numbers of genera and species. Worldwide, the Alismataceae comprise 12 genera and approximately 80 species. The largest genera are *Sagittaria* (32 species), *Echinodorus* (27), and *Alisma* (9). Four genera and 62 species occur naturally in the Western Hemisphere. In tropical America, there are two genera, *Echinodorus* with 26 species and *Sagittaria* with 14 species.

Distribution and habitat. The Alismataceae are cosmopoliton. They occur in temperate as well as tropical climates. The family can be found in the Eastern Hemisphere from South Africa to Russia and China and throughout Australia and in the Western Hemisphere from southern Argentina and Chile to central Canada. *Alisma, Sagittaria,* and *Damasonia* occur in both the Eastern and Western Hemispheres. *Echino-*

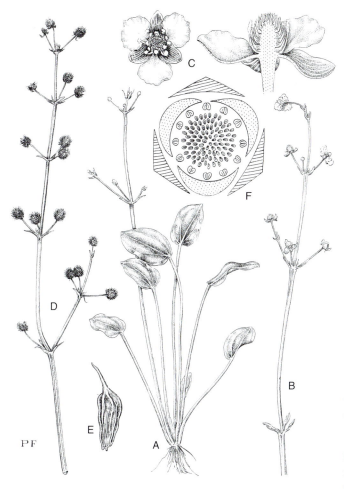

Figure 217. ALISMATACEAE. *Echinodorus berteroi.* **A.** Plant showing roots, leaves, and immature inflorescence (x½). **B.** Inflorescence with open flowers (x⅔). **C.** Apical view (left; x2) and medial section (right; x4) of flower. **D.** Infructescence (x⅔). **E.** Lateral view of fruit (x10). **F.** Floral diagram. Reprinted with permission from Correll and Correll (1982). Artist: Priscilla Fawcett.

Features of the family. Habit: aquatic or wetland herbs; milky sap present; stems either corms or rhizomes, the rhizomes often terminated by tubers (these mostly 0.5 cm diam., rarely reaching 2+ cm diam.). **Leaves** alternate, basal, simple, petiolate or sessile (especially in flowing water); basal sheath present, continuous into petiole, a terminal ligule absent; petiole flattened to triangular to nearly terete in transverse section, usually rigid (immersed leaves), sometimes lax (floating leaves), varying in length from a few centimeter to 0.5+ m; blades oval to elliptic, occasionally ribbonlike (usually submersed leaves), the base ± sagittate or hastate. **Inflorescences** terminal, on short or long scapes, erect (although sometimes floating on water surface), mostly racemose, sometimes branched or in panicles, the flowers in whorls of 3+ per node, the whorls 2–20. **Flowers** actinomorphic, bisexual, from less than 0.5 to 3+ cm diam.; sepals 3, distinct, green; petals 3, distinct, white; androecium of 9 to about 25 stamens, the stamens distinct, the filaments cylindric to dilated, glabrous to pubescent, the anthers basifixed or versatile; gynoecium apocarpous, the carpels 5–100s, the styles terminal or lateral, the stigmas linear; placentation basal, the ovules anatropous. **Fruits** achenes, usually with facial glands, flattened with either lateral or abaxial wings (or both) in *Sagittaria* or nearly terete in cross section (wings absent) with several lateral ribs extending from base to apex in *Echinodorus*. **Seeds** U-shaped.

Natural history. Pollination mechanisms are not well documented, but most species are probably insect-pollinated. Water and animals probably play some roll in disseminating the seeds.

Economic uses. Plants of the Alismataceae are of little economic importance. Tubers, whenever present, may be consumed locally, especially in the Tropics. Some species are used in temperate areas as ornamentals in aquaria.

dorus is endemic to the Western Hemisphere, and the remaining genera are predominantly Paleotropical in distribution.

Species of Alismataceae occur in rivers, lakes, streams, and a wide variety of habitats with saturated soils, at least when the plants begin growing. Most species occupy open areas with full sunlight, although a few are found on the forest floor. Most species are found at lower elevations, but a few extend up Andean slopes to elevations of 2,000 meters.

Family classification. The Alismataceae are placed in the Alismatales by Dahlgren et al. The family is most closely related to Limnocharitaceae, which Dahlgren et al. separated from the Alismataceae. Molecular analyses indicate that within the Alismatales, there are two subclades, the Hydrocharitaceae (including *Najas*) and a sister subclade consisting of the Limnocharitaceae and Alismataceae. The Alismataceae have not been divided into subfamilies.

References. Bogin, C. 1955. Revision of the genus *Sagittaria* (Alismataceae). *Mem. New York Bot. Gard.* 9:179–233. Haynes, R. R., and L. B. Holm-Nielsen. 1994. The Alismataceae. *Fl. Neotrop. Monogr.* 64:1–112. Haynes, R. R., D. H. Les, and L. B. Holm-Nielsen. 1998. Alismataceae. In *The Families and Genera of Vascular Plants*, ed. K. Kubitzki, 4:11–18. Berlin: Springer-Verlag. Les, D. H., and R. R. Haynes. 1995. Systematics of subclass Alismatidae: a synthesis of approaches. In *Monocotyledons: Systematics and Evolution*, eds. P. J. Rudall, P. J. Cribb, D. F. Cutler, and C. J. Humphries, 353–77. Richmond, Surrey, U.K.: Royal Botanic Gardens, Kew. Rataj, K. 1972. Revision of the genus *Sagittaria*. Part II (The species of West Indies, Central and South America). *Annot. Zool. Bot.* 78:1–61. Rataj, K. 1975. Revizion [sic] of the genus *Echinodorus* Rich. *Academia nakladatelství Československé akademie věd Praha.*

ALAN W. MEEROW

Plate 53

- *bulbous herbs*

- *leaves alternate; blades usually sheathing basally, linear*

- *inflorescences pseudo-umbels, borne on scapes*

- *flowers with 6 tepals; stamens 6; ovary superior*

- *fruits loculicidal capsules*

Numbers of genera and species. Worldwide, the Alliaceae comprise 12–15 genera and approximately 600 species. In tropical America, there are three genera and about 20 species.

Distribution and habitat. The greatest generic diversity of Alliaceae is found in the Western Hemisphere, with many small genera concentrated in Chile and Argentina. *Allium*, the largest genus with more than 300 species, is circumboreal in distribution. South American genera are *Gilliesia*, *Ipheion*, *Leucocoryne* (including *Latace* and *Pabellonia*), *Miersia*, *Nothoscordum*, *Schickendantziella*, *Solaria* (including *Ancrumia* and *Gethyrum*), *Speea*, *Trichlora*, and *Tristagma*. Some South American botanists recognize additional segregates of these genera. Among the South American genera, only *Nothoscordum*, *Trichlora*, and perhaps one species of *Leucocoryne* occur within the Tropics; the remaining genera occupy a temperate or Mediterranean-type climate.

Most of the Alliaceae occur in seasonally dry areas. *Trichlora* and the tropical species of *Nothoscordum* are by-and-large mountain dwelling, occurring in grassy *páramos* or meadows, often at high elevation. The one species of *Leucocoryne* from the Tropics grows in deserts.

Family classification. The Alliaceae are placed in the Asparagales by Dahlgren et al. In the past, the family has sometimes been treated as part of either the Liliaceae or the Amaryllidaceae. The most recent classification of Alliaceae, based on molecular data, recognizes three subfamilies: Allioideae (2 genera), Gillesioideae (10, all from South America), and Tulbaghoideae (1). The former tribe Brodiaeeae of Allioideae is recognized as a separate family, the Themidaceae. Molecular data indicates close relationships of Alliaceae to the Agapanthaceae and Amaryllidaceae.

Features of the family. Habit: herbs, perennial, forming bulbs, these surrounded by a papery tunic. Leaves alternate, few, sessile; blades usually sheathing basally (rarely the sheaths prolonged into a pseudostem), linear. Inflorescences pseudo-umbels (reduced helicoid cymes), borne on scapes, the scapes cylindrical or compressed, solid or hollow, subtended by 2 or more spathal bracts enclosing flowers in bud; pedicels lacking bracteoles at base, lacking articulations. Flowers actinomorphic, bisexual; tepals 6, in 2 whorls of 3, distinct or connate, white, green, or purple; corona present in *Leucocoryne*; androecium with 6 stamens in 2 whorls (1 in *Nothoscordum*), the stamens sometimes with only 2–3 fertile, the remainder reduced to staminodes, the filaments, if present, fused to perianth tube or inserted at base of tepals, sometimes fused below, the anthers dehiscing by terminal slits; gynoecium syncarpous, the ovary superior, the carpels 3, the locules 3, the style 1, erect, the stigma capitate or 3-branched (*Trichlora*); septal nectaries present; placentation axile, the ovules 2 or more per locule. Fruits loculicidal capsules. Seeds hard and dry, few to many per locule, roughly triangular, broad with a thick black, phytomelan crust.

Most members of the family contain sulphur compounds such as allyl sulphides, propionaldehyde, propionthiol, and vinyl disulphide. These compounds occur in the essential oils and are the cause of the characteristic onion or garlic odor (though absent from many *Nothoscordum*) of species of this family, especially when plant tissues are wounded. Lactifers are present in all genera. The family is also characterized by the presence of steroidal saponins, which are absent in the Amaryllidaceae; likewise, alkaloids characteristic of Amaryllidaceae are absent in Alliaceae.

Natural history. Little is known about the pollination and dispersal biology or other ecological aspects of Alliaceae.

Economic uses. Many *Allium* are cultivated as food crops, the most important being *A. cepa* (onion), *A. sativa* (garlic), *A. ascalonicum* (shallot), *A. porrum* (leek), and *A. schoenoprasum* (chive). Several *Allium* species are garden ornamentals. Many Alliaceae, especially those with "alliaceous" chemistry, have been used as purgatives and antiseptics by indigenous cultures.

References. FAY, M. F., AND M. W. CHASE. 1996. Resurrection of Themidaceae for the *Brodiaea* alliance, and recircumscription of Alliaceae, Amaryllidaceae and Agapanthoideae. *Taxon* 45:441–51. MEEROW, A. W., M. F. FAY, C. L. GUY, Q-B. LI, F. Q. ZAMAN, AND M. W. CHASE. 1999. Systematics of Amaryllidaceae based on cladistic analysis of plastid *rbc*L and *trn*L-F sequence data. *Amer. J. Bot.* 86: 1325–45. RAHN, K. 1998. Alliaceae. In *Families and Genera of Vascular Plants*, ed. K. Kubitzki 3:70–78, Berlin:

Springer-Verlag. STERLING, C. AND S. HUANG. 1972. Notes on the lacticifers of *Allium, Caloscordum, Nothoscordum, Tristagma* and *Tulbaghia. Pl. Life* 28:43–46. TRAUB, H. P. 1963. *The Genera of Amaryllidaceae*. La Jolla, CA: American Plant Life Society. TRAUB, H. P. 1972. The order Alliales. *Pl. Life* 28:129–32.

ALSTROEMERIACEAE (Alstroemeria Family)

ALAN W. MEEROW

Plate 53

- *herbs or vines, rhizomatous*
- *roots often terminally swollen*
- *leaves alternate (spiral), simple, usually resupinate*
- *flowers with 6 tepals; stamens 6; ovary inferior*
- *fruits loculicidal capsules*

Numbers of genera and species. The Alstroemeriaceae comprise three genera and as many as 280 species restricted to the Western Hemisphere. *Alstroemeria* consists of 60–80 species; *Bomarea*, the largest genus, contains 100–200 species; and *Leontochir* is monotypic. All three genera and about 200 species occur in tropical America.

Distribution and habitat. The Alstroemeriaceae are endemic to tropical and warm-temperate America, ranging from Mexico to Chile, but most diverse in the Andes. *Alstroemeria* is a South American endemic with two main centers of distribution, one in Chile (extending into adjacent Peru, Bolivia, and Argentina) and the second throughout the eastern third of Brazil and adjacent Paraguay and Argentina. *Bomarea* is distributed from southern Mexico to Bolivia, with the greatest diversity in the Andes. *Leontochir ovallei* is found on coastal sands just north of the tropic of Cancer in Chile.

The Chilean species of *Alstroemeria* occur in fog deserts and on the seasonally dry western Andean slopes; only one species, *A. aurea*, has crossed the Andes and occurs in both Argentina and Chile. The Chilean species have warm-temperate ecological requirements. The Brazilian species of *Alstroemeria* are found in a wide variety of habitats, occurring at the margins (rarely the understory) of coastal Atlantic rain forests and inland mesophytic subdeciduous forests; in upland, grassy *campos*; and in seasonally indundated wetlands. However, it is in the *cerrado* and associated gallery forests of the central Brazilian Planalto where the greatest diversity is found. One species, *A. amazonica*, is found in eastern Brazil and the Amazon Basin. Most species of *Bomarea* are confined to margins of montane rain forest, a few can be found in *páramos* at high elevation, and fewer occur at low elevations (e.g., *B. edulis* and *B. rosea*).

Family classification. The Alstroemeriaceae are placed in the Liliales by Dahlgren et al. The family has also been considered part of the Amaryllidaceae (because of its inferior ovary and umbel-like inflorescence) or part of a broadly circumscribed Liliaceae. In the last 30 years, recognition of the group as a distinct family, which dates to 1829, has gained increasing acceptance. Molecular data places the family within the order of colchicoid Liliales, with closest relationships to Colchicaceae and Luzuriagaceae. Although Bayer recognized the segregate genus *Tatalia* for the single annual species *Alstroemeria graminea*, molecular data do not support this separation. The genus *Schickendantzia* is now considered part of *Alstroemeria* by most workers.

No intrafamilial classification for this small family has been proposed.

Features of the family. Habit: erect or scandent herbs (*Alstroemeria* and *Leontochir*, some *Bomarea*) or vines (most *Bomarea*), arising from lateral, branching perennial rhizomes. **Roots** with tuberlike swellings at tips for water and carbohydrate storage, adventitious buds absent. **Stems** unbranched. **Leaves** alternate (spiral), scattered along stem or concentrated in upper half, simple, usually resupinate (inverted) via twisting of leaf base, usually glabrous; blades linear, lanceolate, or elliptic, the base narrow, sometimes appearing petiolate, nonsheathing; simple hairs (some *Bomarea*) present on abaxial (but seemingly adaxial due to resupination) surface. **Inflorescences** terminal, helicoid cymes in umbellate arrangement (cymes in *Alstroemeria* sometimes referred to as a "ray"), the flowers usually few to numerous (to 100+ in some *Bomarea*) per inflorescence, rarely solitary; pedicel short or long; leaf-like bracts usually present. **Flowers** zygomorphic (*Alstroemeria*) or actinomorphic, bisexual; tepals 6, usually distinct, in 2 whorls, the whorls varying from almost similar (*Leontochir*) to different in size, shape, and/or color (especially in *Alstroemeria*), white, red to yellow, pink to purple, or green, the inner whorl often bearing striations or spots; nectaries often present near base of at least 2 inner tepals; androecium of 6 stamens, the stamens in 2 whorls, the anthers pseudobasifixed, oblong; gynoecium syncarpous, the ovary inferior, the carpels 3, the locules 1 (*Leontochir* and one species of *Alstroemeria* by abortion late in development) or 3, the stigma 3-branched; placentation axile (*Alstroemeria, Bomarea*) or parietal (*Leontochir, Alstroemeria pygmaea*), the ovules anatropous. **Fruits** loculicidal capsules, dehiscing explosively in *Alstroemeria*, the apex with a circular scar (from tepals). **Seeds** few per locule, round, the seed coat dry and sometimes warty in *Alstroemeria*, with orange-red, fleshy aril in *Bomarea* and *Leontochir*.

Alstroemeria is characterized by a chromosome number of $2n = 16$; *Bomarea* and *Leontochir* by $2n = 18$.

Bomarea are predominantly vines, though a number of dwarf species occur at high elevations in the Andes.

The plants of *Alstroemeria* and *Leontochir* produce distinct vegetative (sterile) and reproductive (flowering) stems; particularly in *Alstroemeria* the stems can be considerably dimorphic, mostly as a result of the reduction of the leaves on the flowering stems.

Natural history. *Alstroemeria* is pollinated mostly by bees and perhaps some species of butterflies. The somewhat tubular-shaped, often red flowers of *Bomarea* are adapted for hummingbird pollination. The majority of species of *Bomarea* are found at montane elevations where hummingbirds are ubiquitous. The seeds of *Alstroemeria* are dispersed explosively, and the seeds of *Bomarea* are probably dispersed by birds that eat the berries.

Economic uses. *Alstroemeria* hybrids of great commercial importance as cut flowers have been developed from the Chilean species, particularly *A. aurea* (Peruvian-lily), *A. ligtu* (St. Martin's flower), and *A. pelegrina* (Peruvian-lily). A few species of *Bomarea*, especially *B. edulis*, are cultivated throughout Central and South America for their sweet, starchy tubers.

References. Aker, S. A., and W. Healy. 1990. The phytogeography of the genus *Alstroemeria*. *Herbertia* 46(2):76–87. Baker, J. G. 1888. *Handbook of the Amaryllideae*. London: George Bell and Sons. Bayer, E. 1987. Die Gattung *Alstroemeria* in Chile. *Mitt. Bot. Staatssamml. München* 25: 1–362. Bayer, E. 1988. Beitrag zur Cytologie der Alstroemeriaceae. *Mitt. Bot. Staatssamml. München* 27:1–6. Bayer, E. 1998. Alstroemeriaceae In *The Families and Genera of Vascular Plants*, ed. K. Kubitzki, 3:79–83. Berlin: Springer-Verlag. Meerow, A. W., and A. F. C. Tomolato. 1996. The alstroemerias of Itatiaia. *Herbertia* 51:14–21. Rudall, P. J., K. L. Stobart, W.-P. Hong, J. G. Conran, C. A. Furness, et al. 2000. Consider the lilies: systematics of Liliales. In *Monocots: Systematics and Evolution*, eds. K. Wilson and D. Morrison, 347–59. Sydney: CSIRO Press. Uphoff, J.C.T. 1952. A review of the genus *Alstroemeria*. *Pl. Life* 8:37–53. Wilken, P. 1997. *Leontochir ovallei. Bot. Mag.* 14:7–12.

AMARYLLIDACEAE (Amaryllis Family)

Alan W. Meerow

Figure 218, Plate 54

- *bulbous herbs*

- *leaves primarily distichous, rarely spiral, simple; blades mostly linear or strap-shaped, the base often sheathing a short stem, sometimes pseudopetiolate*

- *inflorescences umbels, borne on scapes*

- *flowers with 6 tepals in 2 whorls, usually similar in shape and color; stamens 6; ovary inferior*

- *fruits loculicidal capsules*

Numbers of genera and species. Worldwide, the Amaryllidaceae comprise approximately 60 genera and about 850 species. In the Western Hemisphere, there are 30 genera (29 exclusively) and about 400 species. In tropical America, there are 30 genera and about 350 species. The largest genera in the neotropics are *Hippeastrum* (50–60 species), *Hymenocallis* (about 50), *Zephyranthes* (about 50), and *Clinanthus* (about 30). Four genera contain only a single species.

Distribution and habitat. Although the Amaryllidaceae are cosmopolitan, they are chiefly tropical and subtropical. The family has three main centers of distribution: South America, South Africa, and the Mediterranean of Europe and North Africa. Two genera are found in Central and East Asia and the Australasian region, respectively. A few genera occur in North America and only a single genus, *Crinum*, has species in both the Eastern and the Western Hemispheres.

In the neotropics, the family occurs from Mexico through Central America and the West Indies to Chile and Argentina in South America. Notable areas of diversity throughout this range include eastern Brazil, northern Chile, and the central Andes of Ecuador and Peru.

Hippeastrum is primarily found in the Andes and eastern Brazil, *Hymenocallis* occurs mostly in Mesoamerica, *Clinanthus* is endemic to Peru, and *Zephyranthes* is broadly distributed.

The Neotropical genera of Amaryllidaceae are chiefly adapted for seasonally dry habitats and some prefer truly xeric environments in which their bulbs may remain dormant

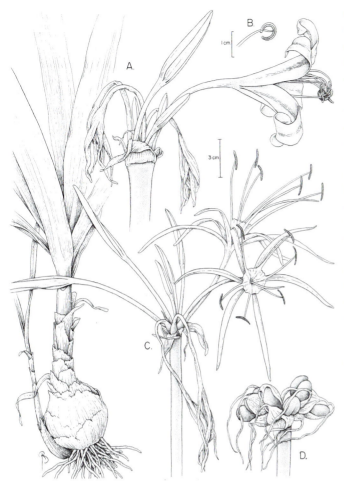

Figure 218. AMARYLLIDACEAE. *Crinum zeylandicum* (A, B), *Hymenocallis caribaea* (C, D). **A.** Base of plant showing roots, bulb, and leaves (left) and inflorescence (right), showing bud, wilted flowers, and lateral view of flower at anthesis. **B.** Apex of stamen showing part of filament and curved anther. **C.** Inflorescence with buds, flowers at anthesis, and wilted flowers. **D.** Infructescence. Reprinted with permission from Acevedo-Rodríguez (1996). Artist: Bobbi Angell.

for a period longer than they are in active growth (e.g., *Leptochiton*, *Paramongaia*, some *Eucrosia*). At the other extreme, species have colonized the understory of rain forests (Eucharideae, *Griffinia*) and aquatic habitats (a number of *Hymenocallis*, *Hippeastrum angustifolium*, and several *Crinum*).

The family has also adapted to the high montane tropical climates of the Andes. Certain genera are primarily found at elevations in excess of 2,000 meters; and *Clinanthus humilis* is found above 4,000 meters. This species has adapted to high elevations by retaining the scape and developing fruit inside the bulb until the seeds are ripe.

Family classification. The Amaryllidaceae are placed in the Asparagales by Dahlgren et al. Families most closely related to the Amaryllidaceae are the Agapanthaceae, Alliaceae, Hyacinthaceae, and Themidaceae.

In the latest classification of the family by Meerow et al.,

the Amaryllidaceae are divided into 15 tribes. These tribes are largely geographically based and six of these are restricted to the American continents (Clinantheae, Eustephieae, Griffineae, Hippeastreae, Hymenocallideae, and Stenomesseae). The only other tribe represented in the Americas is the largely African Amaryllideae (*Crinum*). The six American tribes (and their genera) are: the Stenomesseae (*Caliphruria*, *Eucharis*, *Eucrosia*, *Mathieua* [considered extinct], *Phaedranassa*, *Plagiolirion*, *Rauhia*, *Stenomesson* [including *Pucara*], and *Urceolina*), the Eustephieae (*Eustephia*, *Chlidanthus*, and *Hieronymiella*), the Griffineae (*Griffinia* and *Worsleya*), the Hippeastreae (*Griffiniopsis*, *Habranthus*, *Hippeastrum*, *Phycella*, *Placea*, *Pyrolirion*, *Rhodophiala*, *Sprekelia*, *Traubia*, and *Zephyranthes*), the Hymenocallideae (*Hymenocallis*, *Ismene*, and *Leptochiton*), and the Clinantheae (*Clinanthus*, *Pamianthe*, and *Paramongaia*). Recent evidence using DNA sequence data supports this tribal classification, and indicates that the entirely Neotropical tribes are monophyletic. These data also indicate that recognition of distinct tribes is warranted and that the Eurasian tribes of Amaryllidaceae are more closely related to the Neotropical tribes.

Features of the family. Habit: herbs, perennials, bulbous, the bulbs tunicate. **Roots** of 2 types: contractile and perennial or short-lived and fibrous, both types adventitious, originating from basal plate of bulb. **Leaves** alternate (distichous or rarely spiral), simple, sometimes pseudopetiolate; blades usually sessile, mostly linear or strap-shaped, flat or concave and dorsiventral, less often (a few Hippeastreae) bifacial and nearly terete, the base often sheathing a short stem or, in some genera, the stem variably long, above-ground pseudostem formed by tightly sheathing bases. **Inflorescences** umbellate (apparent umbels composed of 1–several series of reduced cymes), borne on scapes, initiated terminally inside bulb, the scapes variously hollow or solid, either terete or compressed, sometimes sharply 2-edged, sometimes remaining in bulb until fruit is ripe (in some high-elevation *Pyrolirion*, *Stenomesson*, and *Zephyranthes*), bearing 1–40+ flowers, the flowers enclosed in bud by 2 or more bracts; bracts alternately overlapping at margins. **Flowers** zygomorphic or actinomorphic, bisexual, brightly colored, typically lacking scent; tepals 6, in 2 whorls, usually united below into short or long tube, often funnelform, tubular, or crateriform, white, green, and virtually all red and yellow shades, rarely blue (found in only two Neotropical genera, *Griffinia* and *Worsleya*); outgrowths of perianth sometimes present as a corona (*Placea*), a ring of scales (*Hippeastrum*, *Zephyranthes*, *Habranthus*, and *Rhodophiala*) or a callose rim (*Hippeastrum*); androecium of 6 stamens (reduced to 5 in some *Griffinia*), the filaments inserted at throat of floral tube or below, distinct or variously connate or appendaged, connation sometimes forming conspicuous cup or paracorona (Eucharideae, Eustephieae, Hymenocallideae, and Stenomesseae), the anthers dehiscing by lateral slits; gynoecium syncarpous, the ovary inferior, the carpels 3, the locules 3, the style slender, the stigma three-lobed (sometimes deeply) or entire; placentation axile, the ovules anatropous, sometimes appearing basal if few in number (e.g., *Ismene* and *Plagiolirion*). **Fruits** loculicidal capsules. **Seeds** numerous or few per locule, fleshy or often dry, flattened and winged (Eustephieae, Hippeastreae, and Stenomesseae), the seed coat typically thin, black or brown (green and fleshy in *Hymenocallis* and *Ismene*).

Species of *Crinum* have fleshy seeds with a thin, corky outer layer. In *Hymenocallis*, *Ismene*, and perhaps *Leptochiton*, the embryo contains starch-storing cells.

Natural history. White, long-tubed, crateriform flowers with conspicuous false coronas formed by the basal fusion of the staminal filaments occur in at least one genus of Eucharideae, Hymenocallideae, and Stenomesseae; this floral type appears to be an adaptation for hawk-moth pollination. Hummingbird visitation has been observed in *Hippeastrum*, and hummingbirds may also be the pollinators of Andean genera such as *Stenomesson* and *Phaedranassa*. The flowers of species of *Sprekelia* are also thought to be adapted to hummingbird pollination. Visitation by euglossine bees has been reported for a species of *Eucharis*, and bat pollination has been reported for *Hippeastrum calyptratum* in Brazil. Most species of Amaryllidaceae have protandrous flowers and do not self-pollinate, but exceptions occur sporadically among the larger genera.

The flattened, winged seeds characteristic of the Neotropical tribes Eustephieae, Hippeastreae, and Stenomesseae are adapted for wind dispersal.

Economic uses. The Amaryllidaceae have economic importance principally as ornamentals. Among the American genera, *Hippeastrum* (e.g., *H. puniceum*, Barbados lily), in particular, has been hybridized extensively and is an important bulb crop in the Netherlands, South Africa, Israel, and Brazil. The mashed bulbs of a number of tropical genera are utilized by indigenous cultures as poultices for treating sores or are boiled and steeped to prepare an emetic tea for stomach ailments. Floral motifs identifiable as Amaryllidaceae (*Ismene*, *Pyrolirion*, and *Stenomesson*) appear on ceremonial Inca drinking vessels called *keros*. There is interest in the medicinal properties, particularly anticancer, of some of the more than 100 "amaryllidaceous" alkaloids that have been identified. Chemical compounds extracted from the floral aromas of some species are used in making perfumes.

References. BAKER, J. G. 1888. *Handbook of the Amaryllideae*. London: George Bell and Sons. CORRERA Q., J. E., AND H. Y. BERNAL. 1989. Amaryllidaceae. In *Especies vegetales promisorias de los países del Convenio Andrés Bello*, Tomo I. Bogotá, D. E., Colombia: Secretaria Ejecutiva del Convenio Andrés Bello. HERBERT, W. 1837. *Amaryllidaceae*. London: J. Ridgeway and Sons. MEEROW, A. W. 1995. Towards a phylogeny of the Amaryllidaceae. In *Monocotyledons: Systematics and Evolution*, eds. P. J. Rudall, P. J. Cribb, D. F. Cutler, and C. J. Humphries, 169–79. Richmond, Surrey, U.K.: Royal Botanic Gardens, Kew. MEEROW, A. W., M. F. FAY, C. L. GUY, Q-B. LI, F. Q. ZAMAN, AND M. W. CHASE. 1999. Systematics of Amaryllidaceae based on cladistic analysis of plastid *rbc*L and *trn*L-F sequence data. *Amer. J. Bot.* 86:1325–45. MEEROW, A. W., C. L. GUY, Q. LI, AND S-L. YANG. 2000. Phylogeny of the American Amaryllidaceae based on nrDNA ITS sequences. *Syst. Bot.* 25:708–26. MEEROW, A. W. AND D. A. SNIJMAN. 1998. Amaryllidaceae. In *The Families and Genera of Vascular Plants*, ed. K. Kubitzki, 3:83–110. Berlin: Springer-Verlag. TRAUB, H. P. 1963. *Genera of the Amaryllidaceae*. La Jolla, CA: American Plant Life Society.

ANTHERICACEAE (Spider-plant Family)

DENNIS WM. STEVENSON

- *terrestrial herbs*

- *leaves alternate, simple, in basal rosettes; blades linear*

- *inflorescence terminal; simple or compound racemes*

- *flowers bisexual; tepals 6; stamens 6; ovary superior; placentation axile*

- *fruits loculicidal capsules*

Numbers of genera and species. Worldwide, the Anthericaceae comprise nine genera and approximately 200 species.

In tropical America, there are six genera and approximately 65 species.

Distribution and habitat. The Anthericaceae have a subcosmopolitan distribution; they are absent in northern Europe and eastern North American and extremely cold climates. The centers of diversity are tropical Asia and Australia. Many genera exhibit disjunct distributions; e.g., *Chlorophytum*, with approximately 150 species, occurs in eastern Asia, the Arabian Peninsula, southern Africa, and South America. *Anthericum*, with about 50 species, occurs in Europe, the Caucasas, tropical and subtropical Africa, and Central America. Four other genera are also found in the neotropics; *Dia-*

mena and *Diora* are endemic to Peru, and *Hagenbachia* and *Echeandia* are endemic to Central and South America.

Species of Anthericaceae are often found in open habitats such as savannas or grasslands. However, in the neotropics, species of *Anthericum* and *Chlorophytum* may grow in more mesic habitats as understory herbs of rain forest. *Hagenbachia* occurs in montane forests with one species, *H. panamensis*, found frequently as an epiphyte.

Family classification. The Antheriacaceae are placed in the Asparagales by Dahlgren et al. The family, which was segregated from Cronquist's Liliaceae, is in itself very heterogeneous. Dahlgren et al. recognized more than 20 genera. Infrafamilial classification of the Anthericaceae, however, is in a state of flux and a more recent classification by Conran has limited the family to nine genera, a treatment followed here.

The placement of Anthericaceae among the monocots is controversial. The data of Dahlgren et al., Stevenson and Loconte, and Takhtajan support a relationship with the Asphodelaceae (Aloe Family), Thorne treats the Anthericaceae as a subfamily within the Aphyllanthaceae, and Chase et. al., based on molecular data, place Anthericaceae with the Herreriaceae.

Features of the family. Habit: herbs, terrestrial, perennial, rhizomatous. **Leaves** alternate (spiral or rarely distichous), often in basal rosettes, simple; blades sheathing basally, flat, linear. **Inflorescences** terminal, simple or compound racemes, spikes, or panicles, sometimes condensed into clusters or heads; pedicels often articulate. **Flowers** actinomorphic (slight variation in tepal size and shape leads to minor zygomorphy in some *Chlorophytum*), bisexual; tepals 6, equal to subequal, in two whorls of 3, white to pinkish, yellow, blue, or violet; androecium of 6 stamens, the filaments distinct or fused basally (*Echeandria*), the anthers introrse, basifixed (*Anthericum, Chlorophytum, Diamena,* and *Diaora*) or dorsifixed and versatile (*Echeandria* and *Hagenbachia*); gynoecium syncarpous, the ovary superior, the carpels 3, the locules 3, the style simple, the stigma 3-lobed or simple, dry; septal nectaries present; placentation axile, the ovules 2 or more per locules. **Fruits** loculicidal capsules. **Seeds** 2–numerous per locule, often bearing conspicuous elaiosome.

Natural history. Many genera of Anthericaceae, particularly the Australian taxa, grow in dry areas and exhibit adaptations such as semisucculent, stiff and firm, or much reduced leaves. The flowers of Anthericaceae indicate insect pollination. In Costa Rica, buzz pollination by bumblebees has been observed in species of *Echeandia*.

The seeds in most members of the family are reported to be more or less ballistically dispersed when the fruits dehisce. In some species of *Chlorophytum* (e.g., *C. comosum*), the seeds germinate while they are still on the parent plant.

Economic uses. Species of *Anthericum* and *Chlorophytum* are cultivated as ornamentals and *C. comosum* (spider plant) is a popular house plant because young plantlets grow from the inflorescences and root easily. Many cultivars of this species, including numerous variegated forms, are commercially available.

References. CONRAN, J. 1998. Anthericaceae. In *The Families and Genera of Vascular Plants*, ed. K. Kubitzki, 3:114–21. New York: Springer-Verlag.

ARACEAE (Aroid or Philodendron Family)

THOMAS B. CROAT

Figure 219, Plate 54

- *herbs*
- *aerial roots often present*
- *leaves alternate, simple*
- *flowers small, densely congested into spadix, subtended by a leaflike spathe*

Numbers of genera and species. Worldwide, there are 105 genera and about 3,200 species of Araceae. In tropical America, there are 39 genera (including three introduced) and 2,372 species. Thirty-three genera and about 800 species are endemic. The largest genus is *Anthurium* with about 1000 species, followed by *Philodendron* with about 750 species. Many Neotropical genera possess more than 35 species; e.g., *Stenospermation* (110 species), *Dieffenbachia* (114), *Monstera* (60), *Rhodospatha* (67), *Spathiphyllum* (60), *Chlorospatha* (55), *Xanthosoma* (45), and *Syngonium* (36). The following genera have 20 species or less: *Caladium* (17), *Dracontium* (18), *Heteropsis* (13), *Homalomena* (9), *Montrichardia* (2), *Pistia* (1), and *Urospatha* (20).

Distribution and habitat. The Araceae occur on every continent except Antarctica, but are predominantly tropical, with only six genera (each with one or a few species) occurring in northern temperate areas. *Calla, Symplocarpus,* and *Lysi-*

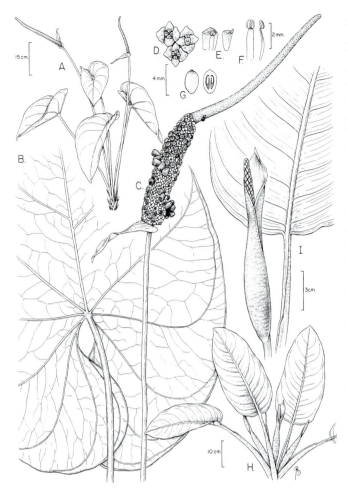

Figure 219. ARACEAE. *Anthurium cordatum* (A–G), *Dieffenbachia seguine* (H, I). **A.** Plant showing leaves and inflorescences. **B.** Abaxial view of part of leaf blade. **C.** Infructescence showing spathe, spadix, and fruits. **D.** Apical view of flowers. **E.** Adaxial (left) and lateral views (right) of perianth segments with stamens. **F.** Adaxial (left) and lateral (right) views of stamens. **G.** Lateral view (left) and medial section (right) of ovaries. **H.** Plant showing leaves and inflorescence. **I.** Inflorescence (left) and detail of leaf base (right). Reprinted with permission from Acevedo-Rodríguez (1996). Artist: Bobbi Angell.

chitum are boreal and, along with *Arisaema*, occur in both hemispheres. In the Southern Hemisphere, the family ranges south to central Argentina, southern Africa, and to New South Wales in Australia. Aroid genera are largely endemic to major continental areas and only *Pistia* is pantropical. Nine genera occur in both the Eastern and the Western Hemispheres, 24 genera occur in North America, 36 genera in South America, and nine genera with relatively few species occur in the West Indies. *Homalomena, Schismatoglottis,* and *Spathiphyllum* occur in both South America and in tropical Asia. Africa and Asia share *Arisaema, Amorphophallus, Eminium, Pistia, Pothos, Raphidophora, Remusatia,* and *Sauromatum.*

Tropical Asia and tropical America are two major centers of species diversity, with nearly an equal number of indige-

nous genera, 43 for Asia and 42 for America. Of these, 33 genera are endemic to the American Tropics or subtropics while 32 genera are endemic to Asia. Africa, a less important center of species diversity, has only 19 indigenous genera of which 12 are endemic. While the paleotropics have more genera than the neotropics (60 versus 37), the neotropics contain roughly two-thirds of the world's Araceae species. There are 18 genera endemic to South America but none range farther south than 30°, whereas in North America and Asia several genera range to 40–50°N.

Araceae occupy a wide variety habitats, extending from tropical dry to rain forest, but also into subarctic marshes, tropical swamps, cloud forests, cold, windswept montane plains, and semiarid to arid coastal plains. The family has many species that will not tolerate any degree of frost or cold, such as *Anthurium brownei*, and others, like *Symplocarpus foetidus* that actually emerge from snow-covered ground.

Family classification. The Araceae are placed in the order Arales by Dahlgren et al. Comparative chloroplast DNA studies by French et al. suggest an affinity with the Lemnaceae and some authors place these two families in a more broadly defined Araceae.

The family is divided into two major groups and seven subfamilies: group one, the Proto-Araceae, with two subfamilies, Gymnostachioideae (monospecific) and Orontioideae (three genera with five species total), and group 2, the true aroids, with five subfamilies, Pothoideae (four genera), Monsteroideae (12 genera), Lasiodeae (10 genera), Calloideae (one genus), and Aroideae (74 genera). All except the Gymnostachioideae (with a single endemic species in Australia) occur in the neotropics. The most recent classification by Mayo et al. was based on a cladistic analysis and made use of the extensive chloroplast DNA studies by French et al. In a major change from the traditional systems of classification, this system abandons subfamilies Colocasioideae and Philodendroideae and incorporates all monoecious genera into the Aroideae.

Features of the family. Habit: herbs, terrestrial, epiphytic or hemiepiphytic, or epilithic, rarely aquatic (free-floating or rooted), often glabrous; sap clear, milky, or dark and taniniferous. **Roots** often aerial, used for prop, attachment, or nutrient uptake. **Stems** creeping, subterranean and rhizomatous (as in *Spathiphyllum* and *Homalomena*) or tuberous (as in *Caladium* and *Dracontium*), or aerial and erect (as in *Dieffenbachia* and *Rhodospatha*), appressed-climbing, frequently scandent, rarely erect, hardened, and armed (*Montrichardia*); cataphylls often variously ribbed and persistent, may remain intact or weather into fibers. **Leaves** alternate, sometimes distichous, simple, basal or cauline, rarely solitary (as in *Dracontium*); petioles often elongate, sheathed at least basally, the apex often geniculate, the attachment scars distinct and conspicuous (e.g., *Philodendron* subg. *Meconostigma*), or obscured by cataphylls; blades often oblong, cordate, sagittate to hastate, sometimes perforated, the margins entire, or pinnately to palmately lobed; main veins often radiate from petiole attachment, rarely parallel, the primary lateral veins (in some families referred to as secondary veins) pinnate, sometimes joining into collective veins along margins, the lesser veins parallel or reticulate. **Inflorescences** terminal or axillary, solitary or clustered in axils, an unbranched spadix subtended by a single spathe; spathe herbaceous, distinct or adnate to spadix, spreading, reflexed, or convolute, sometimes constricted below middle and differentiated into tube below and blade above, often persistent, sometimes (especially when convolute) reclosing over spadix after anthesis, the blade sometimes deciduous (in *Syngonium* or *Xanthosoma*), green, or blade and tube of spathe differently colored (as in *Syngonium* and *Philodendron*); spadix often cylindric, flowers dense, the lower part often pistillate, this part often protected by accrescent spathe tube until maturity of fruits, some parts with sterile flowers or without flowers, the upper part often staminate, this part (e.g., *Syngonium* and *Xanthosoma*) often caducous, the apex frequently tapered, less often clavate or ellipsoidal; bracts absent. **Flowers** small, bisexual or unisexual (the plants usually monoecious, except *Arisaema*, which is sequentially dioecious), sessile, 2–3-merous; perianth (=perigone) lacking in unisexual flowers (subfamily Aroideae); tepals 4–6, usually distinct, rarely united, often cucullate at apex; androecium of 3–6(9) stamens, the stamens distinct or united into synandria, the thecae terminal or lateral, extrorse, dehiscent by longitudinal slits or apical pores; staminodes sometimes present, distinct or united into synandria; gynoecium syncarpous, the ovary usually superior, sessile or immersed in spadix often entire, rarely lobate, the carpels 1–47, the locules 1–3, rarely more, the style often lacking or short, simple, terminal, the stigma terminal, discoid, pulvinar, or capitate, sometimes sessile along apex of ovary, linear-oblong or rarely lobate; placentation axile or parietal, the ovules 1–many per locule, often with funicle, less often sessile. **Fruits** baccate, sometimes juicy, free or rarely fused into syncarp (e.g., *Syngonium*), often colorful. **Seeds** 1–many; endosperm copious, the embryo located in center of endosperm, curved when endosperm lacking.

Among the characters considered primitive for Araceae are a rhizomatous or caulescent growth habit; simple, cordate leaf blades with parallel venation; a simple, green spathe; bisexual, perigonate flowers with trilocular ovaries and axile placentation; anatropous, crassinucellate ovules; elongate stamens with longitudinal anther dehiscence; a base chromosome number of $x = 7$ or 14, and monosulcate, reticulate, binucleate pollen lacking starch.

Petiole cross-sectional shape is diverse and taxonomically significant, especially in the larger genera; e.g., *Anthurium* and *Philodendron*.

When the flowers are unisexual, the plants are usually monoecious, with the lower flowers pistillate and the upper flowers staminate (rarely intermixed). The pistillate and staminate zones are either contiguous or separated by an intermediate zone.

Natural history. The most interesting aspect of the family's ecology is its diversity of adaptive life forms, ranging from submerged or free-floating aquatics to emergent aquatics to plants that are terrestrial, epilithic, or epiphytic. The latter group includes true epiphytes and hemiepiphytes. Hemiepiphytism itself is diverse, with some species (secondary hemiepiphytes) beginning their lives as terrestrial seedlings and then growing toward darkness until they arrive at the nearest host tree (usually a relatively large one that casts a dark shadow). A physiological change takes place there, and they begin growing toward light. Such species grow as appressed epiphytes on trees or as vines in the canopy. Primary hemiepiphytes begin their lives as true epiphytes, but convert to hemiepiphytes by producing long, dangling roots that reach the forest floor. Some species, especially members of subfamily Monsteroideae, have distinct juvenile and adult stages with different leaf and stem morphologies. Juvenile plants may produce small terrestrial rosettes of leaves and then grow rapidly, producing a few small leaves on long internodes. The preadult leaves of the first hemiepiphytic phase of such plants are often very distinct from the adult leaves. Many such species are able to change from adult growth (consisting of short, thick internodes) back to juvenile growth (with elongate internodes bearing smaller leaves). This may be either to establish more adult plants with rosettes of leaves or to survive the dynamics of an ever-changing forest caused by falling trees and branches.

Pollination of Araceae is diverse; some species produce heat and are beetle-pollinated (*Philodendron*, *Syngonium*, *Monstera*, *Rhodospatha*), and others are bee-pollinated (*Anthurium* and *Spathiphyllum*) or fly-pollinated (*Dracontium*). Berries are dispersed by birds (*Anthurium*), mammals, including bats (*Monstera*), or water (*Urospatha*).

Economic uses. The Araceae have long been used as food plants, and some claim that *Colocasia esculenta* (taro) is the world's oldest cultivated crop. Because the majority of Araceae possess acrid saps and needlelike crystals of calcium oxalate when fresh, they must be cooked or processed before they can be used for human consumption. The underground corms, tubers, and rhizomes are rich in starch and, hence, are the parts most commonly consumed. These products are most commonly utilized in tropical areas in ways similar to the use of potatoes in temperate climates. In the Hawaiian Islands, a paste is made from the boiled corms of taro to make poi, which can be eaten fresh or fermented. In taro, the large central corm of one variety yields dasheen and another variety, with a smaller main corm and larger, more numerous cormlets, is the source of eddo. Species of *Xanthosoma* and *Alocasia* are commonly used for their starch rich rootstocks. The leaves of these genera are also employed as a spinach-like vegetable. Those of taro, for example, are rich in vitamin C, vitamin A, calcium, potassium, phosphorus, and protein. In the West Indies, the leaves of dasheen and eddo are combined with coconut milk to make calaloo soup. Few species of Araceae are utilized for their fruit; the exception is *Mon-*

stera deliciosa, the pineapple-flavored ripe spadix of which is eaten raw or used to flavor ice cream.

The aerial roots of some species of *Heteropsis* and *Philodendron* are used as a fiber for making ropes and baskets. The long roots, descending from epiphytes in the canopy, are pulled from the plants, coiled for transport, and eventually split into long segments for use in basketry and even furniture making. The stems of *Montrichardia linifera* are the source of a fiber that can be used to make paper.

Almost all species of Araceae are more or less caustic. Touching, tasting, and even smelling aroids can produce corrosive burns to the skin and internal tissues caused by calcium oxalate crystals. The most frequent cases of aroid toxicity are caused by contact with the commonly cultivated ornamental dumb cane (species of *Dieffenbachia*, but especially *D. seguine*). Biting into the leaves, but especially the stem, of a dumb cane causes a burning sensation and swelling of the mouth and throat that is sometimes so severe that speech (hence dumb cane) and breathing are impaired.

Poultices prepared from the leaves and tubers of species of Araceae have been employed to treat external healing of stings, wounds, skin ailments, and arthritis. It is, however, inadvisable to employ aroids in this manner because of the dermatitis often caused by contact with these plants. In addition, extracts of Araceae have been reported to be used as expectorants, decongestants, contraceptives, sedatives, and as anticarcinogens. There are numerous reports of aroids used to cure parasitic infections.

Many species of tropical Araceae are employed as landscape plants or as household ornamentals. Commonly cultivated species belong to *Aglaonema*, *Alocasia*, *Anthurium*, *Caladium*, *Colocasia*, *Dieffenbachia*, *Epipremnum*, *Homalomena*, *Monstera*, *Philodendron*, *Rhaphidohora*, *Schismatoglottis*, *Schindapsus*, *Spathiphyllum*, *Syngonium*, *Xanthosoma*, and *Zantedeschia*. Some species of Araceae, especially *Anthurium andraeanum* and *Zantedeschia aethiopica*, are sold as cut flowers because of their showy spathes.

References. Bown, D. 2000. *Aroids. Plants of the Arum Family*. Portland, OR: Timber Press. Bunting, G. S. 1960. A revision of the genus *Spathiphyllum* (Araceae). *Mem. New York Bot. Gard.* 10:1–54. Correra Q., J. E., and H. Y. Bernal. 1989. Araceae. In *Especies vegetales promisorias de los países del Convenio Andrés Bello*, Tomo I. Bogotá, D. E., Colombia: Secretaria Ejecutiva del Convenio Andrés Bello. Croat, T. B. 1979. The distribution of Araceae. In *Tropical Botany*, eds. K. Larsen and L. B. Holm-Nielsen, 291–308. London: Academic Press. Croat, T. B. 1981(1982). A revision of *Syngonium* (Araceae). *Ann. Missouri Bot. Gard.* 68(4):565–651. Croat, T. B. 1983. A revision of the genus *Anthurium* (Araceae) of Mexico and Central America. Part 1: Mexico and Middle America. *Ann. Missouri Bot. Gard.* 70(2):211–417. Croat, T. B. 1986. A revision of the genus *Anthurium* (Araceae) of Mexico and Central America. Part 2: Panama. *Monogr. Syst. Bot. Missouri Bot. Gard.* 14:1 204. Croat, T. B. 1988. Ecology and life forms of Araceae. *Aroideana* 11(3 4):4–56. Croat, T. B. 1991. A revision of *Anthurium* section *Pachyneurium* (Araceae). *Ann. Missouri Bot. Gard.* 78(3):539–855. Croat, T. B. 1997. A revision of *Philodendron* subgenus *Philodendron* (Araceae) for Mexico and Central America *Ann. Missouri Bot. Gard.* 84:314–704. French, J. C., M. Chung, and Y. Hur. 1995. Chloroplast DNA phylogeny of Ariflorae. In *Monocotyledons: Systematics and Evolution*, eds. P. J. Rudall, P. J. Cribb, D. F. Cutler, and C. J. Humphries, 255–75. Richmond, Surrey, U.K.: Royal Botanic Gardens, Kew. Grayum, M. H. 1990. Evolution and phylogeny of Araceae. *Ann. Missouri Bot. Gard.* 77:628–77. Grayum, M. H. 1996. Revision of *Philodendron* subgenus *Pteromischum* (Araceae) for Pacific and Caribbean Tropical America. *Syst. Bot. Monogr.* 47:1–233. Mayo, S. J. 1991. A revision of *Philodendron* subgenus *Meconostigma* (Araceae). *Kew Bull.* 46(4):601–81. Mayo, S. J., J. Bogner and P. C. Boyce. 1997. *Genera of Araceae*. Richmond, Surrey, U.K.: Royal Botanic Garden, Kew. Ray, T. S. 1987. Diversity of shoot organization in the Araceae. *Amer J. Bot.* 74:1373–87. Strong, D. R., and T. S. Ray. 1975. Host tree location behavior of a tropical vine (*Monstera gigantea*) by scototropism. *Science* 190:804–80. Zhu, G. H. In press. The systematics of *Dracontium* L. (Araceae). *Ann. Missouri Bot. Gard.*

ARECACEAE or PALMAE (Palm Family)

Andrew Henderson

Figure 220, Plate 55

- *tree- or shrublike, less often lianas*
- *leaves always plicate, often split*
- *inflorescences axillary*
- *flowers usually small and numerous, mostly 3-merous*
- *fruits drupelike, the endocarp often bony*

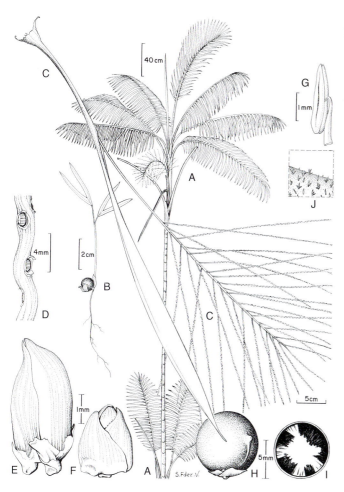

Figure 220. ARECACEAE. *Prestoea ensiformis*. **A.** Plant with basal sprouts, stem, inflorescence, bracts, and leaves. **B.** Lateral view of seedling. **C.** Inflorescence and subtending bract. **D.** Part of the rachilla from inflorescence. **E.** Lateral view of staminate flower. **F.** Lateral view of pistillate flower. **G.** Lateral view of stamen. **H.** Lateral view of fruit. **I.** Transverse section of fruit showing ruminate endosperm. **J.** Detail of trichomes on rachilla. Reprinted with permission from Henderson and Galeano (1996). Artist: Silvio Fernández.

Numbers of genera and species. Worldwide, the Arecaceae comprise 189 genera and more than 2,000 species. In tropical America, there are 67 genera and about 550 species. The largest genera are *Bactris* (75 species), *Chamaedorea* (77), and *Geonoma* (51). In the Western Hemisphere, 18 genera are monospecific.

Distribution and habitat. Palms occur throughout tropical areas of the world. A few species reach as far north as subtropical areas in the United States (e.g., *Sabal palmetto* at 34°N) and other areas in Europe and Asia. In the Southern Hemisphere, they extend into northern Argentina and central Chile (e.g., *Jubaea chilensis* at 36°S) and other areas in Africa, Australia, and New Zealand. Palm genera are mostly endemic to major continental areas, and none are pantropical. Notable exceptions are the coconut, *Cocos nucifera*, widely cultivated in the Tropics, and *Raphia* and *Elaeis*, which are shared by America and Africa. Except for a few widespread genera (e.g., *Acrocomia*, *Bactris*, *Chamaedorea*, *Desmoncus*, *Euterpe*, *Geonoma*, and *Prestoea*), genera of the Western Hemisphere are mostly confined to, or most diversified in, specific regions (e.g., the Caribbean, Andes, Amazon, or Atlantic coastal forest).

Palms occupy a variety of habitats, from desert to mangrove swamps but are most abundant in lowland and montane moist forests. In the neotropics, most species occur at low elevations, but a few reach 3,200 meters on Andean slopes.

Family classification. The Arecaceae are placed in the monofamilial Arecales by both Dahlgren et al. and Cronquist. Traditionally, the Arecaceae have been further placed near families such as the Araceae, Pandanaceae, and Cyclanthaceae. Modern analyses of both morphological and molecular data show the Arecaceae to be an isolated family on a long branch, unrelated to these families. Sister group relationships are currently unclear, but most authors place the Arecaceae in a commelinoid clade, a large group of families that includes the Poaceae, Juncaceae, Cyperaceae, Zingiberaceae, and Bromeliaceae.

The Arecaceae are divided into six subfamilies: Calamoideae, Nypoideae, Phytelephantoideae, Ceroxyloideae, Arecoideae, and Coryphoideae. The latter three are now not considered to be monophyletic. All except Nypoideae occur in the Western Hemisphere.

Features of the family. Habit: treelike or shrublike, less often lianas. **Stems** solitary or clustered, often spiny. **Leaves** spiral or rarely distichous, usually clustered near stem apex, palmate (i.e., fan-shaped) or pinnate (i.e., feather-shaped), or simple (then venation always pinnate); blades plicate, the folds induplicate (V-shaped in cross section) or reduplicate (Λ-shaped in cross section), often split; venation palmate, or pinnate (in simple and pinnately compound leaves). **Inflorescences** axillary, interfoliar or infrafoliar, usually solitary at a node, rarely multiple, spicate or branched to 7 orders; prophyll and one to many peduncular bracts present. **Flowers** actinomorphic, bisexual or unisexual (then plants monoecious, andromonoecious, or dioecious), often borne in clusters (commonly a triad of one pistillate and two staminate flowers), small, numerous; perianth usually biseriate, variously colored but mostly whitish; sepals (2)3(+), imbricate or valvate; petals (2)3(+), imbricate or valvate; androecium with 6–many (to 1,200 in the phytelephantoid *Ammandra*) stamens; staminodes and pistillodes often present in unisexual pistillate and staminate flowers, respectively; gynoecium apocarpous or syncarpous, sometimes pseudomonomerous, the carpels 1–4 (apocarpous species), 3 or rarely more (syncarpous species), the locules usually equal to number of carpels, the stigmas usually sessile; placentation axile, apical-axile, or basal-axile, the ovules 1 per fertile locule. **Fruits** drupelike, the endocarp often bony. **Seeds** 1–several.

Natural history. Pollination, long thought to be carried out by wind, is now known to be predominantly effected by insects. Beetles in the families Nitidulidae and Curculionidae are particularly important pollinators and have evolved an intricate association with palms. Recently staphylinid beetles have been shown to have a highly evolved relationship with some phytelephantoid palms. Bees, flies, and wasps are also important pollinators. *Calyptrogyne* is pollinated by bats.

A wide variety of animals disperse palm fruits, including birds, bats, other mammals, fish, and insects.

Economic uses. Date (*Phoenix dactylifera*), coconut (*Cocos nucifera*), and oil palms (*Elaeis guineensis*) are internationally important crop plants, and the latter two are grown widely in tropical America. The palm family is one of the most useful in the neotropics. Some pre-Columbian cultures relied almost completely on palm products. Currently, there are several major uses. Palm stems are very widely used in house construction; the leaves are employed for thatching and the split trunks are used as floor boards; and the fruits of most species are edible. Certain species are important in local areas. For example, *Euterpe oleracea* for *palmito* (palm heart) and fruits in the Amazon estuary; *Mauritia flexuosa* for edible fruits in the Peruvian Amazon; *Geonoma deversa* for thatching material in the Bolivian Amazon; and *Bactris gasipaes* in Central America and elsewhere for edible fruits and *palmito*. Palms are also popular street trees in many countries. Leaf fibers of many species, especially those of *Mauritia flexuosa* and species of *Astrocaryum*, are woven into baskets, mats, and hammocks.

References. BALICK, M., AND H. BECK. 1990. *Useful Palms of the World. A Synoptic Bibliography.* New York: Columbia University Press. BERNAL, H. Y., AND J. E. CORRERA Q. 1998. Palmae (Arecaceae) (*Bactris gasipaes*). In *Especies vegetales promisorias de los países del Convenio Andrés Bello*, Tomo XII. Santafé de Bogotá, D. E., Colombia: Secretaria Ejecutiva del Convenio Andrés Bello. BORCHSENIUS, F., AND R. BERNAL. 1996. *Aiphanes* (Palmae). *Fl. Neotrop. Monogr.* 70:1–95. HENDERSON, A. 1986. A review of pollination studies in the Palmae. *Bot. Rev.* 52:221–59. HENDERSON, A. 1990. Arecaceae. Part I. Introduction and the *Iriarteinae. Fl. Neotrop. Monogr.* 53:1–100. HENDERSON, A. 1994. *The Palms of the Amazon.* New York: Oxford University Press. HENDERSON, A. 2000. *Bactris* (Palmae). *Fl. Neotrop. Monogr.* 79:1–181. HENDERSON, A. 2002. *Evolution and Ecology of Palms.* Bronx, NY: New York Botanical Garden Press. HENDERSON, A., AND F. BORCHSENIUS. 1999. Evolution, variation, and classification of palms. *Mem. New York Bot. Gard. Vol. 83*:1–324. HENDERSON, A., AND G. GALEANO. 1996. *Euterpe, Prestoea,* and *Neonicholsonia* (Palmae). *Fl. Neotrop. Monogr.* 72:1–90. HENDERSON, A., G. GALEANO, AND R. BERNAL. 1995. *A Field Guide to the Palms of the Americas.* Princeton, NJ: Princeton University Press. MORAES R., M. 1996. *Allagoptera* (Palmae). *Fl. Neotrop. Monogr.* 73:1–35. UHL, N., AND J. DRANSFIELD. 1987. *Genera Palmarum.* Lawrence, KS: Allen Press. ZONA, S. 1996. *Roystonea* (Arecaceae: Arecoideae). *Fl. Neotrop. Monogr.* 71:1–36. ZONA, S., AND A. HENDERSON. 1989. A review of animal-mediated seed dispersal of palms. *Selbyana* 11:6–21.

BROMELIACEAE (Bromeliad Family)

BRUCE K. HOLST AND HARRY E. LUTHER

Figure 221, Plate 55

- *herbs, often epiphytic*
- *usually with rosette growth form*
- *leaves alternate, simple, the margins often spiny; conspicuous peltate foliar trichomes often present*
- *inflorescences frequently showy and bracteate*
- *flowers with 3 sepals; petals 3; stamens 6; stigmas 3*

Numbers of genera and species. The Bromeliaceae comprise 56 genera and approximately 2,900 species, with all but one species restricted to the Americas. Genera with more than 100 species are *Aechmea* (231 species), *Dyckia* (125), *Guzmania* (184), *Neoregelia* (109), *Pitcairnia* (357), *Puya* (199), *Tillandsia* (544), and *Vriesea* (250). Twenty-six genera have 10 species or less, and eight of those have a single species.

Distribution and habitat. The Bromeliaceae are found from Virginia in the southeastern United States through Arizona, Central America, and the West Indies to Patagonia in South America. *Tillandsia usneoides*, one of the world's widest-ranging flowering plants, is the northern and southern most representative of the family. A single species, *Pitcairnia feliciana*, occurs on rock outcrops in Guinea in western Africa.

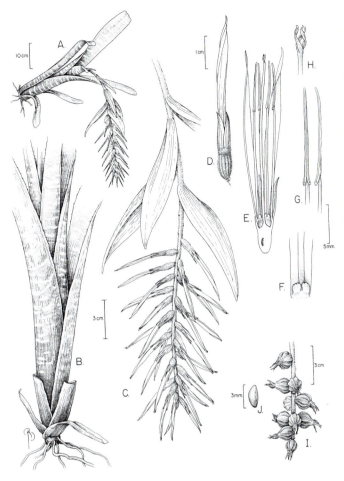

Figure 221. BROMELIACEAE. *Billbergia violacea*. **A.** Plant showing roots, leaves, and inflorescence. **B.** Base of plant. **C.** Inflorescence. **D.** Lateral view of flower. **E.** Medial section of flower. **F.** Detail of scales at base of stamens. **G.** Adaxial (left) and lateral (right) views of anthers and apices of filaments. **H.** Lateral view of stigma. **I.** Part of infructescence. **J.** Seed. Reprinted with permission from Mori et al. (1997). Artist: Bobbi Angell.

The regions with the greatest species diversity in the family are the Andes, the Guayana Shield, and southeastern Brazil. All of the large genera have broad Neotropical distributions with the exception of *Puya*, which is largely restricted to the Andes, and *Dyckia*, which is mostly found in southern South America. Eleven medium-sized genera have much more restricted ranges: *Navia* (90 species), *Lindmania* (38 species), and *Brocchinia* (20) are endemic to the Guayana Shield; *Cryptanthus* (54), *Encholirium* (31), *Orthophytum* (30), and *Nidularium* (45) are mostly found in eastern Brazil; *Deuterocohnia* (15 species), *Fosterella* (25), and *Greigia* (32) are most diversified in the Andes, with the latter two extending into montane Central America; and *Hechtia* (51) is found from southern Texas to northern Central America.

Bromeliaceae occupy a wide range of habitats and are one of the most characteristic elements of Neotropical forests. They occur from arid to very wet regions, from sea level to above 4,000 meters in the Andes, and from rich volcanic soils to nutrient-poor white-sand savannas. The largely terrestrial (90%) Pitcairnioideae are mostly found in open, rocky areas, with greatest concentrations in the Guayana Shield and the Andes. Bromelioideae, with approximately 36 percent terrestrial species and 64 percent epiphytic, are most diverse in southeastern Brazil, particularly the Atlantic rain forest. The predominantly epiphytic (90%) Tillandsioideae are most diverse in the dry forests of Mexico and Central America and humid montane forests of the northern Andes.

Family classification. The Bromeliaceae are placed in the Bromeliales by Dahlgren et al. The Rapateaceae are the likely sister group to the Bromeliaceae. The family is traditionally divided into three subfamilies, though there is considerable debate over their composition and position within the family: the Tillandsioideae, with 9 genera and 1,164 species, the Bromelioideae, with 31 genera and 775 species, and the Pitcairnioideae, with 15 genera and 971 species. The Bromelioideae have fleshy, indehiscent fruits, unappendaged seeds, and mostly spiny leaves; the Pitcairnioideae have dry, capsular fruits, mostly entire-appendaged seeds, and mostly spiny leaves; and the Tillandsioideae have dry, capsular fruits, divided-appendaged seeds, and entire leaves. The largely terrestrial Pitcairnioideae are usually considered the most primitive of the family, though recent analyses shows the subfamily to be polyphyletic, with one clade being primitive in the family and another not. The Bromelioideae and Tillandsioideae are often considered to be more recently evolved. The circumscription of the genera in all three subfamilies has been changing in the past 15 years, and will likely be further modified as a result of much needed broad-based molecular surveys.

Features of the family. Habit: herbs, often obligate terrestrial or epiphytic, sometimes facultative epiphytes, minute (3 cm tall in some epiphytic *Tillandsia*) to massive (nearly 10 m tall in *Puya raimondii*), the growth form often in 1–many sessile rosettes, some species with elongated vinelike stems; roots always adventitious, greatly reduced (some atmospheric, gray species of *Tillandsia*) to merely serving as holdfasts (many epiphytic and saxicolous species) or fully developed (many terrestrial species); stolons present in some species (particularly in *Bromelia* and *Neoregelia*), these short to elongate. **Leaves** alternate, often in rosettes, simple, consisting of sheath and blade, evergreen or more rarely deciduous, membranaous to succulent; sheaths usually entire, often with different color and texture than blades, sometimes enlarged to aid in water retention, with dense layer of absorptive trichomes to facilitate water and nutrient uptake (in tank-forming species); blades ligulate or triangular, or less often elliptic when narrowed basally to form a pseudopetiole, the margins with spines in most Pitcairnioideae and Bromelioideae, these absent in Tillandsioideae, the spines minute to large and formidable; venation mostly of equal-sized, parallel veins, some *Pitcairnia* and *Aechmea* with thickened midrib; trichomes present, commonly radial, peltate, multicelled, sometimes linear or stellate in Pitcairnioideae and Bromelioideae. **Inflorescences** terminal (with few exceptions), sessile or scapose, simple (racemes, spikes, heads, or solitary pseudolateral flowers) or compound (panicles of racemes and spikes, compound heads), glabrous or lepidote, small and inconspicuous or sometimes hidden among leaves, to several meters long, exceeding leaves, and showy, the main axis (or scape) erect or curved, the axes bearing flowers distichously or polystichously, secund flowers common in some genera (e.g., *Pitcairnia, Fosterella, Werauhia,* and *Vriesea*); bracts usually present on main axis, compound inflorescences bearing primary bracts at bases of main branches, a series of large upper-scape bracts (involucral bracts) present in some species, these serving to protect developing inflorescence or, when brightly colored, to attract pollinators; floral bract subtending each flower; pedicels present or absent. **Flowers** actinomorphic to strongly zygomorphic, usually bisexual, sometimes unisexual (plants dioecious in *Androlepis, Catopsis, Cottendorfia,* and *Hechtia* or andromonoecious in *Cryptanthus*); sepals 3, distinct or partially connate, equal or unequal in size (rarely 1 reduced), aestivation either convolute (most genera), with left side of each sepal overlapping right side of next one, or imbricate (some Pitcairnioideae), with sepal opposite floral bract overlapped on both sides by adjacent sepals; petals 3, distinct or partially connate, variously colored; appendages present in some genera, basal to petals; androecium of 6 stamens, the stamens in 2 series, basal to ovary or adnate to petals, the filaments distinct or basally connate, the anthers dehiscing longitudinally or rarely poricidally (some *Navia*); gynoecium syncarpous, the ovary ranging from superior (all Tillandsioideae except *Glomeropitcairnia* and some Pitcairnioideae) to fully inferior (all Bromelioideae and some Pitcairnioideae), the carpels 3, the locules 3, the style terminal, 3-parted, the stigmas 3; placentation axile, the ovules usually numerous. **Fruits** septicidal or loculicidal capsules (rarely indehiscent), berries, or multiple fleshy fruits (*Ananas*). **Seeds** 1–many per locule, winged, caudate, or plumose in most capsular species, or unappendaged in baccate species; endosperm copious, the embryo small to large, borne at base of endosperm.

Vegetative reproduction is common in the Bromeliaceae, with most species producing offshoots from dormant axillary buds at the time the parent shoot becomes reproductive. As the parent shoot produces seeds and dies, the offshoot gradually takes over to repeat the cycle (serial monocarpy).

Natural history. Epiphytic Bromeliaceae rely on two main methods of obtaining water and nutrients: gathering them in tanks formed by overlapping leaf bases or absorbing them directly from the atmosphere through absorptive trichomes. The tank-forming species, which commonly are found in mesic, montane forests, are important sources of water, food, and shelter for canopy-dwelling animals. These animals, in turn, provide additional nutrients for the plants through their activities. The nontank-forming epiphytic bromeliads (only subfamily Tillandsioideae) are often grayish in appearance due to the dense cover of foliar trichomes and are found in dry forests or in the hot, uppermost levels of the canopy in mesic forests. These true atmospheric bromeliads also often have a compact habit and inrolled, relatively short leaves. Along with other succulent, xerophytic, terrestrial species, they use crassulacean acid metabolism to minimize water loss. Terrestrial, nontank-forming Bromeliaceae have well-developed root systems for obtaining water and nutrients. A few species of *Tillandsia, Aechmea, Brocchinia,* and *Neoregelia* house ants in their swollen, bulbous bases formed by enlarged leaf sheaths, and some species of *Aechmea* are epiphytes of ant-nest gardens.

Several bromeliads have been reported to be passive carnivores, most notably *Brocchinia reducta,* which has leaves that form a tight, tubular rosette greatly resembling the pitchers found in other carnivorous, pitfall-type plants. Other adaptations for carnivory in *B. reducta* include light yellow-green leaves that are lined on the inside with a slippery, powdery coating; a highly acidic fluid in the tank; and a sweet smell that emanates from the tank.

The flowers usually are pollinated by birds and insects, less often by bats, and possibly by wind in a few species. Seeds typically are dispersed by wind or gravity in the capsular-fruited Pitcairnioideae and Tillandsioideae and by birds, mammals, or less commonly insects in the fleshy-fruited Bromelioideae.

Economic uses. The pineapple (*Ananas comosus*), cultivated pantropically since the 1500s for its edible fruits, is by far the most commercially important species of Bromeliaceae. Several other bromeliads, particularly species of *Aechmea, Bromelia,* and *Greigia,* have edible fruits but are consumed only locally. The protein-digesting enzyme, bromelain, is extracted from pineapple fruits for use in meat tenderizers and as an anti-inflammatory. *Aechmea magdalenae, Ananas lucidus, Neoglaziovia variegata,* and several *Bromelia* species are, or have been, cultivated for the long, strong fibers in their leaves that are used to make hammocks, fishing nets, and twine. Bromeliads with strong foliar spines (especially species of *Bromelia*) are used as living fences.

Horticulturally, the Bromeliaceae have achieved an important role in the specialty plant market and are now used widely for landscaping in warm climates or as houseplants in cold climates. Local peoples also use the plants or colorful inflorescences for decoration or religious ceremonies. *Tillandsia usneoides* (Spanish moss) was harvested widely in the southeastern United States during the mid-1900s for use as upholstery stuffing.

References. BAENSCH, U., AND U. BAENSCH. 1994. *Blooming Bromeliads.* Nassau: Tropic Beauty Publishers, Ulrich and Urgila Baeusch. BENZING, D. H. 2000. *Bromeliaceae: Profile of an Adaptive Radiation.* Cambridge, U.K.: Cambridge University Press. BROWN, G. K., AND A. J. GILMARTIN. 1989. Stigma types in Bromeliaceae—a systematic survey. *Syst. Bot.* 14:110–32. CRAYN, D. M., R. G. TERRY, J. A. C. SMITH, AND K. WINTER. 2000. Molecular systematic investigations in Pitcairnioideae (Bromeliaceae) as a basis for understanding the evolution of Crassulacean Acid Metabolism (CAM). In *Monocots: Systematics and Evolutions*, eds. K. L. Wilson and D. A. Morrison, 569–79. Melbourne: CSIRO. GIVNISH, T. J., K. J. SYTSMA, J. F. SMITH, W. J. HAHN, D. H. BENZING, AND E. M. BURKHARDT. 1997. Molecular evolution and adaptive radiation in *Brocchinia* (Bromeliaceae: Pitcairnioideae) atop *tepuis* of the Guayana Shield. In *Molecular Evolution and Adaptive Radiation*, eds. T. J. Givnish and K. J. Sytsma, 259–311. New York: Cambridge University Press. HORRES, R., G. ZIZKA, G. KAHL, AND K. WEISING. 2000. Molecular phylogenetics of Bromeliaceae: evidence from *trn*L (UAA) intron sequences of the chloroplast genome. *Pl. Biol.* 2(2000):306–15. LUTHER, H. E. 2000. *An Alphabetical List of Bromeliad Binomials*. Newberg, OR: Bromeliad Society, Inc. ROBINSON, H. 1969. A monograph of foliar anatomy of the genera *Connellia*, *Cottendorfia* and *Navia* (Bromeliaceae). *Smithsonian Contr. Bot.* 2:1–41. SMITH, L. B., AND R. J. DOWNS. 1974. Pitcairnioideae (Bromeliaceae). *Fl. Neotrop. Monogr.* 14(1):1–658. SMITH, L. B., AND R. J. DOWNS. 1977. Tillandsioideae (Bromeliaceae). *Fl. Neotrop. Monogr.* 14(2):663–1492. SMITH, L. B., AND R. J. DOWNS. 1979. Bromelioideae (Bromeliaceae). *Fl. Neotrop. Monogr.* 14(3):1493–2142.

BURMANNIACEAE (Burmannia Family)

ANDREW HENDERSON AND DENNIS WM. STEVENSON

Figure 222, Plate 56

- *saprophytic or hemisaprophytic herbs, small, often delicate*
- *mostly achlorophyllous, then whitish, yellowish, purplish, or reddish*
- *flowers often orchidlike*
- *seeds very small, dustlike*

Numbers of genera and species. Worldwide, the Burmanniaceae comprise 13 genera and approximately 130 species. In tropical America, there are 10 genera and about 54 species. The largest are *Burmannia* (63 species), *Gymnosiphon* (24), and *Thismia* (32).

Distribution and habitat. The Burmanniaceae are widespread in tropical areas of the world but also reach warm temperate regions. Several genera are found in both the Western and the Eastern Hemispheres and *Burmannia*, *Gymnosiphon*, and *Thismia* are pantropical. Some taxa have puzzling disjunctions. *Thismia americana* is known only from an area near Chicago in the United States, where it was last seen in 1917, while its supposed sister species, *T. rodwayi*, is found in Australia, Tasmania, and New Zealand.

Species are found in the understory of lowland and montane moist forests, but also occur in gallery forest, sandy open areas, savannas, swamps, or on rock outcrops.

Family classification. The Burmanniaceae are placed in the Burmanniales by Dahlgren et al. They have traditionally been associated with the orchids, mostly because of their very small, dustlike seeds, but recent cladistic analyses do not support a sister group relationship between the two families. The Burmanniaceae (including the Thismiaceae) is thought to be close to the Corsiaceae and recent analyses suggest that it has affinities with the Dioscoreaceae and Taccaceae. Two tribes are recognized: the Burmannieae and the Thismieae, separated by differences in the number of locules and stamens.

Features of the family. Habit: herbs, small, often delicate, annual or perennial, mostly achlorophyllous, saprophytic, rarely hemisaprophytic, the saprophytes whitish, yellowish, purplish, or reddish, the hemisaprophytes green. **Rootstock** rhizomatous, sometimes with small tubers, the roots thin, branched, creeping. **Stems** usually unbranched. **Leaves** alternate, simple, sessile, usually rather small, narrowly ovate to linear, amplexicaulous in non-saprophytes, reduced to scale leaves in the saprophytes. **Inflorescences** terminal, cymes or of solitary flowers, the cymes 1-many, often bifurcate. **Flowers** usually actinomorphic, bisexual; tepals basally connate into tube, the lobes 6, erect, spreading, or variously modified into elaborate reflexed appendages, sometimes glandular; androecium of 3 (Burmannieae) or 6 (Thismieae, but 3 in *Oxygyne*) stamens, the filaments short, adnate to perianth tube, recurved to pendant (Thismieae); gynoecium syncarpous, the ovary inferior, the carpels 3, the locules 1 or 3, the stigmas sometimes with appendages; nectaries sometimes present, either apical on ovary or in upper part of septae; placentation parietal (locule 1) or axile (locules 3), the ovules numerous. **Fruits** capsular, dehiscing irregularly or by longitudinal or transverse slits, rarely fleshy (*Thismia*). **Seeds** numerous, very small, dustlike, the testa usually extended at each end of seed.

Figure 222. BURMANNIACEAE. *Apteria aphylla* (A–D), *Dictyostega orobanchoides* subsp. *parviflora* (E–H), *Hexapterella gentianoides* (I–M), *Gymnosiphon divaricatus* (N–T). **A.** Plant showing roots, leaves, and inflorescences. **B.** Lateral (left) and opened (right) flowers. **C.** Adaxial view of stamen. **D.** Lateral view of immature fruit enveloped by withered perianth. **E.** Part of plant showing leaves and inflorescences. **F.** Lateral view of flower (right) and opened portion of corolla apex showing adnate stamens (left). **G.** Adaxial view of stamen. **H.** Lateral view of three-parted stigma. **I.** Part of plant showing leaves, bud, and flower. **J.** Lateral view of bud. **K.** Lateral view of flower opened along one side. **L.** Adaxial view of stamen. **M.** Oblique-apical view of stigma with surrounding apices of stamens. **N.** Part of plant showing leaves, buds, and flower with detail of scalelike leaf (left). **O.** Lateral view of bud. **P.** Apical view of flower. **Q.** Lateral view of flower opened along one side (left) and medial section of ovary (right). **R.** Adaxial view of stamen. **S.** Lateral view of three-parted stigma showing filiform appendages. **T.** Lateral view of fruit crowned by persistent perianth. Reprinted with permission from Mori et al. (1997). Artist: Bobbi Angell.

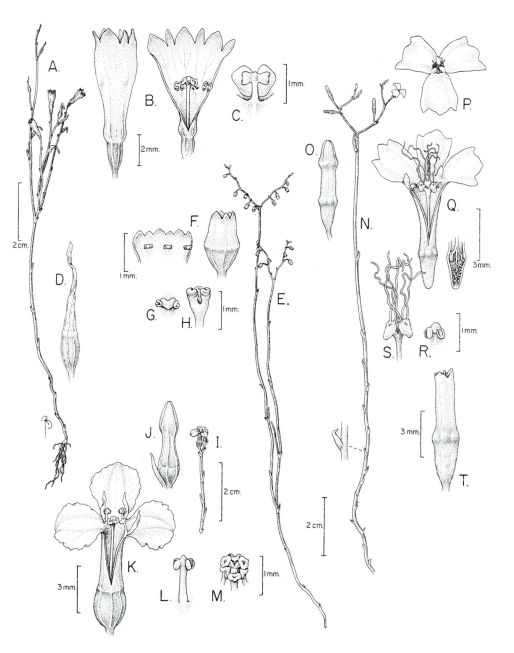

In many species, the modifications of the tepals give the flowers a bizarre, orchidlike appearance.

Natural history. These small, easily overlooked plants, especially the saprophytic species, are poorly known ecologically. Roots of saprophytic species form a symbiotic relationship with mycorrhizal fungi, and plants thus are dependent on the fungi for nutrition. The green-leaved Burmanniaceae are mycorrhizal hemisaprophytes that form a transition between truly autotrophic and truly heterotrophic plants. One nonsaprophytic species, *Burmannia kalbreyeri*, is epiphytic on trees and other vegetation in the Andes and Central American at elevations to 2,300 meters. Pollination has not been studied, but the colorful, variously shaped flowers, often with septal nectaries, indicate insect pollination. Pollination by minute insects (e.g., fungus gnats) has been suggested for *Thismia*. The close proximity of anthers and stigmas in several species also suggests self-pollination. The tiny, dustlike seeds, may be dispersed by wind or water.

Economic uses. No economic uses are known for this family.

References. JONKER, F. 1938. A monograph of the Burmanniaceae. *Meded. Bot. Mus. Herb. Rijks Univ. Utrecht* 51: 1–279. MAAS, P., H. MAAS-VAN DE KAMER, J. VAN BENTHEM, H. SNELDERS, AND T. RÜBSAMEN. 1986. Burmanniaceae. *Fl. Neotrop. Monogr.* 42:1–189. MAAS-VAN DE KAMER, H. 1998. Burmanniaceae. In *The Families and Genera of Vascular Plants*, ed. K. Kubitzki, 3:154–64. Berlin: Springer-Verlag. RASMUSSEN, F. 1995. Relationships of Burmanniales and Orchidales. In *Monocotyledons: Systematics and Evolution*, eds. P. Rudall, P. Cribb, D. Cutler, and C. Humphries, 227–41. Richmond, Surrey, U.K.: Royal Botanic Gardens, Kew.

CALOCHORTACEAE (Mariposa Lily Family)

DENNIS WM. STEVENSON

- *bulbous herbs; bulbs tunicate*

- *plants with 1(2) basal leaves, the flowering axis with 1 or more small leaves*

- *leaves alternate (spiral), simple; blades narrow*

- *flowers with inner tepals cuneate to clawed, pubescent basally, with depressed basal gland; anthers pseudobasifixed*

- *fruits septicidal capsules*

Numbers of genera and species. Worldwide, the Calochortaceae comprise five genera with approximately 100 species. In tropical America, there is one genus, *Calochortus*, and seven to nine species.

Distribution and habitat. The Calochortaceae are mainly north temperate across North America, Europe, and Eastern Asia with outlying species of *Calochortus* in Mexico and Central America. *Calochortus* is primarily found from western North America to Central America, where it occurs mostly in dry, open-desert habitats and occasionally in forests and meadows. Within the neotropics, *Calochortus* is found from tropical Mexico to Guatemala in dry habitats with calcareous soils, especially in oak forests.

Family classification. Historically, the Calochortaceae and related genera have been subjected to numerous disparate treatments. The Calochortaceae as circumscribed by Dahlgren et al. are monogeneric and placed in the Liliales. In contrast, Tamura extended the boundaries of the family to include *Prosartes*, *Scoliopus*, *Streptopus*, and *Tricyrtis*. He recognized two tribes: Calochorteae with *Calochortus* and Tricyrtideae with the remaining four genera. Recent analyses of combined morphological and molecular data sets indicate that the family and its tribes as treated by Tamura are a paraphyletic assemblage at the base of the Liliaceae. These studies suggest that the Calochortaceae may be better placed within the Liliaceae, as was done by Cronquist.

Features of the family. Habit: bulbous herbs; bulbs tunicate; roots contractile. **Leaves** alternate (spiral), simple; plants with 1(2) basal leaves, these well developed; blades narrow. **Inflorescences** terminal, flowering axis scapiform or bearing small leaves, simple to sparingly branched, terminated by 1–3 flowers. **Flowers** actinomorphic, bisexual, campanulate, erect; tepals 6, distinct, in 2 whorls, the outer whorl lavender, the inner whorl white, larger than outer whorl, the tepals cuneate to clawed, the base pubescent, with an obvious depressed basal gland; androecium of 6 stamens, the stamens free, inserted at tepal bases, the anthers pseudobasifixed, latrorse; gynoecium syncarpous, the ovary superior, the carpels 3, the locules 3, the stigma sessile, trifid; placentation axile, the ovules numerous in each locule. **Fruits** septicidal capsules, 3-angled. **Seeds** several per fruit, flat.

Natural history. Nectar-feeding bees pollinate *Calochortus*, and its light, flat seeds suggest wind dispersal.

Economic uses. Species of *Calochortus* are highly prized as ornamentals by bulb collectors, even though they do not do well in cultivation; as a result, some are threatened because of overcollection. The bulbs of *Calochortus* were used as an alternative food source in times of short food supply by native North Americans and early settlers.

References. OWENBY, M. 1940. A monograph of the genus *Calochortus*. *Ann. Missouri Bot. Gard.* 27:371–560. RUDALL, P., K. STOBART, W. HONG, J. CONRAN, C. FURNESS, ET AL. 2000. Consider the lilies: systematics of Liliales. *Monocots: Systematics and Evolution*, eds. K. Wilson and D. Morrison, 347–57. Melbourne: CSIRO. TAMURA, M. 1998. Calochortaceae. In *The Families and Genera of Vascular Plants*, ed. K. Kubitzki, 4:164–75. New York: Springer-Verlag.

CANNACEAE (Canna Family)

DENNIS WM. STEVENSON AND JANICE WASSMER ST

Figure 223, Plate 56

- *Herbs, rhizomatous; aerial shoot well developed, with distinct internodes*

- *leaves alternate, spirally arranged, simple, sheath open*

- *flowers asymmetric; stamen 1, the theca 1; staminodes 1–4, petal-like, one sometimes recurved and called the labellum; ovary inferior*

- *fruits loculicidal, tuberculate capsules, with persistent sepals*

- *seeds many, subglobose, black, very hard*

Numbers of genera and species. Worldwide, the Cannaceae comprise a single genus, *Canna*, and 10 species that originally occurred only in tropical America. All Asiatic and African Canna species are introduced from the New World.

Distribution and habitat. *Canna* is found all over the Tropics of the New World. The center of diversity of the genus is in western South America.

Species of *Canna* preferentially grow in humus-rich soils of lowland, wet, subtemperate to tropical forests where they are often found along river and stream margins. Some species grow in swampy and/or boggy areas. They occur from sea level up to 2,800 meters in the Andes.

Family classification. The Cannaceae are placed in the Zingiberales by Dahlgren et al. Originally, the Cannaceae and Marantaceae were considered a single family, the Cannaceae. Most recent workers recognize both families but acknowledge their close relationship by placing them in the Zingiberales along with the Costaceae, Heliconiaceae, Marantaceae, Musaceae, Strelitziaceae, and Zingiberaceae. In contrast, Takhtajan established the Cannales to accommodate the Cannaceae and Marantaceae. The close relationship of Cannaceae and Marantaceae is supported by cladistic analyses of morphological data and combined morphological and molecular data.

Features of the family. Habit: herbs (to 5 m tall); rhizome horizontal, branched, with short internodes, tuberlike, the aerial shoot well developed, with distinct internodes. **Leaves** alternate (spiral), simple; leaf sheath open. **Inflorescences** terminal; thyrse composed of few-flowered cymes; bracts green, inconspicuous. **Flowers** asymmetric, bisexual; perianth in 2 whorls of 3; sepals 3, much shorter than petals, free, greenish to purple; petals 3, 1 shorter than others, often

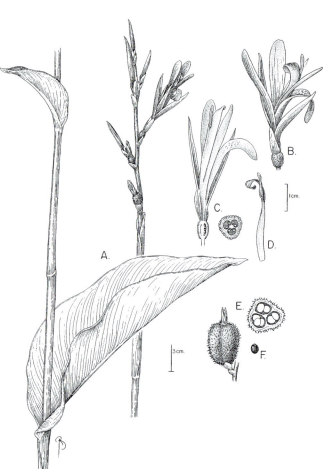

Figure 223. CANNACEAE. *Canna indica.* **A.** Part of stem with leaves (left) and inflorescence (right). **B.** Lateral view of flower. **C.** Medial section of flower (left) and transverse section of ovary (right). **D.** Lateral view of stamen. **E.** Lateral (left) and transverse section of fruits (right). **F.** Seed. Reprinted with permission from Mori et al. (1997). Artist: Bobbi Angell.

yellow to white, basally more or less connate; androecium of 2 whorls of 3: stamen 1, petal-like, the theca 1, the pollen presented secondarily; staminodes 1–4, petal-like, one sometimes recurved and called the labellum, the outer whorl with median staminode always missing; gynoecium syncarpous, the ovary inferior, tuberculate, 3-locular, the style 1, expanded into fleshy, petaloid structure, the stigma on apical margin; septal nectaries present; placentation axile, the ovules many, in 2 rows per locule. **Fruits** loculicidal capsules, the wall tuberculate, with persistent sepals. **Seeds** many, hard, globose, black, with imbibition lid; aril absent, but funicles densely covered with hairlike structures.

Natural history. The often showy flowers and presence of nectar in most species of *Canna* suggest hummingbird pollination. *Canna liliiflora* (= *C. brittonii*), however, is bat-pollinated. The fragrant, night-flowering *C. flaccida* may be moth-pollinated. Little is known about dispersal biology; however, the seeds are thought to fall to the ground when the fruit dehisces or after the breakdown of the fruit wall. The seeds are apparently dispersed by gravity and are known to remain dormant and viable for up to 600 years!

Economic uses. The hybrid *Canna* (often called *C. indica* or *C. generalis*) has large flowers that vary from yellow to red, orange, or purple and showy, red-brown leaves. Because of these features, it is commonly grown as a tropical ornamental. The edible *C. indica* (often misidentified as *C. edulis*) originated as a crop plant some 4,500 years ago in the northern Andes. Its tubers yield an easily digestible starch and it is now grown as a food crop in the Pacific, parts of Asia, and Australia under the names "purple arrowroot" or "Queensland arrowroot." In Andean South America, the rhizomes of *Canna* yield a fine-textured starch known as *achira*, which is used in baking. The shoots and leaves of some species are used locally for their medicinal properties, the leaves are used to wrap food for cooking, and the seeds are used in necklaces and rosaries.

References. BERNAL, H. Y., AND J. E. CORRERA Q. 1990. Cannaceae. In *Especies vegetales promisorias de los países del Convenio Andrés Bello*, Tomo IV. Bogotá, D. E., Colombia: Secretaria Ejecutiva del Convenio Andrés Bello. GROOTJEN, C. J., AND F. BOUMAN. 1988. Seed structure in Cannaceae: taxonomic and ecological implications. *Ann. Bot.* 61: 363–71. KRESS, J. 1990. The phylogeny and classification of the Zingiberales. *Ann. Missouri Bot. Gard.* 77:698–721. KRESS, J. 1995. Phylogeny of the Zingiberanae: morphology and molecules. In *Monocotyledons: Systematics and Evolution*, eds. P. Rudall, P. Cribb, D. Cutler, and C. Humphries, 2:443–60. Richmond, Surrey, U.K.: Royal Botanic Gardens, Kew. KUBITZKI, K. 1998. Cannaceae. In *The Families and Genera of Vascular Plants*, ed. K. Kubitzki, 4:103–[1]06. New York: Springer-Verlag. LINDER, H. P., AND E. A. KELLOGG. 1995. Phylogenetic patterns in the commelinid clade. In *Monocotyledons: Systematics and Evolution*, eds. P. Rudall, P. Cribb, D. Cutler, and C. Humphries, 473–96. Richmond, Surrey, U.K.: Royal Botanic Gardens, Kew. SEGEREN, W. AND P.J.M. MAAS. 1971. The genus Canna in northern South America. *Acta Bot. Neerl.* 20:663–80. TANAKA, N. 2001. Taxonomic revision of the family Cannaceae in the New World and Asia. *Makinoa*, n.s, 1:1–74.

COMMELINACEAE (Spiderwort Family)

CHRISTOPHER R. HARDY AND ROBERT B. FADEN

Figure 224, Plate 56

- *herbs, somewhat succulent, with mucilaginous sap*

- *leaves alternate, simple, entire, with a closed basal sheath; often with involute ptyxis*

- *inflorescences of scorpioid cymes, often in thyrses*

- *flowers trimerous, actinomorphic or zygomorphic, without nectar*

- *fruits usually loculicidal capsules, rarely indehiscent*

Numbers of genera and species. Worldwide, the Commelinaceae comprise approximately 42 genera and 650 species. Twenty-three genera and at least 225 species are native to or naturalized in the Western Hemisphere and 23 genera and about 200 species occur in the neotropics. The largest genera in the Western Hemisphere are *Tradescantia* (70 species), *Dichorisandra* (25), *Tripogandra* (22), and *Callisia* (20). Although much more diverse in tropical Africa, *Commelina* is represented in the Western Hemisphere by at least 25 species.

Distribution and habitat. Species of Commelinaceae are found throughout the warm-temperate and tropical regions of the world. None, however, is native to Europe. Major centers of diversity are Mexico and northern Central America, tropical Africa (including Madagascar), and tropical Asia. Only the following six genera occur in both the Eastern and Western Hemispheres: *Aneilema*, *Buforrestia*, *Commelina*, *Floscopa*, *Murdannia*, and *Pollia*. These all have fewer species in the Western Hemisphere than in the Eastern Hemisphere.

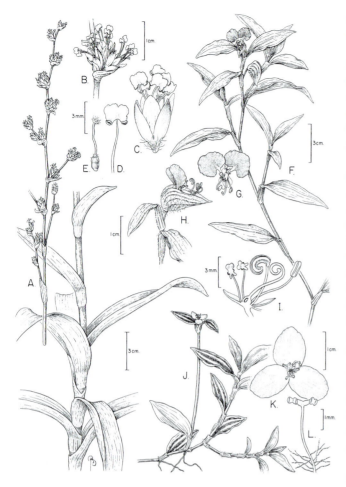

Figure 224. COMMELINACEAE. *Callisia fragrans* (A–E), *Commelina erecta* (F–I), *Tradescantia zebrina* (J–L). **A.** Inflorescence (left) and stem with leaves (right). **B.** Part of inflorescence. **C.** Lateral view of flower. **D.** Adaxial view of stamen. **E.** Lateral view of gynoecium. **F.** Stem with leaves and flowers. **G.** Apical view of flower. **H.** Inflorescence with subtending bract. **I.** Medial section of flower. **J.** Plant showing roots, leaves, and flower. **K.** Apical view of flower. **L.** Adxial view of stamen. Reprinted with permission from Acevedo-Rodríguez (1996). Artist: Bobbi Angell.

In the Western Hemisphere, Commelinaceae are most diverse in Mexico and northern Central America. Species of *Callisia*, *Commelina*, *Tradescantia*, and *Tinantia* extend into temperate regions of North America. Tropical South America, although poorer in species, has the endemic genera *Elasis*, *Geogenanthus*, and *Siderasis*, and most species of *Dichorisandra* are also endemic to this region.

Commelinaceae are found in a variety of habitats and at a wide range of elevations. They occur from tropical rain forest to semiarid grassland and bushland. A few species are aquatics. Neotropical members of the family occur from sea level to above 3,800 meters. Genera confined to high elevations include *Weldenia* in Mexico and Guatemala and *Elasis* in Ecuador. The species of *Murdannia* native to South America grow in seasonally flooded grassland. Species of *Cochliostema*, the only epiphytes of the family in the West-

ern Hemisphere, are native to northwestern South America and contiguous Central America.

Family classification. The Commelinaceae are placed in the Commelinales by Dahlgren et al. where they are allied with the Mayacaceae, Rapateaceae, and Xyridaceae. However, molecular data support a closer alliance to the Pontederiaceae, Philydraceae, Haemodoraceae, and Hanguanaceae.

The family is divided into two subfamilies: Cartonematoideae, with two genera (*Cartonema*, with 11 species in Australia and *Triceratella*, with 1 species in south tropical Africa), and Commelinoideae, with 39–40 genera and more than 630 species worldwide. In the Western Hemisphere, genera and species belong to subfamily Commelinoideae, which comprises two tribes, Tradescantieae and Commelineae. Tribe Tradescantieae is composed of both Eastern Hemisphere and the majority of Western Hemisphere species in the family. Tribe Commelineae is mainly Eastern Hemisphere, although six genera have some Western Hemisphere species. Significant changes in the delimitation of genera in the tribe Tradescantieae have been made recently. The new genera *Matudanthus* and *Thyrsanthemum* have been described from Mexico and *Elasis* from Ecuador, whereas *Campelia*, *Cymbispatha*, *Rhoeo*, *Separotheca*, *Setcreasea*, and *Zebrina* have been synonymized under *Tradescantia* and *Aploleia*, *Cuthbertia*, *Hadrodemas*, *Leiandra*, *Leptorhoeo*, and *Phyodina* have been placed in *Callisia*.

Features of the family. Habit: herbs, perennial or less commonly annual, somewhat succulent, usually terrestrial, rarely epiphytic (only species of *Cochliostema*, these usually with a bromeliad-tank habit), usually small to medium-sized (some erect species of *Dichorisandra* may reach 2.5 m); rhizomes sometimes present; stems erect to spreading (occasionally twining; e.g., some *Dichorisandra*), sometimes very compact in rosette plants. **Leaves** alternate (spiral or distichous), simple; sheath closed; blades often narrowed basally into a pseudopetiole, occasionally purple abaxially, the margins entire; ptyxis involute in many genera (e.g., *Dichorisandra*, *Geogenanthus*), supervolute in others (e.g., *Callisia*, *Gibasoides*, *Murdannia*, *Thyrsanthemum*, *Tripogandra*), of both types in some genera (e.g., *Tradescantia*, *Commelina*). **Inflorescences** terminal or axillary, sometimes borne at or near base of stem (*Geogenanthus* and a few *Dichorisandra*), commonly panicle-like thyrses composed of several to many scorpioid cymose branches (cincinni), sometimes reduced to pair of sessile cincinni (e.g., *Callisia*, *Tradescantia*, *Tripogandra*), a single cincinnus (e.g., *Matudanthus*), or rarely a solitary flower (as in the Cuban *Sauvallea*); bract usually subtending cincinni, rarely absent. **Flowers** actinomorphic (e.g., *Callisia*, *Gibasis*, and *Tradescantia*) or zygomorphic (e.g., *Aneilema*, *Commelina*, and *Tinantia*), bisexual or rarely unisexual (then plants andromonoecious; e.g., some *Dichorisandra* and many *Commelina*), ca. 0.5–5 cm diam. (the largest in *Cochliostema*); calyx of 3 sepals, usually free but united in *Welde-*

nia; corolla of 3 deliquescent petals, usually dissimilar from calyx, usually blue to purple, violet, or white; petals usually free, less commonly basally united (e.g., *Weldenia*, *Cyanotis*, and some *Tradescantia*), the margins glabrous, rarely fringed with moniliform hairs (*Cochliostema* and *Geogenanthus*); androecium of 6 stamens, the stamens in 2 whorls, often some of one or both whorls reduced to staminodes (e.g., *Cochliostema*, *Commelina*, and some *Tripogandra*) or entirely lacking (1 stamen lacking in most *Geogenanthus* and some *Dichorisandra* species; all 6 stamens lacking in pistillate flowers of *Callisia repens*), the filaments glabrous (e.g., *Dichorisandra*, *Siderasis*, *Commelina*) or some (e.g., *Cochliostema*, *Tinantia*, most *Geogenanthus*, most *Tripogandra*) or all (*Gibasis*, most *Tradescantia*, and some *Callisia*) bearded, rarely united (e.g., the 3 fertile stamens in *Cochliostema*), the anther dehiscence longitudinal, less commonly poricidal (e.g., most *Dichorisandra*); gynoecium syncarpous, the ovary superior, the carpels 3, the locules (2)3, the style simple, terminal, the stigma capitate to 3-lobed; placentation axile, the ovules 1–16 per locule. **Fruits** usually loculicidal capsules, rarely indehiscent (e.g., the crustaceous, metallic blue fruit of *Pollia*, the blue or white fruit of some *Commelina*, and the purple, berrylike fruit of *Tradescantia zanonia*). **Seeds** usually uniseriate (biseriate in *Cochliostema*, *Dichorisandra*, *Geogenanthus*, *Pollia*, and *Siderasis*), 1–16 per locule in capsules, 1–24 in indehiscent fruits, ca. 1–7 mm long, exarillate or rarely (in *Dichorisandra*) with orange, red, or white aril; embryotega present.

Natural history. The flowers of Commelinaceae are nectarless, so pollen is typically the only reward for pollinators. The flowers are pollinated mainly by bees and flies or are autogamous. Buzz pollination by euglossine bees has been reported in *Dichorisandra*, which possesses anthers that dehisce through pores. The yellow moniliform hairs on the filaments of some Commelinaceae are thought to mimic masses of pollen that attract pollinators. *Callisia repens* is wind-pollinated.

The seeds of most species have no obvious means of dispersal. *Dichorisandra*, however, has seeds that are covered by an orange, red, or white aril, which are displayed prominently in the dehisced capsules still attached to the infructescences. Birds presumably eat and disperse these seeds. The fruits of *Pollia* resemble berries and also are probably bird-dispersed. Dispersal by water is likely for species of *Commelina* and *Floscopa* that grow in or alongside water. In some rosette genera, such as *Cochliostema*, seed dispersal is evidently limited, and most of the seeds and capsules are dropped alongside or within the leaf axils of the maternal plant and germinate there. This often results in dense clusters of presumably closely related individuals.

Economic uses. Some are grown as ornamentals for their delicate, yet showy flowers or their purple or varie-gated foliage. Ornamentals include species of *Commelina* (dayflower), *Tradescantia* (spiderwort, wandering-Jew, Moses-in-the-cradle, purple-heart), *Aneilema*, *Callisia*, *Cyanotis*, *Palisota*, *Siderasis*, *Tinantia*, *Dichorisandra*, *Geogenanthus* (seersucker plant), and *Cochliostema*. In the Tropics, plants sometimes are collected as fodder for domestic animals, especially at the end of the rainy season when livestock is confined because of high water. *Tradescantia* has been used in biology classes both to demonstrate cytoplasmic streaming, because the cells of the hairs on the stamen filaments are easy to mount on a microscope slide and their contents are translucent, and to teach chromosome counting because some species have low chromosome numbers and large chromosomes. It also has been used as a bioassay in the detection of a wide variety of environmental mutagens. In Japan, the blue pigment extracted from the petals of *Commelina communis* is employed as a dye. Images of *Tradescantia* sometimes appear on Japanese ceramics.

Commelinaceae in the Tropics have local medicinal uses, but none of these has been incorporated into Western pharmacopoeias. The liquid extracted from the spathes of some *Commelina* is used to treat eye infections, both in Africa and in South America, but its efficacy has not been investigated. Chimpanzees in Africa have been observed to ingest various Commelinaceae, apparently for self-medication.

The family is of no major agricultural importance, but species of *Commelina*, *Cyanotis*, *Murdannia*, and *Tradescantia* may occur as weeds among crops or in gardens. *Tradescantia fluminensis* has invaded the hammock vegetation in Florida and *Commelina benghalensis* is listed as a noxious weed by the United States Department of Agriculture.

References. BERNAL, H. Y., AND J. E. CORRERA Q. 1990. Commelinaceae. In *Especies vegetales promisorias de los países del Convenio Andrés Bello*, Tomo IV. Bogotá, D. E., Colombia: Secretaria Ejecutiva del Convenio Andrés Bello. CHASE, M. W., D. W. STEVENSON, P. WILKEN, AND P. J. RUDALL. 1995. Monocot systematics: a combined analysis. In *Monocotyledons: Systematics and Evolution*, eds. P. J. Rudall, P. J. Cribb, D. F. Cutler, and C. J. Humphries, 685–730. Richmond, Surrey, U.K.: Royal Botanic Gardens, Kew. FADEN, R. B. 1992. Floral attraction and floral hairs in the Commelinaceae. *Ann. Missouri Bot. Gard.* 79:46–52. FADEN, R. B. 1998. Commelinaceae. In *The Families and Genera of Flowering Plants*, ed. K. Kubitzki, 4:109–28. Berlin: Springer-Verlag. SIGRIST, M. R., AND M. SAZIMA. 1991. Polinização por vibração em duas espécies simpátricas de *Dichorisandra* (Commelinaceae). In *Resumos, 42nd Congresso Nacional de Botânica*, 20–26 January 1991, p. 484. Goiânia, Brasil: Universidade Federal de Goiás Sociedade Botânica do Brasil. VOGEL, S. 1978. Evolutionary shifts from reward to deception in pollen flowers. In *The Pollination of Flowers by Insects*, ed. A. J. Richards, p. 89–104. Linnean Society Symposium Series No. 6. New York: Academic Press.

CONVALLARIACEAE (Lily-of-the-Valley Family)

DENNIS WM. STEVENSON

- *herbs*

- *leaves distichous; petiole often short; blades lanceolate to ovate; venation parallel*

- *flowers with 6 tepals; stamens 6; locules 3*

- *fruits berries, red, 1–4 seeded*

Numbers of genera and species. Worldwide, the Convallariaceae comprise 17 genera and approximately 130 species. In tropical America, there is a single genus, *Maianthemum*, with eight to 10 species. Originally, all the Neotropical species were described as species of *Smilacina*; however, *Smilacina* is now included within *Maianthemum*.

Distribution and habitat. The Convallariaceae is a Northern Hemisphere family found primarily in temperate Europe, Asia, and North America. However, a few species occur in tropical to subtropical regions of India, Malesia, and Central America. In tropical America, *Maianthemum* ranges from Mexico through Guatemala and Costa Rica.

In the neotropics, the Convallariaceae generally grow at moderate elevations in the understory of cloud forests. At least two species, *M. amoenum* in Central America and *M. scilloideum* in southern Mexico, can occur as epiphytes in cloud forest.

Family classification. The Convallariaceae are placed in the Asparagales by Dahlgren et. al., in a broadly defined Liliaceae by Cronquist, and as a subfamily within the Asparagaceae by Thorne. Morphological and molecular analyses suggest that the Convallariaceae are near the Dracenaceae, Ruscaceae, and Nolinaceae, and some authors place these families in a broadly defined Ruscaceae. As treated by Dahlgren et al., the Convallariaceae contained 19 genera placed into four tribes. More recently, Conran and Tamura have limited the family to 17 genera within three tribes: Polygonateae, with four genera, including *Polygonatum* and *Maianthemum*; Ophiopogoneae, with three genera, including *Liriope* and *Ophiopogon*; and Convallarieae, with 10 genera, including *Convallaria* and *Aspidistra*. Conran and Tamura have also followed LaFrankie and included all species of *Smilacina* (false Solomon's seal) within *Maianthemum* (may lily), a conclusion supported by morphological and molecular data.

Features of the family. Habit: herbs, usually terrestrial, sometimes epiphytic, rhizomatous, the rhizomes horizontal and near surface or vertical (e.g., *Maianthemum paludicola*

in Costa Rica), the roots fibrous or tuberous, the aerial shoots annual or perennial, unbranched, determinate, with sympodial growth. **Leaves** alternate (distichous), simple; petiole usually short; blades lanceolate to ovate, the margins entire; venation parallel. **Inflorescences** terminal, racemes of cymes. **Flowers** actinomorphic, usually bisexual, sometimes unisexual (plants monoecious), erect to pendulous; tepals 6, similar, petal-like, distinct, in 2 whorls; androecium of 6 stamens, the stamens distinct, in 2 whorls, the anthers basifixed, introrse; gynoecium syncarpous, the ovary superior, the carpels 3, the locules 3, the style simple, filiform, the stigma capitate or trilobed; placentation axile, the ovules few. **Fruits** berries, red. **Seeds** 1–4 per locule, tan to pale brown.

Natural history. Nothing is known about the pollination of *Maianthemum*. Buzz pollination by bumblebees is known to occur in some species of *Polygonatum*. At least some species of the Asian *Aspidistra*, which have flowers that are subterranean or just at the soil surface, are thought to be pollinated by snails and/or slugs. One species, *A. elatior*, is pollinated by a small terrestrial crustacean (amphipod). The seeds may be dispersed by animals, which are probably consuming the red, fleshy fruits.

Economic uses. Many species in the family are used as ornamentals. *Aspidistra* (cast iron plant) is used as a pot plant; *Ophiopogon* (e.g., *O. japonicus*, lilyturf), *Liriope*, and *Convallaria* (lily-of-the-valley) are grown as outdoor ornamentals in both temperate and tropical areas; and species of *Polygonatum* (Solomon's seal) are commonly cultivated in temperate areas. The fleshy roots of *Ophiopogon* are eaten, and the roots of at least some species of *Liriope* are used medicinally. The rhizomes and young shoots of many species of *Polygonatum*, *Maianthemum*, and *Convallaria* are eaten; however, it is important to note that *C. majalis* is poisonous if ingested. Nevertheless, the rhizome of this species is used for its medicinal properties and its floral aroma is employed as a constituent of perfume.

References. CONRAN, J., AND M. TAMURA. 1998. Convallariaceae. In *The Families and Genera of Vascular Plants*, ed. K. Kubitzki, 3:186–98. New York: Springer-Verlag. LA-FRANKIE, J. V. 1985. Transfer of species of *Smilacina* to *Maianthemum* (Liliaceae). *Taxon* 35:584–89. LAFRANKIE, J. V. 1986. Morphology and taxonomy of the New World species of Maianthemum. *J. Arnold Arb.* 67:371–439. YAMASHITA, J., AND M. TAMURA. 2000. Molecular phylogeny of the Convallariaceae (Asparagales). In Monocots: Systematics and Evolution, 387–400. Melbourne: CSIRO.

CORSIACEAE (Corsia Family)

ANDREW HENDERSON AND DENNIS WM. STEVENSON

- *saprophytic herbs*

- *achlorophyllous*

- *stems unbranched*

- *leaves scalelike*

- *flowers solitary, zygomorphic; tepals 6*

Numbers of genera and species. Worldwide, the Corsiaceae comprise three genera and about 30 species. *Arachnitis* contains two species, *Corsia* about 27, and the newly described *Corsiopsis* is monospecific. In tropical America, there is a single genus, *Arachnitis*, and one species.

Distribution and habitat. *Arachnitis* occurs in Argentina, the Falkland Islands, Chile, and just reaches the neotropics in Cochabamba, Bolivia; *Corsia* is found in New Guinea, the Solomon Islands, and Australia; and *Corsiopsis* occurs in China. In Bolivia, *Arachnitis* grows in montane moist forest up to 2,500 meters; however, in Chile, it is usually found at much lower elevations.

Family classification. The Corsiaceae are placed in the Burmanniales by Dahlgren et al. This order has traditionally been associated with the Orchidales, but recent studies suggest that the two orders are not closely related. These studies also place the Corsiaceae close to Burmanniaceae. There is no subfamilial classification.

Features of the family. Habit: herbs, saprophytic, tuberous, perennial, achlorophyllous. Stems unbranched. Leaves alternate, scalelike, only on lower part of stem, amplexicaulous. Inflorescences terminal, of solitary flowers. Flowers zygomorphic, bisexual; tepals 6, distinct, red-violet, in 2 whorls, the posterior tepal of outer whorl large, enclosing other tepals in bud, the inner tepals linear; androecium of 6 stamens, the stamens in 2 whorls, the filaments short, distinct, the anthers extrorse; gynoecium syncarpous, the ovary inferior, short, the carpels 3, the locule 1, the styles short, thick, the stigmas 3; placentation parietal, the placentas slightly intruded, the ovules numerous. Fruits capsular, the aperture 1, terminal. Seeds numerous, very small, fusiform.

The tepals give the flowers a somewhat orchidlike appearance.

Natural history. The achlorophyllous Corsiaceae have mycorrhizal associations. No information is available on pollination and dispersal biology.

Economic uses. No economic uses are known for this family.

References. MINOLETTI, M. 1986. *Arachnitis uniflora* Phil.: una curiosa monocotiledónea de la flora chilena. *Bol. Soc. Biol. Concepción* 57:7–20. RASMUSSEN, F. 1995. Relationships of Burmanniales and Orchidales. In *Monocotyledons: Systematics and Evolution*, eds. P. Rudall, P. Cribb, D. Cutler, and C. Humphries, 227–41. Richmond, Surrey, U.K.: Royal Botanic Gardens, Kew. RASMUSSEN, F. 1998. Corsiaceae. In *The Families and Genera of Vascular Plants*, ed. K. Kubitzki, 3:198–201. New York: Springer-Verlag. ZHANG, D., R. SAUNDERS, AND C.-M. HU. 1999. *Corsiopsis chinensis* gen. et. sp. nov. (Corsiaceae): first record of the family in Asia. *Syst. Bot.* 24:311–14.

COSTACEAE (Costus Family)

DENNIS WM. STEVENSON AND JANICE WASSMER STEVENSON

Figure 225, Plate 56

- *herbs, rhizomatous, aerial shoot well developed, with distinct internodes*

- *leaves alternate, spiromonostichous, simple; sheath closed, ligulate*

- *inflorescence generally a terminal spike, bracts and flowers often brightly colored*

- *flowers zygomorphic; stamen 1, petal-like, the thecae 2; staminodes 5, together forming petal-like labellum; ovary inferior*

- *fruits loculicidal capsules, with persistent calyx*

- *seeds many; aril generally white*

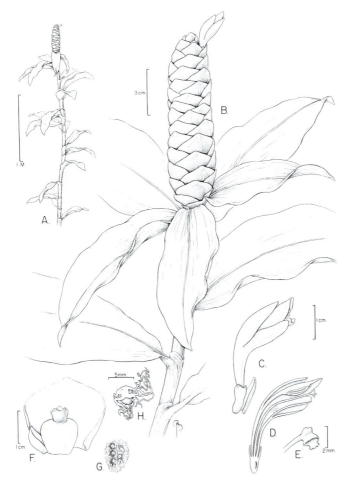

Figure 225. COSTACEAE. *Costus scaber*. **A.** Part of plant showing leaves and inflorescence. **B.** Upper part of stem with inflorescence. **C.** Lateral view of flower with subtending bract. **D.** Medial section of flower. **E.** Oblique-lateral view of stigma. **F.** Lateral view of young fruit subtended by bracts. **G.** Seeds surrounded by arils. **H.** Basal-lateral view of seed surrounded by aril. Reprinted with permission from Mori et al. (1997). Artist: Bobbi Angell.

Numbers of genera and species. Worldwide, the Costaceae comprise four genera and 100–120 species. In tropical America, there are three genera, *Costus* with 60 (ca. 90 worldwide) species, *Dimerocostus* with two species, and *Monocostus* with one species.

Distribution and habitat. The Costaceae are a pantropical family with two of the four genera, *Dimerocostus* and *Monocostus*, endemic to the neotropics. *Dimerocostus* is widespread in Central America and western South America, and *Monocostus* is endemic to eastern Peru. *Costus* is pantropical but with a majority of its species occurring in the neotropics. In the neotropics, *Costus* is represented by species in subgenera *Cadalvena* and *Costus*. A fourth genus, *Tapeinochilos*, is found in eastern Malesia to northeastern Australia, but it is sometimes cultivated in the neotropics.

The Costaceae generally grow in lowland tropical rain forest but may also occur up to 1,000(–2,000) meters in cloud forest. Species are often found at the edges of clearings, especially in areas of slash-and-burn agriculture, and a few species are found in swampy areas or along riverbanks.

Family classification. The Costaceae are placed in the Zingiberales by Dahlgren et al. Historically, the family was considered a subfamily within the Zingiberaceae but all current systems consider it a separate family closely related to the Zingiberaceae. This is supported by morphological and molecular data.

Features of the family. Habit: herbs (to 8 m), terrestrial; rhizome horizontal, branched, with short internodes (often tuberlike); aerial shoots well developed, with distinct internodes. **Leaves** alternate, spiromonostichous, simple; leaf sheath closed, ligulate. **Inflorescences** terminal on leafy shoot or sometimes on separate leafless scape, a strobilus-like spike or flowers solitary in leaf axils (*Monocostus*); bracts conspicuous, leathery, imbricate, green to bright red. **Flowers** zygomorphic, bisexual; perianth in 2 whorls of 3, often brightly colored; calyx tubular, 3-lobed; corolla much longer than calyx, the petals 3, connate at base, unequal, white, yellow, orange, or red, the lateral petals shorter than dorsal petal; androecium composed of 2 whorls of 3: stamen 1, the filament flattened, often petal-like and somewhat succulent, the anther often with connective crest, the thecae 2; staminodes 5, fused into petal-like labellum; labellum large and horizontally spreading or small and tubular; gynoecium syncarpous, the ovary inferior, 3-locular, the style 1, filiform, placed in furrow of filament and held between thecae, the stigma bifid, sometimes with dorsal appendage; septal nectaries present; placentation axile, the ovules many per locule. **Fruits** loculicidal capsules, often irregularly and tardily dehiscent, with persistent calyx. **Seeds** many, angular-ovoid, black or brown, hard, operculate; aril present, white to yellow.

Natural history. In *Dimerocostus* and species of *Costus* with short, wide floral tubes, a white to yellow, often red-striped labellum, and green bracts pollination is by euglossine bees. Neotropical species of *Costus* with narrow, thick-walled floral tubes and red bracts are pollinated by hummingbirds. The pollinators are attracted to the flowers by nectar secreted by the septal nectaries into the tubular perianth.

As the fruits ripen, the bracts of several species of Costus spread out, exposing the white capsules against the red inner side of the bracts. These species are probably dispersed by birds. In *Monocostus uniflorus* and species of *Costus* subgenus *Cadalvena*, the fruiting pedicels elongate, thereby exposing the fruits beyond the bracts. The seeds are held together by their arils and discharged explosively as a unit. In some species of Costaceae found in temporarily inundated areas or along stream banks, the seeds are apparently water-dispersed.

Economic uses. *Costus* has beautiful inflorescences and flowers, and, therefore, species are cultivated as ornamentals in the Tropics and in temperate greenhouses. The stems of species of Costus are sucked for their sour sap; hence the name *cana agria*. The exudate of the stems of *Dimerocostus* is used to treat kidney ailments, *Costus spicatus* is known for its diuretic properties, and extracts from other species of *Costus* are used to cure various kinds of infections. The rhizomes of *C. speciosus* are used locally as a starch source, and the large, succulent flowers of some species are sometimes used locally in salads.

References. KRESS, J. 1990. The phylogeny and classification of the Zingiberales. *Ann. Missouri Bot. Gard.* 77: 698–721. LARSEN, K. 1998. Costaceae. In *The Families and Genera of Vascular Plants*, ed. K. Kubitzki, 4:128–32. New York: Springer-Verlag. MAAS, P.J.M. 1972. Costoideae (Zingiberaceae). *Fl. Neotrop. Monogr.* 8:1–139. MAAS, P.J.M. 1977. Costoideae (Additions). *Fl. Neotrop. Monogr.* 18:162–218. TOMLINSON, P. 1969. Commelinales-Zingiberales. In *Anatomy of the Monocotyledons*, ed. C. R. Metcalfe, Vol. 3. Oxford, U.K.: Clarendon Press.

CYCLANTHACEAE (Cyclanth or "Panama" Hat Family)

HANS T. BECK

Figure 226, Plate 57

- *usually epiphytic herbs or root-climbing lianas, less frequently terrestrial herbs*

- *leaves alternate (spiral or distichous), simple; blades usually bifid, sometimes fan or palmlike; venation parallel or parallel-pinnate*

- *inflorescences spadices, subtended by bracts*

- *flowers unisexual (plants monoecious); staminodes often filiform*

- *fruits indehiscent, fleshy, often coalescent, forming syncarps*

Numbers of genera and species. Endemic to tropical America, the Cyclanthaceae comprise 12 genera and 180 species. *Asplundia* (80–82 species), *Dicranopygium* (40–44 species), and *Sphaeradenia* (38–40 species) are the largest genera. The remaining genera are *Stelestylis* (4 species), *Carludovica* (3 species), *Ludovia* (2 species), *Cyclanthus* (2 species), and the monotypic *Evodianthus, Dianthoveus, Thoracocarpus, Pseudoludovia*, and *Schultesiophytum*.

Distribution and habitat. The Cyclanthaceae occur throughout the neotropics in moist or wet forest or along streams. Species diversity is greatest below 1,500 meters in coastal, montane, and Amazonian habitats. In the Andes, some species of *Sphaeradenia* are found up to 3,000 meters. Many species are endemic to lowland and cloud forests in northwestern South America.

Family classification. The Cyclanthaceae are placed in the monofamilial Cyclanthales by Dahlgren et al.

There are two subfamilies, the Cyclanthoideae containing only *Cyclanthus*, and the Carludovicoideae. The fundamental distinction between the subfamilies rests on flower, fruit, and leaf-blade structure. In *Cyclanthus*, the inflorescences are composed of alternating circular bands of staminate and pistillate flowers; the flowers are not distinct; and the leaves are bifid, with each segment possessing a strongly developed midrib. In contrast, genera of the Carludovicoideae have inflorescences with spirally arranged flowers; the flowers are distinct with a single pistillate flower surrounded by four male flowers; and the leaves are palmately divided, entire, or bifid, and without a strongly pronounced midrib.

Although the Cyclanthaceae possess leaves similar to those of the Arecaceae, their thick-spicate, unbranched inflorescence (spadix), four-sided female flowers surrounded by male flowers, and syncarpic fruits are unlike those of any palm. Based on molecular date, the Cyclanthaceae are more closely related to the Pandanaceae (screw pines).

Features of the family. Habit: perennial rhizomatous herbs or root-climbing lianas, sometimes shrubs, often epiphytic, less frequently terrestrial. **Stipules** absent. **Leaves** alternate (spiral or less commonly distichous); petioles long, the base

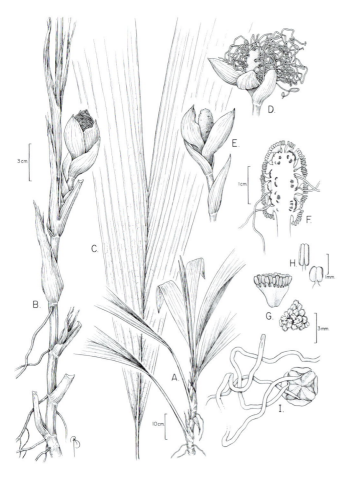

Figure 226. CYCLANTHACEAE. *Asplundia heteranthera*. **A.** Part of stem showing adventitious roots and leaves. **B.** Stem showing adventitious roots and position of inflorescence. **C.** Basal part of leaf. **D.** Lateral view of inflorescence showing long staminodes. **E.** Lateral view of inflorescence after staminodes have fallen; note subtending bracts. **F.** Medial section of inflorescence. **G.** Lateral (above) and apical (below) views of staminate flowers. **H.** Adaxial (above) and abaxial (below) veiws of stamens. **I.** Apical view of pistallate flower showing stigmatic lines and long staminodes. Reprinted with permission from Mori et al. (1997). Artist: Bobbi Angell.

fragrance; gynoecium syncarpous, the ovary half-inferior or inferior, rarely superior, the carpels 4, the locule 1, the style absent or 1, short when present, the stigmas 1–4, very broad; placentation parietal with 4 placentas or apical, the ovules numerous. **Fruits** indehiscent, fleshy, often coalescent, forming syncarps. **Seeds** few to numerous, small; endosperm copious, the embryo small.

Natural history. The flowers of Cyclanthaceae, many of which open at night, are pollinated mostly by beetles. The long staminodia are responsible for emitting aromas that attract the pollinators. Fruit dispersal is often accomplished by birds, bats, or monkeys.

Economic uses. Petiole fibers and older leaves of *Carludovica palmata* are used in basketry and mats, whereas young leaf fibers are woven to make the famous "Panama" hats of Ecuador. Each hat is made from approximately six young leaves, and more than one million hats are exported from Ecuador per year. *Carludovica angustifolia* and *C. sarmentosa* are utilized for making thatched roofs and brooms, respectively. Stems and roots of epiphytic lianas (e.g., species of *Thoracocarpus*), are frequently used by indigenous groups for bindings, in plaited handicrafts, and for making hunting traps. Other species, especially, *Carludovica palmata*, are planted as ornamentals.

References. ACOSTA SOLÍS, M. 1952. *Las fibras y lanas vegetales en el Ecuador*. Quito: Edit. casa de la Cultura Ecuatoriana. DUVALL, M. R., M. T. CLEGG, M. W. CHASE, W. D. CLARK, W. J., KRESS, et al. 1993. Phylogenetic hypotheses for the monocotyledons constructed from *rbc*L sequence data. *Ann. Missouri Bot. Gard.* 80:607–19. HAMMEL, B. E., AND G. J. WILDER. 1989. *Dianthoveus*: a new genus of Cyclanthaceae. *Ann. Missouri Bot. Gard.* 76:112–23. HANNAN, W. 1902. *The Textile Fibres of Commerce. A Handbook on the Occurrence, Distribution, Preparation, and Uses of the Animal, Vegetable, and Mineral Fibres Used in Cotton, Woollen, Paper, Silk, Brush, and Hat Manufactures*. London: C. Griffin. HARLING, G. 1958. Monograph of the Cyclanthaceae. *Acta Horti Berg.* 18:1–428. HARLING, G. 1973. Cyclanthaceae. In *Flora of Ecuador*, eds. G. Harling and B. Sparre, *Opera Botanica* ser. B, no. 1:1–47. Göteborg, Sweden: Department of Systematic Botany, University of Göteborg. JORGENSEN, P. M., AND S. LEÓN-YÁNEX, eds. 1999. Catalogue of the vascular plants of Ecuador. *Monogr. Syst. Bot. Missouri Bot. Gard.* 75:1–1181. VASQUEZ, M. R. 1997. Flórula de las Reservas Biológicas de Iquitos, Perú. *Monogr. Syst. Bot. Missouri Bot. Gard.* 63:1–1046. WENDLAND, H. 1854. *Index Palmarum*. Hannoverae: In Libraria Aulica Hahnii.

sheathing; blades often plicate, usually bifid, sometimes fan or palmlike, or seldom simple and entire; venation parallel or parallel-pinnate. **Inflorescences** terminal or lateral, spadices; 2–several bracts or spathes subtending spadix, these often caducous, the flowers arranged in circular, alternating bands of staminate and pistillate flowers (Cyclanthoideae) or in spirally arranged pistillate flowers surrounded by staminate flowers (Carludovicoideae). **Flowers** actinomorphic, unisexual (plants monoecious). **Staminate flowers:** tepals (0)6; stamens 6–many, the filaments connate at base. **Pistillate flowers:** tepals 0–4; staminodes 4, often filiform, white, with sweet

CYMODOCEACEAE (Manatee-grass Family)

Dennis Wm. Stevenson

Figure 227

- *herbaceous, submerged marine aquatics growing in shallow waters*

- *leaves alternate (distichous), simple*

- *flowers unisexual (plants dioecious); perianth absent; stamens 2, partially fused back to back*

- *fruits indehiscent, small; endocarp stony*

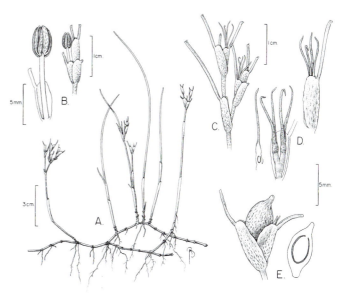

Figure 227. CYMODOCEACEAE. *Syringodium filiforme*. **A.** Plant showing roots, leaves, and inflorescences. **B.** Stamen subtended by bract (left) and part of staminate inflorescence (right). **C.** Pistillate inflorescence. **D.** Medial section of gynoecium (left), lateral view pistillate flower with part of bract removed (middle), and lateral view of intact pistillate flower (right). **E.** Fruit subtended by bract (left) and medial section of fruit (right). Reprinted with permission from Acevedo-Rodríguez (1996). Artist: Bobbi Angell.

Numbers of genera and species. Worldwide, the Cymodoceaceae comprise five genera and 16 species. Of these, two genera, *Halodule* and *Syringodium*, and four species occur in the waters of tropical America.

Distribution and habitat. In general, the family occurs in shallow coastal waters of subtropical and tropical regions. However, *Amphibolis* is restricted to temperate waters of Australia (including Tasmania). Species of *Cymodocea* are disjunct among the East Atlantic and Mediterranean, the Indo-Pacific, and western Australia; *Syringodium* consists of two disjunct species, one in the Caribbean and the other widely distributed in the Indo-Pacific region. *Halodule* is pantropical, with three species endemic to the Western Hemisphere and three others endemic to the Eastern Hemisphere.

The Cymodoceaceae can form extensive submarine meadows in shallow, clear waters with minimal wave action.

Family classification. The Cymodoceaceae are placed in the Najadales by Dahlgren et al. as well as by Cronquist. As a result of recent morphological and molecular studies, however, the Cymodoceaceae are now placed in an expanded Alismatales, which includes both the Najadales and Hydrocharitales. The familial relationships of families within this expanded Alismatales are still unresolved, but it is clear that the previous orders are not monophyletic as circumscribed.

The family has been divided into two apparently monophyletic groups. The first, comprised of *Cymodocea*, *Halodule*, and *Syringodium*, has monopodial, herbaceous rhizomes, and stalked staminate flowers. In contrast, the second, containing *Amphibolis* and *Thalassodendron*, has sympodial, sclerified rhizomes, and sessile, staminate flowers.

Features of the family. Habit: herbs, marine aquatics, submerged, perennial; rhizomes present, creeping. **Leaves** alternate (distichous), simple, with open basal sheath and small ligule, numerous axillary intravaginal squamules present; stomates and trichomes absent. **Inflorescences** borne at end of short, erect shoots, usually of solitary flowers, rarely in cymes. **Flowers** unisexual (plants dioecious); perianth absent. **Staminate flowers:** sessile or stalked; androecium with 2 stamens, the stamens partially fused back to back, each with apical prolongation. **Pistillate flowers:** gynoecium apocarpous, the ovaries superior, the carpels 2, the styles long, slender, often branched, the stigmas inconspicuous in *Halodule* or of 2 stigmatic, stout stylodia in *Syringodium*; placentation apical the ovules 1 per carpel. **Fruits** indehiscent, small; endocarp stony.

Natural history. The pollination biology of Cymodoceaceae has been studied extensively, particularly in Australian species. When released into water, the hydrophobic pollen grains join together into rafts or chains up to 1 millimeter long before being trapped by the branched styles of the pistillate flowers. The nature of the stony endocarp of most species indicates an ability to remain dormant for some time, thus aiding in water dispersal. However, genera such as *Thalassodendron* and *Amphibolis* have scanty seed coats, germinate directly on the parent plant, and are released as seedlings after embryo development.

Economic uses. Species of Cymodoceaceae are important in the stabilization of shallow marine sediments, nutrient recycling, and as food sources for grazing marine animals.

References. Cox, P. A., and C. J. Humphries. 1993. Hygrophilous pollination and breeding system evolution in seagrasses: a phylogenetic approach to the evolutionary ecology of the Cymodoceaceae. *Bot. J. Linn. Soc.* 113:217–26. Hartog, C. den. 1970. The sea-grasses of the world. *Verhandl. Kon. Ned. Akad. Wetensch. Nat.* 59(1): 1–275. Kuo, J., and A. McComb. 1998. Cymodoceaceae. In *The Families and Genera of Vascular Plants*, ed. K. Kubitzki, 4:133–40. New York: Springer-Verlag. Tomlinson, P. B. 1982. Helobiae (Alismatidae). In *Anatomy of the Monocotyledons.* 7:1–522. Oxford, U.K.: Clarendon Press.

CYPERACEAE (Sedge Family)

Wm. Wayt Thomas

Figure 228, Plate 57

- *grasslike herbs*
- *culms usually trigonous, solid*
- *leaves usually 3-ranked; leaf sheaths closed*
- *perianth absent or of 3-many bristles or scales*
- *fruits achenes or achenelike*

Numbers of genera and species. Worldwide, the Cyperaceae comprise 60 genera and about 5,300 species. In tropical America, there are 40 genera and about 1,000 species. The largest genus, *Carex*, has about 2,000 species worldwide. In the neotropics, the largest genera are *Rhynchospora* (250 species), *Carex* (200), *Cyperus* (150), *Eleocharis* (60), *Scleria* (60), and *Bulbostylis* (50).

Distribution and habitat. The Cyperaceae are cosmopolitan. Some large genera are most diverse in temperate regions (i.e., *Carex*) while others are predominantly tropical (i.e., *Cyperus* and *Rhynchospora*).

Sedges occur in almost all Neotropical habitats and can be dominant or of great ecological importance in: marshes and other open wetlands such as the Pantanal of Brazil and the *llanos* of Venezuela; grasslands such as the *cerrado* of Brazil; savannas throughout tropical America; and open, high-altitude vegetation such as the *páramos* of the Andes, the *tepui* summits of the Guayana Highland, and the *campos rupestres* and *campos de altitude* of Brazil.

Family classification. While the resemblance of Cyperaceae to the Poaceae and Juncaceae has been noted for years, the relationships among the three families has been in dispute. Cronquist believed that their vegetative similarity, the unilocular and uniovulate ovary, and the compatible chemistry argued for the grasses and sedges to be placed together in a single order, the Cyperales, within the subclass Commelinidae.

Most others, notably Dahlgren et al., believe that common

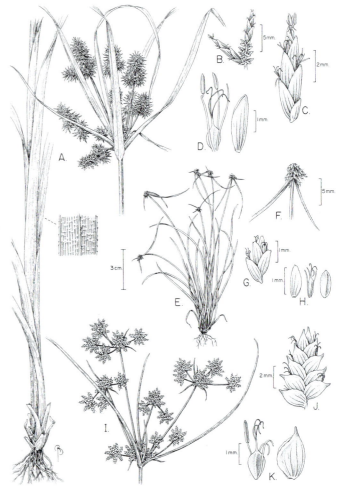

Figure 228. CYPERACEAE. *Cyperus ligularis* (A–D), *C. nanus* (E–H), and *C. elegans* (I–K). **A.** Base of plant showing roots and leaf bases (left), detail of abaxial leaf blade surface (middle), and inflorescence (right). **B.** Part of inflorescence showing spikelets. **C.** Lateral view of spikelet. **D.** Lateral view of flower (left) and lateral view of subtending scale (right). **E.** Plant showing roots, leaves, and inflorescences. **F.** Inflorescence. **G.** Lateral view of spikelet. **H.** Lateral view of scale (left), flower (center), and fruit (right). **I.** Inflorescence with spikelets. **J.** Lateral view of spikelet. **K.** Lateral views of flower (left) and scale (right). Reprinted with permission from Acevedo-Rodríguez (1996). Artist: Bobbi Angell.

characters—including tristichous leaves, paracytic stomates, pollen tetrads, diffuse centromeres, Onagrad-type embryo development, and shared fungal parasites—support the grouping of the Cyperaceae with the Juncaceae and the closely related Thurniaceae in the order Cyperales within a superorder Commeliniflorae. Recent DNA molecular studies by Chase et al. support a close relationship with the Juncaceae.

Interpretation of morphology and homologies of structures are difficult because of the reduced flowers and the highly condensed and often complex inflorescences. Some authors have even viewed the unisexual flowers and partial inflorescence of *Hypolytrum* (and related genera) as evidence of a relationship to Pandanales; following this logic, the apparently simple, bisexual flowers of genera such as *Rhynchospora* and *Cyperus* were interpreted as synanthia. Recent studies, however, show that such a relationship is highly unlikely and support the conclusions of most earlier cyperologists that unisexual flowers in Cyperaceae are derived from bisexual flowers such as are found in Juncaceae.

The reduced flowers and condensed spikes and the resulting differences in morphological interpretation have led to many alternative classifications within the family. The recent classifications of Goetghebeur and Bruhl have many tribes in common and are, in large part, bolstered by the phylogenetic study of *rbc*L DNA of Cyperaceae carried out by Musaya et al. Nevertheless, it is clear that much work needs to be accomplished before relationships among the genera of Cyperaceae are established. Some genera with complex, reduced spikes, and unisexual flowers such as *Hypolytrum* and *Mapania* form a group (corresponding to Goetghebeur's Mapanioideae or Bruhl's Hypolytreae) that is sister to the rest of the Cyperaceae and probably deserves recognition at the subfamilial level. While the balance of the family could be recognized as comprising one subfamily, Goetghebeur recognized four subfamilies, Mapanioideae, Cyperoideae, Sclerioideae, and Caricoideae. Musaya et al. also recognized four "supratribal" groups: a group corresponding to the Mapanioideae as defined above, a group corresponding to Goetghebeur's Sclerioideae (including *Scleria, Becquerelia, Cladium,* and *Schoenus*), a diverse group comprising genera from various tribes (including *Rhynchospora, Carex, Fimbristylis, Eleocharis, Bulbostylis,* and *Isolepis*), and a terminal group comprised primarily of the broadly defined genus *Cyperus* along with *Ascolepis* and *Lipocarpha*.

Although the *Cyperus* group of Musaya et al. is very distinct, their data indicate that the more narrowly defined generic segregates of *Cyperus* (i.e., *Mariscus, Pycreus,* and *Torulinium*) may not be distinct, supporting the taxonomic conclusions of Tucker. Traditionally, the genus *Scirpus* has comprised a heterogeneous group of species. Some researchers, including Van der Veken, believed that the genus was polyphyletic and should be broken up; this view is supported by the work of Musaya et al. Neotropical genera that previously were referred to *Scirpus* include *Bolboschoenus, Isolepis, Oxycaryum, Schoenoplectus, Scirpus sensu stricto,* and *Websteria*.

Features of the family. Habit: grasslike herbs, usually erect or arching, rarely fully submersed aquatics (*Websteria*), or scandent (*Scleria secans*), annual or perennial, caespitose or rhizomatous. **Culms** usually trigonous, solid. **Leaves** basal or cauline, usually 3-ranked, comprising a closed sheath and blade; blades linear to elliptic, occasionally absent (as in *Eleocharis* and a few species of other genera); ligule seldom well-developed (except in some *Carex* and *Scleria*). **Inflorescences** terminal or axillary, panicles, corymbs, clusters, anthelae, or heads, composed of simple spikelets or compound spikes, comprising two or more branching orders within the usually reduced spikelike structure, the simple spikelets with few to many scales (glumes), spirally (e.g., *Bulbostylis, Eleocharis,* and *Rhynchospora*) or distichously (e.g., *Cyperus*) arranged, each scale usually subtending a bisexual flower, the compound spikes (as found in *Hypolytrum, Mapania,* and *Trilepis*) with few to many scales, usually spirally arranged, each scale usually subtending a reduced simple spikelet, the spikelets usually comprising various arrangements of unisexual flowers and their subtending reduced scales; leafy bracts often present, subtending inflorescence. **Flowers** reduced, bisexual or unisexual (then plants mostly monoecious); perianth absent or of 3–many bristles or small scales; androecium usually of 1–3 stamens; gynoecium syncarpous, the ovary superior, the carpels usually 2 or 3, the locule 1, the style short to elongate, the basal portion sometimes persistent, the stigma usually 2 or 3 branched; placentation centrally basal, the ovule 1, anatropous. **Fruits** achenes or achenelike, the style forming a "beak" on fruit (e.g., *Rhynchospora* and *Eleocharis*) when persistent. **Seeds** embedded in endosperm.

In general, bisexual flowers are found in genera with simple spikelets and unisexual flowers are found in genera with compound spikes.

The achenelike fruits are interpreted as comprising a perigynium surrounding and adnate to an achene.

Natural history. In general, pollination of Cyperaceae is accomplished by wind. Species that occur in open areas and have open inflorescences and exserted anthers probably are wind-pollinated; however, many species occur in forests where wind velocities are greatly diminished, and many species of open areas have capitate inflorescences or anthers that are exserted only partially from the spikelet. These species may rely all or in part on insect pollination, and this has been suggested for species of at least 11 genera.

Seeds of aquatic sedges are dispersed by flotation or by animals, particularly waterfowl. Terrestrial species may have seeds dispersed by wind, by attachment to passing animals, or by ingestion and passage through the digestive tracts of animals. Achenes of at least one species of *Rhynchospora* have been observed to be dispersed by ants; it is possible that the persistent style base functions as an elaiosome.

Economic uses. *Cyperus papyrus* (native to the Nile Valley and central Africa), now used horticulturally, is historically important because of its early use in paper making. The Chinese water chestnut, *Eleocharis dulcis* (paleotropics), is farmed commercially. Some sedges, such as the nutgrass, *Cyperus rotundus* (probably native to the paleotropics), are noxious weeds.

In general, however, the economic importance of sedges is less conspicuous. They are used locally in the neotropics in basketry, for making mats, as saddle padding, and to stuff mattresses. Tender shoots of *Cladium jamaicense* have provided as an emergency food source. Many species have medicinal value: Decoctions of several species of *Cyperus*, *Eleocharis*, and *Fimbristylis* are used to alleviate stomach troubles from diarrhea to seasickness; infusions of species of *Bulbostylis*, *Cyperus*, *Fuirena*, and *Rhynchospora*, have been utilized to combat sunstroke; and plants of *Bulbostylis capillaris* are sold to cure venereal disease. Plants of western Amazonian species of *Cyperus*, known as *piri piri*, are sometimes infected by the Ascomycete fungus, *Balansia*. These sterile plants are cultivated by indigenous tribes and the plants, when infected by certain fungi, are used as abortifacients, birth-control agents, and hallucinogens.

Several species of Cyperaceae are used in magical or religious ceremonies. *Piri piri* is supposed to control the souls of the dead and to bring luck in hunting and in love. Plants of certain common species of *Cyperus*, *Rhynchospora*, and *Scleria* are components of Candomblé potions and ceremonies in eastern Brazil.

This ecological importance of Cyperaceae extends beyond biomass and diversity and can influence many levels in the food chain. A study of a Texas marsh showed that three species of Cyperaceae (*Bolboschoenus robustus*, *Cladium jamaicense*, and *Rhynchospora corniculata*) annually produced more than 2,000 kilograms per hectare of seeds, which provided an important part of the diet of many waterfowl.

References. BRUHL, J. J. 1995. Sedge genera of the world: relationships and a new classification of the Cyperaceae. *Austral. Syst. Bot.* 8:125–305. CHASE, M. W., et al. 2000. Higher-level systematics of the monocotyledons: an assessment of current knowledge and new classification. In *Monocots: Systematics and Evolution*, eds. K. L. Wilson and D. A. Morrison, 3–16. Collingwood, Australia: CSIRO. CLARKE, C. B. 1908. New genera and species of Cyperaceae. *Bull. Misc. Inf., Kew*, Add. Ser. 8:1–196. EITEN, L. T. 1976. Inflorescence units in the Cyperaceae. *Ann. Missouri Bot. Gard.* 63:81–112. GOETGHEBEUR, P. 1986. Genera Cyperacearum. Dr. Sci. Thesis, State Univ. Ghent. KOYAMA, T. 1961. Classification of the family Cyperaceae (1). *J. Fac. Sci. Univ. Tokyo* III 8: 37–81. MORTON, J. F. 1981. *Atlas of Medicinal Plants of Middle America*. Springfield, IL: Charles C. Thomas Publ. MUSAYA, A. M., J. J. BRUHL, D. A. SIMPSON, A. CULHAM, AND M. W. CHASE. 2000. Suprageneric phylogeny of Cyperaceae: a combined analysis. In *Monocots: Systematics and Evolution*, eds. K. L. Wilson and D. A. Morrison, 593–601. Collingwood, Australia: CSIRO. RAMEY, V. 1999. Wildlife, wetlands, and those "other plants." *Aquaphyte* 19(1): 1–5. THOMAS, W. W. 1984. The systematics of *Rhynchospora* section *Dichromena*. *Mem. New York Bot. Gard.* 37: 1–116. TUCKER, G. C. 1994. Revision of the Mexican species of *Cyperus* (Cyperaceae). *Syst. Bot. Monogr.* 43: 1–213. VAN DER VEKEN, P. 1965. Contribution à l'embryographie systématique des Cyperaceae-Cyperoideae. *Bull. Jard. Bot. État* 35: 285–354.

DIOSCOREACEAE (Dioscorea Family)

OSWALDO TÉLLEZ-VALDÉS

Figure 229, Plate 57

- *usually vines or lianas*

- *leaves alternate, simple or compound; blades generally cordate; venation campylodromous or actinodromous, the lateral veins anastomosing*

- *flowers with 3 or 6 stamens; staminodia 0, 3, or 6*

- *fruits capsules or samaras*

Numbers of genera and species. Worldwide, the Dioscoreaceae comprise nine genera and 850–900 species. The largest genera are *Dioscorea* with about 800–850 species and *Rajania* with 25 species. The other genera, with five or fewer species each, are *Avetra* (1 species), *Borderea* (2), *Epipetrum* (3) *Hyperocarpa* (3), *Nanarepenta* (5), *Stenomeris* (2), and *Tamus* (5). Only *Dioscorea*, *Epipetrum*, *Hyperocarpa*, *Nanarepenta*, and *Rajania* occur in the Western Hemisphere. With the exception of *Epipetrum*, all genera in the Western Hemisphere and about 430 species occur in the Tropics. However, there are 450 species of *Dioscorea* in the Western Hemisphere, with 35 sections in South America (e.g., Brazil has ca. 250 species and Peru ca. 80 species), three sections in the West Indies, and about 15 sections (95 species) in Mexico and Central America.

Distribution and habitat. The Dioscoreaceae inhabit tropical regions of the world. A few species reach subtropical areas in the United States and other areas of Europe and

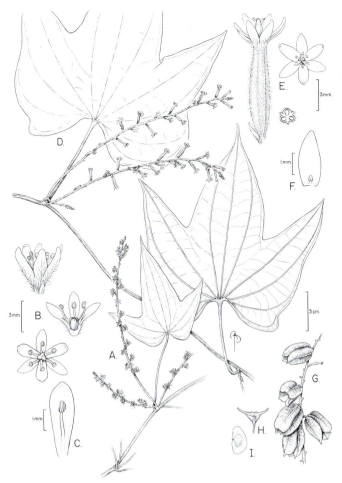

Figure 229. DIOSCOREACEAE. *Dioscorea trifida*. **A.** Stem with leaf and staminate inflorescences. **B.** Lateral (above), lateral with part of perianth removed (middle), and apical (below) views of staminate flowers. **C.** Adaxial view of petal from staminate flower with adnate stamen. **D.** Stem with leaves and pistillate inflorescences. **E.** Lateral (left) and apical (right) views of pistillate flowers and transverse section of ovary (below). **F.** Adaxial view of petal from pistillate flower with vestigial stamen. **G.** Fruits. **H.** Basal view of fruit. **I.** Winged seed. Reprinted with permission from Mori et al. (1997). Artist: Bobbi Angell.

4,200 meters in the Andes, where they are dwarf or prostrate subshrubs (e.g., *Dioscorea ancachsensis* and *D. weberbaueri*).

Family classification. The Dioscoreaceae are placed in the Dioscoreales with families such as the Smilacaceae by Dahlgren et al. However, morphological and molecular data suggest that this order is not monophyletic.

The family is divided into two subfamilies: Dioscoreidoideae and Stenomeridoideae. The Dioscoreidoideae comprise *Borderea*, *Dioscorea*, *Epipetrum*, *Hyperocarpa*, *Nanarepenta*, *Rajania* and *Tamus*, while the Stenomeridoideae is composed solely of *Avetra* and *Stenomeris*. It has been suggested that the genera of the latter subfamily should be treated as separate monogeneric families.

Features of the family. Habit: vines or lianas, occasionally prostrate or erect subshrubs; rhizomes and tubers (the tubers apparently more common in Eastern Hemisphere) present, these sometimes splitting (a form of vegetative reproduction); stems glabrous or pubescent, smooth, occasionally winged, spiny or nonspiny, sometimes with axillary bulbils. Stipules spinescent or foliaceous when present. Leaves alternate, simple or compound; petioles usually long; blades generally cordate, the margins entire or palmately lobate; venation usually campylodromous, or actinodromous, the lateral veins anastomosing; trichomes present, unicellular, glandular, simple, hooked, malphigiaceous, or stellate. Inflorescences axillary or rarely terminal, spikes, racemes, panicles, or cymes, generally with numerous flowers; bracts 2 (1 external and 1 internal, the latter sometimes considered a bracteole). Flowers actinomorphic or rarely zygomorphic, unisexual (plants dioecious or rarely monoecious) or very rarely bisexual, generally small (1–4 mm, although 3 cm in *Dioscorea insignis* from Mexico); tepals 6, distinct or connate, in two whorls; androecium with 6 stamens, the stamens in 2 whorls, the filaments distinct, connate at base, or fused into column, the anthers introrse or extrorse, dehiscing longitudinally; staminodia sometimes present; gynoecium syncarpous, the ovary inferior, the carpels 3, the locules 3, the styles 3, distinct or connate at base, the stigmas 3–6; septate nectaries usually present; placentation axile, the ovules 1 or 4 per locule, anatropous. Fruits capsules or samaras (*Rajania*), the capsules generally dry (*Dioscorea*, *Epipetrum*, and *Hyperocarpa*) or fleshy (*Nanarepenta*). Seeds usually 6 (2 per locule), 1 in *Rajania*, or 12 in *Dioscorea* section *Higinbothamia*, flat (*Dioscorea* and *Hyperocarpa*), ellipsoid (*Nanarepenta*), subsquare (*Epipetrum*), or triangular (*Rajania*), semismooth or reticulate, usually winged, sometimes wingless; embryo small, well differentiated, with a wide subterminal plumule.

Different sexual behaviors occur among species of Dioscoreaceae. For example, *Dioscorea galeottiana* from Mexico, traditionally described as a species with three stamens, produces flowers with 3–6 stamens in the same inflorescence. Diverse species in *Dioscorea* (e.g., *D. convolvulacea*, *D. lepida*, and *D. liebmannii*) can be dioecious and/or monoecious, or, on occasion, the same individual can behave as

Asia. In the Southern Hemisphere, they reach Argentina and Chile, Africa, Australia, and New Zealand. The majority of the genera are endemic to small regions, and only *Dioscorea* is pantropical.

Although *Dioscorea* has a wide distribution, many have limited ranges, for example, 65 percent of the Mexican species are endemic. *Epipetrum* grows in the Chilean Andes; *Hyperocarpa* in western Mexico, Brazil, and Argentina; *Nanarepenta* is endemic to western Mexico; and *Rajania* is endemic to the Caribbean Islands.

The Dioscoreaceae occur in semidesert, temperate, and tropical zones. The family is most abundant, however, in tropical forests where some species grow into the canopy. Numerous species occur at low elevations, but some reach male during one season and as a female the next (*D. lepida*). Bisexual flowers may occur in *D. omiltemensis*.

Natural history. Traditionally, pollination was thought to be by the wind; nevertheless, several species in different genera possess nectar, a light, sweet scent, and brightly colored perianths, anthers, or pollen; features that are generally associated with insect pollination. Bees, thrips, and flies have been observed visiting species of *Dioscorea*, *Nanarepenta*, and *Borderea pyrenaica*, also visited by the same insects, has been reported to be pollinated by ants.

Dispersal of fruits and seeds is mainly by the wind. For example, species of *Dioscorea* have capsules and species of *Rajania* have samaras. Some species of *Dioscorea* have winged seeds, but *Rajania* and other species of *Dioscorea* have wingless seeds. In *Epipetrum*, *Hyperocarpa*, and *Nanarepenta*, dispersal is by gravity, and, therefore, the seeds are not dispersed far from the mother plant.

Economic uses. *Dioscorea alata* (greater yam) and *D. bulbifera* (air-potato, bitter yam, aerial yam) are important edible species worldwide. Although all genera possess rhizomes, the only ones called yams, *names*, and *barbascos* are species of *Dioscorea*. *Dioscorea composita*, *D. floribunda*, *D. gomez-pompae*, *D. mexicana*, and *D. spiculiflora* are the principal sources of steroid compounds (e.g., diosgenin, criptogenin, tokorogenin, and yamogenin) used in the manufacture of hormonal medicines, including birth-control pills. Some American species of *Dioscorea* are of medicinal value; e.g., the tubers of *D. alata* are used to treat tumors, the rhizomes of *D. convolvulacea* provide treatment for abscesses and furuncles, and the rhizomes of *D. composita*, *D. spiculiflora*, and *D. floribunda* are used to treat rheumatism and

sciatica. Extracts from the leaves of *D. convolvulacea* are used as a diuretic, for treating fevers, itching, headaches, dermatitis, and eye infections, and extracts from leaves of *D. mexicana* are used for treating rheumatoid fever.

References. AL-SHEHBAZ, I., AND B. SCHUBERT. 1989. The Dioscoreaceae in the southeastern United States. *J. Arnold Arbor.* 70:57–95. CLARKE, G., AND M. JONES. 1981. The Northwest European Pollen Flora, 23. Dioscoreaceae. *Rev. Paleobot. and Palynol.* 33:45–50. CORRERA Q., J. E., AND H. Y. BERNAL. 1992. Dioscoreaceae. In *Especies vegetales promisorias de los países del Convenio Andrés Bello*, Tomo VII. Santafé de Bogotá, D. E., Colombia: Secretaria Ejecutiva del Convenio Andrés Bello. ERDTMAN, G. 1952. *Pollen Morphology and Plant Taxonomy.* Waltham, MA: Chronica Botanica Co. GARCIA, B., R. ANTOR, AND X. ESPADALER. 1995. Ant pollination of the palaeoendemic dioecious *Borderea pyrenaica* (Dioscoreaceae). *Pl. Syst. Evol.* 198:17–27. GAUSSEN, H. 1965. Revision de *Dioscorea* (*Borderea*) Pyreneens. *Bull. Soc. Hist. Nat. Toulouse* 100:383–99. HUBER, H. 1998. Dioscoreaceae. In *The Families and Genera of Vascular Plants*, ed. K. Kubitzki, 3:216–35. Berlin: Springer-Verlag. JAYASURIYA, A. 1983. A systematic revision of the genus *Dioscorea* (Dioscoreaceae) in the Indian subcontinent. Ph.D. thesis, City N.Y. University. KNUTH, R. 1924. Dioscoreaceae. In *Das Pflanzenreich*, ed. A. Engler, series 4, 43(heft 87):1–388. Berlin: Wilhelm Engelmann. MATUDA, E. 1974. Nueva *Nanarepenta* de Guerrero. *Cact. Suc. Mex.* 19(3):70–71. SCHUBERT, B. 1968. *Aspects of Taxonomy in the Genus Dioscorea.* Publ. Especial 8. Mexico, D.F.: Inst. Nac. Inv. Forestales. ZAVADA, M. 1983. Comparative morphology of monocot pollen and evolutionary trends in apertures and wall structures. *Bot. Rev.* 49(4):331–79.

DRACAENACEAE (Dragon-tree Family)

DENNIS WM. STEVENSON

- *shrubs or rhizomatous herbs*

- *stems of shrubs with distinct vascular bundles, the bundles embedded within fibrous matrix as seen in transverse section*

- *leaves alternate, borne in rosettes, simple; blades distinctly cross-banded (Sansevieria)*

- *flowers with 6 tepals; stamens 6; locules 3*

- *fruits berries with thin fleshy layer, orange*

Numbers of genera and species. Worldwide, the Dracaenaceae comprise two genera, *Dracaena* (60 species, including *Pleomele*) and *Sansevieria* (approximately 100). In tropi-

cal America, only *Dracaena americana* is native. Several species of *Sansevieria* have become naturalized after escape from cultivation.

Distribution and habitat. The Dracaenaceae are found mainly in the subtropical and tropical regions of the Eastern Hemisphere. *Dracaena americana* occurs from southern Mexico to Panama.

The family grows in both tropical rain forests and savannas.

Family classification. The Dracaenaceae are placed in the Asparagales by Dahlgren et al. The family is a segregate from a much larger Agavaceae as defined by Cronquist. As treated here, the Dracaenaceae contains *Dracaena* and *Sansevieria*. In contrast, Thorne combines both Asteliaceae and Nolinaceae with the Dracaenaceae and treats each as subfamilies of a more inclusive Dracaenaceae. Recent work in morphology and molecular systematics supports the recognition of Dracaenaceae, Asteliaceae, and Nolinaceae each with different affinities. Some treatments have included Dracaenaceae within the Convallariaceae. Other analyses suggest that the Dracaenaceae should be placed in a broadly defined Ruscaceae with taxa of the Convallariaceae, Nolinaceae, and Ruscaceae *sensu stricto*. Bos has combined *Sansevieria* and *Pleomele* with *Dracaena*.

Features of the family. Habit: shrubs or rhizomatous herbs (*Sansevieria*), the shrubs sometimes with thick-stemmed, pachycaulous, sparingly branched growth, the stems with distinct vascular bundles, the bundles embedded within fibrous matrix as seen in transverse section. **Leaves** alternate, borne in rosettes at branch apices or in basal rosettes (*Sansevieria*), simple; blades narrowly lanceolate to ovate, completely cylindrical or cylindrical distally and dorsiventral proximally (some *Sansevieria*), distinctly cross-banded (*Sansevieria*), clasping at base. **Inflorescences** terminal or axillary, racemes, panicles, heads, or umbels. **Flowers** actinomorphic, bisexual, articulate with pedicel; tepals 6, equal, petal-like, nearly distinct or slightly connate basally (*Dracaena*), or united into tube for at least ⅓ length of corolla, then lobes distinct (*Sansevieria*); androecium of 6 stamens, the stamens in 2 alternating whorls, inserted at base of perianth lobes, the anthers epipeltate; gynoecium syncarpous, the ovary superior, the carpels 3, the locules 3, the style 1, the stigmas capitate to shallowly 3-lobed; septal nectaries present; placentation axile, the ovules 1 per locule. **Fruits** berries, orange, with thin fleshy layer, the endocarp sometimes woody. **Seeds** generally 3 per fruit, black or brown, covered with papery remnant of endocarp.

All species have a secondary thickening meristem as described for the Nolinaceae. Inflorescences appearing as heads or umbels are derived from racemes.

Natural history. Savanna species exhibit many water-storage features such as pachycaulous trunks, succulent rhizomes, and leaves that are fleshy and sometimes cylindrical. *Sansevieria*, a genus of dry habitats in the paleotropics, has specially thickened cells in the leaves that store water.

Little is known about pollination and dispersal biology; however, the flowers of many species produce nectar and are thought to be pollinated by nocturnal insects. Self-pollination is suspected to occur in species of *Dracaena*.

Economic uses. All genera of Dracaenaceae are cultivated as ornamentals, either as houseplants in temperate regions or as outdoor plants in the subtropics and Tropics. Species of *Dracaena* are popular throughout the world, and many cultivars and variegated leaf forms, particularly of *D. fragrans* and *D. draco* (dragon tree), have been developed. *Dracaena cinnabari*, known as dragon's blood, has been cultivated for centuries as a source of a red resin used in varnishes. Cultivars of species of *Sansevieria* (snake plant, bowstring hemp, or mother-in-law's-tongue) are popular ornamentals and *S. trifasciata* is one of the most commonly grown houseplants. Other species of *Sansevieria* are used in Central Africa as sources of fibers for ropes and bowstrings. Some species are grown as fetish plants in Africa, and many species were introduced into the Americas via the slave trade.

References. Bos, J. 1998. Dracaenaceae. In *The Families and Genera of Vascular Plants*, ed. K. Kubitzki, 3:238–41. New York: Springer-Verlag. Conran, J. 1998. Lomandraceae. In *The Families and Genera of Vascular Plants*, ed. K. Kubitzki, 3:354–65. New York: Springer-Verlag. Rudall, P., and D. Cutler. 1995. Asparagales: a reappraisal. In *Monocotyledons: Systematics and Evolution*, eds. P. Rudall, P. Cribb, D. Cutler, and C. Humphries, 157–68. Richmond, Surrey, U.K.: Royal Botanic Gardens, Kew.

ERIOCAULACEAE (Pipewort Family)

Dennis Wm. Stevenson

Figure 230, Plate 57

- *herbs, often of seasonally wet areas*

- *leaves alternate (spiral), often in dense rosettes, simple*

- *inflorescences borne at apices of long, leafless peduncles, generally headlike, often small*

- *flowers usually with nectar-secreting stylar appendages*

Numbers of genera and species. Worldwide, the Eriocaulaceae contains 10 genera and 700–1,400 species. In tropical America, there are six genera and somewhere between 250 and 500 species.

Distribution and habitat. The Eriocaulaceae are mainly pantropical with a few outlying species in north temperate areas. The greatest concentration of species is in South America and Africa. *Eriocaulon* is widespread with species

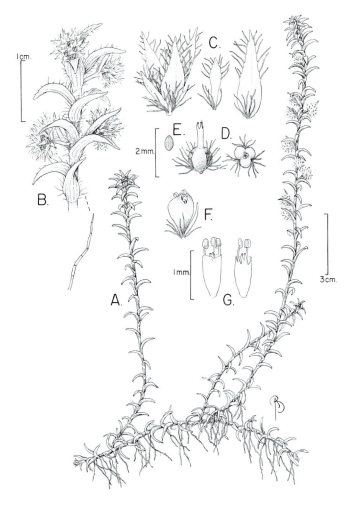

Figure 230. ERIOCAULACEAE. *Tonina fluviatilis*. **A.** Part of plant showing leaves and inflorescences. **B.** Part of stem with inflorescences (above) and detail of hair (below). **C.** Abaxial views of bracts from inflorescence. **D.** Lateral (left) and apical (right) views of pistillate flowers. **E.** Seed. **F.** Lateral view of staminate flower. **G.** Lateral view of intact staminate flower (left) and medial section of staminate flower (right). Reprinted with permission from Mori et al. (1997). Artist: Bobbi Angell.

in Asia, some in western Europe, some in Africa, some in eastern North America, and some in South America. *Lachnocaulon* is confined to the southeastern United States. *Rondonanthus* is restricted to the Guayana Shield in northern South America, *Blastocaulon* to Brazil, and *Tonina* from Brazil northward to the West Indies. *Paepalanthus* and *Syngonanthus* are mainly Central and South American genera, with outlying species in Africa.

The Eriolocaulaceae are found from *páramo* and *tepui* habitats to sea level in the Amazon and West Indies. Species grow mainly on sandy or rocky soils that experience at least some seasonal flooding. A few grow as submerged aquatics (*Tonina*). Some species of Eriocaulaceae are perennial and grow in transient swamp conditions that later become xero-

phytic. These species exhibit a peculiar mix of hydrophyte and xerophyte adaptions.

Family classification. The Eriocaulaceae are placed in the Commelinales by Dahlgren et al., along with Commelinaceae, Mayacaceae, Rapateaceae, and Xyridaceae. Recent evidence indicates that this is an unnatural group, with the Commelinaceae being nearer to the Pontederiaceae and related families. Morphological and molecular evidence suggest that the Eriocaulaceae, Mayacaceae, Xyridaceae, and perhaps the Rapateaceae are related to taxa in the Poales. Traditionally, the Eriocaulaceae have been divided into two subfamilies. The Eriocauloideae, with two genera (*Eriocaulon* and *Mesanthemum*), are distinguished by having two series of stamens and inner perianth segments with an apical gland; the Paepalanthoideae, with eight genera, are distinguished by having one series of stamens and inner perianth segments without an apical gland.

Features of the family. Habit: herbs, annual or perennial, usually terrestrial, sometimes aquatic, generally short in stature, single-stemmed or rarely with branching vertical or horizontal rhizomes, stolons, or with stout trunks to 1 m, the stems densely rooted at base or arising from along rhizomes. **Leaves** alternate (spiral), often in dense rosettes, simple; blades linear (grasslike), filiform when submerged (aquatic forms) or thick and coriaceous (xeric forms). **Inflorescences** occurring singly or in clusters at ends of vegetative branches, borne at apices of long, leafless peduncles, generally head-like, sometimes subcylindrical, often small, with 10–1,000+ flowers, pistillate and staminate flowers generally occurring in same inflorescence, the staminate flowers peripheral, the pistillate flowers central (the reverse condition rare); numerous involcral bracts present; pedicels absent or short. **Flowers** actinomorphic or zygomorphic, unisexual (plants usually monoecious) or rarely bisexual in a few *Syngonanthus*; outer perianth with 2 or 3, sepal-like, membranous tepals, the inner perianth with 2 or 3, petal-like tepals, the tepals often white, sometimes fused into tube, the lobes short, the apices sometimes with nectar-secreting glands. **Staminate flowers**: androecium of 4–6 stamens, the stamens in 1–2 series, the filaments adnate to inner perianth, opposite inner perianth when in 1 series, the anthers basifixed to dorsifixed, introrse; pollen with spiral aperture. **Pistillate flowers**: gynoecium syncarpous, the ovary superior, the carpels 2 or 3, the locules 2 or 3, the style singular, usually with nectar secreting appendages present, the stigmas 2 or 3; placentation basal, the ovule 1 per locule, orthotropous. **Fruits** loculicidal capsules. **Seeds** 3 per fruit, the ornamentation tuberculate or recticulate.

Natural history. Flies and beetles have been observed as pollinators; however, the details remain unknown. In *Eriocaulon*, entire infructescences are released from the inflorescence and dispersed by wind and/or water. In other genera, such as *Paepalanthus*, the sepal whorl dries in a manner that catapults the fruit as far as 2 meters.

Economic uses. The slender inflorescence stalks with their terminal heads are often dyed and sold as everlastings for floral arrangements. Increased market demand has led to overcollecting, especially from Brazil, so some species are now endangered.

References. RUHLAND, R. 1930. Eriocaulaceae. In *Die Natürlichen Pflanzenfamilien*, A. Engler and K. Prantl, 2nd ed. 15a: 39–57 Leipzig: Wilhelm Engelmann. STÜTZEL, T. 1998. Eriocaulaceae. In *The Families and Genera of Vascular Plants*, ed. K. Kubitzki, 4:197–207. New York: Springer-Verlag.

HAEMODORACEAE (Bloodwort Family)

DAVID L. LENTZ

Figure 231, Plate 58

- *herbs*
- *rhizomes often with red pigment*
- *leaves equitant, simple; blades linear*
- *flowers with 6 tepals; locules 3*
- *capsules loculicidal, 3-valved*

Numbers of genera and species. Worldwide, the Haemodoraceae comprise 14 genera and about 80 species. In tropical America, there are four genera and five species: *Xiphidium caeruleum*, *X. xanthorrhizon*, *Lachnanthes caroliniana*, *Pyrrorhiza neblinae*, and *Schiekia orinocensis*.

Distribution and habitat. The Haemodoraceae are native to South Africa, Australia, Southeast Asia, and the Americas. In the Western Hemisphere, the family ranges from the United States to southern Amazonia.

In tropical America, *Lachnanthes caroliniana* and *Xiphidium xanthorrhizon* are endemic to western Cuba. *Lachnanthes caroliniana* grows in wet, open habitats whereas *Xiphidium xanthorrhizon* is found only in dry savannas. *Xiphidium caeruleum* is found in the West Indies and from central Mexico to southern Amazonia, where it is widespread in moist forest and open savannas to 1,500 meters. *Schiekia orinocensis* is found from Venezuela to southern Brazil, where it grows in a variety of habitats ranging from lowland rain forest (*S. orinocensis* subspecies *silvestris*) to open marshes (*S. orinocensis* subspecies *orinocensis*). *Pyrrorhiza neblinae* has been collected only on Cerro de la Neblina in Venezuela, where it grows from 1,680 to 2,100 meters in areas without tree cover.

Family classification. The Haemodoraceae are placed in the Haemodorales by Dahlgren et al. Monophyly of the family is supported by its production of arylphenalenones, a chemical unique to the Haemodoraceae. Based on DNA sequence data, the family appears to be closely related to the Pontederiaceae, Philydraceae, and Commelinaceae.

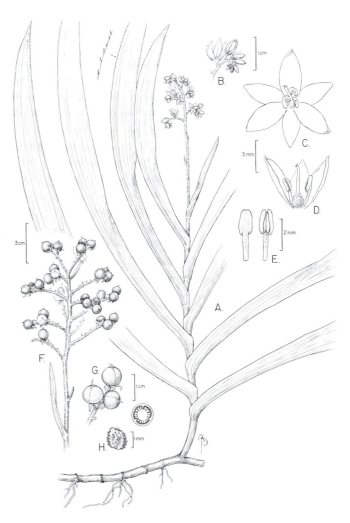

Figure 231. HAEMODORACEAE. *Xiphidium caeruleum*. **A.** Part of plant showing roots, leaves, and inflorescence with detail of leaf margin (above left). **B.** Part of inflorescence. **C.** Apical view of flower. **D.** Lateral view of flower with three tepals removed. **E.** Abaxial (left) and adaxial (right) views of stamens. **F.** Infructescence. **G.** Fruits (left) and transverse section of fruit (right). **H.** Seed. Reprinted with permission from Mori et al. (1997). Artist: Bobbi Angell.

Traditionally, the family has been divided into two tribes: the Conostylideae and the Haemodoreae. The Conostylideae is composed of six genera endemic to western Australia. The Haemodoreae consists of three African genera, one genus from Australia and New Guinea, and *Lachnanthes*, *Pyrrorhiza*, *Schiekia*, and *Xiphidium* from the Americas.

Features of the family. Habit: herbs, erect, perennial. **Rhizomes** frequently present, short, bearing red pigment in the form of arylphenalenone haemocorin, sometimes producing corms. **Leaves** equitant, simple; blades linear, ensiform, sheathing one another at base; venations parallel. **Inflorescences** terminal, cymes, racemes, or panicles, bracteate, covered with simple hairs; pedicels short. **Flowers** actinomorphic or zygomorphic, bisexual; tepals 6, petal-like, imbricate, distinct or connate at base, subequal, persistent, in 2 whorls; androecium with 3 or 6 stamens, the stamens inserted at base of inner tepals, the filaments short, glabrous, the anthers basifixed, dehiscing longitudinally; staminodes 2 in *Schiekia* and *Pyrrorhiza*, attached at base of outer tepals (representing outer staminal whorl in *Schiekia*) or inner tepals (representing inner staminal whorl in *Pyrrorhiza*); gynoecium syncarpous, the ovary superior or inferior, the carpels 3, the locules 3, the styles filiform, persistent, the stigmas simple to three-lobed; placentation axile, the ovules 2–many per locule, anatropous; nectaries present, septile (except in *Xiphidium*). **Fruits** loculicidal capsules, 3-valved. **Seeds** tomentose or glabrous, tuberculate; endosperm copious, the embryo small.

Natural history. Flowers in the Haemodoraceae are pollinated by insects, primarily bees or butterflies. Most species provide a nectar reward, but *Xiphidium* relies only on pollen as an attractant for its bee pollinators. The tiny seeds are wind-dispersed.

Economic uses. A tea made from the crushed leaves and roots of *Schiekia orinocensis* subspecies *silvestris* is used by the Kubeo Indians of Colombia for medicinal purposes. *Lachnanthes caroliniana* roots are utilized by Native Americans as sources of red dye and a tincture that serves as a tonic with narcotic effects. In Panama, *Xiphidium caeruleum* provides a remedy for stomachache and skin disorders; in Colombia, the plant is used to make soap; and in Guyana and Suriname, it is employed in foot remedies. *Xiphidium caeruleum* and, to a lesser degree, *X. xanthorrhizon* are grown as ornamentals throughout the neotropics.

References. HOPPER, S. D., M. F. FAY, M. ROSSETTO, AND M. CHASE. 1999. A molecular phylogenetic analysis of the bloodroot and kangaroo paw family, Haemodoraceae: taxonomic, biogeographic and conservation implications. *Bot. J. Linn. Soc.* 131:285–99. LÓPEZ-FERRARI, A. R. 1996. *Flora de Veracruz*, fasc. 92:1–7. Xalapa, Mexico: Instituto de Ecologia, A. C. MAAS, P.J.M., AND H. MAAS-VAN DE KAMER. 1993. Haemodoraceae. *Fl. Neotrop. Monogr.* 61:1–44. SIMPSON, M. G. 1998. Haemodoraceae. In *The Families and Genera of Vascular Plants*, ed. K. Kubitzki, 4:212–22. Berlin: Springer-Verlag.

HELICONIACEAE (Heliconia Family)

DENNIS WM. STEVENSON AND JANICE WASSMER STEVENSON

Figure 232, Plate 58

- *Herbs, rhizomatous; pseudostems formed by overlapping leaf sheaths or aerial shoots well developed, with distinct internodes*

- *leaves alternate, distichous, simple; sheath open*

- *inflorescences terminal, with large, conspicuous, brightly colored bracts*

- *flowers zygomorphic; stamens 5, the thecae 2 per anther; staminode 1, very small; ovary inferior*

- *fruits red or blue drupes; seeds 3*

Numbers of genera and species. Worldwide, the Heliconiaceae comprise a single genus, *Heliconia*, and 200 species.

Distribution and habitat. *Heliconia* is primarily a Neotropical genus with a few species found in the Old World Tropics in Malesia and Melanesia.

Species of *Heliconia* generally grow in moist tropical forests where they either form extensive stands or are found as scattered individuals. They also grow in open disturbed areas in forests where they frequently form extensive stands as pioneer species.

Family classification. Traditionally, the Heliconiaceae were placed in the Musaceae. Recent workers recognize both families while acknowledging their close relationship by placing them in the Zingiberales. Takhtajan established an order, the Musales, containing only the Musaceae, the Heliconiaceae, and the Strelitziaceae. The close relationship of these families is supported by cladistic analyses of morphological data

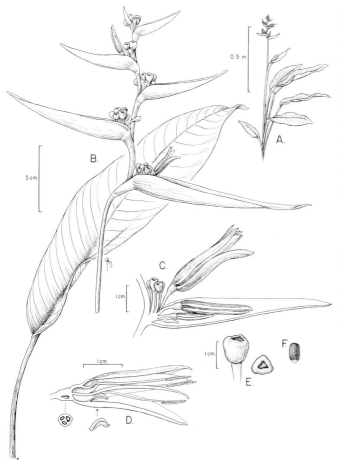

Figure 232. HELICONIACEAE. *Heliconia acuminata* subsp. *acuminata*. **A.** Plant showing leaves and erect inflorescence. **B.** Leaf and inflorescence with one open flower. **C.** A unit of the inflorescence with part of the subtending bract removed. **D.** Medial section of flower (above), transverse section of ovary (below left), and detail of staminode (below right). **E.** Lateral (left) and apical (right) views of fruits. **F.** Seed. Reprinted with permission from Mori et al. (1997). Artist: Bobbi Angell.

and combined morphological and molecular data. Andersson recognizes five subgenera of *Heliconia*.

Features of the family. Habit: herbs (to 10 m); rhizomes creeping and branched; aerial shoot a pseudostem of overlapping leaf sheaths or well developed with distinct internodes. **Leaves** alternate, distichous, simple; sheath tubular, open; petiole long. **Inflorescences** terminal, large, erect or pendent; thyrse composed of many-flowered cymes, each cyme subtended by a bract; bracts large, distichously or spirally arranged, boat-shaped, laterally flattened, often coriaceous,

usually bright red, orange, or yellow. **Flowers** zygomorphic, bisexual; perianth in 2 whorls of 3, basally more or less connate; sepals 3, the median sepal free; petals 3; 2 lateral sepals and 3 petals connate to form floral tube; androecium composed of stamens and staminode in 2 whorls of 3, the stamens 5, free, the filaments slender, adnate to perianth tube, the anthers elongate, the thecae 2, the staminode 1, very small, adnate to base of floral tube; gynoecium syncarpous, the ovary inferior, 3-locular, the style 1, the stigma capitate; placentation axile or basal, the ovule 1 per locule; septal nectaries present. **Fruits** drupes, the outer layer fleshy, bright blue or red at maturity. **Seeds**, three pyriform, gray, brown, or black, hard, operculate; aril absent.

Natural history. In the American Tropics, hummingbirds are the principal pollinators of species of *Heliconia*, while nectar-feeding bats pollinate Old World species. The conspicuous red to orange bracts and the copious nectar of Neotropical species of *Heliconia* are adaptations for hummingbird pollination. Because the staminode seals the slit between the free median sepal and the other fused perianth segments, the flower retains more nectar than would otherwise be possible. Species of *Heliconia* growing in large clumps in more or less open areas are pollinated by territorial hummingbirds, while those growing as separate individuals in the forest understory are pollinated by trap-lining hermit hummingbirds. Although most species of *Heliconia* are self-compatible (i.e., a flower will produce fruit if pollinated with pollen from a flower of the same plant), pollinators moving pollen from one flower to another account for most seed set. The seeds of *Heliconia* are dispersed by birds.

Economic uses. Because of their attractive foliage and inflorescences, species of *Heliconia* are becoming more common as cultivated ornamentals. In contrast to the blue fruits of Neotropical species, those of Old World species are red. *Heliconia* has limited local medicinal uses; e.g., the leaves are used to make poultices or dressings.

References. ANDERSSON, L. 1981. Revision of Heliconia sect. Heliconia (Musaceae). *Nordic J. Bot.* 1: 759–84. ANDERSSON, L. 1998. Heliconiaceae. In *The Families and Genera of Vascular Plants*, ed. K. Kubitzki, 4:226–30. New York: Springer-Verlag. BERRY, F., AND J. KRESS. 1991. *Heliconia. An Identification Guide*. Washington and London: Smithsonian Institution Press. KRESS, W. J. 1984. Systematics of Central American Heliconia (Heliconiaceae) with pendant inflorescences. *J. Arnold Arbor.* 65:429–532. STILES, F. G. 1975. Ecology, flowering phenology, and hummingbird pollination of some Costa Rican *Heliconia* species. *Ecology* 56:285–301.

HERRERIACEAE (Herreria Family)

Andrew Henderson and Dennis Wm. Stevenson

- *scandent subshrubs, lianas, or sometimes herbs*
- *stems with internodes often bearing prickles*
- *leaves alternate, simple, clustered on short shoots*
- *flowers with 6 tepals*
- *fruits septicidal capsules*

Numbers of genera and species. Worldwide, the Herreriaceae comprise two genera and about 10 species. *Herreria* contains approximately seven species and *Herreriopsis* two. In tropical America, there is a single genus, *Herreria*, and two species.

Distributon and habitat. *Herreria* is found in southern South America in Argentina, Bolivia, Brazil, Chile, Paraguay, and Uruguay and *Herreriopsis* occurs in Madagascar.

Species of *Herreria* grow in relatively dry, strongly seasonal regions, especially the Planalto of Brazil and *Chacó* of Bolivia and Paraguay; however, one species, *Herreria sarsaparilla*, is common in lowland moist forests of eastern Brazil.

Family classification. The Herreriaceae are placed in the Asparagales by Dahlgren et al. which is supported by recent molecular analyses. *Herreria* has also been included within the Liliaceae. There is no subfamilial classification.

Features of the family. Habit: scandent subshrubs, lianas, or sometimes herbs. Rhizomes present, subterranean. Stems branched, twining, the internodes elongate, often bearing prickles. **Leaves:** alternate, simple, clustered on short shoots; blades sessile, narrowly linear to broadly elliptic. **Inflorescences** axillary in leaves of lateral branches, racemes or panicles, the panicles with many branches. **Flowers** actinomorphic, bisexual; tepals 6, in 2 whorls of 3; androecium of 6 stamens, the anthers basifixed, dehiscing longitudinally; gynoecium syncarpous, the ovary superior, the carpels 3, the locules 3, the style erect, the stigma capitate; septal nectaries present; placentation axile, the ovules anatropous. **Fruits** septicidal capsules, 3-lobed. **Seeds** few to many, small, flat, black.

Natural history. No information is available on pollination and dispersal biology.

Economic uses. The roots and/or rhizomes of species of *Herreria* have local uses as a stimulant, to reduce fever, and for the treatment of venereal disease. In Santa Cruz, Bolivia, the stems are used for tying cheeses.

References. Conran, J. 1998. Herreriaceae. In *The Families and Genera of Vascular Plants*, eds. K. Kubitzki, J. G. Rohwer, and V. Bittrich, 3:253–55. Berlin: Springer-Verlag.

HYDROCHARITACEAE (Frog-bit Family)

Robert Haynes

Figure 233, Plate 59

- *aquatic herbs*
- *leaves basal, alternate, opposite, or whorled, simple; basal sheath present*
- *inflorescences subtended by 1–2 bracts*
- *sepals and petals usually 3; ovary inferior*
- *fruits berrylike*

Numbers of genera and species. Worldwide, the Hydrocharitaceae comprise 18 genera and approximately 115 species. Twelve genera and about 35 species occur naturally in the Western Hemisphere; of these, five genera and seven species are naturalized. In tropical America, there are 10 genera: *Apalanthe* (1 species), *Egeria* (2), *Elodea* (2), *Halophila* (3), *Hydrilla* (1), *Limnobium* (1), *Najas* (7), *Ottelia* (1), *Thalassia* (1), and *Vallisneria* (1). Two species, *Hydrilla verticillata* and *Najas graminea* are naturalized in the neotropics.

Distribution and habitat. The Hydrocharitaceae occur in all but the coldest climates. The centers of generic and specific diversity, however, are in tropical regions. Most genera are endemic to one or two continental areas, although several have been introduced fairly widely throughout the world. Five genera have become naturalized in the Americas, all in North America, with one, *Hydrilla*, extending into Central America.

Najas is near cosmopolitan, with 11 species in the Western Hemisphere. The genus is widespread throughout the neotropics. *Egeria* is native to southeastern Brazil, but one species, *E. densa*, has been become established in North America. *Elodea* is a Western Hemisphere genus, with three species in North America and two species widespread in the Andes and temperate South America. *Halophila*, a genus of nine species, occurs in warm marine waters throughout the world to a depth of 90 meters. The three Neotropical species of this genus occur in the Caribbean and along the Atlantic coast of northern South America.

Western Hemisphere genera range from northern Canada and Alaska south to central Argentina. All genera native to the Western Hemisphere are native to the neotropics, although the natural distribution of six genera (*Elodea, Limnobium, Vallisneria, Thalassia, Halophila,* and *Najas*) extends into North America.

Species of the Hydrocharitaceae occupy streams, rivers, lakes, bays, and oceans. Three genera are strictly marine (*Halophila* and *Thalassia* in the Western Hemisphere), the rest occupy freshwater habitats.

Family classification. The Hydrocharitaceae are placed in the Alismatales by Dahlgren et al. The family appears to be most closely related to the Alismataceae and Limnocharitaceae. Morphological, flavonoid, and molecular studies support this relationship.

Dahlgren et al. separates the Najadaceae from the Hydrocharitaceae. Shaffer-Fehre, based upon the presence of endotegmen tuberculae (subcellular protuberances from the inner tegmen layer of the seed coat) proposed combining the Najadaceae and the Hydrocharitaceae. These endotegmen tubercules are found only in *Najas* and most genera of Hydrocharitaceae *sensu stricto*. Les and Haynes summarized differences and similarities of the two families and also concluded that Najadaceae and Hydrocharitaceae should be combined. That classification is herein accepted.

The family is so diverse in its vegetative morphology that several different subfamilial classifications have been proposed. Ascherson and Gürke, for example, divided the family into four subfamilies based upon number of carpels, presence or absence of petals, and arrangement of leaves. Hutchinson accepted three subfamilies based upon pollinating mechanisms, as did Shaffer-Fehre, but her classification was based upon seed-coat structure. There are several similarities between the two systems, but there are also many differences. Cook and Les et al. do not recognize subfamilies

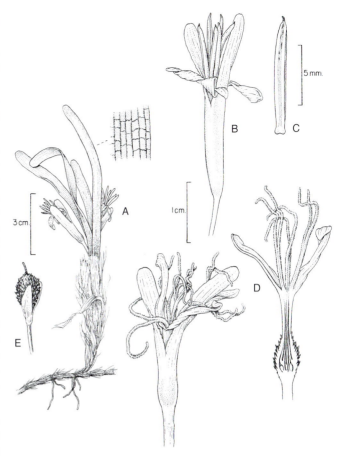

Figure 233. HYDROCHARITACEAE. *Thalassia testudinum.* **A.** Plant showing roots, leaves, flowers, and detail of leaf venation (above right). **B.** Lateral view of staminate flower. **C.** Abaxial view of stamen. **D.** Lateral view (left) and medial section (right) of pistillate flowers. **E.** Lateral view of fruit. Reprinted with permission from Acevedo-Rodríguez (1996). Artist: Bobbi Angell.

in the Hydrocharitaceae, recognizing "groups" instead. Unfortunately, their groups are not the same. In short, classification between the family level and the generic level is not understood for the Hydrocharitaceae.

Features of the family. Habit: aquatic herbs, sometimes emergent, stems stoloniferous or erect, corms often present when stems stoloniferous. **Leaves** basal, alternate, opposite, or whorled, simple, sessile or petiolate; basal sheath present, distinct from blade or petiole, tubular; blades linear (when leaves sessile) or expanded (when leaves petiolate); aerenchyma present in abaxial part of leaf in *Hydrocharis* and *Limnobium*. **Inflorescences** often complex, of 1–many flowers, sessile in leaf axils or terminal on long scapes, subtended by 1–2 bracts, the scapes occasionally with up to 10 longitudinal ridges or wings. **Flowers** actinomorphic, bisexual (often cleistogamous) or unisexual (plants dioecious), sessile or pedicellate in staminate flowers or mostly sessile in pistillate flowers, the pedicels often long and filiform in staminate flowers (elongated hypanthium often gives impression of pedicel in carpellate flowers); hypanthium present; perianth often united to form hypanthium; sepals (2)3; petals (absent or 2)3; androecium of 2–13 stamens (when present), the stamens in several whorls of mostly 3, the filaments distinct or united, the anthers basifixed or dorsifixed; gynoecium syncarpous, the ovary inferior (if present), the carpels 3–20+, the locules 1 or falsely 6–9, the styles 1–9, sometimes bifid, the stigmas linear, dry, papillose; placentation laminar. **Fruits** berrylike, dehiscing irregularly or breaking up at maturity. **Seeds** 3–numerous, ellipsoid to cylindric or fusiform.

Natural history. Pollination is diverse in the family. Some genera are insect-pollinated, either with or without enticement. In some species, pollen is liberated on the water surface or below the surface and floats up; then wind and wave action move the pollen until it contacts a stigma. Examples of this type of pollination include species of *Elodea*. In other species pollinated at the water surface, staminate flowers are liberated underwater and float to the surface or on the water surface itself. The staminate flowers then are moved around by wind or wave action until an anther contacts a stigma to accomplish pollination. Examples of this mode of pollination include *Vallisneria* (a freshwater plant) and *Enhalus* (a marine plant). *Hydrilla* and *Limnobium* transfer their pollen through the air. In the former, the staminate flower buds are released underwater; they rise to the surface, and decreasing water pressure causes them to open explosively. As they do so, pollen is thrown into the air, some of it potentially landing on a stigma and thereby effecting pollination. *Limnobium* is adapted for self-pollination. Both staminate and carpellate flowers are emersed, and the staminate usually are positioned above the carpellate. When pollen is released from the anthers, it drops through the water onto the stigma of a pistillate flower below. *Najas*, *Thalassia*, and possibly *Halophila* are also pollinated underwater. Pollen of *Najas* is released from staminate flowers, which usually are higher on the stem axis than the pistillate flowers. The pollen slowly falls through the water column, possibly contacting a stigma. *Halophila* and *Thalassia* both release their pollen underwater in long chains. However, the pollen in at least some species is buoyant and rises to the surface.

The fruits, like those of most other aquatic plants, must remain moist for the seeds to stay viable. Fruits produced from sessile flowers remain underwater without any modification. Those produced at the tips of scapes often are on the water surface or projected out of the water at anthesis. The scapes bend or coil following pollination, pulling or pushing the developing fruit below the water surface. Such fruits then develop fully submersed and, consequently, remain moist.

Economic uses. Species of the family are of limited economic value. Many species of *Vallisneria*, *Egeria*, and *Elodea* are sold in pet stores for use in aquaria. *Egeria* is also a fixture in general biology laboratories for demonstrating cytoplasmic streaming in plant cells. In Southeast Asia, the leaves of a few species of *Ottelia* are consumed locally. Far more importantly, however, is the invasive nature of many species. *Egeria densa* and *Hydrilla verticillata* have been introduced into the southeastern United States, where they have become major pests, often totally clogging waterways.

References. ANCIBOR, E. 1979. Systematic anatomy of vegetative organs of the Hydrocharitaceae. *Bot. J. Linn. Soc.* 78:237–66. ASCHERSON, P., AND M. GÜRKE. 1889. Hydrocharitaceae. In *Die Natürlichen Pflanzenfamilien* 2(1):238–58. Leipzig: Wilhelm Engelmann. COOK, C.D.K. 1982. Pollinating mechanisms in the Hydrocharitaceae. In *Studies on Aquatic Vascular Plants*, eds. J. J. Symoens, S. S. Hooper, and P. Compère, 1–15. Brussels: Royal Botanical Society of Belgium. COOK, C.D.K. 1998. Hydrocharitaceae. In *The Families and Genera of Vascular Plants*, ed. K. Kubitzki, 4: 234–48. Berlin: Springer-Verlag. HAYNES, R. R. 1977. The Najadaceae in the southeastern United States. *J. Arnold Arbor.* 58:161–70. LES, D. H., AND R. R. HAYNES. 1995. Systematics of Alismatiflorae: a synthesis of molecular and non-molecular approaches. In *Monocotyledons: Systematics and Evolution*, eds. P. Rudall, P. Cribb, D. Cutler, and C. Humphries, 353–77. Richmond, Surrey, U.K.: Royal Botanic Gardens, Kew. LES, D. H., M. A. CLELAND, AND M. WAYCOTT. 1997. Phylogenetic studies in Alismatidae, II: evolution of marine angiosperms (seagrasses) and hydrophily. *Syst. Bot.* 22:443–63. LOWDEN, R. M. 1986. Taxonomy of the genus *Najas* L. (Najadaceae) in the neotropics. *Aquatic Bot.* 24:147–84. SHAFFER-FEHRE, M. 1991 The endotegmen tuberculae: an account of little-known structures from the seed coat of the Hydrocharitoideae (Hydrocharitaceae) and *Najas* (Najadaceae). *Bot. J. Linn. Soc.* 107:169–88. SHAFFER-FEHRE, M. 1991 The position of *Najas* within the subclass Alismatidae (Monocotyledones) in the light of new evidence from seed coat structures in the Hydrocharitoideae (Hydrocharitales). *Bot. J. Linn. Soc.* 107:189–209.

HYPOXIDACEAE (Star-grass Family)

Dennis Wm. Stevenson

Figure 234

- *herbs*

- *tuberous rhizomes present*

- *leaves generally 3-ranked, simple; young leaves generally plicate*

- *flowers with 6 white to yellow tepals; stamens 6; ovary inferior, the locules 3*

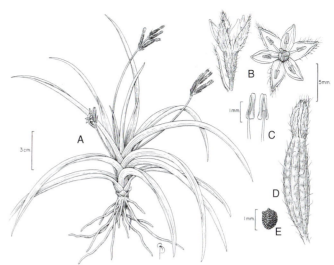

Figure 234. HYPOXIDACEAE. *Hypoxis decumbens.* **A.** Plant showing roots, leaves, and inflorescences. **B.** Lateral (left) and apical (right) views of flower. **C.** Lateral (left) and abaxial (right) views of stamens. **D.** Lateral view of fruit. **E.** Seed. Reprinted with permission from Acevedo-Rodríguez (1996). Artist: Bobbi Angell.

Numbers of genera and species. Worldwide, the Hypoxidaceae comprise nine genera and 100–200 species, of which, 50–100 species are in *Hypoxis.* In tropical America, there are two genera, *Hypoxis*, with 5–10 species, and *Curculigo*, with 2–5 species.

Distribution and habitat. The Hypoxidaceae are a pantropical family with centers of distribution in southern Africa, Australia, the coastal regions of Asia, and South America. The genera *Hypoxis* and *Curculigo* are cosmopolitan within this area. In the Western Hemisphere, the family occurs from the Atlantic coastal region of the southeastern United States to the West Indies and southward through the neotropics to Uruguay.

Generally the Hypoxidaceae are found in grasslands, chaparral, or on sandy soils that frequently experience alternating wet and dry periods. *Curculigo* can be found in wet understory habitats.

Family classification. The Hypoxidaceae are placed in the Asparagales by Dahlgren et al. Both Thorne and Takhtajan also recognized this family as distinct; however, Cronquist included members of the Hypoxidaceae in the Amaryllidaceae. The Hypoxidaceae are a rather isolated family, but recent evidence indicates a relationship with the Orchidaceae. There is no subfamilial classification.

Features of the family. Habit: herbs; tuberous rhizomes present, the rhizomes covered with persistent fibrous leaf bases. **Leaves** generally 3-ranked, simple; petiole absent or short in *Curculigo*; blades generally plicate when young, linear to elliptic to lanceolate. **Inflorescences** axillary, occurring singly at nodes, leafless spikes, racemes, or umbels, or in some species, reduced to a single flower (e.g., some *Curculigo*), pubescent. **Flowers** actinomorphic, bisexual; tepals 6, equal, white or yellow, distinct above ovary; androecium of 6 stamens, inserted at base of perianth lobes, in 2 alternating whorls; nectaries absent; gynoecium syncarpous, the ovary inferior, pubescent, the carpels 3, the locules 3, the style short, 3-branched at apex; placentation axile, the ovules 6–8 per locule. **Fruits** loculicidal capsules opening apically by short vertical slits (*Hypoxis*) or indehiscent and berrylike (*Curculigo*), the perianth persistent. **Seeds** 15–20, small, globose, the seed coat with thick, black, phytomelan crust, the raphe prominent, strophiole at raphe in *Curculigo.*

Species of Hypoxidaceae often are mistaken for palm seedlings because of their strongly plicate (folded), simple leaves.

Natural history. Very little information is available on pollination and dispersal biology of Neotropical Hypoxidaceae. The yellow flowers of *Hypoxis*, however, suggest bee pollination.

Economic uses. Species of *Curculigo* are often cultivated as ornamentals.

References. Nordal, I. 1998. Hypoxidaceae In *The Families and Genera of Vascular Plants*, ed. K. Kubitzki, 3:286–94. New York: Springer-Verlag.

IRIDACEAE (Iris Family)

Paula Rudall

Figure 235, Plate 59

- *herbs*

- *leaves equitant, usually basal, simple; blades typically ensiform, unifacial distally, bifacial proximally; styloid crystals usually present*

- *Flowers with 6 tepals, these generally petal-like; stamens usually 3, opposite outer tepals; ovary inferior*

- *fruits capsules*

Numbers of genera and species. Worldwide, the Iridaceae comprise approximately 70 genera and 1,750 species. Twenty-seven genera and about 280 species occur naturally in the Western Hemisphere, including one genus of Irideae (*Iris*), three genera of Mariceae (ca. 42 species), six genera of Sisyrinchieae, and about 10 genera of Tigridieae (ca. 125 species), of which the largest genus is *Tigridia*, with about 35 species. The largest genus of Iridaceae in the Western Hemisphere is *Sisyrinchium* (ca. 60 species), although a few species of the large, mainly Eastern Hemisphere genus *Iris* (>200 species) occur in North America. In tropical America, there are approximately 20 genera and 170 species.

Distributon and habitat. Iridaceae are a cosmopolitan family. The majority of genera occur in the Southern Hemisphere (South America, sub-Saharan Africa, and Australasia), but there are also numerous taxa in Eurasia and central and north America. The taxa in the Western Hemisphere all belong in subfamily Iridoideae, tribes Mariceae, Tigridieae, Irideae, and Sisyrinchieae. Mariceae and Tigridieae are widespread in South and Central America, although some genera have restricted distributions; for example, *Pseudotrimezia* (Mariceae) is restricted to Minas Gerais, Brazil. Irideae are mainly African, but species of *Iris* occur in both Eurasia and North America. Within Sisyrinchieae, two genera, *Libertia* and *Orthrosanthus*, occur in both Australasia and South America, and *Olsynium*, *Sisyrinchium*, *Solenomelus*, and *Tapeinia* are American. The distribution of the American Sisyrinchieae ranges from Greenland and northern Canada to Tierra del Fuego and the Falkland Islands. Some species have a restricted distribution, such as *Sisyrinchium galapagense*, an endemic to the Galápagos Islands. Other species occupy a wide range of habitats and cover a much larger area: e.g., *S. iridifolium* ranges from the southern United States to Tierra del Fuego. The mainly South American-Australasian distribution of Sisyrinchieae indicates that the large genus *Sisyrinchium* originated in the Southern Hemisphere and spread northward over the equator, especially as most

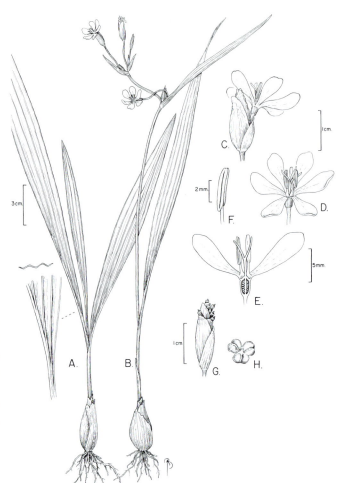

Figure 235. IRIDACEAE. *Eleutherine bulbosa.* **A.** Plant showing roots, bulb, leaves (right), detail of leaf blade base (below left), and transverse section of lower part of leaf blade (above left). **B.** Plant showing roots, bulb, leaf, and inflorescence. **C.** Lateral view of flower subtended by bract. **D.** Apical-lateral view of flower. **E.** Medial section of flower. **F.** Lateral view of apex of stamen. **G.** Part of young infructescence. **H.** Apical view of open fruit without seed. Reprinted with permission from Mori et al. (1997). Artist: Bobbi Angell.

of the high polyploids occur in North America. However, ploidy level is related to altitude as well as latitude in *Sisyrinchium*.

Species of Iridaceae are most commonly found in seasonally dry regions but occupy a range of habitats including tropical forests (e.g., species of *Neomarica* and *Eleutherine*) and wet upland meadows (e.g., species of *Tigridia*).

Family classification. The Iridaceae are placed in the Liliales by Dahlgren et al. Recent analyses place the family in the Asparagales, together with Orchidaceae and many other smaller families such as Asphodelaceae, Hypoxidaceae, and Tecophilaeaceae. Goldblatt subdivided Iridaceae into four subfamilies: Isophysidoideae, Nivenioideae, Iridoideae, and Ixioideae, of which all the Neotropical taxa occur in the Iridoideae, the most diverse subfamily. The Iridoideae were further divided into the tribes Irideae, Mariceae, Tigridieae, and Sisyrinchieae. Goldblatt's classification was reviewed by Reeves et al., who presented a combined multigene analysis of Iridaceae; their results supported the monophyly of all subfamilies except Nivenioideae, which formed a grade in which Ixioideae were embedded.

The Mariceae include *Pseudotrimezia*, *Neomarica*, and *Trimezia*. Tigridieae are closely related to Mariceae, although distinguished by their bulbs, distinctly plicate leaves, and chromosome number based on $x = 7$. The flowers of some Tigridieae, such as *Cypella*, are almost indistinguishable from those of *Trimezia*. Goldblatt subdivided Tigridieae into two subtribes: Tigridiinae and Cipurinae, but this classification requires review following the reduction of some genera to synonymy. Within the tribe Irideae, only some species of *Iris* subgenus *Limniris* (the beardless irises) occur in the Western Hemisphere. If *Bobartia* and *Diplarrhena* are excluded from Sisyrinchieae, the remaining genera include *Libertia*, *Orthrosanthus*, *Solenomelus*, *Tapeinia*, and *Olsynium* (including two former sections of *Sisyrinchium*: *Eriphilema* and *Nuno*, and the former small genera *Chamelum*, *Ona*, and *Phaiophleps*), and *Sisyrinchium*.

Features of the family. Habit: herbs, perennating underground stems usually present, these usually rhizomes or sometimes bulbs (Tigridieae). **Leaves** equitant, usually basal, simple; blades typically ensiform, unifacial distally, bifacial proximally; styloid crystals usually present. **Inflorescences** usually terminal, rhipidia or spikes. **Flowers** normally actinomorphic, bisexual; tepals 6, in 2 whorls, generally petal-like, varying in color; nectariferous glands or elaiophores sometimes present on inner tepals (e.g., some Tigridieae and Mariceae); androecium of 3(2 in *Diplarrhena*) stamens, the stamens opposite outer tepals, the filaments distinct or fused, slender in Tigridieae and Mariceae, the anthers mostly extrorse; gynoecium syncarpous, the ovary inferior, the carpels 3, the locules 3, the style branches sometimes petal-like (especially in Iridoideae; e.g., *Iris* and *Tigridia*); placentation axile, the ovules numerous. **Fruits** capsules. **Seeds** usually black (phytomelan in seed coat), varying in shape; e.g., spherical in *Libertia* and *Sisyrinchium* or angular in *Orthrosanthus*.

Some species of *Sisyrinchium* are annuals. *Trimezia* and its allies have bulblike, short, vertical rhizomes.

Adventitious roots often become contractile, and pull the perennating organs deeper underground.

The presence of styloid crystals and the absence of raphides is a characteristic feature of Iridaceae, although styloids are absent from *Olsynium* and *Sisyrinchium* (Sisyrinchieae). Other leaf anatomical characters are also significant in delineating genera in Iridaceae; e.g., although in most genera sclerenchyma is present at the phloem poles of many vascular bundles, in *Olsynium*, *Solenomelus*, and *Sisyrinchium* subgenus *Sisyrinchium* sclerenchyma occurs mainly at the xylem poles.

There is considerable variation in leaf morphology. Among the taxa in the Western Hemisphere, some species have laterally flattened leaves without a pseudomidrib (e.g., *Neomarica*, *Sisyrinchium*, and species of *Trimezia* section *Trimezia*), and other species have plicate (all Tigridieae) or terete leaves (*Olsynium*, *Solenomelus*, *Pseudotrimezia*, and some species of *Trimezia* section *Juncella*).

In the Western Hemisphere, some Iridaceae, especially *Sisyrinchium*, *Neomarica*, and species of *Trimezia* (e.g., *T. paradoxa*), have "winged" or flattened inflorescence axes.

The flowers of the Iridaceae have many different color variations, sometimes with mottled or spotted patterns; e.g., within the Mariceae, species of *Neomarica* and *Trimezia* have large, showy, yellow, white, or blue flowers, with contrasting markings, whereas *Pseudotrimezia* has small, mostly unpatterned, yellow flowers.

Natural history. The showy flowers of Iridaceae, often ornamented with nectar guides and emitting subtle but sweet aromas, and the production of pollinator rewards such as nectar and oil are adaptations for animal pollination. Some temperate species of *Iris* are pollinated by bees attracted to one of the three functional pollination units of the flower, each consisting of an inner tepal, a showy style, and a stamen. As the bee enters the flower, its weight forces the stigmatic surface against the pollen-bearing surface of the bee. Upon retreating from the flower, a new supply of pollen is placed on the bee in such a way that it is not redeposited onto the stigma of the same flower. Flowers of Neotropical Iridaceae with *Iris*-like flowers may also be pollinated by bees, but beetles and flies have also been reported to pollinate Iridaceae in other parts of the world. In addition, *Rigidella flammea* of the Western Hemisphere is pollinated by hummingbirds, and some African species of Iridaceae are known to be visited by sunbirds. Little is known about the dispersal of Neotropical species of Iridaceae, but a few species have apparent adaptations for fruit and seed dispersal other than simply falling out of the capsules to the ground from which they can be dispersed by gravity and water. A few reports of seed appendages in temperate species of *Iris* suggest that ants may play a role in the dispersal of these species.

Economic uses. Many genera of Iridaceae, including *Crocus*, *Iris*, *Sisyrinchium*, and *Tigridia*, are of horticultural importance because they are hardy in north temperate regions and have attractive flowers. The Mexican species, *Tigridia pavonia*, was cultivated by the Aztecs for its showy flowers and edible starchy bulbs. In tropical America, *Eleutherine bulbosa* is used medicinally as, for example, an astringent and to treat dysentery. The saffron crocus (*Crocus sativus*) of the Eastern Hemisphere provides a worldwide source for the spice saffron. The fragrant, powdered rhizomes of several species of *Iris*, especially *I. florentina*, are the source of orris, a fixative used in perfumery and potpourris.

References. GOLDBLATT, P. 1982. Chromosome cytology in relation to suprageneric systematics of neotropical Iridaceae. *Syst. Bot.* 7:186–98. GOLDBLATT, P. 1990. Phylogeny and classification of Iridaceae. *Ann. Missouri Bot. Gard.* 77: 607–27. GOLDBLATT, P. 1998. Iridaceae. In *The Families and Genera of Vascular Plants*, ed. K. Kubitzki, 3:295–333. Berlin: Springer-Verlag. GOLDBLATT, P., P. RUDALL, AND J. E. HENRICH. 1990. The genera of the *Sisyrinchium* alliance (Iridaceae: Iridoideae): phylogeny and relationships. *Syst. Bot.* 15:497–510. HENRICH, J. A., AND P. GOLDBLATT. 1987. A review of the New World species of *Orthrosanthus* sweet (Iridaceae). *Ann. Missouri Bot. Gard.* 74:577–82. MATHEW, B. 1981. The Iris. London: Batsford Ltd. MOLSEED, E. 1970. The genus *Tigridia* (Iridaceae) of Mexico and Central American. *Univ. Calif. Publ. Bot.* 54:1–113. REEVES, G., M. W. CHASE, P. GOLDBLATT, P. J. RUDALL, M. F. FAY, ET AL. 2001. Molecular systematics of Iridaceae: evidence from plastid DNA regions. *Amer. J. Bot.* 88:2074–87. RUDALL, P. 1994. Anatomy and systematics of Iridaceae. *Bot. J. Linn. Soc.* 114:1–21. RUDALL, P. J., A. Y. KENTON, AND T. J. LAWRENCE. 1986. An anatomical and chromosomal investigation of *Sisyrinchium* and allied genera. *Bot. Gaz.* 147:466–77.

JUNCACEAE (Rush Family)

HENRIK BALSLEV

Figure 236

- *usually grasslike herbs, terrestrial or sometimes aquatic*
- *leaves alternate (tristichous or distichous), simple, sheathing at base*
- *flowers with 6 tepals; stamens 6*
- *fruits capsular*

Numbers of genera and species. Worldwide, the Juncaceae comprise seven genera and about 300 species, excluding the monotypic *Prionium*, which is now treated as its own family. In tropical America, there are six genera and 55 species. The largest genera are *Juncus* with 220 species worldwide and 41 in the neotropics, and *Luzula* with 75 species worldwide and eight in the neotropics. The remaining genera represented in the neotropics are *Rostkovia* (2 species, 1 Neotropical), *Oxychloe* (6 species, 1 Neotropical), *Distichia* (3 Neotropical), and *Patosia* (1 Neotropical).

Distribution and habitat. The Juncaceae are cosmopolitan.

The family is most diverse in the north temperate zone. In the neotropics, Juncaceae occur in mountain ranges along the Pacific Ocean and in the mountains and lowlands of southeastern Brazil. A few species are found on the islands of the Caribbean.

Species of Juncaceae usually occupy open grass lands or swamps. Several species of *Juncus* are halophytic. The cushion forming genera *Distichia*, *Oxychloe*, and *Patosia* are adapted to harsh diurnal freezing and thawing in the high Andes and sometimes reach the altitudinal limit of vegetation.

Family classification. The Juncaceae are placed in the Cyperales by Dalhgren et al. Morphology and molecular analyses support the placement of Juncaceae with the Cyperaceae and Thurniaceae.

The family has not been formally divided into tribes or subfamilies, but they do form three natural groups: 1) the Andean cushion forming genera *Distichia*, *Oxychloe*, and *Patosia* all have single axillary flowers and are dioecious except for one species of *Oxychloe*; 2) two trans-Pacific genera, *Rostkovia* and *Marsippospermum*, have single terminal flowers, tapering stigmatic branches, and mucronate anthers; and 3) the mainly north temperate *Juncus* and *Luzula* are herbaceous but generally not cushion forming, and they have many-flowered inflorescences and emucronate anthers.

Features of the family. Habit: usually grasslike herbs, terrestrial, semiaquatic, or sometimes aquatic, the plants solitary or forming flat or bulging cushions in *Distichia*, *Oxychloe*, *Patosia*, and some *Luzula*, or forming mats by means of densely branching rhizomes. **Leaves** alternate (tristichous or distichous), simple, sheathing at base; sheath open or closed, often terminating in 2 membranous or scarious auricles; blades lanceolate, linear, or filiform, rarely short and ± conical (*Distichia*), the margins pubescent in *Luzula*; sheathing bracts (cataphylls) often present at base of flowering stem. **Inflorescences** variable: 1) solitary flowers, originating in axils of foliar leaves near shoot apices in *Distichia*, *Oxychloe*, and *Patosia*, the peduncles subtended by 2-keeled adaxial prophyll, the flowers clasped by 1–4 bracts, 2) of solitary terminal flowers on long aerial culms in *Rostkovia*, or 3) many-flowered and variously branched in *Juncus* and *Luzula*, the flowers often congested and the inflorescence then headlike. **Flowers** actinomorphic, bisexual in *Juncus*, *Luzula*, *Rostkovia*, and a single species of *Oxychloe*, or unisexual (plants dioecious); tepals 6, distinct, usually less than 7 mm long, lanceolate, green, dull colored, castaneous, or almost black, in 2 whorls, the margins often membranous, the outer whorl often slightly longer, thicker, and more rigid than inner whorl; androecium of 6 stamens, the stamens dis-

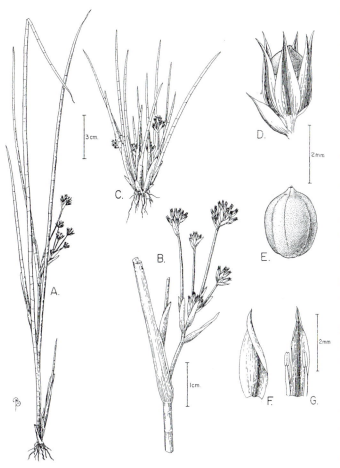

Figure 236. JUNCACEAE. *Juncus breviculmis.* **A.** Plant showing roots, septate leaves, and inflorescences. **B.** Lateral view of stem and inflorescence. **C.** Smaller plant showing roots, septate leaves, and inflorescences. **D.** Lateral view of flower subtended by floral bract. **E.** Lateral view of fruit. **F.** Outer tepal. **G.** Inner tepal and adaxial views of stamens. Reprinted with permission from Balslev (1983). Artist: Bobbi Angell.

tinct, alternate with tepals, the filaments filiform or flattened, the anthers basifixed, dehiscing by longitudinal slits, the connectives apically mucronate and exceeding thecae in *Distichia*, *Oxychloe*, *Patosia*, and *Rostkovia*; gynoecium syncarpous, the ovary superior, globular to oblong, the carpels 3, opposite outer tepals, the locule(s) 1 or 3, the style with 3 filiform or tapering stigmatic branches; placentation usually axile, sometimes with intruding placentas, the ovules many, or 3 and basal in *Luzula*, anatropous, bitegmic, weakly crassinucellate. **Fruits** capsular, globular or ovoid to obovoid, sometimes beaked, terete to trigonous or 3-keeled, dehiscing loculicidally or dehiscence less well defined and sometimes circumscissile in *Distichia*, *Oxychloe*, and *Patosia*. **Seeds** 3 in *Luzula* or 15–120, 0.3–2.5 mm long or sometimes fusiform and to 4 mm long, the testa smooth to reticulate; endosperm starchy, abundant, the embryo small, straight, cylindrical to conical, located medially near micropyle, the cotyledon 1.

Natural history. Wind pollination is predominant in the Juncaceae. The flowers have prominent stigmatic surfaces, abundant pollen, and smooth pollen. Temporal separation of pollen release and stigmatic receptivity (the latter often occurring first) is common. However, self-fertilization is frequent, and cleistogamy occurs in *Juncus bufonius*. Insect pollination is known in some central European species of *Luzula* with bright, white flower heads and in some *Juncus* species in the Himalayas. Insects may visit flowers of species of *Juncus* to collect pollen.

Vegetative propagation by means of the proliferation of rhizomes is common in many species, especially in *Juncus*. Dispersal is otherwise by seeds. The mucilaginous seeds of some species are adapted to external animal dispersal and their small size and ability to adhere to the feet of migrant birds may explain the wide and discontinuous distributions of many species. Carunculate seeds of *Luzula* are dispersed by ants. The swelling of the seed coat upon moistening in some species appears to cause capsule dehiscence.

Economic uses. Few economic uses of Juncaceae are known. In Costa Rica and Guatemala, mats are woven from leaves of *Juncus effusus*. In Colombia and Ecuador, leaves of *J. ramboi* and *J. arcticus* are utilized for weaving baskets. In the highlands of Peru, blocks of the cushion-forming *Distichia muscoides* are cut for use in making fires. *Luzula racemosa* is considered a magic plant near Huancabamba in Peru. In Chihuahua, Mexico, roots of *Juncus marginatus* are used to stupefy fish. *Juncus tenuis* and *J. bufonius* are dispersed by humans and have become weedy.

References. BALSLEV, H. 1979a. Juncaceae. In *Flora of Ecuador*, eds. G. Harling and B. Sparre, 11:1–45. Göteborg, Sweden: Department of Systematic Botany, University of Göteborg. BALSLEV, H. 1979b. On the distribution of *Rostkovia magellanica* (Juncaceae), a species newly rediscovered in Ecuador. *Brittonia* 31:243–47. BALSLEV, H. 1983. New taxa and combinations in neotropical *Juncus* (Juncaceae). *Brittonia* 35:302–08. BALSLEV, H. 1988. Two new rushes (*Juncus*, Juncaceae) from Chiapas, Mexico. *Ann. Missouri Bot. Gard.* 75:379–82. BALSLEV, H. 1996. Juncaceae. *Fl. Neotrop. Monogr.* 68:1–168. BALSLEV, H. 1998. Juncaceae. In *The Families and Genera of Vascular Plants*, ed. K. Kubitzki, 4:252–60. Berlin: Springer-Verlag. BALSLEV, H., AND S. LAEGAARD, 1986. *Distichia acicularis* sp. nov.—a new cushion forming Juncaceae from the high Andes of Ecuador. *Nordic J. Bot.* 6:151–55. BARROS, M. 1953. Las Juncáceas de la Argentina, Chile y Uruguay. *Darwiniana* 10:279–460. BUCHENAU, F. 1906. Juncaceae. In *Das Pflanzenreich*, ed. A. Engler, series 4, 36:1–284. Berlin: Wilhelm Engelmann. CUTLER, D. F. 1969. Juncales. In *Anatomy of the Monocotyledons*, ed. C. R. Metcalfe, 4:1–358. Oxford, U.K.: Clarendon Press. MUNROE, S. L., AND H. P. LINDER. 1998. The phylogenetic position of *Prionium* (Juncaceae) within the order Juncales based on morphological and *rbc*L sequence data. *Syst. Bot.* 23:43–55.

JUNCAGINACEAE (Arrow-grass Family)

ROBERT R. HAYNES

Figure 237

- *aquatic herbs, emergent, grasslike*
- *leaves alternate, basal, simple, sessile; sheath present; blades linear*
- *inflorescences on scapes, terminal spikes or of solitary axillary flowers*
- *flowers with perianth absent, or tepals 1, or 6 in 1 or 2 series*
- *fruits schizocarps or nutlets*

Numbers of genera and species. Worldwide, the Juncaginaceae comprise four genera and about 15 species. The largest genus, *Triglochin* has about 12 species, whereas the remaining genera have one species each. In tropical America, there are two genera, *Triglochin* with three species and *Lilaea* with one species.

Distributon and habitat. The Juncaginaceae are subcosmopolitan in distribution. In the Western Hemisphere, species range from the Falkland Islands and Tierra del Fuego north to the Arctic Circle in Canada and Alaska. *Triglochin* is subcosmopolitan, the remaining genera are limited to one or two continental areas.

Plants of Juncaginaceae occupy a variety of habitats. *Lilaea* can be found in high montane wet meadows from the central Andes to the Rocky Mountains of southern Canada. *Triglochin* usually occurs in marshes that are brackish or have high concentrations of marl. Plants are often extremely abundant in soils so heavily laden with marl or salts that the soil surface is white, especially on high plateaus.

Family classification. The Juncaginaceae are placed in the Najadales by Dahlgren et al. The family is morphologically and chemically most closely related to the Scheuchzeriaceae. The Juncaginaceae have not been divided into subfamilies.

Features of the family. Habit: aquatic herbs, emergent, grasslike, underground rhizomes and erect stems usually present. **Leaves** alternate, basal, simple, sessile; tubular sheath present, adnate proximally to blade; ligule present at apex of sheath (a few millimeters long); blades linear, terete to dorsiventrally flattened. **Inflorescences** terminal on elongate scapes, spikes, solitary pistillate flowers present in *Lilaea* (in addition to spikes), these axillary. **Flowers** actinomorphic or zygomorphic, bisexual or sometimes unisexual in *Lilaea* (plants polygamous); perianth absent, or tepals 1, or 6 in 1–2 series, distinct; androecium of 1, 4, or 6 stamens, sometimes

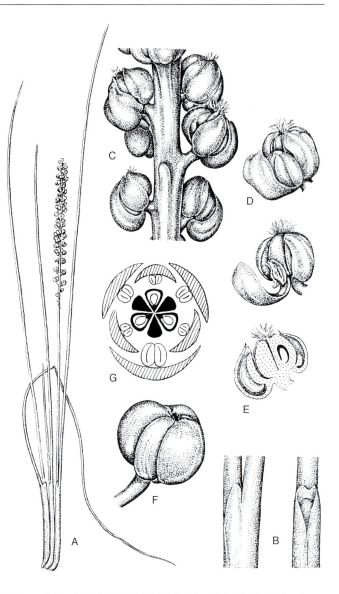

Figure 237. JUNCAGINACEAE. *Triglochin striata.* **A.** Plant showing leaves and inflorescence (x1). **B.** Lateral (left) and adaxial (right) views of leaf sheath (x8). **C.** Part of inflorescence (x16). **D.** Lateral view of intact flower (above) and flower with one perianth segment opended to show anther (below; x16). **E.** Medial section of flower (x16). **F.** Apical-lateral view of fruit (x16). **G.** Floral diagram. Reprinted with permission from Correll and Correll (1982). Artist: Priscilla Fawcett.

absent, the anthers sessile or subsessile; gynoecium weakly connate in *Triglochin*, the ovaries superior, the carpels 3 or 6 (fertile) in *Triglochin*, or 1 in *Lilaea*, 3 sterile carpels alternating with fertile carpels when only 3 fertile carpels present (in *Triglochin*), the styles absent in *Triglochin* and present in *Lilaea*; placentation basal, the ovules 1 per carpel. **Fruits** schizocarps, the 3 or 6 fertile carpels eventually separating into 1-seeded nutlets, the nutlets 3-winged in *Lilaea*. **Seeds** solitary; embryo straight.

Lilea has up to four types of flowers on one plant. These include perfect flowers with tepals present; staminate flowers with tepals present; pistillate flowers with tepals present and the style 0.5–2 mm long or without tepals and the style 0.2–30 cm long. The latter type is solitary in the leaf axils. The remaining ones are in spikes.

Natural history. Pollinating mechanisms have not been studied in the family, but wind pollination is probably most common. No published data exist on dispersal mechanisms, but wading birds probably play an important part in moving plants over short distances.

Economic uses. Plants of the family are of limited economic value. Leaves and rhizomes of some species are edible. A few species contain hydrogen cyanide, which may poison livestock that graze in marshes.

References. AGRAWAL, V. S. 1952. The embryology of *Lilaea subulata* H. B. K. with a discussion on its systematic position. *Phytomorphology* 2:15–29. HAYNES, R. R., D. H. LES, AND L. B. HOLM-NIELSEN. 1998. Juncaginaceae. In *The Families and Genera of Vascular Plants*, ed. K. Kubitzki, 4: 260–63. Berlin: Springer-Verlag. LARSEN, K. 1966. Cytotaxonomical note on *Lilaea. Bot. Not.* 119:496–97. LES, D. H., AND R. R. HAYNES. 1995. Systematics of Alismatiflorae: a synthesis of molecular and non-molecular approaches. In *Monocotyledons: Systematics and Evolution*, eds. P. Rudall, P. Cribb, D. Cutler, and C. Humphries, 353–77. Richmond, Surrey, U.K.: Royal Botanic Gardens, Kew. LOOMAN, J. 1976. Biological flora of the Canadian prairie provinces IV. *Triglochin* L., the genus. *Canad. J. Pl. Sci.* 56:725–32. LÖVE, A., AND D. LÖVE. 1958. Biosystematics of *Triglochin maritium* Agg. *Naturaliste Canad.* 85:156–65. THIERET, J. W. 1988. The Juncaginaceae in the southeastern United States. *J. Arnold Arbor.* 69:1–23.

LAXMANNIACEAE (Wire Lily Family)

DENNIS WM. STEVENSON

- *shrubs*
- *leaves alternate, borne in compact whorls at stem apices, simple, the emerging leaves conduplicate*
- *flowers with 6 tepals; stamens 6, epipeltate; locules 3*
- *fruits loculicidal capsules*

Numbers of genera and species. Worldwide, the Laxmanniaceae comprise 14 genera and about 180 species. In tropical America, there is a single confirmed species, *Cordyline dracaenoides. Tricopetalum plumosum* may occur in northern Chile and reach southern Peru.

Distribution and habitat. The Laxmanniaceae are primarily distributed in subtropical and tropical regions of the Eastern Hemisphere. The family is centered in western Australia where one-half of the genera are endemic to arid and semi-arid areas. The other more widespread genera are found from New Zealand to Southeast Asia and Madagascar, where they occur in a variety of habitats ranging from tropical rain forests to woodlands, dunes, and heathlands. *Cordyline dracaenoides* is known from Bolivia, Paraguay, and Argentina, where it is found in forests and shrub-dominated vegetation form 1,400 to 2,000 meters.

Family classification. The Laxmanniaceae are placed in the Asparagales. The family is a segregate from the Agavaceae *sensu* Cronquist. According to both Conran and Bos, *Cordyline* is placed in the Laxmanniaceae. In contrast, Dahlgren et al. align *Cordyline* in the Asteliaceae and Thorne combines the Asteliaceae and Nolinaceae as subfamilies of a more inclusive Dracaenaceae. Recent morphological and molecular data supports including *Cordyline* in the Laxmanniaceae, but this placement is subject to debate.

Features of the family. Habit: shrubs, sparingly branched. **Leaves** alternate, borne in compact whorls at stem apices, simple, clasping at base, more or less subpetiolate, the emerging leaves conduplicate; blades lanceolate. **Inflorescences** terminal, racemes or panicles. **Flowers** actinomorphic, bisexual; tepals 6, equal, petal-like, slightly connate basally; androecium of 6 stamens, the stamens inserted at base of perianth lobes, in 2 alternating whorls, the anthers epipeltate; gynoecium syncarpous, the carpels 3, the locules 3, the short filiform style 1, stigma capitate to trilobed; septal nectaries present; placentation axile, the ovules 2–20 per locule. **Fruits** loculicidal capsule. **Seeds** smooth, rounded, black.

The stems of Laxmanniaceae have considerable secondary growth from a meristem that continuously produces additional parenchyma internally in which new vascular bundles and fibers develop.

Natural history. Pollination by bees is known for some species of *Cordyline*, buzz pollination by bees occurs in species of extra-Neotropical *Thysanotus* and *Arthropodium* with poricidal anthers, and beetles pollinate some species of extra Neotropical *Lomandra*. Many species of *Cordyline*, including *C. dracaenoides*, are dispersed by birds.

Economic uses. Some genera of the Laxmanniaceae (e.g., species of *Thysanotis*, *Lomandra*, *Arthropodium*, and *Cordyline*) are cultivated as ornamentals, either as houseplants in temperate regions or as outdoor plantings in the subtropics and Tropics. Many cultivars of *C. terminalis* are available with brightly colored leaves. Traditionally, *Cordyline* leaves have served as sources of fiber and medicine and have been used to wrap food in eastern Asia and Polynesia. In New Zealand and Indonesia, the fleshy roots, leaves, and young fruits of *C. australis* are eaten. In the Amazon, *C. dracae-noides* is used to make soap because it contains steroidal saponins. Seeds of *C. australis* are considered to have economic potential as sources of linoleic and oleic acids as well as fructan.

References. Bos, J. 1998. Dracaenaceae. In *The Families and Genera of Vascular Plants*, ed. K. Kubitzki, 3:238–41. New York: Springer-Verlag. Conran, J. 1998. Lomandraceae. In *The Families and Genera of Vascular Plants*, ed. K. Kubitzki, 3:354–65. New York: Springer-Verlag. Rudall, P., and D. Cutler. 1995. Asparagales: a reappraisal. In *Monocotyledons: Systematics and Evolution*, eds. P. Rudall, P. Cribb, D. Cutler, and C. Humphries, 157–68. Richmond, Surrey, U.K.: Royal Botanic Gardens, Kew.

LEMNACEAE (Duckweed Family)

Wayne Armstrong

Figure 238

- *aquatic herbs, float on surface of ponds*
- *plant body reduced, 1–10 mm long, ovoid or thalluslike*
- *commonly in pairs or clusters of 2–4*
- *roots absent or 1–several hairlike roots on undersurface*
- *flowers greatly reduced, in floral cavity on upper surface or within lateral budding pouch*

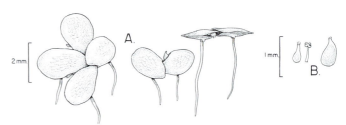

Figure 238. LEMNACEAE. *Lemna aequinoctialis.* **A.** Apical (left and middle) and lateral views (right) of plants. **B.** Lateral views of pistillate (left) and staminate (center) flowers and fruit (right). Reprinted with permission from Acevedo-Rodríguez (1996). Artist: Bobbi Angell.

Numbers of genera and species. Worldwide, the Lemnaceae comprise five genera and 38 species, including *Lemna* (14 species), *Landoltia* (1), *Spirodela* (3), *Wolffia* (11), and *Wolffiella* (10). In tropical America, there are five genera and 18 species. Les and Crawford have proposed a fifth genus, *Landoltia*, containing the single species *L. punctata* (formerly *Spirodela punctata*), thus reducing the number of species in *Spirodela* to two.

Distribution and habitat. The Lemnaceae are widely distributed throughout temperate and tropical regions of the world. They are readily introduced into lakes and ponds by waterfowl, and some species, (e.g., *Spirodela polyrrhiza* and *Lemna aequinoctialis*) are pantropical. A few species (e.g., *Lemna turionifera* and *L. trisulca*) extend north to Canada and Eurasia. River currents and transportation on the feet of waterfowl probably explain the disjunct and widespread distribution of many species. Tropical America is probably the center of origin for the majority of species occurring in North America, and several North American species were originally described from tropical American collections. Re-markable distribution patterns, such as the introduction of the Asian *Wolffia globosa* into southern Florida and California, may be related to the shipment of fish and aquarium cultures or to the cultivation of rice and exotic tropical aquatic species. In the southeastern United States, there are records of plants of species of *Wolffia* being carried by a tornado, and they have even been reported enclosed in hailstones. Because they are very small and generally poorly collected, new species are occasionally discovered in poorly explored regions of tropical America. For example, *Wolffiella caudata* was described by Landolt in 1992 from a collection in the Bolivian Amazon region.

Species of Lemnaceae are found floating on or below the surface of quiet streams and ponds, often forming dense, homogeneous clonal populations.

Family classification. The Lemnaceae are placed in the Arales by Dahlgren et al. Most botanists consider the family to be closely related to the Araceae, and comparative chloroplast DNA studies by French et al. have confirmed this affinity.

The Lemnaceae are divided into two subfamilies, Lemnoideae and Wolffioideae. The Lemnoideae, including *Spi-*

rodela, *Landoltia*, and *Lemna*, have a flattened plant body bearing one to several roots on the undersurface. The Wolffioideae, including *Wolffia* and *Wolffiella*, have a minute ovoid or flattened, thalluslike, rootless plant body. Because of their degree of reduction, Landolt considers the diminutive genera *Wolffia* and *Wolffiella* to be the most recently evolved members of Lemnaceae. *Wolffia* has the fewest shared characters with the presumed ancestral *Spirodela*. The monotypic *Landoltia* is morphologically intermediate between *Lemna* and *Spirodela*. The subdivision of the family into two subfamilies, five genera and 38 species has been substantiated by Les et al. using cladistic analysis of chloroplast DNA.

Since flowers and fruits are rarely observed, most taxonomic keys to the Lemnaceae are based on relatively few vegetative characteristics, and these may vary under different environmental conditions. This often makes precise identification of some species difficult, or in some cases, practically impossible. Minor traits that might seem insignificant in morphologically complex plants have assumed greater importance in the Lemnaceae.

Features of the family. Habit: minute aquatic herbs, commonly in pairs or clusters of 2–4, reduced to fleshy or flattened plant body (not differentiated into stem or leaf), the plant body 1–10 mm long, ovoid or thalluslike, bearing 1–several hairlike roots on undersurface (*Lemna*, *Landoltia*, and *Spirodela*) or roots absent, often containing 1–several layers of conspicuous aerenchyma and 1–several veins; small daughter plants (buds) produced vegetatively in cavity or budding pouch at basal end of plant, often remaining attached to parent plant by short stipe; pouches 1, flattened and triangular (*Wolffiella*) or funnel-shaped (*Wolffia*), or pouches 2, lateral and flattened (*Spirodela*, *Landoltia*, and *Lemna*); turions produced by some species in budding pouch (these sink to bottom and overwinter), rootless (or very short-rooted), starch-filled. Inflorescences solitary, within minute dorsal floral cavity not producing budding daughter plants, or in paired lateral budding pouches. Flowers greatly reduced, bisexual, usually protogynous; sepals absent; petals absent; androecium of 1–2 stamens, the filaments short, the anthers unilocular or bilocular, dehiscing transversely or apically; gynoecium with 1 superior ovary, produced in floral cavity on upper surface (*Wolffiella* and *Wolffia*) or in membranous saclike spathe within lateral budding pouch (*Spirodela*, *Landoltia*, and *Lemna*), the locule 1, the style short, the stigma circular, concave, often secreting a fluid droplet at anthesis; placentation basal, the ovules 1–several. Fruits utricles, indehiscent, bladderlike, prominent operculum present. Seeds 1–several, smooth or longitudinally ribbed.

Duckweeds are the smallest and structurally simplest of all angiosperms, with greatly reduced vascular tissue limited to the veins of the plant body, filaments of the stamens, and the roots of some species.

The plant body of duckweed is quite unlike that of other flowering plants because it does not have stems or leaves. It represents the ultimate in reduction of an entire vascular plant. The terms "frond" and "thallus" are sometimes used in the literature, but these terms are not appropriate because the plant body of duckweed is not homologous to the fronds of ferns or the body of fungi and algae. Although the body of duckweed does have paired guard cells and stomates on its upper surface and superficially resembles a leaf (particularly the flattened duckweeds *Spirodela*, *Landoltia*, and *Lemna*), it is morphologically and embryonically completely different. In *Spirodela*, *Landoltia*, and *Lemna* it is a flattened structure with slender, hairlike roots on the undersurface. *Spirodela* is unique among duckweeds because of a minute, membranous scalelike leaf at the basal end. This basal portion and its connecting stalk correspond to a condensed shoot. *Wolffia* and *Wolffiella* are reduced to minute, rootless spheres or flattened ribbons. *Wolffia* has a minute globose or ovoid body 1 mm or less long. In *Wolffiella* the thalluslike body is transparent and flattened, with the free ends often curved downward in the water. Although widespread in the neotropics, vegetative plants of species of *Wolffiella* are not commonly observed because they float submersed below the water surface, often under other aquatic vegetation.

Turions are especially evident in species that reach the northern latitudes and higher elevations where ponds freeze over during the winter months.

It should be noted that some botanists consider duckweeds to be monoecious with staminate flowers (consisting of 1 or 2 stamens) and a pistillate flower (consisting of a single pistil) on the same plant body. This is consistent with taxonomic affinities between the Lemnaceae and Araceae, particularly the genus *Pistia*.

Natural history. Two of the smallest species of Lemnaceae and the undisputed smallest flowering plants on earth are the Australian/Malaysian *Wolffia angusta* and the Asian *W. globosa*. The plant body of these remarkable species may be only 0.6 millimeters long, small enough to slip through the eye of a sewing needle. A dozen plants in full bloom will fit easily on the head of a pin. These plants also produce the smallest seed-bearing fruits. The mature fruit of *W. angusta* has the general shape of an edible fig, but it is only about 0.4 millimeters long and weighs about 100 micrograms, roughly equivalent to the weight of one or two grains of table salt.

Each plant produces up to a dozen daughter plants during its lifetime of usually 1–2 months. The daughter plants repeat the budding history of their clonal parents, resulting in exponential growth. It has been estimated that the Indian *W. microscopica* may reproduce by budding every 30 hours under optimal growing conditions. At the end of four months, a single individual theoretically could give rise to about one nonillion plants (one followed by 30 zeros), occupying a total volume roughly equivalent to the planet Earth!

Because species of Lemnaceae reproduce vegetatively at an exponential rate under ideal conditions, they are essential producers in aquatic food webs, providing an important source of food for a variety of microfauna, fish, and waterfowl. The animal grazers, in turn, help to limit the exponential population growth of the duckweeds. In addition, Lemnaceae have a positive effect in eutrophic water because they absorb ammonia, which is toxic to fish in high concentrations. Sometimes, the delicate balance between producers and grazers is upset by the inflow of excessive fertilizers (especially phosphorus and nitrogen), causing massive population explosions or "blooms" of duckweeds. The chemical herbicides used to control them may be toxic to animal life through biological magnification and provide only a temporary reduction in the duckweed populations. Herbicides containing heterocyclic compounds, urea derivatives, and quaternary ammonium compounds are the most toxic to duckweeds. *Wolffiella* species appear to be especially sensitive to detergents, polluted water, and concrete flood-control channels and have disappeared from urbanized areas of the southwestern United States.

Although flowers are observed rarely in most species, all duckweeds bloom and reproduce sexually. Some populations in small ponds, however, may be clones of each other and not able to produce viable seeds. Because the flowers typically have a receptive stigma before the anther is mature, the plants must be cross-pollinated by genetically different individuals with mature pollen-bearing anthers in synchronization with the receptive stigmas. The sweet stigmatic secretions and spiny pollen grains suggest that certain species are pollinated by insects. In fact, the pollen has been detected on flies, aphids, mites, and small spiders. With floral organs that project from the surface or lateral budding pouches, many duckweed species may simply be contact-pollinated as they bump together or become piled up in windrows along the edges of ponds and lakes.

Species of Lemnaceae are dispersed by water currents and waterfowl (e.g., tucked under a duck's body during short flights).

Economic uses. Because they can be grown easily under controlled conditions with limited space, duckweeds have been called the "fruit flies of the plant kingdom." They are used in a variety of botanical research, including ecological, physiological, and cytogenetic studies, and for testing the toxicity of herbicides. Their astronomical vegetative growth

and the ability of some species to grow in stagnant, polluted water make some duckweeds well suited for water reclamation and livestock-feeding programs. The duckweeds readily absorb minerals and pollutants from the water. Some species thrive on manure-rich water, and can be fed to livestock, thus completing the recycling process. In addition, some species (such as in *Wolffia*) are potential sources of food for humans because they contain about 40 percent protein (dry weight) and are equivalent to soybeans in their amino acid content (with high levels of all essential amino acids except methionine). Species of *Lemna* and *Spirodela* are also high in protein but contain high concentrations of potentially toxic calcium oxalate crystals in their cell vacuoles. *Wolffia globosa*, known locally as *khai-nam* or water-eggs, is eaten by people in Southeast Asia. Evidence also indicates that certain duckweeds were consumed by pre-Columbian cultures of Central and South America.

References. FRENCH, J. C., M. CHUNG, AND Y. HUR. 1995. Chloroplast DNA phylogeny of Ariflorae. In *Monocotyledons: Systematics and Evolution*, eds. P. J. Rudall, P. J. Cribb, D. F. Cutler, and C. J. Humphries, 255–75. Richmond, Surrey, U.K.: Royal Botanic Gardens, Kew. LANDOLT, E. 1986. The family of Lemnaceae: a monographic study (vol. 1). *Ver. Geobot. Inst. E.T.H., Stiftung Rübel* 71: 1–566. LANDOLT, E. 1992. *Wolffiella caudata*, a new Lemnaceae species from the Bolivian Amazon region. *Ber. Geobot. Inst. E.T.H. Stiftung Rübel* 58:121–23. LANDOLT, E. 1994. Taxonomy and ecology of the section *Wolffia* of the genus *Wolffia* (Lemnaceae). *Ber. Geobot. Inst. E.T.H. Stiftung Rübel* 60:137–51. LANDOLT, E. 1998. Lemnaceae. In *The Families and Genera of Vascular Plants*, ed. K. Kubitzki, 4:264–70. New York: Springer-Verlag. LANDOLT, E., AND R. KANDELER. 1987. The family of Lemnaceae: a monographic study (vol. 2). *Ver. Geobot. Inst. ETH, Stiftung Rübel* 95:1–638. LES, D. H., AND D. J. CRAWFORD. 1999. *Landoltia* (Lemnaceae), a new genus of duckweeds. *Novon* 9:530–33. LES, D. H., D. J. CRAWFORD, E. LANDOLT, J. D. GABEL, AND R. T. KIMBALL. 2002. Phylogeny and systematics of Lemnaceae, the duckweed family. *Syst. Bot.* 27:221–40. MCCLURE, J. W., AND R. E. ALSTON. 1966. A chemotaxonomic study of Lemnaceae. *Amer. J. Bot.* 53:849–60.

LIMNOCHARITACEAE (Water-poppy Family)

ROBERT R. HAYNES

Plate 59

- *aquatic herbs*
- *milky sap present in vegetative structures and fruits*
- *leaves alternate, sometimes basal, simple; basal sheath present; petiole long; blade ovate to oval*
- *inflorescences umbels on short to elongate scapes*
- *flowers with perianth parts in 3s*
- *fruits follicles*

Numbers of genera and species. Worldwide, the Limnocharitaceae comprise three genera and eight species. In tropical America, there are two genera, *Hydrocleys* with five species and *Limnocharis* with two species.

Distribution and habitat. The Limnocharitaceae are widespread throughout the Tropics. *Hydrocleys* and *Limnocharis* occur naturally in the neotropics and *Butomopsis* is restricted to the paleotropics.

Species of the Limnocharitaceae occur in lakes, pools, and slow-moving streams, mostly at low elevations.

Family classification. The Limnocharitaceae are placed in the Alismatales by Dahlgren et al. The family is most closely related to the Alismataceae. Molecular analyses indicate that within the Alismatales, there are two subclades, the Hydrocharitaceae (including *Najas*) and a sister subclade consisting of the Limnocharitaceae and Alismataceae. The Limnocharitaceae have not been divided into subfamilies.

Features of the family. Habit: aquatic herbs, perennial, emergent or floating, the stems underground rhizomes or corms; milky sap present in vegetative structures and fruits. **Leaves** alternate, sometimes basal, simple; basal sheath present, without distinct ligule; petioles long, rigid and without septae in *Limnocharis* (projecting blades above water), or flexible and septate in *Hydrocleys* (floating on water); blades ovate to oval, the base ± rounded or cordate. **Inflorescences** on short to elongate scapes, umbels of 3–10+ flowers, the scape rigid and without septae in *Limnocharis* (projecting above water) or flexible and septate in *Hydrocleys* (floating on water). **Flowers** actinomorphic, bisexual; sepals 3, distinct, green; petals 3, distinct, usually larger than sepals (equal or shorter than sepals in some species of *Hydrocleys*), yellow to white; androecium with 3–numerous stamens, the stamens distinct, in several whorls when numerous, the outer 2 or 3 whorls often modified into staminodes, the filaments longer than anthers, the anthers basifixed; staminodes normally of filaments without anthers; gynoecium with superior ovaries, the carpels 3–numerous, distinct but sometimes cohering at least near base, in a single whorl, forming ring when numerous, the ring with obvious middle opening (much like a doughnut), the stigmas linear, sessile or subsessile; placentation laminar, the ovules few to numerous. **Fruits** follicles, fusiform and terete in *Hydrocleys* and obovate and flat in *Limnocharis*. **Seeds** several to many, U-shaped, attached to carpel wall (unlike Alismataceae), ornamented with hairs (*Hydrocleys*) or transverse ridges (*Limnocharis*).

Natural history. Some species have an unusual method of vegetative reproduction in which a vegetative bud forms in the inflorescence. The peduncle eventually bends enough for roots from the bud to contact the substrate. The new plant takes root and grows enough to become self-sustaining. The connection to the original inflorescence may be severed, resulting in a new, genetically identical individual.

Nothing is known about pollination and dispersal.

Econonomic uses. The family is of little economic importance. A few species are grown as ornamentals (e.g., *Hydrocleys nymphoides* and *Limnocharis flava*). *Limnocharis flava* is eaten as a vegetable in tropical Asia, where it has become naturalized.

References. ARGUE, C. L. 1973. The pollen of *Limnocharis flava* Buch., *Hydrocleis nymphoides* (Willd.) Buch., and *Tenagocharis latifolia* (Don) Buch. (Limnocharitaceae). *Grana* 13:108–12. HAYNES, R. R., AND L. B. HOLM-NIELSEN. 1992. The Limnocharitaceae. *Fl. Neotrop. Monogr.* 56:1–34. HAYNES, R. R., D. H. LES, AND L. B. HOLM-NIELSEN. 1998. Limnocharitaceae. In *The Families and Genera of Vascular Plants*, ed. K. Kubitzki, 4:271–75. New York: Springer-Verlag. LES, D. H., AND R. R. HAYNES. 1995. Systematics of Alismatiflorae: a synthesis of molecular and non-molecular approaches. In *Monocotyledons: Systematics and Evolution*, eds. P. Rudall, P. Cribb, D. Cutler, and C. Humphries, 353–77. Richmond, Surrey, U.K.: Royal Botanic Gardens, Kew. WILDER, G. J. 1974. Symmetry and development of *Butomus umbellatus* (Butomaceae) and *Limnocharis flava* (Limnocharitaceae). *Amer. J. Bot.* 61:379–94.

MARANTACEAE (Prayer-Plant Family)

DENNIS WM. STEVENSON AND JANICE WASSMER STEVENSON

Figure 239, Plate 59

- *herbs, rhizomatous*
- *leaves alternate, distichous, simple; sheath open, petiole pulvinate at apex; blade often asymmetrical*
- *flowers asymmetric; stamen 1, the theca 1; staminodes 2–4, usually petal-like; ovary inferior*
- *fruits loculicidal capsules or dry and indehiscent (Thalia), with persistent sepals*
- *seeds 1–3, arillate*

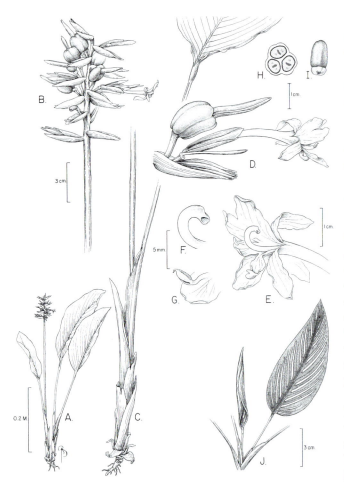

Figure 239. MARANTACEAE. *Calathea elliptica*. **A.** Plant showing roots, leaves, and inflorescence. **B.** Inflorescence. **C.** Base of plant showing roots, part of stem, and sheathing leaf bases. **D.** Part of inflorescence showing lateral views of flower (below) and fruit (above). **E.** Lateral view of apex of flower. **F.** Lateral view of upper part of style and stigma. **G.** Lateral view of stamen. **H.** Transverse section of fruit. **I.** Lateral view of seed with basal aril. **J.** Juvenile plant showing variegated leaf. Reprinted with permission from Mori et al. (1997). Artist: Bobbi Angell.

Numbers of genera and species. Worldwide, the Marantaceae comprise 31 genera and approximately 550 species. In tropical America, there are 13 genera and approximately 350 species. By far the most species rich genus is *Calathea* (300 species), followed by *Ctenanthe* (15), *Ischnosiphon* (35), *Maranta* (25), *Monotagma* (37), *Saranthe* (10), *Stromanthe* (20), and *Thalia* (5). Genera with fewer than five species are *Hylaenthe*, *Koernickanthe*, *Monophyllanthe*, *Myrosma*, *Pleiostachya*, and *Sanblasia*.

Distribution and habitat. The Marantaceae are mainly pantropical, with a few species extending into temperate areas of the New World. A majority of the species and genera are Neotropical, with a few representatives in West Central Africa and Asia, mainly in the Indomalesian region.

In the neotropics, there are four principal areas of distribution: 1) the Pacific lowlands and western Andean slopes and Central America north to Guatemala and southern Mexico, 2) the eastern Andean slopes and western Amazon Basin from Bolivia to central Colombia, 3) the Guianas and the eastern Amazon Basin, and 4) the coastal rain forests of southeastern Brazil.

Plants of the family generally grow in tropical rainforest from sea level to 1,000 meters. Most species prefer areas of natural disturbance (i.e., light gaps caused by tree falls and storms) and very few actually grow as understory herbs under closed canopies.

Family classification. The Marantaceae are placed in the Zingiberales by Dahlgren et al. Originally, the Marantaceae and Cannaceae were placed in the same family, the Cannaceae. Recent workers recognize both families but acknowledge their close relationship by placing them in the same order. Takhtajan has established an order, the Cannales, containing only the Cannaceae and Marantaceae. The close relationship of the Cannaceae and Marantaceae is supported by cladistic analyses of morphological data and combined morphological and molecular data.

Five informal groups have been recognized within the Marantaceae. The *Donax* and *Phrynium* groups, together with 11 genera, are found only in Africa and Asia. The *Calathea* and *Myrosma* groups are primarily endemic to the New World Tropics. Of the genera in these groups, *Calathea* is by far the largest and economically most important. The *Maranta* group, with five genera, is found in the neotropics, Africa, and the Réunion and Comoro Islands. The two paleotropical genera of the *Maranta* group, *Marantochloa* and *Afrocalathea*, form a subgroup, whereas the three Neotropical genera, *Maranta*, *Monophyllanthe*, and *Koernickanthe*, form another subgroup.

Features of the family. Habit: herbs, the rhizomes horizontal, branched, with short internodes (tuberlike in appearance) or elongated with thin ephemeral scalelike leaves; aerial shoots short or long and branched, sometimes scandent. **Leaves** alternate, distichous, simple; sheath open; petiole pulvinate at apex; blades often asymmetrical, sometimes with striking colored patterns. **Inflorescences** terminal or terminating a lateral branch, thyrses composed of few-flowered cymes; bracts green and often conspicuous. **Flowers** asymmetric, bisexual, often in pairs; perianth in 2 whorls of 3; sepals 3, free, rather inconspicuous, green; petals 3, much longer than sepals, often yellow to white to purple, basally fused into tube, the median petal often longer than others; androecium with 1 stamen, the filament narrow to partly expanded and petallike, the theca 1; staminodes 2–4, petal-like, the outer whorl usually composed of 1–2 staminodes, the inner whorl composed of a stamen and 2 staminodes, 1 hoodlike (the cucullate staminode) and the other fleshy and firm (the callose staminode), all staminodes together fused to form a tube, the tube basally connate to petals; gynoecium syncarpous, the ovary inferior, 3-locular, often appearing 1-locular because 2 locules empty and compressed (e.g., *Ischnosiphon* and *Maranta*), the style 1, slender, the stigma slightly expanded apically, funnel-shaped; septal nectaries present; placentation axile or nearly basal, the ovules 1 per locule, often absent in 1–2 locules. **Fruits** usually loculicidal capsules, sometimes dry and indehiscent (*Thalia*). **Seeds** 1–3, subglobose to pyramidal, hard, operculate; aril present in dehiscent-fruited species.

Natural history. The apical pulvinus of the petiole allows the leaf blade to orient to light throughout the day, thereby allowing species of Marantaceae to utilize light coming from different angles. Most Neotropical species of *Calathea* are pollinated by bees, especially euglossines, but there are reports of visiting hummingbirds, which rob nectar from the flowers, as well as effect pollination. In the species of *Calathea* and *Thalia* that have been studied, the pollination mechanism is described as explosive secondary pollen presentation. Before the flowers open, sticky pollen is deposited in a stylar depression behind the stigma. At anthesis the style is included in the cucullate staminode held under tension by a pressure-sensitive spur (appendage of the cucullate staminode). When a pollinator strikes the spur, the style is released and pollen is transferred from the pollinator onto the stigma, and in the same movement a new load of pollen is placed from the stigma onto the pollinator. In a study of *Thalia geniculata*, bees triggered most flowers they visited, hummingbirds triggered about 50 percent of the flowers, and butterflies did not trigger any flowers. Species with arillate seeds appear to be dispersed by ants; e.g., in *Calathea micans*, *C. microcephala*, and *C. ovandensis*, the seeds drop to the ground when the fruits are ripe and ants, especially ponerines, carry them away to subsequently consume the lipid-rich appendages. Some species of *Calathea* with bright blue seeds may be bird-dispersed, but this has not been documented.

Economic uses. *Maranta arundinacea* (West Indian arrowroot) is a widely cultivated crop whose rhizomes contain an easily digestible starch, and the tubers of *Calathea allouia* (topee-tampoo) are eaten like potatoes in the West Indies. Some species of *Calathea* have inflorescences that are consumed by natives of Central America. Species of *Maranta* and *Calathea* are grown as indoor ornamental plants because of their showy and often variegated foliage. *Calathea* leaves are used for roofing, lining basketry, and as food wraps in the preparation of tamales and baked fish. The abaxial surfaces of the large leaves of *C. lutea* yield a commercial wax, the split stems of *Ischnosiphon arouma* are used to make baskets, and the hollowed out stems of other species of *Ischnosiphon* are employed by Amazonian Indians to blow snuff into their noses.

References. ANDERSSON, L. 1998. Marantaceae. In *The Families and Genera of Vascular Plants*, ed. K. Kubitzki, 4:278–93. New York: Springer-Verlag. BERNAL, H. Y., AND J. E. CORRERA Q. 1994. Marantaceae. In *Especies vegetales promisorias de los países del Convenio Andrés Bello*, Tomo X. Santafé de Bogotá, D. E., Colombia: Secretaria Ejecutiva del Convenio Andrés Bello. DAVIS, M. A. 1987. The role of flower visitors in the explosive pollination of *Thalia geniculata*. *Bull. Torrey Bot. Club* 114:134–38. KENNEDY, H. 1978. Systematics and pollination of the "closed-flowered" species of *Calathea*. Univ. Calif. Publ. Bot. 71:1–90. KRESS, J. 1990. The phylogeny and classification of the Zingiberales. *Ann. Missouri Bot. Gard.* 77:698–721. KRESS, J. 1995. Phylogeny of the Zingiberanae: morphology and molecules. In *Monocotyledons: Systematics and Evolution*, eds. P. Rudall, P. Cribb, D. Cutler, and C. Humphries, 2:443–60. Richmond, Surrey, U.K.: Royal Botanic Gardens, Kew. LINDER, H. P., AND E. A. KELLOGG. 1995. Phylogenetic patterns in the commelinid clade. In *Monocotyledons: Systematics and Evolution*, eds. P. Rudall, P. Cribb, D. Cutler, and C. Humphries, 473–96. Richmond, Surrey, U.K.: Royal Botanic Gardens, Kew.

MAYACACEAE (Mayaca Family)

DENNIS WM. STEVENSON

Figure 240, Plate 59

- *rooted aquatic herbs; plants appearing mosslike*

- *leaves alternate (spiral), simple; blades small, narrow, the apices commonly bidentate*

- *flower parts in 3s; anthers poricidal; ovary superior*

- *fruits loculicidal capsules*

Numbers of genera and species. Worldwide, the Mayacaceae comprise a single genus, *Mayaca*, and four to 10 species. In tropical America, there are three to nine species.

Distribution and habitat. The Mayacaceae are disjunct with one species, *Mayaca baumii*, occurring in Zaire, Angola, and Zambia in West Africa, and the other three to nine

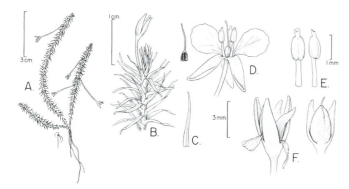

Figure 240. MAYACACEAE. *Mayaca sellowiana*. **A.** Plant showing roots, leaves, and flowers. **B.** Apex of stem with flower. **C.** Adaxial view of leaf. **D.** Lateral view of flower with one petal removed (right) and medial section of gynoecium (left). **E.** Adaxial (left) and lateral (right) views of stamens showing poricidal dehiscence of anthers via an apical tube. **F.** Lateral views of fruits surrounded by old floral parts (left) and with all but two sepals (right). Reprinted with permission from Mori et al. (1997). Artist: Bobbi Angell.

species ranging from the southeast United States through the West Indies and Central America to Paraguay.

Seeds of *Mayaca* are resistant to desiccation, and species are often found in water along riverbanks and lake margins that experience seasonal drying. Plants generally grow on depleted sandy soils that are devoid of other vegetation, indicating that species of *Mayaca* do not do well in competition with other plants.

Family classification. The Mayacaceae are placed in the Commelinales by Dahlgren et al. Cronquist, Takhtajan, and Dahlgren et al. place the Mayacaceae near to the Commelinaceae, although the former two authors suggest that a relationship with Xyridaceae is possible. Recent morphological and molecular data have placed *Mayaca* as sister to *Xyris* within the Xyridaceae.

Features of the family. Habit: rooted aquatic herbs, mosslike. **Leaves** alternate (spiral), simple; petioles absent; blades linear or nearly filiform, the apices commonly bidentate. **Inflorescences** axillary, of solitary flowers. **Flowers** actinomorphic, bisexual, the calyx and corolla strongly differentiated; sepals 3, distinct, green; petals 3, distinct, basally constricted, white (occasionally with lavender); androecium of 3 stamens, the stamens alternating with petals, the anthers dehiscing by apical pores; gynoecium syncarpous, the ovary superior, the carpels 3, the locule 1, the style simple, terminal, the stigma short capitate or slightly trifid; placentation parietal, the ovules several to numerous, arranged in 2 rows on each of 3 placentas, bitegmic, orthotropous. **Fruits** loculicidal capsules, with 3 lines of dehiscence, each midway between two placentas. **Seeds** several to numerous per fruit, ovoid to globose, with longitudinal ridges and an operculum.

Natural history. The poricidal dehiscence of the anthers indicates buzz pollination by bees and the dehiscent fruits and proximity to water suggest water dispersal.

Economic uses. *Mayaca* is sold as an aquarium plant, but is very rarely cultivated successfully. The plants apparently require low nutrients, require some drying out, and do not compete well with other aquarium plants.

References. LOURTEIG, A. 1952. Mayacaceae. *Notul. Syst. (Paris)* 14:234–48. STEVENSON, D. 1998. Mayacaceae. In *The Families and Genera of Vascular Plants*, ed. K. Kubitzki, 4:294–96. New York: Springer-Verlag. THIERET, J. W. 1975. The Mayacaceae in the southeastern United States. *J. Arnold Arbor.* 56:248–55. VENTURELLI, M. AND F. BOUMAN. 1986. Embryology and seed development in *Mayaca fluviatilis* (Mayacaceae). *Acta. Bot. Neerl.* 35:497–516.

MELANTHIACEAE (Bunch Flower Family)

DAWN FRAME

Figure 241

- *lilylike herbs*

- *rhizomes, bulb-rhizomes, or bulbs present*

- *leaves spirodistichous to distichous, mostly basal; blades linear and grasslike*

- *inflorescences racemes or panicles*

- *flowers with 6 tepals*

Numbers of genera and species. Worldwide, the Melanthiaceae comprise more than 20 genera and well above 100 species. In tropical America, there are five genera and about 31–33 species: *Nietneria* (Nartheciae) accounts for two species, *Schoenocaulon* (Melanthieae) 22, *Stenanthium* (Melanthieae) one, *Tofieldia* [= *Isidrogalvia*] (Tofieldieae) three to five, and *Zigadenus* (Melanthieae) three.

Distribution and habitat. The family is essentially north temperate, but has some extensions into tropical eastern

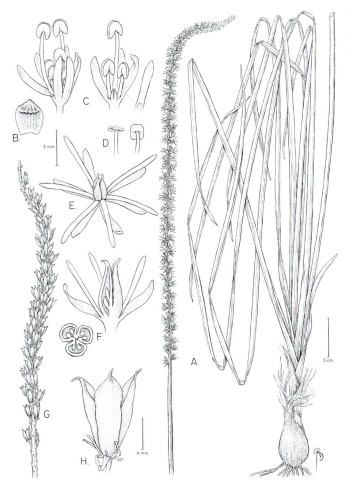

Figure 241. *Schoenocaulon officinale* (A–F, Tillett 839–55; G–H, Lawrence 888). **A.** Plant showing roots, bulb, and leaves (right) and inflorescence (left). **B.** Bract. **C.** Lateral view of flower (left), view of distal, functionally staminate flower with 3 tepals and 3 stamens removed (right) and close-up of tepal showing distinct nectary at base (lower right). **D.** Views of dry stamens. **E.** Oblique-apical view of bisexual flower after anthers have fallen. **F.** Medial section of bisexual flower (right) and transverse section of ovary (left). **G.** Infructescence. **H.** Lateral view of fruit. Original. Artist: Bobbi Angell.

Asia, Malaya, Borneo (the saprophytic, achlorophyllous genera *Petrosavia* and *Protolirion*: Petrosaviaeae), Mexico, Central America, and northern South America. This anomalous distribution pattern may be explained by the fact that the members represent several ancient liliaceous lineages, as well as there being disparate elements included in the family as circumscribed by Dahlgren et al. The members of the three tribes, Narthecieae, Melanthieae, and Tofieldieae, which are found in tropical America, are unquestionably extensions of north-temperate lineages. This is reflected in the fact that all tropical American species outside of Mexico grow in upland locations, usually above 1,000 meters.

With the exception of *Schoenocaulon officinale* (see below) and *Zigadenus volcanicus* (which grows as far south as Guatemala), tropical members of the Melanthieae remain

within the borders of Mexico, and *Schoenocaulon* has its center of diversity there. The single, poorly known Neotropical species of *Stenanthium*, *S. frigidum*, is endemic to pine forests of central Mexico from 2,700 to 3,700 meters.

Schoenocaulon officinale is the most widespread of all tropical American Melanthiaceae, growing from central Mexico to Colombia, Venezuela, and Peru where it is often found in grassy savannas from 1,000 to 2,000 meters.

Species of *Tofieldia* are endemic to the *páramos* of western Venezuela, Colombia, Ecuador, and Peru or the *tepuis* of southern Venezuela and northern Brazil, and *Nietneria* has one species endemic to tops of *tepuis* and another to savannas in neighboring Roraima. In *Tofieldia*, South American species more closely resemble one another than they do their North American congeners, although in sum the differences between the northern and southern species are minor and merely a matter of degree.

Family classification. The Melanthiaceae are placed in the Melanthiales by Dahlgren et. al., and the family as defined by these authors comprises six tribes: Petrosavieae, Melanthieae, Narthecieae, Tofieldieae, Chiongraphideae, and Xerophylleae. With exception of the inclusion of the Petrosavieae, this is fairly standard treatment. The three Neotropical tribes, Melanthieae, Narthecieae, and Tofieldieae, form a natural group, with Narthecieae and Tofieldieae more closely related to each other than to Melanthieae. Additionally, Melanthieae is the most clearly circumscribed tribe of all lilies. However, within Melanthieae, and excepting *Schoenocaulon*, which is distinct, recent proposals to unite genera merit consideration.

Both *Tofieldia* and *Nietneria* are rhizomatous, whereas, the first appearance of the bulb among archaic liliaceous plants occurs in the tribe Melanthieae. In this tribe there are rhizomes, bulb-rhizomes, and bulbs. The bulbs that characterize Liliaceae *sensu stricto* are better developed and have a greater amount of storage material in the leaf bases than do those found in Melanthieae, and it is likely that Liliaceae *sensu stricto* has its evolutionary "roots" in Melanthieae. In recent years, there has been massive inflation of taxonomic rank in Liliaceae *sensu lato*, hence previously recognized genera have become families, and some subfamilies and families have become orders, obscuring natural relationships. Further, phylogenetic analyses based on the very limited morphological characters available in lilies and/or molecular data have produced very complicated and unstable evolutionary trees.

Features of the family. Habit: perennial herbs, lilylike, rhizomes often present, or bulb-rhizomes to bulbs (Melanthieae) present. **Leaves** spirodistichous or distichous, mostly basal; blades linear, grasslike, unifacial or bifacial. **Inflorescences** emerging from leaf bases, either racemes or panicles. **Flowers** actinomorphic, bisexual or sometimes unisexual (often functionally so), small, 3-merous; tepals 6, distinct or nearly so, in 2 whorls (appearing as a single whorl because segments inserted in a tight, condensed spiral); simple nectaries often present at base of tepals, or in seams between carpels; androecium of 6 stamens, the stamens usually distinct, sometimes pubescent (as in *Narthecium*), in 2 whorls; gynoecium with semi-inferior to superior ovaries, the carpels 3, distinct or fused to varying degrees, the styles topping carpels, cohesion varying according to carpel cohesion; placentation marginal to axile, the ovules few to many. **Fruits** often capsules, variously dehiscent. **Seeds** few to many, sometimes winged.

Natural history. *Schoenocaulon officinale* is recognized easily by its graceful plumelike inflorescence. Unlike most other species of Melanthiaceae, it can grow successfully in disturbed habitats. Other than occasional observational notes recorded on herbarium specimens indicating that the flowers are fragrant and that Hymenoptera and Lepidoptera have been observed visiting them, not much is known about the pollination biology of this and other Melanthiaceae. As far as known, Neotropical Melanthiaceae possess no special seed-dispersal mechanisms, and their seeds simply fall to the ground near the parent plant. Asexual propagation is almost always an option in the family, and of particular importance in bunch-forming rhizomatous species.

Economic uses. An important character uniting the Melanthieae (also known as the Veratreae) is the presence of steroidal alkaloids, among the most complex chemical substances produced by plants and of very limited occurrence. *Schoenocaulon* is characterized by the presence of cerveratrum alkamines, which are used to treat high blood pressure and as powerful insecticides. The dried, powdered seeds of *S. officinale* held an important place in the Mexican, Central American, and northern South American aboriginal and later European pharmacopoeias. Commonly known as *sabadilla* or *cebadilla*, its uses were enumerated by Nicolos Monardes in the late sixteenth century. He described it as looking like barley, probably because of its spikelike raceme, and it is likely to have been an object of trade among the Amerindians. Indigenous American people commonly used the powdered dried seeds for controlling lice and worms. They also

may have been aware of its strong insecticidal activity and may even have applied it to crops. Thus, *sabadilla* may represent one of the earliest known natural plant-derived insecticides. Today, *sabadilla* is found sold as an insecticide for use in organic gardening and in the homeopathic pharmacopeia as a treatment for hay fever. The colonists gradually recognized that it possessed properties similar to veratrine, a European drug usually extracted from the rhizome of *Veratrum* and used for treatment of heart and blood-pressure ailments. Europeans eventually learned that the source of the New World drug was the *sabadilla* seed, and it was exported to Europe. This handsome plant adorns the slopes of Avila that rise above Caracas, Venezuela, where it was planted in great numbers during World War I for use in treating infestations of lice, which were rampant in the trenches.

References. CRUDEN, R. W. 1991. A revision of *Isidrogalvia* (Liliaceae): recognition for Ruiz and Pavón's Genus. *Syst. Bot.* 16:270–82. FRAME, D. 1989. *Schoenocaulon* A. Gray. In *Flora Novo-Galiciana*, R. McVaugh, 15:263–75. FRAME, D. M. 1990. A revision of *Schoenocaulon* (Liliaceae: Melanthieae). Ph.D. diss., City University of New York. FRAME, D., A. ESPEJO, AND A. R. LOPEZ-FERRARI. 1999. A conspectus of Mexican Melanthiaceae including a description of new taxa of *Schoenocaulon* and *Zigadenus*. *Acta Bot. Mex.* 48:27–50. KUPCHAN, S. M., J. H. ZIMMERMAN, AND A. AFONSO. 1961. The alkaloids and taxonomy of *Veratrum* and related genera. *Lloydia* 24:1–26. RUDALL, P. J., K. L. STOBART, W-P. HONG, J. G. CONRAN, C. A. FURNESS, ET AL. 2000. Consider the lilies: systematics of Liliales. In *Monocots: Systematics and Evolution*, eds. K. I. Wilson and D. A. Morrison. Collingwood, Australia: CSIRO. STEYERMARK, J. A. 1951. Contributions to the flora of Venezuela. *Fieldiana, Bot.* 28:153–54. ZOMLEFER, W. B., N. H. WILLIAMS, W. M. WHITTEN, AND W. S. JUDD. 2001. Generic circumscription and relationships in the tribe Melanthieae (Liliales, Melanthiaceae), with emphasis on *Zigadenus*: evidence from ITS and *TRNL-F* sequence data. *Amer. J. Bot.* 88:1657–69.

MUSACEAE (Banana Family)

DENNIS WM. STEVENSON AND JANICE WASSMER STEVENSON

- *large to giant herbs, rhizomatous; pseudostems formed by overlapping leaf sheaths*
- *leaves alternate, spirally arranged, simple; sheath open*
- *inflorescences terminal, massive, pendent, with purple bracts, the pistillate flowers proximal, the staminate flowers distal*
- *flowers zygomorphic, functionally unisexual (plants monoecious); ovary inferior*
- *fruits elongate berries with leathery, yellow to red pericarps*
- *seeds usually absent in Neotropical plants.*

Numbers of genera and species. Worldwide, the Musaceae comprise two genera, *Musa* (including *Musella*) with approximately 35 species and *Ensete* with six species. There are no native American species, and, generally, only cultivated hybrids of *Musa* are found in tropical America.

Distribution and habitat. The Musaceae are a widespread Paleotropical family ranging from Africa to East Asia, Australia, and the Pacific Islands. They generally prefer lowland tropical forests but also grow in cloud forests. The "banana," *Musa X sapientum*, and the "plantain," *Musa X paradisiaca*, are both widely cultivated in the neotropics, where they were introduced from Africa and/or Asia. Species of *Ensete* are widespread in Central Africa to Ethiopia, the Transvaal, and throughout Southeast Asia to New Guinea and Java.

Family classification. The Musaceae are placed in the Zingiberales by Dahlgren et al. Takhtajan established an order, the Musales, containing only the Musaceae, Heliconiaceae, and Strelitziaceae. The close relationship of these families is supported by cladistic analyses of morphological data and combined morphological and molecular data. *Ensete* is considered distinct from *Musa* mainly because it lacks a petiole between the sheath and the lamina of its leaves and because it does not sprout from the base. *Musa lasiocarpa*, an endemic of China, has been separated from *Musella* based on its sessile inflorescence, but this segregate is generally not accepted.

Features of the family. Habit: large to giant herbs; rhizome cormlike; pseudostem of overlapping leaf sheaths, enclosing peduncle of large terminal inflorescence. **Leaves** alternate, spirally arranged, simple; petiole usually 1 to several meters long; sheath open; blades with parallel venation, the veins joining at margins to form conspicuous marginal vein, with age, the leaves often tear between veins and appear ragged. **Inflorescences** terminal, massive, becoming pendent, thyrses of many-flowered cymes, each cyme subtended by boat-shaped, purple bract, the proximal cymes of pistillate flowers, the distal ones of staminate flowers. **Flowers** zygomorphic, functionally unisexual; perianth in 2 whorls of 3, the median sepal free, curved downward, the 5 remaining tepals basally connate; androecium with parts in 2 whorls. **Staminate flowers**: stamens generally 5, the filaments slender, adnate to perianth tube, the anthers long, the thecae 2; staminode 1 (sometimes absent), representing median stamen of inner whorl. **Pistillate flowers**: staminodes 5, median staminode of inner whorl absent; gynoecium syncarpous, ovary inferior, 3-locular, the style 1, terminal, the stigma undivided; septal nectaries present; placentation axile, the ovules many, occurring in 2 rows per locule. **Fruits** elongate berries, the pericarp leathery, yellow to red, the interior pulp homogeneous, fleshy. **Seeds** many, or absent in hybrids of neotropics (aborted ovules appearing as black specks), subglobose, black, hard, operculate; aril absent, but seeds sometimes provided with basal tuft of hairs (in ornamental and agriculturally introduced species of neotropics).

Natural history. In their native habitats of the Old World, some species of *Musa* are bat-pollinated, and others have been reported to be bird-pollinated. The bat-pollinated species have pendent inflorescences with flowers that are open for only one night, whereas those that appear to be bird-pollinated have erect inflorescences with flowers that are open for more than one day. Edible bananas and plantains are triploids and thus are sterile. The fruits develop without fertilization, and the black dots in them are the remnants of abortive ovules. Because they have no seeds and produce no vegetative runners, cultivated bananas are not able to spread beyond the area of their original planting. They are cultivated extensively, however, by offshoots of the rhizome and are found widely in previous sites of human habitation.

Economic uses. *Ensete ventricosum* has edible flower heads and seeds, and the leaf sheaths yield a useful fiber. *Musa*, the banana genus, provides a staple food of great importance in the Tropics and in international trade. Most fruit bananas belong to the hybrid *Musa X sapientum* and vary greatly in size, shape, color, and sugar content of the fruits. Some bananas with smaller fruit are cultivated in temperate greenhouses. Plantains, or starch bananas, often are referred to as *Musa X paradisiaca*. They are cooked as a vegetable in the Tropics and often constitute a major carbohydrate source. The leaves of *Ensete* and *Musa* are used as sources of fiber; e.g., *M. textilis* from the Philippines is manila hemp. The leaves of *Musa X sapientum* make up the outer wrap of some "bidi" cigarettes of India and southeastern Asia.

References. ANDERSSON, L. Musaceae. In *The Families and Genera of Vascular Plants*, ed. K. Kubitzki, 4:296–301. New York: Springer-Verlag. CHASE, M., D. STEVENSON, P. WILKEN, AND P. RUDALL. 1995. Monocot systematics: a combined analysis. In *Monocotyledons: Systematics and Evolution*, eds. P. Rudall, P. Cribb, D. Cutler, and C. Humphries, 685–730. Richmond, Surrey, U.K.: Royal Botanic Gardens, Kew. FISHER, J. B. 1978. Leaf-opposed buds in *Musa*: their development and a comparison with allied monocotyledons. *Amer. J. Bot.* 65:784–91. HALLÉ, F., R. OLDEMAN, AND P. TOMLINSON. 1978. *Tropical Trees and Forests: An Architectural Analysis*. Berlin: Springer-Verlag. SIMMONDS, N. W. 1966. *Bananas*. 2nd ed. London: Longmans. START, A. N., AND A. G. MARSHALL. 1976. Nectarivorous bats as pollinators of trees in west Malaysia. In *Tropical Trees, Variation, Breeding and Conservation*, eds. J. Burley and S. Styles, 141–50. London: Academic Press. STEVENSON, D. W., AND H. LOCONTE. 1995. Cladistic analysis of monocot families. In *Monocotyledons: Systematics and Evolution*, eds. P. Rudall, P. Cribb, D. Cutler, and C. Humphries, 543–78. Richmond, Surrey, U.K.: Royal Botanic Gardens, Kew. TOMLINSON, P. 1969. Commelinales-Zingiberales. In *Anatomy of the Monocotyledons*, ed. C. R. Metcalfe, vol. 3. Oxford, U.K.: Clarendon Press.

NOLINACEAE (Pony-tail Plant Family)

DENNIS WM. STEVENSON

- *stems generally pachycalous*

- *leaves alternate, in rosettes, simple; blades linear, fibrous*

- *inflorescences terminal, panicles, often highly branched and profusely flowered*

Numbers of genera and species. The Nolinaceae comprise four genera, *Beaucarnea, Calibanus, Dasylirion,* and *Nolina,* and 50 species endemic to the Western Hemisphere. All four genera and the majority of species occur in tropical America and northern Mexico.

Distribution and habitat. The family is found from the southwestern United States to central Mexico. Plants of the Nolinaceae generally grow in arid habitats on rocky or sandy soils.

Family classification. The Nolinaceae are placed in the Asparagales by Dahlgren et al. and recent molecular data supports this view. Within this Asparagales, the Nolinaceae are probably most closely related to the Convallariaceae, Dracaenaceae, and Ruscaceae. Some authors place these families in a broadly defined Ruscaceae. The presence of the rare flavanol, 3-O-methyl-8-C-methylquercetin, distinguishes the Nolinaceae from the Agavaceae and other related families.

Features of the family. Habit: generally large, arborescent, the stem generally pachycalous, woody, sometimes somewhat succulent, simple or sparingly branched, to 10 meters tall, bearing terminal rosettes of leaves. **Leaves** alternate, in rosettes, simple, sessile; blades linear, fibrous, the margins entire to serrate (*Nolina*) or armed with curved prickles (*Dasylirion*), up to 2 m long. **Inflorescences** terminal, panicles, often highly branched and profusely flowered. **Flowers** actinomorphic, bisexual or unisexual (plants polygamodioecious or dioecious), articulate with pedicel; tepals 6, petal-like, distinct, equal; androecium of 6 stamens, the stamens in 2 alternating whorls, the anthers epipeltate; gynoecium syncarpous, the ovary superior, the carpels 3, the locule(s) 1 in *Dasylirion, Beaucarnea,* and *Calibanus* or 3 in *Nolina,* the style short, the stigma 3-lobed; septal nectaries present;

placentation parietal in unilocular genera and axile in 3-locular genera, the placentas 3 in *Dasylirion, Beaucarnea,* and *Calibanus,* the ovules 2 (3–6 in *Dasylirion*) per locule. **Fruits** more or less dry, 3-angled, globose and indehiscent in *Calibanus,* 3-winged samara (1-seeded) in *Beaucarnea,* bursting irregularly in *Nolina,* dehiscing by 3 valves in *Dasylirion.* **Seeds** 1–3, globose to almost triangular, straw colored to almost black, phytomelans absent.

The stems of Nolinaceae have considerable secondary growth from a meristem that continuously produces additional parenchyma internally in which new vascular bundles and fibers develop.

Natural history. The stems of some species (e.g., *Beaucarnea recurvata,* the pony tail plant) develop swollen bases that store water. Various insects, especially small bees but also beetles, flies, butterflies, and wasps, are known to visit the flowers of Nolinaceae, most likely attracted by nectar and pollen. The winged or inflated and winged fruits of *Beaucarnea, Dasylirion,* and *Nolina* suggest wind dispersal.

Economic uses. The leaves of *Beaucarnea, Nolina,* and *Dasylirion* are used for thatching and basketry. The pulp of the young shoots of *D. texanum* has been utilized by indigenous people as a source of sugar and for making a drink called *sotol.* Swollen stems and leaf bases of *Dasylirion* have been roasted and eaten as a source of starch. *Beaucarnea recurvata* is a common houseplant.

References. BOGLER, D. 1998. Nolinaceae. In *The Families and Genera of Vascular Plants,* ed. K. Kubitzki, 3:392–97. New York: Springer-Verlag. RUDALL, P. 1991. Lateral meristems and stem thickening growth in monocotyledons. *Bot. Rev.* 57:150–63. YAMASHITA, J., AND M. TAMURA. 2000. Molecular phylogeny of the Convallariaceae (Asparagales). *In Monocots: Systematics and Evolution,* 387–400. Melbourne: CSIRO.

ORCHIDACEAE (Orchid Family)

Eric Christenson

Figures 242, 243; Plate 60

- *herbs, the majority epiphytes*

- *roots thick, surrounded by white velamen; stems often modified as pseudobulbs*

- *flowers zygomorphic, one petal modified into a lip often highly ornamented with callus, keels, or false stamens*

- *sexual structures fused into a central column; mostly 1 fertile anther but sometimes 2 (Cypripedioideae) or 3 (Apostasioideae).*

- *pollen usually fused into pollinia with associated delivery systems of caudicles, stipes, and viscidia*

Numbers of genera and species. Worldwide, the Orchidaceae is considered to be the largest family of flowering plants, with best estimates of at least 20,000 species in about 700 genera. The larger genera with estimates of their species richness are the pantropical *Bulbophyllum* (1,500) and *Habenaria* (600); *Dendrobium* (900) and *Eria* (500) of the Eastern Hemisphere; and *Epidendrum* (800), *Lepanthes* (460), *Maxillaria* (420), *Oncidium* (420), and *Pleurothallis* (1,120) of the Western Hemisphere.

Distribution and habitat. Orchids are found in virtually every place on the planet where vascular plant life exists, from above the Arctic Circle to equivalent areas of the Southern Hemisphere. They reach their zenith in diversity in montane tropical regions where abundant rainfall allows for the maximum growth of epiphytes. In the Western Hemisphere, the greatest diversity occurs in the Andes from Colombia to Peru, with each country estimated to have more than 3,000 species. Several large genera are pantropical (e.g., *Bulbophyllum, Habenaria, Malaxis,* and *Vanilla*). Individual species range from narrowly restricted endemics to widespread, often common plants. Only two species are pantropical, *Liparis nervosa* and *Polystachya concreta*. A number of orchids are adapted to colonizing disturbed habitats and have become naturalized outside their original range. In particular, *Arundina graminifolia, Oeceoclades maculata, Spathoglottis plicata,* and *Zeuxine strateumatica* have emigrated with humans from the Eastern to the Western Hemisphere.

Family classification. The Orchidaceae are placed in the Liliales by Dahlgren et al. Recent analyses suggest the Orchidaceae are a basal group within the Asparagales, near families such as the Iridaceae and Hypoxidaceae.

Dressler proposed the most widely followed overall scheme for the family with five subfamilies, the Apostasioideae, Cypripedioideae, Epidendroideae, Orchidoideae, and Spiranthoideae. The Apostasioideae, sometimes separated as the distinct family Apostasiaceae, comprises two Eastern Hemisphere genera with actinomorphic flowers, *Apostasia* and *Neuwiedia*. These so-called "primitive" orchids have two or three fertile anthers that are mostly free from the stigma unlike the reductions and fusions found in the other subfamilies. Unlike other orchids, *Apostasia* and *Neuwiedia* are buzz-pollinated by bees and bear powdery pollen that is not aggregated into pollinia.

The Cypripedioideae, sometimes separated as the distinct family Cypripediaceae, comprises four or five genera known as lady's slipper orchids because of their pouchlike lips. They bear two fertile anthers with sticky, glutinous pollen beneath a column terminated by a generally shield-shaped staminode. *Cypripedium* is a circumboreal genus with subtropical species in southern China and Mexico. *Paphiopedilum*, a genus of the Eastern Hemisphere, commonly cultivated and hybridized. The other two genera, *Phragmipedium* and *Selenipedium*, are Neotropical and range from southern Mexico to Bolivia.

The Orchidoideae and Spiranthoideae are casually called the terrestrial orchids since most of their genera and species are terrestrial. The Orchidoideae is characterized by bearing an anther with a basal viscidium; i.e., the apex of the anther is terminal on the column and the viscidium is beneath it. In contrast, the Spiranthoideae is characterized by bearing an anther with a viscidium terminal on the column. Both subfamilies are cosmopolitan in distribution. Commonly seen members of the Orchidoideae include *Platanthera* in temperate North America and *Habenaria* in the Tropics. Commonly seen members of the Spiranthoideae include *Goodyera*, the North American rattlesnake plantains, and *Spiranthes*, the temperate lady's tresses.

The Epidendroideae, referred to casually as the epiphytic

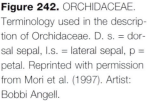

Figure 242. ORCHIDACEAE. Terminology used in the description of Orchidaceae. D. s. = dorsal sepal, l.s. = lateral sepal, p = petal. Reprinted with permission from Mori et al. (1997). Artist: Bobbi Angell.

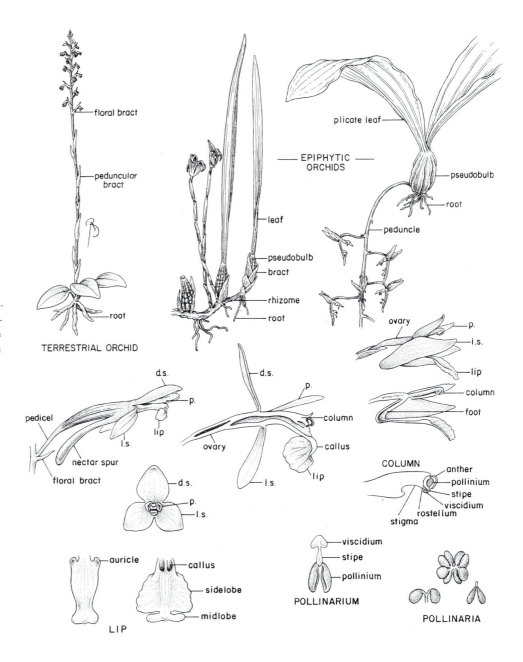

orchids because it includes most of the epiphytic orchid genera and species, comprise most popularly cultivated orchids such as *Cattleya, Cymbidium, Dendrobium, Oncidium, Phalaenopsis,* and *Vanda.* The Epidendroideae are considered the most highly evolved group of orchids, exhibiting the widest range of floral diversity. The pollen of this subfamily is always in hard masses called pollinia. The pollinia may be essentially naked, associated with simple caudicles, or be part of a pollinarium, the collective term for pollinia accompanied by a stipe and viscidium.

One anomalous group, including *Vanilla,* possesses "primitive" characters such as a thickened seed coat and fleshy fruits and was once proposed as a separate family, the Vanillaceae. Coincidentally, this group includes the Asiatic genus *Galeola,* known as the world's largest saprophyte, with some species growing to many meters tall.

Features of the family. Habit: terrestrial, lithophytic, or epiphytic herbs exhibiting sympodial or monopodial growth, sometimes saprophytic, rarely subterranean. **Roots** fleshy, with a specialized absorptive layer (velamen), sometimes modified into tubers, tuberoids, or dactyloid structures, sometimes fasciculate and villose, basal and penetrating the substrate or aerial. **Rhizomes** absent or present, short to elongate, horizontal to ascending, often stout and somewhat woody. **Stems** short to elongate, terete to swollen into pseudobulbs, with 1–many nodes, leafy or naked. **Leaves** usually alternate, sometimes opposite, whorled, or all basal, simple, 1–many, sometimes absent, usually with an abscission layer, conduplicate or plicate, thin-textured to rigid-leathery, sometimes terete, sometimes patterned. **Inflorescences** axillary, basal, or terminal, sessile to long-pedunculate, of solitary flowers, racemes, or panicles; bracts minute to conspicuous,

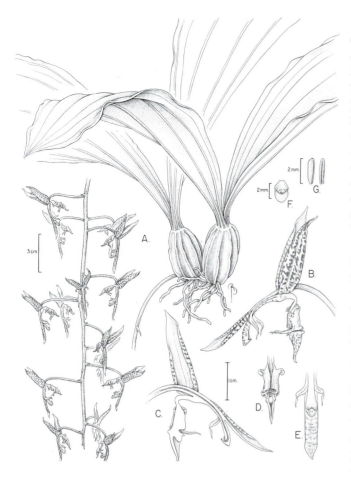

Figure 243. ORCHIDACEAE. *Gongora pleiochroma*. **A.** Base of plant showing roots, pseudobulbs, and leaves (right) and inflorescence (left). **B.** Lateral view of flower. **C.** Medial section of flower. **D.** Adaxial view of lip. **E.** Adaxial view of column. **F.** Anther. **G.** Pollinia. Reprinted with permission from Mori et al. (1997). Artist: Bobbi Angell.

rarely colorful. **Flowers** zygomorphic, usually bisexual, infrequently unisexual (then plants monoecious or dioecious), 1–100s per plant, minute to large and flamboyant, diaphanous to fleshy, in every color (though rarely blue), ephemeral to extremely long-lasting, often fragrant, the sepals and petals similar or distinct, one petal modifed into a lip usually larger and differently colored than other segments, the segments free or variously fused; lip often saccate or spurred, most often with ornamentation of callus, keels, warts, false stamens, pseudopollen, etc.; gynoecium and androecium fused into central column, the structures separated by a specialized flap of tissue (rostellum) that isolates pollinia from stigmatic cavity, the column often with subapical wings, often with a column foot, the foot sometimes incurved and fused to base of lateral sepals forming a mentum; fertile anthers mostly 1 but also 2 (Cypripedioideae) or 3 (Apostasioideae); ovary inferior, the carpels 3, the locule 1; placentation parietal (axile in Apostasioideae), the ovules very numerous, tiny. **Fruits** dry capsules, rarely fleshy and indehiscent. **Seeds** minute, dustlike, lacking endosperm.

Orchids are named after the Greek term for "testicle" because many European genera, including the type genus *Orchis*, bear plants with paired tubers resembling testicles. Believing this was a message from God concerning their intended utility to man, Medieval authors reported the supposed medical benefits of the plant's consumption. Most European terrestrial orchids bear unevenly sized tubers, one shrivelling in the production of the current season's growth and the other growing plump with starch for the subsequent overwintering. A ribald mythology existed that ingesting a decoction of the plump tuber would create a Lothario of truly epic proportions while the accidental ingestion of the shrivelled tuber would lead to a parallel shrivelling of any would-be Don Juan.

Natural history. Orchids have an obligate symbiosis with fungi, and upon germination, the embryo of an orchid is invaded by a symbiotic fungus. In some orchids, especially terrestrial species, this symbiosis is necessary throughout the plant's life span. In other orchids, especially epiphytic species, this symbiosis appears to be required only during early seedling development prior to photosynthesis.

Orchids always have fascinated humans because of their intricate flowers, which are related directly to equally intricate pollination mechanisms. A great truism of orchids is that they practice remarkably deceptive sex, and many species offer no real reward to pollinators. This ensures effective pollination, while avoiding the energy drain of nectar production. In ancient times, the European genus *Ophrys* captivated the imagination because of a pollination mechanism called pseudocopulation. The flowers literally resemble female insects, and, through a combination of colors, textures, and fragrances, lure male insects to attempt mating.

Modern study of orchid pollination has shown a highly complex co-evolution with insects and, to a much lesser extent, birds. Great specificity usually exists between an orchid species and its pollinator. In most cases, only one species of insect pollinates an orchid, and often only one sex of that insect visits the orchid. The rostellum plays an essential role in properly positioning the pollinarium on a potential pollinator. Closely related species of orchids may share a pollinator because they can position their pollinia on different parts of the pollinator (e.g., the leg and the head), which effectively prevents hybridization.

Most lady's slipper orchids are pollinated via a one-way trap method. Bees or flies go into the opening of the pouch and effect pollination when they crawl out of the back of the lip to freedom.

The complexity of these interactions has only been touched upon by biologists. Floral modifications to attract specific pollinators appear to form the primary mode of evolution in orchids, and true genetic barriers are rare. Sporadic natural hybrids occur, and artificial hybrids involving many genera and species are commonplace in horticulture. Even remarkably wide crosses between only distantly related genera from the paleotropics and neotropics have yielded fertile hybrids.

Rather than relying on frequent visits by pollinators, orchids are adapted for the rare, specific, pollination event. When an orchid flower is pollinated, the resulting fruits produce vast numbers of seeds, typically in the tens of thousands. In most cases, the seeds are minute, dustlike, and the small size is partly an adaptation to an epiphytic life among the trees, where wind dispersal is a factor, and partly due to the lack of any endosperm or nutritionally rich support tissue (such as the starch in a kernel of maize).

Economic uses. The flavoring vanilla is derived from the cured seed capsules of a tropical orchid vine (primarily *Vanilla planifolia* and *V. tahitensis*). Production in vanilla plantations is labor-intensive because of the need to hand-pollinate the ephemeral flowers on a daily basis. In Turkey and adjacent regions, the tubers of several terrestrial orchids (mostly species of *Orchis*) are ground into a flavoring called *salep*. The Orchidaceae is one of the few monocot families to have significant numbers of species with alkaloids, so many are used in traditional medicines, especially in China and India. In particular, species of *Flickingeria*, *Liparis*, and *Malaxis* have been utilized, as have most genera with highly patterned leaves, the so-called "jewel orchids" (e.g., *Anoectochilus*, *Goodyera*, and *Macodes*). Although the efficacy of these plants as medicines has not been tested fully, their corresponding alkaloids have been characterized (e.g., Liparidine and Malaxidine).

Other than commercial vanilla, the primary economic use of orchids is floriculture. From corsage flowers (*Cattleya* and *Cymbidium*) to Hawaii's famous leis (*Papilionanthe* hybrids, formerly included in *Vanda*) to Asian cut-flower exports (*Arachnis*, *Aranda*, and *Dendrobium*), orchids constitute an established crop. Orchids, especially *Oncidium* and *Phalaenopsis*, are increasingly mass-marketed as pot plants.

Finally, there is a dynamic network of hobbyist growers who cultivate orchids in home greenhouses, on windowsills, and on and under artificial lights. Orchid fanciers often appreciate obscure genera and species with flowers that one would be hard pressed to describe as showy. Nearly all orchids that can be cultivated are grown by some specialist around the world. Avid collecting for growers who will pay thousands of dollars for rare specimens has endangered some wild populations.

References. ACKERMAN, J. D. 1983. Specificity and mutual dependency of the orchid-euglossine bee interaction. *Biol. J. Linn. Soc.* 20:301–14. ATWOOD, J. T., JR. 1986. The size of the Orchidaceae and the systematic distribution of epiphytic orchids. *Selbyana* 9:171–86. BOCKEMÜHL, L. 1989. *Odontoglossum: monographie und ikonographie*. Hildesheim: Brücke-Verlag Kurt Schmersow. BRAEM, G. J. 1986. *Cattleya*. 2 vols. Hildesheim: Brücke-Verlag Kurt Schmersow. CHASE, M. W. 1986. A reappraisal of the oncidioid orchids. *Syst. Bot.* 11:477–91. CHRISTENSON, E. A. 2001. *Phalaenopsis, a monograph*. Portland, OR: Timber Press. CRIBB, P. J. 1984. A revision of *Dendrobium* section *Latouria* (Orchidaceae). *Kew Bull.* 38:229–306. CRIBB, P. J. 1986. A revision of *Dendrobium* section *Spatulata* (Orchidaceae). *Kew Bull.* 41:615–92. CRIBB, P. J. 1987. *The genus Paphiopedilum*. Richmond, Surrey, U.K.: Royal Botanic Gardens, Kew. DRESSLER, R. L. 1981. *The Orchids, a Natural History and Classification*. Cambridge, MA: Harvard University Press. DRESSLER, R. L. 1993a. *Field Guide to the Orchids of Costa Rica and Panama*. Ithaca, NY: Cornell University Press. DRESSLER, R. L. 1993b. *Phylogeny and Classification of the Orchid Family*. Portland, OR: Dioscorides Press. DUNSTERVILLE, G.C.K., AND L. A. GARAY. 1959–1976. *Venezuelan Orchids Illustrated*. 6 vols. London: Andre Deutsch. DU PUY, D., AND P. J. CRIBB. 1988. *The genus Cymbidium*. Portland, OR: Timber Press. GARAY, L. A. 1972–1974. On the systematics of the monopodial orchids. *Bot. Mus. Leafl.* 23:149–212, 369–75. GARAY, L. A. 1980. A generic revision of the Spiranthinae. *Bot. Mus. Leafl.* 28:278–425. GARAY, L. A. 1986. Olim Vanillaceae. *Bot. Mus. Leafl.* 30:223–37. GARAY, L. A., AND J. E. STACY. 1974. Synopsis of the genus *Oncidium*. *Bradea* 1(40):393–424. LUER, C. A. 1972. *The Native Orchids of Florida*. Bronx, NY: New York Botanical Garden. LUER, C. A. 1975. *The Native Orchids of the United States and Canada Excluding Florida*. Bronx, NY: New York Botanical Garden. LUER, C. A. 1986a. Icones Pleurothallidinarum, I. Systematics of the Pleurothallidinae. *Monogr. Syst. Bot.* 15:1–81. LUER, C. A. 1986b. Systematics of *Masdevallia*. *Monogr. Syst. Bot.* 16:1–63. NILSSON, L. A., L. JONSSON, L. RASON, AND E. RANDRIANJOHANY. 1985. Monophily and pollination mechanisms in *Angraecum arachnites* Schltr. (Orchidaceae) in a guild of long-tongued hawk-moths (Sphingidae) in Madagascar. *Biol. J. Linn. Soc.* 26:1–19. PABST, G.F.J., AND F. DUNGS. 1975–1977. *Orchidaceae Brasiliensis*. 2 vols. Hildesheim: Brücke-Verlag Kurt Schmersow. REEVE, T. M., AND P.J.B. WOODS. 1989. A revision of *Dendrobium* section *Oxyglossum* (Orchidaceae). *Notes Roy. Bot. Gard. Edinburgh* 46:161–305. SCHWEINFURTH, C. 1958–1970. Orchids of Peru. *Fieldiana* (*Bot.*) 30:1–1005, 33: 1–80 (suppl.). SEIDENFADEN, G. 1973. Notes on *Cirrhopetalum* Lindl. *Dansk Bot. Arkiv* 29:1–260. SEIDENFADEN, G. 1979. Orchid genera in Thailand, VIII. *Bulbophyllum* Thou. *Dansk Bot. Arkiv* 33:1–228. SEIDENFADEN, G. 1985. Orchid genera in Thailand, XII. *Dendrobium* Sw. *Opera Bot.* 83:1–295. SEIDENFADEN, G. 1988. Orchid genera in Thailand, XIV. Fifty-nine vandoid genera. *Opera Bot.* 95:1–398. STEWART, J. 1980. A revision of the African species of *Aerangis* (Orchidaceae). *Kew Bull.* 34:239–319. VERMEULEN, J. J. 1987. A taxonomic revision of the continental African Bulbophyllinae. *Orchid Monogr.* 2:1–300. WITHNER, C. L. 1988–2000. *The Cattleyas and Their Relatives*. 6 vols. Portland, OR: Timber Press.

PHORMIACEAE (Bush-flax Family)

Dennis Wm. Stevenson

- *herbs to subshrubs*

- *leaves alternate (distichous), simple; leaf bases strongly keeled*

- *flowers with articulate pedicels; tepals deep blue; anthers elongate*

Numbers of genera and species. Worldwide, the Phormiaceae (as treated here) comprise seven genera and 35 species. In tropical America, there is one genus, *Eccremis*, and one species.

Distribution and habitat. The Phormiaceae grow throughout warmer regions of the Southern Hemisphere. Species are found from Peru to Colombia, New Zealand, Norfolk Island, Madagascar, the Mascrenes, the Seychelles, tropical east Africa, southern Asia, Malesia, Hawaii, the South Pacific Islands, Fiji, New Caledonia, and Australia.

The Phormiaceae grow in a wide variety of habitats from sea level to higher elevations. The only Neotropical species, *Eccremis coarctata*, endemic to Peru and Colombia, grows in high, wet, cold *páramos*.

Family classification. The Phormiaceae are placed in the Asparagales by Dahlgren et al. As circumscribed by Dahlgren et al., the Phormiaceae are a segregate family of the Agavaceae while Cronquist included the Phormiaceae in the Agavaceae. The family has been thought to be closely related to the Doryanthaceae, and this family has even been included as a subfamily within the Phormiaceae by both Takhtajan and Thorne. Morphological and molecular data support a close relationship between Phormiaceae and Hemerocallidaceae and affinities of both with the Doryanthaceae. More recently, Clifford et al. have included the Phormiaceae within the Hemerocallidaceae. The placement of *Eccremis* is itself enigmatic because molecular data places it in the Iridaceae, where it clearly does not belong.

Features of the family. Habit: herbs to subshrubs, the herbs rhizomatous; rhizomes usually thick with clusters of fibrous roots. Leaves alternate (distichous), simple; blades linear, bi-facial, the base strongly keeled. Inflorescences terminal on aerial shoots, sparingly to highly paniculate, thus sparsely to densely flowered; pedicel articulate. Flowers actinomorphic, bisexual; tepals 6, in 2 cycles of 3, equal, deep blue; androecium of 6 stamens, the stamens in 2 cycles of 3, equal, basally fused into ring, 3 adnate to tepals, 3 free from tepals, the anthers elongate, dehiscing longitudinally; gynoecium syncarpous, the ovary superior, the carpels 3, the locules 3, the style narrow, erect, the stigma simple, punctiform; placentation axile, the ovules 4–many per locule. Fruits loculicidal capsules with a septicidal endocarp. Seeds numerous, black; endosperm copious.

Natural history. No information is available on the pollination and dispersal of *Eccremis*. The rather large red flowers of the extra-Neotropical *Phormium* appear to fit the bird pollination syndrome, whereas the blue flowers with poricidal anthers of *Dianella* suggest buzz pollination by insects. The blue fruits of species of *Dianella* are known to be consumed by birds, and the dispersal of the winged seeds of *Phormium* may be aided by wind.

Economic uses. *Phormium tenax* (New Zealand flax) is used by the Maoris in New Zealand as a source of fiber for making cloth. This species is cultivated on a limited scale in the United States, New Zealand, and Central Africa for cordage and for the fabrication of other fibrous materials. The blue fruits of *Dianella* provide a dye source in Hawaii. Varieties of various species of *Phormium* and *Dianella* are cultivated widely as ornamentals.

References. Clifford, H. T., R. J. Henderson, and J. G. Conran. 1998. Hemerocallidaceae. In *The Families and Genera of Vascular Plants*, ed. K. Kubitzki, 3:245–53. New York: Springer-Verlag.

POACEAE or GRAMINEAE (Grass Family)

Jerrold I. Davis

Figures 244, 245; Plate 61

- *herbs, sometimes lignified (the woody bamboos)*

- *stems vertical, usually unbranched, hollow or solid between nodes*

- *leaves alternate, distichous, consisting of sheaths, ligules, and blades*

- *flowers and bracts aggregated into spikelets, each flower enclosed by two bracts (lemma and palea)*

- *flowers mostly wind-pollinated; perianth reduced to absent*

- *fruit a caryopsis (or grain); seed 1 per fruit*

Numbers of genera and species. Worldwide, the Poaceae (also known as Gramineae) comprise approximately 650 genera and 10,000 species, including about 375 genera and 3,300 species in the Western Hemisphere. The largest genera, and the approximate number of species in each, as arranged by subfamily, are: in the Aristidoideae, *Aristida* (250 species); in the Bambusoideae, *Bambusa* (120) and *Chusquea* (200); in Chloridoideae, *Eragrostis* (350), *Muhlenbergia* (160), and *Sporobolus* (160); in the Panicoideae, *Panicum* (470), *Paspalum* (330), *Digitaria* (230), *Andropogon* (100), *Axonopus* (110), *Brachiaria* (100), *Isachne* (100), and *Setaria* (100); and in the Pooideae, *Poa* (500), *Festuca* (450), *Stipa* (300), *Calamagrostis* (270), *Agrostis* (220), *Bromus* (150), *Elymus* (150), and *Helictotrichon* (100). At the other extreme, there are many genera that have only one or a few species. In tropical America, there are a conservatively estimated 267 genera and 2,500 species, including native, naturalized, and widely cultivated taxa.

Distribution and habitat. The Poaceae are widespread and cosmopolitan, with representatives on every continent, including Antarctica. Grasses occur in virtually every terrestrial habitat, including many species of the prairies and savannas, the bamboos (Bambusoideae) of tropical forests; the diminutive, mosslike grasses of equatorial highlands and tundra; and the species of many wetlands. Grasslands, such as the pampas of South America or the prairies of North America, cover large expanses in many parts of the world. Some grasses are common in salt marshes, while others stabilize sand dunes. Perhaps the single most widespread grass is *Phragmites australis* (common reed), which forms large stands in marshy areas throughout the world. The various subfamilies have characteristic habitats and geographic distributions, though there are many exceptions to these general patterns. The Pooideae are abundant and diverse in temperate and boreal regions, as well as in montane tropical habitats. The Panicoideae, Chloridoideae, and Aristidoideae are principally tropical, with the latter two, in particular, occurring in arid habitats. Arundinoideae and Ehrhartoideae usually prefer wetter habitats such as riverbanks and marshes, and a few are truly aquatic. Danthonioideae often occur in mesic to semi-arid habitats, while the five remaining subfamilies (Anomochlooideae, Streptochaetoideae, Pharoideae, Puelioideae, and Centothecoideae), along with Bambusoideae, tend to occur in shaded tropical habitats.

Family classification. The Poaceae are placed in the Poales by Dahlgren et al. This group includes tropical reeds and climbers (Flagellariaceae and Joinvilleaceae), plus a group of families with generalized grasslike structures (Restionaceae, Anarthriaceae, Centrolepidaceae, and Ecdeiocoleaceae). These families are principally confined to the Eastern Hemisphere, but Restionaceae and Centrolepidaceae also occur in South America. Recent phylogenetic studies, based on morphology and DNA sequence data from ndhF and other genes, have confirmed the close relationship among Poaceae and these families and have established a phylogenetic hypothesis for relationships within the family.

Twelve subfamilies currently are recognized in the grass family, four of them large and diverse (Bambusoideae [ca. 1,200 species]), Chloridoideae [ca. 1,400], Panicoideae [ca. 3,300], and Pooideae [ca. 3,300]), and the other eight (Anomochlooideae, Aristidoideae, Arundinoideae, Centothecoideae, Danthonioideae, Ehrhartoideae, Pharoideae, and Puelioideae) with between four and 350 species each. The Bambusoideae include the woody bamboos plus a closely related herbaceous group, the Olyreae, which includes the tropical American genus *Olyra*. Several other herbaceous groups have also been considered "herbaceous bamboos," and often were included within the Bambusoideae, but recent phylogenetic

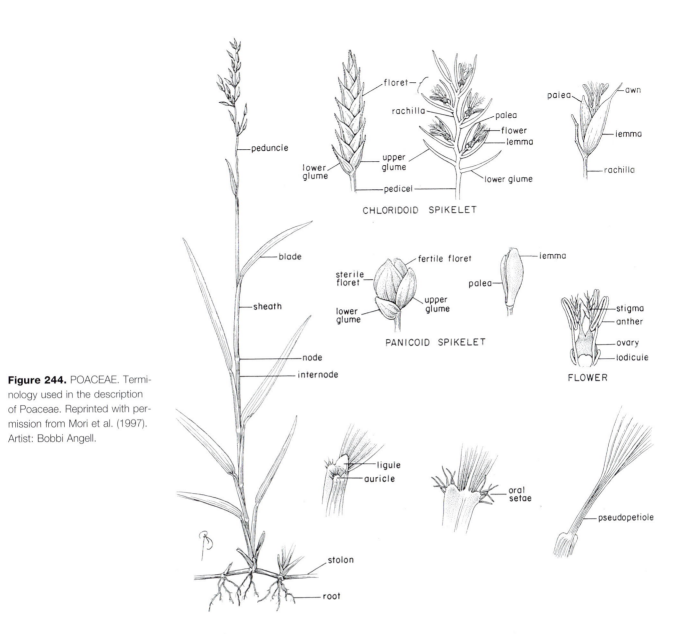

Figure 244. POACEAE. Terminology used in the description of Poaceae. Reprinted with permission from Mori et al. (1997). Artist: Bobbi Angell.

analyses have demonstrated that they are not closely related to the bamboos, and they now constitute four small subfamilies (Anomochlooideae, Ehrhartoideae, Pharoideae, and Puelioideae). Three of these subfamilies are remnants of the earliest-diverging lineages in the grass family: Anomochlooideae, which is endemic to the American Tropics, include *Anomochloa* and *Streptochaeta*; Pharoideae include the tropical American genus *Pharus* and two genera of the Eastern Hemisphere; and Puelioideae are endemic to Africa. The fourth of these small subfamilies, Ehrhartoideae (which has often been called Oryzoideae), include *Oryza* (rice) and related genera (i.e., other genera of tribe Oryzeae) plus two smaller tribes. The Arundinoideae, like the Bambusoideae, recently have been circumscribed more narrowly to reflect current understandings of relationships. Three small groups historically associated with Arundinoideae are now recog-

nized as separate subfamilies: Aristidoideae, including just one genus in the Western Hemisphere, *Aristida*; Danthonioideae, which include *Cortaderia* and other genera; and Centothecoideae, which include the tropical American *Zeugites*. The core Arundinoideae, following the removal of these three groups, include *Phragmites* and several other small genera.

Features of the family. Habit: herbs, short-lived annuals or perennials, a few centimeters or less in height to woody-textured true bamboos (i.e., lignified but lacking secondary growth) reaching 30 m, intercalary meristems present; rhizomes often present, these often profusely branched; vertical stems usually unbranched (above ground, except in inflorescence), hollow between nodes or solid throughout. **Leaves** alternate, distichous, composed of a sheath, ligule, and blade; sheath distinct at margins or less commonly fused, when fused,

Figure 245. POACEAE. *Ichnanthus panicoides* (A–E) and *Lasiacis ligulata* (F–J). **A.** Upper part of stem with leaves and inflorescence. **B.** Detail of part of stem and leaf sheath. **C.** Lateral view of spikelet. **D.** Lateral view of upper glume. **E.** Lateral (left) and adaxial (right) views of upper floret showing appendages and pubescent lemmas. **F.** Part of culm showing leaves and inflorescence. **G.** Detail of part of culm and leaf sheath. **H.** Lateral view of spikelet. **I.** Adaxial view of upper glume. **J.** Lateral (left) and adaxial (right) views of fertile floret showing sterile extension of ligule. Reprinted with permission from Mori et al. (1997). Artist: Bobbi Angell.

forming closed tube surrounding stem and sheaths of other leaves; blades diverging from stem at sheath apex, flattened or inrolled, the narrowed base (present in some grasses) known as a pseudopetiole (this above sheath and ligule); ligule ranging from membranous to a fringe of hairs, or rarely absent; epidermal cells sometimes accumulating silica (shapes of silica bodies often characteristic of tribes or subfamilies). **Inflorescences** compound, consisting of basic units (spikelets) variously arranged in spikes, panicles, and otherwise; bracts present, two-ranked, one pair (glumes) at base of each spikelet and another pair below each flower in spikelet (lemma and palea, these unique to Poaceae). **Spikelets** with

rachilla (short axis), 2 glumes (basal bracts; occasionally more than 2, or only 1, or vestigial), and 1 or more "florets," the glumes and 1 or more florets borne in 2 vertical ranks along rachilla, each succeeding element borne opposite and slightly above preceding one (thus, second glume opposite and slightly above first, and the first floret opposite and slightly above second glume; i.e., directly above first glume), this pattern continuing if more than 1 floret present (thus all odd-numbered florets on same side of rachilla as first glume, and all even-numbered florets on same side as second glume); florets consisting of 1 flower, 1 lemma, and 1 palea (basal bracts), the developing flower enclosed by lemma and palea, the lemma and palea open at anthesis, closing after pollination; awns often present, attached to lemmas, glumes, and rarely paleas. **Flowers** bisexual or unisexual (florets sometimes lacking both androecium and gynoecium), usually consisting of lodicules and reproductive organs; lodicules 2–3, at base of flower (located in position at which petals would occur), positioned just above point of lemma and palea attachment, swelling at anthesis, the swelling causing separation of lemma and palea (like the opening of a clam shell) thus exposing stamens and pistil, shriveling after pollination (the lemma and palea assume original positions and enclose pistil as it matures); androecium usually of 1–3 or 6 stamens (rarely numerous), the filaments usually distinct, the anthers large; gynoecium syncarpous, the ovary superior, the carpels 2–3, the locule 1, the styles 1–3, the stigmas highly branched; placentation variable, the ovule 1. **Fruit** a caryopsis, these thin-walled, indehiscent, the pericarp tightly enclosing and fused to solitary seed. **Seeds** 1 per fruit, the embryo with a scutellum; endosperm usually starchy.

Grasses have intercalary meristems situated near leaf and internode bases. The activity of these meristems allows leaves to elongate from the base, even if apical portions are removed on a regular basis by the grazing of animals or by mechanical mowing, and also allows stems to right themselves. Many grasses of tropical and arid regions, including almost all species of Aristidoideae and Chloridoideae, and most species of Panicoideae, have the moisture-efficient C4 photosynthetic pathway.

Flowers are closely associated with axes and bracts, and there are multiple levels of organization of these aggregations. It is not clear which of these levels corresponds to the inflorescence in related families. At one level there is a characteristic aggregation known as a spikelet, which is found in almost all grasses, yet spikelets are themselves organized into spikes, panicles, and other compound structures. Thus, these and other botanical terms for inflorescence types, and for inflorescence parts, such as pedicel and peduncle, are applied differently in Poaceae than in other families.

A considerable amount of structural variation among grasses is to be seen in variant forms of the spikelet, as well as in the arrangement of the spikelets. In the Panicoideae, for example, there are typically two florets per spikelet; the upper floret has a pistil, and eventually produces a fruit, while the lower floret lacks a pistil, and often lacks stamens as well. Within the Pooideae, in *Triticum* (wheat) and its closest relatives, spikelets are themselves aggregated in a spikelike arrangement (i.e., a spike of spikelets).

In most grasses, the ripened fruit is dispersed in association with the lemma and palea, and sometimes also with the glumes and other portions of the inflorescence, collectively called the "chaff."

Natural history. Tropical forests were the cradle of early grass evolution. The earliest lineages within the family, represented today by *Anomochloa* and *Streptochaeta* (Anomochlooideae), Puelioideae, and Pharoideae, possibly coexisted with the dinosaurs during the late Cretaceous. In the Tertiary, as the climate changed, grasses diversified into more open habitats, where they became successful and even dominant, because of their intercalary meristems, wind pollination, and capacity for vegetative reproduction. These adaptations allowed grasses to withstand fire and grazing and even to thrive under disturbance regimes. The abilities to establish and maintain a sod and to regenerate leaf tissue indefinitely together contribute to the widespread occurrence of grasses as ecological dominants in a variety of grassland formations such as prairies, steppes, and pampas. An additional factor, particularly in tropical regions, is the occurrence of C4 photosynthesis. The silica that grasses take up from the soil and deposit in their leaves and stems is thought to provide some protection from herbivorous insects.

The bamboos are the only major group of grasses adapted to the forest habitat, where they evolved special strategies for competing with trees for light. The woody bamboos produce large, lignified stems that grow rapidly to their full height and then branch extensively; these "tree grasses" typically occur in forest clearings or margins, where their aggressively rhizomatous growth habit serves to stabilize the soil after disturbance. The gregarious, monocarpic flowering characteristic of so many woody bamboos may play a role in the long-term forest dynamics by allowing regeneration after the death of the adult bamboos. Many animals, including giant pandas, and a number of frogs, birds, and insects, as well as fungi and microorganisms, associate with bamboos and, in some cases, rely on bamboos as a source of food or as habitat. The small herbaceous bamboos known as the Olyreae, in contrast, have adapted to the low-light conditions of the forest floor, and some exhibit insect pollination.

Although most grasses are wind-pollinated, several fruit dispersal mechanisms are found within the family. The caryopsis normally falls with the lemma and palea attached, but many grasses are modified so that groups of florets or spikelets or segments of the larger infructescence fall together. Although wind dispersal may occur, the lemma often has awns, hairs, or even hooks, through which dispersal on the fur or feathers of animals is effected. In other grasses, a structure at the base of the floret contains oils that attract ants, which carry off the fruits. Still other grasses have a sharp floret or spikelet base that, in combination with the motion of the twisted awn when it absorbs moisture, serves to bury the seed in the ground. Although annual grasses must reproduce from seed every year, perennial grasses rely upon a combination of seed production and vegetative growth by rhizomes or stolons to maintain their populations.

Economic uses. The three principal food plants of the world, rice (*Oryza sativa*), wheat (*Triticum aestivum* and *T. durum*), and maize (*Zea mays*), are grasses. Other grasses cultivated for human consumption included barley (*Hordeum*), oats (*Avena*), rye (*Secale*), sorghum (*Sorghum*), sugar cane (*Saccharum*), tef (*Eragrostis*), wild rice (*Zizania*), and several genera with species known as millets (e.g., *Pennisetum* and *Setaria*). The Poaceae also include numerous other species that are maintained or planted for various purposes. Those grown as range and pasture grasses for animal forage include bent grass (*Agrostis*), foxtail (*Setaria*), orchard grass (*Dactylis*), pampas grass (*Cortaderia*), ryegrass (*Lolium*), speargrass (*Heteropogon*), timothy (*Phleum*), and wild rye (*Elymus*). Beach grass (*Ammophila*) and sea oats (*Uniola*) are utilized for erosion control. Those grown as lawn grasses include bluegrass (*Poa*), brome (*Bromus*), fescue (*Festuca*), and zoysia (*Zoysia*). Lemon grass (*Cymbopogon*) and vetiver (*Vetiveria*) are aromatics. Ornamental grasses include bamboos (e.g., *Bambusa*, *Phyllostachys*, and *Rhipidocladum*) and miscanthus (*Miscanthus*). The grass family also includes numerous weeds. Industrial applications include uses of bamboos and the common reed (*Phragmites*) in paper making and bamboo stems (*Bambusa*, *Guadua*, and *Phyllostachys*) in the construction of a variety of articles, including baskets, furniture, houses, musical instruments, and scaffolding.

References. BAILEY, L. H. 1949. *Manual of Cultivated Plants*. New York: Macmillan. CLARK, L. G., AND R. W. POHL. 1996. *Agnes Chase's First Book of Grasses*. Washington, D.C.: Smithsonian Institution Press. CLARK, L. G., WEIPING ZHANG, AND J. F. WENDEL. 1995. A phylogeny of the grass family (Poaceae) based on ndhF sequence data. *Syst. Bot.* 20:436–60. CLAYTON, W. D., AND S. A. RENVOIZE. 1986. *Genera Graminum: Grasses of the World*. Richmond, Surrey, U.K.: Royal Botanic Gardens, Kew. FARRELLY, D. 1984. *The Book of Bamboo*. San Francisco, CA: Sierra Club Books. GRASS PHYLOGENY WORKING GROUP. 2001. Phylogeny and subfamilial classification of the grasses (Poaceae). *Ann. Missouri Bot. Gard.* 88:373–457. JUDZIEWICZ, E. J., L. G. CLARK, X. LONDOÑO, AND M. J. STERN. 1999. *American Bamboos*. Washington, D.C.: Smithsonian Institution Press. MCCLURE, F. A. 1966. *The Bamboos*. Washington, D.C.: Smithsonian Institution Press. SORENG, R. J., AND J. I. DAVIS. 1998. Phylogenetics and character evolution in the grass family (Poaceae): simultaneous analysis of morphological and chloroplast DNA restriction site character sets. *Bot. Rev.* 64:1–85.

PONTEDERIACEAE (Water Hyacinth Family)

Spencer C. H. Barrett

Figure 246, Plate 61

- *aquatic herbs*
- *leaves alternate, simple, petiolate; basal sheath present*
- *flowers actinomorphic to moderately zygomorphic; androecium often with dimorphic stamens; gynoecium often tristylous or enantiostylous*
- *fruits usually capsules*

Number of genera and species. Worldwide, the Pontederiaceae comprise six to nine genera and 35–40 species. In tropical America, there are three or four genera and 25–30 species. The majority of species occur in *Eichhornia* (8 or 9 species, all except the African *E. natans* from tropical America), *Heteranthera* (10–12, all except the African *H. callifolia* from tropical America), *Monochoria* (7 or 8, all from the Eastern Hemisphere), and *Pontederia* (6, all from the Western Hemisphere and largely from tropical America). Several small segregate genera include *Eurystemon* (1 species), *Hydrothrix* (1), *Scholleropsis* (1), and *Zosterella* (1–2), all allied with *Heteranthera*, and *Reussia* (2–3), allied with *Pontederia*.

Distribution and habitat. Pontederiaceae are tropical in distribution with a primary concentration in lowland South America, especially Brazil. Modes of dispersal associated with their aquatic existence provide substantial opportunities for long-range migration, hence many Neotropical species show striking disjunct distributions (e.g., *Eichhornia paradoxa*). North American taxa in general appear to be more morphologically apomorphic than those in tropical South America, suggesting that they may have migrated north after intercontinental contact in the Miocene.

Species of Pontederiaceae are found in a wide variety of freshwater habitats, including lakes, rivers, streams, marshlands, bogs, fens, seasonal pools, drainage ditches, low-lying pastures, and rice fields.

Family classification. The Pontederiaceae are placed in the Pontederiales by Dahlgren et al., but molecular evidence suggests that they are better aligned with the redefined Commelinales of Chase et al. Molecular evidence supports monophyly of the family. Both multigene analysis of the chloroplast genome (Sean W. Graham, unpubl.) and pollen ultrastructure support the Haemodoraceae as sister to the Pontederiaceae. Various lines of evidence also support Commelinaceae, Philydraceae, and Hanguanaceae as close relatives of Pontederiaceae and Haemodoraceae.

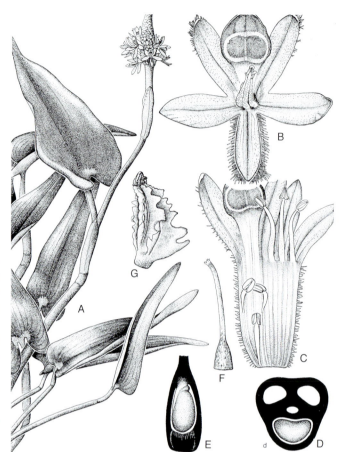

Figure 246. PONTEDERIACEAE. *Pontederia cordata.* **A.** Plant showing leaves and inflorescence (x½). **B.** Apical view of flower (x6). **C.** Corolla tube split open to show adnate stamens (x6). **D.** Transverse section of ovary showing one fertile and two empty locules (x24). **E.** Longitudinal section of ovary showing single, pendulous ovule (x12). **F.** Lateral view of gynoecium (x6). **G.** Lateral view of fruit (x3). Reprinted with permission from Cronquist (1981). Artist: William S. Moye.

No modern subfamilial classification is available for the Pontederiaceae. Phylogenetic reconstruction of the family based on morphological and molecular evidence from the chloroplast genome indicate that *Heteranthera sensu lato*, *Monochoria* and *Pontederia sensu lato* are monophyletic, whereas *Eichhornia* is not. Two phylogenetically distinct clades of *Eichhornia* are evident in most reconstructions; this distinction has important taxonomic implications for the genus as currently circumscribed.

Features of the family. Habit: aquatic herbs, annual or perennial, stems rhizomatous, stoloniferous, submerged, floating, or creeping, the plant with sympodial growth. **Stipules** usually present. **Leaves** alternate, simple, glabrous, petiolate; basal sheath present; blades linear to orbicular, the base cuneate or cordate. **Inflorescences** determinate, terminal (often appearing to be lateral), of 1–2 flowers, spikelike, or paniculate-like (to several hundred flowers in *Eichhornia paniculata*), often showy. **Flowers** actinomorphic or moderately zygomorphic, bisexual, non-dichogamous, 3–40 millimeters wide; perianth tubular or lobed almost to base, blue, purple, magenta, white or yellow, often with prominent yellow or green nectar guide on banner tepal, the lobes usually 6 (4, or rarely 3 in *Scholleropsis*); androecium of 1 (*Hydrothrix*), 3 (*Heteranthera*), or 6 (*Eichhornia*, *Monochoria*, and *Pontederia*) stamens, the stamens dimorphic (heterantherous); gynoecium syncarpous, the ovary superior, the carpels 3, the locules 3(2 aborting in *Pontederia*), the styles elongate, persisting in fruit, tristylous in some *Eichhornia* and *Pontederia*, enantiostylous in *Heteranthera* (including *Eurystemon*) and species of *Monochoria*, the stigmas apical, capitate or 3-lobed; placentation axile or parietal, the ovules numerous (1 per locule in *Pontederia*). **Fruits** capsules or nutlets (*Pontederia* and *Reussia*). **Seeds** many per capsule.

Species of the family display a wide range of aquatic life forms ranging from the emergent habit, which is most common, through procumbent and floating-leaved taxa, to submersed and free-floating forms. Increasing commitment to a fully aquatic existence is associated with specialized vegetative adaptations, as exemplified by the curious threadlike whorls of leaves in the submersed *Hydrothrix gardneri* and swollen air-filled petioles that provide buoyancy in the free-floating *Eichhornia crassipes* and to a lesser extent in *Monochoria australasica* and *Pontederia subovata*.

Characteristic leaf pulvini regulate leaf-blade orientation in species of *Pontederia*. Prominent spongy tissue (aerenchyma) in the petioles of *Eichhornia crassipes* facilitates flotation.

Natural history. Permanent aquatic habitats (e.g., large lakes and extensive marshlands) such as in Amazonia, Mato Grosso, and the *llanos* (Venezuela) favor long-lived, large, outcrossing, clonal taxa such as *Eichhornia azurea* and species of *Pontederia*, whereas seasonal pools, rice fields, and other ephemeral habitats commonly are colonized by self-compatible annuals, such as *Eichhornia diversifolia* and species of *Heteranthera*.

Floral syndromes involve either animal pollination or self-pollination, with none of the adaptations associated with water pollination that occur in many other exclusively aquatic families. Anthesis of individual flowers is short-lived, lasting from four to eight hours, during which pollination is accomplished mostly by bees and, to a lesser extent, butterflies. In *Pontederia* and *Eichhornia*, the flowers are moderately zygomorphic, and cross-pollination is mediated primarily by long-tongued, solitary bees that feed on nectar (species of *Bombus*, *Megachile*, and *Melissodes* in the former and species of *Ancyloscelis* and *Florilegus* in the latter). Populations of three *Eichhornia* and five *Pontederia* species are tristylous and have three floral morphs that differ in the relative lengths of their styles and stamens. This sexual polymorphism is associated with a system of self- and intra-morph incompatibility that is strong in *Pontederia* but only weakly developed in *Eichhornia*. Experimental studies of tristylous taxa of these two genera have confirmed that floral polymorphism increases the proficiency of cross-pollination within populations. In *Heteranthera* and *Monochoria*, floral visitors are mostly pollen-collecting bees. Some members of these genera possess mirror-image flowers with either left- or right-bending styles (enantiostyly), a single, cryptically colored, "pollinating" stamen reflexed in a lateral position opposite the stigma, and the remaining, yellow, "feeding" anthers centrally located. In most taxa, both flower types are produced on a single plant. In *Heteranthera multiflora*, however, individual plants produce either left- or right-handed flowers and the control of style orientation is governed by a single Mendelian locus with right deflection dominant to left. The functional significance of enantiostyly has yet to be fully elucidated, but like tristyly, it is most likely an adaptation that promotes more effective pollen dispersal among plants. In several taxa, especially in *Heteranthera*, flowers are produced that develop entirely underwater and, hence, are completely self-fertilized, a phenomenon common in aquatic plants.

After flowering, rapid downward bending of the floral axis results in maturation of the infructescences underwater in *Eichhornia* and *Pontederia*.

Apart from *Pontederia* and *Reussia*, which are relatively large seeded, all species have small seeds produced in large numbers (20–200) and shed onto mud or into the water. Dispersal occurs on the feet of birds or via water currents. In some cases, long-distance dispersal can be achieved by stem fragments (*Eichhornia azurea*) or rosettes (*E. crassipes*) that act as floating vegetative propagules.

Economic use. Members of Pontederiaceae are of minor economic use. The leaves occasionally are eaten as a vegetable or fed to farm animals, and several species (e.g., *Eichhornia azurea*, *E. crassipes*, and *Pontederia cordata*) are sold as pond ornamentals in North America and Europe. The most economically important member of the family is the notorious water hyacinth (*E. crassipes*), which often is considered the world's most serious aquatic weed. Attempts to eradicate its extensive floating mats from reservoirs, lakes, and irrigation canals in many countries result in considerable annual expenditure. Water hyacinth is also used as a fodder for animals and to treat polluted water. Several other species (e.g., *Monochoria vaginalis* and species of *Heteranthera*) are common as weeds of flooded rice fields.

References. BARRETT, S.C.H. 1988. Evolution of breeding systems in *Eichhornia*: a review. *Ann. Missouri Bot. Gard.* 75:741–60. BARRETT, S.C.H. 1993. The evolutionary biology of tristyly. *Oxford Surv. Evol. Biol.* 9:283–326. BARRETT, S.C.H. 1997. Adaptive radiation in the aquatic plant family Pontederiaceae. In *Molecular Evolution and Adaptive Radiation*, eds. T. J. Givnish and K. J. Sytsma, 225–58.

Cambridge, U.K.: Cambridge University Press. CASTELLA-NOS, A. 1959. Las Pontederiaceae de Brazil. *Arq. Jar. Bot. Rio de Janeiro* 16:147–236. CHASE, M. W., D. W. STEVEN-SON, P. WILKEN, AND P. J. RUDALL. 1995. Monocot system-atics: a combined analysis. In *Monocotyledons: Systematics and Evolution*, eds. P. J. Rudall, P. J. Cribb, D. F. Cutler, and C. J. Humphries, 685–730. Richmond, Surrey, U.K.: Royal Botanic Gardens, Kew. COOK, C.D.K. 1998. Pontederiaceae. In *The Families and Genera of Vascular Plants*, ed. K. Kubitzki, 4:395–403. Berlin: Springer-Verlag. GRAHAM, S. W., AND S. C. H. BARRETT. Phylogenetic systematics of Pontede-riales: implications for breeding-system evolution. In *Mono-cotyledons: Systematics and Evolution*, eds. P. Rudall, P.

Cribb, D. Cutler, and C. Humphries, 415–41. Richmond, Surrey, U.K.: Royal Botanic Gardens, Kew. KOHN, J. R., S. W. GRAHAM, B. R. MORTON, J. J. DOYLE, AND S.C.H. BARRETT. 1996. Reconstruction of the evolution of reproduc-tive characters in Pontederiaceae using phylogenetic evidence from chloroplast DNA restriction-site variation. *Evolution* 50:1454–69. LOWDEN, R. M. 1973. Revision of the genus *Pontederia* L. *Rhodora* 75:426–87. SCHULTZ, A. G. 1942. Las Pontederiaceas de la Argentina. *Darwiniana* 6:45–82. SCHWARTZ, O. 1930. Pontederiaceae. In *Die Natürlichen Pflanzenfamilien*, A. Engler and K. Prantl, 2nd ed., 15a:181–88. SIMPSON, M. G. 1990. Phylogeny and classification of Haemodoraceae. *Ann. Missouri Bot. Gard.* 77:722–84.

POTAMOGETONACEAE (Pondweed Family)

ROBERT R. HAYNES

- *aquatic herbs*

- *leaves usually alternate, simple, submersed or floating; "stipular" sheath present*

- *inflorescences spikes*

- *flowers with 4 tepals; stamens 4; gynoecium apocarpous*

- *fruits drupes*

Numbers of genera and species. Worldwide, the Potamo-getonaceae comprise three genera and about 80 species. In tropical America, there are two genera, *Potamogeton* with 17 species and *Stuckenia* with three. *Groenlandia* (1 species) is restricted to northern Europe.

Distribution and habitat. The Potamogetonaceae occur in aquatic habitats throughout the world. They are especially abundant in temperate regions, and range from Tierra del Fuego to north of the Arctic Circle in the Western Hemi-sphere and from South Africa to north of the Arctic Circle in the Eastern Hemisphere.

In the neotropics, the species occur at all elevations, but they are especially common in the higher Andes. Of the 17 Neotropical species of *Potamogeton*, nine are endemic. The remaining eight species extend northward into North America, with three having near-cosmopolitan distributions. The three Neotropical species of *Stuckenia* are also found in North America, with two being nearly cosmopolitan.

Species occur at depths of a few centimeters to several meters in rivers, streams, lakes, reservoirs, and temporary pools with conditions varying from very soft acidic waters to very hard calcareous waters. Most species are restricted either to acidic or basic waters (the majority occur in acidic waters), but a few can exist in the full spectrum. Species range from sea level to above 4,000 meters.

Family classification. The Potamogetonaceae are placed in the Najadales by Dahlgren et al. The family is most closely related to the Zannichelliaceae. The Potamogetonaceae have not been divided into subfamilies.

Features of the family. Habit: aquatic herbs, typically pe-rennial, rooted in substrate; rhizomes sometimes present; stems erect, ± reaching water surface. **Leaves** alternate or occasion-ally opposite distally, simple, submersed leaves present in all species (although sometimes decayed), these petiolate or sessile, floating leaves present in some species, these nearly always petiolate; "stipular" sheath always present, distinct from petioles or blades (floating leaves) or occasionally ad-nate (submersed leaves); distinct ligule usually present when stipular sheath distinct; blade shape similar or dissimilar in floating and submersed leaves of same plant, expanded (in floating leaves and in most petiolate and occasionally sessile submersed leaves) or linear (many submersed sessile leaves), flattened without groove in *Potamogeton* or semiterete with channel or groove along one side in *Stuckenia*; cuticle evi-dent on adaxial surface of floating leaves, absent in sub-mersed leaves. **Inflorescences** terminal or axillary, spikes, the terminal spikes usually emersed or floating on surface, the axillary spikes usually submersed, rarely with both emersed and submersed spikes on same plant; peduncles rigid in *Potamogeton* (having considerable supporting tissue) allowing for emersion (when peduncle long enough) or non-rigid and never emersed in *Stuckenia*, this sometimes resulting in spikes lying at water surface; spikes consisting of 1–20+ flower whorls, the flowers mostly 3 per whorl. **Flowers** actinomorphic, bisexual; tepals 4, clawed; androecium of 4 stamens, the filaments each adnate to tepal claw, the anthers extrorse; gynoecium apocarpous, the ovaries superior, the carpels 4, the styles short, the stigmas capitate; placentation marginal, the ovule 1 per carpel. **Fruits** drupes, oval to obovoid, 2–5 mm, green during maturation, dull red to green to brown when fully mature, the abaxial surface mostly rounded, a keel or wing present along this surface in a few species, sometimes the angle between fruit face and abaxial surface with obvious keel or wing. **Seeds** 1 per fruit; embryo coiled.

The distance between flower whorls mostly varies with the species, but it usually is about the same from top to bottom of an individual spike. A few species in both genera have gaps of a few millimeters to 1 cm or more between groups of whorls. A spike with such gaps is called a moniliform spike. Presence of moniliform spikes is species specific.

Fruits provide the most important features in separating species of the family; consequently one should always collect fruiting specimens.

Natural history. Pollination of inflorescences that are projected above the water surface is mostly by wind. That of submersed or floating spikes is not understood fully, but most studies indicate that pollen is transferred from anthers to stigmas along the margin of air bubbles, which are released from the anthers as they dehisce underwater.

Dispersal is by stem fragments or fruits, both of which may be carried by water currents or by animals. Pondweed drupes are significant food sources for waterfowl, and research has indicated that many seeds pass through their digestive tracts intact. Such seeds have an extremely high germination rate.

Economic uses. The Potamogetonaceae include some of the most important foods for waterfowl and some also are grown in aquaria. Environmentally, the plants are immensely important in substrate stabilization and in removing particles from the water column. A detrimental effect of some species is that they occasionally clog water bodies, which then serve as breeding grounds for mosquitoes.

References. HAGSTRØM, J. O. 1916. Critical researches on the potamogetons. *Kongl. Svenska Vetenskapsakad. Handl.* 55(5):1–281. HAYNES, R. R. 1975. A revision of North American *Potamogeton* subsection *Pusilli* (Potamogetonaceae). *Rhodora* 76:564–649. HAYNES, R. R. 1978. The Potamogetonaceae in the southeastern United States. *J. Arnold Arbor.* 59:170–91. HAYNES, R. R. 1985. A revision of the clasping-leaved *Potamogeton* (Potamogetonaceae). *Sida* 11:173–88. HAYNES, R. R., D. H. LES, AND L. B. HOLM-NIELSEN. 1998. Potamogetonaceae. In *The Families and Genera of Vascular Plants*, ed. K. Kubitzki, 4:408–15. New York: Springer-Verlag. HOLUB, J. 1997. *Stuckenia* Börner 1912—the correct name for *Coleogeton* (Potamogetonaceae). *Preslia* 69:361–66. LES, D. H., AND R. R. HAYNES. 1995. Systematics of Alismatiflorae: a synthesis of molecular and non-molecular approaches. In *Monocotyledons: Systematics and Evolution*, eds. P. Rudall, P. Cribb, D. Cutler, and C. Humphries, 353–77. Richmond, Surrey, U.K.: Royal Botanic Gardens, Kew. PRESTON, C. D. 1995. *Pondweeds of Great Britain and Ireland*. BSBI Handbook No. 8. London: Botanical Society of the British Isles. TUR, N. 1982. Revisión del género *Potamogeton* L. en la Argentina. *Darwiniana* 24:214–65.

RAPATEACEAE (Flower-of-Maroa Family)

DENNIS WM. STEVENSON

Figure 247, Plate 62

- *herbs, usually terrestrial, often in wet places*

- *trichomes producing copious amounts of clear mucilage*

- *leaves simple, usually ensiform*

- *inflorescence borne on long, naked scapes, subtended by bracts*

- *flowers with poricidal anthers*

Numbers of genera and species. The Rapateaceae comprise 16 genera and about 80 species, with all but *Maschalocephalus dinklagei* restricted to tropical America.

Distribution and habitat. The Rapateaceae occur mainly from Panama to Bolivia. The greatest diversity occurs in the lowlands of the Guayana-Amazon region with two disjunct genera, *Maschalocephalus* restricted to West Africa and *Epidryos* to Panama and the Chocó of Colombia. *Kunhardtia*, *Rapatea*, and *Stegolepis* have species in both the low-

Figure 247. RAPATEACEAE. *Rapatea saülensis*. **A.** Basal (left) and apical (right) parts of leaf. **B.** Lateral view of inflorescence showing pair of subtending bracts. **C.** Lateral view of part of inflorescence showing bracteoles subtending flowers. **D.** Adaxial view of bracteole from inflorescence. **E.** Adaxial view of opened calyx. **F.** Corolla opened to show adnate stamens. **G.** Lateral view of stamens surrounding style. **H.** Lateral (left), adaxial (middle), and abaxial (right) views of stamens. **I.** Lateral view of gynoecium. **J.** Lateral view of open fruit among bracteoles. **K.** Lateral view of dehisced fruit. **L.** Seed. Reprinted with permission from Mori et al. (1997). Artist: Bobbi Angell.

lands and the highlands. The highland *Amphiphyllum*, *Marahuacaea*, and *Phelpsiella*, are each endemic to a single *tepui*.

In the neotropics, the Rapateaceae occur in a variety of habitats such as forest understory, shrublands, seasonally flooded savannas, and open rock and bog formations. Highland taxa occur in bogs and on sandstone substrates, while lowland taxa are commonly found in wet sandy soils, e.g., the species found in the Gran Sabana of Venezuela and along seasonally flooded river margins in Amazonian *caatinga*. *Epidryos* is an epiphyte found in the mountains of Panama.

Family classification. The Rapateaceae share many anatomical, embryological, and palynological features with the Commelinaceae, Xyridaceae, and, to a lesser extent, the Eriocaulaceae and the Mayacaceae, and are thus placed with them in the Commelinales by Dahlgren et al.

The Rapateaceae are divided into two subfamilies: Rapateoideae with two tribes, Rapateeae and Monotremeae, and Saxofridericioideae, with two tribes, Saxofridericieae and Schoenocephalieae. Recent studies indicate that only the Schoenocephalieae, Rapateoideae, and Rapateeae are monophyletic.

Features of the family. Habit: herbs, perennial, terrestrial, or rarely epiphytic, the leaves from fleshy, vertical, rhizomes, branching occurring from axillary buds when rhizome terminates in an inflorescence; uniseriate trichomes present, 2- to 6-celled, located in axils of leaves and bracts, the trichomes secreting copious amounts of mucilage, the mucilage clear, covering emerging leaves and young inflorescences. **Leaves** simple, distichous; petioles, when present, often bearing short prickles; ligule occasionally present; blades usually ensiform. **Inflorescences** axillary or terminal, borne on long, naked scapes, racemes of cymes or cymes of cymes, subtended by bracts; peduncle long, nonappendaged; bracts 2+, the number and fusion variable. **Flowers** actinomorphic to slightly zygomorphic, bisexual, calyx and corolla strongly differentiated; sepals 3, green; petals 3, white, yellow, or red, occasionally spotted; androecium of 6 stamens, the stamens basally fused, sometimes basally adnate to corolla, in 2 alternating whorls, the anthers dehiscing by 1, 2, or 4 apical to subapical pores; gynoecium syncarpous, the ovary superior, the carpels 3, the locules 3 (occasionally 1 by abortion); placentation axile, the ovules 1–8 per locule, bitegmic, anatropous. **Fruits** septicidal capsules. **Seeds** 2–10, prismatic or oblong, occasionally bearing appendages.

Two kinds of inflorescences occur: those with an indeterminate main axis and determinate lateral axes (a raceme of cymes) and those with both a determinate main axis and determinate lateral axes (a cyme of cymes). The spikelets composing the cymes bear numerous spirally arranged coriaceous bracts and a terminal flower. The number of spikelets is variable, and some genera may have inflorescences with 70 spikelets (*Saxofridericia* and *Spathanthus*) or only 1–3 spikelets per inflorescence (*Stegolepis* and *Monotrema*). The position of the inflorescences varies among tribes. Thus, in Saxofridericieae, the inflorescences are axillary; in Schoenocephalieae, they are terminal with a dormant axillary bud at the base; and in Rapateeae, they are axillary with a proximal axillary vegetative bud.

Natural history. Many species of the Rapateaceae are pollinated by insects or birds. The presence of anthers with pores or a similar mode of dehiscence strongly suggests buzz pollination, which has been observed in species of *Stegolepis*. The Schoenocephalieae are reported to be pollinated by hummingbirds. No information is available on dispersal biology.

Economic uses. Because the floral bracts are so colorful and last well into fruiting, the inflorescences are used locally in floral arrangements.

References. MAGUIRE, B., AND J. WURDACK 1958. Rapateaceae. In The botany of the Guayana Highland. Part III. *Mem. New York Bot. Gard.* 10:19–49. MAGUIRE, B., AND J. WURDACK. 1965. Rapateaceae. In The botany of the Guayana Highland. Part VI. *Mem. New York Bot. Gard.* 12: 69–102. PILGER, R. 1930. Rapateaceae. In *Die Natürlichen Pflanzenfamilien*, A. Engler and K. Prantl, 2nd ed., 15a:1–5. Leipzig: Wilhelm Engelmann. STEVENSON, D., M. COLELLA, AND B. BOOM. 1998. Rapateaceae. In *The Families and Genera of Vascular Plants*, ed. K. Kubitzki, 4:415–24. New York: Springer-Verlag. TIEMANN, A. 1985. Untersuchungen zur Embryologie, Blütenmorphologie und Systematik der Rapateaceen und der Xyridaceen-Gattung *Abolboda* (Monocotyledonae). *Dissertationes Botanicae*, Band 52. J. Cramer, Vaduz.

RUPPIACEAE (Ditch-grass Family)

ROBERT R. HAYNES

Figure 248

- *submersed aquatic herbs*

- *leaves alternate, simple, sessile, sheathed at base*

- *flowers actinomorphic, bisexual; perianth absent; stamens 2, sessile; gynoecium apocarpous*

- *fruits drupes*

Numbers of genera and species. Worldwide, the Ruppiaceae comprise a single genus, *Ruppia*, and seven or eight species. In tropical America, there are four species.

Distribution and habitat. The Ruppiaceae are subcosmopolitan in distribution. Most species occur in temperate or subtemperate regions, although a few extend into the Tropics. In the Western Hemisphere, *Ruppia maritima* (nearly cosmopolitan in distribution) and *R. cirrhosa* (also in Europe) range from southern South America to northern North America; *R. filifolia* is endemic to the crater lakes of the high Andes; and *R. didyma* is endemic to the Caribbean Islands and Central America.

Species of Ruppiaceae are found in brackish to marine waters. Those species that occur inland, *R. cirrhosa* and *R. filifolia*, inhabit waters that have high salt contents. Individuals are found at depths from a few centimeters to more than a meter, depending on the clarity of the water.

Family classification. The Ruppiaceae were combined with the Potamogetonaceae (Najadales) by Dahlgren et al. More recent evidence, especially molecular, indicates that the two families should be separated. Les and Haynes and Haynes et al. have summarized the evidence. Morphologically, Ruppiaceae lack a perianth, have 2 stamens, and nuclear endosperm development, whereas Potamogetonaceae have a perianth, 4 stamens, and helobial endosperm development. Molecular

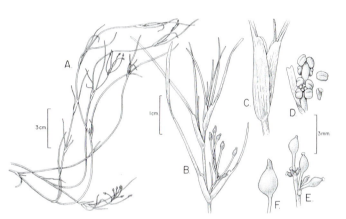

Figure 248. RUPPIACEAE. *Ruppia maritima*. **A.** Plant showing leaves and inflorescences. **B.** Detail of part of stem with inflorescence. **C.** Part of stem with inflorescence hidden by leaf sheaths. **D.** Lateral view of inflorescence (left), anther (above right), and lateral view of carpel (below right). **E.** Infructescence. **F.** Lateral view of fruit. Reprinted with permission from Acevedo-Rodríguez (1996). Artist: Bobbi Angell.

data suggest that Ruppiaceae are more closely related to the Cymodoceaceae and Posidoniaceae, both marine plants, than to the Potamogetonaceae. The Ruppiaceae have not been divided into subfamilies.

Features of the family. Habit: aquatic herbs, submersed, mostly annual (occasionally surviving winter as underground rhizome). **Leaves** alternate, simple, sessile, sheathed at base, the sheaths fused for entire length; ligule absent; blades linear, the margins entire, except at apex, the apex irregularly serrate; venation of midrib only. **Inflorescences** terminal, 1- to few-flowered spikes, the spikes first enclosed by 2 subopposite foliage leaves; peduncle varying in length (by species), projecting inflorescence to water surface (where pollination occurs). **Flowers** actinomorphic, bisexual; perianth absent; androecium of 2 sessile stamens, the anthers dehiscing by longitudinal slits, each bearing a broad connective with a dorsiventral outgrowth; gynoecium apocarpous, the ovaries superior, the carpels (2)4(16), stalked, the stigma sessile or nearly so; placentation marginal distally, the ovule 1 per carpel, ± pendulous near apex of carpel. **Fruits** drupes, nearly spherical, stalked, the endocarp rigid. **Seeds** 1 per fruit, the seed coat permanently attached to endocarp.

Natural history. All species of Ruppiaceae grow to the water surface at time of flowering. In species of *Ruppia*, the two subopposite leaves separate and the peduncle begins to elongate, eventually projecting the inflorescence to just below the water surface. The 2 anthers split, releasing the pollen grains, which then float to the water surface in end-to-end chains. These chains are moved along the water by wind and wave action. Following pollen release, the peduncle continues to grow, eventually raising the stigmas to the water surface, where they potentially can be contacted by a pollen chain. Following pollination, the whole inflorescence is drawn below the water surface by contractions of the peduncle.

The fruits of *Ruppia* float for a short period of time and then sink, becoming buried in the substrate.

Economic uses. The Ruppiaceae are of minor importance as food for animals of aquatic ecosystems. In addition, species are useful in stabilizing substrates and aiding in removing suspended particles from the water column.

References. GAMERRO, J. C. 1968. Observaciones sobre la biología floral y morfología de la potamogetonácea *Ruppia cirrhosa* (Petg.) Grande (= "*R. spiralis*" L. ex Dum.). *Darwiniana* 14:575–608. HAYNES, R. R. , L. B. HOLM-NIELSEN, AND D. H. LES. 1998. Ruppiaceae. In *The Families and Genera of Vascular Plants*, ed. K. Kubitzki, 4:445–48. New York: Springer-Verlag. LES, D. H., AND R. R. HAYNES. 1995. Systematics of Alismatiflorae: a synthesis of molecular and non-molecular approaches. In *Monocotyledons: Systematics and Evolution*, eds. P. Rudall, P. Cribb, D. Cutler, and C. Humphries, 353–77. Richmond, Surrey, U.K.: Royal Botanic Gardens, Kew. NOVELO, R. A. 1991. *Ruppia didymia* (Potamogetonaceae) en México y las Antillas. *Anales Inst. Biol. Univ. Nac. Auton. Mexico Bot.* 62:173–80.

SMILACACEAE (Greenbrier or Sarsaparilla Family)

JOHN D. MITCHELL

Figure 249, Plate 62

- *lianas or vines*

- *stems often armed with prickles*

- *stipular tendrils present*

- *leaves alternate, simple; venation acrodromous*

- *flowers with 6 tepals*

- *fruits berries*

Numbers of genera and species. Worldwide, the Smilacaceae comprise three genera and more than 300 species. In tropical America, there is a single genus, *Smilax*. Worldwide there are approximately 300 species of *Smilax*, but it is difficult to estimate the number of species in the neotropics. The genus has been treated in various country and regional floras and checklists, but the opinions about what constitutes a species vary widely.

Distribution and habitat. The Smilacaceae are widespread in tropical and temperate regions of the world. In tropical America, *Smilax* is particularly widespread in both wet and drier habitats of the lowlands to 1,500 meters, including tropical wet and dry forests, gallery forests, and savannas. Occa-

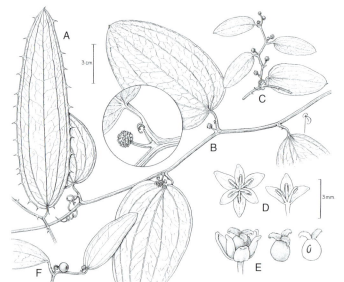

Figure 249. SMILACACEAE. *Smilax coriacea.* **A.** Leaf with spiny margins. **B.** Fertile main stem with leaves and inflorescences; inset showing stipular tendrils and old infructescence after fruits have fallen. **C.** Lateral stem showing leaves and axillary pedicels after fruits have fallen. **D.** Apical (left) and lateral with three of tepals removed (right) views of staminate flowers. **E.** Lateral view of pistillate flower (left) and lateral view (middle) and medial section (right) of gynoecia. Reprinted with permission from Acevedo-Rodríguez (1996). Artist: Bobbi Angell.

sionally, *Smilax* occurs at much higher elevations. A few species, such as *S. brasiliensis*, *S. goyazana*, and *S. oblongifolia*, are subshrubs of the *cerrados* and *campos rupestre* of central and eastern Brazil.

Family classification. The Smilacaceae are placed in the the Dioscoreales by Dahlgren et. al., the Liliales by Cronquist, and the Smilacales by Takhtajan. Recent molecular evidence supports the inclusion of Smilacaceae in the Liliales. The family is divided into two subfamilies by Dahlgren: the Smilacoideae with two genera, the widespread *Smilax* and the East Asian *Heterosmilax* (including *Pseudosmilax*), and the monogeneric Ripogonoideae (*Ripogonum*), which occurs from Australia to New Guinea and New Zealand.

Feature of the family. Habit: lianas or vines, often armed with prickles. **Roots** fibrous, tuberous, or xylopodiumlike rhizomes (some subshrubs of *cerrados* and *campos rupestre*). **Stipules** present, forming sheath, the sheath usually terminating in pair of tendrils. **Leaves** alternate, simple; blades broadly ovate to lanceolate, glabrous or pubescent, the margins entire or armed with prickles; venation acrodromous, usually with 3–9 veins, the midrib sometimes armed with prickles, the tertiary venation typically reticulate. **Inflorescences** axillary or emerging from apices of branchlets, umbellate or racemose; peduncules often terminating in a thickened, bracteate, receptacle; pedicels present. **Flowers** actinomorphic, unisexual (plants dioecious), tepals 6, petal-like, greenish, white, or cream-colored. **Staminate flowers:** stamens 6, in 2 whorls, the filaments distinct or sometimes ± fused into tube, the anthers basifixed, dehiscing longitudinally, introrse or latrorse. **Pistillate flowers:** staminodes 0–6; ovary superior, globose, usually compound, the carpels 3, the locules 3, the styles usually absent, the stigmas papillate; placentation axile, the ovules 1 or 2 per locule. **Fruits** berries, globose, fleshy, orange, red, blue, or black. **Seeds** 1–3(6) per fruit, often very hard; endosperm present.

Several of the tropical forest species of *Smilax* are robust lianas that climb high into the canopy.

Natural history. Species of *Smilax* are probably pollinated by insects. The only species that has been studied in detail is *S. herbacea*, a perennial geophyte from temperate eastern North America that is pollinated principally by andrenid and halictid bees and anthomyiid and stratomyiid flies.

The fleshy berries of *Smilax* are dispersed primarily by birds.

Economic uses. The young shoots, leaves, and tendrils of some species of *Smilax* are used as salad greens or cooked vegetables. A powder made from the dried roots of some species is used as a gelatin substitute or boiled with sugar to make jelly. The dried roots also can be pounded into flour to make bread or used as a thickener for soups. The berries of some West Indian species are occasionally eaten raw.

Smilax longifolia has been reported to be the source of true "sarsaparilla." Several other species of *Smilax*, however, are also referred to as sarsaparilla and may contain a similar mixture of active ingredients. In the past, the dried roots of sarsaparilla were exported from South America in large quantities for the treatment of syphilis. Sarsaparilla is also used as a flavoring agent in beverages and medicinals. Decoctions of dried root from various *Smilax* are often combined with other plant and animal products by indigenous peoples to treat many ailments, including rheumatism, fevers, menstrual cramps, labor pains, menopause, venereal diseases, anemia, stomach cramps, colic, skin diseases, and parasitic worms. Species of *Smilax* are used occasionally in the preparation of aphrodisiacs. An unusual aphrodisiac recipe prepared by the Palikur of French Guiana consists of a decoction of dried *Smilax* and *Ptychopetalum olacoides* (Olacaceae) roots, a white-hot nail, and the penis of the coatimundi (*Nasua nasua*). The mixture is chilled, filtered, and stored in a bottle for a week, and then a teaspoon a day is taken. Root extracts of *Smilax* are also used in the preparation of abortifacients, blood tonics, and diuretics. An extract of the leaves of *S. quinquenervia* has been reported to have analgesic properties.

References. ANDREATA, R.H.P. 1997. Revisão das espécies brasileiras do gênero *Smilax* Linnaeus (Smilacaceae). Pesquisas, Bot. 47: 7–243. DUCKE, A. 1930. Plants nouvelles ou peu connues de la région amazonienne. *Arq. Jard. Bot., Rio de Janeiro* 5: 101–02. GUAGLIONE, E. R., AND S. GATTUSO. 1991. Estudios taxonomicos sobre el genero *Smilax* (Smilacaceae). *Bol. Soc. Argent. Bot.* 27(1–2): 105–29. HOWARD, R. A. 1979. Smilacaceae. In Flora of the Lesser Antilles, ed. R. A. Howard, Vol. 3. Monocotyledoneae, 463–67. Jamaica Plain, MA: Arnold Arboretum, Harvard University. HUFT, M. J. 1994. Smilacaceae. In *Flora Mesoamericana*, ed. G. Davidse, Mario Sousa S., and A. O. Chater. Vol. 6. Alismataceae a Cyperaceae, 20–25. MITCHELL, J. D. 1997. Smilacaceae (Greenbrier family). In *Guide to the Vascular Plants of Central French Guiana*. Part 1: Pteridophytes, Gymnosperms, and Monocotyledons. eds. S. A. Mori, G. Cremers, C. Gracie, J.-J. de Granville, M. Hoff, and J. D. Mitchell, 362–65. Mem. N.Y. Bot. Gard. 76(1). SAWYER, N. W., AND G. J. ANDERSON. 1998. Reproductive biology of the carrion-flower, *Smilax herbacea* (Smilacaceae). *Rhodora* 100:1–24. VANDERCOLME, E. 1947. Historia botânica e terapêutica das salsaparrilhas. *Revista Flora Med.* 14(7): 317–524.

STRELITZIACEAE (Bird-of-Paradise Flower Family)

Dennis Wm. Stevenson and Janice Wassmer Stevenson

Figure 250, Plate 62

- *giant herbs, rhizomatous; aerial shoot semiwoody*

- *leaves alternate, distichous, simple; sheath open*

- *flowers zygomorphic, large, cream-colored; stamens 5, the thecae 2 per anther; staminodes absent; ovary inferior*

- *fruits loculicidal, green, woody capsules*

- *seeds many, with an orange, red, or blue fibrous aril*

Numbers of genera and species. Worldwide, the Strelitziaceae comprise three genera and six or seven species. In tropical America, there is a single native species, *Phenakospermum guyannense*. Of the remaining genera, *Strelitzia* has four or five species and *Ravenala* one species. *Strelitzia reginae* is commonly cultivated and naturalized in some areas in the neotropics. *Ravenala madagascariensis* (traveler's palm) is also commonly cultivated in the neotropics.

Distribution and habitat. *Phenakospermum* is found only in tropical South America, *Ravenala* is endemic to Madagascar, and *Strelitzia* is native to South Africa. *Phenakospermum guyannense* generally grows along river margins, in swamp forests, or in disturbed areas.

Family classification. Originally, the Strelitziaceae were placed in the Musaceae. Recent workers recognize both families while acknowledging their close relationship by placing them in the same order, the Zingiberales (e.g., Dahlgren et al.). Takhtajan established an order, the Musales, containing only the Musaceae, Heliconiaceae, and Strelitziaceae. The close relationship of these families is supported by cladistic analyses of morphological data and combined morphological and molecular data. *Strelitzia* and *Phenakospermum* appear to be more closely related to each other than either is to *Ravenala*, thus the family has been divided into two tribes, the Strelitzieae and the Ravenaleae.

Features of the family. Habit: giant herbs (to 10 m tall); rhizome short and massive, cormlike; aerial shoot semiwoody with peripheral massive fibrous layer, unbranched. **Leaves** alternate, distichous, simple; sheath open; petiole long. **Inflorescences** terminal or lateral; thyrse composed of many-flowered cymes, each cyme subtended by a bract; bracts distichously arranged, large, boat-shaped, stiff, green to greenish yellow, filled with mucilage. **Flowers** zygomorphic, bisexual, large (to 28 cm long), mostly cream-colored; perianth in 2 whorls; sepals 3, distinct, subequal; petals 3, bas-

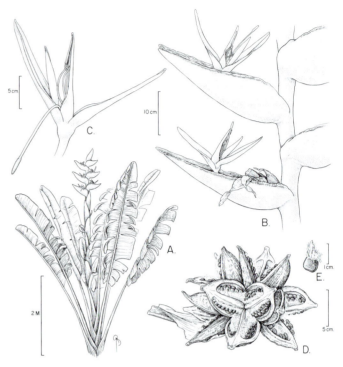

Figure 250. STRELITZIACEAE. *Phenakospermum guyannense.* **A.** Apical part of plant showing leaves and inflorescence. **B.** Lateral view of part of inflorescence showing open flowers subtended by bracts. **C.** Lateral view of flower showing exserted, lax style. **D.** Lateral view of part of infructescence with apical view of dehisced fruits showing arillate seeds. **E.** Seed with aril. Reprinted with permission from Mori et al. (1997). Artist: Bobbi Angell.

ally connate, unequal; androecium of 5 or 6 stamens, the filaments slender, adnate to perianth tube, the anthers linear, the thecae 2; staminode lacking; gynoecium syncarpous, the ovary inferior, 3-locular, the style 1, long, filiform, the stigma conical; septal nectaries present; placentation axile, the ovules many, in 4 rows per locule. **Fruits** loculicidal capsules, woody. **Seeds** many, black; aril of dense red, orange, or blue threadlike structures.

Natural history. *Phenakospermum guyannense* is pollinated primarily by nectar-feeding bats of the genus *Phyllostomus*. The nocturnal flowers are also visited by the marsupial *Caluromys philander* (bare-tailed wooly opossum), which robs nectar but does not effect pollination. *Strelitzia* is bird-pollinated, with the birds transferring pollen primarily with their feet, and *Ravenala* is pollinated by the ruffed lemur (*Varecia variegata*), a nonflying mammal.

The presence of a brightly colored aril indicates animal, probably bird, dispersal.

Economic uses. *Ravenala madagascariensis*, the traveler's palm or traveler's tree, holds rainwater in its flower bracts and leaf bases, which can be used as emergency drinking water. The strictly distichous leaves borne on the trunk also contribute to the common name, because they were thought to be aligned north-south, and, thus, indicate direction to travelers. This plant is cultivated widely in the Tropics because of its stately appearance. Some species of *Strelitzia*, especially *S. reginae* (bird-of-paradise flower), are cultivated in the Tropics and in temperate greenhouses.

References. ANDERSSON, L. 1998. Strelitziaceae. In *The Families and Genera of Vascular Plants*, ed. K. Kubitzki, 4: 451–55. New York: Springer-Verlag. FISHER, J. B. 1978. Leaf-opposed buds in *Musa*: their development and a comparison with allied monocotyledons. *Amer. J. Bot.* 65:784–91. KRESS, W. J., AND D. E. STONE. 1993. Morphology and floral biology of *Phenakospermum* (Strelitziaceae), an arborescent herb of the neotropics. *Biotropica* 25:290–300. KRESS, W.J. ET AL. 1994. Pollination of *Ravenala madagascariensis* (Strelitziaceae) by lemurs in Madagascar: evidence for an archaic coevolutionary system? *Amer. J. Bot.* 81(5): 542–51. MAAS, P., AND H. MAAS-VAN DE KAMER. 1997. Strelitziaceae. In *Guide to the Vascular Plants of Central French Guiana*, eds. S. A. Mori, G. Cremers, C. A. Gracie, J.-J. de Granville, S. V. Heald, et al. *Mem. New York Bot. Gard.* 76(part 1):365, 367–68. PROCTOR, M., AND P. YEO. 1973. *The Pollination of Flowers*. London: Collins. TOMLINSON, P. 1969. Commelinales-Zing[iber]ales. In *Anatomy of the Monocotyledons*, ed. C. R. Metcalfe, 3: Oxford, U.K.: Clarendon Press.

TACCACEAE (Tacca Family)

DENNIS WM. STEVENSON

Plate 63

- *herbs, rhizomatous*

- *inflorescences cymes, with two conspicuous subtending bracts*

- *flowers with incurved, purplish anthers*

- *seeds reniform, with conspicuous longitudinal ridges*

Numbers of genera and species. Worldwide, the Taccaceae comprise a single genus, *Tacca*, and approximately 10–15 species. In tropical America, there is a single species, *T. sprucei*.

Distribution and habitat. The Taccaceae are primarily Paleotropical and centered in Indomalesia, Southeast Asia, and the Solomon Islands. *Tacca sprucei* is widespread from southern Mexico to the Guianas and the Amazon Basin of South America. This disjunction between Asia and the neotropics is rare among flowering plants.

Species of *Tacca* generally grow as understory plants in rain forests. In Brazil and Colombia, *T. sprucei* is commonly found growing on white sand along riverbanks.

Family classification. The Taccaceae are placed in the Dioscoreales by Dahlgren et al. Traditionally, the family has been recognized as a very distinct group closely related to the Dioscoreaceae. Evidence from phylogenetic analyses of both molecular and morphological data support its inclusion within the Dioscoreaceae. The Taccaceae are monogeneric, although one species has historically been segregated as the genus *Schizocapsa*; recent studies have suggested that *Schizocapsa* should be combined with *Tacca*.

Features of the family. Habit: herbs, perennial, acaulescent, the leaves and inflorescences from rhizomes, the rhizomes with copious starch, ± thickened. **Leaves** alternate along rhizome, simple; petiole long; blades narrowly elliptic to narrowly lanceolate, the margins entire. **Inflorescences** axillary, long, naked peduncle terminated by a cyme; bracts 2, enclosing cyme; bracteoles present. **Flowers** actinomorphic, bisexual; perianth of 6 tepals, the tepals fused into very short broad tube above ovary, dull, dark brown to purplish; stamens 6, in 2 alternating whorls of 3, inserted at base of perianth lobes, the filaments short, broad, adnate to perianth except for inflexed margins, the anthers incurved toward stigma, purplish, basifixed, introrse; ovary inferior, syncarpous, the carpels 3, the locule 1, the style simple, three-winged, the stigmas 3, broad, appearing almost petal-like; placentation parietal, the placentas 3, intrusive, the ovules numerous. **Fruits** berrylike, dull, dark purple to black, pendulous. **Seeds** numerous, dark purple, reniform, with conspicuous longitudinal ridges.

Natural history. Pollination and dispersal biology of *Tacca sprucei* are not known. The dark purple to almost black flowers and bracts and tubular perianth suggest fly pollination, and there are some reports that species from the Eastern Hemisphere are pollinated by flies. The fruits of some species from the Eastern Hemisphere are known to have the capacity to float for many months, thereby adapting them to water dispersal.

Economic uses. The tubers of some species from the Eastern Hemisphere, especially *Tacca leontopetaloides*, are a source of starch used for making bread after the bitter princi-ple, taccalin, has been removed. In the Eastern Hemisphere, the leaves are woven into hats and those of the Malesian *T. palmata* are used locally as a poultice.

References. DRENTH, E. 1976. Taccaceae. In *Flora Malesiana*, ed. C.G.G. Van Steenis, ser. 1, 7(4):806–19. Alphen Aan Den Rijn, Netherlands: Sijthoff and Noordhoff International Publishers. KUBITZKI, K. 1998. Taccaceae. In *The Families and Genera of Vascular Plants*, ed. K. Kubitzki, 3: 425–28. New York: Springer-Verlag.

TECOPHILAEACEAE (Tecophila Family)

DENNIS WM. STEVENSON

- *herbs*
- *corms usually covered with persistent leaf bases*
- *leaves basal or subbasal, simple*
- *flowers with 6 tepals, these deep blue*
- *fruits loculicidal capsules*

Numbers of genera and species. Worldwide, the Tecophilaeaceae comprise eight genera and about 25 species. In the Western Hemisphere, there are four genera; *Conanthera* (5 species), *Odontostomum* (1), *Tecophilaea* (2), and *Zephyra* (1).

Distribution and habitat. Of the four genera in the Western Hemisphere, three (*Conanthera*, *Tecophilaea*, and *Zephyra*) are distributed in coastal Peru and Chile and one (*Odontospermum*) occurs in the western United States. *Tecophilaea*, however, is the only one to enter the neotropics in northern Chile and coastal Peru. Four other genera are endemic to sub-Saharan Africa and Madagascar.

The family often grows in very dry areas. In the neotropics, *Tecophilaea* is found at low elevations in very dry areas; e.g., the *lomas* of coastal Peru and Chile. In Chile, species of Tecophilaeaceae occur in cordilleras up to 3,000 meters.

Family classification. The genera of the Tecophilaeaceae have been shuffled among the Liliaceae, Amaryllidaceae, Haemodoraceae, and Hypoxidaceae. The family is currently placed in the Asparagales by Dahlgren et al., but recently it has been suggested that it, along with Cyanastraceae, Eriospermaceae, and Ixioliriaceae, should be placed in a separate order, the Tecophilaeales. In particular, the family is thought to be close to the South African Cyanastraceae and has been combined with it, a classification followed here. Recently, *Lanaria*, a South African endemic, has been ex-cluded from Tecophilaeaceae and placed in its own family, the Lanariaceae, within the Asparagales.

Features of the family. Habit: herbs. Corms present, ellipsoid to globose, usually covered with persistent leaf bases, the leaf bases membranous to fibrous. Leaves 2, simple, basal, the outer leaf non-photosynthetic, tubular; blades with base sometimes sheathing, linear-lanceolate. Inflorescences terminal, solitary or few flowered racemes; bracteoles present. Flowers slightly zygomorphic (tepals only), bisexual; tepals 6, shortly connate at base, deep blue; androecium with 3 fertile stamens and 3 staminodes, the anthers dehiscing apically by pores, appendage present at base; gynoecium syncarpous, the ovary semi-inferior, the carpels 3, the locules 3, the style elongate, the stigmas papillate; placentation axile, the ovules numerous. Fruits loculicidal capsules. Seeds numerous, ellipsoid.

Natural history. The poricidal anthers indicate buzz pollination by bees. No information is available on dispersal biology.

Economic uses. Species are sometimes cultivated as ornamentals and are so sought after by bulb growers that some species are threatened with extinction as a result of overcollecting.

References. BRUMMITT, R., H. BANKS, M. JOHNSON, K. DOCHERTY, K. JONES, ET AL. 1998. Taxonomy of Cyanastroideae (Tecophilaeaceae): a multidisciplinary approach. *Kew Bull.* 53:769–803. RUDALL, P., M. CHASE, D. CUTLER, J. RUSBY, AND A. DE BRUIJN. Anatomical and molecular systematics of Asteliaceae and Hypoxidaceae. *Bot. J. Linn. Soc.* 126:431–52. SIMPSON, M., AND P. RUDALL. 1998. Tecophilaeaceae. In *The Families and Genera of Vascular Plants*, ed. K. Kubitzki, 3:429–36. Berlin: Springer-Verlag.

THEMIDACEAE (Brodiaea Family)

ALAN W. MEEROW

- *herbs with corms*
- *leaves alternate (spiral), sheathing, simple*
- *inflorescences pseudoumbels, borne at apex of a scape*
- *flowers with 6 tepals; stamens 6; ovary commonly borne on stipe or gynophore*
- *fruits loculicidal capsules*

Numbers of genera and species. The Themidaceae comprise 11–12 genera and 60 species. In tropical America, there are five genera and 13–15 species. *Milla* is the largest, with perhaps six species; *Dandya* comprises five; *Bessera* has two; and *Petronymphe* and *Jaimehintonia* are monotypic.

Distribution and habitat. The Themidaceae are restricted to the Western Hemisphere, where they are found chiefly in western North America but occur as far south as Guatemala. The tropical genera of the family are almost all endemic to Mexico. The remaining genera are found in the western United States, some extending into contiguous Mexico (e.g, *Dichelostemma* and *Muilla*).

Most of the Themidaceae occur in seasonally dry areas. The tropical species are often found on cliffs and steep slopes where the long, fragile leaves, and wiry inflorescences hang pendulously.

Family classification. Until recently, the Themidaceae were treated as part of Alliaceae (Asparagales *sensu* Dahlgren et al., tribe Brodiaeeae) or within Liliaceae or Amaryllidaceae when a separate Alliaceae was not recognized. Molecular data indicate that Themidaceae are distinct from the rest of Alliaceae and are actually most closely related to the Hyacinthaceae. The Mexican species have been treated as a distinct subtribe in the past.

Features of the family. Habit: herbs, perennial, with corms, these surrounded by parallel or reticulate fibers. **Leaves** alternate (spiral), simple; blades sheathing about base, terete (or nearly so) and hollow or flattened and solid. **Inflorescences** pseudoumbels (reduced helicoid cymes), borne at apex of a scape; scapes leafless, cylindrical, slender, hollow; spathelike bracts 3 or more, distinct, subtending inflorescence, not enclosing buds; bracteoles present at base of pedicels in at least lower portions of inflorescence. **Flowers** actinomorphic, bisexual, usually articulate with pedicel, a noticeable joint present; tepals 6, in 2 whorls, the tepals distinct or fused into long tube, white to blue, violet, purple, red, pink, or yellow-green; androecium of 6 stamens, the stamens in 2 whorls, the filaments adnate to floral tube (if present), sometimes connate basally into staminal cup, the cup toothed along rim (*Bessera*), the anthers versatile, dehiscing introrsely by terminal slits; gynoecium syncarpous, the ovary superior, commonly borne on stipe or gynophore of variable length, the carpels 3, the locules 3, the style 1, hollow, the stigma 3-lobed, the lobes short or long; septal nectaries present; placentation axile, the ovules 2 or more per locule. **Fruits** loculicidal capsules. **Seeds** 2 to several per locule, small, angular, rarely flattened and obscurely winged, with a thick black, phytomelan crust.

The family lacks alliaceous sulphur compounds and alkaloids. Lactifers are never present.

Natural history. Little is known about pollination and dispersal biology or other ecological aspects of the family.

Economic uses. The Themidaceae are economically important only because of a few species that are sometimes cultivated as ornamentals.

References. FAY, M. F., AND M. W. CHASE. 1996. Resurrection of Themidaceae for the *Brodiaea* alliance, and recircumscription of Alliaceae, Amaryllidaceae and Agapanthoideae. *Taxon* 45:441–51. HOWARD, T. M. 1970. Some bulbous and cormous plants of Mexico and Guatemala. *Pl. Life* 26:14–32. MEEROW, A. W., M. F. FAY, C. L. GUY, Q-B. LI, F. Q. ZAMAN, AND M. W. CHASE. 1999. Systematics of Amaryllidaceae based on cladistic analysis of plastid *rbc*L and *trn*L-F sequence data. *Amer. J. Bot.* 86: 1325–45. MOORE, H. E. 1953. The genus *Milla* (Amaryllidaceae-Allieae) and its allies. *Gentes Herb.* 8:262–94. RAHN, K. 1998. Themidaceae. In *Families and Genera of Vascular Plants*, ed. K. Kubitzki 3: 436–41, Berlin: Springer-Verlag. TRAUB, H. P. 1963. *The genera of the Amaryllidaceae*. La Jolla, CA: American Plant Life Society. TRAUB, H. P. 1972. The order Alliales. *Pl. Life* 28:129–32. TURNER, B. L. 1993. *Jaimehintonia* (Amaryllidaceae: Allieae), a new genus from northeastern Mexico. *Novon* 3:86–88.

THURNIACEAE (Thurnia Family)

DENNIS WM. STEVENSON

Figure 251, Plate 63

- *herbs of wet areas*

- *leaves alternate (tristichous), simple; blades V-shaped in transverse section, the margins often with inconspicuous but sharp teeth*

- *inflorescences spherical heads of sessile flowers subtended by several leafy bracts*

- *fruits loculicidal capsules*

- *seeds pointed at both ends, the seed coat with small, hooked prickles*

Numbers of genera and species. Restricted to tropical America, the Thurniaceae comprise a single genus, *Thurnia*, and three species.

Distribution and habitat. *Thurnia* is known only from tropical lowland Venezuela, the Guianas, and Brazil. Species of *Thurnia* generally grow in sandy soils along and in rivers and streams, at lake margins, and in swamps.

Family classification. The Thurniaceae are placed in the Cyperales by Dahlgren et al., along with the Cyperaceae (sedges) and Juncaceae (rushes). This placement is well supported by morphological and molecular data. Within the order, the Thurniaceae are more closely related to Juncaceae than to Cyperaceae and may even be a member of the former.

Features of the family. Herbs, perenial, rhizomatous, the rhizomes large, subterranean, bearing short aerial shoots with rosettes of leaves, the branching from axillary buds when vertical leafy shoot terminates in inflorescence. **Leaves** alternate (tristichous), simple; blades long, coriaceous, V-shaped in transverse section, the base sheathing, the margins often with inconspicuous, sharp teeth. **Inflorescences** terminal (1 per shoot), a spherical headlike structure, borne at apex of long peduncle; bracts 2+, leaflike. **Flowers** actinomorphic, bisexual, sessile; tepals 6, in 2 series of 3, brown, spotted; androecium of 6 stamens, the stamens in 2 alternate series of 3, the filaments slightly adnate to base of tepals, the anthers basifixed, introrse; gynoecium syncarpous, the ovary superior, the carpels 3, the locules 3, the styles united and very short, the stigmas 3, elongate, dry; placentation basal, the ovules 1–several per locule, bitegmic, anatropous. **Fruits** loculicidal capsules, the lines of dehiscence 3. **Seeds** 1 per locule, pointed on both ends, the seed coat bearing many small, hooked prickles.

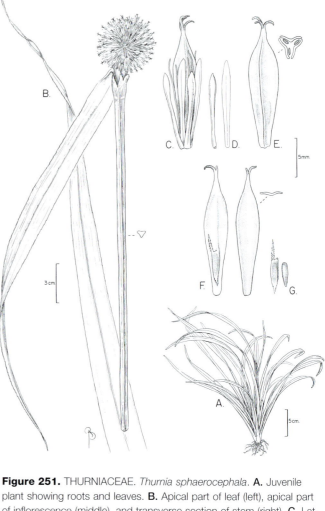

Figure 251. THURNIACEAE. *Thurnia sphaerocephala.* **A.** Juvenile plant showing roots and leaves. **B.** Apical part of leaf (left), apical part of inflorescence (middle), and transverse section of stem (right). **C.** Lateral view of flower after filaments have shed their anthers. **D.** Lateral (left) and adaxial (right) views of tepals. **E.** Lateral view of gynoecium (left) and transverse section of ovary (upper right). **F.** Adaxial (left) and abaxial (middle) views and transverse section (upper right) of fruit valves. **G.** Lateral view of seed with awnlike appendage (left) and lateral view of embryo (right). Reprinted with permission from Mori et al. (1997). Artist: Bobbi Angell.

The family resembles sedges in their vegetative morphology. Leaf anatomy is unusual because the veins occur in pairs with their phloem facing each other.

Natural history. Aquatic species of *Thurnia* are rooted in the substrate and are often submerged, at least seasonally, but their inflorescences are always produced well above the surface of the water. No information is available on pollination and dispersal biology.

Economic uses. No economic uses are known for the family.

References. KUBITZKI, K. 1998. Thurniaceae. In *The Families and Genera of Vascular Plants*, ed. K. Kubitzki, 4:455–57. New York: Springer-Verlag. SIMPSON, D. 1995. Relationship within Cyperales. In *Monocotyledons: Systematics and Evolution*, eds. P. Rudall, P. Cribb, D. Cutler, and C. Humphries, 497–509. Richmond, Surrey, U.K.: Royal Botanic Gardens, Kew.

TRIURIDACEAE (Triurid Family)

MARIA A. GANDOLFO

Figure 252, Plate 63

- *saprophytic herbs*
- *chlorophyll absent*
- *leaves scalelike*
- *flowers with 3–6 tepals; stamens 2–6; carpels 10+, distinct*
- *fruits achenes or follicles*

Numbers of genera and species. Worldwide, the Triuridaceae comprise eight genera and approximately 50 species. In tropical America, there are six genera and 16 species. *Sciaphila* is the largest genus, with approximately 32 species, eight occurring in the neotropics. The remaining Neotropical genera are *Peltophyllum* (2 species), *Triuris* (3), and *Soridium*, *Lacandonia*, and *Triuridopsis* (all monotypic).

Distribution and habitat. Triuridaceae are found in tropical and subtropical areas of the world. Species, except for some *Sciaphila*, are found in very restricted areas. Neotropical species of *Sciaphila* occur in Guatemala, Belize, Honduras, and northern South America. Five genera are restricted to the neotropics. *Lacandonia* in the Lacandona region of Mexico; *Triuridopsis*, in the Loreto Province in Peru; *Soridium*, from Panama to southern Amazonia Brazil; *Triuris*, from Guatemala to southeastern Brazil, but predominantly in Amazonia; and *Peltophyllum*, in southeastern Brazil. *Hyalisma*, *Seychellaria*, and some species of *Sciaphila* are restricted to the Eastern Hemisphere.

Triuridaceae are terrestrial saprophytes most common in lowland rain forests. *Sciaphila purpurea* (Neotropical) and *S. arfakiana* (Australasian) grow on termite nests.

Family classification. The Triuridaceae are placed in the Triuridales by Dahlgren et al. Based on molecular studies, the family was placed in the Pandanales, and additional work based on combined morphological and molecular data confirms this position. These analyses, however, include only *Sciaphila* and *Triuris* for the Triuridaceae. Although cladistic analyses have related the Triuridaceae with the Pandanaceae,

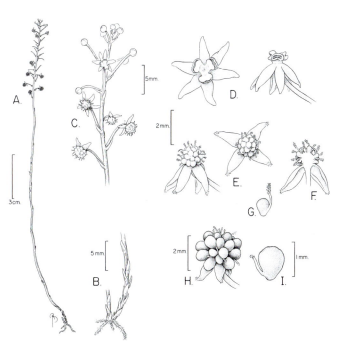

Figure 252. TRIURIDACEAE. *Sciaphila albescens*. **A.** Plant showing roots, scalelike leaves, and inflorescence. **B.** Basal part of plant showing roots and scalelike leaves. **C.** Apical part of stem showing inflorescence. **D.** Apical (left) and lateral (right) views of staminate flowers. **E.** Lateral (left) and apical (right) views of pistillate flowers. **F.** Medial section of pistillate flower. **G.** Lateral view of gynoecium. **H.** Head of fruits. **I.** Lateral view of fruit. Reprinted with permission from Mori et al. (1997). Artist: Bobbi Angell.

Cyclanthaceae, Velloziaceae, and Stemonaceae, more analyses including additional genera of Triuridaceae are needed to confirm the family's relationships. Based on morphological similarities, the family was initially thought to be related to the Alismataceae.

Traditionally the Triuridaceae are divided into two tribes, Sciaphileae and Triurideae. Sciaphileae are characterized by unappendaged tepals and a basal style and comprise *Sciaphila*, *Soridium*, *Hyalisma*, and *Seychellaria*, whereas Triurideae are characterized by appendaged tepals and a lateral style and comprise *Lacandonia*, *Triuris*, *Peltophyllum*, and *Triuridopsis*.

Features of the family. Habit: saprophytic herbs, chlorophyll absent, mycorrhizal, roots reduced, rhizomes present, usually creeping or occasionally erect, covered by scalelike leaves, stems slender, 2–30 cm tall (*Sciaphila purpurea* can reach 1.4 m), unbranched, commonly white or yellow, less frequently red, purple, or hyaline. **Leaves** alternate (usually spirally arranged), scalelike, sessile, triangular, very small (1–2 mm long), number of leaves per stem 0–2 (in *Peltophyllum* and *Triuris*) or 1–15 (in *Soridium* and *Sciaphila*); stomates absent. **Inflorescences** 1 per plant, racemes, elongate, with 1–16 (in *Triuris*, *Lacandonia*, and *Peltophyllum*) to many (50+ in some *Sciaphila*) flowers, the staminate flowers in upper part of inflorescence, always more than pistillate flowers; pedicels evident, sometimes recurved in fruit. **Flowers** actinomorphic, unisexual (dioecious or, in Sciaphileae, monoecious) or bisexual in *Lacandonia* and some *Sciaphila*; tepals 3(4) or 6 (*Soridium*), connate at base, triangular to deltoid, the adaxial surface sometimes covered by papillae, the apex sometimes bearded or bearing glandular knobs (*Sciaphila*) or tail-like appendages (*Triuris* and *Peltophyllum*); androecium with 2 (*Soridium*), 3 (remaining genera), or 6 (*Triuris*) stamens, the stamens generally epitepalous, sessile or with filaments, an androphore present in *Triuris*, the anthers extrorse (introrse in *Peltophyllum luteum*), sometimes with well-developed connective extension, dehiscing longitudinally, diagonally, or transversally; staminodes present in some *Sciaphila*; gynoecium apocarpous, the carpels 10 to numerous in bisexual flowers, immersed in receptacle, the styles terminal or lateral (then almost basal), the stigmas papillate to penicillate or glabrous; placentation basal, the ovules 1 per carpel, anatropous. **Fruits** achenes or follicles.

The vascular tissue consists of a poorly differentiated stele. The staminate flowers of *Triuridopsis* bear a central projection described as a pistillode. *Lacandonia* is characterized by the arrangement of the sexual organs, with the 3 stamens surrounded by the carpels, constituting the only case among the living angiosperms in which the carpels are located out-side the anthers. For this reason, it is sometimes placed in its own family, the Lacandoniaceae.

Natural history. The Triuridaceae live symbiotically with mycorrhizal fungi and frequently are associated with other saprophytes. At present, no data on pollination or dispersal are available; however, the morphology of the tepals and the production of fragrance suggest that they are visited by insects. Some evidence points to animals, wind, and water as methods of dispersal.

Economic uses. No economic uses for the Triuridaceae are known.

References. GOLDBERG, A. 1989. Classification, evolution, and phylogeny of the families of Monocotyledons. *Smithsonian Contr. Bot.* 71:1–74. MAAS, P.J.M., AND T. RÜBSAMEN. 1986. Triuridaceae. *Fl. Neotrop. Monogr.* 40:1–55. MAAS-VAN DE KAMER, H. 1995. Triuridiflorae—Gardner's delight? In *Monocotyledons: Systematics and Evolution*, eds. P. Rudall, P. Cribb, D. Cutler, and C. Humphries, 287–301. Richmond, Surrey, U.K.: Royal Botanic Gardens, Kew. MAAS-VAN DE KAMER, H., AND P.J.M. MAAS. 1994. *Triuridopsis*, a new monotypic genus of Triuridaceae. *Pl. Syst. Evol.* 192: 257–62. MAAS-VAN DE KAMER, H., AND T. WEUSTENFELD. 1998. Triuridaceae. In *The Families and Genera of Vascular Plants*, ed. K. Kubitzki, 3:452–58. Berlin: Springer-Verlag. MARTINEZ, S. E., AND C. H. RAMOS. 1989. Lacandoniaceae (Triuridales): una nueva familia de México. *Ann. Missouri Bot. Gard.* 76:128–35. MEERENDONK, J.P.M. VAN DE. 1984. Triuridaceae. In *Flora Malesiana*, ser. 1, 10:109–21. Alphen Aan Den Rijn, Netherlands: Sijthoff and Noordhoff International Publishers. RÜBSAMEN-WEUSTENFELD, T. 1991. Morphologische, embyologische und systematische Untersuchungen un Triuridaceae. *Biblioth. Bot.* 140:1–61.

TYPHACEAE (Cat-tail Family)

DENNIS WM. STEVENSON

Figure 253

- *herbs, aquatic, rhizomatous*

- *rhizomes with large air canals*

- *leaves alternate (distichous), simple; blades long, linear*

- *inflorescences terminal, cylindrical, spikelike*

- *flowers unisexual, highly reduced; ovule 1 per locule, pendulous*

Numbers of genera and species. Worldwide, the Typhaceae comprise two genera, *Typha* with 8–13 species and *Sparganium* with 14 species. In tropical America, there is a single genus, *Typha*, and four species.

Distribution and habitat. The Typhaceae are cosmopolitan, with centers of distribution in North America and Eurasia. Species of Typhaceae are found in damp areas and in shallow water, in marshes, ponds, lakes, and river margins. The Typhaceae are often aggressive colonizing weeds, form-

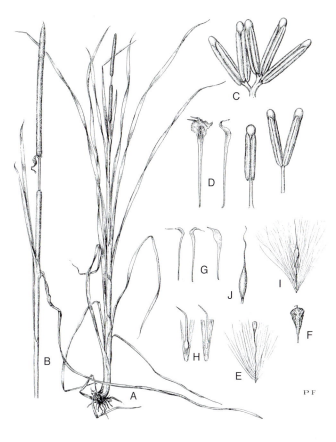

Figure 253. TYPHACEAE. *Typha domingensis*. **A.** Plant showing roots, leaves, and inflorescence (x⅛). **B.** Stem with inflorescence (x⅓). **C.** Stamens with five anthers (above), one anther (below left), and two anthers (below right) (x12). **D.** Adaxial (left) and lateral (right) views of staminate bracts. **E.** Lateral view of flower with aborted ovary (x6). **F.** Lateral view of aborted ovary with rudimentary style (x12). **G.** Pistillate bracts (x12). **H.** Intact immature pistillate flower (left) and medial section of pistillate flower (right) (x12). **I.** Lateral view of mature pistillate flower subtended by coma (x6). **J.** Lateral view of mature gynoecium (x12). Reprinted with permission from Correll and Correll (1982). Artist: Priscilla Fawcett.

ing extensive stands in shallow, slow-moving water and roadside ditches.

Family classification. The Typhaceae are placed in the Typhales by Dahlgren et al. with the Sparganiaceae. Both Dahlgren et al. and Thorne place the Typhaceae near the Bromeliaceae, and Takhtajan aligns the family near the Pandanaceae and Cyclanthaceae. Cronquist places it in the Commelinidae near the Poaceae and Cyperaceae. Recent morphological and molecular studies align the Typhales with the Commelinidae near or within the Poales. Kubitzki places *Typha* and *Sparangium* together in one family, the Typhaceae, which may better reflect the close relationship of these two genera.

Features of the family. Habit: herbs, aquatic, perennial, rhizomatous; rhizomes subterranean, starchy, with large air canals, producing only scale leaves, the aerial shoots terminated by an inflorescence, the renewal growth from axillary bud of scale leaf. **Leaves** alternate (distichous), simple; blades long, linear, very spongy as a result of well-developed air canals. **Inflorescences** terminal, cylindrical, spikelike, of 2 superposed regions with short sterile band between them, the lower bearing pistillate flowers, the upper staminate flowers. **Flowers** actinomorphic, unisexual, highly reduced; perianth of 1–several scales and/or thin bristles, inserted in 1+ diffuse whorls, the scales inconspicuous, membranous. **Staminate flowers** with androecium of (1)3(8) stamens, the anthers basifixed. **Pistillate flowers** with gynoecium stalked, syncarpous, the carpels 3, 2 failing to mature, the style persistent, the stigma 1, dry, somewhat spatulate; placentation apical, the ovule 1 per locule, pendulous. **Fruits** follicles, with tuft of basal hairs, dehiscing after dispersal. **Seeds** minute.

Natural history. Species of Typhaceae are wind-pollinated and thus produce copious quantities of pollen. Similarly, they are wind-dispersed and, therefore, produce large inflorescences with numerous, small, light fruits. In *Typha*, the dispersal unit is the entire female flower because the perianth functions as a parachute that facilitates wind dispersal. The ripe fruits of *Sparganium* have spongy outer parts that allow them to float and be dispersed by water.

Economic uses. *Typha* has a long and diverse history of uses. The starchy rhizomes, the young inflorescences, and pollen are edible. The leaves are used to make baskets, mats, and chair seats. *Typha angustifolia* (cat-tail), for example, is the primary source of "rush" fiber in North America. The female part of the inflorescence was used as padding in pillows and mattresses by indigenous people.

References. KUBITZKI, K. 1998. Typhaceae. In *The Families and Genera of Vascular Plants*, ed. K. Kubitzki, 4:457–61. New York: Springer-Verlag.

VELLOZIACEAE (Vellozia Family)

RENATO DE MELLO-SILVA

Figure 254, Plate 63

- *herbs and shrubs, common in rocky or sandy habitats*

- *stems covered by persistent leaf sheaths and adventitious roots*

- *leaves whorled, tristichous or spirotristichous, simple, clustered at branch apices*

- *flower with a hypanthium; tepals 6; ovary usually inferior*

- *fruits capsules*

Numbers of genera and species. Worldwide, the Velloziaceae comprise about seven genera and approximately 250 species. In tropical America, there are four genera and about 220 species. The largest genera are *Vellozia* and *Barbacenia sensu lato*, both exclusively Neotropical, and each with a little more than 100 species. *Barbaceniopsis*, has only four known species, and *Nanuza* (*N. plicata*) is monotypic.

Distribution and habitat. Species of Velloziaceae are found in tropical South America, Africa, and Madagascar. Most species occur in the mountains of central Brazil, but a few inhabit the eastern foothills of the Andes (*Barbaceniopsis*) and the Guayana Highlands. The widespread *Vellozia tubiflora* reaches the mountains of Panama. *Xerophyta* and *Talbotia* are found in the Eastern Hemisphere, predominantly in Africa and *Acanthochlamys* occurs in China.

Most species of Velloziaceae occur in full sun in relatively dry, rocky, or sandy habitats, at elevations ranging from 700 to 2,000 meters.

Family classification. The Velloziaceae are placed in the Velloziales by Dahlgren et al. and in the Pandanales by the Angiosperm Phylogeny Group. Traditionally, the family has been associated with several families of Liliales *sensu lato*; e.g., the Agavaceae, Aloeaceae, Amaryllidaceae, Haemodoraceae, Hypoxidaceae, and Bromeliaceae. Recent morphological analyses have shown that the Velloziaceae are related to the Bromeliaceae and Hypoxidaceae. Molecular studies, however, have indicated unexpected relationships with the Pandanaceae and Cyclanthaceae. Combined analyses suggest a relationship with the Stemonaceae. *Acanthochlamys*, a monotypic genus originally placed in the Velloziaceae, has been segregated as the Acantochlamidaceae, which, according to some botanists, is sister to the Velloziaceae. Because of this, the Angiosperm Phylogeny Group has retained *Acanthochlamys* in the Velloziaceae.

Figure 254. VELLOZIACEAE. *Vellozia glabra* (A, Irwin et al. 21823; B–E, Maguire et al. 44369; F, Maguire 49048). **A.** Upper part of stem showing leaf bases, leaves, flower, and immature fruit. **B.** Upper part of plant showing branched stem with persistent leaf bases, leaves, flowers, immature fruit, and detail of leaf blade apex (above). **C.** Medial section of flower (left) and transverse section of ovary (right). **D.** Lateral view of stamen. **E.** Apical-lateral view of stigma and upper part of style. **F.** Lateral view of fruit. Original. Artist: Bobbi Angell.

The Velloziaceae are divided into two subfamilies: Vellozioideae, including both American and African species, and the exclusively Neotropical Barbacenioideae. Recent morphological analyses indicate that this division is paraphyletic and that *Barbaceniopsis* should be included in *Xerophyta* to form a monophyletic group. These analyses show *Nanuza* and *Talbotia* as independent clades, thereby supporting their treatment as separate genera. Finally, among the genera included in *Barbacenia sensu lato* (*Aylthonia*, *Barbacenia sensu stricto*, *Burlemarxia*, and *Pleurostima*), *Aylthonia* seems to be polyphyletic and *Barbacenia sensu stricto* may not be monophyletic.

Features of the family. Habit: herbs and shrubs, *Dracaena*-like, ranging from a few centimeters (*Vellozia abietina* and

V. mimima) to more than 6 m (*V. gigantea*), the stems sparsely branched, aerial, ca. 1–2 cm diameter, covered by persistent leaf sheaths, adventitious roots, and sometimes marcescent leaves (thereby increasing diam. to as much as 50 cm). **Leaves** whorled (tristichous or spirotristichous), simple, clustered at branch apices, ranging from a few centimeters to almost 1 meter long; leaf sheaths present, well developed; blades narrowly lanceolate, straight or curved, deciduous with abscission line at sheath junction or marcescent and reflexed, the margins serrate or entire. **Inflorescences** terminal, fasciculate, with 1–many flowers (to 12 in *Barbacenia polyantha* and 15 in *Vellozia tubiflora*). **Flowers** actinomorphic, bisexual or rarely unisexual in *Barbaceniopsis* (plants dioecious), often large and showy; hypanthium present, usually prolonged into conspicuous tube beyond apex of ovary, smooth or with small glandular or nonglandular protuberances; tepals 6, purple in most species of *Vellozia*, white in *Nanuza*, purple, white, or yellow in *Barbaceniopsis*, or red, orange, yellow, white, green, purple, or a combination in *Barbacenia sensu lato*; corona of petalar origin present in *Barbacenia sensu lato*; androecium with 6 (−76 in *Vellozia*) stamens, lacerated staminal appendages often present in *Vellozia*, the filaments free (*Vellozia* and some *Barbacenia*) or absent, then anthers adnate to corona lobes or hypanthium (*Barbacenia sensu lato* and *Barbaceniopsis*); gynoecium syncarpous, the ovary inferior or rarely semi-inferior (*Vellozia hemisphaerica* group), the carpels 3, the locules 3, the stigmas peltate-trilobed (*Vellozia*), capitate, clavate, linear, or subapical (*Barbacenia sensu lato* and *Barbaceniopsis*); septal nectaries conspicuous; placentation axile, the ovules numerous. **Fruits** capsules, loculicidal or dehiscent by apical, basal, or longitudinal slits. **Seeds** numerous.

The anatomical structure of the leaf blade is variable and of importance in the taxonomy of the family. Especially useful features are the presence of furrows, aquiferous parenchyma, and the structure of the fibrovascular bundles.

Most species of *Vellozia* and *Nanuza plicata* are diploid, species of *Barbacenia sensu lato* are tetraploid, and species of *Xerophyta* and *Talbotia elegans* are hexaploid.

Natural history. Species of *Barbacenia sensu lato* apparently flower almost continuously throughout the year, whereas species of *Vellozia* have relatively short flowering seasons. Some species may flower after the frequent dry-season fires of central Brazil.

Pollination mechanisms in Velloziaceae have been studied extensively in Minas Gerais, Brazil, where most species of *Vellozia* are pollinated by bees; *V. leptopetala* is pollinated by birds, and species with white flowers and long hypanthial tubes are pollinated by moths. Species of *Barbacenia sensu lato*, with their colorful flowers and large amounts of nectar, are typically pollinated by birds, but bats might be pollinators of a few species (e.g., *B. vandellii*).

The seeds are small and numerous but there have been no studies on their dispersal. In many species of *Vellozia*, the seeds possess an external layer of empty cells with spiral thickenings on the walls, the function of which has not been determined. Vegetative propagation, especially well developed in *Vellozia prolifera*, is common in some species.

Economic uses. Species of Velloziaceae are not commercially exploited on a large scale, but they are frequently used by local populations. The resinous stems of many species are utilized as fire lighters, especially those of *Vellozia sincorana* (*candombá*), which are found for sale in local markets of Bahia, Brazil. The stems of *V. furcata* and *V. glabra* are used as primitive paint brushes for whitewashing houses. Recently, a large quantity of dried stems of *V. glabra* and *V. compacta* from Minas Gerais, has been harvested and sent to cities throughout Brazil where they are sold for decorative purposes. Many species are well adapted to cultivation, and *Nanuza plicata* was used widely by Brazilian landscaper Burle Marx in his gardens. In the interior of Bahia, *V. canelinha* is said to be an effective remedy for liver and kidney problems. A few Brazilian and African species have been studied because of their supposed anticancer potential.

References. ALVES, R.J.V. 2002. Two new species of *Nanuza* (Velloziaceae) from Brazil. *Novon* 12(1):12–17. AYENSU, E. S. 1973. Biological and morphological aspects of the Velloziaceae. *Biotropica* 5(3):135–49. GOLDBLAT, P., AND M. E. POSTON. 1988. Observations on the chromosome cytology of Velloziaceae. *Ann. Missouri Bot. Gard.* 75:192–95. IBISCH, P. L., C. NOWICKI, R. VÁSQUEZ, AND K. KOCH. 2001. Taxonomy and biology of Andean Velloziaceae: *Vellozia andina* sp. nov. and notes on *Barbaceniopsis* (including *Barbaceniopsis castillonii* comb. nov.). *Syst. Bot.* 26(1):5–16. KUBITZKI, K. 1998. Velloziaceae. In *The Families and Genera of Vascular Plants*, ed. K. Kubitzki, 3:459–67. Berlin: Springer-Verlag. MELLO-SILVA, R. 1991. The infra-familial taxonomic circumscription of the Velloziaceae. A historical and critical analysis. *Taxon* 40:45–51. MELLO-SILVA, R. 2000. Partial cladistic analysis of *Vellozia* and characters for the phylogeny of Velloziaceae. In *Monocots: Systematics and Evolution*, eds. K. L. Wilson and D. A. Morrison, 505–22. Melbourne, Australia: CSIRO. MELO, N. F., M. GUERRA, A. M. BENKO-ISEPPON, AND N. L. MENEZES. 1997. Cytogenetics and cytotaxonomy of Velloziaceae. *Pl. Syst. Evol.* 204:257–73. MENEZES, N. L. 1980. Evolution in Velloziaceae with special references to androecial characters. In *Petaloid Monocotyledons: Horticultural and Botanical Research*, eds. C. D. Brickell, D. F. Cutler, and M. Gregory, 117–39. London: Academic Press. MENEZES, N. L., R. MELLO-SILVA, AND S. MAYO. 1994. A cladistic analysis of the Velloziaceae. *Kew Bull.* 49(1):71–92. SALATINO, A., M.L.F. SALATINO, R. MELLO-SILVA, M. A. SLUYS, D. E. GIANNASI, AND R. A. PRICE. 2001. Phylogenetic inference in Velloziaceae using chloroplast *TrnL*-F sequences. *Syst. Bot.* 26(1):92–103. SMITH, L. B., AND E. S. AYENSU. 1974. Classification of the Old World Velloziaceae. *Kew Bull.* 29(1):181–205. SMITH, L. B., AND E. S. AYENSU. 1976. A revision of American Velloziaceae. *Smithsonian Contr. Bot.*, no. 30:i–viii, 1–172.

XYRIDACEAE (Yellow-eyed Grass Family)

Lisa M. Campbell

Figure 255, Plate 64

- *herbs*
- *leaves usually basal, sometimes cauline, often distichous, often equitant*
- *inflorescences usually on scapes*
- *flowers bisexual, ephemeral, corolla conspicuous, often zygomorphic; staminodia with moniliform hairs (Xyris)*
- *fruits loculicidal capsules*

Numbers of genera and species. Worldwide, the Xyridaceae comprise five genera and about 375 species. In tropical America, there are five genera and about 250 species. *Xyris* includes about 350 species, of which more than 200 occur in the neotropics; *Abolboda* comprises 21 species, all Neotropical; and *Achlyphila*, *Aratitiyopea*, and *Orectanthe* are monotypic and restricted to northern South America.

Distribution and habitat. *Xyris* is the most widely distributed genus in the family, with species occurring in Australia, through Indonesia to southern Asia, Africa, and the Americas where they range from southern Ontario, Canada, to southern Brazil. The greatest concentration of species of *Xyris* is in the neotropics and the number of species decreases with increasing latitude. The genera of Xyridaceae occur only in northern South America, where they are mostly endemic to the Guayana Shield, especially the *tepuis* of the Roraima formation. The monotypic *Achlyphila* and *Aratitiyopea* are known from only a few *tepuis*.

Xyridaceae occur in seasonally or permanently wet or moist grasslands and savannas, or on rock faces, such as sandstone and granitic outcrops, and other exposed habitats. In the neotropics, they are often a component of ephemeral wet-season and postfire floras.

Family classification. The Xyridaceae are placed in the Commelinales by Dahlgren et al. Recent evidence suggests that the Xyridaceae, Eriocaulaceae, Mayacaceae, and perhaps the Rapateaceae, are more closely related to the Poales. Xyridaceae are often considered related to Eriocaulaceae or to Rapateaceae, and it has been suggested that the monogeneric Mayacaceae should be included in the Xyridaceae. Two families or subfamilies have been recognized: Xyridaceae (*Xyris*) and Abolbodaceae (including *Orectanthe*), but most authors recognize a single diverse family.

Features of the family. Habit: herbs, perennial or annual, iridoid. Ligule sometimes pronounced, appearing as continu-

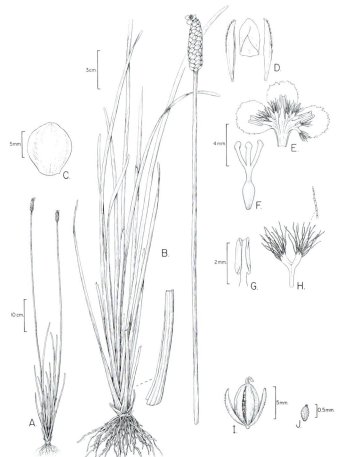

Figure 255. XYRIDACEAE. *Xyris laxifolia*. **A.** Plant showing roots, leaves, and inflorescences. **B.** Basal part of plant (left), detail of leaf sheath (middle), and apical part of stem with inflorescence (right). **C.** Abaxial view of bract from inflorescence. **D.** Lateral (left and right) and abaxial (middle) views of sepals, the medial sepal cucullate. **E.** Sympetalous corolla opened to show adnate stamens and staminodes. **F.** Lateral view of gynoecium. **G.** Adaxial view of stamen. **H.** Adaxial view of staminode with detail of ultimate hairlike division (above right). **I.** Lateral view of fruit. **J.** Seed. Reprinted with permission from Mori et al. (1997). Artist: Bobbi Angell.

ation of leaf margin (*Achlyphila* and some *Xyris*). **Leaves** basal or cauline, distichous and often equitant (*Achlyphila* and most *Xyris*) or polystichous. **Inflorescences** usually on scapes, spikes or heads, rarely thyrsoid, many to few flowered; bracts firm. **Flowers** actinomorphic or zygomorphic, bisexual, showy; sepals (2)3; petals 3, distinct or united, yellow (in *Xyris*, *Achlyphila*, and *Orectanthe*), blue or white (in *Abolboda*), pink-magenta or white (in *Aratitiyopea*); androecium with 3 stamens, the stamens epipetalous (except in *Achlyphila*); staminodia often present (in most *Xyris* and some *Abolboda*), usually branched and with apical moniliform hairs in *Xyris*; gynoecium syncarpous, the ovary superior, the carpels 3, the locules 1 or 3 (sometimes incomplete), the style with well-developed to reduced lateral or basal appendages (*Abolboda*, *Aratitiyopea*, and *Orectanthe*), the apex branched or funnelform (capitate in *Achlyphila*), usually papillate; placentation axile or free-central (*Xyris*) or axile (all remaining genera). **Fruits** loculicidal capsules. **Seeds** numerous.

Natural history. The corollas of Xyridaceae are delicate and often last only a few hours. Bee pollination is reported in *Xyris* and bird pollination in *Orectanthe*, but nectar is not produced. Dispersal takes place by gravity when the seeds fall from the dehiscing fruits.

Economic uses. A few aquatic species of *Xyris* are sold for aquaria, and other species of this genus are used in dried flower arrangements.

References. KRAL, R. 1992. A treatment of American Xyridaceae exclusive of *Xyris*. *Ann. Missouri Bot. Gard.* 75:522–722. KRAL, R. 1998. Xyridaceae. In *The Families and Genera of Vascular Plants*, ed. K. Kubitzki, 4:461–69. Berlin: Springer-Verlag. LINDER, H. P., AND E. A. KELLOGG. 1995. Phylogenetic patterns in the commelinid clade. In *Monocotyledons: Systematics and Evolution*, eds. P. Rudall, P. Cribb, D. Cutler, and C. Humphries, 473–96. Richmond, Surrey, U.K.: Royal Botanic Gardens, Kew. MAGUIRE, B. 1958. Xyridaceae. In The botany of the Guayana Highland—part III. *Mem. New York Bot. Gard.* 10(1):1–19. MAGUIRE, B., AND J. J. WURDACK. 1960. Xyridaceae. In The botany of the Guayana Highland—part IV. *Mem. New York Bot. Gard.* 10(2):11–15. RUDALL, P. J., AND M. G. SAJO. 1999. Systematic position of *Xyris*: flower and seed anatomy. *Int. J. Plant Sci.* 160:795–808.

ZANNICHELLIACEAE (Horned Pondweed Family)

ROBERT R. HAYNES

- *submersed aquatic herbs*

- *leaves subopposite or subwhorled, simple; blades linear*

- *inflorescences axillary*

- *flowers unisexual; stamen 1; gynoecium apocarpous*

- *fruits drupes*

Numbers of genera and species. Worldwide, the Zannichelliaceae comprise four genera and perhaps 12 species. In tropical America, there is a single genus, *Zannichellia*, and two species.

Distribution and habitat. The Zannichelliaceae are nearly cosmopolitan. Only *Zannichellia* is known from the Western Hemisphere.

Individuals of Zannichelliaceae are submersed in fresh, cold waters of spring-fed streams or brackish waters of bays. In the neotropics, *Zannichellia palustris* occupies habitats at lower elevations, whereas *Z. andina* is limited to cold, high-elevation streams.

Family classification. The Zannichelliaceae are placed in the Najadales by Dahlgren et al. The family is most closely related to the Potamogetonaceae. The Zannichelliaceae have not been divided into subfamilies.

Features of the family. Habit: submersed aquatic herbs, annual. **Leaves** subopposite or subwhorled (often on same individual), simple, sessile; basal sheaths present, adnate to blade base, extending into ligule; blades linear to filiform; venation essentially of midrib. **Inflorescences** axillary, of 1 staminate and 1 pistillate flower per axil. **Flowers** actinomorphic, unisexual (plants monoecious). **Staminate flowers:** located directly behind pistillate flowers (in same leaf axis); androecium of 1 stamen, the filament to 3 cm long, the anther directly above stigmas. **Pistillate flowers:** perianth a closed tubelike structure; gynoecium apocarpous, the ovaries superior, the carpels 1–8, surrounded basally by perianth, the stigmas funnel-shaped, exserted from perianth tube; placentation apical, the ovules 1 per carpel, pendulous. **Fruits** drupes, the endocarp prickly. **Seeds** 1 per fruit; embryo strongly curved.

Natural history. Pollination mechanisms have been studied in *Lepilaena* and *Zannichellia*. Both genera release the pollen from the anther in a gelatinous matrix. In *Lepilaena*, the gelatinous matrix with the enclosed pollen rises to the water surface, where pollination is accomplished. In *Zannichellia*, however, pollen sinks after release from the anthers, presumably still within the gelatinous matrix, and contacts the funnel-shaped stigmas below the anther, presumably in the same leaf axis.

Various waterfowl consume fruits of horned pondweeds, and some of the seeds pass through the digestive tracts intact, after which they germinate readily.

Economic uses. Other than serving as occasional food for waterfowl, members of the Zannichelliaceae are of little economic value. They rarely, if ever, form populations large enough for substrate stabilization or to impact human use of waterways.

References. Cox, P. A. 1988. Hydrophilous pollination. *Annual Rev. Ecol. Syst.* 19:261–80. Cox, P. A., and R. B. Knox. 1989. Two-dimensional pollination in hydrophilous plants: convergent evolution in the genera *Halodule*, (Cymodoceaceae), *Halophila*, (Hydrocharitaceae), and *Lepilaena* (Zannichelliaceae). *Amer. J. Bot.* 76:164–75. Haynes, R. R., and L. B. Holm-Nielsen. 1987. The Zannichelliaceae in the southeastern United States. *J. Arnold Arbor.* 68:259–68. Les, D. H., and R. R. Haynes. 1995. Systematics of Alismatiflorae: synthesis of molecular and non-molecular approaches. In *Monocotyledons: Systematics and Evolution*, eds. P. Rudall, P. Cribb, D. Cutler, and C. Humphries, 353–77. Richmond, Surrey, U.K.: Royal Botanic Gardens, Kew. Vierssen, W. van. 1982. The ecology of communities dominated by *Zannichellia*-taxa in western Europe I. Characterization and autecology of the *Zannichellia* taxa. *Aquatic Bot.* 12:103–55. Vierssen, W. van, R. J. Wijk, and J. R. Van Der Zee. 1982. On the pollination mechanism of some eurysaline Potamogetonaceae. *Aquatic Bot.* 14:339–47.

ZINGIBERACEAE (Ginger Family)

Dennis Wm. Stevenson and Janice Wassmer Stevenson

Figure 256, Plate 64

- *herbs, aromatic, rhizomatous; pseudostem formed by overlapping leaf sheaths*

- *leaves alternate, distichous, simple; sheath open, ligulate*

- *flowers zygomorphic; staminodes 5, the inner 2 fused to form petal-like labellum; stamen 1, the thecae 2; ovary inferior*

- *fruits dry or fleshy capsules; calyx persistent*

- *seeds with orange to white aril*

Numbers of genera and species. Worldwide, the Zingiberiaceae comprise 46 genera and approximately 1,300 species. In tropical America, there is a single native genus, *Renealmia*, with 55 species, and four introduced and naturalized genera, *Alpinia*, *Curcuma*, *Hedychium*, and *Zingiber*.

Distribution and habitat. The Zingiberaceae are a pantropical family with the greatest concentration of genera and species in Southeast Asia. Three tribes, Hedychieae, Globbeae, and Zingibereae, collectively with 24 genera, are found only in the paleotropics from Australia to tropical Asia and Africa. The fourth tribe, Alpinieae with 21 genera, is found primarily in the paleotropics with one genus, *Renealmia*, occurring in the neotropics. *Renealmia* contains about 75 species, 20 of which are found in Africa, with the others occurring in the West Indies, Mexico, and tropical Central and South America. Other species, for example *Alpinia purpurata* and *A. zerumbet*, are frequently cultivated in the neotropics and may occasionally appear to be native.

Generally, the Zingiberaceae grow in wet tropical forests as understory herbs in well-illuminated areas such as clearings caused by tree falls. A few species of *Renealmia* are found at elevations up to 2,500 meters in the Andes.

Family classification. The Zingiberaceae are placed in the Zingiberales by Dahlgren et al. Historically, the Zingiberaceae were divided into two subfamilies, the Costoideae and the Zingiberoideae. Although the Costoideae were considered a subfamily in the Zingiberaceae, all current systems recognize two distinct but related families, the Zingiberaceae and the Costaceae based on both morphological and molecular data. Moreover, there is support for a group within the Zingiberales that includes one clade with the Zingiberaceae-Costaceae and another clade with the Cannaceae-Marantaceae. Together these two clades form a larger more inclusive group.

The 46 genera of Zingiberaceae have been, until recently, placed into four tribes, the Alpinieae, Globbeae, Hedychieae, and Zingibereae of which only the latter is native to the neotropics. Kress et al., however, divide the family into four subfamilies and six tribes: Siphonochiloideae (Siphonochileae), Tamijioideae (Tamijieae), Alpinioideae (Alpinieae, Riedelieae), and Zingiberoideae (Zingibereae, Globbeae).

Features of the family. Habit: herbs (to 8 m tall), aromatic, the rhizome horizontal, branched, with short internodes (often tuberlike in appearance); aerial shoot a pseudostem, formed by overlapping leaf sheaths. **Leaves** alternate, distichous, the plane of distichy perpendicular to rhizome in Alpinieae, or parallel to rhizome in Hedychieae, Globbeae, and Zingibereae, simple; leaf sheath open, ligulate; petiole distinct, short. **Inflorescences** terminal, on separate leafless scape or rarely on leafy shoot, thyrses, of 1–few-flowered cymes, the cymes congested, globose to cylindrical or strobilus-like and lax. **Flowers** zygomorphic, bisexual; perianth in

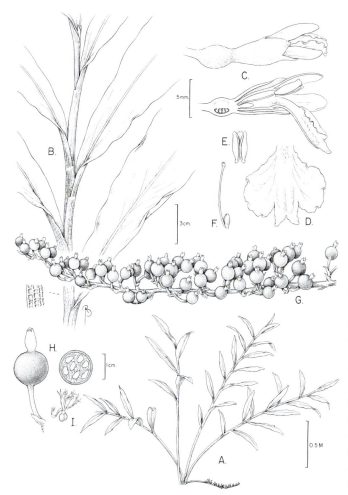

Figure 256. ZINGIBERACEAE. *Renealmia floribunda.* **A.** Apical part of plant showing leaves and inflorescence. **B.** Part of stem with detail of pattern on leaf sheath (below left). **C.** Lateral view (above) and medial section of flower (below). **D.** Adaxial view of labellum. **E.** Adaxial view of anther. **F.** Lateral view of style showing basal glands. **G.** Apical part of infructescence. **H.** Lateral view of intact fruit (left) and transverse section of fruit (right). **I.** Seed with aril. Reprinted with permission from Mori et al. (1997). Artist: Bobbi Angell.

2 whorls of 3; calyx tubular, 3-lobed, sometimes split on 1 side; petals 3, basally connate, white, yellow, or red, longer than calyx, the median petal often longer than lateral ones; androecium composed of 2 whorls of 3: the outer whorl of 2 lateral tooth- to petal-like staminodes and a reduced median staminode, the inner whorl composed of a stamen and 2 lateral staminodes (the lateral staminodes fused into a variable labellum); stamen 1, with 2 thecae and short filament (*Renealmia*); gynoecium syncarpous, the ovary inferior, 3-locu-lar, the style 1, in furrow of filament and between thecae, the stigma funnelform, sometimes variously ciliate; septal nectaries present; placentation axile, the ovules several to many per locule. **Fruits** dry or fleshy, loculicidal or indehiscent capsules, sometimes with persistent calyx. **Seeds** several to many per fruit, black to brown, hard, operculate; aril generally lacerate or lobed, orange to white.

Natural history. The nectar-producing tubular flowers last for one day and are pollinated by hummingbirds, various species of bees, hawkmoths, and butterflies. The infructescences of *Renealmia* often trail along the ground, and the fruits open to expose black seeds subtended by orange arils, suggesting dispersal by birds or terrestrial animals, including ants.

Economic uses. Numerous genera of the family have beautiful flowers and are cultivated in the Tropics and in temperate greenhouses. The torch ginger (*Etlingera elatior*); ginger lilies (species of *Hedychium*, especially *H. coronarium*); the red ginger (*Alpinia purpurata*); and the shell ginger (*A. zerumbet*), among others, are found in most botanical gardens throughout the neotropics.

Species of this family have ethereal oils in their cells, and, therefore, include many important spice plants of Old World origin such as turmeric (*Curcuma longa*), cardamom (*Elettaria cardamomum*), and ginger (*Zingiber officinale*). *Curcuma angustifolia* (East Indian arrowroot) yields an edible starch, and *C. aromatica* and *C. longa* are the source of dyes. The seeds of *Aframomum melegueta* (grains of paradise) and other species of the genus are utilized as spices. *Hedychium spicatum* (abir) and *Alpinia galanga* (greater galangal) yield rhizomes rich in aromatic compounds used in perfumery. Species of the family are employed locally as medicinals that range from *A. officinarum* for treating aching teeth to *Zingiber officinale* for alleviating travel sickness.

References. KRESS, J. 1990. The phylogeny and classification of the Zingiberales. *Ann. Missouri Bot. Gard.* 77:698–721. KRESS, J., L. M. PRINCE, AND K. J. WILLIAMS. 2002. The phylogeny and a new classification of the gingers (Zingiberaceae): evidence from molecular data. *Amer. J. Bot.* 89(11): 1682–96. LARSEN, K. 1998. Costaceae. In *The Families and Genera of Vascular Plants*, ed. K. Kubitzki, 4:128–32. New York: Springer-Verlag. LARSEN, K., J. M. LOCK, H. MAAS, AND P.J.M. MAAS. 1998. Zingiberaceae. In *The Families and Genera of Vascular Plants*, ed. K. Kubitzki, 4:474–95. New York: Springer-Verlag. MAAS, P.J.M. 1977. *Renealmia* (Zingiberaceae-Zingiberoideae. *Fl. Neotrop. Monogr.* 18:1–161.

ZOSTERACEAE (Eel-grass Family)

Dennis Wm. Stevenson

- *intertidal to marine aquatic herbs*
- *flowers unisexual, both sexes on same spadix; perianth absent*
- *staminate flowers of a single stamen; pistillate flowers with ovary with 1 locule; pollen released in long, filamentous strands*
- *fruits achenes*

Numbers of genera and species. Worldwide, the Zosteraceae comprise three genera and at least 18 species. Species of all three genera, *Heterozostera*, *Phyllospadix*, and *Zostera*, occur in subtropical waters, and, hence may marginally reach the Tropics.

Distribution and habitat. In general, the family occurs in shallow coastal waters of temperate to subtropical regions. *Zostera* is widely distributed in both hemispheres and in the North Atlantic extends southward to subtropical areas. *Heterozostera*, with only a single species, is found on the coasts of Australia and Chile. *Phyllospadix* is found mostly in temperate waters of the North Pacific, but *P. torreyi* has been collected from the waters of Baja California, Mexico. The perennial plants can form extensive stands (often called submarine meadows) in shallow brackish and saltwater areas with clear water and minimal wave action.

Family classification. The Zosteraceae are placed in the Najadales by Dahlgren et al. and recent molecular analyses support this placement. *Zostera* has been divided into two subgenera, *Zostera* and *Zosterella*. Recent evidence from molecular analyses indicates that the genus *Phyllospadix* is more closely related to subgenus *Zostera* than either is to subgenus *Zosterella*, indicating these two genera will eventually be combined. Similarly, the recognition of *Heterozostera* is problematic.

Feature of the family. Habit: perennial, rarely annual herbs, usually submerged, a few species intertidal and periodically exposed to air; rhizomes with monopodial branching. **Leaves** alternate (distichous), simple, linear. **Inflorescences** borne on simple or branched, erect spadices, the flowers in 2 rows, enclosed by spathe. **Flowers** unisexual (monoecious in *Heterozostera* and *Zostera* or dioecious), highly reduced; perianth absent. **Staminate flowers** with 1 stamen, the anthers with 2 distinct, bilocular thecae, longitudinally dehiscent; pollen shed in long, filamentous strands. **Pistillate flowers** with ovary with 1 locule, the stigmas 2, long; ovule 1. **Fruits** achenes. **Seeds** without endosperm; hypocotyl enlarged.

Natural history. In intertidal species, chains of the pollen grains are released on the surface of the water where they contact the stigmas, whereas the pollination of submerged species occurs underwater. The dispersal of the fruits is by water. Vegetative propagation also occurs by rhizome branching, which often results in the formation of extensive stands. Some of the rhizome branches may become detached and root at new sites.

Economic uses. Members of this family are important in the stabilization of shallow marine sediments, and as a food source for grazing marine animals, including the commercially important blue crab. Dried plants of *Zostera marina* have been used as packing material.

References. HARTOG, C. DEN. 1970. The sea-grasses of the world. *Verh. Kon. Ned. Akad. Wetensch., Afd, Natuurk., Tweede Sect.* 59(1):1–275. KUO, J., AND A. MCCOMB. 1998. Zosteraceae. In *The Families and Genera of Vascular Plants*, ed. K. Kubitzki, 4:496–502. New York: Springer-Verlag. TOMLINSON, P. B. 1982. Helobiae (Alismatidae). In *Anatomy of the Monocotyledons* vol. 7. Oxford, U.K.: Clarendon Press.

GLOSSARY

See the features of leaves (figure 257) and the features of flowers (figure 258) illustrations at the end of the glossary.

a-—A prefix meaning "without."

abaxial—Referring to the side of an organ situated away from the axis; i.e., the morphologically lower surface of a leaf. Opposite of adaxial and same as anterior, dorsal, and lower.

abortion—The process of arrested development.

abscission—The process by which plant parts, such as leaves, are shed.

acanthophyll—A hook derived from a modified leaf or leaflet; e.g, in *Desmoncus* spp. (Arecaceae).

acaulescent—Stemless or appearing stemless. Opposite of stemmed or caulescent.

accrescent—Enlarging with age, usually referring to parts of an inflorescence or a flower; e.g., the spathe of some Araceae and the calyx of *Chaunochiton kappleri* (Olacaceae).

achene—A small, dry, indehiscent, one-seeded fruit derived from a superior ovary with the seed attached to the fruit wall at one point only; e.g., species *Ranunculus*. Compare with cypsela.

achlorophyllous—Without chlorophyll; i.e., not green; a feature of saprophytes such as the species of *Voyria* (Gentianaceae), some species of orchids, the Triuridaceae, and the Burmanniaceae and of some parasites such as *Helosis cayennensis* (Balanophoraceae).

acicular—Needle-shaped.

acrodromous—Referring to a type of leaf venation in which two or more primary or strongly developed secondary veins arch upward from the base or close to it; perfect acrodromous is used when these veins converge near the apex; e.g., *Strychnos* (Loganiaceae); imperfect acrodromous is used when these veins do not converge at the apex.

acropetalous—Developing from the base toward the apex. Opposite of *basipetalous*.

acroscopic—Facing or directed toward the apex. Opposite of basiscopic.

actinodromous—Referring to a type of leaf venation in which three or more primary veins diverge radially from a single point.

actinomorphic—Capable of being divided, in more than one plane, into two equal parts that are mirror images; usually applied to flowers; e.g., in *Gustavia* (Lecythidaceae) and species of Myrtaceae. Opposite of zygomorphic and same as regular and radially symmetrical.

aculeate—Covered with aculei (prickles).

aculeus—A prickle or a spine.

acumen—Apex.

acuminate—Gradually tapering to an acute apex with the sides being concave. Compare with acute.

acute—Sharp; usually referring to the apex of a flattened structure (such as a leaf) in which the two sides are straight and, when they meet, form an angle that is always less than 90°. Compare with acuminate and obtuse.

ad-—A prefix meaning "to" or "toward."

adaxial—Referring to the side of an organ facing toward the axis; i.e., the morphologically upper surface of a leaf. Opposite of abaxial and same as ventral.

admedial—Toward the axis of any structure, especially used to describe leaf venation. Opposite of exmedial.

adnate—Referring to the fusion of one type of structure to another type of structure, as the stamens to the corolla or the stipules to the petiole. Compare with connate.

adventitious embryony—Referring to the production of embryos and, subsequently, plants without the fusion of sperm and eggs.

adventitious—Referring to an organ arising from an unusual position, especially buds or roots; e.g., the aerial roots of species of Araceae.

andropodium—In the Podostemaceae, a stalk formed as the result of fusion of the filaments.

adventitious roots—Roots arising directly from the stem.

adventive—Referring to a plant or animal that has become established in a region to which it is not native.

aerenchyma—Tissue with large, intercellular, air-filled spaces; e.g., in the petioles of many species of Araceae and in the roots, stems, and leaves of many aquatic plants.

aerial roots—Adventitious roots of lianas and hemiepiphytes in the forest canopy that ultimately anchor in the ground or some other substrate; e.g., in some species of *Clusia* (Clusiaceae) and *Philodendron* (Araceae).

aestivation—The arrangement of the parts of the perianth in the floral bud.

aggregate fruit—A fruit formed by the coalescence of carpels that were distinct in the flower; e.g., *Rubus* or blackberry.

alate—Winged.

albumen—General term for the nutritive tissue of the seed located between the embryo and seed coat.

albuminate (albuminous)—With albumen

aliform—Winglike; e.g., the seeds of many Bignoniaceae.

alternate—Arising from an axis singly at each node; e.g., leaves from a stem. Compare with opposite and whorled.

alveolate—Like a honeycomb; i.e., with angular pits separated by thin, ridgelike partitions.

alveolus (plural = alveoli)—A small, angular pit like those of a honeycomb.

ament—See catkin.

amphitropous—Referring to an ovule with a curved embryo sac in which the stalk (funicle) is curved such that the tip of the ovule and the base of the stalk are near one another. Compare with anatropous.

amplexicaul—Clasping the stem, such as the base of a leaf.

anadromous—Referring to a venation pattern in which the first vein in a given segment arises on the side toward the apex. Compare with catadromous and isodromous.

anastomosing—United to form a network; e.g., leaf veins or some aerial roots (e.g., strangler figs).

anatropous—Referring to an ovule with the ovule curved downward such that the micropyle is close to the funicular attachment. Compare with amphitropous ovule.

anchoriform—Shaped like an anchor.

ancipitous—Two-edged, the edges sharp.

androdioecious—Referring to the sexual condition of a species that bears only staminate flowers on some plants but staminate and pistillate flowers or bisexual flowers on other plants.

androecial hood—A prolongation on one side of the androecium that forms a hoodlike structure in the zygomorphic-flowered species of Lecythidaceae.

androecium—The collective term for the staminate structures of the flower; the stamens as a unit. Compare with gynoecium.

androgynophore—A stalk that is elevated above the point of perianth attachment and supports the androecium and gynoecium; e.g., species of Passifloraceae.

androgynous—Referring to inflorescences with both staminate and pistillate flowers, e.g., the inflorescences of *Mabea* (Euphorbiaceae) with one or a few pistillate flowers at the base and numerous staminate flowers distally.

andromonoecious—Referring to the sexual condition of a species that bears staminate and bisexual flowers on the same plant; in the Mimosaceae, referring to the presence of staminate and pistillate flowers in the same cluster.

androphore—A stalk elevated above the point of perianth attachment and supporting the stamens; e.g., the united filaments of species of Menispermaceae and Myristicaceae.

anemochorous—Referring to a fruit or seed adapted for dispersal by wind.

aneuploidy—Referring to a process in which chromosome numbers arise that are more or less than, but not exact multiples of the base chromosome number for that group of organisms.

angiosperm—A flowering plant; a plant whose seeds are borne within a fruit derived from a carpel or carpels.

angulate—Angled.

anisocotylous—Referring to seedlings in which the cotyledons differ in shape and/or size.

anisomorphic—With two different forms of an organ.

anisophyllous—With two leaves of a pair differing in shape and/or size.

annotinous—Referring to structures (e.g., inflorescences) arising from branches of the previous year's growth.

annual—Plant with a life cycle of one year or less from seed to maturity and death. Compare with biennial and perennial.

annular—In the form of a ring.

anomalous secondary growth—A general term referring to types of secondary growth that differ from the more familiar or standard kinds; e.g., that of many lianas.

antepetalous—Referring to structures, usually stamens, inserted opposite or facing the petals.

anterior—See abaxial.

antesepalous—Referring to structures, usually stamens, inserted opposite or facing the sepals.

ant garden—A ball of roots that forms in certain species of epiphytic plants and is inhabited by ants.

anthelae—The panicle of some Cyperaceae and Juncaceae in which the upper branches are overtopped by the lower ones.

anther—The pollen-bearing part of the stamen.

antheriferous—Bearing anthers.

anther sac—See theca.

anthesis—The expanding and opening of a flower.

anthocarp—A type of fruit in which some part of the flower other than the pericarp persists (e.g., the perianth on the fruit of Nyctaginaceae).

anthocyanic—Containing anthocyanins (water-soluble blue or red pigments).

antidromous—Referring to an organ twisted alternately in one direction at one node and in another direction at the next node; e.g., the capsules of *Caiophora* (Loasaceae).

antrorse—Directed upward or forward. Opposite of retrorse.

aperture (aperturate)—Referring to an opening into an organ; e.g., pollen grains with pores are aperturate and those without them are inaperturate.

apetalous—Without petals.

apex—The tip or distal end of a structure such as a stem or leaf.

apical—Toward the apex.

apical placentation—A type of placentation in which the ovules are attached at the apex of the locule. See placentation.

apical pore—An opening at the apex of a structure; e.g., the flower of some species of Monimiaceae or the anthers of some species, such as, *Gustavia augusta* (Lecythidaceae).

apiculate—Terminating abruptly in a short, sharp point or apiculus.

apiculus—A short, sharp point.

apocarpous—Referring to a gynoecium of distinct carpels; e.g., many species of Annonaceae and Menispermaceae. Compare with syncarpous.

apomixis—In the broad sense, any form of asexual reproduction, and, in the narrow sense, seed production without fertilization.

apomorphic—Referring to a feature of a plant that is derived from an ancestral character state, i.e., an evolutionary advanced character state that helps define taxonomic groups.

apophysis—A projection or protuberance.

apotropous—Referring to an ovule with a ventral raphe.

appendage—A secondary structure attached to a main structure; e.g., the outgrowths on anthers of Melastomataceae.

appendaged—Bearing an appendage. Same as appendiculate.

appendicular—Of or relating to appendages.

appendiculate—Bearing appendages. Same as appendaged.

apposition—Two plant structures placed side by side or against each other.

appressed—Lying flat against a surface or axis; e.g., trichomes, leaves, or bracts.

aquatic—Growing in water.

arachnoid—Like a spider's web, usually because of a pubescence of fine, entangled hairs.

arborescent—Treelike.

arbusculiform—See dendritic.

arcuate—Curved like a bow, often used to describe venation.

areolate—Possessing areoles; in mimosoid and caesalpinioid legumes, referring to seeds with a pleurogram.

areole (areola)—A flattened spot, circular or elliptic in outline, often on the apex of the seeds of some Violaceae (e.g., *Rinorea*); the smallest area of an organ (e.g., a leaf), enclosed by united veins; the spine-bearing area in the leaf axils of Cactaceae.

aril—An outer, often fleshy and brightly colored covering or appendage on a seed derived from the funicle, which aids in dispersal by animals. Compare with elaiosome and sarcotesta.

arillate—Possessing an aril.

arilloid—An aril-like structure seed.

aristate—Bearing an elongate, narrow appendage at the apex of a structure (organ); e.g., the lemmas of some species of Poaceae.

armed—Provided with prickles, spines, or thorns.

article—A joint or segment; e.g., a segment of a fruit (loment) of *Desmodium* spp. (Fabaceae).

articulate—Having nodes or joints or constrictions, often of the pedicel, where a part of a structure will naturally break off.

ascending-cochleate—Referring to a type of corolla aestivation in the Acanthaceae in which one petal, being larger than the others covers the other petals in bud.

asexual reproduction—Referring to the production of new plants not involving the fusion of sperm and eggs, e.g., vegetation reproduction by buds or runners.

asymmetrical—Referring to a structure that cannot be divided into mirror-image halves; unequally developed on the opposite sides of an axis. Opposite of symmetrical.

attenuate—Tapering very gradually to a narrow tip.

aureole—See eyespot.

auricle—An ear-shaped appendage.

auriculate (auricled)—Referring to an organ or structure, such as a leaf blade, with earlike lobes, which usually are situated at the base.

autogamy—Referring to fertilization resulting from the union of a sperm and an egg from the same plant.

autotrophic—Capable of synthesizing complex organic substances from simple inorganic substrates. Opposite of heterotrophic.

awn—A bristle or hairlike appendage; e.g., the terminal extension of the midvein of the glume, palea, or lemma in the Poaceae.

axil—An angle formed at the junction of two structures; e.g., the petiole of the leaf and the stem, or a secondary vein of a leaf and the midrib.

axile—Relating or belonging to the axis of a structure.

axile placentation—A type of placentation in which the ovules arise from the central or axile wall of the locule. See placentation.

axillary—Arising from an axil.

baccate—Berrylike. See berry.

ballistic dispersal—A type of dispersal in which seeds are ejected from the fruits upon dehiscence.

banner—See standard.

barbate (diminutive = barbellate)—Bearded or tufted with hairs.

bark—All tissue of the trunk or stem external to the vascular cambium. See inner bark, outer bark, and periderm.

basal placentation—A type of placentation in which the ovules arise from the base of the locule. See placentation.

basal stoppers—Valves in the woody pericarp of *Parinari* (Chrysobalanaceae) that allow for the escape of the seedling. Same as obturamenta.

base—The bottom or proximal end of a structure such as a stem, leaf blade or flower.

basifixed—Attached at the bottom or the base; e.g., the anthers of many plants.

basipetalous—Developing from the apex toward the base. Opposite of acropetalous.

basiscopic—Facing or directed toward the base. Opposite of acroscopic.

basitonic—Referring to a type of branching in which the shoots nearest the base of the stem show the greatest development, as in the inflorescences of Hydrangeaceae.

beak—A narrow or prolonged tip; often used to describe the apices of fruits or seeds.

berry—A usually soft, fleshy or juicy, multiseeded, indehiscent fruit (e.g., *Solanum* spp., Solanaceae).

bi-—A prefix meaning "two."

biennial—A plant that completes its life cycle in two seasons. Compare with annual and perennial.

bifacial—Referring to an organ with the opposite surfaces differing in color, texture, or structure; e.g., the anthers of Gronoviaceae, or to a leaf with two different types of tissue on each side, as observed in a transverse section.

bifarious—Arranged in two vertical rows, such as ovules in an ovary or seeds in a fruit.

bifid—Cleft into two generally equal parts.

bifoliolate—Referring to a compound leaf with two leaflets.

bifurcate—Splitting into two equal parts at the apex; forked.

bilabiate—Two-lipped, usually referring to zygomorphic calyces and corollas such as those found in the Lamiaceae.

bilabiate capitulum (head)—Inflorescence of Asteraceae with at least some bilabiate flowers. Restricted to tribe Mutisieae.

bilaterally symmetrical—See zygomorphic.

bilocular—Having two locules.

binucleate pollen—Referring to pollen grains that have two nuclei when shed from the anthers. Compare with trinucleate pollen.

biofilm—A thin layer of living tissue found between a plant and the substrate upon which it grows.

biota—The totality of organisms found in a given environment.

bipartite—Split into two parts.

bipinnate—Twice-pinnate; e.g., leaves of many species of Mimosaceae. See pinnate.

biseriate—Composed of two whorls or rows; e.g., a perianth with both calyx and corolla or a hair with two rows of cells. Compare with uniseriate.

bisexual—Referring to a flower with functional stamen(s) and a functional gynoecium. Same as perfect.

bitegmic—Referring to ovules with two integuments.

biternate—Twice ternate, in two groups of three each; e.g., the leaves of some species of *Serjania* (Sapindaceae).

blade—The expanded portion of an organ such as a leaf, bract, sepal, or petal. Same as lamina and limb.

blaze—See slash.

bole—See trunk.

boreotropics—A former tropical region around the earth at the level of the southern United States, Caribbean, Southeast Asia, and southern Europe, which lasted until about 38 million years ago, when the climate got cooler.

bostryx (plural = bostryches)—See helicoid cyme.

brachyblast—A short, leafless, lateral axis of limited growth that bears inflorescences.

bract—A reduced and frequently otherwise differentiated leaf often associated with inflorescences and sometimes subtending a flower.

bracteate—Provided with bracts.

bracteole—A small bract usually inserted on the pedicel.

brochidodromous—Referring to a type of leaf venation in which the secondary veins do not terminate at the margin but join to form a series of prominent arches. Compare with eucamptrodromous.

bud—A young shoot from which leaves or flowers may develop.

budding pouch—A cavity found at the basal end of the plant body of Lemnaceae in which flowers or vegetative buds are produced.

bud scale—A reduced leaf that encloses a bud.

bulb—A short, underground stem covered by enlarged and fleshy leaf bases.

bulbil—A small bulblike structure that functions in asexual reproduction, usually formed in axils or sinuses of leaves.

bulbous—Swollen like a bulb.

bullate—Blistered on the surface.

buttress—An outgrowth at the base of a tree trunk. See also flying buttress, plank buttress, and running buttress.

buzz pollination—A type of pollination in which bees vibrate their indirect flight muscles to cause the release of pollen, usually from poricidal anthers; e.g., in many species of *Solanum* (Solanaceae).

caatinga—A Portuguese term referring to a vegetation type of low forest or savanna on sandy soil in the Brazilian Amazon; a Portuguese term referring to a dry, thorn-scrub, deciduous vegetation of northeastern Brazil.

caducous—Falling off early. Same as fugacious.

caespitose (cespitose)—Growing in dense clumps or tufts; e.g., the growth form of some species of Poaceae and Cyperaceae.

callose—Bearing a callus; hard or thick.

callus—A thickened part of an organ; e.g., in some Orchidaceae, the fleshy outgrowth of the labellum, or in the Poaceae, the hardened base of the spikelet or floret just above the point of disarticulation.

calycine—Belonging to the calyx; e.g., in species of Lecythidaceae, the calycine rim, or line of scars left by the calyx.

calycophyll—An expanded sepal of some Rubiaceae that functions to attract pollinators or to aid in wind dispersal.

calyculate—Referring to species of Asteraceae (especially Senecioneae) possessing a secondary series of bracteoles subtending the primary phyllaries.

calyculus—Rimlike calyx of Loranthaceae.

calyptrate—Bearing a lid- or caplike structure; e.g., the apex of the connate calyx of *Calyptranthes* (Myrtaceae) that falls intact from the flower at anthesis.

calyx (plural = calyces)—The outer circle or first whorl of floral parts; a collective term for the sepals.

calyx tube—In Ericaceae with inferior ovaries, the proximal portion of the calyx fused with the ovary wall; same as hypanthium in other flowering plants.

CAM—See Crassulacean acid metabolism.

cambium—The actively dividing tissue or lateral meristem located between the xylem and the phloem, which produces xylem to the inside and phloem to the outside. Compare with cork cambium; same as vascular cambium.

campanulate—Broadly bell-shaped with a wide mouth; usually used to describe a corolla.

campo rupestre—A Portuguese term referring to a rocky kind of savanna, usually at midelevations in Brazil. Species of several plant families; e.g., Velloziaceae and Turneraceae, are characteristic of this vegetation.

campos de altitude—A Portuguese term referring to savanna or prairielike vegetation at high altitudes in Brazil.

camptodromous—Referring to a type of leaf venation in which the secondary veins do not terminate at the margin; several variations include brochidodromous and eucamptodromous.

campylodromous—Referring to a type of leaf venation in which a series of more or less equal primary veins originate from a common point at the base, arch upward, and reunite toward the apex; e.g., species of *Aristolochia* (Aristolochiaceae).

campylotropous—Referring to an ovule in which the axis is at an approximately right angle to its stalk (funicle).

canaliculate—With a channel or groove.

candelabra—A type of stellate hair in which the divisions are arranged in several tiers; e.g., in some species of Buddlejaceae.

Candomblé—A religious celebration performed by Afro-Brazilians, most commonly in the state of Bahia.

cane—The stem of large grasses (e.g., bamboos) and small palms.

canescent—Gray in color because of a covering of dense hairs.

canopy—A hypothetical stratum in the forest consisting of the crowns of trees, which form a ± continuous layer commonly at a maximum height of about 25–35 meters in the neotropics. Compare with understory and emergent.

capitate—Shaped like a head; having or growing in a head (capitulum).

capitellate—Referring to a plant with small, headlike structures.

capitulum (plural = capitula)—A dense headlike inflorescence such as that of the Asteraceae and some Cyperaceae, Lamiaceae, and Rubiaceae.

capsule—A dry, dehiscent fruit that develops from a syncarpous ovary; it can open in the middle of the locules (loculicidal), along the septa (septicidal), or around the circumference (circumscissile).

carina—A keel or ridge.

carinate—Having a keel, ridged like the bottom of a boat. Same as keeled.

carnose—Thick and fleshy.

carnosulose—Thick and fleshy but not marked so.

carpel—The fundamental unit of the gynoecium, often considered to be a folded, specialized leaf. The number of carpels comprising the gynoecium is sometimes indicated by the number of locules or the number of valves of the ovary and/or by the number of divisions of the style or stigma.

carpophore—A prolongation of the receptacle to which the carpels are attached; e.g., the expanded red structure bearing the fruits in *Ouratea* (Ochnaceae); the central axis of a fragmenting fruit (schizocarp) to which the separate parts are attached; e.g., the fruits of Apiaceae and some species of Sapindaceae (in this sense, same as columella).

carpopodium—Differentiated base of the cypsela (Asteraceae), commonly zygomorphic and occasionally sculptured.

caruncle—An appendage or outgrowth at the point of attachment of the seed to the funicle. Compare with aril.

carunculate—Possessing a caruncle. Compare with strophiole.

caryopsis—A dry, hard, one-seeded, indehiscent fruit unique to the Poaceae in which the pericarp is adnate to the seed coat. Same as grain.

castaneous—Chestnut-colored; grayish brown to moderately reddish brown.

catadromous—Referring to a venation pattern in which the first vein in a given segment arises on the side toward the base. Compare with anadromous and isodromous.

cataphylls—Scalelike bracts on the proximal part of a newly expanded vegetative or reproductive shoot.

cat-claw tendril—A tendril with the distal part divided into three equal, conspicuously recurved, spiny parts; e.g., in *Macfadyena unguis-cati* and *Parabignonia steyermarkii* (Bignoniaceae).

catkin—A spike with closely congested, often apetalous, unisexual flowers; e.g., staminate inflorescences of species of Betulaceae. Same as ament.

cauda—A tail-like appendage.

caudate—Terminating in a tail-like appendage.

caudex—A short, vertical, usually woody and persistent stem at or just below the surface of the ground.

caudicle—See translator.

caulescent—With a stem.

cauliflorous—Producing flowers on the main stem or trunk and/or leafless branches; e.g., *Theobroma cacao* (Sterculiaceae). Compare with ramiflorous.

cauline—Of or relating to the main stem or trunk.

caustic—Capable of causing a burning sensation; e.g., the sap of *Hura crepitans* (Euphorbiaceae).

caviform—Hollow.

cellular endosperm—A type of endosperm development in which cell walls develop starting with the first cell division.

cephalium (plural = cephalia)—An enlargement with a dense covering of hairs at the apex of the stem in some Cactaceae.

ceraceous—Waxy in texture or appearance.

cernuous—Drooping or nodding.

cerrado—A Portuguese term referring to a savanna-like vegetation best developed in central Brazil but also found in patches in the Brazilian Amazon.

Chacó—A Spanish term referring to a dry, thorn-scrub, deciduous vegetation found mostly in Paraguay and known as pantanal in adjacent Brazil.

chaff—Thin, dry scales or bracts.

chalaza—The part of an ovule or seed opposite to the micropyle and adjacent to the attachment of the funicle; the basal portion of the nucellus of an ovule.

chaparral—A mild, temperate region with cool, moist winters and long, dry summers dominated by sclerophyllous, evergreen shrubs.

chartaceous—Having the texture of paper.

chasmogamous, chasmogamy—Referring to flowers that open before fertilization and usually are cross-pollinated. Compare with cleistogamous.

chlorophyll—The green pigment in plant cells that plays an essential role in photosynthesis.

choripetalous—See polypetalous.

ciliate (diminutive = ciliolate)—Fringed on margin with straight trichomes finer than those of a fimbriate margin.

cincinnus (plural = cincinni)—A type of helicoid cyme, usually characterized by short internodes.

cinereous—Ash-colored or light gray.

circinate (circinotropous)—Coiled from the tip downward, as in the fiddlehead of a fern, but also characteristic of some inflorescences; e.g., in Plumbaginaceae or Boraginaceae.

circumaustral—Referring to a plant or animal distributed around the high latitudes of the southern hemisphere.

circumboreal—Referring to a plant or animal distributed around the high latitudes of the northern hemisphere.

circumscissile—Dehiscing via a line around a fruit with the top usually falling off like the lid of a jar; e.g., the fruit of many Lecythidaceae.

cirrhose (= cirrose)—Resembling a tendril.

cirrus—A whiplike extension of the leaf rachis that is armed with reflexed spines and aids in climbing; e.g., in species of *Desmoncus* (Arecaceae).

clade—A monophyletic evolutionary line.

cladode—A flattened, green, photosynthetic stem; e.g., in some Cactaceae.

cladodromous—Referring to a type of leaf venation in which the secondary veins branch freely before they reach the margin.

clasping—At least partially enclosing the axis; e.g., the base of a leaf that partially surrounds the stem on which it is borne. Same as amplexicaul.

class—A unit of classification. A phylum is divided into classes; e.g., the Liliopsida (monocots) and Magnoliopsida (dicots) are the two classes of Magnoliophyta (flowering plants) in the system of Cronquist (1981).

clathrate—Latticelike in appearance.

clavate—Club-shaped.

clavuncle—See style head.

claw—A markedly narrowed base of a petal; e.g., in Malpighiaceae or some legumes.

clawed—Having a claw. Same as unguiculate.

cleistogamous, cleistogamy—Referring to flowers that do not open and usually are self-fertilized. Compare with chasmogamous.

clinandrium—In the Orchidaceae, the portion of the column upon which the anther is borne; the columnar tissue surrounding or covering the anther.

clone—A population of plants produced by asexual reproduction resulting in individual members with the same genetic composition.

coccus (plural = cocci)—One of the parts of a dry fruit that breaks into usually 1-seeded segments; e.g., the fruit of *Serjania* spp. (Sapindaceae); in the Euphorbiaceae, one of the sections of the wall of a dry dehiscent fruit.

cochleariform—Concave like a spoon.

cochleate—Shaped like a snail shell.

coeval—Originating or existing during the same period of time.

coevolution—A reciprocal process in which adaptations of one organism promote adaptations in another; e.g., the nocturnal anthesis of a cup-shaped flower and the elongated snout of a bat that pollinates that flower.

coherent—Clinging together of like parts without fusion. Compare with connate and connivent.

Coleoptera—The order of insects including the beetles and weevils.

collar—An ringlike expansion around a structure. See stylar collar.

collateral—Situated side by side; e.g., the ovules in a locule.

collective vein—A vein running along the leaf margin, such as in many species of *Anthurium* (Araceae).

colleter—In the Rubiaceae, a simple or branched, glandlike structure in the axil of stipules; in the Apocynaceae a gland, located along the interpetiolar lines or in the leaf axil, which is sometimes mistaken for a stipule.

colporate pollen—Referring to a pollen grain with composite apertures, each consisting of a furrow and a pore.

colpus (plural = colpi)—An elongated aperture in the wall of a pollen grain.

columella—See carpophore; the central axis within the fruit; e.g., in Lecythidaceae.

column—In the Orchidaceae, the structure formed by the fused androecium and gynoecium.

column foot—In the Orchidaceae, the fleshy continuation of the base of the column, often more prominent in fruit.

coma—A tuft of hairs.

combretaceous hairs—Referring to long, sharp pointed, unicellular, and very thick-walled hairs with a conical internal compartment at the base; characteristic of Combretaceae.

commissure—In the Apiaceae, the face by which two carpels join one another.

comose—Tufted with long trichomes; usually applied to a wind-dispersed seed with a tuft of trichomes at one end.

complanate—Flattened.

complete flower—A flower with all whorls of floral parts; i.e., calyx, corolla, stamen(s), and gynoecium. Compare with incomplete flower.

compound—Referring to an organ, such as a leaf, which is divided into smaller units; i.e., leaflets. Opposite of simple.

compound pistil—A gynoecium of more than one carpel.

concave—Curved inward or hollowed out, as the surface of a saucer. Opposite of convex.

concolorous—Of uniform color.

conduplicate—Referring to the lateral margins of a structure that are bent inward toward the axis; i.e., folded together lengthwise; usually used to describe embryos or leaves when in bud.

condyle—In the drupe of Menispermaceae, the inward wing or projection of the endocarp around which the embryo or endosperm is folded.

conflorescence—The aggregation of several inflorescences into one; e.g., some species of Proteaceae.

confluent—Running together; e.g., two veins.

conglutinate—As though stuck or glued together; e.g., the seeds and dissepiments of some species of Commelinaceae.

conic—Cone-shaped.

conjugate—United or joined together; coupled.

connate—Referring to similar structures fused to each other, such as the petals of a sympetalous corolla. Same as coherent and connivent. Compare with adnate.

connective—The tissue connecting the thecae of the anther and sometimes prolonged beyond its apex.

connivent—Coming into contact but not fused; e.g., the anthers of species of Asteraceae. Compare with coherent and connate.

contorted—Twisted; in reference to aestivation.

contractile—Referring to a root that contracts, usually to keep a bulb, corm, or rhizome at a certain level in the ground.

contraligule—In Cyperaceae, a projection at the summit of the leaf sheath opposite the insertion of the leaf blade.

convex—Curved outward, as the exterior surface of a sphere. Opposite of concave.

convolute—Referring to a type of aestivation in which one margin of a petal or sepal is always to the outside of the adjacent one and the opposite margin is always to the inside of the adjacent one.

coppice—Leafy shoots produced from the base of a tree; e.g., the multiple stems of *Euterpe oleracea* (Arecaceae).

coralline—Referring to a structure (e.g., corona) that appears like a corolla.

coralloid—Coral-like.

cordate (cordiform)—Heart-shaped; e.g., the shape of a leaf blade.

cordulate—Somewhat cordate.

coriaceous—Having the texture of leather.

cork—See periderm.

cork cambium—The actively dividing tissue that produces cork to the outside and phelloderm to the inside. See phellem and periderm.

corneous—With a horny texture.

corniculate—Bearing a small, hornlike projection.

cornucopia—A flowering strategy in which abundant flowers are produced each day for a few weeks to more than a month.

cornute—Bearing a hornlike projection.

corolla—The second whorl of floral parts; the collective term for the petals.

corona—A structure located between the petals and the stamens of some flowers and derived from either of these organs; e.g., in *Passiflora* (Passifloraceae), some Apocynaceae subfamily Asclepiadoideae, and some Melastomataceae.

coroniform—Shaped like a crown.

corpus—Body; e.g., the main part of the style head in Apocynaceae.

corpusculum—A structure connecting the two translators of the pollinia of Apocynaceae subfamily Asclepiadoideae, sometimes referred to as the "gland."

cortex—The tissue in a stem or root between the epidermis and the vascular tissue.

corymb—A more or less flat-topped, indeterminate inflorescence.

costa—A rib, usually used to describe the midrib of a leaf or leaflet.

costate—Possessing a costa or rib.

cotyledon—The leaves (one in monocots and two in dicots) of an embryo.

craspedium—A legume pod in which the valves separate at maturity from the persistent sutures or replum, and, as a rule, simultaneously break into one-seeded segments.

craspedodromous—Referring to a type of leaf venation in which the secondary veins terminate at the margin.

crassinucellar—Referring to a nucellus with well-developed tissue between the epidermis and embryo sac. Compare with tenuinucellar.

Crassulacean acid metabolism—A photosynthesis pathway characteristic of plants that grow in water or carbon dioxide limited environments, most prevalent in species of Bromeliaceae, Cactaceae, Crassulaceae, and Orchidaceae.

crassulate—Thick.

crateriform—Cup- or bowl-shaped.

crenate (diminutive = crenulate)—Referring to margins with rounded teeth.

crepuscular—Appearing during the twilight hours of dusk and dawn.

cretaceous—Chalky or chalky white in appearance; the color caused by a waxy layer.

cristate—Crested.

cross section—See transverse section.

crown—The top of a tree; i.e., all but the trunk.

crownshaft—A conspicuous cylinder formed by the tubular leaf sheaths of some palms; e.g., the royal palms (*Roystonea* spp., Arecaceae).

cruciform (cruciate)—Cross-shaped.

crustaceous (crustose)—Hard, thin, and brittle.

cryptocotylar—A type of seed germination in which the cotyledons remain within the seed coat. Compare with phanerocotylar.

cryptogam—A plant that does not produce seed; e.g., a moss or a fern. Compare with phanerogam.

cucullate—Hood-shaped.

culm—The stem of a grass or sedge.

cuneate (cuneiform)—Wedge-shaped; usually referring to the base of a two-dimensional organ (such as a leaf blade) of which the angle formed by meeting of the margins is less than 90°.

cupulate—Bearing a cupule.

cupule—A cup-shaped structure that usually subtends a fruit; e.g., that of many species of Lauraceae or some Cyperaceae.

cushion plant—The growth from of a plant, usually of high altitudes, in which numerous stems are congested together resulting in a low, pillow- or cushionlike structure.

cusp—A short, sharp, abrupt point usually at the tip of a leaf or other organ.

cuspidate—Bearing a cusp.

cyanobacteria—Blue-green bacteria resembling eukaryotic algae in many ways.

cyathiform—Cup-shaped.

cyathium (plural = cyathia)—An inflorescence consisting of several naked staminate flowers accompanied by usually one naked pistillate flower and subtended and mostly enclosed by a cup-shaped involucre, characteristic of *Euphorbia* (Euphorbiaceae).

cymbiform—Boat-shaped.

cyme—A determinate inflorescence in which growth of the central axis is terminated by a flower that opens first and each branch or pair of branches subtending this flower then is terminated by a single flower. This pattern, when repeated several times, often results in a somewhat flat-topped inflorescence.

cymose—Cymelike.

cymule—A small cyme.

cypsela (plural = cyselae)—A dry, indehiscent fruit derived from an inferior, bicarpellate ovary; e.g., in Asteraceae. Similar to an achene, but derived from an inferior ovary.

cystolith—A crystal typically of calcium carbonate ($CaCO_3$) located in the epidermal cells at the surface of leaves of certain plants (e.g., Acanthaceae) and appearing as a light-colored streak or protuberance.

dbh—Diameter of a tree trunk measured at breast height (i.e., 1.3 ms above the ground).

deciduous—Falling at some season or some stage in the life cycle of a plant; e.g., leaves shed in the dry season or petals after flowering. In the case of leaves, the opposite of evergreen.

declinate—Curved downward; e.g., the filaments of some species of Lamiaceae.

decompound—More than once-compound.

decumbent—Growing horizontally along the ground but with the apex ascending or erect.

decurrent—Extending down and adnate to an axis; e.g., the blade of a leaf onto the petiole, the leaf blade onto the stem, or the secondary veins onto the midvein in some species of Anacardiaceae, Lauraceae, and Monimiaceae.

decussate—Referring to opposite leaves arranged with each succeeding pair at right angles to the pair below it.

deflexed—Bent downward.

dehiscent—Opening to discharge or display contents, as fruits or anthers do. Opposite of indehiscent.

deliquescent—Tending to rapidly wilt, lose rigidity, and dissolve into semiliquid; e.g., perianth parts.

deltoid—Shaped like an equilateral triangle.

dendritic—Branched in a treelike fashion; often used to refer to the form of hairs.

dentate (diminutive = denticulate)—Toothed; having a margin with sharp teeth oriented at right angles to the central axis of the structure bearing them. Compare with serrate and erose.

determinate—A type of inflorescence in which the terminal or central flower opens first.

dextrorse—Twisted from the left to the right as viewed from above (clockwise); e.g., the petals in a floral bud. Opposite of sinistrorse.

diadelphous stamens—Stamens united into two, often unequal, sets; e.g., those of many Fabaceae, which have nine stamens in one set and one stamen in the other.

diaphanous—Translucent.

diaspore—See propagule.

dichasial—Referring to a cyme with lateral branches on both sides of the main axis.

dichogamous, dichogamy—Referring to a flower in which pollen is released and stigmas are receptive at different times. See protandrous and protogynous.

dichotomous—In morphology, forking into two more or less equal parts; a type of taxonomic key that progressively presents two alternative choices.

diclesiuim—A type of indehiscent anthocarp in which the perianth encloses or is accrescent arount the pericarp and aids in dispersal.

dicliny, diclinous—Referring to species with separate staminate and pistillate flowers. See dioecious and monoecious. Compare with monocliny.

dicotyledon (dicot)—One of the two classes of angiosperms usually characterized by having two cotyledons, net-veined leaves, and flower parts generally in fours or fives. In the classification of Cronquist (1981), this class is called Magnoliopsida. Compare with monocotyledon (monocot).

didynamous—With two pairs of stamens of unequal length.

digitate—Arranged as fingers on a hand; in the Cyperaceae and Poaceae, referring to such an arrangement of spicate branches of an inflorescence; for application to leaves, see palmate.

dimidiate—Divided into two halves such that the smaller half is almost lacking; e.g., the leaflet blades of *Dimorphandra* (Fabaceae).

dimorphic—Occurring in two forms; e.g., in the Mimosaceae, different flower shapes in the same inflorescence. Compare with heteromorphic and monomorphic.

dioecious, dioecy—Describing a sexual condition of a species that bears only functionally staminate flowers on some plants and only functionally pistillate flowers on other plants. Compare with monoecious.

diplostemonous—With two series of stamens; those of the outer series inserted opposite the sepals, those of the inner series inserted opposite the petals. Compare with obdiplostemonous.

Diptera—The order of insects that includes the flies.

disc (disk)—A fleshy, lobed, or annular nectariferous structure found within flowers; the position can be either outside or within the stamens. Not to be confused with disk flower.

disciform capitulum (head)—Inflorescence of Asteraceae with marginal actinomorphic, pistillate flowers and central disk flowers.

discoid—In the shape of a thin, flat, circular plate.

discoid capitulum (head)—Inflorescence of Asteraceae with only disk flowers.

discolorous—Of two different colors (including different shades of green), often referring to the difference in color between the adaxial and abaxial surfaces of a leaf blade.

disk flower—An actinomorphic flower with a tubular corolla found in Asteraceae. Compare with ray flower.

dissepiment—See septum.

distal—Remote from the place of attachment. Opposite of proximal.

distichous—Two-ranked or in two rows; usually referring to the way in which leaves or bracts are inserted on an axis. Compare with polystichous and tristichous.

distinct—Referring to parts of the same organ not fused with one another; e.g., separate petals are said to be distinct. Compare with free.

distyly, distylous—A type of heterostyly in which flowers with both long and short styles occur in different individuals of the same species.

diurnal—Appearing during the day.

divaricate—Widely diverging or spreading.

divergent—Referring to an organ, such as a flower, that spreads away from the axis to which it is attached.

division—See phylum.

dolabriform—Pick-shaped; e.g., the trichomes of some species of Boraginaceae.

domatium (plural = domatia)—A cavity, an enclosed chamber, or a cluster of trichomes, often found in the axils of secondary veins, such as, *Ticorea foetida* (Rutaceae), or at the base of the leaf blade, such as, *Maieta guianensis* (Melastomataceae); all may be inhabited by mites or insects, especially ants.

dorsal—Same as abaxial.

dorsifixed—Attached at the back; e.g., as in some anthers.

dorsiventral—Having an upper and lower surface.

double margin—Referring to a calyx with the apex folded over to give the impression that two calyx margins are present; e.g., species of *Amphilophium* (Bignoniaceae).

drepanium—A cymose inflorescence shaped like a sickle.

drupaceous—Like a drupe.

druparium (plural = druparia)—A cluster of drupelike fruits derived from the carpels of an apocarpous ovary; e.g., in the Simaroubaceae.

drupe—A single-seeded, indehiscent fruit with three distinct layers, the often fleshy exocarp and mesocarp, and the often woody or bony endocarp.

e-—A prefix meaning "without."

ecarinate—Lacking a keel.

echinate—Covered with prickles.

ectoaperture—The external part of the opening into a pollen grain. Compare with endoaperture.

edaphic—Of or relating to soil.

effuse—Widely spreading.

ektexine—The outermost layer of the wall of a pollen grain.

elaiophore—An outgrowth of the flower that secretes oils collected by pollinators.

elaiosome—A fleshy, oily outgrowth of the seed coat that often attracts ants for dispersing the seeds. Compare with aril and sarcotesta.

ellipsoid—A solid (three-dimensional) structure or organ with an elliptical outline in longitudinal section.

elliptic—Referring to the outline of essentially two-dimensional structures, such as leaves, bracts, petals, and sepals, which are widest at or near the middle.

emarginate—Markedly notched, such as the apex of a leaf or other structure.

embryo—The young sporophytic plant.

embryo sac—The female gametophyte of angiosperms (flowering plants). Same as megagametophyte.

embryotega—A small circular thickening near the seed scar on the seeds of some plants; e.g., Commelinaceae.

emergent—Forest tree with its crown emerging above the canopy; an aquatic plant with parts emerging above the surface of the water.

enantiostylous—Referring to flowers whose styles protrude alternately to the right and to the left of the main axis; i.e., to opposite sides of the axis.

enation—A projection or outgrowth from the surface of an organ.

endemic—Native to and restricted to a given geographic region.

endoaperture—The internal part of the opening into a pollen grain. Compare with ectoaperture.

endocarp—The innermost layer of the fruit wall. Compare with pericarp.

endophyte—A plant living partially or entirely within another plant.

endosperm—The energy-rich food supply that is formed by the fusion of the sperm and polar nuclei of the female gametophyte, initially surrounds the embryo, and is often apparent in the seed.

ensiform—Sword-shaped.

entire—Referring to a margin of a leaf, sepal, or petal that is not interrupted by teeth or lobes.

eophyll—The first true leaf of a seedling; i.e., the first leaf to appear after the cotyledon(s).

ephemeral—Lasting a short time. Same as evanescent.

epi-—A prefix meaning "upon."

epicalyx—A whorl of bracts on the pedicel, similar to sepals, and inserted below the calyx.

epicarp—See exocarp.

epichile—In the Orchidaceae, the apical portion of a complex lip.

epicortical roots—In some Eremolepidaceae and Loranthaceae, roots that develop from the cortex of the stem to form secondary points of attachment to the host.

epicotyl—That part of the stem of a seedling above the point of attachment of the cotyledons.

epidermis—The outer layer of cells of a plant.

epigeal—Referring to a type of seed germination in which the cotyledons are held at or above the ground. Compare with hypogeal.

epigeous—Referring to the above-ground parts of a plant.

epigynous—Referring to a flower in which the floral parts appear to arise from the summit of the ovary. Compare with hypogynous and perigynous.

epilithic—Growing on rocks. Same as epipetric.

epipeltate anther—An anther with the filament attached above the base and with the part of the anther that is prolonged downward facing toward the center of the flower; e.g., in the Dracaenaceae.

epipetric—See epilithic.

epiphyllous—Growing from or on leaves; e.g., the inflorescences of Phyllonomaceae.

epiphyte—A plant that grows upon, but does not parasitize, another plant. Compare with hemiepiphyte and parasitic plant.

epitropous—Referring to a type of anatropous ovule in which the raphe is next to the placenta when the ovule is pendulous or away from the placenta when the ovule is ascending.

equator—In a pollen grain, the area midway between the poles.

equisitoid—Referring to a plants that resemble *Equisetum* (horsetails).

equitant—Usually applied to distichous leaves with overlapping leaf blades that are flattened in the plane of the axis; often appearing fan-shaped; e.g.; in many Iridaceae and some Orchidaceae.

ericoid—Like some members of the Ericaceae in some feature;

e.g., the small leaves without typical venation in some species of Melastomataceae.

erose (diminutive = erosulose)—Having a margin that is irregularly jagged. Compare with dentate and serrate.

erostrate—Without a beak.

estipulate—Without stipules. Same as exstipulate.

ethereal oils—Aromatic compounds especially common in the vegetative tissue of dicotyledons such as Annonaceae, Myristicaceae, Canellaceae, Lauraceae, and Piperaceae.

eucamptodromous—Referring to a type of leaf venation in which the secondary veins do not reach the margin and do not form a series of prominent arches. Compare with brochidodromous.

eukaryote, eukaryotic—Referring to an organism that has cells with a nucleus separated from the cytoplasm by a membrane.

eugenioid embryo—A type of embryo found in the Myrtaceae in which the cotyledons are thick, separate, and plano-convex (like those of a bean) and the hypocotyl is a short protrusion, or the cotyledons are fused partially or completely into a single mass and the hypocotyl is not distinguishable. Compare with myrcioid embryo and myrtoid embryo.

evanescent—See ephemeral.

even-pinnate—See paripinnate.

evergreen—Bearing viable leaves at all times of the year. Opposite of deciduous.

ex-—A prefix meaning lacking (e.g., exstipulate), outside of (e.g., exocarp), or away from (e.g., exmedial).

exalbuminous—Without albumen.

exine—The outer layer of the two-layered wall of a pollen grain. Compare with intine.

exmedial—Away from the leaf axis.

exocarp—The outermost layer of the fruit wall. Same as epicarp; compare with pericarp.

exostome—That part of the seed coat surrounding the micropyle.

exserted—Extending beyond, as stamens beyond the corolla. Opposite of included.

exstipulate—Same as estipulate.

extra-—A prefix meaning outside of, beyond, apart from, besides, in addition to.

extrafloral nectary—A structure that secretes nectar and is located on a part of the plant other than the flower; e.g., the glands on the petioles of many mimosoid legumes.

extrastaminal—Outside of the stamens; e.g., the discs of Sapindaceae.

extrorse—Directed outward (abaxially), as the dehiscence of an anther. Compare with introrse and latrorse.

exudate—Any liquid substance emitted from a plant when it is cut; e.g., latex, sap, or resin.

eyespot—A more or less circular mark, usually on a petal that may serve as a nectar guide; e.g., often found on the standard of species of Fabaceae.

f—Abbreviation for forma (form). See forma.

falcate—Sickle-shaped.

false fruits—Fruits that develop from more than just the ovary; e.g., the outermost layer may be derived from a hypanthium.

farinaceous—Containing starch or starchlike substances.

farinose—With a mealy appearance.

fascicle—A tight cluster or bundle of roots, stems, leaves, flowers, or other structures arising from the same point.

fasciculate—Arranged in fascicles.

faucal appendages—Scalelike structures located in the throat of the corolla of species of Boraginaceae subfamily Boraginoideae.

fenestrate—Pierced with holes; e.g., the trunk of *Minquartia guianensis* (Olacaceae) or leaves of *Monstera* spp. (Araceae).

ferruginous—Rust-colored.

few—In botanical descriptions, meaning 10 or fewer in number.

fiber—An elongated, usually tapering, sclerenchyma cell found in wood.

fibrous roots—A root system characteristic of monocots in which all of the branches are approximately equal in diameter. Compare with taproot.

filament—The stalk of the stamen that is terminated by the anther.

filiform—Threadlike or very slender.

fimbriate—Fringed on the margin with trichomes coarser than those of a ciliate margin.

flabellate (flabelliform)—Fan-shaped; i.e., broadly wedge-shaped.

flag—See standard.

flagellate (flagelliform)—Whiplike.

flagelliflorous—A plant with a whiplike inflorescence that usually hangs below the crown.

flexuous—Bent alternately in opposite directions.

floccose (diminutive = flocculose)—Covered with tufts of wool-like hairs that often rub off easily.

floral cavity—A minute cavity on the dorsal side of *Wolfia* and *Wolfiella* (Lemnaceae) in which flowers are produced; note that vegetative buds are not produced in this cavity.

floral tube—A tube formed by the fusion of sepals, petals, or both, or as an outgrowth of the hypanthium. Nectar often accumulates within the floral tube.

floret—In the Asteraceae, a small flower characteristically found in a head; in the Poaceae, the term includes the lemma and palea as well as the enclosed flower.

fluted—Same as sulcate.

flying buttress—Buttress of a tree trunk that is elevated above the ground. Compare with plank buttress and running buttress.

fodder pollen—A type of pollen that cannot germinate and serves as a pollinator reward; e.g., in *Lecythis zabucajo* (Lecythidaceae) and *Swartzia* spp. (Fabaceae).

foliaceous—Leaflike.

foliolate—With leaflets; e.g., 3-foliolate or trifoliolate is a leaf with three leaflets.

follicetum—An aggregate of follicles formed from an apocarpous gynoecium.

follicle—A dry or somewhat fleshy or leathery, dehiscent fruit formed from a single carpel and opening along a ventral suture; e.g., the fruit of Apocynaceae subfamily Asclepiadoideae.

forked—Same as furcate.

forma—A taxonomic rank used to indicate a minor variant of a species, subspecies, or variety.

formicarium (plural = formicaria)—An ant domatium.

fornicate—Arched.

foveolate—Pitted.

fractiflex—Zigzagged; referring to a structure that is bent alternately in opposite directions much more sharply than is implied by the term flexuous.

free—Not fused to other parts; e.g., petals not adnate to any other floral parts. Compare with distinct.

free-central placentation—A type of placentation in which the ovules are borne on a central column in a unilocular ovary. See placentation.

free nervation—Leaf veins that do not unite to form a network. Compare with anastomosing and reticulate.

friable—Brittle; e.g., the bark of Chrysobalanaceae, which breaks into many small pieces when cut with a machete.

frondose—Leafy; used to describe inflorescences bearing numerous, leaflike bracts, a condition especially common in the Rubiaceae.

fugacious—See caducous.

fulvous—Dull yellowish brown.

funicle (funiculus)—The stalk of the ovule.

funnelform—In the shape of a funnel; i.e., gradually widening upward. Same as infundibular.

furcate—Forked, separating into two divisions.

furfuraceous—Scurfy or flaky.

fusiform—Spindle-shaped; i.e., narrowed toward both ends from a swollen middle.

galeate—Helmet- or hood-shaped, as the upper lip of some bilabiate corollas.

gall fruits—In *Ficus* (Moraceae), the seedless fruits that develop from ovaries parasitized by wasps.

gamete—A haploid (n) reproductive cell, two of which fuse to form a diploid (2n) zygote.

gametophyte—The gamete producing, haploid phase (n) of a plant's life cycle. Compare with sporophyte.

gamopetalous—See sympetalous.

gamosepalous—See synsepalous.

gap—Any opening in the canopy of the forest produced by the death of trees or by the fall of branches.

geitonogamous, geitonogamy—Referring to the fertilization of the ovules of a flower by pollen from another flower of the same plant. Compare with xenogamous.

geminate—Arranged in pairs.

gemma (plural = gemmae)—A specialized vegetative bud that often separates from the parent plant to produce a new plant.

gemmiferous—Bearing gemmae.

geniculate—Abruptly bent like a knee.

geophyte—A herbaceous plant that perennates by means of underground parts; i.e., at least part of the plant's life cycle is spent below the ground, usually to avoid environmental stresses such as prolonged dry periods.

geotropic—Referring to a shoot or root that responds positively to the pull of the earth's gravity.

geoxylic suffrutices—Shrubs, often found in cerrado habitats, that produce a woody trunk below the ground and only branches above the ground.

gibbous—Pouched or swollen on one side.

glabrate—Becoming glabrous.

glabrescent—Becoming glabrous or nearly glabrous.

glabrous—Smooth, devoid of trichomes (hairs).

gland—A secretory structure such as a floral or extrafloral nectary; a glandlike body whether it is secretory or not; e.g., the body connecting, via translators, the two pollinia of Apocynaceae subfamily Asclepiadoideae.

glaucous—Covered with a whitish substance that can be rubbed off.

globally symmetrical pollen—In the Malpighiaceae, pollen with the pores not all in the same plane and the ectoapertures, if present, variously oriented.

globose—Spherical.

glochid—A very thin and usually deciduous, barbed spine characteristic of some Cactaceae (Opuntioideae).

glochidiate—Barbed; bearing glochids.

glomerate—Referring to a structure, such as an inflorescence, composed of very densely clustered units; e.g., flowers.

glomerule—A tightly congested cymose inflorescence, usually with sessile flowers; e.g., in the Asteraceae.

glume—A bract at the base of a spikelet in the Poaceae.

grade—A level of evolutionary organization and advancement.

grain—See caryopsis.

granulate (granulose)—Appearing as if covered by very small grains; minutely or finely mealy.

ground tissue—Plant tissue other than the vascular tissue, the epidermis, or the periderm.

Guayana—A phytogeographic region corresponding to the Guayana Shield and including the Guianas and parts of northern Amazonian Brazil, Amazonian Colombia, and Amazonian Venezuela, not to be confused with Guyana, the country, or the Guianas, a political term that encompasses Guyana, Suriname, and French Guiana.

Guayana Shield—A geographic region in northern South America corresponding with Precambrian bedrock.

gymnosperm—A vascular plant with seeds not enclosed in an ovary.

gynobasic—Referring to a style arising from the base of the ovary; e.g., in species of Chrysobalanaceae, Rhabdodendraceae, and Lamiaceae.

gynodioecious, gynodioecy—Referring to a sexual condition of a species that bears pistillate flowers on some plants and bisexual flowers or staminate flowers as well as pistillate flowers on other plants.

gynoecium—The collective term for the pistillate structure of the flower. Compare with androecium.

gynomonoecious, gynomonoecy—Referring to a sexual condition of a species that bears pistillate flowers and bisexual flowers on the same plant.

gynophore—Stalk of the ovary; e.g., in Capparaceae and Simaroubaceae. Same as stipe.

gynostegial corona—A corona derived from the gynostegium.

gynostegium—The structure formed by the fusion of the stamens and the stigmatic region of the gynoecium in the Apocynaceae subfamily Asclepiadoideae. Compare with column in the Orchidaceae.

gynostemium—In the Aristolochiaceae, a structure formed by the fusion of the stamens to the style and stigma.

habit—The growth form of a plant; e.g., herb, tree, or shrub.

habitat—The place where a plant grows; e.g., wet soils along small streams, rain forest, or savanna.

hair—See trichome.

halophyte (halophytic)—A plant adapted to growing in saline soils. (referring to a plant growing in saline soils)

hapaxanthic—See monocarpic; opposite of pleionanthic.

haplostemonous—Referring to an androecium with a single series of stamens in one whorl.

hapter (plural = haptera)—Disclike or irregularly formed lateral outgrowths of roots (rarely shoots) that affix plants of many Podostemaceae to the substrate. Same as holdfast.

hastate—In the shape of an arrowhead but with the basal lobes spreading at more or less right angles to the long axis.

haustorium (plural = haustoria)—The tissue-penetrating and food-absorbing organ of a parasitic plant.

head—See capitulum.

helicoid cyme—A sympodial, determinate inflorescence whose lateral branches all develop from one side; it usually appears coiled and bears secund flowers. Same as bostryx.

heliophile—Lover of sunlight; a plant that thrives under conditions of high light intensity.

helobial endosperm—A type of endosperm in which two unequal cells develop differently, the larger one in a noncellular manner (see nuclear endosperm) and the smaller one in various ways.

hemiepiphyte—A plant that grows for part of its life on other plants without connection to the ground and for part of its life with a connection to the ground. A primary hemiepiphyte (e.g., *Clusia* spp., Clusiaceae) begins life without a connection with the ground but later develops aerial roots that reach the ground. A secondary hemiepiphyte (e.g., various species of Araceae) grows from the ground onto its support and later loses its connection with the ground. Compare with epiphyte.

hemiparasite—A plant that both photosynthesizes and extracts some of its nutrition from a host; e.g., Loranthaceae and Viscaceae.

hemisaprophyte—A saprophyte with chlorophyll in some of its tissue.

herb—A nonwoody plant. Large as well as small plants may be herbaceous; the largest native herb in the neotropics is *Phenakospermum guyannense* (Strelitziaceae).

herbaceous—With annual, nonwoody stems as opposed to perennial, woody stems.

herbarium (plural = herbaria)—A collection of dried, mounted, and permanently preserved specimens of plants from which scientific information may be obtained.

hermaphrodite—See bisexual; in the Mimosaceae, referring to the presence of both staminate and pistillate flowers in the same inflorescence.

hesperidium—A berrylike fruit with tough or coriaceous outer rind, e.g., the fruit of most species of *Citrus* (Rutaceae).

heterantherous—See heteromorphic stamens.

hetero-—A prefix meaning different or other.

heteroblastic—Referring to a plant with juvenile forms that are morphologically distinct from adult forms; often used to describe leaves changing from compound to simple as the plant passes from juvenile to adult.

heterochlamydeous—Referring to a flower with differentiated calyx and corolla. Compare with monochlamydeous.

heterogamous—Having flowers of two or more different types; e.g., the heads of certain Asteraceae with both ligulate and disk flowers.

heteromorphic—Referring to structures or organs within a species or individual that differ in form or size; e.g., the simple juvenile and pinnately compound leaves of *Syagrus inajai* (Arecaceae). Compare with dimorphic and monomorphic.

heteromorphic stamens—Stamens of two distinct types; one type usually bears fertile pollen and the other type bears sterile or fodder pollen; e.g., *Lecythis zabucajo* (Lecythidaceae) and species of *Senna* (Fabaceae).

heterophyllous—Referring to species or individuals with leaves that differ in size or shape. See heteromorphic.

heterosporous—Producing two different kinds of spores; e.g., those giving rise to the microgametophytes and megagametophytes of the flowering plants.

heterostyly, heterostylous—A condition in which the style and stamen lengths vary among individuals of the same species; e.g., in *Coussarea racemosa* (Rubiaceae), with flowers with long styles and short stamens and flowers with short styles and long stamens in different trees of the same population. Opposite of homostyly.

heterotrophic—Unable to synthesize organic compounds from inorganic substrates. Opposite of autotrophic.

hilar—Of or relating to the hilum.

hilum—A scar on the seed indicating where the funicle was attached.

hippocrepiform—Horseshoe-shaped.

hippuriform—Shaped like a horse's tail; e.g., the inflorescences of species of *Oenocarpus* (Arecaceae).

hirsute (diminutive = hirtellous)—With rough or coarse hairs.

hispid (diminutive = hispidulose)—With dense, stiff trichomes.

holdfast—See hapter.

holoparasite—An achlorophyllous parasitic plant that derives all of its nutrition from its host; e.g., species of Rafflesiaceae.

homo-—A prefix meaning "the same."

homoecious—Describes a species of plant that bears only bisexual flowers.

homogamous—Possessing flowers of one kind; e.g., the heads of certain Asteraceae with only disk flowers; referring to flowers in which the anthers release pollen at the same time as the stigma(s) is (are) receptive.

homophyllous—See isophyllous.

Homoptera—The order of insects including the cicadas and leaf hoppers.

homosporous—Producing a single kind of spore; e.g., as in most species of fern.

homostyly—A condition in which the style and stamen lengths are more or less the same in all individuals of a species. Opposite of heterostyly.

honey guide—Same as nectar guide.

hood—One of five hollow chambers of the corona of some species of Apocynaceae subfamily Asclepiadoideae.

hoop mark—A raised ring caused by bud scale scars that may partially or completely encircle the trunk of a tree; e.g., *Cecropia* spp. (Cecropiaceae).

horn—An appendage shaped like an animal's horn; e.g., the horn of the corona of Apocynaceae subfamily Asclepiadoideae.

humifuse—Referring to a growth form in which the plant is spread out over the ground.

hyaline—Very thin almost to the point of being colorless and transparent; often applied to leaf, sepal, or petal margins.

hybrid—The result of a cross between genetically dissimilar individuals.

hydathode—A structural modification, usually in leaves, that permits the release of water through an opening in the epidermis.

hydrophobic—Not combining or mixing well with water; e.g., the pollen grains of Cymodoceaceae.

hydropote—In the Myrsinaceae, a multicellular, epidermal structure, often of leaves, serving for the absorption of water and mineral salts. When young, hydropotes consist of a basal stalk and a group of cap cells, but at maturity the superficial structure breaks off and the remaining depression often regulates water as a hydathode.

hygrochastic—Referring to a type of plant caused by the absorption of water; e.g., the opening of capsular fruits as the result of taking in moisture from the air.

hygroscopic—Readily taking up and retaining moisture; structures sometimes change in position as a result of alternating gain and loss of water.

hypanthium—An often cup-shaped tube from which the calyx, corolla, and stamens are borne, usually formed from the fusion of calyx, corolla, and androecium but sometimes formed from the receptacle; in Ericaceae with inferior ovaries, the proximal portion of the calyx fused with the ovary wall.

hypha (plural = hyphae)—The tubular filament of a fungus.

hypocarp—The swollen pedicel that subtends the fruit of *Anacardium* (Anacardiaceae).

hypochile—The basal portion of a complex lip in Orchidaceae.

hypocotyl—The part of the stem of a seedling between the cotyledonary node and the roots.

hypocrateriform—See salverform.

hypogeal—Referring to a type of seed germination in which the cotyledons are retained below the ground. Compare with epigeal.

hypogynium—A disc or cuplike structure below the ovary of some Cyperaceae.

hypogynous—Referring to a flower in which the floral parts arise beneath the ovary or to a structure arising from below the ovary; e.g., the flowers of Ranunculaceae or the bristles of some species of *Rhynchospora* (Cyperaceae). Compare with epigynous and perigynous.

hypopeltate anther—Referring to an anther with the filament attached above the base and with the part of the anther that is prolonged downward facing away from the center of the flower.

-iform—A suffix indicating similarity to another structure.

igapó—A Portuguese term referring to periodically flooded forests located along the banks of black-water rivers and streams in Amazonia.

imbibition lid—In the Cannaceae, a lid on the raphe of the seed that covers a pore through which water passes into the seed.

imbricate—Referring to a type of aestivation in which the sepals or petals overlap at the adjacent edges or to the overlapping leaf bases as found in some species of Bromeliaceae.

immersed—Embedded in the substance of a structure. Compare with impressed.

imparipinnate—Pinnate with an uneven number of leaflets, i.e., with a terminal leaflet. Same as odd pinnate; compare with paripinnate.

imperfect—See unisexual.

impressed—Sunk below the surface as if pressed in; e.g., some leaf veins in relation to the rest of the leaf surface. Compare with immersed.

inaperturate—Without openings, often used to refer to pollen grains.

incerta sedis—Referring to a taxon whose relationships are not known with certainty.

included—Not protruding from a structure, such as the stamens from the corolla. Opposite of exserted.

incomplete flower—A flower with at least one of the whorls of floral parts missing; i.e., calyx, corolla, stamen(s), or gynoecium. Compare with complete flower.

indehiscent—Not opening; usually applied to fruits that remain closed at maturity. Opposite of dehiscent.

indeterminate—Referring to an inflorescences whose main axis continues to grow; i.e., is not terminated by a flower (e.g., a raceme); referring to the compound leaf of *Guarea* (Meliaceae) in which the tip of the rachis has the potential to continue growing.

indument (indumentum)—A covering of hairs.

induplicate—In Arecaceae, referring to leaflets that are V- or trough-shaped in transverse section. Opposite of reduplicate.

indurate—Hard.

indusium—Usually referring to the protective covering of the sporangia of some ferns, but sometimes used to refer to other structures; e.g., the stylar outgrowth of species of Goodeniaceae.

inferior ovary—An ovary in which the floral parts (calyx, corolla,

and stamens) arise from the summit; e.g., in Rubiaceae and Asteraceae. Same as epigynous; compare with superior ovary.

inflexed—Bent inward.

inflorescence—The structure in which the flower or flowers are displayed on a plant.

infra-—A prefix meaning "beneath" or "below" or "not quite reaching"; e.g., "infraterminal" means below the apex, an inframarginal vein is one that does not quite reach the margin, and an infrageneric classification is one in which the species of a genus are placed in groups of lesser rank.

infrafoliar—Borne below the leaves; e.g., the position of the inflorescence of certain Arecaceae such as, *Euterpe* spp. and *Oenocarpus bacaba*.

infructescence—The structure in which fruits are displayed on a plant.

infundibular—See funnelform.

inner bark—The functional phloem that occupies the region between the most recent periderm and the vascular cambium.

inrolled—Rolled inward.

inserted—Joined to or placed on; e.g., the stamens inserted on the corolla of Rubiaceae.

inside—See adaxial.

integument—The outer covering of the ovule that develops into the testa or seed coat; it may be composed of two layers, the inner and outer integuments.

inter-—A prefix meaning between or among.

intercalary—Inserted between adjacent tissues or structures.

interfoliar—Borne among the leaves; e.g., the inflorescence of *Attalea* (Arecaceae).

internode—The part of the stem between nodes.

interpetiolar—Located between the petioles of two opposite leaves; e.g., the stipules of Rubiaceae.

interpetiolar glands—Excretory structures located between the petioles of some plants; e.g., species of Bignoniaceae.

intersecondary vein—A leaf vein that is intermediate in size between secondary and tertiary veins and often runs parallel to a secondary vein.

interseminal sinuses—The spaces between the seeds in a legume pod.

intervenium—The space between the veins of a leaf.

intine—The inner layer of the two-layered wall of a pollen grain. Compare with exine.

intra-—A prefix meaning within.

intramarginal vein—A vein close to and parallel to the margin of a leaf.

intrastaminal—Placed inside of the stamens; e.g., the discs of most Anacardiaceae and Meliaceae.

intravaginal squamules—Scalelike structures found in the axils of the leaves of Alismataceae, Araceae, and Cymodoceaceae.

introrse—Directed inward, as the dehiscence of an anther. Compare with extrorse and latrorse.

intruded placenta—A parietal placenta that penetrates into the locule such that the placentation appears to be axile; e.g., in some species of Flacourtiaceae.

involucre (diminutive = involucel)—A series of fused or overlapping bracts that subtend inflorescences; e.g., in some Apiaceae, many Asteraceae, and *Euphorbia* (Euphorbiaceae).

involucrum—An adherent group of hairs arising from the style head in the Apocynaceae and often forming a ring that closes off the corolla. Sometimes called the ring.

involute—With the margin inrolled toward the adaxial surface as in the leaves of many Commelinaceae (e.g., *Dichorisandra*) and some Araceae such as *Anthurium jenmanii*. Compare with revolute and supervolute.

iridoid—Like an iris or a member of the iris family (Iridaceae).

irregular—See zygomorphic.

iso-—A prefix meaning equal or like.

isocotylous—Referring to seedlings in which both cotyledons are similar in shape and size. Compare with anisocotylous.

isodiametric—Referring to cells with equal diameters throughout; i.e., approximately spherical in shape.

isodromous—Referring to a venation pattern in which the first two veins in a given leaf segment arise opposite one another. Compare with anadromous and catadromous.

isomorphic—Referring to structures or organs in species or individuals that are similar in form and size. Opposite of heteromorphic and anisomorphic.

isophyllous—Having leaves all of one shape and size. Same as homophyllous.

isthmus—A thin, constricted connection between parts of an organ or structure.

iteroparous—See polycarpic.

jaculator—A hooklike structure derived from the funicle of many Acanthaceae that aids in dispersal by ejecting the seed from the fruit. Same as retinaculum.

jugum (plural = juga)—A pair of leaflets on a pinnately compound leaf.

keel—The two lower, united petals of the flower of most species of Fabaceae.

keeled—Bearing a keel. See carinate.

keystone species—A species that plays a role in the survival of other species, such as by providing a source of food; e.g., species of *Ficus* (Moraceae).

labellum—A liplike petal, such as the lower petal (lip) of the flower of Orchidaceae; in the Costaceae and Zingiberaceae, a petaloid structure derived from staminodes.

labiate—Lipped; i.e., referring to plant parts that are shapped like lips; of or pertaining to the Lamiaceae (mint family).

lacerate—Torn, irregularly cut or divided.

laciniate—Cut into narrow divisions.

lageniform—Gourd-shaped.

lamellate—Made up of small, thin plates.

lamina—See blade.

laminar—Expanded into a flattened or bladelike structure.

laminar placentation—A type of placentation in which the ovules arise along the surface (rather than the margins) of the carpels. Compare with marginal placentation; see placentation.

laminate (laminated)—Arranged in layers.

laminiform—Bladelike.

lanate—Woolly.

lanceoid—Referring to a three-dimensional structure that is lance-shaped when viewed from the side (wider at the base than at the middle).

lanceolate—Referring to a leaf, sepal, petal, or other flat structure that is wider at the base than at the midpoint, tapers toward the apex, and has a length-to-width ratio of 3:1 or more.

lanuginose—Woolly or cottony.

lateral dehiscence—Referring to the anthers of many flowering plants that open along the side.

lateral vein—See secondary vein.

latex—Opaque, white, creamy, or yellow, free-flowing exudate, usually observed from a wound in a plant.

laticifer—A latex-producing cell or series of cells.

latrorse—Directed toward the side, as the dehiscence of an anther. Compare with extrorse and introrse.

latticed—Cross-barred; e.g., the trunks of *Swartzia polyphylla* (Fabaceae), which are sulcate with connections between the ridges.

lax—Loose, not congested; term often used to describe the density of flowers in an inflorescence.

leaf gap—A region of parenchyma in the vascular tissue of a stem that is located above the level where a leaf trace diverges from the stem toward the leaf.

leaflet—A division of a compound leaf.

leafstalk—In legumes, the main axis of the leaf from its attachment to its apex; i.e., the petiole plus the rachis.

leaf trace—That part of a vascular bundle extending from the vascular cylinder of the stem into the base of the leaf.

leftcontor—Referring to a type of corolla aestivation in the Acanthaceae in which one petal is wholly rolled up to the left of another petal.

legume—A fruit that is derived from a single carpel, dehisces along two sutures, and is usually dry and several-seeded; informally, a member of the legume family *sensu lato* (Fabaceae).

lemma—The lower of the two bracts that enclose the floret of the Poaceae. Compare with palea.

lenticel—A spongy area in the bark of roots, trunks, and stems that allows the interchange of gases.

lenticellate—Possessing lenticels.

lenticular—Lens-shaped.

lepanthiform—Referring to tubular sheaths of leaves in the Orchidaceae that are flared and usually ciliate at the apex.

Lepidoptera—The order of insects including the butterflies and moths.

lepidopylls—Scalelike leaves found at the apical meristems of stems and rhizomes of Gunneraceae.

lepidote—Covered with small, peltate scales.

leprose—See scurfy.

leptocaulous—Referring to a much-branched growth form in which the higher order branches and stems are markedly more slender. Compare with pachycaulous.

liana—A woody climbing plant. Compare with vine.

ligneous—Woody.

lignified—Transformed into wood.

ligulate—Furnished with a ligule.

ligulate capitulum (head)—Inflorescence of Asteraceae with only ligulate flowers.

ligulate flower—A zygomorphic flower with a straplike corolla found in the Asteraceae tribe Lactuceae. Differing from a ray flower by having five instead of three lobes.

ligule—A strap-shaped organ; e.g., the blade of the corolla of a ray flower of some Asteraceae; the thin projection from the apex of the leaf sheath such as that of the Cyperaceae, Poaceae, and Zingiberaceae; an outgrowth from the petal of some Bromeliaceae; or an adaxial outgrowth of the corona of some Apocynaceae.

Liliopsida—The scientific name of the class of vascular plants that produce embryos and seedlings with a single cotyledon, also known as the monocotyledons.

limb—See blade.

limen—In some Passifloraceae, a ring or a cup-shaped membrane more or less closely surrounding the base of the gynophore.

linear—Referring to a structure such as a leaf, sepal, or petal that is narrowly oblong and has a length-to-width ratio of 10:1 or more.

linguliform, ligulate—Tongue-shaped.

lip—Either one of the two divisions of a bilabiate corolla; same as labellum in the Orchidaceae.

lithophyte—A plant growing on rocks.

llanos—A Spanish term referring to large expanses of plains found mostly in Colombia and Venezuela.

lobulate—Lobed.

locellus (plural = locelli)—A small, secondary compartment.

locular (loculate)—Divided into locules, such as an ovary or an anther.

locule—A chamber or cavity, such as that of an ovary or fruit that contains the ovule(s) or seed(s).

loculicidal capsule—See capsule.

lodicule—A small, colorless scale appressed to the ovary of most Poaceae that may represent a vestige of the perianth.

loma—A Spanish term referring to the dry vegetation found along the coast of Peru.

loment—A type of legume fruit in which each single-seeded segment breaks away from adjacent segments; e.g., in *Desmodium* (Fabaceae).

lomentiform—Like a loment.

longitudinal section—A cut along the long axis of an organ but not necessarily through the middle of the organ. Compare with medial section.

lophate—Referring to a type of pollen ornamentation in which the exine is raised in a network of ridges surrounding depressions.

lorate—Strap-shaped.

lower—See abaxial.

lunate—Crescent-shaped.

lustrous—Shiny.

lutescent—Becoming yellow.

lysigenous—Referring to an intercellular space caused by the dissolution of cells.

Macaronesia—The geographic region including five island groups off the northwest coast of Africa: Azores, Madeira, Canary Islands, Cape Vorde Islands, and Salvages.

macrophyte—A plant large enough to be seen with the naked eye; usually used to distinguish between vascular and nonvascular aquatic plants.

macropodial embryo—A solid embryo without differentiated cotyledons; e.g., in *Lecythis* spp. (Lecythidaceae) and *Monstera* spp. (Araceae).

Magnoliophyta—The scientific name of the phylum of vascular plants that bear flowers.

Magnoliopsida—The scientific name of the paraphyletic class of vascular plants that produce flowers and seeds usually with two cotyledons, also known as the dicotyledons.

Malesia—The geographic region including six southeastern Asian countries: Indonesia, Malaysia, Singapore, Brunei Darussalam, the Philippines, and Papua New Guinea.

malpighiaceous trichomes—Hairs that are unicellular, appressed, and attached by the middle; common in the Malpighiaceae, in which they can be T-shaped or Y-shaped.

many—In botanical descriptions, meaning more than 10. Same as numerous.

marcescent—Withering but persisting.

marginal placentation—A type of placentation, of a gynoecium of a single carpel, in which the ovules arise along the margins of the carpel. Compare with laminar placentation; see placentation.

marginate—Very narrowly winged; e.g., the rachis of the leaf of a number of species of *Inga* (Fabaceae).

marginicidal dehiscence—See septifragal dehiscence.

marmorate—Marblelike in appearance.

Mata Atlântica—A Portuguese term referring to rain forest running along the Atlantic coast of Brazil from the state of Rio Grande do Norte to the state of Rio Grande do Sul in a band from 120 to 160 kilometers wide. This band may be interrupted in various places by other types of vegetation.

mauve—Pinkish blue.

medial section—A cut along the long axis and through the middle of an organ. Compare with longitudinal section.

median—Of the middle.

medifixed—Referring to an organ that is attached in the middle.

mega-—A prefix meaning large.

megagametophyte—See embryo sac.

megaphyll—A leaf with more than one vein; characteristic of ferns, gymnosperms, and flowering plants. See microphyll.

megasporangium (plural = megasporangia)—A structure in which megaspores are formed.

megaspore—A spore that develops into a female gametophyte.

megasporophyll—A leaf bearing a megasporangium.

membranous—Thin and flexible.

mentum—In some Orchidaceae, a lateral (sometimes nectariferous) projection from the base of the column.

mericarp—A part of a schizocarp.

meristem—Undifferentiated plant tissue from which new cells arise.

-merous—A suffix referring to the number of parts of an organ; e.g., 5-merous flowers have their floral parts in fives or multiples of fives.

mesic—Referring to a habitat intermediate in moisture or water supply; i.e., not too dry and not too wet.

mesocarp—The middle layer of the fruit wall. Compare with pericarp.

mesochile—The central portion of a complex lip in Orchidaceae.

micro-—A prefix meaning small.

microgametophyte—See pollen.

microhabitat—A specialized habitat usually created by living organisms such as trees; e.g., the habitats found within the crown or in the shade of a tropical rain-forest tree.

microphyll—A leaf with a single vein, characteristic of Lycopodiaceae and Selaginellaceae and not found in the flowering plants. Compare with megaphyll.

micropyle—An opening in the integuments of the ovule through which the pollen tubes generally penetrate.

microsporangium (plural = microsporangia)—A structure in which microspores are formed.

microspore—A spore that develops into a male gametophyte.

microsporophyll—A reduced leaf bearing one or more microsporangia.

midnerve—See midrib.

midrib—The primary vein of a leaf, bract, sepal, or petal. Same as costa, midnerve, and midvein.

midvein—See midrib.

mitra-shaped—Shaped like a bishop's hat; i.e., broadest at the base and tapered equally on each side to the apex.

modified steady state—A flowering strategy in which a few flowers are produced each day over long periods of time but for shorter periods than in steady state species.

monad—A pollen grain that occurs singly. Compare with tetrad.

monadelphous—Referring to stamens united by their filaments into a single group.

moniliform—Cylindric but constricted at regular intervals and, thus, appearing like a string of beads; e.g., the staminal hairs of Commelinaceae.

mono-—A prefix meaning one.

monocarp—A unit of the fruit of apocarpous Annonaceae; e.g. *Guatteria* spp. and *Unonopsis* spp., Menispermaceae, Monimiaceae, and Ochnaceae.

monocarpic—Referring to plants that die after a single episode of flowering and fruiting; e.g., many bambusoid Poaceae and *Tachigali* (Fabaceae). Same as hapaxanthic and opposite of iteroparous, pleionanthic, or polycarpic.

monochlamydeous—Referring to a flower with a single whorl of perianth parts. Compare with heterochlamydeous.

monoclinous, monocliny—A species with functionally bisexual flowers. Compare with dicliny.

monocolpate—A pollen grain with a single colpus.

monocotyledon (monocot)—One of the two classes of angiosperms usually characterized by having one cotyledon, parallel-veined leaves, and flower parts most often in threes. In the classification of Cronquist (1981), this monophyletic class is called Liliopsida. Compare with dicotyledon.

monoecious, monoecy—Referring to the sexual condition of a species of plant that bears staminate and pistillate flowers on the same plants. Compare with dioecious.

monogeneric—Referring to a plant family with a single genus.

monograph—A scientific publication that includes all information known about a group of plants throughout its geographic range; e.g., *Flora Neotropica Monographs*.

monographer—A botanist who prepares a monograph.

monomorphic—Referring to structures or organs within a species or individual that do not differ distinctly in form or size. Compare with dimorphic and heteromorphic.

monophyletic—A group derived from the same ancestral taxon.

monopodial—Referring to plants with indeterminate growth along one axis.

monospecific—Referring to a higher taxonomic unit, such as a genus or family, composed of a single species.

monosulcate pollen—Referring to a pollen grain with one groove or furrow.

monothecous—Referring to an anther with a single theca.

monotypic—Referring to a genus with a single species.

morph—A phenotypic or genetic variant.

mucilage—A sticky, viscous liquid; e.g., that present among the leaf bases of Rapateaceae.

mucro—A sharp point at the apex of a leaf or a similar structure.

mucronate—Bearing a mucro.

Muellerian (Müllerian) bodies—Glycogen-rich food bodies located on fuzzy pads (trichilia) at the base of the petiole of some species of *Cecropia* (Cecropiaceae). Compare with pearl bodies.

multiple big bang—A flowering strategy in which abundant flowers are produced each day for a few days at several different times of the year. Compare with big bang.

multiple fruit—A fruit formed from the ovaries of more than one flower, such as that of the pineapple, equal to a compact infructescence.

muricate—Rough because of the presence of short, often stiff, protuberances.

muticous—Blunt, without a point.

mycelium—The totality of hyphae that compose the body of a fungus.

mycorrhiza (plural = mycorrhizae)—A symbiotic relationship between certain fungi and the roots of many species of plants.

myrcioid embryo—A type of embryo found in the Myrtaceae in which the cotyledons are normally thin, leafy, and folded, and the narrow, cylindrical hypocotyl is about the same length as the cotyledons and encircling them. Compare with eugenioid embryo and myrtoid embryo.

myristicaceous branching—A growth form found in the plant family Myristicaceae in which the main trunk is orthotropous and with spiral phyllotaxy, and the branches are plagiotropous with distichous phyllotaxy.

myrtoid embryo—A variable type of embryo found in the Myrtaceae in which the hypocotyl is the same length or much longer than the cotyledons; in genera with hard seed coats, the embryo is C-shaped; in genera with membranous or submembranous seed coats, the hypocotyl often is greatly swollen, and sometimes the whole embryo forms a spiral. Compare with eugenioid embryo and myrcioid embryo.

myxocarpy—The production of mucilage by fruits, which often aids in seed dispersal.

napiform—Turnip-shaped.

nastic—Referring to plant movement in response to a stimulus.

naturalized—Referring to an organism that is established and reproducing in areas outside of its native range.

navicular, naviculiform—Boat-shaped.

nectar—A sugar solution of varied composition produced by nectaries within flowers to attract pollinators or by extrafloral nectaries to attract insects that protect the plant from predation.

nectar guide—A marking on a flower that apparently serves to guide pollinators to the nectar. Some are visible to humans, but others are apparent to humans only through ultraviolet photography.

nectar ring—In some Passifloraceae, a low narrow ring situated below the operculum.

nectariferous disc—A more or less fleshy and elevated part of the receptacle, situated between the perianth and the stamens or between the stamens and the gynoecium, which functions in the production of nectar. Also referred to simply as a disc.

nectary—A tissue or structure that produces nectar.

niche—The ecological role of a species in a community.

nigrescent—Becoming black.

nitid—Shiny or lustrous.

nocturnal—Appearing at night.

node—The part of the stem where buds, leaves, and or adventitious roots are produced.

nomenclature—The process of naming plants.

nucellus—Tissue of the ovule in which the embryo sac develops.

nuciform—Nut-shaped.

nuclear endosperm—Endosperm development in which many nuclei develop before cell walls are formed.

numerous—See many.

nut—A hard, indehiscent, unilocular, single-seeded fruit arising from a simple or compound ovary.

nutant—Nodding.

nutlet—A small nut; often used to refer to one of the four parts of the mature fruit of some species of Boraginaceae, Lamiaceae, and Verbenaceae.

ob-—A prefix meaning opposite or against.

obcompressed—Vertically (rather than laterally) compressed.

obdiplostemonous—With two series of stamens: those of the outer series inserted opposite the petals and those of the inner series inserted opposite the sepals. Compare with diplostemonous.

oblanceolate—Referring to a leaf, bract, sepal, petal, or other structure in which the greatest width is distal to the midpoint and the length-to-width ratio is 3:1 or more.

oblate—Spheroidal but flattened at the ends; i.e., slightly broader than long.

oblique—Referring to a leaf base or similar structure in which the two sides are unequal.

oblong—Referring to a leaf blade or similar structure of which the greatest width extends throughout a zone where the margins are parallel.

obovate—Referring to a leaf blade or similar structure in which the greatest width is distal to the midpoint and the ratio of length to width is less than 3:1.

obturamenta (singular = obturamentum)—See basal stoppers.

obturators—In the Styracaceae, outgrowths of the placental wall that partly cover the ovules.

obtuse—Blunt, usually referring to the apex of a flattened structure (such as a leaf) in which the two sides are straight and, when they meet, form an angle greater than 90°. Compare with acute.

ochraceous—Ocher-colored, yellow-brown.

ochroleucous—Yellowish white.

ocrea (plural = ocreae)—A structure formed of stipules fused into a sheath and surrounding the stem; i.e., a diagnostic character of the Polygonaceae; in palms, an extension of the leaf sheath beyond the petiole insertion, a kind of ligule.

odd pinnate—See imparipinnate.

-oid—A suffix meaning like or resembling.

olid—Emitting a smell.

oligotrophic—Referring to habitats low in nutrients.

ontogenetic—Referring to ontogeny.

ontogeny, ontogenic—The course of growth and development of a living organism from inception to maturity.

operculate—Possessing an operculum.

operculum—The lid of the fruit of species with circumscissilely dehiscent fruits, in many Lecythidaceae; a valvelike opening into the stony endocarp of the fruit of some species (e.g., Humiriaceae); referring to a seed with an opening covered by a lid (e.g., Zingiberaceae) or the membranous cover of the nectary in *Passiflora* (Passifloraceae).

opposite—Arising from an axis, such as leaves from a stem, in pairs at the same node. Compare with alternate and whorled.

oral setae—Coarse, bristlelike appendages present at the summit of the leaf sheaths of some grasses.

orbicular—Referring to a two-dimensional structure with a circular outline.

orthotropous—Referring to a straight ovule in which the micropyle is positioned in a straight line and opposite the funicular attachment or to a growth habit in which the growing apex is oriented vertically. Compare with anatropous and plagiotropous.

osmophore—Tissue, often associated with flowers, from which aromas emanate.

ostiole—The opening into the syconium (fig) of Ficus (Moraceae).

outer bark—Dead tissue surrounding branches, trunks, and roots that includes all tissue from the innermost periderm outward.

outside—When used to indicate position, same as abaxial.

ovariodisc—In the Burseraceae, a single, parenchymatous structure representing the ontogenetic fusion of the nectary disc and the pistillode.

ovary—The part of the gynoecium containing the ovules.

ovate—Referring to the shape of a leaf blade or other structure in which the axis of greatest width is basal to the midpoint and the ratio of length to width is less than 3:1.

ovipositor—The egg-laying apparatus of an insect.

ovoid—Egg-shaped; the three-dimensional version of ovate.

ovule—The organ that after fertilization becomes the seed. The ovule in angiosperms contains the embryo sac with its egg cell and is enclosed within the locule of the ovary.

pachycaulous—Referring to a growth form in which the branching is sparse and the higher-order branches and stems are not markedly diminished in thickness. Compare with leptocaulous.

palate—In the Lentibulariaceae and Scrophulariaceae, the space at the throat and limb of the corolla used by pollinating insects as a landing platform.

pale—A bract found in the head of Asteraceae.

palea—The upper of the two bracts that enclose the floret in the Poaceae. Compare with lemma.

paleate (paleaceous)—Possessing pales.

paleoherbs—A hypothesized clade of flowering plants including the Aristolochiales, monocots, Nymphaeales, and Piperales.

pallid—Pale in color.

palmate—Referring to leaf venation in which the main veins of the blade radiate from a common point near the base or to compound leaves in which all leaflets radiate from a common point. See digitate.

palmately lobed, palmatilobate, palmatisect—Digitately divided; arranged like the fingers of a human hand.

pampas—A Spanish term referring to grass-dominated plains, especially those found in eastern Argentina.

pandurate—Fiddle-shaped.

pantanal—See *Chacó*.

papilionaceous corolla—The zygomorphic corolla of most species of papilionoid legumes.

papilionoid—Referring to flowers similar to those of Fabaceae subfamily Papilionoideae; e.g., those of the Polygalaceae.

papillae—Minute, rounded protuberances that typically cover a surface.

papillate—Bearing papillae.

pappus—A modified calyx of hairs, scales, or bristles typical of many Asteraceae.

papyraceous—Papery.

parallel-veined (parallel-nerved)—Generally applied to secondary or higher-order veins that are parallel to each other and to the margins of the leaf, sepal, or petal in which they occur.

páramo—A Spanish term referring to a high-elevation, humid, Andean vegetation ranging from Venezuela to northern Peru.

paraphyletic—A taxonomic group encompassing some but not all of the descendants of its most recent common ancestor.

parasitic plant—A plant that obtains its food and water from another plant; i.e., the plant that does not photosynthesize; e.g., *Helosis cayennensis* (Balanophoraceae).

parenchyma—Ground tissue composed of mostly isodiametric, thin-walled cells that usually retain the ability to divide.

parietal placentation—A type of placentation found in compound, unilocular ovaries in which the ovules arise from placentae inserted on the wall of the locule near the sutures. See placentation.

paripinnate—Pinnate with an even number of leaflets; i.e., without a terminal leaflet. Same as even-pinnate; compare with imparipinnate.

patelliform—Shaped like a kneecap; e.g., the glands of some species of *Diospyros* (Ebenaceae).

patent—Spreading.

pearl bodies—Glycogen-rich food bodies on the surfaces of the leaves of species of *Pourouma* (Cecropiaceae). Compare with Muellerian bodies.

pectinate—Pinnately divided into many more or less parallel segments and resembling the teeth of a comb.

pedaliform—Resembling the sole of a foot in shape.

pedate—Palmately divided with the lateral divisions 2-cleft.

pedatisect—Pedately divided with the sinuses nearly reaching the middle. Compare with pedate.

pedicel—The stalk supporting some flowers.

pedicellate—Possessing a pedicel.

peduncle—The primary stalk of some inflorescences; in the Marantaceae, the common stalk of the flower pair; and in the Mimosaceae, the stalk of the capitulum (the latter two are actually secondary peduncles).

peduncular bract—A bract on the peduncle in Arecaceae located on the main axis of the inflorescence between the prophyll and the first bract of the rachis; any bract associated with the peduncle; e.g., in the Orchidaceae.

pedunculate—Possessing a peduncle.

pellucid dots—Dots that transmit light when held against a light source, often observed on the leaves of some species of Myrtaceae and Rutaceae.

peltate—Shield-shaped; e.g., a leaf or scale attached to a stalk by its lower surface rather than its margin.

pendent, pendulous—Hanging.

penicillate—Shaped like an artist's brush; e.g., the stigma of some species of *Turnera* (Turneraceae).

pepo—A fleshy, indehiscent, many-seeded fruit with a rigid exocarp typical of many species of Cucurbitaceae.

percurrent growth—In the Viscaceae, the longitudinal pattern of shoot growth through continued activity of the apical meristem.

percurrent veins—Veins of the same order that run parallel to each another between veins of a higher order; e.g., tertiary veins and their orientation between secondary veins.

perennate—Referring to an organ; e.g., an inflorescence, persisting for more than one flowering period.

perennial—A plant that lives for 3 or more years. Compare with annual and biennial.

perfect—See bisexual.

perforate—Provided with holes; e.g., the leaves of some species of *Monstera* (Araceae).

pergameneous—With the texture of parchment.

perianth—The collective term for the calyx and the corolla, even when they are not differentiated (i.e., represented by tepals)

pericarp—The wall of the fruit, which is usually made up of three layers: exocarp, mesocarp, and endocarp.

pericarpel—In the Cactaceae, the part of the receptacle fused to the ovary.

periderm—Protective tissue located on the outside of stems, branches, and roots, consisting of the phellogen or cork cambium, the phellem or cork to the outside, and the phelloderm to the inside.

perigon—A reduced perianth found in the flowers of some species of Araceae, Monimiaceae, and Siparunaceae.

perigoniate—Having a perigon.

perigynium—A saclike structure surrounding the ovary of some Cyperaceae. Same as utricle.

perigynous—Referring to a flower in which the floral parts arise from the rim of a cuplike hypanthium. Compare with hypogynous and epigynous.

peripheral filaments—Protein filaments associated with sieve-element plastids.

perisperm—Food-storage tissue derived from the nucellus of some flowering plants.

persistent—Referring to a structure that remains attached. Opposite of deciduous.

personate—Referring to a bilabiate corolla with an expansion on the lower lip that blocks entry into the tube; e.g., in some species of Acanthaceae.

perula (plural = perulae)—A scale of a leaf bud.

perulate—Referring to buds covered with scales.

petal—A segment of the corolla.

petaloid—Petal-like.

petiole—The stalk of a leaf; in compound leaves, the stalk between the leaf attachment and the insertion of the first leaflets.

petiolule—The stalk of a leaflet. Several different orders of petiolules may exist in leaves twice or more compound; those in a palmately compound leaf radiate from a common central point.

phanerocotylar—A type of seed germination in which the cotyledons emerge from the seed coat. Compare with cryptocotylar.

phanerogam—A plant that produces seed; the gymnosperms and angiosperms are phanerogams. Compare with cryptogam.

pharmacopoeia—A collection or stock of drugs possessed by different cultures.

phellem—A layer of suberized cells produced outwardly by the cork cambium.

phelloderm—A layer of parenchyma produced inwardly by the cork cambium.

phellogen—See cork cambium and periderm.

phenology—The timing of vegetative and reproductive events in plants and the relationship of these events with abiotic and biotic factors.

phenotype—The sum total of the observable structures and functional characteristics of a living organism.

phenotypic plasticity—The capacity for marked variation in the phenotype; i.e., variation in character states.

pherophyll—Leaflike bract found in frondose inflorescences.

phloem—The food-conducting tissue of vascular plants. In most woody plants, the inner bark is phloem.

phloem arm—A segment of cross-shaped or star-shaped phloem as seen in transverse section in some lianas, especially species of Bignoniaceae.

-phore (-phorus)—A suffix meaning bearing.

photosynthate—The product of photosynthesis.

photosynthesis—The process by which green plants produce carbohydrates from carbon dioxide and water utilizing radiant energy from the sun.

phyllary—One of a series of overlapping bracts that subtends the capitula of Asteraceae.

phylloclade—A branch that has taken on the form and function of a leaf.

phyllode—A petiole that has taken on the form and function of a leaf; e.g., in certain species of *Acacia*.

phyllotaxy—Three-dimensional arrangement of leaves on a stem.

phylogenetic—Referring to a classification based on the evolutionary relationships of the organisms involved.

phylum (plural = phyla)—A unit of classification. The plant kingdom is divided into phyla of which the Magnoliophyta are treated in this book. Same as division.

phytomelan—A carbonaceous, opaque material that usually covers the seed coat to give it a black appearance, common in certain monocot families.

pilose (diminutive = pilosulous)—Bearing a covering of long, soft, simple trichomes.

pin flower—One of two types of flowers found in some species in which the style is long and the stamens are short. Compare with thrum flower; see heterostyly.

pinna (plural = pinnae)—The primary division of a compound leaf.

pinnate, pinnately compound—Bearing leaflets in pairs or alternately along a common axis or rachis. See paripinnate and imparipinnate.

pinnate venation—A type of venation pattern in which the secondary veins run parallel to each other from the midrib to the margin.

pinnatifid—Pinnately divided with the sinuses extending halfway or more to the midrib but not reaching it.

pinnatisect—Pinnately divided with the sinuses reaching the rachis. The segments of pinnatisect leaves or fronds are not stalked; i.e., they lack petiolules.

pioneer—A species of plant that colonizes a barren or disturbed area; e.g., many species of *Cecropia* (Cecropiaceae).

pistil—The female part of the flower composed of the ovary, style, and stigma.

pistillate—Referring to unisexual flowers with functional gynoecia but without functional stamens (staminodes may be present).

pistillode—A rudimentary, sterile gynoecia.

pith—The spongy ground tissue occupying the center of many stems.

placenta (plural = placentae)—The structure in the ovary to which the ovules are attached.

placental obturator—A massive outgrowth of the placenta. In the Styracaceae, the micropyle of each ovule opens upon an obturator; the obturators may or may not be connate.

placentation—The arrangement of ovules within the ovary. See axile, basal, free-central, and parietal placentation.

plagiotropous—Referring to a growth habit in which the growing apex is oriented horizontally. Compare with orthotropous.

planalto—A Portuguese and Spanish word referring to a flat area usually at higher elevations; e.g., the planaltos of central Brazil and the Andes.

planar—Flat.

plane—Flat, even, level; i.e., without any projections; usually referring to leaves with veins at same level as leaf blade surface.

plank buttress—A vertically flattened, boardlike buttress. Compare with flying buttress and running buttress.

plano-compressed—Compressed such that the sides are flat.

plano-convex—Flat on one side and curved outward on the other; often refers to cotyledons.

pleio-—A prefix meaning more.

pleiochasium—Referring to a cyme in which each of the main axes produces more than two branches.

pleionanthic—See polycarpic.

pleiothyrse—A complex thyrse; e.g. those of some species of Apocynaceae subfamily Asclepiadoideae.

pleisiomorphic—Referring to a feature of a plant that is an ancestral character state; i.e., an evolutionarily primitive character state that does not help define taxonomic groups.

pleurogram—A line or crack, sometimes shaped like a horseshoe, found on the lateral faces of the seed coat of some legumes.

pliant—Flexible.

plicate—Folded into lengthwise plaits, like a fan.

pliveined (plinerved)—Referring to leaf blade venation in which the midvein is accompanied by several nearly equal secondary veins arising at or near the base; e.g., in many Ericaceae and some Euphorbiaceae.

plumose—Feathery or bearing featherlike hairs or bristles.

plumule—The upper portion of the embryo that develops into the primary shoot.

pneumatophore—An erect, aerial, "breathing root," common in species of mangrove habitats.

pneumatorhiza (plural = pneumatorhizae)—A short, specialized, lateral, cone-shaped rootlet produced on aerial roots and pneumatophores.

pock marks—Small circular depressions on the external surface of bark.

pod—The most common fruit of the Fabaceae; see legume.

polar nuclei—Two nuclei that migrate to the center of the embryo sac and fuse with the male nucleus to form the primary endosperm nucleus.

pollen—Male reproductive structures contained within the anther of the stamen and usually released at anthesis. Same as microgametophytes.

pollinarium (plural = pollinaria)—The pollen-bearing structure of Orchidaceae composed of a viscidium, a stipe, and pollinia.

pollinium (plural = pollinia)—An aggregate pollen mass characteristic of Orchidaceae and those Apocynaceae formerly considered Asclepiadaceae.

poly-—A prefix meaning many.

polyandrous—Referring to an androecium with numerous stamens.

polycarpic—Referring to plants that flower repeatedly; i.e., those that do not die after a single flowering. Same as iteroparous and pleionanthic; opposite of hapaxanthic and monocarpic.

polycolpate pollen—Referring to a pollen grain with more than one colpus or furrow.

polygamodioecious—Referring to the sexual condition of a species that bears staminate and bisexual flowers on some plants and pistillate and bisexual flowers on other plants.

polygamomonoecious—Referring to the sexual condition of a species that bears staminate, pistillate, and bisexual flowers on the same plant. Same as trimonoecious.

polygamous—Referring to the sexual condition of a species that bears bisexual and unisexual flowers on the same plant.

polymorphic—The occurrence of different forms of the same organ within the same species.

polypetalous—Having petals free from one another. Opposite of sympetalous; same as choripetalous.

polyphyletic—The inclusion of more than one evolutionary line in a taxonomic group.

polyploidy—Referring to a process in which more than two sets of chromosome numbers are present. This is often the result of hybridization.

polyporate—Having numerous apertures; e.g., pollen grains.

polystelic—Referring to a stem with more than one vascular bundle.

polystemonous—Having many stamens.

polystichous—Inserted in many series around an axis. Contrast with distichous and tristichous.

pore—A small opening, usually round.

poricidal dehiscence—Opening via pores; usually applied to anthers that shed their pollen via terminal apertures; e.g., *Gustavia* spp. (Lecythidaceae) and *Solanum* spp. (Solanaceae).

porrect—Directed outward and forward; perpendicular to the surface of origin.

posterior—On the side toward the axis; used in this book to describe the position of some of the sepals of Bromeliaceae. Same as adaxial.

posterior rib—In Araceae, the connate or apparently united portion of the basal veins (those primary veins that join the midrib at the petiole attachment).

praemorse—With a jagged, irregular apex, appearing as if bitten off; e.g., the apices of the leaflets of *Socratea exorrhiza* (Arecaceae).

prairie—A treeless, grass-dominated vegetation found scattered throughout the neotropics.

prickle—A sharp, pointed outgrowth of the superficial tissue of a stem; e.g., on the trunk and branches of *Ceiba pentandra* (Bombacaceae), *Hura crepitans* (Euphorbiaceae), and *Jacaratia spinosa* (Caricaceae), and on the stems of *Smilax* spp. (Smilacaceae). Compare with spine and thorn.

primary vein—See midrib; all the nearly equal first-order veins of most species of Melastomataceae (excluding species of *Mouriri* and *Tovomita*); two or more primary veins of a leaf that are not distinguishable from one another; e.g., the higher-order veins of *Smilax* spp. (Smilacaceae).

proboscis—The slender, tubular, feeding structure of some insects.

proliferous—Producing offshoots or buds capable of forming other plants.

prominent (diminutive = prominulous)—Raised above the surface; e.g., the veins of a leaf.

propagule—A unit of dispersal of a plant; it can be vegetative or sexual. Same as diaspore.

pro parte—A Latin word meaning in part, usually referring to a situation in which only part of a taxon possesses a given feature; often abbreviated as p.p.

prophyll—In monocots, the first leaf produced on a branch and located between the branch and the main axis; usually two-keeled.

prop roots—Aerial, adventitious roots that are circular in transverse section; e.g., in *Socratea exorrhiza* (Arecaceae). Same as stilt roots.

prostoma (plural = prostomata)—An indented and/or membranous area through which the queens of plant-associated ants bore into the hollow chambers of the trunks and stems; e.g., in many species of *Cecropia* (Cecropiaceae).

prostrate—Lying flat on the ground.

protandrous, proterandrous—Referring to a flower in which the pollen is shed before the stigma is receptive. Compare with protogynous.

proteoid roots—In the Proteaceae, small, lateral roots of limited growth that form dense clusters on "ordinary" roots.

protogynous, proterogynous—Referring to a flower in which the stigma is receptive before the pollen is shed. Compare with protandrous.

proximal—Near to the place of attachment. Opposite of distal.

pruinose—Having a bloom or whitish cast on the surface.

pseudanthium (plural = pseudanthia)—A false flower; e.g., the inflorescence of species of Asteraceae and *Dalechampia* (Euphorbiaceae).

pseudaril—In Burseraceae, soft aril-like tissue that covers part or all of the pyrene and attracts dispersal agents.

pseudo-—A prefix meaning false.

pseudobulb—In Orchidaceae, a specially modified stem that is variously swollen and stores food and water.

pseudocarp—A fruit with accompanying parts, such as that of *Siparuna* (Siparunaceae), in which the separate carpels are surrounded by a fleshy hypanthium.

pseudodisc—In some Menispermaceae, the button-shaped fleshy whorl of petals.

pseudomonomerous—Referring to a structure that appears to consist of one unit but has been derived from the fusion of more than one unit; e.g., a gynoecia with one locule derived from more than one carpel and with no obvious indication that it was derived from more than one carpel.

pseudomonopodial—Referring to a plant having a primary stem with sympodial growth and secondary stems with monopodial growth.

pseudopetiole—The narrowed portion of the leaf located between the ligule(s) and the blade in many Bambuseae, in other Poaceae such as *Pharus*, and in some Cyperaceae.

pseudospikelet—A group of indeterminate, spikeletlike structures that develop from buds, are subtended by glumelike, sterile bracts, and are found in some Bambuseae and a few other Poaceae.

pseudostaminodia (singular = pseudostaminodium)—In the Amaranthaceae, referring to sterile, filamentous, entire to fimbriate processes as long as or longer than the stamens and alternating with them.

pseudostem—The apparent stem of *Musa* (Musaceae), *Phenakospermum* (Strelitziaceae), and some other monocots which is actually a cylinder formed by overlapping leaf bases.

pseudostipule—A leaf (e.g., in some species of Aristolochiaceae) or leaflet (e.g., in some species of *Trichilia*, Meliaceae) that resembles a stipule; in some Bignoniaceae, a bud scale derived from the axillary buds that resembles a stipule.

pseudosyncarpous—In the Annonaceae, referring to fruits in which the carpels seem to be connate, but in reality are free or almost free (e.g., species of *Duguetia* in the Annonaceae).

pterophyll—Expanded sepal (usually white or green) of some Rubiaceae that usually are expanded fully after anthesis and aid in wind dispersal.

ptyxis—Referring to the way a leaf is folded within a bud.

puberulent, puberulous—Minutely pubescent.

pubescence—A covering of short, soft trichomes.

pubescent—Covered with short, soft trichomes.

pulverulent—Appearing dusty or powdery.

pulvinate—Possessing pulvini.

pulvinule—An enlargement of a portion of the petiolule.

pulvinus (plural = pulvini)—An enlargement of a portion of the petiole, without an apparent function (e.g., *Protium*, Burseraceae) or sometimes controlling the orientation of the leaf or leaflet (e.g., *Mimosa polydactyla* and *M. pudica*, Fabaceae).

puna—A Spanish term referring to a high altitude, rather dry, Andean vegetation dominated by grasses and ranging from Peru southward.

punctate—Covered with translucent dots, glands, or pits.

punctation—A glandular dot such as found in the leaves of Myrtaceae.

punctiform—Dotlike, reduced to a mere point.

purpureus—Red-violet but closer to red than blue.

pyramidate—Pyramid-shaped.

pyrene—The nut or nutlet in a drupe; i.e., the hardened part of the drupe containing the seeds, sometimes referred to as the stone; in the Burseraceae, part of the fruit surrounding a seed or seeds that is derived from the endocarp and is sometimes surrounded by a pseudaril.

pyriform—Pear-shaped.

pyxidium, pyxidiate—A capsular fruit with circumscissile dehiscence.

quadrate—Square.

quaternate—Referring to a type of leaf arrangement in which four leaves are found at each node.

quincuncial—Referring to a type of imbricate aestivation of five sepals or petals, two with both margins inside, two with both margins outside, and one with one margin inside and the other margin outside.

raceme—An indeterminate inflorescence with a single axis, the flowers borne on pedicels of more or less equal length, and the uppermost flower the youngest. Compare with spike.

racemose—Racemelike.

rachilla—A secondary axis of an inflorescence; e.g., the axis of the spikelet in Poaceae or the axis that bears the flowers in Arecaceae.

rachis (rhachis)—The axis of a compound leaf (excluding the petiole) or of an inflorescence (excluding the peduncle); in legumes, that part of the leaf axis bearing leaflets of any order.

radially symmetrical—See actinomorphic.

radially symmetrical pollen—In the Malpighiaceae, referring to pollen with pores on the equator and colpi, if present, oriented at right angles to the equator.

radiate capitulum (head)—Inflorescence of Asteraceae with marginal ray flowers and central disk flowers.

radicant—Rooting, usually referring to a prostrate or aerial stem giving rise to roots at the nodes.

radicle—The lower portion of the embryo that develops into the root.

ramicaul—Secondary stem of some Orchidaceae.

ramiflorous—Producing flowers on leafless branches or leafless parts of stems; a special type of cauliflory. Compare with cauliflorous.

ranalean odor—See ethereal oils.

rank, ranked—A vertical row; e.g., leaves that are in two vertical rows are said to be 2-ranked.

raphe—A ridge on a seed formed by the fusion of the funicle to the seed coat.

raphide—A needle-shaped crystal of calcium oxalate found in the cells of some plants.

ray—A radial band of tissue in the wood of vascular plants that allows movement of water, nutrients, and photosynthate in stems and trunks; in Cyperaceae, a secondary axis of a compound inflorescence; in *Solanum* (Solanaceae), a division of a stellate hair.

ray flower—A zygomorphic flower with a straplike corolla found in Asteraceae. Compare with disk flower.

*rbc*L—A chloroplast gene that encodes the large subunit of the photosynthetic enzyme ribulose-1,5-bisphosphate carboxylase/oxygenase.

receptacle—The more or less expanded apex of the axis beyond the pedicel upon which the floral parts are borne.

receptacular throat—In the Cactaceae, the part of the receptacle above the receptacular tube.

receptacular tube—In the Cactaceae, the broadened part of the receptacle between the summit of the ovary and the point at which the receptacle begins to broaden. Same as epigynous hypanthium.

recurved—Curved backward.

reduplicate—In Arecaceae, referring to leaflets that are upside down, V-shaped in transverse section. Opposite of induplicate.

reflexed—Abruptly bent backward or downward.

regular—See actinomorphic.

reniform—Kidney-shaped.

repand—Undulate, usually referring to the margins of leaves or other structures.

repent—Creeping, usually referring to stems growing along the ground that produce roots at their nodes.

replum—Persistent structure along the suture of a legume pod that persists after the seeds have been dispersed; partition between the two compartments of the fruits of many Brassicaceae.

resin—Transparent or nearly transparent, colorless or colored, viscous exudate.

restinga—Portuguese term referring to a diverse array of vegetation found in sandy soil in a narrow band along the Brazilian coast between the high-tide mark and taller forests farther inland.

resupinate—Turned 180° in development; e.g., flowers of the Orchidaceae in which the lip originates in the uppermost position but is lowermost at anthesis.

reticulate—Netted, like the veins of many leaves.

retinaculum (plural = retincula)—In the Orchidaceae, the structure connecting the pollinia; in the Acanthaceae, see jaculator.

retrorse—Directed downward or backward. Opposite of antrorse.

retuse—Notched slightly at the apex.

revolute—With the margin inrolled toward the abaxial surface. Compare with involute.

rhipidium (plural = rhipidia)—An alternately branching fan-shaped cyme with axes in one plane.

rhizoid—A rootlike structure lacking xylem and phloem.

rhizomatous—Bearing rhizomes.

rhizome—A prostrate stem below the ground that sends off rootlets and, at the apex, vertical stems or leaves; in the Poaceae, lateral underground stems that collectively constitute a "sod" from which leafy stems emerge.

rhombic—Diamond-shaped; i.e., referring to a four-sided plane figure with the opposite sides parallel and equal.

rhomboid—Nearly rhombic but with the adjacent sides unequal.

rimose—Fissured or cracked, as the bark of some trees.

riparian—Growing along streams or rivers.

rosette—An arrangement of leaves radiating from the base of the stem and usually placed close to the ground.

rostellum (plural = rostella)—The portion of the stigma in Orchidaceae that separates the fertile part from the pollinia and aids in gluing the pollinia to the pollinators; a small beak.

rostrate—With a beak.

rostrum—Beak.

rosulate—Referring to a cluster of leaves arranged in a rosette.

rotate—Disk-shaped or flat and circular, usually referring to a sympetalous corolla with a short tube and very widely spreading lobes.

rudimentary—Referring to a structure or organ arrested at an early stage of development.

rufous (rufescent)—Reddish brown (becoming reddish brown).

rugose (diminutive = rugulose)—Having a wrinkled surface.

ruminate endosperm—Testa or seed coat folded into the endosperm; e.g., that of many species of Annonaceae, Myristicaceae, and Arecaceae.

runner—A slender stolon.

running buttress—A thick, rounded buttress that extends along the ground several meters or more from the trunk. Compare with flying buttress and plank buttress.

rupicolous—Dwelling among rocks.

saccate—Bag-shaped.

sagittate—Shaped like an arrowhead.

salient—Raised from the surface, usually referring to veins of leaves.

salverform—Referring to the shape of a sympetalous corolla in which the tube is slender and the lobes are abruptly spreading and flat. Same as hypocrateriform.

samara—An indehiscent, winged fruit; e.g., that of *Machaerium* spp. and *Vataireopsis* spp. (Fabaceae).

sap—A free-flowing exudate that can be translucent, colorless, yellow, orange, or red.

saprophyte—Heterotrophic plant that is without chlorophyll, lives on decayed plant material and usually depends on a symbiotic relationship with a fungus to obtain food.

sapwood—The outer functional part of the xylem.

sarcotesta—A fleshy layer of the integument of the seed that aids in dispersal by animals. Compare with aril and elaiosome.

sarmentose—Referring to a plant that produces long, slender runners.

saxicolous—Same as epilithic.

scabrous—Rough to the touch.

scalariform—Arranged as in the rungs of a ladder; ladderlike.

scale—Any thin, scarious bract, usually a vestigial leaf; e.g., that of some saprophytes such as species of *Voyria* (Gentianaceae) or the bracteole subtending a flower or spikelet in the Cyperaceae.

scallop marks—Irregular, shallow depressions on the external surface of bark.

scandent—Climbing.

scape—A leafless, often bracteate peduncle that arises from near the base of the plant; e.g., in *Xyris* (Xyridaceae).

scapose—Having scapes or scapelike structures.

scarious—Parchmentlike; thin and dry.

schizocarp—A dry, dehiscent fruit that splits into several parts (each called a mericarp), each usually with a single seed; e.g., in Apiaceae, most lianas of Malpighiaceae, and *Serjania* spp. (Sapindaceae).

sclereid—A thick-walled, lignified cell that is variable in form.

sclerenchyma—Tissue composed of dead, thick-walled cells, such as stone cells and fibers.

scorpioid cyme—A determinate inflorescence that has the lateral flowers developing on alternate sides of the axis and often appears coiled.

scree—The rocky base of steep slopes or inclines.

scrobiculate—Minutely pitted.

scurfy—Scaly. Same as leprose.

scutellum—A small plate or scalelike appendage; e.g., on the calyx of *Scutellaria* (Lamiaceae); in the seeds of Poaceae, a flattened lateral structure between the endosperm and embryo.

secondary growth—Vegetation that develops after disturbance by humans or forces of nature; plant tissue derived from lateral meristems.

secondary pollen presentation—The presentation of pollen to the pollinator in a place other than the anther; e.g., on the style of Vochysiaceae.

secondary vegetation—Same as secondary growth.

secondary vein—A leaf vein arising from the midrib or primary vein. Same as lateral vein.

sectile—Referring to the aggregate clumps of granular pollen found in some Orchidaceae.

secund—Referring to leaves, branches, flowers, or other structures that arise or seem to arise from one side of an axis; e.g., the flowers of *Heliotropium* (Boraginaceae).

seed—The mature ovule that contains the embryo.

seed coat—The outer covering of a seed. Same as testa.

self-compatible—Referring to a plant in which pollen from a plant can fertilize eggs of the same plant; i.e., a plant that can be self-fertilized. Compare with self-incompatible.

self-incompatible—Referring to a plant in which pollen from a plant cannot fertilize ovules of the same plant. Compare with self-compatible.

semelparity—A flowering strategy in which flowers are produced only once, usually in massive numbers after many years, and then the plant dies; e.g., species of *Agave* (Agavaceae).

semi-—A prefix meaning half, partly, or almost.

seminiferous—Bearing seeds.

sensu lato—A Latin term meaning in the broad sense; e.g., the legumes when considered as a single family rather than three separate families.

sensu stricto—A Latin term meaning in the narrow sense; e.g., the genus *Cassia* when *Chamaecrista* and *Senna* (Fabaceae) are excluded.

sepal—A segment of the calyx.

sepaline—Referring to sepals.

sepaline tails—Long extensions of the sepals.

sepaloid—Resembling a sepal.

septal nectary—A nectary developing in the septal regions of the ovary.

septal region—That part of the ovary associated with the septa.

septate—Referring to a structure divided into chambers by partitions (septa); e.g., septate hairs.

septicidal capsule—See capsule.

septifragal dehiscence—Referring to a type of fruit dehiscence in which the valves break away from the septa, e.g., in species of *Paullinia* (Sapindaceae). Same as marginicidal dehiscence.

septum (plural = septa)—A partition or cross wall; a wall of a locule of an ovary or fruit (then same as dissepiment).

sericeous—Silky; i.e., with long, soft, slender, somewhat appressed hairs.

serrate (diminutive = serrulate)—Having a margin with sharp teeth oriented toward the apex of the structure bearing them. Compare with dentate and erose.

sessile—Stalkless, as leaves, inflorescences, flowers without petioles, peduncles, or pedicels.

seta (plural = setae)—Stiff bristle or hair.

setose (diminutive = setula)—Covered with bristles.

several—In botanical descriptions, more than two or three but not more than 10.

sheath—Tubular, inrolled base of a leaf blade or petiole that surrounds the node and a portion of the internode; e.g., in the Cyperaceae, Poaceae, and many other monocotyledons.

shingle leaves—Broadly overlapping, simple, juvenile leaves that are markedly different from adult leaves of the same species;

e.g., in certain species of Araceae and *Marcgravia* spp. (Marcgraviaceae).

shrub—A woody plant that is branched at the base or unbranched but less than 2 meters tall. The difference between unbranched shrubs and treelets is sometimes unclear. Compare with treelet and tree.

sigmoid—S-shaped.

silicle—A fruit similar to a silique but scarcely, if at all, longer than wide, characteristic of some species of Brassicaceae. Compare with silique.

silique—An elongate (usually more than twice as long as wide), capsular fruit with two seed chambers and a persistent replum, characteristic of some species of Brassicaceae. Compare with silicle.

siltation—The deposition of silt.

simple—Referring to an organ, such as a leaf, that is not divided into smaller units. Opposite of compound.

simple pistil—A gynoecium composed of a single carpel.

sinistrorse—Twisted from the right to the left (counterclockwise) as viewed from above; e.g., the petals in a floral bud. Opposite of dextrorse.

sinuate—See undulate.

sinus—The space or recess between two lobes of a leaf, petal, or other expanded organ.

slash—A tangential cut through the outer and inner barks that exposes many characters useful in tree identification. See blaze.

sordid—Of a dull, dingy, or muddy color.

sp. (plural = spp.)—Abbreviation for species.

spadix (plural = spadices)—A congested spike with very small flowers that often is subtended by a spathe; e.g., the inflorescences of Araceae.

spathaceous—Spathelike; in the Bignoniaceae, referring to the split calyx found in some species.

spathe—A conspicuous bract that subtends or surrounds a spadix; in the Araceae, the lower part is called the tube and the upper part the blade; in Arecaceae the large, often woody bract derived from either the prophyll or peduncular bract.

spathella—Saclike covering of the young flowers of Podostemaceae.

spatulate (spathulate)—Shaped like a spatula, rounded above and narrowed to the base.

spicate—Referring to a spikelike inflorescence or a plant with a spikelike inflorescence.

spike—An indeterminate, unbranched inflorescence with sessile flowers and the uppermost flowers the youngest. Compare with raceme.

spikelet—A small secondary spike, such as the basic unit of the inflorescence of Cyperaceae and Poaceae; a spikelike branch of a compound inflorescence of the Bromeliaceae.

spine—A sharp-pointed modified leaf or part of a leaf; e.g., in some species of Cactaceae; in Arecaceae all sharp outgrowths, regardless of origin, are called spines. Compare with prickle and thorn.

spirally arranged—Referring to alternate leaves or other organs inserted at intervals around a stem or some other axis.

spirodistichous—Referring to a type of leaf arrangement in which the leaves are initially distichous but later appear spirally arranged.

spiromonostichous—Leaves inserted in a continuous spiral; typical of the Costaceae.

spirotristichous—Referring to a type of leaf arrangement in the Velloziaceae in which the leaves are initially tristichous but later appear spirally arranged.

splinter hair—A modified, barbed hair with a sharp, retrorsely barbed tip.

sporangium (plural = sporangia)—A chamber in which spores are produced.

spore—A reproductive cell.

sporogenous—Bearing or producing spores.

sporophyll—A leaf on which are borne sporangia.

sporophyte—The spore-producing, diploid (*2n*) phase of a plant's life cycle. Compare with gametophyte.

spur—A tubular, usually nectar-producing outgrowth of a part of a flower; e.g., the sepal in some Vochysiaceae.

squama (plural = squamae)—A scale.

squamate—Covered with scales.

squamella (plural = squamellae)—A small scale.

ssp—See subsp.

stamen—The male part of the flower comprised of the filament and the anther.

staminate—Referring to unisexual flowers with functional stamens but without functional gynoecia (pistillodes may be present).

staminode, staminodium (plural = staminodia)—A sterile stamen, sometimes modified such that it does not resemble a stamen; e.g., Cannaceae.

standard—The upper, broad petal of Fabaceae. Same as banner, flag, and vexillum.

steady state—A flowering strategy in which a few flowers are produced each day over a long period of time.

stele—The vascular cylinder of the stem or root.

stellate—Star-shaped, usually referring to trichomes.

stemonozone—In the Mimosaceae, a tube formed by the adnation of the corolla and filaments.

stenopalynous—Referring to plant taxa characterized by only slight variation in pollen forms; e.g., Gunneraceae.

stick-tight—A fruit or seed that adheres to substrates such as fur or clothing.

stigma—The part of the gynoecium receptive to pollen.

stilt roots—See prop roots.

stipe—See gynophore; in some Orchidaceae, a nonsticky tissue derived from the column and connecting the pollinia to the viscidium.

stipel—Stipule of a leaflet, such as found in some legumes; an outgrowth at the base of the leaf blade in some species of Euphorbiaceae; e.g., *Aparisthmium cordatum*.

stipellate—Bearing stipels.

stipitate—Having a stipe.

stipulate—Possessing stipules.

stipule—A reduced leaflike or bractlike appendage, either solitary or paired, inserted at the base of the petiole and variable in morphology.

stipule cap—In some Rubiaceae (e.g., *Duroia*), the structure formed by the fusion of the stipules; it covers the apical buds and usually falls off as soon as the bud develops.

stipule persistence—In the Rubiaceae, the persistency of the stipules provides a useful character for identifying genera and subgenera. Readily caducous stipules are present only when the leaves are in bud; caducous stipules are present during leaf development but fall before the leaves fall; and persistent stipules are still present after the leaves of their node fall.

stolon—A horizontal stem that is located above the ground and usually produces adventitious roots and vertical stems at the nodes.

stoloniferous—Bearing stolons.

stomatal crypt—A pit, usually on the abaxial leaf surface, in which the stomates of some species occur.

stomate—A small opening, usually in the abaxial surface of leaves, through which gases utilized and produced in photosynthesis pass into and out of the plant.

stone—See pyrene.

stone cell—A short, roughly isodiametric sclereid.

stramineous—Strawlike or straw-colored.

strangler—A plant that grows upon another plant in such a way that its roots surround the host and eventually cause it to die; e.g., in various species of *Ficus* (Moraceae).

striate—With fine striations.

striation—A fine longitudinal line, ridge, or groove.

strigose (diminutive = strigulose)—With sharp, stiff, often basally swollen, appressed, straight hairs.

strobiliform—Resembling a strobilus, often referring to an inflorescence.

strobilus (plural = strobili)—A compact cluster of sporophylls that are well differentiated from the vegetative leaves.

strophiole—A seed appendage located near the hilum or raphe. Compare with caruncle.

stylar collar—An annular expansion on the style; e.g., in some species of Melastomataceae and *Lecythis zabucajo* (Lecythidaceae).

style—The part of the gynoecium between the ovary and the stigma.

style head—The expanded distal part of the style, including the stigma, in some species of Apocynaceae. Same as clavuncle.

styloid—Slender and pointed, needlelike.

stylopodium—An enlargement at the base of the style as in some species of Apiaceae and Lamiaceae.

sub-—A prefix meaning "below," "less than," or "subordinate."

subclass—A unit of classification, a subdivision of a class; e.g., the Magnoliidae and Asteridae are two of the six subclasses of the class Magnoliopsida, according to the system of Cronquist (1981).

subshrub—A plant that is intermediate between a herb and a shrub and slightly woody only at the base; a perennial plant woody only at the base. Same as suffrutex.

subsp—Abbreviation for subspecies; e.g., *Heliconia acuminata* subsp. *acuminate* (Heliconiaceae). Same as ssp.

subulate—Awl-shaped.

succulent—Fleshy and juicy.

sucker—A secondary shoot arising from the base of a tree or shrub or from the bases of many monocots.

suffrutescent—Adjectival form of suffrutex.

suffrutex (plural = suffrutices)—See subshrub.

sulcate—Furrowed or grooved; e.g., the trunk of some species of *Aspidosperma* (Apocynaceae). Same as fluted.

sulcus (plural = sulci)—A furrow or groove.

superior ovary—An ovary of a hypogynous or perigynous flower in which the floral parts arise from beneath or around the ovary or from the rim of a hypanthium. Compare with inferior ovary.

superposed—One structure placed over another.

supervolute—Referring to a type of leaf vernation in which the blade margins are unequally inrolled adaxially such that one of the margins overlaps the other. Compare with involute.

suture—A line of fusion (e.g., the valves of the carpels of an ovary) or a line of dehiscence (e.g., the lines along which anthers or fruits open).

syconium (plural = syconia)—A hollow, fruitlike receptacle lined by tiny achenes, characteristic of figs (*Ficus* spp., Moraceae).

symbiotic—Referring to two different organisms living together in close association.

symmetric—Referring to a structure that can be divided into mirror-image halves. Opposite of asymmetric; compare with actinomorphic and zygomorphic.

sympatric—Referring to species that have overlapping geographic ranges.

sympetalous—Having petals united for at least part of their length. Opposite of polypetalous. Same as gamopetalous.

sympodial—Referring to a branching pattern in which the terminal bud ceases to grow and growth is continued from a lateral bud; e.g., in most arborescent Combretaceae.

synandrium (plural = synandria)—The structure resulting from the cohesion of the anthers of separate male flowers in some Araceae; an androecium with united filaments; e.g., Campanulaceae.

synandroidium (plural = synandroidia)—A structure formed by the coherence of staminodes of separate flowers in some Araceae.

synandrous—Having united anthers.

synapomorphic—Referring to a derived feature shared by two or more taxa that indicates common ancestry.

syncarp—A type of multiple fruit resulting from the fusion of numerous ovaries.

syncarpous—Composed of connate carpels.

syncephalous—Referring to an inflorescence of fused capitula.

synflorescence—A number of separate inflorescences clustered such that they appear as a single inflorescence; e.g., in *Monotagma* spp. (Marantaceae).

syngynesious anthers—Anthers cohering in a ring; e.g., in the Asteraceae.

synsepalous—Having sepals united for at least part of their length. Same as gamosepalous.

tanniferous—Containing or yielding tannin.

tannin—General term for a heterogeneous group of secondary, water-soluble plant compounds derived from phenols that often give a dark appearance to the cells in which they are found.

taproot—A large primary root, markedly larger than other roots arising from it, that may persist in adult plants and is characteristic of dicots. Compare with fibrous roots.

taxon (plural = taxa)—A taxonomic unit regardless of rank, such as family, genus, or species.

tendril—A usually coiled extension of a stem or part of a leaf or inflorescence that assists in climbing.

tendrillate—Bearing tendrils or tendril-like structures.

tenuinucellar—Referring to a nucellus composed of the epidermis and an embryo sac. Compare with crassinucellar.

tepal—A segment of a perianth in which the sepals and petals are not clearly differentiated; a segment of a perianth whose origin as either sepal or petal is not known. Sometimes staminodes resemble tepals or petals (e.g., Aizoaceae)

tepui—A Spanish term referring to the flat-topped mountains of Venezuela, Colombia, Guyana, and Suriname that are dominated by a highly endemic flora.

terete—Circular in transverse section.

ternate—In groupings of three; e.g., the ternately compound leaves of some species of Sapindaceae.

terra firme—A Portuguese term referring to land not subject to periodic flooding.

terrestrial—Growing upon the ground, referring to a plant with its root system anchored in the ground.

tessellate—Arranged in small squares or patterned like a checkerboard.

testa—See seed coat.

tetra-—A prefix meaning four.

tetrad—A group of four units, such as pollen grains.

tetradynamous—Having four long stamens and two short stamens; e.g., in Brassicaceae.

tetragonal—Four-angled.

thalloid—A generalized term used to describe the prostrate axis of a plant when demarcation into stem, leaf, and root is not obvious.

theca (plural = thecae)—The chamber of an anther in which the pollen is produced.

thorn—A sharp-pointed, aborted branch that is woody and has vascular tissue. Compare with prickle and spine.

three-ranked—See tristichous.

thrum flower—One of two types of flowers found in some species in which the style is short and the stamens are long. Compare with pin flower; see also heterostyly.

thyrse—An inflorescence in which the main axis is indeterminate and the lateral axes are determinate; i.e., a raceme of cymes.

thyrsiform—Like a thyrse.

tomentose (diminutive = tomentellous)—Densely woolly; with a soft, wool-like pubescence.

tomentum—A covering of short, soft, matted, or tangled hairs.

torus—The receptacle of a flower or head of flowers.

translator (translator arm)—In the Apocynaceae subfamily Asclepiadoideae and Orchidaceae, the structure connecting the pollinia to the gland. Same as caudicle.

translucent—Transmitting light.

transverse section—A cut at right angles to the axis of an organ. Same as cross section.

trap line pollination—Movement of a pollinator from the flowers of one plant to the flowers of another plant on a specific route.

trapeziform—In the shape of a four-sided figure with only two parallel sides (a trapezoid).

tree—An erect, usually single-stemmed, woody plant 5 centimeters or more dbh; some trees may have multiple trunks but at least some of them are 5 centimeters or more in diameter. Compare with treelet.

treelet—An erect, single-stemmed, woody plant less than 5 centimeters dbh and more than 2 meters tall; differences between treelets and unbranched shrubs or trees are sometimes unclear. Compare with shrub and tree.

tri-—A prefix meaning three.

triad—In palms, a group (structurally a short cincinnus) of two lateral staminate flowers and a central pistillate flower.

trichilium (plural = trichilia)—A pad of densely clustered trichomes located at the abaxial base of the petiole of some species of *Cecropia* (Cecropiaceae) and containing Muellerian bodies that are a source of food for ants.

trichome—A hairlike outgrowth of the epidermis.

trichosclereid—A branched schlerenchymatous cell with thin, hairlike extensions into the intercellular spaces.

trichotomy—A division into three parts.

tricolpate—Referring to a pollen grain with three colpi.

tricolporate—Referring to a pollen grain with three pores situated within three colpi.

tridioecious—Referring to the sexual condition of a species that bears only staminate flowers on some plants, only pistillate flowers on some plants, and staminate plus pistillate flowers or bisexual flowers on other plants.

trifid—Split into three parts.

trifoliolate—With three leaflets.

trigonous—Three-angled.

trilocular—With three locules; e.g., an ovary.

trimonoecius—See polygamomonoecious.

trinucleate pollen—Referring to pollen grains that have three nuclei when shed from the anthers. Compare with binucleate pollen.

triplivenation—With three ± equal, longitudinal veins.

triquetrous—Triangular in transverse section.

trisect—Divided into three parts.

tristichous—Three-ranked or in three rows. Compare with distichous and polystichous.

tristyly (tristylous)—The condition in which three different style lengths and corresponding stamen lengths are found in the same species.

trullate—Trowel-shaped.

truncate—Referring to an apex or base that terminates abruptly in a nearly straight horizontal edge.

trunk—In trees, the unbranched portion of the stem. Same as bole.

tube—A chamber formed by the fusion of separate parts; e.g., the corolla tube or the tube of the spathe in Araceae.

tuber—An underground, swollen part of a stem that functions in food storage.

tubercle—The modified and persistent style base of some Cyperaceae.

tuberculate—Covered with warty outgrowths; e.g., the fruit of *Canna indica* (Cannaceae).

tunic—the outer, dry and papery covering of a bulb or corm.

tunicate—Possessing a tunic.

turbinate—Obconical or top-shaped.

turion—An underground bud or shoot characteristic of aquatic plants that enables them to overwinter.

two-ranked—See distichous.

-ulate—A suffix serving as a diminutive modifier of an adjective; e.g., mucronulate is the diminutive of mucronate.

umbel—A flat-topped or convex-topped inflorescence with all pedicels arising from the same point. Compound umbels are typical of the Apiaceae and some species of Araliaceae and Smilacaceae.

umbellate—Like an umbel.

umbo—A relatively small protrusion usually in the middle of a structure; e.g., the operculum of a fruit.

umbonate—Referring to a structure that possesses an umbo.

uncinate, uncate—Hooked at the apex.

understory—A hypothetical stratum in the forest consisting of the crowns of trees found below the canopy and usually less than 20–25 meters tall at maturity.

undulate—Wavy.

unguiculate—See clawed.

uni-—A prefix meaning one.

unifacial—Referring to a leaf with the same type of tissue on each side as observed in a transverse section.

unifoliate—Referring to a plant with one leaf.

unifoliolate—With a single leaflet (sometimes appearing as a simple leaf).

unilocular—With a single locule.

uniseriate—Occurring in a single whorl or row such as a perianth composed of either the calyx or the corolla; e.g., that of Thymelaeaceae.

unisexual—Referring to a flower with either functional stamens or functional gynoecia but not both. Same as imperfect.

unitegumic—Referring to ovules with one integument.

upper—See adaxial.

urceolate—Urn-shaped.

urticaceous stamens—Stamens that spring forward to release pollen at anthesis; typical of the flowers of the Urticaceae and some related families.

urticant—Causing itching or stinging when touched.

utricle—A small, one-seeded, somewhat inflated, usually indehiscent fruit; e.g., in some species of Caryophyllaceae, Lemnaceae, and Plumbaginaceae; the inflated basal chamber formed by the perianth of *Aristolochia* (Aristolochiaceae); in Cyperaceae, see perigynium.

utriculate—In the shape of a bladder.

vacuole—A space or cavity within the cell.

vaginate—Possessing a sheath; e.g., used to describe the petiole base of some species of *Piper*.

valvate—A type of aestivation in which the edges of the sepals and petals meet exactly and do not overlap (compare with imbricate); referring to the opening of an anther by small flaps; e.g., in Lauraceae.

var—Abbreviation for variety, a subdivision of species.

variegated—Having streaks, marks, or patches of different colors; e.g., the immature leaves of some species of *Calathea* (Marantaceae) and several species of *Psychotria* (Rubiaceae), and the mature leaves of *Cyclopogon olivaceus* (Orchidaceae).

várzea—A Portuguese term referring to forest growing in areas periodically indundated by alkaline, café au lait-colored water.

vascular—Referring to the xylem and phloem.

vegetative—The nonfloral parts of a plant; a nonsexual means of reproduction.

veinlet—See venule.

velamen—A spongy covering of one or two layers of cells on roots; e.g., Orchidaceae and Araceae.

velum—Membranous flap of tissue; in *Siparuna* (Siparunaceae), a perforated flap of tissue at the apex of the flower.

velutinous—Velvety; covered with short, soft, spreading hairs.

ventral—See adaxial.

ventricose—Inflated or swollen on one side.

venule—A small vein. Same as veinlet.

vermiform—Wormlike.

vermifuge—A substance that expels intestinal worms.

vernation—The arrangement of leaves in the bud.

verrucose (diminutive = verruculose)—Warty.

versatile anthers—Anthers that can be moved freely on the apices of their filaments.

verticil—A whorl of structures; e.g., leaves or bracts.

verticillaster—A pair of cymes arising from the axils of opposite leaves or bracts such that they falsely appear to be in a verticil; e.g., in some Acanthaceae and Lamiaceae.

verticillate—See whorled.

vesicle—Small bladderlike structure; e.g., the formicaria of some some Melastomataceae.

vesicular—Of or pertaining to vesicles.

vestigial—Rudimentary.

vestiture—The epidermal outgrowths or coverings.

vexillum—See standard.

villous—Provided with long, soft hairs.

vine—A nonwoody, climbing plant; some authors do not distinguish between liana and vine. Compare with liana.

violaceous—Blue-red but nearer to blue than to red.

virgate—Long, slender, and straight like some twigs.

viscid—Sticky.

viscidium—In the Orchidaceae, a sticky part of the rostellum that is removed with the pollinia as a unit and serves to attach the pollinia to the dispersal agent.

viscin—A sticky substance surrounding the seeds of some plants (e.g., species of Eremolepidaceae and Viscaceae) or found in threads associated with pollen (e.g., Ericaceae and Onagraceae).

viscous—Having a relatively high resistance to flow; thick and usually sticky.

vitta (plural = vittae)—An oil tube in the ovary walls of fruits of Apiaceae.

viviparous—Germinating while still attached to the parent plant.

voucher—A herbarium specimen used to document the identification of a species of plant in anatomical, ecological, economic, medicinal, and taxonomic studies.

whorled—Arising from an axis in groups of more than two at the same node; e.g., leaves from a stem. Same as verticillate. Compare with alternate and opposite.

wing—Either of the two lateral petals of a flower of Fabaceae; a thin, flattened outgrowth from stemes, petioles, fruits, or seeds.

witch's broom—A type of fungal infection that causes the host to produce anomalous growth that bears a remote resemblance to a broom.

within—When used to indicate position equals adaxial. See adaxial.

without—When used to indicate position equals abaxial. See abaxial.

xenogamous, xenogamy—Referring to the fertilization of the ovules of a flower by pollen from a flower on a different plant. Compare with geitonogamous.

xeric—Referring to dry habitats.

xylem—The water- and mineral-conducting tissue of plants.

xylopodium (plural = xylopodia)—An underground, woody, storage organ derived from stems or roots and common in cerrado vegetation.

zygomorphic—Capable of being divided only into two equal parts; a structure (e.g., a flower) in which a line drawn through the middle will produce a mirror image of one side of the line to the other side. Opposite of actinomorphic; same as bilaterally symmetrical and irregular.

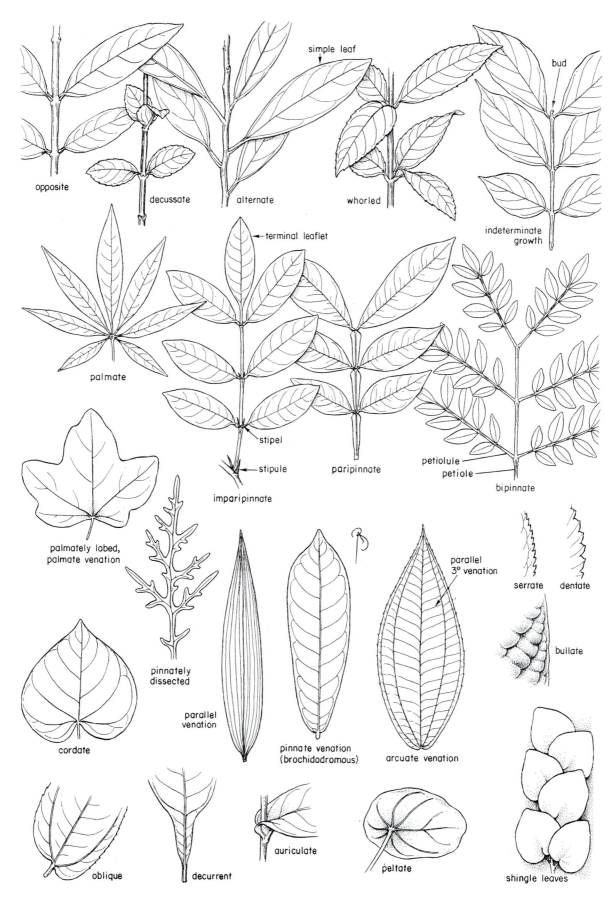

Figure 257. Features of leaves of the flowering plant families of the American Tropics.

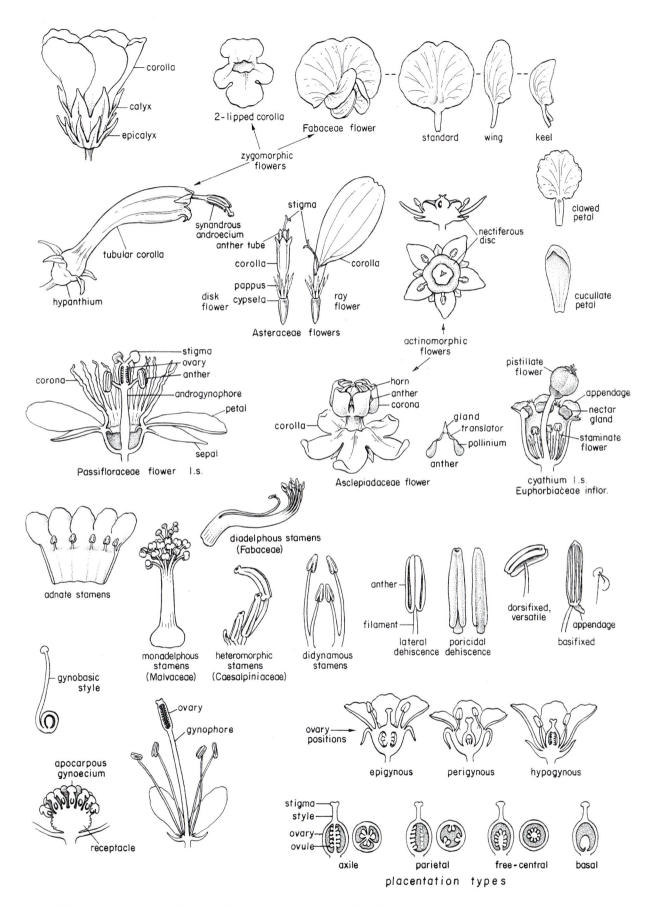

Figure 258. Features of flowers of the flowering plant families of the American Tropics.

LITERATURE CITED

ACEVEDO-RODRÍGUEZ, P. 1996. Flora of St. John. US. Virgin Islands. *Mem. New York Bot. Gard.* 78:1–581.

———. In press. *Bejucos y plantas sarmentosas de Puerto Rico y Islas Virgenes.*

ANGIOSPERM PHYLOGENY GROUP (APG). 1998. An ordinal classification for the families of flowering plants. *Ann. Missouri Bot. Gard.* 85:531–43.

AUBLET, C. F. 1775. *Histoire des plantes de la Guiane Françoise*, 4 vols. Paris: Dido.

BALICK, M. J., AND P. A. COX. 1996. *Plants, people, and culture. The science of Ethnobotany.* New York: Scientific American Library.

BALSLEV, H. 1983. New taxa and combinations in Neotropical *Juncus* (Juncaceae). *Brittonia* 35(3):302–08.

BELL, A. D. 1991. *Plant Form: An Illustrated Guide to Flowering Plant Morphology.* New York: Oxford University Press.

BERNAL, H. Y., AND J. E. CORRERA Q. 1989. *Especies vegetales promisorias de los países del Convenio Andrés Bello*, Tomo II. Bogotá, D. E., Colombia: Secretaria Ejecutiva del Convenio Andrés Bello.

———. 1990. *Especies vegetales promisorias de los países del Convenio Andrés Bello*, Tomo IV. Bogotá, D. E., Colombia: Secretaria Ejecutiva del Convenio Andrés Bello.

———. 1991. *Especies vegetales promisorias de los países del Convenio Andrés Bello*, Tomo VI. Santafé de Bogotá, D. E., Colombia: Secretaria Ejecutiva del Convenio Andrés Bello.

———. 1992. *Especies vegetales promisorias de los países del Convenio Andrés Bello*, Tomo VIII. Santafé de Bogotá, D. E., Colombia: Secretaria Ejecutiva del Convenio Andrés Bello.

———. 1994. *Especies vegetales promisorias de los países del Convenio Andrés Bello*, Tomo X. Santafé de Bogotá, D. E., Colombia: Secretaria Ejecutiva del Convenio Andrés Bello.

———. 1998. *Especies vegetales promisorias de los países del Convenio Andrés Bello*, Tomo XII. Santafé de Bogotá, D. E., Colombia: Secretaria Ejecutiva del Convenio Andrés Bello.

BORROR, D. J. 1985. *Dictionary of Word Roots and Combining Forms.* Palo Alto, CA: Mayfield Publishing Company.

BRIDSON, G.D.R., AND E. R. SMITH, eds. 1991. *Botanico-Periodicum-Huntianum/Supplementum.* Pittsburgh: Hunt Institute for Botanical Documentaion, Carnegie Mellon University.

BROWN, J. H., AND M. V. LOMOLINO. 1998. Biogeography, 2nd ed. Sunderland, MA: Sinauer Associates, Inc.

CHASE, M. W., D. E. SOLTIS, R. G. OLMSTEAD, D. MORGAN, D. H. LES, ET AL. 1993. Phylogenetics of seed plants: an analysis of nucleotide sequences from the plastid gene *rbc*L. *Ann. Missouri Bot. Gard.* 80:528–80.

CHASE, M. W., D. E. SOLTIS, P. S. SOLTIS, P. J. RUDALL, M. F. FAY, ET AL. 2000. Higher-level systematics of the monocotyledons: an assessment of current knowledge and a new classification. In *Monocots: Systematics and Evolution*, eds. K. L. Wilson and D. A. Morrison, 3–16. Collingswood, Victoria, Australia: CSIRO Publishing.

CHASE, M. W., D. W. STEVENSON, P. WILKEN, AND P. RUDALL. 1995. Monocot systematics: a combined analysis. In *Monocotyledons: Systematics and Evolution*, eds. P. Rudall, P. Cribb, D. Cutler, and C. Humphries, 685–730. Richmond, Surrey, U.K.: Royal Botanic Gardens, Kew.

CLIFFORD, H. T., AND P. F. YEO. 1985. *The Families of Monocotyledons: Structure, Evolution and Taxonomy.* New York: Springer-Verlag.

CORRELL, D. S., AND H. B. CORRELL. 1982. *Flora of the Bahama Archipelago (Including the Turks and Caicos Islands).* Vaduz: J. Cramer.

CORRERA Q., J. E., AND H. Y. BERNAL. 1989. *Especies vegetales promisorias de los países del Convenio Andrés Bello*, Tomo I. Bogotá, D. E., Colombia: Secretaria Ejecutiva del Convenio Andrés Bello.

———. 1990. *Especies vegetales promisorias de los países del Convenio Andrés Bello*, Tomo V. Bogotá, D. E., Colombia: Secretaria Ejecutiva del Convenio Andrés Bello.

———. 1992. *Especies vegetales promisorias de los países del Convenio Andrés Bello*, Tomo VII. Santafé de Bogotá, D. E., Colombia: Secretaria Ejecutiva del Convenio Andrés Bello.

———. 1993. *Especies vegetales promisorias de los países del Convenio Andrés Bello*, Tomo IX. Santafé de Bogotá, D. E., Colombia: Secretaria Ejecutiva del Convenio Andrés Bello.

———. 1995. *Especies vegetales promisorias de los países del Convenio Andrés Bello*, Tomo XI. Santafé de Bogotá, D. E., Colombia: Secretaria Ejecutiva del Convenio Andrés Bello.

CRONQUIST, A. 1981. *An Integrated System of Classification of Flowering Plants.* New York: Columbia University Press.

———. 1988. *The Evolution and Classification of Flowering Plants.* New York: The New York Botanical Garden.

DAHLGREN, R.M.T. 1980. A revised system of classification of the Angiosperms. *Bot. J. Linn. Soc.* 80:91–124.

DAHLGREN, R.M.T., H. T. CLIFFORD, AND P. F. YEO. 1985. *The Families of the Monocotyledons.* Berlin: Springer-Verlag.

DOYLE, J. A., M. J. DONOGHUE, AND G.E.A. ZIMMER. 1994. Integration of morphological and ribosomal RNA data on the origin of angiosperms. *Ann. Missouri Bot. Gard.* 81:419–50.

EHRENDORFER, F., F. KRENDL, E. HABELER, AND W. SAUER. 1968. Chromosome numbers and evolution in primitive angiosperms. *Taxon* 17:337–53.

ENDRESS, P. K. 1994. *Diversity and Evolutionary Biology of Tropical Flowers.* Cambridge, U.K.: Cambridge University Press.

———. 1995. Major evolutionary traits of monocot flowers. In *Monocotyledons: Systematics and Evolution*, eds. P. Rudall, P. Cribb, D. Cutler, and C. Humphries, 43–80. Richmond, Surrey, U.K.: Royal Botanic Gardens, Kew.

ESAU, K. 1977. *Anatomy of Seed Plants*, 2nd ed. New York: John Wiley & Sons.

FAEGRI, K., AND L. VAN DER PIJL. 1979. *The Principles of Pollination Ecology*, 3rd. rev. ed. Oxford, U.K.: Pergamon Press.

FRODIN, D. G. 2001. *Guide to Standard Floras of the World: An Annotated Geographically Arranged Systematic Bibliography of the Principal Floras, Enumerations, Checklists, and Chorologi-*

cal Atlases of Different Areas, 2nd. ed. Cambridge, U.K., and New York: Cambridge University Press.

GENTRY, A. H. 1993. A Field Guide to the Families and Genera of Woody Plants of Northwest South America (Colombia, Ecuador, Peru). Chicago, IL: The University of Chicago Press.

GIFFORD, E. M., AND A. S. FOSTER. 1989. Morphology and Evolution of Vascular Plants. New York: W. H. Freeman and Company.

GLEDHILL, D. 2002. The Names of Plants, 3rd ed. New York: Cambridge University Press.

GÓMEZ-LAURITO, J., AND L. D. GÓMEZ P. 1989. Ticodendron: A new tree from Central America. Ann. Missouri. Bot. Gard. 76(4): 1148–51.

HAMMEL, B. E., AND N. A. ZAMORA. 1993. Ruptiliocarpon (Lepidobotryaceae): a new arborescent genus and tropical American link to Africa, with a reconsideration of the family. Novon 3(4): 408–17.

HARRIS, J. G., AND M. WOOLF HARRIS. 1994. Plant Identification Terminology. An Illustrated Glossary. Spring Lake, UT: Spring Lake Publishing.

HENDERSON, A., AND G. GALEANO. 1996. Euterpe, Prestoa, and Neonicholsonia (Palmae). Fl. Neotrop. Monogr. 72:1–89.

HEYWOOD V. H. (consult. ed.). 1993. Flowering Plants of the World. New York: Oxford University Press.

HEYWOOD, V. H., AND S. D. DAVIS. 1997. Introduction. In Centres of Plant Diversity, eds. S. D. Davis, V. H. Heywood, O. Herrera-MacBryde, J. Villa-Lobos, and A. C. Hamilton. Cambridge, U.K.: The World Wide Fund for Nature.

HICKEY, M., AND C. KING. 2000. The Cambridge Illustrated Glossary of Botanical Terms. Cambridge, U.K.: Cambridge University Press.

HILL, A. F. 1937. Economic Botany: A Textbook of Useful Plants and Plant Products. New York: McGraw-Hill.

HOEHNE, F. C., M. KUHLMANN, AND O. HANDRO. 1941. O jardim botânico de São Paulo. Secretário da Agricultura, Indústria e Comércio de São Paulo, Brazil.

HUTCHINSON, J. 1926. The Families of Flowering Plants. Vol.1, Dicotyledons. London: Macmillan.

———. 1959. The Families of Flowering Plants. 1. Dicotyledons, ed. 2. London: Oxford University Press.

———. 1967. The Genera of Flowering Plants. Volume 2. Oxford, U.K.: Clarendon Press.

———. 1973. The Families of Flowering Plants. Oxford, U.K.: Clarendon Press.

———. 1980. Genera of Flowering Plants, vol. II. Koenigstein, Germany: Otto Koeltz Science Pub.

HUTCHINSON. V. H. 1993. Flowering Plants of the World. New York: Oxford University Press.

JACQUIN, N.J.F. VON. 1760. Enumeratio systematica plantarum, quas in insulis Caribaeis vicinaque Americes continente detexit novas, aut jam cognitas emendavit. Lugduni Batavorum.

JUDD, W. S., C. S. CAMPBELL, E. A. KELLOGG, P. F. STEVENS, AND M. J. DONOGHUE. 2002. Plant Systematics: A Phylogenetic Approach, 2nd ed. Sunderland, MA: Sinauer Associates, Inc.

JUDD, W. S., R. W. SANDERS, AND M. J. DONOGHUE. 1994. Angiosperm family pairs: preliminary phylogenetic analysis. Harvard Pap. Bot. 5:1–51.

KELLER, R. 1996. Identification of Tropical Woody Plants in the Absence of Flowers and Fruits: A Field Guide. Boston, MA: Birkhäuser.

KIGER, R. W., AND D. M. PORTER. 2001. Categorical Glossary for the Flora of North America Project. Hunt Institute for Botanical Documentation. Pittsburgh: Carnegie Mellon University.

KUBITZKI, K. 1998a. The Families and Genera of Vascular Plants. Vol. 3. Flowering Plants, Monocotyledons: Lilianae (except Orchidaceae). Berlin: Springer-Verlag.

———. 1998b. The Families and Genera of Vascular Plants. Vol. 4. Flowering Plants, Monocotyledons: Alismatanae and Commelinanae (except Gramineae). Berlin: Springer-Verlag.

KUBITZKI, K., AND C. BAYER, EDS. 2003. The families and genera of vascular plants. Vol. 5. Flowering plants, Dicotyledons: Malvales, Capparales and non-betalain Caryophyllales. Berlin: Springer-Verlag.

KUBITZKI, K., J. G. ROHWER, AND V. BITTRICH, EDS. 1993. The Families and Genera of Vascular Plants. Vol. 2. Flowering Plants, Dicotyledons: Magnoliid, Hamamelid and Caryophyllid Families. Berlin: Springer-Verlag.

KUIJT, J. 1969. The Biology of Parasitic Flowering Plants. Berkeley and Los Angeles: University of California Press.

LAWRENCE, G.H.M. 1951. Taxonomy of Vascular Plants. New York: The Macmillan Company.

LAWRENCE, G.H.M., A.F.G. BUCHHEIM, G. S. DANIELS, AND H. DOLEZAL, EDS. 1968. Botanico-Periodicum-Huntianum. Pittsburgh, PA: Hunt Botanical Library.

LINNAEUS, C. 1775. Plantae Surinamenses 17. Uppsala, Sweden.

LONDOÑO, A. C., E. ALVAREZ, E. FORERO, AND C. M. MORTON. 1995. A new genus and species of Dipterocarpaceae from the neotropics. I. Introduction, taxonomy, ecology, and distribution. Brittonia 47(3):225–36.

MAAS, P.J.M., AND Y. TH. WESTRA. 1998. Neotropical Plant Families: A Concise Guide to Families of Vascular Plants in the Neotropics, 2d ed. Koenigstein, Germany: Koeltz Scientific Books.

MABBERLEY, D. J. 1993. The Plant-book. Cambridge, U.K.: Cambridge University Press.

MAGUIRE, B. 1972. Bonnetiaceae. In The botany of the Guayana highland—Part IX, B. Maguire and collaborators. Mem. New York Bot. Gard. 23:131–65.

———. 1978. Sarraceniaceae. In The botany of the Guayana highland—Part X, B. Maguire and collaborators. Mem. New York Bot. Gard. 29:36–62.

MAGUIRE, B., AND J. A. STEYERMARK. 1981. Tepuianthaceae, Sapindales. In The botany of the Guayana highland—Part XI, B. Maguire and collaborators. Mem. New York Bot. Gard. 32:4–21.

———. 1989. Cunoniaceae. In The Botany of the Guayana Highland—Part XIII, Maguire and collaborators. Mem. New York Bot. Gard. 51:117–18.

MARCGRAVE, G. 1648. In G. Piso and G. Marcgrave, Historia naturalis brasiliae, auspicio et benefico illustris I. Mauritii Com. Nassau, Leiden.

MARTIUS, K.F.P. VON. 1860–1906. Flora brasiliensis. München, Wien, Leipzig.

MITCHELL, J. D. 1997. Anacardiaceae. In Flora of the Guianas, eds. A.R.A. Görts-van Rijn and M. J. Jansen-Jacobs, ser. A, 19: 1–47.

MORI, S. A., G. CREMERS, C. GRACIE, J.-J. DE GRANVILLE, S. V. HEALD, ET AL. 2002. Guide to the vascular plants of central French Guiana. Part 2. Dicotyledons. Mem. New York Bot. Gard. 76(2):1–900.

MORI, S. A., G. CREMERS, C. GRACIE, J.-J. DE GRANVILLE, M. HOFF, AND J. D. MITCHELL. 1997. Guide to the vascular plants of central French Guiana. Part 1. Pteridophytes, gymnosperms, and monocotyledons. *Mem. New York Bot. Gard.* 76(1):1–422.

MORI, S. A., AND J. A. KALLUNKI. 1977. A revision of the genus *Phyllonoma* (Grossulariaceae). *Brittonia* 29:69–84.

MORI, S. A., AND G. T. PRANCE. 1990. Lecythidaceae—Part II: the zygomorphic-flowered New World Genera (*Couroupita, Corythophora, Bertholletia, Couratari, Eschweilera, & Lecythis*). With a study of the secondary xylem of Neotropical Lecythidaceae by Carl de Zeeuw. *Fl. Neotrop. Monogr.* 21:1–376.

NEE, M. 1994. A new species of *Talauma* (Magnoliaceae) from Bolivia. *Brittonia* 46(4):265–69.

———. 1996. A new species of *Acanthosyris* (Santalaceae) from Bolivia and a key to the woody South American Santalaceae. *Brittonia* 48(4):574–79.

NORMAN, E. 1982. Buddlejaceae. In *Flora of Ecuador*, eds. G. Harling and B. Sparre. 16:1–24. Göteborg, Sweden: Department of Systematic Botany, University of Göteborg.

PARRA-O., C. 2000. A new species of *Morella* (Myricaceae) from Bolivia and Argentina. *Brittonia* 52(4):320–24.

PIJL, L. VAN DER. 1982. *Principles of dispersal in higher plants*, 3rd rev. ed. Berlin: Springer-Verlag.

PLANT NAMES PROJECT, THE. 1999. International Plant Names Index. Published on the Internet; http://www.ipni.org.

PROCTOR, M., P. YEO, AND A. LACK. 1996. *The Natural History of Pollination*. Portland, OR: Timber Press.

RIBEIRO, J. E. DA S., M. J. G. HOPKINS, A. VICENTINI, C. A. SOTHERS, M. A. DA S. COSTA, ET AL. 1999. *Flora da Reserva Ducke. Guia de identificação das plantas vasculares de uma floresta de terra-firme na Amazônia central*. The numerous images of Amazonian plants make it useful for the identification of Amazonian plant families. Manaus, Brazil: INPA.

RIDLEY, H. N. 1930. *The Dispersal of Plants Throughout the World*. Ashford, Kent, U.K.: L. Reeve & Co., Ltd.

ROOSMALEN, M.G.M. VAN. 1985. *Fruits of the Guianan Flora*. Utrecht: Institute of Systematic Botany.

RUDALL, P., P. CRIBB, D. CUTLER, AND C. HUMPHRIES. 1995. *Monocotyledons: Systematics and Evolution*. Richmond, Surrey, U.K.: Royal Botanic Gardens, Kew.

SAVOLAINEN, V., M. W. CHASE, S. B. HOOT, C. M. MORTON, D. E. SOLTIS, ET AL. 2000a. Phylogenetics of flowering plants based on combined analysis of plastid *atp*B and *rbc*L gene sequences. *Syst. Biol.* 49:306–62.

SAVOLAINEN, V., M. F. FAY, D. C. ALBACH, A. BACKLUND, M. VAN DER BANK, ET AL. 2000b. Phylogeny of the eudicots: a nearly complete familial analysis based on *rbc*L gene sequences. *Kew Bull.* 55:257–309.

SCHERY, R. W. 1972. *Plants for Man*, 2nd ed. Englewood Cliffs, NJ: Prentice-Hall, Inc.

SIMPSON, B. B. 1989. Krameriaceae. *Fl. Neotrop. Monogr.* 49:1–108.

SIMPSON, B. B., AND M. C. OGORZALY. 1995. *Economic Botany: Plants in Our World*, 2d ed. New York: McGraw-Hill, Inc.

SMITH, N. J. H., J. T. WILLIAMS, D. L. PLUCKNETT, AND J. P. TALBOT. 1992. *Tropical Forests and Their Fruits*. Ithaca, NY: Cornell University Press.

SOLTIS, D. E., P. S. SOLTIS, M. W. CHASE, M. E. MORT, D. C.

ALBACH, ET AL. 2000. Angiosperm phylogeny inferred from 18S rDNA, *rbc*L, and *atp*B sequences *Bot. J. Linn. Soc.* 133:381–461.

STAFLEU, F. A., AND R. S. COWAN. 1976–1988. *Taxonomic Literature*, 2nd ed. Utrecht: Bohn, Scheltema & Holkema.

STEARN, W. T. 1992. *Botanical Latin Newton Abbot*, [England] David & Charles Publishers.

STEVENSON, D. W., AND H. LOCONTE. 1995. Cladistic analysis of monocot families. In *Monocotyledons: Systematics and Evolution*, eds. P. Rudall, P. Cribb, D. Cutler, and C. Humphries, 543–78. Richmond, Surrey, U.K.: Royal Botanic Gardens, Kew.

STEVENS, P. F. (2001 onwards). Angiosperm Phylogeny Website. Version 3, May 2002. http://www.mobot.org/MOBOT/research/APweb/.

STEYERMARK, J. A., AND J. L. LUTEYN. 1980. Revision of the genus *Ochthocosmus* (Linaceae). *Brittonia* 32(2):128–43.

TAKHTAJAN, A. 1980. Outline of the classification of flowering plants (Magnoliophyta). *Bot. Rev.* 46:225–359.

———. 1997. *Diversity and Classification of Flowering Plants*. New York: Columbia University Press.

THORNE, R. F. 1992. *Classification and Geography of the Flowering Plants. Bot. Rev.* 58:225–348.

———. 2001. The classification and geography of the flowering plants: dicotyledons of the class angiospermae (subclasses Magnoliidae, Ranunculidae, Caryophyllidae, Dilleniidae, Rosidae, Asteridae, and Lamiidae). *Bot. Rev.* 66(4):441–647.

TODZIA, C. A. 1988. Chloranthaceae: *Hedyosmum. Fl. Neotrop. Monogr.* 48:1–139.

TOMLINSON, P. B. 1980. *The Biology of Trees Native to Tropical Florida*. Allston, MA: Harvard University Printing Office.

TROPICOS. Missouri Botanical Garden. http://mobot.mobot.org/W3T/Search/vast.html.

UPHOF, J.C.T. 1968. *Dictionary of Economic Plants*. 2nd ed. New York: Lehre, J. Cramer.

VOGEL, S. 1968. Chiropterophilie in der neotropischen Flora. *Neue Mitt. I. Flora, Abst. B* 157: 562–602.

———. 1969. Chiropterophilie in der neotropischen Flora. *Neue Mitt. III. Flora, Abst. B* 158: 289–323.

WATSON, L., AND M. J. DALLWITZ. 1992 onward. The Families of Flowering Plants: Descriptions, Illustrations, Identification, and Information Retrieval. Version: 14 December 2000. http://biodiversity.uno.edu/delta/.

WEBERLING, F. 1981. *Morphology of Flowers and Inflorescences*. Cambridge, U.K.: Cambridge University Press.

WEIGEND, M., AND M. BINDER. 2001. A revision of the genus *Ribes* (Grossulariaceae) in Bolivia. *Bot. Jarhrb. Syst.* 123 (1): 111–34.

WIELGORSKAYA T., AND A. TAKHTAJAN. 1995. *Dictionary of Generic Names of Seed Plants*. New York: Columbia University Press.

WIERSEMA, J. H., AND B. LEÓN. 1999. *World Economic Plants: A Standard Reference Guide*. New York: CRC Press.

WILLIS J. C. 1973 *A Dictionary of the Flowering Plants and Ferns*, 8 ed., revised by H. K. A. Shaw. Cambridge, U.K.: Cambridge University Press.

YATSKIEVYCH, G., AND C. T. MASON. 1986. A revision of the Lennoaceae. *Syst. Bot.* 11(4):531–48.

APPENDIX I

Classification of Dicotyledons *sensu* Cronquist (1981) (Including annotations relative to *Flowering Plants of the Neotropics*)

- Families in bold are treated in *Flowering Plants of the Neotropics*.
- Families not in bold are not native to tropical America and, with exception of Casuarinaceae, Nelumbonaceae, and Pedaliaceae, not treated in *Flowering Plants of the Neotropics*.
- Italicized notes refer to differences between the family circumscriptions of Cronquist and *Flowering Plants of the Neotropics*.

Class **Magnoliopsida**
Subclass 1. **Magnoliidae**
  Order 1. **Magnoliales**
    Family
      1. WINTERACEAE
      2. DEGENERIACEAE
      3. HIMANTANDRACEAE
      4. EUPOMATIACEAE
      5. AUSTROBAILEYACEAE
      6. MAGNOLIACEAE
      7. LACTORIDACEAE
      8. ANNONACEAE
      9. MYRISTACEAE
      10. CANELLACEAE
  Order 2. **Laurales**
    Family
      1. AMBORELLACEAE
      2. TRIMENIACEAE
      3. MONIMIACEAE (*includes taxa in Siparunaceae*)
      4. GOMORTEGACEAE
      5. CALYCANTHACEAE
      6. IDIOSPERMACEAE
      7. LAURACEAE
      8. HERNANDIACEAE
  Order 3. **Piperales**
    Family
      1. CHLORANTHACEAE
      2. SAURURACEAE
      3. PIPERACEAE
  Order 4. **Aristolochiales**
    Family
      1. ARISTOLOCHIACEAE
  Order 5. **Illiciales**
    Family
      1. ILLICIACEAE
      2. SCHISANDRACEAE
  Order 6. **Nymphaeales**
    Family
      1. NELUMBONACEAE (*locally naturalized in tropical America*)
      2. NYMPHAEACEAE
      3. BARCLAYACEAE
      4. CABOMBACEAE
      5. CERATOPHYLLACEAE
  Order 7. **Ranunculales**
    Family
      1. RANUNCULACEAE
      2. CIRCAEASTERACEAE
      3. BERBERIDACEAE
      4. SARGENTODOXACEAE
      5. LARDIZABALACEAE
      6. MENISPERMACEAE
      7. CORIARIACEAE
      8. SABIACEAE
  Order 8. **Papaverales**
    Family

      1. PAPAVERACEAE
      2. FUMARIACEAE

Subclass 2. **Hamamelidae**
  Order 1. Trochodendrales
    Family
      1. TETRACENTRACEAE
      2. TROCHODENDRACEAE
  Order 2. **Hamamelidales**
    Family
      1. CERCIDIPHYLLACEAE
      2. EUPTELIACEAE
      3. PLATANACEAE
      4. HAMAMELIDACEAE
      5. MYROTHAMNACEAE
  Order 3. Daphniphyllales
    Family
      1. DAPHNIPHYLLACEAE
  Order 4. Didymelales
    Family
      1. DIDYMELACEAE
  Order 5. Eucommiales
    Family
      1. EUCOMMIACEAE
  Order 6. **Urticales**
    Family
      1. BARBEYACEAE
      2. ULMACEAE
      3. CANNABACEAE
      4. MORACEAE
      5. CECROPIACEAE
      6. URTICACEAE
  Order 7. Leitneriales
    Family
      1. LEITNERIACEAE
  Order 8. **Juglandales**
    Family
      1. RHOIPTELEACEAE
      2. JUGLANDACEAE
  Order 9. **Myricales**
    Family
      1. MYRICACEAE
  Order 10. **Fagales**
    Family
      1. BALANOPACEAE
      2. FAGACEAE
      3. BETULACEAE
  Order 11. **Casuarinales**
    Family
      1. CASUARINACEAE (*introduced to tropical America*)

Subclass 3. **Caryophyllidae**
  Order 1. **Caryophyllales**
    Family
      1. PHYTOLACCACEAE
      2. ACHATOCARPACEAE

      3. NYCTAGINACEAE
      4. AIZOACEAE
      5. DIDIEREACEAE
      6. CACTACEAE
      7. CHENOPODIACEAE
      8. AMARANTHACEAE
      9. PORTULACACEAE
      10. BASELLACEAE
      11. MOLLUGINACEAE
      12. CARYOPHYLLACEAE
  Order 2. **Polygonales**
    Family
      1. POLYGONACEAE
  Order 3. **Plumbaginales**
    Family
      1. PLUMBAGINACEAE

Subclass 4. **Dilleniidae**
  Order 1. **Dilleniales**
    Family
      1. DILLENIACEAE
      2. PAEONIACEAE
  Order 2. **Theales**
    Family
      1. OCHNACEAE
      2. SPHAEROSEPALACEAE
      3. SARCOLAENACEAE
      4. DIPTEROCARPACEAE
      5. CARYOCARACEAE
      6. THEACEAE (*includes taxa in Bonnetiaceae & Ternstromiaceae*)
      7. ACTINIDIACEAE
      8. SCYTOPETALACEAE
      9. PENTAPHYLACEAE
      10. TETRAMERISTACEAE
      11. PELLICIERACEAE
      12. ONCOTHECACEAE
      13. MARCGRAVIACEAE
      14. QUIINACEAE
      15. ELATINACEAE
      16. PARACRYPHIACEAE
      17. MEDUSAGYNACEAE
      18. CLUSIACEAE
  Order 3. **Malvales**
    Family
      1. ELAEOCARPACEAE
      2. TILIACEAE
      3. STERCULIACEAE
      4. BOMBACACEAE
      5. MALVACEAE
  Order 4. **Lecythidales**
    Family
      1. LECYTHIDACEAE
  Order 5. **Nepenthales**
    Family
      1. SARRACENIACEAE
      2. NEPENTHACEAE

3. DROSERACEAE

Order 6. **Violales**

Family

1. **FLACOURTIACEAE** (*includes taxa in Muntingiaceae*)
2. PERIDISCACEAE
3. **BIXACEAE**
4. **CISTACEAE**
5. HUACEAE
6. **LACISTEMATACEAE**
7. SCYPHOSTEGIACEAE
8. STACHYURACEAE
9. **VIOLACEAE**
10. TAMARICACEAE
11. **FRANKENIACEAE**
12. DIONCOPHYLLACEAE
13. ANCISTROCLADACEAE
14. **TURNERACEAE**
15. **MALESHERBIACEAE**
16. **PASSIFLORACEAE**
17. ACHARIACEAE
18. **CARICACEAE**
19. **FOUQUIERIACEAE**
20. HOPLESTIGMATACEAE
21. **CUCURBITACEAE**
22. DATISCACEAE
23. **BEGONIACEAE**
24. **LOASACEAE**

Order 7. **Salicales**

Family

1. **SALICACEAE**

Order 8. **Capparales**

Family

1. **TOVARIACEAE**
2. **CAPPARACEAE** (*includes taxa in Setchellanthaceae*)
3. **BRASSICACEAE**
4. MORINGACEAE
5. RESEDACEAE

Order 9. **Batales**

Family

1. GYROSTEMONACEAE
2. **BATACEAE**

Order 10. **Ericales**

Family

1. **CYRILLACEAE**
2. **CLETHRACEAE**
3. GRUBBIACEAE
4. EMPETRACEAE
5. EPACRIDACEAE
6. **ERICACEAE** (*includes taxa in Monotropaceae & Pyrolaceae*)
7. PYROLACEAE (*included in Ericaceae*)
8. MONOTROPACEAE (*included in Ericaceae*)

Order 11. Diapensiales

Family

1. DIAPENSIACEAE

Order 12. Ebenales

Family

1. **SAPOTACEAE**
2. **EBENACEAE**
3. **STYRACACEAE**
4. **LISSOCARPACEAE**
5. **SYMPLOCACEAE**

Order 13. Primulales

Family

1. **THEOPHRASTACEAE**
2. **MYRSINACEAE**
3. **PRIMULACEAE**

Subclass 5. Rosidae

Order 1. **Rosales**

Family

1. **BRUNELLIACEAE**
2. **CONNARACEAE**
3. EUCRYPHIACEAE
4. **CUNONIACEAE**
5. DAVIDSONIACEAE
6. DIALYPETALANTHACEAE
7. PITTOSPORACEAE
8. BYBLIDACEAE
9. **HYDRANGEACEAE**
10. **COLUMELLIACEAE**
11. **GROSSULARIACEAE** (*includes taxa in Escalloniaceae, Phyllonomaceae, & Pterostemonaceae*)
12. GREYIACEAE
13. BRUNIACEAE
14. **ANISOPHYLLEACEAE**
15. ALSEUOSMIACEAE
16. **CRASSULACEAE**
17. CEPHALOTACEAE
18. **SAXIFRAGACEAE** (*includes taxa in Lepuropetalaceae*)
19. **ROSACEAE**
20. NEURADACEAE
21. CROSSOSOMATACEAE
22. **CHRYSOBALANACEAE**
23. **SURIANACEAE**
24. **RHABDODENDRACEAE**

Order 2. **Fabales**

Family

1. **MIMOSACEAE** (*placed within Fabaceae*)
2. **CAESALPINIACEAE** (*placed within Fabaceae*)
3. **FABACEAE** (*including taxa from Mimosaceae & Caesalpiniaceae*)

Order 3. **Proteales**

Family

1. ELAEAGNACEAE (*not treated but introduced to the American Tropics*)
2. **PROTEACEAE**

Order 4. **Podostemales**

Family

1. **PODOSTEMACEAE**

Order 5. **Haloragales**

Family

1. **HALORAGACEAE**
2. **GUNNERACEAE**

Order 6. **Myrtales**

Family

1. SONNERATIACEAE
2. **LYTHRACEAE** (*includes taxa in Alzateaceae*)
3. PENAEACEAE
4. CRYPTERONIACEAE
5. **THYMELAEACEAE**
6. TRAPACEAE
7. **MYRTACEAE**
8. PUNICACEAE (*not treated but cultivated in the American Tropics*)

9. **ONAGRACEAE**
10. OLINIACEAE
11. **MELASTOMATACEAE** (*including taxa from Memecylaceae*)
12. **COMBRETACEAE**

Order 7. **Rhizophorales**

Family

1. **RHIZOPHORACEAE**

Order 8. **Cornales**

Family

1. ALANGIACEAE
2. **NYSSACEAE**
3. **CORNACEAE**
4. **GARRYACEAE**

Order 9. **Santalales**

Family

1. MEDUSANDRACEAE
2. DIPENTODONTACEAE
3. **OLACACEAE**
4. **OPILIACEAE**
5. **SANTALACEAE**
6. MISODENDRACEAE
7. **LORANTHACEAE**
8. **VISCACEAE**
9. **EREMOLEPIDACEAE**
10. **BALANOPHORACEAE**

Order 10. **Rafflesiales**

Family

1. **HYDNORACEAE**
2. MITRASTEMONACEAE (*taxa included in Rafflesiaceae*)
3. **RAFFLESIACEAE** (*includes taxa in the Mitrastemonaceae*)

Order 11. **Celastrales**

Family

1. GEISSOLOMATACEAE
2. **CELASTRACEAE**
3. **HIPPOCRATEACEAE**
4. STACKHOUSIACEAE
5. SALVADORACEAE
6. **AQUIFOLIACEAE**
7. **ICACINACEAE**
8. AEXTOXICACEAE
9. CARDIOPTERIDACEAE
10. CORYNOCARPACEAE
11. **DICHAPETALACEAE**

Order 12. **Euphorbiales**

Family

1. **BUXACEAE**
2. SIMMONDSIACEAE
3. PANDACEAE
4. EUPHORBIACEAE

Order 13. **Rhamnales**

Family

1. **RHAMNACEAE**
2. LEEACEAE
3. **VITACEAE**

Order 14. **Linales**

Family

1. **ERYTHROXYLACEAE**
2. **HUMIRIACEAE**
3. **IXONANTHACEAE**
4. **HUGONIACEAE**
5. **LINACEAE**

Order 15. **Polygalales**

Family

1. **MALPIGHIACEAE**

2. **VOCHYSIACEAE**
3. **TRIGONIACEAE**
4. TREMANDRACEAE
5. **POLYGALACEAE**
6. XANTHOPHYLLACEAE
7. **KRAMERIACEAE**

Order 16. **Sapindales**
Family
  1. **STAPHYLEACEAE**
  2. MELIANTHACEAE
  3. BRETSCHNEIDERACEAE
  4. AKANIACEAE
  5. **SAPINDACEAE**
  6. **HIPPOCASTANACEAE**
  7. **ACERACEAE**
  8. **BURSERACEAE**
  9. **ANACARDIACEAE**
 10. JULIANIACEAE
 11. **SIMAROUBACEAE** (*includes taxa in Picramniaceae*)
 12. **CNEORACEAE**
 13. **MELIACEAE**
 14. **RUTACEAE**
 15. **ZYGOPHYLLACEAE**

Order 17. **Geraniales**
Family
  1. **OXALIDACEAE** (*includes Hypseocharis & taxa in Lepidobotryaceae*)
  2. **GERANIACEAE**
  3. LIMNANTHACEAE
  4. **TROPAEOLACEAE**
  5. **BALSAMINACEAE**

Order 18. **Apiales**
Family
  1. **ARALIACEAE**
  2. **APIACEAE**

Subclass 6. **Asteridae**
Order 1. **Gentianales**
Family

1. **LOGANIACEAE** (*includes taxa in Desfontainiaceae & Gelsemiaceae*)
2. RETZIACEAE
3. **GENTIANACEAE**
4. SACCIFOLIACEAE (*taxa placed in Gentianaceae*)
5. **APOCYNACEAE** (*includes taxa in Asclepiadaceae* sensu *Cronquist & Plocospermataceae* sensu *Flowering Plants of the Neotropics*)
6. *ASCLEPIADACEAE* (*taxa placed in Apocynaceae*)

Order 2. **Solanales**
Family
  1. **DUCKEODENDRACEAE**
  2. **NOLANACEAE**
  3. **SOLANACEAE**
  4. **CONVOLVULACEAE**
  5. **CUSCUTACEAE**
  6. **MENYANTHACEAE**
  7. **POLEMONIACEAE**
  8. **HYDROPHYLLACEAE**

Order 3. **Lamiales**
Family
  1. **LENNOACEAE**
  2. **BORAGINACEAE**
  3. **VERBENACEAE** (*includes taxa in Avicenniaceae*)
  4. **LAMIACEAE**

Order 4. **Callitrichales**
Family
  1. HIPPURIDACEAE
  2. **CALLITRICHACEAE**
  3. HYDROSTACHYACEAE

Order 5. **Plantaginales**
Family
  1. **PLANTAGINACEAE**

Order 6. **Scrophulariales**
Family
  1. **BUDDLEJACEAE**
  2. **OLEACEAE**

3. **SCROPHULARIACEAE**
4. GLOBULARIACEAE
5. **MYOPORACEAE**
6. **OROBANCHACEAE**
7. **GESNERIACEAE**
8. **ACANTHACEAE** (*includes taxa in Mendonciaceae*)
9. **PEDALIACEAE** (*includes taxa in Martyniaceae; family as treated in* Flowering Plants of the Neotropics *is introduced*)
10. **BIGNONIACEAE**
11. MENDONCIACEAE (*taxa included in Acanthaceae*)
12. **LENTIBULARIACEAE**

Order 7. **Campanulales**
Family
  1. PENTAPHRAGMATACEAE
  2. **SPHENOCLEACEAE**
  3. **CAMPANULACEAE**
  4. STYLIDIACEAE
  5. DONATIACEAE
  6. **BRUNONIACEAE**
  7. **GOODENIACEAE**

Order 8. **Rubiales**
Family
  1. **RUBIACEAE**
  2. THELIGONACEAE

Order 9. **Dipsacales**
Family
  1. **CAPRIFOLIACEAE**
  2. ADOXACEAE
  3. **VALERIANACEAE**
  4. **DIPSACACEAE**

Order 10. **Calycerales**
Family
  1. **CALYCERACEAE**

Order 11. **Asterales**
Family
  1. **ASTERACEAE**

APPENDIX II

Dahlgren, Clifford, and Yeo's (1985) Monocotyledon Classification (Including annotations relative to *Flowering Plants of the Neotropics*)

- Families in bold are treated in *Flowering Plants of the Neotropics*.
- Families not in bold are not native to tropical America and, with exception of Musaceae, are not treated in *Flowering Plants of the Neotropics*.
- Italicized notes refer to differences between the family circumscriptions of Dahlgren et al. and *Flowering Plants of the Neotropics*.

Superorder **Liliiflorae**
Order **Dioscoreales**
Family
  Trichopodaceae
  Dioscoreaceae
  Taccaceae
  Stemonaceae
  Trilliaceae
  Smilacaceae
  Petermanniaceae
Order **Asparagales**
Family
  Philesiaceae

Luzuriagaceae
Convallariaceae
Asparagaceae
Ruscaceae
Herreriaceae
Dracaenaceae
Nolinaceae
Asteliaceae (*includes taxa in Laxmanniaceae*)
Hanguanaceae
Dasypogonaceae
Calectasiaceae
Blandfordiaceae

Xanthorrhoeaceae
Agavaceae
Hypoxidaceae
Tecophilaeaceae
Cyanastraceae
Eriospermaceae
Ixioliriaceae
Phormiaceae
Doryanthaceae
Hemerocallidaceae
Asphodelaceae
Anthericaceae
Aphyllanthaceae

Funkiaceae
Hyacinthaceae
Alliaceae (*includes taxa in Themida-
   ceae*)
Amaryllidaceae
Order **Melanthiales**
   Family
      Melanthiaceae
      Campynemaceae
Order **Burmanniales**
   Family
      Burmanniaceae
      Thismiaceae
      Corsiaceae
Order **Liliales**
   Family
      Alstroemeriaceae
      Colchicaceae
      Uvulariaceae
      Calochortaceae
      Liliaceae
      Geosiridaceae
      Iridaceae
   Orchids
   Family
      Apostasiaceae
      Cypripediaceae
      Orchidaceae
Superorder **Ariflorae**
   Order **Arales**
      Family
         Araceae
         Lemnaceae
Superorder **Triuridiflorae**
   Order **Triuridales**
      Family
         Triuridaceae
Superorder **Alismatiflorae**
   Order **Alismatales**
      Family
         Aponogetonaceae
         Butomaceae

Limnocharitaceae
Alismataceae
Hydrocharitaceae
Order **Najadales**
   Family
      Scheuchzeriaceae
      Juncaginaceae
      Potamogetonaceae (*includes taxa in
         Ruppiaceae*)
      Posidoniaceae
      Zosteraceae
      Zannichelliaceae
      Cymodoceaceae
      Najadaceae
Superorder **Bromeliiflorae**
   Order **Velloziales**
      Family
         Velloziaceae
   Order **Bromeliales**
      Family
         Bromeliaceae
   Order **Philydrales**
      Family
         Philydraceae
   Order **Haemodorales**
      Family
         Haemodoraceae
   Order **Pontederiales**
      Family
         Pontederiaceae
   Order **Typhales**
      Family
         Sparganiaceae
         Typhaceae
Superorder **Zingiberiflorae**
   Order **Zingiberales**
      Family
         Lowiaceae
         Musaceae (*introduced to tropical
            America*)
         Heliconiaceae
         Strelitziaceae

Zingiberaceae
Costaceae
Cannaceae
Marantaceae
Superorder **Commeliniflorae**
   Order **Commelinales**
      Family
         Commelinaceae
         Mayacaceae
         Xyridaceae
         Rapateaceae
         Eriocaulaceae
   Order **Hydatellales**
      Family
         Hydatellaceae
   Order **Cyperales**
      Family
         Juncaceae
         Thurniaceae
         Cyperaceae
   Order **Poales**
      Family
         Flagellariaceae
         Joinvilleaceae
         Poaceae
         Ecdeiocoleaceae
         Anarthriaceae
         Restionaceae
         Centrolepidaceae
Superorder **Cyclanthiflorae**
   Order **Cyclanthales**
      Family
         Cyclanthaceae
Superorder **Areciflorae**
   Order **Arecales**
      Family
         Arecaceae
Superorder Pandaniflorae
   Order Pandanales
      Family
         Pandanaceae

APPENDIX III

Families treated in *Flowering Plants of the Neotropics* but not recognized by Cronquist (1981) or Dahlgren, Clifford, and Yeo (1985)

Dicotyledon families not recognized by Cronquist (1981)

ALZATEACEAE (*taxa from Lythraceae* sensu *Cronquist*)
AVICENNIACEAE (*taxa from Verbenaceae* sensu *Cronquist*)
BONNETIACEAE (*taxa from Theaceae* sensu *Cronquist*)
DESFONTAINIACEAE (*taxa from Loganiaceae* sensu *Cronquist*)
ESCALLONIACEAE (*taxa from Grossulariaceae* sensu *Cronquist*)
GELSEMIACEAE (*taxa from Loganiaceae* sensu *Cronquist*)
LEPIDOBOTRYACEAE (*taxa from Oxalidaceae* sensu *Cronquist*)
LEPUROPETALACEAE (*taxa from Saxifragaceae* sensu *Cronquist*)
MARTYNIACEAE (*taxa from Pedaliaceae* sensu *Cronquist*)
MEMECYLACEAE (*taxa from Melastomataceae* sensu *Cronquist*)

MUNTINGIACEAE (*taxa from Flacourtiaceae* sensu *Cronquist*)
PHYLLONOMACEAE (*taxa from Grossulariaceae* sensu *Cronquist*)
PICRAMNIACEAE (*taxa from Simaroubaceae* sensu *Cronquist*)
PLOCOSPERMATACEAE (*taxa from Apocynaceae* sensu *Cronquist*)
PTEROSTEMONACEAE (*taxa from Grossulariaceae* sensu *Cronquist*)
SETCHELLANTHACEAE (*taxa from Capparaceae* sensu *Cronquist*)
SIPARUNACEAE (*taxa from Monimiaceae* sensu *Cronquist*)
TERNSTROEMIACEAE (*taxa from Theaceae* sensu *Cronquist*)
TICODENDRACEAE (family described after 1981)

Monocotyledon families not recognized by Dahlgren et al. (1985)

Laxmanniaceae (*taxa from Asteliaceae* sensu *Dahlgren* et al.)
Ruppiaceae (*taxa from Potamogetonaceae* sensu *Dahlgren* et al.)
Themidaceae (*taxa from Alliaceae* sensu *Dahlgren* et al.)

APPENDIX IV

Families of angiosperms as treated by Judd et al. (Boldface families are treated in *Flowering Plants of the Neotropics* = FPN) (Families grouped within each order are not necessarily in evolutionary order)

Basal families
  Amborellales
    AMBORELLACEAE
  Nymphaeales
    NYMPHAEACEAE
  Austrobaileyales
    ILLICIACEAE
    Schisandraceae
  Placement uncertain
    Chloranthaceae
Magnoliid complex
  Magnoliales
    MAGNOLIACEAE
    ANNONACEAE
    MYRISTICACEAE
    DEGENERIACEAE
  Laurales
    LAURACEAE
    CALYCANTHACEAE
    HERNANDIACEAE
    MONIMIACEAE
    SIPARUNACEAE
  Canellales
    WINTERACEAE
    CANELLACEAE
  Piperales
    PIPERACEAE
    ARISTOLOCHIACEAE
    LACTORIDACEAE
    SAURURACEAE
    HYDNORACEAE
  Placement uncertain
    CERATOPHYLLACEAE
MONOCOTS
  Acorales
    ACORACEAE
  Alismatales
    ARACEAE (includes **LEMNACEAE**)
    ALISMATACEAE (includes **LIMNO-CHARITACEAE**)
    HYDROCHARITACEAE
    POTAMOGETONACEAE
    BUTOMACEAE
    CYMODOCEACEAE
    POSIDONIACEAE
    RUPPIACEAE
    TOFIELDIACEAE (*FPN places within* **MELANTHIACEAE**)
    ZANNICHELLIACEAE
    ZOSTERACEAE
  Liliales
    LILIACEAE
    "UVULARIACEAE"
    COLCHICACEAE
    SMILACACEAE
    MELANTHIACEAE
    TRILLIACEAE
    ALSTROEMERIACEAE
    CALOCHORTACEAE
  Nartheciales
    NARTHECIACEAE

  Asparagales
    ASPARAGACEAE
    RUSCACEAE (includes **CONVALLA-RIACEAE, NOLINACEAE, DRACAENACEAE**)
    AGAVACEAE
    HYACINTHACEAE
    ALLIACEAE
    AMARYLLIDACEAE
    ASPHODELACEAE
    IRIDACEAE
    ORCHIDACEAE
    AGAPANTHACEAE
    HEMEROCALLIDACEAE (includes **PHORMIACEAE**, JOHNSONIA-CEAE)
    HYPOXIDACEAE
    THEMIDACEAE
    XANTHORRHOEACEAE
  Dioscoreales
    DIOSCOREACEAE
    BURMANNIACEAE
    TACCACEAE
Commelinoid clade
  Arecales
    ARECACEAE
  Commelinales
    COMMELINACEAE
    HAEMODORACEAE
    PONTEDERIACEAE
    PHILYDRACEAE
  Poales
    BROMELIACEAE
    TYPHACEAE (includes SPARGANIA-CEAE)
    ERIOCAULACEAE
    XYRIDACEAE
    JUNCACEAE
    CYPERACEAE
    RESTIONACEAE
    POACEAE
    FLAGELLARIACEAE
    JOINVILLEACEAE
    MAYACACEAE
  Zingiberales
    ZINGIBERACEAE
    MARANTACEAE
    CANNACEAE
    COSTACEAE
    HELICONIACEAE
    MUSACEAE
    STRELITZIACEAE
EUDICOTS (TRICOLPATES)
  "Basal Tricolpates"
  Ranunculales
    MENISPERMACEAE
    RANUNCULACEAE
    BERBERIDACEAE
    PAPAVERACAE (includes FUMARI-ACEAE)
    LARDIZABALACEAE

  Proteales
    PLATANACEAE
    PROTEACEAE
    NELUMBONACEAE
  Other "Basal Tricolpates"
    TROCHODENDRACEAE (includes TETRACENTRACEAE)
    BUXACEAE
Core Eudicots ("Core Tricolpates")
  Caryophyllid clade (includes Caryophyllales and Polygonales)
  Caryophyllales
    CARYOPHYLLACEAE
    PHYTOLACCACEAE
    NYCTAGINACEAE
    AMARANTHACEAE (includes **CHENOPODIACAE**)
    AIZOACEAE
    "PORTULACACEAE"
    CACTACEAE
    PETIVERIACEAE (*FPN places within* **PHYTOLACCACEAE**)
    SIMMONDSIACEAE
  Polygonales
    DROSERACEAE
    POLYGONACEAE
    PLUMBAGINACEAE
    NEPENTHACEAE
  Santalales
    LORANTHACEAE
    VISCACEAE
    "OLACACEAE"
    "SANTALACEAE"
    MISODENDRACEAE
    OPILIACEAE
    SCHOEPFIACEAE
  Rosid Clade
  Saxifragales
    SAXIFRAGACEAE
    CRASSULACEAE
    HAMAMELIDACEAE
    ALTINGIACEAE
    CERCIDIPHYLLACEAE
    GROSSULARIACEAE
    HALORAGACEAE
    ITEACEAE
    PAEONIACEAE
  Vitales
    VITACEAE
    LEEACEAE
  Geraniales
    GERANIACEAE
  Eurosids I
  Zygophyllales
    ZYGOPHYLLACEAE
    KRAMERIACEAE
  Oxalidales
    OXALIDACEAE
    CEPHALOTACEAE
    CUNONIACEAE
  Celastrales

CELASTRACEAE (includes **HIPPO-CRATEACEAE**)
PARNASSIACEAE
Malpighiales
MALPIGHIACEAE
EUPHORBIACEAE
PHYLLANTHACEAE (*FPN places within* **EUPHORBIACEAE**)
CLUSIACEAE
RHIZOPHORACEAE
VIOLACEAE
PASSIFLORACEAE
SALICACEAE (includes **FLACOUR-TIACEAE**)
ACHARIACEAE
CHRYSOBALANACEAE
PICRODENDRACEAE
PODOSTEMACEAE
PUTRANJIVACEAE
Fabales
FABACEAE
POLYGALACEAE
SURIANACEAE
Rosales
ROSACEAE
RHAMNACEAE
ULMACEAE
CELTIDACEAE (*FPN places within* **ULMACEAE**)
MORACEAE
URTICACEAE
CANNABACEAE
CECROPIACEAE
Cucurbitales
CUCURBITACEAE
BEGONIACEAE
DATISCACEAE
Fagales
FAGACEAE
BETULACEAE
CASUARINACEAE
MYRICACEAE
JUGLANDACEAE
NOTHOFAGACEAE
RHOIPTELEACEAE
TICODENDRACEAE
Myrtales (placement uncertain; either in Eurosides I or II)
LYTHRACEAE (includes SONNERA-TIACEAE, TRAPACEAE, PUNICA-CEAE)
ONAGRACEAE
COMBRETACEAE
MYRTACEAE
MELASTOMATACEAE
MEMECYLACEAE
VOCHYSIACEAE
Eurosides II

Brassicales
BRASSICACEAE (includes **CAPPA-RACEAE**)
BATACEAE
CARICACEAE
MORINGACEAE
RESEDACEAE
Malvales
MALVACEAE (includes **TILIA-CEAE, STERCULIACEAE, BOM-BACACEAE**)
CISTACEAE
DIPTEROCARPACEAE
THYMELAEACEAE
Sapindales
RUTACEAE
MELIACEAE
SIMAROUBACEAE
ANACARDIACEAE (includes JULI-ANACEAE)
BURSERACEAE
SAPINDACEAE (includes **ACERA-CEAE, HIPPOCASTANACEAE**)
Asterid Clade (=Sympetalae)
Cornales
HYDRANGEACEAE
CORNACEAE (includes **NYSSA-CEAE**)
LOASACEAE
Ericales
SAPOTACEAE
EBENACEAE
PRIMULACEAE
MYRSINACEAE
THEACEAE
ERICACEAE (includes PYROLA-CEAE, MONOTROPACEAE, EM-PETRACEAE, EPACRIDACEAE)
SARRACENIACEAE
LECYTHIDACEAE
POLEMONIACEAE
ACTINIDIACEAE
BALSAMINACEAE
CLETHRACEAE
CYRILLACEAE
FOUQUIERIACEAE
STYRACACEAE
SYMPLOCACEAE
TERNSTROEMIACEAE
THEOPHRASTACEAE
Euasterids I
Garryales
GARRYACEAE
Solanales
SOLANACEAE (includes **NOLANA-CEAE**)
CONVOLVULACEAE (includes **CUS-CUTACEAE**)

BORAGINACEAE (includes **HYDRO-PHYLLACEAE**, in part; **LEN-NOACEAE**)
HYDROLEACEAE
Gentianales
RUBIACEAE
GENTIANACEAE
APOCYNACEAE (includes ASCLEPI-ADACEAE)
GELSEMIACEAE
LOGANIACEAE
Lamiales
OLEACEAE
GESNERIACEAE
PLANTAGINACEAE (includes **CAL-LITRICHACEAE, SCROPHULA-RIACEAE** in part)
SCROPHULARIACEAE
OROBANCHACEAE (includes **SCROPHULARIACEAE**, parasitic species)
BIGNONIACEAE
ACANTHACEAE (includes MEN-DONCIACEAE)
LENTIBULARIACEAE
VERBENACEAE
LAMIACEAE (includes many genera typically treated as **VERBENA-CEAE**)
AVICENNIACEAE
BUDDLEJACEAE
CALCEOLARIACEAE
MYOPORACEAE
PHRYMACEAE
Euasterids II
Aquifoliales
AQUIFOLIACEAE
HELWINGIACEAE
Apiales
APIACEAE (includes **ARALIA-CEAE**, HYDROCOTYLACEAE)
PITTOSPORACEAE
Dipsacales
CAPRIFOLIACEAE (includes DIPSA-CACEAE, **VALERIANACEAE**, DIERVILLACEAE, LIN-NAEACEAE)
ADOXACEAE (includes *Sambucus, Viburnum*)
Asterales
CAMPANULACEAE (includes LOBE-LIACEAE)
ASTERACEAE
CALYCERACEAE
GOODENIACEAE
MENYANTHACEAE
STYLIDIACEAE

APPENDIX V

Aids to Identification

Introduction

The following aids are designed to help with the identification of Neotropical plants to family. These keys account only for taxa that exhibit the most common characteristics within each family, and, therefore, will not lead to a correct identification for all plants. In most cases, leaves, flowers, and rarely fruits must be present to efficiently use the keys. The keys will lead to a single family or to a list of possible families that share the same or similar characters. The treatments within this book should then be used to confirm the family identification or to help narrow down possible taxa to a single family within a given list. Some plants can cause severe dermatitis if touched and many of them belong to the family Anacardiaceae and have alternate, pinnately compound leaves; however, there are exceptions to this, and there are other families as well that can cause contact dermatitis or have stinging or irritating hairs on their stems, leaves, or fruits. For this reason, it is important to be cautious when handling unfamiliar plants. In addition, extreme care must be used when tasting plants as some may be poisonous. When taste is mentioned in the key, this does not mean that the unknown plant should be eaten. Instead, only the tip of the tongue should briefly touch the unknown plant.

The information within this appendix was compiled from numerous sources, the most important being the family treatments presented in this book. Other references used were Cronquist (1981, 1988), Gentry (1993), Mori et al. (1997, 2002), Ribeiro et al. (1999), and Takhtajan (1997).

Key 1. Dicotyledons vs. Monocotyledons (From Cronquist, 1988)

1. Leaves usually net-veined. Flower parts, when of definite number, typically borne in sets of 5, less often 4, seldom 3 (carpels often fewer). . . . . Key 2. Dicotyledons.
1. Leaves mostly parallel-veined. Flower parts, when of definite number, typically borne in sets of 3, seldom 4, almost never 5 (carpels often fewer). . . . . Key 3. Monocotyledons.

Key 2. Dicotyledons

1. Leaves absent or reduced to scales. . . . . Subkey 1 (p. 536).
1. Leaves present, not reduced to scales.
  2. Leaves whorled, not in basal rosettes. . . . . Subkey 2 (p. 536).
  2. Leaves opposite or alternate, sometimes in basal rosettes.
    3. Leaves in basal rosettes. . . . . Subkey 3 (p. 538).
    3. Leaves not in basal rosettes (arising from along stems).
      4. Leaves opposite.
        5. Leaves compound.
          6. Leaves palmate (> 3 leaflets). . . . . Subkey 4 (p. 539).
          6. Leaves pinnate (including trifoliolate). . . . . Subkey 5 (p. 539).
        5. Leaves simple. . . . . Subkey 6 (p. 540).
      4. Leaves alternate.
        7. Leaves compound.
          8. Leaves palmate (> 3 leaflets). . . . . Subkey 7 (p. 546).
          8. Leaves pinnate (including trifoliolate). . . . . Subkey 8 (p. 547).
        7. Leaves simple. . . . . Subkey 9 (p. 550).

Key 3. Monocotyleons

1. Plants aquatic. . . . . Subkey 10 (p. 559).
1. Plants not aquatic.

2. Plants saprophytic or hemisaprophytic herbs. Leaves often absent or reduced to scales. . . . . . . Subkey 11 (p. 560).
2. Plants not saprophytic or hemisaprophytic herbs. Leaves present, not reduced to scales.
   3. Plants climbing or scandent. . . . . Subkey 12 (p. 560).
   3. Plants not climbing or scandent.
      4. Plants appearing woody (shrub-like or tree-like) or herbaceous and > 5 meters tall. . . . . Subkey 13 (p. 560).
      4. Plants herbaceous, < 5 meters tall.
         5. Leaf blades broad (not linear, lanceolate, grass-like, ensiform, or terete). . . . . Subkey 14 (p. 561).
         5. Leaf blades linear, grass-like, lanceolate, ensiform, or terete, never broad. . . . . Subkey 15 (p. 561).

DICOTYLEDONS

Subkey 1. Dicotyledon. Leaves absent or reduced to scales.

1. Chlorophyll present in stems.
   2. Stems usually with spines, thorns, or prickles. . . . . *Cactaceae*.
   2. Stems without spines, thorns, or prickles.
      3. Plants growing in or near saltwater. Stems jointed. *Chenopodiaceae* (*Salicornia*).
      3. Plants not growing in or near salt water. Stems sometimes jointed.
         4. Plants growing on stems or roots of other woody dicotyledons. . . . . *Viscaceae*.
         4. Plants not growing on stems or roots of other woody dicotyledons. . . . . Casuarinaceae (*Casuarina*).
1. Chlorophyll absent in stems, or appearing absent (also see Monocotyledon families without chlorophyll: *Burmaniaceae, Corsiaceae, Orchidaceae, Triuridaceae*).
5. Plants not terrestrial, growing within trunk or stem of tree. . . . . *Rafflesiaceae*.
5. Plants terrestrial, not growing within trunk or stem of tree (though sometimes on roots of another plant).
   6. Plants climbing or scandent.
      7. Anthers dehiscing by hinged flaps. . . . . *Lauraceae* (*Cassytha*).
      7. Anthers not dehiscing by hinged flaps. . . . . *Cuscutaceae* (*Cuscuta*).
   6. Plants not climbing or scandent.
      8. Plants mushroom-like.
         9. Scale-like leaves present.
            10. Perianth present, sympetalous more than basally.
               11. Flowers zygomorphic. . . . . *Orobanchaceae*.
               11. Flowers more or less actinomorphic. . . . . *Lennoaceae*.
            10. Perianth present or absent, when present, never sympetalous more than basally.
               12. Scale-like leaves whorled around base or solitary flower or flowering stem. Perianth always present.
                  . . . . *Rafflesiaceae*.
               12. Scale-like leaves spiral around inflorescences and stem; Perianth present or absent. . . . .
                  . . . . *Balanophoraceae*.
         9. Scale-like leaves absent.
            13. Inflorescences of solitary flowers. . . . . *Hydnoraceae* (*Prosopanch*).
            13. Inflorescences of numerous flowers. . . . . *Balanophoraceae*.
      8. Plants not mushroom-like.
         14. Plants of moist forests, usaully associated with *Abies*, *Pinus*, and *Quercus*, from Mexico to southwestern Colombia. Perianth parts distinct. . . . . *Ericaceae* (*Monotropa*).
         14. Plants of seasonally dry climates to moist lowland rain forests, in many regions, usually not associated with *Abies*, *Pinus*, and *Quercus*. Perianth sympetalous.
            15. Locules ≥ 10. . . . . *Lennoaceae*.
            15. Locule 1. . . . . *Gentianaceae* (*Voyria, Voyriella*).

Subkey 2. Dicotyledon. Leaves whorled (not in basal rosettes).

1. Plants usually aquatic.
   2. Leaves bearing insectiverous "bladders" or traps (these sometimes very small). Corolla 2-lipped. . *Lentibulariaceae*.
   2. Leaves not bearing insectiverous "bladders" or traps. Corolla not 2-lipped.

3. Flowers with inferior ovary; stamens 4 or 8. . . . . *Haloragaceae.*

3. Flowers with superior ovary; stamens 2–numerous.

   4. Pistillate flowers with 1 locule, the ovule 1. . . . . *Ceratophyllaceae.*

   4. Pistillalte flowers with (2)3–5 locules, the ovules numerous. . . . . *Elatinaceae.*

1. Plants usually not aquatic (some aquatics in families under this couplet).

   5. Leaves usually aromatic when crushed, the smell lemon-like, and/or leaves glandular-punctate.

      6. Leaves often aromatic when crushed, glandular punctate or not glandular punctate.

         7. Leaves glandular punctate. . . . . *Rutaceae.*

         7. Leaves not glandular punctate. . . . . *Siparunaceae.*

      6. Leaves not aromatic when crushed, glandular punctate. . . . . *Clusiaceae.*

   5. Leaves infrequently aromatic when crushed (if aromatic, the smell not lemon-like), leaves not glandular punctate.

      8. Plants with inflorescences in capitula. Fruits cypselae. . . . . *Asteraceae.*

      8. Plants usually without inflorescences in capitula. Fruits not cypselae.

         9. Latex present.

            10. Flowers in cupular cyathium of connate bracts. . . . . *Euphorbiaceae (Euphorbia).*

            10. Flowers not in cupular cyathium of connate bracts.

                11. Flowers zygomorphic. . . . . *Campanulaceae.*

                11. Flowers actinomorphic.

                    12. Stamens usually numerous, never forming part of gynostegium, often aggregated into groups ("bundles"). . . . . *Clusiaceae.*

                    12. Stamens 5, sometimes forming part of gynostegium, never aggregated into groups ("bundles"). . . . . *Apocynaceae.*

         9. Latex absent.

            13. Inflorescences dense spikes. Perianth absent. . . . . *Piperaceae.*

            13. Inflorescences not dense spikes. Perianth present.

                14. Leaves succulent. . . . . *Crassulaceae.*

                14. Leaves not succulent.

                    15. Stamens and carpels arranged inside receptacles. . . . . *Monimiaceae, Siparunaceae.*

                    15. Stamens and carpels not arranged inside receptacles.

                        16. Indument of 2-branched hairs. Petals clawed. . . . . *Malpighiaceae.*

                        16. Indument not of 2-branched hairs. Petals usually not clawed.

17. Flowers with zygomorphic corollas.

    18. Petal and stamen 1 per flower. . . . . *Vochysiaceae.*

    18. Petal and stamen > 1 per flower.

        19. Petals distinct, not 2-lipped or forming a tube. . . . . *Polygalaceae.*

        19. Petals connate, 2-lipped or forming a tube, at least basally.

            20. Leaves bearing insectiverous "bladders" or traps (these sometimes very small). . . . . . . *Lentibulariaceae.*

            20. Leaves not bearing insectiverous "bladders" or traps.

                21. Stipules present. Ovary inferior. . . . . *Rubiaceae.*

                21. Stipules absent. Ovary usually superior.

                    22. Fruits usually capsules. Seeds usually numerous per fruit.

                        23. Placentation axile. . . . . *Scrophulariaceae.*

                        23. Placentation parietal. . . . . *Gesneriaceae.*

                    22. Fruits usually achenes or splitting into single-seeded sections (mericarps, pyrenes).

                        24. Style usually gynobasic. . . . . *Lamiaceae.*

                        24. Style not gynobasic. . . . . *Verbenaceae.*

17. Flowers with actinomorphic corollas.

    25. Flowers with uniseriate perianth, multiseriate perianth but sepals and petals not distinguishable (tepals), or sepals and petals distinguishable but the petals very reduced.

        26. Perianth forming connate tube basally. . . . . *Nyctaginaceae.*

        26. Perianth not forming connate tube basally.

            27. Stamens opposite perianth lobes. . . . . *Proteaceae.*

            27. Stamens (or outer series of stamens) alternate perianth lobes.

                28. Gynoecium apocarpous. Fruits follicles, the follicles aggregated into star-like clusters. *Brunelliaceae.*

                28. Gynoecium syncarpous or carpel 1 per flower. Fruits variable, not aggregated into star-like clusters.

                    29. Fruits capsules. Seeds usually numerous per fruit. . . . . *Molluginaceae.*

29. Fruits achenes. Seeds 1 per fruit. . . . . *Polygonaceae.*
25. Flowers with biseriate perianth, the sepals and petals distinguishable (tepals not present), not reduced.
    30. Ovary inferior.
        31. Hypanthium present. . . . . *Onagraceae.*
        31. Hypanthium absent.
            32. Stamens clearly opposite petal lobes. . . . . *Loranthaceae.*
            32. Stamens not clearly opposite petal lobes. . . . . *Rubiaceae.*
    30. Ovary superior.
        33. Gynoecium apocarpous or carpels slightly fused at base. . . . . *Coriaraceae.*
        33. Gynoecium fully syncaropus.
            34. Corolla forming tube. . . . . *Gesneriaceae.*
            34. Corolla not forming tube.
                35. Petals distally segmented. . . . . *Rhizophoraceae (Sterigmapetalum).*
                35. Petals not distally segmented
                    36. Stamens ≤ 10. . . . . *Caryophyllaceae.*
                    36. Stamens > 10.
                        37. Ovary with 1 locule, the style 1. . . . . *Cistaceae.*
                        37. Ovary with > 1 locule, the styles > 1. *Quiinaceae.*

Subkey 3. Dicotyledon. Leaves in Basal Rosettes.

1. Vegetative and floral parts with secretory cavities (appearing as red or brownish lines or dots). . . . . *Primulaceae.*
1. Vegetative and floral parts without secretory cavities.
    2. Leaves tubular, forming a "pitcher." . . . . *Sarracenniaceae.*
    2. Leaves not tubular, not forming a "pitcher."
        3. Leaves succulent. Gynoecium apocarpous. . . . . *Crassulaceae.*
        3. Leaves not succulent. Gynoecium syncarpous.
            4. Apical meristem protected by scale-like leaves (lepidophylls). . . . . *Gunneraceae.*
            4. Apical meristem not protected by scale-like leaves (lepidophylls).
                5. Flowers with stamens opposite petals; styles 5 or stigmas 5. . . . . *Plumbaginaceae.*
                5. Flowers without combination of stamens (or outer series of stamens) opposite petals and 5 styles or 5 stigmas.
                    6. Flowers in compact heads, capitula, spikes, or umbels.
                        7. Flowers in compact heads, capitula, or umbels.
                        8. Gynoecium with 2-branched style or 2-lobed stigma.
                            9. Ovary inferior. . . . . *Apiaceae, Asteraceae.*
                            9. Ovary superior. . . . . *Plantaginaceae (Plantago).*
                        8. Gynoecium without 2-branched style or 2-lobed stigma. . . . . *Calyceraceae.*
                      7. Flowers in spikes.
                        10. Perianth present. . . . . *Plantaginaceae (Plantago).*
                        10. Perianth absent. . . . . *Saururaceae.*
                    6. Flowers usually in cymes, panicles, racemes, or solitary.
                      11. Flowers sympetalous, the petals fused more than basally, or synsepalous when corolla absent or reduced to scales.
                        12. Flowers hightly zygomorphic, sometimes with spurred perianth part; corolla often 2-lipped.
                          13. Leaves bearing insectiverous "bladders" or traps (these sometimes very small). . . . .
                            . . . . *Lentibulariaceae.*
                          13. Leaves not bearing insectiverous "bladders"or traps. . . . . *Scrophulariaceae.*
                      12. Flowers more or less actinomorphic, spurred perianth part absent; corolla not 2-lipped.
                        14. Inflorescences usually helicoid or scorpioid cymes, rarely of solitary flowers.
                          15. Ovary usually with 1 locule (or < 4 locules). Fruits capsules. . . . . . *Hydrophyllaceae.*
                          15. Ovary with 4 locules. Fruits drupes or mericarps (nutlets). . . . . *Boraginaceae.*
                      14. Inflorescences not helicoid or scorpioid cymes, the flowers solitary. . . . *Lepuropetalaceae.*
                  11. Flowers apopetalous, or the petals sometimes fused basally, or aposepalous when corolla absent.
16. Leaves covered with sticky glandular hairs. . . . . *Droseraceae.*
16. Leaves not covered with sticky glandular hairs.

17. Flowers with spurred perianth part. . . . . *Volaceae.*
17. Flowers without spurred perianth part.
    18. Flowers with stamens in 5 epipetalous fascicles of 10–15 each. . . . . *Loasaceae (Caiophora).*
    18. Flowers without stamens in 5 epipetalous fascicles of 10–15 each.
        19. Ovary often deeply lobed. . . . . *Saxifragaceae.*
        19. Ovary not deeply lobed.
            20. Petals 4; stamens 6 (rarely 2 or 4). . . . . *Brassicaceae.*
            20. Petals not 4, or if 4, stamens not 6.
                21. Nodes not swollen. Leaves often compound, tasting of oxalic acid. . . . . *Oxalidaceae.*
                21. Nodes often swollen. Leaves always simple, not tasting of oxalic acid. . . . . . . *Caryophyllaceae.*

Subkey 4. Dicotyledon. Leaves Opposite, Palmately Compound (> 3 leaflets).

1. Flowers actinomorphic.
    2. Leaves usually with entire or crenate leaflets. Flowers large, > 5 cm diam., nocturnal; stamens fused at base into ring. Fruits indehiscent. . . . . *Caryocaraceae (Caryocar).*
    2. Leaves usually with distinctly serrate leaflets. Flowers smaller, < 2 cm. diam., diurnal; stamens not fused at base into ring. Fruits dehiscent. . . . . *Cunoniaceae (some Lamanonia).*
1. Flowers zygomorphic.
    3. Ovules >1 per locule. Fruits dehiscent. Seeds winged. . . . . *Bignoniaceae (Tabebuia and relatives).*
    3. Ovules 1 per locule. Fruits not dehiscent. Seeds not winged. . . . . *Verbenaceae (Vitex).*

Subkey 5. Dicotyledon. Leaves Opposite, Pinnately Compound.

1. Leaves bipinnate; petioles pulvinate. . . . . *Fabaceae.*
1. Leaves only pinnately compound; petioles infrequently pulvinate.
    2. Lianas. Tendrils present. . . . . *Bignoniaceae.*
    2. Trees or shurbs. Tendrils absent.
        3. Petiole and rachis conspicuously winged. Flowers with 8 stamens and 2 styles. . . . . *Cunoniaceae (Weinmannia).*
        3. Petiole and rachis not conspicuously winged. Flowers usually without the combination of 8 stamens and 2 styles.
            4. Flowers with uniseriate or reduced perianth.
                5. Stipules present.
                    6. Plants often aromatic. Flowers with perianth reduced to 2 sepals; ovary inferior. . . . .
                        . . . . *Juglandaceae (Alfaroa, Oreomunnea).*
                    6. Plants not aromatic. Flowers usually with perianth of 5–7 sepals (never 2); ovary superior.
                        7. Stamens usually 10 or 12, always < 20. Gynoecium apocarpous. . . . . *Brunelliaceae.*
                        7. Stamens ≥ 20. Gynoecium usually syncarpous. . . . . . . *Cunoniaceae (some trifoliolate Lamanonia).*
                5. Stipules absent.
                    8. Gynoecium apocarpous. . . . . *Ranunculaceae (Clematis).*
                    8. Gynoecium syncarous. . . . . *Aceraceae (Acer negundo), Oleaceae (Forestiera and Fraxinus).*
            4. Flowers with biseriate perianth.
                9. Flowers zygomorphic.
                    10. Flowers with petals connate for much of corolla length. . . . . *Bignoniaceae, Verbenaceae (Vitex).*
                    10. Flowers with petals distinct or fused only basally.
                        11. Flowers with 6–8 stamens; ovary with 3 locules. . . . . *Hippocastanaceae.*
                        11. Flowers usually with 10 stamens (never 6–8); ovary with 1 locule. . . . . *Fabaceae.*
                9. Flowers actinomorphic.
                  12. Ovary inferior. . . . . *Caprifoliaceae (Sambucus).*
                  12. Ovary superior.
                      13. Inflorescences spikes or densely capitate. . . . . *Fabaceae* subfam. *Mimosoideae.*
                    13. Inflorescences not spikes or densely capitate.
                        14. Gynoecium apocarpous. . . . . *Quiinaceae (Froesia).*
                        14. Gynoecium syncarpous.

15. Flowers unisexual or bisexual, the staminate flowers with numerous stamens, the bisexual flowers with numerous stamens and 4 or more styles. . . . . *Quiinaceae* (*Touroulia*).

15. Flowers usually bisexual, if unisexual then never with combination of numerous stamens and multiple styles.

   16. Flowers with 4 petals or petal lobes; stamens usually 2; gynoecium with 2 locules, the styles 2. . . . . *Oleaceae*.

   16. Flowers without the combination of 4 petals or petal lobes, 2 stamens, 2 locules, and 2 styles.

      17. Flowers usually with 10 stamens and 5 locules. . . . . *Zygophyllaceae*.

      17. Flowers with 5 stamens and < 5 locules. *Staphyleaceae*.

Subkey 6. Dicotyledon. Plants with Opposite, Simple Leaves.

1. Plants aquatic.
   2. Flowers unisexual.
      3. Leaves with peltate and/or linear scales. Flowers without perianth; stamen 1; ovary 4-lobed. . . . *Callitrichaceae*.
      3. Leaves without peltate or linear scales. Flowers with perianth; stamens > 1; ovary not 4-lobed. . . . .
      . . . . *Haloragaceae* (*Laurembergia*).
   2. Flowers bisexual.
      4. Submersed leaves opposite, floating leaves alternate and peltate. Flowers with 3–numerous stamens; gynoecium apocarpous. Seeds ≤ 5 per fruit. . . . . *Cabombaceae*.
      4. Submersed leaves also opposite, floating leaves never alternate or peltate. Flowers with 2–10 stamens; gynoecium syncarpous. Seeds > 5 per fruit. . . . . *Elatinaceae*.
1. Plants usually not aquatic (some aquatics in families under this couplet).
   5. Plants trees of mangroves, with conspicuous pneumatophores or prominent aerial roots.
      6. Plant with prominent aerial roots, pneumatophores absent. . . . . *Rhizophoraceae* (*Rhizophoreae*).
      6. Plants without prominent aerial roots, pneumatophores present.
         7. Petioles basally grooved, the furrow lined with black hairs. . . . . *Avicenniaceae* (*Aveicennia*).
         7. Petioles not basally grooved, the furrow not lined with black hairs. *Crombretaceae* (*Laguncularia racemosa*).
   5. Plants not trees of mangroves, without conspicuous pneumatophores or aerial-roots.
      8. Plants hemiparasitic on stems of another woody plant.
         9. Flowers often bisexual, often showy; perianth biseriate, the calyx reduced to rim. . . . . *Loranthaceae*.
         9. Flowers unisexual, often inconspicuous; perianth uniseriate, the calyx absent.
            10. Stamens adnate to perianth. . . . . *Viscaceae*.
            10. Stamens not adnate to perianth. . . . . *Eremolepidaceae*.
      8. Plants terrestrial or epiphytic, never hermiparisitic on stems of another woody plant.
         11. T-shaped trichomes present on petioles and young stems.
            12. Leaves glandular-punctate. . . . . *Myrtaceae*.
            12. Leaves not glandular-punctate. . . . . *Malpighiaceae*.
         11. T-shaped trichomes absent on petioles and young stems.
            13. Inflorescences capitula. . . . . *Asteraceae*.
            13. Inflorescences not capitula.
14. Colored exudate present (white or milky, red, yellow, orange, brown).
   15. Plants lianas. Exudate red. Leaves (sub)opposite. . . . . *Hippocrateaceae* (*Prionostemma aspera*).
   15. Plants herbs, shrubs, trees, vines, or lianas. Exudate variable in color. Leaves opposite.
      16. Exudate white to light brown. Leaf blades cordiform. Conspicuous stipule present at stem apex. Inflorescences globose or spicate. . . . . *Moraceae* (*Bagassa*).
      16. Exudate variable in color. Leaf blades variable in shape. Conspicuous stipule absent at stem apex. Inflorescences not globose or spicate.
         17. Exudate white. Corolla sympetalous; anthers connate.
            18. Ovary inferior. . . . . *Campanulaceae*.
            18. Ovary superior or semi-inferior. . . . . *Apocynaceae*.
         17. Exudate variable in color. Corolla not sympetalous; anthers not markedly connate.
            19. Exudate white. Petals distinctly clawed. . . . . *Malpighiaceae*.
            19. Exudate variable in color. Petals not distinctly clawed.

20. Exudate milky. Leaves often anisomorphic. Perianth uniseriate. . . . . *Urticaceae.*

20. Exudate variable in color. Leaves not anisomoprhic. Perianth biseriate.

 21. Exudate usually yellow, sometimes orange or white. Leaves often with close secondary veins. Flowers often showy; stamens usually numerous; carpels and locules usually 2–5; style 1. . . . . *Clusiaceae.*

 21. Exudate usually white. Leaves with secondary veins variable. Flowers usually not showy; stamens usually 5–15; carpels and locules usually 3; styles > 1. . . . . *Euphorbiaceae.*

14. Colored exudate absent.

 22. Plants woody. Leaves giving off citrus-like smell when crushed.

  23. Leaves glandular-punctate. . . . . *Rutaceae.*

  23. Leaves not glandular-punctate.

   24. Petiole bases connate, forming sheath. . . . . *Chloranthaceae.*

   24. Petiole bases not connate, not forming a sheath. . . . . *Siparunaceae.*

 22. Plants woody or herbaceous. Leaves not giving off citrus-like smell when crushed.

  25. Vegetative and floral parts with secretory cavities (appearing as red or brown lines or dots) or leaves glandular-punctate.

   26. Plants mostly herbaceous. Leaves not glandular-punctate. Leaves and floral parts with secretory cavities. . . . . *Primulaceae.*

   26. Plants mostly woody. Leaves glandular-punctate. Leaves and floral parts without secretory cavities. . . . . *Myrtaceae.*

  25. Vegetative and floral parts without secretory cavities, not glandular punctate.

   27. Inflorescences often stroboloid or in spikes. Perianth absent.

    28. Plants herbaceous. . . . . *Piperaceae (Peperomia).*

    28. Plants woody.

     29. Plants sub-shrubs of ocean shores. Leaves without connate petioles. . . . . *Bataceae (Batis).*

     29. Plants not growing on ocean shores. Leaves with connate petioles.

      30. Leaves aromatic when crushed. . . . . *Chloranthaceae.*

      30. Leaves not aromatic when crushed. . . . . *Garryaceae.*

   27. Inflorescences not stroboloid, sometimes spikes. Perianth usually present.

    31. Flowers arranged inside receptacles, the receptacles often colorful and recurved or disc-like at maturity. Fruits displayed on well-developed receptacles. . . . . *Monimiaceae.*

    31. Flowers not arranged inside receptacles. Fruits usually not displayed on well developed, colorful, and recurved or disc-like receptacles at maturity.

     32. Inflorescences helicoid or scorpioid cymes.

      33. Ovary usually with 1 locule (or < 4). Fruits capsules. . . . . *Hydrophyllaceae.*

      33. Ovary with 4 locules. Fruits drupes or mericarps (nutlets). . . . . *Boraginaceae.*

     32. Inflorescences not helicoid or scropioid cymes.

34. Gynoecium apocarpous or appearing so.

 35. Plants herbaceous. Stems and leaves succulent. Carpels usually 5. . . . . *Crassulaceae.*

 35. Plants herbaceous or woody. Stems and leaves usually not succulent. Carpels variable in number.

  36. Perianth uniseriate. . . . . *Brunelliaceae.*

  36. Perianth multiseriate.

   37. Corolla sympetalous, campanulate, or funnelform. . . . . *Nolanaceae.*

   37. Corolla of distinct petals or petals only fused basally, not companulate or funnelform.

    38. Large glands present on sepals. Petals distinctly clawed. . . . . *Malpighiaceae.*

    38. Large glands not present on sepals. Petals usually not distinctly clawed.

     39. Plants trees. Stamens >10; carpels 3, never fused basally. . . . . *Quiinaceae (Froesia).*

     39. Plants herbs or shrubs. Stamens ≤ 10; carpels not 3, fused basally.

      40. Shrubs. Carpels 5–10. . . . . *Coriariaceae.*

      40. Herbs. Carpels usually 2. . . . . *Saxifragaceae.*

34. Gynoecium syncarpous or appearing so.

 41. Flowers with uniseriate perianth or the calyx and corolla not distinct in appearance.

  42. Lateral branchlet apices forming spines. . . . . *Geraniaceae (Rhynchotheca).*

  42. Lateral branchlet apices not forming spines.

   43. Stamens adnate to perianth, or, if stamens absent, perianth borne on apex of floral tube.

    44. Floral tube present.

45. Locule 1 per ovary. . . . . *Thymelaeaceae.*

45. Locule > 1 per ovary. . . . . *Lythraceae* (petals caducous).

44. Floral tube absent.

  46. Ovary superior. . . . . *Proteaceae.*

  46. Ovary inferior. . . . . *Loranthaceae* (*Gaiadendron*).

43. Stamens not adnate to perianth, perianth never borne on apex of floral tube.

  47. Anthers dehiscing by hinged flaps. . . . . *Lauraceae.*

  47. Anthers not dehiscing by hinged flaps.

    48. Plants trees. Flowers with perianth parts fused, the lobes 5; locules 2; styles 2. Fruits winged schizocarps. . . . . *Aceraceae.*

    48. Plants herbs, shrubs, trees, vines, or lianas. Flowers without combination of 5-lobed perianth, 2 locules, 2 distinct styles, and winged schizocarps.

      49. Anther connectives conspicuous, heart-shaped, petal-like, becoming exserted between calyx lobes at anthesis. . . . . *Alzateaceae.*

      49. Anther connectives not conspicuous, not heart-shaped or petal-like, not exserted between calyx lobes at anthesis.

        50. Stamens > 10.

          51. Stamens inserted on surface or margin of disc. . . . . *Elaeocarpaceae.*

          51. Stamens not inserted on surface or margin of disc. . . . . . *Flacourtiaceae* (*Abatia*).

        50. Stamens usually ≤ 10.

          52. Ovary usually with 3 locules; styles usually 3. . . . . *Buxaceae, Euphorbiaceae.*

          52. Ovary usually with combination of 1 locule and varying number of styles, but usually not 3.

            53. Perianth connate more than basally. . . . . *Nyctaginaceae, Caryophyllaceae, Polygonaceae.*

            53. Perianth distinct or connate only basally.

              54. Principal leaf veins often 3, arising from base of blades. Stamens opposite tepals, inflexed in bud, forcibly ejecting pollen at anthesis. . . . . *Urticaceae, Ulmaceae* (*Lozanella*).

              54. Principal leaf veins usually not 3, usually not arising from base of blades. Stamens opposite or alternate tepals, not inflexed in bud, not forcibly ejecting pollen.

                55. Plants herbs or subshrubs. Flowers usually bisexual; placentation axile; ovules and seeds often numerous (or at least 5) per fruit.

                  56. Plants succulent herbs or shrubs. Stamens (outermost) sometimes petal-like; ovary with 5 locules. . . . . *Aizoaceae.*

                  56. Plants sometimes slightly succulent. Stamens never petal-like; ovary multi-locular below, often 1-locular above. . . . . . . *Molluginaceae.*

              55. Plants woody or herbaceous. Flowers bisexual or unisexual; placentation basal, apical, or free-central; ovules and seeds often 1, less often few or numerous per fruit. . . . . *Amaranthaceae, Caryophyllaceae, Chenopodiaceae, Polygonaceae, Urticaceae, Ulmaceae* (*Lozanella*).

41. Flowers with perianth biseriate, the calyx and corolla distinct in appearance.

  57. Flowers sympetalous, petals fused more than just at base, frequently forming long tube.

    58. Corolla only appearing sympetalous; petals forming tube but truly distinct, or petals distinct and borne on apex of floral tube (the petals sometimes very small and/or caducous). . . . . *Alzateaceae, Combretaceae, Lythraceae, Loranthaceae* (*Gaiadendron*), *Thymelaeaceae.*

  58. Corolla truly sympetalous.

    59. Corolla zygomorphic.

      60. Nodes distinctly swollen on young stems. Cystoliths sometimes present in leaves (visible along margins with 10x lens). Inflorescences often with leaf-like bracts. . . . . *Acanthaceae.*

      60. Nodes not distinctly swollen on young stems. Cystoliths usually not present/visible in leaves. Inflorescences sometimes with leaf-like bracts.

        61. Opposing leaves anisophyllous. . . . . *Gesneriaceae.*

        61. Opposing leaves not anisophyllous.

62. Ovary inferior or semi-inferior.
    63. Stipules present. . . . . *Rubiaceae.*
    63. Stipules absent.
        64. Stamens 3. Fruits achenes. . . . . *Valerianaceae.*
        64. Stamens 4 or 5. Fruits capsules or berries.
            65. Plants often herbaceous. Fruits usually capsules. . . . . *Gesneriaceae.*
            65. Plants usually woody. Fruits berries. . . . . *Caprifoliaceae.*
62. Ovary superior.
    66. Leaves aromatic when crushed.
        67. Style usually gynobasic. Fruits 1–4 mericarps. . . . . *Lamiaceae.*
        67. Style terminal. Fruits capsules, schizocarps, or of mericarps.
            68. Fruits drupes or schizocarps (splitting into mericarps). . . . . *Verbenaceae.*
            68. Fruits capsules.
                69. Capsules with 2 distinct, sharp, curved projections. . . . . *Martyniaceae.*
                69. Capsuels often with projections but never just 2. . . . . *Pedaliaceae.*
    66. Leaves not aromatic when crushed.
        70. Leaves with blade margins spinulose. Stamens 5; locules 3. . . . . *Polemoniaceae (Loeselia).*
        70. Leaves with blade margins variable. Stamens sometimes 5; locules never 3.
            71. Ovary usually deeply 4-lobed; style usually gynobasic. Fruits composed of 1–4 mericarps. . *Lamiaceae.*
            71. Ovary not deeply 4-lobed; style not gynobasic. Fruits sometimes composed of mericarps.
                72. Fruits not capsules.
                    73. Fruits berries. Seeds numerous.
                        74. Leaves sessile, clasping stems. Placentation axile. . . . . . . *Scrophulariaceae (Leucocarpus).*
                        74. Leaves variable. Placentation parietal. . . . . *Gesneriaceae.*
                    73. Fruits drupes or schizocarps splitting into single seeded segments. Seeds not numerous. . . . .
                    . . . . *Acanthaceae, Verbenaceae.*
                72. Fruits capsules.
                    75. Plants shrubs or small trees, known from southern Mexico and Guatemala. Stamens 5. Seed apices with tufts of hairs. . . . . *Plocospermataceae.*
                    75. Plants herbs, shrubs, trees, vines, or lianas, found in many regions. Stamens usually 2 or 4, infrequently 5, rarely 3. Seed apices lacking tufts of hairs.
                        76. Plants usually woody. Seeds usually with distinct wings. . . . . *Bignoniaceae.*
                        76. Plants usually herbaceous. Seeds infrequently winged.
                            77. Stamens 2 or 4. Seeds subtended by hook-shaped retinaculum or jaculators. . . . .
                            . . . . *Acanthaceae.*
                            77. Stamens 2–5. Seeds never subtended by hook-shaped retinaculum or jaculators.
                                78. Plants usually scandent or creeping. Placentation parietal. . . . . *Gesneriaceae.*
                                78. Plants usually erect. Placentation axile. *Scrophulariaceae.*

            59. Corolla actinomorphic (or nearly so).
                79. Nodes distinctly swollen on young stems. Inflorescences often with leaf-like bracts. . . . .
                . . . . *Acanthaceae.*
                79. Nodes not distinctly swollen. Inflorescences variable.
                    80. Tendrils present, coiled in single plane, thick. Venation often acrodromous. . . . .
                    . . . . *Loganiaceae (Strychnos).*
                    80. Tendrils absent. Venation variable.
                        81. Opposing leaves often anisophyllous. . . . . *Gesneriaceae.*
                        81. Opposing leaves usually not anisophyllous.
                            82. Flowers usually with deeply 4-lobed ovary; style usually gynobasic. Fruits 1–4 mericarps. . . . . *Lamiaceae.*
                            82. Flowers usually without deeply 4-lobed ovary; style not gynobasic. Fruits usually not mericarps.
83. Ovary inferior or semi-inferior.
    84. Stipules present on young stems. . . . . *Rubiaceae.*
    84. Stipules absent on young stems or appearing as interpetiolar lines or extrafloral nectaries.
        85. Leaves needle-like, united at bases. . . . . *Buddlejaceae (Polypremum).*

85. Leaves not needle-like, not united at bases.
    86. Stamens 3. . . . . *Valerianaceae.*
    86. Stamens 4 or 5.
        87. Fruits capsules. . . . . *Loganiaceae.*
        87. Fruits berries. . . . . *Caprifoliaceae* (*Viburnum*).
83. Ovary superior.
    88. Plants mostly restricted to arid regions of the Pacific Coast of South America. Flowers with carpels fused only basally; styles gynobasic. . . . . *Nolanaceae.*
    88. Plants found in many regions. Flowers with carpels completely fused; styles not gynobasic.
        89. Flowers with 5 stamens.
            90. Leaf blade margins with spine-like teeth. . . . . *Desfontainiaceae* (*Desfontainia spinosa*).
            90. Leaf blade margins without spine-like teeth.
                91. Colleters usually present in leaf axils and adaxial base of calyx. Interpetiolar lines or ocrea connecting leaf bases often present.
                    92. Stigma twice dichotomously divided. . . . . *Gelsemiaceae.*
                    92. Stigma not twice dichotomously divided. . . . . *Gentianaceae, Loganiaceae.*
                91. Colleters absent. Interpetiolar lines rarely present; ocreas absent.
                    93. Style with 3 stigmatic branches. . . . . *Polemoniaceae.*
                    93. Style without 3 stigmatic branches.
                        94. Flowers with ovary usually 1 locular. Fruits not schizocarps. Seeds numerous. . . . . *Gesneriaceae.*
                        94. Flowers with ovary usually 5-locular, never 1-locular. Fruits schizocarps. Seeds 1 to few per mericarp. . . . . *Nolanaceae.*
        89. Flowers with 2–4 stamens.
             95. Colleters usually present in leaf axils and adaxial base of calyx. Interpetiolar lines or ocrea connecting leaf bases often present. . . . . *Gentianaceae, Loganiaceae.*
            95. Colleters absent. Interpetiolar lines sometimes present; ocreas absent.
                96. Seeds subtended by hook-shaped retinaculum or jaculators. *Acanthaceae.*
                96. Seeds not subtended by hook-shaped retinaculum or jaculators.
                    97. Ovary with 1 or few ovules. Fruits with 1 or few seeds.
                        98. Young stems often square. Stamens usually 4. . . . . *Verbenaceae.*
                        98. Young stems not square. Stamens usually 2. . . . . *Oleaceae.*
                    97. Ovary with numerous ovules. Fruits with numerous seeds.
                        99. Plants usually herbaceous. Stems often sprawling with age. Young stems with uniseriate and glandular trichomes. . . . . *Gesneriaceae.*
                        99. Plants usually woody. Stems erect. Young stems and flowers often with stellate and glandular trichomes. . . . . *Buddlejaceae.*

57. Flowers with distinct petals or rarely, at least 2, but not all petals fused together beyond base, flowers not forming long tube.
    100. Flowers with conspicuous hypanthium or floral tube; perianth parts (usually corolla) at apex of hypanthium or floral tube.
        101. Petals crinkled. . . . . *Lythraceae.*
        101. Petals not crinkled. . . . . *Combretaceae, Melastomataceae, Onagraceae, Rosaceae.*
    100. Flowers without conspicuous hypanthium or floral tube; perianth parts not at apex of hypanthium or floral tube.
        102. Flowers zygomorphic.
            103. Flowers with 1 sepal or 1 petal spurred, or with 1–2 petals appearing saccate or carinate (boat-shaped).
                104. Flowers with 1 sepal or 1 petal spurred, the petals not saccate or carinate.
                    105. Plants trees. Flowers with one stamen. *Vochysiaceae.*
                    105. Plants herbs. Flowers with 5 stamens. *Balsaminaceae.*
                104. Flowers without 1 sepal or 1 petal spurred, 1or 2 petals saccate or carinate (boat-shaped).
                    106. Stipules or stipular scars present. Petals 5. . . . . *Trigoniaceae.*
                    106. Stipules absent. Petals 3. . . . . *Polygalaceae.*
            103. Flowers without spurred sepals or petals, the petals never saccate or carinate.

107. Leaf venation variable, usually without 3 or more primary veins ascending from near blade base. Flowers with large glands on sepals; petals distinctly clawed; anthers longitudinally dehiscent, without appendages. . . . . *Malpighiaceae.*

107. Leaves usually with 3 or more primary veins ascending from or near blade base. Flowers without large glands on sepals; petals usually not distinctly clawed; anthers apically dehiscent, often with appendages. . . . . *Melastomataceae.*

102. Flowers actinomorphic.

108. Plants covered in glochidiate or scabrid hairs. Leaves opposite below, alternate above (opposite leaves often absent in mature plants); blade margins often lobed or serrate. . . . . . .
. . . . *Loasaceae.*

108. Plant indumentum variable. Leaves never alternate above; blade margins variable.

109. Plants herbs, non-climbing.

110. Leaves with 3 or more primary veins ascending from or near base. Flowers bisexual; anthers apically dehiscent by pores. . . . . *Melastomataceae.*

110. Leaves infrequently with 3 or more primary veins ascending from or near base. Flowers bisexual or unisexual; anthers not apically dehiscent.

111. Trichomes covering entire plant. Sepals and petals serrate. . . . . *Loasaceae (Caiophora).*

111. Trichomes absent or present but rarely covering entire plant. Sepals and petals never serrate.

112. Gynoecium often deeply 2-lobed. . . . . *Saxifragaceae* (opposite leaves rare).

112. Gynoecium not deeply 2-lobed.

113. Ovary inferior. . . . . *Onagraceae.*

113. Ovary superior.

114. Stamens with filaments basally connate into tube. *Linaceae.*

114. Stamens with filaments sometimes connate basally, but not forming tube.

115. Flowers with stamens adnate to petals; locules 2. Fruits circumscissile capsules. . . .
. . . . *Oleaceae (Menodora).*

115. Flowers without stamens adnate to petals; locules never 2. Fruits often capsules, but not circumscissile.

116. Plants often in wet areas or near water. Stamens adnate to petals; ovary with (2)3–5 locules apically. . . . . *Elatinaceae.*

116. Plants usually not in wet areas. Stamens sometimes adnate to petals; ovary usually with 1 locule apically. . . . . *Caryophyllaceae, Molluginaceae.*

109. Plants trees, shrubs, or herbaceous or woody climbers.

117. Plants usually montane. Leaves with punctations. Stamens adnate to petals. . . . . *Loranthaceae (Gaiadendron).*

117. Plants sometimes montane. Leaves without punctations. Stamens sometimes adnate to petals.

118. Leaves often but not always with 3 or more primary veins ascending from or near base. Anthers apically dehiscent by pores, or dehiscing by short slits and then connectives dorsally bearing concave glands. . . . .
. . . . *Memecylaceae, Melastomataceae.*

118. Leaves infrequently with 3 or more primary veins ascending from near base. Flowers without apically dehiscent anthers or concave glands on connectives.

119. Large glands present on sepals; petals distinctly clawed. . . . . *Malpighiaceae.*

119. Large glands not present on sepals; petals infrequently clawed.

120. Flowers with extrastaminal disc (the disc entire or composed of septate glands); intrastaminal disc not present.

121. Plants often lianas. Leaf blade margins commonly crenulate or serrate. Stamens usually 3, rarely 5. . . . . *Hippocrateaceae.*

121. Plants always trees. Leaf blade margins always entire. Stamens 5 or more. . . . .
. . . . *Tepuianthaceae.*

120. Flowers without extrastaminal disc; intrastaminal disc sometimes present.

122. Stamens inserted on disc, often but not always numerous; style 1 per flower. . . . .
. . . . *Elaeocarpaceae.*

122. Stamens not inserted on disc, usually not numerous. Style number variable, often > 1.

123. Stamens opposite petals; intrastaminal disc present. . . . . *Rhamnaceae.*

123. Stamens not opposite petals or, if opposite petals; intrastaminal disc absent.

124. Prominant intrastaminal disc usually present. Ovary superior. Seeds often arillate. . . . . *Celastraceae.*

124. Prominant intrastaminal disc usully not present when ovary superior. Seeds usually not arilllate.
    125. Anther connective with large dorsal appendages. . . *Violaceae* (*Rinorea*).
    125. Anther connectives without dorsal appendages.
126. Ovary inferior.
    127. Plants with petal-like bracts or "sterile flowers" surrounding fertile flowers.
        128. Plants trees. Leaf, when torn, held together by secondary xylem (appearing like mucilage), the bases never clasping. Stamens always 4; intrastaminal disc usually present. . . . . *Cornaceae* (*Cornus*).
        128. Plants shrubs or lianas. Leaves not held together by secondary xylem when torn, the bases usually clasping in lianas. Stamens ≥ 4; intrastaminal disc absent. . . . . *Hydrangeaceae*.
    127. Plants without petal-like bracts or "sterile flowers" surrounding fertile flowers. . . *Hydrangeaceae, Onagraceae*.
126. Ovary superior.
    129. Petals usually apically fringed, cleft, or notched.
        130. Style 1. . . . . *Rhizophoraceae*.
        130. Style never 1. . . . . *Caryophyllaceae*.
    129. Petals usually not apically fringed, cleft, or notched.
        131. Plants usually halophytic. Salt glands present on stems, leaves, and calyces. Leaf pairs united at base. Flower petals clawed; ovary usually trigonous. . . . . *Frankeniaceae*.
        131. Plants usually not halophytic. Salt glands absent. Leaf pairs usually not united at base. Flower petals usually not clawed; ovary sometimes trigonous.
            132. Ovary usually 3 lobed; styles usually 3. . . . . *Euphorbiaceae*.
            132. Ovary usually not 3-lobed; styles variable in number.
                133. Conspicuous interpetiolar stipules usually present. Venation craspedodromous. Stamens ≥ 9. . . . . *Quiinaceae*.
                133. Stipules absent or small. Venation variable. Stamens usually < 9.
                    134. Stamens usually 2. . . . . *Oleaceae*.
                    134. Stamens never 2. . . . . *Aquifoliaceae*.

Subkey 7. Dicotyledon. Leaves Alternate, Palmately Compound (> 3 leaflets).

1. Colored exudate present.
    2. Exudate white. Stipules absent. Inflorescences not spikes or globose heads. Flowers unisexual. Fruits berries, not surrounded by fleshy floral parts. . . . . *Caricaceae*.
    2. Exudate drying blackish. Stipules present. Inflorescences often spikes or globose heads. Flowers bisexual. Fruits achenes, surrounded by fleshy floral parts. . . . . *Cecropiaceae*.
1. Colored exudate absent.
    3. Stipules present. Ovary superior.
        4. Plants trees or shrubs.
            5. Perianth uniseriate.
                6. Plants with hollow stems, these often inhabited by ants. Stipule scars completely surrounding stem. Inflorescences spikes. Fruits achenes, surrounded by fleshy flower parts. *Cecropiaceae*.
                6. Plants without hollow stems, not inhabited by ants. Stipule scars not completely surrounding stem. Inflorescences not spikes. Fruits capsules, not surrounded by fleshy flower parts. . . . . . . *Sterculiaceae* (*Sterculia*).
            5. Perianth biseriate.
                7. Flowers usually > 1 cm diam.; nectary disc absent.
                    8. Gynophore present. . . . . *Capparaceae*.
                    8. Gynophore absent.
                        9. Petals fall as unit at anthesis. Fruits indehiscent. . . . . *Caryocaraceae* (*Anthodiscus*).
                        9. Petals usually fall separately after anthesis. Fruits dehiscent. . . . . *Bombacaceae*.
                7. Flowers usually < 1 cm diam.; nectary disc present. . . . . *Sapindaceae* (*Allophyllus*).
        4. Plants vines, lianas, or herbs.
            10. Plants vines or lianas.
                11. Plants lianas, climbing with aid of tendrils. Flowers usually < 5 mm diam. . . . . *Vitaceae*.

11. Plants vines, usually climbing with aid of twining petioles. Tendrils absent. Flowers usually > 10 mm diam. . . . . *Tropaeolaceae.*

  10. Plants herbs.

    12. Flowers zygomorphic. . . . . *Fabaceae* subf. *Faboideae* (*Desmodium*).

    12. Flowers actinomorphic.

      13. Gynophore present. . . . . *Capparaceae.*

      13. Gynophore absent.

        14. Leaves often tasting of oxalic acid. . . . . *Oxalidaceae.*

        14. Leaves not tasting of oxalic acid. . . . . *Rosaceae.*

3. Stipules absent. Ovary superior or inferior.

  15. Ovary inferior.

    16. Plants trees. . . . . *Araliaceae.*

    16. Plants herbs. . . . . *Apiaceae.*

  15. Ovary superior.

    17. Plants trees or shrubs.

      18. Flowers with petals fused into tube. . . . . *Bignoniaceae.*

      18. Flowers with petals distinct.

        19. Leaves with punctuations, often aromatic when crushed. . . . . *Rutaceae.*

        19. Leaves without punctuations, usually not aromatic when crushed.

          20. Gynophore present. . . . . *Capparaceae.*

          20. Gynophore absent. . . . . *Sapindaceae.*

    17. Plants vines, lianas, or herbs.

      21. Plants vines or lianas.

        22. Plants lianas, climbing with aid of tendrils.

          23. Tendrils from leaf axils. Flowers usually < 5 mm diam., bisexual; ovary superior. . . *Vitaceae.*

          23. Tendrils from side of node at right angle to leaves. Flowers usually > 10 mm, unisexual; ovary inferior. . . . . *Cucurbitaceae.*

        22. Plants vines, usually climbing with aid of twining petioles. Flowers usually > 10 mm diam. . . . . *Tropaeolaceae.*

      21. Plants herbs.

        24. Leaves with punctuations, often aromatic when crushed. . . . . *Rutaceae.*

        24. Leaves without punctuations, usually not aromatic when crushed.

          25. Ovary with carpels distinct. . . . . *Ranunculaceae.*

          25. Ovary with carpels connate.

            26. Leaves often tasting of oxalic acid. . . . . *Oxalidaceae.*

            26. Leaves not tasting of oxalic acid. . . . . *Rosaceae.*

Subkey 8. Dicotyledon. Leaves Alternate, Pinnately Compound (including trifoliolate).

1. Plants aquatic. Leaves often highly dissected.

  2. Leaves bearing insectiverous "bladders" or traps (these sometimes very small). Corolla 2-lipped. . *Lentibulariaceae.*

  2. Leaves not bearing insectiverous "bladders" or traps. Corolla not 2-lipped. . . . . *Brassicaceae* (*Nasturtium*), *Haloragaceae* (*Laurembergia, Proserpinaca*), *Podostemaceae.*

1. Plants not aquatic. Leaves usually once or sometimes > once pinnate.

  3. Colored exudate present.

    4. Exudate red. Flowers zygomorphic, with petals differentiated into standard, keel, and wings. . . . . *Fabaceae.*

    4. Exudate usually milky white. Flowers actinomorphic, or if zygomorphic, petals not differentiated into standard, keel, and wings.

      5. Paired tendrils present at base of inflorescences. Flowers with extrastaminal disc. . . . . *Sapindaceae.*

      5. Paired tendrils absent at base of inflorescences. Flowers without extrastaminal disc.

        6. Flowers with filaments fused into tube for all of length. . . . . *Meliaceae* (*Trichilia havanensis*).

        6. Flowers without filaments fused into tube for all of length.

          7. Flowers with 1 ovule per locule. . . . . *Anacardiaceae.*

          7. Flowers with 2 ovules per locule. . . . . *Bursuraceae.*

3. Colored exudate absent.

8. Plants woody. Leaves > once pinnate.
    9. Ovary inferior. . . . . *Araliaceae.*
    9. Ovary superior. . . . . *Fabaceae* subfam. *Mimosoideae* or subfam. *Caesalpinioideae.*
8. Plants woody or herbaceous. Leaves only once pinnate.
    10. Tendrils present.
        11. Tendrils leaf-opposed. . . . . *Vitaceae* (*Cissus*).
        11. Tendrils not leaf-opposed.
            12. Terminal leaflet modified into tendril, the tendrils not paired, not present at base of inflorescences.
            . . . . *Polemoniaceae* (*Cobaea*).
            12. Terminal leaflet not modified into tendril, the tendrils paired, present at base of inflorescences. . . .
            . . . . *Sapindaceae.*
    10. Tendrils absent.
        13. Leaves glandular-punctate, often aromatic when crushed. . . . . *Rutaceae.*
        13. Leaves not glandular-punctate, sometimes aromatic when crushed.
            14. Plants herbs, with scorpioid inflorescences. . . . . *Hydrophyllaceae* (*Phacelia*).
            14. Plants sometimes herbs, without scorpioid inflorescences.
                15. Perianth uniseriate or absent.
                    16. Inflorescences catkins. Flowers unisexual; perianth absent or of 4 sepals; stamens not obviously opposite perianth (when perianth present). . . . . . . *Juglandaceae* (*Carya, Juglans*).
                    16. Inflorescences raceme-like. Flowers usually bisexual; perianth uniseriate. Stamens opposite 4 tepals. . . . . *Proteaceae.*
                15. Perianth biseriate (the calyx sometimes only appearing as small lobes).
                    17. Flowers with hypanthium, actinomorphic. . . . . *Rosaceae.*
                    17. Flowers without hypanthium, actinomorphic or zygomorphic.
18. Flowers with extrastaminal disc.
    19. Plants without rank odor. Petals usually 5. . . . . *Sapindaceae.*
    19. Plants with rank odor. Petals > 5. . . . . *Tovariaceae*
        20. Ovary on long gynophore. . . . . *Capparaceae* (*Crateva*).
        20. Ovary not on long gynophore.
18. Flowers without extrastaminal disc.
    21. Flowers with apocarpous gynoecium or carpels weakly united.
        22. Flowers with gynobasic styles. . . . . *Surianaceae* (*Recchia*).
        22. Flowers without gynobasic styles.
             23. Flowers with styles basally united. . . . . *Simaroubaceae.*
             23. Flowers without styles basally united.
                24. Herbs. . . . . *Ranunculaceae.*
                24. Trees, shrubs, or lianas. . . . . *Connaraceae.*
    21. Flowers with syncarpous gynoecium or with only 1 carpel.
        25. Ovary inferior.
            26. Plants usually covered with glochidiate or scabrid hairs, these sometimes stinging. Inflorescences not umbels or heads. Flowers often showy; style 1. . . . . *Loasaceae.*
            26. Plants with variable indumentum, the hairs or prickles never stinging. Inflorescences usually umbels or heads. Flowers usually inconspicuous; styles 2.
                27. Plants usually herbaceious. . . . . *Apiaceae.*
                27. Plants woody. . . . . *Araliaceae.*
        25. Ovary superior.
28. Androecium of > 10 stamens, or stamens few to numerous and filaments connate into tube of various lengths.
    29. Stamens few to > 10, the filaments connate into tube.
        30. Flowers highly to slightly zygomorphic, the corolla of a dorsal (the standard), 2 lateral (the wings), and 2 lower (keel) petals.
            31. Plants often herbs. Flowers highly zygomorphic, the lateral petals enclosed by standard petal in bud, the ventral petals ± fused into keel; stamens 10, usually diadelphous. . . . . *Fabaceae* subfam. *Faboideae.*
            31. Plants usually trees or shrubs. Flowers slightly zygomorphic, the wings covering standard in bud, the ventral petals not fused into keel; stamens (5)10, not diadelphous. . . . .
            . . . . *Fabaceae* subfam. *Caesalpinioideae.*

30. Flowers actinomorphic or slightly zygomorphic, the corolla not of a dorsal, 2 lateral, and 2 lower petals.
    32. Inflorescences usually spicate or capitate. . . . . *Fabaceae* subfam. *Mimosoideae*.
    32. Inflorescences not spicate or capitate.
        33. Bark often with spicy or sweet scent when cut. Petioles without swollen pulvinus at each end. Anthers with 2 thecae. . . . . *Meliaceae*.
        33. Bark lacking spicy or sweet scent when cut. Petioles with swollen pulvinus at each end. Anthers often with 1 theca. . . . . *Bombacaceae*.
29. Stamens > 10, the filaments distinct or only connate at base.
    34. Plants usually herbs or subshrubs, covered entirely in glochidiate or scabrid hairs, the hairs sometimes stinging. . . . . *Loasaceae*.
    34. Plants usually trees, shrubs, or lianas, usually not covered in glochidiate or scabrid hairs.
        35. Inflorescences usually spicate or capitate. *Fabaceae* subfam. *Mimosoideae*.
        35. Inflorescences not spicate or capitate.
            36. Corolla calyptrate. . . . . *Caryocaraceae* (*Anthodiscus*).
            36. Corolla not calyptrate. . . . . *Ochnaceae* (*Rhytidanthera*).
28. Androecium of ≤ 10 stamens, the filaments not connate into tube.
    37. Flowers zygomorphic.
        38. Flowers with combination of 2 fertile stamens and 3 staminodes. . . . . *Sabiaceae*.
        38. Flowers without combination of 2 fertile stamens and 3 staminodes.
            39. Flowers with 2 petals, one on each side of ovary, modified into oil-secreting structures. Fruits round capsules, variously covered with barbs. . . . . *Krameriaceae* (*Krameria cytisoides*).
            39. Flowers without 2 petals modified into oil-secreting structures. Fruits legumes, never round and covered with barbs. . . . . *Fabaceae*.
    37. Flowers actinomorphic.
        40. Stipules or stipular glands present.
            41. Inflorescences often spikes or heads. . . . . *Fabaceae* subfam. *Mimosoideae*.
            41. Inflorescences not spikes or heads. . . . . *Staphyleaceae*, *Zygophyllaceae* (*Morkillia mexicana*).
        40. Stipules and stipular glands absent.
            42. Flowers usually with petals connate > 1/2 length of corolla. . . . . *Solanaceae*.
            42. Flowers with petals distnct or basally connate.
                43. Interstaminal disc or gynophore present.
                    44. Plants usually herbs or subshrubs, often covered with glochidiate or scabrid hairs, the hairs sometimes stinging. . . . . *Loasaceae*.
                    44. Plants usually trees, shrubs, or lianas, usually not covered with glochidiate or scabrid hairs.
                        45. Leaflets with transparent glandular lines or dots. . . . . *Meliaceae*.
                        45. Leaflets without transparent glandular lines or dots.
                            46. Flowers with carpels weekly united, the styles united basally. . . . . *Simaroubaceae*.
                            46. Flowers with carpels completely united or appearing so (carpel sometime only 1 per flower), the styles variously united.
                                47. Flowers with 3–5 stamens, the stamens opposite petals. . . . . *Picramniaceae*.
                                47. Flowers with ≥ 5 stamens, the stamens alternate with petals.
                                      48. Flowers with 1 ovule per locule. *Anacardiaceae*.
                                      48. Flowers with 2 ovules per locule. *Burseraceae*.
                43. Interstaminal disc and gynophore absent.
                    49. Flowers with punctate petals. . . . . *Connaraceae* (*Connarus*).
                    49. Flowers without punctate petals.
                      50. Leaves often tasting of oxalic acid. Flowers with 5 sepals, petals, stamens, locules, and styles. . . . . *Oxalidaceae*.
                      50. Leaves not tasting of oxalic acid. Flowers without combination of 5 sepals, petals, stamens, locules, and styles.
                        51. Perianth of calyx only; staminodes 6, petal-like; stamens 6. . . *Berberidaceae* (*Mahonia*).
                      51. Perianth usually of calyx and corolla; staminodes sometimes present, not petal-like; stamens usually 5–10; disc present but inconspicuous.
                            52. Flowers with 1 ovule per locule. . . . . *Anacardiaceae*.
                            52. Flowers with 2 ovules per locule. . . . . *Burseraceae*.

Subkey 9. Dicotyledon. Plants with Alternate, Simple Leaves.

(Some families with unifoliolate leaves are not included: e.g., *Staphyleaceae*. Other families not included in this key that rarely have alternate simple leaves: *Aizoaceae*, *Caryophyllaceae*, *Oleaceae* [*Jasinum*])

1. Plants aquatic or semi-aquatic.
  2. Leaves peltate (at least floating leaves).
    3. Sepals and petals 3 each. . . . . *Cabombaceae.*
    3. Sepals and petals > 3 each. . . . . *Nymphaeaceae.*
  2. Leaves not peltate.
    4. Leaves bearing insectiverous "bladders" or traps (these sometimes very small). Corolla 2-lipped. . . . . *Lentibulariaceae.*
    4. Leaves not bearing insectiverous "bladders"or traps. Corolla not 2-lipped.
      5. Perianth absent. Flowers terminal spikes subtended by petal-like bracts. . . . . *Saururaceae.*
      5. Perianth usually present. Flowers never terminal spikes, not subtended by petal-like bracts.
        6. Petal margins distinctly fringed. . . . . *Menyanthaceae (Nymphoides).*
        6. Petal margins not distinctly fringed.
          7. Perianth parts > 8.
            8. Carpels embedded in turbinate, spongy recepticle. . . . . *Nelumbonaceae (Nelumbo).*
            8. Carpels not embedded in a turbinate, spongy recepticle.
              9. Styles forming expanded disc. . . . . *Nymphaeaceae.*
              9. Styles not forming expanded disc. . . . . *Podostemaceae.*
          7. Perianth parts ≤ 8.
            10. Ovary inferior. . . . . *Haloragaceae.*
            10. Ovary superior. . . . . *Podstemaceae.*
1. Plants mostly non-aquatic (some aquatics in families under this couplet).
  11. Plants hemiparasitic on stems of another woody plant.
    12. Flowers unisexual, usually small; stamens not adnate to perianth. . . . . *Eremolepidaceae.*
    12. Flowers usually bisexual, sometimes showy; stamens adnate to perianth. . . . . *Loranthaceae.*
  11. Plants not hemiparasitic on stems of another woody plant.
13. Colored exudate present in trunk, stems, leaves, or flowers (*Anacardiaceae* & *Urticaceae* not treated here).
  14. Conspicuous conical stipule usually present, covering apical bud. Inflorescences usually racemes, spikes, globose heads, or embedded on or within receptacle.
    15. Exudate milky white. . . . . *Moraceae.*
    15. Exudate black or red. . . . . *Cecropiaceae.*
  14. Conspicuous conical stipule absent. Inflorescences variable, never embedded on or within receptacle.
    16. Hypanthium present; style gynobasic. . . . . *Chrysobalanaceae.*
    16. Hypanthium absent; style never gynobasic.
      17. Exudate milky white. Flowers resupinate, zygomorphic; corolla tubular; stamens 5, the anthers connate, the "lower" anthers often covered with hairs or scales; ovary inferior. . . . . *Campanulaceae.*
      17. Exudate variable in color. Flowers not resupinate, more or less actinomorphic; corolla sometimes tubular; stamens variable in number, the anthers never connate, not covered with hairs or scales; ovary usually superior.
        18. Exudate red or reddish. Flowers often small; perianth uniseriate. . . . . *Myristicaceae.*
        18. Exudate or sap usually white (rarely yellow). Flowers large or small; perianth uniseriate or multiseriate.
          19. Stamens, at least outer series, opposite petals or corolla lobes, adnate to perianth.
            20. Placentation free-central. Fruits drupes, often subtended by accrescent and colorful calyx. . . . . *Olacaceae.*
            20. Placentation axile. Fruits usually berries, not subtended by accrescent and colorful calyx. . . . . *Sapotaceae.*
          19. Stamens, at least outer series, alternate petals or corolla lobes or orientation not obvious because stamens numerous, sometimes adnate to perianth.
           21. Flowers unisexual.
            22. Glands absent on leaves. Stamens 10; ovary usually with 1 locule, the style 1, the stigmas 5. . . . . *Caricaceae.*
            22. Glands sometimes present on leaves (check petiole and leaf base). Stamens (1)5–15 (nu-

merous); ovary usually with 3 locules, the styles usually 3, the stigmas entire to multifid.
. . . . *Euphorbiaceae*.

21. Flowers bisexual.
    23. Petals usually connate (at least at base); stamens 5.
        24. Plants usually herbaceous or woody climbers, rarely trees or shrubs. . . . .
        . . . . *Convolvulaceae*.
        24. Plants usually trees or shrubs. . . . . *Apocynaceae*.
    23. Petals usually distinct; stamens numerous. . . . .
    . . . . *Bixaceae, Bonnetiaceae, Clusiaceae, Papaveraceae*.
13. Colored exudate absent in trunk, stems, leaves, and flowers.
  25. Tendrils present.
    26. Stipular sheath terminating in pair of tendrils. . . . . *Smilacaceae* (monocot).
    26. Stipular sheath not terminating in pair of tendrils.
      27. Tendrils axillary.
        28. Petiolar or leaf nectaries usually present. Flowers with extrastaminal corona and androgynophore. . . .
        . . . . *Passifloraceae*.
        28. Petiolar or leaf nectaries absent. Flowers without extrastaminal corona or androgynophore. . . . .
        . . . . *Rhamnaceae* (*Gouania*).
      27. Tendrils not axillary.
        29. Tendrils leaf-opposed. . . . . *Vitaceae*.
        29. Tendrils subopposite to leaf node. . . . . *Cucurbitaceae*.
  25. Tendrils absent.
    30. Vegetative and/or floral parts with secretory cavities (appearing as lines or dots) or glandular-punctate leaves.
      31. Plants with glandular punctations or secretory cavities in leaves.
        32. Plants herbaceous. . . . . *Primulaceae*.
        32. Plants woody.
          33. Flowers zygomorphic; staminode 1, bearded, adnate to upper corolla lip. . . . . . . *Myoporaceae*.
          33. Flowers actinomorphic; staminode absent, never adnate to upper corolla lip.
            34. Flowers bisexual; stamens > 10; style gynobasic. . . . . *Rhabdodendraceae*.
            34. Flowers bisexual or unisexual; stamens < 5 to > 10; style not gynobasic.
              35. Leaves aromatic when crushed. Anthers dehiscing by hinged flaps. . . . . *Lauraceae*.
              35. Leaves sometimes aromatic when crushed. Anthers never dehiscing by hinged flaps.
                36. Placentation parietal.
                  37. Leaves aromatic when crushed. Stamens fused into tube, the anthers attached to
                  outside of tube. . . . . *Canellaceae*.
                  37. Leaves not aromatic when crushed. Stamens usually not united into tube, the
                  anthers not attached to outside of tube if tube present. . . . . . . *Flacourtiaceae*.
                36. Placentation free-central or axile.
                  38. Placentation free-central. . . . . *Myrsinaceae*
                  38. Placentation axile.
                      39. Stamens usually 4–10, rarely numerous, the filaments sometimes fused into
                    tube. . . . . *Rutaceae, Meliaceae* (*Trichilia*, unifoliolate).
                    39. Stamens usually > 10, the filaments never fused into tube. . . . .
                    . . . . *Humiriaceae, Ternstroemiaceae, Myrtaceae*
                    (cultivated *Lepstospermoideae*).
      31. Plants with or without glandular punctations or secretory cavities in leaves, these present on floral parts.
        40. Plants herbaceous. . . . . *Primulaceae*.
        40. Plants woody.
          41. Stamens 10. . . . . *Connaraceae* (*Connarus*, plants unifoliolate).
          41. Stamens ≤ 5. . . . . *Myrsinaceae*.
    30. Vegetative and floral parts without secretory cavities or glandular-punctate leaves.
      42. Plants with inflorescences in capitula. Ovary inferior. . . . . *Asteraceae*.
      42. Plants without combination of inflorescences in capitula and inferior ovary.
43. Gynoecium apocarpous or very deeply lobed (then carpels only fused basally), the carpels never 1 per flower.
  44. Hypanthium present . . . . *Rosaceae*.

44. Hypanthium absent.
    45. Plants herbaceous, never climbing.
        46. Corolla campanulate or funnelform. . . . . *Nolanaceae.*
        46. Corolla not campanulate or funnelform.
            47. Gynoecium deeply lobed, "stylar beaks" 2. . . . . *Saxifragaceae.*
            47. Gynoecium sometimes lobed, "stylar beaks" absent.
                48. Stems succulent. Leaves succulent Perianth never uniseriate; carpels usually 5. . . . *Crassulaceae.*
                48. Stems not succulent. Leaves somewhat succulent or not succulent. Perianth uniseriate or multiseri-
                ate and composed of tepals; carpel number few to numerous.
                    49. Inflorescences terminal. . . . . *Ranunclulaceae.*
                    49. Inflorescences rarely terminal. . . . . *Phytolaccaceae.*
    45. Plants woody, or herbaceous and climbing.
        50. Flowers minute, clustered in dense, ball-like structures. . . . . *Platanaceae.*
        50. Flowers not minute, not clustered in dense, ball-like structures.
            51. Styles gynobasic. . . . . *Surianaceae.*
            51. Styles not gynobasic.
                52. Gynophore or androgynophore present.
                    53. Gynophore present. . . . . *Ochnaceae.*
                    53. Androgyphore present. . . . . *Sterculiaceae (Sterculieae).*
                52. Gynophore or androgynophore absent.
                    54. Plants often with thorns. Styles basally united. . . . . *Simaroubaceae (Castela).*
                    54. Plants usually without thorns. Styles not basally united.
                        55. Flowers uniseriate.
                            56. Ovules 1 per carpel. . . . . *Phytolaccaceae.*
                            56. Ovules usually > 1 per carpel. . . . . *Sterculiaceae.*
                        55. Flowers biseriate or multiseriate.
                            57. Corolla campanulate or funnelform; stamens 5. . . . . *Nolanaceae.*
                            57. Corolla not campanulate or funnelform; stamens often numerous.
58. Carpels ≥ 8.
    59. Plants with conspicuous terminal stipule, the stipules leaving conspicuous scars around stem. Petioles often conspic-
    uously grooved. . . . . *Magnoliaceae.*
    59. Plants without terminal stipule, the stipules not leaving conspicuous scar around stem. Petioles variable.
        60. Fibrous bark present. Perianth parts in whorls of 3; stamens and carpels usually tightly packed together. . . . .
        . . . . *Annonaceae.*
        60. Fibrous bark absent. Perianth parts variable, often numerous; stamens and carpels variable, usually not packed
        tightly together.
            61. Plants trees or shrubs. Leaf blades often coriaceous, usually glaucous abaxially. Fruits berries. . . . .
            . . . . *Winteraceae (Drymes).*
            61. Plants trees, shrubs, or lianas. Leaf blades sometimes coriaceous, not glaucous abaxially. Fruits not berries.
                62. Plants trees or shrubs. Flowers bisexual. Fruits follicles. . . . . *Illiciaceae.*
                62. Plants lianas. Flowers unisexual. Fruits drupes. . . . . *Menispermaceae (some Sciadotenia).*
58. Carpels < 8.
    63. Plants often lianas. Flowers unisexual. . . . . *Menispermaceae, Dilleniaceae (Tetracera).*
    63. Plants trees or lianas. Flowers bisexual.
        64. Lowland plants, usually lianas. . . . . *Dilleniaceae.*
        64. Montane trees or shrubs. . . . . *Winteraceae.*

43. Gynoecium syncarpous or carpel 1 per flower.
    65. Perianth absent, uniseriate, or multiseriate and composed of tepals. (*Apiaceae, Araliaceae, Combretaceae* may
    appear uniseriate).
        66. Perianth absent and/or flowers minute, numerous, and in dense heads, ball-like structures, catkins, spikes, or
        embedded in a receptacle.
            67. Conspicuous terminal stipule present (do not confuse with lepidophylls). . . . .
            . . . . *Araliaceae, Moraceae, Cecropiaceae.*
            67. Conspicuous terminal stipule absent.
                68. Plants shrubs or small trees. Nodes swollen. . . . . *Piperaceae.*

68. Plants herbs, shrubs, or trees. Nodes not swollen.
    69. Plants herbaceous.
        70. Plants often small and scandent or climbing. Inflorescences dense, slender spikes. Perianth absent. . . . . *Piperaceae.*
        70. Plants usually not scandent or climbing. Inflorescences usually not dense, slender spikes. Perianth present.
            71. Apical meristem protected by scale-like leaves (lepidophylls). . . . . *Gunneraceae.*
            71. Apical meristem not protected by scale-like leaves (lepidophylls).
                72. Ovary superior; styles 1 per flower. . . . . *Amaranthaceae.*
                72. Ovary inferior; styles 2 per flower. . . . . *Apiaceae.*
    69. Plants woody.
        73. Inflorescences dense, ball-like heads.
            74. Plants trees, often in or near salt water. Conspicuous stipules absent. . . . . *Combretaceae (Conocarpus).*
            74. Plants trees or shubs, not near salt water. Conspicuous stipules often present. . . . . *Araliaceae, Hamelidaceae, Platanaceae.*
        73. Inflorescences catkins or spicate. . . . . *Araliaceae, Betulaceae, Fagaceae, Myricaceae, Salicaceae, Santalaceae, Ticodendraceae.*
66. Perianth present and/or flowers not minute, not in heads, catkins, spikes, or receptacles.
    75. Fibrous bark present.
        76. Floral tube present. . . . . *Thymelaeaceae.*
        76. Floral tube absent.
            77. Stellate hairs often present on young stems and leaves. Leaf blade bases often asymmetrical. Stamens usually > 5; locules often > 1. . . . . *Sterculiaceae, Tiliaceae.*
            77. Stellate hairs absent on young stems and leaves. Leaf blade bases usually symmetrical. Stamens ≤ 5; locule 1.
                78. Stigmas 1. Fruits achenes. . . . . *Urticaceae.*
                78. Stigmas 2. Fruits not achenes. . . . . *Ulmaceae.*
    75. Fibrous bark absent.
        79. Young stems often succulent, chlorophyllous. Spines often present. Flowers often showy; tepals distinct; stamens numerous. . . . . *Cactaceae (Pereskia).*
        79. Young stems not succulent, not chlorophyllous. Spines sometimes present. Flowers usually without the combination of showy, distinct tepals, and numerous stamens.
            80. Plants shrubs. Spines present. Flowers yellow, with 6 stamens and 6 petal-like staminodes; locule and style 1. . . . . *Berberidaceae (Berberis).*
            80. Plants woody or herbaceous. Spines absent. Flowers variable in color, without combination of 6 stamens, 6 petal-like staminodes, 1 locule, and 1 style.
81. Ochrea present. . . . . *Polygonaceae.*
81. Ochrea absent.
    82. Conspicuous terminal stipule present. . . . . *Moraceae, Cecropiaceae.*
    82. Conspicuous terminal stipule absent.
        83. Leaves with petioles pulvinate at both ends; blades triveined, with large abaxial pit in axil of each of basal lateral veins. . . . . *Peridiscaceae.*
        83. Leaves without combination of petioles pulvinate at both ends, triveined blades, and large abaxial pits in axil of each lateral vein.
            84. Plants often but not always climbing. Perianth forming zygomorphic tube; gynostemium present. Fruits often dehiscing acropetally. . . . . *Aristolochiaceae.*
            84. Plants usually not climbing. Perianth not forming zygomorphic tube; gynostemium absent. Fruits not dehiscing acropetally.
                85. Plants usually herbs. Leaf blade bases asymmetrical; venation palmate. Flowers zygomorphic, unisexual. Fruits 3-lobed, usually winged. . . . . *Begoniaceae.*
                85. Plants trees, shrubs, herbs, vines, or lianas. Leaf blades bases usually symmetrical; venation sometimes palmate. Flowers mostly actinomorphic, bisexual or unisexual. Fruits not 3-lobed or 3-lobed, not winged or winged.
86. Ovary inferior.
    87. Leaves aromatic when crushed. Filaments with basal appendages; anthers dehiscing by valves. . . *Hernandiaceae.*

87. Leaves not aromatic when crushed. Filaments without basal appendages; anthers not dehiscing by valves.
    88. Stamens opposite tepals. . . . . *Santalaceae.*
    88. Stamens not opposite tepals.
        89. Ovary with 1 locule. . . . . *Combretaceae.*
        89. Ovary with > 1 locule.
            90. Plants usually vines. Leaf blades often cordate; venation often palmate. Perianth 2 whorls of 3 tepals each; stamens 6. . . . . *Dioscoreaceae* (monocot).
            90. Plants not vines. Leaf blades not cordate; venation not palmate. Perianth not 2 whorls of 3 tepals each; stamens variable in number, but usually not 6. . . . . *Onagraceae.*
86. Ovary superior or semi-inferior.
    91. Leaves aromatic when crushed. Anthers dehiscing by hinged flaps. . . . . *Lauraceae.*
    91. Leaves usually not aromatic when crushed. Anthers not dehiscing by hinged flaps.
        92. Plants vines. Pistillate flowers with 1 sepal, 1 petal, and 1 carpel. . . . . *Menispermaceae* (*Cissampelos*).
        92. Plants usually not vines. Pistillate flowers, when present, without 1 sepal, 1 petal, and 1 carpel.
            93. Ovary with > 1 locule. . . . . *Buxaceae, Euphorbiaceae, Flacourtiaceae, Hamamelidaceae, Molluginaceae, Phytolaccaceae.*
            93. Ovary with 1 locule.
                94. Stamens usually alternate with tepals; styles ≥ 2. . . . . *Achatocarpaceae, Basellaceae, Chenopodiaceae, Lepuropetalaceae, Molluginaceaen, Nyctaginaceae, Phytolaccaceae.*
                94. Stamens often opposite tepals; style 1. . . . . *Amaranthaceae, Basellaceae, Lacistemataceae, Opiliaceae, Proteaceae, Santalaceae, Urticaceae.*

65. Perianth biseriate, calyx and corolla present (calyx sometimes inconspicuous).
    95. Flowers subtended by bracts modified into nectaries. . . . . *Marcgraviaceae.*
    95. Flowers not subtended by bracts modified into nectaries.
96. Corolla sympetalous, never with some petals distinct, the petals connate > basally, frequently forming long tube or cup, or petals appearing distinct and inserted on rim of hypanthium or "floral tube/cup"; stamens often adnate to corolla.
    97. Flowers with hypanthium or floral tube (*Styracaceae* not treated here).
        98. Plants herbaceous, in hemispherical tufts. Leaves spatulate, usually with lines of reddish glands. . . . .
        . . . . *Lepuropetalaceae.*
        98. Plants herbaceous or woody, not in hemispherical tufts. Leaves usually not spatulate, with or without lines of reddish glands.
            99. Plants with fibrous bark. . . . . *Thymelaeaceae.*
            99. Plants without fibrous bark.
                100. Androgynophore present. . . . . *Malesherbiaceae.*
                100. Androgynophore absent.
                    101. Gynobasic style present. . . . . *Chrysobalanaceae.*
                    101. Gynobasic style absent.
                        102. Petals clawed; stamens often opposite and enveloped by petals. . . . . *Rhamnaceae.*
                        102. Petals clawed or not clawed; stamens not opposite and enveloped by petals.
                            103. Styles > 1 per flower.
                                104. Flowers usually showy; styles 3, with brush-like stigmas. . . . . *Turneraceae.*
                                104. Flowers showy or not showy; styles often > 3, without brush-like stigmas. . . .
                                . . . . *Rosaceae.*
                            103. Style 1 per flower.
                                105. Style bifid. . . . . *Grossulaceae.*
                                105. Style simple or lobed, not bifid. . . . . *Onagraceae.*
    97. Flowers without hypanthium or floral tube.
        106. Leaves clasping stems. Flowers with 3 stamens opposite corolla lobes; ovary inferior. Fruits with accrescent, hairy or plumose, persistent calyx. . . . . *Valerianaceae.*
        106. Leaves sometimes clasping stems. Flowers never with combination of 3 stamens and inferior ovary. Fruits sometimes with persistent calyx, the calyx usually not hairy or plumose.
            107. Corolla zygomorphic.
                108. Inflorescences usually borne on petioles. Flowers with > 1 style. . . . . *Dichapetalaceae* (*Tapura*).
                108. Inflorescences not borne on petioles. Flowers with 1 style. . . . . . . *Bignoniaceae, Gentianaceae, Gesneriaceae, Martyniaceae, Pedaliaceae, Scrophulariaceae, Solanaceae.*

107. Corolla actinomophic.
    109. Plants in arid regions of Mexico. Petiolar spines present. . . . . *Fouquieriaceae.*
    109. Plants in many regions. Petiolar spines usually not present.
        110. Plants in Sierra de la Neblina *tepui* complex. Leaves hood-shaped. . . . .
        . . . . *Gentianaceae* (*Saccifolium*).
        110. Plants in many regions. Leaves not hood-shaped.
            111. Inflorescences helicoid or scorpiod cymes. . . . . *Boraginaceae,*
            Hydrophyllaceae, Solanaceae.
            111. Inflorescences not helicoid or scorpiod cymes.
112. Plants herbaceous and non-climbing.
    113. Ovary inferior or semi-inferior.
        114. Inflorescences capitulate, resembling those of Asteraceae. . . . . *Calyceraceae.*
        114. Inflorescences spikes, not resembling those of Asteraceae. . . . . *Sphenocleaceae.*
    113. Ovary superior.
        115. Inflorescences spikes or heads, on terminal scapes. Flowers inconspicuous; petals scarious. . . . .
        . . . . *Plantaginaceae.*
        115. Inflorescences often racemes, cymes, or solitary flowers, not spikes or heads, usually not on terminal scapes.
        Flowers usually conspicuous; petals usually not scarious.
            116. Style with 3 stigmatic branches. . . . . *Polemoniaceae.*
            116. Style without 3 stigmatic branches.
                117. Sepals distinct. . . . . *Convolvulaceae.*
                117. Sepals fused, at least basally.
                    118. Gynoecium with 1 locule. . . . . *Plumbaginaceae.*
                    118. Gynoecium with 2 locules. . . . . *Solanaceae.*
112. Plants woody or climbing.
    119. Inflorescences borne on petiole. Stamens sessile at apex of corolla tube. . . *Dichapetalaceae* (*Stephanopodium*).
    119. Inflorescences not borne on petiole. Stamens position variable, but usually not sessile at apex of corolla
    tube.
        120. Corona present in throat of corolla. . . . . *Lissocarpaceae.*
        120. Corona not present in throat of corolla.
            121. Stamens > 10. . . . . *Caryocaraceae* (*Anthodiscus*).
            121. Stamens ≤ 10.
                122. Flowers with appendages alternating with petal lobes; stamens opposite petal lobes; placentation
                free-central. . . . . *Theophrastaceae.*
                122. Flowers without the combination of appendages alternating with petal lobes, stamens opposite
                petal lobes, and free-central plancetation.
                    123. Corollas with lobes as long as corolla tube, the lobes never inconspicuous.
                        124. Stamens twice as many as corolla lobes, the filaments fused with corolla basally,
                        often forming connate tube above corolla tube. . . . . *Styracaceae.*
                        124. Stamens usually equal to number of corolla lobes, the filaments often fused with
                        corolla basally, not forming a connate tube above corolla tube. . . . . *Aquifoliaceae.*
                    123. Corolla with lobes shorter than corolla tube, the lobes sometimes inconspicuous.
                      125. Inner bark black. Dark glands present on lower surface of leaf. Corolla lobes convo-
                      lute (contorted). Fruits berries, with enlarged calyx. . . . . . *Ebenaceae* (Diospyros).
                      125. Inner bark not black. Dark glands not present on lower surface of leaf. Corolla lobes
                      sometimes convolute. Fruit not berries, without enlarged calyx.
                        126. Flowers with contorted corolla lobes; style 1; stigmatic branches 3. . . . .
                        . . . . *Polemoniaceae.*
                      126. Flowers without the combination of contorted corolla lobes, 1 style, and 3 stig-
                      matic branches.
                        127. Plants usually in cool, moist, montane forests. Young leaves often reddish.
                        Corolla urceolate to tubular, often brightly colored (red to orangish); an-
                        thers often with 2 distal tubules or 2–4 awns and dehiscing by pores or
                        clefts. . . . . *Ericaceae.*
                      127. Plants in various habitats including in cool, moist, montane forest. Young
                      leaves usually not reddish. Corolla and anthers variable, the anthers with-

out distal tubules and awns, but sometimes dehiscing by pores. . . . .
Convolvulaceae, Duckeodendraceae, Olacaceae (*Brachynema, Schoepfia*),
Polygalaceae (*Diclidanthera*), *Solanaceae.*

96. Corolla apopetalous or partially sympetalous, if sympetalous then some petals always distinct or all petals connate only basally, never forming tube or cup, the petals never inserted on rim of hypanthium or "floral tube/cup"; stamens infrequenlty adnate to corolla.

    128. Plants with T-shaped hairs on petioles and young stems. Flowers with clawed petals. . . . . *Malpighiaceae.*

    128. Plants without the combination of T-shaped hairs on petioles and young stems and clawed petals.

        129. Inflorescences borne on petioles. . . . . *Dichapetalaceae.*

        129. Inflorescences not borne on petioles.

            130. Principle leaf veins often but not always arising from base of leaf blades. Filaments and/or anthers fused into androphore, androgynophore, staminal tube, large staminal ring or staminal hood (*Rutaceae* not included here), the filaments usually fused well above base, or, if only fused basally then stamens in fascicles. Gynophore sometimes present (*Fabaceae* not included here).

                131. Flowers unisexual; androphore present. . . . . *Menispermaceae.*

                131. Flowers usually bisexual; androphore not present.

                    132. Fibrous bark present. Leaf venation often basal. Gynophore or andgynophore infrequently present.

                        133. Stamens fused basally into actinomophic ring (not long tube), this sometimes extended into zygophorphic hood, the filaments not grouped into fascicles. . . . .
. . . . *Lecythidaceae.*

                        133. Stamens fused into long staminal tube, or filaments fused basally and grouped in fascicles, not fused into actinormorphic ring or extended into zygomorphic hood.

                            134. Stamens grouped in fascicles basally, the filaments not forming elongated tube.
. . . . *Bombacaceae, Tiliaceae.*

                            134. Stamens fused into an elongated tube, the filaments sometimes grouped in fascicles above tube.

                                135. Plants usually shrubs or subshrubs, sometimes herbs, rarely trees. Flowers often subtended by epicalyx. . . . . *Malvaceae.*

                                135. Plants usually trees, sometimes shrubs, subshrubs, or herbs. Flowers usually not subtended by epicalyx. . . . . *Bombacaceae, Sterculiaceae.*

                    132. Fibrous bark not present. Leaf venation usually not basal. Gynophore or androgynophore present. . . . . *Brassicaceae* (e.g., *Cremolobus*), *Capparaceae, Ochnaceae, Setchellanthaceae, Sterculiaceae* (*Helicteres*, some *Ayenia*).

            130. Principle leaf veins infrequently arising from base of leaves. Filaments and/or anthers not fused into androphore, androgynophore, large staminal ring or staminal hood, the filaments sometimes fused basally into ring. Gynophore absent.

136. Extrastaminal disc present.

    137. Plants commonly cultivated. Androecium often with 1 fertile stamen larger than other stamens. . . . .
. . . . *Anadcardiaceae* (*Mangifera indica*).

    137. Plants usually not cultivated. Androecium without 1 fertile stamen larger than other stamens.

        138. Plants often lianas. Flowers usually with 3 stamens (rarely 5). . . . . *Hippocrateaceae.*

        138. Plants shrubs, trees, or lianas. Flowers with > 3 stamens.

            139. Plants trees, known from Guayana region of Venezuela, Brazil, and Colombia. Disc of of 5 to 10 fleshy glands, the glands glabrous abaxially, usually densely pubescent adaxially. . . *Tepuianthaceae.*

            139. Plants shrubs, trees, or lianas, known from many regions. Disc usually without above combination of characters. . . . . *Flacourtiaceae, Sapindaceae* (unifoliolate).

136. Extrastaminal disc absent.

    140. Plants herbaceous, never climbing.

        141. Corolla zygomorphic.

            142. Flowers often unisexual; petals 2, usually small; stamens 1 or 2. . . . . *Gunneraceae.*

            142. Flowers usually bisexual; petals > 2; stamens usually > 2.

                143. Leaves highly pinnatifid. Androecium of 5 fertile stamens and 5 staminodes; locules 5. . . . . . .
. . . . *Geraniaceae* (*Erodium*).

                143. Plants without combination of highly pinnatifid leaaves, 5 stamens, 5 staminodes, and 5 locules.

144. Flowers usually only slightly zygomorphic; ovary often deeply lobed, with 2 stylar "beaks." . . . . *Saxifragaceae.*

144. Flowers highly zygomorohphic; ovary not deeply lobed, without stylar "beaks."

    145. Flowers with one perianth member spurred or saccate.

        146. Plants insectivorous. Stamens 2. . . . . *Lentibulariaceae.*

        146. Plants not insectivorous. Stamens 5. . . . . *Violaceae, Balsaminaceae.*

    145. Flowers without perianth member spurred or saccate.

        147. Corolla with 2 petals on each side of ovary modified into oil-secreting structures; stamens 3–4. Fruits with barbs. . . . . *Krameriaceae.*

        147. Corolla without 2 petals on each side of ovary modified into oil-secreting structures; stamens usually 10. Fruits usually without barbs. . . . . *Fabaceae* subfam. *Faboideae, Polygalaceae.*

141. Corolla actinomorphic.

    148. Plants insectiverous. Leaves with sticky, red, glandular hairs. . . . . *Droseraceae.*

    148. Plants not insectiverous. Leaves without sticky, red, glandular hairs.

        149. Inflorescences umbels or less often heads. Gynoecium with inferior ovary, the styles 2. . . . . *Apiaceae.*

        149. Inflorescences usually not umbels or heads. Gynoecium without combination of inferior ovary and 2 styles.

            150. Sepals, petals, and stamens 5; styles 3, the stigmas brush-like. . . . . *Turneraceae.*

            150. Sepal, petals, and stamens sometimes 5, styles not 3 when stamens 5, the stigmas not brush-like.

                151. Stamens > 10. . . . . *Bixaceae, Cistaceae, Loasaceae, Portulacaceae, Tiliaceae* (*Corchorus*).

            151. Stamens ≤ 10.

                152. Flowers with 4 petals; stamens usually 6, often tetradynamous (outer 2 shorter than inner 4). . . . . *Brassicaceae.*

                152. Flowers without the combination of 4 petals and 6 tetradynamous stamens.

                    153. Stamens opposite petals.

                        154. Intrastaminal disc present. . . . . *Rhamnaceae* (*Crumenaria*).

                        154. Intrastaminal disc absent.

                            155. Leaf blades not succulent. Styles often 5, variously fused; ovules 1 per ovary. . . . . *Plumbaginaceae.*

                            155. Leaf blades often succulent. Styles variously clefted, often in 3 parts, usually not 5; ovules > 1 per ovary. . . . *Portulacaceae.*

                    153. Stamens not opposite petals.

                      156. Gynoecium with > 1 style.

                        157. Filaments connate basally; styles 2–5. . . . . *Linaceae.*

                        157. Filaments not connate basally; styles usually 2. . . . . *Saxifragaceae.*

                    156. Gynoecium with 1 style.

                      158. Stigmas 5. . . . . *Geraniaceae.*

                      158. Stigma 1. . . . . *Loasaceae.*

140. Plants woody, or herbaceous and climbing.

    159. Corolla zygomorphic.

        160. Plants common along seashores. Corolla fan-like; specialized stylar outgrowth (indusium) present. . . . . *Goodeniaceae* (*Scaevola*).

        160. Plants growing in numerous habitats. Corolla not fan-like; specialized stylar outgrowth (indusium) not present.

            161. Plants known from Guayana Shield of southern Venezuela and bordering countries. Petals 3, spatulate, clawed; androecium with stamens and staminode united into split tube. . . . . *Euphroniaceae.*

            161. Plants occurring in many regions. Petals not 3, not spatulate, not clawed; androecium without stamens and staminode united into split tube.

                162. Perianth member spurred.

                    163. Anterior petal spurred. . . . . *Violaceae.*

163. Calyx spurred. . . . . *Tropaeolaceae (Tropaeolum).*
162. Perianth member not spurred.
  164. Flowers with 2–3 petals connate, forming keel or lip.
    165. Lianas, known only from Espírito Santo in southeastern Brazil. Fruits trigonous.
      . . . . *Trigoniaceae (Trigoniodendron).*
    165. Plants shrubs, trees, lianas, or vines, occurring throughout tropical America. Fruits usually not trigonous.
      166. Stamens 10. . . . . *Fabaceae* subfam. *Faboideae.*
      166. Stamens < 10.
        167. Flowers with 2 petals, one on each side of ovary, modified into oil-secreting structures; stamens 3–4; style often curved, protruding from flower. Fruits covered with barbs. . . . . *Krameriaceae.*
        167. Flowers without 2 petals, one on each side of ovary, modified into oil-secreting structures; stamens usually 8. Fruits not coverd with barbs. . . . . *Polygalaceae.*
  164. Flowers without petals forming keel or lip. . . . .
    . . . . *Icacinaceae, Polygalaceae, Sabiaceae, Violaceae.*
159. Corolla more or less actinomorphic.
  168. Inflorescences on leaves. . . . . *Phyllonomaceae.*
  168. Inflorescences not on leaves.
    169. Leaves, when torn in half, held together by secondary xylem (appearing like mucilage). . . . . .
      . . . . *Cornaceae.*
    169. Leaves, when torn in half, not held together (conspicuously) by secondary xylem.
      170. Filaments flattened, often abruptly constricted at apex. . . . . *Symplocaceae.*
      170. Filaments usually not flattened, not abruptly constricted at apex.
171. Ovary inferior.
  172. Flowers unisexual; style > 1.
    173. Petals often fringed or divided; stamens usually 8; styles (3)4. . . . . *Anisophylleaceae.*
    173. Petals not fringed or divided; stamens 5; styles 2. . . . . *Apiaceae.*
  172. Flowers usually bisexual; style 1.
    174. Plants endemic to central and southern Mexico. Flowers with 5 stigmas. . . . . *Pterostemonaceae.*
    174. Plant in many regions. Flowers without 5 stigmas.
      175. Stamens > 15. . . . . *Loasaceae, Muntingiaceae (Neotessmannia,).*
      175. Stamens ≤ 15. . . . . *Escalloniaceae, Loasaceae, Nyssaceae* (usually unisexual), *Onagraceae.*
171. Ovary superior or semi-inferior.
  176. Stamens > 12.
    177. Leaf blade bases often asymmetrical; venation palmate.
      178. Sepals distinct.
        179. Stamens inserted on surface of disc. . . . . *Elaeocarpaceae.*
        179. Stamens not inserted on surface of disc.
          180. Stamens often in conspicuous fascicles. . . . . *Tiliaceae.*
          180. Stamens usually not in conspicuous fascicles. . . . . *Bixaceae.*
      178. Sepals fused at least basally.
        181. Petioles with swollen pulvinus at each end. . . . . *Bombacaceae.*
        181. Petioles without swollen pulvinus at each end.
          182. Stamens often in conspicuous fascicles. . . . . *Tiliaceae.*
          182. Stamens not in conspicuous fascicles. . . . . *Muntingiaceae (Dicraspidia, Muntingia).*
    177. Leaf blade bases not markedly asymmetrical; venation usually not palmate.
      183. Leaf blades usually coriaceous, secondary venation often closely spaced. . . . . *Bonnetiaceae,*
        Ericaceae, Clusiaceae, Ternstroemiaceae, Theaceae.
      183. Leaf blades usually not coriaceous; secondary venation usually not closely spaced.
        184. Styles > 1, sometimes fused basally. . . . . *Actinidiaceae, Flacourtiaceae, Hugoniaceae,*
          Dilleniaceae (Curatella, Pinzona).
      184. Style 1.
        185. Plants trees. Leaves with involute vernation; blades sometimes with longitudinal striations

running lengthwise, often punctate-glandulose near petiole or margin. Placentation axile. . . . . *Humiriaceae.*

185. Plants trees or shrubs. Leaves without involute vernation, without longitudinal striations running lengthwise, not punctate-glandulose near petiole or margin. Placentation often parietal. . . . . *Cistaceae, Dipterocarpaceae, Loasaceae.*

176. Stamens ≤ 12.
    186. Plants trees of mangroves. . . . . *Pellicieraceae.*
    186. Plants not trees of mangrove.
        187. Shrubs from eastern Cuba. Flowers yellow, sepals, petals, stamens, and locules 3. . . . . *Cneoraceae (Cneorum).*
        187. Plants occurring throughout Neotropics. Flowers never yellow with above combination of sepals, petals, stamens, and locules 3.
            188. Intrastaminal disc present.
                189. Stamens inserted on surface of disc. . . . . *Elaeocarpaceae.*
                189. Stamens not inserted on surface of disc. . . . *Anacardiaceae, Celastraceae, Humiriaceae, Ixonanthaceae, Loasaceae, Rhamnaceae.*
            188. Intrastaminal disc absent.
                190. Cataphylls often present on stems. Leaves with involute vernation, sometimes imprinting 2 parallel lines and/or distinct central panel on abaxial surface. Petals with appendages; stamens fused basally; styles 3. . . . . *Erythroxylaceae.*
                190. Cataphylls absent on stems. Leaves without involute vernation, not imprinted with parallel lines and/or central panal on abaxial side. Flowers without combination of petals with appendages, stamens basally fused, and styles 3.
                    191. Plants usually with palmate venation; blade bases often asymmetrical. Stamens often in fascicles. . . . . *Tiliaceae.*
                    191. Plants lacking combination of palmate venation, asymmetrical blade bases, and stamens in fascicles.
                        192. Flowers with stamens opposite petals; styles or stigmas 5. . *Plumbaginaceae.*
                        192. Flowers never with the combination of stamens opposite petals (at least outer whorl of stamens) and styles or stigmas 5.
                            193. Anther connectives with conspicuous appendages. . . . . *Violaceae.*
                            193. Anther connectives without conspicuous appendages. . . . *Anacardiaceae (Anacardium, introduced Mangifera), Aquifoliaceae, Berberidaceae, Clethraceae, Cyrillaceae, Dipterocarpaceae, Ericaceae, Flacourtiaceae, Hugoniaceae, Icacinaceae, Sabiaceae, Ternstroemiaceae, Tetrameristaceae, Violaceae.*

MONOCOTYLEDONS

Subkey 10. Monocotyledon. Plants fully aquatic.

1. Plants growing in saltwater or brackish habitats. . . . . *Cymodoceaceae, Hydrocharitaceae, Juncaginaceae, Ruppiaceae, Zosterace.*
1. Plants growing in freshwater habitats.
    2. Plant body reduced. . . . . *Lemnaceae.*
    2. Plant body not reduced.
        3. Plants with milky exudate. . . . . *Alismataceae, Limnocharitaceae.*
        3. Plants without milky exudate.
            4. Leaves 3-ranked. . . . . *Cyperaceae, Juncaceae.*
            4. Leaves not 3-ranked.
                5. Internodes often hollow. Leaf sheaths ligulate. . . . . *Poaceae.*
                5. Internodes usually solid. Leaf sheath not ligulate.
                    6. Inflorescences dense, spikelike, usually subtended by spathe or scar left by fallen spathe. Flowers unisexual, the pistillate flowers usually basal to staminate flowers. . . . . *Araceae, Typhaceae.*

6. Inflorescences usually not dense, spikelike, Flowers bisexual or unisexual, then pistillate flowers usually not basal to staminate flowers. . . . . *Eriocaulaceae, Hydrocharitaceae, Juncaceae, Juncaginaceae, Mayacaceae, Pontederiaceae, Potamogetonaceae, Thurniaceae, Zannichelliaceae.*

Subkey 11. Monocotyledon. Plants saprophytic or hemisaprophytic herbs. Leaves often absent or reduced to scales.

1. Flowers with sexual parts fused into central column. . . . . *Orchidaceae.*
1. Flowers without sexual parts fused into central column.
   2. Flowers unisexual, the carpels distinct. . . . . *Triuridaceae.*
   2. Flowers bisexual, the carpels connate.
      3. Tepals basally connate into tube. . . . . *Burmanniaceae.*
      3. Tepals distinct. . . . . *Corsiaceae.*

Subkey 12. Monocotyledon. Plants climbing or scandent.

1. Roots surrounded by white velamen. Flowers with sexual structures fused into central column. . *Orchidaceae (Vanilla).*
1. Roots not surrounded by white velamen. Flowers without sexual structures fused into central column.
   2. Stems 3-ranked. . . . . *Cyperaceae.*
   2. Stems not 3-ranked.
      3. Prickles often present on stems and leaves. Tendrils present, derived from stipules. . . . . *Smilacaceae.*
      3. Prickles sometimes present on stems and leaves. Tendrils absent.
         4. Leaves pinnately compound, spiny. . . . . *Arecaceae (Desmoncus).*
         4. Leaves not pinnately compound, not spiny.
            5. Internodes often hollow. Leaf sheath ligulate. . . . . *Poaceae.*
            5. Internodes usually solid. Leaves sheath not ligulate.
               6. Leaves petiolate.
                  7. Leaf blades bifid or sometimes simple. Inflorescences of many flowers, each pistillate flower surrounded by staminate flowers. . . . . *Cyclanthaceae.*
                  7. Leaf blades never bifid. Inflorescences of few to many flowers, never with staminate flowers surrounding each pistillate flower.
                    8. Plants hemiepiphytes, usually not vines. Inflorescences of spathe and spadix. . . . . *Araceae.*
                    8. Plants not hemiepiphytes, vines. Inflorescences not of a spathe and spadix. . . . . . *Dioscoreaceae.*
               6. Leaves sessile.
                 9. Stems often bearing prickles. Leaves clustered on short shoots, not resupinate. . . . . *Herreriaceae (Herreria).*
                 9. Stems not bearing prickles. Leaves not clustered on short shoots, usually resupinate. . . . . *Alstroemeriaceae.*

Subkey 13. Monocotyledon. Plants appearing woody (shrub-like, tree-like) or herbaceous and vegetative growth > 5 meters tall.

1. Plants giant herbs (because of size, sometimes interpreted as woody), vegetative growth > 5 meters.
   2. Leaves spiral. . . . . *Musaceae (Musa).*
   2. Leaves distichous.
      3. Internodes usually hollow. Leaves ligulate; blades sessile. . . . . *Poaceae.*
      3. Internodes not hollow. Leaves not ligulate; blades on long petioles. . . . . *Strelitziaceae.*
1. Plants shrub-like to arborescent, never giant herbs with vegetative growth > 5 meters.
   4. Stems not branching; internodes usually hollow. Leaf sheaths ligulate. . . . . *Poaceae.*
   4. Stems branching or not branching; internodes usually not hollow. Leaf sheaths not ligulate.
      5. Leaves whorled. . . . . *Velloziaceae.*
      5. Leaves not whorled.
         6. Leaves compound; blades plicate. . . . . *Arecaceae.*

6. Leaves simple; blades plicate or not plicate.
    7. Leaf blades plicate. . . . . *Arecaceae.*
    7. Leaf blades not plicate. . . . . *Dracaenaceae, Laxmanniaceae, Nolinaceae.*

Subkey 14. Monocotyledon. Plants herbaceous, not climbing, scandent, or fully aquatic. Leaf blades broad.

1. Leaves spiromonostichous. . . . . *Costaceae.*
1. Leaves not spiromonostichous.
    2. Leaves 3-ranked. . . . . *Cyperaceae, Hypoxidaceae.*
    2. Leaves not 3-ranked.
        3. Tertiary veins exposed along margin when leaf blade torn. . . . . *Marantaceae.*
        3. Tertiary veins not exposed along margin when leaf blade torn.
            4. Leaves bifid or palm-like. . . . . *Cyclanthaceae.*
            4. Leaves not bifid or palm-like.
                5. Leaves in basal rosettes; blades coriaceous or fleshy, the apex gradually tapering into sharp point. . . . .
                  . . . . *Agavaceae.*
                5. Leaves never in basal rosettes; blades sometimes coriaceous or fleshy; the apex never tapering into sharp point.
                  6. Internodes often hollow. Leaf sheaths ligulate. . . . . *Poaceae.*
                  6. Internodes usually solid. Leaf sheaths not ligulate.
                      7. Flowers with sexual parts fused into central column. . . . . *Orchidaceae.*
                      7. Flowers without sexual parts fused into central column.
                          8. Inflorescences of spathe and spadix. . . . . *Araceae.*
                          8. Inflorescences not of spathe and spadix.
                              9. Flowers actnomorphic or zygomorphic, perianth parts 6; stamens often 6.
                                  10. Perianth with outer and inner parts different in appearance (with sepals and petals). . . . . . .
                                    . . . . *Commelinaceae.*
                                  10. Perianth with outer and inner parts similar in appearance (with tepals). . . . .
                                    . . . . *Alstroemeriaceae, Convallariaceae, Herreriaceae.*
                            9. Flowers zygomorphic, without combination of 6 perianth parts and 6 stamens.
                                11. Leaves spiral.
                                  12. Plants monoecious. Inflorescences very large, the units subtended by large, boat-shaped bracts. Flowers unisexual. . . . . *Musaceae.*
                                  12. Plants hermaphroditic. Inflorescences not very large, the units not subtended by large, boat-shaped bracts. Flowers bisexual. . . . . *Cannaceae.*
                                11. Leaves distichous.
                                  13. Stamens 1 per flower; staminodes 2–5, petal-like.
                                    14. Plants aromatic. Thecae 2 per anther. . . . . *Zingerberaceae.*
                                    14. Plants not aromatic. Thecae 1 per anther. . . . . *Marantaceae.*
                                13. Stamens > 1 per flower, usually 5; staminodes absent or 1, not petal-like. . . . .
                          . . . . *Heliconiaceae, Strelitziaceae* (small *Phenakospermum*).

**Subkey 15. Monocotyledon. Plants herbaceous, not climbing or scandent, not fully aquatic.
Leaf blades linear, grass-like, lanceolate, ensiform, or terete.**

1. Plants terrestrial. Leaves in basal rosettes; blades succulent, the apex gradually tapering into sharp point. . *Agavaceae.*
1. Plants terrestrial or epiphytic. Leaves sometimes in basal rosettes; blades infrequently succulent, the apex never tapering into sharp point.
    2. Leaves 3-ranked. . . . . *Cyperaceae, Hypoxidaceae, Juncaceae.*
    2. Leaves not 3-ranked.
        3. Leaves equitant. . . . . *Haemodoraceae, Iridaceae, Orchidaceae, Xyridaceae.*
        3. Leaves not equitant.
             4. Internodes often hollow. Leaf sheaths ligulate. . . . . *Poaceae.*
             4. Internodes usually solid. Leaf sheaths not ligulate.

5. Plants with mucilage covering emerging leaves and young inflorescences. . . . . *Rapateaceae.*

5. Plants without mucilage covering emerging leaves and young inforescences.

    6. Small rainforest herbs, often in white sand along riverbanks. Inflorescences cymes, subtended by 2 long conspicuous bracts. . . . . *Taccaceae (Tacca).*

    6. Plants small or large, in many habitats. Inflorescences without combination of cymes subtended by 2 long conspicuous bracts.

        7. Roots surrounded by white velamen. Flowers with sexual parts fused into central column. . . . . *Orchidaceae.*

        7. Roots not surrounded by white velamen. Flowers without sexual parts fused into central column.

            8. Plants with extremely fibrous leaves. Leaf blades often with alternating horizontal bands of lighter and darker colors. . . . . *Dracaenaceae (Sansevieria).*

            8. Plants usually without extremely fibrous leaves. Leaf blades usually not with alternating horizontal bands of lighter and darker colors.

                9. Perianth of sepals and petals.

                    10. Ovary inferior. . . . . *Bromeliaceae.*

                    10. Ovary superior.

                        11. Inflorescences often heads or spikes. . . . . *Eriocaulaceae, Xyridaceae.*

                        11. Inflorescences not heads or spikes. . . . . *Commelinaceae.*

                9. Perianth of tepals.

                  12. Ovary inferior.

                    13. Leaves usually resupinate. . . . . *Alstroemeriaceae*

                    13. Leaves not resupinate. . . . . *Amaryllidaceae, Velloziaceae*

                12. Ovary superior or semi-inferior. . . . . *Alliaceae, Anthericaceae, Calochortaceae, Convallariaceae, Herreriaceae, Juncaceae, Melanthiaceae, Phormiaceae, Tecophilaeaceae, Themidaceae, Thurniaceae, Velloziaceae.*

INDEX TO SCIENTIFIC NAMES

The index to scientific names is prepared from the dicotyledon and monocotyledon sections only. Family names are set in capitals and families covered in the book are in **bold**. The page number at which a family treatment starts is in **bold**, and pages with botanical line illustrations are indicated by asterisks(*). As plates are not on numbered pages, color images are referred to by their plate (Pl.) numbers.

Bambusoideae (Poaceae), 470
Banara, 160
Banisteriopsis, 229
  caapi, 232
  muricata, 229
Baptisia, 155
Barbacenia, 490, 491
  polyantha, 491
  vandellii, 491
Barbacenioideae (Velloziaceae), 490, 490
Barbaceniopsis, 490, 491
Barbeuioideae (Phytolaccaceae), 293
Barclayoideae (Nymphaeaceae), 271
Barleria
  cristata, 6
  lupulina, 6
Barnadesia arborea, Pl. 5B
Barnadesieae (Asteraceae), 33, 35, 36, 38
Barnadesiinae (Asteraceae), 36
Barnadesioideae (Asteraceae), 33, 36
Barneoudia, 320
Barnebya, 231
Bartonia, 167
Bartsia, 348, 349
Basananthe, 286
Basella, 44, 45
  alba, 44*, 45
  paniculata, 44
BASELLACEAE, 44*, 311
Basistemon, 349, 350
Bastardiopsis, 234
BATACEAE, 45, 46*, 97
Batales, 45
Batis, 46
  argillicola, 45
  maritima, 45, 46*
Battus, 32
Bauera, 123
Bauhinia macranthera, 153
BAUERACEAE, 122
Bdallophyton, 318, 319
  americanum, 319
  bambusarum, 319
Beaucarnea, 464
  recurvata, 464
Becquerelia, 435
Begonia, 46, 47
  glabra, 47*
BEGONIACEAE, 46, 47*, 116, 120
Begoniella, 47
Beilschmiedia, 204
Beiselia, 67, 68
  mexicana, 67
Bejaria, 142
Bellendenoideae (Proteaceae), 314
Belliolum, 398
Belonanthus, 385
BERBERIDACEAE, 48, 49*, 247, 285, 320
Berberidineae (Berberidaceae), 48
Berberis, 48, 49
  bumeliifolia, 49*
Bergenia, 348
Bergia, 138, 139
  arenarioides, 138
  capensis, 138
  suffruticosa, 138, 139
  texana, 138

Berlinianche, 318
Bernardinia, 112, 113
Bernoullia, 56, 360
Berrya, 376
Bertholletia, 207, 208
  excelsa, 207, 208, 209
Bertolonieae (Melastomataceae), 242
Beschorneria, 405
Besleria, 171
Beslerieae (Gesneriaceae), 171
Bessera, 485
Beta, 97
Betula, 50
BETULACEAE, 46, 50*, 90, 157, 196, 374
Betuleae (Betulaceae), 50
Bicuiba, 261
Bidens, 38, 39
Bieberstinia, 169
BIGNONIACEAE, 51, 52*, 53, 202, Pl. 6
Bignonieae (Bignoniaceae), 52, 53
Billbergia violacea, 419*
Billia, 182
  columbiana, 182
  hippocastanum, 182
  rosea, 182, Pl. 23B1, B2
Biophytum, 283, 284
Bixa, 54, 55
  orellana, 54*, 55, Pl. 6D
BIXACEAE, 54*, 103, 159, 200, 290, 291,
  Pl. 6
Blakea, 241, 242
Blakeeae (Melastomataceae), 242
Blastemanthus, 275
Blastocaulon, 440
Bleasdalea, 314
Blechum, 4, 6
Blennosperma, 38
Blighia, 341
Blossfeldia liliputana, 75
Blumenbachia, 217
Bobartia, 449
Bocagea, 19
Bocageopsis, 19
Bocconia, 284, 285
  frutescens, Pl. 35C
Boehmeria, 384, 385
Boerhavia, 269, 270
  diffusa, 269
  erecta, 269
  hirsuta, 271
  tuberosa, 271
Bolboschoenus, 435
  robustus, 436
Boldoa, 270
Boldoeae (Nyctaginaceae), 270
Bomarea, 409, 410
  edulis, 409
  pardina, Pl. 53D
  rosea, 409
BOMBACACEAE, 55, 56*, 137, 233, 234,
  235, 360, Pl. 7
Bombacoideae (Bombacaceae), 55, 56, 57,
  235
Bombacopsis, 56
Bombax, 56
Bombus, 137, 240, 475
Bonamia, 113, 114

Bonnetia, 58, 59
  celiae, 58*
  sessilis, Pl. 7D
BONNETIACEAE, 58*, 106, Pl. 7
Bonnetioideae (Bonnetiaceae), 58, 370
Bonplandia, 305
  geminiflora, 306
Bontia daphnoides, 258, 259*
Bonyunia, 220, 221
Boopis, 77, 78
BORAGINACEAE, 59, 60*, 61, 62, 113, 190,
  202, 210, 305, 355, 356, Pl. 7
Boraginales, 60, 190
Boragineae (Boraginaceae), 59, 60, 61
Boraginoideae (Boraginaceae), 59, 60, 61
Borago, 59, 60
Borderea, 436, 437
  pyrenaica, 438
Borojoa, 328
  patinoi, 332
  sorbilis, 332
Borreria, 328
Boswellia sacra, 70
Bouchea, 387
Bougainvillea, 270
Bougueria, 297
Bourreria, 59
  rubra, 61
  succulenta, 62
Boussingaultia, 44
Bouvardia, 333
Bowlesia, 29
Boykinia, 347
Brabejum, 314
Brachiaria, 470
Brachycereus, 74
Brachychiton, 361
Brachymyrmex heeri, 332
Brachynema, 276
Brachyotum, 241
Brachyphylla, 172
Bracteanthus, 353
Brasenia, 72, 73
  schreberi, 72, 73*
Brassavola martiana, Pl. 60E
Brassica, 63, 64, 225
  juncea, 64
  napus, 64
  oleracea, 64
  rapa, 64
BRASSICACEAE, 46, 62, 63*, 82, 377
Brassicales, 85, 379
Brassiceae (Brassicaceae), 63
Bravaisia, 5
Brayopsis, 64
Bredemeyera, 307
  floribunda, 308
Bretschneidera, 379
Brexia, 175
Brocchinia, 419, 420
  reducta, 420
Brodiaeeae (Alliaceae), 408, 485
Bromelia, 419
BROMELIACEAE, 417, 418, 419*, 420, 489,
  490, Pl. 55
Bromeliales, 419
Bromelioideae (Bromeliaceae), 419, 420

Cereus, 74
  jamacaru, 75
Cerinthe, 61
Ceriops, 325
Ceropegia, 25
Ceroxyloideae (Arecaceae), 417
Cervantesia, 338
  tomentosa, 338
Cespedesia spathulata, 275
Cestroideae (Solanaceae), 355, 356
Cestrum, 134, 355
Ceuthostoma, 90
Chaenactideae (Asteraceae), 36
Chamaecrista, 151
Chamaedorea, 417
Chamaesyce, 146, 148
  amplexicaulis, Pl. 19C
Chamelum, 449
Chamerion, 280
  angustifolium, 280
Champereia, 282
Chaunochiton, 276, 277
Cheiloclinium, 183, 184
Cheilodromes, 28
Chelidonioideae (Papaveraceae), 285
Chelonanthus, 167
  alatus, 166*, 167
Cheloneae (Scrophulariaceae), 349
CHENOPODIACEAE, 13, 46, **97**, 98*, 270,
  293
Chenopodium, 98
  album, 98
  ambrosioides, 98*
  berlandieri variety nuttaliae, 98
  quinoa, 98
Chichicaste, 217, 218
Chimantaea mirabilis, Pl. 5E
Chimarrhis, 331, 332
  microcarpa, 330*
  turbinata, 329*
Chiococceae (Rubiaceae), 331
Chionanthus, 278
  compacta, 278*
Chiongraphideae (Melanthiaceae), 461
Chiranthodendron, 360, 361
Chiranthofremontia
  lenzii, 360
Chironia, 167
Chironieae (Gentianaceae), 166, 167
Chlidanthus, 411
Chloantheae (Verbenaceae), 388
Chloanthoideae (Verbenaceae), 388, 389
CHLORANTHACEAE, **99***, Pl. 13
Chloranthus, 99
Chloridoideae (Poaceae), 470, 472
Chlorocardium, 204
  rodiei, 206
Chlorophytum, 412, 413
  comosum, 413
Chlorospatha, 413
Choisya, 333
Chomelia, 328
Chorisepalum, 167
Chorisia, 56
Chosenia, 337
Chromolaena, 33, 39
  odorata, 39

Chromolucuma, 342
Chrysanthemum, 39
  coccineum, 39
CHRYSOBALANACEAE, **100**, 101*, 128,
  143, 150, 152, 321, 378, 397, Pl. 13
Chrysobalaneae (Chrysobalanaceae), 101
Chrysobalanus, 100, 101, 102
  icaco, 100, 101, 102
Chrysochlamys, 105, 106
Chrysolepis, 157
Chrysophylleae (Sapotaceae), 342
Chrysophyllum, 342, 343
Chrysosplenium, 346, 347
Chrysothemis pulchella, Pl. 22C
Chusquea, 470
Chytropsia, 330
Cichoraceae (Asteraceae), 36
Cichorieae (Asteraceae), 36
Cichorioideae (Asteraceae), 36
Cichorium intybus, 39
Cienfuegosia, 233
Cinchona, 199, 331, 332
Cinchoneae (Rubiaceae), 330, 331, 332
Cinchonoideae (Rubiaceae), 330, 332
Cinnamodendron, 81
Cinnamomum, 204, 205
  zeylanicum, 206
Cipurinae (Iridaceae), 449
Circaea, 280
Cissampelos, 248
  pareira, 248*
Cissus, 394, 395
  erosa, 395*, Pl. 51D
  erosa subspecies erosa, 395
  quadrangularis, 394
  striata subspecies striata, 394
CISTACEAE, 54, **102**, 103*, 159, 257,
  351
Cistales, 103
Cistus, 104
  incanus subspecies creticus, 104
  ladanifer, 104
  salviifolius, 104
Citharexyleae (Verbenaceae), 388
Citharexylum, 388, 390
Citroideae (Rutaceae), 333
Citronella, 192, 193
  mucronata, 192
Citrus, 334, 335
  aurantifolia, 335
  limon, 335
  paradisi, 335
  sinensis, 335
Cladium, 435
  jamaicense, 436
Cladocolea, 221
Clarisia ilicifolia, 254
Clarkia, 280
Clavija, 371, 372
  lancifolia subspecies chermontiana,
  371*
Clematis, 320, 321
  bahamica, 320*
Clematoclethra, 9
Cleome, 82, 83
  hasslerana, 83
  spinosa, 83

Cleomoideae (Capparaceae), 63, 82, 83,
  377
Clerodendreae (Verbenaceae), 388
Clerodendrum, 202, 387, 389, 390
Clethra, 104, 105
  section Clethra, 104, 105
  section Cuellaria, 104, 105
  section Cuellaria subsection Cuellaria, 104
  section Cuellaria subsection Pseudocuellaria, 104
  acuminata, 105
  alnifolia, 105
  arborea, 105
  barbinervi, 105
  pringlei, Pl. 13C1, C2
CLETHRACEAE, **104**, 125, 141, Pl. 13
Cleyera, 367, 368
  ochnacea, 368
Clibadium, 39
Clidemia, 242
Cliftonia, 125, 126
Clinantheae (Amaryllidaceae), 411
Clinanthus, 410, 411
  humilis, 411
Cliococca, 215
Clitoria amazonum, Pl. 20C
Clusia, 12, 105, 106, 107
  candelabrum, Pl. 14A
  columnaris, 107
  criuva, 107
  microstemon, Pl. 14B
  nemorosa, Pl. 14C
  palmicida, 106*
  rosea, 107
  schomburgkiana, 107
CLUSIACEAE, 12, 58, **105**, 106*, 107, 138,
  302, Pl. 14
Clusieae (Clusiaceae), 106
Clusiella, 106
Clusioideae (Clusiaceae), 106, 107
Clytostoma, 53
CNEORACEAE, **108**, 352
Cneoridium, 333
Cneorum, 108
  pulverulentum, 108
  tricoccon, 108
  trimerum, 108
Cnestidium, 112
  guianense, 112*
Cnidoscolus, 146, 147, 148, 149
  aconitifolius, 149
  urnigerus, 148
Coaxana, 21
Cobaea, 305, 306
  scandens, 305*, 306
Cobaeoideae (Polemoniaceae), 305
Coccoloba, 308, 309, 310
  parimensis, 309*
  uvifera, 310
Coccolobeae (Polygonaceae), 309
Cochliostema, 426, 427
COCHLOSPERMACEAE, 54
Cochlospermum, 54, 55
  subgenus Cochlospermum, 54
  subgenus Diporandra, 54
  vitifolium, 54*, 55
Cocos nucifera, 417, 418

Euglypha, 31
Euonymus, 96, 192
Eupatorieae (Asteraceae), 33, 35, 36, 37
Eupatorium, 33, 37
Euphonia affinis, 258
Euphorbia, 146, 147, 148, 149, 210
  subgenus Poinsettia, 148
  antisiphylitica, 149
  pulcherrima, 149
EUPHORBIACEAE, 127, 143, **146**, 147*,
  148*, 149*, 159, 200, 210, 230, 372, 381,
  Pl. 19
Euphorbiales, 71, 147
Euphorbieae (Euphorbiaceae), 147, 148, 149
Euphorbioideae (Euphorbiaceae), 146, 147,
  148, 149
Euphrasieae (Scrophulariaceae), 349
Euphronia, 150, 151, 397
  acuminatissima, 150, 151
  guianensis, 150, 151, Pl. 19D
  hirtelloides, 150, 151
EUPHRONIACEAE, 150, Pl. 19
Euplassa, 314, 315
  pinnata, 314*
Euploca, 59
Eupodostemeae (Podostemaceae), 303
EUPOMATIACEAE, 262
Euptoieta hegesia, 381
Eurosidae, 147
Eurosids, 95
Eurosids I, 87, 186, 391, 215
Eurya, 368
Eurystemon, 474, 475
Euscaphis, 358
Eustephia, 411
Eustephieae (Amaryllidaceae), 411, 412
Eustoma, 166
  grandiflorum, 167
Euterpe, 417
  oleracea, 418
Euthemideae (Ochnaceae), 275
Eutrema wasabi, 64
Euverbeneae (Verbenaceae), 388
Euxylophora paraensis, 335
Evea, 330
Evodianthus, 431
  funifer, Pl. 57C
Evolvulus, 113, 114
  glomeratus, 115
Exaceae (Gentianaceae), 167
Exacum affine, 168
Exellodendron, 100, 101
Exospermum, 398
Exostema, 332

FABACEAE, 148, **151**, 152*, 153*, 154*,
  155*, 187, 198, 306, 328, 364, Pl. 20, Pl.
  21
Fabales, 152, 306, 306, 364
Faboideae (=Papilionoideae; Fabaceae), 151
Facheiroa, 74
FAGACEAE, 46, 50, 90, **156**, 157*, 158, 196,
  374, Pl. 21
Fagales, 50, 157, 196
Fagoideae (Fagaceae), 157
Fagonia, 400, 401
Fagopyrum esculentum, 310

Fagraea, 167
Fagus, 156, 157, 158
  mexicana, 157
Faramea, 328, 331
  anisocalyx, Pl. 41B
  guianensis, 329*
Farsetia, 64
Fauria, 249
Fendlera, 188, 218
Ferdinandusa paraensis, 329*
Ferocactus, 76
Ferula, 20
Festuca, 470, 473
Fevillea cordifolia, 121
Ficeae (Moraceae), 254
Ficus, 94, 253, 254, 255, 256
  carica, 255, 256
  glabrata, 256
  gomelleira, 255, Pl. 31E
  nymphaeifolia, 255
  schultesii, 255
Fimbristylis, 435, 436
Fioria, 233
Firmiana, 361
Fittonia, 6
Flacourtia, 159
  indica, 160
FLACOURTIACEAE, 54, 82, 137, 143, **158**,
  159*, 160, 161, 200, 201, 235, 257, 286,
  290, 291, 337, 372, 375, 376, 381, Pl. 21
Flacourtieae (Flacourtiaceae), 160
FLAGELLARIACEAE, 470
Flickingeria, 468
Flindersioideae (Rutaceae), 333
Florilegus, 475
Floscopa, 425, 427
Floydia, 314
Fockea, 23
Foetidioideae (Lecythidaceae), 207, 208
Forchhammeria, 63, 82
Forestiera, 278
  eggersiana, 278*
Formanodendron, 157
Forsythia, 279
Fosterella, 419, 420
Fothergilleae (Hamamelidaceae), 179
Fouquieria, 161, 162
  subgenus Bronnia, 162
  subgenus Fouquieria, 162
  subgenus Idria, 162
  columnaria, 162
  formosa, 161
  splendens, 161, 162*
FOUQUIERIACEAE, **161**, 162*, 305
Fouquieriales, 162
Frailea, 74
Francoa, 347
Frankenia, 163
  chilensis, 163
  ericifolia, 163
  gypsophila, 163
  laevis, 163
  margaritae, 163
  salina, 163
  triandra, 163
FRANKENIACEAE, 163
Frankia, 260

Franklinia altamaha, 370
Fraxinus, 278, 279
Fremontieae (Sterculiaceae), 360, 361
Fremontodendron, 360
Frezieria, 367, 368
Froesia, 317, 318
Fryxellia, 233
Fuchsia, 279, 280
  paniculata, Pl. 34C
Fuertesia, 217, 218, 219
Fuirena, 436
FUMARIACEAE, 285
Funastrum clausum, 25
Funifera, 373
Furcraea, 405
Fusaea, 19, 20
  longifolia, Pl. 3A
  peruviana, 19
Fusispermoideae (Violaceae), 391
Fusispermum, 390, 391

Gaiadendron, 222
  punctatum, 223
Galeandra devoniana, Pl. 60D1, D2
Galegeae (Fabaceae), 152
Galeola, 466
Galipea jasminiflora, 335
Galipeinae (Rutaceae), 334
Galium, 328, 330, 331, 332
Gallesia, 293, 294
Galphimia, 231
  glauca, 232
  gracilis, 232
Galpinia, 224
Galvezia, 349, 350
Gamanthera, 204
Gambelia, 349
Gamocarpha, 77
Gamochaeta, 39
Gamotopea, 330
Garcinia, 105, 106, 107
  gummi-gutta, 107
  mangostana, 107
Gardenia, 332
Gardenieae (Rubiaceae), 331, 332
Gardneria, 220
Garrya, 164
  subgenus Fadyenia, 164
  subgenus Garrya, 164
  elliptica, 164
  fremontii, 164
  veatchii, 164
GARRYACEAE, 117, **164**
Garryales, 192
Garuga, 68
Gastonia, 28
Gaultheria, 140
Gaylussacia, 140, 142
Gazania, 39
Geissanthus, 262, 263
Geissoieae (Cunoniaceae), 122
Geissois, 123
GELSEMIACEAE, 164, 165*, 220, 300
Gelsemieae (Gelsemiaceae), 165, 300
Gelsemium, 165
  rankinii, 165
  sempervirens, 165*

Geniostoma, 220, 221
GENIOSTOMACEAE, 220
Genipa, 332
  americana, 332, Pl. 42C
Genisteae (Fabaceae), 152
Genlisea, 211, 212
Gentiana, 166, 167, 168
GENTIANACEAE, 109, **166***, 167, 220, 249,
  Pl. 22
Gentianales, 127, 165, 167, 220, 249, 300, 328,
  330, 355
Gentianeae (Gentianaceae), 166, 167
Gentianella, 166, 167, 168
  cernua, Pl. 22B
Gentianinae (Gentianaceae), 167
Geoffrea, 155
Geogenanthus, 426, 427
Geonoma, 417
  deversa, 418
GERANIACEAE, **168**, 169*, 358, 379
Geraniales, 43, 122, 169, 213, 283, 379
Geranieae (Geraniaceae), 169
Geranium, 168, 169, 170
  carolinianum, 169*
Gerascanthus, 59
Gerbera, 39
Gesneria, 171, 173
GESNERIACEAE, 66, 109, **170**, 171*, 172,
  173, 220, Pl. 22
Gesnerieae (Gesneriaceae), 171
Gesnerioideae (Gesneriaceae), 171, 172,
  173
Gethyrum, 408
Geum, 326
Geunsia, 389
Gevuina, 314, 315
  avellana, 315
Gibasis, 426, 427
Gibasoides, 426
Gilia, 305
  incisa, 306
Gillenieae (Rosaceae), 326
Gillesioideae (Alliaceae), 408
Gilliesia, 408
Ginoria, 223, 224, 225
Glandularia, 390
  teucriifolia, 388
Glaucidium, 320
Glaucioideae (Papaveraceae), 285
Gleasonia, 328, 330, 331
Gleditsia, 152, 155
Glinus, 251
Globbeae (Zingiberaceae), 494
Gloeospermum, 390, 391, 392
Glomeropitcairnia, 420
Glossocalyx, 353, 354
  longicuspis, 354
Glossophaga, 172
  soricina, 258
Gloxinieae (Gesneriaceae), 171, 172
Glyricidia, 155
Gmelina arborea, 390
Gnaphalieae (Asteraceae), 35, 36, 37
Gochnatia, 33, 35
Goetzea, 355
GOETZEACEAE, 355
GOMORTEGACEAE, 205, 354

Gomphrena, 13
  globosa, 14
Gomphrenoideae (Amaranthaceae), 13
Gongora pleiocrhoma, 467*
GONYSTYLACEAE, 372
Gonzalagunia, 328
Goodenia, 173, 174
GOODENIACEAE, 36, 78, **173**, 174*, 249,
  Pl. 22
Goodyera, 465, 468
Gordonia, 369
Gordonieae (Theaceae), 370
Gossypieae (Malvaceae), 233, 234
Gossypioides, 233
Gossypium, 233, 234
  arboreum, 234
  bardadense, 234
  herbaceum, 234
  hirsutum, 234
Gouania, 323
  domingensis, 324
  lupuloides, 324
Goupia, 95, 96
  glabra, 95*, 96
GOUPIACEAE, 95, 391
Graffenrieda, 241
Grahamia, 312
GRAMINEAE, **470**
Grammadenia, 262
Graptopetalum, 118
Gratioleae (Scrophulariaceae), 349
Greigia, 419, 420
Grevilleoideae (Proteaceae), 314, 315
Grewia, 375
Grewieae (Tiliaceae), 375
Grias, 207, 208
  cauliflora, 207
  haughtii, 209
  neuberthii, 209
  peruviana, 209
Griffineae (Amaryllidaceae), 411
Griffinia, 411
Griffiniopsis, 411
Grindelia, 38
Griselinia, 29
GRISELINIACEAE, 29
Groenlandia, 476
Gronovia, 217, 218
  longiflora, 218
Gronovioideae (Loasaceae), 217, 218
Grossularia, 175
GROSSULARIACEAE, 117, 145, 146, **174**,
  175*, 316, 347
GRUBBIACEAE, 141
Grumilea, 330
Guadua, 473
Guaiacum, 400, 401
  angustifolium, 401
  officinale, 400*, 401
  sanctum, 401, Pl. 52E1, E2
Guapira, 269, 270
  opposita, 269
Guarea, 243, 244, 245
  cristata, 245
  guidonia, 245

  kunthiana, 243
  michel-moddei, 245*
  pubescens, 244
Guatteria, 18, 19
  punctata, Pl. 3C
  scandens, 19
Guazuma, 360, 361
  ulmifolia, 361
Guettarda, 328
Guettardeae (Rubiaceae), 331, 332
Guilfoylia, 364
Guizotia abyssinica, 125
Gundelieae (Asteraceae), 36
Gunnera, 42, 176, 177, 178
  subgenus *Misandra*, 176, 177
  subgenus *Ostenigunnera*, 176
  subgenus *Panke*, 176, 177
  atropurpurea, 177
  brephogea, 177
  colombiana, 176, 177
  herteri, 176
  insignis, 177*, Pl. 23A1, A2
  lobata, 176, 177
  macrophylla, 177
  magellanica, 176, 177
  magnifica, 177
  manicata, 177
  pilosa, 177
  tinctorea, 177
GUNNERACEAE, 42, **176**, 177*, 178, Pl. 23
Gunneroideae (Gunneraceae), 176, 178
Gurania, 120, 121
  subumbellata, Pl. 16C1–C3
Gustavia, 207, 208, 209
  hexapetala, 207*
  longifolia, Pl. 26B
  speciosa, 209
Guttiferae, 138
Guzmania, 418
  nicaraguensis, Pl. 55E
Gymnocalycium, 74
Gymnocladus, 152, 155
Gymnopodium, 308, 309, 310
Gymnosiphon, 421
  divaricatus, 422*
Gymnosporia, 96
Gymnostachydoideae (Araceae), 414
Gymnostoma, 90
Gynopleura, 228
Gynotrocheae (Rhizophoraceae), 325
Gynoxys, 33, 175
Gypsophila, 88, 90
Gyranthera, 56, 57
Gyrocarpoideae (Hernandiaceae), 180, 181
Gyrocarpus, 180, 181
  americanus, 181
  jatrophifolius, 181
GYROSTEMONACEAE, 45

Habenaria, 465
Habranthus, 411
Hackelia, 59, 61
Hadrodemas, 426
Haematoxylum campechianum, 156
HAEMODORACEAE, 426, **441***, 442, 474,
  484, 490, Pl. 58
Haemodorales, 441

Homalium, 159, 160
  racemosum, 161
Homalomena, 413, 414, 416
Hopea, 131
Hordeum, 473
Hornschuchia, 19
Horsfordia, 234
Hortia arborea, Pl. 42D
Hortonia floribunda, 252
Hortonioideae (Monimiaceae), 252
Hosta, 405
Hoya, 25
Hualania, 306, 307
Huberodendron, 56
Hudsonia, 102
Huertea, 358, 359
Hugonia, 184, 185
HUGONIACEAE, 143, **184**, 185*, 186, 215, Pl. 24
Humbertiodendron, 378
  saboureaui, 377
Humiria
  balsamifera, 185, 186, 187
HUMIRIACEAE, 143, **185**, 186*, Pl. 24
Humiriastrum, 185, 186, 187
Humirioideae (Humiriaceae), 186
Humulus, 254
Hunnemannia, 284, 285
Huodendron, 363
Hura, 149
  crepitans, 149
Hureae (Euphorbiaceae), 149
Huthia, 305
HYACINTHACEAE, 405, 411, 485
Hyalisma, 487
Hybanthus, 390, 391, 392
Hydnocarpus, 160
Hydnora, 187, 188
HYDNORACEAE, 32, **187**, 296, Pl. 24
Hydnorales, 42
Hydrangea, 188, 189
  section Cornidia, 188, 189
  section Cornidia subsection Monosegia, 188
  section Cornidia subsection Polysegia, 188
  integrifolia, 188
  peruviana, 189*
HYDRANGEACEAE, 109, 117, **188**, 189*, 218, 347
Hydrangeeae (Hydrangeaceae), 188
Hydrangeoideae (Hydrangeaceae), 188
Hydrastis, 320
Hydrastoideae (Ranunculaceae), 320
Hydrilla, 444, 445, 446
  verticillata, 444, 446
Hydrocera, 43
Hydrocharis, 445
HYDROCHARITACEAE, 407, **444**, 445*, 457, Pl. 59
Hydrocharitales, 433
Hydrocleys, 457
  nymphoides, 457, Pl. 59C
Hydrocotyle, 20, 21, 22
Hydrocotyloideae (Apiaceae), 21, 29
Hydrogaster, 375, 376
Hydrolea, 190, 191
  spinosa, 190, 191
  zeylanica, 190

Hydroleae (Hydrophyllaceae), 190
HYDROPELTIDACEAE, 72
Hydropeltidales, 72
Hydropeltoideae (Cabombaceae), 72
HYDROPHYLLACEAE, 60, 113, **190**, 191*, 210, 300, 305, 355, 356, Pl. 24
Hydrophylleae (Hydrophyllaceae), 190
HYDROSTACHYACEAE, 76, 302
Hydrothrix, 474, 475
  gardneri, 475
Hyeronima, 146, 147
Hylaenthe, 458
Hylenaea, 183, 184
Hylocarpa, 186, 187
Hylocereus, 75
  trigonus, 74*
  undatus, 75
Hymenaea, 153, 155
  coubaril, 155
Hymenocallideae (Amaryllidaceae), 411
Hymenocallis, 410, 411, 412
  caribaea, 411*
Hypelate, 341
HYPERICACEAE, 106, 138
Hypericeae, 302
Hypericoideae (Clusiaceae), 106, 302
Hypericopis, 163
Hypericum, 105, 106, 107
  laricifolium, Pl. 14D
Hyperocarpa, 436, 437, 438
Hypocyrta, 172
Hypoestes, 5
  phyllostachya, 6
Hypolytreae (Cyperaceae), 435
Hypolytrum, 435
  pulchrum, Pl. 57D
HYPOXIDACEAE, **447***, 448, 465, 484, 490
Hypoxis, 447
  decumbens, 447*
Hypseocharis, 168, 169, 170, 283
Hypsipyla, 245
Hyptis, 201, 202, 203
  lanceolata, 202*

Iberis, 64
Ibetralia surinamensis, 329*
Ibicella, 239
Icacina, 192
  oliviformis, 193
  senegalensis, 193
ICACINACEAE, **192***, 193, Pl. 25
Icacineae (Icacinaceae), 192
Ichnanthus panicoides, 472*
Ichthyothere, 39
Icicopsis, 69
Idesia, 337
Idria, 162
Ilex, 26, 96
  aquifolium, 26, 27
  cissoidea, 27
  colchica, 27
  cornuta, 27
  crenata, 27
  cymosa, 27
  dimorphophylla, 26
  dipyrena, 26
  guayusa, 27

latifolia, 27
  mitis, 27
  opaca, 27
  paraguariensis, 26
  petiolaris, Pl. 4F
  purpurea, 27
  tarapotina, 27
  urbaniana, 27*
  vomitoria, 27
  yunnanensis variety eciliata, 27
ILLICIACEAE, **193**, 194*, 398
Illiciales, 193, 398
Illicium, 193, 194
  anisatum, 194
  cubense, 193
  floridanum, 193, 194*
  parviflorum, 193, 194
  verum, 194
Illigera, 180
Impatiens, 43
  bakeri, 43
  balsamina, 43
  mexicana, 43
  sodenii, 43
  turrialbana, 43
  walleriana, 43
Indigofera, 151, 155
Indorouchera, 184
Inga, 154
Ingeae (Fabaceae), 152, 154
Inuleae (Asteraceae), 35, 36
Iochroma, 357
Iodeae (Icacinaceae), 192
Ipecacuanha, 330
Ipheion, 408
Ipomoea, 113, 114, 115
  series Pharbitis, 114
  alba, 114, 115
  aquatica, 113
  arborescens, 114
  batatas, 115
  carnea subspecies fistulosa, 114
  eggersii, 114*
  nil, 115
  pescaprae, 113, 115
  purpurea, 115
  repanda, 114*
  setifera, Pl. 15D
  tricolor, 115
  triloba, 114*
Ipomoeeae (Convolvulaceae), 114
Ipomopsis, 305, 306
Iresine, 13
IRIDACEAE, **448***, 449, 465, Pl. 59
Irideae (Iridaceae), 448, 449
Iridoideae (Iridaceae), 448, 449
Iris, 448, 449
  subgenus Limniris, 449
  florentina, 449
Irlbachia, 166, 167
IRVINGIACEAE, 352
Irvingioideae (Simaroubaceae), 352
Iryanthera, 261, 262
Isachne, 470
Isatis, 64
Ischnosiphon, 458, 459
  arouma, 459

Nerium oleander, 25
Nesaea, 223, 224
Nesaeeae (Lythraceae), 224
Neuburgia, 220
Neurada, 54
NEURADACEAE, 54
Neurolaena, 39
Neurotheca, 167
Neuwiedia, 465
Nicandra, 356
Nicotiana, 42, 355
  sylvestris, 356
  tabacum, 356
  tomentosiformis, 356
Nidularium, 419
Nietneria, 460, 461
Nigella sativa, 321
Nitraria, 401
NITRARIACEAE, 401
Nivenioideae (Iridaceae), 449
Noisettia, 391, 392
  orchidiflora, 392*
Nolana
  subgenus *Nolana*, 268
  subgenus *Alona*, 268
  galapagensis, Pl. 32F
NOLANACEAE, **268**, 355, Pl. 32
Nolina, 464
NOLINACEAE, 439, 453, **464**
Nonatelia, 330
Norantea, 236, 237, 238
  guianensis, 237*, 238, Pl. 29A1, A2
Noranteoideae (Marcgraviaceae), 237
Norrisia, 221
Nostoc, 176
  punctiforme, 177
Notaphila, 73
NOTHOFAGACEAE, 157, 196, 374
Nothofagus, 156, 157
Nothoscordum, 408
Notobuxus, 71
Notopleura, 328, 330
Notopora schomburgkiana, 142
Nototriche, 233
Nuphar, 271, 272
  advena, 271
Nupharoideae (Nymphaeaceae), 271
NYCTAGINACEAE, 210, 251, **269***, 270, Pl. 33
Nyctagineae (Nyctaginaceae), 270
Nymphaea, 271, 272
  subgenus *Hydrocallis*, 272
  caerulea, 271
  capensis, 271
  lotus, 271
  mexicana, 272
NYMPHAEACEAE, 96, 194, **271**, 272*, Pl. 33
Nymphaeales, 72, 96, 267, 271
Nymphaeoideae (Nymphaeaceae), 271, 272
Nymphoides, 249, 250
  aquatica, 250
  fallax, 249
  flaccida, 249, 250
  grayana, 249, 250*
  humboldtiana, 249
  indica, 249, 250, Pl. 31C
  peltata, 250

Nypoideae (Arecaceae), 417
Nyssa, 274
  aquatica, 274
  sylvatica, 273*, 274
  talamancana, 273
NYSSACEAE, 117, **273***

Obolaria, 167
Ochna, 274
OCHNACEAE, 54, 200, **274**, 275*, 317, Pl. 33
Ochneae (Ochnaceae), 274
Ochnoideae (Ochnaceae), 274, 275
Ochoterenaea, 14, 16
Ochroma, 56, 57
  pyramidale, 57, Pl. 7B
Ochthephilus, 241
Ochthocosmus, 195
  attenuatus, 195, 196
  longipedicellatus, 195*, 196
  roraimae variety *parvifolius**, 195
Ocimum basilicum, 203
Ocotea, 204, 205
  caparrapi, 205
  diffusa, Pl. 25F
  tenera, 206
Odonellia, 113, 114
Odontocarya, 247
Odontonema
  cuspidatum, 6
  tubiforme, 6
  strictum, 6
Odontonemeae (Acanthaceae), 3
Odontostomum, 484
Oeceoclades maculata, 465
Oecopetalum, 192, 193
Oedematopus, 105
Oenothera, 279, 280
  biennis, 280
Okenia, 210, 270
OLACACEAE, **276***, 277*, 481, Pl. 34
Oldfieldioideae (Euphorbiaceae), 146, 147, 148
Olea europaea, 279
OLEACEAE, 109, **277**, 278*, 279
Oleales, 278
Oleeae (Oleaceae), 278
Oleoideae (Oleaceae), 278, 279
OLINIACEAE, 12
Olmediella, 159
Olsynium, 448, 449
Olyra, 470
Olyreae (Poaceae), 470, 473
Ombrophytum, 41, 42
  subterraneum, 42
Omphalea, 149
Omphalocarpeae (Sapotaceae), 342
Omphalodes, 60, 61
Ona, 449
ONAGRACEAE, 109, 224, **279***, 280, Pl. 34
Onagreae (Onagraceae), 280
Oncidium, 465, 466, 468
Oncotheca, 26
Onosma, 59
  echioides, 62
Onychopetalum amazonicum, 19

Operculina, 113, 114
Ophiocaryon, 335
  paradoxum, 335
Ophiocolea, 52
Ophiopogon, 428
  japonicus, 428
Ophiopogoneae (Convallariaceae), 428
Ophrys, 467
Ophthalmoblapton, 149
OPILIACEAE, 276, **281***, 338
Oplopanax, 28
Opuntia, 74, 76
  dillenii, Pl. 9C1, C2
  ficus-indica, 75
  fragilis, 74
  macrorrhiza, 75
Opuntioideae (Cactaceae), 74, 75
ORCHIDACEAE, 328, 447, 448, **465**, 466*, 467*, Pl. 60
Orchidales, 429
Orchidoideae (Orchidaceae), 465
Orchis, 467, 468
Orectanthe, 492, 493
Oreithales, 320
Oreocallis, 314, 315
Oreomunnea, 196, 197, 198
Oreomunneoideae (Juglandaceae), 196
Oreomyrrhis, 21
Oreopanax, 28, 29, 30
  capitatus, 28*, 29, 30
  dactylifolius, 29
  echinops, 29
  peltatus, 30
  sanderianus, 29
  xalapensis, 29, 30
Origanum, 203
Orites, 314, 315
Oritrophium, 35, 38
Ormosia, 154, 155
OROBANCHACEAE, 202, **282**, 298, 349, Pl. 34
Orobanche, 282
Orontioideae (Araceae), 414
Oroxyleae (Bignoniaceae), 52
Orthion, 391
Orthomene prancei, Pl. 31A
Orthophytum, 419
Orthopterygium, 15, 16
Orthosanthus, 448, 449
  chimboracensis, Pl. 59B
Oryctanthus, 222, 223
Oryza, 471
  sativa, 473
Oryzeae (Poaceae), 471
Oryzoideae (Poaceae), 471
Osbeckieae (Melastomataceae), 242
Osa pulchra, Pl. 42A
Oserya, 303
Osmanthus, 278
  americanus, 278
Osteophloeum, 261, 262
Ostrya, 50, 51
  virginiana, 50, 51
Ostryopsis, 50
Otoba, 261, 262
Ottelia, 444, 446
Ottoa, 22

Ottoschultzia, 192
Ouratea, 274, 275
  section *Kaieteuria*, 275
  litoralis, 275*
  poeppigi, Pl. 33C
Ourisia, 349, 350
Ovidia, 372
OXALIDACEAE, 122, 169, 213, **283***, 284,
  Pl. 35
Oxalidales, 65, 122
Oxalis, 283, 284
  barrelieri, 283*
  corniculata, 283, 284
  debilis, Pl. 35B
  tuberosa, 284
Oxandra, 19, 20
  lanceolata, 20
Oxycaryum, 435
Oxychloe, 450, 451
Oxygyne, 421
Oxysporeae (Melastomataceae), 242
Oyedaea wurdackii, Pl. 5D

Pabellonia, 408
Pachira, 56, 57
  aquatica, Pl. 7A
  glabra, 56
  insignis, 56
  quinata, 57
Pachycereus, 74, 76
Pachyphytum, 118
Pachysandra, 71
Pachystachys, 3, 6
  coccinea, 6, Pl. 1A
  lutea, 6
  ossolaea, 5
  puberula, 5
  spicata, 5, 6
Paeonia, 320
Paepalanthoideae (Eriocaulaceae), 440
Paepalanthus, 440
  bifidus, Pl. 57F
Pagamea, 328, 331
Pakaraimaea, 130, 131
  dipterocarpacea, 130
Pakaraimoideae (Dipterocarpaceae), 130, 131
Palaquium, 344
Palicourea, 328, 330, 331, 332
  crocea, Pl. 42B
Palisota, 427
PALMAE, **416**
Palmeria, 252
Pamianthe, 411
Pamphilia, 363
Panax, 28
  ginseng, 30
  quinquefolius, 30
PANDACEAE, 147
PANDANACEAE, 417, 431, 487, 489, 490
Pandanales, 487, 490
Panicoideae (Poaceae), 470, 472
Panicum, 470
Panopsis, 314, 315
  rubescens, 314, 315
Papaver, 284, 285
PAPAVERACEAE, 48, 247, **284**, 285*, 320,
  Pl. 35

Papaverales, 285
Papaveroideae (Papaveraceae), 285
Paphiopedilum, 465
Papilionanthe, 468
Papilionoideae (Fabaceae), 151, 152, 153, 154,
  155, 198, Pl. 20
Papuodendron, 56
Paracaryum, 59
Parachimarrhis, 332
Paraia, 204
Paramongaia, 411
Pararistolochia, 31, 32
Parathesis, 262, 263
Parentucellia viscosa, 350
Parides, 32
Parietales, 381
Parinari, 100, 101, 102
  montana, 101*
  obtusifolia, 101, 102
Parinarieae (Chrysobalanaceae), 101
Parkia, 154
  discolor, Pl. 21A
Parnassia, 214, 347
Parnassiales, 214
Parodia, 74
Parodianthus, 388
Parodiodendron, 147
Paronychioideae (Caryophyllaceae), 89
Paropsieae (Passifloraceae), 159, 286
Parrotia, 180
Parthenium, 39
Parthenocissus, 394, 395
  quinquefolia, 394
Paspalum, 470
  repens, Pl. 61B
Passiflora, 286, 287
  caerulea, 286
  coriacea, 287
  costata, Pl. 36B
  edulis, 286*, 287
  foetida, 286*
  incarnata, 286, 287
  laurifolia, 286*
  lutea, 286
  mexicana, 287
  mollissima, 287
  quadriglandulosa, Pl. 36A
  tarminiana, 287
PASSIFLORACEAE, 143, 159, 200, 228,
  230, **286***, 287, 290, 291, 381, Pl. 36
Passifloreae (Passifloraceae), 286
Patagonula, 59, 61, 62
  americana, 61
Patima guianensis, 332
Patinoa, 56, 57
Patosia, 450, 451
Patrinia, 386
Paullinia, 339, 341
  cupana, 341
  pinnata, 339, Pl. 43A
  rubiginosa, 340*
  tricornis, Pl. 43D
Paulownia, 51
PAULOWNIACEAE, 51
Pausynistalia yohimbe, 332
Pavonia, 233, 234
  section *Typhalea*, 234

paludicola, 233
kearneyi, 233
Paypayrola, 390, 391, 392
  grandiflora, 392
Paypayrolinae (Violaceae), 391
Peckia, 319
Pectocarya, 59
PEDALIACEAE, 239, **288***, 289, Pl. 36
Pedalieae (Pedaliaceae), 288
Pedalium, 288
Pedicularis, 349
Pedilanthus, 148
PEGANACEAE, 401
Peganum, 401
Pehria, 223, 224, 225
Pelargonium, 169, 170
  grossularoides, 170
Pelletiera, 312, 313
Pelliciera, 289, 290, 324
  rhizophorae, 289, Pl. 36D1, D2
PELLICIERACEAE, 237, **289**, Pl. 36
Peltaea, 233
Peltanthera, 66, 67
Peltogyne paniculata, 155
Peltophyllum, 487, 488
  luteum, 488
PENAEACEAE, 12
Pennisetum, 473
Pentaclethra macroloba, Pl. 21C
Pentamerista, 289, 368
  neotropica, 369*
Penstemon, 348, 349, 350
Pentacalia, 33
  subgenus *Pentacalia*, 35
Pentadesma, 106, 107
Pentagonia, 331
Pentaplaris, 375, 376
Pentas lanceolata, 332
Pentasetmonodiscus, 89
Penthorum, 347
Peperomia, 296, 297
PEPEROMIACEAE, 296
Peplis, 223
Pera, 147, 148
  distichophylla, Pl. 19A
Perameae (Rubiaceae), 330
Perckiamya, 319
Pereae (Euphorbiaceae), 146
Perebea, 255
Perseeae (Lauraceae), 205
Pereskia, 74, 75
  grandiflora, Pl. 9A
  lychnidiflora, 75
  portulacifolia, 75
  weberiana, 75
Pereskiodieae (Cactaceae), 74, 75
Pereskiopsis, 75
PERIDISCACEAE, **290**, 291, Pl. 37
Peridiscus, 290, 291
  lucidus, 290, Pl. 37A
Peripentadenia, 136
Periplocoideae (Apocynaceae), 23
Periptera, 234
Peritassa, 184
  campestris, 183
Perityle emoryi, 38
Perityleae (Asteraceae), 36

Tepualia, 264, 265
  stipularis, 264
TEPUIANTHACEAE, **366***
Tepuianthus, 366
  auyantepuiensis, 366, 367
  aracensis, 367
  colombianus, 366*
  savannensis, 366
Terminalia, 110, 111
  australis, 110
  amazonia, Pl. 15A
  buceras, 110*, 111
  catappa, 111
  lucida, 110
  molinetii, 111
Terminaliinae (Combretaceae), 110
Ternstroemia, 367, 368
  japonica, 368
  parvifolia, 368
  peduncularis, 367*
  pungens, Pl. 48C
TERNSTROEMIACEAE, 87, 237, 289, 365, **367***, 368, Pl. 48
Ternstroemieae (Ternstroemiaceae), 368
Ternstroemioideae, 368, 370
Tessaranda, 278
Tessaria integrifolia, 39
Tessmannianthus, 242
Tetracarpaea, 175
Tetracera, 129
Tetracoccus, 147
Tetradiclis, 400, 401
Tetragastris, 68
  altimssima, 68*
Tetragonia, 10
  tetragonioides, 11
Tetragonioideae (Aizoaceae), 10
Tetralocularia, 113
TETRAMELACEAE, 116
Tetrameranthus, 19
Tetramerista, 368
TETRAMERISTACEAE, 237, 289, 368, 369*
Tetramerium, 5
Tetranema, 349, 350
  roseum, 350
Tetrapanax, 28, 29, 30
  papyrifer, 30
Tetrapterys, 228
Tetrastigma, 394
Tetrataxis, 224
Tetrazygia elaeagnoides, 241*
Tetrorchidium, 146, 147, 149
Teucrium, 203
Thalassia, 444, 445, 446
  testudinum, 445*
Thalassodendron, 433
Thalia, 458, 459
  geniculata, 459
Thalictroideae (Ranunculaceae), 320
Thalictrum, 320, 321
Thamnosma, 333
Thaumatocaryum, 59
THEACEAE, 9, 58, 87, 159, 192, 237, 289, 368, **369**, 370
Theales, 9, 58, 87, 106, 130, 138, 237, 274, 289, 317, 362, 365, 368, 370

Theeae (Theaceae), 370
Thelesperma megapotamica, 38
Theligonieae (Rubiaceae), 332
THEMIDACEAE, 405, 408, 411, **485**
Theobroma, 360, 361
  cacao, 361, Pl. 47A1, A2
  velutinum, 360*
Theoideae (Theaceae), 370
Theophrasta, 372
THEOPHRASTACEAE, 262, 313, **371***, 372, Pl. 48
Thesium, 338
Thespesia, 233
  populnea, 233*, Pl. 28C
Thevetia, 24
  peruviana, 25
Thibaudia, 140
Thiloa, 110
Thismia, 421
  americana, 421
  rodwayi, 421
THISMIACEAE, 421
Thismieae (Burmanniaceae), 421
Thoracocarpus, 431
Thornea, 106
Thottea, 31, 32
Thouinia, 341
Thraupis, 319
Thunbergia, 4, 5, 6
  alata, 5
  coccinea, 5
  erecta, 5
  fragrans, 5
  grandiflora, 5
Thunbergioideae (Acanthaceae), 4, 5
Thurnia, 486
  polycephala, Pl. 63B
  sphaerocephala, 486*
THURNIACEAE, 435, 450, **486***, Pl. 63
THYMELAEACEAE, 103, **372**, 373*, Pl. 49
Thymelaeales, 127
Thymelaeoideae (Thymelaeaceae), 372
Thymus, 201, 203
Thyrsanthemum, 426
Thyrsodium, 14, 15
Thysanostemon, 106
Thysanotus, 453, 454
Tiarella, 348
Tibouchina, 241, 242
Tibouchineae (Melastomataceae), 242
TICODENDRACEAE, 157, 196, **374***
Ticodendron, 374
  incognitum, 374*
Tigridia, 448, 449
  pavonia, 449
Tigridieae (Iridaceae), 448, 449
Tigridiinae (Iridaceae), 449
Tilesia baccata, 38
Tilia, 375, 376
TILIACEAE, 136, 137, 159, 233, 235, 257, **375***, 376, Pl. 49
Tilieae (Tiliaceae), 375
Tillaea, 118
Tillandsia, 418, 419, 420
  usneoides, 418, 420
Tillandsioideae (Bromeliaceae), 419, 420

Tinantia, 426, 427
Tipuana, 155
Tiquilia, 59, 60, 61, 210
Tirpitzia, 215
Titanotricheae (Gesneriaceae), 171
Tococa, 242
Toddalioideae (Rutaceae), 333, 334
Tofieldia, 460, 461
Tofieldieae (Melanthiaceae), 460, 461
Toisusu, 337
Tolmiea menziesii, 348
Tonina, 440
  fluviatilis, 440*
Tontelea, 183, 184
  cylindrocarpa, 183*
  micrantha, 183
  nectandrifolia, 184
Toona sinensis, 243
Topobea, 241, 242
Torulinium, 435
Tournefortia, 59, 60, 61
  argentea, 62
  bicolor, Pl. 7F
  maculata, 61
  volubilis, 61
Tournonia, 44
  hookeriana, 44
Touroulia, 317, 318
Tourretia lappacea, 52
Tourrettieae (Bignoniaceae), 51, 52
Tourrettia lappacea, 53
Tovaria, 376, 377
  diffusa, 376
  pendula, 376, 377*, Pl. 49D
TOVARIACEAE, 46, **376**, 377*, Pl. 49
Tovomita, 105, 106
Tovomitopsis, 105
Toxicodendron, 15, 16
Tradescantia, 425, 426, 427
  fluminensis, 427
  zanonia, 427
  zebrina, 426*
Tradescantieae (Commelinaceae), 426
Tragia, 146
Tragopogon porrifolius, 39
TRAPACEAE, 224
Trapella, 288
TRAPELLACEAE, 288
Trattinnickia, 68, 69
Traubia, 411
Trema, 382, 383
  micrantha, 382, 383*, Pl. 50B
TREMANDRACEAE, 122
Tresanthera, 331
Trevoa
  quinquenervia, 324
  trinervia, 324
Trianthema, 10
  portulacastrum, 11*
Tribuloideae (Zygphyllaceae), 401
Tribulus, 210, 400, 401
  cistoides, 400
  longipetalus, 400
  terrestris, 400, 401
Triceratella, 426
Trichanthera, 5

Veronieae (Scrophulariaceae), 349
Verrucularia, 231
Vetiveria, 473
Viburnum, 83, 84
Vicieae (Fabaceae), 152
Victoria, 271
  amazonica, 271, 272*, Pl. 33B
  cruziana, 271, 272
Viguiera, 33
Villadia, 118
Villarsia, 249
Vinca
  major, 25
  minor, 25
Viola, 390, 391, 392
  odorata, 392
VIOLACEAE, 101, 143, 159, 200, 230, 290, 381, **390**, 391*, 392*, Pl. 51
Violales, 47, 54, 82, 85, 103, 120, 137, 159, 161, 163, 200, 218, 228, 286, 290, 291, 351, 381, 391
Violeae (Violaceae), 391
Violoideae (Violaceae), 391
Vireo flavoviridis, 160
Virola, 6, 261, 262
  michelii, Pl. 32A
  surinamensis, 262
  sebifera, 261*
  venosa, Pl. 32B
VISCACEAE, 222, **393***, 394, Pl. 51
Viscainoa, 400
  geniculata, 401
Viscum album, 394
Vismia, 105, 106
VITACEAE, 129, 323, **394**, 395*, Pl. 51
Vitales, 394
Vitex, 202, 387, 388, 389, 390
  cymosa, 388
  excelsa, 389
  triflora, 389*
Vitica, 131
Viticeae (Verbenaceae), 388
Viticoideae (Verbenaceae), 387, 388, 389
Vitis, 394, 395
  labrusca, 395
  rotundifolia, 395
  vinifera, 394, 395
Vitoideae (Vitaceae), 394
Viviania, 169
Vochysia, 396, 397, 398
  apopetala, 397
  herbacea, 397
  pacifica, 397
  pumila, 397
  surinamensis, 396*
  venezuelana, Pl. 52C
VOCHYSIACEAE, 150, 265, 378, **396***, 397, Pl. 52
Vochysieae (Vochysiaceae), 396, 397
Votomita, 242, 246, 247
Votschia, 371
Vouacapoua americana, 155
Voyria, 167
  acuminata, Pl. 22A

Voyrieae (Gentianaceae), 167
Voyriella, 167
Vriesea, 418, 420

Wallacea, 275
  insignis, Pl. 33D
Wallenia, 262
Waltheria, 360, 361
Warneckea, 246
Warszewczia, 331, 333
  coccinea, Pl. 41A
Websteria, 435
Weddellina, 302, 303
Weddellineae (Podostemaceae), 302
Weigeltia, 262
Weinmannia, 122, 123, 145
  neblinensis, 122*
  tinctoria, 123
Weldenia, 426, 427
Wellstedioideae (Boraginaceae), 60
Wendtia, 168, 169
Wendtiae (Geraniaceae), 169
Werauhia, 420
Wercklea, 233
Werneria, 35
Whittonia, 290, 291
  guianensis, 290
Wigandia, 191
  caracasana, 191
  kunthii, 191
  urens variety *caracasana*, Pl. 24D
Williamodendron, 204
Wimmeria, 96
WINTERACEAE, 81, **398**, 399*, Pl. 52
Winterales, 398
Withania, 355
Witheringia maculata, Pl. 46A
Wolffia, 454, 455, 456
  angusta, 455
  globosa, 454, 455, 456
  microscopica, 455
Wolffiella, 454, 455, 456
  caudata, 454
Wolffioideae (Lemnaceae), 454, 455
Woodfordia, 224
  fruticosa, 225
Worsleya, 411
  rayneri, Pl. 54A

Xanthium, 38
Xanthorrhoea, 405
Xanthosoma, 413, 415, 416
Xerophylleae (Melanthiaceae), 461
Xerophyta, 490, 491
Ximenia, 276
  americana, 277
Xiphidium, 442
  caeruleum, 441*, 442, Pl. 58A1, A2
  xanthorrhizon, 441, 442
Xolocotzia, 387
Xylonagra, 280
Xylopia, 18, 19
  aromatica, Pl. 3B
  benthamii, 19

Xylopodia, 218
Xylosma, 159, 160
XYRIDACEAE, 426, 440, 460, 478, **492***, 493, Pl. 64
Xyris, 460, 492, 493
  blepharophylla, Pl. 64B
  laxifolia, 492*

Yucca, 405, 406
  aloifolia, 405*, 406
  filifera, Pl. 53A
Yuccoideae (Agavaceae), 405

Zannichellia, 493
  andina, 493
  palustris, 493
ZANNICHELLIACEAE, 476, **493**
Zanonioideae (Cucurbitaceae), 120
Zantedeschia, 416
  aethiopica, 416
Zanthoxylum, 333, 334
  flavum, 335
Zea mays, 473
Zebrina, 426
Zenia, 152
Zephyra, 484
Zephyranthes, 410, 411
  cearensis, Pl. 54B
Zeugites, 471
Zeuxine strateumatica, 465
Zigadenus, 460
  volcanicus, 461
Zingiber, 494
  officinale, 495
  spectabile, Pl. 64D
ZINGIBERACEAE, 417, 424, 430, 458, **494**, 495*, Pl. 64
Zingiberales, 424, 430, 442, 463, 482, 494
Zingibereae (Zingiberaceae), 494
Zingiberoideae (Zingiberaceae), 494
Zinnia, 39
Zinowiewia, 95, 96
Zizania, 473
Ziziphus, 323, 324
  chloroxylon, 324
  cinnamomum, 323*, 324
  mauritiana, Pl. 40A
  mistol, 324
  spina-cristi, 324
Zostera, 496
  subgenus *Zostera*, 496
  subgenus *Zosterella*, 496
  marina, 496
ZOSTERACEAE, 496
Zosterella, 474
Zoysia, 473
Zygogynum, 398
ZYGOPHYLLACEAE, 108, 198, 210, **400***, 401, Pl. 52
Zygophylloideae (Zygphyllaceae), 401
Zygophyllum, 400, 401
  dumosum, 401